Encyclopedia of Islamic Civilisation and Religion

Encyclopedia of Islamic Civilisation and Religion

Edited by
Ian Richard Netton

Routledge
Taylor & Francis Group

LONDON AND NEW YORK

First published 2008
by Routledge
2 Park Square, Milton Park, Abingdon, Oxon, OX14 4RN

Simultaneously published in the USA and Canada
By Routledge
270 Madison Avenue, New York, NY 10016, USA

Routledge is an imprint of the Taylor and Francis Group, an informa business

© 2008 Ian Richard Netton

Typeset in Times New Roman and Optima
by Taylor & Francis Books
Printed and bound
by MPG Books Ltd, Bodmin

British Library Cataloguing in Publication Data
A catalogue record for this book is available from the British Library

Library of Congress Cataloging in Publication Data
A catalog record for this book has been requested

ISBN13: 978-0-7007-1588-6

Contents

Introduction

This *Encyclopedia of Islamic Civilisation and Religion* celebrates diversity in unity: the diversity lies within the framework of one of the world's great monotheistic religions, Islam, which itself declares the oneness and unity of God whom it knows in Arabic as Allah. The founder-Prophet of Islam, Muhammad b. Abdallah was born in c. AD 570. By the time of his death in AD 632, the seeds had been sown of a mighty religion and civilisation whose speed and articulation would encompass the rise and fall of many diverse Islamic empires.

It is a truism that today Islam is rarely out of the news. It is equally true that this is a religion that is frequently misinterpreted, unconsciously or, at times, deliberately, by a media voracious for a sensationalist story or striking image. In the process, reality and truth are often the first casualties. In an age of globalisation that prides itself on the accumulation of knowledge and knowledge transfer, too little is known about Islam among non-specialists and non-Muslims.

This *Encyclopedia*, designed to be of use both to the scholar and the non-expert, intends to remedy that. In *sura* (chapter) 20 of the sacred text of Islam, the Holy Qur'an (a word that means simply 'recitation'), there is an invocation that the Lord will increase the suppliant in knowledge. Throughout its history, the Islamic religion, and the diverse civilisations and empires to which it gave birth, have fostered the idea that knowledge is key, knowledge is a necessary end. The great medieval collectors of traditions, from and about the Prophet Muhammad, travelled thousands of miles in search of knowledge. That search could be an adjunct of the pilgrimage (*hajj*) to Mecca itself. A saying attributed to the Prophet Muhammad urges the believer to seek knowledge even as far as China. Whatever one may believe about the ultimate authenticity of this tradition, there is no ignoring the fact that it underlines the radical enthusiasm for knowledge accumulation that was so characteristic of the medieval Islamic world.

In our present electronic age, epistemological horizons have exploded by virtue of the Internet and e-mail. Renaissance Man, epitomised in such intellectual giants as an Erasmus or a Sir Thomas More, has been replaced by 'specialist man'. Knowledge is all around us; how do we gain access to it in manageable form?

This *Encyclopedia* attempts to facilitate this for the world of Islam. It embraces both the medieval and the modern ages. The author of each entry is responsible for his or her own script. One may speak from a deeply Muslim perspective; others may prefer a more dispassionate phenomenological approach. All, however, have attempted to inform their entries with good scholarship and lucidity. Each entry illustrates my initial remark that Islam is not a narrow theological monolith but a religion with a diversity of articulations and approaches, while focusing in a unified manner on certain key and inalienable doctrines like the Five Pillars.

In this *Encyclopedia* the curious reader will find coverage of a host of themes, personages, doctrines, and events. The material is organized in an A to Z format for ease of use, and the coverage includes Arab and Islamic texts, art and architecture, biography, caliphs, cities and geography, dynasties, history, Islam in West Africa, law, movements, origins, philosophy, Qur'an, science, Sufism, *tafsir*, and theology.

It cannot be totally comprehensive and the Editor is well aware that a favourite game of the book reviewer and critic is 'spot the omissions'. However, it does aim to facilitate that search for knowledge so characteristic of the medieval Islamic paradigm. The mystical dimension is here in all its multifaceted splendour; so is the rational dimension of Islam because Islam, as well as being a religion of revelation, also prides itself on being a religion of reason that makes reasonable demands on its worldwide community (*umma*).

Here, too, are the problems that have vexed the minds of the medieval Islamic sages, philosophers, and theologians alike, like the transcendence and immanence of the Deity, the attributes of God, the reconciliation of free will and predestination, authority and leadership as well as more modern topics like the role of women, education, interpretation of medieval texts in a modern age, the use of independent judgement (*ijtihad*), and the potential and actual clashes of theocracy with democracy. It will be recognised that these problems are by no means unique to Islam but have beset and vexed many of the other great world religions as well.

The many diverse entries in this *Encyclopedia* may not provide definitive answers to age-old questions; they will, at least, provide information about them. The reader's search is also aided by blind entries naming alternate terminology and, at the end of entries, references and 'See alsos'. There is a Thematic Bibliography preceded by contributor-linked bibliographies. Just as the scholarship is diverse, so too is the citation style in academia worldwide. For this reason, in an effort to be user-friendly to the non-specialist, diacritics have been omitted.

There are many encyclopedias, dictionaries and reference books in the market-place today that deal with Islam and the volatile arena that is the Middle East. This is not surprising and, indeed, such riches are to be applauded. All these reference works, whether designed and written for the specialist scholar or the informed lay reader, serve to quench the fires of ignorance that have raged for far too long, fuelled by suspicion, cynicism and outright fear. So, it may be asked, how does this particular encyclopedia of Islamic civilisation and religion differ from its rivals?

First, the focus is primarily on a whole civilisation and culture, rather than just religion or theology, narrowly interpreted. It recognises the indivisibility of the Islamic way of life where, classically, no division should be made between secular and sacred. All creation is designed to submit, to be in that state of submission to the will of Allah that we call *Islam*. 'Submission' is the meaning and essence of that word.

Sometimes, however, a division will be detected in these entries between secular and sacred for the sake of clarity or emphasis. That does not, and should not, undermine the classical paradigm.

Second, Islam is the religion of a worldwide community, the *umma* as it is called in Arabic, whose leaders are, and have been throughout history, important as at least theoretical bearers and proponents of the message. So there is an emphasis in this encyclopedia on the prosopographical, especially in its provision of brief biographies of nearly all the rulers of three of Islam's greatest dynasties, the Umayyads, the 'Abbasids and the Ottomans.

Third, Islam fosters a notion of sacred space in its great mosques and its great cities. Location is of both historical and contemporary importance. Thus, there are entries on mosque architecture as well as on some of the great cities of Islam such as Cairo and Mecca.

Finally, we have chosen to include a large number of entries that have a particular reference to the development of Islam in West Africa. This illustrates the fact that Islam, although it grew to fruition in the Near and Middle East, in the Arabian cities of Mecca and Medina to be precise, is nonetheless a universal and global religion of global significance, relevance and importance in our twenty-first-century universe. And whether or not there is a 'clash of civilisations' as Samuel P. Huntington would have us believe, we all need to be aware that Islam flourishes powerfully outside the cockpit of the Near and Middle East. It is worth repeating the salient statistic here that the country with the largest Muslim population in the world is Indonesia, not Arabia. As I have already stated, the views of the author of each entry in this encyclopedia remain his or her own and are not necessarily shared by the editor.

Each entry is individually signed by the author. Some have contributed more entries than others. I thank all for their hard work and contribution in bringing this volume to birth. I shall not single out any by name except to pay a special tribute to Professor Edward Hulmes who, when – as is inevitable during an endeavour of this size – some contracted contributors were unable to fulfil their commitment, stepped into the breach and supplied splendidly scholarly and seemingly effortless copy in a very short space of time. Edward, I thank you from the bottom of my heart. I am most grateful to the following distinguished scholars who provided valuable comment on the initial choice of entries at the beginning of this project. Needless to say, they are not responsible for any lacunae in the final choice of entries: Professor Michael Cook, Dr Yasin Dutton, Professor Anoush Ehteshami, Dr Andrew Newman, Professor Andrew Rippin. I would also like to pay particular tribute to my editor in New York, Kate Aker, Director of Development at Routledge, New York, who has helped keep me sane during an uphill editorial process and been a beacon of good sense, inspiration and, above all, patience with this editor's manifold foibles! Finally, I thank most warmly my UK editors at Routledge, in particular Gerard Greenway, Jason Mitchell and Fiona Maclean. They have become friends as well as colleagues during this endeavour.

Professor Ian Richard Netton
Professor of Arabic Studies
University of Leeds
Spring 2007

Contributors

Hussein Abdul-Raof
University of Leeds

C. E. Bosworth
Formerly University of Manchester

Ronald Paul Buckley
University of Manchester

Peter Clark
Formerly British Council

Mawil Izzi Dien
University of Wales, Lampeter

Maha El-Kaisy Friemuth
Trinity College, Dublin

Robert Gleave
University of Exeter

H. P. Goddard
University of Nottingham

Derek Hopwood
Formerly University of Oxford

Edward Hulmes
Formerly University of Durham

Colin Imber
University of Manchester

Michael E. Marmura
University of Toronto

Leslie McLoughlin
University of Exeter

Sean McLoughlin
University of Leeds

Simon Murden
Britannia Royal Naval College, Dartmouth

Ian Richard Netton
University of Exeter

Andrew J. Newman
University of Edinburgh

Patrick S. O'Donnell
Santa Barbara City College

Gavin Picken
School of Oriental and African Studies, University of London

Lloyd Ridgeon
University of Glasgow

Andrew Rippin
University of Victoria, Canada

Sajjad H. Rizvi
University of Exeter

Jennifer Scarce
University of Dundee

Janet Starkey
University of Durham

Paul Starkey
University of Durham

Tony Street
University of Cambridge

David Thomas
University of Birmingham

Martin Whittingham
Edinburgh

List of entries – alphabetical

LIST OF ENTRIES – ALPHABETICAL

AARON

See: **Harun**

'ABBAS I B. MUHAMMAD KHUDABANDA (r. 1587–1629)

The greatest of the Safavid shahs. He maintained the integrity of Iran by warding off his Sunni enemies, the Ottomans to the west and the Ozbegs to the north-east, whilst preserving friendly relations with the Mughals. He moved the capital from Qazvin to Isfahan and set about beautifying the latter with splendid buildings and gardens. The shrines of his ancestors at Ardebil in Azerbaijan, and that of the Eighth Shi'ite Imam at Mashhad, were much visited by him, as head of the Safavid order, but he was in many respects tolerant of non-Muslims. Contacts with Europe were opened, and English, Spanish and Portuguese envoys visited his court, although the hoped-for alliance against the mutual enemy, the Ottomans, never materialised.

References

Gibb and Bosworth (1960–2003), Roemer (1986: 268–78), Savory (1980: 76–119).

C. E. BOSWORTH

'ABBAS II B. SAFI (r. 1642–66)

The second most able Safavid ruler after Shah 'Abbas I. He preserved his frontiers and gained territory in Afghanistan, and was likewise a builder at Isfahan and follower of his forebear's tolerant policy towards the Armenians and other Christians, though he bore down harshly on the Jews. His successors were men of lesser calibre, and the decline of the empire was manifest after his death.

References

Gibb and Bosworth (1960–2003), Roemer (1986: 288–304), Savory (1980: 231–9).

C. E. BOSWORTH

1

'ABBASIDS (AD 750 –1517)

These formed the second line of caliphs in Islam following the Umayyads, with their capital in Iraq, principally at Baghdad. They derived their legitimacy through descent from Muhammad's uncle, al-'Abbas, regarding this connection as superior to that of 'Ali and his descendants, the Shi'ite imams. Under their rule, mainstream Sunni Islam developed its body of law and theology, with the caliphs as the embodiments of moral authority and as protectors of the Muslim frontiers and as Imams who might at times claim to interpret Islamic law and belief. It was under the 'Abbasids that the four main law schools of Sunni Islam arose and that the body of Muslim theologians ('ulama') and lawyers (fuqaha') acquired a corporate identity within Islamic society. The 'Abbasids maintained the boundaries of the Islamic world as established by their predecessors, but found their territories reduced in extent as autonomous or independent lines arose in the provinces, and although there was a revival of caliphal power in the later twelfth century, this was cut short by the eruption into the Islamic lands of the Mongols, who sacked Baghdad in 1258 and killed the caliph. The last 'Abbasids eked out an existence in Cairo (1261–1517) as puppet rulers, with no authority but a moral one, until the Ottoman conquest of Egypt ended them.

References

Bosworth (1996: No. 3), Gibb and Bosworth (1960–2003), Kennedy (1981, 1986: 124–99)

See also: **Buyids; Saffarids; Saljuqs; Samanids**

C. E. BOSWORTH

'ABD

'Slave', and that part of a Muslim's proper name combined with one of the names of Allah to denote such a relationship to Allah, for example 'Abd al-Rahman ('slave of the Merciful').

References

Gibb and Bosworth (1960–2003).

See also: **ninety-nine names of God**

ANDREW J. NEWMAN

'ABD AL-'AZIZ I B. MUHAMMAD (r. 1765–1803)

Son of Muhammad b. Su'ud, Amir in eastern Arabia of the first Su'udi state. He was already prominent during his father's lifetime as a military leader, and as *amir*, their sheikhdom of Dir'iyya in Najd became vigorously expansionist. Su'udi control was established on the Gulf seaboard, and the island of Bahrayn temporarily occupied. There were uneasy relations with the Sharifs of Mecca over the admission of Wahhabi pilgrims to the Holy Places, after 'Abd al-'Aziz's death, his son Su'ud was in 1803 to enter Mecca and destroy what Wahhabi rigorists regarded as un-Islamic accretions at the shrines. Wahhabism was even more hostile to Shi'ism, with its veneration of the House of 'Ali, and in 1801 or 1802 the shrine of Husayn at Karbala' in Iraq was bloodily sacked.

References

Gibb and Bosworth (1960–2003), Vassiliev (1998: 85–102), Winder (1965).

See also: **Su'udis**

C. E. BOSWORTH

'ABD AL-'AZIZ II B. 'ABD AL-RAHMAN, called IBN SU'UD (1902–52)

Founder of the third Su'udi state and eventually king of the greatest state in the Arabian peninsula. The second phase of Su'udi power had ended in internal dissensions and eclipse by the rival Rashidi family of Ha'il. Ibn Su'ud struggled to recover authority in Najd from these last and their supporters, the Ottomans. In 1915, he entered into treaty relations with Britain, receiving an annual subsidy and a promise of military assistance if ever required. He finally crushed the Rashidis (1921) and in 1924 invaded the Hijaz, wresting it from the Hashimite Sharifs, enabling him in 1926 to assume the title of King of the Hijaz and Najd and, in 1932, King of Su'udi Arabia. An able and impressive figure, Ibn Su'ud brought his kingdom into the first stages of modernity, with Sa'udi Arabia assuming a position of world significance through possession of the oil deposits of eastern Arabia.

References

Gibb and Bosworth (1960–2003), Vassiliev (1998: 210–327).

C. E. BOSWORTH

'ABD AL-JABBAR
(c. AD 935–1025)

The last great thinker of the school of the Mu'tazila in the classical period of Islamic thought. He was born in western Iran and went to study in Basra, where he changed his allegiance from the Ash'ari school to the Mu'tazila, and he then moved to Baghdad. In AD 978 he was appointed chief qadi (judge) of the city of Rayy (near modern Tehran), where he spent most of the rest of his life. His largest work the *Kitab al-Mughni* (literally 'The Book which makes sufficient') was rediscovered in Yemen in 1950, and his shorter one-volume summary of the teachings of the Mu'tazila, the *Sharh al-Usul al-Khamsa* (Exposition of the Five Principles: the unity of God, His justice,

the 'promise and threat' (in the afterlife), the intermediate position (as outlined earlier by Wasil ibn 'Ata'), and 'commanding what is right and forbidding what is wrong') is an accessible introduction to the ideas of the school.

References

Hourani (1971), Martin, Woodward and Atmaja (1997), Peters (1976).

HUGH GODDARD

'ABD AL-MALIK B. MARWAN
(AD 685–705)

Son and successor of the Umayyad caliph Marwan b. al-Hakam. The Umayyad dynasty, with its capital in Damascus, reached the high point of its power and glory under the rule of 'Abd al-Malik and his immediate successors. 'Abd al-Malik's main task was to restore the unity of the empire and reassert the control of the Umayyad caliphate founded by Mu'awiya b. Abi Sufyan. Assisted by his loyal and able governor of Iraq and the east, al-Hajjaj b. Yusuf, 'Abd al-Malik was able to crush serious uprisings by the Khawarij and a major Shi'ite revolt in Kufa led by al-Mukhtar (d. AD 687). The final defeat of Ibn al-Zubayr took place in AD 692, an event that marked the end of the second *fitna* in Islam.

'Abd al-Malik's answer to the crumbling state administration established by Mu'awiya was to begin a political and administrative centralisation of government in which power was concentrated in the caliph and backed up by the military might of the Syrian army. Among the measures introduced was the Arabicisation of the administration which entailed changing the official language used in the public bureaux to Arabic, the beginnings of a rationalised Islamic system of taxation, the minting and circulation of a specifically Arabic coinage and a postal service between Damascus and the provincial capitals. In this way, the structure of the caliphal state began to take shape.

'Abd al-Malik's nomination of his son al-Walid as successor was not challenged, and al-Walid inherited a united and peaceful empire.

References

Hitti (1970: 205–7), Kennedy (1996: 93–103), Shaban (1971: 93–117), al-Tabari (1985–95: XX, 153–4, 159–60; XXI; XXII).

RONALD PAUL BUCKLEY

'ABD MANAF

The pre-Islamic heathen name, 'Abd Manaf, is part of the appellation of Abu Talib, the father of 'Ali, the cousin of the Prophet Muhammad. The fact that Muslim historians were prepared to use the pagan name, 'Abd Manaf, suggests that he was not a legendary figure. One of the advantages enjoyed by Muhammad was that, although his social position in Meccan society was initially relatively uninfluential, he could always claim to be a Qurashi and a member of the prestigious Banu Hashim branch of the noble house of his ancestor, 'Abd Manaf. This family link ensured that he was never without the protection of his extended family. The ancient custom in Arabia of the cessation of hostilities during the four forbidden months was strictly observed by the House of 'Abd Manaf. The four months in question most probably came to be Muharram, Rajab, Dhu'l-Qa'da and Dhu'l-Hajj.

See also: **calendar, Islamic (*al-taqwim al-islami*, *al-hijri*); months, Islamic; Muhammad ibn 'Abdallah, the Prophet of Islam**

EDWARD D. A. HULMES

'ABD AL-MUTTALIB

As a member of the important clan of Hashim, and hence a prominent social and political figure in Meccan society, 'Abd al-Muttalib was the paternal grandfather of the Prophet Muhammad. 'Abd al-Muttalib's son 'Abdallah, the father of Muhammad, died before the boy Muhammad was born. 'Abd al-Muttalib then assumed the responsibility of caring for the boy. Many stories about his generosity, probably legendary, circulated about 'Abd al-Muttalib, whose uncle is said to have brought him to Mecca. The best attested historical fact about him, however, is that he undertook the task of helping the orphan Muhammad.

See also: **Mecca; Muhammad ibn 'Abdallah, the Prophet of Islam**

EDWARD D. A. HULMES

'ABD AL-NASIR, JAMAL (1918–70)

Usually known as Gamal Abd al-Nasser or Nasser, Egyptian soldier and leader.

He was born into a lower-middle-class family and lived for sometime in the village of Bani Murr in upper Egypt where he observed at first hand the daily life of the *fellahin* (peasants) with its poverty and unremitting toil, and yet with the dignity of labour and the solidarity of family and village life. He went to school later in Cairo where he became acquainted with two other sides of Egyptian life – urban poverty and overcrowding – and the activities of different kinds of politics aimed against the British occupation. He took part in anti-British demonstrations in the streets, was arrested on one occasion, and became committed to the cause of expelling the hated occupier. He entered the Military Academy in 1937 as an officer-cadet as soon as it was opened to the sons of peasants. In 1943 he was appointed an instructor at the Academy and during this time he was able to make contact with other young Egyptian officers who, like him, were fired with the idea of liberating their country.

The Arab defeat in Palestine in 1948 had a deep effect on 'Abd al-Nasir and his colleagues (the Free Officers) who felt that the corrupt regime in Egypt was responsible for the defeat. They began secretly to plan the overthrow of the Monarchy and Government. They carried out their almost bloodless coup on 23 July 1952 and forced King Faruq to abdicate and his government eventually to resign. General Najib (Naguib) was the figurehead of the coup but 'Abd al Nasir was the real power behind him. In July he became president of the Revolutionary Command Council with defacto power. He negotiated a treaty with the British for their withdrawal, survived an assassination attempt and slowly became the established leader with an admired reputation throughout the Third World.

To underline Egypt's new independent status, in 1956 he announced the nationalisation of the Suez Canal in retaliation for the USA withdrawing its offer of a loan to help to build the Aswan High Dam. The British Prime Minister Anthony Eden, in particular, reacted strongly to this move and, together with France and Israel, Britain embarked on the disastrous Suez war – an attempt to regain control of the canal. The defeat of this undertaking (ostensibly by Egypt but really because of US pressure) added to 'Abd al-Nasir's prestige and he was tempted into various schemes the success of which he believed his personality alone could guarantee, thus the short-lived union with Syria (1958–61), the disastrous war in Yemen and the even more disastrous war against Israel in 1967.

In internal affairs he did not hold strongly to any ideology but under the influence of Third World leaders and of the Soviet Union he introduced Arab socialism into Egypt together with nationalisation, central planning and an attempt at land reform. He did not like to delegate his authority and the Arab Socialist Union was designed largely as a means of ensuring centralised control with no real democracy. He had built himself a position that seemed unassailable yet after leading the country into the 1967 defeat he offered to resign. The people, having lost the war, could not face losing him as well and took to the streets to reject his resignation. He agreed to continue but in a weakened state. His prestige was diminished, a fifth of the country occupied, the canal closed and his army shattered. There was little he could do at home or abroad. He toyed with two policies, those of introducing more political freedom and of moving towards some negotiations with Israel. He did not have any time left, however, and died of a heart attack in September 1970.

He had dominated Egyptian and Arab politics for over two decades and had guided his country through the difficult post-colonial period. He was the symbol to many in the Arab and Third Worlds of resistance to the West and of post-colonial regeneration.

References

Stephens (1971).

DEREK HOPWOOD

'ABD SHAMS

The son of 'Abd Manaf and brother of Hashim, the great-great-grandfather of the Prophet Muhammad. 'Abd Shams had a son, Umayya, who was the eponymous ancestor of the Umayyad dynasty.

See also: **Umayyads**

EDWARD D. A. HULMES

'ABDALLAH B. YASIN
(d. AD 1058)

Moroccan scholar who came to reside with the Lamtuna Berbers of the western Sahara and enforced amongst them a strict Maliki view of the *shari'a*, allegedly from the base of a *ribat* or hermitage in what is now Mauritania or Senegal. Under his leadership, these so-called *murabitun* gradually secured control of the western Sahara, with 'Abdallah providing the administrative expertise and spiritual fervour for the expansion northwards into Morocco of the Lamtuna chiefs who were to become the Almoravid dynasty.

References

Bosch (1956), Gibb and Bosworth (1960–2003), Norris (1982: 105–56).

C. E. BOSWORTH

'ABDALLAH IBN 'ABD AL-MUTTALIB

The father of the Prophet Muhammad bore the name *'Abd-Allah,* which means 'the slave, or the worshipper of God'. The Prophet was born after his father's death. Apart from the distinction of paternity, nothing is known about 'Abdallah. The name *'Abd-allah* was highly respected in pre-Islamic Arabia, especially by the Quraysh of Mecca. They addressed prayers to *Allah*, a word contracted from the Arabic *al-ilah,* meaning 'the God', to refer to what appears to have been their tribal deity.

See also: **Muhammad ibn 'Abdallah, the Prophet of Islam**

EDWARD D. A. HULMES

'ABDUH, MUHAMMAD (1849–1905)

Born in Egypt and educated at al-Azhar, the leading institution of Islamic learning in that country, 'Abduh became a disciple of Jamal al-Din al-Afghani during the period that he was in Egypt in the 1870s. When the British occupied Egypt in 1882 'Abduh found himself first in prison and then in exile, joining al-Afghani in Paris. In 1885, however, he moved to Beirut, where he delivered some lectures on theology which became the basis for his most important work the *Risalat al-Tawhid* (*The Theology* [lit. *Letter*] *of Unity*). In 1888 he returned to Egypt, having come to a pragmatic acceptance of the reality of British rule, and during the remaining years of his life he progressed through the legal and religious institutions of Egypt, becoming a member of the Council of al-Azhar in 1895 and Chief Mufti (Legal Official) in 1899. He also began the publication of a radically new type of commentary on the Qur'an, which appeared in a journal, *al-Manar* (*The Lighthouse*), and which attempted to relate the message of the scripture directly to contemporary issues. Like al-Afghani 'Abduh was concerned about defending the world of Islam from European encroachment and Islam itself from European influences, and he therefore sought to purify and revive Islamic practice but, in contrast, to al-Afghani he laid far less stress on political action and far more on educational and social reform, and he was readier to reformulate traditional Islamic doctrine in the light of modern thought.

References

'Abduh (1966), Badawi (1978: Chapter 2), Kedourie (1966), Kerr (1966).

HUGH GODDARD

'ABDUL-'AZIZ (r. 1861–76)

Ottoman Sultan, son of Mahmud II. On his accession 'Abdul-'Aziz faced rebellions in Montenegro, Hercegovina, and Crete. The troubles in Montenegro were suppressed in 1862. In 1868, new regulations set up a special administration in Crete. A year before, however, Serbia gained effective independence, and the Sultan recognised the independence of Romania. In 1875, there were insurrections in Hercegovina and Bosnia, which threatened to spread to Bulgaria. The situation led to a conference of Germany, Russia and Austro-Hungary, demanding reforms in these provinces. 'Abdul-'Aziz was deposed before receiving the memorandum.

'Abdul-'Aziz and his ministers carried forward the *Tanzimat*. The 1860s saw further reorganisation of the provinces and the education system, a commission was established to draw up a civil code, the army was re-organised and re-equipped with German advice, the navy with English advice, railway building advanced, and the telegraph network established. By 1875, however, the Government was unable to meet its debt repayments. This crisis, together with insurrections in the Balkans, led the Sultan's ministers – Midhat Pasha, Rusdu; Pasha and Huseyin Avni Pasha – to engineer his dethronement in May, 1876. He died a few days later.

References

Dumont (1989: 509–15).

COLIN IMBER

'ABDUL-HAMID (r. 1876–1909)

Ottoman Sultan, son of 'Abdul-Mecid. He came to the throne at a period of crisis, with rebellions in Bulgaria, Hercegovina and Bosnia, and a declaration of war by Serbia and Montenegro. Russian intervention deprived the Sultan of victory in this war. In December, a congress of the powers assembled in Istanbul, to find itself pre-empted by the declaration of the Constitution, which, if implemented, would meet the powers' demands. The establishment of a parliament followed. In the meantime Russia used Ottoman refusal to implement all the powers' demands as a *casus belli*. By 1878, the Russians had advanced to within a few miles of Istanbul, where they forced large concessions. This treaty was unacceptable to the other powers, and revised at the Congress of Berlin. The Congress resulted in the creation of a Bulgarian principality, the Russian annexation of Kars and Ardahan, an award of territory to Greece, the Austro-Hungarian occupation of Bosnia-Hercegovina, and the cession of Cyprus to Britain. This experience persuaded 'Abdul-Hamid to avoid military confrontation and to attempt to maintain the Empire's integrity by diplomacy. Nonetheless, the French occupied Tunis in 1881 and the British occupied Egypt in 1882. Success in a war with Greece in 1897 merely produced great power intervention which gave autonomy to Crete.

The war of 1877–8 provided 'Abdul-Hamid with a pretext to abrogate the Constitution, inaugurating a period of personal rule. Throughout his reign, internal rebellion and the growth of nationalism threatened the integrity of the Empire. To foster the loyalty of his Muslim subjects, he emphasised his claims to the caliphate. Rebellions by non-Muslim subjects, especially of the Armenians in 1894–5 were met with brutal suppression. Nonetheless, non-Muslims and especially Armenians continued to play important roles in his government, and the educational developments of his reign were secular. The reign also saw an inflow of foreign capital: 'Abdul-Hamid saw the development of railways and communications, which required foreign investment, as a means of reinforcing his authority in the provinces.

During the 1880s and 1890, 'Abdul-Hamid saw Germany as the only power without territorial designs and, beginning with a German military mission in 1882, German military experts became instructors in the Ottoman Military Academy. By 1900, Germany was a monopoly supplier of arms.

'Abdul-Hamid's autocratic style of government led to opposition not only from separatists, but also from the German-trained officers who believed that his autocracy and passivity in the face of the powers was leading to ruin. In particular, the officers of the Macedonian army formed cells of opposition. In 1908, this organisation – the Committee of Union and Progress – rebelled, forcing 'Abdul-Hamid to restore the Constitution. In 1909, there was a counter-coup. In the face of these events, the commander in Macedonia, Mahmud Sevket Pasha, mobilised his forces and occupied Istanbul. Under this pressure, the Parliament declared 'Abdul-Hamid deposed. He was exiled to Salonica and, in 1912, returned to Istanbul, where he died in 1918.

References

Deringil (1998), Georgeon (1989: 523–76), Yasamee (1996).

COLIN IMBER

'ABDUL-HAMID I (r. 1774–89)

Ottoman Sultan, son of Ahmed III. He came to the throne after defeat in the war with Russia which had continued since 1768. The war ended with the treaty of Kucuk Kaynarca in 1774, which terminated Ottoman overlordship of the Crimea, ceded adjoining territory to Russia, gave the Russians the right to 'protect' Orthodox subjects in Istanbul and to navigate freely in the Black Sea. After the war, 'Abdul-Hamid attempted to reform the army and navy with the help of foreign advisers, and to restore order in the provinces. In 1784, the Sultan recognised the Russian occupation of the Crimea, but the Russian conquest of Georgia in 1788 led to war.

References

Mantran (1989c: 421–5).

COLIN IMBER

'ABDUL-MECID (r. 1839–61)

Ottoman Sultan, son of Mahmud II. He came to the throne following the capture of his fleet by Muhammad 'Ali of Egypt and the defeat of his army by Muhammad Ali's son, Ibrahim Pasha. The intervention of Britain and Russia ended the crisis, with the Treaty of London in 1841 granting Muhammad Ali the hereditary governorship of Egypt. Crises continued elsewhere. Insurrections broke out in Crete. The Grand Vizier Mustafa Resid Pasha secured a temporary halt to sectarian warfare in Lebanon. However in 1860, fighting erupted again, to be settled by a conference of the powers in Istanbul which gave part of Lebanon autonomous status under the tutelage of France. There were further revolts in Kurdistan in 1847, and in Bosnia and Montenegro in the 1850s. The control of Moldavia and Wallachia remained a matter of dispute between Russia and the Ottoman Empire which together with Russian claims over the Holy Places, led to the outbreak of the Crimean War in 1853 and the Ottoman alliance with France and England. The union of the Danubian principalities in the aftermath of the Crimean war, and Ottoman recognition of their autonomy in 1861 was a step in the creation of independent Romania.

Throughout his reign, 'Abdulmecid continued his father's reforms, the Decree of Gulhane of 1839 initiating the period remembered as the *Tanzimat*. Most notably the decree gave equal status to all Ottoman subjects regardless of religion; the second reform decree of 1856, reiterated this principle. The reforms of the Sultan and his ministers, notably Mustafa Resid Pasha included the reorganisation of the army, the introduction of new secular schools, the reorganisation of the provinces, and new criminal, commercial and land codes.

References

Dumont (1989: 459–64).

COLIN IMBER

ABLAQ (PIEBALD)

A decorative technique of Roman and Byzantine inspiration found mainly in western Islamic architecture where alternating courses, stripes and shapes of stone in different colours create dramatic contrasts such as black and white, cream and dark red. It was used to striking effect in mosques of Egypt and Syria of the twelfth to fifteenth centuries to embellish *mihrabs* and outline entrances. Here the *mihrab* of the *mosque-madrasa* of al-Muayyad Shaykh (1412–22) in Cairo is a fine example inlaid with zigzags, palmettes, radiating interlaced foliage bands and stylised calligraphy. Borders of alternating radial blocks of cream and red also outline the interiors of the domes and vaults of Ottoman mosques of the sixteenth century such as the Suleymaniye in Istanbul and the Selimiye in Edirne.

References

Goodwin (1987), Hautecoeur and Wiet (1932–4).

JENNIFER SCARCE

ABLUTION (*GHUSL, WUDU', TAYAMMUM*)

The Arabic words shown above refer to three kinds of ablution in Islam. Each of them serves to restore the believer to a state of ritual purity in preparation for the fulfilment of a religious duty, especially that of ritual prayer and worship. Choice of the form of ablution to be used depends upon the personal circumstances of the worshipper and on local conditions.

The first kind of ablution is *ghusl* (the 'greater ablution'), which requires the ritual washing of the entire body. It is required on conversion to Islam. Thereafter, it is prescribed whenever a state of major ritual impurity (*junub*) arises. For example as a consequence of sexual activity, menstruation and childbirth. The believer must ensure that the whole body, including the hair, is cleansed of every impurity by water. The *ghusl* should also be performed before undertaking *Hajj* and before the *Jummah* prayer and the *Eid* prayer.

The second kind of ablution is known as *wudu'* (the 'lesser ablution'), which is the usual form of ablution made before performing ritual prayer and worship (*salat*). This is enjoined in the Qur'an:

> O ye who believe! When ye prepare for Prayer, wash your faces, and your hands (and arms) to the elbows, rub your heads (with water), and (wash) your feet to the ankles. If ye are in a state of ceremonial impurity, bathe your whole body. But if ye are ill, or on a journey, or one of you cometh from offices of nature, or ye have been in contact with women, and ye find no water, then take for yourselves clean sand or earth, and rub therewith your faces and hands, God doth not wish to place you in a difficulty, but to make you clean, and to complete His favour to you, that ye may be grateful.

(Q.5:6)

Partial ablution thus involves ritualistic rinsing of the hands to the wrist, mouth, nostrils, face, forearms to the elbow, top of the head, ears, nape and, feet to the ankles, using water if it is available. It serves to cleanse the worshipper from those 'impurities' known as *ahdath*, which are caused by for example natural bodily functions, by a period of sleep or unconsciousness, or by touching a dog.

The third kind of ablution is known as *tayammum* (dry ablution). It may be used in the absence of water, or when water is scarce, or when the use of water might involve a risk to health. In this case, the hands are dipped in clean earth or sand, or brought into contact with a piece of unworked stone. The earth or sand is rubbed off the hands, which are then applied to the face and forearms.

The 'lesser ablution' (*wudu'*) is held to be sufficient for the recitation of the five daily prayers throughout the day.

References

Gibb (1955: 55, 73), Hitti (1973: 131–2), Tritton (1968: 23–4,157).

EDWARD D. A. HULMES

ABORTION (*IJHAD, ISQAT*)

The protection of the foetus, the unborn child, is a duty that is placed upon all Muslims although abortion, not specifically mentioned in the Qur'an, is not forbidden in Islam except after the moment when 'a child' is formed in its mother's womb. In the light of recent developments in the study of human embryology, Muslims are obliged to decide just when this moment occurs. In discussing the moment when a foetus becomes fully *human* in the womb, Islamic theologians traditionally distinguished between non-existence and existence, between what is potential and what is actual. The critical moment was the 'ensoulment' of the foetus, which was said to take place 120 days after conception. The *shafi'i* jurist *al-Nawawi* (1233–77) recorded a *hadith* which refers first to the sperm (*nutfa*) planted in the mother's womb, then to the developing blood clot (*'alaq*), and then to the tiny configuration of flesh into which an angel blows the breath of life. Only then did the foetus become a human being. For this reason, abortions were permitted up to the fourth month, although there was no universal agreement about the acceptability of the practice before or after that time. In recent years, anti-abortion sentiments are being forcefully expressed by some Muslims, who take the view that conception marks the beginning of Allah's unchallengeable creative activity (see Q.40:67). Nothing is created by accident or chance. If Allah wills it, it is not for any of His human creatures to attempt to prevent the birth of a child. The right to life is inalienable. From conception to death the lives of human beings are in the hands of Allah who, nevertheless, gives His creatures the freedom to obey or to disobey what is commanded.

References

Bouhdiba (1985: 159–60), Omran (1992: 7–9, 228–9).

EDWARD D. A. HULMES

ABRAHA

In AD 525 the Christian Negus (*Najashi*, ruler) of Abyssinia dispatched an army across the Red Sea, first to assist and then to subdue the Arabians in the Yemen. The force was led by Abraha, who succeeded in establishing control in the principality of Saba'. He became the Abyssinian viceroy of the region, under whose patronage a splendid cathedral was built in what became the capital city, San'a. Tradition records that he was also responsible for having the irrigation system and the great dam of Ma'rib repaired. It was Abraha who commanded an attack on the city of Mecca in AD 570, the year of the birth of the Prophet Muhammad. The date is known in Islamic tradition as 'the Year of the Elephant' (*'am al-fil*). It appears that the elephants in Abraha's invading force impressed the Meccans, who had not been confronted by such animals before. A passage in the Qur'an (Q.105:1–5) records the miraculous way in which Abraha's invading army was routed by 'the small baked stones' (*sijjil*), hurled at them by passing birds. Other sources attribute the city's deliverance to the outbreak of smallpox that afflicted the invading troops. In AD 575 the Persian Sasanids ended Abraha's rule in the Yemen.

See also: **Mecca; Muhammad ibn 'Abdallah, the Prophet of Islam**
EDWARD D. A. HULMES

ABRAHAM

See: **Ibrahim**

ABU AL-'ABBAS

He was a great-great grandson of al-'Abbas ibn-'Abd-al-Muttalib ibn-Hashim, the uncle of the Prophet Muhammad. Born in AD 722 he was the first of the 'Abbasid dynasty, who ruled from AD 750 until his death four years later. He came to power after the 'Abbasids were able to depose the Umayyad dynasty, which had ruled the Islamic empire from Damascus since AD 661. The Umayyads were weakened progressively by corruption and decadence. The 'Abbasids were to rule in their stead for another 500 years. Two years after leading a successful revolt against Umayyad rule in

AD 748, abu al-'Abbas assumed the caliphate and began to hunt down his opponents and rivals. In his first statement of intent, a *khutba* delivered in the mosque in Kufa in Iraq, he described himself as *al-Saffah*, 'the shedder of blood'. The subsequent persecution and execution of his enemies confirmed the appropriateness of the sobriquet. During his caliphate he succeeded in setting up a stable administrative and legal system for his successors, the first of whom moved the capital of the empire from Damascus to Baghdad.

References

Hitti (1973: 288–362).

See also: **'Abbasids; Umayyads**
EDWARD D. A. HULMES

ABU BAKR AL-SIDDIQ

On the death of Muhammad in AD 632, it was one of the Prophet's fathers-in-law, the ageing Abu Bakr, who was appointed as Muhammad's successor (*khalifa*). Born in the year AD 573, Abu Bakr was caliph for only two years. He died in AD 634. The Prophet Muhammad appears to have left no explicit instructions about the identity of the man who was to take his place, as a result of which the eventual succession was disputed. There were other claimants to the succession, but it was Abu Bakr, one of the first in Mecca to believe in the mission of the Prophet and to accept Islam, who assumed responsibility for leading the Islamic community in Medina. According to Ibn Ishaq, the early biographer of Muhammad, Abu Bakr was honoured by the epithet, *al-Siddiq*, for his piety and uprightness, and subsequently known as the first of the four rightly guided (*al-rashidun*) Caliphs'. Gentle of character, he gave constant support to

Muhammad throughout the most difficult period of the Prophet's mission in Mecca, believing him to be the divinely appointed Messenger of God. When others, especially the unbelieving Quraysh, were sceptical about the revelations of the Qur'an that Muhammad claimed to have received, or questioned (for example, the reality of the Prophet's 'Night Journey', to Jerusalem), Abu Bakr entertained no doubts about their authenticity. Islamic tradition records him as the man who accompanied Muhammad on the secret move from Mecca to Medina in the year of the *hijra*, AD 621, when the mockery and persecution of the Muslims in Mecca made the journey prudent as well as timely. This incident and the choice of Abu Bakr as a companion on this epoch making migration are recalled in the Qur'an (Q.9:40), where he is described as 'the second of two', a title that he afterwards bore with pride. A small group of Meccan Muslims, 'emigrants' (*muhajirun*), had already gone on before to Yathrib, situated some 280 miles (450 kilometres) north-east of Mecca, and renamed *Madinat al-Nabi* ('city of the Prophet') after Muhammad's arrival. Rather than take refuge in Abyssinia under the protection of the Christian Negus in AD 615 with the small number of Muslims who left Mecca because of persecution, Abu Bakr chose to stay near to Muhammad in Mecca until the local opposition to the Prophet's mission necessitated the migration to Medina. Abu Bakr is said to have used his considerable personal wealth for charitable purposes and to have retained little of it after the *hijra*. Shortly after this migration to Medina, the Prophet married again. On this occasion he took as wife a child bride, Abu Bakr's young daughter 'A'isha, who was to become Muhammad's favourite wife. Characteristically, Abu Bakr, set up a modest dwelling for his family in Medina and remained a constant and loyal companion of the Prophet. He was able to reconcile and keep together in the common cause those who held different opinions. It may have been this gift above all that led to his speedy nomination as the leader of the Islamic community and the Prophet's successor in AD 632.

During Abu Bakr's brief caliphate, from AD 632–4, it was necessary for him to ensure that the de-facto recognition of Muhammad's temporal political and military pre-eminence in the Arabian peninsula was transformed into an acknowledgement of his *de jure* spiritual authority as the Prophet of Islam as well. Many had been prepared to accept the former whilst denying the latter, so Muhammad's death provided the opportunity for a loosening of the alliances that had been established during his lifetime. It was not only the political stability of the region that was threatened by the potential disintegration of the newly organised Islamic state. A reversion to polytheism presented a challenge to the strict monotheism proclaimed by the Prophet. It fell to Abu Bakr to counter these threats, in particular, the threat of apostasy (*riddat 'an al-islam, irtidad*). The action taken by Abu Bakr became known as the *ridda* wars, i.e., the wars against apostasy and, thus, the secession from central Islamic authority. Tribes in distant parts of Arabia objected to the rising power of the Islamic community (*umma*) that was increasingly centralised in Medina and Mecca in the *Hijaz,* and refused to pay tax (*al-zakat*). Abu Bakr issued orders that such opposition be ended by military means. He appointed Khalid ibn al-Walid to lead the force that effectively defeated the 'seceders' in central Arabia within a period of a few months. Further campaigns were led by other Muslim generals in the Yemen, Hadramawt,

'Uman and al-Bahrayn, the intention of which was to bring everyone into the household of Islam (the *dar al-islam*). The successful conclusion of the *ridda* wars by AD 633 owes much to the determination of Abu Bakr, who was thus able to ensure that the future expansion of Islam under the leadership of his successors could proceed apace, once the previously warring tribes in the Arabian peninsula had been united. The warlike spirit of the tribes was not eliminated, however. It was harnessed under the banner of Islam in the subsequent campaigns and conquests that were to take Islam north into the Fertile Crescent to Syria and Iraq and west into Egypt and North Africa. At the instigation of his successor as caliph, 'Umar ibn al-Khattab, Abu Bakr is credited as one who encouraged the early followers of the Prophet to collect together the revelations of the Qur'an received by Muhammad. These scattered fragments of bone and parchment along with memorised verse were brought together under the supervision of Zaid and 'Umar to form the received text of the Qur'an.

See also: **'Ali ibn Abi Talib; Muhammad ibn 'Abdallah, the Prophet of Islam; Pillars of Islam; 'Umar ibn al-Khattab; 'Uthman ibn 'Affan; wives of the Prophet Muhammad**

EDWARD D. A. HULMES

ABU DA'UD (AD 817–89)

The compiler of one of the authoritative books of *hadith* reports in Sunni Islam. Sulayman ibn al-Ash'ath Abu Da'ud al-Sijistani was born in AD 817 in Sijistan, lived in Basra, and died there in AD 889. He is reported to have travelled widely and learned at least 500,000 *hadith* reports. He incorporated 4,800 of the reports in his collection called *Kitab al-Sunan*. That book is considered to have been less stringent in its criteria for inclusion of traditions than that in other *hadith* collections. Abu Da'ud placed most of his critical attention on the plausibility of the *isnad* transmission chain rather than the text (*matn*) of the report. He often included explanatory comments supporting his decision to include less than totally authenticated reports and he discussed the relative value of reports. He also added remarks about the various transmissions of the reports, including variant readings and traditions.

References

Goldziher (1971a: II, 229–34), Siddiqi M. Z. (1993: 61–3).

ANDREW RIPPIN

ABU HANIFA

Abu Hanifa (full name Nu'man b. Thabit) (*c.* AD 699–767) was the eponym of the Hanafi school of Islamic thought. He was born in Kufa, Iraq to a family of Persian origin who were involved in the trading of textiles. He was taught by a number of scholars, including Hammad b. Abu Sulayman, the Kufi (d. AD 737/8). This teacher was important to Abu Hanifa because he provided him with a scholastic link with the generation of the Prophet's Companions. Hammad was the top scholar of Islamic law and the Mufti of Kufa at the time of Abu Hanifa's association with him, a relationship that was to endure for ten years.

Subsequent to this, he felt sufficiently equipped to start his own study circle. However, Abu Hanifa was hesitant to do so and he felt that such an action might not meet the approval of his master. When he met the master in the mosque, he decided not to do so and to continue being a student. Only after having been deputised to stand in for the master as a result of a two-month absence did Abu Hanifa begin to pass judgement on his own cases and record the relevant procedures. On his return, the master enquired about sixty of the cases that Abu Hanifa made in his absence and only forty of them were passed. As a result he vowed to remain with his master until the latter's death.

An interesting question arises from the above story. How did Abu Hanifa accurately record his *fatwas* in order to have them verified by his master. Did he do that by writing or simply memorise each *fatwa*? It seems very likely that he recorded these *fatwas* in writing. This conclusion differs from the common opinion that Abu Hanifa did not write any of his *fatwas* and that his students documented all his procedures and produced them in a written format.

Abu Bakr al-Baghdadi, the author of *Tarikh Baghdad*, cites an occasion when the 'Abbasid Caliph, Mansur, requested that Abu Hanifa divulge the source of his knowledge. He replied, 'I learned about 'Umar through his companions and likewise about 'Ali and 'Abdallah b. 'Abbas from their respective companions'. Mansur, himself reported to be a scholar, replied, 'Indeed you have authenticated your learning'. Abu Hanifa's methodology in approaching and understanding law had a profound impact not only on his students, but also on the entire discipline of Islamic law. His teaching methods did not adhere to the classical format of 'teacher-led' classes in which the students listened and took notes; rather he employed a more active approach that entailed discussion, debate and opportunity to air opinion. His workshop-style classes enabled his students to develop analytical and deductive skills that were to stand them in good stead for future examining of legal cases.

Abu Hanifa's own deduction of legal problems was based on the principles within the Qur'an, *sunna* and the consensus of scholars. He is reported to have stated that these were his primary legal sources, which would then be followed with reference to selected statements of the Prophet's Companions. Only after having explored all these avenues would he resort to individual opinion.

His establishing of the foundation of the legal dialectic between the text and the practical life of society highlights the value of his ability to deduce legal injunctions in a critical way. However, despite his respect for the text, Abu Hanifa did venture into exercising reason in some cases if he felt that particular circumstances warranted this. In order to exemplify his vision of the relationship between text and practice, his opinion regarding the subject of laughter during prayer can be cited. According to Abu Hanifa, the prayer of an individual who laughed would be rendered invalid, as indicated in a weak prophetic tradition, yet one may expect him to have resorted to reason, whereby laughter would not constitute the violation of prayer on the ground that the act may have been unintentional. However he preferred to rely on a weak *hadith*, as in this case related to worship and thus had no effect on the practical aspect of an individual's life. If it had related to a contract of marriage or of sale, then the interest of the individual would have been taken into account in deducing the appropriate injunction. Hence, when considering the subject of ritual, Abu Hanifa adhered to the text, giving it preference over analysis.

Despite what has been said it can be observed that Abu Hanifa did in fact exercise his own opinion in certain areas of ritual such as the case of waving a hand to salute others during prayer. Such an action according to some scholars including the Prophet's companion Abu Hurayra, would nullify the validity of that prayer. However, in the light of the statement of Suhayb, another companion of the Prophet, the Prophet himself would wave in salutation when praying, Abu Hanifa maintained that such an action would not invalidate prayer. He respected both opinions and concluded that hand waving should only constitute a distasteful practice, rather than a forbidden one that merited penalty.

A further distinctive feature of Abu Hanifa's jurisprudence lies in his utilisation of legal tricks *hiyal*, a method of skirting round the law but not actually breaking it. For example, someone who swears not to enter into a contract with a certain person could nominate a third party to act on his behalf, thus achieving his aim without abrogating his original oath. This methodology has received criticism because of its potential for unethical reformatting of the concept, in order to practise that which is not allowed. However, Abu Hanifa's method here was controlled by the general principles of Islam and he aimed to achieve justice, particularly in cases that entailed the upholding of Islamic law within the framework of legal contracts. Abu Hanifa died in Baghdad in AD 767 but his mosque remains famous in the city and contains a venerable manuscript library. Sadly, many esteemed works were lost during the 2003 American invasion of Iraq.

References

Coulson (1964: 50–2), Izzi Dien (2004: 3–20), Schacht and Bosworth (1974: 360), Wahabi (1999: 130, 137).

MAWIL IZZI DIEN

ABU HURAYRA (d. *c.* AD 678)

Prominent companion of Muhammad to whom many *hadith* reports are attributed. He converted to Islam in the year 7 after the *hijra* (AD 629), Abu Hurayra was a poor man who was later appointed Governor of Bahrayn and then the caliph's representative in Medina. He died around AD 678 when he was seventy-eight years old. He was a prolific transmitter of *hadith* reports, despite the short time with which he was associated with Muhammad. Some 800 people are credited with transmitting from him and many of the reports found their way into the collections of al-Bukhari and Muslim ibn al-Hajjaj, having been judged to be sound and reliable transmissions.

References

Gibb and Bosworth (1960–2003: I, 129).

ANDREW RIPPIN

ABU JAHL

Abu Jahl was a prominent critic of Muhammad's mission in Mecca in the years after the Prophet's call to be the Messenger of God in AD 610. Like others in the city he considered that the Prophet and the message of Islam he preached were threats to the stability and economic prosperity of Mecca. In AD 616 Abu Jahl led the opposition of members of the Quraysh who objected to the protection offered by clan loyalty to Muhammad. This protection enabled the Prophet to continue his public ministry. Opposition to his mission continued but he survived the vilification and persecution endured by the small group of Muslims in Mecca. After the move from Mecca to Medina (*hijra*) Abu Jahl continued to lead opposition to Muhammad. There were skirmishes between the Meccans and the Muslims of Medina, the most significant of which proved to be the Battle of Badr, which was fought in AD 624. The Muslims gained a victory that was seen as a vindication of Muhammad's prophetic claims. Abu Jahl and seventy of his men were killed in the battle and many leading men from Mecca were taken prisoner.

See also: **Badr, Battle of; Mecca; Muhammad ibn 'Abdallah, the Prophet of Islam**

EDWARD D. A. HULMES

ABU LAHAB

The Arabic sobriquet of an uncle of the Prophet Muhammad means 'Father of Flame'. Abu Lahab and his wife were fierce opponents of Muhammad's mission. The 111th *sura* of the Qur'an bears this uncle's nickname. The verses of the *sura* employ puns to spell out in fiery terms what kind of fate awaits him and his wife ('the collector of firewood') for their opposition to the Prophet. Abu Lahab died in AD 624, shortly after learning of Muhammad's success at Badr.

See also: **Badr, Battle of**

EDWARD D. A. HULMES

ABU MUSLIM, 'ABD AL-RAHMAN IBN MUSLIM AL-KHURASANI (d. AD 753/4)

Leader of the revolutionary movement in Khurasan that brought the 'Abbasid dynasty to power in AD 750. Few details are known of the life of Abu Muslim, who was probably a slave of Persian origin, until he was sent by the Imam Ibrahim ibn Muhammad to Khurasan in AD 745/6 to direct the 'Abbasid insurrection there. At first, he encountered some hostility, especially from Sulayman ibn Kathir who had been in charge of local organisation, but Sulayman's objections were quickly overcome and on 15 June 747, under Abu Mus-

lim's leadership, the black banners of the 'Abbasids were raised for the first time – a symbolic act that continued to reverberate through Islamic history. From that date the 'Abbasids began to gain support in most provinces of the Umayyad Empire. Abu Muslim's army succeeded in capturing Merv (Marw) in December AD 747 or January AD 748, and from there the general Qahtaba ibn Shabib pursued the Umayyad forces towards the west. The defeat of the Umayyad forces under Marwan II at the Battle of the Great Zab River in Mesopotamia in AD 750 marked the collapse of the Umayyad dynasty, though one survivor, 'Abd al-Rahman, succeeded in escaping and established himself in Spain (AD 756), founding the dynasty of the Umayyads of Cordoba.

Following the accession of al-Saffah as the first 'Abbasid caliph, Abu Muslim continued to serve as Governor of Khurasan, where he suppressed a Shi'ite revolt in Bukhara in AD 750/1, and from where he mounted further expeditions towards the east. His relations with the new dynasty quickly became strained, however, and in AD 753/4, following the accession of al-Mansur, he was tricked into appearing at the caliph's court in Baghdad, where he was killed.

References

Shaban (1970, 1971), Wellhausen (1963).

PAUL STARKEY

ABU SUFYAN

He was a bitter opponent of Muhammad in Mecca (AD 610–21) and for most of the following decade, when the Prophet moved to Medina to establish the Islamic community there. Abu Sufyan was a prominent Qurashi of the family of 'Abd Manaf and a wealthy entrepreneur, who frequently led caravans of merchandise from Mecca, to and from Syria. His initial opposition to the mission of Muhammad may have stemmed from the threat posed by Islam to the business and pilgrimage interests of the Quraysh in Mecca. It was whilst Abu Sufyan was in charge of the great caravan on his way back to Mecca in AD 624 that a Medinan force led by Muhammad threatened to attack. Abu Sufyan sent to Mecca for help. A Meccan army of some 1,000 men under the command of Abu Jahl was despatched from the city to relieve the caravan. They outnumbered the Medinan Muslims by three to one in the battle of Badr, which took place in the month of Ramadan but victory went to Muhammad. Abu Jahl and seventy of his men perished in the battle. Abu Sufyan's son, Hanzala, was also among those killed. Abu Sufyan assumed command of the Meccan forces after the Battle of Badr and led them against Muhammad on several occasions, for instance at Uhud. For reasons that may have been more pragmatic than idealistic, Abu Sufyan's attitude to the Prophet changed. In AD 630 the Meccan Quraysh attacked a tribe protected by an agreement with the Muslims. The fragile truce agreed at Hudaybiyya was broken. Muhammad promptly led a large army against the pagan Meccans. After making peace with the Prophet and accepting Islam, Abu Sufyan returned to Mecca with the promise that if the Prophet met with no opposition to his entrance no one would be harmed. Muhammad's triumphant entry was peaceful and virtually bloodless. Thereafter the city became the centre for Islamic pilgrimage and devotion. In subsequent campaigns Abu Sufyan served the cause of Islam. The first of the Rightly Guided Caliphs, Abu Bakr, made him Governor of Najran and the Hijaz. Abu Sufyan was also a progenitor of the Umayyad caliphate through his son, Mu'awiya. The date of Abu Sufyan's death is disputed, but the prevailing view is that he died in AD 652 at the advanced age of eighty-three.

References

Hitti (1973: 117, 140, 189–93), Momen (1985: 6, 19, 34).

See also: **Badr, Battle of; Al-Hudaybiyya, the treaty of; Tabuk; Uhud, Battle of; Umayyads; Yarmuk, Battle of**

EDWARD D. A. HULMES

ABU TALIB

Abu Talib 'Abd Manaf ibn 'Abd al-Muttalib was a paternal uncle of the Prophet Muhammad and the father of 'Ali, the fourth of the rightly guided (*al-rashidun*) caliphs. On the death of Muhammad's paternal grandfather, 'Abd al-Muttalib, it was Abu Talib who assumed responsibility for the welfare and protection of the orphan, Muhammad. Tradition records that the boy accompanied his uncle on caravan business journeys north from Mecca to and from Syria. His uncle continued to protect Muhammad from detractors and opponents in Mecca after the Prophet's call to be the Messenger of God in AD 610. In return for this protection, Muhammad is said to have arranged for 'Ali to be brought up in the Prophet's home in Medina. Abu Talib died in AD 619, the same year in which Muhammad's first wife, Khadija died. This double bereavement, first the death of his protector and second the death of his first convert to Islam, occurred in the year known afterwards as the 'Year of Mourning'. Legends soon began to arise about the life and character of Abu Talib, a man who played a key role in the life of his nephew, but who apparently never converted to Islam. Some accounts state that he did become a Muslim before his death. Others insist that he considered Muhammad to have deluded himself about his mission. One story goes as far as to suggest that the Prophet was unable to make an exception in the case of his uncle for the pains suffered in Hell by pagans.

See also: **Muhammad ibn 'Abdallah, the Prophet of Islam**

EDWARD D. A. HULMES

ABU TALIB AL-MAKKI
(d. AD 996)

Al-Makki was a Sufi inspired by the kind of teachings current among the students of Sahl al-Tustari (d. AD 896). He is the author of *Qut al-qulub* (*Nourishment of the Hearts*) which has been described as an apologetic work that attempted to place Sufism firmly within mainstream Sufi opinions. Thus, in addition to copious citations from the Qur'an and *hadith*, there are also substantial sections that deal with Islamic rituals. The Sufi element appears in discussions of the stations (*maqamat*) and states (*ahwal*). *Qut al-Qulub* was an influential work upon other major Sufis including Abu Hamid al-Ghazali who copied large passages of al-Makki's work in his *Ihya' 'ulum al-din* (*Revivification of the Religious Sciences*).

References

Abu Talib al-Makki (1893).

LLOYD RIDGEON

ABU YAZID AL-BISTAMI
(d. AD 874)

Also known as Bayazid Bistami, this Sufi from north-west Iran is famous for his ecstatic sayings (*shatahat*) and descriptions of his mystical ascension that are recorded in the writings of later Sufis. 'Glory be to me how great is my majesty', is his most celebrated ecstatic saying, which mirrors Q.17:1 of the Qur'an: 'Glory be to He [God] who carried His servant [Muhammad] by night from the Holy Mosque to the Farthest Mosque'. Other ecstatic statements of Abu Yazid reveal a concern to uncover the essence of humanity, typified in his utterance of 'My "I" is not "I am"', because I am He, and I am "he is He"'. It is worthwhile noting, however, that at the end of his visionary descriptions, Abu Yazid rejected them all as a deceit. His contribution to the development of Sufism is vital in that in addition to individual piety there is also a visionary element. Western academics have sought to identify the roots of Abu Yazid's worldview, and most noteworthy of all was R. C. Zaehner's opinion that there was an Indian influence.

References

Ernst (1996: 161–7), Zaehner (1960: 198–218).

LLOYD RIDGEON

ABU ZAYD AL-BALKHI, AHMAD (*c.* AD 849–934)

Arab geographer, born in Khurasan, who also, according to Yaqut' wrote on philosophy, astrology and the religious sciences. Although not widely travelled, he is said to have studied in Baghdad with the famous Islamic philosopher al-Kindi.

Al-Balkhi's present reputation depends entirely on a work usually entitled *Suwar al-Aqalim*, but also known as the *Taqwim al-Buldan*, which is lost in its original form, but almost certainly comprised a set of twenty regional maps with commentary; it is likely that, in compiling it, he drew on the work of earlier geographers such as Abu Ja'far al-Khazin. Al-Balkhi's work formed the basis for the work of later geographers of the so-called 'Balkhi' or 'Classical' school, including al-Istakhri, Ibn Hawqal and al-Muqaddasi, though, in the absence of al-Balkhi's original work, the precise relationship between his contribution and that of his successors remains confused. A characteristic feature of al-Balkhi's approach appears to have been an attempt to reconcile the tradition of Ptolemaic cartography with the Islamic tradition as embodied in the Qur'an and *hadith*, thus ensuring a prominent position for the Arabian Peninsula and the Holy Cities of Mecca and Medina.

References

Miquel (1973).

PAUL STARKEY

ABU'L-HUDHAYL AL-'ALLAF (*c.* AD 750–*c.* AD 840)

One of the outstanding thinkers of the school of thought known as the Mu'tazila. Born in Basra, he spent his formative years there, probably moving to Baghdad around AD 818 and then dying there some twenty years later. None of his works survive, but based on their titles and the summaries of his views produced by others he argued for the strict unity and utter transcendence of God, so that He is utterly unlike His creatures, for human free will, because God is not the author of evil actions, and for the created-ness of the Qur'an. He gathered a number of disciples around him, especially in Baghdad, where he chaired a number of religious discussions at the court of the caliph al-Ma'mun, and he was also responsible for a number of polemical works against other religious traditions.

References

Caspar (1998: Chapter 7), Watt (1998: Chapter 8).

HUGH GODDARD

ACRE ('AKKA)

An old Arab town on the Bay of Haifa, now in Israel. It is one of the oldest inhabited towns in the world, founded before 1500 BC. It was a Phoenician city and in 332 was incorporated into the empire of Alexander the Great and then into Ptolemaic Egypt. (It was known as Ptolemais until the Middle Ages.) It was later an important seaport and trading centre under Rome and the Byzantine Empire. Occupied by Arab invaders in AD 638 it retained its importance under the Fatimid dynasty of Egypt. The town came into prominence in European history when it was captured by the Crusaders in AD 1104 and became a central point in the Christian possessions in the Holy Land (known as St Jean d'Acre). It was adorned with walls and fortifications and the splendid church of St Jean built by the Knights of St John. It was recaptured by Saladin (AD 1187), retaken by the Third Crusade and finally by the Muslims after a long siege in 1291 during which the buildings suffered large-scale damage. It was still in ruins when in 1517 it became a minor location within the Ottoman Empire. In the mid-eighteenth century it was partially rebuilt under two local dynasties. It was razed during the period of Ibrahim Pasha and further rebuilt. It fell to the Allied armies in 1918 at the close of the First World War and was subsequently incorporated into the British mandate of Palestine. Acre fell to the Jewish forces in 1948 fighting to establish the state of Israel since when it has been an adjunct to neighbouring Haifa but has developed as the centre of the steel industry.

The old Arab town has been sanitised as a centre for arts and tourism. With its eighteenth-century mosque of al-Jazzar, Arab market, the remains of the crypt of St John and the double walls and fortifications, attractively situated by the

Mediterranean, Acre has become an important tourist centre.

References

Murphy-O'Connor (1992).

DEREK HOPWOOD

'AD AND THAMUD

The 'Ad and the Thamud were the principal groups of ancient and extinct (*ba'id*) peoples, to which the inhabitants of Arabia have traditionally attributed their ancestry and traced their genealogies. They appear to have flourished between the fourth century BC and the middle of the seventh century AD. Thamudic rock inscriptions have been found in central Arabia. Both these groups are mentioned several times in the Qur'an, for example, Q.7:65–72, 73–9; Q.11:61–8, Q.25:38. The Qur'anic references point out the passing nature of worldly power and the fate of the Thamud who, warned by the Prophet Salih to worship Allah, were destroyed because they failed to do so. The cuneiform records of the Assyrian king, Sargon II (d. 705 BC), mention the Thamud, who are said to be the cultural heirs of the 'Ad. The civilisation of the 'Ad is said to have developed in Hadramawt in the southern part of the Arabian Peninsula.

References

Hitti (1973: 30–86).

EDWARD D. A. HULMES

ADAB

The word *adab* suggests urbanity, cultured behaviour, and a refinement of taste. The phrase *adab al-islam* refers to the rules of conduct, good manners, decency, morals, and decorum, to be acknowledged, commended, and observed

by Muslims. Such norms of behaviour are derived from principles outlined in the Qur'an, sanctioned by the example set by the Prophet Muhammad and recorded in the *sunna*, and tested by experience in Islamic society.

References

Bouhdiba (1985), al-Khaysi (1996), Omran (1992).

EDWARD D. A. HULMES

ADAM

According to Islamic teaching Adam was made from clay by Allah, he was the first man and point of origin of Arab genealogies. Allah taught Adam, recognised as a prophet, the names of things (Q.2:28–31). He lived in Eden with Eve/ Hawwa, created from Adam's rib but, beguiled by Iblis, he ate the fruit forbidden by Allah, a sin of giving in to temptation, as for Christians, the point of origin of sin. Adam is believed to have built the structure which the Ka'ba of Ibrahim and Isma'il later rebuilt over the foundations.

References

Rahman (1976: 14).

See also: **Iblis; Isma'il, Son of Ibrahim; Heaven; sin**

ANDREW J. NEWMAN

ADEN ('ADAN)

A port on the Red Sea in southern Yemen and the economic capital of the Republic of Yemen. It is a busy fuelling station for ships on passage through the Suez Canal with a large oil refining facility in Little Aden.

The town was originally an ancient trading centre under Egyptian control, then a Roman colony in 24 BC that was conquered both by the Ethiopians and the Persians. It fell to the invading Arabs in the seventh century and became associated with north Yemen. The whole country came under a number of Muslim dynasties including the Ayyubids (thirteenth century), Rasulids (fifteenth century), and Tahirids (sixteenth century). Despite repeated attacks by the Zaydi imams of Yemen, Aden and the surrounding areas were never fully integrated into the north.

The discovery of the sea route to India and the rise of Ottoman power (Ottoman occupation 1538) marked the beginning of a decline in the trade of Aden. On the very fringes of the Ottoman Empire, Aden was occupied by the British Empire in 1839 as a strategic asset. It was administered from India and grew in importance after the opening of the Suez Canal in 1868. It became a crown colony in 1937 and developed as an important military base particularly during the Second World War.

After the war Britain planned to retain Aden as an important base in the Middle East. However, nationalist resentment against the British grew encouraged by Nasser's Egypt. After a prolonged and bloody struggle, the British finally withdrew and Aden gained independence in 1967 as the capital of the Marxist state of the People's Democratic Republic of South Yemen. It did not prosper under communism and in 1970 merged with the Yemen Arab Republic to become part of the Republic of Yemen.

Amongst the mosques of Aden the most celebrated is that of Abu Bakr al-'Aydarus, the patron of the town.

References

Burrowes (1995).

DEREK HOPWOOD

'ADL

'Justice, just-ness'. One of the five key doctrines of the Mu'tazilites, that given the Justness of Allah, man possessed the free will to choose between good and evil actions.

References

Watt (1973: 231–48).

See also: **free will and predestination**

ANDREW J. NEWMAN

ADULTERY AND FORNICATION

Zina' is a word that means both adultery and fornication, sexual intercourse of persons not in a legal state of matrimony or concubinage. *Zina'* is defined as the sexual act outside of marriage and takes place between a man and a woman, whereby normal penetration of the woman occurs with the mutual consent of the parties. The text specifies that *zina'* constitutes full penetrative sex and not other modes of physical contact. However, homosexuality within either gender is considered as *zina'*, on the basis of a *hadith* that states homosexual practice to be equal to adultery. The philosophy that seems to lie behind the prohibition of extra marital sexual intercourse is to protect against the conceiving of illegitimate children, who would doubtless come to face future hardships. Islam considers the welfare of children to be of paramount importance, thus stable cohesion of the family unit is prescribed.

The punishment for proven fornication between unmarried couples would be 'lashing' and for adultery (between consenting married couples) it would be death by 'stoning'.

The severity of the punishment reflects the firm Islamic attitude towards sexual morality within society. However, the punishment for *zina'* require the fulfilment of the most stringent conditions before it can be implemented. There must be four male witnesses who are willing to testify that they have seen the couple in the act of fornication and that the genitals of the accused have been visible to them. The witnesses must be mukallaf (of the accepted age of maturity) and of an accepted responsible status. They must also be primary witnesses and not merely passing on the information from another source. All four witnesses must agree on the time and place of the alleged fornication and statements must be made at one time, separate testimonies not being valid. A variety of issues, such as the impotency of either party, must be investigated to ensure that the fornication was feasible or likely in the first place. Thus the fulfilling of these rigorous conditions for *zina'* appear to have been put in place as deterrents and are aimed more at couples who have sexual relations in public.

References

al-Zuhayli (1985: 23–49).

See also: **divorce**

MAWIL IZZI DIEN

AL-AFGHANI, JAMAL AL-DIN (1839–97)

The details of al-Afghani's early life are rather opaque in that although he claimed to have been born in Afghanistan (hence his title, al-Afghani) he was almost certainly born in Iran, and thus came from a Shi'i background. He first appears on the public stage in Afghanistan, however, as an adviser to the King, whom he sought to warn against British expansionist ambitions. He was expelled, however, in 1868, and over the next

few years he spent time in Istanbul, Cairo, India, Paris, Iran, Russia, Iran once again, and then finally Istanbul, where he died. In each of these places he caused controversy for either his political or his religious views (or both), and this was the reason for his often having to move from one place to another. In politics he sought to arouse both rulers and people in the Muslim world to the dangers of European, and especially British, expansion, and to call the Muslim world to unite under the banner of Islam in order to resist this process. This unity, he suggested, this 'pan-Islam', should not only transcend existing political boundaries but also include both Sunni and Shi'i Muslims. With respect to his religious views al-Afghani called for a return to the two earliest sources of religious guidance, the Qur'an and the *hadith*, and the proper practice of Islam on this basis, he suggested, would bring about the revival of both the faith of Islam and the political fortunes of its adherents. Islam was also, in his view, a supremely modern and rational religion, and in sharp contrast to Sayyid Ahmad Khan, against whom he wrote strongly while he was in India, it did not need to be reformulated in order to make it so; it was only necessary to interpret the two earliest sources properly.

References

Badawi (1978: Chapter 1), Keddie (1972, 1983), Kedourie (1966).

HUGH GODDARD

AFLAQ, MICHEL (1910–89)

Arab political thinker. Aflaq was born in Damascus into an Orthodox Christian family. He spent his early years in the city at a time when ideas of Arab nationalism were taking hold at the end of the Ottoman Empire. He lived through Faysal's

Arab kingdom in Syria and then saw the imposition of the French mandate. In the 1930s he was a student in Paris together with Salah al-Din Bitar (a fellow activist) and returned to teach in secondary schools for ten years until he resigned in 1942 to take up full-time political activity. He began to expound his vision of Arab nationalism to small audiences in Syria. Gradually a political movement developed that became a party which 'Aflaq called *Hizb al-Ba'th al-'Arabi* (the party of the Arab awakening). It was officially founded in 1947 with a constitution and executive committee. It propagated pan-Arab nationalism with the motto 'One Arab nation with an eternal mission'. It excluded all national attachments to smaller units, local or religious, and included all Arab countries on the same footing. It laid emphasis on the role of Islam in Arab nationalism and on the need for social revolution. 'Aflaq was secretary general and he edited its newspaper *al-Ba'th*. He was an inspirational leader and a good teacher though not fitted for the rough and tumble of Arab politics. He only held office once, briefly as Minister of Education in Syria in 1949.

Ba'thism was very popular amongst young nationalist Arabs in the 1950s and 1960s and was a rival to Nasserism. It was hijacked by the military in Syria and 'Aflaq resigned in 1965 and went into exile in Iraq in 1966. There he was caught up in the rivalry between the two Ba'th parties of Syria and Iraq. He became Secretary General in Baghdad, ironically of a split party devoted to Arab unity. He stayed until his death in 1989. He was one of the most influential theorists of Arab nationalism.

References

Devlin (1976), Hopwood (1989: 85–9).

DEREK HOPWOOD

AGENCY OF GOD, THE

The question of the agency of God gained importance within the discussion on Qadar, predestination and free will. It was discussed among the early theologians, known as *al-Mutakallimun,* and also raised among the Arab philosophers in their discussions on causality. The questions examined here were: what is the role of God in the world and how decisive is His control over all events and human behaviour? Wolfson mentions that John of Damascus, the late seventh-century Christian theologian, explained that the question between the Christians and Muslims on the issue of causality is that Christians believe that after God created the world, a process of sequential events took place through intermediate causes, while Muslims believe that each event is created directly by God. This early Islamic belief was, no doubt, influenced by many verses in the Qur'an such as: 'it is God who ... sendeth down rain from the skies and with it bringeth out fruits wherewith to feed you: it is He who hath made the ships subject to you, that they may sail through the sea by His command' (Q.14:32 and similarly Q.36:82, Q.35:38, Q.80:25–32, etc.) This belief was also supported by the Umayyad rulers in order to strengthen their control. Later, two main concepts were adopted among the two main theological schools, the Ash'arite and Mu'tazilite: the Ash'arites believed that God determines all events through His eternal knowledge and will. In addition, human beings cannot act by their own power but acquire the power to act through will, *isti'a'a*, which God creates in them at the time of acting. This concept is known as *kasb*, through which the Ash'arites attempt to attribute some kind of freedom of action to humans but only according to God's will and knowledge. In contrast, the Mu'tazilites consider that actions and events produce a series of events which function as causes. This concept is known as the concept of *tawlid*. Thus, the agency of God here functions through intermediate series of causes. In addition, God's justice, in their view, requires the bestowal of free will to all humans in order to have a just judgment on the last day.

The Muslim philosophers, for their part, followed Aristotle in his concept of necessary causes. They discussed this concept in the branch of philosophy which they called cosmology. Here they studied the series of causes which leads to the formation of all events and phenomena. Many Arab philosophers, e.g., Ibn Sina and al-Farabi, confirmed that God is the first and efficient cause but not the direct cause of each event. God, they think, acts through the intermediate intellects (sometimes also called angels) who, through the power they receive from God, are able to carry on the process of evolution. The questions that theologians asked of the philosophers were: are these series of causes connected through God's power and His divine will or through natural necessity? Is there a possibility that events might be reversed? Thus the question of the agency of God seems to have different importance among the different Islamic schools.

References

Wolfson (1976: 518–93).

See also: **alienation**

MAHA EL-KAISY FRIEMUTH

AGHA KHAN

The Agha Khan is the leader of the Nizari branch of the Isma'ili Shi'ites. The split between the Nizaris and the Musta'lis can be traced to the dispute over the succession to the Fatimid caliph and Imam al-Mustansir (r. AD 1036–94). Generally Isma'ilis within the Fatimid empire (primarily Egypt) adhered to the Caliph al-Musta'li, those outside adhered to al-Musta'li's older brother Nizar. These Nizari Isma'ilis established castles from which they conducted rebel actions against both the 'Abbasids and the Fatimids. Along with the 'Abbasids, their power base was wiped out by the Mongol invasions in the mid-thirteenth century, and the Nizari Isma'ilis survived as religious minorities in various parts of the Muslim world. They were particularly numerous in Iran, and the Nizari imam was, for much of the later period, based in Mahallat in central Iran. In the nineteenth century, the imam Hasan 'Ali Shah was given the title of Agha Khan (Prince) by Fath 'Ali Shah Qajar (r. 1797–1834), the Shah of Iran. Hasan 'Ali, the first Agha Khan, had developed a close relationship with Fath 'Ali Shah, in part exploiting the indebtedness Fath 'Ali Shah may have felt following the murder of Hasan 'Ali's father in 1817. The first Agha Khan probably recognised that Isma'ilis needed some sort of royal protection as they were a minority in a Twelver Shi'ite state. His incorporation into the Qajar state was enhanced even further by his marriage to one of Fath 'Ali Shah's numerous daughters. His close relationship with the Qajar monarchy did not, however, outlast the reign of Fath 'Ali Shah. Soon into the reign of Muhammad Shah Qajar (r. 1834–48), attempts were made by the court to depose him from the governorship of Kerman. In 1838, he rebelled against Qajar rule. The rebellion led to a fourteen-month siege of the walled town of Bam to which Hasan 'Ali had retreated. He was eventually captured and imprisoned. He was released on the condition he retired from military endeavours, however, once again Hasan 'Ali set about building up a military force, and in 1840 he began to lead rebellions against Qajar power. He was decisively defeated in 1842 in Kerman, and, with many of his followers, left Iran, going first to Afghanistan in 1843, and then to India. At first he had wished to return to Iran, but this became clearly impossible, and Hasan 'Ali settled on Bombay as the seat of the Agha Khan. From there, he commanded the spiritual allegiance of the Nizari Isma'ilis. The seat of the Nizari imam was moved to Paris in the 1950s by the current Agha Khan.

Hasan 'Ali died in 1881 and was succeeded for a short time by his son 'Ali Shah (d. 1885), then by his grandson, Sultan Muhammad Shah (d. 1957, who gained sufficient international prominence to be president of the League of Nations in 1937), and then by Sultan Muhammad Shah's grandson, the current imam, Karim Khan. Agha Khan Karim Khan is then the fourth imam to hold the title Agha Khan, though he is considered by Nizaris to be the forty-ninth imam after imam 'Ali, the Prophet's cousin and son-in-law.

The nature of the Agha Khan's authority has certainly changed as the Nizaris have moved into modernity. Isma'ili theories of the imamate normally attribute sinlessness ('isma) and infallibility to their imam. The Isma'ili conception of imam was also embellished during the Fatimid period with the incorporation of Neoplatonic ideas into Isma'ilism and the development of complex Isma'ili cosmologies. The current Agha Khan clearly wishes his rulings to be considered authoritative for his followers, but not to the exclusion of other perspectives from other Muslim traditions or from modern Western thought. His extensive resources have enabled Isma'ilism to 'modernise' with education and research programmes which are respected in Western acade-

mia, and development programmes which have improved the quality of life of the poorest communities of the world. Doctrinally, the Nizari Isma'ilis are still in conflict with the 'traditional' Sunnis (and, to a lesser extent, the Twelver Shi'ites), the reverence displayed towards the Agha Khan is just one element of the dogmatic conflict between the Nizaris and other Muslim groups. With respect to other Isma'ili traditions (the Da'udi and Sulaymanis, for example), the current Agha Khan has attempted to pursue a policy of Isma'ili 'ecumenism', though this has not solved the doctrinal differences between the different Isma'ili groups and has not yet resulted in the Agha Khan being recognised as a spokesman for all Isma'ilis, let alone all Muslims.

References

Algar (1969), Daftary (1990: 435–548), Dumasia (1903).

ROBERT GLEAVE

AGHLABIDS (AD 800–909)

These were a line of Arab governors of Ifriqiya (modern Tunisia) who, from their great distance from Baghdad, enjoyed de-facto autonomy from the 'Abbasids whilst continuing to acknowledge them as overlords. Under their rule, the conquest of Sicily and Malta was undertaken, with both islands to be held for some two centuries until the Norman reconquest, whilst Kairouan in central Tunisia was built up as the spiritual capital of eastern Maghribi Sunni traditions and of the Maliki law school throughout North Africa and Spain.

References

Bosworth (1996: No. 12), Gibb and Bosworth (1960–2003), Talbi (1966).

C. E. BOSWORTH

AGRICULTURE (*AL-FILAHA, AL-ZIRA'A*)

The management of the various branches of agriculture and horticulture owes much to the early researches conducted by Muslims as they developed (for example) botanical studies of flora and fauna, irrigation experiments in hydrology, and the observation of tides, floods, seasons and weather conditions. After the expansion of Islam from Arabia in the seventh century AD, and on the basis of their experience of primitive methods gained in the ancient Near and Middle East, Muslims began to work on the taxonomy, the naming of species in Arabic, and the sexual differences of crops, plants, herbs and simples. Work was done on the cultivation of varieties of grain, citrus fruits and vegetables such as the aubergine. In medieval Spain, this work continued on rice, cotton, and sugar ('the sweet cane from a far country'). The development of newer and more sophisticated irrigation systems became a priority. A classic work on the subject of agriculture, with the title *Kitab al-Filaha* (*Book of Agriculture*), was written by Abu- Zakariya' Yahya ibn Muhammad ibn al-'Awwam in twelfth-century AD Seville. The ancient traditional methods of subsistence farming are still practised in many parts of the Near and Middle East alongside new high technology methods, which are revolutionising the development of agriculture throughout the modern world.

References

Lord (1979), Schacht and Bosworth (1979: 210–18).

See also: **astronomy (*'ilm al-falak, 'ilm al-nujum*); gardens, Islamic; irrigation (*al-siyaqa*); Nile, the river**

EDWARD D. A. HULMES

AHKAM AL-ARADI (LAND LAW)

This Arabic term generally represents a group of Islamic codes pertaining to the regulation of land, whether that acquired by Muslims through war or that already inhabited by them, such as Mecca and Medina. The first classification, conquered land, is categorised into three types: land taken by force, by truce and by acquisition resulting from its having been abandoned by the original owners. The land taken by force is considered to be Muslim public property, thus, it has become subject to Islamic law and must be distributed accordingly as the State sees fit. Usage of land acquired through truce (*sulh*) is controlled by the treaty of the truce between the Muslim army and the previous owners. This can be according to any arrangement agreed upon by the two parties, such as remaining under the control of the original owners who can then pay any financial dues to the Muslim treasury. However the land taken over as a result of the abandonment of its owners (*fay'*) would become the sole property of the Muslim treasury and it could be allocated to individuals for management. They are then responsible for its maintenance and the payment of rent to the treasury. Land that is already inhabited by a Muslim population falls under Islamic law and has existing rules to regulate the individually owned sections (*mamluk*) and those that are classified as public trust (*mubah*). No one has the right to do anything to the former without written consent from the owner, unless the state perceives otherwise. Islam recognises dead land (*al-ard al-mawat*) that is situated away from habitation and not owned by any individual. This kind of wasteland may be developed for either agricultural or construction purposes if the ruler sees fit. Permission is generally granted for any reasonable development so long as there is no good reason for refusal.

References

Izzi Dien (2000: 37–45), al-Zuhayli (1985: 531–42, 545).

MAWIL IZZI DIEN

AL-AHKAM AL-SULTANIYYA

This book is among the earliest theoretical accounts of the Islamic state, and maybe the single most influential. It is the best-known work of the political theorist and man of public affairs Abu 'l-Hasan 'Ali b. Muhammad al-Mawardi (974–1058 CE). Its full title, *Al-Ahkam al-Sultaniyya wa'l-Wilayat al-Diniyya*, can be translated as 'The Ordinances of Government and the Institutions of Faith'.

Concerning the circumstances in which he composed the work, al-Mawardi says in his short preface that he has written 'in compliance with the wishes of one to whom obedience is incumbent on me'. This leaves little doubt that he wrote at the request of the Caliph himself, which is not altogether surprising as he was a close companion and diplomatic representative of both al-Qadir (991–1031) and al-Qa'im (1031–1074). It has been suggested that the *Ahkam al-Sultaniyya* was a theoretical justification of the state or a contribution to current debates; a practical defence of the Sunni caliphate against the Shi'i counter claims of the Buyids, who increasingly sought recognition that matched their power, and of the Fatimids; and an attempt to legitimise current administrative practices by inserting them into the *shari'a*. It is difficult to ignore the fact that throughout the work al-Mawardi appears to be conferring divine validation upon a structure that has been debilitated by internal and external forces, and forcing himself to recognise the pragmatic realities around him. So there is at least an element of rationalisation of the status quo in this exemplification of the perfect Islamic state.

Following the brief and straightforward preface, the *Ahkam al-Sultaniyya* consists of twenty chapters, *abwab*, beginning with the imamate, chief ministers, governors and war leaders, continuing with legal officials, prayer leaders and organisers of the annual pilgrimage and alms tax, and concluding with the rules governing chancery, crimes and market trading. It brings into hierarchical relationship the institutions of the state, both in theory and in practice, and shows how they are interdependent and legitimised by scripture and the precedent of the first Muslim community.

The apex of the whole state structure and point from which it issues is the caliph or, as al-Mawardi calls him, the imam. And the first chapter is the most important in the book, because 'The Imamate is intended as the vicarate of the prophethood, *khilafat al-nubuwwa*, in upholding the faith and managing the affairs of the world'. The primary duty of the imam is to guard the faith and defend it against heretics, so that it should 'remain pristine and the nation free from error'. In addition, al-Mawardi identifies nine other duties, culminating in the imam's personal responsibility to manage public policy rather than delegate this to others 'while he is preoccupied with worship or pleasure'.

He carries out his duties through four categories of deputies: those appointed to general jurisdiction without specification, the ministers; those appointed to jurisdiction in specific domains, such as governors of provinces and towns; those appointed to specific jurisdiction but over unlimited territory, such as the chief judge and the commander-in-chief of the army; and those appointed to specific jurisdiction in particular territory, such as local judges or commanders of particular garrisons. These actually execute the power delegated by the imam, and so the remaining nineteen chapters of the *Ahkam al-Sultaniyya* detail their responsibilities and duties.

These chapters set out the same ideal requirements for each office-holder as the first chapter on the imamate, establishing them on Qur'anic and prophetic bases and explaining how each official should execute his responsibilities within the overall hierarchy. But they are far from mere theory, and al-Mawardi repeatedly, and not without some wit, shows his seasoned grasp of realpolitik. This is exemplified eloquently in Chapter 3, on the Appointment of Provincial Governors, in his depiction of the position of those who usurp the position of governor. The caliph, he says, gives them a decree of appointment, so that they become autonomous controllers of political power while he transforms their lawlessness into legality, upholding the sacred law while surrendering the ideal. He somewhat wryly observes, 'decisions that would normally be unacceptable in regular appointment based on choice are permissible under usurpation and necessity, owing to the difference between ability and incapacity'.

This quality of realism balances the theoretical presentation of the structures of state throughout the work. And al-Mawardi knows when not to attempt a final judgement where this is impossible, whether on the balance of actual power between the caliph and his vizier – if both make appointments to the same office 'we should find out whose appointment was made earlier' – or on the blood money to be exacted for a Jew or Christian – Abu Hanifa said the same as for a Muslim, Malik said half, and al-Shafi'i said a third. Thus the *Ahkam al-Sulta-*

niyya is as valuable for its repertory of information and circumspect pragmatism as for its vision of the divinely ordained state.

The value of the work was recognised within years of its appearance, when the Hanbali Abu Ya'la Ibn al-Farra' (d. 1066) copied it almost *verbatim* in his own *Ahkam al-Sultaniyya* with some additions from his own school. It was acknowledged as an authoritative source by a succession of political writers, among them Ibn Khaldun, and has continued to be employed by writers on political thought to the present day.

The *Ahkam al-Sultaniyya* has been published in many editions. It has been translated into French by Fagnan (1915) and into English by Wahba (1996).

DAVID THOMAS

AHL AL-DHIMMA

See: **dhimmis**

AHL AL-HADITH

'People of Tradition'. The term is generally used to refer to those who saw themselves as upholding the authority of the *sunna* of Muhammad as based upon the *hadith* material as opposed to those who undertook theological speculation among the Ash'aris and the Mu'tazila. Such tendencies, often associated with the Hanbali school of law, are characterised as conservative and anti-intellectual.

In contemporary times, a group in India has come to be known as the *Ahl-i hadith* (it appears to have earlier been called 'Wahhabi' especially by their opponents). It holds to need to re-evaluate the basis of law through a re-examination of the *hadith* material. Its position is characterised as being opposed to the established legal schools, arguing that the Islamic attitude of reliance upon the *sunna* has been replaced by reliance on legal scholars. It is associated with people such as the theologian Sayyid Nadhir Husayn of Delhi (d. 1902).

References

Gibb and Bosworth (1960–2003: I, 259).

ANDREW RIPPIN

AHL AL-JAMA'A

The phrase *ahl al-jama'a* ('people of the community') is often used in Muslim texts as an abbreviation of *ahl al-sunna wa'l-jama'a* ('the people of the *sunna* and congregation'), the formal name of the Sunni Muslims. The abbreviation *ahl al-sunna* is used more frequently. The term is sometimes used as a synonym for *umma* and both refer to the 'community of believers' (*jama'at al-mu'minin*). The meaning of the term *jama'a* connotes a gathering together, and the phrase *ahl al-jama'a* implies a community, bound together by a common, unified belief. This 'bound' community is, of course, the ideal picture of the Muslims found in theological texts. *Ahl al-jama'a* can also refer to the people who congregate for daily prayer (*salat al-jama'a*, to be distinguished from *salat al-jum'a* which refers specifically to the Friday noon prayer). The jurists (*fuqaha'*) make a distinction between the obligatory nature of the daily prayers, and the recommended (*mandub*) nature of gathering in congregation for these prayers. Hence, for most Muslims, it is preferable that one gathers with others for the daily prayers, but not essential for the fulfilment of the duty of prayer.

References

Calder (2000: 66–86), Melchert (1997).

ROBERT GLEAVE

AHL AL-KITAB

'The people of the Book', i.e., Jews and Christians who had received the revelation before Islam and who believe in God and the final judgement. Zoroastrians are sometimes included (Q.22:17) as are some other, unspecified groups which also had received the revelation prior to Islam (Q.10:47, Q.40:78). These are not to be converted by force (Q.2:256) and are entitled to protection in Islam but are to pay a head tax (Q.9:29) and, later, the *kharaj*, a land tax. Also called *ahl al-dhimma*, or *dhimmis*.

References

Rahman (1979: 26–8).

See also: **compulsion, religious**

ANDREW J. NEWMAN

AHL AL-RA'Y

'The people of opinion'. In contrast to *ahl al-hadith*, who strictly adhered to the tradition of the Prophet and would limit their methodology of legislative deduction to the text and concepts derived directly from it. The scholars of opinion did not hesitate to utilise individual opinion in the deducing of legislation and perceived this practice as valid if there was no available injunction in the text. The justification for this methodology lay in their notion that Islamic law can be rationalised and that the human mind is capable of understanding the reasoning and objectives behind the achievement of human interest. They maintained that some of the Prophet's Companions including 'Umar and 'Ali, and 'Abdallah b. Mu'adh, would apply such a method by examining the reasons behind the injunctions and then applying them to other similar cases. This school of opinion flourished in Kufa, whilst the school of text flourished in

Medina, the latter reflecting its proximity to the nucleus of Islamic law. The differing nature of each town and the emphases placed by the various scholars who resided there, influenced the assimilation of these contrasting schools of thought.

References

Izzi Dien (2004: 11, 25–7), Khallaf (1986), Zaydan (1991: 115).

MAWIL IZZI DIEN

AHL AL-SUNNA

More fully *ahl al-sunna wa'l-jama'a*, 'the people of the *sunna* and community', usually called Sunnis (and as distinguished from the *ahl al-bayt* or the Shi'a). The group is nominally defined as those who follow the four accepted schools of law and align themselves with al-Ash'ari or al-Maturidi in theology. The name appears to have evolved both in opposition to other groupings in the formative period of Islam and also as a way of designating the one correct group which, according to a report stemming from Muhammad, would survive after the community split into seventy-three sects.

References

Gibb and Bosworth (1960–2003: II, 411–12).

ANDREW RIPPIN

AHMAD B. HANBAL, 'THE IMAM OF BAGHDAD', AD 780–855

Distinguished theologian, jurist and one of the most influential scholars on the formation of Islamic law. He was born in Baghdad and studied with many well-known scholars, such as Abu Yusuf (d. AD 798), and *Al-Shafi'i* student, Abd

al-Rahman b. Mahdi (AD 752–813/14). Ibn Hanbal would not teach without being asked specific questions which he would use as a starting point for his lectures. He would refer only to authentic references to compile his lecture. His son 'Abdallah states that one of the characteristic feature of his lessons is that Ibn Hanbal would not rely on memory only and would often use written materials to avoid possible error of narration. He was the eponym of the fourth school of Islamic law and was celebrated as a top scholar of his time because of his deep and independent knowledge of the *sunna*. His most renowned work is *Al-Musnad*, a compilation of more than 40,000 *hadith*, which were collated from his lectures by his own son Abdallah. Ibn Hanbal interpretation of Islamic law, relies heavily on the Qur'an and *sunna*. From Ibn Hanbal's perspective, these texts overrule the individual views of any scholar, no matter how knowledgeable. A correct *hadith* could be overturned neither by the actions of the people of Medina, nor by analogy, nor by the statements of the Prophet's Companions nor even by consensus. Subsequent to consultation of the text, Ibn Hanbal tended to resort to the legal opinion of the Prophet's Companions, on the proviso that none had disagreed with them. On occasions where the Companions had disputed certain issues, then he would refer to the texts and choose according to the preferred injunction that was closest to the matter in hand. It is interesting to note that he would refer to a weak Hadith in preference to analogy regarding such a narration as neither false nor emanating from an unreliable narrator, but rather giving this type of *hadith* a specific class of its own. Analogy as a source of reference was always a last resort for Ibn Hanbal, and utilised only when all other channels of enquiry had been exhausted.

At times Ibn Hanbal was reluctant even to offer his opinion, if he felt that the available evidence was conflicting. The reason for his unfaltering recognition of the views of the Companions of the Prophet lay in his assertion that they of all people had practised the injunctions of the text in a more precise manner than other generations. In addition to this, just prior to his death, the Prophet himself had recommended referral to their views and practices as well as to his own. Ibn Hanbal's attitude to tradition and strict adherence to the text was inextricably linked to his doctrine of ethics, the latter maintaining that the objective of all action is the serving of God. To Ibn Hanbal the concept of faith was inherent in words, deeds, intention and attachment to the *sunna*.

He was constantly consulted on questions, *masa'il*, of all sorts relating to dogma, ethics or law. Although he may not have prohibited the writing down of his opinions as formally as certain traditions assert, it is certain that he warned his questioners against the danger of codifying his thought, which might then replace the principles of conduct traced by the Qur'an and the *sunna*, he himself, in contrast to *Al-Shafi'i*, never sought to present it systematically as a body of doctrine. The fundamental purpose of his teaching is to be seen as a reaction against the codification of the law.

References

Coulson (1964: 71), al Diqr (1999: 43, 46, 58), Izzi Dien (2004: 22–6).

MAWIL IZZI DIEN

AHMADIS (AL-AHMADIYYA)

A breakaway-Islamic sect affiliated with its founder Mirza Ghulam Ahmad (1835–89) of Qadiyan and who are consequently commonly known as Qadiyanis (al-Qadiyaniyya) or Mirza'is. Born in the small town of Qadiyan in the Punjab in the early 1850s, Mirza Ghulam Ahmad began writing down his thoughts at around the age of forty, shortly after which he claimed that he was receiving revelations and hence claimed prophethood. Further to this he also claimed that he was not only a prophet (*nabi*) but also that he was the messiah (*al-masih*) and the promised one (*al-mahdi*). The sect has advanced its views through various forms of literature, especially commentaries of the Qur'an, to the extent that they have even established a satellite channel in the UK to promote their thought. As for the beliefs proposed by Mirza Ghulam Ahmad, regarding Divine attributes, he states that Allah, fasts, prays, sleeps, wakes up, writes, makes mistakes and has sexual intercourse. In addition to his own claim to prophethood, he also claimed that Jesus escaped death on the cross only to travel to Kashmir, where he died and was buried in Srinagar. Regarding the practical aspects of Islamic law, he invalidated the concept of *jihad* and, in addition, also permitted the drinking of alcohol and the taking of drugs. Ahmadis do not consider anyone a believer – including 'Muslims' – until they accept the aforementioned sectarian views. It should also be noted that the Ahmadis themselves are split regarding the nature of Mirza Ghulam Ahmad: a section of his adherents believe him to be a prophet and are referred to as 'Qadiyanis', whereas another group believe him to be no more than a reformer (*mujaddid*) and are generally termed 'Lahoris'.

References

Al-Johani (1999: 416–20), Netton (1997: 23–4), Zahir (n.d.).

See also: **Shi'ism; Sunnism**

GAVIN PICKEN

AHMED I (r. 1603–17)

Ottoman Sultan, son of Mehmed III. Ahmed suceeded at a time of war with Austria, a war with Iran and rebellions in Anatolia. On the eastern front between 1603 and 1606 the Ottomans lost all the territory gained from Iran between 1578 and 1590. The war with Austria ended in stalemate with the treaty of Zsitvatorok in 1606. Ahmed's attempt to lead a campaign against the rebels in 1605 was a fiasco. By 1609, the Grand Vizier Kuyucu Murad Pasha had defeated the rebels in Anatolia, and crushed the attempt by Canbuladoglu of Aleppo to gain independence. In celebration of this success, Ahmed commissioned the mosque in Istanbul that bears his name.

References

Griswold (1983), Imber (2002: 71–7), Mantran (1989a: 228–33).

Colin Imber

AHMED II (r. 1691–5)

Ottoman Sultan, son of Ibrahim. In the war of the Holy League, the Austrians defeated and killed his Grand Vizier Koprulu Mustafa Pasha at Slankamen in 1691, and the Venetians occupied Chios. Peace proposals failed in the face of the Sultan's opposition.

References

Mantran (1989a: 248).

Colin Imber

AHMED III (r. 1703–30)

Ottoman Sultan, son of Mehmed IV. On his accession, Ahmed suppressed the rebellion which had forced Mustafa II's abdication. Mustafa's reforms had initiated a period of prosperity and a peace which lasted until 1709. From this year, the Grand Vizier Silahdar Ali Pasha sought to reverse the losses of the wars between 1683 and 1699. In 1709, he opened hostilities with Russia. The treaty of Edirne of 1713 forced Peter the Great to restore most of his gains of 1699. In 1714–15, the Ottomans reconquered the territories that Venice had won. However, war with Austria from 1716 led to the loss, by the treaty of Passarowitz in 1718, of Belgrade, northern Serbia, Temesvar and part of Wallachia. In the east, the collapse of the Safavid dynasty in 1723 allowed the Ottomans to occupy parts of western Iran and the Caucasus. After the treaty of Passarowitz, the Grand Vizier Damad Ibrahim Pasha maintained peace with the European powers.

Ahmed was an important patron of the arts, which flourished during his reign, also showing the first signs of European, especially French, influence. It was in part the extravagances of his court that provoked the rebellion of the Janissary Patrona Halil that forced the execution of Damad Ibrahim Pasha and the abdication of Ahmed.

References

Mantran (1989: 271–6), Quataert (2000: 74, 75, 85).

Colin Imber

AHWAL

A term used by the Sufis to denote their mystical experiences or 'unveilings'. Often translated as 'states', the *ahwal* (singular *hal*) were believed to be bestowed by God in contrast to the station (*maqam*, pl. *maqamat*) which were achieved on the basis of the individual's own effort. The *ahwal* are described as the intimate feelings experienced by the

Sufi that range from ecstatic joy and happiness to deep depression and fear.

References

Netton (1993).

LLOYD RIDGEON

'A'ISHA

'A'isha (*c.* AD 614–78), the daughter of Abu Bakr, was born in Mecca. The Prophet Muhammad's first wife, Khadija, died in AD 619, the 'Year of Sadness'. Until her death she had been his only wife. Her loss left him inconsolable. Muhammad was charmed by 'A'isha, then only a six-year-old child. He asked Abu Bakr for permission to marry her. Her father eventually agreed, but the child was already betrothed to another. After this arrangement was ended, she was free to marry Muhammad. The marriage was contracted after the payment of a dowry (*mahr*), a year or two before the *hijra*, the migration from Mecca to Medina in AD 621. The young girl took her toys with her to the house of her husband who, already over forty years her senior, is reported to have joined in her games. According to tradition, the marriage was not consummated until after the move from Mecca to Medina. The Prophet's affection for 'A'isha was clear. She was to become his favourite wife, but their relationship suffered after an incident in which Muhammad believed, wrongly in the event, that she had dallied with a young man on a journey back to Medina in AD 628 after Muhammad had gone on ahead without her, unaware that she was not with his company. One of the Prophet's closest associates, his son-in-law (married to Fatima) and cousin, 'Ali ibn abi Talib, advised him to divorce her, but after the incident was investigated she was exonerated. A passage in the Qur'an (Q.24:1–20), which

may have helped to resolve this case, considers what is to be done when a case of adultery is suspected and charged, what is to count as evidence, and how many are to be called as witnesses. The enmity that arose between 'A'isha and 'Ali as a result of his advice to Muhammad persisted. Still only eighteen years old when the Prophet died, she sought to influence the choice of his successor. Throughout the caliphates of 'Umar ibn al-Khattab (AD 634–44), and 'Uthman ibn 'Affan (AD 644–56), her dislike of 'Ali was undiminished, so that when he was elected as the fourth caliph in AD 656 she supported a rising intended to displace him. The attempt failed. From her detailed knowledge of Muhammad's words and actions, she was able to contribute over 2,000 contributions to what were ultimately to become the collections of *hadith*. As Muhammad's widow, she is said to have received an annual pension of 12,000 dirhams from the public treasury.

See also: **hadith; marriage; al-Rashidun ('the rightly guided Caliphs'); wives of the Prophet Muhammad**

EDWARD D. A. HULMES

AJAL

Appointed time, e.g., of one's time on earth, as such known only to God (Q.46:3).

ANDREW J. NEWMAN

AJNADAYN, BATTLE OF

After the death of the Prophet Muhammad in AD 632, Muslim forces under the leadership of Khalid ibn al-Walid, who had already proved himself to be a capable military commander under the Prophet's leadership, moved north into Syria. Having engaged in skirmishes with Christian forces in the neighbourhood

33

of Damascus, Khalid moved south into Palestine, where he inflicted a decisive defeat on them at Ajnadayn in July AD 634. The victory opened the rest of Palestine up to conquest. Jerusalem fell to the Arabs in AD 638.

EDWARD D. A. HULMES

AKBAR B. HUMAYUN (r. 1556–1605)

The greatest ruler of the Mughal dynasty in India and the creator of the most powerful state of Muslim India. To his original territory in the Ganges valley he added by conquest much of central India and the northern Deccan, Gujarat, Kashmir, Baluchistan, and Bengal. He was a great administrator as well as a soldier, and under him there evolved a hierarchy of civil and military officials, *mansabdars*, supported on land grants, the bedrock of the empire till the early eighteenth century. Though a convinced Muslim, Akbar realised the importance of securing the loyalty of the Hindu majority of his subjects. Like most of his line, he took Hindu wives, and he abolished the poll tax on non-believers. His interest in religion in general and his genuine belief in toleration led him to patronise debates between Muslim *'ulama'* and scholars from other faiths, and to initiate an eclectic 'divine faith', the *Din-i Ilahi*, with roots in certain strains of contemporary Sufism, including an illuminationist veneration of the sun and light as divine forces, and with certain other features resembling those of other faiths. It was only meant by Akbar for a small circle of almost wholly Muslim adepts, and did not survive his death, but it had a lasting significance in the strongly traditionalist reaction which it provoked in India, seen in the orthodox Naqshbandiyya Sufi order and in the Ahl-i Hadith movement.

References

Gibb and Bosworth (1960–2003), Richards (1993: 12–94), Rizvi (1975).

See also: **Jizya**

C. E. BOSWORTH

'ALAWIS (1631–)

The Shorfa of Morocco, who had long enjoyed an influential social position there, were able in the early sixteenth century to use their messianic leadership, with an ardour intensified by the Christian attacks on the coastlands, to establish a ruling dynasty, the Sa'dian Sharifs. In the next century, another line of Sharifs came to power as the 'Alawis or Filalis, with centres at Fez and Meknès. But they were always beset by internal revolts, and by Spanish and Portuguese, and then French also, pressures from without, culminating in the French Protectorate of 1912. The sultans nevertheless remained as heads of state, and when Morocco achieved full independence in 1956, they became and remain the present kings of Morocco.

References

Bosworth (1996: No. 21), Gibb and Bosworth (1960–2003), Terrasse (1949–50: II, 239–406).

See also: **Idrisids**

C. E. BOSWORTH

ALCHEMY (*AL-KIMIYA'*)

The ancient art and pseudo-science of alchemy was already a subject of independent inquiry from the fifth century BC in China and India, and the third century BC in Greece and Egypt (notably in Alexandria, where the notion of 'the philosopher's stone' may have originated). In the centuries that followed, the investigations of alchemists were motivated by the dream of transmuting base metals such as lead into silver or gold, of discovering the elixir of life, and of preparing a universal medical panacea. Gold was considered to be the perfect metal and the symbol of perfection. In pursuit of these aims alchemists sometimes resorted to deception, producing metal alloys which appeared to be what they were not. Alchemy began to degenerate into an esoteric craft debased by spurious mysticism, superstition and magic. It began to flourish once more among the Arabs in the twelfth and thirteenth centuries. By the twelfth century AD, translations of Arabic alchemical texts, many of them written in cryptic language, were being studied in Europe, notably in Prague. In medieval times scholars of the calibre of Albertus Magnus (c. AD 1200–80) showed an interest in them. Best known for his efforts in harmonising theology and Aristotelianism as the foundation of scholasticism, he appears in legend as a magician. The English philosopher Roger Bacon (c. AD 1214–92) and the Swiss physician, Paracelsus (1493–1541) also gave the subject careful attention. The latter believed that alchemy would eventually provide the answers needed to restore youth and to prolong human life. The study of alchemy declined in Europe with the coming of the Renaissance. The alchemists, who worked hard to protect their secrets, continued to benefit from the patronage of the wealthy, but they failed in their stated aims. Their experiments over the years, such as those designed to extract medicinal juices from plants, were acknowledged to have some scientific merit and value. Experimental apparatus included the *kerotakis*, used for sublimation and the alembic (*al-anbiq*) used for distillation. The modern science of chemistry may be said to owe something at least to the work of the alchemists.

References

Burland (1967), Mostyn and Hourani (1988: 267–9), Schacht and Bosworth (1979: 443–5).

See also: **astrology (*'ilm al-tanjim*); astronomy (*'ilm al-falak, 'ilm al-nujum*); magic and talismans.**

EDWARD D. A. HULMES

ALCOHOL (*KUHL*)

The Arabic word *al-kuhl*, from which the word 'alcohol' is derived, refers to a preparation of refined and pulverised antimony used cosmetically for darkening or colouring the eyelids. In English it is sometimes called *kohl*. In another sense, probably unused in the early Islamic period in Arabia, it came to be applied to intoxicating liquors and spirits that are manufactured by processes of fermentation, rectification, and distillation. As such these products fall under the Islamic proscription of intoxicating drink (Q.2:219, 5:93). Though wine (*khamr, nabidh*) is associated with life-enhancing and spiritually elevating properties in Paradise, it does not have similar associations in this world (Q.47:15). Here on earth, wine intoxicates, in the life to come it does not. In medieval times, physicians and surgeons mixed wine with herbs to prepare anaesthetics. Despite the proscription, however, alcohol is often available in Islamic societies, principally for non-Muslim residents and visitors. Penalties for the consumption of consciousness-changing substances vary from the relatively mild to the severe. This includes 'drugs of choice' but excludes drugs used for medicinal purposes. Therefore strict adherence to Islamic principles requires abstinence from the consumption of alcohol and drugs, which cloud the mind, weaken the body, and thus make an individual incapable of following 'the Straight Path' (*sirat al-mustaqim*) of Islam.

EDWARD D. A. HULMES

ALEPPO (HALAB)

Second city of Syria situated in the north of the country. It is one of the oldest continuously inhabited cities in the world and no other place that is still inhabited can boast a comparable history. The early city had relations with the Hittites and on their fall it owed its recovery to Alexander the Great. The Seleucids built on the site the city of Beroia following a regular plan, some of whose characteristics remain today. It was incorporated into Roman Syria in 64 BC and new markets were built. Christians settled early there. It became the greatest trading centre between Europe and the east and was a resting place for Arab caravan trains. The city fell to the Arabs in AD 636. The Great Mosque was built under Walid I and remained the chief place of worship until recent times. Aleppo flourished under numerous Muslim dynasties and under the Hamdanids became the capital of a state. In AD 962 it was pillaged by Nicephorus Phocas (later a Byzantine emperor). The city was then quarrelled over by many rival factions until the Crusaders besieged and damaged but did not occupy it in AD 1123. It was restored under the Zangids (AD 1183) who built many mosques, madrasas and restored the citadel, one of the most splendid works of military art in the Middle Ages. It was then sacked and occupied by the Mamluks, captured by the Mongol Hulagu (AD 1260) and by Tamerlane (1400). In the fifteenth and sixteenth centuries Aleppo became an important staging post on the caravan route between Europe and the East, especially for the silk trade with Venice. As an Ottoman *wilaya* (from 1514) it suffered from factional struggles yet developed commercially as European consuls and traders settled there. Mosques, *zawiyas*, *suqs* and *khans* were built. The Ottoman *khans* are among the best-preserved monuments of the contemporary city.

In the second half of the nineteenth century, a new town grew alongside the old. It developed as an agricultural trading centre and site of small industries after being incorporated into present-day Syria in 1918. The old and new towns exist side by side, with the former dominated by its citadel surrounded by a moat and enclosed by a medieval wall.

References

Fugelstad-Aumerier (1991–4).

DEREK HOPWOOD

ALEXANDER THE GREAT (356–323 BC)

King of Macedonia (336–323 BC) and great military adventurer. Alexander was bequeathed a powerful army by his assassinated father, Philip II of Macedonia (359–336 BC), and he went on to consolidate Greek civilisation. In 334 BC, he crossed into Asia and won a series of victories over the Achaemenid Persian Empire at Granicus (334 BC), Issus (333 BC) and Guagamela (331 BC). In 332 BC, he took control of Egypt and made Alexandria its principal seaport. Following the fall of the Persian Empire, Alexander went on to Afghanistan and India, but his army eventually refused to campaign further. Returning to Babylon, Alexander fell ill and died at the age of thirty-two. His glorious reputation endured in Europe, while he continued to be associated with infamy in much of Asia.

References

Bosworth (1998: 27–30), Keay (2000: 70–7).

SIMON W. MURDEN

ALEXANDRIA (AL-ISKANDARIYYA)

Second city of Egypt situated on the Mediterranean coast in the Nile delta, one of the few important seaports on the African coast. It was one of the greatest cities of the classical world, founded by Alexander the Great in 332 BC, with regular streets, temples, and other public buildings including the great library that contained the largest collection of books in the ancient world. It was best known, however, for the harbour with its large mole and the famous Pharos lighthouse, one of the seven wonders of the ancient world. Under the Egyptian Ptolemies Alexandria became a literary, scientific and commercial centre but one that gradually lost its importance after the foundation of Constantinople.

The Arabs besieged and captured the city in AD 646. The library that had been previously damaged by fire on several occasions was finally destroyed by them. The city declined in importance under the Muslims as Cairo grew in importance, particularly after the fall of the Fatimids. It continued as a trading centre between East and West and numerous foreign merchants resided there. Wealthy Muslim merchants endowed the city with mosques, schools and religious foundations.

Napoleon occupied the city in 1798 and therewith began a long period of European influence. The modern city developed as a thriving Levantine centre where Europeans lived alongside the Egyptians. Greek culture flourished again and well-known literary figures lived there, such as Cafavy, Lawrence Durrell and E. M. Forster. After the Egyptian revolution of 1952, the foreign population departed and Alexandria began to suffer from decline and overpopulation. It is still an attractive seaside resort where many Egyptians like to spend the summer. An interesting development was the opening in 2002 of a large purpose-built public library in homage to the original institution.

DEREK HOPWOOD

ALF LAYLA WA-LAYLA

No work written in Arabic has exerted more influence on the popular imagination the world over than the *Alf Layla wa-Layla* (*The Thousand and One Nights*). Many of its characters and stories are universally known, and have inspired entertainers, musicians and authors to recast them for audiences who have little idea of their origins or of the corpus from which they have emerged.

The history of *The Thousand and One Nights*, known also as *The Arabian Nights*, is long and complicated. In the Arab world its existence is attested in the ninth century AD by the earliest written fragment of its stories that has survived. And as early as the tenth century AD there are references to collections of stories that may have formed its core. Al-Mas'udi in the *Muruj al-Dhahab* refers to a book translated from Persian, the *Hazar Afsana*, 'which in Arabic means "thousand tales", for "tale" is in Persian *afsana*. The people call this book *Thousand Nights*. This is the story of the king and the vizier and his daughter and her servant-girl, who are called Shirazad and Dinazad'. Al-Nadim in the *Fihrist* mentions this same Persian book and gives similar details about the main characters, and also says that an earlier contemporary of his, Abu 'Abdallah b. 'Abdus al-Jahshiyari, had begun a collection of 1,000 stories from Arab, Persian, Greek and other sources, but died before completing it. These references, and especially the details that parallel elements in the frame story of *The Thousand and One Nights*, suggest it must have been known in some form in early 'Abbasid times. They also indicate that the stories themselves were gathered from a range of much earlier sources, rather than being composed by a single Arab storyteller.

The mention of a collection of tales entitled *The Thousand and One Nights* by the late Fatimid historian al-Qurti in the twelfth century AD, and versions of single or groups of tales from the fifteenth century AD and earlier parallel to those in the collection as it later became, are evidence that it was in circulation in some form at this time. And it is possible to discern the shape and character it may then have borne from the first extant manuscript of the *Nights*, which dates from the fourteenth century AD (Bibliothèque Nationale: 3609–11). Here, the story begins 'long ago' with the Sasanid King Shahriyar's discovery of his wife's infidelity and his decision to marry each night a virgin and have her killed the next morning. Eventually his vizier, unable to find any more virgins in the town, gives him his daughter Shaharazad, whose sister Dinarazad accompanies her to the palace, and on her instruction asks her each night to tell a story. They continue for 282 nights, not 1001, until finally Shahriyar declares his deep love for his wife and they live happily ever after. This is the framework in which all the tales are set, and its continuity and energy are generated by Shaharazad's ingenuity by which the King is so pleased that he preserves her life in return for more tales.

It has been suggested by D. Pinault that the motif presented here of warding off violence through telling of stories thematically links many of the tales in this early collection, and that tales of marital violence function as commentaries on the frame story. Thus, the whole is given unity as themes recur and are treated in varied ways, and irony and tension are imparted to the frame story as Shahriyar is imagined listening to implicit criticisms of himself and yet delaying his wife's execution in order to hear more.

The presence of these common themes in many of the tales suggests the guiding influence of one or more master storytellers, and also that tales which had previously circulated independently were subtly modified in detail and structure as they were chosen for inclusion. In fact, the survival of some tales in their original form makes possible a comparison of the *Nights* and independent versions.

This fourteenth-century AD collection, which has been shown by its editor M. Mahdi to be Syrian in origin, is an early representative of the core structure to which all subsequent collections can be related, because it can be shown that later collectors habitually followed its order as far as it went and then added whatever additional stories they were able to find. In this way the original core became the ancestor of the two main branches of the *Nights*, the Syrian and Egyptian. In the eighteenth century it was employed by scholars in Cairo to produce a greatly enlarged text that eventually covered the 1,001 nights of the work's title. In turn this text, which is known as the Zotenberg Egyptian Recension after the nineteenth-century scholar H. Zotenberg who identified it, became the basis of the main published editions of the *Nights*, and of many manuscripts of the work that found their way into European libraries.

So the development of *The Thousand and One Nights* into its modern form was slow and lengthy, from early cycles that may have been linked by a frame story (as suggested by al-Mas'udi and Ibn al-Nadim), to the fourteenth-century AD Syrian collection that closely represents the core structure on which later versions are built, and onwards to two main families of collections centred on Syria and Egypt, culminating in the Zotenberg Egyptian Recension. The more recent versions incorporated stories and cycles that were circulating independently, subordinating them to the original structure and dividing them into nightly units, though without the internal modification detectable in the early Syrian collection to link them thematically with one another and with the frame story.

The subsequent textual history of the *Nights* is largely of printed versions. The most important are the Egyptian State Printing Office edition printed at Bulaq in 1835 and frequently since, and the second Calcutta edition edited by W. H. MacNaughten in 1839–42. Both of these are editions of Zotenberg's Egyptian Recension, which forms the basis of the translations of the *Nights* that have made it familiar, if not always known in its exhilarating rawness, in the past two centuries. Among English translations, that of E. W. Lane, *The Arabian Nights' Entertainments*, 1839–41, comprises part of the Bulaq original, with much of its raciness toned down or removed, and that of Sir Richard Burton, *Book of the Thousand Nights and a Night*, 1885–8, which is indebted to an earlier translation of the Bulaq edition by J. Payne, is a complete translation of the Calcutta edition into an idiosyncratic style, together with copious notes that often reflect the translator's personal experience in the Islamic world. These were the main sources of imitations and retellings of the *Nights* stories by English-speaking authors. There have also been many translations into other languages, most notably A. Gallard's important French translation of the Syrian collection (the MS of which he owned) together with other stories he heard from a Syrian Christian, *Les Mille et Une Nuits*, 1704–17, which first introduced the stories to

European readers, and E. Littmann's German translation of the Calcutta edition, together with a number of stories from other MSS and editions, *Die Erzählungen aus den tausendundein Nächten*, 1921–8, which is regarded as the most reliable. The fact that some of these translations add material to the printed editions on which they are based serves to emphasise the amorphous form of the *Nights* corpus, and to underline the danger in attempting to identify any stable set of stories from which it is constituted.

But it is in the nature of the *Nights* not to be reducible to a single set of stories, since it has always been at least as much a body of oral literature as written. As such, it has varied in contents over time and place and according to the talent and memory of individual tellers, and each tale has been retold and gradually changed to suit occasions and audience expectations. Thus, the language frequently reflects that of the street rather than the literary essay, and the originals frequently contain the repetitions that characterise oral recitation. Further, the tales themselves are intended to kindle emotions that sober authors composing written narratives with an eye to the judgement of posterity might not dare: there is explicit sexual activity from the very opening, mixed moral motives attributed to supposed heroes, and scatological humour of the most deliciously embarrassing kind. This is colourful storytelling rather than high literature.

Collected as they are from a range of sources, Indian, Greek, Persian, Turkish, Arabic, and also ancient Babylonian, the *Nights* embrace a number of literary genres, including fairy tales, popular romances, legends, parables and humorous anecdotes. There are also many passages of poetry which, though added by redactors from separate sources, often perform functions integral to the narrative by echoing themes of the tales in which they appear or by moving the main action forward.

It is paradoxical that while figures such as Sindbad the Sailor, Aladdin and Shahrazad herself have become familiar throughout the world to children and their parents, they and the stories of their exploits were long shunned in polite Arab circles as the currency of market-place storytellers. They were first taken seriously in the twentieth century, when leading authors such as Taha Husayn and Najib Ma'fuz retold some of them and brought out their often latent moral elements and darker implications. The tales remain childhood romances for European audiences, many of whom would be shocked to discover the true adult characters of the figures they laugh at in pantomimes.

The fourteenth-century AD Syrian manuscript of the first-known collection of the *Nights* has been edited by Mahdi (1984), and translated by Haddawy (1990). As well as the editions and translations of the later collections mentioned previously, Dawood (1973) can be recommended as a selection of the main stories that evokes much of the atmosphere of the original.

References

Marzolph *et al.* (2004), Meisami and Starkey (1998).

DAVID THOMAS

ALGERIAN CIVIL WAR

The rebellion led by Islamic militants against the secular state after 1991. By the 1980s, the Front de Libération Nationale regime was discredited, and in many poorer neighbourhoods its appeal had been superseded by the Front Isla-mique du Salut (FIS). Reforms initiated by President Chadli Benjedid backfired, and when the FIS appeared close to winning parliamentary elections in December 1991, the army intervened. Benjedid resigned, further voting can-celled, and the FIS banned and its leaders imprisoned. Civil war ensued, with organisations like the Groupe Isla-mique Armé waging a ruthless terrorist campaign. The security forces respon-ded in kind, but neither side prevailed. In 1999, President Abdelaziz Bouteflika sought reconciliation, but the conflict dragged on.

References

Owen (2000: 160–2), Roy (1994: 75–88), Spencer (1996: 93–107).

SIMON W. MURDEN

ALHAMBRA

The Alhambra is the only fully pre-served palace which has survived from the medieval Islamic world whose beauty has generated many romantic legends which have tended to obscure its true history and significance as a serious work of architecture. In fact it is an outstanding example of a fortified royal city strategically located on a spur of the Sierra Nevada mountains overlooking Granada, the capital of the Nasrids, the last Muslim rulers of Spain from 1232 to 1492. The site had been occupied since the ninth century by a fortress which was later enlarged until it became a vir-tually self-contained complex of palaces, mosques and gardens whose history from the thirteenth to fourteenth cen-tury is documented in both literary sources and site inscriptions. Among the seemingly confusing progression of buildings, courts and water channels two main palaces define the Alhambra. Yusuf I (AD 1333–54) began an ambi-tious programme of expansion and decoration which resulted in the construction of the Comares palace complex with a massive entrance, a private audience chamber – the Hall of the Ambassadors, royal apartments and the so-called Court of the Myrtles where a graceful colonnade encloses a pool and flowering plants. The principal patron, however, was Muhammad V (AD 1361–92) who built the second palace complex whose masterpiece is the Court of the Lions. This is a private courtyard where the garden focuses on a central fountain supported on twelve marble lions which spout water into a canal and four channels. The court in turn opens into domestic quarters including the Hall of the Two Sisters, decorated with a spectacular ceiling of pendant stalactites – *muqarnas*. Apart from the plan the outstanding features of the Alhambra are the proportions of its architecture and the richness of its decoration. The buildings themselves are structurally simple based on arcades and domed chambers supported on slender columns of white marble. They are lavishly decorated with friezes and panels of glazed mosaic tiles, carved plaster, interlocking units of wood in a kaleidoscope of geometrical motifs and lacelike foliage all further enriched by the play of light filtered through the courtyards, windows and porches.

References

Grabar (1978), Irwin (2004).

JENNIFER SCARCE

'ALI, ABDULLAH YUSUF (1872–1953)

The translation of the Holy Qur'an by Abdullah Yusuf Ali is one of the best known among anglophone Muslims and non-Arab students of Islam. Majestic and with a sensitivity to the cadences of English, the translation is accompanied by the translator's own *tafsir* and a running commentary in English verse. But the translator was also public servant, educationalist and scholar.

Yusuf Ali was born on 4 April 1872 at Swat in Gujerat, the younger son of an official in the police force. He showed early intellectual prowess and promise and was reading the Qur'an in Arabic from the age of five. He was educated in Bombay, first at the Anjuman-e-Islam school and then at Wilson's School. The first school was chosen to improve his Islamic education. The second had strong Church of Scotland connections. He went on to study Latin and Greek history at the University of Bombay, graduating with a first-class Bachelors Degree in 1891 at the age of nineteen. His British education was crowned with a scholarship to continue his studies in the United Kingdom. He spent three years at St John's College Cambridge graduating with a second-class degree.

He was successful in the open competition to enter the Indian Civil Service and embarked on a nineteen-year career as imperial official. His activity extended beyond his legal and administrative duties. In the pattern of many a British servant of the Raj he published in 1900 an ethnological monograph, on *Silk Fabrics Produced in the North West Province and Oudh*. His identification with the British became personal with marriage in 1900 in a Bournemouth church to Teresa Shalders, a marriage that was half-concealed from his superiors and was not to last, in spite of the rapid production of four children.

Further posts in rural areas followed. He built up a reputation as a financier and became Acting Under Secretary for Finance for the Indian government in 1907, the year he published a second book, *Life and Labours of the People of India*. But the following year a promising career suffered a setback. Some kind of a nervous breakdown led to nine months medical leave in Britain. The breakdown accompanied the collapse of his marriage.

He returned to India to a post in Kanpur where, in 1912, the municipality demolished the ablution area of the mosque. This led to Muslim anger and riots directed against the Government. Yusuf Ali found himself having to defend an unpopular decision in the face of his co-religionists. This experience probably led to a sense of frustration. He resigned from the service in early 1914 on the pretext of wishing to spend more time with his family in Britain. He retired with an annual pension of 800 pounds.

He spent the war years in London and threw himself into war propaganda with articles and speeches, and lectures at the new School of Oriental Studies. Work for the Ministry of Information included a tour of Sweden. He identified with the ally whose misfortunes had triggered off the war, Serbia, publishing in 1916 *Mestrovic and Serbian Sculpture*. During these years he expressed a fervent loyalty to the King and became one of the first holders of the honour of Commander of the Order of the British Empire (CBE) and accompanied the Secretary of State for India to the Peace Conference in Paris. All this alienated him further from the activist Muslim Indian mainstream.

His personal life continued to be turbulent. His children rejected him and he married a second Englishwoman, Gertrude Mawby, who embraced Islam and produced a son. But the marriage was not to endure.

Yusuf Ali returned to India in 1920 and spent two years in Hyderabad, in financial administration and planning the Osmania University. An advocate of the Urdu language, he wrote a handbook on Urdu orthography. He moved

to Lucknow and practised law and also researched Mughal history and issues of Muslims in the contemporary world. Then in Lahore he became Principal of the Islamia College in 1925, a post that brought him little tranquillity. He travelled regularly to Britain during the 1920s and 1930s, but was also prolific with his pen. One rigorous work of scholarship was a new edition of *Wilson's Anglo-Muhammadan Law*.

But there was a growing isolation. Although a friend and admirer of the poet Iqbal, he was alienated from the Muslim League, sympathising rather with the princely states. He was active in the All-India Muslim Council, set up to undermine the League, and dismissed the idea of Pakistan as 'a student's scheme'.

During the 1930s he found consolation in his great work of translating the Qur'an. Yusuf Ali's knowledge of Arabic was limited: he never spoke it, but he was sensitive to the literature and succeeded in producing a translation that was a work of English literature. The translation appeared first in Lahore in instalments over the course of three years. As a book it was published in two volumes by Muhammad Ashraf of Lahore in 1938.

Yusuf Ali's Islam was a personal faith, quietist rather than activist. It was not the sole determining factor in his public life. He was deeply interested in other cultures, especially classical Europe, and other faiths. During his lengthy and frequent visits to Britain where he would stay at the National Liberal Club rather than with his second family, he became a pioneer of inter-faith dialogue and was active in the World Congress of Faiths.

He was in his late sixties when the Second World War broke out. Exhausted and prematurely aged he undertook some more propaganda work. The last decade of his life was sad. He accepted the Muslim League analysis of the threat to Indian Muslims, but not Indian independence. Senile decay set in after the war. His last years were sad and lonely and he became increasingly frail. At the age of eighty-one he was found destitute in a Westminster doorway and died, alone, in hospital on 10 December 1953.

PETER CLARK

'ALI AL-HADI

The Twelver Imams (*ithna 'ashariya*) trace their ancestry and the legitimacy of their claim to the spiritual leadership to the fourth of the rightly guided (*al-rashidun*) Caliphs', 'Ali ibn abi Talib, through his son, al-Husayn. The tenth of their number, born in Medina in AD 827, was Abu'l-Hasan 'Ali ibn Muhammad, who was known as 'the guided one' (*al-hadi*). Born in Medina *c.* AD 827, the son of a Moroccan slave woman, he was also to become known as 'the distinguished one' (*al-naqi*). He spent some twenty years in Samarra, the 'Abbasid capital near Baghdad, virtually a prisoner of the Caliph Mutawakkil. 'Ali al-Hadi died in AD 868.

References

Hitti (1973: 440–1), Momen (1985: 43–4).

See also: **Shi'ism; Twelver Imams**

EDWARD D. A. HULMES

'ALI AL-RIDA

Abu'l-Hasan 'Ali ibn Musa, the eighth of the Twelver Shi'i Imams was born in Medina in AD 765. He was known by his title, 'the approved one' (*al-rida*). As in the case of the other Twelver Imams (*ithna 'ashariya*) his ancestry and the legitimacy of his claim to spiritual leadership is traced to the fourth of the rightly guided (*al-rashidun*) Caliphs', 'Ali ibn abi

Talib, through his son, al-Husayn. His years as Imam saw the death of the caliph Harun al-Rashid and the division of the Islamic empire between the caliph's two sons, Amin and Ma'mun. For reasons never fully understood, the latter appointed 'Ali al-Rida to be his heir, an arrangement that enjoyed neither the approval of the Imam nor the favour of the 'Abbasid family, who chose a rival caliph. Fatima, the sister of al-Rida, died at Qumm on her way to visit him in Khurasan. Successive generations have added to the imposing shrine built in her honour. Her brother is said to have died as a result of poison, reputedly administered in Tus in AD 818 by the Caliph Ma'mun.

References

Hitti (1973: 439–41), Momen (1985: 41–2).

See also: **Shi'ism; Twelver Imams**

EDWARD D. A. HULMES

'ALI IBN ABI TALIB

'Ali was the son of Abu Talib and the cousin and son-in-law of the Prophet Muhammad. He was born in Mecca *c.* AD 600. Tradition suggests that he was only ten years old when he became the second person in Mecca to believe in Muhammad's mission and to accept Islam. The Prophet's wife Khadija was the first. Muhammad was to include him as one of the ten Muslims who would enter Paradise. He married the Prophet's daughter, Fatima in Medina after the *hijra*. She bore him two sons, al-Hasan and al-Husayn. 'Ali, somewhat reluctantly, became the fourth of the rightly guided (*al-rashidun*) caliphs', holding the office from 656 to AD 661, after the murder of the third caliph, 'Uthman ibn 'Affan. 'Ali is honoured by Shi'i Muslims as the man whose claim to

43

be the legitimate successor of the Prophet Muhammad in AD 632 was rejected at that time by the intrigues of his opponents, who refused to believe that during, or immediately after, the Farewell Pilgrimage to Mecca in AD 631/2 Muhammad actually named 'Ali as his successor. 'Ali, who did not at first accept the authority of the man who did succeed the Prophet, Abu Bakr, declined to press his own case. 'Ali's years as caliph were beset with problems that arose, not least, from what he considered to be the neglect of Islamic principles of faith and justice. His attempts to end this neglect were opposed by the leading figures in Mecca, whose personal wealth was growing as the Islamic empire was extended beyond the borders of the Arabian Peninsula. One of his most bitter opponents was 'A'isha, the daughter of Abu Bakr and the widow of Muhammad. Still harbouring a grudge against 'Ali because on one occasion he had advised Muhammad to divorce her on grounds of a suspected adulterous liaison with another man, she and others instigated a rebellion against 'Ali. The attempt to displace him failed. A second insurrection, led by Mu'awiya, then the Islamic Governor of Syria, ended when he avoided defeat at the hands of 'Ali's force during the Battle of Siffin by appealing for, and being allowed, arbitration. The outcome was disastrous for 'Ali. By AD 660 he had lost control of much of the empire, from Egypt to Syria. Mu'awiya, the founder of the Umayyad dynasty, was about to become the new caliph.

'Ali was killed in AD 661 on his way to the mosque in his capital city, Kufa, in Iraq. His assailant was said to be a one of the 'seceders' (khawarij), a man named 'Abdul-Rahman ibn Muljam, whose intention was to avenge the deaths of the khawarij killed in the fight against 'Ali at Nahrawan in AD 658. 'Ali died almost three days after the poisoned sword of his assassin inflicted fatal head wounds. He was buried in Kufa. Shi'i Muslims regard him as a martyr and a saint. Some have even believed him to be not only *wali Allah* (the close friend of God) but also an incarnation of divinity. By means of this phrase he is to be distinguished from Muhammad who, in accordance with the strictest Qur'anic prescriptions against *shirk* (associating the creature with the Creator) is described as the pre-eminent, but still only human, *nabi* and *rasul* (Prophet and Messenger) of God. Hitti (1973: 162) commented that 'Ali was held to be the 'friend and vice-regent of Allah, just as Muhammad had been the Prophet of Islam and the Messenger of God'. 'As a canonised martyr' the dead man proved to be more effective than when he was alive. Despite of, or perhaps because of his reputation, 'Ali remains a focus for divisions among Muslims. There are still unresolved hostilities between the two main branches of Islam that arose after his initial failure to become caliph, and which intensified after his assassination. The household of Islam has been divided ever since into the *Shi'i* (from the Arabic *shi'at 'Ali*, i.e. 'the party of 'Ali) and the *Sunni* (from the Arabic *sunna*, i.e., 'the custom' [of the Prophet Muhammad]). There are many legends about 'Ali's saintly character and his selflessness. One describes how he slept in the Prophet's bed at the time of the *hijra* from Mecca to Medina, impersonating him, when enemies were seeking Muhammad to kill him. It was only when news came of Muhammad's safe arrival in Medina that 'Ali chose to go there himself. Another story describes how he stayed behind in Mecca for a few days in order to return monies deposited with Muhammad before his move to Medina. 'Ali fought alongside the Muslim troops at the

Battles of Badr, Uhud (where he is reported to have received sixteen wounds) and 'the Ditch' (al-Khandaq). It was he who carried the Prophet's banner at Khaybar. 'Ali's piety, courage, generosity and self-denial are considered to be exemplary. His zeal for the cause of Islam is exemplified by his actions in destroying the pagan idols in the Ka'ba when the hitherto hostile Meccans led by Abu Sufyan accepted the authority of Muhammad and submitted to Islam with a minimum amount of bloodshed in AD 630. Ali remained loyal to the memory of Muhammad, contributing several hundred details about the Prophet's words and actions for possible inclusion in the collections of *hadith* (traditions). He is also regarded as one of the founders of the study of Arabic grammar, and credited with establishing the authentic style of Qur'anic recitation. In addition he is reported to have helped to organise the oral revelations that were received and transmitted by Muhammad into the written form of the Qur'an. The collection of 'Ali's writings, the *Nahj al-Balagha* (*The Path of Eloquence*), compiled by Abu'l-Hasan Mujammad, Sharif al-Radi, is held by some Muslims to be second in importance only to the Qur'an itself. The suggestion that the year of the *hijra* be officially made the first year of the Islamic era was made by 'Ali to the second caliph, 'Umar ibn al–Khattab.

References

Hitti (1973: 178–86), Momen (1985: 12–16, 23–6, *et passim*).

See also: **ahl al-sunna**; **'A'isha**; **Muhammad ibn 'Abdallah, the Prophet of Islam**; **Shi'isma (al-Shi'a)**

EDWARD D. A. HULMES

ALIENATION

Alienation, the separation between God and the world, is a concept which is extensively discussed in al-Ghazali's well-known book *Tahafut al-Falasifa*. In this book he refuted many concepts of the Arab philosophers, Ibn Sina and al-Farabi, for their adoption of many Greek concepts without considering their consequences. The concept of the eternity of the world in addition to that of the eternity of God obliterate the belief that God is the actual creator, *al-sani'*, for if the world is eternal then it does not need a creator and consequently there is a separation between God and the world. The second concept which creates alienation between God and the world is their concept of God's universal knowledge, which cannot perceive contingent events. In order to uphold the unity of God's nature, the philosophers considered that God can only know universal concepts which govern the world system, since to know every transitory event would cause a change in His nature. This second concept made God seem alone as a being that, because of His essential oneness, is not able to have real communication with the world and therefore transcends all the different qualities of the world: while the world has plurality, God is absolutely one, and while the world is changing, God is eternal, in a single constant state. Consequently, al-Ghazali believes, God for the philosophers is only the First Cause, He neither influences the events of the world, nor does He know all its changes. This, from al-Ghazali's stand point, creates a real alienation between God and the world, a concept which endangers the importance of revelation and the Holy Scriptures.

References

al-Ghazali (1961), Leaman (1999: 24–6, 37–9).

See also: **creation *ex nihilo*; God's knowledge**

Maha El-Kaisy Friemuth

ALLAH

'The God', 'Allah'. In the pre-Islamic period *ilah* (god) referred to any god, though there was always a notion of a single superior, omnipotent being above such gods. In this period, referred to as 'the Period of Ignorance (*al-Jahiliyyah*)', the Ka'ba in Mecca contained a number of idols to such gods identified with cults based in Mecca and further afield which were brought to the city with the effect of both encouraging regional trade and asserting Meccan predominance thereof. Islam proclaimed the unique supremacy of Allah as creator – as seen in the Muslim profession of faith, 'There is no god but Allah and Muhammad is his prophet' – and, at Muhammad's conquest of Mecca in AD 630, these idols were destroyed.

Islam also proclaimed the unity (*tawhid*) of Allah (Q.20:14, Q.37:4, Q.52:39, Q.43, Q.73:9, 112) as distinct from these idols but also in contrast with the Christian concepts of God as triune and Jesus as God's son, both of which are rejected in the Qur'an. Indeed, Allah had sent messengers and prophets before but their messages and previous revelations (including the Torah, for example) had been either distorted or misunderstood.

The earliest-revealed, more eschatological, verses of the Qur'an also proclaimed the imminence of the Day of Judgement which was known to Allah alone and cast Muhammad in his role of 'warner' (Q.79:42–6) but also portrayed Allah as merciful and forgiving (Q.25:70) who would reward good deeds but punish the disobedient.

The essence, attributes, majesty and beauty of Allah are described in passages of the Qur'an which form the basis for the 'ninety-nine names' by which Allah is often known, and which are called 'the Most Beautiful Names' (Q.7:180). Thus, for example, the two references to Allah in the *basmalah* ('In the name of Allah, the Merciful [*ar-Rahman*], the Compassionate [*ar-Rahim*]'), which formula Muslims often repeat before undertaking any lawful action, both derive from the Qur'an (Q.55:1 and Q.2:143, respectively). The term 'slave' (*'abd*) is prefixed to some of these names to form a Muslim's proper name.

Early in Islamic history these, together with references in the Qur'an to Allah's face (e.g., Q.28:88), hands (e.g., Q.38:75) and such verses as Q.32:4 ('He mounted the throne'), encouraged debates about the possibly anthropomorphic nature of Allah and, therefore, of the nature of the Qur'an itself as Allah's own speech. Both the Hanbalis and Ash'arites and their adversaries the Mu'tazilites denied the existence of the human attributes of Allah, albeit for different reasons, but disagreed on the createdness of the Qur'an.

References

Tafsir ibn Kathir (http://www.tafsir.com/), Waines (1995).

See also: **'abd; anthropomorphism; attributes of God; 'Isa; judgement on the *yawm al-qiyama*; ninety-nine names of God; *tawhid*; al-Tawrat**

Andrew J. Newman

ALMOHADS (AD 1130–1269)

The Almohads (*al-Muwahhidun*, 'those who proclaim God's unity') represented a Berber protest, led by a *mahdi* or charismatic leader, Muhammad Ibn Tumart, against the Maliki legalism and the laxness of the later Almoravids. They built up a powerful state in the

Maghrib, extending also into Muslim Spain, directed by the Almohad caliph and a hierarchy of spiritual advisers, but latterly, they lost most of their Spanish territories to the resurgent Christians, whilst North Africa passed to new powers like the Marinids and Hafsids. Although the Almohad grip on society within their dominions was a fierce and intolerant one, with repression of Muslim dissidence and persecution of the Christian and Jewish *dhimmi*s or 'protected peoples', within the narrow court circle intellectual speculation was allowed, permitting a late flowering of Islamic philosophy under figures like Ibn Rushd (Averroes) and Ibn Tufayl (Abubacer).

References

Bosworth (1996: No. 15), Gibb and Bosworth (1960–2003), Huici Miranda (1956–7), Le Tourneau (1969), Terrasse (1949–50: I, 261–367).

C. E. BOSWORTH

ALMORAVIDS (AD 1062–1147)

The Almoravids (*al-Murabitun*, 'those who dwell in frontier posts, *ribats*') arose from a wave of spiritual exaltation amongst the Berbers of the north-western Sahara under the leadership of 'Abdallah b. Yasin. Their warriors took over Morocco and much of what is now Algeria, founding a capital at Marrakesh and furthering the conservative Maliki law school, now dominant in North Africa after the defeat of Kharijism there, and in AD 1086 invaded Spain, introducing a fiercely puritanical form of Islam there. They were replaced some decades later by the Almohads, but a lasting legacy of theirs was the impetus to Islamisation within the Sahara and as far as the Sahel region of west Africa.

References

Bosch (1956), Bosworth (1996: No. 14), Gibb and Bosworth (1960–2003), Terrasse (1949–50: I: 211–60).

C. E. BOSWORTH

ALMS-GIVING (*ZAKAT, SADAQA, WAQF*)

The Arabic terms given refer to three complementary aspects of almsgiving in Islam, each of which contributes in a specific way to the welfare of an Islamic community. The first of these is *zakat*, the obligatory giving of alms, which is one of the five religious duties of a Muslim. Payment of the tax helps to 'purify' the giver, as the root meaning of the word *zakat* suggests. In the earliest days of Islam *zakat* was payable following an assessment of the value of crops, livestock, and other possessions. These included grapes and dates, camels, cattle, sheep, goats and horses, gold and silver, and merchandise of various kinds. From the beginning *zakat* was assessed at 2.5 per cent and levied annually. With the spread of Islam worldwide, the development of modern economies, and the growing disparity between the rich and the relatively poor in many parts of the Islamic world, a more realistic assessment of the percentage to be charged seems appropriate. The resources thus collected are used to help finance actions that 'serve the cause of Islam', support the efforts of those involved in *jihad*, help to redeem slaves and free prisoners taken in war, help to build and maintain mosques and to promote other specific charitable objectives. Only Muslims are called upon to pay. Non-Muslims living in an Islamic society do not. The tax payable by 'client' peoples, namely, Jews and Christians, took the form of a 'tribute' or a 'poll tax', known as *jizya*. Muslims whose circumstances render them incapable of paying in cash or kind are freed from the obligation to pay *zakat* and numbered instead among its beneficiaries. Provision for the needs of those who collect the tax is also made from what is collected. The word *adaqa*, implying 'truthfulness', 'righteousness', appears in Q.2:263: 'Kind words and forgiveness are better than *sadaqa* (almsgiving) followed by injury. God is rich [in mercy] and clement'. The word is used for charitable giving that is not strictly required by Islamic law. The third term to be considered here is *waqf*, literally 'standing still', 'halting'. In this context, however, it means 'religious endowment'. The word bears a legal significance, referring to donations made for charitable purposes intended to further the cause of Islam. Large gifts, such as those that make possible the building of a mosque, for instance, fall under this category. Once given, the gift is inalienable and cannot be recovered. Once prayers are said in a mosque built with the help of such an endowment, the benefactor relinquishes any claim to ownership of the property. An unrelated meaning of the word *waqf* may also be mentioned. It is used to indicate places where one who recites from the Qur'an is to make a full pause in reading aloud. Such places are indicated in the text by the letters *qf*.

References

Hitti (1970: 132), Momen (1985: 77, 179, 207), Tritton (1968: 25–6).

EDWARD D. A. HULMES

ALP ARSLAN B. CHAGHRI BEG DAWUD (r. AD 1063–73)

Great Saljuq sultan in succession to his childless uncle Toghril Beg. He maintained a strong frontier in the eastern parts of his realm against the Ghaznavids and Qarakhanids, but his most celebrated exploits were in the west, where he hoped to push back the Fatimids from Syria but was, in the event, caught up in warfare with the Byzantines and achieved a great victory at Mantzikert/ Malazgird in eastern Anatolia in 1071, capturing the Emperor Romanus Diogenes and laying open the whole of Asia Minor to Turkmen raiders who were eventually to establish there the Saljuq sultanate of Rum.

References

Bosworth (1968: 54–66), Gibb and Bosworth (1960–2003).

C. E. BOSWORTH

AMAL

Sh'ia Muslim organisation in Lebanon. The acronym of the group's title, *Afwaj al-Muqawama al-Lubnaniyya* (Lebanese Resistance Detachments), also means 'hope' in Arabic. The group was established by Sh'ia cleric, Imam Musa al-Sadr, in 1974–5, although he was to disappear during a trip to Libya in 1978. After the Israeli invasion in 1982, the secular-minded leadership of Nabih Berri prompted those militants who wanted an Iranian-style Islamic revolution to set up a separate group, *Hizballah*. Under Nabih Berri, Amal became an important Syrian client. With the end of the civil war, Amal members were absorbed into the new political settlement.

References

Roy (1994: 52, 186–7, 191), Zisser (1997: 90–110).

SIMON W. MURDEN

AMIN, AHMAD (1886–1954)

The author of a noted work of autobiography in the context of Egypt in the first half of the twentieth century, which includes a memorable description of his feelings on being enrolled as a student in al-Azhar, the oldest institution of traditional Islamic learning in the world, and having to put on a turban: 'I became prematurely old'. He went on to be Professor of Arabic Literature in Cairo University from 1936–46 and to produce a three-volume history of the Islamic world until the year 1000, which was the first such work in Arabic to make use of critical method.

References

Amin A. (1968).

HUGH GODDARD

AMIN, QASIM (1863–1908)

Born in Alexandria, Amin studied law in Cairo and then Paris, and there, under the influence of Muhammad 'Abduh, he became convinced that the main reason for the relative backwardness of Muslim societies compared with Europe was simply ignorance, which began in the family. The main solution, he therefore suggested, was to raise the living conditions and educational attainments of women, by ending their seclusion and veiling, declaring polygamy and unilateral divorce to be illegal, and giving women the opportunity to work, all of which, he insisted, was not contrary to Islamic law but rather a more correct interpretation of it.

References

Amin Q. (2000).

HUGH GODDARD

AMINA

She was the mother of the Prophet Muhammad. She died when her son was about six years old. Little is known about her except that she belonged to the clan of Zuhra and probably had family connections with Yathrib, the place that was renamed 'City of the Prophet' (*Madinat al-Nabi*) after the *hijra*. Muhammad's father, Abdallah ibn 'Abd al-Muttalib died before the boy was born.

See also: **Muhammad ibn 'Abdallah, the Prophet of Islam**

EDWARD D. A. HULMES

AMIR AL-HAJJ

'Leader', 'commander' of the 'greater' pilgrimage, the journey to and performing of a series of rites at and near Mecca's Grand Mosque over ten days each Muslim calender year, obligatory for those believers who can 'make their way' (Q.3:97).

References

Hourani (1991: 222), Waines (1995: 91–2).

ANDREW J. NEWMAN

AMIR AL-MU'MININ

'Commander of the faithful', traditionally referring to the caliph's role as military leader but also a term used by the Shi'a to refer to 'Ali.

References

Halm (1991: 8).

ANDREW J. NEWMAN

AL-'AMIRI, ABU AL-HASAN MUHAMMAD

Al-'Amiri, a philosopher and Sufi, is considered the last follower of the al-Kindi school of Baghdad. He was born in Nishapur at the beginning of the tenth century. He studied under the well-known philosopher and follower

49

of al-Kindi Abu Zayd al-Balkhi (d. AD 934) in Khurasan. Al-'Amiri, like most philosophers of the time, travelled to many towns of the Islamic empire, al-Tawhidi mentions his two important visits to Baghdad, in which he took part in some of the important *majlis* and led influential discussions and debates. Al-'Amiri also spent five years in Rayy at the court of the Buyid wazir al-'Amidi, who also was a philosopher and patron of philosophers. There al-'Amiri met Miskawayh, the librarian of the *wazir*. That al-Amiri and Miskawayh had similar views can be seen from Miskawayh's work *al-Fawz al-'Aghar*, which also demonstrates that they shared some sources.

Al-'Amiri's main concern, in most of his books, was to reconcile philosophy and Islamic dogmas, attempting to find a thread between the five most important Greek philosophers: Empedocles, Pythagoras, Socrates, Plato and Aristotle and the prophetic tradition in his work *On the Afterlife*. Here he considers that the Qur'anic revelation is the continuation of what Greek philosophy was not able to discover without divine revelation, mainly the question of bodily resurrection. In addition, in his work the *Deliverance of Mankind from the Problem of Predestination and Free Will,* he attempts to find a middle position between the Greek concept of human freedom and the *jabr* of the Ash'arite and Hanbalite school reaching the Hanafite concept of denying divine absolute constraint, *jabr*, and the unrestricted human delegation of power, *tafwid.* In most of his twenty-five works known to us, al-'Amiri was concerned to show the important role of Islam in the field of philosophical speculation as two inseparable ways of thought.

Towards the end of his life, al-'Amiri enjoyed the favour of the Samanid rulers of Bukhara and died peacefully in his native town Nishapur in AD 992.

References

Rowson (1996).

Maha El-Kaisy Friemuth

AMMAN ('AMAN)

Capital city of the Kingdom of Jordan and the country's commercial, administrative and industrial centre. The site has been occupied since prehistoric times and was the biblical city of Rabbath Ammon, capital of the Ammonites on the citadel hill site. In the third century BC it was captured by Philadelphus of the Ptolemies and named Philadelphia in his honour. Remains of that period are still visible. In the first century AD it became the leading city of a Roman province, then fell to the Byzantines and was captured by the Arabs in the seventh century. It had fallen into decline by about 1300 and become little more than a small village. Its fortunes began to revive when it was settled by a group of Circassian refugees in 1878. It was captured by the Arab and Allied forces in 1918 and chosen as the capital of the newly founded Hashimite state of Transjordan. The site has spread over the surrounding hills and the population was swollen by the influx of large numbers of Palestinian refugees after 1948 and 1967.

References

Northedge (1992).

Derek Hopwood

AL-AMR BI'L-MA'RUF

'The command to do what is known to be good', the first part of Q.3:104, which continues 'and enjoin against what was known to be evil', and is held to be obligatory on the part of Muslims.

References

Cook (2000).

ANDREW J. NEWMAN

AL-ANDALUS

Modern Andalusia, the southernmost part of Spain, consists of eight *provincias*: Almeria, Cadiz, Cordova, Granada, Huelva, Jaén, Malaga and Seville. The region is bounded by Portugal to the west, by the Atlantic to the south-west, and by the Mediterranean to the south and the south-east. The Iberian peninsula was known to the Arabs as *al-Andalus*, a term which probably meant 'the land of the Vandals', a Germanic group, who came as marauding invaders in the fifth century AD. Carthaginians, Greeks and Romans took an interest in the region centuries before Muslims from the north-African littoral came to establish Islamic culture and religion in *al-Andalus*. In the eighth century AD, having pushed westwards towards the Atlantic after clearing the Byzantines from North Africa west of Carthage, Arabs set out across the narrow strip of water at the western end of the Mediterranean. Among the first to enter Spain were Berbers, a few foot soldiers and mounted men, who landed on the southernmost tip of the peninsula in AD 700. A year later, the Umayyad governor of North Africa, Musa ibn Nusayr, sent 7,000 troops into Spain under the leadership of the Berber, Tariq ibn Ziyad. His soldiers landed close to the rock that bears his name, *jabal tariq*, 'mountain of Tariq' (Gibraltar). The etymology is disputed, however. The term *al-Andalus* eventually came to mean the area of Spain conquered and held by Muslims (Moors),

an area that promised to be 'the south-western gate to Europe', despite the increasing opposition in the fifteenth century AD to Islamic expansion from Christians in the north. Fresh vigour was injected into Moorish Spain by the presence of Almoravids and later Almohads between the eleventh and the thirteenth centuries AD. Over time, a diverse culture arose in the region as Jews, Christians and Muslims lived together under the generally tolerant eyes of Islamic rulers. The founding of a Talmudic school in Cordoba in the Umayyad period stimulated the culture of the Andalusian Jewish community. Architecture flourished in Cordoba, Granada and Seville, together with philosophy and many other branches of learning. Cordoba's cathedral/mosque and the Alhambra (*al-qal'a al-hamra'*, 'the red fortress') in Granada are among the finest architectural examples. Work on Greek and Arabic texts prepared the way for subsequent studies in the sciences and the humanities by Europeans during the Renaissance. Spanish Jews enjoyed enhanced legal status. They adopted Arab dress, spoke and wrote in Arabic. The Arabs introduced the cultivation of apricots, almonds and sugar cane. Plans for irrigation schemes were drawn up and implemented. Islamic influence declined until Andalusia became part of the Christian kingdom of Castile in 1492. The Jews were expelled from Spain in that year. The *Moriscos* (Spanish Muslims, whose ancestors had been Christians), were expelled in 1609. An exemplary era of cultural diversity and religious tolerance in the history of Spain was ended. In recent times Muslim fundamentalists, headed by members of al-Qa'ida have made the recovery of the Islamic kingdom of southern Spain, lost to Christians in 1492, a frequently repeated aim.

References

Hitti (1973: 493–60), Hourani (1991: 41–3), Johnson (1987: 221–30).

See also:**Almohads; Almoravids; Berbers**
EDWARD D. A. HULMES

ANGELS

A hierarchy of beings believed to be created of light and immune from human desires and needs, including, at their head, four great angels – Jibril (Gabriel), Israfil, Izra'il and Mikal (Michael). These were ordered by Allah to bow down to Adam, pictured as superior thereto, at his creation by Allah. All did except Iblis who was thereupon banished. Angels are accorded the status of *rasul*.

See also: ***dahr*; Iblis; *rasul***

References

Waines (1995).

ANDREW J. NEWMAN

ANKARA

Ancrya (classical), Anguriyah (Persian), Ankira, Ankuriyya (Arabic), Enguriye, Enguri, Enguru (Turkish), national capital and province in Turkey, district of Galatia. Ankara was a central fortress (Kal'at al-Salasil, according to Arabic geographers), an important market at cross roads for caravans. A Hittite settlement over 4,000 years ago, an important Phrygian sanctuary (1200–1700 BC), conquered by Alexander the Great in 334 BC and capital of the Galatian Tectosage tribe in the third century BC and of the Roman province of Galatia (25 BC). This Byzantine commercial centre was attacked frequently by Arabs in AD 654, by Harun al-Rashid (AD 806), and *c.* AD 1073 by Saljuq Turks but reconquered by Raymond IV of Toulouse in 1101; then controlled by the Saljuqs (AD 1143) until the collapse of the Saljuq empire (AD 1308). There are five existing Seljuq mosques including the 'Ala' al-Din mosque (*minbar* dated AD 1198) and the Arslan-Khane mosque (*minbar* dated AD 1290).

From 1308, Ankara was a protectorate of the Mongol Ilkhan empire of Iran, then the Eretnids. The Akhi order controlled the city until the Ottomans took power under Murad I (AD 1361). Ankara remained an Ottoman base for conquests in eastern Anatolia until it was besieged in 1402 by Timur who defeated Bayazid (r. AD 1389–1402). Ankara became an important Ottoman commercial city with its cloth market (*c.* 1470) and mohair production (Turk. *tiftik*). Over twelve Ottoman mosques still stand, including one built in 1429 (by a temple of Augustus that was converted into a Byzantine church) by the founder of the Dervish Bayramiyya order, Haci Bayram Wali (1352–1429/30), the 'Imaret Djami' (1427–8) and Djenabi Ahmad Pasha built by Sinan (1565–6).

In 1919 Mustafa Kemal (Ataturk) used Ankara at the centre of his resistance movement against the Ottoman sultan and he declared Ankara capital of Turkey on 13 October 1923. The town plan was designed by Hermann Jansen in 1926. In the face of Islamic convention, sculpture and painting of human and animal forms was encouraged, yet some of the early nationalist buildings retained traditional Saljuq or Moorish styles. From 1928, Turkey has been a secular state with religion seen as a personal matter.

References

Cross and Leiser (2000).

JANET STARKEY

AL-ANSAR

Two groups of Muslims are credited with assisting the Prophet Muhammad to establish the Islamic community in Medina after the *hijra*. The Muslims who welcomed him when he arrived in Medina are known as *Ansar al-Nabi,* 'the Helpers' or 'supporters' of the Prophet (cf. Q.9:117). The Muslims who left Mecca to join him in Medina are known as *al-Muhajirun,* 'the emigrants' (cf. Q.9:100). When Muhammad died in AD 632 several parties claimed the right to decide who was to succeed him. Among them were the supporters and the emigrants. The former insisted that they had offered the Prophet asylum in Medina and that without their help he would never have been able to survive and prosper. The latter claimed that they belonged to the Prophet's family and that they had joined him in Mecca from the outset of his mission. The descendants of *al-Ansar,* who were never able to see one of their number assume the caliphate, continued to play a part in the history of Islam until their political influence was ended during the Umayyad dynasty. They were famed alike for their piety, their devotion to the Prophet's memory and their military prowess in the campaigns of Islamic expansion.

See also: **al-Muhajirun**

EDWARD D. A. HULMES

ANTHROPOMORPHISM

The Ash'ari school, which in the eleventh century became the dominant school of theology among Sunni Muslims, maintained that Qur'anic references to Allah's face and hands, his seeing, speaking, hearing and sitting on a throne referred literally, for example, to the face and hands of Allah. However, given the divine transcendence, Ash'aris maintained that these attributes of Allah could not be likened to the human face and hands so as to ascribe to Allah any anthropomorphic qualities. Thus also

Allah's acts, including the divine will, existed but were beyond all human comprehension. The transcendent nature of their reality was to be accepted without question and further speculation was to be avoided.

References

Fakhry (1983: 209–10), Rahman (1979: 85–6), Waines (1995: 117–22), Watt (1973: 316).

See also: **attributes of God;** *bila kayfa***; free will and predestination**

ANDREW J. NEWMAN

ANTUN, FARAH (1874–1922)

A Lebanese journalist, born into the Greek Orthodox Christian community, who spent a number of years in New York and was also well versed in the French intellectual tradition, with a particular partiality for the ideas of Ernest Renan, whose *Life of Jesus* he translated into Arabic. In 1903 he published (in Arabic) a study of the Islamic philosopher Ibn Rushd which also reflected Renan's influence as in it Antun argued that Ibn Rushd's ideas represented reason, science and civilisation, and that the European model of equality between religions and the development of a secular state was the way forward for Middle Eastern societies. Antun's former friend, Muhammad 'Abduh, wrote a strong riposte to his views.

References

Hourani (1983: Chapter 10).

HUGH GODDARD

APOSTASY (*RIDDA 'AN AL-ISLAM, IRTIDAD*)

A decision to forsake Islam and convert to another religion is considered by Muslims to be an act of wilful apostasy and thus a betrayal that has the most serious consequences for the individual concerned. A *murtadd* is 'one who turns back'. Muhammad is reported to have said: 'Every infant is born *'ala 'l-fitra* (i.e. in the state of nature that accords with God's creative will and purpose)'. This natural disposition ensures that created beings inherit at birth the true religion, Islam. It is for Muslims to safeguard this inheritance (Q.30:30). Whether or not children continue to enjoy their rightful spiritual patrimony depends upon their parents and the influences of the society in which they grow up. The Islamic community (*umma*), promotes the social, political, economic, and religious integration of its members. For this reason apostasy has been interpreted as a betrayal, for which the authoritative schools of Islamic jurisprudence prescribed the death penalty for apostate males and confinement until repentance for females and children. The disposition of an apostate's personal possessions and wealth is decided according to local law and custom. Islamic marriage is automatically annulled by the apostasy of either partner. The apostasy of someone of unsound mind or in a state of intoxication is discounted.

References

Tritton (1968: 141–2).

See also: **ilhad**

EDWARD D. A. HULMES

'AQABA, PLEDGES OF

In the year AD 620, shortly before the Prophet Muhammad's migration (*hijra*) to Yathrib, he met six or seven men from that city. Members of the Khazraj tribe, they were persuaded to become Muslims. A year later, five of them returned to meet the Prophet at a pass known as 'Aqaba, not far from Mecca, bringing a further group of their number with them. These men pledged that they would obey Muhammad, although they did not go as far as to offer to fight for him. In addition, they pledged that they would oppose the worship of idols, refrain from adultery, cease making false accusations, eschew theft, and prevent infanticide. They went back to Yathrib, where their account of meetings with the Prophet helped to convince other leading figures in the city that Muhammad was the man they needed to reconcile the dissident factions among them. The result was that seventy-two men and three women from Yathrib visited Mecca in AD 621 to pledge their allegiance to the Prophet. The way was thus clear for him and his fellow Muslims, who were living under considerable difficulty among the hostile Quraysh in Mecca, to migrate some 280 miles (450 km) to the northeast to Yathrib, which was renamed in honour of his arrival a few months later, *Madinat al-Nabi,* 'the City of the Prophet', Medina.

EDWARD D. A. HULMES

'AQA'ID (sing. *'aqida*)

'Beliefs', 'creeds', referring to the systematic statements of belief on the basis of which both heresies and opposing schools of theology were refuted.

References

Gibb and Bosworth (1960–2003).

ANDREW J. NEWMAN

AQALIM (sing. *iqlim*)

'Areas', 'regions'. The word is used of the countryside and the provinces, as distinct from the city or urban area. It is sometimes used in a derogatory sense.

More specifically it refers to administrative districts, as for example, to the provinces of the Islamic empire under the Umayyads and the 'Abbasids, namely, Africa to the west of the Libyan desert and Sicily, Egypt, Syria and Palestine, central Arabia, southern Arabia. These provinces were known as *al-aqalim al-maghrib* ('the western provinces'). Provinces to the east, including al-Bahrayn and 'Uman and other territories extending to western Asia, the river Indus and north-east to Samarkand, were known as *al-aqalim al-mashriq* ('the eastern provinces'). In medieval Arabic geography the word indicated a 'climate' or 'zone', of which there were traditionally seven, covering the inhabited earth. Compare the Persian *keshwar* system of six great kingdoms surrounding the seventh, namely, Iran.

References

Gibb and Bosworth (1960–2003: III, 1076–8), Hitti (1973: 330–1).

EDWARD D. A. HULMES

'AQILA

Male relatives who pay the blood money *diya*. The word means 'restrainers' in reference to those individuals who restrain men from shedding blood. (*'aql* itself has many meanings including the human mind which restrains from doing or taking the wrong action or decision).

References

Coulson (1964: 39, 93), al-Zuhayli (1985: 318–19).

MAWIL IZZI DIEN

'AQIQA

See: **naming ceremony of a child**

ARAB REVOLT

The Arab insurrection from 1936–9 against the British Mandate. In April 1936, an Arab High Committee was formed to coordinate opposition to Jewish encroachment. Sectarian violence followed. The Arab resistance was eventually broken by British and Jewish forces, and Arab leaders went on to fight amongst themselves. Amid international events in 1939, Britain reined in Jewish expansion and the conflict quietened until the end of the Second World War.

References

James (1997: 407–10), Salibi (1976: 958).

SIMON W. MURDEN

ARABIC IN THE MODERN WORLD

Arabic is the principal Semitic language and a language of ritual in religion. It is the everday spoken language of some 300 million people in the Arab world, Christian and Muslim. Arabic is also the official language of the twenty-two states of the Arab League, including Comoros, Djibouti, Mauritania and Somalia.

Arabic script may be the most widely used script after Latin, used in Iran, Afghanistan, Pakistan, and India as well as in other Islamic countries in Asia and Africa. Arabic is one of the six UN working languages. It is broadcast worldwide through radio, satellite television, and related web sites. It is in connection with Islam, however, that Arabic is a truly international language. There are some 1,200 million Muslims in the world.

Muslims believe that the Qur'an ('Recital') exists from all eternity and is the final revelation to mankind of the true religion, Islam, through the Prophet Muhammad (AD 570–632). Born in

Mecca, Muhammad began from AD 610 to receive revelations in Arabic through the angel Gabriel. The Qur'an frequently emphasises Arabic's unique qualities which, for Muslims, make it impossible to convey in any other language the Word of God. The Qur'an is meant to be heard, not simply studied.

Muslims are summoned five times daily in Arabic to say their prayers in Arabic towards Mecca. Consequently, there has been remarkable stability and continuity in the language. We have a good idea of how Arabic has sounded from the seventh century AD. Compare contemporaneous Anglo-Saxon: we have almost no idea of its sound.

It is the fact that Arabic is so intimately related to Islam through prayer and the Qur'an that explains the situation of Arabic in the modern world.

The Qur'an gave a unique status to Classical Arabic (CA) and is quoted by grammarians to show correct usage. CA was codified by 'schools' of grammarians, between the eighth and ninth centuries AD to ensure that the new non-Arab Muslims would receive accurately the Word of God in Arabic.

From the Qur'an there is a direct line of descent to the modern written language. The script is practically identical, syntax and morphology are strikingly similar and above all both use the same feature, the Semitic triliteral root.

The triliteral root of 'Islam', for example, is s-l-m meaning 'peace or submission'. When a 'pattern' is imposed on the root a real word is produced. Hence a believer in submission to the will of God is a 'mu-s-li-m' while the verb 'sa-lla-ma' means' to say to someone 'Peace be upon you', i.e. 'to greet'. (Hebrew has a cognate root, 'shalom' = 'peace').

Modern written Arabic (MWA) is a simplified version of CA developed for the needs of journalism in the nineteenth century, principally in the Levant and in Egypt. MWA is not a debased form of CA. It is a medium for literary creativity in the form of poetry, novels and essays and for serious thought and research. It has a fully elaborated grammar and vocabulary and the difference can be described as being the difference between modern sophisticated English and a more elaborate form of stylised English, orotund or even florid in its formulations, discursive and clearly modelled on more ancient forms.

Of the connection between CA and MWA there can be no doubt because Muslims tampering with the language that conveyed the Word of God to mankind is inconceivable. Because of the reverence felt for Arabic as a sacred language there exists in the Arab world a situation of diglossia, or triglossia, or even quadriglossia.

MWA is the language used in the spoken media, radio and television and on the Internet. It is completely standard throughout the Arab world: Arabic news bulletins and commercial advertisements are understandable from the Gulf to the Atlantic and from Syria to deep into Africa.

The spoken form of MWA is not a natural medium for native speakers to use actively, although all have a good understanding of it. It is used actively only by those who are 'professionals' in language, such as broadcasters, lecturers, and teachers (lay and religious). This form of spoken language is sometimes advocated – by Arabs and non-Arabs – as being the ideal for foreigners to use because in the twenty-two countries of the Arab League there are such wide variations of dialectal Arabic. In the wider Islamic world MWA is a lingua franca, as is CA.

In the Arab world, everyday speech is not CA, nor is it MWA in its spoken form. It is dialectal Arabic which varies enormously because of geography, being used throughout twenty-two countries in Africa and Asia.

Time also has affected Arabic dialects, which have developed over at least fifteen centuries. Hence eastern and western Arabic sound so different that some specialists in linguistics have called for the establishment of national languages based on the dialects. For them, Arabic is like Latin, formerly the language of Empire and of Church, which did indeed develop into the Romance languages. CA, however, has retained its elevated status as a sacred language. It is this which has prevented the dialects from becoming national languages. Today, therefore, a foreigner wishing to be totally conversant with Arabic in a particular Arab country would have to be familiar with, at least, three forms of Arabic. CA is heard in sermons in the mosque, live and broadcast, as well as in poetry, ancient and modern – poetry has a place in Arabic everyday life which it would be difficult to exaggerate. MWA is found in books and newspapers and is heard on radio and television and in lectures. Colloquial Arabic ('Coll. A') is used by the populace, both educated and illiterate.

It is also possible to speak of a fourth type of spoken Arabic, educated spoken Arabic. This is less formal than MWA but is clearly different from the dialectal Arabic of the villages and towns. It is said to be spoken between native Arabic speakers from different dialect areas but its features are an ongoing area of research.

Coll. A is used at home, in the *suq* and in everyday communication. It is also a medium in popular theatre, in particular in slapstick comedy. It is also found in some countries' local commercial advertisements on radio and television, although hardly at all on hoardings. Coll. A is the medium used in radio and television plays, particularly in 'soaps'. In these it tends to lack the richness of genuine speech, which uses wise sayings, proverbs, plays on words, references to God, quotes from the Qur'an and poetry and non-verbal devices such as hand gestures. Coll. A is supposed never to be written since this is considered to be demeaning to the status of the language of the Qur'an. In practice, Coll. A is found in comic books and in cartoons in the press. A growing use of Coll. A is in text messaging. Arabic speech is so varied that two nearby villages can be said to have different dialects (as in the novels of Amin Maalouf, based on Lebanese usage).

Palestine gave the world the word 'shibboleth' (see Judges 12:16). There, pronunciation was used to detect people's origins. Thousands died for giving a variant pronunciation of 'sunbula', which is still the Arabic word for 'an ear of corn'.

With so many dialects some suggest a broad categorisation of areas such as Gulf and Peninsular, Egyptian, Levantine, Iraqi, Sudanese, and Maghrebi. Other analyses are possible: Yemeni Arabic may be a totally separate case.

How written Arabic works:

1. The Semitic triliteral root is basic, on which 'patterns' are imposed. The consonants 'n-S-r' convey 'victory'. The pattern 'aa-i' conveys the meaning of 'the person doing the action' and so 'naaSir' (Nasser) means 'He who gives victory', which is one of the ninety-nine 'Most Beautiful Names of God'.

2. In modern books, only the consonants are written because syntax and morphology make the vowelling mostly predictable. Only the Qur'an and the Bible are written with full vowelling, as are children's books.

3. The script is alphabetic with twenty-eight consonants, all lower-case,

57

and is cursive in both handwriting and printing.

4. The fourth Caliph, 'Ali b. Abi Talib, is reported to have said that 'The Arabic language is three things: the noun, the verb and the particle. So, walk along this path (naHw)'. 'naHw' is still the Arabic word for 'syntax'.

5. The verb system is both simple and highly complicated.

    (a) There are only two tenses, past (conjugated with suffixes) and non-past (conjugated with prefixes (see (f) later)).

    (b) There are no 'irregular' verbs.

    (c) Any verb in the active voice ('he wrote'/kataba) can be made passive ('It was written') by imposing the pattern 'u-i': hence: 'kutiba'.

    (d) A verb such as 'sallama' is of the 'second derived form' out of the ten most-used derived forms. In these a pattern is imposed on the original 'first form verb', such as 'salima'.

        (i) For each derived form's meaning there is a high degree of predictability once the pattern is imposed, and the root's meaning is known.

        (ii) For each derived form the conjugation of the verb is predictable.

In contrast ...

    (e) Verbs have not only two genders but also three numbers.

    (f) These are singular, plural and dual, making thirteen separate 'persons'

for each verb (of which, in the non-past, nine have both prefixes and suffixes).

Arabic uses few words of foreign origin as the root-and-pattern system generates words for new concepts and inventions. For the hybrid 'automobile' Arabic uses the word that can only mean 'something-which-moves-of-itself', a word found in the Qur'an but with the meaning of 'planet'. Hence, manuals of information technology, nuclear physics, medicine, etc., can use only Arabic words. Far from importing foreign words, Arabic has exported many hundreds of words, particularly to Spanish and Portuguese, influenced by Arabic in the Iberian Peninsula for 800 years.

Arabic is clearly related to ancient Semitic languages. The Hebrew alphabet is almost the same as the Arabic, although the order differs. Similarly, the Aramaic spoken by Jesus at the Crucifixion is clearly Semitic 'Eloi, Eloi, lamma sabachtani' ('My God, my God, why has thou forsaken me?'). Similar features can be found in Syriac, a dialect which became a language of Christian ritual.

Arabic inscriptions have been found from before Islam. Probably the Bible was translated in part into Arabic for the Arabic-speaking Christian tribes, such as Ghassan, living in what is modern Syria.

As seen above CA is a highly developed form of a Semitic dialect, the dialect spoken in Mecca at the time of Muhammad by his tribe, the Quraysh, who were then dominant. The origins of Arabic speech are lost in Arab mythology which associates northern Arabic with an eponymous ancestor Adnan and southern Arabic with Qahtan. It was northern Arabic, and more particularly that of Mecca, which became the dominant form of written Arabic, enshrined in the Qur'an.

Arabic is spoken by some 300 million native speakers of whom many millions are Christian, in Palestine, Jordan, Egypt, Lebanon, Syria, Iraq, and Sudan. Arabic is the language of prayer for some 1.2

billion Muslims for whom only the Arabic text of the Qur'an is valid. The modern language is clearly related to CA, the language of the Qur'an and of a rich literature in prose and poetry. Indeed all the dialects can be related to MWA and CA, especially in vocabulary.

A medieval Arabic writer said, 'Wisdom has alighted on three things: the brain of the Franks, the hand of the Chinese, and the tongue of the Arabs'.

And finally, it is a pious belief that those who attain Paradise will there speak Arabic.

LESLIE MCLOUGHLIN

ARABIC LANGUAGE, ELEMENTS OF

Arabic is a south-central Semitic language spoken by over 300 million people, principally in the countries of the Middle East and North Africa. It is also the liturgical language of Muslims throughout the world, whatever their native language may be. The Holy Book of Islam, the Qur'an, is written and recited in Arabic. The elegance and beauty of its language, normative for classical Arabic, is the basis for the development of the modern literary language which is used in the media throughout the Arabic-speaking world. Arabic is written from right to left, using an alphabet which consists of twenty-eight consonants or radicals. In normal use (the Qur'an being the notable exception, because there must be no room for ambiguity in its private or public lection) the written language appears in vowel-less, that is in unpointed format. The three basic vowels are represented by *fatha* ('a' in the English word pat), *kasra* ('i' as in pit), and *damma* ('u' as in put), each of which may be shown as short or long vowels. With few exceptions Arabic words are derived from 'simple roots', which consist of groups of three consonants. So, for example, the many words derived from groups such as *DRS*, *KSR* and *KTB* suggest aspects of 'studying', 'breaking' and 'writing' respectively. The normal word order in Arabic is verb, subject, object. The tense structure of the Arabic verb is derived from the same basic root system, with the addition of prefixes, intermediary letters and suffixes to indicate completed or uncompleted action. Colloquial Arabic is spoken in many local dialects in different parts of the world. In the Middle Ages, Arabic was the language into which ancient works on astronomy, geography, history, medical theory and practice, philosophy and religion were translated and preserved before many of the originals were lost. English-speaking students, who are interested in deepening their knowledge and understanding of Islamic civilisation, may be guided through the intricacies of Arabic vocabulary, grammar and syntax by the books mentioned in the Reference section.

References

Abboud *et al.* (1976), Abdul-Rauf (1977), Kapliwatsky (1975), Middle East Centre for Arab Studies (1974), Wehr (1961).

EDWARD D. A. HULMES

ARABIC SYLLOGISM

After Aristotle's *Prior Analytics* and a number of important commentaries on it had been translated from the Greek, a process which took a little over 200 years, syllogism became an object of intensive study and disputed interpretation. Broadly speaking, two schools of interpretation emerged, one which may be termed Farabian (after al-Farabi, d. AD 950), the other Avicennan (after Avicenna, d. AD 1037). Aristotle's original system of the *Prior Analytics* always constituted the focus of study of the Farabian school, whereas Avicenna's revised system came to be the focus of study of the Avicennan school – in the Avicennan school, in fact, after Avicenna Aristotle ceased to figure as a point of reference.

Syllogistic was investigated in Islamic realms generally from one of four main points of interest: (1) the analysis of juristic arguments in terms of syllogism; (2) the 'matter' of syllogisms, and how it determines the kind of argument produced; (3) the relation between the categorical and the hypothetical syllogistics; and (4) the modal syllogistic. Each of these points will be treated briefly in what follows.

Analysis of juristic arguments in terms of syllogism. One of al-Farabi's concerns was to find a place for logic alongside the Islamic disciplines (such as jurisprudence, Koranic interpretation, grammar) which were, in the early tenth century, acquiring their classical formulation. An important strategy in advancing a case for logic in this way was to show that the argument-technique used in juristic and theological reasoning, analogy, depended for its theoretical justification on the syllogism. Al-Farabi wrote a text, translated as the *Short Commentary on the Prior Analytics*, in which he analysed the structure of these arguments as ultimately syllogistic. Whatever the logical merits in this effort, it was taken up by Ibn Hazm (d. AD 1064) and, more importantly, by Abu Hamid al-Ghazali (d. AD 1111), who went so far as to preface his juridical summa, *The Distillation of the Principles of Jurisprudence*, with a short treatise on Aristotelian logic presenting precisely this kind of analysis.

The 'matter' of syllogisms. Another point of discussion had to do with the analysis of syllogistic matter, that is, the epistemic level of each premise making up the syllogism. A valid syllogism with certain premises is a demonstration, one with premises agreed on for the sake of argument is dialectical, one with premises that are merely persuasive is rhetorical, and one with premises that excite the imagination is poetical. This arrangement of stretches of discourse is Alexandrian in origin, but characterises all later Avicennan texts, including, for example, the much-studied *Logic for Shamsaddin* by Najm al-Din al-Katibi (d. AD 1276).

The relation between the categorical and hypothetical syllogistics. Farabian logicians tended to disregard the hypothetical syllogistic, considering it something Aristotle had rightly neglected. Avicenna, by contrast, had argued that Aristotle had written a text on hypothetical syllogisms that had been lost, and devoted a large part of his treatment of the syllogistic to what we would call hypothetical syllogisms. He also went on – and he claimed this as his own innovation – to divide syllogisms into those in which the conclusion is only present in the premises potentially (the *iqtirani*, this would include what we call a categorical syllogism) and those in which the conclusion or its contradictory is present in the premises actually (the *istithna'i*). This means that inferences like 'if P, then all As are Bs, but all Bs are Cs, therefore if P, then all As are Cs' are for Avicenna *iqtirani*. Avicenna analysed the proof for Baroco (some Js are not Bs, all As are Bs, therefore some Js are not As) into *iqtirani* and *istithna'i* syllogisms:

Iqtirani: When it is not the case that some Js are not As, then all Js are As, but all As are Bs, therefore when it is not the case that some Js are not As, then all Js are Bs.

Istithna'i: When it is not the case that some Js are not As, then all Js are Bs, but it is not the case that all Js are Bs, therefore it is not not the case that some Js are not As. (QED).

This analysis was the subject of much later discussion and dispute. The hypothetical syllogistic was extended and explored in other ways by writers after Avicenna.

The modal syllogistic. A primary point of interest of the tenth and eleventh-century logicians was in making sense of Aristotle's notoriously complex modal syllogistic. Numerous strategies were investigated by the Farabian school, the most important for subsequent Western discussions being one which turned on a distinction between *per se* and *per accidens* readings. More interesting – and much more important for the Islamic world – was the alternative system proposed by Avicenna. One important aspect of the system is that it is built on the necessity-contingency layers of the syllogistic, rather than on the assertoric syllogistic as Aristotle's is. Another aspect is Avicenna's investigation of propositions in the descriptional (*wasfi*) reading (all As are Bs while As) and how they contribute to inferences. Later Avicennan logicians extended the number of propositions investigated, and introduced repairs to the original Avicennan system; they also evinced entire indifference to square what they did with the Aristotelian text.

The only work on the syllogistic done in Arabic which had any impact on the Latin West was the work on the modal syllogistic of the Farabian school. This was a consequence of the difference in textual focus between the Farabian and Avicennan schools; the Farabian school could have real impact on Christian and Jewish scholars of the medieval West who were working on Aristotelian texts. Avicenna's system, by contrast, just seemed incommensurable with the *Prior Analytics*, and was ignored by the translators.

References:

Lagerlund (2000), Lameer (1994), Rescher and Van Der Nat (1974), Shehaby (1973), Street (2002).

TONY STREET

ARAB–ISRAELI WARS (THE WARS STEMMING FROM THE CREATION OF ISRAEL)

Following the declaration of the State of Israel on 14 May 1948, the armies of Egypt, Transjordan, Syria, Lebanon and Iraq invaded, but by 7 January 1949 Israeli troops had pushed them back beyond the area granted by the UN Partition Plan of 1947. In 1956, Israeli forces attacked Egypt as part of an Anglo-French plan to control the Suez Canal and overthrow the Nasser regime. Israeli forces triumphed, but withdrew leaving Sinai to UN peacekeepers. In June 1967, Israel again attacked following an ill-conceived Arab diplomatic campaign. The Egyptian Air Force was destroyed on 5 June, and Israeli troops went on to conquer the Sinai, the West Bank, east Jerusalem, and the Golan Heights. The Six Day War marked a turning point. The future of the Occupied Territories now dominated the conflict, as the frontline Arab states gradually gave up on the aim of destroying Israel and instead sought to bargain a 'land-for-peace' deal. The October War of 1973, launched by Egypt and Syria during the Jewish festival of Yom Kippur, was a limited war. The attack on 6 October caught Israel off guard as did Arab fighting abilities, but Israeli forces eventually prevailed, crossing the Suez Canal and menacing Damascus. Superpower intervention forced an end to the fighting, although the related Arab oil embargo would have lasting consequences. The Egyptian regime went on to negotiate a separate peace deal with Israel in 1978–9.

References

Perrett (1996: 120–1, 270–2, 283–4), Salibi (1976: 960–1, 964–5).

SIMON W. MURDEN

A'RAD (sing. *'arad*)

A'rad is the plural of the word *'arad* which means what is not substantial but accidental and changing. The word *'arad* is usually translated into English as 'accident'. The Muslim theologians, *al-Mutakallimun,* used this word in order to explain the nature of the change in everything. Most of them adopted the Greek theory of atomism. All bodies or material things, for them, consist of very small parts or atoms. These atoms in themselves do not have any attributes except of being in existence and occupying space. Their qualities, however, derive from some attributes which come to inhere in the atoms for a long or a short period. These attributes, which causes change in all beings, they call *a'rad.* Thus *a'rad* are the powers which cause change and activity in the things. It is possible to compare *a'rad* with the Aristotelian concept of *form* which actualises matter, however, the Arabic concept *a'rad* is more complex because the activity of each moment is explained and interpreted as an inherent quality of a certain *'arad* (accident) at a certain moment. *A'rad* are also distinguished from the Aristotelian form by being created by God at the time when they inhere in the atom and only God can make them disappear. However, the Mu'tazilites consider the possibility of the existence of *a'rad* as a consequence of human ability and will, for example, a teacher creates the *'arad* of knowledge in his pupils by the power of his teach-

ing, or generates the *'arad* of pain by beating someone.

References

Dhanani (1994).

MAHA EL-KAISY FRIEMUTH

AL-A'RAF

'The Heights' (Q.7:46–7), a place between paradise and hell where believers may be relegated, without suffering, if their good and bad deeds are equal. They will eventually enter Paradise.

ANDREW J. NEWMAN

'ARAFAT, YASIR (1929–2004) PALESTINIAN LEADER

'Arafat was born either in Egypt or in Jerusalem and was raised in Jerusalem, Egypt and Gaza. In 1948 he moved to Cairo after the foundation of the state of Israel and in 1956 took an engineering degree at Cairo University where he became involved in student political activities, chairing the Palestinian Students' Union. In the early 1960s he helped to found Fatah – the Palestinian guerrilla movement dedicated to the elimination of Israel and to the foundation of a Palestinian state. In 1968 he took Fatah into the Palestinian Liberation Organisation (PLO), the umbrella body for all Palestinian groups. Under him, Fatah began to make raids into Israel mainly from Jordan and became the most powerful of the PLO groups. In 1969 he was made Chairman of the PLO executive committee and Commander-in-Chief, i.e., he became the recognised leader of the Palestinian national movement. Through thick and thin he remained as such. The PLO was not a state and neither was it a fully fledged liberation movement and, consequently, it found it difficult to play an effective role. In Jordan it acted in defiance of the legitimate government and King Husayn tried to suppress it in 'Black September' 1970. 'Arafat was forced to leave Amman for Beirut. For several years the Arab world could not reach agreement on whether to support him until in 1974 the Arab League recognised the PLO as the sole legitimate representative of the Palestinian people. At the United Nations he famously appeared with an olive branch and a gun and called for the creation of a Palestinian state threatening a violent response if this did happen. Several years of hijackings, assassinations and bombings followed.

In Beirut the PLO set up a large bureaucracy that provided welfare, support and some education for the Palestinian refugees. In 1982 Israel invaded Lebanon in an attempt to liquidate the PLO and 'Arafat had to flee again, this time to Tunis. His power decreased but he stayed on and in 1988 he renounced military opposition to Israel which he recognised as a legitimate state. He inexplicably backed the Iraqi invasion of Kuwait and lost much credibility, some of which he regained when he moved towards peace negotiations with Israel. In September 1993 in Washington he and Prime Minister Rabin signed a peace agreement. They (together with Israeli foreign minister Peres) received the Nobel peace prize.

The Palestinian Authority was created on a small part of the occupied West Bank and 'Arafat and the PLO took control of Jericho. In December 1995 under the Oslo Agreement Israeli forces withdrew from the main West Bank towns. However, after the assassination of Rabin and the subsequent election of hardliner Binyamin Netanyahu, the peace process stalled. He opposed the Oslo Agreement and continued to build settlements in the occupied areas. 'Arafat was placed in a dilemma. He wanted peace and stability yet could not stand idly by in face of continued Israeli expansion into his lands. Hamas (an extreme Islamic resistance group) continued attacks against the Israeli population and he was continually pressured into condemning them.

Under President Clinton negotiations restarted as the Israeli position hardened. 'Arafat and Netanyahu met twice and signed the Wye Memorandum by which Israel was supposed to withdraw further and Palestine to cease terrorist attacks. Prime Minister Ehud Barak met 'Arafat in 1999 but they could not agree over settlements and territory. Unrest continued in the Palestinian areas while 'Arafat's popularity wavered. Some thought him too ready to make concessions and others criticised his autocracy and the way he handled the final status talks. In July 2000 he met Barak again at Camp David where they could reach no agreement. Everything was put into the melting pot when General Sharon provocatively visited the Haram (Temple Mount) with an armed guard in September 2000. The second Palestinian *intifada* (uprising) broke out. Sharon – now Prime Minister – sought to quell it and to prevent suicide bombings in Israel by reoccupying Palestinian areas and by severe retaliatory measures against people and property. 'Arafat was rendered virtually helpless by being confined to his HQ in Ramallah and Sharon and President George W. Bush refused to negotiate him as they considered him a terrorist leader.

'Arafat was largely ineffective under Israeli pressure. He nevertheless remained the representative of his people although accused of autocracy, corruption and violation of human rights.

References

Hart (1989), Hopwood (1989).

DEREK HOPWOOD

ARKAN

See: **Pillars of Islam**

AL-'ARSH, ISTAWA 'ALA

From such verses as Q.7:54 and Q.32:4, 'He mounted the throne'. The followers of Ahmad ibn Hanbal and the Ash'ari school understood this and references to Allah's face and hands as literal descriptions of the attributes of Allah.

References

Watt (1973: 310).

See also: **attributes of God;** *tashbih*

ANDREW J. NEWMAN

'ASABIYYA

In Arabic historical texts, the term *'asabiyya* refers to the internal loyalty of a group (normally a tribe), or the loyalty of an individual to that group. Arab tribes are said to have had a 'strong' *'asabiyya*: the tribal factions of Qays and Kalb for example had, according to some sources, 'strong tribal loyalty' *shadid al-'asabiyya*, as did many Arabian tribes in both the *jahiliyya*, and Islam. Individuals also had this quality, which meant at times the quality of tribal loyalty, and at other times the ability to inspire tribal loyalty (through leadership or through reciting poetry in which the tribes exploits are described). The Prophet Muhammad is said to have condemned *'asabiyya*, claiming it had no place in Islam, because the believers' loyalty was to the Muslim community (*umma*) as a whole and not to any remnant of pre-Islamic tribal lineage.

Perhaps the most impressive pre-modern analysis of *'asabiyya* is that of the great Muslim historian Ibn Khaldun (d. AD 1382). Ibn Khaldun sees *'asabiyya* as one of the processes operating in human history, influencing the rise and fall of dynasties and empires. *'Arabiyya*, he argued, was the driving force behind the territorial expansion of political units, falling away as the tribal group which has gained dominance seeks to secure their power through other means. The implication is that whilst the Muslim empire was built up through *'asabiyya*, it was maintained through the establishment of a coherent ideology. This remarkable 'modern' insight into the processes of power formation and maintenance has its parallels in later Western sociology (such as Weber's theory of the necessary 'routinisation' of charisma and the establishment of a 'rationality' by the dominant power group). Ibn Khaldun did not conceive of *'asabiyya* in purely biological or racial terms, loyalty could find its roots in blood-ties between individuals, but more importantly it could be manufactured through 'affiliation' (*wala'*). *Wala'* was a legal process whereby one individual (normally a slave) becomes 'bonded' to another (normally the slave's former master). The slave is loyal to his master because his master 'owns' him, the manumitted slave is loyal because of the tie of *wala'* – the slave, and his descendants, continue to be indebted to the one who freed them. This allegiance is displayed in their *'asabiyya*. In the early period, non-Arab converts to Islam acquired an affiliate tribe to which they regularly displayed devout loyalty in battles and internal conflicts.

The Prophet's condemnation of *'asabiyya* is often cited as evidence that the new religion of Islam did not recognise race or lineage as important elements in the assessment of an individual. The issue of racial purity, though, obviously troubled some early Muslims more than others (the *hadiths* relating to this topic probably reflect disputes between Arab 'purists' and those who placed less emphasis on race). Race undoubtedly played a part in the unfolding Islamic empire. Non-Arab converts to Islam (*mawali*) were crucial to the success of the 'Abbasid revolution, as they felt excluded from the Arab Umayyad power structures. The issue of the superiority of Arabs over the non-Arabs plagued the early Muslim community and led to internal tensions within the Empire. In religious literature, the importance of lineage was also stressed in various elements of law: the caliph must be from the Quraysh (according to most Sunni jurists), an Arab should not marry a non-Arab (a popular element of Sunni marriage law). Perhaps the most widespread phenomenon linked to racial and lineage purity can be found in the belief of the Shi'a groups that only a member of the *ahl al-bayt* (the 'people of the house' of the Prophet) could lead the Muslim community. Later, in Shi'i thought, it was only through a member of the *ahl al-bayt* that religious knowledge could be gained. The believers, under such a scheme, affiliate themselves to the imam, and thereby, it might be said, show '*asabiyya* to the line of descendants of the Prophet Muhammad.

References

Crone (1987, 1994), Mahdi (1957).

ROBERT GLEAVE

AL-ASAD, HAFIZ (1928–2000) PRESIDENT OF SYRIA

Asad was born in the Syrian village of Qardahah near Latakia of a poor peasant family of the 'Alawi sect, an esoteric minority whose religion is an amalgamation of pre-Islamic, extreme Shi'ism and Christian elements. They claim to be Muslim but some strict Sunnis do not recognise them as such. They gained importance when, later, Asad

and his entourage took power. Growing up under the French mandate, Asad, like other politically minded students, was drawn into anti-French activities. In the 1940s his political awakening coincided with the birth of the Ba'th party which, with its secularist nature, attracted members of the marginal communities. However, he first entered the Homs Military Academy in 1951 and was trained there and in the Soviet Union. He became a combat pilot in 1954. He remained so committed to Ba'thi politics that during the union with Egypt (1958–61) he and other officers were sent to Cairo to be kept under Egyptian control. While there, he and other officers formed a committee that aimed to take Syria out of the union and to replace those Syrian Ba'thi leaders who had originally formed it. He returned to Syria after the break-up of the United Arab Republic and helped to carry out a coup in 1963. He became Minister of Defence 1966–70 during which period Syria suffered its disastrous defeat in the 1967 war with Israel and lost the Golan Heights territory. After he and a group of colleagues seized power in 1970 he became Prime Minister and was elected President in 1971.

In foreign affairs he was committed to the cause of pan-Arabism, was firm in opposition to Israel and played a role in stabilising the Middle East. Because of the bitter rivalry between the Ba'th parties of Syria and Iraq, Asad supported Iran in the Iran–Iraq war. At home he showed indifference to human rights and democracy and tolerated official corruption until his later years and presided over a long period of economic stagnation. He was the target of attempted coups and sent the army to Hama in 1982 to brutally crush an uprising there led by the Muslim Brothers.

He supported President Sadat of Egypt during the 1973 war but rejected

Egypt's agreements with Israel in the later 1970s. He sought rather a total agreement by which Syria would regain the Golan Heights.

One of his main preoccupations was relations with Lebanon which Syria never really recognised as an independent state. Civil war there and the Israeli intervention threatened Syria's stability and in 1986 he sent troops into Lebanon and brokered a cease fire in 1987. In 1990, Asad sent Syrian troops to Saudi Arabia to support the coalition against Iraq in the Gulf War. For this and despite his previous close relations with USSR he was looked upon with more favour by the West. This did not mean he would make peace with Israel as he still insisted on the unconditional return of the Golan. He did agree, however, to attend negotiations but these stalled under the hard line Israeli Prime Minister Netanyahu. They were resumed under Barak but were cut short by Asad's death. The West accused him of supporting the Hizbollah in south Lebanon and of allowing Palestinian resistance groups freedom to act from Syria.

At home in his later years he allowed a little liberalisation, some privatisation was introduced, and the Ba'th won control at elections. In 1999 the People's Assembly voted him a fifth term of office as President. He was succeeded by his son Bashar.

References

Seale (1990).

DEREK HOPWOOD

ASBAB AL-NUZUL

'Occasions of revelation'. Muslim tradition speaks of the Qur'an being revealed to Muhammad over a period of twenty-three years in discrete sections. Theoretically, each of those revelations may be connected to a time and space within the life of Muhammad and, sometimes, that situation is seen to have a causal connection to the contents of the text. That connection is sometimes very direct as in specifying who the particular revelation was directed to (for example, Muhammad's wives as in Q.33), and sometimes more oblique, as in simply providing the name of someone referred to in the text. *Asbab al-nuzul* reports were gathered together by Muslim exegetes and formed into an independent genre of texts within the interpretative tradition. The most famous of its type is by al-Wahidi who died in AD 1076, entitled simply *Kitab Asbab al-Nuzul*, it gathers all the reports together following the order of the text of the Qur'an. In many instances variant accounts are provided, often differing significantly in their content (for example, whether the audience being addressed is the Jews or the pre-Islamic Arabs). Al-Suyuti (d. 1505) revised al-Wahidi's work and imposed a more systematic definition of what constituted an 'occasion of revelation' as compared (for example) to a mere identification of referents.

The traditions on the 'occasions of revelation' provide a sense of the historical underpinnings of the Qur'an, although in most cases they are quite vague about specific historical details such as date, time and place. Rather, the traditions provide a narrative interpretation of a verse embedded within the historical account through the careful use of textual glosses. Al-Wahidi, for example, was not concerned to identify a single historical circumstance, but rather was quite prepared to accommodate rival accounts of the historical context within the text. This emphasises the point that history is not what is at stake in these traditions, but rather exegesis. A number of reports simply indicate to whom the verse was addressed, such comments are crucial for interpretation but have little to do with a historical or chronological determination.

References

Calder *et al.* (2003: §4.4), Rippin (1988: 1–20).

ANDREW RIPPIN

AL-ASH'ARI (*c.* AD 873–935)

The founding father of one of the main schools of thought in Islamic theology, which still exists today, along with that of al-Maturidi. Al-Ash'ari was born in Basra and studied there in the school of the Mu'tazila. Around AD 912, however, he claims to have had a series of dreams during the month of fasting, Ramadan, in which he saw the Prophet Muhammad, who commanded him first to adhere to tradition, which al-Ash'ari at first understood to be a command to abandon *kalam* (rational theology); later, however, the Prophet told him not to abandon *kalam*, and this al-Ash'ari came to understand as being a call to defend tradition but using the methods of *kalam*. Whatever the nature of these experiences they accurately describe his intellectual pilgrimage as after AD 912 he adopted the views of the traditionists with reference to such things as the nature of God's attributes and of the Qur'an even if he sought to continue to use *kalam*-style arguments to defend these positions. He thus came to occupy a kind of intermediate position between the Mu'tazila on the one hand and the traditionists on the other hand. He also further developed the idea of *kasb* (acquisition) first proposed by Dirar ibn Amr whereby human actions were ultimately created by God but human beings acquired the responsibility for them.

References

Caspar (1998: Chapter 8), McCarthy (1953), Watt (1994: Chapter 10).

HUGH GODDARD

ASH'ARISM (AL-ASH'ARIYYA/ AL-ASHA'IRA)

A school of scholastic theology (*'ilm al-kalam*) belonging to the Sunni denomination attributed to its founder Abu 'l-Hasan 'Ali al-Ash'ari (AD 873–935). His life is said to have undergone three stages. First, a period spent studying under the Mu'tazilite master Abu 'Ali al-Jubba'i (d. AD 915) until he himself became a renowned scholar of this school. The second phase of his life includes his rejection of this theological school and his interpretation of Islamic texts in a manner that he considered to be in agreement with an intellectual approach. In the third stage he rejected this method also and reverted to the understanding of the earliest Muslim generations, which was to believe in all the Divine attributes amodally or 'without stating how' (*bi la kayf*). He wrote extensively on matters of theology and the resulting sectarianism that occurred because of the different approaches to this discipline, the most famous of his works being *Maqalat al-Islamiyyin*, *al-Luma'* and *al-Ibana fi Usul al-Diyana*. After his death many scholars explained and commentated upon his works, thus developing his thought to a new and quite different teaching, resulting from their application of scholastic theology (*'ilm al-kalam*) and philosophy (*falsafa*). This later development of the school then became identified with being 'Ash'ari' until it became synonymous with it. These later scholars included such luminaries as Abu Bakr Muhammad al-Baqillani (AD 950–1013), Abu

Muzaffar Shahfur al-Isfarayini (d. AD 1027), Abu 'l-Ma'ali 'Abd al-Malik al-Juwayni (AD 1027–85), Abu Hamid Muhammad al-Ghazali (AD 1058–1111) and Fakhr al-Din al-Razi (AD 1150–1210), who all played significant roles in the development of this school. As a result of the departure of this school from the earlier generations in its methodology, the school differs in a number of issues, which relate directly to tenets of faith. The use of the intellect (*al-'aql*) in dealing with such issues has caused them to approach tenets of faith generally and the certain divine attributes of Allah (*al-sifat*) in a particular way. Therefore regarding such Divine attributes as Allah having a face (*wajh*), hand (*yad*) and foot (*qadam*), many of the later Ash'arites reinterpret the attribute utilising metaphorical interpretation (*ta'wil*), as such divine attributes, as far as they are concerned, are 'intellectually incomprehensible' with regard to Allah. In this sense they have differed from the earliest generations as these Muslims saw no distinction, nor contradiction between the intellect and revelation and in all cases, revelation takes precedence, whether is it is 'intellectually comprehensible' or not, as for them this was the meaning of having true faith. Despite this however, they developed a theological discourse that directly countered the onslaught of Mu'tazilite rationalism, defending the 'traditional' position and as such, make up a large proportion of the Sunni Muslim community until the present day.

References

Hanafi (1980: 71–6), al-Johani (1999: 83–94), Netton (1997: 41), Watt (1948: 135–64; 1997: 64–8, 75–97; 2002: 303–16).

See also: **Mu'tazilism (al-Mu'tazila); Salafis; Sunnism**

GAVIN PICKEN

ASHAB AL-KAHF

The 'Companions of the Cave'. Mentioned in Q.18:9–26 (in a chapter called *Surat al-Kahf*, after this story), the account is a rendition of the Christian story of the 'Seven Sleepers' of Ephesus. According to the legend, seven young Christian men took refuge in a cave near Ephesus during the time of the persecution of Christians under the Emperor Decius (ruled AD 249–51). They fell into a miraculous sleep for over a century and awoke during the rule of Emperor Theodosius – either the Great (AD 379–95) or the Younger (AD 408–50). They were discovered and shortly thereafter died. Their grave was considered, since the beginning of the sixth century, a place of worship.

In the Qur'an, the story is appropriately Islamicised. The youths fled in order to be able to preserve their faith in the one God. Their sleep lasted 309 years but it seemed like only a day to them. They were discovered when one of them used an antiquated coin in the neighbouring city. Just how many youths there were is uncertain according to the Qur'an, although it is known that there was a dog with them who counts as one of their number.

References

Gibb and Bosworth (1960–2003: I, 691).

ANDREW RIPPIN

AL-ASMA' AL-HUSNA

See: **beautiful names of God**

ASSASSINS (HASHISHIYYA)

The Assassins (Hashishiyya) were a sect of the Nizari Isma'ilis, active between the eleventh and thirteenth centuries, and operating mainly in northern Iran.

The Nizaris' origins are to be found in the dispute over the succession to the Fatimid caliph and Isma'ili Imam, al-Mustansir bi'llah (d. AD 1094). When al-Mustansir died, his second son Ahmad 'al-Musta'li' was proclaimed caliph and imam inside Fatimid territory. Hasan-i Sabbah, the Isma'ili missionary in Iran however recognised al-Mustansir's older son, Nizar as imam. From then on (and to this day) the Isma'ilis divided between Musta'lis and Nizaris. Hasan-i Sabbah, who had led the force which captured the fort of Alamut, near Qazvin in 1090, set up an alternative Isma'ili structure with himself as 'proof' (*hujja*) or representative of the (now hidden) Nizar. He saw the outside world as hostile and full of unbelief, and sent out missionaries to parts of Iran in order to gain disciples and lead uprisings. Many of these were successful and even before the split with Fatimid Egypt, Hasan had established a network of Isma'ili agents across Iran. After the split, Hasan set about making his Nizari disciples loyal spies, who would be willing to attack and kill prominent 'Abbasid and Fatimid figures. Legend has it that Hasan and his successor 'proofs' drugged Nizari disciples with hashish, promised them the delicacies of heaven in reward for loyalty, and then sent them out to commit political murder. For this reason they were called the *hashishin* (*hashish*-users), from which the term 'assassin' is derived.

Amongst the victims of the Nizari assassins were Nizam al-Mulk (in AD 1092), the Fatimid caliph, al-Amir (AD 1130), the 'Abbasid caliph al-Mustarshid (AD 1135), Shihab al-Din (the vizier to the Zangid ruler of Aleppo in AD 1177) and, most interestingly, Marquis Conrad of Montferrat (King of Jerusalem in AD 1192). As can be seen, these murders were carried out (primarily) for political purposes. Sunnis, the Isma'ili Fatimids and even Christian crusaders were prey to Nizari killers. In northern Iran, Hasan and his successors set about establishing an effective Isma'ili state. They had captured a number of castles before the split with the Fatimids, and they continued this expansion despite Saljuq attempts to rein in Nizari activity. Apart from Alamut and the other fortresses in the Elburz mountains, the Nizaris captured or built castles in Quhistan and near Isfahan. Nizaris in Syria also sought to establish fortress bases and they did achieve recognised status (of a sort) in Damascus when they were allowed to operate the fortress at Banyas and, later, a number of other castles. The 'Assassins' were eventually crushed by the Mongols in 1256, and whilst the Nizaris continued to exist as a religious community (living under Mongol and later Safavid rule), the activities for which the Assassins had become famous came to an end.

References

Daftary (1994), Hodgeson (1955), Ivanow V. (1960), Lewis (1968).

ROBERT GLEAVE

ASTROLABE (*AL-ASTURLAB*)

Astrolabes were in use in the early Middle Ages in the Islamic world and Europe. These compact scientific instruments were once employed by astronomers for their observations of celestial bodies, by mariners for calculating the latitude and longitude of their positions at sea, and even by astrologers for their predictions. By observing the altitude of the sun or a star above the horizon, an observer could also establish the local time. An astrolabe could also be used for terrestrial surveying, for example, to measure the height of a mountain. The simplest form consisted of a flat disc with the degrees of a circle marked round its circumference. A pivoting pointer, known to Arab astronomers as the 'alidade' (al-'idad), was positioned in the centre of the disc. Observers were able to align a chosen object in the sky along its length and then take measurements with reference to the network of lines engraved on the disc. Astrolabes were made of wood, iron or brass. The planespheric astrolabe, a more sophisticated and sometimes elaborately decorated instrument, enabled observers to work out the position of the sun and other stars in relation to the celestial sphere. Its disc bore a 'climate' (a star 'map') and the circle of the zodiac. Seafarers began to use the sextant instead of the astrolabe from the late fifteenth century AD, at a time when their voyages of discovery called for a more reliable navigational instrument.

References

Mostyn and Hourani (1988: 268–9).

EDWARD D. A. HULMES

ASTROLOGY (*'ILM AL-TANJIM*)

In the Middle East, the pseudo-science of astrology dates back at least as far as the second millennium BC. The Assyrians and the Chaldaeans were among the first to employ a system of divination that was based upon astronomy and numerology rather than on worship of the gods and goddesses of the sky. In India and China, the origins of astrology are lost in history. Astrologers claim to be able to predict future events after studying the motion and positions of the Sun, Moon, planets, stars and other celestial bodies. Interpreting the course of human existence in the light of historical, contemporary and future cosmic and climatic occurrences became a subject of increasing popular interest with the invention of the horoscope in Hellenistic times. Astrologers still use the device, with its twelve signs of the Zodiac, to reveal what is likely to happen to an individual from birth. Astrology arrived in medieval Europe from the Arabs. Among the Arab astronomer/astrologers was the tenth-century Abu Ma'shar Ja'far b. Muhammad al-Balkhi. Claims that the movements and phases of heavenly bodies determine what happens on Earth do not accord with Islamic tradition. As a means of divining the future, astrology has been condemned in Islam as dangerous to the soul, although in an age when the distinction between astrology, astronomy and mathematics was not clearly drawn, astrology was widely practised in the Islamic world, as elsewhere. Monotheists, whose worldviews are predicated on the contingency of the universe, affirm the sovereignty of the Creator, whose will and purpose for the creation is progressively revealed. For Muslims this revelation is already 'written' (*maktub*) and literally *prescribed*. Speculation about the course of future events must, therefore, give way to patient effort to acquire knowledge of what has been ordained by divine *fiat*. This is implied by Islamic belief in God's eternal knowledge. In the exercise of 'choice' and 'free-will' Muslims are inevitably constrained by divine decrees.

References

Mostyn and Hourani (1988: 266–7), Schacht and Bosworth (1979: 441–3).

See also: **astronomy (*'ilm al-falak, 'ilm al-nujum*); iman; magic and talismans; mathematics**

EDWARD D. A. HULMES

ASTRONOMY ('ILM AL-FALAK, 'ILM AL-NUJUM)

As in the study of other natural sciences, the development of astronomy in the world of Islam was influenced in the first instance by work already done in other countries, notably during the florescence of the ancient cultures of China, Egypt, Greece, India and Mesopotamia. Few works from this scholarly corpus were more important for the researches of Arabic speaking astronomers than those of Indian provenance dealing with aspects of mathematics. These and many other scientific treatises and texts in discrete disciplines began to be translated into Arabic (and subsequently into Latin) from Sanskrit and the languages of Byzantium and Asia Minor. Without this labour of translation into Arabic many classical astronomical and mathematical texts would be unknown today because the originals have been lost. The significance of this scientific legacy was assimilated by Arabs who soon instituted inquiries of their own in the years following the rapid expansion of Islam from Arabia into the surrounding countries in, and after, the seventh century AD. This scientific research continued as an integral part of Islamic culture into the fourteenth and fifteenth centuries AD. Observatories were built by Muslims, notably in Baghdad, Cairo, Delhi, Istanbul and Samarkand. The fruits of this work on the ancient texts and the results of original observations were passed on to Europe. The journeys of discovery made by European mariners were helped by navigational instruments such as the astrolabe, the designs of which were refined in the light of observations made by the astronomers. Spanish-Arab astronomers detected and corrected observational errors in the ancient astronomical and astrological treatises. In Andalusia astrology served as a handmaid to astronomy because the prediction of astral influences on human behaviour and destiny called for the more precise positioning of celestial as well as terrestrial bodies. Muslim astronomers were not inhibited by tradition, however, from casting critical eyes on the cosmological theories of Ptolemy, challenging his misrepresentation of the movements of stars, Sun, Moon and planets. It may be said that in this respect they helped to prepare the way for Copernicus (1473–1543), whose observations led to the replacement of a geocentric theory of the universe by a heliocentric theory. Evidence of the work done by Islamic astronomers is to be found in the names by which some of the more prominent stars in the heavens are still popularly known. Among these are Aldebaran (*al-dabaran*) in the constellation Taurus, Algol (*al-ghul*) in Perseus, Betelgeuse (*bayt al-jawz*) and Rigel (*al-rijl*) in Orion, Deneb (*al-dhanab*) in Cygnus. Technical terms derived from the Arabic include albedo (*al-bayda'*, 'whiteness'), azimuth (*zawiyat al-sumut*, 'the direction of the paths'), nadir (*nazir al-samt*, 'the opposite of the direction'), zenith (*samt al-ra's*, 'the direction of the head').

References

Mostyn and Hourani (1988: 266–7), Schacht and Bosworth (1979: 461–4).

See also: **al-Andalus; astrolabe (*al-asturlab*); astrology ('ilm al-tanjim); mathematics; Ptolemy (Claudius Ptolomaeus)**

EDWARD D. A. HULMES

ATATURK, MUSTAFA KEMAL (1881–1938)

Turkish soldier, statesman and President. Ataturk was born in Salonika (Thessaloniki), the son of a minor official and timber merchant. He first went to military schools and then in 1899 entered the Military Academy in Istanbul. He was an outstanding student and soon became interested in politics. He joined the Young Turk movement of army officers that was founded to work against the autocratic Ottoman government that he believed was responsible for the ills of the Ottoman Empire. He was posted to Syria in virtual exile where, ever the activist, he founded the Fatherland and Freedom Society (1906). On transfer to Salonika he joined the important revolutionary body the Committee of Union and Progress dedicated to the overthrow of the Government. In 1908 it carried out the Young Turk revolution in which Ataturk played no active part. He continued his life as an efficient soldier in Libya, the Dardanelles and Bulgaria until the outbreak of the First World War in which Turkey allied itself with the Germans. He took a notable part in the defence of Gallipoli against the Allied invasion in 1915. He later served in the Caucasus and in Syria where he was put in charge of an army group that was unable to prevent the final defeat of the Turkish forces there.

After the armistice of October 1918 the Greek army foolhardily attempted to occupy Anatolia – the remaining heartland of Turkey after the demise of the Ottoman Empire. Ataturk, who had been appointed inspector of the Third Army in Anatolia, immediately rallied his forces to repel the Greeks. He was opposed to the existing government in Istanbul which he thought had weakly acquiesced in the Allied occupation of the capital and the possible partition of Turkish territory. He set up a separate nationalist government in Ankara in April 1920 that was able eventually to expel the Greeks from Turkish territory in 1922.

He now turned to internal affairs and proclaimed the birth of the Turkish Republic in October 1923 with himself as President. The sultanate in Istanbul was abolished and the capital transferred to Ankara. He embarked on a series of reforms to transform Turkey into a modern, secular Western type state. He established a single party regime (the Republican People's Party), introduced Western law, calendar, dress and alphabet and abolished many Islamic institutions. In 1928 Islam was removed as the state religion. Although not everyone welcomed all his reforms he was able to pursue his singular vision on the basis of his great prestige. Few were minded to oppose him. He eliminated all political rivals and ruled as a dictator with support from the army and other sections of the population. His ideology – named Kemalism – was recognised as the foundation of the new state and still remains honoured.

References

Kinross (1964), Mango (2000).

DEREK HOPWOOD

ATOMISM

Most Muslim theologians have adopted the theory that all bodies consist of several parts, the smallest of which they called atoms or *jawahir*. Badawi considers the Mu'tazilite Abu al-Hudhayl to be the earliest to adopt the theory of atoms and accidents. He was probably influenced by the ancient Greek atomists who, however, considered that the smallest part of the body, the atom, existed eternally. Yet the Greeks seem to believe that atoms function through their own qualities, while Muslim theologians consider that movements, convergence, warmth, coldness, and all other attributes do not belong to the atoms but come to inhere in them. Muslim theologians, in addition, considered that atoms are created and destroyed by God. Atoms in themselves have only two properties – of existence and occupying space. All their other activities are produced by the inherence of accidents which cause their movement and change. The version of atomism adopted by the Sunni Ash'arite school is used to explain their concept of God's decree for everything. God creates all accidents and atoms and also decrees their moment of dissolution. Therefore, they are considered to uphold an occasionist position in which nothing is considered to have a permanent character, but everything is subjected to change according to God's will. Thus, God determines the character of all things, rather than any natural law. This is considered the scientific explanation of the Qur'anic verse: 'Nor is hidden from the Lord the weight of an atom in earth or in heaven' (Q.10:61, Q.34:3).

References

Wolfson (1976: 466–86).

MAHA EL-KAISY FRIEMUTH

'ATTAR, FARID AL-DIN
(d. AD 1220)

One of the major Sufi poets of the medieval period, 'Attar composed much of his work in long couplet-poems (mathnawi) which were didactic in nature and in which the main narrative is complemented by incidental stories. His last and perhaps most well-known poem is the *Mantiq al-Tayr* (Conference of the Birds) in which 'Attar describes how all the birds join together to undertake an arduous journey, seeking the *Simurgh* who is their lord and master. The birds have to cross seven valleys, symbolic of seven stages in the quest for God. One by one the birds fall by the wayside until thirty birds are left, and when

they finally reach their destination they come to realise that they themselves, the thirty birds (*si murgh*), are the *Simugh*. 'Attar's other poetic works include *Asrar-nama* (*The Book of Secrets*), *Ilahi-nama* (*The Book of God*) and *Musibat-nama* (*The Book of the [Mystical] Goal*). He is also the author of a prose work of anecdotes and sayings about major Sufis called *Tadhkirat al-awliya'* (*Memorial of the Saints*).

References

Arberry (1964), Avery (1998).

LLOYD RIDGEON

ATTRIBUTES OF GOD

Such references in the Qur'an to Allah's face (e.g., Q.28:88), hands (e.g., Q.38:75) and such verses as Q.32:4 ('He mounted the throne') were understood by the followers of Ahmad ibn Hanbal (d. 855) and 'Ali al-Ash'ari (d. 935) as literal descriptions of the attributes of Allah which are separate and distinct from the divine essence. Together with their belief in the uncreatedness of the Qur'an the Hanbalis and Ash'arites opposed the recourse to philosophy and deductive reasoning practised by the Mu'tazilite school. The latter, whose origins lay in the wake of the disputes over the succession to the prophet and the promotion of the claims of latter's cousin and son-in-law 'Ali and his descendants over those of the Umayyad clan, maintained the validity of recourse to philosophy, the createdness of the Qur'an and the free will of man. The Mu'tazilites also denied the existence of the attributes of Allah on the grounds that it contradicted the oneness (*tawhid*) of Allah by suggesting that Allah's qualities were distinct from the divine essence. In the early ninth century, the 'Abbasid dynasty struggled to assert the legitimacy of its claim to authority by supporting the pro-'Alid aspects of Mu'tazilism. Thus in AD 827 the 'Abbasid caliph al-Ma'mun declared the createdness of the Qur'an official doctrine and Ibn Hanbal himself was scourged for his belief in the Qur'an's eternal nature. In the eleventh century, however, Ash'arism became the dominant theology among Sunni Muslims.

References

Fakhry (1983), Rahman (1979: 85–6), Waines (1995: 115–16), Watt (1973).

See also: **anthropomorphism;** *al-'arsh*, *istawa 'ala*; *mihna*; **ninety-nine names of God**; *tashbih*; *tawhid*

ANDREW J. NEWMAN

AVERROISM

Averroism refers to the adoption of Ibn Rushd's Aristotelian philosophy, it is a concept that flourished in Western culture from the end of the thirteenth century. Abu Walid Muhammad b. Ahmad b. Rushd, known in Latin as Averroes, was born in Cordoba in AD 1126 and died in Marrakesh in AD 1198. He was one of the most important Muslim philosophers in Spain. However, since he called for a revival of the strict and direct Aristotelian tradition and criticised the Neoplatonic tendency of the Arab philosophers, his books were not popular among the Eastern schools of philosophy. Most of his Arabic books are lost but, fortunately, survived in their Hebrew and Latin translations. The first Jewish philosopher who admired and paid great attention to Ibn Rushd's works was Moses Maimonides. Ibn Rushd's book of *Fasl al-Maaal* was studied carefully by many of the Jewish scholars of the time. They considered his arguments for the reconciliation between philosophy and religion to be strong and convincing. However, Leaman maintains that the term 'Averroist' should be applied only to those scholars who perceived the Aristotelian basis of Ibn Rushd's arguments. Averroism, in fact, flourished among Western scholars because of Averroes' contribution to the reviving of the true nature of Aristotle's thought. Ibn Rushd wrote commentaries on most of Aristotle's works with the aim of disentangling Aristotle from various misinterpreted versions and restoring his ideas in their purity. Many Western scholars have used his works to argue against the authority of the church, which supported Neoplatonic doctrines more than those of Aristotle. Ibn Rushd's philosophy also emphasises the role of humanity in receiving knowledge, based on the concept that matter has in itself the potential for form and that form and matter can exist independently without any divine force. This demonstrates that humans have in themselves the potential for receiving and creating knowledge, but their knowledge of the divine is received from the active intellect. This occurs when the active intellect unites itself with the human intellect for some moments and throws light upon it. Thus, Latin Averroism could possibly be the philosophical starting point of Western humanism.

References

Corbin (1986), Leaman (1996: 769–79).

See also: **double truth; Ibn Rushd, Abu al-Walid Ibn Ahmad (Averroes)**

MAHA EL-KAISY FRIEMUTH

AVICENNA

See: **Ibn Sina, Abu 'Ali al-Husayn**

AWLIYA'

'Saints', from Q.10:62 where it is usually translated as 'the friends of Allah'.

Though often disdained by traditional *'ulama'* as incompatible with the notion of the unity (*tawhid*) of Allah, the veneration of saints worship has been common in Islamic history and saints' tombs can be found in many Muslim countries.

References

Hourani (1991: 155–7).

See also: **wali**

ANDREW J. NEWMAN

AWRANGZIB B. SHAHJAHAN (r. 1658–1707)

Mughal ruler under whom the empire reached its maximum extent, swallowing up the remaining Shi'ite states of south India until only the Hindu kingdom of Vijayanagara remained in the southwestern tip of the Deccan. But within a few decades of Awrangzib's death, the Mughal empire disintegrated, receiving a death-blow from the Persian conqueror Nadir Shah's attack on Delhi in 1738–9 and the pressures of the resurgent Marathas and Sikhs. Traditionalist Muslims have regarded Awrangzib as a model Islamic ruler, one who endeavoured to assert the otherness of Islamic faith and culture within the surrounding sea of non-Islamic populations. He reversed the traditions of tolerance of his forebears, reimposing the poll tax on Hindus, and opposing the Shi'ites and the more syncretistic and immanentist of the Sufi orders in favour of the conservative Naqshbandiyya. Keenly interested in religion and learning, he commissioned a compendium of Hanafi law, the *Fatawa-yi 'Alamgiriyya*, which became canonical in Muslim India.

References

Gibb and Bosworth (1960–2003), Richards (1993: 151–252).

See also: **Akbar b. Humayun**

C. E. BOSWORTH

AWTAD

Four individuals within the hierarchy of Friends of God discussed by Sufis who inform the *qutb* (the pillar, or spiritual pole of the universe) about any imperfection in the universe.

LLOYD RIDGEON

AYA

A 'sign' or 'wonder' of God, specifically a verse of the Qur'an. The word is used in the Qur'an as a referent of the wonders of nature (as in lightning and rain in Q.30:24), of the more generalised 'signs' of God to which humans should pay attention (e.g., Q.6:124) and of the units of the Qur'anic recitation (Q.2:252: 'These are the verses of God which We recite to you'). Muslim tradition developed a system of verse separation and numbering for the text of the Qur'an based upon the rhyme words and assonance (sometimes ignoring the sense of the text), frequently resulting from the use of certain grammatical forms and endings that occur in Arabic. The resultant length of verses varies tremendously throughout the text. Such versification schemes resulted in variations emerging in the counting of the number of verses, with different traditions being associated with different geographical areas. Thus, the total number of verses in the Qur'an is calculated to be in the tradition of Kufa 6236, Basra 6204 or 6205, Damascus 6226, Hims 6232, Mecca 6219, and Medina 6210 or 6217. Some of these differences may be seen in the variation of verse numberings between translations of the text, especially when those from India are compared with those based upon the recent Egyptian printing of the Qur'anic text. Variation is especially to be noted as to whether the *basmala*, 'The name of God, the Merciful, the Compassionate' counts as a verse or not. The European tradition stemming from the 1834 printed text done by Gustav Flugel does not appear to follow any established Muslim tradition but is found in some translations. Tables of verse equivalences are found in many reference works on the Qur'an.

References

Spitaler (1935), Watt (1970).

ANDREW RIPPIN

AYATALLAH

'A sign of Allah' (e.g., Q.3:112, Q.40:4, Q.41:53). An honorific title, which appeared in the twentieth century, referring to a high-ranking Twelver Shi'i cleric.

References

Momen (1985: 248–9, 295–6).

See also: **Hujjat al-Islam; marji' al-taqlid; mujtahid**

ANDREW J. NEWMAN

'AYN AL-QUDAT AL-HAMADANI (AD 1098–1131)

The most accessible work of this mystic who wrote in both Arabic and Persian is probably *Tamhidat* (*Preparations*) in which he discusses the nature of faith and infidelity. The working of some themes in this book resemble some of those in Hallaj's *Tawasin*, notably the rehabilitation of Satan who is presented as a loyal monotheist for not bowing to Adam, but whose infidelity consists in his refusal of God's command to do so. In fact, it is the analysis of faith and infidelity that is central to *Tamhidat*, as infidelity is portrayed as a longing for union in which the individual must pass beyond the self. It is the stage where true faith and unity (*tawhid*) commence. The reasons for 'Ayn al-Qudat's execution are not entirely clear, although he was accused of claiming divinity, incarnationism and speaking of God in the language of the philosophers.

References

Arberry (1969), Lewisohn (1993).

LLOYD RIDGEON

AL-AYS WA 'L-LAYS

Al-ays wa 'l-lays are early form of terms which were used to refer to the existent beings, *ays*, and the non-existent, *lays*. The problem around the existent and non-existent flourished mainly among the Mutakallimun theologians, in their discussion of creation and the existence of the void in their theory of atomism. An early term which also expressed non-existence was *al-ma'dum* which Wolfson considers to have been used since John of Damascus, who introduced to the Arabs the formula of creation *ex nihilo*: *al-khalq min al-'adam*. The discussion about whether *al-ma'dum* is nothing or something, flourished mainly among the Mu'tazilite theologians. This discussion first concerned the existence of a void between all atoms and whether this void is itself non-existent or something which exists, *shay'*. The Greek Democritus, an early proponent of this theory, considers that the void is in no way less existent than anything else. However, this discussion seems to gain importance in the context of whether creation occurred *ex nihilo*. Wolfson considers that the Mu'tazilite concept that of *al-ma'dum* is something, *shay'*, is influenced by the above Greek doctrine, however, it seems that they later used the term *la min shay'* to express 'the nothing' *al-lays*, in order to avoid this confusion.

The Arab philosophers, in contrast, considered that 'nothing', *al-lays,* cannot exist because it would be impossible for it to do so since the world exists eternally, the possibility of existence must always have existed. Nevertheless, al-Kindi, who was known as the first philosopher of the Arabs, presented numerous arguments for the thesis that God has created the world from nothing, *lays.* This he calls *ibda',* origination, which proves God's ability to create and originate things from nothing, *lays* or *la min shay'.*

References

Wolfson (1976: 359–73).

MAHA EL-KAISY FRIEMUTH

AYYUB

The prophet Job, whose trials are mentioned in Q.21:83, and Q.38:41–2.

See also: **nabi**

ANDREW J. NEWMAN

AYYUBIDS (1169–later fifteenth century)

The Ayyubids were of Kurdish military origin, and their real founder Salah al-Din (Saladin) established their rule in Egypt after the death of the last Fatimid caliph in AD 1171. Other branches of the family arose in Syria, based on Damascus and other towns, in Upper Mesopotamia and even in distant Yemen, certain of these minor lines lingering on for several centuries. Salah al-Din restored Sunni tradition in Egypt after two centuries of Shi'ite rule, and he and his family began a policy of building and endowing Sunni mosques and *madrasas* all over the Near East. He recovered Jerusalem from the Crusaders in AD 1187, to lasting acclaim in the Islamic world. More than any other power, it was the Ayyubids who wore down the Crusader principalities of the Levant and reduced them to the coastland. Internal rivalries plus the appearance of the Mongols in the Near East led to their decline and replacement by the Mamluks.

References

Bosworth (1996: No. 30), Chamberlain (1998: 211–41), Gibb and Bosworth (1960–2003), Holt (1986: 46–81), Humphreys (1977).

C. E. BOSWORTH

AL-AZHAR

The name of the Azhar mosque (*al-Jami' al-Azhar*) and university, is derived from an Arabic root that also gives the word *al-zahra'* ('the shining one'), a sobriquet associated with Fatima, the youngest daughter of the Prophet Muhammad and wife of the fourth 'rightly guided Caliph', 'Ali. The 'Great Mosque' was built AD 972 by Jawhar al-Siqilli in al-Qahira (modern Cairo), which he planned and which became the new capital city of the Fatimid dynasty in Egypt a year later. By the end of the tenth century, al-Azhar was a leading centre of higher Islamic education and learning. Since then it has maintained a unique continuous tradition of teaching and research, earning a reputation as the most prestigious centre of Islamic learning in the world. Islamic scholars (*'ulama'*) are trained there for work throughout the Muslim world. From the beginning the curriculum included the Arabic language, Islamic law (*shari'a*), Islamic traditions (*hadith*), theology (*kalam*), the Qur'an, and commentary (*tafsir*) on its text. For a time, medicine and philosophy were also included, until both subjects were removed in deference to strict orthodox religious opinion. The study of philosophy (*falsafa*) was reinstated in the nineteenth century at the instigation of Jamal al-Din al-Afghani (1839–97), the political reformer who insisted that there could be no conflict between Islam and the broadening spectrum of knowledge. In the twentieth century, women were admitted as students in segregated academic departments, which now include the social sciences.

References

Hourani (1962: 103–29, 183–4, 336–7 *et passim*).

EDWARD D. A. HULMES

B

BABISM (AL-BABIYYA)

A pseudo-Islamic sect usually associated with the Shi'ite denomination, being attributed to its founder Mirza 'Ali al-Shirazi (1819–50) who was termed 'al-Bab', literally meaning 'the door' but used here to mean 'the gateway to divine enlightenment'. In 1844, he announced that he was the new 'Bab' and messenger of God in the same way that Musa (Moses), 'Isa (Jesus) and Muhammad were messengers of God. To this extent he claimed that the 'cycle of prophethood' had ended and a new one begun, with the implication that all the revelation revealed to the Prophet Muhammad, including the Qur'an and the Islamic law (*shari'a*), was now abrogated by a new revelation which had been revealed to him. As a result such basic concepts as *jihad* and the Islamic code dress for women were repealed. It is also interesting to note that this sect also fragmented after the execution of the 'Bab' for claiming physical and actual divine incarnation, this further schism being caused by the dispute between his appointed heir apparent Mirza Yahya 'Ali (d. 1912), known as 'Subh Azal' and his brother Mirza Husayn 'Ali (1817–92), known as 'Baha' Allah'. The former thus became the funder of the Azaliyya subsect whereas the latter founded the Bahai faith (al-Baha'iyya).

References

al-Johani (1999: 409–15), Netton (1997: 48), Zahir (n.d.).

See also: **Shi'ism; Sunnism**

GAVIN PICKEN

BABUR (r. 1526–30)

The Turco-Mongol descendant of Timur and the first implanter of Mughal power in north-western India. His early years were spent in central Asia vainly trying to restore his family's fortunes there, until he decided to seek his fortune at Kabul and then in India, against the Lodi line of Delhi sultans, laying the foundations for the achievement of his son Humayun. Babur was a considerable scholar and poet, writing in both Persian and his native Turkish, he left behind a *diwan* of poetry but, above all, his own autobiography, the *Babur-nama*, valuable both as a historical source and as a great work of Chaghatay Turkish literature.

References

Gibb and Bosworth (1960–2003), Richards (1993: 6–9).

C. E. BOSWORTH

BADR, BATTLE OF

Badr, a small village south-west of Medina, was the place where a force of 300 Muslims under the command of the Prophet Muhammad defeated about 1,000 Meccan Quraysh, led by Abu Jahl, in Ramadan, AD 624, the second year after the *hijra*. The Meccans had been sent to protect a wealthy caravan on its return from the north from an attack by the Medinan Muslims. Abu Jahl and seventy of his men were killed in the ensuing battle. In reality it was little more than a military skirmish, but it has assumed lasting significance in the life of the Islamic community. The fact that so few Muslims were able to defeat a much larger force of the pagan Quraysh, was seen as a confirmation of Muhammad's divine mission. Any challenge to his temporal authority or spiritual pre-eminence in Medina was thus set aside by this victory in the face of overwhelming odds. The military reverse suffered a year later at Uhud, brought about chiefly by the indiscipline of the Muslims on the Medinan side, caused only a temporary halt in the growing momentum of Muhammad's success. Questions were raised by these engagements. How legitimate is the prosecution of war during the months of truce? How are prisoners

taken in battle to be treated? How is booty to be distributed among the victors? Under what circumstances is *jihad* permissible? What is the fate of those who fall in battle? What provision is to be made for the widows of those who fall? After Badr the embryonic Islamic community needed the kind of guidance and regulation prescribed in the Medinan suras of the Qur'an. Badr and Uhud, respectively, continue to illustrate what the consequences of discipline and indiscipline can be for Muslims in following 'the Straight Path' of Islam. The Battle of Badr is seen in retrospect by Muslims as a deliverance similar to that of the Israelites under the Prophet Moses from the pursuing Egyptians. Reference is made (Q.8:41) to this day of 'testing' (*furqan*), this distinction between good and evil, which helped to vindicate Muhammad's prophethood and to confuse the pagan world.

References

Q.3:13, Q.8:5–19, Watt (1956: 13).

See also: **Uhud, Battle of;** *umma*

EDWARD D. A. HULMES

BAGHDAD

Capital of Iraq situated on the river Tigris in the centre of the country. It was founded by the Caliph al-Mansur in AD 762 near ancient Babylon and called Madinat al-Salam (city of peace). It was built on the plan of a round city surrounded by three concentric walls. It reached a peak of prosperity under Harun al-Rashid and it spread to the east bank of the river, the area which later became the heart of the city adorned with splendid Islamic buildings. It continued to prosper for four centuries after Harun as capital of the 'Abbasid Empire, the fabled city of the

The Thousand and One Nights. Its decline began when it was sacked in 1258 by Hulagu, grandson of Chingiz Khan, thereby putting an end to the 'Abbasid caliphate. The Mongols burnt down many mosques, shrines and city quarters but spared it from complete devastation. It lost its central importance, however, and was later (1401) sacked by Tamerlane, before falling successively under the control of the Persians (1508), and the Ottomans (1534), although Mamluks controlled it during part of the latter period. It remained a provincial city, seat of an Ottoman governor until it fell during the First World War to Anglo-Indian forces in 1917. It was chosen in 1921 as capital of the new state of Iraq, seat of government and of the monarchy. Since the revolution of 1958, the city has spread into many new areas. New roads, monuments, government and commercial buildings have been erected. It is the centre of manufacturing industry, of education and of culture. Few ancient Islamic buildings remain although some have been restored or rebuilt such as the al-Mustansiriyya College. The splendid mosque of al-Kazhimayn is in the suburbs. It was heavily bombed during the Anglo-American invasion in 2003.

References

Baghdad (1969), Hitti (1973).

DEREK HOPWOOD

BAHIRA

In the company of his uncle and protector, Abu Talib, the young Muhammad is said to have gone on a caravan journey to Syria. The story of this episode in the twelve-year-old boy's life tells how he met a Christian monk, to whom legend has given the name Bahira (an Aramaic word meaning 'chosen'), and who lived in a cell near Busra. The legend, recounted by Ibn Hisham (d. AD 834) goes on to say that when the caravan stopped near him, Bahira saw a cloud about one of the travellers, who was sitting shaded by the newly sprouted branches of a tree. The sight prompted Bahira to invite the travellers to share a meal with him. Muhammad was left to look after the caravan, but the monk sent for him, having noticed that the boy's features were those of the one appointed to be the last of the prophets of God. In response to questioning, and eschewing worship of pagan deities, the boy gave answers that confirmed Bahira's intuition about him. The monk then advised Abu Talib to guard the boy with special care.

EDWARD D. A. HULMES

AL-BAKRI, ABU 'UBAYD (d. AD 1094)

Arab geographer, theologian, poet and lexicographer, together with al-Idrisi, one of the two most important representatives of the 'post-classical' Arab geographical work *al-Masalik wa'l-mamalik*, a work which, in addition to the sort of basic geographical information implied by its title, is distinguished by its author's methodical approach to a wide variety of historical, political and social detail. Although this work no longer survives in its entirety and there are difficulties in determining its precise original scope, the sections on west Africa, Spain and eastern Europe contain much useful and detailed historical and ethnographic information, and his accounts of the Idrisids and origins of the Almoravids remain among the most reliable sources of information on these dynasties. Of particular importance is the section on west Africa (*bilad al-sudan*), which appears to have been widely known and used by his successors, probably as a self-standing work; this section remains an important source for the history of the spread of Islam in sub-Saharan Africa. Al-Bakri's account of the Slavs and Russians is also of considerable interest.

Despite the precision of many of his descriptions, there is no evidence that al-Bakri ever undertook any significant travels of his own, and his work appears to rely on a combination of oral accounts and works by previous authors, in particular the *al-Masalik wa'l-Mamalik* by Muhammad ibn Yusuf al-Warraq, whom he mentions several times.

In addition to his *al-Masalik wa'l-Mamalik*, al-Bakri also compiled a work entitled *Mu'jam ma 'sta'jam*, an alphabetical listing of place names occurring in Jahili poetry and the prophetic *hadiths*, often accompanied by comments on their etymology and quotations of appropriate verses of poetry. The work represents probably the earliest example of its type. Although it had few if any immediate successors, it may be regarded as paving the way for later genuine gazetteers such as the *Mu'jam al-Buldan* of Yaqut al-Hamawi.

As well as the two important geographical works described previously, al-Bakri is also said to have written a number of works on theology, botany and philology, many of which are now lost.

References

el-Hajji (1968), Hashim (1963–5), Krachkovsky (1957), Wüstenfeld (1876–7).

PAUL STARKEY

AL-BALADHURI, AHMAD IBN YAHYA (d. AD 892)

'Abbasid historian, probably of Persian origin. Though he travelled widely in the course of his career, al-Baladhuri's career was mainly spent in Baghdad, where he was prominent in the court of the caliph al-Mutawakkil. His reputation rests on two major historical works: *Futuh al-Buldan* (also known as *Umur al-Buldan*) and *Ansab al-Ashraf*. The first of these works is an annalistic history of the early Arab conquests, for which it remains one of the most valuable sources: it begins with the campaigns undertaken by the Prophet Muhammad, followed by an account of the *ridda*; the work is then arranged on the basis of individual provinces, providing accounts of the conquest of Syria, the Arabian Peninsula, Armenia, Egypt, the Maghrib, Iraq and Persia. In addition to the strictly historical narrative, the work contains much valuable information on administration, culture and social customs. The second, and more substantial, work – which remained unfinished – is a biographical history of famous men arranged according to tribe; it begins with the Prophet Muhammad himself, followed by the 'Alids, the 'Abbasids, and the 'Abd Shams. A notable feature of al-Baladhuri's work is his concern with the personalities of the Umayyad caliphs and their court, and his work is also a valuable source for the history of the Kharijites.

In compiling his accounts, al-Baladhuri used a wide variety of both written and oral sources, albeit on a very selective basis, and had no hesitation in incorporating into his own text substantial portions of the works of earlier writers, most notably those of his teacher al-Mada'ini. Although his accuracy has sometimes been questioned, and much of his work was to some extent superseded by the more detailed and extensive history of his younger contemporary al-Tabari, al-Baladhuri's works remain important sources for the Arab conquests and the history of early Islam.

References

Duri (1983), Hitti and Murgoten (1916–24), Khalidi (1994).

PAUL STARKEY

BALAT AL-SHUHADA' (POITIERS), BATTLE OF

The battle of Poitiers in October AD 732 was the event that effectively halted the Muslim ingress into Christian Europe. In Arabic sources it is called the battle of Balat al-Shuhada' – 'the Pavement of the Martyrs' – because of the large number of Muslim casualties. The Muslim forces began their campaign into mainland Europe when the Berber Tariq b. Ziyad, a client (*mawla*) of the great Arab military commander Musa b. Nusayr (d. AD 716–17), landed at Gibraltar (Jabal Tariq) in AD 711. Over the next twenty years, the Muslim forces proceeded through the Iberian peninsula and, later, into southern France (Gaul). 'Abd al-Rahman al-Ghafiqi, the governor of Muslim Spain and a respected and pious 'successor' (i.e. of the second generation of Muslims after the Prophet Muhammad), led an expedition from the Muslim-occupied area into Frankish Christian territory. The disunity of the Christians had lead to the collapse of any effective Spanish resistance to the Muslim invaders. In response to the growing Muslim threat to Europe, the western Frankish forces rallied around Charles Martel. In AD 732, al-Ghafiqi lead an army into Gaul with the aim of capturing the town of Tours, and in particular the basilica of St Martin, a famous landmark of the town. Al-Ghafiqi met his first Christian resistance at Bordeaux. There his army easily beat the forces of Eudo, Prince of Aquitaine. Eudo was forced to flee, and according to some Latin sources he asked for Charles Martel (Charles 'the Hammer') for help. Charles Martel prepared his army and went to meet al-Ghafiqi outside Poitiers. Charles's forces were better organised and successfully routed the Muslims. Al-Ghafiqi was killed in battle and his men fled. The Austrian Fredegar, one of Charles's household records that 'with Christ's help [Charles] overthrew [the Muslims'] tents and hastened after them in the battle to destroy them'. Another Latin source records that Charles 'collected the spoils and returned with great triumph and glory to Francia'.

With al-Ghafiqi dead, the Muslim forces retreated to the town of Narbonne (Arbuna in Arabic sources). After the battle of Poitiers, Muslim forces were unable to maintain any firm footing in Gaul and were restricted to shaky alliances with local dukes, or booty-raids into Gaulish territory. The area of southern France under Muslim control was gradually reduced as Christian forces regained momentum, first under Martel and later under Pepin the Short.

Two aspects of Balat al-Shuhada' are of interest here: first the term Balat al-Shuhada' (i.e. when and how it came to be applied to the contest at Poitiers by Muslim historians), and second, the religio-historical interpretation of the battle by Western historians. First, the term 'balat', perhaps coming from Latin *platea* ('paved road' or 'paved area'), is used in place names (such as Albalat in Spain, and al-Balat in northern Syria). The battle between al-Ghafiqi and Martel is only named Balat al-Shuhada' in Arabic texts written some two or three centuries after the event, and even then it took time to become common currency in historical writings. Earlier texts refer merely to the 'martyr's death' of 'Abd al-Rahman al-Ghafiqi in his battle with the 'infidel'. The lack of stability in the name of this battle indicates, perhaps, that it was considered more important for Western Christian writers than it was for Muslim historians. This leads on to the second point: Poitiers is seen as the high watermark of Muslim military achievement in western

Europe, and has been portrayed as the battle in which western Europe was saved from Muslim domination.

References

Fredegarius (1888: 175), Lévi-Provençal (1950: 60–2), al-Maqqari (1949: I, 350–68).

ROBERT GLEAVE

BALFOUR DECLARATION

The policy statement made by the British Foreign Secretary, Arthur Balfour, sent in the form of a public letter to the leader of the British Zionist Federation on 2 November 1917, supporting the creation of a Jewish homeland in Palestine.

References

Hiro (1996: 47–8), Hourani (1991: 318), James (1997: 398–9, 404, 406), Salibi (1976: 958).

SIMON W. MURDEN

AL-BANNA, HASAN (1906-1949)

Egyptian Muslim leader. Al-Banna was an Egyptian schoolteacher from a small town in the Nile Delta who was inspired to found an Islamic reform movement. In 1928 he founded a small social club that became known as the Ikhwan al-Muslimun (the Muslim Brothers). He was a gifted religious leader with talents both as preacher and organiser. He quickly built a following and a movement organised under himself as General Guide with nationwide cells, battalions, youth groups and a secret apparatus for undercover activities. The aims of the Society were the formation of an Islamic system that would reform civic, social, family and educational organisations that he believed had been corrupted by the influence of the West and by

materialism. Islam was seen by him as a total system, complete in itself and the final arbiter of life in all its aspects. Reform entailed fighting two kinds of imperialism – external, the brute force of the occupying power, and internal, those elements that by deliberate neglect or by indifference to the needs of the Muslim community served the interests of that power. He did not advocate the overthrow of the Government but considered anyone or any group that opposed his ideals to be an enemy.

The methods he used to further his aims were good organisation, propaganda, regular meetings and a militancy which was rationalised in the concept of *jihad* or struggle against non-believers or opponents. *Jihad* meant both intellectual and physical struggle culminating in death and martyrdom if necessary. The secret apparatus was formalised as the instrument for the defence of Islam and of the Society. He linked his creed to Egyptian nationalism and inspired great devotion amongst his followers who came the urban middle classes, students, and peasants. At its peak it had about 2,000 branches and a membership of some 500,000.

Volunteer squads from the Ikhwan fought well in the battle against the new state of Israel in 1948 and al-Banna was horrified by the defeat that to him meant the loss of Muslim territory to non-believers. There were disturbances in Cairo against Jewish and foreign inhabitants encouraged by the Ikhwan. The Government ordered the suppression of the movement which retaliated by assassinating the Prime Minister. The new Premier confronted them and detained thousands of them in concentration camps. In 1949 al-Banna himself was assassinated, probably by agents of the security branch of the Government. His inspiration lived on and the movement or derivatives of it spread throughout the Muslim world.

References

Mitchell (1969), Wendell (1978).

DEREK HOPWOOD

BANU MUSA

In line with his convictions about the need for both faith and reason in the profession of religious belief, the caliph al-Ma'mun established the *Bayt al-Hikma* ('House of Wisdom') in his capital, Baghdad in AD 830. This institution became famous for the work of scholars engaged in the sciences and in translating Greek texts into Arabic. Among these scholars were three brothers, Ahmad, Hasan and Muhammad, who were renowned as mathematicians and linguists. They were also known as *Banu Musa Shakir*.

References

Hitti (1973: 310, 373, 410).

EDWARD D. A. HULMES

BANU NADIR

The oasis city of Yathrib (renamed *Madinat al-Nabi,* 'the City of the Prophet', Medina, after the *hijra*), was inhabited by two prominent Jewish tribes, the Banu Nadir and the Banu-Qurayza. The former were forced into exile from Medina for opposing Muhammad after his arrival in the City and his efforts to establish the Islamic community there. After the Battle of the Trench (*al-khandaq*) a year later in AD 627, 600 male members of the Banu-Qurayza were executed before the rest were expelled from Medina, ostensibly for assisting the 'Confederates' (*al-ahzab*) against the Muslims.

References

Hitti (1973: 116–18).

EDWARD D. A. HULMES

BANU QAYNUQA'

In pursuit of his aim to establish and expand the Islamic community (*umma*) in Medina, the Prophet Muhammad succeeded in making alliances with several neighbouring Bedouin tribes. He was unsuccessful, however, in persuading Jews or Christians in and around Medina to accept him as the Messenger of God or to submit to Islam. Having failed to secure their cooperation in the cause of Islam, he saw them as enemies not potential allies. In a number of military engagements he defeated the Jewish clans and had many of their males executed before the rest were expelled from Medina. One of these Jewish clans was that of the Banu Qaynuqa'.

See also: **Banu Nadir; Banu Qurayzah**

EDWARD D. A. HULMES

BANU QURAYZAH

Among the Jewish clans in Medina who opposed the Prophet Muhammad and refused to submit to Islam, were the Banu Qurayza. After the Battle of the Trench (*al-khandaq*) in AD 627, Muhammad accused them of supporting the attack on Medina by the 'confederates' (*al-ahzab),* the Meccans and their Bedouin and Abyssinian mercenaries. The attackers withdrew after a siege that lasted for a month, after which 600 of the men of the Banu Qurayza were beheaded by way of reprisal. The remaining members of the Jewish clan were expelled from Medina.

References

Q.33:25–7.

See also: **Banu Nadir; Al-Khandaq, Battle of; Khaybar**

EDWARD D. A. HULMES

BAQA'

A term used by the Sufis to describe a situation in which the individual remains or subsists in God. The Sufis came to describe *baqa'* as a spiritual stage beyond that of *fana'* (annihilation) in which the obstacles that separate the individual from God are removed.

References

Izutzu (1994).

LLOYD RIDGEON

AL-BAQILLANI (d. AD 1013)

A significant theologian in the Ash'ari school of Islamic theology, and its first systematiser after al-Ash'ari himself. He was born and educated in Basra and when he was about thirty he was summoned to Shiraz in Iran to take part in theological discussions at the court of the Shi'i ruler of the day, of the Buyid dynasty. In AD 982 he took part in a diplomatic mission to the Byzantine Empire, and the rest of his life was then spent in Baghdad. His most important work, the *Kitab al-Tamhid* (literally *The Book of Introduction*) is the earliest example of a complete work of systematic Islamic theology, which includes discussion of the existence and names of God, refutation of other religions, and refutation of non-traditionalist groups within the Islamic community. He also wrote a classic work on the *i'jaz* (inimitability) of the Qur'an.

References

Haddad (1995: 82–94), McCarthy (1957), Von Grunebaum (1950), Watt (1985, Chapter 12).

HUGH GODDARD

BARELWI, AHMAD (1786–1831)

Indian reformer and activist. In his early years Barelwi was a disciple of 'Abd al-'Aziz, the son and successor of the reformist thinker Shah Waliullah, but in his later years, due largely to changing political circumstances in India, his thought moved in a more conservative and activist direction. He worked first to organise a *jihad* against the Sikhs, against whom he enjoyed some success but by whom he was in the end defeated and killed, as a result of which he was given the title *shahid* (martyr) by some of his followers, and second to oppose the expanding influence of the British. This theme was taken up by some of his followers after his death, and became one of the forces behind the Indian Mutiny of 1857.

References

Ahmad (1964: Chapter 9), Metcalf (1982: Chapter 2).

HUGH GODDARD

BARELWIA (AL-BARAYLWIYYA)

An Islamic sect attributed to its founder Ahmad Rida Khan Baraylwi (1856–1921) – the term Baraylwi being an adjective deriving from the city of Barielly (Barayli) in Uttar Pradesh. The sect does not use this term to describe itself but in fact its adherents consider themselves to be the 'true' Sunnis, who directly oppose all reform-minded Muslims in general and their antithesis, the Deobandis in particular. In reality, however, they are an extreme manifestation of Sufism, which is made apparent in their veneration of the Prophet in particular and Sufi 'saints' (*wali*, pl. *awliya'*), such as 'Abd al-Qadir al-Jilani and Mu'in al-Din Chisti, in general.

Consequently, they lay great emphasis on celebrating the Prophet's birthday (*mawlid*), the visiting of shrines and tombs to seek the intercession of such dead luminaries, the spiritual authority of *pirs* or *shaykhs* and the widespread use of amulets (*ta'widh*). In addition, they are strong adherents to the concept of 'the light of Muhammad' (*nur Muhammad*), which is thought to be derived from divine light and from which all creation was made – a concept that is based on fabricated *hadith*. They attribute other divine qualities to the Prophet also, such as his knowledge of the unseen (*'ilm al-ghayb*), his ability to intervene in the affairs of the worlds as he wishes and a concept termed *al-hadir wa al-nazir*, which essentially means that he is present and can see the actions of all the creation at once, in any time or place. As a result of the fact that they regard themselves as the 'true' Sunnis, they do not hesitate to remove anyone who denies such concepts from the fold of Islam and refer to them as 'infidels' (*kafir*, pl. *kuffar*).

References

al-Johani (1999: 298–303), Netton (1997: 52–3), Sirriyeh (1999: 49).

See also: **Deobandis (al-Diyubandiyya); Wahhabism**

GAVIN PICKEN

BARELWISM

Barelwism takes its name from Bareilly, the town in Uttar Pradesh where the movement's central figure, Ahmad Riza Khan (1856–1921), was based during late nineteenth- and early twentieth-century India. However, those who follow Riza reject the term 'Barelwi' in favour of Ahl al-Sunna wa'l-Jama'a, underlining their claim to be authentic representatives of traditional Sunni Islam. Riza was a Hanafi *'alim* and Qadiri Sufi whose precocious talents saw him follow his father and grandfather into the study of *fiqh*. One of the main functions of Riza's scholarship was to defend many of the more customary aspects of religious practice that were being criticised as un-Islamic innovations (*bid'a*) by reformist movements of the period. Unlike the Deobandis for example, he distinguished between 'good' and 'bad' innovations. In this respect the Ahl al-Sunna are often seen as representing resistance to Islamic revivalism. Nevertheless, as Usha Sanyal argues in *Devotional Islam and Politics in British India*, it is clear that Riza saw himself as reviving the Prophet's *sunna* amongst 'forgetful' Muslims in an attempt to recreate the 'moral climate' of early Islam.

The Barelwis under discussion here are to be distinguished from the 'anti-Sufi' *jihad* movement of Sayyid Ahmad Barelwi (1785–1831). While the latter sought to organise Muslims against the British and the Sikhs, Riza adopted a largely apolitical response to the *raj*, rejecting pan-Islamic ideals and viewing the political arena as basically 'amoral'. In the aftermath of the so-called 'Indian Mutiny' of 1857, by which time virtually all military resistance to the British was crushed, the Ahl al-Sunna were one of a number of neo-traditionalist *'ulama'*-led movements which 'turned inwards' to reaffirm the authority of the past. Like their great rivals, the Deobandis, they accepted British rule in so far as it did not interfere in Muslim religious affairs. However, at the same time, the Ahl al-Sunna actively sought to create an alternative world to that of the non-Muslim state.

The Ahl al-Sunna places great stress on devotion to, and veneration of, the Prophet Muhammad. It emphasises the Sufi concept of the 'light of Muhammad' (*nur Muhammad*) which, rather like the Christian *logos*, is said to have existed from creation and is derived from God's own light (*nur khuda*). According to Barelwi scholars, Muhammad is no mere mortal. He possesses *'ilm al-ghayb* (knowledge of the unknown) and is the primary focus for *tawassul* (intercession) with God. Indeed, the Prophet is understood to be a continuous presence in the life of Muslims. Riza, for example, wrote devotional poetry in praise of Muhammad (*na't*) and always discussed him in the present tense. Similarly, during the celebration of the Prophet's birthday (*mawlid*), when Muhammad's birth is recalled and blessings are called down upon him (the *salat al-salam*), Barelwis stand believing that the Prophet's spirit is present among them.

The Ahl al-Sunna are also distinguished by the intensity of their respect for the *awliya'* (literally 'friends of God', Sufi *pirs* or saints). In the same way that one cannot reach God except through the Prophet, so too, Barelwis believe that one cannot expect to reach the Prophet unless one has access to the intercession of a holy person. As Riza suggests, the *pir* is the '*qibla* of the soul'. The resulting devotion to the *awliya'*, and the desire for their charismatic blessing (*baraka*), finds popular expression in local and regional cults of saints. The characteristic institution of such cults is the *mazar* (shrine) or *dargah* (more revealingly, 'court'), where people make their *ziyara* (visitation) to supplicate one of God's friends. It is believed that, although dead, the saints are spiritually alive and retain their power of intercession after death. Indeed, the celebration of a saint's *'urs* (death anniversary, literally 'wedding'), when the soul of the deceased is 'married' to God, can be one of the main celebrations of the year.

In the literature it is usual to see reference to Barelwism as drawing much of its support from the rural masses in south Asia for whom Sufi saints and shrines remain as important as ever. However, the leadership of the Ahl al-Sunna consisted mainly of *'ulama'* and only those *pirs* who were self-consciously reformist in character. Moreover, this leadership was drawn mainly from the prosperous and landowning families of small agricultural towns and larger urban settlements. Therefore while the Ahl al-Sunna was happy to 'represent' ordinary Muslims, rural shrines were not 'Barelwi' as such. The Ahl al-Sunnat *'ulama'* may have been sympathetic to 'popular' ritual worship, denying any absolute opposition between the shrine and the mosque. However, Ahmad Riza Khan was first and foremost a Hanafi *'alim*. He was part of a long tradition of reformed Sufism which condemns the extravagances of folk Islam, especially those which reject the *shari'a* or exhibit evidence of Hindu–Muslim syncretism.

The Barelwis' beliefs and practices drew them into polemical conflicts with their fellow Sunni Muslims, especially the Deobandis, Tablighi Jama'at, Ahl-i Hadith and the Nadwat al-'Ulama'. It was not unusual for Riza to publicly attack an opponent as a *kafir* (unbeliever). He refused to have any social relations with Shi'ites and condemned Deobandis for their lack of respect for the *awliya'*. Moreover, he would correspond with Sunni *'ulama'* in Mecca and Medina, where he had long-standing contacts and some authority, seeking wider endorsement for his rulings. In turn, Riza's opponents would retort that Barelwi beliefs and practices were 'backward' and 'ignorant'. Such controversies were played out very publicly during preaching tours, oral disputations and in an increasingly elaborate sectarian literature. This provided the main medium for educated Muslims to debate their faith towards the end of the nineteenth century. For example, the 1880s witnessed a massive increase in the number of printing presses in India and the Ahl al-Sunna published around 1000 of Riza's Urdu *fatwa* in newspapers, pamphlets and books. They also produced a monthly journal and their own annual newspaper.

Such activities were supported by the subscriptions of the educated and affluent core of the Ahl al-Sunna's membership, which included some of the old aristocracy, the newer professions and those working in the British administration. For this reason, Sanyal contests the common misperception that Riza and the Ahl al-Sunna did not promote the 'modern' turn towards a more self-conscious and individualised religious identity evident amongst other movements. Like the Deobandis and others, the emergence of the Ahl al-Sunna reflected a time when the State provided no symbolic focus for ideas about Muslim 'community'. Sanyal considers that Riza's major achievement in this respect was in creating an overarching identity for an expression of Islamic belief and practice which is naturally diverse and fragmented. Indeed, compared to the Deobandis, the Barelwis were much slower in developing educational institutions and achieved a much less centralised, and generally less well-organised, structure than their rivals. To this day, so-called 'Barelwis' will identify most closely with an individual Sufi *pir* or *tariqa* rather than any *'ulama'* or organisation.

After, Riza's death, and as movements for Indian independence gathered pace in the early to mid-twentieth century, some members of the Ahl al-Sunna, came to support the communalist project of a Muslim homeland as eventually advocated by the secular-nationalist elites of the Muslim League. This represented quite a shift from Riza's uncompromising position of refusing to engage with those Muslims he regarded as being in error on matters of religion. Of course, some Barelwis held fast to such a stance and did not leave India for Pakistan when Partition finally came in 1947. Others stayed simply because they had a *dargah* to look after. However, once in Pakistan, the Barelwi *'ulama'*, represented by Jami'at-i 'Ulama'-i Pakistan (JUP), became increasingly active in the political arena, forming an *'ulama'* party, as did the Deobandis. This was at least in part a response to the activism of a new rival, Mawdudi's Islamist organisation, Jama'at-i Islami (JI). Like JI, these *'ulama'* parties have been courted at times by Pakistan's rulers, all keen to have their policies 'Islamically' endorsed. For example, during the 'Islamisation' of Pakistan by General Zia (r. 1977–88), there was state-sponsorship for a huge expansion in *madrasa* numbers. Zaman, for example, shows that the number of Barelwi institutions grew from under 100 in 1971 to over 1,000 in 1994. However, Zia's interventions escalated sectarian competition, conflict and violence both between Sunnis and Shi'ites and between Sunnis of different persuasions. Since the 1980s, the JUP has split into different factions and an expanding urban middle class has seen support grow for the Deobandis, especially, at the expense of the Barelwis.

References

Sanyal (1996), Zaman (2002).

See also: **Deobandism; Muslim League**

SEÁN MCLOUGHLIN

BARMAKIDS

Barmakids, also known as Barmecides (Arabic al-Baramika), a prominent family of state viziers and secretaries under the early 'Abbasid caliphs. Their name was derived from *barmak*, the custodian of a former Buddhist shrine at Balkh in eastern Khurasan. A member of the family, Khalid ibn Barmak, took part in the 'Abbasid insurrection that originated in Khurasan and which led eventually to the overthrow of the Umayyads in AD 750, and Khalid's family, who saw themselves as successors to the Sasanian administrative tradition, quickly rose to prominent positions under the new 'Abbasid dynasty.

Khalid himself, who died in AD 781/2, had served under the first 'Abbasid caliphs in various administrative capacities, holding at different times the important positions of governor of Fars and governor of Tabaristan. The family's influence at the caliphal court reached its peak, however, with the accession in AD 786 of Harun al-Rashid, who appointed Khalid's son Yahya as vizier with unlimited powers, and gave Yahya's two sons, al-Fadl and Ja'far, charge of the caliph's personal seal. For the next decade at least, the family had effective control of the 'Abbasid empire. Ja'far in particular, Harun's favourite, became known for his love of worldly pleasures and seems rarely to have left the court. The family's influence finally came to an end in AD 803, when Ja'far was executed – parts of his body being displayed on the bridges of Baghdad. Yahya and al-Fadl died in prison in AD 805 and AD 808 respectively.

The sudden and brutal 'fall of the Barmecides' was much debated by later historians, anxious either to discredit or to uphold their reputation as efficient administrators, generous patrons of the arts, or vain self-servers as the case might be. Whatever specific accusations might have been leveled against them at the time, the most likely explanation for their downfall seems to be that their influence, which certainly involved a high degree of manipulation, had simply become too much for the ruling caliph to bear. Such a sudden reversal of fortune, however, held an obvious attraction for later writers and narrators, and has ensured that the name of the Barmecides has continued to live on in the *Thousand and One Nights* and other literary works.

References

Kennedy (1981), Sourdel (1959–60).

PAUL STARKEY

BARQUQ, SAYF AL-DIN, called AL-MALIK AL-ZAHIR (r. 1382–9, 1390–9).

Mamluk sultan in Egypt and Syria and the first of the second and final line of rulers, the Burjis (so-called because these troops, mainly Circassians, were quartered in the Citadel (*Asl'aa*) of Cairo), replacing the previous Bahri line. From being marshal of the troops (*atabak al-'asakir*), Barquq seized the throne. His reign was largely filled with struggles against rival amirs, one of whom managed temporarily to wrest the throne from him in 1389. But he had to take defensive precautions in Syria against the threat, already directly felt in lands further east, posed by the Turco-Mongol conqueror Timur, and in 1394 a confrontation, in fact peaceful, took place between armies on the Euphrates; but more ominous for the future of the Mamluks was the appearance for the first time of the Ottomans on the fringes of Syria.

References

Garcin (1998: 290–1), Gibb and Bosworth (1960–2003), Holt (1986: 127–9), Northrup (1998: 288–9).

C. E. BOSWORTH

BARSBAY, SAYF AL-DIN, called AL-MALIK AL-ASHRAF (r. 1422–38)

Mamluk sultan of the Burji line, whose reign formed something of an Indian summer before the onset of Mamluk decay from economic decline and the ravages of plague. Like his predecessors, he was careful to maintain the Mamluk protectorate over the Holy Places in the Hijaz against Timurid rivals and at the same time control trade through the Red Sea from the Orient. He defended northern Syria and adjacent parts of Anatolia from the Turkmen Aq Qoyunlu, and quarrelled with the Timurid sultan Shah Rukh over the right to supply the *kiswa* or covering for the Ka'ba in Mecca, but above all, he carried on the tradition of Mamluk *jihad* by mounting three expeditions against Frankish Cyprus, almost the last Christian outpost in the eastern Mediterranean, reducing its Lusignan king to vassal status, before dying in an epidemic that swept Egypt.

References

Garcin (1998: 293–5), Gibb and Bosworth (1960–2003), Holt (1986: 184–8).

C. E. BOSWORTH

AL-BARZAKH

In different contexts, the Arabic word may mean 'interval', 'gap', 'break', 'partition', 'bar', 'obstruction', 'isthmus'. The word appears in the Qur'an, 23:100: 'Before them is a Partition, Till the Day they are raised up' (see also Q.25:53 and Q.55:20). The term is used here with reference to a 'partition', which separates human beings in this world from their future life in the next. The word *barzakh* is also taken by Muslims to refer to a place, or a state, in which individuals will find themselves in the quiescent interval between death and the Day of Judgement. Islamic commentators have not associated the word with a kind of purgatory in which even the faithful are subjected to refining punishment. When death supervenes, some people will spend their time asleep in this state until they are awakened to give an account of the fidelity at the Last Day. In a mystical interpretation, 'the Perfect Man' (*al-insan al-kamil*), is *barzakh*, in the sense that he bridges the gap between God and mankind as an intermediary, as one among God's creatures who expresses for the benefit of mortals the perfection of divinity and humanity.

References

Tritton (1968: 150–2).

EDWARD D. A. HULMES

BASMALA

The formula 'In the Name of Allah, the Merciful, the Compassionate' spoken in Arabic before, for example, commencing any lawful action.

See also: **tasmiyya.**

ANDREW J. NEWMAN

BASRA (AL-BASRA)

Main port of Iraq in the south-east of the country on the Shatt al-'Arab. Oil terminal and refining centre. Old Basra (now marked by the site of the village of Zubayr) was founded by 'Umar ibn al-Khattab in AD 636 as a military camp (*misr*). It reached its height of development as a trading and cultural centre in the eighth/ninth centuries but declined after the fall of the 'Abbasids. By the fourteenth century it was largely in ruins after visitations by the Mongols. After the Ottoman occupation of the area the Pasha of Baghdad was satisfied with minimum respect and tribute from

Basra. A local dynasty opened the port to the ships of Europe and through the eighteenth and nineteenth centuries it remained the metropolis of southern Iraq, the only port and centre of the date trade. Europeans established consulates, trading posts and missions in the town. It looked south towards the Gulf and India and was a centre for local tribes. The period 1832–1914 was one of slow development. It became an Ottoman *wilaya* in 1850 with an (disputed) interest in Kuwait. Anglo-Indian forces occupied the town in 1914 at the beginning of the invasion of Mesopotamia and under the British it was transformed into a modern port with new roads and harbour. It became the leading port of the Gulf. It was damaged during the Iran–Iraq war and bombed during the Gulf wars in 1991 and 2003.

References

Michell (1995).

DEREK HOPWOOD

BA'THISM

The brand of Arab nationalism stemming from the Ba'th Party (Renaissance Party). It emerged in Syria in the 1940s in the political activism of Michel Aflaq and Salah al-Din Bitar. Ba'thism was anti-imperialist, pan-Arabist and socialist, with particular emphasis on the importance of a vanguard elite. The party was adept in organising cells within Arab officer corps. Following indecisive periods in power, Ba'thists seized Iraq in 1968 and Syria in 1970, but divisions always prevented the pan-Arab ideal coming to fruition. In Iraq, Ba'thism was hijacked by Saddam Husayn, and it became an adjunct to his clan-based totalitarianism and military adventurism. The rule of Husayn and the Ba'th Party in Iraq was overthrown in 2003

following the war launched by the US and UK against the regime.

References

Bill and Springborg (1994: 39–40, 73–5, 103, 260), Bulloch and Morris (1991: 50–73), Owen (2000: 155–60).

SIMON W. MURDEN

BATIN AND *ZAHIR*

The 'inner' and 'outer' sense of the text of the Qur'an respectively. The terms have several applications, all hermeneutical in purpose. Within the early juristic-grammatical tradition of Qur'anic interpretation, the *zahir* was asserted to be the accepted, authoritative sense of the text and the *batin* had the sense of that which was understood by those who went against the consensus. In this usage, the opposition is not necessarily that the 'outer' meaning is literal and the 'inner' sense figural, but rather there is an ethical and authoritative impulse behind the assertion that something was *zahir*. However, the literal–figural bifurcation of the terms did take hold especially among the Shi'is and the Sufis, with the figural sense becoming preferred and seen as a source of spiritual insight. The notion that God is called *al-batin* (Q.57:3) reinforced the validity of this sense of the text but did not allow the denial of the *zahir*, because God is termed that as well, in parallel to Him being the First and the Last.

References

Böwering (2003: 346–65), Gibb and Bosworth (1960–2003: XI, 389–90).

ANDREW RIPPIN

BAY'

Bay' is an Arabic word designating 'buying'. The word could mean both parts of the contract of selling and buying. *Safqa* is another word that designates selling and buying although it literally refers to 'striking hands together'.

References

Izzi Dien (1997).

MAWIL IZZI DIEN

BAY'A

'Pact', 'oath' made between, for example, a ruler and his subjects, or between the novice and master of a Sufi order.

References

Waines (1995: 231).

ANDREW J. NEWMAN

BAYBARS I AL-BUNDUQDARI, called AL-MALIK AL-ZAHIR (r. AD 1260–77)

Supremely energetic Mamluk sultan in Egypt and Syria, of the so-called Bahri line (from the situation of their barracks on an island in the Nile, al-Bahr, near Cairo), mainly Turks. Baybars secured the throne through the assassination of his predecessor Qutuz, after having commanded the Egyptian army that repelled the Fifth Crusade and captured Louis IX of France. As Sultan, his great concern was to extend Mamluk power over Syria after the repulse from it of Hulegu's Mongols. The remaining Ayyubid princes were removed or reduced to vassal status, and the state of coexistence between Muslims and Franks during the later Ayyubid period now replaced by an aggressive policy, with the Mamluks projecting themselves as the spearhead of Islamic *jihad*. From AD 1263 onwards, the Crusader fortresses in Palestine were reduced, and Antioch

captured after some 170 years of Frankish rule, so that Baybars achieved the reputation of a second Saladin, and in the year of his death he led an invasion into Anatolia, defeating the Mongol Il-Khanids.

References

Gibb and Bosworth (1960–2003), Holt (1986: 89–98), Irwin (1986: 37–61), Northrup (1998: 250–2).

C. E. BOSWORTH

AL-BAYDAWI, 'ABDALLAH IBN 'UMAR ABU'L-KHAYR (d. *c.* AD 1286)

al-Baydawi (d. *c.* AD 1286 but perhaps as late as AD 1316), best known for his commentary on the Qur'an, *Anwar al-Tanzil wa Asrar al-Ta'wil* (*The Lights of Revelation and the Secrets of Interpretation*). That work, plus a commentary on it by al-Khatib al-Karuni (d. 1553), has continued to be an important element in the course of studies at the Muslim religious university al-Azhar in Cairo. Al-Baydawi's text is short and succinct, but is exhaustive at the same time. It presents the essence of Sunni doctrine and has attracted a large number of other commentaries as well. While clearly dependent upon al-Zamakhshari, although avoiding those points of Mu'tazili doctrine that he deemed unacceptable, al-Baydawi was also indebted to a good deal of the general tradition of exegesis that preceded him.

References

Beeston (1963).

ANDREW RIPPIN

BAYEZID I (r. 1389–1402)

Ottoman Sultan, son of Murad I. He succeeded his father, according to Ottoman tradition, on the battlefield of Kosovo, following the execution of his brother Ya'kub. In 1390 he annexed the independent principalities in western Anatolia and, between 1391 and 1400, expanded his borders as far east as Sivas. In 1394, he placed Constantinople under siege. His marriage to a Serbian princess brought Serbia under his lordship and, in 1395, he extinguished the Tsardom of Bulgaria. In the face of growing Ottoman power in the Balkans, the Hungarian king Sigismund called for a Crusade. An army of French and Burgundian knights joined the Hungarians, only to suffer a defeat at Nicopolis in 1396. By 1400, Bayezid's territory bordered on that of the central Asian conqueror, Timur (Tamerlane). Disputes between them led to Timur's invasion and defeat of Bayezid at Ankara in 1402.

References

Imber (1990: 37–54).

COLIN IMBER

BAYEZID II (r. 1481–1512)

Ottoman Sultan, son of Mehmed II. Bayezid's reign began with the defeat and flight to Egypt of his brother Cem. Cem's second attempt to gain the throne ended with his flight to Rhodes, from where the Knights of St John transferred him to captivity in France. In 1489, he came into the custody of the Pope. He died in 1495 as the prisoner of Charles VIII of France. Cem's potential as a weapon in the hands of European powers forced Bayezid before 1495 to pursue peace with his western neighbours.

In 1483 Bayezid led a successful campaign against Moldavia, but pursued an unsuccessful war against the Mamluks in Cilicia between 1485 and 1490. After Cem's death, a war with Venice between 1499 and 1503 secured important coastal fortresses in the Peloponnesos. After 1500, the greatest danger to Bayezid came from the rise of the Safavid Shah Isma'il in Iran who, as the leader of a militant religious order, claimed adherents among Bayezid's subjects. Support for the Safavids was one element in a rebellion which broke out in Anatolia in 1511. Bayezid's infirmity led to conflict between his sons over the succession. In 1512, with Janissary support, his youngest son, Selim, forced him to abdicate. He died shortly afterwards.

References

Imber (2002: 37–44), Vatin (1989).

COLIN IMBER

BAYT AL-HIKMA

Well known for his keen interest in knowledge and science, the 'Abbasid Caliph al-Ma'mun founded in AD 832 the first Arabic centre for scientific and philosophical knowledge in Baghdad. This centre was known as Bayt al-Hikma (the House of Wisdom). It was the most important library and source for rare Greek works, because al-Mamun regularly sent messengers to purchase important Greek manuscripts from the Byzantine Empire. Yahya b. Masawayh, the well-known physician, was the first to be appointed as its director, followed by Hunayn b. Ishaq.

References

Fakhry (1983: 10–13).

MAHA EL-KAISY FRIEMUTH

BAYT AL-MAL

Bayt al-mal is the term comprising two words *bayt*, house, and *mal*, wealth, or property. It means the house of wealth or state treasury that controls the state revenue and expenditure. Not all state revenue belongs to the *bayt al-mal*, but only that which belongs to the community as a whole and the purpose for which it is used depends on the discretion of the imam or his delegate.

References

Izzi Dien (1997: 136), al-Zuhayli (1985: 12, 5, 523).

Mawil Izzi Dien

BEAUTIFUL NAMES OF GOD (*AL-ASMA' AL-HUSNA*)

The words of the Arabic phrase given above may be rendered in English as 'the *most* beautiful names', i.e. of Allah (cf. Q.7:179 and Q.59:24). These ninety-nine 'divine names', 'qualities', or 'attributes' of God are commonly committed to memory by devout Muslims and often recited with the aid of an Islamic rosary, a *misbaha*, or *subha*, as an act of piety. The repetition of the 'Names' encourages a Muslim to concentrate attention on the glorification (*tasbih*) of Allah by constantly calling God to mind. The practice of repeating the 'Names', common in the litanies recited by members of Sufi orders of Islamic mystics, is claimed to help Muslims to transcend the limits of time and space in their contemplation of God. Some of the ninety-nine names come directly from the Qur'an. Others come from passages in the Qur'an that suggest the appropriateness of the chosen name. Others are not contained in the Qur'an, coming instead from the accumulation of tradition. This has given rise to differences in the ninety-nine listed, but the following, divided into three groups of thirty-three, are commonly used.

The Merciful (*al-Rahman*), the Compassionate (*al-Rahim*), the King (*al-Malik*), the Holy (*al-Quddus*), the Peace (*al-Salam*), the All Faithful (*al-Mu'min*), the Guardian (*al-Muhaimin*), the Mighty (*al-'Aziz*), the Compeller (*al-Jabbar*), the Imperious (*al-Mutakabbir*), the Creator (*al-Khaliq*), the Evolver (*al-Bari'*), the Fashioner (*al-Musawwir*), the Forgiving (*al-Ghaffar*), the Subduer (*al-Qahhar*), the Bestower (*al-Wahhab*), the Provider (*al-Razzaq*), the Opener (*al-Fattah*), the Knowing (*al-'Alim*), the Constrictor (*al-Qabid*), the Expander (*al-Basit*), the Abaser (*al-Khafid*), the Exalter (*al-Rafi'*), the Honourer (*al-Mu'izz*), the Dishonourer (*al-Mudhill*), the All Hearing (*al-Sami'*), the All Seeing (*al-Basir*), the Judge (*al-Hakam*), the Just (*al-'Adl*), the Gracious (*al-Latif*), the Well-informed (*al-Khabir*), the Clement (*al-Halim*), the Magnificent (*al-'Azim*),

The Forgiver (*al-Ghafur*), the Grateful (*al-Shakur*), the High One (*al-'Ali*), the Great (*al-Kabir*), the Preserver (*al-Hafiz*), the Sustainer (*al-Muqit*), the Reckoner (*al-Hasib*), the Sublime (*al-Jalil*), the Generous (*al-Karim*), the Watchful (*al-Raqib*), the Responsive (*al-Mujib*), the All-Embracing (*al-Wasi'*), the Wise (*al-Hakim*), the Loving (*al-Wadud*), the Glorious (*al-Majid*), the Resurrector (*al-Ba'ith*), the Witness (*al-Shahid*), the Truth (*al-Haqq*), the Trustee (*al-Wakil*), the Strong (*al-Qawi*), the Firm (*al-Matin*), the Protecting Friend (*al-Wali*), the One Worthy of Praise (*al-Hamid*), the Accounter (*al-Muhsi'*), the Originator (*al-Mubdi'*), the Restorer (*al-Mu'id*), the Giver of Life (*al-Muhyi*), the Slayer (*al-Mumit*), the Living (*al-Hayy*), the Self-Subsistent (*al-Qayyum*), the Finder (*al-Wajid*), the Noble (*al-Majid*), the Unique (*al-Wahid*),

The One (*al-Ahad*), the Eternal (*al-Samad*), the Capable (*al-Qadir*), the One Possessing Power (*al-Muqtadir*), the Expediter (*al-Muqaddim*), the Delayer (*al-Mu'akhir*), the First (*al-Awwal*), the Last (*al-Akhir*), the Manifest (*al-Zahir*), the Hidden (*al-Batin*), the Governor (*al-Wali*), the Most Exalted (*al-Mu'ta'ali*), the Beneficent (*al-Barr*), the Acceptor of Repentance (*al-Tawwab*), the Avenger (*al-Muntaqim*), the Pardoner (*al-'Afuw*), the Gentle (*al-Ra'uf*), the Owner of the Kingdom (*Malik al-mulk*), the One Full of Majesty and Bounty (*Dhu'l-jalal wa'l-ikram*), the Equitable (*al-Muqsit*), the Gatherer (*al-Jami'*), the Self-Sufficient (*al-Ghani*), the Enricher (*al-Mughni*), the Preventer (*al-Mani'*), the Afflicter (*al-Dar*), the Propitious (*al-Nafi'*), the Light (*al-Nur*), the Guide (*al-Hadi*), the Incomparable (*al-Badi'*), the Everlasting (*al-Baqi*), the Inheritor (*al-Warith*), the Guide to the Straight Path (of Islam) (*al-Rashid*), the Forebearing (*al-Sabur*).

References

Friedlander (1977: 13–143).

EDWARD D. A. HULMES

BEGIN, MENACHEM
(1913–92)

Israeli politician and Prime Minister. Begin was born in Russia and from an early age became involved in Zionist youth organisations. When sixteen he joined the activist group *Betar* that advocated a more forceful policy than did mainstream Zionism. He received a degree from Warsaw University in 1935 and in 1938 became head of Betar. He fled back to Russia from Poland on the Nazi invasion in 1939 but was imprisoned in concentration camps by the Soviets until he was allowed to join the Polish army in 1941. He left for Palestine the next year. There he took charge of the Irgun Zvai Leumi, an underground terrorist group dedicated to expelling the British Mandate authorities. In 1946 they bombed the King David hotel in Jerusalem which was also the British army's headquarters. Ninety-one people died, most of them civilians. Begin was unrepentant, describing his tactics as 'turning Palestine into a glass-house with the world looking in'. Wanted by the British for his terrorist activities, he went into hiding until the proclamation of the Jewish state. In 1949 he founded the Herut party and entered the Knesset. He favoured an aggressive expansionist Israeli policy and was too extreme for Prime Minister Ben Gurion to accept him into the Government. Begin helped to negotiate a merger of Herut with Gahal – a more liberal group – which helped to make his views more acceptable amongst the middle classes.

Begin was leader of the opposition in the Knesset until 1967 when he joined Levi Eshkol's government. He resigned in 1970 after a disagreement over returning territory captured in the Six Day War. In opposition again he helped found the right-wing Likud party of which he became leader.

When they won the elections in 1977, Begin became Israel's first non-socialist prime minister. A year later he surprised the world by receiving President Sadat of Egypt in Jerusalem and later signing with him a peace treaty in 1979. Israel was recognised by Egypt but the Arabs got very little in return. Israel evacuated the Sinai Peninsula occupied in 1967 but continued to build illegal settlements on the West Bank of the Jordan. He maintained an aggressive foreign policy, ordering the destruction of the Iraqi nuclear facility in 1981 and the invasion of Lebanon in 1982. When this latter dragged on unsuccessfully Begin seemed to become disillusioned and resigned in September 1983. He spent the rest of his life out of the public eye.

References

Perlmutter (1987), Temko (1987).

DEREK HOPWOOD

BEIRUT

Capital of Lebanon and Mediterranean port. Beirut was one of the most important cities of Phoenicia and became a Roman colony. Conquered by the Arabs in AD 635 it prospered under their early rule. During the Crusader occupation, the Hospitallers built the Church of St John the Baptist, later converted into the mosque of al-'Umari. The Muslims finally retook the town in AD 1291 and it became subservient to Damascus under the Mamluk dynasty. It remained an important trading centre in the Middle Ages particularly with Venice. Incorporated into the Ottoman Empire in 1516, by the mid-eighteenth century it was the most populous coastal city after Tripoli. The nucleus of the population being Maronite Christian, the city and Mount Lebanon remained of interest to the European powers. Missionaries, traders, teachers and consuls came to city and endowed it with a cosmopolitan atmosphere. Under the French mandate it became capital of Greater Lebanon. It expanded during the mandate and after independence (1943) as a centre of trade, banking, culture and tourism. In a relatively free atmosphere, Arabic journalism and literature, in particular, flourished. The city grew in unplanned fashion with great divisions amongst religious groups and between wealth and poverty. The situation exploded into prolonged civil war (1975–91) during which much of the central area was destroyed. The city was divided into two sections: Christian and Muslim. Since the end of fighting, attempts have been made at reconstruction and at re-establishing Beirut as the important commercial and cultural centre it once was.

References

Debbas (1986), Jidejian (1973).

DEREK HOPWOOD

BEKTASHIYA

The origins of the Bektashiya Sufi order are traced to Hajji Bektash Wali who lived in Anatolia in the thirteenth century. The order has been noted for its Shi'ite tendencies, the consumption of wine in certain rituals and the full participation of women in its rituals.

References

Birge (1937).

LLOYD RIDGEON

BELL, GERTRUDE (1868–1926)

British archaeologist, writer and government official. Bell was born in County Durham of a rich manufacturing family and was educated at Oxford where she was the first woman to take a first-class degree in history. She was a lively, even self-opinionated, student who had no wish to settle down to domestication. She took to travelling, exploring and alpine climbing, almost exclusively in male company.

Bell became deeply attracted to the Near East particularly after a visit to Tehran in 1892–3. She translated Persian poetry and settled in Jerusalem for a while to study Arabic. In 1905 she undertook extensive travels through Syria which she described in her book *The Desert and the Sown*. She also took part in archaeological excavations in the area where she met T. E. Lawrence with whom she had (as with many men) a prickly relationship. She was a women active in an exclusively men's world. In 1913 she travelled further through northern Arabia and reached Baghdad in 1914. Through her travels she gained a deep knowledge of Arabian politics and personalities.

At the beginning of the First World War Bell worked for the Red Cross in London and was then sent to Cairo to join the group of British Near East experts in the newly formed Arab Bureau. She put to use her knowledge of Arabia in drawing up intelligence reports. She was then sent to Basra, which British forces had recently occupied, in order to join the staff of Percy Cox who became civil commissioner in Iraq. She worked as his oriental secretary and later for his successor A. T. Wilson. She helped him to set up the government of the newly formed state of Iraq in 1921 and was close to the King Faysal. She stayed on in mandated Iraq and worked in establishing the archaeological museum. She died in 1926, possibly from an overdose, after the failure of an earlier love affair and perhaps feeling that her work was finished in Iraq.

References

Wallach (1996), Winstone (1993).

DEREK HOPWOOD

BEN GURION, DAVID (1886–1973)

Israeli statesman and Prime Minister. Born in Russia, Ben Gurion became committed to the Zionist cause early in life. He studied in Warsaw where he joined the socialist workers party, Po'alei Zion, which propagated ideas of settling Palestine through collective labour. He moved to Jaffa in Palestine in 1906 to work as a farmer. He was also active in labour politics. He worked as a journalist in Jerusalem and then moved to the University of Constantinople to study law, graduating in 1914. He returned to Palestine and continued to help to organise trade unions. The Ottoman Government exiled many Zionists from the country and he spent some time in the USA. In 1917, after the British had issued the Balfour Declaration, Ben Gurion joined the Jewish Legion which

assisted the British in their fight against the Turks in the First World War.

After the war, he returned to politics and quickly became a leading figure. He helped to found the Histadrut (Federation of Labour Unions) and the Ahdut Ha'avodah (labour party) which became Mapai (Workers Party). He was dedicated to the foundation of an Israeli state, which he believed would be achieved through a conciliatory policy towards the British Mandate authorities. From 1935 to 1948 he was chairman of the executive committee of the Jewish Agency. During the Second World War he supported the Allied cause while still working for a Jewish state. At a Zionist conference in New York he helped to secure the adoption of the Biltmore programme which called for the creation of a Jewish commonwealth and for greater Jewish immigration into Palestine.

After the war he too supported a more activist policy towards the British and on their withdrawal in 1948, he declared the birth of Israel. He was the obvious choice as prime minister. His first task was to repel the invasion of the new state by Arab armies. This he did by bringing together existing armed groups into the Israel Defence Forces. He encouraged the large-scale immigration of Jews from Europe and the Middle East, and developed education and the institutions of state. He quarrelled with other politicians over the signing of a reparations agreement with West Germany and in 1953 voluntarily retired to a *kibbutz* in the Negev to rest from the rigours of his long career. He returned to office in 1955 after a scandal in the Government and as Prime Minister led Israel into collusive action with Britain and France in the disastrous Suez War in 1956. He continued in office, however, until 1963 when he resigned as Prime Minister, while remaining in the Knesset. He formed a new party Rafi which had limited success. He left the political scene in 1970. He may truly be considered the father of Israel.

References

Bar-Zohar (1978).

DEREK HOPWOOD

BENIN, THE EMPIRE OF

The Empire of Benin was one of the most important in the history of the peoples and states of the West African coast. Its fame is based not only on its political and economic power but on the works of sculpture created by its artists. The city of Benin served as the capital of this black African kingdom, the beginnings of which are lost in history. The kingdom was probably founded in the thirteenth century and it flourished from the fourteenth to the seventeenth century. Its ruler was the Oba. Human sacrifices were made to him and to the members of his family. At first, Benin was a trading settlement and later a city in the Niger Delta on the coast of west Africa. The first rulers of Benin were the Ogiso. The Edo people of Benin, influenced by the political and economic advances made by their Yoruba neighbours, grew impatient with their own traditional rulers. They sent to Oduduwa, the Oni of Ife, asking him to send one of his sons as to be the ruler of Benin. This son, Oranmiyan, presided over the beginning of a new period in the life of the Empire in the early fifteenth century, during which Benin grew in importance. The Empire was built up and extended on trade. In the sixteenth century the Oba ruled over an area stretching from what is now Lagos to the Niger Delta. The Portuguese made contact with Benin in 1486 and were soon impressed by the extent of the Empire and by its ruler's authority. The royal traditions of Benin were compiled by Chief Jacob Egharevba. One of the most famous Obas was Ewuare, who came to the throne in the mid-fifteenth century. He presided over political changes that led to the institution of a state council, a centralised government and an efficient bureaucracy. From the late fifteenth century, Benin engaged in trade with European merchants. In return for cash, trinkets, other goods, alcohol and guns, African slaves were delivered for shipment in crowded and inhuman conditions to the Americas on board the European vessels employed for the transatlantic passage. Benin also traded in ivory, pepper and works of art despatched to European markets. In the early sixteenth century the Oba sent an ambassador to Lisbon. The King of Portugal responded by sending Catholic missionaries to Benin. The kingdom of Benin declined after 1700 but revived in the nineteenth century with the development of trade in palm oil, palm kernels and timber, products which were eagerly sought by European entrepreneurs. The British conquered and burned the city of Benin in 1898 after conflicts arose between African and European traders along the coast. British colonial rule followed. Benin is famous for its artefacts of cast iron work and carved ivory, but best known for the bronze portrait busts, some of which date from as early as the thirteenth century. These pieces of sculpture are considered to be among the finest works of art produced in Africa and are in great demand in the museums of the world.

See also: **Dahomey; slavery and the slave-trade in west Africa**

EDWARD D. A. HULMES

BERBERS

The Berbers inhabit land that lies along the North African littoral from Egypt to the Atlantic Ocean and between the Sahara desert and the Mediterranean. They constitute a large part of the population of Morocco, Algeria and Libya. Apart from the nomadic Tuaregs they live as craftsmen and farmers in their independent settlements. Their products include pottery and earthenware, embroidered cloths, artefacts made of lead, iron and copper. They are Sunni Muslims, speaking a variety of languages in the Hamitic group. Many also speak Arabic, the language of their religion. Their origins are uncertain. Theories have been advanced which relate them to the Celts, the Phoenicians, ancient Canaanites, and the Basques. Many were Christian at a time when the Church in Africa was disturbed by the proliferation of heresy, notably Donatism, which arose when the appointment of Caecilian as Bishop of Carthage was opposed.

It was alleged that during the persecution of Diocletian (*c.* AD 303) Caecilian had been a *traditor* (one who surrendered the Holy Scriptures on the orders of the Emperor). In the seventh century, the Berbers were conquered by Muslim Arabs, under whose tutelage they were Islamicised, subsequently forming key elements in the Arab armies which conquered southern Spain. Helped by Berbers, the Fatimids built up an empire that stretched from Palestine to Tunisia in the tenth and eleventh centuries, with its capital in Cairo. The Almoravids and Almohads were Berber movements which established dynasties in the western Sudan in the eleventh and twelfth centuries. When the French and Spanish occupied much of North Africa in the nineteenth century, the Berbers in the mountains offered fierce resistance.

References

Davidson (1977: 20, 70–1, 183n), Levtzion (1973: 114–15, 118).

See also: **Almoravids**

EDWARD D. A. HULMES

BID'A

'Innovation', referring to a practice or belief not present in the Qur'an or the traditions and, hence, un-Islamic. An innovation which does not challenge the essentials of the faith may be acceptable.

References

Hallaq (1997: 66).

ANDREW J. NEWMAN

BILA KAYFA

'Without question', 'without asking how', referring to acceptance of certain of the revelation which may appear to contradict human comprehension. The latter include, for example, references in the Qur'an to the apparently human attributes of Allah.

References

Hourani (1991: 65), Waines (1995: 123, 281).

See also: **anthropomorphism**; *'al-'arsh, istawa 'ala'*

ANDREW J. NEWMAN

BILQIS

The name given by Arabic literary tradition to the Queen of Sheba who is referred to, but not named, in Q.27:15–44. The story focuses on the Queen, her encounter with the biblical King Solomon, and her conversion from sun worship to belief in the one true God. It is based very loosely on the biblical account found in I Kings 10:1–13. Solomon is pictured in the Qur'an as a great and wealthy king who has power over birds, animals and the *jinn*. He is brought a message by a hoopoe that there is a Queen ruling in Sheba who is very wealthy, yet she and her people worship the sun. Solomon sends her a letter, summoning her to Islam. Her response is to send him a present. Solomon then threatens the Queen and orders her throne brought to him. The Queen then comes to Solomon and is astonished at the sight of her throne and of a palace paved with glass such that she accepts the faith of Solomon. Muslim literature as found in the genre of the 'stories of the prophets' (*qisas al-anbiya'*) develops the story substantially and fills in the missing gaps from the Qur'an with the final conclusion of the developed story being that Solomon marries Bilqis.

References

Lassner (1993), Watt (1974: 85–103).

ANDREW RIPPIN

BIMARISTAN (HOSPITAL)

Also known as a *maristan, timarhane, darussifa*. The development of medical theory and practice is one of the great intellectual achievements of Islamic science which studied and transmitted the classical Greek texts. Outstanding physicians such as the Iranian Ibn Sina (Avicenna) (AD 980–1037) compiled an encyclopaedic *Canon of Medicine* which in Latin translation was the principal textbook in European medical schools from the twelfth to sixteenth centuries. Hospitals were founded by the early ninth century in Baghdad, well equipped with dispensaries and medical reference libraries. Some of the great mosque complexes of the Otto-

man Empire often included a hospital and medical school as part of their charitable foundation. Here one of the most extensive is the complex of Bayazit II (1481–1512) built by the architect Hayrettin between 1484 and 1488. The hospital, asylum and medical school are domed structures located at the east side of the courtyard. According to the terms of the charitable trust, the hospital was staffed with three doctors, two eye specialists, two barber surgeons and a dentist, while music therapy was prescribed for the insane.

References

Campbell (1926).

JENNIFER SCARCE

BIRTH CONTROL (*TAQLIL AL-NASL*)

Artificial birth control is neither forbidden nor encouraged in Islam. In Islamic belief, children are considered to be gifts of God, although in Islamic tradition the approach to pregnancy is accommodating and pragmatic. So, for example, in Muslim's *Book of Marriage* (*Kitab al-Nikah* 3883) when a male asked for advice about having intercourse with a slave-girl without wanting her to conceive a child, Muhammad is reported to have answered: 'Use *coitus interruptus* ('*azl*) if that is your wish, but that which is decreed for her will come about'. The tradition goes on to record that on hearing that the girl had become pregnant by the man Muhammad observed: 'I told you that what was decreed for her would come about'. To safeguard the health of the mother, or in recognition of the economic conditions of the parents concerned, it is considered to be acceptable to use birth control to

101

postpone pregnancy, but not to do so indefinitely.

References

Bouhdiba (1985: 43–57, 159–211), Omran (1992: 7–9, 59–183, 228–9).

EDWARD D. A. HULMES

BIRTHDAY OF THE PROPHET MUHAMMAD

See: *mawlid (milad) al-nabi*

AL-BIRUNI, ABU AL-RAYHAN MUHAMMAD IBN AHMAD (AD 973–*c.* 1050)

Scientist and polymath. Little is known of the life or family circumstances of al-Biruni. A native of Khwarizm, he spent time in the service of the Khwarizm-shahs and the ruler of Gorgan before moving early in the eleventh century to the court of Mahmud of Ghazna. He accompanied Mahmud as an astrologer on his expeditions to India in AD 1017–30 and apparently acquired some knowledge of Sanskrit during this period. After Mahmud's death in 1030, he successively served Mahmud's sons, Mas'ud and Mawdud, until *c.* AD 1049.

A prolific writer, al-Biruni was the author of some 146 titles, including nearly 100 on mathematical astronomy and related subjects and around fifty on subjects as varied as history, literature, religion, philosophy and pharmacology. Not all have survived. Among his more important extant works are:

1. *al-Athar al-Baqiya 'an al-Qurun al-Khaliya*, a unique attempt to record the rites, traditions and customs of the various nations of ancient and medieval times, from the Assyrians and Babylonians through to the Islamic caliphs, with particular attention devoted to their calendars and the astronomical notions underlying them;

2. *Tahqiq ma li 'l-Hind min Maqula Maqbula fi'l-'Aql aw Mardhula*, a comprehensive account of Indian life around 1030, deriving both from his own direct observations of Indian society and from Arabic translations of Sanskrit sources;

3. *al-Qanun al-Mas'udi,* a comprehensive astronomical handbook, of considerable interest to the historian of Islamic astronomy and mathematics in the light of the author's pioneering use of new mathematical concepts and computational techniques;

4. *al-Tafhim li-Awa'il Sina'at al-Tanjim*, the most comprehensive surviving astronomical handbook in Arabic.

Despite the wide-ranging nature of al-Biruni's works, not all of which have yet been studied adequately, there is some evidence that he was not regarded by his contemporaries or successors as an intellectual figure of the first order and that, whatever his accomplishments in the field of mathematics, he had little aptitude for more general philosophical questions. This view is supported by a text known as *al-As'ila wa'l-Ajwiba*, a set of correspondence between al-Biruni and the philosopher Ibn Sina, in which al-Biruni apparently offended Ibn Sina through his excessively harsh language. In more modern times, controversy has also surrounded some of his accomplishments, for example the extent of his knowledge of languages other than Arabic and Persian. Despite that, al-Biruni's works continue to be of major importance for the historian of the Islamic sciences and his reputation as one of the leading Islamic scientists of the 'Abbasid period seems assured.

References

Sachau (1879, 1888), Young *et al.* (1990: 405–23).

PAUL STARKEY

BLACK DEATH

The global pandemic of bubonic and pneumonic plague between 1333 and 1350. Carried by fleas hosted on rats, it produced fever-like symptoms and blackened swellings of the lymph nodes, known as 'buboes'. It began in China, spreading across the Mongol realm into the Middle East and Europe. Genoese traders carried the plague into Europe where it may have killed a third of the population, but its devastating impact appears to have been greater and longer lasting in the Middle East. Plague outbreaks recurred throughout the fourteenth century.

References

Fernandez-Armesto (1995: 108–100).

SIMON W. MURDEN

BLACK STONE (*AL-HAJR AL-ASWAD*)

This stone, a sacred object to Muslims, is lodged in the wall at the south-east comer of the Ka'ba, the cubic-shaped edifice in the centre of the Sacred Mosque (*al-Masjid al Haram*) in Mecca, which is circumambulated seven times in anticlockwise direction by Muslim pilgrims during the course of the annual pilgrimage (*hajj*). The stone marks the place where the circumambulation (*al-tawaf*) of the Ka'ba begins and ends. Pilgrims attempt to touch or kiss the stone as they pass by, believing that by so doing they will receive a special blessing (*baraka*). The stone is 12 inches (30.5 centimetres) in diameter and set in silver. It is the only remaining relic of the original shrine, which Muslims believe to have been erected by Ibrahim and his son Isma'il after it was sent to them by the Angel Jibril. In pre-Islamic times, erratic rocks of volcanic or meteoric origin were used at places where pagan deities were worshipped. The Black Stone was purged of any such association with polytheism, in accordance with the strict monotheism of Islam. Among the accounts of its origin is the legend that it was sent to Earth when Adam, the first man, was created.

See also: *Al-Hajj*

EDWARD D. A. HULMES

BLYDEN, EDWARD WILMOT (1832–1912)

E.W. Blyden, the black American, author, educator, explorer, *savant*, racial theorist, theologian, politician and diplomat, never became a Muslim himself but throughout his career he did much to bring to the attention of Europeans and Americans the rich history and culture of Islam in West Africa. More specifically, perhaps, he focused on West African Islam, that is to say, on the ways in which Islam had been (and was continuing to be) inculturated in that religiously diverse region. He was a man who lived between two worlds in more than one sense. On the one hand he was 'a Negro of ebony hue' (his own words), who understood the fears and aspirations of a subject race (again, his word), and who sought to use his talents to improve their lot. He explored Islamic life and thought with a growing conviction that Islam rather than Christianity provided the key to the social, economic, political and spiritual emancipation of black Africans, whom he consistently referred to as *Negroes*. At the same time he was at home in the intellectual world of Europe's dominant colonial administrators. He belonged to the *new* world of the Americas by virtue of his birth and early education. He belonged to the *old* world of European civilisation and culture by virtue of his intellectual interests and achievements. In another sense he belonged neither to Europe nor to America, because his 'Negro roots' were in Africa. His was a complex character. He was a Christian who came to admire Islam, chiefly because he saw in it a coherent system of belief and practice which could satisfy the *present* needs of Negroes. He was a strong critic of the work of Christian missionary activity in West Africa. He admired the work of Muslim scholars and teachers in West Africa who, down the centuries, had exerted a sustained and stabilising influence on local communities. Intellectually he was an elitist, drawn to the European classical tradition. Emotionally, he identified with black African aspirations.

The third of seven children, Blyden was born on 3 August 1832 to free black parents on the island of St Thomas in the West Indies. He died on 7 February 1912 in Freetown, Sierra Leone, alone, in retirement, and in comparative penury. A full account of his remarkable life is given in Hollis R. Lynch (1970). Blyden's career was to take him first to Liberia, established in 1821 by the American Colonisation Society for the benefit of black people who wished to return to the West African coast. After pressure by Britain the colony was declared independent in 1847. He subsequently travelled to Britain, to Egypt and the Levant, and on several occasions he returned to the USA, where he consistently and vigorously exhorted freed slaves to emigrate to Liberia. In this project he enjoyed little success. His posts were to include senior educational, academic and administrative appointments in Liberia. He was also appointed to diplomatic and ambassadorial posts abroad. In England he met several leading humanitarians, including W. E. Gladstone, with whom he continued to correspond, sharing with the British Prime Minister an interest in the classical literatures of Greece and Rome. It was almost as if Blyden felt more at home in the company of European and American intellectuals, yet he continued to work for the emancipation of the 'Negro' from the economic and cultural dominance of Europe. In 1877 he served as Liberia's first Minister to the Court of St James in London, where he was lionised by society hostesses and put up for membership of the Athenaeum and St George's. In the 1990s he moved to Lagos in Nigeria, where he was welcomed with a eulogy in the *Lagos Weekly Times* of 27 December 1890 which included an adapted quotation: 'Africa's destiny lay hid in night. God said, "Let Blyden be!", and all was light'. His curious racial theories, in which he sought to defend the purity of the 'Negro race', lie beyond the scope of this entry but it may be noted that his insistence on the *inferiority* of individuals of mixed black and white parentage was diametrically opposed to the universalist teachings of Christianity and Islam, precepts that he professed to honour.

His interest in the diversity and antiquity of African culture led to his increasing awareness of the spiritual values enshrined in African traditional religion and in Islam. His knowledge of Arabic enabled him to study the primary sources of an Islamic literature that was already centuries old and virtually unknown outside west Africa. In an article called 'Mohammedanism in Western Africa', published in the *Methodist Quarterly*

Review of January 1871, he refers to the pioneer efforts of European scholars such as Noeldeke, Muir, Spanger and Deutsch to interpret Islam in a less hostile way. Blyden's attitude to Islam was illuminated by the conviction that a system 'which has had so widespread an influence upon mankind', could not be wholly bereft of truth and goodness. Paradoxically, in view of his own personal beliefs about the needs for racial purity, Blyden could not fail to notice that discrimination within the Islamic community on grounds of race and colour was forbidden. He noted that, rightly or wrongly, Christianity had become associated with white European ascendancy. Above all, Negroes wanted to be free from white domination, colonial dependency, and a sense of cultural inferiority. Blyden insisted that Islam not only promised but had demonstrated that it was able to provide this measure of emancipation.

What was the nature of the benefits that the coming of Islam had secured for Africans? Blyden cites the absence of caste distinctions among Muslims and mentions the resilient self-confidence which characterises the Muslim's approach to life. This makes a Muslim a willing communicator to non-Muslims of the liberating effects of Islam. Degrading drunkenness is virtually eliminated from society by the Islamic proscription of intoxicating liquor at a time when white Europeans were encouraging the consumption of alcohol in West Africa in the pursuit of trading interests. The spread of Islam was, in Blyden's view, a relatively peaceful process. He noted the thoroughness with which Muslims provide systematic education based upon Islamic principles for their children in schools and later in centres of higher learning. First, they were taught to read letters and vowel marks, and then to read the text itself. Understanding was

imparted as the words of the text were committed to memory. This learning process provided students with a knowledge of 'the acts of Mohammed', 'the duties of fasting, prayer, alms, corporal purification', 'the mystical tradition', and '[Islamic] history and chronology'. A board of 'imams and ulemas' tested candidates in a seven-day examination, by means of which, young men who wished to be 'enrolled among the ulemas' demonstrated their knowledge, understanding and insight. In recording what he witnessed, Blyden noted that successful candidates in this examination were presented with a sash or scarf, usually of fine white cloth and of local manufacture, which they were entitled to wind around their caps, with one end hanging down behind, 'as a sort of Bachelor of Arts diploma'. They were then led round the town on horseback to receive the congratulations of the local population.

The study of the Qur'an was thorough and regular in the ancient centres of learning in the interior of West Africa, where Muslims had access to other Islamic books and manuscripts. On his travels to these remote areas Blyden had seen:

> extensive manuscripts in poetry and prose. One showed us at Boporo, the Makamat of Hariri, which he read and expounded with great readiness, and seemed surprised that we had heard of it. And it is not to be doubted that some valuable Arabic manuscripts may yet be found in the heart of Africa.
> (Blyden 1967: 179)

Blyden summarised his impressions of the impact of Islam on West African societies by drawing attention to the existence of ancient centres of civilisation, learning, commerce and industry, all of which owed their culture to Islam.

He singled out the Nigerian cities of Kano and Sokoto, the history of which were virtually unknown to the white inheritors of Mediterranean culture, who presumed to speak about Africa as 'the dark continent'. The free movement of Arabic- and Hausa-speaking Muslims across the vast tracts of the Sahara made for a creative exchange of ideas as well as trade. In spite of this general praise for the contribution of Islam to the life of the peoples of West Africa, Blyden's attitude to Islam does not amount to unqualified approval. As already noted, he never became a Muslim. Even though his formal links with institutional Christianity were effectively broken when he resigned as a Presbyterian minister in 1886, he seems to have retained the belief that *ultimately* Islam was only a preparation for the Gospel of Christ, and that the Negro's true spiritual destiny was to be found within the fellowship of a refined Christianity, purged of white domination and European cultural accretion.

References

Blyden (1967: 178–9), Hulmes (1990: 44–65), Lynch (1970).

EDWARD D. A. HULMES

BOHORAS

The Bohoras are a subdivision of the Isma'ili Musta'lians, being known as Tayyibis, because their support for al-Musta'li bi-llah's grandson al-Tayyib. This latter subdivision was prominent in Yemen and their teachings were successfully propagated among Hindus upon the arrival of the first *da'i* s (religio-political missionaries) in India. This *da'wa* was particularly successful among the artisan class of Gujarat, who were known later as *bohra/bohora*, which is said to be derived from the Gujarati word *vohorvu*, meaning 'to trade'. The sect itself seems to be similar to the generality of Muslims in belief and practice but at the same time adopts a typical Isma'ili/Batini approach, in the sense that their real belief is 'hidden'. However the main difference with the Bohoras is that the emphasis is on their imam, al-Tayyib, who is now considered to be 'concealed'. It is also worth mentioning that this sect is also subdivided into further two subsects, which arose because of a dispute concerning succession to the office of *da'i*, one group supporting Dawud Burhan al-Din (d. 1612) and another, who supported Sulayman b. Hasan. The former group, known as Dawudis, represent the majority of the Tayyibis and are found primarily in India, whereas the latter group, known as the Sulaymanis constitute the minority and mostly found in Yemen.

References

Daftary (1998: 2–3, 185–93), al-Johani (1999: 386–9), Netton (1997: 58).

GAVIN PICKEN

BOOKS, JUDGEMENT WITH

One of two types of judgement exercised on the Day of Judgement (Q.84:7–12).

See also: **judgement on the *yawm al-qiyama*; *najat*; scales, judgement with; *yawm al-qiyama***

ANDREW J. NEWMAN

BOURGUIBA, HABIB (1901/3–2000)

Statesman and first President of the Republic of Tunisia. Bourguiba was born in the southern coastal town of Monastir in 1901 or 1903 (sources vary although the earlier date seems more likely). He spent his early days there in a typical Tunisian family and was closely attached to his mother. He was sent alone, however, to Tunis at an early age to study in the Sadiki College. He did not shine to begin with and the death of his mother in 1913 was a heavy blow. He fell ill and left the college to recuperate in the mountain resort of Le Kef. His stay there transformed him and he returned in 1921 to the French Lycée Carnot where he determined to outshine all the other pupils, Tunisian and European. This he did and in 1924 he went to the Sorbonne in Paris to obtain degrees in law and international finance. He fell heavily under the influence of French life and culture and married a Frenchwoman, Mathilde, with whom he had a son, Habib junior.

Back in Tunisia in 1927 he worked as a lawyer but also threw himself in political journalism which brought him to the notice of the French colonial authorities. He joined the Destour party, a nationalist organisation devoted to the expulsion of the French. In 1934 at a famous meeting in Ksar Hellal he and a group of friends formed a splinter group – the Neo-Destour – dedicated to a more active programme than that of the more careful older members. For this he was arrested by the French and imprisoned in exile in the desert under harsh conditions. Released in 1936 by the left-wing Paris Government he embarked on a demanding round of speaking engagements, building up his political base and widening his popular appeal. Arrested once again in 1938 he was sent to the French mainland where he was released from prison in Lyons by the Nazi commandant Klaus Barbie in 1943. The Axis powers thought they could manipulate him as a collaborator. He was sent back to Tunis by the Italians from where he escaped to Egypt. He moved around the Arab world and the USA, all the time making the case for Tunisian independence. He dared to return to Tunisia but was arrested for the third time in 1952. However, the political climate was now changing and the French were eventually forced to negotiate with him as the acknowledged leader of his country.

He returned in triumph in 1955 and became President in 1956 of the independent state. He introduced a very progressive series of reforms in the areas of law, women's rights and education. He was a political moderate in foreign affairs and on occasions alienated his fellow Arab leaders by advocating, for example, the recognition of Israel. He clung to power despite increasing age and continual ill health. He made himself president for life in 1974. He became ever more arbitrary and unpredictable, and in 1987, much to his and the country's surprise, he was overthrown by Zayn al-'Abidin Ben 'Ali. He died in Monastir, still a respected figure as the father of his country but one who had not known when to relinquish power.

References

Hopwood (1992).

DEREK HOPWOOD

BREAKING OF THE FAST (*'ID AL-FITR*)

This is the first of the two festivals in Islam. It is sometimes known as 'the lesser feast' (*'Id al-Saghir*), as distinct from 'the great feast', 'the Feast of the Sacrifice' (*'Id al-Adha*). These two feasts are the most important holidays in the Islamic calendar. The feast of Breaking of the Fast is celebrated for up to three days from the first day of the month of Shawwal. Celebrations begin after the first sighting of the new moon following the fasting during the month of Ramadan. Special attention is given to charitable giving (*sadaqat al-fitr*). Food is provided for those in need of it. Not surprisingly, after the preceding period of austerity, Muslims observe the feast with considerable verve and community spirit, putting on new or best clothes, visiting friends and relatives, and exchanging presents. Special *'id* prayers for forgiveness and in thanksgiving are recited in mosques, at an outdoor *musallan*, and in homes. Cemetaries are visited, and the departed remembered. A special payment of alms (*zakat al-fitr*) is to be made by Muslims by the end of the first day of the feast. The alms collected are then distributed among the poor of the community.

References

al-Khaysi (1996: 113–16), Noss (1974: 511, 534), Tritton (1968: 25).

EDWARD D. A. HULMES

BRIDGE, BATTLE OF THE

Khalid ibn al-Walid, one of Muhammad's most successful generals, continued to lead Muslim troops in the campaigns that followed the Prophet's death in AD 632. Two years later he led his troops swiftly south-west from al-Hira in Iraq to the neighbourhood of Damascus in Syria, where he inflicted defeat on a Byzantine force, thus opening up Palestine to Islamic conquest. The Bedouin chief, al-Muthanna ibn Haritha of the Banu Shayban, was left in charge of the eastern front. On 26 November AD 634 a Persian force attacked and almost destroyed the Muslims at the Battle of the Bridge near al-Hira. The success was short lived. A year later the reinforced al-Muthanna gained the victory at al-Buwayb on the river Euphrates. The victory prepared the way for the conquest of Persia.

See also: **Ajnadayn, Battle of**

EDWARD D. A. HULMES

BRITISH MANDATE IN PALESTINE

Following the First World War, the Allied powers agreed at San Remo to grant a mandate for Britain and France to supervise parts of the defeated Ottoman Empire; this was authorised by the League of Nations. Britain took responsibility for Palestine, Transjordan and Iraq, and France for Syria and Lebanon. In Palestine, proposals to devolve authority failed, and British rule was increasing destabilised by Arab–Jewish sectarian conflict. Following the Second World War, British forces were again attacked by Arab and Jewish insurgents. In April 1947, Britain turned to the United Nations which produced a partition plan that was approved by the General Assembly on 29 November 1947. Britain declared an end to the Mandate on 15 May 1948 and withdrew its remaining troops. The Arab–Israel war of 1948–9 followed.

References

Hourani (1991: 315–32), James (1997: 399), Salibi (1976: 958–60).

SIMON W. MURDEN

BUKHARA

Already an ancient city in central Asia when it was captured by the Arabs in AD 709 Bukhara was to grow as a centre of Islamic civilisation and learning in Transoxania, the region to the east of the river Oxus (*Amu Darya*). The river was the traditional border between the Persian-speaking and Turkish-speaking peoples. Strategically located in present-day Uzbekistan, Bukhara remains an important centre for transcontinental trade along the major highway which leads from Baghdad in the west to Samarkand and China to the east. The city is famed for the production of intricate gold embroidery, quality silks, soft furnishings, carpets, prayer rugs and metalwork. Several important mosques and buildings dating from tenth to the seventeenth century AD, such as the City Fortress and the mausoleum of Ismail Samani, remain in the old city. In the mid-twentieth century the economy and prosperity of the city were boosted by the discovery of substantial reserves of natural gas in the region. The city was the birthplace of Ibn Sina (Avicenna).

In the ninth and tenth centuries AD Bukhara was the capital of the Samanid dynasty. In AD 1220 the city was captured and devastated by Cingiz Khan (AD 1155–1227). A century and a half later, in AD 1370, it fell to Timur (Tamerlane). He was the Islamic leader, feared for the violence of his conquests from the shores of the Mediterranean to India. In the sixteenth century, Bukhara became the capital of the Uzbeki Shaybanids, whose khanate extended to include Afghanistan and northern Persia. Bukhara later became the capital of an independent emirate, which was annexed by Russia in 1868. Soviet troops occupied the city in 1920 and four years later the Bukharan Soviet People's Republic was incorporated into the USSR as the Uzbek Soviet Socialist Republic. Uzbekistan gained independence in 1991.

References

Arberry (1953: 104, 361–3), Schacht and Bosworth (1979: 116–30).

See also: **Ibn Sina, Abu 'Ali al-Husayn (Avicenna); Samarqand**

EDWARD D. A. HULMES

AL-BUKHARI, MUHAMMAD IBN ISMA'IL (AD 810–70)

al-Bukhari, who lived from 810 to AD 870, a compiler of one of the six authoritative books of *hadith* in Sunni Islam. Born in Bukhara, he spent much of his life in Nishapur; he later returned to Bukhara and then went to Samarkand towards the end of his life.

Al-Bukhari is said to have travelled throughout the Middle East in order to hear *hadith* reports from as many sources as possible, he is said to have listened to some 1,000 transmitters. He is reported to have had an astounding memory which he cultivated from a young age and to have accumulated some 600,000 reports which he reduced to about 2,762 distinct traditions (although there are 7,397 entries in the work when one includes the duplicated traditions) that he considered reliable enough according to his own strict criteria for inclusion in his book. Organised by subject matter, al-Bukhari's *al-Sahih* is considered to be the most reliable collection of authenticated reports along with that of Muslim ibn al-Hajjaj, as a pair, these works are considered by Sunni Muslims as second only to the Qur'an in authority. The work, which took sixteen years to compile, is organised according to books (of which there are ninety-seven) and chapters (3,450 in total), following the established agenda of juristic and theological problems of the time.

References

Goldziher (1971a: II, 216–26), Siddiqi (1993: 53–8).

ANDREW RIPPIN

BUKHTISHU

Bukhtishu is the name of a family of Nestorian Christian physicians who had a leading position in the school of Jundishapur in the eighth century.

Twelve members of this family served the 'Abbasid Caliphs as physicians and advisers in scientific matters. They also worked on translating scientific texts and contributed to some medical treaties. Jurji b. Jira'il b. Bukhtishu was the first physician to be called to the service of the 'Abbasid Caliph al-Mansur. After his return to Jundishapur, where he died in AD 768, his son took his place in Baghdad in AD 787, serving also the Caliph Harun al-Rashid. The different members of the Bukhtishu family continued to be court physicians to the 'Abbasid Caliph al-Mutawakkil.

References

Gibb and Bosworth (1960–2003: I, 1298).

MAHA EL-KAISY FRIEMUTH

BULUGH (PUBERTY)

According to Islam, puberty is recognised as having been reached when one of its natural processes is observed – i.e., female menstruation or male ejaculation of sperm. However, the majority of Muslim scholars concur that fifteen is the accepted age of puberty, a condition that is stipulated in the Majallah (Articles 985 and 986). Other scholars, and in particular Abu Hanifa, take into consideration the variation of development rates between the genders and consider puberty to have been reached at seventeen years for girls and eighteen years for boys.

References

al-Bustani (n.d.), al-Zuhayli (1985: 122–5).

MAWIL IZZI DIEN

BURAQ

The animal mentioned in the *hadith* as ridden by Muhammad on his Night Journey to Jerusalem.

See also: **isra'**

ANDREW J. NEWMAN

BURDA

Muslims have expressed their devotion to the Prophet Muhammad in varied ways throughout Islamic history, starting in his own lifetime. Most famous among the poems in praise of him is the *Qasidat al-Burda*, 'The Mantle Poem', of the thirteenth-century Berber Sufi Sharaf al-Din Abu 'Abdallah Muhammad al-Busiri (d. AD 1294). This has come to occupy a position of central importance in celebrations of the Prophet, and in many popular minds has taken on quasi-supernatural powers of protection: verses are worn as charms, written on walls of houses, and recited at funerals.

Al-Busiri, a Shadhili Sufi who worked under the Mamluks in Egypt, reputedly composed the *Burda*, the full title of which is *Kawakib al-Dursiyya fi Madh Khayr al-Barriyya*, 'Glittering Stars in Praise of the Most Excellent of Creatures', after he had recovered from illness when the Prophet appeared to him in a dream and laid over him his mantle, *burda*. He seems to have been consciously echoing the incident in which the Prophet had laid his mantle over the poet Ka'b Ibn Zuhayr as a sign of forgiveness. Ka'b had been a critic, but then composed a poem in praise of him, also called the *Burda*.

Al-Busiri's *Burda* consists of 164 verses, each rhyming on the letter *mim*, maybe a reminiscence of the first letter of Muhammad's name. Al-Busiri begins with the conventional lament for unrepaid love that is usual in classical Arabic odes, and a self-conscious plea for his tears to be tolerated. But he gradually turns from this unrestrained surrender to passion and the tricks of evil, and recalls his religious responsibilities. So he begins to remember the abstinence of the Prophet and his surpassing qualities, and reflects on his unique supremacy over all other creatures:

> Muhammad, Lord of the two Worlds, and of the two species having weight, [humans and jinn, both with physical forms]
>
> And of the two groups, Arabs and non-Arabs ...
>
> He surpassed the prophets in physical and moral qualities,
>
> Nor did they approach him in either knowledge or magnanimity.
>
> All of them seek to obtain from the Apostle of Allah
>
> A ladle-full from the ocean or a sip from the continuous rains.
>
> (34, 38, 39)

Such thoughts lead him further in his wonder about the Prophet's excellences, and he sees that these are in fact without limit, so that ordinary mortals cannot grasp his true nature and perfection: 'Like a flower in delicate freshness, like the full moon in splendour / Like the sea in bountifulness, and like time in aspiration' (58). This verse is especially famous as a summary of the Prophet's pre-eminence.

Reflections on the Prophet's sublimity and universal significance lead al-Busiri to remember his life, and how what is known about him concurs with this timeless perfection. At his birth portents presaged the end of the old regimes and heralded his coming, and miraculous signs confirmed his prophetic status: 'How many a diseased person has been cured by the touch of his palm / And how many a madman loosed from his fettering knots' (88). Above all, the verses of the Qur'an stand out as a miracle of eloquence:

> They are clear, leaving no room for ambiguousness,

> From which the doubter could take profit, nor do they need any arbiters.
>
> Never have they been combated without the combatant retiring.
>
> Even the most inimical of their enemies have sued for peace.
>
> (97, 98)

And their teachings convey justice, with such obvious power to save from damnation that only the envious would deny their meaning. This miracle is complemented by Muhammad's Night Journey and Ascension:

> Thou wast called, as one exalted, as though one unique, unequalled,
>
> That thou mightest enjoy union – what a [mystery] hidden
>
> From eyes! And a secret – what a hidden thing!
>
> Thus hast thou taken to thyself every glory without any partner,
>
> And surpassed every rank, without any contestant.
>
> (115–17)

Here the poet imagines the unique communion between Muhammad and God himself, and, overcome by the thought of the Prophet uniquely enjoying the immediate presence of God, he is lost for words. A concluding aspect of this perfect life is the Prophet's victorious campaigns against his enemies as the power of his message overcame all wrong, and Islam was firmly established. Therefore, al-Busiri feels confident that despite his own weaknesses and the wrongdoings of his youth, Muhammad sustains him in his faith and will grant him his favour unceasingly. Even after his death, the Prophet will assist him if he stumbles when crossing the Bridge at the Judgement, so he can feel confident of God's mercy when death approaches. The *Burda* ends with a prayer for blessing on Muhammad, his family and his followers.

111

This sustained meditation on the singular virtues of the Prophet and the unique achievements of his life has exerted a powerful influence. It was already popular soon after al-Busiri's own time, (Ibn Khaldun was among those who wrote commentaries on it), and it later became common practice to interweave one's own lines with it (this was customary with religious poems), particularly by inserting three lines between two of its original lines to make a five line stanza, *takhmis*. Its powers to heal and bless are considerable and, for example, lines 23 and 24 are often thought to give comfort to the distressed if recited at dawn:

> Let the tears pour down freely from an eye which has taken its fill of forbidden sights, and cling close to the protectiveness of repentance.
>
> Go contrary to both the soul and Satan, disobey them both,
>
> And if that pair pretend sincere affection in advising thee, be suspicious.

The *qasida* has become the common property of Muslims throughout the world. It has been translated into Persian, Malay, Swahili, Turkish, Urdu and other languages, versions of which are published together with the Arabic original so as not to lose mystical power. And recitations of it often form the high points of ceremonies to mark the Prophet's birth, when it is heard in the different styles developed among the communities that cherish it.

There are many published versions of the *Qasidat al-Burda*, often accompanied by one of the many commentaries that have been written on it. And it has been translated into a number of European languages. The most accessible English translation is by Jeffery (1962: 606–20) from which the quotations above are taken. It is also available in recorded form with English voice-over.

References

Jeffrey (1962), Schimmel (1985, Chapter 10).

DAVID THOMAS

BURHANIYYA

This Sufi order has been traced to Ibrahim ibn 'Abi 'l-Majd al-Dasuqi who was an Egyptian mystic of the thirteenth century. His followers spread his message in to Arabia and Syria and it is one of the six main Sufi orders in Egypt today.

References

Trimingham (1971: 46, 275).

LLOYD RIDGEON

BURQU' (BURQA)

This is the long veil worn in public places by Muslim women which leaves only the eyes exposed. It takes various forms according to local custom. It may even extend to the ground. In some places, notably, the Gulf states, it is a leather mask with slits for the eyes. It is not universally required throughout the Islamic world as a mark of female modesty, but in recent years it has been seen more frequently in some Islamic communities in which a stand is taken against what is considered to be the baleful influences of the secular permissiveness tolerated in non-Islamic societies.

References

Bouhdiba (1985: 233–7), Omran (1992: 40–58).

See also: *hijab*

EDWARD D. A. HULMES

BURSA

Previously called Brusa, Burusa and Khodavendi kyar, capital of Bursa province in north-west Turkey, which extends from the Sea of Mamara and includes Iznik, famous for its faience tiles from the Ottoman period. Like many Turkish towns it enjoys prestige as a provincial centre. The city, in the foothills of the Ulu Dag, fed by thermal springs, was probably founded by a Bithynian king in the third century BC. It prospered in the Byzantine empire as Justinian I (r. AD 527–65) had a palace there. It was attacked by Saljuq Turks, then by Crusaders in the eleventh century. After the fall of Constantinople in AD 1204, Bursa became the centre for Byzantine resistance until about AD 1308. The founder of the Ottoman dynasty, 'Uthman I (r. 1281–c. AD 1324), and his son, Orkhan (c. AD 1324–60), are buried on terraces overlooking the city. Okhran captured Bursa (AD 1326), churches were converted to mosques and new mosques built, including Ulu-Djami' (AD 1399, restored 1421) with twenty domes and fine calligraphic decoration. The Yesil Turbe is the tomb of Sultan Mehmed I (1403) and other sultan family tombs are found in the fifteenth-century Muradiye Cami complex. The beautifully tiled Yesil Cami (1421) houses a famous theological college, library, and ablutions fountain. Dar al-Shifa, the first Ottoman hospital, was built in Bursa. The first Ottoman capital until AD 1367, then occupied by Timur (1402); afterwards the capital (*dar al-saltana*) of the Ottoman State was transferred to Adrianople (Edirne). Bursa recovered under Murad II and expanded under the Ottomans with a mixed population including Greeks, Jews, Circassians from 1864, Armenians and Muslims. By 1892 there were 165 mosques, fifty-seven schools, twenty-seven *madrasas*, seven *'imarets*, seven churches, three synagogues, forty-nine caravanserais and thirty-six factories. As one of closest Muslim centres to Christian Europe, it prospered as an international centre for silk, spices, dyes, soap, sugar and perfumes from India, Persia, Syria, Arabia and Egypt. The city opposed Mustafa Kemal in 1919.

References

Naval Intelligence Division (1943: II, 28–34), Stewig (2004).

JANET STARKEY

BUYIDS (AD 932–1062)

From the Daylam region of north-western Iran, the Buyids rose to power in western and central Iran; hence, their emergence is one aspect of the appearance of hitherto-submerged peoples of Iran like the Daylamis and Kurds. As Zaydi Shi'ites, the Buyids had a role in encouraging existing Shi'ite communities in Iran and their scholars. Entering Baghdad in AD 945, they exercised tutelage over the 'Abbasid caliphs in Baghdad, but were themselves content with the title of *Amir al-Umara'* 'Supreme Commander'. There were three component branches of the Buyid family, so that their rule was something like a confederation, but in the mid-eleventh century they went down before the incoming Saljuqs.

References

Bosworth (1996: No. 75), Busse (1969, 1975: 250–304), Gibb and Bosworth (1960–2003).

C. E. BOSWORTH

BYZANTINE EMPIRE

The Qur'an speaks not of Byzantines as such, but of 'Rum', a usage which does not appear to discriminate between the various elements of Christendom. The *Surat al-Rum* (Q.30) consists of sixty verses. The early part of the chapter mentions the Byzantines, or 'Rum': 'Rum has been defeated, in a nearby land, after this defeat, though, they will be conquerors [again]' (Q.30:2 and 3), supposedly referring to the loss of Syria and Palestine to the Persians, and the prediction of future Byzantine victories. The future victories are interpreted as referring to victories of Heraclius against the Persians.

It is clear that Rum is the term used for the imperial manifestation of Christianity and not the faith itself. The most common appellation of Christians is *nasara* ('Nazarenes'). The appellation 'Rum' derives from 'Rome' (both the city and empire), though it came to mean the eastern empire only, and more precisely, Asia Minor, 'the Rum' was used to refer to 'the people of the land of Rum', ie the population of Asia Minor. The term *Bazantiya* is also known (from the Greek, 'Byzantion') though was less commonly used in Muslim religious literature.

Early Muslim knowledge of the Byzantines was quite extensive. Contacts between the pre-Islamic Arabs and the Byzantines were established through trade, but also through military alliance. The most famous of these alliances was with the Christian Ghassanid division of the Arab tribal group al-Azd. The Ghassanids were, however, Monophysites, believing Christ to have had only one divine nature. The Orthodox Byzantines (believing Christ to have had a nature which was both human and divine) were wary of those they regarded as heretics, but they depended on the Ghassanids for their claim to suzerainty over Syria and Jordan. Ghassanid power collapsed in the face of the Persian invasion in AD 613–14. The Persians in turn lost control of the area to the Arab-Muslim forces,

as the Persian Sassanian forces were driven out of Iraq following the famous battle of al-Qadisiyya sometime between 635 and AD 637.

After the emergence of the Arab-Muslim empire, the Near East was almost entirely conquered and came under Arab-Muslim control. The Byzantines were restricted to a rather shaky power base in Anatolia. The desire to capture Constantinople, perceived to be the centre of the Christian faith, became a goal of the Muslims. The desire to control it gave rise to a number of apocalyptic traditions: conquering Constantinople was seen as a precursor to the drama of the end times, signalling the imminent arrival of al-Dajjal, the Anti-Christ. When Constantinople did, eventually, fall to the Ottoman Turks in 1453, the event was greeted with millenarian hopes in some quarters of the Muslim world.

The Byzantine Empire in Syria crumbled under the military advances of the Arabs whose successes under the second caliph 'Umar (r. AD 634–44) are described in detail in Muslim chronicles. At the Battle of Yarmuk in AD 636, the Byzantine forces suffered a resounding defeat by the Arab-Muslim forces under the leadership of the general Abu 'Ubayda al-Jarrah. The defeat meant that the Byzantines lost their major fighting force in Syria, and was a sign of the loss of all of Syria to the Muslims. The Byzantines retreated to Anatolia (Asia Minor), where they established firmer defences. The Arab desire to conquer Constantinople continued to give rise to Arab raids in Anatolia, and attacks on Byzantine ships. These continued, though without any dramatic success, and by the time of the Umayyad caliph 'Umar b. 'Abd al-'Aziz (r. AD 717–20), the desire to capture Constantinople had waned somewhat. The last serious Arab attempt was made by Harun (later the 'Abbasid caliph, Harun al-Rashid) in AD 781–2. He did not, however, vigorously pursue the prize, as he agreed to desist from attacking for the payment of tribute from the Byzantine Empress, Irene.

Anatolia, on the whole, remained in the hands of Christians until the eleventh century. The relationship between the Byzantines in Asia Minor and the Arabs (both Umayyads and 'Abbasids) was one of relatively peaceful coexistence, punctuated by Arab raids into Byzantine territory. As the 'Abbasids began to lose the central caliphal control they had enjoyed in the early part of their reign, Muslim dynasties, formally allied with the caliphate but effectively operating as independent states, began to develop throughout the Muslim empire. Ethnic groups began to assert their independence. In particular the Turkish Saljuq clan established a Sunni dynasty first in Iran and Iraq, and later Syria and Anatolia. The Saljuq ingress into Byzantine Anatolia was characterised by a gradual heightening of military activities and raids by Saljuq clan members in the late eleventh century. The Byzantine Empire was fragmented and weakened by internal dispute and the Saljuq Sulayman b. Qutalmish was able to make Izniq (Iznik or Nicaea) his capital in 1081. The town was, however, recaptured by western European crusaders in 1097. The success of the crusaders signalled yet another threat to the Byzantine Empire. Whilst the Muslim forces to the east were gradually gaining ground, the adventurous crusaders, most of whom viewed the Byzantines as heretics, began to establish states in Anatolia. Byzantine attention was divided between two foes: the Muslims and the crusaders. On a number of occasions over the next two centuries, Byzantine losses can be traced to having to deal with these two different threats.

Sulayman, in the capture of Iznik, had demonstrated that incursions into Byzantine territory need not be mere temporary raids. Through the work the Saljuq Mas'ud the First (r. AD 1118–55), a permanent capital at Konya was established. Mosques and *madrasas* were constructed, and Konya became a thriving intellectual and commercial centre. From there, Saljuq Muslim control over formerly Byzantine lands was established. The main threat came, not from the Byzantines, but from crusading armies. Frederick Barbarossa's army, for example, plundered Konya in AD 1190. The Byzantines also suffered from the crusading armies, most ignominiously in the sack of Constantinople of 1204 and the establishment of Frankish crusader states on formerly Byzantine soil. The intricacies of the diplomatic relations between Frankish, Byzantine, Muslim and Italian states and potentates in Anatolia and Greece need not be examined in detail here. The principal lesson to be drawn is that religious creedal divisions were not always of paramount importance when alliances were made or broken. The Muslims acted with the Byzantines against the crusaders on occasions, and against the Byzantines at other times.

The Mongol invasions of the central Muslim lands in the thirteenth century did not remove the Saljuqs from power, but merely made them a vassal state of the new Mongol khanate. Through them the remaining areas of Byzantine control in Anatolia came under Muslim control. The Byzantines were effectively left with their Greek territories, ruling them precariously from Constantinople. As central control within the Muslim Empire gradually collapsed once more in the thirteenth century, states began to appear on the edges of the areas under Muslim control. A number of these emerged in Anatolia, one of which, the 'Osmanli (Ottomans) was to eventually bring an end to the Byzantine Empire. The Ottomans, originally from the central Asian Turkish Oghuz people, developed a power base in Bithynia in north-west Anatolia in 1299. From there, their power expanded as they conquered rival Muslim powers in Anatolia, and expanding into the Balkans in the fourteenth century, instituting an 'Turkification' policy. As they secured power in the Balkans and Anatolia, the Ottomans gradually encircled the Byzantines, permitting them to maintain power, but conquering them when they were too troublesome. The Ottomans themselves faced threats from the Muslim East, demonstrated most impressively by the victory of Timur (Tamerlane) over the Ottoman Sultan near Ankara in 1401. This led the Ottomans to concentrate their power in formerly Greek Byzantine territory. In particular, they established themselves at Adrianople (or Edirne in Turkish) and from there, the Empire was effectively run. Ottoman patience with the remnants of the Byzantine empire finally ran out and Sultan Mehmet II (r. 1444–6 and 1451–81) ordered his troops into the city of Constantinople on 29 May 1453. The city was taken in a day, and Emperor Constantine IX was killed in battle. The Ottomans now occupied the city which had been the desire of the Muslim Arabs since the time of the second caliph in the seventh century. It was renamed Istanbul. The remains of the Byzantine Empire were mopped up by the Ottomans. The Byzantine 'Despotate' of Morea fell in 1460, and the Comnenus Byzantine rule of Trebizond was ended by Mehmet II's forces in 1461.

The collapse of the Byzantine Empire did not, of course, mean the end of a thriving Christian community in the area. The Orthodox Church continued to operate, and whilst the population of Asia Minor was primarily Muslim, Greece (Morea and neighbouring areas) remained Orthodox. Formerly Byzantine institutions, such as monasteries and churches established a *modus vivendi* with the Ottomans. When Greece (with the help of the great powers) freed itself from Ottoman control in the 1820s, Orthodox identity had freed itself from reliance on the existence of a Byzantine state. Constantinople however, retains its importance (symbolic and otherwise) for Orthodox Christians as the historic centre of the Byzantine Empire.

References

Babinger (1978), Nicol (1993), Runciman (1977).

ROBERT GLEAVE

BYZANTINES (AD 330–1453)

Byzantium, the Christian 'Second Rome' at Constantinople, was for some eight centuries the great rival of the Muslims for control of the Near East, the only Christian power with which the Arabs were compelled to treat on equal terms. There were in the early centuries some cultural and artistic interchanges, and one report says that the Byzantine emperor sent mosaicists, at the Umayyad caliph's request, to work on the Prophet's tomb at Medina. With the initial expansion of the Arabs, Byzantium lost most of its outlying territories in the Mediterranean basin, but maintained a much-fought-over frontier with the Muslims along northern Syria and Mesopotamia, until after the eleventh century the Turkish invaders subtracted much of Anatolia from Greek control. It was nevertheless not until 1453 that the Ottomans captured Constantinople and extinguished the empire, after 1,000 years' life, shortly afterwards.

References

Gibb and Bosworth (1960–2003), Shahid (1995–2002), Vasiliev (1952).

C. E. BOSWORTH

C

CAIRO

Capital of Egypt and largest city in Africa. Situated on both banks of the river Nile at the foot of the delta. It is difficult to separate the city from the surrounding areas, although the river together with several islands is the core of its life. The site has been settled for more than 6,000 years, originally as ancient Egyptian Memphis and then as Roman Babylon on the east bank of the Nile. The Arabs founded the settlement (*misr* – Arabic for camp and the name used both for Cairo and for the whole country) of Fustat in AD 641. The next important development was the founding of a new city by the Fatimid dynasty from North Africa in AD 969 that they called Misr al-Qahira (the victorious city) and which became an important Islamic centre with the founding of al-Azhar mosque and university (AD 988). In the twelfth century the crusaders attacked Cairo but were defeated by Salah al-Din (known to the West as Saladin) who founded the powerful Ayyubid dynasty. Saladin built the citadel and the Mamluks (a long reigning dynasty from the thirteenth to the sixteenth centuries – descendants of slaves) built numerous mosques, madrasas and fortifications. Cairo was a provincial Ottoman city from 1517 to 1798 and capital again of the semi-independent Muhammad 'Ali dynasty (1805–1953) after the brief interregnum of the Napoleonic French occupation (1798–1801). Egypt and Cairo were opened to European influence by the Khedive (ruler) Isma'il and new quarters were built with straight avenues and Parisian-style buildings. The city continued to expand under the British occupation and, after independence, it became a large and sprawling Third World city with attendant problems of great poverty, inadequate infrastructure, poor transport and overpopulation. Surrounding rural areas have been overwhelmed by the city although its centre is still the Nile and its islands. The regular flooding of the river has been tamed since the building of the Aswan High Dam.

Cairo is a vibrant city that seems able to cope with its problems, home of the institutions of government, education, culture and tourism that create a dense pattern of constant activity. The centre of the city is Tahrir Square which contains the Egyptian National Museum, the headquarters of the Arab League and the Mugamma' – a notorious government bureaucratic building. Medieval Cairo is centred around al-Azhar and is an ensemble of narrow alleys, *suqs*, mosques and city gates. The large City of the Dead at the foot of the Muqattam hills has been taken over by the living as permanent dwellings. To the south is Old Cairo with its Coptic churches, the original site of Fustat. Further out are the suburbs of Heliopolis and Helwan and other newer developments.

References

Abu-Lughod (1971).

DEREK HOPWOOD

CALENDAR, ISLAMIC (*AL-TAQWIM AL-ISLAMI, AL-HIJRI*)

The Islamic calendar dates from the *hijra*, the 'migration' or 'departure' of the Prophet Muhammad from Mecca to Yathrib (Medina) in AD 622. Sixteen years later, in AD 637 'Umar ibn al-Khattab, the second of the four Rightly Guided Caliphs, established the year 622 as the first year of the Islamic era, namely, 1 AH (*anno hejirae*). The Hejiran calendar, as it is sometimes called, is a lunar calendar, in which the year is divided into twelve months based upon the orbits of the moon around the earth and the observations of the phases of the moon as seen from the earth. In the early days of Islam physical sightings of the new moon determined the start of another month. This practice gave way

long ago to calculations based upon astronomical observations of the moon's reappearance, but there is still a reminder of the older tradition when the physical sighting of the new moon marks the beginning and the ending of the month of Ramadan, the month of the annual period of fasting in Islam.

Each lunar (synodic) month consists of approximately twenty-nine and a half days, a period that elapses between the appearance of one new moon and the next. The days of the week begin and end at sunset. Beginning with Muharram ('the sacred month'), the Islamic calendar consists of six months of thirty days alternating with six months of twenty-nine days, making a total of 354 days. The months are Muharram, Safar, Rabi' al-Awwal, Rabi Akhir, Jumada al-Ula, Jumada al-Akhira, Rajab, Sha'ban, Ramadan, Shawwal, Dhu'l-Qa'da, Dhu'l-Hijja. The solar year, based upon the time it takes the earth to orbit the sun, consists of approximately 365 days with an additional day added every fourth, or 'leap', year. In simple terms this means that an Islamic new year begins eleven days earlier than a year of the solar, Gregorian, calendar. In consequence, the lunar months regress through the seasons. The month of Ramadan ('the month of great heat'), for example, moves throughout the seasons from summer to winter during the course of some thirty-three solar years, thus making the observance of the Islamic fast an even greater trial when it occurs during the hottest period of the year.

A somewhat laborious method of calculating the number of a Gregorian year from the number of an Islamic year is as follows. Multiply the *hijri* year by 970.224. Count six places from the right and insert a decimal point. Add 621.5774. The number to the left of the decimal point gives the year of the Gregorian calendar. If the decimal fraction is then multiplied by 365, the result is the number of the day in the Gregorian calendar on which the Islamic year began. So, for example the Gregorian year 2002 is the Islamic year AH 1424. Many almanacs and diaries in the non-Islamic world include the date and number of the new Islamic year.

Among the most important dates in the Islamic calendar are the celebration of *ra's al-sana*, New Year on 1 Muharram, *'ashura'* on 10 Muharram, *mawlid* (*milad*) *al-nabi* (the birthday of the Prophet Muhammad on 12 Rabi' al-Awwal), *laylat al-mi'raj* (the Night Journey, on 27 Rajab), *laylat al-qadr* (the Night of the Descent of the Qur'an between the 21 and 27 Ramadan), *'Id al-fitr* (the Breaking of the Fast, during three days at the end of Ramadan), *'Id al-adha* (the Feast of the Sacrifice, at the end of the pilgrimage to Mecca in the month of Dhu'l-Hijja).

References

Hitti (1973: 176), Hourani (1991: 149).

EDWARD D. A. HULMES

CALENDAR, LUNAR

See: **months, Islamic**

CALIPHATE

The origins of the Caliphate are to be found in the events that occurred immediately after the death of the Prophet Muhammad in AD 632. Given the fact that he did not appear to have designated his successor (*khalifa*), despite reports that he had mentioned the name of 'Ali ibn abi Talib, it was inevitable that different interested parties would contend with each other for the honour of appointing that successor. References to these disputes are made in the ency-

clopaedia entries mentioned below. The key dispute was between the supporters of the first caliph, Abu Bakr, and the supporters of the man who was to become the fourth, 'Ali. The consequences of this bitter disagreement remain to this day, in the division of the household of Islam into Sunnis and Shi'is. The former group opposed the election of 'Ali. The latter worked to secure it. The situation was made more complex when, from an early date, succession in the Caliphate became hereditary and dynastic instead of elective. Further complexity arose when the imamate developed in Shi'i Islam. The fourth caliph 'Ali, is considered by Shi'is to be their first imam. The distinction between the two terms is that a caliph is elected by consensus, as an exemplary *primus inter pares*. An imam, designated by his predecessor without any appeal to consensus, is the spiritual guide of the Islamic community, and nominated by divine ordinance (*nass*). The historic Caliphate, per se, was ended when the Mongols destroyed Baghdad in AD 1258. The Ottoman Caliphate was abolished by the new Turkish Republic in the 1920s.

References

Hourani (1991: 22–62), Momen (1985: 18–22, 147–60).

See also: **'Abbasids; Abu Bakr al-Siddiq; 'Ali ibn abi Talib; Fatimids; Muhammad ibn 'Abdallah, the Prophet of Islam; Shi'ism; Sunnism; 'Umar ibn al-Khattab; Umayyads; 'Uthman ibn 'Affan**

EDWARD D. A. HULMES

CALL TO PRAYER (*ADHAN*)

Muslims are summoned to prayer and worship five times each day, and to congregational worship in the mosque at noon on Fridays, by the *mu'adhdhin*, who 'announces' the hours of prayer from the precincts of the mosque. Soon after his arrival in Medina (AD 623), and disliking the sound of the wooden clappers and bells used for the purpose of calling the faithful to worship in Christian churches, Muhammad adopted the *adhan* as the formal call to prayer for members of the Islamic community. The first *Mu'adhdhin* ('one who calls to prayer') was Muhammad's Abyssinian slave Bilal, whose stentorian voice made him well suited for the task. In the earliest days the call was made from the rooftop or the doorway of a mosque. Later, when leadership of the Islamic community passed from Medina to Damascus under the Umayyads, the *adhan* was intoned from the balcony of a minaret (*manara*, 'lighthouse', 'watchtower'). It was at this time that the minaret became a distinctive feature of the architecture of a mosque. In modern times, the voice of the *mu'adhdhin* is often amplified electronically to make the call to prayer heard above the noises of a busy town or city.

For Sunni Muslims the *adhan* consists of seven statements, the sixth of which repeats the first:

1. 'Allah is most great!' (or 'Allah is greater [i.e. than anything else])'.
2. 'I bear witness that there is no god other than Allah'.
3. 'I bear witness that Muhammad is the messenger of Allah'.
4. 'Come to prayer!'
5. 'Come to salvation!'
6. 'Allah is most great!'
7. 'There is no god other than Allah'.

The first of the seven statements is uttered four times, the second to sixth are uttered twice, the seventh is voiced only once. At the time of morning prayer (*salat al-subh*) the words 'Prayer is better than sleep' are added. The *adhan* of Shi'i Muslims is slightly differ-

ent in two respects, namely, it adds an eighth statement, 'Come to the best work!', between the fifth and sixth, and voices the final statement twice. A Muslim who observes the five daily hours of prayer alone, or with his family, and beyond the range of the intonations of a *mu'adhdhin*, is required to pronounce the formulas of the *adhan* 'in a loud voice', but there is no single way of intoning the words. The words of the final statement *la ilaha illa'llah* (there is no god other than Allah) are whispered into the right ear of a newborn child, partly to guard the child against the wiles of the rebellious among the *jinn* (the unsubdued spirits hostile to man), but chiefly because the words express the first of the two affirmations in a Muslim's Profession of Faith.

References

Hitti (1973: 118, 259n), Momen (1985: 178, 237).

EDWARD D. A. HULMES

CALLIGRAPHY

Calligraphy was the most respected art in the Islamic world as the means of recording the Arabic of the Qur'an, the literal word of Allah, in the most beautiful manner possible. The Qur'an itself speaks of Allah teaching the use of the pen (Q.96:4–5). Many styles of calligraphy have developed from the earliest dated example in the Dome of the Rock of AD 692 written in blue angular Kufic script against gold. Early manuscripts of the Qur'an were also written in Kufic in bold contrasts of black letters on cream-coloured vellum or gold on blue. Classic rounded scripts – *naskh* and *thuluth* – which had evolved during the tenth to eleventh centuries eventually replaced Kufic in manuscripts. Other script forms include the graceful cursive *taliq* and *nastaliq* developed by Iranian calligraphers. Calligraphy adorns all media – carved stone, wood and stucco, mosaic and painted tilework, glazed ceramics, woven and embroidered textiles, engraved metalwork – as well as illuminated manuscripts. Apart from the Qur'an and other religious texts, fine calligraphy is used in volumes of poetry, historical chronicles and official documents.

References

Safadi (1978), Welch (1979).

JENNIFER SCARCE

CAUSALITY

Causality (*al-sababiyya*) was at the center of both Islamic philosophical and theological thought. From the vast and varied literature treating it, one can discern some of the essential features that typify the respective views of the Islamic philosophers, the *falasifa*, and the theologians (*the mutakallimun*), particularly those belonging to the dominant school of Islamic theology (*kalam*), the Ash'arite, that takes its name after its founder al-Ash'ari (d. AD 935). The Ash'arite Ghazali, (d. AD 1111), levelled severe logical criticisms at the philosophical systems of two of Islam's major philosophers, Al-Farabi (Alfarabi) (d. AD 950) and Ibn Sina (Avicenna) (d. AD 1037). At the heart of these criticism was his different conception of causality.

For the philosophers' treatment of causality, it is perhaps best to turn to the thought of Ibn Sina who discussed it extensively and perceptively. As expected, he adopted Aristotle's doctrine of the four causes, the material, the formal, the efficient and the final. In the terrestrial world, all these are needed to explain change. He also followed Aristotle's causal doctrine as it pertained to demonstrative logic. At the same time,

he expanded on Aristotle's causal views and affected changes. The changes are perhaps most evident in the Neoplatonic metaphysics he developed, according to which the world proceeds from God in a series of emanations. Thus, while in the terrestrial realm, the effect that follows the cause is motion in one of its forms, this is not entirely the case with divine causality. To be sure, God as the teleological cause is ultimately the cause of the motion of the spheres. However, for Ibn Sina, he is more than this. He is the cause that bestows existence on everything that emanates from him. Probably, to safeguard his system from a drift towards pantheism, Ibn Sina insisted that the effect is always other than its cause.

Another feature of Ibn Sina's causal theory is his differentiation between the essential and accidental cause. The essential cause is prior to its effect in essence, not in time. The accidental cause, in contrast, precedes the effect in time. This distinction is basic to the proof of God's existence because the essential cause coexists with its effect and hence any series of such coexisting causes and effects cannot be infinite – otherwise they would constitute an actual infinite, deemed impossible by Ibn Sina. Hence, the series must have a beginning, a First Cause, namely, God. The accidental causes, contrarily, can be infinite, because, for Ibn Sina (and the majority of the Islamic philosophers) they do not form an actual infinite.

Ibn Sina held that the inferential relation between cause and effect is reciprocal, only, however, when certain conditions are fulfilled. In the case of the terrestrial efficient cause, for example, the efficient cause must be the proximate cause, the other three Aristotelian causes must also exist, the recipient of the effect must exist and must have the disposition for such a reception, and there must also be

121

no impediment. What, then, if an effect has more than one cause? The inferential relation is no longer reciprocal. It becomes reciprocal when a common element among the different causes is isolated and identified as the one proximate cause.

If cause and effect coexist, and the inferential relation between them is reciprocal, then logically each would constitute the necessary and sufficient condition for the other. How can one then determine which is the cause and which is the effect? In his analysis of this problem, Ibn Sina differentiated between the existence of cause and effect in external reality, their existence in the mind and 'the indication' to the mind of their existence in reality. Thus, he held that when either cause or effect exists in the mind, then the other must also exist in the mind, and that when the existence of either cause or effect in reality is present to the mind, the mind necessarily infers the existence of the one or the other in reality. In external reality, however, it is only the cause that brings about the existence of the effect – the effect can only be removed when the cause is removed.

Within this system all existents other than God, are necessitated by their causes. Ultimately, God necessitates the existence of all things, acting, however, through intermediary causes that in turn necessitate their effects. In the terrestrial natural realm, while all events are ultimately, the necessitated effects of divine causality, terrestrial natural things are endowed (through emanation) with causal powers that necessitated their effects. How can one know this? Ibn Sina was well aware that sheer observation of regularities in nature shows only concomitance, not necessary causal connections. Still, he maintained that the regularities observed in nature must have a reason. Taking his cue from

Aristotle's statement about chance (*Physics*, ii, 5, 196b, 10–11), Ibn Sina argued that in addition to the observation of regularities, there is always 'a hidden syllogism' to the effect that if such regularities were accidental or coincidental they would not have continued. He concluded that these regularities derive from the inherent causal nature of things. Despite it being open to the criticism that it is circular (since by definition the coincidental and the accidental are irregular occurrences), the argument became well known in Islam and the Latin West.

Turning to theology, the early (first important) school of theology, *kalam*, the Mu'tazilite, tended to allow causal action in natural things. This was expressed in their doctrine of generation (*al-tawallud*). But there were differences in their understanding of this doctrine and there was a tendency among a few of them to move towards the occasionalist position that denied causal efficacy in things, attributing all causal action to God. According to this doctrine, the events we ordinarily regard as causes are simply the occasions (also created by God) accompanying divine action. This became the general doctrine of the Ash'arite school that gradually replaced the Mu'tazilite as the dominant school of *kalam*. Ash'arite predecessors of Ghazali argued on empirical grounds that the belief in causal efficacy in created beings is not provable. It was Ghazali, however, who gave their argument its most forceful expression.

In his *Incoherence of the Philosophers,* directed largely against Ibn Sina, Ghazali declared that the connection in observable things between what are habitually believed to be causes and effects is not necessary. Their connection is as a result of God's decree, who creates them concomitantly. Then, taking as his example the piece of cotton that is brought to fire, he argued that all that we observe is the burning occurring with the cotton's contact with the fire, not its burning by the fire. The one who enacts the burning, he maintained is God. Now, the purpose of his argument against necessary causal connections in nature is to show that certain miracles reported in the scriptures, whose possibility was denied by the philosophers, are in fact possible. He further tried to show that even if one accepts with some modification the philosophers' causal theory, one can still show that such miracles are possible. In works written after the *Incoherence*, it becomes clear that this concession to the philosophers was done for the sake of argument. In these works he affirmed the occasionalist position.

This occasionalist view opposed the doctrine that God acts by necessity, which meant for Ghazali the denial of the attribute of will. For the Ash'arites, the attributes of life, knowledge, will and power, though subsisting in the divine essence, are 'additional' to it. God has eternally willed all happenings in His creation. They are necessary only because of this. They have no inherent necessity and are not the necessary consequence of the divine essence. God could have willed things other than what they are. Connected with this doctrine of the divine will is the Ash'arite belief in the habitual course of events decreed by the divine will. It is this which gives nature its uniformity. Disruptions of this uniformity occur when God creates miracles. When a miracle takes place, God removes momentarily our knowledge of this uniformity, creating in its stead knowledge of the miracle.

As Ghazali sees it, this doctrine of the uniformity of nature, can accommodate Ibn Sina's causal patterns, divesting them, however, of real causal powers and of any inherent necessity. What Ibn Sina

regards as causes and effects, are not real causes and effects, but behave as though they are. As such, Ghazali suggests that one can make causal inferences from them, proceeding in accordance with the Aristotelian canons of demonstration. In effect, he attempted to reinterpret Aristotelian demonstrative science in occasionalist terms, an attempt that is not without philosophical interest. One of the virtues of this attempt is that it brings home the point that the basic premise underlying scientific endeavors is the belief in nature's uniformity.

References

Al-Ghazali (2000), Anawati (1978-85: I, 210–11), Bouyges (1930), Fakhry (1958), Marmura (2004: 231–60; 273–99; 301–34; 2005: IV, Chapter 1), Van Der Bergh (1954).

MICHAEL E. MARMURA

CHANGE

Change is a concept that is closely connected to movement and time. It is, indeed, the first effect of the internal or external movement of things. Accordingly, there are two kinds of change: change that happens within something of itself and change that is caused by the movement of a thing from one place to another. The concept of change in metaphysics indicates the difference between the nature of the material and immaterial worlds. The former is signified by its property of being in a state of continuous change, while the latter is eternal and unchangeable. Plato was the first to draw a clear distinction between these two worlds, he considered that the material world is only an imitation and a shadow of the divine unchangeable world. God's nature, to theologians and philosophers, has the attributes of immateriality and is therefore unchangeable and eternal. Thus, following Plato, the theologians and philosophers used the notion of change in order to identify the essential nature of the material world and to draw a clear distinction between the essence of the divine and that of the human.

References

Gibb and Bosworth (1960–2003: III, 169–72), Ibn Sina (1960), Wolfson (1973).

See also: **time; movement and motion**
MAHA EL-KAISY FRIEMUTH

CHILDREN (*ATFAL, AWLAD*)

Muslims recognise that children are among the greatest of God's gifts to humankind, acknowledging that a great responsibility devolves upon those to whom the nurture of children is thus delegated. A key verse in the Qur'an for the guidance of Muslims is Q.2:233, which speaks of the mutual obligations of parents to their children and to each other. The creation of all that exists (and the ultimate destiny of all that is created) is in the hands of *Allah*. If God wills that children ('male or female') be born (Q.42:49–50), Muslims are not at liberty to prevent it. For this reason, artificial birth control, though not forbidden in Islam under certain circumstances, is considered to be an unlawful means of interfering with the creative purposes of God. The pagan practice of exposing unwanted female children in pre-Islamic Arabia, leaving them to die, was forbidden by the Qur'an. In some Islamic societies where *shari'a* prevails, sexual intercourse outside lawful marriage may carry the penalty of death. The paternity of a child from such an illicit union may be contested, but the child is not to be stigmatised as illegitimate or deprived of its rights in Islamic law.

In Islam there is no doctrine of 'original sin'. On the contrary, every newborn child, whether born to Muslim parents or not, is born innocent and in a state of *fitra*, that is, in a state of natural harmony between the Creator and creation, such as existed between God and Adam in the Garden of Eden. In Islam this gives rise to the belief that everyone is born a Muslim, an inheritor of the true religion prescribed by Allah. It follows that children who are not brought up as Muslims by Muslims are deprived of their natural spiritual patrimony, which is Islam. The Qur'an contains little by way of specific prescription for the nurture of children. Islamic tradition, however, is replete with instruction and guidance for parents about the progressive education of children according to Islamic principles.

References

Bouhdiba (1985: 88, 212–30), Omran (1992: 27–39).

See also: **abortion; birth control; circumcision; education, Islamic; naming ceremony of a child**
EDWARD D. A. HULMES

CHINGIZ KHAN (d. AD 1227) (GENGHIS KHAN)

A title probably meaning in Mongolian 'Terrible, Ferocious Khan', originally named Temujin, Mongol chief and world conqueror. He established his hegemony over the local tribes and led them outside Mongolia in a series of expansionist campaigns, first into northern China, sacking Peking in AD 1215, and then in AD 1219 turning westwards into central Asia and attacking the Muslim Khwarazm-Shahs. Transoxania, Afghanistan and eastern Iran were devastated, until in AD 1221 Chingiz returned to Mongolia, leaving others of his family to continue the conquests further.

References

Gibb and Bosworth (1960–2003), Ratchnevsky (1991).

See also: **Mongols**

C. E. BOSWORTH

CHISHTIYYA

The founder of this Sufi order was Khwajah Mu'in al-Din Hasan (d. AD 1236) although the Chishti shaykh Nizam al-Din Awliya' (d. AD 1325) is perhaps more famous. The order is known for its non-elitist approach and the respect and veneration accorded to the *pir*. The order practices the usual Sufi rituals such as *dhikr* but it also focused on controlled breathing, reminiscent of some practices of Indian yogis.

References

Rizvi (1991).

LLOYD RIDGEON

CIRCUMCISION (*KHITAN, TAHUR*)

Circumcision, commonly practised by Jews and Muslims, is the surgical removal of all, or part, of the foreskin of the penis. It is normally performed on newborn babies. Islamic tradition recognises that circumcision was a pre-Islamic institution, widely practised throughout the Middle East and Africa as a rite of social and religious initiation. Accounts of the origin of the rite are conjectural. Following the example of the biblical Abraham, the Hebrews considered male circumcision to be a sign of the covenant relationship between God and man (cf. Genesis 17:10). For Christians, the rite was not deemed to be necessary for membership of the community, as the record of the Council of Jerusalem in Chapter 15 of the Acts of the Apostles shows. No reference to circumcision is found in the Qur'an, but the practice clearly survived the changes introduced by the Prophet Muhammad's reforms. It was regarded as part of the *millat Ibrahim* ('the religion of Abraham'). The *Malikii* school of Islamic jurisprudence commends it, the *Shafi'i* school holds that it is a duty, the neglect of which is to be punished. Islamic tradition reveals that Muhammad himself was circumcised, thus providing an example for all devout Muslims to follow. 'Umar (AD 634–44), the second of the four rightly guided successors of the Prophet Muhammad, and admired in Islamic tradition as one who possessed all the Islamic virtues, did not require converts to Islam to be circumcised. The circumcision of male children is lawful seven days after birth, but it is normally performed some years later, before a child reaches the age of twelve. Converts to Islam are not expected to undergo this painful rite of passage.

More controversially in the modern world, perhaps, is the rite of female circumcision, clitoridectomy (the removal of the *labia minora* and/or the clitoris), which is still practised in some Islamic communities. In modern times, the claim that circumcision brings certain medicinal benefits remains unproven. It is clear, however, that the practice often leads to complications in childbirth and to consequent disease in children.

EDWARD D. A. HULMES

COLONIALISM

The expansion of one people at the expense of another. Colonialism involves an act of domination as emigrants from the dominant group establish settlements in their new realm.

Colonialism is an ancient practice, but is most associated with the era of European colonialism after the sixteenth century. In the eighteenth and nineteenth centuries, the Muslim world was encroached upon by the European empires, notably by the British in Egypt, Sudan, the Persian Gulf, and Indian subcontinent, the French in North Africa and Lebanon, and the Russians in the Caucasus. In the Middle East, the Ottoman Empire limited European penetration until the end of the First World War. During the twentieth century, the European empires largely disappeared and settler-colonialism became illegal in international law. A notable exception was the settler-colonialism practised by Jews and the State of Israel during and after its foundation in 1948. The long-running conflict stemming from the Israeli occupation of the West Bank, Gaza and Golan Heights after the Six Day War of 1967 was a colonial struggle.

References

Ayubi (1995: 86–123), Hourani (1991: 315–32), James (1997: 169–83, 200–16, 269–87, 386–411), Owen (2000: 8–22).

SIMON W. MURDEN

COMMUNITY, ISLAMIC

See: *umma*

COMPULSION, RELIGIOUS

Forced conversion to Islam of Jews and Christians as people of the Book is not permitted in the Qur'an and indeed their practitioners are guaranteed their faith (e.g., Q.2:256, 109:6).

See also: *ahl al-kitab*; **conversion**; *Devirshirme*

ANDREW J. NEWMAN

CONTEMPLATION

Contemplation to the Arab philosophers means the process by which God produces the first being – the first Intellect, *al-'aql* – by contemplating Himself. The Intellect, in turn, produces other beings by contemplating God and completing itself. Thus contemplation is the divine intellection which produces the creation of the world. In their epistemological discipline, however, these philosophers consider contemplation as the attempt of the human intellect to establish a connection to the divine intellects, also called angels. Al-Farabi in his psychology explained that the human intellect in its highest development is able to make contact with the active intellect, also known among philosophers as the Angel Jibril, who has the function of illuminating the human mind. At this stage stands also the Prophet, who alone is able to receive divine knowledge all at once. Ibn Sina adopted this theory but added an important modification. For him the human intellect is not able to reach any universal concepts by its own merits but is always in need of communicating with the active intellect. Thus, this communication occurs at the first stage of perceiving theoretical knowledge and not at the end. This communication he calls also *hads,* intuition. Intuition, however, is a talent which is possessed only by the few, the masses usually learn from the knowledge which is poured upon their teachers or great masters. In his last encyclopaedic work, *Remarks and Admonitions, al-Isharat wa 'l-Tanbihat*, Ibn Sina demonstrated another kind of contemplation. This contemplation aims at mystic communication directly with the light of God which unveils the divine *tajalli,* the presence of God. This communication illuminates the human soul which, through different stages, *maqamat*, ascends to the same rank as the divine intellects or the angels. Thus, the human soul in Ibn Sina's philosophy can reach the ranks of the divine and have the same privileges as the Intellects through its philosophical mystical contemplation.

References

Davidson (1992).

MAHA EL-KAISY FRIEMUTH

CONTRACEPTION (*MAN' AL-HAML*)

See: **birth control (*taqlil al-nasl*)**

CONVERSION

See: *ahl al-kitab*; **compulsion**; *Devshirme*

CORDOBA (CORDOVA)

Situated south of the Sierra Morenan *massif* in Andalusia in southern Spain, the city of Cordoba lies on the northern bank of the Guadalquivir River, some 75 miles (120 kilometres) north-east of Seville. Cordoba is the capital of the province that bears its name. The city was occupied by the Romans in 152 BC. It fell to the Visigoths in 572 and in AD 711 to the Arab Moors. During the years of the Umayyad dynasty, Cordoba became the administrative and cultural centre of an independent emirate (a de-facto caliphate), which extended to include most of Islamic Spain. In AD 1078 after the fall of the Umayyads the city was subject to Seville. Cordoba gained a reputation for the way in which Islamic and Jewish culture flourished side by side. Among the most distinguished men to be born there were the Jewish philosopher Maimonides (AD 1135–1204) and the Spanish-Arab philosopher Averroes (Ibn Rushd, AD 1126–98). The city became known for the quality of its lea-

therwork, jewellery, brocades, silk, gold and silver. Its architects created many notable houses, palaces and mosques. The most famous of the latter is the Great Mosque, work on which began in the eighth century AD. Additional pillars, arches and domes were added subsequently until the structure was completed *c.* AD 987. It was built to rival the two Islamic sanctuaries in al-Quds (Jerusalem) and Mecca, and described by some as the Ka'ba of the West. In AD 1238, the mosque became a Christian cathedral after Ferdinand III of Castile took the city by conquest and it remained a Christian stronghold in the struggle against the Islamic kingdom of Granada. When Granada fell in 1492 Cordoba began to decline as a centre of vigorous cultural activity. It was attacked by the French in 1808 for giving support to the cause of rebels against Napoleonic rule. In the Spanish Civil War of 1936–9 it was occupied by the Falangist forces of Franco.

References

Hitti (1973: 499–525), Michell (1984: 212–15), Schacht and Bosworth (1979: 79–100 *passim*).

See also: **al-Andalus; Granada; Ibn Rushd, Abu al-Walid IBN Ahmad (Averroes); Seville**

EDWARD D. A. HULMES

COSMOLOGY

The study of cosmology is connected to the branch of philosophy which the Greeks call metaphysics and most of the Arab philosophers call *al-ilahiyat*. Metaphysics, as is defined by Ibn Sina, is the subject which searches the universal principles of the physical world, such as motion, rest, time and existence, and their relation to the immaterial world of the divine beings. Cosmology is the branch of metaphysics that examines the principles of the material world and provides different doctrines of relating this world to its First Cause, while theology, another branch, searches the features of the immaterial world and defines God as the goal of metaphysics. It is the science that inquires into the doctrines which attempt to find the link between the existence of the world and the First Cause. Many Arab and Muslim philosophers have adopted the theory of emanation as an explanation for the existence of the world. However, the Isma'ili philosophers attempted to link the theory of creation *ex nihilo* with Neoplatonic emanation, while al-Kindi, the first Arab philosopher, preferred creation *ex nihilo* as the cosmological theory which explains the existence of the world.

References

Leaman (1996: I, 783–802).

See also: **creation *ex nihilo*; emanation**
MAHA EL-KAISY FRIEMUTH

CREATION *EX NIHILO*

The concept of creation is a way of clarifying the relationship between the First Cause (God), the physical world and the immaterial world. One way of doing so is to consider that the First Cause is not only the immediate cause of the motion of the world but also its absolute creator. There two different ways of understanding this theory: the first is to argue that the process of creation is not restricted to a certain moment but is perpetual and timeless. The second is to relate the process of creation not only to a certain historical moment but also to consider that creation began from nothing – nothing other than God, that is. The latter interpretation is

that which is known as creation *ex nihilo*. This concept is, indeed, a religious concept which demonstrates God's omnipotence and will. For theologians, Muslim, Christian and Jewish, the world is the product of God's will, is made according to His knowledge and is under His absolute control. God wills the world as it is and created it for a certain purpose. For Muslim theologians, God created the world in order to reward those who follow His divine law. God also from the theological standpoint did not create the world out of any other eternal substance, as God is the First cause, then He is the only eternal principle. Al-Ghazali in his *Tahafut al-Falasifa* condemned philosophers for supposing the world to be eternal, for if it were then it would be impossible neither to consider God as its maker, *sani'*, nor as its First Cause.

References

Leaman (1999: 24–6), Wolfson (1976: 466–86).

See also: **emanation**
MAHA EL-KAISY FRIEMUTH

CREED, ISLAMIC

See: **shahada**

CREMATION (*AL-HARAQ*)

See: **death and burial**

CROWTHER, SAMUEL AJAYI (*c.* 1806–91)

In his day, Crowther was a pioneer in the field of Christian–Muslim relations. In 1864 he became the first black African to be consecrated bishop in the Anglican communion. An entry under his name appears in this volume by virtue of his pioneering efforts in the nineteenth century to engage with the religious beliefs and practices of Muslims in West Africa. His short monograph, *Experiences with Heathens and Mohammedans in West Africa*, was published posthumously in London in 1892.

He was born *c.* 1806, 'a pure Yoruba' in Oshogun, a town situated in the south-western region of what is now Nigeria. He was nurtured in the traditional religious beliefs and customs of his people. In 1821 the town was attacked by Yoruba Muslims. Men, women, and children (including Crowther) were roped by the neck and herded south to a place on the coast, which at that time was a centre of the Portuguese slave trade. During the trek he attempted to commit suicide. On 18 April 1822, the Portuguese slave-ship carrying him and the other slaves was heading for the Americas when it was intercepted by two British naval anti-slavery patrol ships. The captives were released and taken to safety in Sierra Leone where, in Bathurst, Crowther was placed in the care of Church Missionary Society missionaries, Mr and Mrs Davey. Under their guidance, he proved himself to be a willing and able student. On 11 December 1825 he was baptised, received into the Christian church, and given the names Samuel Crowther to add to his African name, *Ajayi*. His 'English' names were those of the then vicar of Christ Church, Newgate Street, London, who was one of the founding committee members of the Church Missionary Society. It was common for liberated slaves to be given such names. On 16 August 1826 Crowther landed at Portsmouth with the Daveys. It was his first visit to Britain. For eight months he attended the parochial school in Islington before returning with his mentors to Sierra Leone, where he became one of the first to enrol as a student at the newly established Fourah Bay College. Two years later he was given permission to marry a liberated slave, who was given the names Susan Thompson at her baptism.

In 1834 he returned to Fourah Bay College as a tutor. He had a gift for languages and pursued his studies with considerable vigour. In 1841 he joined 145 Europeans on the ill-fated Niger Expedition, the purposes of which were 'to promote trade, to link up with local chiefs, and wherever possible to conclude treaties with them, to establish a model agricultural farm, to survey the principal languages, to introduce western medicine, to build roads and canals, and to introduce the printing press'. Forty of the Europeans on board the three iron vessels that set out up the Niger died of malaria. In June 1843 Crowther was ordained as an Anglican deacon in London. He was the first black African to be ordained for service with the Church Missionary Society, returning to Freetown in December that year to be greeted by Muslims and adherents of African traditional religion as well as by Christians. He then began to translate the Gospels into Yoruba. Within a few months he was Acting Principal of Fourah Bay College. In December 1844 he left Freetown to visit his Yoruba homeland for the first time since he was taken into slavery. In Abeokuta he was reunited with his mother, whom he baptised as his first convert in 1848, giving her the name Hannah, the mother of the biblical Samuel.

On a visit to England in 1851, he was presented to Queen Victoria and Prince Albert. Hearing of his work on the translation of the Bible into Yoruba, the Queen asked him to repeat the words of the Lord's Prayer 'in the Yoruba'. Crowther did. His words pleased the Queen, who commented on 'the soft and melodious language' of his native tongue. Another Niger Expedition set out in 1854 to explore the Niger and Benue rivers. It was not a missionary venture, but Crowther used the opportunity to locate suitable sites for missionary activity. The expedition was successful. The Niger Mission was established in 1857. What was needed was a bishop, but not necessarily a white man. On 29 June 1864 (St Peter's Day) Crowther was consecrated bishop in Canterbury Cathedral with the title Bishop of Western Equatorial Africa beyond the Queen's Dominions. From the outset, and sometimes incurring the opposition of white expatriate members of the church, he sought to understand the beliefs and practices of local Muslims. He did this in order to prepare the way for missionary work among them, but in doing so he prepared the way for a more ecumenical approach to Islam. His approach to Muslims was not approved by some of his white missionary contemporaries and their leaders in London. A critical report of his leadership of the Niger Mission was published in October 1880. It came out only a few days after the death of his wife, to whom he had been married for fifty years. The criticisms of his motives clouded his last years. He died on 31 December 1891. He was able to use the knowledge acquired in his encounters with Muslims and followers of African traditional religion in the writing of a short monograph with the title *Experiences with Heathens and Mohammedans in West Africa*. It was published in London in 1892 by the Society for Promoting Christian Knowledge (SPCK) as a posthumous tribute to him.

References

Ajayi (1967: 289–316), Page (1908).

See also: ***Experiences with Heathens and Mohammedans in West Africa***

EDWARD D. A. HULMES

CRUSADES

The Crusades (*hamlat salibiyya*) were undertaken between the eleventh and fourteenth centuries AD by European Christians, whose aim was to recover the Holy Land of Palestine from the Muslims and to retain it. Muslims had captured Jerusalem in AD 638. From a Christian point of view, the problem arose when Christian pilgrims were denied access to the Holy Places and increasingly persecuted for their mere presence in the area. Control of Jerusalem passed from the Egyptians to the less tolerant Saljuq Turks in AD 1072. In an address he gave to the Council of Claremont in 1095, Pope Urban II appealed for Christians to fight for the recovery of the Holy Sepulchre in Jerusalem. The First Crusade began in the same year and lasted until 1099, when Godfrey de Bouillon took Jerusalem and was appointed Defender of the Holy Sepulchre. The Latin Kingdom of Jerusalem, with its Latin patriarch, dates from that year. It was to last until AD 1291. The crusaders, known to Muslims simply as 'infidels' or 'Franks', adopted the words *deo le vult* ('God wills it') as their motto. The crosses distributed to them at that time gave the crusaders their name. St Bernard of Clairvaux preached the Second Crusade, which lasted from 1147 to AD 1149. Unlike the first, this military expedition failed. In AD 1187 the Kurdish Muslim leader Salah al-Din Yusuf ibn Ayyub (Saladin) captured Jerusalem. This led to the Third Crusade (AD 1189–92), which was preached by Pope Gregory VIII. Among the leaders were the Holy Roman Emperor, Frederick I and the English king, Richard I. Jerusalem was recovered, but the crusaders withdrew after quarrels broke out between their leaders. Richard, having organised the fortification of Jaffa and the rebuilding of Ascalon, established a three-year truce with Saladin in 1192, at which point he left the Holy Land and the crusade ended. The Fourth Crusade lasted from 1202 to AD 1204. It began near Venice and was led by French and Flemish noblemen. It was an abortive venture. The attention of the 'crusaders' was diverted from the Holy Land to Constantinople by domestic political and economic pressures. Constantinople was stormed and sacked. The spoils were divided among the Venetian sponsors of the venture. There were to be six other minor crusades, including the pathetic 'Children's Crusade' in AD 1212 that was led by youngsters hoping to rectify the failures and betrayals of their elders. Some of these children were captured and sold into slavery. None of the later crusades were motivated by the same ideals and enthusiasms that led to the First Crusade. From the beginnings in AD 1095 to the end in the fourteenth century, these campaigns were conducted occasionally, when the seasons allowed. In the interim periods the crusaders and their camp followers met amicably with members of the local population. Intermarriage between Christians and Muslims, between European Christians and Arab Christians was common. The descendants of these unions are to be found throughout the Near East. In recent times Muslims have used the word 'crusade' pejoratively with reference to any actual or perceived attack made on Islamic values and polity by non-Muslims from the West.

References

Runciman (1951-4), Schacht and Bosworth (1979: 187–208).

EDWARD D. A. HULMES

D

DAHOMEY

Dahomey (now known as Benin) is located on the Bight of Benin in the Gulf of Guinea. It is bordered on the east by Nigeria, on the north by Niger and Burkina Faso (formerly Upper Volta), and on the west by Togo. The largest ethnic group is the Fon, who make up some 40 per cent of the total population in the south. French is the official language. Little is known about the origins of Dahomey, which was to become known as the independent Republic of Dahomey from 1960–75 and thereafter as Benin. In the twelfth or early thirteenth centuries AD members of the Aja tribe founded the village of Allada, which subsequently became the capital of the state of Great Ardra. The kings ruled with the consent of the elders.

Great Ardra attained the peak of its power and prestige at the end of the sixteenth century and the early years of the seventeenth. In 1625, a dispute about who should be king divided a family of three brothers. One retained control of Great Ardra, the second founded the town of Abomey, the third founded the town of Ajatche, which was later called Porto Novo by Portuguese merchants. Abomey boasted a centralised administration and a standing army. In the late seventeenth century the Dahomeyans raided their neighbours for the purpose of securing slaves for shipment to the Americas. The trade with Europeans proved to be lucrative. Some 20,000 slaves were sold annually. King Agaja (1708–32) began to use women as soldiers, conquering much of the south of the country. This brought Dahomey into warring conflict with the powerful Yoruba kingdom of Oyo to the east. The Yorubans captured Abomey in 1738 and forced the Dahomeyans to pay annual tribute. From the seventeenth to the nineteenth century the country derived great wealth from slavery and the slave trade. The coast became known as 'the Slave Coast'. The French established commercial agreements with the kingdom in 1851. They developed the capital of Porto Novo and transport links to the interior. In 1904 Dahomey became a colony in French West Africa. Independence came on 1 August 1960. After twelve years of political instability, in which civil and military governments alternated, the 'colonial' name of Dahomey was abandoned. The Republic of Dahomey became Benin in 1975. Cotonou is the largest city and chief port. It was developed by the French. The chief cash crops of the country are cacao, cassava, cotton, groundnuts, maize, manioc, millet, palm kernels and palm oil, pulses and sorghum.

References

Ajayi and Crowder (1977-8: 129–30), Marty (1926), Thomas (1997: 351–443).

See also: **Benin, the Empire of**

EDWARD D. A. HULMES

DAHR

'Time' but, in reality, a philosophical concept rendered as 'meta-time' inhabited by such unchangeable entities as angels.

References

Waines (1995: 8).

ANDREW J. NEWMAN

DA'I

'He who calls', referring to chief propagandist of a sect.

References

Halm (1991: 193–9).

See also: **da'wa**

ANDREW J. NEWMAN

AL-DAJJAL

'The impostor', a reference in the *hadith* to 'the false messiah', the Anti-Christ in Christian theology, who will appear shortly before Jesus returns to earth and destroys al-Dajjal, which process ushers in the Day of Judgement.

References

Waines (1995: 130).

ANDREW J. NEWMAN

DAMAN

Lexically, *daman* means 'guarantee of any sort'. In Islamic law, *daman* means civil liability in the widest meaning of the term, whether it arises from the non-performance of a contract or from negligence.

References

al-Zuhayli (1985: 277).

MAWIL IZZI DIEN

DAMASCUS

Capital city of the Syrian Arab Republic situated in the south-west of the country on the Barada river, a source of irrigation but otherwise insignificant. A foundation from biblical times, it fought Israel and was occupied successively by the Assyrians, the Seleucids, the Greeks (under Alexander the Great) and the Egyptians. It was a Christian city under both the Romans and the Byzantines. After capture by the Arabs in AD 635 Damascus became capital of a great empire – the Umayyad – and residence of the caliphs who adorned it with numerous mosques, *madrasas* and other public buildings and fortifications. The great Byzantine church of St John in the centre was converted into the Umayyad mosque, the principal building of contemporary Damascus.

After the fall of the Umayyads in AD 762 and the transfer of the capital to Baghdad, Damascus dwindled to the level of a provincial town. It fell under various Turkic and other dynasties until captured by the Fatimids of Cairo in AD 970. More political disturbance followed until the arrival of Nur al-Din of the Zangid dynasty in AD 1154. The master of Aleppo, he unified Syria and Damascus became the capital of a large Muslim state. He built new religious and other buildings and religious and intellectual life flourished. The Ayyubids (founded by Salah al-Din – Saladin) moved the capital to Cairo but Damascus remained important.

The Mamluks ruled the city from 1260 to 1516 during which time it was pillaged by Timur (1401) although it was quickly rebuilt. It began to profit from trade with Europe but merchants rarely settled there because of the hostility of the local population. They took to Europe brocades, inlaid work and glassware. Damascus fell to the Ottomans in 1516 and became a modest *pashalik* within the vast Ottoman Empire. It grew in importance when it became the starting point for the pilgrimage to Mecca (much later in 1908 the terminus for the Hijaz railway). The city's history was radically changed by its occupation by Ibrahim Pasha from Egypt who allowed Christians to settle there. This disturbance of the traditional balance led to massacres and riots and the destruction of the Christian quarters in 1860. European intervention re-established calm and European influence increased. Missionaries, merchants and consuls settled in the city as it became the seat of an important Ottoman governor. New quarters were built together with Ottoman public buildings and the great central market – the Suq Hamidiyya. Damascus became a centre of growing Arab nationalism. It fell to the Allied forces in 1918 and for a short two years was the capital of Faysal's Arab kingdom. In July 1920 France occupied the city and established its mandate. Much unrest followed and during revolts parts of the city were destroyed. Syria finally gained full independence in 1946 and Damascus began to expand as a modern capital.

References

Rihawi (1977).

DEREK HOPWOOD

DAR AL-HARB

'The realm of war', referring to areas in which Islam does not hold sway.

References

Waines (1995: 100–1, 258, 281).

ANDREW J. NEWMAN

DAR AL-ISLAM

Areas in which Islam and Islamic law prevail.

References

Waines (1995: 100–1, 258, 281).

ANDREW J. NEWMAN

DAR AL-SULH

'The realm of peace', referring to areas in which Islam does not predominate but which have agreements and relations with Islamic states, as the Prophet Muhammad had with the Christian state of Najran.

ANDREW J. NEWMAN

DARURA

This word is derived from the lexical root *darar* that signifies 'harm' or 'damage'.

Darura designates both the state of necessity and its cause, *sabab*, which justifies altering a legal injunction on the basis of avoiding imminent harm. In the works of *fiqh* it has a narrow meaning when used to denote such a state of necessity. A person finding himself in a dangerous position is permitted to do something normally forbidden.

References

Izzi Dien (1997), al-Zuhayli (1997: 67–8).

MAWIL IZZI DIEN

DA'UD

'David', the Old Testament king and prophet who received the Psalms (*al-Zabur*) and fought Goliath (Q.2:251–2).

See also: **al-Injil; nabi; al-Tawrat; al-Zabur**

ANDREW J. NEWMAN

DAVID

See: **Da'ud**

DA'WA

'Calling', the invitation to accept Islam, or the doctrines of a specific sect thereof.

References

Halm (1991: 21–3, 166–70).

See also: **da'i**

ANDREW J. NEWMAN

DAY OF JUDGEMENT (*YAWM AL-DIN, YAWM AL-'AKHIR, YAWM AL-HISAB*)

The Arabic phrase *yawm al-din* means 'the day of reckoning', that is, the day on which all will be judged by God (*Allah*) according to what each has done (or not done) during life on earth. Belief in the final judgement is one of the principal articles of Islamic faith (*iman*). No one knows when that day will come, but a sign of its impending arrival will be the widespread incidence of *fitna*, rebellion against the true religion of Islam and against rightful rulers. This climactic day has other names, for instance, 'the last day' (*yawm al-akhir*), and 'the day of reckoning' (*yawm al-hisab*). Muslims believe that although it is not given to human beings to know when the created order will come to an end, they have been made aware of the signs that will herald the imminence of the cataclysmic events towards which the whole of creation is moving (Q.53:55–62). Those who are faithful to the teachings of Islam have 'nothing to fear or regret' when the time for judgement comes (Q.2:62). However, when that day of reckoning does arrive to surprise unbelievers, a more fearful judgement will await those who denied the fearful consequences of opposing the true religion of Islam on the Last Day.

In his public ministry in Mecca (610 to AD 622), Muhammad used vivid language to warn his hearers as much about the fires of Hell that await unbelievers as about the delights of Paradise to which faithful Muslims may look forward. The Qur'an contains descriptions of what is to happen at the final judgement. Q.99 bears the Arabic title *al-Zilzal* ('the convulsion' or 'the earthquake'):

> When the earth is shaken in her final convulsion, when the earth erupts from within, and when man says, What is happening to her?, On that day the earth will declare her tidings, for which your Lord will have given her inspiration. On that day people will come in numbers to be sorted out and shown their deeds. Anyone who

has done an atom's weight of good shall see it, anyone who has done an atom's weight of evil shall see it'.

The consequences of choosing to accept or to reject Islam are presented starkly in Q.101, which bears the title al-Qari'a: 'the [day of] calamity and misfortune: Those whose balance (of good deeds) weighs heavy shall enter the garden of Paradise (al-Janna), but those whose balance is found to weigh light shall be cast into the bottomless pit of hell (al-Jahannam), where there is a fiercely burning fire. Muslims whose good deeds outweigh what they have done amiss will be rewarded with Paradise in a life of good pleasure and satisfaction', those whose misdeeds outweigh what good has been done will be cast into the Abyss, in which the fires of torment burn'.

Despite these vivid pictures of what the day of judgement is going to be like, the Qur'an offers no systematic description of how the final period of human history will work out. Islamic tradition supplies the deficiency, recording what Muhammad is reported to have said. 'The Last Day will not dawn until you [that is, Muslims] have seen the following ten signs that will herald its coming'. The first is that of an overwhelming smoke that will fill the earth. 'The smoke' (al-Dukhan), is the title of Q.44 of the Qur'an. The 'smoke' or 'mist', will continue for forty days. The second sign will be the appearance of the dark impostor, the Anti-Christ (al-Dajjal). This fearsome figure, whose right eye resembles a protruding grape, will confess to belief in Allah, but his profession will deceive many, even though he bears the indelible mark of kafir (unbeliever) on his brow. The third sign is the return to earth of the Islamic prophet Jesus ('Isa). Muhammad is said to have observed that when Jesus returns he will come as a righteous judge, in order to participate in the Final Judgement. The renowned thirteenth-century AD Islamic exegete al-Baydawi taught in gory as well as graphic terms that Jesus will descend in the Holy Land at a place called Afik, with a spear in his hand, he will use the weapon to kill al-Dajjal and enter the city of Jerusalem at the time of morning salat, the leader of the Islamic community, the imam, will offer to give place to him, but Jesus will refuse, merely joining other Muslims at prayer. Jesus will then destroy the cross and slay the swine, he will lay in ruins the synagogues of the Jews and the Christian churches, killing all the Christians who refuse to believe in him for what he truly is. All those who are left will become Muslims. Jesus himself will remain on earth for forty more years, after which – having not yet died as every mortal must – he will die. He will then be buried according to custom, in Medina, where an empty grave lies awaiting him between the graves of Abu Bakr and 'Umar, who succeeded Muhammad as leaders of the Islamic community. The fourth sign is that of Gog and Magog (see 1 Chr. 5:4, Ezek. 38, 39). In the Qur'an, the names of Gog and Magog are identified as representing two peoples of uncertain origin, possibly wild tribes from central Asia, who create havoc on earth (Q.18:94). The fifth sign of the end is the appearance of a monster from within the earth. It will accuse human beings of their unbelief (Q.27:82). The sixth sign is that the sun will rise in the West. The seventh sign is that a great conflagration will break out in al-Hijaz in western Arabia. Signs 8, 9, and 10 will be cataclysmic collapses of the surface of the earth, one in the east, one in the west, and the third in the Arabian peninsula. Some Islamic traditions refer to al-mahdi, 'the rightly guided one', whose appearance will herald the end. Other traditions state that when knowledge disappears to be replaced by ignorance, when alcoholic drinks are widely consumed, and when adultery is commonly practised, the end of the world will not be far away.

References

Brown and Palmer (1987: 62–87), Momen (1985: 177–8).

See also: **al-barzakh**

EDWARD D. A. HULMES

DAYS OF IGNORANCE

See: **Jahiliyya**; **pre-Islamic Arabia**

DEATH AND BURIAL (*MAWT, DAFN, JINAZA*)

Death occurs at the moment decided by God: 'Nor can any soul die except by God's permission. The term of every life is fixed, as it were, in writing' (cf. Q.3:139, 145). On the death of a Muslim, the body is given 'the greater ablution' known as *ghusl*, which involves the ritual cleansing of the whole body. This is normally conducted by members of the immediate family or close friends. Males supervise the preparations in the case of a deceased male, women in the case of a deceased female. Relatives and friends visit the bereaved family to express their condolences. The openings in the body of the deceased are plugged with cotton wool. It is then wrapped in a shroud, placed on a bier, and carried to the cemetery for interment, usually the burden being shared by members of the family, relieved from time to time by volunteers as the funeral procession moves through the streets. While the body is borne along on the shoulders of the bearers, the mourners offer prayers and repeat the words of the *shahada*: 'There is no god but God (Allah), and Muhammad is the Messenger of God'. These are the first words to be whispered into the ear of a newborn child and the last to be uttered consciously by a dying person. Burial (*dafn*) usually follows quickly on the same day as death, before the sun sets. The body is lowered into the grave on its right side, with the face turned in the direction of Mecca. The use of coffins is not forbidden, but it is more usual for the body to be buried in the simple winding-sheet. Cremation (*haraq*) is not practised in Islam. Special prayers are said during the funeral procession (*jinaza*), which may also be said later in a mosque. 'Martyrs' (*shuhada*', sing. *shahid*), who meet their deaths 'in the cause of God' (*fi sabil-llah*), are buried unwashed, wearing the clothes in which they died, and with their wounds bearing mute testimony to their sacrifice and faith.

An Islamic tradition, grounded in the belief that the dead will be raised on the Last Day and called to account on the *yawm al-din* (Day of Judgement) for their deeds and misdeeds, states that the grave is but the first step on the road to eternal life. Compared with the life to come that is promised to the faithful Muslim, the life of this world offers only illusion and deception (cf. Q.3:185). Remembering the dead is a matter of local use and custom. The words 'God be merciful to him (or her)' are frequently repeated, especially during a period of some forty days of mourning following the death, when special prayers in memory of the dead are recited privately or in a mosque. The period of mourning is not to be unnecessarily protracted, however, because death is considered to be the gateway to another life, in which those who now grieve hope to be reunited with all those who have died as faithful Muslims.

References

Brown and Palmer (1987: 204), al-Khaysi (1996).

EDWARD D. A. HULMES

DELACROIX, EUGÈNE
(1798–1863)

French Orientalist painter. Born near Paris, Delacroix's father was politically active during the French Revolution and his early childhood was marked by upheavals and violence. His subsequent painting is often heroic and presents man as a battleground of conflicting ideals and passions. His early paintings were denounced for their violence and darkness. Delacroix became an admirer of contemporary English painting and his own work gained a certain transparency and elegance. The exotic appeal of the Near East gained a hold on him and he took many of his themes from Byron and Walter Scott, for example, *The Crusaders Entering Jerusalem.* In 1832 he satisfied a long-held ambition by visiting Algeria and Morocco where he found a nobility and beauty in its peoples not found in France. The vibrant nature and the beauty of the horses, the Arabs and their flowing robes also attracted him. He filled his sketchbooks and journals with visual and verbal impressions. Major paintings resulted including *The Women of Algiers in their Apartments* (1834), *The Fanatics of Tangier* (1838) and *The Jewish Wedding* (1839). He continued to paint Arab subjects almost until the end of his life. The light, colour and energy of his work contributed to their popularity and to nineteenth-century (mis)conceptions of the 'Orient'.

References

Diehl (1967).

DEREK HOPWOOD

DELHI

For centuries, the dominant religious systems in India ('Hindustan' as the Greeks named it after their incursions into the Indus valley) were Hinduism and Buddhism. The first Muslims to arrive in the subcontinent were Arab traders who began to arrive on the south-western Malabar coast soon after the death of the Prophet Muhammad in the year AD 632. Together with their trading interests they brought to the region a readiness to extend the social and political influence of Islam. From the eleventh century AD Muslim conquerors began to arrive much further north in the subcontinent. They were not known for their tolerance of religious diversity. By the end of the twelfth century AD Islamic rule had been extended under the control of the Delhi sultanate (1206–1555) throughout most of India. The most renowned Islamic rulers were the Mughals, who were of mixed Mongol and Turkish decent. Their sovereignty in India was established in 1526. It flourished until the eighteenth century. Delhi was made the capital of the Mughal Empire by the Emperor Shah Jehan in 1638. The Red Fort, which housed the imperial palace, was built under his supervision. Mughal religion and culture was distinctively Islamic, but they gained a reputation for religious tolerance in their dealings with the majority of their Hindu subjects. Islam played an increasingly important, though ultimately divisive, role in the rise of modern India. Islamic presence in the cities, towns and villages centred round the mosques and law-courts. Islamic teachers and peripatetic Sufis helped to further the appeal of popular Islam among the non-Muslim population, but the antipathy between Hindus and Muslims brought matters to a crisis after the end of the Second World War. What were euphemistically described at the time as 'communal problems' between Hindus and Muslims led to the establishment of the separate independent states of India and Pakistan following the partition of India after independence from British rule was gained on 15 August 1947. Old Delhi is the walled city on the River Jumna. New Delhi, a little further south, is the seat of the government of India.

References

Schacht and Bosworth (1979: 135–9), Spear (1965: II, 221–2).

EDWARD D. A. HULMES

DEOBAND

In Saharanpur district, Uttar Pradesh, Deoband contains the unrivalled Muslim theological centre (*madrasa*) in India, with over 1,500 residential students from all over the Muslim world. A place of great antiquity, with buildings dating back to the early Pathan period. Shaykh 'Ala' al-Din, a pupil of Ibn al-Djawzi is buried here and extant mosques date to the reigns of Sikandar Lodi (1489–1517), Akbar (1556–1605) and Awrangzib (1658–1707). The House of Learning, the *dar al-'ulum*, where religious leaders are trained, was founded by Hajji Muhammad 'Abid Husayn in 1867. He was influenced by the eighteenth-century Muslim reformer Shah Wali Allah and his Dihli school of *muhaddithini* and the early nineteenth-century puritanical Indian Wahhabiya. The *dar al-'ulum* contains a mosque, lecture halls and a library of over 67,000 Arabic, Persian and Urdu printed books and manuscripts. Instruction is traditional and includes Qur'anic exegesis (*tafsir*) and *hadith*, jurisprudence (*fiqh*), scholastic theology ('*ilm al-kalam*) and philosophy (*falsafa*) in order to concentrate on enhancing religious personality rather than concerns with issues of the modern world, yet many of their scholars have embraced national struggles for freedom, ranging from very eminent scholars such as Mawlana Rashid Ahmad Ganguhi, Sayyid Husayn Ahmad Madani,

Mawlana Muhammad Ya'kub, and even members of the Afghan Taliban. The ideological base of the *djami'at 'ulama'-i Hind*, the influential organisation of Indian '*ulama*', is provided by the *dar al-'ulum*.

References

Hashmi (1989), Metcalf (2002).

JANET STARKEY

DEOBANDIS (AL-DIYUBANDIYYA)

Adherents to an Islamic educational and reformist movement, affiliated to the place where it was first established, Deoband, a small town in the Saharanpur district of Uttar Pradesh. Originally formed to withstand the onslaught of British colonialism in India, a group of Indian scholars in this area created a system of learning in their institutions, termed *dar al-'ulum* (lit. 'the abode of knowledge'), which would become the blueprint of academic centres throughout the Indian subcontinent. With the goal of producing a future generation of Islamic scholars ('*ulama*') to serve the Muslim community, they designed a curriculum that focused in particular on the study of *hadith* and although there was some emphasis on Arabic and Persian, the language of instruction was Urdu. In addition to the emphasis on *hadith*, all the other tradition Islamic disciplines were also taught, including philosophy and logic. With regard to religious practice the Deobandis adhere zealously to the Hanafi school of law and adopt the Maturidi school of theology, regarding tenets of faith. A more surprising attachment, however, bearing in mind their strong aversion to the practices of popular religion and its manifestation in the practice of the Barelwis in particular, is their emphasis on Sufism, as it is not uncommon to find them affiliated to a number of Sufi orders (*tariqa*, pl. *turuq*), including the Qadiri, Naqshabandi, Chishti and Suhrawardi orders. In addition, it should be also noted that this method of teaching is not confined only to the Indian sub-continent and as such, the *dar al-'ulum* system can be readily found in South Africa and Britain, as well as other parts of the world.

References

al-Johani (1999: 304–9), Netton (1997: 69), Sirriyeh (1999: 46–8).

GAVIN PICKEN

DEOBANDISM

Until Barbara Metcalf completed her seminal work, *Islamic Revival in British India*, Deobandism had not been much studied by scholars of South Asian Islam. She suggests that the movement, founded in the late nineteenth century, proved relatively inconspicuous compared to modernist elites such as Sayyid Ahmad Khan. Indeed, the founders of Deoband-ism did not deliberately engage with the colonial state. Therefore, the movement has sometimes been caricatured as con-structing an introverted Islamic com-munity, one which locates authority in an unchanging past. However, Metcalf argues that Deobandism is more properly seen as engaging in a self-conscious reas-sessment of Muslim belief and practice, drawing upon the norms and resources of the Islamic tradition itself. Deoband-ism, then, is a movement of moral pur-ification which argues for continuity with the past even if it cannot avoid adapting to the present. It looks not to the West or modernism for inspiration but back to the prophetic era. The emphasis is on renewal (*tajdid*) and 'turning within' rather than 'without'.

In the wake of the so-called Mutiny of 1857, known by some Indians as the First War of Independence, resistance to the British Raj often assumed a more quietist form than the *jihad* movements of the early nineteenth century. Muslims, Hindus and Sikhs all returned to their religious roots to identify a sense of cul-tural pride and eventually to articulate a possible route to resurgence. With the terminal decline of the Mughal Empire, Islam's traditional religious specialists, the '*ulama*', found that they had no state to serve. Many retreated from the large cities to urban country towns such as Deoband, which is 90 miles (145 kilo-metres) north-east of Delhi. Less tou-ched by British rule, Deoband became a centre for the preservation of Muslim culture under the influence of two Islamic scholars, Muhammad Qasim Nanutvi (1833–77) and Rashid Ahmad Gangohi (1829–1905).

In the face of highly organised Christian missionary institutions, Nanutvi and Gangohi's contribution was to revolu-tionise traditional Islamic education. While Deobandi mosques and schools were built, their signature institution became the *dar al-'ulum* or *madrasa* (Islamic seminary), the first of hundreds being established in 1867. Metcalf explains that the *madrasa* does not appear to have been a major institution in the pre-colonial period. Those who wished to be religious specialists would sit at the feet of one or more teachers, often tra-velling from place to place seeking a certificate signalling completion of par-ticular books and studies. At Deoband, by contrast, students received a more formalised education which produced a newly professionalised scholarly class holding degrees for the first time. Instead of being trained for specific state functions, as would have been the case under Muslim rule, they became teachers, writers and public preachers.

In building up their educational institutions, Nanutvi and Gangohi refused any assistance from the colonial government, preferring instead the popular patronage and contributions of a self-sufficient Muslim community. At Deoband, Muslims could receive a traditional Islamic education without reference to the English language or Western subjects. Indeed, as a bastion of conservative orthodoxy, the Islamic university at Deoband has long been considered second only to al-Azhar in Cairo.

In their *madaris* the Deobandis sought to create a new kind of religious personality. Given the absence of an Islamic state to regulate Muslim lifestyles, there was an attempt to embody a self-conscious Islamic character within individuals. The Deobandi message was therefore one of a disciplined adherence to the divinely ordained *shari'a* as interpreted by the Hanafi *madhhab* (school of law). So, while students were provided with their education and basic necessities free of charge, there was a strict regime in terms of cultivating a disciplined personal morality and correct ritual practice. This was based on an intensive study of the Qur'an and *hadith* that was relatively unknown under the Mughals. Accordingly, there was also a renewed emphasis on the Prophet Muhammad as the most perfect model of how Muslims should live. Indeed, the Deobandis saw themselves as deputies of Muhammad, moral exemplars who practised the religion of individual responsibility that they preached and published about so vigorously.

Deobandism's main vehicle for communicating this 'proper' teaching and behaviour was the *fatwa* (legal opinion). Indeed, by the end of the nineteenth century, the chief *mufti* of the seminary was increasingly disseminating his opinions and advice in print. For all their reassertion of traditional norms of Islamic authority, the Deobandis undoubtedly exposed a new, more broadly based, Muslim audience to reformist ideas. In an age of unprecedented technological advance, a new industry grew up around the printing and distribution, not only of *fatawa,* but also religious books and pamphlets via the postal service and railways. Arabic classics were also being translated into the lingua franca of Urdu as opposed to Persian. Moreover, courtesy of travel companies such as Thomas Cook, far greater numbers of Indian Muslims were going on the *hajj* and encountering new religious ideas.

The scripturalism and universalism of Deobandi Islam appealed to those people most caught up with the social changes of an increasingly globalising world. It brought a certain respect and status to the upwardly mobile given its association with increased literacy and rationality. Some have even suggested that Deobandism represents a privatised, 'Protestant', form of Islam. Certainly it 'travelled' much more readily than a popular Islam based around parochial cults. Nanutvi and Gangohi were reformist Sufis in the Chistiyya tradition, but sharing Shah Wali Allah's affiliation to the Naqsbandiyya, they advocated a combination of both spiritual guidance and restrained devotional practice. Optional rites and 'innovations', thought to be introduced into Indian Muslim practice by Shi'ites and Hindus, but in no sense sanctioned as obligatory in the *hadith*, were actively discouraged by the Deobandis. Such rituals included the celebration of a saint's death anniversary (*'urs*) and customs associated with weddings.

In defending their position, the Deobandis engaged in highly polemical disputes with opponents, something that continues to this day. For example, whilst itself a Muslim reform movement with an emphasis on *hadith*, Barelwism has traditionally defended many of the customary practices that the Deobandis disdain. Barelwis routinely label Deobandis as 'Wahhabis' despite the fact that Deobandism does not represent an absolute rejection of Sufism. Indeed, at Deobandi seminaries many of the teachers initiated students into traditional Sufi disciplines and meditations. In the Indian subcontinent it is actually the Ahl-i Hadith, with their uncompromising approach to *taqlid* and Sufism, that perhaps come closest to the ideas of Ibn 'Abd al-Wahhab.

Since Partition, Metcalf maintains that the Deobandis in India have remained largely moderate and apolitical. However, it is Zaman's argument that in Pakistan the activities of the Deobandi *'ulama'* have become increasingly public and political. Lower ranking *'ulama'* especially have had a key role in sectarian activism and violence at the grassroots level since the 1980s. This is the product of a number of interlinking factors including General Zia's attempts at 'Islamisation' from the late 1970s. This, in turn, represented a threat to the Shi'ite community in Pakistan, itself politically emboldened by the Iranian revolution of 1979. It was against this context of Shi'ite radicalisation that a radical Sunni organisation, the Sipah-i Sahaba (Soldiers of the Prophet's Companions), was founded in 1985 (banned 2002). An offshoot of the Jami'at-i 'Ulama-i Islam (JUI), itself a minority group formed when Deobandis split over the desirability of Pakistan as a Muslim homeland, the Sipah-i Sahaba sought to combat Shi'ite 'influence', especially in the countryside where a mixture of Sunni, Sufi and Shi'ite practice still prevails. Zaman suggests that while the highest-ranking Deobandi *'ulama'* restricted their criticisms of Shi'ism to 'moral' and 'intellectual' levels, more 'peripheral' *'ulama'* were often seen, and

saw themselves, as receiving implicit sanction to attack the minority community. This drawing of the *'ulama'* into radical politics has seen Deobandism thrive at the expense of the Barelwis and Jama'at-i Islami, especially amongst a growing, recently urbanised, middle class. Indeed, it also expanded outside Pakistan, most notably in the JUI *madaris* on the Pakistan–Afghanistan border. When law and order effectively broke down after the expulsion of the Soviets from Afghanistan in 1989, it was a Deobandi-related movement that eventually intervened from 1994 to 2001. The Taliban (*madrasa* 'students') imposed a severe and rigorous vision of correct ritual practice and personal behaviour on the country. While Deobandi scholars in Pakistan were not always comfortable with the students' narrow interpretations of Islam, the Taliban undoubtedly raised the movement's profile amongst Muslims and non-Muslims alike.

References

Metcalf (1982, 2002), Zaman (2002).

See also: **Barelwism; The Faith Movement; Taliban; Wahhabisms**

SEÁN MCLOUGHLIN

DEVIRSHIRME

The Ottoman system of drawing a levy of Christian boys to serve as officials and soldiers. Periodically, young men would be taken from their communities for re-education in the Ottoman capital, including conversion to Islam. Many served in the elite Janissary corps. One of the greatest Ottoman architects, Sinan (1489–1588), whose designs included the mosque of Suleyman the Magnificent in Istanbul, was conscripted from Greek Orthodox parentage in 1512 and initially trained to work as a construction officer in the Ottoman army. The system was abandoned in 1637.

References

Lapidus (1999: 316–18, 334).

SIMON W. MURDEN

DHABIHA

See: **sacrifice**

AL-DHAHABI, SHAMS AL-DIN MUHAMMAD IBN AHMAD (AD 1274–1348)

Shafi'ite *hadith* scholar, historian and biographer, born in Damascus, where he also died. As a young man, al-Dhahabi studied in Damascus and Cairo and travelled widely in the central Islamic world studying the science of *hadith* and related disciplines. He later taught *hadith* in Damascus, where he acquired the sobriquet *muhaddith al-'asr* (*hadith* relater of the age). He was struck by blindness several years before his death.

Al-Dhahabi's most significant work is almost certainly the immense *Ta'rikh al-Islam*, which aimed to provide comprehensive biographies for the first seven centuries of the Islamic era within a chronological framework based on decades. The work begins with the genealogy of the Prophet Muhammad and ends in the author's lifetime with the year AD 1300/1. It contains both a series of obituary notices and a general narrative, with increasing emphasis being given to the general narrative as the work proceeds. For the first three centuries, the author relied heavily on the work of al-Tabari. Al-Dhahabi's work provides a valuable supplement to the accounts of other historians such as Ibn al-Athir, as he records events ignored by other writers. His account

was later continued by a number of other hands, and several abridgements were made, including more than one by al-Dhahabi himself.

Among al-Dhahabi's other works may be mentioned his *Tadhkirat al-Huffaz*, later continued and abridged by al-Suyuti under the title *Tabaqat al-Huffaz*, *Mizan al-i 'tidal fi Naqd al-Rijal*, on tradition, *Siyar A'lam al-Nubala'*, and *Mukhtasar li-Ta'rikh Baghdad li 'bn al-Dubaythi*, a synopsis of the earlier author's history of Baghdad.

Although al-Dhahabi's reputation, even among his contemporaries, was a slightly mixed one, his main works remain useful sources of information for the historian until the present day.

References

Rosenthal (1968), Somogyi (1932: 815–55).

PAUL STARKEY

DHAWQ

Dhawq is a technical term of the Sufis denoting the experience of the divine. It has been rendered into English as 'tasting', 'mystical intuition' and 'unveiling'.

References

Chittick (1989: 212–31).

LLOYD RIDGEON

DHIKR

The *dhikr* (recollection of God) is an important Sufi ritual that resembles a mantra found in many of the world's religious traditions. It can take the form of the *shahada* repeated thousands of times. Sometimes the *shahada* is shortened in the process of *dhikr* recitation to 'huwa' or He. Great variety is found among Sufi orders concerning the performance of the *dhikr*. Some prefer an audible *dhikr*, while others practise a non-verbal form under the breath, and there are some Sufis who engage in rhythmical movements of the head and body during recitation.

References

Elias (1995: 119–34), Nakamura (1990), Sviri (1997), Waley (1993: 501–18).

LLOYD RIDGEON

DHIMMIS

Members of the 'the people of the covenant, or obligation' (*ahl al-dhimma*), were originally the members of the religious communities, Jews, Christians, Sabians (and later Zoroastrians and Manichaeans), who were tolerated as 'clients' (*mawali*) in an Islamic society. Until the Jews and Christians in and around Medina failed to accept the mission of the Prophet Muhammad and to submit to Islam, members of other religious communities in receipt of a revealed scripture were called 'people of the Book' (*ahl al-kitab*) along with Muslims. This latter description remains to emphasise what Jews, Christians and Muslims have in common, but from an early date a significant juridical distinction has been made in Islam between Muslims and non-Muslims. The *ahl al-dhimma* were non-Muslims living in an Islamic society, who were accorded client status. They were afforded protection and a measure of freedom to worship according to their various religious beliefs, and to conduct their affairs in accordance with the canon laws administered by their religious leaders. But these privileges fell short of full religious freedom, because a non-Muslim, by definition, remained outside the unique privileges and responsibilities prescribed by Islamic law. This client status effectively reduced those so designated to the status of second-class citizens. In return for the protection offered to them, non-Muslim adult males were required to pay a *per capita* tax, the *jizya*, introduced by the Prophet Muhammad in the ninth year after the *hijra*. An additional form of tribute, *kharaj*, a land-tax raised on 'the yield of the fields', also became payable by client non-Muslims. Payment of the poor tax, *zakat* remained substantially a religious obligation for Muslims, however. With notable exceptions *dhimmis* were excluded from holding the higher administrative offices in Islamic state. Nor were they permitted to serve in the army.

EDWARD D.A. HULMES

DHU 'L-NUN (d. AD 859)

Little is known of the Egyptian Dhu 'l-Nun's life or writings except for what is found in Sufi hagiographic literature. The scarcity of information makes it difficult to establish whether Dhu 'l-Nun was a visionary mystic rather than just a pious, ascetic believer.

References

Schimmel (1975: 42–7), Smith (1931: 191–7, 230–6).

LLOYD RIDGEON

DHU NUWAS

Dhu Nuwas was a Jew and the last of the Himyarite kings in the Yemen in pre-Islamic Arabia. After the creation of the State of Israel in 1948, thousands of Jews living in the Yemen moved north to settle in Israel.

EDWARD D. A. HULMES

DHU'L-QARNAYN

'Of the two horns', a term often taken to refer to Alexander the Great whom

Allah empowers to erect a barrier to separate mankind from Gog and Magog, representations of chaos. See Q.18:83.

References

Waines (1995: 130).

ANDREW J. NEWMAN

DIKKA

The *dikka* is a flat platform usually supported on columns reached by a narrow staircase which is positioned before the main *mihrab* in a congregational mosque. It is strictly practical in function, a place where reciters can repeat the postures and responses of prayer in order to relay them to a full congregation. The *dikka* is a special feature of the Mamluk mosques of Cairo and the Ottoman imperial mosques of Istanbul and Edirne as a handsome structure built of finely worked marble.

References

Goodwin (1987).

JENNIFER SCARCE

DIRAR IBN 'AMR (*c.* 730–800 or AD 820)

Little is known about Dirar ibn Amr's life beyond the fact that he spent most of his life in Basra, Iraq, but he made a huge contribution to the development of Islamic thought, partly as a result of the fact that he composed a book on the Aristotelian notion of substances and accidents, one of the first demonstrations of Muslim knowledge of this material as a result of its translation into Arabic in this period, and partly because of the richness of his own thought. He supported the use of rational arguments in theology, like the Mu'tazila, but his own conclusions tended to differ from those

of the Mu'tazila so that, for example, he argued that all human actions are determined by God. Human beings thus do not have free will, even if Dirar argued that humans did acquire responsibility for their actions, the idea of *kasb* (acquisition), an idea which was later taken up and developed by al-Ash'ari.

References

Caspar (1998: Chapter 7), Watt (1994: Chapters 7 and 8).

HUGH GODDARD

DIVORCE (*TALAQ, INFISAL, KHUL'*)

The root meaning of *talaq* is 'being made free from a bond', the meaning of *infisal* is 'separation'. In Shi'i law divorce is permitted under the strict conditions of the *talaq al-sunna*, but not under the 'easier' conditions of 'innovated divorce' (*talaq al-bid'a*) favoured by some Sunnis. In sura.65 of the Qur'an (*Surat al-talaq*) guidelines on divorce are provided for the partners of a lawfully contracted Islamic marriage. The chapter makes provision for the welfare of women (and their children), who are involved in divorce. Although marriage is the basis of stable family relationships, it is acknowledged that divorce may become a practical necessity under certain conditions because of human weakness and impiety. In the *Sunan* (13.3), Abu Dawud (d. AD 888) mentions a *hadith* in which the Prophet Muhammad is recorded as saying: 'Of all the things permitted by Law the most hateful in the sight of *Allah* is divorce'. Divorce is, thus, not lightly undertaken even though the process begins with a simple thrice repeated statement of repudiation on the part of the husband, who says to the wife: 'I divorce you'. If, however, this statement is made by the man in a state of anger or intoxication, it is invalid. If divorce follows the non-consummation of the marriage, the wife retains her dowry (*mahr*).

The plain statement of intent by the husband may be made three times in rapid succession, but it is deemed to be more fitting for it to be uttered once in each of three successive months, during which time man and wife must abstain from sexual intercourse with each other. The statement is not to be made when the woman is menstruating. This male initiative is sufficient to facilitate divorce, provided that the wife is not pregnant. If the wife is carrying a child, the divorce cannot be finalised until after the baby is born. The father is legally (and, it may be thought, morally) obliged to provide for the needs of mother and child. The reasons for initiating divorce proceedings are many and varied. If proven, allegations of the adultery (*zina'*) of either partner may have serious consequences in Islamic law beyond the ending of the marriage contract. Over the centuries Islamic law has developed to take account of local (and sometimes pre-Islamic) custom, but the words of Q.2:229 serve as a general caution. They include a reference to 'the limits of God', which are not to be transgressed.

The time of waiting after the initial repudiation of a marriage is known as *'idda*. It gives time not only for finding out whether or not a woman is already pregnant by her husband (and thus for establishing the paternity of the unborn child), but also for allowing the partners to be reconciled. Divorce proceedings during the *'idda* can be stopped by the husband by pronouncing a statement to that effect. If reconciliation takes place after the period of waiting, it is to be acknowledged through remarriage. The bride price (*mehr*) paid by the husband to the wife at the time of the marriage becomes the wife's personal property. It remains hers after the divorce unless the marriage is dissolved before it is consummated, in which case half the bride price is to be repaid to the husband (see Q.4:4). In recent times, the male prerogative in the initiation of divorce is being questioned by women on the grounds that Islam claims to recognise the equality of the sexes. One form of divorce by mutual consent dates from pre-Islamic times. It is known as *khul'* (release) and requires a woman to repay the bride price to the husband and gain her freedom from the marriage contract. There is no doubt that for Muslims, both men and women, Western secular values increasingly challenge the traditional values and practices of Islam, not least with regard to divorce and remarriage. In many cases the Islamic prescriptions are effectively ignored by those most intimately concerned.

References

Bouhdiba (1985: 14–18, 19–22, 30–42), Momen (1985: 182–3, 338n), Omran (1992: 15–26, 40–58).

See also: **marriage;** *mut'a*
EDWARD D. A. HULMES

DIWAN

'Book', a Persian reference to a collection of, for example, poetry or an account book and, hence, the department in which accounting records were kept.

References

Hourani (1991: 217, 13).
ANDREW J. NEWMAN

DIYA

Blood money. Islamic law holds that compensation must be paid for the taking of the life of another person. The practice is pre-Islamic and it is justified within Islam under the broad provision of 'retaliation' as stipulated in Q.5:45 and in the specific implementation of the ruling in Q.4:92:

> Never should a believer kill a believer except by mistake. If one kills a believer by error, it is ordained that he should free a believing slave, and pay *diya* to the deceased's family, unless they remit it freely. If the deceased belonged to a people at war with you, and he was a believer, the freeing of a believing slave is enough. If he belonged to a people with whom ye have treaty of mutual alliance, *diya* should be paid to his family, and a believing slave should be freed. For those who find this beyond their means, then prescribed is a fast for two months running: God's turning, God is All-knowing, All-wise.

Islamic law developed structures which served to define precisely when *diya* was obligatory or optional, whether a homicide was intentional or deliberate, and the extent to which other bodily injuries could result in *diya* being payable.

References

Gibb and Bosworth (1960–2003: II, 340).

ANDREW RIPPIN

DOME

The dome is a rounded vault forming the roof of a building or structure already well-established in Roman, Parthian, Sassanian and Byzantine architecture, which the Islamic world modified to great distinction. Domes in mosques were constructed singly over the chamber which housed the *qibla*, and in series over courtyard arcades. This is seen in the brick domes of Seljuk Iran and to

spectacular effect in the stone multiple domes of the Ottoman imperial mosques. Domes also covered funerary monuments such as Oljeitu's mausoleum in Iran built between 1307 and AD 1313, the tombs of the Mamluks in Cairo and the Taj Mahal. In civil architecture they are found in palaces, baths, bazaars and caravanserais.

References

Goodwin (1987), Gye (1988).

JENNIFER SCARCE

DOME OF THE ROCK, JERUSALEM

The earliest example of monumental Islamic architecture which has survived in its original form is the Dome of the Rock commissioned by the Umayyad Caliph 'Abd el-Malik (AD 685–705) in AD 692 who lavished the tax revenues of Egypt for seven years to pay for it. The Dome is located in the centre of a large platform in the south-east corner of the old city of Jerusalem on the site of Solomon's Temple which the Romans destroyed in AD 70. The Rock is of great religious and symbolic importance to Jews, Christians and Muslims as the grave of Adam, the location of the Temple, the place where Abraham/Ibrahim prepared to sacrifice his son Isaac/Isma'il and the point where the Prophet Muhammad began his Night Journey (*mi'raj*) to Heaven (Q.17). It is, thus, the holiest site in Islam after Mecca and Medina. The building is octagonal and ascends to a single gold-plated, centrally placed dome interpreting a plan used in Christian baptisteries and commemorative structures. Within an outer circle of eight piers and an inner circle of four piers support the enclosure. Brilliant mosaic decoration lines the interior in shades of green and blue further enriched with mother-of-pearl and gold inlay in designs of acanthus scroll, vines, palm trees and garlands influenced by the repertoire of Byzantine and Sassanian iconography. A continuous band of Qur'anic inscriptions in angular Kufic script stresses the unity of God as against the Christian Trinity and Incarnation. The Dome of the Rock has survived both turbulent events, repairs and restorations. When the Knights Templar controlled Jerusalem in the twelfth century AD, they converted the Dome into a church. Later Saladin after his reconquest of Jerusalem in 1187, returned the Dome to Muslim use. Inevitably the building suffered with the destruction of the stone and glass mosaic that had also covered the external walls. The Ottoman Sultan Suleyman I (1520–66) commissioned polychrome Iznik tiles to restore this decoration between 1545 and 1552.

References

Brend (1991), Grabar (1978, 1990).

JENNIFER SCARCE

DOUBLE TRUTH

Double truth is a concept that emerged in Ibn Rushd's discussion of the reconciliation between philosophy and religion in his book *Fasl al-Maqal*. However, the first one who proposed reconciling religion and philosophy was al-Kindi who, after the theologians attacked him for adopting Greek philosophy in his theology, called for the truth to be sought in all kinds of knowledge. Al-Farabi and Ibn Sina after him considered that the revelation which is given to the prophets is, in its essential message, not different from philosophical knowledge but it is only formulated in figurative and symbolic terms to suit the understanding of the masses. The concept of 'double truth', however, was formulated by Ibn Rushd to explain that religion and philosophy are arguing in two different ways which cannot be reconciled. Nevertheless, they are both aiming at the same thing – to unveil the principles behind the world. Philosophy and reason argue through demonstrative methods, while religion discusses its concepts through symbolic language and presents explanations which are accepted and understood by many different types of people, not only by scientists and philosophers. Both disciplines are presenting the truth but in two different formulations and methodologies, hence, the question of which is the better discipline should not be asked. Thus, the double truth means for Ibn Rushd expressing the same truth in two different systems which are not comparable.

References

Ibn Rushd (1972), Leaman (1999: 144–8).

MAHA EL-KAISY FRIEMUTH

DOUGHTY, CHARLES MONTAGU (1843–1926)

British writer and traveller. Doughty was born in Suffolk and went to a preparatory school for the navy but was rejected for service on medical grounds. He later graduated from the University of Cambridge in natural sciences but became deeply interested in English language and literature, particularly Chaucer and Spenser and their style of using language. He also began to travel through Europe and beyond and in 1874 reached Acre in Palestine. He wandered further throughout Syria and Egypt. He planned to enter Arabia where he wished to look at the inscriptions in the pre-Islamic city of Medain Salih. Against the will of the Turkish authorities he joined the *hajj* caravan to Mecca in the guise of a Christian Arab,

Khalil, after he had spent a year learning Arabic. He spent twenty-one months travelling alone across central Arabia ending up in Jiddah in 1878 on the Red Sea. He was often in danger and faced hostility from the Muslim Arabs and yet never renounced his Christian identity. He eventually returned to England with his health broken by his ordeals. He settled down to compile a detailed account of his wanderings which he published as *Arabia Deserta* written in an ornate language influenced by his study of Elizabethan literature. It was not an immediate success but eventually was recognised as the classic work of desert travel and an authoritative account. He spent the rest of his life engaged in writing and research in English language and history.

DEREK HOPWOOD

DOWRY

See: **marriage**

DREAMS (*AL-AHLAM*)

The interpretation of dreams has been a feature of life in Semitic, as in other, societies for centuries. Accounts of events and visions perceived by the mind during periods of sleep have been interpreted from ancient times by individuals who have claimed the power and the authority to do so. Islamic tradition speaks of dreams as 'one fortieth part of prophecy'. When asleep we are not distracted by normal experiences, so the mind is said to be more receptive to communications emanating from another, higher, world. Muslims have traditionally distinguished between dreams which are self-explanatory because they are God given and those which are difficult to interpret without assistance. The deeper significance of dreams and visions

may not be immediately apparent. Deciding whether or not a dream or a vision reveals an aspect of truth presents even the most subtle interpreters with a problem. As traditionally interpreted, a nightmare (*hulm mufzi'*, or *kabus*) is the work of a malevolent spirit. The classic example of a dream/vision with universal and timeless moral significance, is contained in the twelfth sura (*Yusuf*) of the Qur'an, where it is described in the third verse as 'the most beautiful of stories'. The occasion of the dream, its unfolding in the lives of the individuals immediately concerned, its subsequent interpretation and its implications for all human beings are subjects of continuing reflection for faithful Muslims.

References

Ali (1934: 548–600), Tritton (1968: 149–50).

See also: **astrology (*'ilm al-nujum*); magic and talismans; pre-Islamic Arabia**

EDWARD D. A. HULMES

DRESS

Dress is universally important as a cultural statement that transmits powerful messages about a wearer's rank, occupation, wealth, race, religious affiliation, gender, family and marital status and personal worth. Responses to all these messages are found in the dress traditions of the Middle East which are of such diversity that they defy containment. Survivals from their pre-Islamic heritage are seen in the draped and unstructured wraps and cloaks of Roman origin which are worn in North Africa and in the long-sleeved tunics and trousers based on Parthian and Sassanian prototype which were worn by the Umayyad caliphs of the seventh to eighth centuries AD. The main principle of Islamic ornament is that it is a versatile art of surface decoration ideally suited to textile design. The traditional silk wedding belts of Fez, for example, are woven with repeated geometric and foliage motifs. Sources for a study of Middle Eastern dress are rich, varied and uneven in coverage but are more plentiful for urban upper- and middle-class clothing. Surviving garments are relatively few as textiles are perishable and also vulnerable to hazards of political turmoil and war. Written sources including official records in Middle Eastern languages and European trade documents and travel accounts are when interpreted critically very informative. Visual sources, which are relatively limited and fragmentary for the early Islamic world, require an understanding of their pictorial treatment. Wall paintings, manuscript illustration of historical and literary texts, representation on other media such as ceramics, metalwork, ivory, wood and textiles, European drawings, engraving prints and from the nineteenth century onwards photographs all have stylistic conventions and degrees of realism which need to be understood.

A broad overview of the sources highlights some of the major developments. They reveal the existence of a sophisticated court dress code and flourishing textile industries to supply the necessary fabrics and accessories. The Caliph Harun al-Rashid's (AD 786–809) serious interest in clothes is seen in the wardrobe inventory listed by his son al-Amin which includes the vast numbers of coats, robes, shirts, etc., required for the layering of garments which is the main sartorial feature of Middle Eastern dress for both men and women. Among the enterprises which catered in medieval Islam for the demand for textiles were the *tiraz* factories especially in Baghdad and Alexandria which produced luxurious silk robes woven or embroidered with inscription bands usually along the shoulders and upper sleeves giving such valuable documentation as the names of the ruler, workshop, city and date. While most of these garments were for exclusive court use some of the factories catered for admittedly wealthy private clients. During the long rule of the Mamluks in Egypt from the thirteenth to early sixteenth centuries dress fashions continued the tradition of layers of garments, combining robes of plain and lavishly patterned fabrics codified and accessorised at court level according to a hierarchy of ruler, senior officials, and a supporting civil and military administration. Foreign influence also entered the basic Middle Eastern dress tradition, especially from China. They are seen in Iranian paintings of the fourteenth century onwards in the introduction of cloud collars and fabrics patterned with repeated motifs of flying cranes, phoenix and dragons to the robes worn by men and women. The most comprehensive record of Middle Eastern dress consists of the garments of the Ottoman Turkish rulers and their families, which are preserved in the collections of the Topkapi Palace Museum in Istanbul ranging in date from the late fifteenth to early twentieth century. The record is not complete and there are some problems of correct attribution and date but the range of garments – shirts, trousers, kaftans for both men and women – when studied together with the representations of dress illustrated in Ottoman historical chronicles and supplemented by archival material give a detailed picture of fabric, cut and construction, decoration and Ottoman taste. Workshops in Bursa and Istanbul supplied the textiles – velvets in deep crimson and green, silks in complex weaves often embellished with gold and silver thread worked in brilliant multicoloured designs based on repeated motifs of stars, rows of foliate scrolls and schemes of foliage interwoven with tulips, peonies, carnations and lotus comparable with those on Iznik ceramics and tiles of the sixteenth century. Such heavyweight densely patterned fabrics require the simplest of cut and construction methods and were therefore made into long-sleeved full-length robes based on a combination of rectangular main pieces with triangular sections added at sides and front to produce a well-fitting shape. They were mainly layered over plain robes in complementary or contrasting colours. Elaborately wound turbans decorated according to rank, leather shoes and accessories of finely worked belts and daggers completed an Ottoman courtier's dress. The latest additions to the Topkapi's collections were the uniforms of the last sultans of the early twentieth century, which indicates the changes which had affected the Middle Eastern dress traditions during the nineteenth century when the elites of Turkey, Tunisia, Morocco, Egypt and Iran adopted European civilian and military styles.

References

Atasoy *et al.*. (2001), Scarce (2002), Stillman (2000).

JENNIFER SCARCE

DRUZE (DURUZ)

A religious sect with its roots in the Isma'ili Shi'a sect and taking its origins from the belief that the sixth Fatimid caliph Abu 'Ali al-Mansur, commonly known as al-Hakim bi Amri-llah (AD 985–1021), is in fact divine. This notion was promoted primarily by the architects of the doctrine, Hamza b. 'Ali b. Muhammad al-Zuzani (985–1039) and Muhammad b. Isma'il al-Durzi (d. 1020), who gave the movement its name. Their doctrine is complex and the structure of their community is hierarchical, being divided into *'uqqal* (lit. the 'intellectual') and the *juhhal* (lit. 'the ignorant'). Their exclusion from the general precepts of Islam is sufficiently substantiated by their belief in the incarnation of al-Hakim bi Amri-llah alone, however they also believe in reincarnation, that the Qur'an and all other religions have been abrogated and consider all of the Prophets and Messengers to be 'devils' (cf. Sunnism). Despite their beginnings being in Egypt, they are most commonly found today in Lebanon, Syria and Palestine.

References

al-Johani (1999: 397–402), Netton (1997: 74–5).

See also: **Shi'ism; Sunnism**

GAVIN PICKEN

E

EDUCATION, ISLAMIC

Education plays a uniquely important role in Islam as the means by which Muslims learn to understand and appreciate aspects of their heritage of faith, duty and culture. Evidence of the richness of Islamic educational theory and praxis is provided by the words used to express this diversity. Five Arabic words may be cited in support of this. The word *ta'lim* connotes instruction, information, direction, schooling, the word *ta'dib* suggests good manners, urbanity, refined taste, the word *tarbiya* is associated with upbringing, teaching, instruction, good breeding, the word *tathqif* is linked with the cultivation of the mind and the processes of enculturation, the word *ma'rifa* suggests a deeper kind of intuitive, mystical knowledge.

Although it is not possible in this entry to do more than acknowledge the original contributions made by Islamic scholars down the centuries to the common store of human knowledge, the principles upon which these and other Muslims predicated their search for knowledge can be mentioned briefly. For Muslims the universe is already, or potentially, a source of revelation, knowledge and insight because it is the work of the God who, as its Creator, is self-evidently its 'Lord' (Q.1:2). All that is worth knowing is. of God in two senses, first because it comes *from* God and second because it is ultimately *about* God. To gain knowledge of God from whatever source is, thus, the responsibility of all Muslims. The acquisition of such knowledge is the *raison d'être* of Islamic education, the principles of which are not the same as those in a secular Western society. The key word in Arabic is *'ilm*. It is not a generic word for all that we may know or come to know, but a specific term for 'knowledge of God'. In short, everything that is worth knowing reveals the hand of God at work in his creation. The purpose of Islamic education is to identify this knowledge and to make its acquisition possible. In this

152

sense, 'religious' education can never be the 'separate subject' in an Islamic curriculum in the way in which it has recently been defined in Britain, for instance. This is because in Islamic education each 'subject' contributes integrally to the education of a Muslim. All that constitutes *'ilm* may lead the student to acknowledge the revealed will of God for His creation.

The Qur'an speaks about the source of true knowledge:

> [God] taught Adam the names of all things and then set them before the angels, saying: 'Tell Me the names of these, if what you say be true'. 'Glory to You', they replied, 'we have no knowledge except that which You have given us. You alone are all-knowing and wise'.
>
> (Q.2:32).

The injunction to learn the ways of God is explicit: '[O my] Lord increase my knowledge ['*ilm*]'. (Q.20:114). God's power to illuminate the minds of human beings is shown in the following passage:

> God is the light of the heavens and the earth. His light may be compared to a niche that enshrines a lamp, the lamp within a crystal of star-like brilliance. It is lit from a blessed olive tree neither eastern nor western. Its very oil would almost shine forth, though no fire touched it. Light upon light, God guides to His light whom He will. God speaks in metaphors to men. God has knowledge of all things.
>
> (Q.24:35)

A Muslim is encouraged to commit the words of the Qur'an to memory in the disciplined effort to become a *hafiz* (one who 'preserves' substantial parts of the Qur'an, if not the whole of it, in the memory). The Word of God is thus interiorised. To assist younger children to begin this arduous task is one of the principal aims of a Qur'anic school (*kuttab*). More modern systems of education in Islamic communities require children in upper schools to study a broader curriculum, though clearly not in a secular Western sense. Tensions exist in the Islamic world between those who favour a traditional approach to education and those who favour reform. The mosque is an important centre for local Islamic education. The *madrasa* is an institution for further study, which in some cases provides students with residential facilities. Courses of study include logic, Qur'anic exegesis (*tafsir*), jurisprudence (*fiqh*), literature, mathematics, and medicine.

It has been said that the most admirable quality in a Muslim scholar (*'alim*) is not critical acumen but a good memory. This reflects a quite different approach to education in the West, where the training of the memory has long ceased to be a major objective of secular education, in which the difference between perfunctory 'learning by rote' and the interiorising of *knowledge* through 'learning by heart' is often overlooked. Islamic tradition (*hadith*) records many sayings of varying authenticity attributed to the Prophet Muhammad on the question of knowledge and its acquisition. The following examples can be cited: 'The quest of knowledge is obligatory for every Muslim', 'Truly, the men of knowledge are the inheritors of knowledge', 'Seek knowledge from the cradle to the grave, even as far as China', 'Whomsoever Allah intends to do good, He gives right understanding of religion . . . Knowledge is maintained only through teaching', 'Acquire knowledge, for he who acquires it in the way of Allah performs an act of piety, he who speaks of it, praises the Lord, he who seeks after it adores God, he who dispenses instruction in it bestows alms, and he who imparts it to others performs an act of devotion to Allah'.

From an Islamic point of view the following points about education can be summarised. The chief (one might say, the *only*) purpose of education, not just in school but throughout life, is to provide individuals with a secure knowledge of Islam and the proper ordering of human affairs according to Islamic principles. Children, in particular, should be taught the meaning and purpose of life, their place in the created order, the doctrines of the Unity (*tawhid*) of God and the unique prophethood of Muhammad. They should be taught about the life after death and the judgement of God which precedes it. Islamic religious duties, beliefs, and moral values are to be inculcated and exemplified. Islamic culture is to be appreciated and defended. Education is to be the means by which men and women are enabled to acquire conviction about the Islamic ideals and the universal Islamic community (*umma*). Yet this does not mean that education proceeds in terms of indoctrination. Mature Muslims are to be individuals who are capable of leading useful and fulfilling lives guided by Islamic principles. They are to be witnesses to the Truth, and, thus, human beings who know and understand what needs to be known and understood about the plan and purposes of God. For all of this the Qur'an is the supreme educational guide and the unique source of inspiration and knowledge. The fact is that the Qur'an is the mainspring of all knowledge. Nor is the study of its contents merely for discrete periods of 'religious education'. On the contrary, the Qur'an offers guidance for everyone who seeks knowledge, whatever 'subject' is being studied. Muslims believe that knowledge is ultimately indivisible. The aim of the Islamic teacher is to demonstrate the integrity of knowledge.

References

Ahmad (1968: 16–22), Hulmes (1989: 28–53), Tibawi (1972: 19–87).

EDWARD D. A. HULMES

EMANATION

Most Muslim philosophers, following the Neoplatonists, believed in the existence of two worlds: the physical/material and the divine/immaterial. They defined the task of metaphysics as looking for a possible relationship between these two worlds and also for their relation to their First Cause (God). Plotinus interpreted this relationship as a necessary process which mirrors the nature of the divine as an emanating being whose perfection flows over other things and causes their existence. Muslim and Arab philosophers adopted the latter theory but considered it to be a late Aristotelian interpretation because of the attribution to Aristotle of a Neoplatonic work, which includes the Enneads (Books IV–VI) of Plotinus. This work was known among the Arabs as the *Theologia Aristotelis*. Plotinus explains here that the process of producing the world was a necessary one and required neither a will nor an act from God, for these might suggest a need for another or confirm plurality in His essence. However, God has emanated only the universal intellect, and the universal intellect emanated the universal soul. This trinity of Plotinus is clearly different from the Christian trinity because he attributed different ranks to the three persons. God stands in the highest rank, then comes the universal intellect, and then the universal soul in lower ranks, which in turn produced the world. Most Muslim and Arab philosophers adopted different versions of this theory and, therefore, presented different contributions and enrichments of it. Al-Farabi developed from the trinity of Plotinus a series of ten intellects ordered in rank and presented an intermediate world of intellects standing between God and the material world. Ibn Sina, though he adopted al-Farabi's theory, tried to present a direct connection between God and the world by explaining that God bestows existence (which can be understood as life) directly on each thing in the world, because He is the only giver of existence. This theory is known as 'essence and existence'.

In another version of the emanation theory, some Isma'ili philosophers attempted to combine the religious belief in creation *ex nihilo* with emanation. Al-Nasafi was the first to present an attempt to show how the creation of the first intellect happened through the word of God, which became separate from Him and caused the existence of the universal intellect, which he called *al-sabiq*. Thus this first existence happened as an absolute innovation *ibda'* from God without the use of any other substance outside Him. The world, however, proceeded from the universal intellect in a process of emanation. Al-Sijistani also believed in the double process of the origin of the world through creation and emanation. However, he applied many items of Qur'anic vocabulary and Isma'ili images to this theory, such as identifying the First Intellect with the sun and *al-Kursi*, the throne, while the universal soul is the moon or the divine throne *al-'arsh*.

References

Netton (1989).

MAHA EL-KAISY FRIEMUTH

ENOCH

See: **Idris**

ESCHATOLOGY

The beliefs referring to the last days before the Day of Judgement in which Gog and Magog, the *mahdi* and 'The Impostor' appear, after which Jesus returns.

References

Waines (1995: 51–2, 129–30).

See also: **al-Dajjal;** *yawm al-qiyama*

ANDREW J. NEWMAN

ESSENCE

Essence can be seen as the translation of the word *dhat*, which means the permanent element in things that determines its character. Essence is used in logic as the element which differentiates one thing from all others. The essence of a human being, for example, is that he is an animal capable of talking. In theological terms, essence determines the attributes which are permanent and defines the person (or God) as he (He) really is. These are known as *sifat al-dhat*. Muslim philosophers refer to essence also as the *jawhar*, by which they mean the basic elements of a thing which determine its nature. Thus the philosophers consider the essence of a thing to be its basic natural characteristics, while *dhat* for the theologians means the created elements which determine the character of the thing. The only essence which is not created for the theologians is the essence of God.

References

Dhanani (1994), Peters (1976).

MAHA EL-KAISY FRIEMUTH

ETHICS

The study of ethics did not leave major traces among the Muslim philosophers.

Most of them classify it with practical knowledge, following Aristotle, who, in his division of knowledge into theoretical and practical, placed ethics and politics under practical knowledge. For him, the aim of ethics is the human welfare and that of society, which can be achieved through secular laws. In contrast, Plato in his *Republic* explains that the ultimate happiness of humanity is in contemplating the divine world and imitating divine goodness and perfection. The philosopher therefore is the only person who possesses true goodness and virtue. For Plato, then, the ideal ruler who can lead society to a state of well-being is the philosopher. Al-Farabi followed the concepts of the *Republic* but emphasised the role of the philosopher as a political leader and a prophet. For him, religion is the simplified divine law which is received by the philosopher-prophet who has the political ability to lead the masses. Thus, the philosopher, in the view of al-Farabi, has to have a practical role and function in society, which he portrays symbolically in the cave myth of Plato, the philosopher is the one who returns to the cave and tells the people within about the light. Ibn Tufayl, in contrast, believes only in the theoretical role of the philosopher and accepts the fact that he has to live in seclusion from the public. Ibn Rushd in his commentary on Plato's *Republic* takes the same position as al-Farabi and emphasises the important role which the philosopher has to play for the welfare of society. Therefore, it seems that Muslim philosophers consider that ethics can be studied as a branch of theoretical knowledge as well as a branch of practical, attempting to reconcile the opinion of Aristotle with that of Plato.

The Ash'arite Muslim theologians do, indeed, believe in the practical role of ethics but they emphasise that the only way to receive the rules of ethics is through the divine revealed law. Only God, they believed, can reveal what is good and evil, human knowledge cannot measure the distinction between them. In contrast the Mu'tazilites believed in an objective ethics, declaring that human beings possess a necessary knowledge which distinguishes good clearly from evil.

References

al-Farabi (1985), Leaman (1999: 108–14).

MAHA EL-KAISY FRIEMUTH

EVLIYA CELEBI (1611–*c*. 1694)

Also known as Dervis Mehmed Zilli, Ottoman traveller. Born in Constantinople (Istanbul), Evliya received a traditional Islamic education before attracting the attention of the Ottoman Sultan Murad IV, under whose patronage he entered the palace school, where he received further instruction in Arabic, calligraphy, music and *tawhid*. Under the patronage of the court, he subsequently embarked on a series of travels and voyages throughout the Ottoman Empire and neighbouring lands that lasted in all over forty years. These travels, on some of which Evliya acted as an official representative of the Ottoman Government, formed the basis for his celebrated work, the *Seyahatname*. This work, in ten parts, not only provides a unique, 'insider' account of the history, geography and ethnography of the Ottoman Empire and neighbouring regions but also contains interesting and useful information on the Ottoman system of government; unfortunately, it has yet to appear in a complete critical edition printed in the original script.

The *Seyahatname* begins with a description of Istanbul and its environs followed by an account of the author's travels through the various provinces of the Ottoman Empire in Europe and the Near East; the last two books describe, *inter alia*, a pilgrimage to Mecca, and journeys in Sudan, Abyssinia and Egypt, where he is thought to have spent eight or nine years. The last date mentioned in his work is 1676. He appears to have spent the last year of his life in Istanbul editing his work, though it is clear from the text that has come down to us that he did not complete this task.

Evliya's work was clearly designed to entertain as well as instruct, and his approach to his subject, which includes the use of anecdotes for comic effect, is well calculated to hold the attention of the reader. Like many other travellers of the period, however, he has a marked taste for the fantastic and unusual, and he occasionally lets his imagination run away with him, describing places that he is unlikely to have visited or events that cannot possibly have occurred: an obvious example is the expedition of 10,000 Tatars through Austria, Germany and Holland to the North Sea recorded in Book 5.

References

Dankoff (1991), Dankoff and Elsie (2000), Pallis (1951).

PAUL STARKEY

EXPERIENCES WITH HEATHENS AND MOHAMMEDANS IN WEST AFRICA

This is the title of a short monograph written by the black Christian bishop, Samuel Ajayi Crowther. It was published posthumously in London in 1892 by the Society for Promoting Christian Knowledge as a tribute to his memory. It is of interest in the history of Islam in West Africa for the references its author makes to inter-religious encounters in the region between himself, the adherents of African traditional religion, Muslims and other Christians. In his dealings with Muslims he was thoroughly biblical and evangelical, always seeking opportunities to explain and to share his own faith with them, but by adopting a more eirenic approach to differences of religious belief and practice he was ahead of his time in the promotion of inter-faith dialogue. Crowther's short book was certainly intended to serve as an introductory manual for Christian missionaries working among Muslims, but it also shows the readiness of many followers of Islam to listen to what a Christian like Crowther had to say.

References

McKenzie (1976), Page (1908).

See also: **Crowther, Samuel Ajayi**

EDWARD D. A. HULMES

F

FAITH AND ACTION

The prophet is quoted as saying faith entails action.

References

Waines (1995: 103–11).

See also: *irja'*

ANDREW J. NEWMAN

THE FAITH MOVEMENT

The Faith Movement (in Urdu Tahrik-i Iman), more widely known as Tablighi Jama'at, is one of the most significant grassroots religious movements in the Muslim world today. It was founded near Delhi in 1926 by Maulana Muhammad Ilyas (1885–1944), an *'alim* and Sufi in the Deobandi tradition. For this reason the movement is perhaps best regarded as an example of neo-traditionalist Islamic activism. While little researched by academics until recently, the foremost scholar of Deobandism, Barbara Met-

calf, suggests that Tablighi Jama'at is like other Deobandi-related movements in that it has emphasised reforming the individual Muslim personality above all else. However, unlike its parent organisation, which focuses on education in the *madrasa*, the Faith Movement has prioritised preaching directly to the Muslim masses. Tending not to engage other movements in polemics, it professes only to promote 'correct' ritual and individual behaviour as defined by the *sunna* and *shari'a*.

Tablighi Jama'at emerged against the heightened communalism in late British India, a context which saw the 'hardening' of discrete religious identities and boundaries, culminating in Partition. In particular, the movement can be seen as a modern Islamic response to Hindu missionaries such as the Shuddhis, who sought to 'reconvert' Muslim peasants to the putative tradition of their ancestors. Maulana Ilyas's response to this situation, and the persistence of many 'Hindu' customs amongst 'Muslims',

158

was to organise the building of mosques and religious schools to educate his co-religionists about matters such as worship, morality and dress. However, he soon realised that, on their own, the bookish 'ulama' and their institutions could not reach out effectively to this constituency. To counteract the influence of the Hindus, what was needed was a rival preaching movement that could address the masses face to face and on their own terms. It was at this point that Maulana Ilyas resigned his teaching post at a *madrasa* in Saharanpur and moved to Delhi, assuming the new role of a peripatetic missionary.

Maulana Ilyas's first mission was to Mewat on the Indo-Gangetic plains southwest of Delhi, a place where a people known as the Meos were settled. Although Muslim by name, the Meos's religious beliefs and practices were essentially syncretic. As Maulana Ilyas discovered, they worshipped Hindu deities and celebrated Hindu festivals but could not even recite the *shahada*. By the time of his death, however, Tablighi Jama'at had achieved huge success amongst the Meos as thousands of missionaries joined him to proselytise in Mewat. Indeed, hundreds of new mosques and dozens of *madrasas* were built, reflecting a process of religious revival that would eventually spread throughout north India and beyond. Ilyas organised a unit (*jama'at*) of ten missionaries to go out to each village where Muslims would be invited to assemble, usually at the local mosque if one existed. There, those gathered, would be invited to become 'good Muslims', a message usually summarised in terms of a demand that they:

1. be able to recite the *shahada*;
2. know how to perform *salat*;
3. become 'knowledgeable Muslims', namely by reading the Qur'an in

Arabic as well as seven Tablighi tracts (today published as the *Tablighi Nisab/Tablighi Curriculum*);
4. have respect for each Muslim, a basic requirement of *da'wa* work;
5. cultivate a sincere and honest personality for the pleasure of God
6. volunteer for preaching to spread God's message.

In addition, the literature suggests that Maulana Ilyas later added the injunction that any Tablighi should avoid time-wasting and activities that might lead to sinfulness.

Tablighi Jama'at, then, is based on the principle that any sincere believer can teach a fellow Muslim about their faith. Against the context of faltering colonial rule and an emerging mass society, it invited the 'lay' Muslim to take a lead in the obligation of preaching, something once the preserve of religious specialists and the State they served. In terms of a commitment to preaching, a pattern emerged of calling participants to spend one evening per week, a few days per month, forty continuous days a year, and a least 120 days once in a lifetime, engaged in missionary work.

Metcalf argues that, for its predominantly semi-urban lower middle-class constituency, this emphasis on disciplined individual piety and mission represented a lifestyle choice that sought to revive the sense of a moral community associated with the Prophet's time. Moreover, the Tablighis do not simply idealise preaching as a male activity. Women are responsible for their own piety and, in theory at least, have the right to decline other duties in favour of mission amongst other women. Occasionally Tablighi women will travel with their partners or male family members on longer tours.

Tablighis define their work as part of the 'greater' *jihad*, the struggle for

159

self-purification. Therefore, preaching is considered a blessing that transforms the missionary at least as much as the missionised. Preachers can endure all sorts of difficulties including rejection, which is said to cultivate a humble dependency on God. Tablighis also dress in simple clothes, use simple language and perform menial tasks, from cooking and cleaning to mending clothes. As Metcalf remarks, in south Asia especially, these are activities usually associated with women and the 'lower born'. Therefore, going on *tabligh* can be seen as temporarily suspending various social hierarchies. Moreover, viewed against the Sufi context informing much Tablighi work – Maulana Ilyas was a *shaykh* of the Sabiriyya branch of the Chistiyya order and encouraged the practice of restrained *dhikr* – these characteristics also reveal deeply religious values such as the idea of *khidma* (service). Indeed, Metcalf has made the intriguing observation that in Tablighi Jama'at, 'the holiness of the *pir* is in many ways defused into the charismatic body of the *jama'at* so that the missionary group itself became a channel for divine intervention'.

Tablighis do not tend to seek prominent positions in public life. Political activities are banned amongst activists, although, in places such as Pakistan, the movement often provides a solid base of support for 'religious' parties such as the Jama'at-i 'Ulama'-i Islam. A largely privatised approach to religion and an emphasis on the responsibilities of Muslims as citizens, would also seem to have aided adaptation in the West where Tablighi Jama'at has been able to operate with great success. Despite this, some outsiders do claim that the movement is secretly political. Indeed, its larger gatherings have recently come under scrutiny in the USA as being possible, if innocent, recruitment grounds for radical Islamists. At the same time, however, the movement has been attacked for being apolitical by Muslims impatient with its 'obsession' with matters of individual religious practice such as the *sunna* of how long one's trousers should be.

For all these debates, the Faith Movement today remains an informal association with no written constitution. There is an *amir* (chief) elected for life who appoints a *shura* council (consultative body) for advice. Since Partition in 1947, the centre of the movement has moved from India to Raiwind near Lahore in Pakistan. Annual convocations there can attract as many as 2 million for the three-day meeting, representing perhaps the second largest gathering of Muslims worldwide after the *hajj*. Since the 1950s and 1960s especially, the movement has spread beyond South Asia to 100 countries in South-East Asia, the Middle East, Africa, Europe and North America. Indeed, outside South Asia and its diaspora, Tablighi Jama'at has begun to transcend its Deobandi Indian origins, creating a vision of Islamic renewal that is increasingly cosmopolitan. However, despite a growing interest from Moroccans and other Maghribians, the movement has yet to command a significant following amongst Arab Muslims.

References

Anwarul Haq (1972), Masud (2000), Metcalf (1996, 2002), Zakariyya (1987).

See also: **Deobandism**

SEÁN McLOUGHLIN

FAKHR AL-DIN AL-RAZI (AD 1149–1207)

Fakhr al-Din al-Razi is one of the last encyclopaedic writers of Islamic philosophy in its relation to theology who followed the footsteps of Abu Hamid al-Ghazali. He was born in Rayy in AD 1149 and, like the scholars of the medieval period, he travelled extensively to different towns in Persia. Finally he settled in Herat where he enjoyed the favour and admiration of 'Ala' al-Din Khwarizm and worked in his court. His teachers include important and influential scholars such as Majd al-Din al-Jili and Suhrawardi. He was most influenced by Ibn Sina (AD 1037), Abu 'l-Barakat al-Baghdadi (AD 1168) and Abu Hamid al-Ghazali (d. AD 1111).

Al-Razi left many philosophical and theological works. His most important theological books are *al-Arba'in fi Usul al-Din* and *al-Muhassal*. Among his important philosophical works are the three commentaries on Ibn Sina's works: *al-Isharat, 'Uyun al-Hikma* and *al-Mabahith al-Mashriqiyya*. In the latter work al-Razi comments on many metaphysical issues also from *al-Shifa'*, but mainly in Avicennan style. In this work he, following al-Ghazali, criticises Ibn Sina's concept of emanation. He found no logical ground for the concept that the One can produce only one entity, which is considered one of the basics of the Neoplatonic concept of emanation. He also criticises Ibn Sina's view that God cannot know particulars. He sees no ground for considering that the act of knowing should be unified with the knowable which would entail multiplicity in the divine knowledge. Knowledge, for him, is an especial relationship to the object known and therefore causes, not multiplicity, but rather a relationship to the world. This argument, in fact, mainly reflects al-Ghazali's concept of God's knowing the world through an eternal knowledge which does not change but includes all kinds of knowledge (knowledge of the particular and of the universal). However, while al-Razi's refutation of Ibn Sina is considered more thorough and less aggressive than that of al-Ghazali, it

does not surpass it. After leading an active productive life, al-Razi died in Herat in AD 1207.

References

Fakhry (1983: 319–23).

MAHA EL-KAISY FRIEMUTH

FALASIFA

The Greek term 'philosophy' is translated by the early Arab and Syrian translators as *falsafa*, and they turned the word philosopher into *faylasuf*, of which the plural is *falasifa*. Philosophy was learned in different Greek and Syriac centres before the spread of the Arab peoples over the Middle East. Most of the Greek works were already translated, as early as the fifth century, into Syriac and later into Arabic. Philosophy at the beginning of the ninth century was mainly discussed among the translator scholars, who were mostly Christians or with a Zoroastrian background, in the halls of Harun al-Rashid and al-Ma'mun. However, they were also allowed to teach their scientific and philosophical knowledge to Arab students. The first Arab scholar who was called *faylasuf* by many biographers was al-Kindi (d. AD 866). This title was given to scholars who had done their main scholarly work in the natural sciences and/or in Greek philosophy, such as Abu Bakr al-Razi, al-Farabi and Ibn Sina. In many different periods the *falasifa* were condemned for heterodoxy and some of them had their books burnt. The reason mainly was that the *falasifa* were more like free thinkers who respected Islam and even wrote many treatises on the reconciliation between religion and philosophy. They considered that the messages of revelation are meant to present truth in a simple form for the masses, while philosophy presents truth through demonstrative methods. Thus, for them, religious truth can be included in philosophical truth. In their eyes religion is the divine law which is given for sake of the masses.

The *falasifa* were by no means in harmony with the *Mutakallimun*, the Muslim theologians. Al-Ghazali in his famous book the *Incoherence of the Philosophers* attacks the main philosophical concepts of al-Farabi and Ibn Sina. He accuses them in twenty-four charges and in three of these they are held to be infidels. These three issues are: their belief in the eternity of the world as well as the eternity of God; the belief of the universal nature of God's knowledge as opposed to His knowledge of the particulars; and the rejection of the resurrection of the body.

References

Leaman (1999: 1–13).

See also: **God's knowledge**

MAHA EL-KAISY FRIEMUTH

FALSAFA

An Arabic term that renders the Greek *philosophia* and is used to describe the Graeco-Arabic tradition of philosophy and the wider classical Islamic tradition. The impetus for philosophical speculation in Islam is a much debated issue. Whether one wishes to see solely Hellenic roots for philosophy in the 'Abbasid period or one searches as a confessional statement for philosophical inspiration in the Qur'an and the tradition of the Prophet is largely a matter of ideology. The origins of philosophy are far too complex to be reduced to a singular causality. What is clear is that in the 'Abbasid period, the speculative desire to understand the nature of the Qur'an, and the relationship between believer

and cosmos, community and individuals was increasingly articulated in arguments of a systematic nature. The standards of argumentation, partly as a result of the need to find a neutral set of rules that could apply in disputation with non-Muslims who did not accept the validity of the Qur'anic revelation, was Aristotelian logic and especially the *Topics* (translated into Arabic in this period as the Book of Dialectic or *al-jadal*). Recently, it has also been suggested that the 'Abbasids encouraged philosophical and scientific speculation, complemented by translations from Greek works as an expression of their imperial ideology. A translation movement developed in the capital Baghdad, fuelled by money from the court and produced mainly by Arab Christian theologians familiar with Greek and with the Syriac tradition of translating the works of Aristotle, Plato and other Hellenic thinkers into scholarly Near Eastern vernaculars. The works were kept in the library of the chancellery in Baghdad and named Bayt al-Hikma (House of Wisdom). This movement intersected with a key intellectual circle associated with arguably the first Muslim philosopher Abu Yusuf Ya'qub al-Kindi (d. AD 870). Thus, translations and arguments that joined Hellenic debates and took them into fresh avenues of inquiry were largely coeval.

Important translators such as Hunayn ibn Ishaq (d. AD 873) and Yahya ibn 'Adi (d. AD 974) coordinated translations first of the Aristotelian *organon* to establish rules of disputation and standards of rational discourse, and later the metaphysical, natural philosophical and psychological works of the Stagirite. Aristotle was the philosopher par excellence, and the Neoplatonic curriculum that Islam inherited began the study of philosophy with Aristotle. What they also inherited was the desire to harmonise the work of Plato and Aristotle. Yahya is supposed to have translated Plato's *Timaeus*, the key cosmological text of the Neoplatonic curriculum, and Porphyry's *Isogoge* or introduction to Aristotelian logic was incorporated into the study of logic. Harmonisation led to the proliferation of pseudo-Aristotelian works attributed to the Stagirite that were actually of Neoplatonic provenance. Foremost amongst them were the *Theology of Aristotle*, a paraphrastic epitome of Plotinus' Enneads IV–VI and *Kitab fi Mahd al-Khayr* (*Liber de Causis*), a work that draws upon Proclus' *Stoikeiosis Theologike* (*Elements of Theology*). The result was that the main thrust of the Hellenic influence that shaped early Islamic philosophy was Aristoteliaic Neoplatonism.

The push eastwards brought Muslims in contact with Persian and Indian thought and science and, from early on, astronomical and medical works were translated from Pahlavi and Sanskrit. The scientist and philosopher al-Biruni (d. AD 1048) also had the *Yogasutra* of Patanjali translated from Sanskrit, the only major work of Indian philosophy available in the classical period. Persian texts on *moralia* were transformed into a work such as *Javidan Khirad* (*Eternal Wisdom*) of Miskawayh (d. AD 1030). But the most enduring and striking legacy of the East was the physics of atomism that became a central feature of theological speculation about the nature of the cosmos, and the significance and influences of the celestial bodies upon the earth.

If rational discourse is a standard for judging *falsafa*, then much of the *kalam* tradition ought to be considered to be philosophical. While the philosophical nature of much of the debate among theologians (*mutakallimun*) is indubitable such as arguments about occasionalism, atomism, freewill and determinism,

there was a tension from an early period between them and philosophers. Theology remained an apologetic defence of dogma as discerned in the Qur'an and the prophetic tradition, whilst *falsafa* was an attempt at a rational speculation about some more abstract notions about reality. Although it did not fail to serve as the handmaiden of theology when need arose, the Neoplatonic Aristotelianism of the philosophers (*falasifa*) was considered to be in contravention with sound belief. The famous classical theologian al-Ghazali (d. AD 1111) in his *Tahafut al-Falasifa* (*Incoherence of the Philosophers*) revealed the ambivalence of theology towards philosophy. He was quite willing to coopt Aristotelian logic as a standard for argumentation and use philosophical styles of discourse, but quite averse to the metaphysics to which they committed the practitioner. In this work, al-Ghazali condemned twenty doctrines expressed by philosophers such as Ibn Sina and held them to be incompatible with Muslim dogma, whilst providing rather philosophical refutations of those positions. On three specific issues, he regarded the philosophers as being guilty of heresy since belief in those doctrines was unbelief. These were the notions that the world was coeternal with God because it was only a logical and not a temporal consequent of him, that God did not known particulars but only knew universals, and that that there was no bodily resurrection. That al-Ghazali was willing to use philosophical arguments to refute philosophy and that he wrote other works that seemed to acknowledge Avicennan cosmology did contribute to his losing the case. One must not accept condemnations of philosophical as a universal distaste for rational discourse in Islam. The cultural history of the classical period actually suggests that philosophy was far from being a pursuit marginal to intellectual Muslim society.

The philosophical tradition survived al-Ghazali's assault. Ibn Rushd (d. AD 1198) wrote a successful refutation of it. But the real success of *falsafa* led to its naturalisation within the theological tradition of *kalam*. The rise of philosophical theology meant that discourse not only commenced with philosophical logic, but also with its epistemological foundations concerning the nature of knowledge and its metaphysical foundations concerning existence and its divisions. Works of *falsafa* included extensive discussions about the nature of God, his attributes and his relationship with the world and included both the *kalam* cosmological proof for his existence and the Avicennan proof of God as the necessary existent. Avicennan *falsafa* won the day.

References

Adamson and Taylor (2005), Afnan (1964), Badawi (1946), Corbin (1964), Daiber (1999), Endress (1990), Endress and Kruk (1997), Fakhry (1983), Gutas (1998, 2002), al-Jabiri (1982–98), Leaman (1985), Mattock (1989: 73–102), Nasr and Leaman (1996), Peters (1968), Rosenthal (1975), Steinschneider (1960), Tarabishi (1998), Walzer (1962).

SAJJAD H. RIZVI

FANA'

Translated as 'annihilation', *fana'* is a term used by Sufis to describe the passing away of a certain human state. Sufis have interpreted *fana'* in a number of ways, some speak of '*fana'* in the *shaykh*', while others have discussed '*fana'* in the prophet', and yet others have elaborated on *fana'* in God. Underlying the notion of *fana'* is the leaving behind of the baser human emotions and desires that serve to obstruct man from the divine. Sufis often spoke of a higher stage above

fana', namely *baqa'*, or subsistence (in God).

References

Izutsu (1994).

LLOYD RIDGEON

AL-FARABI, ABU NASR MUHAMMAD IBN UZLUGH (AD 870–950)

A pivotal figure in the history of Islamic philosophy, born around AD 870 in Farab in Transoxania. He studied and taught at Baghdad until AD 942. In Baghdad he was associated with Christian Aristotelians. The Arabic sources mention the Nestorian, Yuhanna Ibn Hylan (d. AD 910) as his teacher. One source mentions the famous translator Abu Bishr Matta (d. AD 940), who belonged to al-Farabi's circle, as also being his teacher. We know that al-Farabi studied Arabic grammar with Ibn al-Sarraj, the leading grammarian of the period. It is also known that he dedicated his great book on music to one of the viziers of the 'Abbasid caliphs.

The Baghdad of this period was undergoing political instability as it was subject to the whims of military adventurers. The Baridi brothers, tax farmers, acquired military support and in AD 942 invaded Baghdad, their soldiery looting and causing havoc. Whether or not al-Farabi left Baghdad before this occurred, because of it or for some other reason is not known. He immigrated to Syria and received support from the Hamdanid Arab ruler of Aleppo, Sayf al-Dawla, and died in Damascus in AD 950.

Al-Farabi wrote commentaries on Aristotle's *Organon* as well as on other works, also criticisms of such thinkers as Galen and al-Razi. He was the foremost logician of his time and was referred to as the second teacher; the first being

Aristotle. He was, however, a great metaphysician in his own right, developing an emanative system that was very influential. Among his many achievements were his works on music. He is generally reckoned as the foremost musical theorist of his time and a musicologist of calibre. There are indications that he was also a skilful performer.

Apart from his commentaries and writings on logic, which had a determining influence on the development of Islamic philosophy, it is perhaps as a metaphysician and, above all, as the founder of a Platonic theory of the state that he was most influential. His political philosophy, in its essentials, was adopted and elaborated by such subsequent philosophers as Ibn Sina (Avicenna) (d. AD 1037), Ibn Bajja (Avempace) (d. AD 1138), Ibn Tufayl (d. AD 1194) and Ibn Rushd (Averroes) (d. AD 1198).

Following Aristotle, al-Farabi defines metaphysics as knowledge of the existent in as much as it is an existent – this in contradistinction to physics, the study of the existent in as much as it is in motion and mathematics, the existent in as much as it is quantified. Underlying his definition of metaphysics is a doctrine of real essence, namely that things have objective specific natures. This, as we shall see, is relevant to his political philosophy. What is also relevant to this philosophy is his emanative metaphysics.

This metaphysics is linked to the geocentric astronomical view. Revolving around our earth are the heavenly spheres, the closest being the spheres of the moon, followed by the spheres of Mercury, of Venus, the sun, Jupiter, Saturn, the sphere of the fixed stars and finally an outermost spheres without stars. Al-Farabi's emanative scheme relates all these to each other. Accordingly, there is to begin with an overflow from God of a first intelligence. This intelligence undergoes eternally two acts of cognition, knowl-

edge of God and knowledge of itself. These are creative acts from which two things respectively result, another intelligence and the outermost sphere. The second intelligence undergoes a similar cognitive act, resulting in the emanation of another intelligence and the sphere of the fixed stars. The process is repeated by the successive intelligences resulting in the existence of the planets, the sun, and the moon. The last of the intelligences is the active intellect which governs the sublunar world and provides human rational souls with the intelligibles. Al-Farabi suggests that this world comes into being through the action of the celestial bodies that endow it with substantial forms.

The cosmos is hierarchical, the existents closer to God are more perfect than their successors. Moreover, it is harmonious and rational, each of the celestial spheres being governed by an intellect, by reason. In the terrestrial world, man being endowed with the freedom of the will, must seek to establish a political order that is rational and harmonious. The model for this is the celestial realm. Within the terrestrial world, there is a hierarchical order. The human, being endowed with a rational soul, stands highest in the scale of value. But humans vary in their rationality. Some are incapable of abstract thought and among those capable of it there is variance.

The human rational soul at first is a potentiality, having a disposition to become actually rational. It begins its process of actualisation with the reception of sensory images which, in the case of those capable of abstract thought, become transformed by the illuminating action of the Active intellect and become abstract. Such souls now attain an immaterial status and are capable of cognising themselves. Having attained immateriality, these souls become separable from the body after death. The separated rational 'good' souls live an eternal blissful life of contemplating the intelligences and God. The destiny of souls that have not attained immateriality, and those that have not fully actualised their potentialities depends largely, as will be noted, on the type of political state to which they belonged.

In the terrestrial hierarchical scheme of things, the highest in the scale of value is the philosopher-prophet, whose existence is a necessary condition for the realisation of the good state, 'the virtuous city'. The prophet-philosopher receives knowledge from the active intellect directly. His rational soul, in both its theoretical and practical parts, becomes inundated with the intelligibles that overflow on it from the active intellect. Among the inner faculties of the human soul, the imaginative is incapable of abstract thinking. It has the ability, however, to imitate abstract thought. Al-Farabi insists that the prophet must also be endowed with a most powerful imaginative faculty that imitates abstract knowledge, 'translating' it, so to speak, into none abstract terms. Its imitations of the intelligibles that inundate the prophet's rational faculty constitute either particular instances of universal knowledge, or that which symbolises them. For al-Farabi, this is the revealed word, conveyed in the language that the non-philosophic majority of humans can understand. Religion is thus defined as 'the imitation of philosophy' as it conveys philosophical truth in symbolic terms. It does not contradict philosophy. This theory of the reception of prophetic knowledge is basic for understanding Al-Farabi's political philosophy. The 'virtuous' state is the one that strives after happiness which is the good in itself. Happiness consists in the actualisation of one's rational potentialities. It is ideally attained within a state that functions harmoniously and is guided by reason. Such a state, as with Plato, is hierarchical, divided into different social levels, each having a leader, all functioning harmoniously, guided by reason and by law. The bringer of this law is the prophet who is also a philosopher. Ideally, subsequent rulers should also be philosophers, though not necessarily, prophet-philosophers. Sometimes, however, a ruler may be one who is well versed in the law, but not a philosopher – he must follow what has been revealed to the Prophet. The ideal ruler must also be endowed with practical wisdom to adapt the law to new circumstances. But above all, he must have knowledge of the nature of true happiness, its specific objective nature, alluded to earlier. It is when rulers fail to have such knowledge that the result is the rise of various types of ignorant cities, namely, the indispensable, the vile, the timocratic, the despotic, and the democratic. Al-Farabi also discusses the immoral states and the erring cities.

In the case of the ignorant cities, the leadership lacks knowledge of the true nature of happiness. It mistakes happiness either for mere survival, wealth, pleasure, honour, or liberty. The souls of those who live the lives of these ignorant cities do not separate after death from their bodies. Their souls become part of the process of generation and corruption. With the immoral cities, both leader and citizens have knowledge of what true happiness is, but deliberately forsake it for pleasure or power and so on. In the hereafter, their souls are deprived from contemplating the intelligences and God and live in the torment of such deprivation. The erring cities are those whose leader alone knows what true happiness is, but does not pursue it. His soul alone survives death and is punished.

Returning to the theory that religion is an 'imitation' of philosophy, there are two things to be noted. The first is its elitism – only the philosopher is allowed to interpret religion philosophically. The second is that it includes a tendency towards ecumenism. As images and languages differ from one culture and another, Al-Farabi suggests that it is possible that the differences in religions may be only differences in symbolisation, not in what is being symbolised.

References

Bouyges (1938), Galston (1990), Hyman (1973: 215–21), Kutch and Morrow (1960), Lerner and Mahdi (1963: 24–57), Mahdi (1961, 1968a, 1968b, 1969, 2000), Najjar (1964), Netton (1992), Rosenthal and Walzer (1943), Walzer (1985), Zimmerman (1981).
MICHAEL E. MARMURA

FARA'ID

Fara'id is an Arabic term designating the plural of *fard* religious duty, which indicates an injunction which is prescribed by the text in a specific manner. In the case of inheritance it refers to the method of disposing of the estate of a deceased person according to the stipulation of shares of inheritance in the Qur'an (4:11). Accordingly, the Islamic inheritance law appears to have developed into an entire discipline whereby the shares of each individual are assessed on the basis of the Qur'an and *sunna*. Inheritance may not be assessed on analogy or individual opinion, unless approved by all Muslim scholars in the form of consensus *ijma'*. Normally *fara'id* focuses on three aspects, the deceased, the beneficiary and the legacy, all of which must be addressed according to the text and *ijma'*.

References

Ibn Manzur (n.d.), al-Zuhayli (1985: 234–47).
MAWIL IZZI DIEN

FASTING (*SAWM, SIYAM*)

Fasting during Ramadan, the ninth month of the lunar Islamic calendar is one of the five 'pillars', or religious duties of Islam. It is obligatory for all adult Muslims to fast during that period unless there are special circumstances for which a temporary dispensation is made. Muslims who are unable to fast at the prescribed time are expected to honour their obligation when the circumstances allow. Muslims who wilfully ignore the fast are guilty of failing to take part in a corporate act of spiritual cleansing that serves to unite members of the Islamic community throughout the world. For this failure they will be held accountable when the 'Day of Judgement' comes. The Arabic word for the fast is *sawm* (*siyam*). It derives from a root which expresses the notion of 'being at rest'. To be thus disposed is to be prepared for spiritual effort, by means of which a relationship with God and with other Muslims may be reviewed over the prolonged period of the thirty day month. During Ramadan self-denial (*imsak*, 'abstinence'), is undertaken for the specific purpose of concentrating on the significance of *islam* – the fundamental meaning of which is 'personal surrender to the revealed will of God'. The time of fasting is designed to renew faith and to strengthen Islamic action. It is to assist Muslims to free themselves from worldly thoughts and habits, to distance themselves from what is ephemeral, and to help them to subject their bodily needs to the discipline of self-denial. Muslims believe that fasting will purify the soul and give them the strength to conquer evil.

Fasting for religious reasons was known in pre-Islamic Arabia before the birth of the Prophet Muhammad (*c.* AD 570), whose journeys brought him into contact with Jews and Christians, for whom fasting was already customary. He was in the habit of withdrawing into the desert for fasting and meditation. It was there, aged forty, that he received the call to be the Messenger of God in the year AD 610. In the same year, during the night of the of *Ramadan* – a night to be remembered later as *laylat al-qadr*, 'the Night of Power' (see Q.97 and Q.44:3) – he received the first of the revelations of the Qur'an (Q.96:1–5) from the Angel Jibril. At first, Muslims kept the *'ashura'* voluntary day of fasting as observed by Jews in connection with the Jewish Day of Atonement (Lev. 16). After the Battle of Badr (AD 624), in which the Muslim forces under Muhammad gained a celebrated victory over the Meccans, his attitude hardened to Jews who would not accept Islam or his leadership. After Muhammad's mission was rejected by the followers of these two other monotheistic religions, the Qur'an instituted fasting during the month of Ramadan as a specific religious duty for Muslims.

Fasting begins at the first appearance of the new moon and ends thirty days later as soon as the next new moon is sighted. The references to fasting in the Qur'an (Q.2:183–7) provided the basis for the regulation of *sawm*. From dawn until dusk, in either case at the moment when a white thread can be distinguished from a black thread, 'full-grown' (*baligh*) and physically fit (*qadir*) Muslims are obliged to abstain from eating, drinking, rinsing the mouth with water, smoking and sexual intercourse. Children are expected to fast from their tenth year and are sometimes compelled to do so. Some Islamic authorities have even forbidden the swallowing of saliva, insisting that it is to be ejected from the mouth. Voluntary fasting at other times is meritorious. Muslims who are especially devout in their practice, or who desire to do penance for bad deeds, may under-

take additional periods of fasting. This practice is desirable rather than obligatory, and it counts as earning merit. An additional fast is recommended, for instance, on the day of *'ashura'*, or for six days during the month of Shawwal, the lunar month that follows Ramadan. Fasting is forbidden during the main festivals of the Breaking of the Fast and of Sacrifice. The expression of excessive zeal through self-mortification is forbidden.

For fasting to be valid, it must begin with an expression of intention (*niyya*) to perform the fast faithfully according to custom. There is no universal agreement among Muslims about whether this is to be done daily or just at the beginning of the period of fasting. One who fasts, a *sa'im*, must be in a reasoning frame of mind (*'aqil*). Women must be free from menstruation and from bleeding in childbirth. The keeping of the fast has important social consequences. The rhythm of daily life is governed by the requirements of the fast. The usual patterns of life are disrupted. Offices and shops close earlier, but more normal life begins at the end of each day's fasting, when believers may eat anything that is lawful, up to ninety minutes before the fast for the next day begins. Special recitations from the Qur'an are chosen. In addition, times for prayer during the nights of the month (*salat al-tarawih*), bring Muslims together in the mosques. After sunset anything that it is lawful to eat or drink may then be consumed. During the hours of darkness, after the sun has set, generous provision is often made for eating and drinking (even for the consumption of alcohol by non-Muslims in some places). After the days of fasting there comes *'id al-fitr*, 'the Festival of the Breaking of the Fast'.

The rigorous laws about fasting during Ramadan may be relaxed. Those who are excused from keeping the fast include young children, elderly people, the sick, pregnant and nursing women, those engaged in heavy manual labour, military personnel on active service, students (who are presumed to be 'striving in the way of God' as they seek to acquire knowledge), travellers, and those of unsound mind. Those for whom the rules of fasting are relaxed are deemed to be in danger of suffering damage to life if subjected to the rigours of the fast, but when their circumstances change they are expected to make up for the fasting they have been spared, day for day. Those who cannot endure the pangs of hunger or thirst as a result of fasting may seek temporary respite, but there remains a 'ransom' for those unable to fast at all. This is 'paid' by helping to feed those who are poor and without sufficient means to provide for themselves. These rules have been subjected to local interpretation and application, although the general position is clear. Although God does not make the fast too burdensome for anyone, those who break it wilfully must subsequently make reparation with a sixty-day fast of repentance, or by purchasing the freedom of a slave, or by paying alms. For one who dies whilst there is still an obligation on him to fast, a near relative must undertake to complete it. There are certain sins for the cleansing of which additional fast-days are sometimes prescribed (Q.5:98). Yet this pious hope remains a somewhat vague one, given that God is perfectly free to act as He chooses with regard to His judgement and His forgiveness.

EDWARD D. A. HULMES

FATIMA (*c.* AD 605–33)

Fatima was the youngest and the favourite daughter of the Prophet Muhammad, and the only one of his children to survive him. Her mother was Khadija, the first wife of the Prophet. Fatima became the wife of 'Ali ibn Abi Talib, the fourth of the rightly guided (*al-rashidun*) caliphs. Her two sons were al-Hasan and al-Husayn. The Shi'i Fatimid caliphs, who ruled in Egypt, North Africa, Syria and Palestine from AD 909–1171, are reputed to be the lineal descendants of Fatima and 'Ali through al-Husayn.

References

Hitti (1973: 617–31).

See also: **Fatimids**

EDWARD D. A. HULMES

FATIMIDS (AD 909–1171)

The Fatimids began in North Africa as a messianic religious movement under 'Ubaydallah al-Mahdi, with claims to represent the line of 'Ali through his wife Fatima, daughter of the Prophet. It seems likely, in fact, that his movement had its roots in radical Shi'ite circles of the Muslim East, Isma'ili groups in Syria and Iraq, whence propaganda was carried to the Maghrib. After AD 969, the dynasty was established in Egypt and Syria, with their newly founded capital of Cairo (*al-Qahira*, 'The Victorious'). The Fatimids had assumed the title of caliphs in rivalry with the Sunni 'Abbasids of Baghdad, and for over two centuries, their empire was the most powerful and most brilliant state within the whole Islamic world. It is from this time that there dates the primacy of Cairo in Arab culture. There was an elaborate Isma'ili hierarchy in Cairo, and missionaries proselytised energetically for the cause in regions as distant as Yemen, Iran and Sind, in parallel with the more activist Isma'ili movement centred on Syria and Iran of the so-called Assassins. In the eleventh century, Fatimid vigour declined, and the Ayyubid Salah al-Din (Saladin) had little difficulty in AD 1171 in restoring Egypt to its old Sunni allegiance.

References

Bosworth (1996: No. 27), Gibb and Bosworth (1960–2003), Sanders (1998), Walker (1998).

See also: **Hasan-i Sabbah**

C. E. BOSWORTH

FATRA

An Arabic word signifying a brief interval of time, a period of transition. Classically it was used for the interval between the Call of the Prophet Muhammad to become the Messenger of God during the *laylat al-qadr*, 'the Night of Power', or 'the Night of the Descent of the Qur'an', when, as tradition records, the first *sura* to be revealed to Muhammad (Q.96) was brought to him by the Angel Jibril. The commemoration of this night was subsequently fixed towards the end of the Islamic month of Ramadan. The interval between this first revelatory vision and the second is known as a *fatra*.

EDWARD D. A. HULMES

FATWA

Fatwa is an opinion on a point of law. Law, in Islam, is any civil or religious matter. *Fatwas* may only be given by a qualified scholar, magistrate or similar authority.

See also: ***mufti***

MAWIL IZZI DIEN

AL-FAZAZI (d. AD 1229/30)

The thirteenth-century Moroccan poet and mystic al-Fazazi wrote a poetic eulogy of the Prophet Muhammad, which became a popular addition to the genre of prophetic panegyric, particularly in north and west Africa and in Egypt. In virtue of its verse structure it was known as 'The Twenties'. It was a work of uncritical adulation, including such lines as: '[Muhammad] is not to be compared with the full moon, which lasts but half way through the month, because its effulgence does not outlast its prescribed time, whereas his effulgence lasts for ever'.

The poet proceeded to paraphrase some of the significant events in Muhammad's life, basing his verses on passages in the Qur'an which refer, *inter alia*, to the miraculous *laylat al-isra' wa'l-mi'raj* (Night Journey). The Prophet is singled out for special praise because it was he who was favoured with an ascent into the seventh heaven that took him to within 'two bow-lengths' of the divine throne. The result of such panegyric was to foster a belief that it was really the Prophet Muhammad, rather than Jibril or the other angels, who was the chosen intermediary between God and His human creatures.

References

Nicholson (1953: 326–7).

EDWARD D. A. HULMES

FEAST OF THE SACRIFICE (*'ID AL-ADHA*)

This feast is considered by Muslims to be the more important of the two holy feasts in Islam, the other one being 'the Feast of Breaking of the Fast'. 'The Feast of Sacrifice' is also known as 'the great feast' (*'Id al-kabir*). In Turkey it is known as *kurban bayram*. The feast takes place on the tenth day of Dhu 'l-Hijja, the month during which the *hajj*, the annual pilgrimage to Mecca, is made. The animal sacrifice concludes the pilgrimage, marking the completion of the rites and duties of the *hajj* in accordance with the injunctions contained in the

Qur'an (Q.2:26–38). The place at which Muslim pilgrims make their sacrifice is *Mina*, some 4 miles (6 kilometres) south-east of Mecca. It is here that the three pillars are stoned three times by the pilgrims, each of whom casts at least forty-nine pebbles. The ritual is a reminder of the way in which Satan vainly attempted three times to make Abraham disobey God's command. The ritual sacrifice of an animal is made at this time in commemoration of the sacrifice of the ram that was offered up by Ibrahim (Abraham) instead of his son. Muslims believe that the son was Isma'il (Ishmael), although the name of the boy is not mentioned in the Qur'an. The biblical account of Abraham's sacrifice of the ram records how the life of his named son Isaac was spared providentially by God as a result of Abraham's faith and obedience to a divine ordinance (Gen. 22). The fact that the father was prepared to sacrifice his son in obedience to God's call when there was little hope that he would ever see another son, given his advanced age and that of his wife, is taken by Jews and Christians as well as Muslims to be evidence of Abraham's exemplary faith in and submission to God. The Feast of the Sacrifice is observed by Muslims throughout the world at the same time as their co-religionists are ending the pilgrimage to Mecca. The only other occasion when an animal sacrifice is made by Muslims is that of the *'aqiqa*, an event taking place when the child is seven days old during which the baby is shaved and named. The sacrifice is made to seal the bond that the child will be raised as a Muslim and will be protected from evil.

References

Brown and Palmer (1987: 116–17), Gibb (1955: 42, 56), Tritton (1968: 26–7).

EDWARD D. A. HULMES

FESTIVALS, ISLAMIC

The two major festivals in Islam are *'Id al-fitr* (the Festival of the Breaking of the Fast) and *'Id al-adha* (the Feast of the Sacrifice). These festivals are community celebrations, in which Muslims join together in order to mark the fulfilment of two of their primary religious duties, namely, the end of the Fast during the month of Ramadan and the completion of the pilgrimage to Mecca (*hajj*). Other festivals considered in separate entries in this volume are: *laylat al-qadr* (the Night of Power, or Destiny), *mawlid* (*milad*) *al-nabi* (the birthday of the Prophet Muhammad).

References

Momen (1985: 238–9).

EDWARD D. A. HULMES

FEZ

The city of Fez, or Fès (*Fas*) is situated north of the Great Atlas mountains, 100 miles (160 kilometres) east of Rabat (*ribat al-fath*), the present capital of Morocco. Fez was the capital of the Idrisid state, founded in AD 808 by Idris ibn 'Abdallah (Idris II) and sometimes described as the first Shi'i state in the history of Islam. Its medieval character has been largely preserved. The new city was founded in AD 1276. In AD 1062 Fez lost its status as capital city to Marrakesh (whence the name Morocco), when the latter was made the capital of their empire by the Almoravids. Other dynasties followed during the Middle Ages. Of the 100 or so mosques in Fez, two are especially renowned. The first contains the shrine of Idris II. A place of pilgrimage, it remains one of the holiest Islamic sites in Morocco. The second is the Qayrawiyin mosque, which dates from AD 859. The mosque became the centre of the ancient Islamic university of Fez. Many saints and scholars are associated with the city. Their reputations help to attract large numbers of pilgrims to Fez. The collection of the lives of the saints of Fez is known as *Salawat al-Anfus*. The red round hat, with its tasselled, flat-topped, brimless hat made of felt or cloth, is said to have taken its name from Fez. The hat, also known in Arabic as a *tarbush*, became a characteristic headgear of males in the Middle East. Fez is famous for its textiles, carpets and leather goods.

References

Hitti (1973: 450–51, 546–9), Michell (1984: 216), Mostyn and Hourani (1988: 76–8).

See also: **Almohads; Almoravids**

EDWARD D. A. HULMES

FI 'L-FALSAFAT AL-ULA

Abu Yusuf Y'aqub b. Is'aq al-Kindi (d. AD 870) was the first major exponent of philosophy in Islam, and *Fi 'l-Falsafat al-Ula* (*On First Philosophy*) is his main surviving work on the nature of this new discipline. As al-Kindi addresses it to the Caliph al-Mu'tasim bi-llah (r. AD 833–42), it can be dated to the period when he enjoyed success and respect at the 'Abbasid court in Baghdad and was close to the Caliph and his family, before his fall from favour under al-Mutawakkil (r. AD 847–61). It is one of a multitude of philosophical works for which he is known, themes from many of which it echoes and parallels.

Although al-Kindi's position as the earliest philosopher of Islam is generally acknowledged in the title 'philosopher of the Arabs', his precise position with regard to philosophy and theology is a matter of ongoing discussion. This is because his thought reflects elements of both Aristotelian and Neoplatonic philosophy and also rationalist Mu'tazilite theology. But this eclecticism that has been detected in his thinking is maybe symptomatic of his times, when the thought of the ancient world was being introduced into the Islamic empire at the very time that Muslim intellectuals were systematising the teachings of their own scriptural resources. *Fi 'l-Falsafat al-Ula* displays the different currents that interested and influenced al-Kindi as much as any of his known works.

In its present form the treatise comprises four *funun*, 'chapters'. The first does not bear a title, but the titles of all the other three specifically refer to the fact that they are within 'the first part' of the overall work, Chapter 2 is the fullest, '*Al-Fann al-Thani, wa-Huwa al-Juz' al-Awwal fi 'l-Falsafat al-Ula*', (The Second Chapter of the First Part of *On First Philosophy*). These references raise the expectation that there may have been more than one part in the original work, which the concluding sentence of the whole makes clear, '*tamma al-juz' al-awwal min kitab Ya'qub b. Ishaq al-Kindi*', 'The First Part of Ya'qub b. Ishaq al-Kindi's Book Concludes'. A brief paragraph quoted by Ibn Hazm that may well have come from elsewhere in the work confirms there were further parts, though nothing substantial from these has come to light, and there is no indication in the extant part of what may have followed. At the outset this part states that the object of first philosophy is the First Cause, and this is what is accomplished.

The first chapter contains an explanation of philosophy as 'knowledge of the First Truth, who is the cause of all truth', together with a brief account of the analytical method it employs, and also a defence and justification of its seeming independence from revelation. As philosophy in its long history has brought undeniable progress in knowledge of truth, anyone who sincerely seeks truth would be wrong to ignore this valuable source, although the ancient philosophers must be adapted to new conditions. Further, the detractors of philosophy (unidentified, but clearly Muslims who wrongly deny that anyone but themselves possesses knowledge) know little about what they condemn and do this for selfish ends, unaware that philosophy and revelation teach the same things.

In Chapter 2, al-Kindi begins to develop his central theme. After a methodological justification of inference as a means of arriving at truth, he shows that corporeal being cannot be eternal and, thus, that the body of the universe must be finite and necessarily subject to time and motion, which themselves cannot be eternal. In Chapter 3 he goes on to demonstrate that existent things must be brought into being by a cause outside themselves, and then argues that since all phenomenal entities are composite, even though some may loosely be termed 'one', they must have a cause that gives unity to their multiplicity. This cause must be absolutely One. In Chapter 4, al-Kindi inquires into this One, and concludes that it is unlike anything else:

> [It] has neither matter, form, quantity, quality, or relation, is not described by any of the other intelligibles, and has neither genus, specific difference, individual, property, common accident or movement, and it is not described by any of the things which are denied to be one in truth. It is, accordingly, pure and simple unity.

> Derived unities and the multiplicities to which they give rise are ultimately emanations from the One, and can be said to be created. This completes the argument of the first part of the Book.

Al-Kindi presents here a One that is both beyond all conception, though also intimately related to the contingent world. In order to explain it he employs both Aristotelian and Neoplatonic elements, although he does not explore the full consequences of either in this part of his work. In fact, the divinity whom he portrays in largely negative terms is as reconcilable with the God of Islamic revelation as with that of either philosophical tradition.

The text of the *Fi 'l-Falsafat al-Ula* is published in Abu Rida, *Rasa'il*, and also, accompanied by a French translation, in Rashed and Jolivet (1998). Ivry (1974) presents an annotated English translation.

References

Atiyeh (1966), Fakhry (1983: Chapter 3), Netton (1989: Chapter 2).

DAVID THOMAS

FIHRIST

This work (*The Index* or *The Catalogue*), is the main composition of Abu 'l-Faraj Muhammad b. Abi Ya'qub Ishaq al-Warraq, known as al-Nadim, 'the court companion'. (He is called both al-Nadim and Ibn al-Nadim by Muslim authors, and Ibn Abi Usaybi'a uses both names. A warrant for 'al-Nadim' is given by Chester Beatty MS 3315, one of the main authorities for the work, where the title appears as *Kitab al-Fihrist li-'l-Nadim*.) It is an invaluable bibliography of works known up to the late tenth century AD in Baghdad that supplies irreplaceable information about lost writings from earlier times and adds to the picture of fervent intellectual activity in the formative centuries of Islam.

Al-Nadim himself states that he was engaged in the first parts of the *Fihrist* in December AD 987; he probably finished it in the next year or so, though he did not complete every detail, because some items such as dates of birth and death, and some elements in names are occasionally left blank. The fact that he did not supply these subsequently suggests that he died not long after finishing his work (dates between 995 and AD 998 are given by later authors).

As al-Nadim briefly summarises it in his introduction, the *Fihrist* is 'a catalogue of the books of all peoples, Arab and foreign, existing in the language of the Arabs, as well as of their scripts, dealing with various sciences, with accounts of those who composed them and the categories of their authors' and, most valuably, supplying details of their lives and characters. Thus it is effectively a bio-bibliographical dictionary of the major scholars who wrote in Arabic in the first four centuries of Islam. It is divided into ten chapters, *maqalat*, all except the last subdivided into sections, *funun*. The subjects treated in each are as follows:

1. languages, scriptures and the Qur'an;
2. grammar;
3. histories, biographies and genealogies;
4. pre-Islamic and Islamic poetry;
5. theological groups and sects;
6. law schools;
7. philosophy and Greek sciences;
8. 'evening recountals', fables, magic and juggling;
9. doctrines and beliefs of dualist sects and of Indian, Chinese and other sects;
10. alchemy.

These represent both the Islamic and the 'foreign' sciences. A number of the sections are introduced by an explanation of the subject treated within them, frequently in the form of histories of their origin and development. Thus, Chapter I, Section 1 begins with an account of Arabic and other scripts, together with samples of alphabets, Chapter VII, Section 1 begins with an account of Greek philosophy and the way in which it reached the Arabic-speaking world, and Chapter IX, Section 1 begins with a detailed account of the beliefs and practices of the Sabians of Harran. Following these in each section come systematic lists of the major groups that held distinctive views about the subject of the section, and then brief biographical notices of individual authors and the works ascribed to them. As most of these works are no longer extant and many of them are not recorded elsewhere, their titles serve as instructive indications of intellectual and cultural life in the early Islamic centuries.

The *Fihrist* has not survived in any single manuscript, and published editions have had to be reconstructed from a number of authorities. Nevertheless, it is quite clear from al-Nadim's introduction that he conceived the work with the ten-chapter structure outlined previously. On the basis of Istanbul MS Koprulu 1135, however, which contains only the Introduction and Chapters I Section 1, VII, VIII, IX and X, it has been suggested that in addition to the full edition, al-Nadim also published a shorter version that was concerned solely with non-Islamic subjects. In support, it has been pointed out that these particular chapters are more elaborate than the others and less like unadorned bibliographical lists. The existence of such an edition is not attested anywhere else, however, and so whether this abbreviated edition was in fact the work of al-Nadim or some later editor who excerpted what was originally intended as a single edition, remains a matter of debate.

The best edition of the *Fihrist* is Rida-Tajaddud (1971) (this is more complete than that by Flugel (1871–2)). There is an English translation by Dodge (1970).

References

Gibb and Bosworth (1960–2003).

DAVID THOMAS

AL-FIQH AL-AKBAR

This is the title given to a number of summaries of belief that are associated with the great jurisprudents Abu Hanifa and al-Shafi'i, though their true authorship cannot be fixed with any certainty. The title can be taken to mean 'The greater understanding of matters of faith', or more technically 'The supreme religious law'.

The *Fiqh Akbar I* (as it is designated by A. J. Wensinck) is a short summary comprising ten statements about points of belief over which there were open differences within the early Muslim community. In al-Nadim's *Fihrist*, from the tenth century, a *Fiqh Akbar* is ascribed to Abu Hanifa (d. AD 767) and this *Fiqh* is traditionally identified as his work. It certainly fits into the period of his activity, and evidence from the very similar *Fiqh Absa*, which comprises answers on points of religion that can be reliably attributed to him, indicates that it closely reflects his own views. So the *Fiqh Akbar I* can be dated to the first half of the eighth century AD.

This was a period of ferment among Muslim groups, who adopted opposing positions over major questions of Islam that were emerging in debates about the fundamentals of faith and action. The *Fiqh Akbar I* represents a summation of views that temper more extreme attitudes, and advocates some latitude in belief as an advantage and a blessing: Difference of opinion in the community of Islam is a token of divine mercy (Article 7).

The ten articles of this creed, *'aqida*, appear to fall into two groups: Articles 1–6 are general statements about aspects of Islam that state positively what is acceptable within the bounds of orthodoxy, implicitly giving judgements about current points of difference, Articles 8–10, coming after the latitudinarian statement of the boundaries of orthodoxy in Article 7, anathematise those who hold views that patently contradict teachings of the Qur'an.

Closer study of the *Fiqh* shows that it engages fully with the opinions of the major groups active in the first two centuries of Islam. Article 1, for example, can be seen as contradicting the rigorist Khawarij; Article 2 the predestinarian Jabriyya; Article 3 the Qadariyya who supported independent human responsibility; Articles 4 and 5 the supporters of 'Ali and his descendants and the Khawarij. These were all advocating exclusive views, and threatening to divide the community irreparably. Hence, the positive though implicitly critical tone of Article 1: 'We do not consider anyone to be an infidel on account of sin, nor do we deny his faith', which somewhat rebukes those who intolerantly link sinful acts with lack of faith and thus exclude sinners from Islam. Or the recommendation to refrain from hasty judgement in Article 5: 'We leave the question of 'Uthman and 'Ali to Allah, who knows the secret and hidden things', which counsels against dissension between the early Shi'a and their opponents, and tacitly condemns the hasty action of arrogating to humans God's position as judge. These statements are characteristic of the Murji'a.

After Article 6, which ranks piety above intellectual accomplishment, and the general all encompassing statement of Article 7, come three Articles that condemn particular views: Article 8 against those who exclude Moses and

175

Jesus from the line of messengers from God; Article 9 against those who refuse to say where God exactly is; and Article 10 against those who deny knowledge of punishment after death. Each of these contrary positions violates an explicit teaching of the Qur'an and, in declaring these condemnations, the author of the *Fiqh* reveals the boundary of his definition of orthodoxy. Although he allows latitude in discussion of the teachings of the Qur'an, even the intolerant views of the Khawarij, he rejects outright divergence from what it explicitly contains.

Although the *Fiqh Akbar I* is classed among the Islamic creeds, it does not bear the basic features of a creed in that it says nothing direct about the fundamental beliefs of Islam, such as the oneness of God, the apostleship of Muhammad or the Qur'an. It reflects more a mean position between contradictory views, and maintains broad acceptance in the face of mutual anathematisation between hostile groups. Thus, it appears to represent a stage in the development towards orthodoxy rather than the firm statement of what orthodox faith comprises.

The *Fiqh Akbar II* (as Wensinck calls it) is much longer than its counterpart, containing twenty-nine articles mostly of considerable length. It bears traces of the different views about the characterisation of God that emerged in the ninth century AD, such as the statement in Article 4: 'His hand is his quality, without [asking] how, *bila kayfa*. Likewise his wrath and his good pleasure are two of his qualities without [asking] how', which seeks to assert that the Qur'an's depictions of God must be accepted as they are rather than in an allegorical interpretation, without inquiring into the mode of their attribution. This, and such other features as the formula that explains the mode of existence of God's attributes in Article 2, 'from eternity he

knows by virtue of his knowledge, knowledge being an eternal quality', and the reference in Article 6 to acquisition, *kasb*, of acts created by God, are emblematic of the teachings of Abu 'l-Hasan al-Ash'ari (d. AD 935), who set out rational defences of traditional teachings. And so Wensinck connects the *Fiqh* with him, though he goes no further than to say it bears signs of his influence and must therefore have originated no earlier than the tenth century AD. W. M. Watt points to certain features in the creed that show it must date from the late tenth century AD, and also that it bears Hanafi characteristics which could not have come from the defender of Hanbali teachings al-Ash'ari, who was linked with the Shafi'iyya but not the Hanafiyya. Both Wensinck and Watt agree that it should not be dated later than the tenth century AD, because it still reflects differences that were current around the beginning of that century, and lacks the more systematic treatment of points of belief typical of works from a later time. However, this cannot be taken as convincing evidence of a *terminus ad quem*, because it presupposes uniform development in theological thinking throughout the Islamic world. While its Ash'arite features suggest that it cannot be earlier than the tenth century AD, the precise date of its composition must remain an open question.

Wensinck detects some coherent arrangement at the beginning of the *Fiqh Akbar II*. Following the opening statement of faith in Article 1, Articles 2–7 refer to the being and actions of God, and Articles 8–10 continue with statements about the prophets, Muhammad and his successors. After this point, however, the arrangement loses clarity, and articles on the community, observances, eschatology and so on succeed one another haphazardly, with some which are clearly related to earlier ones, for example Articles 22 and 26 which refer to 3 and 6 respectively, occurring at a distance from them.

The *Fiqh Akbar III* is given this title by Wensinck because it bears a direct relation to the *Fiqh Akbar II*. It was traditionally known as the *Fiqh Akbar* of al-Shafiʻi, but far from having any connection with the great jurist it dates from the eleventh century AD, and lists the descriptive statements of a catechism, similar to many composed in later times, rather than the categorical declarations of a creed. Wensinck suggests a date of composition around the beginning of the eleventh century, and identifies its author as an Ashʻarite.

The thirty-three articles of the *Fiqh Akbar III* form a clear progression from the importance of acquiring knowledge through arguments for the existence of God, the being of God, his activity in creating the world, his sending prophets, the response of faith, eschatology and judgement, and ending with the imamate. The latter feature, which has not appeared in the earlier *Fiqhs*, links the *Fiqh Akbar III* with systematic treatises of faith that survive from the tenth century onwards, such as the *Kitab al-Tamhid* of the Ashʻarite Abu Bakr al-Baqillani which concludes with a long discussion on the imamate. This *Fiqh* is more like a summary of the main points of such works than the statements of orthodoxy and condemnations of heresy that are found in earlier credal formulations.

The major work on the *Fiqh Akbar* is Wensinck (1932). This contains translations of the *Fiqh Akbar I* and *Fiqh Akbar II*, and a summary of the *Fiqh Akbar III*.

References

Van Ess (1991–7), Watt (1973).

DAVID THOMAS

FINANCE

See: **Islamic banking**

FIRʻAWN

Pharaoh of Egypt at the time of Moses and Aaron. Depicted as an evil denier of God, he is named over seventy times in the Qurʼan. The focus of the attention to Pharaoh is derived from the Bible, specifically Exodus 1–14. The highlights of that story are all touched upon, including the oppression of the Children of Israel, the birth of Moses, the mission of Moses and Aaron, the hardening of the heart of Pharaoh, Moses' miracles, the plagues, the Exodus, the crossing of the Red Sea and the drowning of Pharaoh. This story is told within the literary patterning of the Qurʼan, not as an overall narrative but as an example of the struggle of the prophets against communities which resisted the message of God, the most extended treatments are Q.7:103–41, Q.20:49–69, Q.26:10–51 and Q.40:23–46. The treatment of Pharaoh is perhaps unique in the sense that the focus is on the resistance of a single person who becomes a symbol of evil. This is a metaphor which has been employed throughout history, with Pharaoh being a political power who resists the implementation of the *shariʻa*. This may especially be seen in the work of the Egyptian Sayyid Qutb in his attitude to modern political leaders.

References

Johns (1990: 143–70).

ANDREW RIPPIN

FIRDAWSI (ABU AL-QASIM MANSUR) (*c.* AD 935–*c.* 1020)

Firdawsi, also spelled Ferdowsi, pseudonym of Abu al-Qasim Mansur (*c.* 935–*c.*

177

1020), Persian poet and author of the Persian national epic, the *Shahnameh*. Little is known of the life of Firdawsi, who was born near Tus, Iran. He began work on his epic around AD 980 and completed it around AD 1010, dedicating the final version to Sultan Mahmud of Ghazna who had acquired a reputation as a patron of the arts, though Firdawsi apparently failed to collect his expected reward. The sources on which the poet drew for his masterwork are not known for certain, but in addition to oral tradition and folklore, they certainly included the prose *Shahnameh* of Abu Mansur and the poetic work of Daqiqi (d. *c.* AD 977), who had already commenced a verse *Shahnameh* on the orders of the Samanid monarch in Bukhara.

Firdawsi's *Shahnameh* itself is divided into fifty chapters of varying length and consists of about 60,000 couplets rhyming in pairs, in a uniform metre. It begins with the creation of the world and the earliest heroes of Iranian antiquity, Guyumart, Hushang and Tahmurath, then continues through the Iranian dynasties in chronological order, beginning with the mythical Pishad dynasty and ending with Yazdagerd III, the last ruler of the Sassanian dynasty before the Arab invasion. The narrative is a mixture of historical fact, myth and legend, usually centred on individual heroes, of whom the Iranian national hero, Rostam, is the most illustrious of all. The overriding theme of the work is the struggle between good and evil, a theme with obvious Zoroastrian overtones which finds expression in the struggle of the settled Iranians against the nomads of central Asia, but the work also includes many romantic scenes and descriptions of nature. Despite its enduring status as the national epic of Iran, the work has frequently been criticised for its monotonous metre and repetitive passages. Also it is compared frequently, if not always favouably, to the classical epics of Homer and Virgil, though the conception of the work is in fact fundamentally different: the poem is essentially a collection of self-contained scenes extending over a long period, loosely strung together to form an epic poem.

The lyric poems sometimes attributed to Firdawsi are of doubtful authenticity, and it has now been shown that the attribution to Firdawsi of the epic poem *Yusof o Zolikha* in particular is mistaken.

References

Arberry (1958: 42–52), Davis (1993), Massé (1935).

PAUL STARKEY

FIRST WORLD WAR (1914–18)

The war engulfing all the major European powers between 1914 and 1918. Western Europe was the principal front, but the conflict soon spilled over. Turkey's alliance with Germany led to its involvement. With the Western Front deadlocked by the end of 1914, Britain and France attacked the Gallipoli Peninsula in February 1915, with the aim of forcing the Bosporus Straits and assaulting Constantinople. The campaign was badly conceived and met stiff Turkish resistance that was commanded by German general, Limon von Sanders, and Mustafa Kemal (later Ataturk). Gallipoli was evacuated in January 1916.

British forces also campaigned in the regions of Sinai, Palestine and Hijaz as well as in Mesopotamia. Turkish resistance was strong. A British-Indian division commanded by Major-General Charles Townshend was besieged and lost at Kut-al-Amara by April 1916, while a relief force under Lt. Gen. Sir Fenton Alymer was repeatedly turned back.

General Murray's Egypt-based army also suffered a serious setback against Turkish forces in Gaza in April 1917. The British liaison officer, T. E. Lawrence, in Hijaz was more successful in encouraging a Hashemite-led Arab rebellion. The arrival of General Sir Edmund Allenby in July 1917 was a turning point, although not until the middle of 1918 were the necessary forces in place. Allenby won major victories at Gaza and Megiddo, and took Jerusalem, Damascus and Aleppo. Arab irregulars reached Damascus, but their hopes of establishing an independent Arab state were dashed. In Mesopotamia, a British army took Baghdad and swept up as far as Mosul. The war ended the Ottoman Empire.

References

Lawrence (1955), Liddell-Hart (1997: 157–82, 269–73, 306–7, 432–40), Perrett (1998: 117, 164, 203–4).

SIMON W. MURDEN

FITNA

'Strife', 'rebellion', referring to any rising against a lawful ruler.

References

Waines (1995: 46–7).

ANDREW J. NEWMAN

FITRA

The word is used to refer to the original and natural state of human beings when they are born into the world. It signifies the manner in which all things are created by God. An Islamic tradition records that: 'Every child is born [a Muslim] in the *fitra*. Its parents make it into a Jew, a Christian, or a Magian'. The implication is that children who grow up to be anything other than Muslims have been deprived of their natural spiritual patrimony. There is no doctrine of original sin in Islam. Children come into the world with their primordial nature unsullied, in short, as natural Muslims, whether or not they are born into a family of believing Muslims, into an Islamic community, or into a society in which Islam is neither known nor recognised.

EDWARD D. A. HULMES

FLYING-MAN ARGUMENT

The flying-man or suspended-man argument is a critical pivot of Ibn Sina's psychology and functions as a proof for the separability and independence of the soul/intellect from the body that prefigures the famous Cartesian *cogito*. This thought experiment that Ibn Sina presented in the *De Anima* of *al-Shifa'* (*The Cure*) and repeated in *al-Isharat wa'l-Tanbihat* (*Pointers and Reminders*) and other works can be interpreted in at least four ways: as a proof for the mind–body dualism, the existence of the soul, the self-awareness of the soul and the substantiality of the soul. The core point made is that the soul exists and that one can be self-aware of this fact without recourse to any empirical observation mediated through physical sensation.

The argument set out in the beginning of the *De anima* is the following. An intelligent individual can imagine the following. Suppose that an individual perfectly formed is suspended in the air but has no sensory perception nor does the substance of the air touch him. He then reflects upon whether he can affirm the existence of his essence, his soul. He can indubitably. He cannot affirm the existence of his body or limbs as he has no sensation of them, and even if he were to imagine them, he would not suppose them to be either part of his essence or an accidental accretion to his essence. What he can affirm (his

179

essence or soul) is thus distinct from what he cannot affirm (his body). Thus, he understands that he is identical to that knowing suspended essence. His soul, and not his body, is his true identity and reality.

Whether this argument may be used to affirm the existence of the self in Ibn Sina is open to question (as indeed is the wider question of whether it makes sense to speak of self rather than soul in pre-modern psychology). What it does affirm is that humans have a core being or essence that is uniquely available and identical to them and can be known indubitably through self-knowledge.

The success of the argument, especially given its Neoplatonic origins in the separability of the soul from the body and the privileging of intellectual intuition and immediate self-knowledge over sensory perception and acquired knowledge, was such that it was continuously cited in psychological works both in medieval scholasticism and in philosophical traditions in the Islamic East.

References

Arnaldez (1972: 341–9), Crabbe (1999), Druart (1988: 27–48), Furlani (1927: 53–72), Galindo-Aguilar (1958: 279–95), Marmura (1986: 384–95), McTighe (1988: 51–4), Nadir (1998).

SAJJAD H. RIZVI

FODIO, SHEHU USUMAN DAN (1754–1817)

In 1804, the learned Fulani theologian and pious Sufi, Shehu (*shaykh*) Usuman dan Fodio (Fodiye), declared a *jihad* against the King of Gobir and the Habe kings of Hausaland, which lasted until 1811. He was born in 1754 and died in 1817. The Arabic for his Hausa name is 'Uthman ibn Fudi. He soon gained the support of disaffected Fulanis. He and his supporters set out to reform the practice of Islam, which had grown lax, so much so that the rulers of Hausaland were accused by the Shehu of being pagans, even though they professed to be Muslims. Usuman dan Fodio claimed that the provisions of Islamic law (*shari'a*) were not being observed. Within the space of a few years, most of Hausaland came under the effective control of the jihadists. In Sokoto, their new capital, they began to reform the administration of the territories they now controlled. Society was henceforth to be regulated in accordance with the *shari'a*. Like reformers in other religious traditions they sought to return to the origins of their religion – to the sources of Islamic belief and polity. From their point of view this involved the purifying of Islam by stripping it of inauthentic historical accretions. The key to this was a return to the days of the first four Rightly Guided Caliphs (*al-Rashidun*), who ruled the Islamic world from the death of the Prophet Muhammad in 632 to the assassination of 'Ali in AD 661. Usuman dan Fodio did not claim to be other than a *mujaddid*, that is to say, a 'renewer' of religion, a forerunner of the messianic figure of *al-mahdi*, 'the rightly guided one'. He and his supporters based their actions on 'the commanding of what is approved and the forbidding of what is disproved'. That which constituted innovation (*bid'a*), namely, that which was not contained in the revelations of the Qur'an, was to be rigorously excluded from the life of society. A puritanical sensibility was transformed into a purifying religious zeal, which began to interfere with long established custom. Music dancing, drumming were all proscribed. In time this was to lead to open opposition to such measures and thus to weaken the course of the reform movement. The reformers insisted on strict adherence to Islamic commercial law, as outlined in the *shari'a*. This was being disregarded by Hausa farmers and traders, who continued to conduct their business according to the rules of the market. The reformers imposed unpopular taxes on cattle and property. Relationships between the sexes had grown lax, regulated less by Islamic principles than by ancient African custom. The reformers demanded the rejection of traditional forms of African tribal polity, which were to be replaced by a universal caliphate on the pattern instituted by the aforementioned Rightly Guided Caliphs. Shehu Usuman established the Sokoto caliphate, the rule of which he left to his brother and his son. After his death in 1817, his son Muhammad Bello gained sole control, became the first caliph of Sokoto, and founded the Fulani empire.

References

Davidson (1977: 267–73), Hiskett (1973), Last (1967: 1–29).

See also: **jihad**, **Sokoto caliphate**.

EDWARD D. A. HULMES

FOOD AND DRINK

'O, you people, eat of that which is lawful and good on earth' (Q.2:168). In Islam there are strict rules about what it is lawful (*halal*) to eat and what is forbidden (*haram*). Swine flesh is forbidden. So too is 'dead meat', that is to say carrion, the flesh of an animal that is not expressly slaughtered for the purpose.

> O, you who believe! Eat of the good things that We have provided for you, and be grateful to God if you truly worship him. He has forbidden you only dead meat, the blood and the flesh of swine, and that on which any other name than that of Allah has been invoked.
>
> (Q.2:172–3)

Interestingly, the next part of the verse quoted here makes a virtue of a necessity, because if no *halal* food is available a Muslim is permitted to take food prepared by others. Scavenging animals are forbidden food. The position with regard to the different species of shellfish is not clear. As scavengers they would appear to be forbidden, but as food from the sea (*al-bahr*) some have pointed to the words of Q.5:96 as legitimising their consumption. Game is *halal*, provided that the words of dedication are uttered when it is shot and its carcass retrieved by a trained dog. It is lawful to eat fish that are caught alive. Consistency in the application of dietary rules is complicated by local custom. Animals are to be ritually slaughtered by a Muslim. First comes a declaration of intent (*niyya*) to perform an act of ritual slaughter. This is followed by the invocation of the Divine name in the formula: 'In the Name of God, God is Most Great', the two 'Names of Mercy', *al-rahman*, *al-rahim*, being omitted. The animal's throat is cut, severing the jugular vein and the windpipe. The blood, which is not acceptable as a food in Islam, must be drained from the animal. In Judaism, the blood is identified with the life force, and is also not to be consumed. With regard to drink, it should be remembered that alcohol in the form of wines and spirits is forbidden. That which inebriates is not permitted, and the same proscription applies in the case of consciousness-altering drugs that are used 'recreationally'. The use of prescribed medical drugs is not forbidden.

References

Brown and Palmer (1987: 210–16), al-Khaysi (1996).

See also: **alcohol**, **sacrifice**.

EDWARD D. A. HULMES

FORTY HADITH

In addition to the six collections of *hadith* made in the ninth century AD that gradually came to be recognised as the most reliable compilations of the Prophet's sayings and actions, Muslims made numerous other collections both earlier and later than these. A favourite form was the selection, and among these the type known as the *Arba'in*, '*The Forty*' was extremely popular. One of the best known and most widely read was al-Nawawi's *Kitab al-Arba'in*, which appeared in the thirteenth century AD. The Syrian scholar Muhyiddin Abu Zakariyya' Yahya b. Sharaf al-Nawawi (AD 1233–77) in his comparatively brief life composed authoritative works on a number of subjects, including jurisprudence, *hadith*, Arabic grammar and mysticism. Among many works for which he is remembered, and upon which later authors commentated, is his *Kitab al-Arba'in*. Curiously, the work comprises forty-two prophetic sayings, together with ascriptions to their original sources and al-Nawawi's own comments on them.

In a brief preface al-Nawawi explains his inspiration and purpose: 'Whoever memorises and preserves for my people forty *hadiths* relating to their religion, Allah will resurrect him on the Day of Judgement in the company of jurists and religious scholars'. He goes on to say that he intends his collection to be an essential summary of the faith, almost a primer in prophetic spirituality, for he limits himself to the *sahih hadiths* alone, with the majority from al-Bukhari and Muslim, and, whereas earlier selections had chosen sayings about a single category of belief or action, he himself has decided to cover all aspects of Islam: 'Each of these *hadiths* is a major fundamental of religion, described by the scholars as "a pivot of Islam", or "half of Islam" or a third or the like'. Furthermore, he has only included the text, *matn*, of each *hadith* and the Companion who acts as its guarantor, 'in order to make memorising them easier and to make the benefit of them wider'. For 'every person wishing to attain the Hereafter should become acquainted, *ya'rifu*, with these *hadiths*'.

The *hadiths* in the selection include one *hadith qudsi* (no. 24), and twelve from sources other than al-Bukhari and Muslim. They generally focus on individual belief and action, for example: 'Part of someone's being a good Muslim is his leaving alone that which does not concern him' (No. 12); 'None of you believes until his inclination is in accordance with what I have brought' (No. 41), and there are many reminders about God's pervasive awareness of what individuals do: 'Fear Allah wherever you are, and follow up a bad deed with a good one and it will wipe it out, and behave well towards people' (No. 18); 'Allah the Almighty has said: O son of Adam, so long as you call upon me and ask of me, I shall forgive you for what you have done, and I shall not mind' (No. 42 in part).

The last provides a comforting conclusion to the collection. Not all the *hadiths* are as pithy as these, but they each contain some striking phrase, image or short sentence that can easily be remembered. In fact, this quality may have governed al-Nawawi's choice of the particular *hadiths* as much as considerations about the reliability of their derivation.

The selection has been published many times. Recent editions are by Ibrahim and Johnson-Davies (1976) and Zarabozo (1999). These both contain the texts of the *hadiths* and al-Nawawi's introduction in Arabic and English, in the latter accompanied by an extensive commentary by the editor. Pouzat (1982) contains the full text of the *Arba'in*, including al-Nawawi's notes, in Arabic and French.

DAVID THOMAS

FREE WILL AND PREDESTINATION

One of the five key elements of Mu'tazilite doctrine was belief in the free will of man based itself on the belief in the justice (*'adl*) of Allah, that nothing could occur that Allah opposed and that Allah would not impose Evil but, having willed Evil to exist, allows man to choose between Good and Evil acts but stipulates the price for such decisions as salvation or damnation. On the two extremes, the Qadariyya maintained man was absolutely a free actor whereas the Jabariyya held man's acts were completely predetermined. Ultimately Ash'arism became the dominant school of Sunni theology. Initially al-Ash'ari (d.941 or 945) himself was a Mu'tazilite but ultimately his methodology combined aspects of theology based on revelation and reason. Ash'arism itself maintained that man was free to make choices based on which he would consigned to Heaven or Hell but, although such choices are based on combinations of cause and effect ultimately, Allah knows what is to happen. Ash'aris maintain that one's sins could even be forgiven in Hell and that, although it was possible, Allah would not send a pious man to hell, and that Allah can change a man's heart. However, man is absolutely free only to choose to accept or reject the reality of Allah.

References

Fakhry (1983: 43–50), Rahman (1979: 85–6), Watt (1973: 4–5, 82, 85, 94, 97–8, 117, 116, 118, 189, 234–8).

See also: **'adl**; **attributes of God; judgement on the *yawm al-qiyama***

ANDREW J. NEWMAN

FREEDOM

'Hurriya' in Arabic. Following the French Revolution in 1789, contemporary Muslim writers at first equated Western notions of 'civil', 'political' and especially individual freedom and liberty, with anarchy and licentiousness. As key Western political documents became available in translation over the nineteenth century, such concepts were identified with 'the rule of law' and certain constitutional arrangements and, especially, parliamentarian institutions. The Egyptian Rifa'a al-Tahtawi (d. 1873), who lived in Paris from 1826 to 1831, argued the aims of such institutions were compatible with classical Islamic concepts of justice, especially as these focused on preventing the ruler from undertaking arbitrary acts against a subject. Al-Tahtawi limited himself to addressing socio-economic and legal rights, not the 'political' rights of the individual *per se*. Subsequent Middle Eastern experiments with consultative councils and parliaments in fact only enhanced the authority of the state institutions. In the late 1860s and 1870s the Young Ottomans identified 'freedom' with the establishment of political sovereignty in the people and the State's respect for individual political rights, with such institutions as parliaments acting to safeguarding such rights as freedom of expression and worship. In the same period also some Arab authors living in Ottoman territory also addressed such issues. The Egyptian Ahmad Lutfi al-Sayyid (d. 1963) addressed issues of individual freedom and their being safeguarded by fixed arrangements and institutions, at the same time rejecting Arab nationalism and pan-Islamism in favour of emphasis on the nation-state and its freedom from foreign rule and domestic absolutism. In the post-colonial period, however, freedom has mainly been understood more in the context of freedom of the nation-state from foreign political, economic and cultural dominance than in terms of individual rights, although the Islamic Republic of Iran has recently witnessed very public disputes over such issues as freedom of the press and personal expression.

References

Hourani ((1970:) esp 67–8, 170–1).

See also: **Marxism and Islam; modernity; secularism; socialism**

ANDREW J. NEWMAN

FRIDAY SERMON IN THE MOSQUE

See: *khutba*

FULANI EMPIRE

See: **Fodio, Shehu Usuman dan**

FUNDAMENTALISM

Religious 'fundamentalism' is routinely associated with a range of character-istics including the absolute authority of scripture and an active, indeed pur-itanical, approach to the regulation of individual lifestyles. At the same time, 'fundamentalists' are generally seen as exhibiting a commitment to social transformation, although such an impulse may involve a distancing from, as well as attempts to take control of, the established political order.

Shepard shows that the term 'funda-mentalism' was originally applied to a conservative, evangelical brand of Pro-testant Christianity determined to fight the liberal and modernist rationalism undermining the truth claims of doc-trines such as the Inerrancy of Scripture and the Virgin Birth. Today, however, 'fundamentalism' is variously used to characterise individuals and movements across the world's religions and beyond. Some such as Parekh would confine fundamentalism to religions 'of the book' such as Judaism, Christianity and Islam, while others such as Bhatt include in their analysis the so-called 'Hindu nationalism' evident in modern Indian politics. Others still, such as Akhtar, have even spoken of 'liberal fundamentalism' in contexts where the public recognition of Muslim minorities in the West has provoked an uncompromising reaction to the seeming de-secularisation of public space. However, it must be acknowl-edged that religious believers themselves rarely use the term 'fundamentalism' and commentators have long argued that it perpetuates stereotypes, not least in the Western media. As Parekh has noted, 'like the term terrorism the term fundamentalism is increasingly becom-ing a polemical hand-grenade to be thrown at those we detest and fear and defeat with a clear conscience' (1992: 9).

Scholars working outside Islamic Studies such as Gray, Bhatt and others often view 'Islamic fundamentalism' as essentially a product of modernity, an utopian ideology of liberation and pur-ity which both mimics, and articulates alternatives to, Western '-isms'. While usefully illuminating contemporary manifestations of the phenomenon, in particular 'Islamism' (see later), more longstanding patterns of 'fundamentalist' revival can also be discerned in pre-modern Islam. Understood by Calder and Rippin, for example, as a timeless attempt to 'contract' the 'expansive' tendency of tradition, 'fundamentalism' can be seen as a pervasive theme in Islamic history from the early secessio-nists, the Khawarij, to pre-modern movements such as Wahhabism. What perhaps distinguishes modern expressions from those of previous periods is that the emphasis on 'contraction' over 'expansion', say, in the conservative 'Salafism' of the Syrian scholar, Rashid Rida (1865–1935), has increasingly moved from the margins towards the centre of Islamic discourse. For Rahman, modernists and traditionalists alike have been forced to respond to – and even to mimic – 'fundamentalist' arguments such is the power of their appeal to 'authenticity'.

Revivalism in Islam has flourished during times of decline, with a perceived loss of religious and moral 'purity' often linked to social and political crisis. In both pre-modern and modern times the twin targets of such revivalists have been (i) the rigidity of the *'ulama'* and the legal schools (where *taqlid* or imitation of previous generations eventually leads to the stagnation of tradition); and (ii) the corruption associated with such 'un-Islamic' innovation (*bid'a*) as visitation at Sufi saints' tombs, intercession and participation in ecstatic rituals. By contrast, strategies of revival have suggested a 'return' to the scriptural 'simplicity' of the Qur'an, *sunna* and the practice of *al-salaf al-salih* (the pious ancestors of the generation after Muhammad). To a greater or lesser extent this has been coupled with *ijtihad* (personal 'effort' in interpretation on matters not covered by the Qur'an or *sunna*), *hijra* (migration) from 'unbelievers' and *jihad*, interior but also more exterior 'struggles' with the self and with society, the latter sometimes culminating in armed political activism.

Since the so-called 'Islamic resurgence' of the 1970s, and especially the Iranian revolution of 1979, 'fundamentalism' has been most often associated with the modern ideology of political Islam or 'Islamism'. Rather than 'modernising' Islam like the liberals of colonial times

they would eventually eclipse, since the early twentieth century Islamists such as Hasan al-Banna' (d. 1949) in Egypt and Sayyid Abul-A'la al-Mawdudi (d. 1979) in the Indian subcontinent have refuted any notion of a Western 'copyright' on modernity. Instead, they have appropriated and 'Islamised' it, 'ideologising religion' and drawing as appropriate on modern forms of political organisation and communications technology. With post-colonial independence and the subsequent failure of corrupt and authoritarian secular-nationalist regimes to deliver 'earthly utopias' to the Muslim masses, Islamists sought to fill the vacuum in political legitimacy with appeals to more 'indigenous' forms of cultural nationalism and identity. While Kemalists and Nasserists looked 'outside' either to capitalism or socialism for inspiration, incorporating tame 'statist' Islamic scholars and repressing Islamist activists as necessary, Islamists themselves typically called for an (equally authoritarian and utopian) Islamic state, *shari'a* alone being sufficient to regulate public life. Kepel and others argue that this appeal to religious certainty has been attractive to young, secularly and especially technically educated, lower middle-class constituencies. In any case, different methodologies have been employed by activists in pursuit of the Islamic state, with 'reformists' having sought power through an accommodation to the established political process, and 'radical revolutionaries' having sanctioned armed uprising.

In the mid-1980s and 1990s, given irreducible social, economic and political realities, 'reforming' elements within Islamist movements such as al-Ikhwan al-Muslimun are widely understood to have institutionalised within the mainstream of nascent Muslim civil societies. Burgat, for example, maintains that reformism's 'fundamentalist core' has been transformed and is embracing much broader and re-intellectualised dynamics in the reconstruction of Muslim identity. Islamists are being credited with fostering some of the conditions necessary for 'democratisation' by bringing previously excluded groups into the political process. However, as Roy suggests, this accommodation has also, in part, created the space for ideologically more conservative but politically more radical 'neo-fundamentalists', including deterritorialised supranational militant *jihadi* Wahhabis, to take up a global religious war against all 'unbelievers'.

References

Akhtar (1989), Bhatt (1997), Burgat (2003), Calder (1993), Gray (2003), Kepel (1994), Parekh (1992), Rahman (1979), Rippin (2005), Roy (n.d.), Sayyid (2003), Shepherd (1987).

See also: **Wahhabism**

SEÁN MCLOUGHLIN

FUNERAL RITES AND PRAYERS

See: **death and burial**

FUQAHA' (sing. *faqih*)

'Legist', specifically someone with knowledge of religious law (*shari'a*) and its canonical derivations (*ahkam* or *furu'*). The term is also used in Twelver Shi'a law to refer to the scholar delegated to assume duties and responsibilities of the Imam during the latter's absence.

References

Waines (1995: 65, 74, 281).

See also: *ghayba*; *mujtahid*

ANDREW J. NEWMAN

FUSUS AL-HIKAM

This allusive and often cryptic work is one of the most important writings of the Andalusian mystic Muhyi 'l-Din Muhammad b. 'Ali b. Muhammad Ibn al-'Arabi (AD 1165–1240). The title has been translated as *The Gems of Wisdom*, *The Bezels of Wisdom* and *The Seals of Wisdom*, though since the contents of the book concern the human bearers of divine knowledge who can be compared with the precious metal setting of a ring that holds the gemstone, the translation *The Settings of Wisdom* is as apt as any.

Ibn 'Arabi (he is often referred to in this abbreviated form) himself explains the genesis of the book at its beginning: 'I saw the Apostle of God in a visitation granted to me during the last ten days of the month of Muharram in the year 627 [AD 1230], in the city of Damascus. He had in his hand a book and he said to me, "This is the *Kitab Fusus al-Hikam*: take it and bring it to men that they might benefit from it"'. The work is thus a product of Ibn 'Arabi's mature years, and has often been seen as a summation of his major teachings, especially those in the much larger *Futuhat al-Makkiyya*, which is mentioned twice in the *Fusus*. Ibn 'Arabi's explanation of its origin uncompromisingly declares that he regards it as a distillation of wisdom from the highest source, and devotees of Islamic mysticism have always looked on it as one of the major works from 'the greatest master', al-Shaykh al-Akbar.

Following the brief preface which explains the book's origin are twenty-seven chapters named after particular individuals, the title of each indicating that it deals with a different aspect of wisdom associated with that figure, though Ibn 'Arabi does not explain why he chooses this number or why each is associated with the particular form of wisdom he is. In part the choice can be explained on Qur'anic grounds, as twenty-five are prophets who appear there, but Seth, Shith, the son of Adam, and Khalid Ibn Sinan, who is mentioned in a *hadith*, are not, while two Qur'anic prophets, Dhu 'l-Kifl (usually identified as Ezekiel) and Alyasa' (Elisha) do not appear among Ibn 'Arabi's names.

This is difficult to account for entirely, as is the order in which the prophets in their chapters appear. The progression from Adam, Seth, Noah and Enoch, Idris, through Abraham, Isaac, Ishmael, Jacob and Joseph generally follows an order of genealogy. But later, after Hud, Saleh, Shu'ayb and Lot, the order of Ezra, Jesus, Solomon, David, Jonah, John, Zakariyya, Elias, Luqman, Aaron, Moses and Khalid, before the culmination in Muhammad, seems arbitrary.

It has been conjectured that the number 27 is intended to correspond with the number of named prophets in the Qur'an, and is also the same as the traditional date in Ramadan of the *Laylat al-Qadr*, the Night of Power, when the first revelation was sent down to the Prophet Muhammad (Chodkiewicz 1993: 86–7). This is attractive, given that Ibn 'Arabi says he received the vision from which the book originated in the last ten days of Ramadan, and suggests that he may have in mind the familiar Islamic idea that the line of prophets together imparts a complete compendium of the aspects of knowledge given as inspiration from God. But it still does not explain the substitution of the two prophets, and cannot be securely linked with the Night of Power when the *hadiths* state that this could be any of the odd nights at the end of the fasting month. Ibn 'Arabi's reason for choosing this number, or indeed his reason for associating some sages with a particular aspect of wisdom, remains enigmatic.

Ibn 'Arabi is not a systematic teacher in a conventional sense, and so the progression of teachings in each chapter is not always immediately obvious. To take a few examples, in the chapter on Abraham he focuses on the theme of mutual penetration in the relation between God and the prophet, and enlarges this to discourse on the relation between God and the contingent order, suggesting a mutuality that seems to strain the traditionally maintained distinction between the two:

> He praises me and I praise Him,
> He worships me and I worship Him.
> In my existence (*hal*) I affirm Him,
> And in my essence (*al-a'yan*) I deny him.

All this arises from the title of Abraham as *khalil Allah*, 'friend of God', which Ibn 'Arabi relates to the meaning of its root verbal form *khalla* as 'to pierce', 'to transfix', and builds his portrayal of the wisdoms of rapturous love, *hikma muyhaymiyya*, on that.

In the chapter on Jesus, Ibn 'Arabi focuses on the concept of spirit, not only as this is related to Jesus himself and his ability to heal and restore to life, but also as it refers to revival from spiritual death by imparting knowledge and the creation of the universe as a manifestation of the breath of God:

> All is essentially in the Breath,
> As light is, in essence, in the dark before dawn.
> Knowledge by proof
> Is like the emergence of daylight to one half asleep.

He concludes with a consideration of the distinction between God and Jesus and the relationship between them as Master and servant. This arises from the resonances of the word *ruh*, spirit, and its relation to the concepts of blowing, impregnating and enunciating, all of which appear in the chapter.

A key to understanding is that the discourse on each figure very often involves close exegesis of the teachings about him in the Qur'an. This provides a first step in attempting to understand the rich fusion of themes from his own thought and that of others that Ibn 'Arabi imparts in his reflections on the various facets of prophethood, and the manner in which these reflect the divine light.

A number of commentaries on the *Fusus* have been written over the centuries, among the most notable being those by 'Abd al-Razzaq al-Kashani (d. AD 1335), Dawud Qaysari (d. AD 1350) and 'Abd al-Ghani al-Nabulusi (d. 1731).

The standard edition of the *Fusus al-Hikam* is by 'Afifi (1946). There is a partial translation by Burckhardt (1975) (translated into English from the French original by A. Culme-Seymour), and a full translation by Austin (1980). Chodkiewicz (1993) discusses aspects of the book's meaning and significance.

DAVID THOMAS

AL-FUTUHAT AL-MAKKIYYA

This is the major work of the Andalusian Sufi Muhyi 'l-Din Abu 'Abdallah Muhammad Ibn al-'Arabi (AD 1165–1240) and, together with his *Fusus al-Hikam*, which repeats most of its ideas in summary form, the most important source of his thought. Its title, which can be translated as 'The Meccan Illuminations', refers to its historical origins and the experiences that led to its conception.

Ibn 'Arabi (his name is often given in this shortened form) made his first pilgrimage to Mecca in AD 1202. Almost immediately he began writing the *Futuhat*, and continued with it until AD 1231 (as is attested in one early manuscript). Three years later in AD 1234 he began a revised version, and completed it in

AD 1238, two years before his death. This is a greatly expanded edition of the earlier, though it closely follows the structure that Ibn 'Arabi outlines in the Introduction to the first version, which he wrote in AD 1202. Both versions circulated in subsequent centuries, though modern editions generally are of the later revised version.

During the two years of his first visit to Mecca, Ibn 'Arabi claimed to receive many visions and dreams. These presumably form the basis of the *Futuhat*, because he himself denies any part in its composition (though he says the same about the *Fusus* and other works): 'I have not written a single letter of this book other than under the influence of divine dictation, sovereign recital and spiritual exhalation into the heart of my being'. And it was to these overwhelming disclosures (another possible interpretation of the term *Futuhat*) that he attributed the abrupt changes in the subject matter of the work. In fact, he rather audaciously compared the fragmentary character of much of the discourse in the work with that of the Qur'an itself.

Ibn 'Arabi divides the *Futuhat* into 560 chapters, *abwab*, arranged in six sections, *fusul*, preceded by a prologue and introduction. Together they comprise a vast and, it is often admitted, difficult compendium of ideas about his insights into esoteric knowledge of the relationship between God and the cosmos and their mutual participation in being.

As though aware of this complexity, Ibn 'Arabi explains in the Introduction the different kinds of knowledge, and defends the 'knowledge of secrets' as the highest: 'it is knowledge of "the inbreathing of the Holy Spirit in the heart", and it is peculiar to prophets and saints'. As such, it should be recognised as superior to intellectual knowledge, and those who impart it should be respected as truthful and infallible. It compels the assent of many more faculties than the intellect alone, and it should not be judged by the criterion of theology, because it is vastly superior in both form and content. In short, Ibn 'Arabi suggests that the teachings he gives here should be humbly accepted as they are rather than being subjected to analysis based upon limited human perceptions.

The 560 chapters of the *Futuhat* combine a host of themes, in which Ibn 'Arabi demonstrates the relationship between his 'knowledge of secrets', human reason and the teachings of the Qur'an and *hadith* of the Prophet. In the seventy-three chapters of the first section, *Fasl al-Ma'arif*, 'Understandings', he treats the metaphysical framework of his thought. Then in the second section, *Fasl al-Mu'amalat*, 'Conduct', in 116 chapters, he shows how each of the 'stations', *maqamat*, of Sufi spiritual advancement must be transcended and left behind if progress is to be real and truth is to be found. Thus, *dhikr*, the remembering of God, must be abandoned because in itself it implies a distinction between the one remembering and the One remembered, and the initiate must move to a point at which this distinction ceases.

In the third section, *Fasl al-Ahwal*, 'States', in eighty chapters, he treats the spiritual states of Sufi experience and shows that while these may be taken as external signs of advancement in holiness on the part of the practitioner, in themselves they are not permanent goals, unlike true knowledge of the One. In the fourth section, *Fasl al-Manazil*, 'Places of descent', in 114 chapters, he discourses on the points of meeting between the human and divine realised through the effects of worship on both the worshipper and the Worshipped. In the fifth section, *Fasl al-Munasalat*, 'Encounters', in seventy-eight chapters,

he explains the successive 'meetings' between God and the human as he follows the path of realisation and increasingly perceives more of the reality of the divine being. Then finally in the sixth section, *Fasl al-Maqamat*, 'Stations', in ninety-nine chapters, he explains the spiritual regions through which the aspirant passes and the knowledge and 'states' appropriate to each. He devotes a large part of this section to the 'poles', *aqtab*, the individual saints and mystics who have embodied the qualities of each station. The last three chapters of the section, on the divine names, 'secrets', and practical advice for the mystical practitioner, bring the *Futuhat* to a conclusion.

The complexity of this progression, and of the discourse in each chapter, should not be understated. A hint of this may be given in a brief summary of Chapter 317 'Concerning the True Knowledge of the Waystation of Trial and its Blessings', from *Fasl al-Manazil*. Ibn 'Arabi begins by touching on one of the major themes of the *Futuhat*, and of his thought in general, the close relationship between God and the cosmos, in which through his manifestation of his light it is held in being. The life of humans is endowed by the spirit within them, and when this departs their bodies die, though these departed spirits inhabit intermediary *barzakh* forms until they are reunited with the bodies at the general resurrection. There is, however, another life in human and other bodies, not endowed by their spirits, but intrinsic within them, through which 'they glorify their Lord constantly, whether or not their spirits are within them', and derived from God's own self-disclosure to them. But while bodies are aware of this, the minds of humans can only know it by reflection and reasoning (angels and *jinn* are in a similar position). This is a mercy from God, so that they have

189

some defence for not having awareness of God and for transgressing his injunction to know him.

Thus God 'is the spirit of the cosmos', and the cosmos is related to God in the same way that the human body is to the spirit that controls it. And through both God's self-disclosure to the bodies of humans, which is not immediately manifest, and the human's potential as a living being to know God, 'there is nothing in what exists, *wujud*, save God, his names, and his acts'. He has given humans the opportunity to perceive him, though there are waverers and the mistaken who do not.

In a word, the world is like a shadow play in which the audience believes the characters act by themselves, though the discerning know that they are moved by the operator: 'God has set this up as a likeness for his servants, in order that they might take heed and come to know that the cosmos is related to God just as these forms are related to their mover, and that the screen is the veil of the mystery of destiny'. And just as the narrator sets the scene at the beginning and describes the play to come, so Adam appeared at the beginning of creation, to give the true meaning of what came after.

In this relatively short chapter of the *Futuhat* the richness of themes and also their disturbing elusiveness is evident. The dominant idea of God's pervasive presence in the phenomenal reality (Ibn 'Arabi's followers would identify this by the term *wahdat al-wujud*, 'unity of being', though he himself did not employ it) repeatedly comes to the fore, to the extent that it almost suppresses the declared subject of the chapter, human testing, which can be discerned as the imposed duty to perceive God. And at the end with the fleeting reference to Adam is an allusion to another favourite theme of Ibn 'Arabi, that of the Perfect Man, of whom all the prophets were instances and supremely Muhammad himself. Further, the whole argument is studded, and to some extent linked together, by quotations from the Qur'an and explanations of them, given as part of the ongoing discussion and fully integrated within it. Ibn 'Arabi is clearly involved in a form of spiritual discourse that has little direct relation to the systematic exposition of *kalam* texts, but speaks to the imagination and the heart as much as to the mind.

Maybe because it is so voluminous, the *Futuhat* did not attract the same attention from commentators in the Ibn 'Arabi tradition as his much briefer *Fusus al-Hikam*. It remains a work that deserves study and explication in order to make it accessible and its discursive insights beneficial to students of spiritual truth.

The *Futuhat al-Makkiyya* is available in an edition published in Cairo, 1911, in four volumes. A new edition, expected to comprise thirty-seven volumes of 500 pages each, has been in preparation since 1972, edited by O. Yahya. Extracts from a number of its chapters have been published in French and English, the fullest being Chodkiewicz (1988). There are further translations (including one of Chapter 317, which were used for this summary) and studies in Hirtenstein and Tiernan (1993).

DAVID THOMAS

G

GALEN (*JALINUS,* CLAUDIUS GALENUS, *c.* AD 130–200)

Graeco-Roman physician, surgeon and author, who adopted, developed and applied the medical teachings of his celebrated Greek predecessor, Hippocrates. Galen was born to Greek parents in Pergamum in Asia Minor. Translated into Arabic, his works were soon absorbed by Arab medical practitioners. Thanks to the efforts of the translators, more of Galen's estimated 500 treatises on aspects of medicine and philosophy are available in Arabic than in the original Greek. One of the most celebrated of the Arab translators of scientific treatises from the Greek was the Baghdad physician and Nestorian Christian, Hunayn b. Ishaq (*c.* AD 808–73).

Galen served in Pergamum as a surgeon in the school of gladiators. From the middle of the second century AD he lived in Rome, where he was appointed physician to the emperor Marcus Aur-elius (AD 121–80). For over 1,000 years his authority was virtually undisputed in medical theory and practice. Once they were translated into Latin, his treatises were used widely for medical education in the new European universities. He considered that the study of anatomy was the basis of medical knowledge and advocated students to use dissection as the means of acquiring such knowledge. Hampered by the prevailing objections to the dissection of human cadavers, he turned to the bodies of monkeys and other animals. Galen is also remembered for notable work on the circulation of the blood, the brain, the nervous system, the spinal cord, and for his use of the pulse for diagnostic purposes.

References

Mostyn and Hourani (1988: 270–2), Schacht and Bosworth (1979: 430–32).

See also: **Hippocrates (*Buqrat*); Ibn Sina, Abu 'Ali al-Husayn (Avicenna); medicine** and pharmacology; al-Razi, Abu Bakr Muhammad Ibn Zakariyya

EDWARD D. A. HULMES

GAMBLING (*MAYSIR*)

The word *maysir* is derived from the verb *yasira* ('to be easy'). It is found in the Q.2:219 and Q.5:90, where gambling (along with the consumption of wine and the worship of idols) is specifically forbidden. The word originally referred to an ancient game, played in pre-Islamic Arabia, in which numbered arrows stripped of their heads and feathers were used for the casting of lots for unequal pieces of a slaughtered animal. In later years the word came to refer to any activity that involved the use of dice or participation in other games of chance. In some cases, games such as backgammon and chess fell under the general interdict on gambling. Despite the Islamic proscription of gambling, however, games of chance are not unknown in Islamic communities, where various kinds of lottery (*ya nasib*) and other forms of betting are to be found. Such diversions may exist in theory to accommodate the foibles of non-Muslim residents and visitors. Responsibility for the incidence of gambling in societies where it is proscribed by Islam is sometimes attributed – disingenuously, it may be thought – to the influence of European colonialists.

References

Gibb (1955: 58), Hitti (1973: 87–108).

EDWARD D. A. HULMES

GARDENS, ISLAMIC

Several Arabic words are used to express the idea of a 'garden'. Among these are *bustan* (orchard), *hadiqa*, *junayna* (little garden), *rawda* (a word suggesting 'taming' by cultivation). The term *janna* is used specifically of the 'Garden' to which faithful Muslims hope to progress after their life on earth is over and they are judged worthy of *Paradise*. In the seventh century AD, Muslim Arabs began to capture territory in Asia Minor and Egypt before moving westwards across the North African littoral as far as Spain. They took with them memories of the gardens they had known in Byzantium, the Fertile Crescent and Persia. For those who had endured the rigours of the desert, water was a special luxury so it is not surprising that efforts were made to provide the enclosed space of a garden with fountains and shallow cement-based channels so that the sounds and the cooling influence of flowing water could soothe the spirit. These pools (often rectangular) and channels were often painted blue to give an impression of depth. Feelings of spaciousness were enhanced under the wide canopy of the sky. In the fourteenth century, the construction of gardens reached a peak of elegance. It is said that there were some 50,000 private gardens in Spain during the Moorish Caliphate of Cordoba. A typically Moorish house was built facing inwards to a patio of simple uncluttered proportions and furnishing. The gardens of the Alhambra Palace in Granada were widely renowned. So, too, were the gardens of the Royal Palace in Isfahan. Systems of irrigation had to be designed, which ensured not only a regulated supply of moisture for flowers, plants and trees but also adequate drainage to avoid water-logging. Screens woven with floral designs were often erected temporarily to afford shelter from the heat of the sun. Deer and game birds were reared in gardens more like parks. Their presence was decorative but they were not always safe from the hunter. In Seville in the twelfth century AD

Abu Zakariya' Yahya ibn-Muhammad ibn al-'Awwam wrote a manual on 'agriculture' with the title *Kitab al-Filaha* which, in view of its contents, might well be translated as *The Book of Gardening*.

Islamic art, of which the garden may be said to be a practical form, has developed within the framework of a general Islamic prohibition, which forbids the representation of human beings and other living creatures. Exceptions in the form of miniatures, for example, can be found, but the principle remains. The proscription accounts for the use of geometrical patterns, not only in the architecture of Islamic buildings but in the design of an Islamic garden. The variety and intricacy of flowers, petals, leaves and other kinds of vegetation have inspired such designs. In the course of time, trees gave shelter from the heat of the sun and from the seasonal hot winds. The environment of the larger mosques, classically, is a place where these amenities are to be found, not merely for ritual ablution but for the delight of worshippers and visitors.

References

Arberry (1953: 259–91), Hitti (1973: 575–6), Lord (1979).

See also: **Cordoba; Granada; irrigation**

EDWARD D. A. HULMES

GHADIR AL-KHUMM

During the rule of the twenty-third 'Abbasid caliph, al-Muti' (AD 946–74), the anniversary of the death of al-Husayn on 10 Muharram was firmly established for Shi'i Muslims as a time of public mourning. So, too, was the celebration of the day on which the Prophet Muhammad was believed to have designated 'Ali ibn abi Talib as his successor (*khalifa*). The date chosen for this celebration was 18 Dhu'l-Hijja. According to Shi'i tradition, it was near the *ghadir al-khumm,* a brook between Mecca and Medina, that the Prophet is reported to have said, 'Of whomsoever I am lord, 'Ali is his lord also ... Be Thou, O God, the supporter of whoever supports 'Ali and the enemy of whoever opposes him'. The event is said to have taken place after the Prophet had performed the rites of his Farewell Pilgrimage to Mecca in AD 632. Together with a large number of Muslims he was returning to Medina, when he stopped the caravan, improvised a pulpit and gave the address that included the quoted words.

References

Momen (1985: 15, 82, 143, 239).

EDWARD D. A. HULMES

GHANA

The ancient kingdom of Ghana, with its capital at Kumbi Saleh situated to the west of the great bend of the river Niger, lay astride the trans-Saharan caravan routes. The kingdom flourished in northwest Africa between the sixth and the thirteenth centuries. It was founded by the Soninke peoples. Life in eleventh-century AD Ghana was portrayed by the Arab geographer al-Bakri, who described a Ghanaian city that was built of stone and wood, not mud. It was divided into a Muslim quarter and a non-Muslim quarter. Its ruler was a Soninke animist, many of whose officials and advisers were Muslims. The Muslims took part in court life but were free to pursue their own Islamic way of life without having to join in polytheistic ritual and worship. The two groups lived apart but they appear to have associated amicably in the pursuit of commercial interests in the extensive operations of the caravan trade, which transported goods – salt, gold and eventually slaves – to the Mediterranean littoral and Egypt in the north and north-east, and south to the coast of West Africa. Like the empire of Mali which followed its demise, the kingdom of Ghana was built up on the prosperity derived from the exaction of local tribute and from trade. Ancient Ghana reached the pinnacle of its power and prestige in the eleventh century AD, when its territory extended to include parts of present-day Senegal, Mauritania and Mali. Internal divisions and an Almoravid invasion in 1076/7 contributed to Ghana's decline. The reforming zeal of the Almoravids (Arabic *al-murabitun*, 'the people of the monastery fortress') led to the conversion of many people in the kingdom of Ghana to Islam. Historians are not yet decided about the timing of Ghanaian conversions to Islam, however. The Almoravids may have encouraged further peaceful conversions in an area in which the profession of Islam was already common. Further conflicts with marauding Berber tribes of the Sahara led to the disintegration and collapse of the kingdom of Ghana in the thirteenth century. Much of its former territory was integrated into the empire of Mali. In pre-colonial times what is now the republic of Ghana consisted of a number of independent kingdoms including Gonja and Dagomba.

The first European fort on the West coast of Africa had been built in 1482 by the Portuguese at Elmina. Intense competition for trade in African gold and African slaves began. This trade involved the Portuguese, the Spanish, the French, the Dutch, the Danes, the Swedes, and the British. In return for the gold shipped to Europe and the slaves shipped to the Americas, European merchant venturers supplied their African contacts with a range of goods including alcohol and guns. The nineteenth century saw the decline and the eventual abolition of the slave trade. The Ashanti (Asante) began to dominate the interior some time before the thirteenth century, when Akan peoples migrated into forest belts of present-day Ghana and established small states near modern Kumasi. By the late seventeenth century, these states had been brought together by members of the Oyoko clan into the Ashanti Confederation, with its capital at Kumasi and an Oyoko chief as king. The confederation came into conflict with British settlements along the west coast. Despite treaties of friendship (1817 and 1820) the Ashanti wars ensued. The Danes (1850) and the Dutch (1872) withdrew from the coastal forts as a result of the increasing attacks by the Ashanti. Britain held on, in alliance with the coastal Fanti against the Ashanti. In 1874 the British defeated the Ashanti and organised the coastal region as the Gold Coast colony. In 1896 there was more fighting between the British and the Ashanti. In fact the British mounted four expeditions against them. In 1901 the British made the kingdom of Ashanti a colony. King Pempeh I was exiled to the Seychelles. The Ashanti were famed for their craftsmanship, for their colourful *kente* cloth, and for the gold-encrusted 'Stool', which had been the symbol of their sovereignty since the seventeenth century. Otumfuo Sir Osei Agyeman, nephew of the deposed Pempeh, was made head of the re-established confederation in 1935 as Pempeh II. The Golden Stool (actually a throne-like chair), was returned to Kumasi in 1935. The king of Ashanti (*Asantehene*) continues to hold ceremonies in which the stool is used. Ashanti artefacts are to be found in The British Museum.

After the First World War the western parts of Togoland, formerly administered by Germany, were taken over by Britain to become part of the Gold Coast colony. Under Kwame Nkrumah and the Convention People's Party (CPP) Ghana, renamed after the medieval West African kingdom, became an independent country within the British Commonwealth on 6 March 1957. In 1960 Ghana became a republic, with Nkrumah the self-appointed President for life. Modern Ghana is bordered to the west by the Ivory Coast. To the north it is bordered by Burkina Faso (formerly Upper Volta). To the east it is bordered by Togo. In the south the population is predominantly Christian, in the north it is mainly Muslim. Followers of African traditional religion are found throughout the modern republic. The biggest cash crop of modern Ghana is cacao. Coffee, palm kernels, palm oil and coconuts are grown extensively. Aluminium smelting has been developed as an important industry. Rich in minerals, the country also produces diamonds, manganese and bauxite as well as gold. Timber is also a major export. The damming of the Volta, the largest river in Ghana, resulted in the creation of the huge Lake Volta on which the hydro-electric station at Akosombo was completed in 1964.

References

Davidson (1977: 20, 34–45), Fage (1959), Levtzion (1973, 1977:114–51), Trimingham (1962).

See also: **Islam and African Traditional Religion; slavery and the slave trade in West Africa**

EDWARD D. A. HULMES

GHASSANIDS (*c.* AD 500–early seventh century)

This line of Arab chiefs in Syria were allies of the Byzantine emperors, enjoying such exalted titles as *patricius* 'patrician', and acted as guardians of the desert frontier against nomadic Arab pressures from the desert. Their strong Monophysite Christian faith led them to build many churches and monasteries, whilst at the same time their strong Arab feeling was expressed in the patronage at their court for many of the leading pre-Islamic Arab poets. The Ghassanids fought for the Byzantines against the Muslim Arab invaders in the AD 630s, but their power was ended by the Arab victory.

References

Gibb and Bosworth (1960–2003), Shahid (1995-2002).

C. E. BOSWORTH

GHAYBA

A term translated as 'occultation', *ghayba* refers to the Shi'ite belief in the physical absence of the Imam from the world. Twelver Shi'ites hold that the Twelfth Imam went into the 'Lesser Occultation' during which time he communicated to his followers through a series of four agents. Then in AD 941 the 'Greater Occultation' commenced, and this is a period during which there is neither direct nor indirect access to the Imam. This state continues to the present day. Shi'ites believe that the Imam is still alive but he is concealed from human eyes, and he will return to establish a brief period of justice just before the Day of Judgement. The doctrine of the *ghayba* has posed the problem of identifying political and spiritual leadership of the community for Shi'ite clerics because such authority and legitimacy pertains to the Imam alone. However, recent writings concerning *ghayba* such as those by Ayatallah Khumayni have argued that in the absence of the

Imam it is the duty of the clerics to perform the functions of the Imam as far as possible.

References

Momen (1985: 161–71).

LLOYD RIDGEON

GHAYLAN AL-DIMASHQI
(d. *c.* AD 737)

One of the early pioneers in Islamic theology (*kalam*) of the idea that human beings have free will, rather than all their actions being determined by God. He was the son of a freed slave of the third caliph, 'Uthman, and served in the administration of the Umayyad caliphs in Damascus. His views on free will, however, made him unpopular with his rulers, not least because a belief in free will suggested that Umayyad rule had not been predestined by God and could therefore be challenged, and after a number of disputes and a period in exile in Armenia he was executed by the caliph Hisham.

References

Caspar (1998: Chapter 6), Watt (1994: Chapter 4).

HUGH GODDARD

AL-GHAZALI, ABU HAMID
(AD 1058–1111)

One of the greatest thinkers of medieval Islam, and also one of the most accessible on account of the availability of his autobiography, in which he outlines the different stages of his intellectual search for the truth, through theology, then philosophy, Shi'i Islam and then finally Sufism. Like his teacher al-Juwayni, he eventually concluded that truth was not perceived by intellectual apprehension but rather by immediate experience and walking in the way of the mystics. Born in Tus, in northeastern Iran, he studied there and in Nishapur before he was called to Baghdad to teach in the Nizamiyya Academy, one of the leading intellectual institutions of the day, but while there he seems to have had some kind of nervous breakdown, as a result of which he left his post and spent a decade travelling around the Middle East, including to Mecca and Medina, and living as a poor Sufi. He was recalled to teaching in 1105, however, but at the time of his death he was once again living in Tus, in a Sufi community. Apart from his autobiography many of his works are still available, perhaps the two most important being the *Tahafut al-Falasifa* (*The Incoherence of the Philosophers*), in which he suggests that Neoplatonic Islamic philosophers such as al-Farabi and Ibn Sina are unbelievers because of their rejection of the ideas of creation, the resurrection of the body, and God's knowledge of specific individuals and actions, and the *Ihya' 'Ulum al-Din* (*The Revival of the Religious Sciences*), in which he outlines his programme for the renewal of the Muslim community.

References

Burrell (1992), Jackson (2002), McCarthy (2001), Marmura (1997), Moosa (forthcoming), Watt (1963, 1994).

HUGH GODDARD

AL-GHAZALI, AHMAD
(d. AD 1126).

Younger brother of the more famous Abu Hamid al-Ghazali, Ahmad al-Ghazali was a celebrated Sufi in his own right. He was the author of *Sawanih*, a book on the psychology of love, and is

196

perhaps the author of a treatise that inspired 'Attar's *Mantiq al-Tayr*.

References

al-Ghazali (1986).

LLOYD RIDGEON

GHAZNAVIDS (AD 977–1186)

This line of sultans arose out of the Turkish slave guards of the Samanids, and the greatest figure of the line, Mahmud of Ghazna, built up the most extensive and powerful military empire of its age, stretching as it did from western Persia to north-western India. Its ethos was strongly Sunni. Isma'ilis and other sectarians were ruthlessly hunted down within his lands, and Mahmud's conquests in northern India earned him a great contemporary reputation as hammer of the infidel Hindus. In reality, these were essentially plunder raids, and it was not until the thirteenth century that there was any widespread, state-directed attempt at implanting Islam in northern India. Later rulers lost their western territories to the Saljuqs and Ghurids, but the Ghaznavids survived for several decades more in north-western India with their capital at Lahore.

References

Bosworth (1963, 1968: 162–97, 1975, 1996: No. 158), Gibb and Bosworth (1960–2003).

C. E. BOSWORTH

GHURIDS (early eleventh century AD–1215)

These petty chiefs of Ghur, in central Afghanistan, challenged the Ghaznavids and eventually drove the last Ghaznavids into the Panjab, building up a mighty empire in the eastern Iranian lands. They went down before a new power arising there, that of the Khwarazm-Shahs, but these last were in turn overwhelmed within a few years by the Mongols. An important feature of the Ghurid period is that it was their commanders who for the first time attempted to implant Islam permanently in northern India, and out of their ranks arose various Turkish and Afghan rulers in Delhi (1206–1555), amongst whom were the Tughluqids.

References

Bosworth (1968: 157–66, 1996: No. 159), Gibb and Bosworth (1960–2003).

C. E. BOSWORTH

GHUSL

See: **ablution**

GIBBON, EDWARD (1737–94)

Edward Gibbon is one of the world's greatest historians. A product of the European Enlightenment, his comprehensive presentation of twelve centuries of post-classical history has formed the minds of west Europeans for over 200 years. Although he never visited the lands of Islam he had a lifelong fascination for the Arab world, from the days of his childhood reading of *The Arabian Nights*.

Gibbon was born in Putney in western London in 1737 to a comfortable middle-class family. He was sickly as a child, but read voraciously in history and literature. He went to Westminster School and on to Magdalen College Oxford with, as he said in his *Memoirs* 'a stock of erudition that might have puzzled a Doctor, and a degree of ignorance of which a school-boy would have been ashamed'. At Oxford he had an unfulfilled wish to study Arabic. Wide reading led him to question his family Protestant beliefs and, at the age of seventeen, he became a Roman Catholic. His horrified father sent him to Switzerland to study under a Calvinistic pastor. This worked and Gibbon returned to the Protestant fold. But he stayed on in Switzerland for five years and became soaked in European classical scholarship. His reading bore fruit in his first book, written in French, an essay on the study of literature, published in 1761.

By now he was back in England, wintering in London and spending the summer on active service with the Hampshire grenadiers. In 1763 he set off for a year's European travel. In Rome, 'musing amid the ruins of the Capitol', he conceived the idea of writing his *History and Decline of the Roman Empire*. This was to occupy most of his energies for the next twenty years. Most, but not all. He became a member of parliament in 1774 and took office in the Government of Lord North, as Commissioner of Trade and Plantations.

The first volume was published in 1776, the year of the US Declaration of Independence and Adam Smith's *Wealth of Nations*. Volumes II and III were published in 1781; the last three volumes in 1788. The work was an instant success and Gibbon enjoyed fame for the rest of his life. He died in London in 1794. His *Memoirs* were published posthumously two years later.

His great history contains a million and a half words. The first four volumes trace Roman history in detail from the late second to the early seventh century. The last two volumes gallop through the next eight centuries to the conquest of Constantinople/Istanbul by the Ottoman Turks in 1453.

Gibbon was a methodical scholar. He relied on printed sources and fitted into a tradition of 'philosophical history'. The antiquary delved among primary sources, the philosopher reviewed their works to present his gentlemanly conclusions

to his public. Gibbon was totally familiar with available sources in English, French, and Latin – history, literature and published documents. He was less assured in other languages – German, Italian, and Greek.

His work is mostly a narrative chronological history, though he breaks off to follow through themes that cross centuries: Roman law, the rise of Sassanid Persia or the rise of Christianity. His two chapters on the rise of the Church angered the established clergy. Gibbon's youthful religious upheavals left him with a deep scepticism about supernatural claims. He applauded the tolerant polytheism of the Roman Empire, where religion was 'considered by the people as equally true, by the philosopher as equally false, and by the magistrate, as equally useful'. Church historians before Gibbon saw the rise of the Christian church as the fulfilment of God's purpose. Gibbon argued that that may be so, but he also attributed secondary causes for the success of the church and examined the social and political context of that success. But he never lost an opportunity to be sarcastic about Christian claims and the frailties of popes and churchmen. His jibes were often in witty and scurrilous footnotes: a literary habit developed by Richard Burton a century later in his translation of *A Thousand and One Nights*.

His warm account of the rise of Islam, 'one of the most memorable revolutions which have impressed a new and lasting character on the nations of the globe', may be seen as part of his habit of belittling Christianity. For his account he relies on translations, usually into French, of Arabic sources, on George Sale's translation of the Qur'an, on English scholars such as Ockley, Prideaux and Pococke, and on the writings of travellers to Islamic lands. The latter, 'in the present decay of religious fervour', were 'edified by the profound humility and attention of the Turks and Persians'.

Gibbon was eloquent on the merits of the Prophet Muhammad.

> His memory was capacious and retentive, his wit easy and social, his imagination sublime, his judgment clear, rapid, and decisive. He possessed the courage both of thought and action, and, although his designs might gradually expand with his success, the first idea which he entertained of his divine mission bears the stamp of an original and superior genius.

As with his account of the rise of Christianity, he does not acknowledge divine favour for Islam's success. He places the Prophet's mission in a social and historical context. But he is cordial towards the tenets of Islamic faith: 'A philosophic theist might subscribe the popular creed of the Mohammedans: a creed too sublime perhaps for our present faculties'. He is generally fair on the philosophical bases of Islam: 'The God of nature has written his existence on all his works, and his law in the heart of man'.

Gibbon's sympathetic treatment of Islam came at an important historical moment. Britain was, in his generation, undertaking political responsibilities for millions of Muslims in India. Writings on Islam in Britain henceforth became, in general, less polemical. Gibbon's rationalism, genial curiosity and majestic prose have had an impact on most historians, many writers and thousands of readers over the last two centuries.

References

Gibbon (1986), Low (1937), Porter (1988).

PETER CLARK

GOD'S KNOWLEDGE

God's knowledge is a subject studied at length among Muslim theologians and philosophers. *Al-Mutakallimun* theologians studied it under God's attributes. They attribute to God an eternal knowledge which is also able to know the changing world in all its details. For the theologians the concept of eternal does not only imply God's knowledge before creation but includes all knowable and unknowable things. Therefore, God, as the Qur'an also states, knows all things in their changes and knows humanity's need for guidance and, therefore, sent to the different nations' prophets with revealed scriptures. The philosophers, however, had a problem with this theological concept. If God has a kind of knowledge which is changing and progressing, this would imply a change in His essence, which conflicts with His eternal being. That is because the *falasifa* define the eternal as unmoveable and unchanging. What is eternal is what remains always the same and never changes. Thus they attributed to God an eternal unchanging knowledge which knows the world in its eternal structure and knows the eternal world, the world of the intellect, in all its detail. Al-Ghazali in his *Tahafut al-Falasifa* accused them of infidelity for this belief since this must lead to rejecting revelation as God's direct message for humanity. Yet Ibn Rushd, in his *Tahafut al-Tahafut*, where he refutes al-Ghazali's attack against the philosophers, considers it absurd that God should have a limited and changing kind of human knowledge in order to fulfill the concept of prophecy.

References

Leaman (1999: 37–9).

MAHA EL-KAISY FRIEMUTH

199

GOG AND MAGOG

In Arabic Ya'juj wa Ma'juj, or Yajuj wa Majuj, Gog and Magog are the people named in the Bible who play a role in the battles at the end of time (Ezek. 38, 39). In the Qur'an, Dhu 'l-Qarnayn is described as erecting a barrier against the people which God will destroy at the end of time (see Q.18:93–8); in Q.21:96, Gog and Magog are a part of the description of events at the end of time, when they will be 'unloosed and they slide down out of every slope'. Many traditions have developed in Islam about these people, whose origins, numbers and physical size are uncertain. Their role is clear, however, because they are directly connected to the coming of the Day of Judgement and their appearance is deemed one of the 'signs of the hour'. The barrier which holds them back has traditionally been seen to be between two mountains (see Q.18:93), perhaps between Armenia and Azerbaijan or perhaps further east in central Asia or even China.

References

Gibb and Bosworth (1960–2003: XI, 231–3).

ANDREW RIPPIN

GRANADA

The ancient city of Granada, founded in the eighth century AD, is situated on the river Genil on the north-western slopes of the Sierra Nevada in Andalusia in southern Spain. It is the capital of the Spanish province that bears its name. Granada is 78 miles (125 kilometres) south-east of Cordoba and 135 miles (217 kilometres) east of Seville. It became the capital and the last stronghold of the Moorish kingdom of Granada, which fell to the Catholic monarchs Ferdinand II and his wife Isabella I in 1492. Once the residence of the Moorish rulers of the city, the Palace of the Alhambra (*al-qal'a al-hamra'*) remains one of Granada's most famous buildings, designated in 1924 as part of a World Heritage Site. The cathedral of Santa Maria de la Encarnacion, numerous churches, convents, monasteries, hospitals and fine houses, add to the city's architectural heritage. Tolerance of religious and cultural diversity came to an end when Jews and Muslims were required to be baptised as Christians. Jewish converts to Christianity (*conversos*) remained in Spain but those who would not convert were expelled in the closing years of the fifteenth century AD. Arabic books and manuscripts on Islam were burned in Granada. Given the choice of conversion to Christianity or expulsion from Spain, many Muslims complied but others refused. The 'Moriscos', Spanish Muslims whose ancestors had been Christians, were among those to be presented with the same choice. The forcible expulsion of Muslims from Spain was authorised by Philip III in 1609.

References

Hitti (1973: 493–556), Johnson (1987: 177–8), Michell (1984: 212–15).

See also: **Almohads; Almoravids; al-Andalus; Cordoba; Seville**

EDWARD D. A. HULMES

GULF WAR (1990–1)

The war launched by a thirty-nation coalition to end the Iraqi occupation of Kuwait. Saddam Husayn's Iraq invaded Kuwait on 2 August 1990, and the US administration responded by deploying over half a million troops to the Gulf. On 29 November 1990, the UN Security Council passed Resolution 678 authorising member states to use 'all necessary means' after a deadline of 15 January. Iraq did not comply, and on 16 January the coalition launched Operation Desert Storm: a six-week air war to dismantle Iraq's military-industrial infrastructure and recapture Kuwait.

Iraq struggled to deal with the size and sophistication of coalition forces. Iraq fired SCUD ballistic missiles at Israel and the Gulf states, but this political strategy ultimately failed in its aim to mobilise the 'Arab street'. Iraq also tried to initiate a land battle at the Saudi town of Khafji, but coalition air power utterly dominated the battlefield. On 24 February, the coalition launched Operation Desert Sabre to recapture Kuwait city and encircle retreating Iraqi troops. As the Iraqis pulled out, they set fire to many oil wells creating huge clouds of smoke. Iraqi forces disintegrated, with tens of thousands becoming prisoners. The war was ended on 28 February 1991 amid scenes of liberation in Kuwait and ones of carnage on the roads back to Iraq.

References

Murden (1995: 222–47, 259–300), Perrett (1996: 165–6).

Simon W. Murden

H

HABIL AND QABIL

The two sons of Adam according to Islamic tradition, although they are not named as such in the Qur'an.

ANDREW J. NEWMAN

HADANA

Responsibility or custody of a child. *Hadana* is considered to be the right of the child and the duty of the guardian and can be enforced even against the will of the individual concerned. For example, in the case where a woman applies for a divorce intending to leave the child with the father and such an action clearly contravenes the interest of that child, then the law can enforce custody on the mother. However this compulsion cannot be exercised on someone who is not recognised by Islamic law as a fitting custodian, some of the detailed conditions for this role being that the woman is the rightful mother and also that she is not guilty of apostasy or corrupt or gravely anti-social behaviour. There is little doubt that Islam views the custody of children to be the mother's right, a claim supported by the tradition of the Prophet and his Companions. The Prophet is reported to have stated that the divorced woman is the one most entitled to the custody of the children unless she remarries. Next in line for custody is the maternal grandmother, and then the older sister of the child followed by the aunt. After the womenfolk come the father, grandfather, brother and so on.

References

Ibn Manzur (n.d.), al-Zuhayli (1985: 7, 719–30).

MAWIL IZZI DIEN

HADD

Hindrance, impediment, limit, boundary or frontier. *Hadd* has come to mean in a narrow, technical sense the legally specified punishment of certain acts according to the text of Qur'an or *hadith* and thereby crimes against religion.

References

Ibn Manzur (n.d.), Subhi Al-Salih (1982).

See also: **hudud**.

MAWIL IZZI DIEN

AL-HADI, MUSA B. AL-MAHDI, ABU MUHAMMAD (AD 785–6)

al-Hadi was the son and successor of the 'Abbasid caliph al-Mahdi. During al-Hadi's brief and relatively untroubled reign of just over one year he did little more than continue the policies adopted by his father, including the religious persecution of the Manicheans (*zanadiqa*). He died in somewhat mysterious circumstances and was succeeded by his far more illustrious brother Harun al-Rashid.

References

Kennedy (1996: 139–41; 1981: 108–13), Muir (1915: 473–5), al-Tabari (1985–95: XXIX, 162–258 *passim*).

RONALD PAUL BUCKLEY

HADITH NABAWI

Hadith reports that contain the words of Muhammad as opposed to *hadith qudsi*, which contain the words of God as reported by Muhammad. Most *hadith* reports are classified as *nabawi*.

References

Siddiqi (1993: 2–5).

ANDREW RIPPIN

HADITH OF GABRIEL

A prominent report found in most major collections of *hadith* reports in which the angel Gabriel (in the guise of an unknown man) discussed the meaning of faith with Muhammad. A popular version of the tradition is found in the 'Book of Faith' in the *sahih* of Muslim as follows:

It is reported that 'Abdallah ibn 'Umar said that his father 'Umar ibn al-Khattab said that one day, while we were with the Prophet a man, with shining white clothes and jet black hair, appeared before us. We could see no evidence of a journey on him and neither did anyone among us know him. He sat with the Prophet such that his knees touched the Prophet's knees, he placed his hands on his legs. He said, 'Muhammad, inform me about *islam*'. The Prophet replied, '*Islam* is that you bear witness that there is no god but God and that Muhammad is the messenger of God, that you establish prayer, that you pay charity, that you fast during Ramadan, and that you undertake the pilgrimage (*hajj*) to the house (of God) if you are able'. He said, 'You are right'.

We were surprised at him. He asked the Prophet a question and then himself verified the Prophet's answer.

Then he said, 'Inform me about *iman*'. The Prophet said, '*Iman* is that you believe in God, His angels, His books, His prophets, and the last day and that you believe that good and bad things are a part of the decree (of God)'. He said, 'You are right'.

Then he said, 'Inform me about *ihsan*'. The Prophet replied, '*Ihsan* is that you serve God as if He was right in front of your eyes, for even if you cannot see Him, He definitely sees you'.

Then he said, 'Inform me about the hour'. The Prophet replied, 'The person who is being asked is no more aware of it than the inquirer'.

Then he said, 'Tell me about its signs'. The Prophet replied, 'That the slave girl will give birth to the free woman, that you shall see these bare-footed, naked, and poor shepherds competing with each other in making high buildings'.

'Umar continued: Then he went away and I kept sitting there for quite some time. Then the Prophet said to me, 'Umar, do you know who this inquirer was?' I said, 'God and His messenger know best'. He said, 'It was Gabriel. He came to you to teach you your religion'.

The report is an early attempt to create a synopsis of the key doctrinal elements of Islam and to provide a solid basis for resolving several matters of intense Muslim debate in the early centuries regarding how to define membership in the community and to understand the relationship between faith and works. The report, in one form or another, is found in most major collections of *hadith*.

References

Amjad (2003).

ANDREW RIPPIN

HADITH QUDSI

Literally, 'sacred reports', being *hadith* reports that, rather than quoting the words or deeds of Muhammad, quote the words of God, usually in the first person, and which are viewed as revelation of a non-Qur'anic status. An example of such a report, found in several of the important collections of *hadith* material including al-Bukhari and Muslim, is the following: The Apostle of God said, 'God said, "I have prepared for My upright servants what neither eye has seen, nor ear has heard, nor has entered into the heart of any person"'.

References

Graham (1977).

ANDREW RIPPIN

HADITH, TECHNICAL TERMINOLOGY OF

An entire 'science of *hadith*' arose in classical Islam in order to authenticate and support the body of *hadith* material which was to be used as the source of the *sunna*. This process involved a rigorous review of the chain of transmission of the individual reports. As a result, an extensive body of terminology emerged in order to classify the various traditions. Among the important terms are the following methods of classifying traditions on the basis of the quality of the *isnad*, the nature of the *matn* and the acceptance or rejection by the early generations of Muslims: *sahih*, 'sound', *hasan*, 'fair', and *da'if*, 'weak'. Weak reports were ranked according to the faults found in the *isnad*. These include: *mu'allaq*, 'suspended', *maqtu'*, 'interrupted', *munqati'*, 'broken', *mursal*, 'incomplete', *musahhaf* ('having a mistake in either the *isnad* or the *matn*'), *shaadh*, 'rare' (a report which has a reliable *isnad* but whose content is not otherwise attested), *mawdu'*, 'forged'.

As a part of the science of *hadith*, the critique of individuals in the *isnad* was important. This science was known as *'ilm al-jarh wa'l-t'adil* and it allowed individuals to be classified by terms such as *thiqa*, 'trustworthy', *mutqin*, 'exact', *thabt*, 'strong', and *'adl*, 'truthful'. The extent of the transmission of a report was also classified: *mutawatir*, 'widespread' (and thus declared to have no possibility of falsification), *mashhur*, 'well known', a tradition that had more limited circulation in the first generation after Muhammad but became more fully transmitted later, *ahad*, 'singular', which stems from fewer transmitters for several generations after Muhammad.

References

Siddiqi (1993: Chapter 7).

ANDREW RIPPIN

HADRAMAWT

Hadramawt was an ancient South Arabian kingdom in what is now south-east Yemen and south-west of the Sultanate of Oman and is also used for a deep valley parallel to the Arabian south coast, Wadi Hadramawt, separating the coastal plain from the Empty Quarter.

An ever-changing series of wars, alliances and coalitions were made with the nearby ancient states of Saba', Qataban, and other South Arabian states, but Hadramawt from its capital Shabwa, a shrine and pilgrimage centre, remained politically independent until the late third century AD. Other important sites include Tarim, Madhab, Mayfa'at, Cane and Shibam. The Hadramawt economy prospered through trade in frankincense and salt. It was incorporated into Saba' until AD 220, initially ruled by King Shamir Yuhar'ish. Shibam was capital of Hadramawt several times between the third century AD and the sixteenth century and contains 500 mud-brick tower-houses many dating to the sixteenth century and several mosques, including its Friday mosque (AD 904) built by Caliph Harun al-Rashid on the site of an earlier one, and the seventeenth-century mosque of Shaykh Ma'ruf. Shibam is now protected by UNESCO.

Muslim sources place the Hadramawt as the homeland of the Kinda nomads. In AD 951 Sayyid Ahmad ibn 'Isa al-Muhajir, a descendant of the Prophet Muhammad, settled in Hajrayn, in the eastern part of the *wadi*, where he established Shafaism. His tomb is still a place of pilgrimage. The sea-port, al-Mukalla (founded AD 1035) contains the al-Rawdha mosque and mosque of 'Umar. In 1488, Kathirids of Hamdanis, a San'a tribe, conquered the Hadramawt and made Tarim and then Say'un its capital. Say'un was a sixteenth-century mosque of al-Haddad and contains the twentieth-century tomb of Habshi. In the fifteenth century, the west of Hadramawt was stabilised by the Qu'aitis, a Yadi'i tribe originally brought to the region by the Kathirids as paid soldiers. The Qu'aiti sultanate was ruled from al-Qatn. Disputes between Qu'aities and Kathirids continued until the mid-1800s when the *wadi* was divided between Say'un and Shibam. The Kathirids remained in power until the 1967 revolution.

Tarim contains the Muhdar mosque, with a 50-metre high square minaret and al-Afqah library, founded in 1972 to preserve spiritual heritage of local Islamic scholarship. It contains over 14,000 volumes and 3,000 antique manuscripts from all over Hadramawt. Its graveyards with uniformly designed sandstone monuments are inscribed with calligraphy in a unique Yemeni style. Many Hadramawtis migrated to south-east Asia and helped to spread Islam into Indonesia and Malaysia. Others migrated to oil-rich Arab states in the twentieth century, including the Bin Laden family.

References

Bujra (1971), Smith (1997), Stark (2003).

JANET STARKEY

HAFEZ, MUHAMMAD SHAMSODDIN (AD 1327–90)

Persian poet, born in Shiraz, where he also died. Little is known with certainty about Hafez's early life, but it appears that his father died when Hafez was a young boy and that his childhood was spent in poverty. His poetic gifts quickly became apparent, however, and by the late 1340s and early 1350s he was dedicating poems to the ruler of Shiraz and other senior officials, probably supplementing his income by working as a copyist at the same time. These early poems had already revealed a tendency towards a liberal interpretation of Islam, and Hafez's subsequent poetic career was highly dependent on the attitudes of the current ruler towards the drinking of wine and other worldly pleasures. Under the ascetic Mobarezoddin (AD 1353–8), Hafez was forced to develop a style of expression in which veiled allusion played a prominent part. His fortunes rose, however, with the accession of Shah Shoja' (AD 1358–84), whose liberal attitudes coincided with Hafez's own, and who was also himself a competent poet. Hafez's close association with Shoja' lasted for only some six years, however, and from 1368 to AD 1374 Hafez was banished from Shiraz. The reason for this banishment is not known for certain, but was probably a combination of jealousy on the part of the ruler and disapproval by the religious authorities. By the time of the death of Shah Shoja' in 1384, Hafez's reputation had already spread widely in the eastern Islamic world, though he wrote little during his final years.

The main general themes of Hafez's poetry may be summarised as wine, love, physical beauty, eulogy of the sovereign, and a mystical vision of the universe that at times verges on pantheism – though such a list can give little idea of the particular flavour of his poetry. Attempts to categorise him, as a mystic or Epicurean, for example, have generally failed. In structural terms, his main achievement lay in extending the potential of the *ghazal* form to embrace a wider and more complex thematic range, and it is this development that accounts for his

enduring reputation as the greatest lyric poet of Persia. In addition to the esteem accorded him in the eastern Islamic world, Hafez's poetry has been widely studied in the West, and used as a source of inspiration by some modern poets, among them Goethe.

References

Arberry (1958: 329–63, 1968, 1994), Levy (1969: 116–34).

PAUL STARKEY

HAFIZ

One who has memorised the Qur'an. The word itself means to 'protect' and this sense is central to all Muslim understandings of the memorisation of the Qur'an. The stories of the transmission of the Qur'an from Muhammad to today emphasise the role of memory in providing the authentication and reliability of the textual tradition. Thus, the active participation of individuals in the memorisation of the text is both essential and highly prized. The traditional Islamic educational system has focused on the memorisation of the Qur'an and provided the basis for the establishment of literacy. However, memorisation has also taken place in many parts of the Muslim world as a rote activity in which the understanding of the text is ignored or de-emphasised. The ability of a young boy to have memorised the Qur'an is highly praised and the significance of the act is often a part of contemporary stories of 'coming of age' in the Muslim world, featured in novels such as Taha Husayn's *An Egyptian Childhood: The Autobiography of Taha Husayn* and Cheikh Hamidou Kane's *Ambiguous Adventure*. The performance of reciting the Qur'an as a ritual act has created a professional class of *huffaz* (sing. *hafiz*) whose trained voices follow certain melodic patterns in recitation.

References

Husayn (1981), Kane (1972), Nelson (2001).
ANDREW RIPPIN

HAFSA (b. *c.* AD 605)

One of the wives of the Prophet Muhammad, born in about AD 605, daughter of 'Umar, the second caliph of the Arab empire. Her marriage to Muhammad (probably his fourth) is portrayed as a strategic one, solidifying his alliance with his powerful convert 'Umar. The two married in AD 625 when she was eighteen: she was already a widow, having been married to Khumays, one of the early emigrants to Abyssinia who died after the Battle of Badr. She played a special role in the preservation of the written text of the Qur'an by participating in the actual collection and then being entrusted with the earliest copy of the text done by Abu Bakr after the death of her father.

References

Gibb and Bosworth (1960–2003: III, 63).
ANDREW RIPPIN

HAFSIDS (1229–1574)

The Hafsids were the most important dynasty of the later medieval period in the eastern Maghrib, political heirs of the Almohads and Marinids. Under their rule the capital Tunis enjoyed a great resurgence of prosperity, having trade links with the Italians and Spanish. It also became a centre for Maghribi culture and spirituality, centred round the Zaytuna Mosque, and it was here that the *madrasa* system of education, already characteristic of the central and eastern

Islamic lands, now developed in the Maghrib. In the sixteenth century the last Hafsids, despite help from Spain, were unable to withstand the Ottoman Turkish maritime expansion into the western Mediterranean.

References

Bosworth (1996: No. 18), Brunschvig (1940–7), Gibb and Bosworth (1960–2003).
C. E. BOSWORTH

HAGAR

Mother of Ishmael/Isma'il by Abraham/Ibrahim. Isma'il is held to be 'the father of the Arabs' as Isaac/Ishaq is held to be that of the Jews. At the latter's birth Ibrahim turned Hagar and Isma'il out into the desert because of the jealousy of his wife Sarah. The Zamzam well near Mecca is held to be the well from which they later drank.

References

Hourani (1991: 150).

See also: **Isma'il, son of Ibrahim**
ANDREW J. NEWMAN

AL-HAJAR, AL-ASWAD

See: **Black Stone**

AL-HAJJ

This, specifically, is the annual pilgrimage to Mecca and its environs. It can only be undertaken by Muslims. Those who complete it are entitled to use the honorific title *al-hajj, al-hajji* (male) or *al-hajja* (female). The Arabic root conveys several related meanings: 'overcoming through effort', 'convincing', 'setting out with a specific purpose in mind'. These intentions motivate those who decide to fulfil what is the fifth of the five obligatory religious duties of a Muslim. The physical focus of the pilgrimage is the tall cubic structure, the Ka'ba, situated in the centre of the Grand Mosque in Mecca (*al-masjid al haram*). The pilgrimage to Mecca is a once-in-a-lifetime obligation for every adult Muslim, man or woman, except for those who are without the means to perform it. With the prior expression of intent it may be performed for another person by proxy. Women must be accompanied by a male relative. To make the pilgrimage, Muslims must ensure before leaving home that all their debts are paid, that they have sufficient money to take them to Mecca and back home without becoming a financial burden to anyone else, and that they have the necessary documentation to prove that they are bona-fide Muslims. In former times, the journey to Mecca could be long and dangerous. The round trip on foot or pack animal and sailing boat could take up to two years. Today a pilgrim may travel by air to Jidda, and thence to Mecca on foot, astride an animal, or in a motor vehicle driven by a local guide.

Before entering Mecca, and still some distance away from the city, everyday clothing is exchanged for pilgrim dress. This consists of two pieces of unsewn woollen or linen white cloth for men, one wrapped around the lower part of the body and the other draped over the shoulders. Women wear simple white gowns and leave their faces unveiled. Entering into a state of ritual purity and consecration, *ihram*, is a necessary preliminary for entry into Mecca. From this point on until the pilgrimage is officially ended, pilgrims are forbidden to hunt, to argue, to cut their hair or their nails or to engage in sexual relations. Once in this dress, all the pilgrims, rich or poor, distinguished or otherwise, are equal before God whatever their station

in life. 'Here I am at your service' (*labbayka*), is the cry that repeatedly goes up from the pilgrims. For their welfare, their health, and the provision of suitable accommodation, the Saudi Arabian authorities assume responsibility. During the annual month of pilgrimage, the twelfth of the lunar year, the influx of pilgrims in Mecca calls for considerable organisational effort on the part of the host nation. The seventy-day pilgrimage season each year begins with the start of the tenth month of the lunar calendar. Entry to the Grand Mosque may be made through the Gate of Peace in order to join other pilgrims intent on performing *al-tawaf,* the prescribed seven anticlockwise circumambulations of the Ka'ba. Pilgrims recite: 'O Lord! Grant this house greater honour, veneration, and awe and grant those who venerate it and make pilgrimage to it peace and forgiveness. O Lord! Thou art the peace. Peace is from Thee. So greet us on the Day of Judgement with the greeting of peace'.

In the south-east corner of the Ka'ba, the Black Stone (*al-hajar al-aswad*) is lodged. It is a rock, 12 inches (30 centimetres) in diameter, and set in silver. It is the only remaining relic from the original structure, which Muslims believe was erected by Ibrahim and his son Isma'il. The stone marks the place where *al-tawaf* starts and ends. Pilgrims strive to touch or kiss it as they pass. A black curtain (*kiswa*) – originally made each year in Egypt, but now in Mecca – is used to cover the Ka'ba. It features Qur'anic inscriptions embroidered in gold letters around its top. It is changed each year. The old *kiswa* is divided and the pieces given to pilgrims. The colour black, mentioned twice here, symbolises the ineffability of that which lies beyond human powers of conception, namely, God. Pilgrims attempt to drink from the near-by well of Zamzam, the miraculous spring which appeared when Hagar, one of the wives of Ibrahim, having been expelled from the household with her infant son, Isma'il, was desperate for water. Muslims believe that this miracle prompted Ibrahim to build the House of God in the vicinity. After the visit to Zamzam pilgrims hasten seven times between the remains of two small hills, Safa and Marwa, enclosed within the Grand Mosque and separated by a distance of 431 yards (394 metres). This rush of activity (al-sa'y) symbolises the search for water made by Hagar.

The eve of the ninth day of the month of pilgrimage is spent in Mina, a village some 4 miles (6.5 kilometres) to the east of Mecca. The pilgrims rest there in preparation for the 'Day of Standing', the day following, when they gather to stand on the Plain of 'Arafat, praying from noon until just before sunset.

By this time Mina becomes a crowded temporary tent city. After dawn prayers, pilgrims proceed in buses, trucks and cars, on the backs of camels and donkeys, or on foot to the Plain of 'Arafat, 8 miles (13 kilometres) further to the east. By midday a vast crowd of pilgrims has congregated on the desert plain in the heat of the sun. Nearby is the place where the Prophet Muhammad, sitting on his camel, delivered his farewell sermon shortly before his death in Medina in AD 632. Personal wealth and position are left behind in the shared acts of praying for salvation. After sunset the pilgrims begin their return to Mecca. An overnight halt is made almost half-way, at the village of Muzdalifa, a short distance to the east of Mina. Prayers are offered, again, just as Muhammad did on his pilgrimage. Pebbles are collected to throw at the three 'Stoning points of Satan' in Mina, to drive the Devil away. Seven pebbles are thrown at each of the three pillars. The pillars at which the stones are cast symbolise the forces

of evil against which the faithful must always contend. The end of the Pilgrimage comes on the tenth day of the month, when pilgrims celebrate 'Id al-adha (Feast of the Sacrifice). Animals are slaughtered and the pieces distributed as pilgrims take food and drink again. After the stoning of the Devil and the Feast of the Sacrifice, pilgrims return to the Grand Mosque in Mecca to repeat the tawaf and the running between the two small hills of Safa and Marwa. The end of ihram is signalled when pilgrims have a lock of hair clipped. The statutory requirements of the hajj are thus completed.

References

Abdul-Rauf (1978: 580–607), Hitti (1973: 100, 133), Hourani (1991:149–51, 222–3), Momen (1985: 180–2).

See also: *'umra*

EDWARD D. A. HULMES

AL-HAJJAJ IBN YUSUF
(*c.* AD 661–714)

Umayyad administrator, best known for his role as governor of Iraq (AD 694–714). Born in Ta'if in humble circumstances, little is known of his childhood or early life. He first came to prominence around AD 691 when his success in restoring order among some mutinous troops attracted the attention of the Caliph 'Abd al-Malik. Shortly afterwards, he distinguished himself during the second civil war by leading his troops to victory over Mus'ab ibn al-Zubayr, the rebel governor of Iraq. Following a further victory over 'Abdallah ibn Zubayr, the 'anti-caliph' of Mecca, in the Hijaz in AD 692, the Caliph 'Abd al-Malik appointed him Governor of Hijaz and the Yemen, where the harshness of his rule, which on occasion led the Caliph himself to intervene, provided a foretaste of the style of government he was later to employ in Iraq. In AD 694 al-Hajjaj was transferred to the governorship of Iraq, among the most important administrative positions in the Umayyad state, to which were quickly added the governorships of Khurasan and Sistan. Al-Hajjaj quickly restored order among the troops, put an end to the Kharijite threat, and succeeded in ensuring a period of relative prosperity and stability that allowed fresh conquests in the east – his efforts to improve the state of agriculture in the area being of particular importance in this connection. He also made efforts to produce a uniform text of the Qur'an, and is said to have been instrumental in ordering the introduction of new vowel points for this purpose.

Despite general agreement that al-Hajjaj was among the most capable administrators of the early Islamic period, the harshness of his rule ensured that his name became a byword for Umayyad oppression and tyranny at the same time. This reputation – together with the oratorical gifts that led al-Jahiz to record many of his speeches and correspondence – has survived until the present day.

References

Hawting (1986), Périer (1904), Wellhausen (1963: 226–57).

PAUL STARKEY

AL-HAKIM I, AHMAD B. AL-HASAN, ABU'L-'ABBAS (AD 1262–1302)

After the Mongol destruction of the 'Abbasid caliphate in Baghdad (AD 1258), al-Hakim, a descendant of al-Mustarshid, was proclaimed as Caliph of Aleppo, Harran and northern Syria (AD 1261) by the Mamluk ruler of Aleppo, Aqush al-Barli. Al-Hakim subsequently joined

forces with al-Mustansir, who had been installed as 'Abbasid caliph in Cairo, with the intention of regaining Iraq from the Mongols. The ensuing battle between the 'Abbasid forces and the Mongols resulted in the death of al-Mustansir. Al-Hakim, however, managed to escape and fled to Cairo. After his genealogy was examined and declared authentic by the chief *qadi*, al-Hakim was chosen by the Mamluk sultan al-Zahir Baybars to replace al-Mustansir. The Sultan was careful not to allow the Caliph to become a rival, however, and al-Hakim was permitted to exercise no political power. For the next two and a half centuries until the Ottoman conquest of Egypt (1517), the descendants of al-Hakim were to be 'shadow' caliphs under the Mamluks. Al-Hakim was succeeded by his son Sulayman b. al-Hakim al-Mustakfi.

References

Arnold (1924: 95–8), Gibb and Bosworth (1960–2003: VII: 729), Ibn Iyas (1975: I, 320–1, 345, 368, 398), Salim (1965: II: 23–5), al-Suyuti (1969: 478–83).

RONALD PAUL BUCKLEY

AL-HAKIM II, AHMAD B. AL-MUSTAKFI, ABU'L-'ABBAS (AD 1341–52)

The 'Abbasid caliph in Cairo, al-Mustakfi, designated his son Ahmad b. al-Mustakfi to succeed him, but the Mamluk sultan al-Nasir b. Muhammad b. Qalawun rejected this and installed instead al-Wathiq I (r. AD 1340–41). Al-Wathiq was subsequently deposed and replaced with Ahmad who was given the honorific 'al-Hakim bi Amr Allah', the same title as his grandfather the caliph al-Hakim I. Although the caliphate was the theoretical source of all authority in the Muslim community and was thus used by the Mamluk sultans to legitimise their rule, it had no secular authority. The Caliph was kept in virtual seclusion and was permitted no influence in political affairs, all secular power being totally usurped by the Mamluks. Al-Hakim II died without designating an heir. He was succeeded by his brother Abu Bakr b. al-Mustakfi al-Mu'tadid I.

References

Ibn Iyas (1975: I: 474, 475, 487, 495, 519, 541, 548, 549), Salim (1965: II, 27–8), al-Suyuti (1969: 490–500).

RONALD PAUL BUCKLEY

AL-HAKIM, AL-MANSUR B. AL-'AZIZ (r. AD 996–1021)

Fatimid caliph in North Africa and Egypt of elusive and enigmatic character, whose reign was characterised by a series of violent and capricious actions, leading to accusations that he was mentally unbalanced, a verdict assisted by the fact of his mysterious end. In AD 1020 he had the whole of Old Cairo burnt down, and his reign was filled with repressive acts and persecution of Christians and Jews, culminating in the destruction in AD 1010 of the Church of the Holy Sepulchre in Jerusalem. He carried to extremes ideas current in certain Isma'ili circles and considered himself the incarnation of God, and it was out of the preaching of one of these Isma'ili extremists that the Druze movement arose in Syria after al-Hakim's death; these ideas may have had a part in his own final disappearance and presumed death.

References

Gibb and Bosworth (1960–2003), Sanders (1998: 152).

C. E. BOSWORTH

AL-HAKIM, AL-TIRMIDHI (d. c. AD 932)

al-Tirmidhi was an important Sufi who lived in the second half of the ninth century. His most significant work was *Sirat al-awliya'* in which he discussed the concept of friendship of God (*walaya*) and the various kinds of friends of God. His thought was more influential after his death, and was discussed by Sufis including Ibn al-'Arabi.

References

Radtke and O'Kane (1996).

LLOYD RIDGEON

HALAL

See: **food and drink; sacrifice**

AL-HALLAJ (d. AD 922)

Al-Hallaj was one of the most controversial of all Sufis because of his statement found in his book *Tawasin* (6:23), 'I am the Truth'. Taken by Muslim scholars and jurists as an insult to God (the Truth), al-Hallaj was ultimately executed. His execution was regarded by many as justified, even by many of those sympathetic to Sufism, such as Abu Hamid al-Ghazali who commented, 'the killing of him who utters something of this kind [i.e. I am the Truth] is better in the religion of God than the resurrection of ten others'. Al-Hallaj enjoyed the companionship of major Sufis of his age including Sahl al-Tustari and 'Amr al-Makki, although sources suggest that they did not altogether approve of their student for his lack of respect and the divulgence of esoteric, Sufi secrets. Moreover, al-Hallaj's family connections with certain circles at the 'Abbasid court may have played some part in his downfall. Al-Hallaj was arrested in AD 913 for 'claiming divine lordship and preaching incarnationism (*hulul*)' and he remained imprisoned until his execution.

References

Massignon (1982).

LLOYD RIDGEON

AL-HAMADHANI, BADI' AL-ZAMAN (968–1008)

'Abbasid writer, best known for his works in the *maqama* genre, of which he is popularly – and probably correctly – supposed to have been the originator. Born in Hamadhan, he began his career at the court of the Buyids, but spent most of his short life in the east of Iran, travelling between one court and the other, until his early death in Herat. His sobriquet ('Wonder of the Age') was given to him at an early age in recognition of his rhetorical accomplishments. Although he was also the author of a number of poems and 'epistles', some of which have been published, his reputation is almost entirely dependent on his surviving *maqamat* ('standings', 'seances'), a literary term that has been much discussed, but which was probably intended in opposition to the *majalis*, or 'sessions', of the 'proper' scholar. Al-Hamadhani began the composition of his *maqamat* around AD 990 and continued to compose them over several years; he is said to have dictated at least 400 in all, although only fifty-two survive. The unfinished impression that the collection presents has been attributed by some scholars to the author's premature death, but probably merely reflects the fact that his *maqamat* were originally oral improvisations.

Sometimes described as the nearest medieval Arabic equivalent to the modern short story, the short narrative units of al-Hamadhani's *maqamat*, which seldom exceed a few pages in length, involve a narrator, 'Isa ibn Hisham, together with (in most cases) a witty vagabond, Abu al-Fath al-Iskandari, who uses his eloquence in order to escape from a tricky situation or to exploit a gullible audience. Composed largely in rhymed prose (*saj'*), interspersed with occasional verse, their principal purpose appears to have been to demonstrate the verbal dexterity of their hero, or author. At the same time, however, they are characterised by a remarkably keen observation on the author's part of his fellow men, as well as by an obvious fascination with the underworld – a preoccupation also evident in a number of other medieval Arab authors from al-Jahiz onwards.

The *maqama* form was subsequently taken up by al-Hariri a century or so later and formed one of the stock genres of Arabic literature, surviving even into the modern era.

References

Beeston (1990), Monroe (1983), Predergast (1915).

PAUL STARKEY

HAMDANIDS (AD 906–1004)

This Shi'ite line, of Bedouin Arab origin, ruled in northern Syria and in Mesopotamia, with centres at Aleppo and Mosul. Their *amirs* played notable roles in the struggle to contain the resurgent Byzantine advance, under the Macedonian emperors into Syria, but latterly they were menaced by the Fatimids. They achieved renown as encouragers of Arabic literature, seen in the Amir Sayf al-Dawla's patronage of the greatest poet of the classical period, al-Mutanabbi.

References

Bosworth (1996: No. 35), Canard (1951), Gibb and Bosworth (1960–2003).

See also: **Byzantines**

C. E. BOSWORTH

AL-HAMIDI, IBRAHIM B. AL-HUSAYN

Al-Hamidi held the highest rank of the second Da'i Mutlaq among the Tayyibi community in Yemen. In AD 1138 he was chosen as the assistant of the first *da'i mutlaq*, Dhu'ayb b. Musa and after the latter's death in AD 1151 he held the highest religious Isma'ili authority (in the absence of the imam). Al-Hamidi lived in San'a' until his death in AD 1162.

Ibrahim introduced the *rasa'il* of the Ikhwan al-Safa' into the Tayybi literature and presented the works of al-Kirmani according to his own interpretation of them. His main work was called *Kitab Kanz al-Walad, The Book of the Youth's Treasure.* In this work he followed al-Kirmani's (Neoplatonic) cosmological system, but attributed human characteristics to different intellects. He also used the myth of the 'Spiritual Adam', which was used by early Christian Gnostic circles, to present the doctrine of salvation through which the tenth intellect acts as the saviour who calls humanity to repentance. Al-Hamidi and his master al-Kirmani are considered to have introduced a kind of Neoplatonism which is mixed with Gnostic myths and produced a new facet of the influence of Neoplatonism on Islamic philosophy.

References

Netton (1989: 229–34).

MAHA EL-KAISY FRIEMUTH

HAMMAM

The *hammam* (bath) with its sequence of cold, warm and hot rooms was inherited from the Romans. As a weekly visit to the *hammam* was required for cleansing before the Friday noon prayer, it was a charitable act for wealthy citizens to commission a public bath. Ottoman Istanbul has baths which are both functional and magnificent examples of architecture. Sultan Suleyman I (1520–66) commissioned in 1556 a *hammam* in the name of his wife Roxelana for the use of the clergy of the Aya Sofya mosque. This is a double bath with separate but identical sections for men and women, each has a great domed entrance vestibule which leads into adjoining suites of rooms. A public *hammam* was an economic asset as its revenues contributed to the upkeep of neighbouring mosques and schools. The palaces of rulers were furnished with luxurious private baths. The Umayyad caliphs of Syria particularly enjoyed this amenity which is well illustrated at the desert hunting lodge built for Walid I (AD 705–15) between 711 and AD 715 at Qusayr Amr. Here the bath suite is decorated with painted scenes of dancing and feasting and the signs of the zodiac.

References

Hillenbrand (1982).

JENNIFER SCARCE

HANIF (pl. *hunafa'*)

The word is found several times in the Qur'an, e.g., Q.3:67, Q.4:125, Q.6:161, instances that refer to the faith of Ibrahim in a way that contrasts the inclination to a transcendent monotheism with that of an immanent polytheism. In Qur'anic terms a *hanif* is thus contrasted favourably with a *mushrik*, i.e., one who 'associates' a creature with the Creator. In Q.10:105 the exhortation (to the Prophet) is to 'turn your face' *li-din hanifan*, i.e., 'towards religion as a man of pure faith'. In this context, the term *hanif* is almost a synonym for *muslim*. By way of an example,

Q.3:67 may be rendered: 'Ibrahim was neither a Jew nor a Christian. He was an upright man, submitted to God [*hanifan musliman*]. He was not among the idolaters [*mushrikin*]'. Before its use in Islam the word *hanif* was probably used to refer to a Christian ascetic or someone in search of a spirituality cleansed of the current accretions of polytheistic superstition. In this sense the *hunafa'* may have been looked on as dissidents, who led a lonely existence in desert places. Temperamentally, they seem to have been monotheists without subscribing to contemporary Jewish or Christian beliefs. From a later Islamic point of view they were, at least, proto-Muslims. The word *hanif* implied no membership of an organised religious group, but rather a natural disposition to the true religion (Islam), which preaches a rigorous revealed monotheism and discourages ascetic practices.

References

Haleem (2004: 135), Watt (1953: 162–4).

EDWARD D. A. HULMES

HARAM

Haram, which can be translated as 'restricted, forbidden, sacred, private' is a concept whose interpretation depends on context. In religious terms, *haram* applies to sacred space, especially focused around the earliest mosques and the tombs of the Prophet Muhammad and his family at Mecca and Medina, and the Dome of the Rock in Jerusalem. Access to these areas is reserved for Muslims only. In social terms, *haram* refers to the private quarters of a household reserved for the women, children and related male members of a family. A *haram* can vary from a simple screened section of a nomad's tent or village house to the magnificently decorated and extensive complex of the Topkapi Palace which resemble a small city in plan and activities of its members.

References

Al-Qaradawi (1985).

JENNIFER SCARCE

HARAQ

See: **death and burial**

HARAT

Also called Herat, Haret, Hara; in old Persian, Haraiva; and in Armenia, Hret, Harat is a capital city and a province (*velayat*) of western Afghanistan, that includes the fertile Hari Rud valley and is bounded by the Hindu Kush. Tadzhiks and Durrani Pashtuns live in the oases, with semi-nomadic Dari-speaking people in the deserts and mountains. Many empires have conquered the region including the Parthians (247 BC–AD 224), Kushans, Sasanids, and Hephthalites. The city (922 m above sea level) on the Hari Rud in the most densely populated oasis of the province, is a major focus for trade from the Mediterranean to Turkmenistan, Iran, China and for surrounding Afghan provinces of Badghisat, Ghowr and Farah. It is the site of earlier ancient cities, including Alexandria in Aria built by Alexander the Great.

Conquered by Muslim Arabs in AD 652 and again in 661, the Umayyad forces and followers of Ibn al-Ash'ath were expelled from Harat in AD 702. Harat was also centre for followers of Ustadhsis. Famous for its textiles during the 'Abbasid caliphate, it was one of the main Muslim centres (with Nishapur, Marv and Balkh) of Iran and central Asia, in which cultural life was dominated by allegiance to pan-Muslim Arabic culture and to local ethnic awareness. Scholars included al-Sam'ani al-Harawi. Arabic and Persian geographers described the city in the tenth century AD. During the Ghazbawid and early Ghurid periods (eleventh century AD), the heretical Karamiyya sect flourished, supported at first by Ghiyath al-Din the Ghurid, who later supported the Sunni *shafi'i* school. Harat prospered under the Ghurid dynasty in the twelfth century AD and the Friday mosque, built by Ghiyath al-Din in AD 1201, is one of finest Islamic buildings in the world. Privately funded *madrasas* specialising in Islamic law (*madhhabs*) developed in the early Saljuq period and a lost city-palace of the Saljuq prince Tughansah was described in detail by Aufi, with its *iwans* and elaborate decoration, located by a lake, and with landscaped terraces.

Captured by the Mongols (AD 1221), its skilled craftsmen fled to the Jazira whilst Harat lay ruined until *c.* AD 1236. In AD 1244 Shams al-Din Kurt was confirmed ruler of Harat for the Mongols and founded a new dynasty that built many mosques and patronised the arts. The Kurt dynasty was overthrown after Timur took Harat (AD 1380) but the city flourished under the Timurid princes, especially under the patronage of Mir 'Ali Shir Nawa'i when it became a centre of science and culture and Timurid capital. Earlier mosques were refurbished, others built, gardens developed and *madrasas* served as centres of education, worship, and community activity. Many contained *mausolea*, such as the Sultan Husayn Baiqara *madrasa*. The tomb of the poet and saint 'Abdallah Ansari was built by Timurid Shah Rukh Mirza (b. AD 1377) and is still highly venerated. Shah Rukh was a patron or the arts centred in Harat and developed an important library. His wife, Gawharshad (d. 1418), constructed fine public buildings, with the Persian architect, Qavam al-Din. The *madrasa* of Gawharshad with its bulbous melon dome (1432–3) was used to bury other members of the dynasty, but four immense broken minarets are all that remains of the *madrasa* that was blown up by visiting British adventurers in 1838. Nearby the Gazargah shrine with tomb of 'Abdallah Ansari (d. AD 1088), Sufi mystic and poet, was rebuilt under Shah Rukh's patronage (*c.* 1425) by architect Zain ud-Din whose tomb, in the form of a crouching dog, is nearby. Following the interests of Shah Rukh, his son Baysunqur Mirza (d. 1433) went on to develop Harat as an important centre of painting that overshadowed the school of Shiraz. Its court artists came from Persia and Afghanistan to paint themes such as the Persian epic *Shah-nameh* (AD 1010, *Book of Kings*) by the Persian epic poet Firdowsi (d. AD 1020). The artists were inspired by the *Khamseh* of Nezami, the work of the poet Sa'di and the Sufi poet Jami and the tradition of miniature paintings, until the Uzbeks sacked the city in 1507.

Between 1507 and 1747 when it became part of a unified Afghanistan, Harat was fought over by Uzbeks, Turkomans, Safawids and Aghans. Between 1837 and 1856 Persians and Afghans fought over the city but it became a provincial capital of Afghanistan by 1863. Controlled by Soviet forces from 1980, then dominated intermittently by the Taliban, fought over by Coalition forces in 2002, it remains culturally associated with Iran.

References

Adamec (1972–85), Farhfidi (1996), Hillenbrand (1994: 414–15), Yarshater (2003).

JANET STARKEY

AL-HARIRI, ABU MUHAMMAD AL-QASIM IBN 'ALI (AD 1054–1122)

Poet, grammarian and man of letters, who wrote in Basra and Baghdad. Although also known for his collected poems and epistles, al-Hariri's continuing reputation has rested on his *Maqamat*, a collection of fifty short narrative pieces in rhymed prose (*saj'*) interspersed with verse, modelled on those of Badi' al-Zaman al-Hamadhani, who is generally considered to have been the first to compose in the genre. Al-Hariri's *maqamat* are structured around a narrator, al-Harith ibn Hammam, and a protagonist, Abu Zayd al-Saruji, who appears (unlike al-Hamadhani's protagonist) in every *maqama*. Apparently modelled on a real person of that name, al-Hariri's Abu Zayd is presented as a confidence trickster whose character includes qualities of wit and erudition, but also a taste for imposture and a tendency to overindulgence in alcohol. Unlike al-Hamadhani's Abu al-Fath al-Iskandari, however, he emerges as a consistent personality throughout the entire fifty *maqamat* – a feature that reinforces the difference between the nature of al-Hamadhani's text, originally composed as a set of oral improvisations, and the more scholarly approach of al-Hariri. A further distinction between the two authors' works lies in al-Hariri's more extensive use of verse, which in al-Hamadhani's work is often incidental and usually undistinguished. Al-Hariri's collection has been regarded by some later critics almost as a picaresque novel, though it lacks the overarching chronological framework necessary for this description, each *maqama* being effectively self-contained.

Al-Hariri's *maqamat*, which quickly eclipsed those of his predecessor, betray their author's profession as a grammarian; their language bristles with puns and obscure vocabulary, and it seems likely that one at least of the author's purposes in composing them was a pedagogic one. In all events, they quickly became regarded as a model of Arabic eloquence; they were used as a school-book for several centuries and sparked

many imitations, including a collection of *maqamat* in Hebrew by a Spanish Jew Judah al-Harizi (AD 1170–1235). Although by general consent al-Hariri's *maqamat* have never been surpassed for their eloquence, the *maqama* form continued to be used intermittently as late as the twentieth century, the last great example being Muhammad al-Muwaylihi's *Hadith 'Isa ibn Hisham*, published in book form in 1906.

References

Beeston (1990: 125–35), Chenery and Steingass (1969), Killito (1978: 18–47).

PAUL STARKEY

HARRAN

From Sumerian/Akkaian 'Harran-U', meaning 'journey', 'caravan' or 'crossroad', also called Haran and Altinbasak, Latin: Carrhae, one of the oldest continuously occupied settlements founded around 2000 BC as a trading post for Ur, now only a village of distinctive beehive mud-brick houses on the Djullab river in Urfa Province, Turkey. Believed to be the birthplace of Abraham, whose family settled in Harran after they left Ur (Gen. 11:31–2) and Jacob, Isaac's son, fled there from the wrath of Esau (Gen. 27:41–29:30). Of strategic importance to the Assyrians on the road from Nineveh to Carchemish, and centre of the cult of Sin, the moon god (1111 BC) until its temple was destroyed by the Byzantine emperor Theodosius in AD 382, its pre-Islamic plan was roughly oval, resembling the moon. The Roman Governor, Crassus, defeated the Parthians in 53 BC at Carrhae and the Persian King Narses defeated Emperor Galerius here in AD 297.

Occupied peacefully by Arabs in AD 640, Harran was an important town to which 'Umar II transferred a school of medicine from Alexandria. Marwan II, the last Umayyad caliph, made Harran his capital (AD 744) until he was overthrown by the 'Abbasids (AD 750). The Umayyad Great Mosque (AD 750) at Harran was square in plan. In AD 830, the 'Abbasid caliph al-Ma'mun forcibly converted the townspeople to Islam. The Sabians (*Sabi'un*), a Neo-Platonic sect regarded as pagans by early Muslims (Q.2:62, Q.5:72, Q.22:17) who worshipped stars and idols, flourished in Harran until the mid-eleventh century. Many were renowned translators of texts on Greek mathematics and astronomy into Arabic and who influenced Muslim 'Abbasid scholars. In the twelfth and thirteenth centuries the city revived under the Numayrids, Fatimids and Saljuqs, who controlled marauding nomads by building massive city walls. From AD 1149 Nur al-Din beautified the city, as did Saladin who enlarged the Great Mosque (AD 1183–6), described by Ibn Jubayr (AD 1184) as being 'of great beauty'. He also mentions Harran's fortified, moated citadel. Muslim numbers increased under the Ayyubids. In AD 1237 the Khwarizmians occupied the town, only for it to be reoccupied by the Ayyubids (AD 1240) until Harran surrendered to the Mongols, who destroyed its mosques, buildings and fortifications in AD 1271. The city was never rebuilt.

References

Creswell (1989: 219–21), Dodge (1967: 59–85), Green (1992), Hillenbrand (1994: 77).

JANET STARKEY

HARUN

'Aaron', the brother of Moses (Musa). See Q.20:30, 92.

See also: **Musa, *nabi*.**

ANDREW J. NEWMAN

HARUT AND MARUT

The two angels responsible for teaching sorcery to men and for creating divisions between husband and wife (Q.2:102).

ANDREW J. NEWMAN

HASAN AL-'ASKARI, ABU MUHAMMAD HASAN IBN 'ALI (*c.* AD 845–74)

Abu Muhammad Hasan ibn 'Ali was born in Medina. He was the eleventh Shi'i Twelver Imam, whose brief period in office lasted from AD 868 until his death six years later. Some of the histories maintain that he was poisoned by the 'Abbasid caliph, al-M'utamid. Hasan became known as *al-'Askari*, presumably because of his lengthy detention under military guard by the 'Abbasids in a camp at Samarra on the Tigris in Iraq. The fact that detention made him almost inaccessible to his followers required him to use messengers in order to communicate with them. His death occasioned a crisis about the succession in the imamate, which gave rise to reports that he had not died but gone into occultation.

References

Hitti (1973: 442), Momen (1985: 44, 59–60, 162).

EDWARD D. A. HULMES

AL-HASAN II, B. MUHAMMAD (r. AD 1162–6)

Called 'Ala Dhikhrihi al-Salam, Grand Master of the Isma'ilis in Alamut. Inaugurated a new phase in Nizari Isma'ilism by proclaiming himself not only *da'i* and *hujja* but also the *khalifa* or representative of God Himself, bringing the messianic *qiyama* or Last Day, to be interpreted symbolically and spiritually, hence requiring of the believer spiritual obedience to the Isma'ili imam rather than mechanical observance of the prescriptions of the *shari'a*.

References

Hodgson (1955: 148–59).

See also: **Hasan-i Sabbah.**

C. E. BOSWORTH

AL-HASAN OF BASRA
(d. AD 728)

An ascetic from Iraq and often included within Sufi chains of initiation, he is known to have criticised the Umayyad rulers, some of whom sought religious guidance from him. Living in a time when some Muslims were amassing great fortunes, Hasan of Basra emphasised spiritual riches rather than earthly rewards.

References

Ritter (1931).

LLOYD RIDGEON

AL-HASAN, IBN 'ALI IBN ABI TALIB (*c.* AD 625–69)

Al-Hasan was the elder son of 'Ali, the fourth of the Rightly Guided Caliphs and Fatima, the daughter of the Prophet Muhammad. He was born *c.* AD 625, a few years after the *hijra* and brought up in Medina in the Prophet's household until Muhammad died in AD 632. The Prophet was clearly fond of his two grandchildren, al-Hasan and al-Husayn, who he is reported to have described on one occasion as 'chiefs of the youths of Paradise', adding on another occasion, 'He who has loved Hasan and Husayn has loved me and he who has hated them has hated me'. In AD 657 Hasan was present at the Battle of Siffin, which was fought on the west

bank of the Euphrates between 'Ali's force of Iraqis and a force of Syrians led by Mu'awiya. Hasan appears to have taken no active part in the battle. When his father was assassinated in Kufa in AD 661, Hasan was thirty-seven years old. He was proclaimed the fifth caliph whilst serving with Muslim troops in Iraq. Pressed by his supporters to engage, in renewed warfare with Syria, he preferred to come to terms with Mu'awiya, soon to be the first Umayyad caliph. Hasan had little interest in exercising political leadership. He gained a reputation for being more at home in the *harem* than in the caliphate. It was not long before he abdicated in favour of Mu'awiya, who guaranteed him an undisturbed retirement in Medina if he renounced the caliphate. Hasan's decision to accept was undoubtedly made easier by a generous settlement of 5 million *dirhams* and an annual pension made up of income from lands in Persia. For his brother, al-Husayn, he succeeded in procuring a settlement of 2 million *dirhams* under the same agreement. The agreement in question is quoted by Hitti (1973) from a copy of the letter Mu'awiya is said to have sent to Hasan after the latter's abdication: 'I admit that because of thy blood relationship thou art more entitled to this high office than I. And if I were sure of thy greater ability to fulfil the duties involved I would unhesitatingly swear allegiance to thee. Now then, ask what thou wilt'. A blank promissory note, which was signed by Mu'awiya, was apparently enclosed with the letter. One account attributes Hasan's death in Medina at the age of forty-five, *c.* AD 669, to natural causes after consumption had taken its course. Among Shi'i Muslims the story is very different. They maintain that he died of poisoning. During his lifetime he is said to have contracted 100 marriages, a feat that gained him the sobriquet *al-mitlaq*, 'the divorcer'. It may be that his marital arrangements brought him any number of personal enemies, who might well have wished him dead. Whatever the truth may be, Shi'i Muslims blame Mu'awiya for the death of Hasan, whom they have elevated to the status of a martyr (*shahid*). Shi'is also describe Hasan as *al-Mujtaba* ('the chosen one'), who became their second imam on his father's death in AD 661. His younger brother al-Husayn succeeded him as head of the house of 'Ali.

References

Hitti (1973: 197), Momen (1985: 26–8).

See also: **al-Husayn, ibn 'Ali ibn Abi Talib; Fatima; Shi'ism; Siffin, Battle of.**

EDWARD D. A. HULMES

HASAN-I SABBAH (d. AD 1124)

Da'i or propagandist and founder of the Nizari branch of the Isma'ilis centred on Alamut in northern Iran. It was Hasan's followers who became known in medieval Christian Europe as Assassins (supposedly from a term for '*hashish*-eaters', because of a popular belief that the daredevil activities of the Assassins were drug induced). In the absence of Nizar, the dispossessed son of the Fatimid Caliph and Imam al-Mustansir, captured by his brother al-Musta'li and imprisoned at Cairo, Hasan assumed the title of *Hujja* 'proof, demonstration of the truth'. Under his leadership, the Isma'ilis spread widely in the mountainous regions of Syria and Iran, achieving a notoriety for their assassination of opponents.

References

Gibb and Bosworth (1960–2003), Hodgson (1955: 37–98).

C. E. BOSWORTH

HASHIM

Muslim genealogies record Hashim as the great-grandfather of the Prophet Muhammad. The ancestry of Hashim is traced back further to Quraysh, whose descendants were divided into ten clans, including that of Hashim, to which Muhammad belonged. The Prophet's uncle, Abu Talib was head of the Banu Hashim and the father of 'Ali, who became the fourth of the Rightly Guided Caliphs in AD 656. It was from the marriage of Fatima and 'Ali, the cousin of the Prophet, that the most honoured line of the Hashim passed through al-Hasan. The 'Alids and the 'Abbasids subsequently claimed legitimacy for their succession to the caliphate and the imamate by linking themselves in direct line of descent to the Prophet Muhammad and the clan of Hashim.

References

Momen (1985: 2–34, 42, 63–4, 70).

See also: **'Abd Manaf; Muhammad ibn 'Abdallah, the Prophet of Islam; Shi'ism**

EDWARD D. A. HULMES

HASHIMITES (1827–1925 in Western Arabia; 1921–58 in Iraq; 1946– in Jordan)

The Hashimite Sharifs of Mecca traced their ancestry back to the Prophet and his clan of Hashim in Mecca. For several centuries they were governors of Mecca for outside powers, and then in the later nineteenth century for the Ottomans Turks. The Sharif Husayn was prominent in the Arab Revolt of 1916 against the Ottomans, and after the First World War members of the family were set up in the newly mandated territories of Iraq and Jordan. The Hashimites lost control of the Hijaz in 1925 to Ibn Su'ud, together with their hopes of reviving for themselves the caliphate, but the branch in Jordan continues today as the Hashimite kings.

References

Bosworth (1996: No. 56), de Gaury (1951), Gibb and Bosworth (1960–2003).

See also: **Su'udis (Saudis)**

C. E. BOSWORTH

HASHIMIYYA

A term used generally to denote the 'Abbasids but used specifically to denote a group seemingly affiliated with early Shi'ism. It is the second usage that concerns us here and in this sense, the term is derived from Abu Hashim (d. AD 716), the son of the celebrated 'Alid Muhammad al-Hanafiyya. This religio-political group is significant as upon the death of Abu Hashim, they believed that the imamate was transferred to Muhammad b. 'Ali b. 'Abdullah b. al-'Abbas and thus to the household of al-'Abbas. Consequently, the 'Abbasids inherited this group and its organisation, which became instrumental in the 'Abbasid propaganda in Khurasan and ultimately, in the overthrow of the Umayyad caliphate.

References

Netton (1997: 99–100), Watt (1997: 14–18).

GAVIN PICKEN

HASHIM, BANU

See: **Hashim**

HAUSA LANGUAGE

The Hausa language is the most important member of the Chad group (centred on Lake Chad), usually assigned to the Hamitic sub family of the Hamito-Semitic family of languages. Hausa is spoken by some 9 million people, three-quarters of whom live in northern Nigeria. Hamito-Semitic languages are spoken in East, Central and West Africa, in the Sahara regions, in the Arabian peninsula, Iraq, Syria, Jordan, Lebanon and Israel. Hausa is also spoken in Benin, the Cameroons, Togo, and other parts of West Africa, where it has been the lingua franca of trade for centuries. For this reason it is learned and used by many non-native Hausa speakers. Hausa employs an alphabet based on Arabic, although in recent times the orthography makes use of Roman characters. The literature of poetry and prose is extensive. The Hausa people are famed for their peripatetic entrepreneurial skills, in the exercise of which individual traders move great distances throughout West Africa in the buying and selling of locally produced goods. They are predominantly Muslim. In the northern provinces of Nigeria they have been among the first to welcome the introduction of Islamic law (*shari'a*).

References

Kirk-Greene (1970).

EDWARD D. A. HULMES

HAUSA STATES, ISLAM IN THE

According to the *Kano Chronicle*, a collection of Hausa traditions written down centuries after the events described, the first s*arki* (king) of Kano was Bogoda, who began to rule in AD 999. The legend of the *Hausa Bakwai*, 'the Hausa Seven', makes special mention of a group of seven dynasties which emerged between the tenth and the thirteenth centuries AD. Five members of this group are generally considered to be the most important of the Hausa states, namely

Daura, Gobir, Katsina, Kano, and Zazzau (Zaria). Sometimes they worked together in the common interest. At other times their interests clashed and quarrels ensued. The Hausa states did not join together in order to form what might be described as the Hausa Empire. They succeeded in retaining their independence until the Fulani conquests of AD 1804–11.

Before the rise of the great kingdoms and empires of the central Sudan, the Hausa peoples were among the most populous in the region. There is little evidence that they were interested in uniting politically with other groups such as the Kanuri, the Bolewa, or the Manga. The Hausas emerge on the scene at the beginning of the second millennium, probably as a result of the intermingling of Berber immigrants from the Sahara and the indigenous Negro population of the savannah. Their homelands were in the central Sudan, a region known as *qasar hausa*, 'the land of the Hausa language'. In time a polity based upon kinship was replaced by one in which authority was based on the control of territory. Independent local communities joined together to form larger groups with centralised administrative arrangements. These moves were no doubt driven initially by common economic and trading interests. Towns and cities, often built on hills for obvious reasons, served local needs. Among them were the great Hausa cities of Dutsen-Turunku, Dutsen-Kufena and Dutsen-Dala.

The city was the seat of the *sarkin qasa*, 'the king of the country'. It provided defence against the raids of marauding tribesmen, enabling neighbouring farmers and peasants to take shelter within its walls as occasion arose. The city provided a market for locally produced produce and for peripatetic traders to sell their wares. The city was also a staging post for much wider trading operations along the trans-Saharan car-avan routes. The government of these emerging states led to creation of burgeoning bureaucracy and a hierarchy of officials, each with title indicating his special function, for example, *sarkin kasuwa*, 'king of the market', *uban farauta*, 'father of hunting', *sarkin noma*, 'king of farming', whose responsibilities included the organising of seasonal religious ritual. At the head of the administration was the *sarkin qasa* (king of the country), whose authority depended to a large extent on his ability to promote the peace and prosperity of his subjects, and on his readiness to reward his supporters from his own resources for services rendered. In colonial times the traditional Hausa and Fulani social and political structures in Nigeria were maintained under the British policy of indirect rule.

Of particular interest in this volume is the question of the rise of Islam in the Hausa states. It is not known for certain when the first Muslims arrived in Hausaland. The spread of Islam in the region gained impetus in the second half of the fifteenth century. Three contemporary kings, Muhammad Korau in Katsina, Muhammad Rabbo in Zazzau, and Muhammad Rumfa in Kano, played an important part in the Islamicisation of the Hausa states. The process was gradual because the Hausa peoples maintained their ancient traditional religious beliefs and practices. Their high god, Ubangiji, was not actively concerned with the day-to-day lives of mortals. More immediately, it was important not to offend the nearer spirits, *iskoki*.

References

Davidson (1977: 274–6).

See also: **jihad**; **Fodio, Shehu Usuman dan**; **Sokoto Caliphate**

EDWARD D. A. HULMES

HAYY IBN YAQZAN

This is the best-known work of the twelfth-century AD philosopher and physician Abu Bakr Ibn Tufayl (*c.* AD 1116–85/6), who served as physician to the Muwah-hid caliph Abu Ya'qub Yusuf for many years. He is credited with introducing Ibn Rushd into the caliph's service, and also with persuading him to compose for Abu Yusuf a set of commentaries on Aristotle. A comment he made in excusing himself from this task gives a hint about the date of *Hayy Ibn Yaqzan*. For he says: 'The only things that prevent me from doing so myself are, as you know, my advanced age, my official responsibilities, and my preoccupation with a project that for me is more important'. It has been suggested that the project he refers to is this book, which means that he must therefore have been engaged with it in the last years before he retired from the Caliph's service in AD 1182. It is thus the fruit of his mature years.

The title *Hayy Ibn Yaqzan*, 'Living, Son of Awake', refers to the protagonist of the book, whose solitary life on a desert island and self-taught wisdom is its subject. But this title, with its clear suggestion that the hero is something of a symbol or archetype, immediately indicates that it is more than a simple tale, and that readers should be alert to multiple layers of meaning. It is borrowed from the allegorical work of the same name by Ibn Sina (d. AD 1037), which is also about a quest for knowledge, but in the form of a journey in which Hayy appears as a supernatural guide for the narrator. Ibn Tufayl acknowledges this earlier story, and the underlying structure of his own account of Hayy's voyage of self-education has correspondences with it. But both the frame of his story and his intention in composing it are quite different from Ibn Sina's tale.

On its narrative surface, the story of Ibn Tufayl's work is not at all difficult to follow. Hayy Ibn Yaqzan lives alone on a deserted island. It is not clear whether he came into existence there spontaneously or whether he was carried there from a nearby island when his mother was forced to abandon him (her marriage to his father Yaqzan was forbidden by her brother the king). He was found and suckled by a doe, and from his youth he learns the secrets of life, the universe and its Maker. The story is about Hayy's discovery of the truths of philosophy and religion without the teachings of either to hand, through nothing more than his own inductive and inferential powers.

Ibn Tufayl traces Hayy's growth and development in seven-year periods, following the received wisdom of Galen. By the age of seven, he learns to make sounds like his doe foster-mother and other animals, to recognise his nakedness and cover it, and to make weapons to defend himself from predators. Then when the doe dies and he cuts her open to find her heart is empty, he realises that whatever was there has left and that this had been the doe of which the body was only an instrument. By investigating the bodies of other animals he comes to see that they too are tools of the vital spirits that direct them but which depart at their deaths.

By the age of twenty-one, in addition to learning about the bodies and spirits of the animals he has dissected, he has also acquired the skills of making clothes, building storehouses near his shelter, hunting and taming wild horses. At this point he begins to see that though animals have many bodily parts they are effectively one, that whole species are also one in certain respects, and that the whole animal kingdom is one. He sees further that plants and animals have common aspects, and that inanimate objects also share certain aspects with them. So he realises that all physical things are one.

Beyond this he comes to see that all beings are made up of physical bodies and spirits, and that the latter are united in what he calls soul. So he concentrates on the latter and begins to realise the world beyond the senses. He also glimpses the Cause behind all things that came into being, and so turns his attention away from the earth to the heavenly bodies. This is his attainment by the age of twenty-eight.

Hayy's reflections and deliberations progress through the realisation that the heavens are in reality one thing, to the point at which he asks whether they are eternal or came into existence at a point in time. He remains baffled by this dilemma for some years, but concludes that the universe must have an ultimate Cause, 'and all are his effects, whether they came to be out of nothing or had no beginning in time'. Thus, by the age of thirty-five he comes to appreciate the nature of this ultimate Being, and sees the effects of his actions all around.

Hayy's attention now fixes on the Being whom he has deduced is the Necessary Existent, and on a means of apprehending him closely. He knows that among physical entities he alone has awareness of this Being, and tries to cultivate this awareness to the exclusion of everything else. Thus he adopts regimes to make himself like the heavenly bodies which are closest to the Necessarily Existent, sometimes spinning around in the way they do. But he goes even beyond this, attempting to resemble the Being by denying his own physicality, until eventually he achieves the point at which he ceases in himself and 'drowned in ecstasy, he witnessed "what no eye has seen or ear heard, nor has it entered into the heart of man to conceive"'. Here he is granted a vision of the universe in its entirety, and from this moment lives on a higher plane, resenting the needs of his body and seeking to enjoy this vision to the exclusion of everything else. So he passes the age of forty-nine.

At this stage in Hayy's progression to the point of uniting with the One, the perfection of his human nature, a sudden change occurs in the story. Just when he yearns to abandon his physical nature, another human comes to invade his transcendent solitude. This is Absal, who with his friend Salaman (both characters from another story by Ibn Sina) lives on a neighbouring island where they follow the faith taught by an ancient prophet. Absal seeks to follow the contemplative religious life, while the other prefers to put the prophet's teaching into practice in community on their island. They part and Absal comes to Hayy's island.

The two meet and after initial fear they begin to communicate (Absal teaches Hayy how to speak), and the autodidact philosopher leads the prophetic disciple into the full truth. For his part, Hayy realises that all Absal tells him about his own faith harmonises with what he himself has seen, though it consists of symbols and makes concessions to the weakness of common people.

The two resolve to return to Absal's island, to teach the truth to its people. But when they arrive and Hayy begins to preach, they realise the ignorance of the people they meet and their indifference to Hayy's words. Hayy perceives that religion serves to help most people to lead decent lives and no more, and that they can cope with no more than the prophets had taught. So the two return to Hayy's island, where they resume their spiritual practices for the rest of their lives.

It is immediately apparent that this fable was written for rather more than the story itself. It contains continual references to philosophical problems of Ibn Tufayl's day and allusions to attempts to resolve them, and also to the wider discussion of the relative merits of philosophical, intuitive and revealed truth. Thus, it is effectively a survey and to some extent synthesis of current debates between proponents of the divine explorations of knowledge in narrative form, an experiment in dramatising intellectual discovery.

This is not to say that the story does not contain narrative finesse. Hayy himself is not altogether implausible as a character; his despair at the loss of his doe foster-mother, and his reassuring if inarticulate signs to Absal when they first meet – he 'patted his head, rubbed his sides, and spoke soothingly to him' – reveal him as a man with feelings, and illustrate Ibn Tufayl's grasp of characterisation. The tension in the narrative, however, lies not in the development of character, but in the manner in which Hayy is plausibly moved through the attainments of knowledge to the highest experience of unitive self-abandonment purely by his own sensory and intellectual efforts. This is the central interest of the story, and it provides the key to understanding what it is about.

The meaning of the story has been seen by some to be an exposition of the fundamental harmony between philosophy and religion as represented by Hayy and Absal. Undoubtedly, this is part of Ibn Tufayl's design, as his repeated quotations from the Qur'an to indicate the equivalents in revelation of Hayy's purely intellectual discoveries amply show. But it has been pointed out by others that this cannot be the main purpose of the story, because its central thrust focuses on Hayy's individual development unaided by scriptural teachings. Thus it is, as Ibn Tufayl himself says at the very outset, an unfolding of 'the secrets of the essential philosophy', by which he means Ibn Sina's teachings about intellectual apprehension of the higher reality and also progressive experience of this until communion is reached. In its deepest meaning it is concerned with rational and mystical ascent to the origin of existence.

It says much about the sophistication of Ibn Tufayl's story that these and other interpretations, among them critiques of formalised Islam (probably in the Maghrib) as represented by the figure of Salaman and his people, and of the alienation of the true seeker from society, have been suggested, and that it continues to be the subject of scholarly inquiry.

The standard edition of *Hayy Ibn Yaqzan* is by Gauthier (1936). Among English translations, Goodman (1972) contains a full introduction and notes. Conrad (1996) is a collection of essays from a group of authors on aspects of the context and intention of the tale. Matar (1998), 98–102 outlines the impact and appeal of work in seventeenth-century England.

DAVID THOMAS

HEAVEN

Al-Janna (the garden) in the Qur'an, referring to the Garden of Eden but also, and especially, Paradise (e.g., Q.61:12, Q.2:23, Q.19:61) and reserved for those who 'repent and believe and do right' (Q.19:60, Q.16:31–2, Q.13:35, also, Q.70:22–35). For synonymous references, see also Q.6:127, Q.10:9, 25, Q.23:11, Q.25:15, Q.29:64, Q.35:35.

Located in Heaven near the 'lote tree on the boundary' (Q.51:22, Q.53:14–15), Paradise is as large as Heaven and Earth together (Q.3:133, Q.57:21), and contains agreeable accommodation (Q.19:72), and dwellings for the Houris (Q.55:72), beings from another world who are kept as virgins and are promised to those in Paradise (Q.44:54, Q.56:22–4, 34–8, 72–4, Q.2:25, Q.3:15, Q.4:57) though Paradise is also populated by families (Q.13:23, Q.36:54–5, Q.40:8, Q.43:70). Paradise features gardens, streams of water, milk, wine, honey and 'every kind of fruit' (Q.47:15). 'As a reward for your deeds' (Q.52:19–20), dwellers in Paradise are also promised wonderful banquets, with every food and drink, the latter never causing drunkenness, silliness or fighting (Q.37:43–9, Q.52:20–4, Q.88:31–5), while being waited on by 'boys of everlasting youth' (Q.76:19, Q.56:17, Q.52:24). Dwellers in Paradise will also be 'resplendent in gazing upon their Lord' (Q.75:22–3). In later revelations, such sensual rewards are held to be allegorical (Q.13:35, Q.47:15) while in Medinan revelations Allah's 'approval' is held to be 'the greater' and 'the supreme Triumph' than such material rewards (Q.9:72).

Qu'ranic references to two gardens (Q.55:46, 62) occur but these are held to be references to the same place.

Although there are no Qur'anic references to a state of Purgatory, Q.7 (The Heights), a late Meccan *sura*, refers to 'dwellers on the heights' who 'call to the dwellers in the Garden' and to 'dwellers in the Fire' (Q.7:46–8).

Prophetic traditions and numerous commentators both expand on and debate these Qur'anic descriptions of Paradise, its rewards and the nature of the vision of Allah which believers would experience. Some explain the Qur'anic descriptions of Paradise's various features as reference to various 'stages' in Paradise. Seven levels (the latter as per Q.17:44, Q.23:86, Q.41:12, Q.65:12) thereof are frequently known.

References

Q.99:60–1, Tafsir ibn Kathir ((http://www.tafsir.com/) .

See also: **al-A'raf; Kafur; al-Kawthar; *al-Nar*; resurrection of the dead; Salsabil; Sidrat al-Muntaha**, **Tasnim**

ANDREW J. NEWMAN

HELL

'Fire'. The term *'al-Nar'* appears more than 100 times in the Qur'an as a reference to Hell, along with such other terms as al-Jahannam (Q.3:12), *al-saqar* ('scorching fire', Q.54:48), *al-Jahim* ('the burning', Q.5:10), *al-Hawiyah* ('the abyss', Q.101:9), *al-hutamah* ('crushing pressure', Q.104:4–5), to which 'those who are rebellious and wicked', 'who turn aside' from the Revelation . . . the criminals' (Q.32:20–2, Q.5:86, Q.7:40), unbelievers and worshippers of idols (Q.21:29, Q.98), blasphemers (Q.39:32), polytheists (Q.40:60, Q.98:6), the Hypocrites (Q.48:6), those who persecute Muslims (Q.85:10) and did not feed the poor (Q.69:34), 'the unbelievers among the people of the Book [Christians and Jews] and the pagans' (Q.98:1–6) are condemned 'for ages' (Q.78:23, also Q.5:37) there they will 'taste the torment of Fire which [they] used to reject as false' (Q.32:20).

The damned are condemned to eating the bitter fruit of the Zaqqum tree (Q.44:43) and to drinking 'boiling water' and the pus of wounds (Q.78:25, Q.14:16). They are fastened with a chain 70 cubits long (Q.69:32). 'The fire of Hell will burn the skin of his head away' (Q.70:15–16). They will be clothed with 'garments of fire' and boiling water 'like boiling oil' will be poured on them 'melting their skins and that which is in their bellies' and they shall be lashed with 'hooked rods of iron' (Q.22:19–23, Q.18:29).

The nineteen angelic guardians of Hell (the Zabaniyya, Q.96:18, Q.74:30–1) are led by Malik (Q.43:77) who will command them to cast the condemned into the fire. Just as there are Qur'anic references to seven heavens (Q.17:44, Q.23:86, Q.41:12, Q.65:12), so Hell has seven gates, for each class of the condemned (Q.15:44). The *jinn* also inhabit Hell (Q.7:38, Q.55:39).

At the same time, *al-nar* has other Qur'anic references. The *jinn* were created out of a 'smokeless fire' (Q.15:27, Q.55:15), for example, and heavenly 'fire' is a proof of prophetic mission (Q.3:183) and a sign of divine power (Q.55:35).

References

Q.96:18, 74:30–1, 15:44, Tafsir ibn Kathir (http://www.tafsir.com/).

See also: **al-A'raf**; *al-Jahim*; **al-Janna**; **judgement on the** *yawm al-qiyama*; **Malik**; **scales, judgement with**; *Sirat al-Jahim*; **Zaqqum, tree of**

ANDREW J. NEWMAN

HELLENISM

Muslim civilisation has been influenced by the intellectual and cultural achievements of Hellenic culture in a number of important ways. When al-Ya'qubi, the great Muslim historian, described the Greeks as 'philosophising sages', he was expressing an important element of traditional Muslim respect for elements of Hellenism. Adopting the Greek classification of sciences (medicine, logic, metaphysics) in the tenth century AD, Muslim philosophers produced a hybrid Graeco-Arabic tradition within Islam which received both admiration and opprobrium amongst Muslim thinkers in subsequent years. The influence of this non-Arab tradition on the Muslim Arab conquerors began with the translation of Greek works into Arabic in initiatives such as the *Bayt al-Hikma* of the 'Abbasid Caliph al-Ma'mun (d. AD 833). The Neoplatonic school of the Mediterranean influenced great Muslim thinkers such as al-Farabi (d. AD 950). The Aristotelian philosophical tradition was adopted by Ibn Rushd (d. AD 1198). However, there was vehement opposition to the adoption of this un-Islamic learning, and this was given expression in a sophisticated manner by al-Ghazali (d. AD 1111). A less sophisticated campaign against Hellenic influence was to be found amongst the Hanabila, though here too, the respect for the Greek tradition of a Hanbali thinker such as Ibn Taymiyya (d. AD 1328) is clear despite his personal dislike of the use of Greek logic in religious sciences. In theology, Hellenic methods of proof can be seen to have been utilised in the dialectic format of *kalam* works, though the primacy of revelation in the Ash'ari tradition has, to an extent, restrained this influence. Further, the principal elements of Islamic mathematics and medicine are almost entirely adaptations of the system laid out by the Hellenic masters such as Euclid and Galen.

References

Gutas (1988), Walzer (1962).

ROBERT GLEAVE

HERESIOGRAPHICAL WORKS

This is the overall name given to works that survey and place in order the beliefs of Muslims and often of non-Muslims as well, though some of them are actually doxographical rather than heresiographical. Their titles frequently include such terms as *milal*, *nihal* and *ahwa'*, which refer to groups possessing different beliefs and opinions and can be employed in complimentary and derogatory ways, or the more impartial *maqalat*, which simply refers to the varying teachings attributed to different groups.

There are records of surveys by Muslim authors of different beliefs from at least the ninth century AD onwards. The little-known figure Abu Ya'la Muhammad al-Misma'i, nicknamed Zurqan (d. *c.* AD 891), wrote a *Kitab al-Maqalat* (*The Book of Teachings*), in which he included the views of Muslims, Aristotle, the people of Harran (often regarded as star-worshippers), Sabians, Hindus and Buddhists, the even more shadowy Abu 'l-'Abbas al-Iranshahri (late ninth century AD) wrote another *Kitab al-Maqalat*, based on al-Misma'i and including the

teachings of the Jews, Christians, Manichaeans, Hindus and Buddhists, and
the better-known independently minded
Abu 'Isa Muhammad b. Harun al-Warraq
(mid-ninth century) wrote a *Kitab
Maqalat al-Nas wa-'khtilafihim* (*People's
Teachings and the Differences between
them*), which included the views of a
number of Christian groups, maybe as
many as seventy, Jewish groups, dualist
groups (this remained a major source of
information for hundreds of years, and
attracted accusations of sympathy on
the part of the author), Muslim groups
and possibly pre-Islamic Arabs. This work
is cited as a source by a number of later
authors, and from comparisons of wording was evidently employed without
attribution by many more. It appears to
have been substantially descriptive in
character, with no sustained arguments
against the many different views it relates,
although by placing the groups in some
order with respect to the teachings about
the nature of God for which they may
well have been included (it is at least
noteworthy that only groups who held
monotheist or related teachings are recorded from the work), al-Warraq may have
been communicating an implicit judgement about them.

While it seems clear that these and
other such works from the ninth century
AD were surveys and presumably classi-
fications or gradings of religious views,
little more can be said about them since
they have not survived. From the end of
the ninth century AD more information
is available. Al-Hasan b. Musa al-Nawbakhti's (d. before AD 922) extant *Kitab
Firaq al-Shi'a* (*The Sects of the Shi'a*),
appeared at this time. He also wrote a
lost *Kitab al-Ara' wa'l-Diyanat* (*Opinions
and Religions*), which is known to have
included references to Greek philosophers,
Indian religions, Sabians and various
Muslims, very much like the earlier
works from this century. But the first

major extant heresiographical work is
the *Maqalat al-Islamiyyin wa'khtilaf al-
Musallin*, (*The Teachings of those who
Belong to Islam, and the Differences
between those who Pray*) of Abu 'l-Hasan
'Ali b. Isma'il al-Ash'ari (AD 873–935),
the eponym of the leading Sunni theological school. In its final form this is a
work of his later years, though it may
incorporate parts which he wrote earlier
when he was still a Mu'tazilite. It is in
two parts, the first a short account of
the historical origins of schism in Islam
and a long patient listing of the major
groups of his day, and the second a
thematic tabulation of the various questions debated among Muslim intellectuals.

Al-Ash'ari's *Maqalat*, like al-Warraq's earlier work, does not contain criticism to any notable degree. As its title
indicates, all those who are included in
the work are regarded as Muslims and
'those who pray', and so the work is a
somewhat impartial survey rather than
an appraisal of correct and incorrect
doctrines. It serves as a handbook of
theological views that might aid the
reader in knowing what particular sects
and individuals thought, and then what
range of opinions was offered on the
various questions debated within theology. Al-Ash'ari also composed a lost
and little-known *Maqalat Ghayr al-Islamiyyin* (*The Teachings of Non-Muslims*),
which may have been organised in this
same twofold way.

The first surviving work in which judgements are offered about the rightness
and wrongness of different beliefs is
the *Farq bayn al-Firaq* (*The Distinction
between the Sects*), of Abu Mansur 'Abd
al-Qahir al-Baghdadi (d. AD 1037), which
is concerned solely with Muslim sects
and those which claim to belong to Islam.
It is divided into five main chapters, the
first two concerned with the reasons
for the divisions in Islam, the third with
erring sects, the fourth with sects that

claim to be Islamic but are not, and the fifth with 'the saved sect', *al-firqa 'l-najiya*, which al-Baghdadi identifies as the *Ahl al-Sunna wa'l-jama'a*. The whole work leads up to the conclusion in which this group is identified.

The key to understanding the *Farq* is given in Chapter 1, where al-Baghdadi explains that the Muslim community divided over doctrinal differences in fulfilment of the saying of the Prophet that the Jews would divide into seventy-one sects, the Christians into seventy-two, and the Muslims into seventy-three sects. This is the informing principle of the work, and it generates both the number of sects identified and the criteria by which their relations to orthodoxy can be judged. But it also raises the question of the correspondence between at least some of the sects that are specified and historical fact. For example, the Mu'tazili sects of the Jahiziyya, Jubba'iyya and so on, named after leading individual scholars, are less likely to have existed as doctrinally distinct groups than to have been the author's own reifications as he strove to arrive at the predicted number of sects. This characteristic of the *Farq* identifies it as a work of theology as much as a record of heresiographical divisions in Islam.

Al-Baghdadi's *Farq bayn al-Firaq* is the earliest of a trio of heresiographical works that show the genre in its full flowering. The second of these is the Andalusian Abu Muhammad 'Ali b. Ahmad Ibn Hazm's (AD 994–1064) *Kitab al-Fisal* (or *Fasl*) *fi 'l-Milal wa'l-Ahwa' wa'l-Nihal* (*The Division between the Religious Groups, the Followers of Fancy and the Sectarians*), a hard-hitting critique of all the errors in those who deviate from the right way. It is a long, diverse work, in the standard published edition divided into five parts.

In the first of these Ibn Hazm scrutinises the views of non-Muslim groups including Jews and Christians, and makes incisive criticisms of their scriptures. In the second he pursues his attack on Christianity and the Gospel, and then turns to the detractors of Islam, and to the Muslim belief in the unity and characteristics of God. He continues in the third part with Muslim beliefs, including the Qur'an, divine omnipotence and human responsibility, the status of unbelievers, and the nature of belief and disbelief. In the fourth part he examines the obedience of the prophets, eschatology, the merits of the early community and the imamate, and then attacks the Shi'a, Khawarij, Mu'tazila and other sects. Then lastly in the fifth part he discusses minor questions discussed among Muslim theologians.

It is clear that for all its diversity (which some have attributed to incorporation of what were originally separate works into some parts) the *Fisal* follows an essentially unified theological line, from basic questions of epistemology and the origin of the world, through the character of God as Creator to true belief in him, and the nature of the correct form of that belief. But Ibn Hazm's argument progresses as much by refutation of those whose teachings conflict with various stages of his demonstration, for example, the Christians on the unity of God, the Jews on prophethood, as by statements of positive beliefs. It is structured according to the traditional teachings of faith as the Zahiri Ibn Hazm holds them, and turns against the particular non-Muslim and Muslim groups where their doctrines become illustrations as counter versions of his own. Thus the *Fisal* is as much a polemical thematic theology as it is a theologically structured heresiography. A significant feature is that some at least of its material is the product of Ibn Hazm's own researches into faith communities of his day and their beliefs, although this is inserted into his preconceived view that his own faith, in his own interpretation, is the only true form.

The third fully developed heresiographical work is Abu 'l-Fath Muhammad al-Shahrastani's (*c.* AD 1087–1153) *Kitab al-Milal wa'l-Nihal*, 'The Book of Religious Groups and Sects', which dates from about AD 1127–8. This is the most comprehensive heresiography known from the Islamic world, covering both religious communities, *milal*, and sects without a God-given basis, *nihal*. Drawing upon a host of named and unnamed previous sources, al-Shahrastani orders the various groups under these two headings, the Muslims with all their subgroups, Jews, Christians, Zoroastrians, dualists and Manichaeans – all claiming a scripture – under the first, and the Sabians, philosophers, *jahili* Arabs and Indians under the second. Within each division and subdivision there is a strict though unobtrusive hierarchical order, from the general to the specific.

Unlike al-Baghdadi and Ibn Hazm, al-Shahrastani refrains from systematic attacks on those with whom he disagrees, allowing himself no more than occasional remarks. It can be inferred that the order of his arrangement is an indication of his judgement, and he does state in the first of his five prefaces that only one group preserves the truth. But he does not identify this, and while it can safely be assumed that it is Muslim, he says no more. Thus the *Milal* has characteristics both of a heresiography and of a religious and historical geography. It remains the most comprehensive work of its kind from the Islamic world.

These works that share the feature of surveying religious groups differ in a number of aspects. Some confine themselves to Islam, while others take in the major religions that could be known in their day, some verge on the polemical, while others appear almost indifferent to the diverse faiths they record, some show how Islam is the supreme embodiment of truth, while others reflect an antiquarian curiosity in details of other people's faiths. But all the examples that are known organise the faiths they treat in one or other way that indicates or at least implies a gradation of some kind (the only exception is possibly al-Ash'ari's *Maqalat*).

This feature raises the question of the intention of the authors. Of course, this must usually be guessed, but with some it is clear that they have set out to establish that only one form of Islamic faith is right by demonstrating the errors in the rest. Others are not so definite, and yet they still tend towards the assumption that Islam or one form of it is correct, and others fail by degrees. Thus, they are all part of the theological enterprise of proving and defending the truth of Islam and its superiority. And in bearing apologetic and polemical features of this kind, they may all be termed heresiographical.

For lost early heresiographies, see Monnot (1986) Thomas (1996: 275–90). Major extant works are as follows: al-Nawbakhti (1931), al-Ash'ari (1930), al-Baghdadi (1910), Ibn Hazm (1926).

See also:*al-Milal wa'l-Nihal*

DAVID THOMAS

HEYERDAHL, THOR (1914–97)

Norwegian ethnologist, adventurer, and prolific writer and documentary filmmaker who recreated a number of ancient journeys. In 1947, he drifted from Peru to Polynesia on his balsa-wood raft, *Kon Tiki*. In 1969–70, his Ra expeditions sailed Egyptian-style papyrus boats from Morocco to the Caribbean. In 1977, he sailed from Iraq to the Horn of Africa in his reed boat, *Tigris*.

References

Ralling (1990).

SIMON W. MURDEN

229

HIJAB

The Arabic word carries a nominal, an adjectival, and a metaphysical meaning. Literally 'veil', and then 'partition', the term *hijab* describes the dress (specifically, the head-covering) worn by a woman in order to present herself in public with due modesty. Whilst requiring a woman to cover every part of her body in public except the hands and face, it is not universally obligatory in Islamic societies for her to wear the veil (cf. Q.24:30–1). The term also expresses the disposition of a Muslim woman to adopt the modest form of dress as defined within the Islamic community in which she lives. The word *hijab* assumes a metaphysical significance when it is used of the 'partition', which divides the created world from the Creator. Islamic mystics have developed the notion of a 'veil' that serves to protect human senses from the otherwise blinding effulgence of the Light emanating from God (cf. Q.4:174, Q.24:35–6). This 'veil' refracts some of this glorious light so that human beings may at times catch a glimpse, but not more, of its source.

References

Bouhdiba (1985: 233–7), Omran (1992: 40–58).

See also: ***burqu'***

EDWARD D. A. HULMES

AL-HIJAZ

Also spelt Hejaz, Hedjaz, al-Hidjaz, meaning 'the barrier', birthplace of the Prophet Muhammad and spiritual home (*al-bilad al muqaddasa*) of Islam, on the mountainous coast of the Red Sea from Jordan to 'Asir, corresponding to the western province of Saudi Arabia. There are three main sections. The north was occupied by Chaldean kings of Babylon who used Tayma' as their summer capital; later it was part of the Nabatean kingdom (10 BC–AD 200) based at Mada'in Salih, and the Damascus–Makka pilgrim route crossed the area. The southern section is mountainous with valleys. Al-Hijaz is served by the Red Sea ports of Jiddah (for Makka) and Yanbu' (for Medina) and major cities are now linked by modern highways. Restrictions to access in al-Hijaz have always been placed on non-Muslims.

The central part is the most important in the history of Islam. Previously famous for its gold mines, from the seventh century onwards the region was the focus of Islamic pilgrimage (*hajj*) to the sacred cities (*harams*) of Makka as the site of the Ka'ba, and Medina al-Munawwara. This is the region of the migration (*hijra*) by the Prophet Muhammad from Makka to Medina (AD 622), where he died in AD 632. After 'Ali transferred the seat of government to Kufa, the Prophet's house in Medina became a sanctuary as the location of Allah's revelations, and was converted to a mosque by AD 674. The Qur'an reflects Hijazi orthography. The region continued to be a source of literary inspiration to Muslim poets, mystics as well as theologians and jurists: for example, Malik ibn Anas (d. AD 796), founder of one of the four major Sunni Islamic law schools, the Maliki, flourished in Medina.

Allegiances and territorial groupings of Bedouin tribes are significant and have relevance beyond al-Hijaz. Muhammad's tribe, the Quraysh, dominated Makka; al-Aws and al-Khazradj were principal tribes in Medina. The Qurashi Banu Shayba are the hereditary guardians of the Ka'ba. Many caliphates derive from the Quraysh including the Rashidun, Umayyads, 'Abbasids and the Hashimids. Those who bear the title of *sharif* (descendants of the Prophet) have been influential throughout the Muslim world. The Harab live between Makka and Medina and other Bedouin groups migrated to

Egypt and the Maghrib (eleventh century AD).

The pilgrimage was under the control of Bahgdad until AD 1258, then controlled by the Egyptians. Al-Hijaz was described by Ibn Jubayr (AD 1145–1217) and Ibn Buttata (d. 1368 or AD 1377), who visited Makka between AD 1326 and 1347. In 1517 al-Hijaz was occupied by the Turks. Nominal rule remained in hands of the *sharifs* of Makka until the early nineteenth century, when Makka and al-Madin were raided by the Wahhabis. After 1845, al-Hijaz was controlled by the Ottomans who built the Damascus–Medina railway (1900–8, 820 miles [1,320 kilometres]) for pilgrims. Sharif Husayn ibn 'Ali proclaimed himself King of al-Hijaz (1916–24) until a Wahhabi invasion. In 1926 Ibn Sa'ud, sultan of Najd, became King of al-Hijaz and by 1932 al-Hijaz, Najd and other districts becamse the Kingdom of Saudi Arabia with Ta'if as its summer capital.

References

Meisami and Starkey (1998: I, 285–6), Ochsenwald (1984), Wohaibi (1973), Yamani (2004).

JANET STARKEY

HIJRA

The term *hijra* (migration) is used by Muslims specifically to refer to the Prophet Muhammad's departure from his native city Mecca (*makka al-mukarrama*, 'Mecca the Blessed') in the year AD 622. He and a small group of his followers moved to Yathrib, some 280 miles (450 kilometres) to the north-east. They were obliged to leave Mecca because of the increasing hostility and persecution faced by the small number of Muslims. For understandable reasons, Muslims dislike the suggestion that the word *hijra* be translated as the 'flight' of the Prophet. To mark his arrival in Yathrib, the place

was renamed 'the City of the Prophet' (*Madinat al-Nabi*), a phrase subsequently shortened to Medina, the name by which it is still known. The exact date of the *hijra* is uncertain, but tradition records it as having taken place in the month of September AD 622. The significance of the Prophet's *hijra* for members of the Islamic community was officially recognised some sixteen years later in AD 637, when the second of the four Rightly Guided Caliphs ('Umar ibn al-Khattab, who died in the year 23 *anno hejirae*), named the year AD 622 as the first year of the Islamic era, renaming it as AH 1. For Muslims the word *hijra* carries an existential as well as a historical significance. In consequence, it refers not merely to an ancient historical event but also to a present personal spiritual experience. The 'migration' or 'departure' of Muhammad from Mecca to Medina marked a new beginning for him and a break with the religion of the past. It marked the beginnings of the expansion of Islam from its geographical roots in Mecca. The decision to become a Muslim, to identify oneself as a member of the Islamic community, marks a spiritual point of departure for anyone prepared to profess Islam. For Muslims generally, and for converts to Islam in particular, the term *hijra* signifies conversion, a decision to make a fresh start in life, and thus to initiate a radical break with the past.

References

Hitti (1973), Momen (1985: 5–8, 116), Tritton (1968: 181).

EDWARD D. A. HULMES

HIKMAT AL-ISHRAQ

This key foundational work of later Iranian philosophy is the major composition of the twelfth-century AD philosopher Shihab al-Din Abu 'l-Futuh Yahya b.

Habash al-Suhrawardi. He was born in Persia but spent his last years in Aleppo, where he composed this work and was executed on the order of the Ayyubid Sultan Salah al-Din in AD 1191, at the age of thirty-six.

The *Hikmat al-Ishraq* (*The Philosophy of Illumination*), which al-Suhrawardi says he completed in AD 1186, enunciates the teaching of illuminationism, or what may be termed the systematisation of the intuitive apprehension of truth. It presents a critique of previous philosophical trends in Islam, despite being deeply indebted to Ibn Sina, and looks back beyond Aristotle to ideas about inspiration found in Plato and earlier thinkers. For this reason, it has been characterised as a theosophical or mystical text, though equally defended as a sound philosophical resolution of ambiguities concerning the axiomatic premises of Peripatetic thought.

The *Hikmat al-Ishraq* stands out from the other major surviving works of al-Suhrawardi, which address conventional Aristotelian topics. It has thus been understood as a departure from them in its exploration of light and the Light of Lights as the source of being, referring back to pre-Islamic Iranian concepts. But it has also been defended, in fact, as a continuation of the Shaykh's earlier works, which themselves expose and criticise ambiguities in Aristotelianism, and as such prepare the way for the new system laid out in this mature work with its own distinctive premises.

The fundamental element in this new system is light as the most immediately apparent entity in existence. This emanates from the supreme source, the Light of Lights, and constitutes part of all material and non-material being. Non-material being comprises the hierarchy of lights which govern the heavenly spheres (al-Suhrawardi's cosmology resembles Ibn Sina's closely here, though he admits many more lights in his system than the ten

Intellects of his predecessor) and thereby control the lower world. They are pure light, and eternally emanate from the Light of Lights. As they contemplate their separation from their source, from them emanate the material entities that make up the heavenly bodies, and from these in turn emanate the bodies of the observable world. Material substance in both the heavenly and earthly realms thus all derives from the same source in the heavenly lights.

An important implication of this system of emanation in which light is intrinsic to the constitution of all entities, is that material existences can apprehend themselves as such and not, as in the Peripatetic school, only by virtue of formally distinguishable essences which participate in higher forms of reality. In this al-Suhrawardi, in contradiction to Ibn Sina, gives primacy to concrete essence over superadded existence.

The *Hikmat al-Ishraq* comprises a brief introduction and two major parts. In the introduction al-Suhrawardi looks back to Plato and earlier Western and Eastern philosophers as his precursors, and asserts that intuitive philosophy, *al-ta'alluh*, has as important a history as discursive philosophy, although its masters have sometimes been hidden. He warns that only those with a modicum of intuitive knowledge will profit from this book.

The first part, 'On the Rules of Thought', is effectively a simple survey and critique of the logical tools of philosophy. It comprises three discourses, *maqalat*: on definitions, in which al-Suhrawardi shows that unless one already has direct knowledge of a thing any definition of it will not avail; on proofs, in which he shows that all syllogisms can be simplified to a basic formula; and on fallacies, in which he shows how to avoid common logical pitfalls. In the third section of this third discourse he develops his criticisms of peripatetic philosophy in a series of ten 'judgements', and concomitantly outlines his own methodology in preparation for the second part of the work.

The second part, 'On the Divine Lights, the Light of Lights, and the basis and order of existence', contains the substantive metaphysical system for which al-Suhrawardi became known. It comprises five discourses. The first explains its basic elements, light and darkness, the forms of light, including the immaterial lights from which other being is derived, and ultimately the Light of Lights which is the uncaused cause of all existence. The second and third discourses deal with the cosmological system of the emanated lights and material existences that descend from the Light of Lights, and then the complex relations between them that give rise to the phenomena of the physical world. Here al-Suhrawardi solves one of the major difficulties of Ibn Sina's cosmology by showing that the One may have knowledge of the particulars in the contingent world simply through their being present to him. This is the supreme instance of his philosophy of knowledge by immediate presence, rather than by the causal relation required in Ibn Sina's system, and an indication of how he systematised his fundamental axiom that true knowledge is imparted intuitively, 'by presence', rather than by the exercise of rational faculties.

The fourth discourse explains how the physical world is founded as light, and the fifth is concerned with topics of religion, such as salvation, the nature of evil, prophecy and visions in dreams. The work concludes with a portrayal of the true seer, who will be like the great philosophers and prophets, immediately aware of the Light of Lights and a commanding presence to those around him.

The *Hikmat al-Ishraq* is obviously related to Ibn Sina's works, and particularly the *Shifa'*. In many respects it actually revises much of the systematic there. But it is far from being simply derivative, as it establishes its whole system on the principle of light, rather than intellect, which produces significantly different consequences. It also resembles mysticism in some ways, but it never loses its philosophical rigour or its distinction between the One and the many.

The work does not appear to have exerted an immediate influence, though individual scholars expounded its teachings and left commentaries upon it. It eventually became popular in Persia in the sixteenth century, and there remained a lasting authority. In the seventeenth century, Mulla Sadra (d. AD 1631) expressed disagreement with a number of its key teachings, and thereby caused a continuing split in Persian illuminationist thought between those who remained faithful to al-Suhrawardi's original conception and those who followed a revised form.

The best edition and translation of the *Hikmat al-Ishraq* is by Walbridge and Ziai (1999).

References

Aminrazavi (1996), Fakhry (1983: Chapter 20), Netton (1989: Chapter 6), Ziai (1990).

DAVID THOMAS

HILAL

From Arabic, *al-hilal* (crescent moon). As an architectural term, *hilal* refers to the metal device of a crescent moon located at the tip of a minaret or at the apex of the dome of a mosque to identify the direction of the *qibla* especially for people praying outside, the centre of the *hilal* especially refers to the *qibla*. The use of the crescent as a symbol of Islam is associated with the Ottoman Turks who both adorned their mosques with golden crescents and displayed the crescent and star on their flags. The moon is also associated with Islam through the calendar which is based on a lunar year of rotating seasons.

References

Goodwin (1987).

JENNIFER SCARCE

HILM

The pre-Islamic Arab virtue of *hilm* ('clemency', 'tranquillity of temperament', 'gentleness', 'forbearance') may be defined as the virtue that enables the soul (*al-nafs*) to remain tranquil in the face of provocation, however dire or protracted. In Islamic times it continued to be cultivated as a *finesse politique*, a rare willingness to pursue one's aims by peaceful means rather than through the use of force. Some of the Arab biographers of the Umayyad leader Mu'awiya (AD 661–80) considered that his ability to achieve his ends and to outwit his opponents without resorting to force (at least on occasions) was attributable to the self-control he was able to show as a man who possessed the virtue of *hilm* to an enviable degree.

References

Hitti (1973: 87–8, 197).

EDWARD D. A. HULMES

HIMA'

Hima is an Arabic term that refers to a protected area of land that is normally under the jurisdiction of the Government, and public usage is prohibited. Often *hima* refers directly to land that individuals are not permitted to graze, except those designated by law. Islam stipulates certain conditions for the classification of land as *hima* in so far as the acreage in question should be limited in size and the restrictions of usage must have been put in place to serve the public interest and not that of one individual or any particular group. The system of *hima* is crucial to Islamic environmental conservation, thus sanctuaries are legalised on this basis in order to prevent misuse of environmentally important land, by tree felling and logging or building etc.

References

Ibn Manzur (n.d.), Izzi Dien (2000: 35–7).

MAWIL IZZI DIEN

HIPPOCRATES (*BUQRAT*)

The theory and practice of medicine in medieval Islam was founded on the Greek systems of Hippocrates and Galen. The classical Greek texts were translated into Arabic when the latter became the language of re-invigorated scientific inquiry. Hippocrates (*c.* 460–370 BC), still known today as 'the Father of Medicine', was the most famous physician to appear in ancient Greece. Little is known of his life. He was born on the island of Kos, where he earned a living practising and teaching medicine. He died at Larissa in Thessaly. His empirical methods in diagnosis, prognosis and treatment promoted an approach to medicine as an independent discipline, separated as never before from the study of philosophy and the influence of superstition. He maintained that sickness and disease are the consequences of an imbalance in the 'humours' or 'fluids' of the body, namely, the blood, the phlegm, the yellow bile and the black bile. Health is to be found when the correct, or natural, balance is restored. He encouraged moderation in eating and drinking, and recommended the beneficial effects of living in places where the air is pure.

Although his name will continue to be associated with the Hippocratic Oath, its authorship has been attributed to him mistakenly. The pledge is still made in several countries, including the United Kingdom, by practitioners about to enter the medical profession, who promise to use their knowledge and skill ethically in the service of patients. Over a period of 200 years the followers of Hippocrates produced the *Corpus Hippocraticum*, a collection of seventy-two works on aspects of medical treatment and surgery. Many of his ideas were adopted, developed and applied by the Graeco-Roman physician, Galen. This legacy of knowledge and experience was to provide the foundation of medical theory and practice in Europe for 1,500 years.

References

Hitti (1973: 367–71), Mostyn and Hourani (1988: 270–2).

See also: **Galen (*Jalinus*, Claudius Galenus), Ibn Sina, Abu 'Ali al-Husayn (Avicenna); medicine and pharmacology; al-Razi, Abu BAkr Muhammad Ibn Zakariyya**

EDWARD D. A. HULMES

HIRA'

The degree of security and leisure afforded to the Prophet Muhammad by his marriage to the wealthy widow Khadija enabled him to spend more time in private meditation. He was often to be seen occupied in penance and solitary thought, wrapped in a mantle, in a cave (*ghar*) in the side of Mount Hira above Mecca. His associates noticed that these periods often left him deeply troubled in spirit. On one occasion in the year AD 610 whilst in the cave he heard the command, 'Recite (*iqra'*) in the name of your Lord, who created man from a clot ('*alaq*) of blood'. This, according to tradition, was mediated to

him by the Angel Jibril. This first revelation, which constituted Muhammad's call to be the Prophet and Messenger of God, appears in Q.96 of the Qur'an. The revelations continued for the next twenty-two years until his death, after which they were collected to form the Qur'an.

References

Haleem (2004: 428), Q.96 and 97.

See also: **Night of the Descent of the Qur'an**
EDWARD D. A. HULMES

HIRABA (HIGHWAY ROBBERY)

The act of standing in a public road and either fighting with a member of the public or stealing his or her property. This is applicable to both single individuals and groups of offenders. If the perpetrator fulfils the usual conditions of sanity and being of accepted maturity, etc. then he or she will be subject to punishment. These conditions are also a prerequisite for incurring the appropriate punishment for other categories of theft, where the value of the stolen goods is also considered before sentence is issued. In the case of highway robbery, which must have occurred in an Islamic state, the committing of the crime incurs the amputation of one hand and one leg from opposite sides of the body. If the life of the victim is taken and there is no theft of property, then the death penalty is incurred. If both property and life are taken, then the offender incurs amputation and subsequently crucifixion. If the highway robber only frightens the victim, then a discretionary punishment and jail sentence will be pronounced.

References

al Dhahabi (1985: 98–100).
MAWIL IZZI DIEN

HISBA

An Arabic term derived from *hisab*, meaning 'calculating'. *Hisba* is an Islamic notion that originated as an ethical practice at the time of the Prophet, whereby he encouraged all Muslims to remonstrate, not only when witnessing the occurrence of something wrong, but also when perceiving the omission of a beneficial action. 'He who sees an evil should remonstrate by his hand, his mouth or within himself, which is the weakest of faith ... '. This ideal developed into a social institution that has come to supervise all behaviour and practice both in the marketplace and other public domains.

There are two categories of *hisba*, the first being related to individual practice that is limited by personal adherence to the law. In other words, a person cannot take the law into his own hands. The second is official *hisba* which is a public service provided by the Government. This is achieved by the appointment of an overseer entitled *muhtasib* who is expected to enjoin good and discourage evil in all matters. His supervisory position demands strength of character that will not waver in the face of any malpractice and he may refer to the police for assistance. The *muhtasib* has a variety of duties such as ensuring that people perform prayer on time and in the correct manner. He must also supervise the proper adherence to ritual by remonstrating with those who break their fast during Ramadan for example. He is also expected to oversee the marketplace and to check for any fraudulent practice, such as traders who cheat their customers by tampering with their wighing scales. The *muhtasib* can command huge respect depending on his approach, and the nature of the conditions for his original appointment dictates that he should not only be knowledgeable, but also possess excellent interpersonal skills. Interestingly, 'Umar appointed the knowledgeable Muslim lady al-Shifa as a *muthasib* in the markets of Medina and despite being known for her severity, she proved to be extremely successful at her job.

References

Izzi Dien (1997: 115), Mawardi (1973: 242), al-Zuhayli (1985: 768).

MAWIL IZZI DIEN

HISHAM B. 'ABD AL-MALIK (AD 724–43)

Hisham succeeded his older brother Yazid II and was the fourth son of 'Abd al-Malik b. Marwan to become Umayyad caliph. After Mu'awiya b. Abi Sufyan and 'Abd al-Malik, Hisham is considered by Muslim historians to be the last statesman of the Umayyad family. He largely continued the fiscal policies inaugurated by 'Umar b. 'Abd al-'Aziz (r. AD 717–20) and which led to increasing conversion to Islam. In contrast to the rule of 'Umar, however, the Government under Hisham began to show a distinct tendency towards absolutism with much of the bureaucracy being controlled centrally from the capital in Syria and with the caliph surrounded by state officials who stood between him and the populace.

Internally, Hisham's reign is notable for being a period of relative peace, despite the ill-fated but potentially serious Shi'ite revolt of Zayd b. 'Ali in Kufa (AD 738). Externally, however, Hisham was faced with many enemies on all frontiers of the empire, these including attacks by the Turgesh tribes in Khurasan and by the Khazar in Adherbayjan and on the Armenian frontier, incursions by the Byzantines, unrest in Egypt, and an extensive Berber revolt which threatened the loss of the whole of North Africa. Showing considerable energy and resourcefulness, Hisham was able to avert all external threats and with his death the empire was comparatively secure and peaceful.

During Hisham's reign and that of his brother al-Walid b. 'Abd al-Malik (r. AD 705–15) the Islamic empire attained its greatest extent, stretching from the Atlantic and the Pyrenees to the Indus and China. With Hisham, however, Muslim expansion more or less came to a halt.

The high point of Umayyad power and glory which had begun under the rule of 'Abd al-Malik came to end with the death of Hisham, the dynasty declining rapidly to its fall. His son and intended successor, Mu'awiya, died before him and Hisham was obliged to recognise his nephew al-Walid, a son of Yazid II, as his heir.

References

Kennedy (1996: 108–12), Muir (1915: 382–404), Shaban (1971: 138–52), al-Tabari (1985–95: XXV, see index; XXVI, see index).

RONALD PAUL BUCKLEY

HIZB

'Group', 'faction', 'party', in the plural *ahzab*, the title of Q.33. In the Qur'an, in the singular, dual and plural, the term appears with negative connotations (Q.23:53, Q.18:12 and Q.13:36). In Q.5:56 and Q.58:22, however, appears the term *hizb Allah* (party of Allah) which has been used by various groups to name their organisations or describe their programme, most recently in Lebanon in 1979.

ANDREW J. NEWMAN

HIZB AL-TAHRIR

In the main study to date of Hizb al-Tahrir al-Islami (HT) – the Islamic Liberation Party – Taji-Farouki explains that its origins can be traced to Jerusalem of the 1940s and the cumulative impact of the end of the Ottoman Empire, the creation of the State of Israel and the

more general political crisis of Muslims in the late colonial/post-colonial period. Taqi al-Din al-Nabhani (1909–77), an al-Azhar-trained scholar who worked first for the Palestinian Ministry of Education, and then eventually as a judge in the courts of law, applied to the Jordanian authorities to form a new political party in 1952. However, al-Nabhani's request was declined because of HT's ideological commitment to the idea of one Islamic state and the perceived incompatibility of this with both Arab nationalism and the monarchy.

For all his Islamist ideology, al-Nabhani was deeply influenced by the secular-nationalist politics that dominated the Middle East in the first half of the twentieth century. In particular, HT reflected the methodology of those parties which emphasised the role of an elite revolutionary vanguard in the education of the masses. Whereas their contemporaries and great rivals, the Muslim Brotherhood, were more inclined towards the populism represented by the Wafd Party, HT shared the Ba'th Party's emphasis on systematic ideology. So, while the reformist Brotherhood began as a bottom-up movement which stressed gradual social and political change, as well as engaging in a range of welfare activities, HT were an avowedly 'top-down' outfit, which addressed every matter only in terms of their ultimate aim, the restoration of the caliphate.

In many ways, then, HT's vision is of an Islamic, as opposed to a secular, utopia, based on the ideal of the Prophet and his Rightly Guided Caliphs. However, what makes the party distinctive is that it has both eschewed revolutionary violence and refused participation in existing political systems (at least since the late 1950s when all opposition was suppressed in Jordan and the West Bank). Rather, HT's approach has been to use propaganda to promote intellectual and political subversion with the aim of creating a constituency sympathetic to any *coup d'état* led by the party. As they do today, activists of the 1950s took advantage of established religious gatherings to distribute their leaflets as well as organising lectures, sermons, study circles and selling books.

In 1953 the party relocated from Jerusalem to Damascus while branches were established in Nablus and Hebron as well as in Kuwait and also Lebanon (where al-Nabham himself eventually settled). Despite the widespread popularity of Nasserism, in the late 1960s and early 1970s HT attempted a number of (failed) coups in Amman, Baghdad, Cairo and Damascus. Thereafter, a downturn in the zeal of activists affected the scale of their activities. At the time of the Islamic Revolution, HT delegations were sent to Iran, to 'advise' on the necessity of a caliph and the implementation of the party's constitution, but, unsurprisingly, they were ignored by Khumayni. Indeed, by the early 1980s, HT had virtually no popular support, and party activists acknowledged that there had been a serious 'delay' in their ultimate goal.

Only in the late 1980s and into the 1990s did the party begin to exploit the worldwide Islamic resurgence to their own advantage. In particular, a series of international crises, including two Gulf wars have provided HT with opportunities to politicise Muslims. The party has reiterated its argument that the only solution to ongoing imperialist conspiracies against Islam is the restoration of the caliphate. In the last decade or so HT has also maintained a presence in the West, especially in the UK, where Taji-Farouki notes that the party has enjoyed fairly unrestricted freedom of speech. Nevertheless, after September 11th, 2001 especially, the party's alleged links to militants overseas has come under increasing scrutiny.

It is Taji-Farouki's conclusion that HT has failed to win the large following it initially anticipated. It was eclipsed by Nasser's pan-Arabism and then by gradualist and more radical Islamist trends. Nevertheless, she suggests that, having been almost universally proscribed, the party's survival in the Middle East, North Africa, South-East Asia and now Europe, is nothing short of remarkable. This qualified success Taji-Farouki attributes to the commitment and discipline of party activists.

References

Taji-Farouki (1996).

SEÁN MCLOUGHLIN

HOLY WAR

See: *jihad*

HUD

A pre-Islamic prophet mentioned seven times by name in the Qur'an (Q.7:65, Q.11:50–60, Q.11:89, Q.26:124), sent to the people of 'Ad. The ancient history of Arabia becomes featured in the story of Hud. According to the Qur'an, the people of 'Ad were those who built 'monuments in tall places', the remnants of which would likely have been known by the Arabs of Muhammad's time. The story of Hud himself follows the stereotyped format of other prophet stories: the prophet is commissioned, he delivers his message to the people (emphasising the benefits God has given the people and the uselessness of idol worship), the people reject him (calling him a liar, mad and having no proof for what he says), the people are destroyed (as the evidence of the ruins testifies), and the prophet himself and those who believe are saved. Despite the extensive passages devoted to Hud in the Qur'an, there is little historical information provided which can help in contextualising the story. Neither the historical period nor the extra location of 'Ad can be determined. The details do suggest that the story was a part of the collective Arab memory of its past.

References

Tottoli (2002: 45–7).

ANDREW RIPPIN

AL-HUDAYBIYYA, TREATY OF

The Treaty, or Peace of al-Hudaybiyya, an encampment some 9 miles (14 kilometres) from Mecca was agreed in AD 628. The people of Mecca, were still voicing opposition to the mission of the Prophet Muhammad. He and a group of Muslims heading on pilgrimage to Mecca that year found their path blocked by Meccans, who were reluctant to allow the Prophet to proceed. He was able to negotiate a compromise that promised to end the conflict between the two groups. Muhammad's group of pilgrims withdrew that year, on the understanding that they would be allowed to travel to Mecca the following year. A ten-year truce offered equal treatment for Muslims and non-Muslims, but within a year it had been broken on the Meccan side. The reconciliation among the Quraysh may have led directly to the recruitment of two men to Muhammad's cause. Khalid ibn al-Walid and 'Amr ibn al-'As joined him at about this time. They were to become successful generals in the campaigns of Islamic expansion.

See also: **al-Khandaq, Battle of; Khaybar**
EDWARD D. A. HULMES

HUDUD

Arabic term indicating crimes that are textually specified (i.e. in the Qur'an and *sunna*) and are accompanied by stipu-lated punishments. Often they are called the grand sins, *kaba'ir*. These include *zina'* (adultery), *qadhf* (slander), *hiraba* (highway robbery), *khamr* (the drinking of alcohol) and *ridda* (apostasy).

References

al Dhahabi (n.d.), Ibn Manzur (n.d.).

MAWIL IZZI DIEN

HUJJAT AL-ISLAM

'The proof of Islam', a title developed within Twelver Shi'ism in the nineteenth century to denote a high-ranking cleric. The term *ayatallah*, which appeared in the last century, denotes a higher rank.

References

Binder (1965).

See also: **ayatallah; Marji' al-taqlid, mujtahid**

ANDREW J. NEWMAN

AL-HUJWIRI (d. *c*. AD 1071)

Al-Hujwiri is famous for his *Kashf al-Mahjub*, a treatise that is probably the first systematic Persian work on Sufism. It discusses among other things twelve different schools of Sufis although it is not clear whether these existed or were invented by Hujwiri in order to elucidate Sufi doctrine.

References

Hujwiri (1911).

LLOYD RIDGEON

HULUL

A term used in a pejorative sense by opponents of Sufis to denote the idea of the indwelling of two spirits (man and God's spirit, i.e., incarnationism) in one body. It was a charge levelled against 'Ayn al-Qudat amongst others, although belief in *hulul* was condemned by major 'orthodox' Sufis.

References

Ernst (1985).

LLOYD RIDGEON

HUMAYUN B. BABUR
(r. 1530–40, 1555–6)

Second Mughal ruler after his father Babur. He faced great difficulties in his efforts to maintain his father's inheritance, and the first period of his rule was largely taken up with struggles against other family members. He was thus unable to withstand the Afghan Suris, who began a short-lived line of sultans in Delhi (1540–55). After a period of exile in other parts of India and then in Safavid Persia, he regained the throne, but died in the next year, having paved the way for the achievement of Akbar, his own sympathies for the Sufi mystics of India and his tolerant attitude towards religion foreshadowing what was to be a major interest of his son.

References

Gibb and Bosworth (1960–2003), Richards (1993: 9–12).

C. E. BOSWORTH

HUMOURS (FOUR)

Greek and Arab philosophers and physicians considered fire, air, water and earth to be the four basic elements of which all bodies are composed. These elements produce four kinds of effect: hot (fire), cold (air), wet (water) and dry (earth). The mixture of these four elements produces plants which are used to feed animals and from this food the four humours are produced. They are blood, phlegm, yellow bile and black bile. Blood is produced in the liver from the juices of the digested food. Its colour is pure red. Phlegm is cold and wet and is the element which remains in the veins in order to nourish the organs. Yellow bile is a fine and pure liquid and is supposed to refine and thin the blood so that it flows regularly into the veins. Black bile is cool and dry, it nourishes the organs and parts of it remain at the entrance to the stomach to stimulate the appetite. These four humours are called the daughters of the elements in which fire corresponds to yellow bile which is hot and dry, air corresponds to blood which is hot and wet, water to phlegm which is cold and wet and earth to black bile which is cold and dry. If these humours are in balance, the person is considered healthy, but if this balance is disturbed illness will ensue.

References

Ullmann (1978: 57–60).

MAHA EL-KAISY FRIEMUTH

HUNAYN IBN ISHAQ

Hunayn Ibn Ishaq is the most prominent and active transmitter of Greek sciences and philosophical works into Arabic. Most important was his clear and practical translation of the medical treatises of Galen and Hippocrates, which contributed to the progress of Arab physicians. He was born in Hira in AD 808, where his father was a pharmacist. His family was among the Arab Christians who remained faithful to the Syriac Nestorian church. In his early youth he mastered both Arabic and Syriac and later he acquired a knowledge of Greek language. This was probably the result of his stay in Alexandria, which lasted for more than two years. The importance of the translations produced by Hunayn and his school lies in the accuracy of his precise and correct Arabic grammar. He is credited with an immense number of translations (about 100) ranging over medicine, astronomy, philosophy, mathematics and even magic. He also edited and revised other translations and supplied a better Arabic version. His main contribution, however, was in producing a new scientific and philosophical Arabic terminology to convey the terms of Greek and Syriac texts.

Hunayn was himself an important physician, he studied under the famous physician Ibn Maswaya. He was appointed chief physician in the court of the Caliph al-Mutawakil and also became the second director of *Bayt al-Hikma* after Ibn Maswaya. Besides his translations, Hunayn also wrote many works mainly on medicine, the most important was *al-Mash'il fi 'l Tibb*, which was written in a question-and-answer form. He also wrote on other subjects, such as philosophy, zoology and even history. Hunayn remained the Chief Physician of the Caliph's court until his death in AD 873.

References

Gibb and Bosworth (1960–2003: III, 578–81), Rosenthal (1937: I, 15–19).

MAHA EL-KAISY FRIEMUTH

AL-HUSAYN, IBN 'ALI IBN ABI TALIB (AD 626–81)

Husayn was born in Medina in AD 626, the elder son of 'Ali ibn Abi Talib and Fatima. He and his elder brother, al-Hasan, were grandsons of the Prophet Muhammad, who is said to have been on affectionate terms with both of them. Their father, 'Ali, is said to have favoured Husayn, who became head of 'Ali's house on the death of Hasan *c.* AD 669. The terms of the agreement made between Mu'awiya and Hasan, in which the latter abdicated as caliph in favour of the former, probably inhibited Husayn from playing a more prominent role in public affairs until after his brother's death (see the entry on al-Hasan). When Mu'awiya died in AD 680, having named his son Yazid as successor, Husayn answered the call of his supporters in al-Kufa to declare himself the legitimate caliph. Shi'is designate Husayn as the third imam. On 10th Muharram 681 Husayn and a small group of his followers were surrounded by a large force of Umayyad troops, at Karbala', 25 miles (40 kilometres) northwest of Kufa. Husayn refused to obey the command to accept the legitimacy of Yazid's succession. Nor was he prepared to surrender. After negotiations in which he was refused permission to withdraw his party, or even to have access to water, he was killed. Tradition records that thirty wounds were inflicted on him by sword-blades, lances and arrows, and that the hooves of horses also left their imprints on his fallen body. Almost all his companions were also killed. His head was cut off and sent to Yazid in Damascus. The head was eventually given back to his sister and it was buried with the rest of the body in Karbala', where the shrine of Husayn is still visited by countless numbers of Muslim pilgrims. Husayn is considered to be a martyr by Shi'i Muslims. More than that, he is known as 'the lord of the martyrs' (*sayyid al-shuhada'*). It is said that Shi'ism began on the day of his death. The schism between Sunni Muslims and Shi'i Muslims, which began after the death of the Prophet Muhammad, and which intensified after the killing of Husayn, remains unsettled. His death may be said to have provided his followers with the historical foundation for a theology of salvation through suffering and martyrdom, a doctrine that has continued to influence the lives of many Muslims to the present day. Husayn's martyrdom is commemorated annually. The first ten days of Muharram are days of mourning and lamentation for Shi'is. Special sermons are preached in the mosques. Wearing signs of mourning, the faithful process through the streets to express their continuing grief. Some of them use the occasion to show their devotion in acts of self-mutilation. A passion play in memory of the day (*'ashura'*) on which the fatal event occurred is performed near to Baghdad at this time each year. In Karbala' another part of the passion play called *The Return of the Head* is performed during the rest of the month of Muharram. In the history of Shi'ism no event has been more significant than the martyrdom of al-Husayn.

References

Hitti (1973: 190–1), Momen (1985: 28–33, 47–9).

See also: **al-Hasan, ibn 'Ali ibn Abi Talib; Fatima; Karbala', Battle of; Shi'ism**

EDWARD D. A. HULMES

HUSAYN, SADDAM (1937–2006)

Iraqi President. Husayn was born to a peasant family in Tikrit, a small town to the north of Baghdad. He was raised by his widowed mother and other relatives. He moved to Baghdad in 1955 and quickly became involved in politics by joining the Ba'th party. His ability and ruthlessness led to his rise in the party and his approach to politics was soon demonstrated by his readiness to help to organise an assassination attempt on the then military president 'Abd al-Karim Qasim. Both Qasim and Husayn were injured and the latter fled to Cairo to study law. He returned to Baghdad in 1963 where he became Assistant Secretary General of the Ba'th. In 1968 the party seized power in a military coup and he became Vice Chairman of the Revolutionary Command Council, the body with absolute power in the country. With the support of a clique of supporters mainly from Tikrit he began to take a leading role in domestic politics and foreign affairs. His career has been marked by a seeming ability to negotiate and compromise and a willingness to use maximum force against those he considers his opponents.

He first negotiated with the Kurds and then turned against them brutally (on one notorious occasion using lethal gas against their villages). In 1975 he negotiated an agreement with Iran which involved Iraqi concessions in return for the cessation of Iranian support of the Kurdish opposition. He led Iraqi opposition to any negotiations with Israel after the Camp David agreement and showed himself in general as a hardliner in the Arab cause.

In 1979 he took over as President from al-Bakr, who had retired, just at the time of the Iranian revolution under Ayatallah Khumayni. Saddam Husayn feared the spread of Islamic fundamentalism from the neighbouring country and in an attempt to overthrow the new regime abandoned the 1975 accord and invaded Iran for the start of a long and bloody conflict. At home he faced opposition from the Kurds, disaffected Shi'is and members of the Ba'th. He ruthlessly eliminated all opposition, however. A ceasefire was negotiated with Iran in 1988 after a war that left Iraq devastated with many casualties and large debts. These did not deter him from further aggressive policies and in 1990 he reopened the Iraqi claim to Kuwait. He then viciously invaded his small neighbour, an action that aroused a large international response. The following Gulf War only lasted a few months and Husayn's troops were evicted by superior forces.

Despite his disastrous policies and Iraq's financial ruin and international isolation and the imposition of sanctions he remained in power, brooking no opposition to his authority. The north and south of his country were put under US/British aerial supervision to prevent his persecution of the Kurds and Shi'is, although in the south he virtually destroyed the environment of the Marsh Arabs. He continuously taunted the international community by allowing and then forbidding UN inspection of sites of the suspected manufacture of chemical and other weapons. Ordinary Iraqis suffered from the lack of food and medicines caused by the sanctions. His regime was ended by the Anglo-US invasion of 2003. He was executed in December 2006.

References

Cockburn (2002).

DEREK HOPWOOD

HUSAYN, SHARIF (1852/4–1931)

Hashimite leader and King. Born in Mecca, the son of 'Ali of the Hashimi family (descendants of the prophet Muhammad), he was kept in exile for the early years of his life in Istanbul by the Ottoman sultan Abdulhamid. After the Young Turk revolution in 1908 he was allowed to return to the Hijaz in Arabia and was appointed Amir of Mecca. There a strong rivalry developed between himself and the up-and-coming ruler of Arabia 'Abd al-'Aziz ibn Sa'ud. In 1914 at the beginning of the First World War he contacted the British High Commissioner in Cairo with an unfulfilled request for help in expelling the Turks from the Hijaz. In 1915 he renewed his request when the British showed greater interest. In return for his support Husayn demanded independence for Arabia under his rulership. The British agreed and conditions were supposedly agreed in the infamous Husayn–McMahon (British High Commissioner) correspondence. However, ever since the exchange of letters between the two there has disagreement over exactly what was agreed. Husayn believed that he had been promised unconditional independence in a large area of Arab land, whereas the British claimed any promises had been hedged about with conditions. Nevertheless, Husayn proclaimed the Arab revolt and demanded that he be proclaimed King of the Arab Lands. The British objected to such an all-embracing title and Husayn was named merely King of the Hijaz in October 1916. The Hashimite family then faithfully supported the revolt and in 1918 T. E. Lawrence and Husayn's son, Faysal, entered Damascus on the heels of the defeated Ottoman Turks.

After the war, Husayn refused to endorse the proposals of the Paris Peace Conference as they included provisions for the mandates in the Arab world instead of the independence he thought he had been promised. Because of this he also turned down British proposals for an Anglo-Hijazi Treaty that would have provided promises of aid and guarantees against outside attack. He would not recognise the mandate arrangements for Iraq, Syria and Palestine and refused to send a delegate to a conference in Kuwait in 1923 to settle border disputes. Instead he proclaimed himself Caliph of Islam without the agreement of any other Islamic leader. This caused anger particularly amongst the Wahhabis of neighbouring Najd. At the same time his territorial dispute with Ibn Sa'ud was worsening and when the Sa'udis attacked Hijaz in 1924, the British refused to come to his aid. Husayn felt he had to abdicate in favour of his son 'Ali. Mecca fell to the invading Sa'udi forces and he escaped to 'Aqaba from where he was taken in 1926 in a British ship to Cyprus. He spent the rest of his life there or with his son 'Abdullah in Transjordan. He died in Amman and was buried in Jerusalem.

References

De Gaury (1951: 257–77).

DEREK HOPWOOD

HUSAYN, TAHA (1889–1973)

Egyptian writer and critic. Husayn was born in Upper Egypt into a modest family and became blind at the age of two. He entered the local village school (*kuttab*) and in 1902 was sent to al-Azhar university in Cairo. He disliked the traditional methods of teaching there and did not settle. He failed his exams and moved to the newly founded National University of Cairo. There he immersed himself in criticism and philosophy under the influence of Western thought. He became the university's first graduate in 1914 and was able to enter the Sorbonne in Paris where in 1918 he wrote a doctorate on the Arab social historian Ibn Khaldun.

He returned to Cairo to work in his old university, was appointed Professor of Arabic Literature in 1925 and became the first Egyptian Dean of the Faculty of Arts. In 1926 he caused great controversy amongst traditional Muslims with the publication of his study *Fi al-shi'r al-jahili* (*On Pre-Islamic Poetry*) in which he questioned the origins of poetry composed before the advent of Islam in a manner that had religious implications. He was dismissed from office in 1932 and spent his time writing until in 1942 he was given a number of educational posts including that of Minister of Education (1950–2). He wrote in all forms (excluding poetry) and was particularly active as a critic. His most popular work is his three-part autobiography *Kitab al-ayyam* (*The Stream of Days*). He was one of Egypt's best loved and greatest writers.

References

Cachia (1956).

DEREK HOPWOOD

I

IBADISM (AL-'IBADIYYA)

The Ibadis are a subsect of the Khawarij, taking their name from their alleged founder 'Abdullah b. 'Ibad al-Tamimi – a seventh-century Kharijite leader. The Ibadis themselves refute the claim that they are a Kharijite group, but they do have a common origin and agree with them on a number of issues; however, it must be said that they are a moderate group within the larger sect. The Ibadis rely on the Qur'an and *sunna* for their doctrine and it is worth mentioning that they have their own book of *hadith*, termed *'Musnad al-Rabi' b. Habib*. They are agreement with the Mu'tazila on a number of issues, namely that the Qur'an is created and that Allah will not be seen in the hereafter. They also metaphorically interpret some of the divine attributes, such as the hand (*al-yad*) and events in the hereafter, such as the scales (*al-mizan*) and the path over hellfire (*al-sirat*). They consider other Muslim who disagree with them to be non-believers (*kuffar*) but not polytheists (*mushrikin*). Similarly, they consider someone who commits a major sin (*kabira*, pl. *kaba'ir*) to be a disbeliever (*kafir*) and if such a person does not repent then they will punished in hell forever. Ibadis can still be found today in North and East Africa and especially in Oman, where Ibadism is the official state doctrine.

References

Al-'Aql (1996: 60–114), al-Johani (1999: 58–63), Netton (1997: 109).

GAVIN PICKEN

IBLIS

From the Greek, a reference to Satan, who refused to bow down to Adam at Allah's command for which Allah cast him from Heaven (Q.18:50). He then tempted Adam and Eve to eat the forbidden fruit.

References

Waines (1995: 29).

See also: **Adam; sin**

ANDREW J. NEWMAN

IBN 'ABD AL-WAHHAB, MUHAMMAD (1703–92)

Hanbali preacher and revivalist in Arabia. Born in al-'Unayna, an oasis in Najd, the central area of Arabia, he studied the Hanbali works of Ibn Qudama with his father and then, following a visit to Mecca, he spent time in Medina, where he was influenced by the ideas of Ibn Taimiyya and Ibn Qayyim al-Jawziyya. He then spent some time in Basra, returning to Najd in 1739. There, in 1744, he entered into an alliance with the local ruler, Muhammad ibn Su'ud, whereby Ibn 'Abd al-Wahhab would provide spiritual guidance and Ibn Su'ud would provide the political and military means to see it implemented. Over the next twenty years or so 'Abd al-Wahhab's message and Ibn Su'ud's political power were together established over much of central Arabia and this process continued after Ibn Su'ud's death in 1765 and that of Ibn 'Abd al-Wahhab in 1792. The message which he preached was one of strict monotheism, with no intermediaries between God and humanity, and this led to harsh condemnations of Sufism and of many of the religious practices widely current in Arabia, which were described as *shirk* (idolatry). Arabia was thus reckoned still to be in a state of *jahiliyya* (spiritual ignorance), from which it needed to be purged. The alliance of these two figures, after a number of vicissitudes in the nineteenth century, provided the foundations of the modern state of Su'udi Arabia, and also the intellectual roots of much revivalist thought across the whole of the Islamic world.

References

Algar (2002), al-Faruqi (1979), Vassiliev (2000: Part I), al-Yassini (1985: Part I).

HUGH GODDARD

IBN 'ADI, ABU ZAKARIYYA YAHYA (AD 893–974)

A Jacobite Christian born in AD 893 in Tikrit in Iraq. Tikrit was a centre of intellectual activity for Christians and a centre for discussion and debate between them and Muslims. He studied, however in Baghdad with the Christian Matta b. Yunus and Abu Nasr al-Farabi. He was a professional amanuensis, copying and collecting philosophical manuscripts. Ibn 'Adi was also a translator and editor of Syriac texts translated into Arabic. He also wrote commentaries on some Aristotelian works such as his commentary on the *Organon* and the *Categoriae*. In the main, he followed the philosophical position of his teacher al-Farabi and is considered to be one of his disciples. He also attempted to interpret Christian concepts in the light of Aristotelian thinking, considering the persons of the trinity to stand for the intellect (the father) the intellectually cognising subject (the son) and the intellectually cognised object (the holy spirit). Ibn 'Adi was also the 'founder' of a philosophical school of which the members included Abu Sulayman al-Sijistani, Abu Hayyan al-Tawhidi, Abu 'Ali Miskawayh and other important philosophers.

Ibn 'Adi died in Baghdad in August AD 974 and was buried in the church of Mar Thomas.

References

Netton (1992: 8–11).

MAHA EL-KAISY FRIEMUTH

IBN 'ARABI (AD 1165–1240)

Muhyi'l-Din Muhammad ibn 'Ali al-'Arabi is perhaps the most influential Sufi of the medieval period and continues to inspire Sufi movements in the contemporary world as well as institutions devoted to him such as the Muhyiddin Ibn 'Arabi Society in Oxford. Popularly known as Ibn 'Arabi, he is often also given the honorific of *al-Shaykh al-Akbar* (The Greatest Sufi Master) because of his influence, his writings, and spiritual authority for Sufis throughout the ages. An Arab of the tribe of al-Tayy, he was born in Murcia in southern Spain in 1165 during the rule of the Almohads. His father may have been a significant courtier of the local ruler Ibn Mardanish and after his fall, entered the service of the Almohad sultan Abu Ya'qub Yusuf in Seville. He later claimed to have experienced visions as an adolescent that inspired him to the Sufi path. In the hagiographical account of his meeting with the philosopher Averroes, an acquaintance of his father, in AD 1180 in Cordoba, he is already presented as a spiritually precocious young man. The philosopher, impressed by his knowledge, embraced him and said, 'Yes'. The young man replied, 'Yes', but seeing the resultant joy on the face of Averroes, said, 'No'. The philosopher's colour changed and he asked, 'What kind of solution have you found through illumination and divine inspiration? Is it just the same as we receive from speculative thought?' Ibn 'Arabi replied, 'Yes and no. Between the yes and the no spirits take flight from their matter and necks break away from their bodies'. This highly stylised account is designed to assert the superior insight of the Sufi in comparison with the philosopher at a time when Ibn 'Arabi had not yet taken a Sufi guide. It also reveals his ambivalence towards philosophy: he always claimed to have mastered philosophy and in his works displayed knowledge of philosophical terms and arguments, but remained critical of the inability of rational speculation to arrive at the truth and reality of existence. Alongside his studies in jurisprudence and theology, he studied the works of Sufis such as Ibn al-'Arif (d. AD 1141) and Ibn Qasi, and began to frequent Sufi masters in Seville, especially Abu'l-'Abbas al-'Uraybi, his first master. He claimed a connection with the famous Maghribi Sufi Abu Madyan (d. AD 1198), both through a spiritual initiation (as he never met him) and through that Sufi's disciple 'Abd al-'Aziz al-Mahdawi in Tunis. In his work *Ruh al-Quds*, he gives an account of his contacts with Sufis including two female spiritual guides, Shams of Marchena and Fatima of Cordoba. In the 1190s, he left Andalusia for the first time to study with Sufi masters in Tunis. He continued his travels in search of knowledge and had further visions of famous Sufis and Prophets. He acquired a companion 'Abdallah al-Habashi who would remain a disciple and scribe. By 1200, he left Andalusia for good, partly due to the political upheavals and headed east. By this time, his fame had spread and he was met in cities like Cairo by Sufis and scholars. He may also have believed in his superior spiritual authority following a vision in 1198, when he realised that he was the seal of Muhammadan sainthood, a rank that would place him at the head of the spiritual hierarchy in the totality of sacred space and time after the Prophet. He set out for the pilgrimage to Mecca and spent a few years there, pivotal years that inspired his *magnum opus*, *al-Futuhat al-Makkiya* (*The Meccan Revelations*), a vast treasury of knowledge, and *Tarjuman al-Ashwaq* (*Interpreter of Desires*), a set of allegorical love poems addressed to Nizam, the daughter of his friend Abu Shuja'. His travels took him to Konya in AD 1210, which established a link later to flourish in the Mevlevi Sufi order that drew upon his teachings. Finally, in AD 1223 on the invitation of the Ayyubid ruler al-Malik al-'Adil, he settled in Damascus, where he died in AD 1240 and was buried in the cemetery of the Banu Zaki.

Ibn 'Arabi affected the apophatic style of many Sufis and often claimed that his experiences were ineffable. Yet, perhaps as a corollary of this claim, he was extremely prolific. He wrote short treatises recounting his views, his 'ascensions', and his understanding of certain key Sufi texts and doctrines. However, the majority of his tradition and scholarship has focused on two texts. The first is his vast compendium *al-Futuhat al-Makkiyya* (*Meccan Revelations*) inspired during his first pilgrimage in AD 1202, the first draft of which was completed in AD 1231 in Damascus, the second draft was later completed and rehearsed with his disciples in the last two years of his life. An autograph copy that was preserved by his disciple Sadr al-Din Qunawi survives and is known as the 'Konya manuscript' because of its provenance. The text is divided into 560 chapters of hugely variance in length, arranged in six sections. The work is prefaced by an introduction that introduces the reader to the epistemological method of Ibn 'Arabi and provides insights into his hierarchy of knowledge. The first section on inspired knowledge (*ma'arif*) includes a chapter on his key notion of the perfect man (*al-insan al-kamil*), chapters on the spiritual reality of Islamic worship, and a key chapter (73) on the spiritual hierarchy and his known of sainthood (*walaya*). The second section on agency and transactions (*mu'amalat*) includes discussions of law, spiritual rank, and station. The following section focuses on spiritual states (*ahwal*) and includes an ontological and spiritual commentary on the vast literature of Sufi works preceding him. The fourth section describes 'points of

ascent' (*manazil*) along the Sufi path and includes his discussion of eschatology. The fifth section on 'mutual points of encounter' (*munazalat*) draws on insights upon Qur'anic and other scriptural texts. The final section on spiritual stations (*maqamat*) includes his commentary on the ninety-nine names of God, the return to God and a recapitulation of the whole work. The text has been studied since the thirteenth century although it does not have an extensive commentary tradition his sixteenth-century Egyptian devotee 'Abd al-Wahhab al-Sha'rani did write an influential summary entitled *al-Yawaqit wa'l-Jawahir fi Bayan 'Aqa'id al-Akabir* (*Rubies and Gems Explaining the Doctrines of the Elders*).

His other main text has spawned a vast commentary culture. In AD 1230, he claims to have encountered the Prophet Muhammad in Damascus who gave him a book to disseminate. This is *Fusus al-Hikam* (*The Ring-Settings of Wisdom*), a work divided into twenty-seven chapters, each one on the particular wisdom associated with one of the prophets mentioned in the Qur'an. As such it can be seen as a metaphysical commentary upon the prophetology of the Qur'an, and even as a mystical exegesis of the Qur'an itself.

Ibn 'Arabi is most famous as the author of the concept of the unity of existence (*wahdat al-wujud*), although he himself never used the term. Consonant with Neoplatonic thinkers, he held that God is utterly transcendent, inaccessible to a communicable experience, a pure being (*al-Wujud al-Mutlaq* or *al-Haqq*) that was devoid of attributes. The cosmos in contrast as a locus of attributes, multiplicities and accidents is impoverished and completely dependent on that pure being. Only God exists really and all that we perceive as existing does so by virtue of being a self-disclosure (*tajalli*) or manifestation (*mazhar*) of the hidden

existence of God. His monism and scepticism about the reality of phenomenal
experience did not entail an otherworldly rejection of life in this world,
but entailed an ethics of community and
moral agency of equivalence across different beings, an idea taken up by his
Indian disciples later on and given the
name *sulh-i kull* (peace to all). While
the universalist intention of this doctrine is
clear (since everything one experiences is
ultimately the 'face of God'), it does not
mean that Ibn 'Arabi was a moral relati-
vist who did not believe in the superiority
of the application of the Law of Islam.

A concomitant of this doctrine is Ibn
'Arabi's influential notion of the perfect
man as an ontological presence and comprehensive microcosmic reality that acts
as an isthmus (*barzakh*) between God
and the cosmos, as he reflects the perfection of the divine, and in his humanity
is their face and hopes oriented towards
God. An alternative name for this notion
is the Muhammadan reality (*al-haqiqa
al-Muhammadiyya*) since this meso-
cosmic property existed in the nature of
the Prophet and his spiritual successors.

The increasingly philosophical sophistication of Ibn 'Arabi's ideas already
began in the work of his disciple and stepson Sadr al-Din al-Qunawi (d. AD 1274),
who entered into a correspondence
with the scientist and philosopher Nasir
al-Din al-Tusi (d. AD 1274). The legacy
of Ibn 'Arabi centred on the teachings of
his major works and commentaries upon
them. Qunawi wrote the first commentary
on the *Ring-Settings*, but it was 'Abd al-
Razzaq Kashani's work that began the
shift to a more philosophically intuitive
understanding of his teachings. Through
the work of the Shi'i Sufi Sayyid Haydar
Amuli (d. after AD 1385), these teachings
entered and influenced Shi'i thought and
were profoundly transformed and nat-
uralised. Major commentaries continued
into the nineteenth century, when Amir

'Abd al-Qadir, who led Algerian resistance to the French, wrote *al-Mawaqif*
(*The Stops*) having settled in Damascus,
and arranged for the publication of the
Meccan Revelations.

But there was also an experiential, Sufi
initiatic inheritance through developing
Sufi orders both in the Maghrib and the
Islamic East. Some Sufi orders such as the
Shadhiliyya in North Africa, Kubrawiyya
in Iran and the Chishtiyya in India
adopted wholescale the metaphysics of
Ibn 'Arabi. Because the focal idea that
they preached was *wahdat al-wujud*, the
monistic unity of existence, they became
known as the *wujudiyya*, a term used
pejoratively by detractors and as a badge
of honour by like-minded individuals.

References

Abu Zayd (1983), Adamson and Taylor
(2005), Addas (1993, 2000), Ashtiyani (1966),
Austin (1971, 1982), De Bustinza (1999),
Chittick *et al.* (1988), Chodkiewicz (1993),
Corbin (1969), Cornell (1996), Elmore (1999),
Al-Hakim (1981), Hirtenstein and Tiernan
(1993), Ibn 'Arabi (1946), Izutsu (1984), Knysh
(1999), Morris (1986: 107, 539–51, 733–56;
1987: 101–19), Nettler (2004), Rosenthal (1988:
1–35), Sells (1994), Takeshita (1987), Winkel
(1997), Yahia (1984).

SAJJAD H. RIZVI

IBN AL-MUNDHIR (d. AD 930)

Abu Bakr Muhammad b. Ibrahim b. al-
Mundhir al-Naysaburi (*c.* AD 856–930)
was an outstanding ninth–tenth century
jurist, renowned for mastery of the
both the fields of jurisprudence (*fiqh*)
and prophetic tradition (*hadith*). Very
little is known about his early life in
terms of his birth, childhood, education
or upbringing except that he was born in
Naysabur (Nishapur), the then capital of
Khurasan. Despite there being no mention of Ibn al-Mundhir's education, we
can assume that he gained a substantial
early education, as Nishapur was a highly

developed centre of Islamic culture at the time. As no record exists of Ibn al-Mundhir's early life, we might expect to find some source describing his journeys in search of knowledge (*talab al-'ilm*), but the answer however, is rather disappointing as there seems to be no record of any such travel, except the history books mention his formative years in Nishapur and his consequent residency in Mecca. It seems however, that despite this, he may have travelled to Egypt as his own comments seem to indicate that he read al-Shafi'i's (AD 767–820) books to his student al-Rabi' b. Sulayman (AD 790–873). He had numerous teachers and even more numerous students including the great *hafiz* Abu Bakr Muhammad b. Ibrahim b. 'Ali Ibn al-Muqri' al-Isbahani (d. AD 991) and Muhammad Ibn Hibban al-Tamimi al-Bistami (d. AD 868).

He also left a rich and voluminous body of works, numbering around twenty-seven works, most of which concerned the discipline of jurisprudence (*fiqh*), including *al-Ijma'* (*Consensus*), *Kitab al-Iqna'* (*The Persuasion*), *al-Ishraf 'ala Madhahib al-'Ulama'* (*The Supervision of Scholarly Methodologies*) and exegetical work *Tafsir al-Qur'an al-Karim* (*An Exegesis of the Noble Qur'an*). Unfortunately however the vast majority of his works have been lost to the ravages of time. Most scholars regard Ibn al-Mundhir as being an independent jurist of the calibre capable of deducing his own legal opinion (*mujtahid mutlaq*). However, al-Shirazi considered Ibn al-Mundhir as a scholar of the *shafi'i madhhab*, mentioning him frequently in his juristic work *al-Muhadhdhab* and commenting on this in his biographical work *al-Tabaqat*. However, it cannot escape the attention of any thorough researcher that despite Ibn al-Mundhir's affiliation to the *shafi'i madhhab*, he did on occasion oppose the opinion of al-Shafi'i himself, making his own personal *ijtihad* regarding the issue in question.

His influence on later jurists, particularly in the field of comparative jurisprudence and jurisprudential dispute (*al-fiqh al-muqarin/al-khilaf*) was immense, and he is frequently mentioned in the most comprehensive works in this field namely: *al-Muhalla* by 'Ali b. Ahmad b. Sa'id Ibn Hazm al-Andalusi (d. AD 1064), *al-Mughni* by Muwaffiq al-Din Abu Muhammad b. 'Abdullah Ibn Qudamah al-Maqdisi (d. AD 1233) and *al-Majmu' Sharh al-Muhadhdhab* by Muhyi al-Din Abu Zakaria Yahya b. Sharaf al-Nawawi (d. AD 1277), as well as the juristic exegesis of Imam Shams al-Din Abu 'Abdullah Muhammad b. Ahmad b. Abu Bakr al-Qurtubi (d. AD 1272), which he entitled *al-Jami'li 'l-Ahkam al-Qur'an*. Historians have differed regarding the date on which Ibn al-Mundhir died, al-Shirazi, Ibn Khallikan and al-Yafi'i claim that he died in Mecca in 921 or AD 922. However, al-Dhahabi concludes, 'What *al-shaykh* Abu Ishaq [al-Shirazi] mentioned about his death is presumption, as he [Ibn al-Mundhir] listened to Ibn 'Ammar in 928 and the historian Ibn al-Qattan al-Fasi, recorded the date of his death as being 930'. Thus, Ibn al-Mundhir died having reached the pinnacle in both the disciplines of *fiqh* and *hadith*, being known as 'the jurist (*al-faqih*) of Mecca' and 'the scholar of the Holy Precincts (*shaykh al-haram*)'. Al-Dhahabi summaries the esteem in which he was held saying: 'Ibn al-Mundhir al-Naysaburi: the guardian (*al-hafiz*), the guidance (*al-dalala*), the jurist (*al-faqih*), the scholar of the holy precincts (*shaykh al-haram*) and the possessor of books the like of which have never been written'.

References

Ibn al-Mundhir (1993: 11–98, 1997: 10–37), Picken (1999: 21–47, 66–70).

GAVIN PICKEN

IBN AL-MUQAFFA'
(early eighth century, d. AD 755 or 756–7).

A Manichean of Persian origin who subsequently converted to Islam, Ibn al-Muqaffa' (originally known as Ruzbih) played a crucial role in the early development of medieval Arabic prose both through his translations from Middle Persian and through his own compositions. He served as secretary to two uncles of the 'Abbasid caliph al-Mansur and was executed as a consequence of a failed revolt in which he was implicated.

Ibn al-Muqaffa' is best known for his translation from Persian of *Kalila wa-Dimna*, a collection of didactic animal fables, mostly of Indian origin, known as the 'Fables of Bidpai'. The name itself is a corruption of the Sanskrit Karataka and Damanaka, the two jackals who appear in the opening story. Much of the work ultimately derives from the celebrated Sanskrit storybook, the *Pancatantra*. In making his translation, Ibn al-Muqaffa' had no hesitation in inserting additional material of his own, and this practice was continued by numerous copyists. Although the text is essentially an early example of the 'Mirrors for Princes' genre, laying down rules of conduct (*adab*) for princes, secretaries and administrators, it has also been read as a children's book, in which capacity it has achieved considerable popularity; unfortunately, as part of this process, a number of copyists and editors have bowdlerised the text to make it more suitable for children's reading, and few of the published versions available today can be said to be based on sound editorial principles.

In addition to *Kalila wa-Dimna*, Ibn al-Muqaffa' also translated from Middle Persian the *Khwadaynamag*, or *Book of Kings*, which was used by al-Tabari and other historians as a source of information on pre-Islamic Iran. He also collected political maxims in his *Kitab al-Adab al-Kabir*, and apparently composed an original work of political counsel in his *Risala fi al-Sahaba*.

Although some lingering doubts were expressed about the genuineness of Ibn al-Muqaffa''s conversion to Islam, his mastery of Arabic prose style was almost universally praised by the Muslim commentators, and his position as the main conduit for the transmission of Indian and Persian ideas into Arabic culture during this early period seems assured.

References

Amir Arjomand (1994: 9–36), Ashtiani *et al.* (1990: 48–77), Beeston (1983: 483–96).

PAUL STARKEY

IBN AL-NADIM, ABU AL-FARAJ MUHAMMAD IBN ISHAQ (before AD 936–990/9)

'Abbasid copyist, bookseller and cataloguer. Little is known of the life of Ibn al-Nadim, beyond the fact that he was an Imami Shi'ite, certainly with wide-ranging contacts among the scholars of his day and probably with access to court circles in Baghdad, where he worked. His fame rests entirely on his *Fihrist*, completed according to his own account in AD 987–8, which is essentially a comprehensive listing by subject and author of all the Arabic books known to the compiler; his listing includes translations from other languages, for which it is a particularly valuable source of information. Although he undoubtedly also consulted earlier sources, Ibn al-Nadim appears to have relied for his index largely on the books to which he had access in the course of his trade; his experience and interests as a bookseller are apparent in the weight that he attaches to describing the books as well as their authors, sometimes including a note of the number of pages or lines.

Two versions of the *Fihrist* exist, a longer and a shorter edition, the prefaces to both bearing the same date; the precise relationship between the two versions remains unclear. The ten subject areas ('discourses') covered in the larger version are:

1. the scriptures of the Jews, Christians and Muslims, with emphasis on the Qur'an;
2. grammar and philology;
3. history and related subjects;
4. poetry;
5. theology;
6. law and tradition;
7. philosophy and other non-religious sciences;
8. legends and magic;
9. the non-monotheistic religions (Sabaeans, Manichaeans, etc.);
10. alchemy.

The first pages are occupied with a description of the different scripts and alphabets employed by fourteen peoples, Arab and non-Arab. Ibn al-Nadim's listings, particularly in the second half of the work, are occasionally filled out with more extensive expositions on particular topics that interested him, among them the Isma'ilis, Plato and Aristotle, the Arabian Nights, and the Egyptian pyramids.

The *Fihrist* remains a unique production in the history of medieval Arabic literature, extensively used by later authors until the present day.

References

Dodge (1970).

PAUL STARKEY

IBN BAJJA (AVEMPACE)

Abu Bakr Muhammad b. Yahya b. al-Sa'igh al-Saraqusti, philosopher and *wazir*. No recorded details of his life survive but it is known that he died at an early age around AD 1139, and he must have been born towards the end of the eleventh century. His native town was probably Saragossa (in Andalusia) where he also became a *wazir* for the Berber governor Abu Bakr b. Ibrahim al-Sahrawi, known as Ibn Tifalwit. He was twice imprisoned: once during a political mission to 'Imad al-Dawla b. Hud, and later when he was accused of heresy. He probably was appointed to a second wazirship under Yahya b. Yusuf b. Tashufin.

Some works of Ibn Bajja survive in their original Arabic but others are in a Hebrew translation. The *Risalat al-Wada'* and his later *Risalat Ittisal al-'aql bi 'l-Insan* and the Hebrew version of *Tadbir al-Mutwahhid*, are the important works which reveal his philosophical thought. The principle of the conjunction of the human intellect with the active intellect is his most influential concept. He considers that the human intellect, in its highest stage of knowledge, is able to have light from and conjunction with God and therefore to become an active intellect. This idea is probably derived from a treatise of Alexander of Aphrodisias. In his *Tadbir*, he introduces an ethical theory which is influenced by al-Farabi's *al-Siyasa*. Here he explains that philosophers must have a leading position in bringing society to an ideal state and therefore must take part in working towards an utopian state, similar to the position of the philosopher in the Plato's *Republic*.

Ibn Bajja died in Fez probably as a result of eating a poisoned fruit provided by a servant of Abu al-'Ala' b. Zuhr, in May AD 1139.

References

Nasr and Leaman (1996: I, 294–313).

MAHA EL-KAISY FRIEMUTH

IBN BATTUTA (AD 1304–68/9 or 1377).

Arab traveller of Maghribi origin, born in Tangier. Ibn Battuta's account of his travels, which has sometimes been compared with that of his near-contemporary Marco Polo, provides what is probably the most famous example of travel (*rihla*) literature in the medieval Arabic tradition. Setting out from Tangier in AD 1325 on a pilgrimage to Mecca, his subsequent travels included not only the central regions of the Islamic world but also India, Sri Lanka, East Africa, the Maldives, South-East Asia, China and, less certainly, the Russian steppes. During his residence in Delhi, he served as chief *qadi* for several years. Returning home in AD 1349, after having completed not merely one but several pilgrimages, he rested for only a few months before embarking on a further journey to Granada, Niger and adjoining regions of Africa. His travels have been estimated at some 75,000 miles (120,700 kilometres). He died in Morocco, probably in AD 1377, having extended the concept of *rihla* literature from the traditional account of a pilgrimage to Mecca and the Holy Places to what was in effect a description of much of the civilised world.

Ibn Battuta's account of his travels was dictated to his scribe Ibn Juzayy, who edited his text for publication. Ibn Battuta's dictation was completed in 1357, and the text appeared shortly afterwards, under the title *Tuhfat al-Nuzzar fi Ghara'ib al-amsar wa-'Aja'ib al-Asfar*. Although generally authentic, Ibn Battuta's account clearly underwent some reordering and reconstruction during the process of editing, as may be inferred from the inconsistencies of style that characterise the text. He was almost certainly indebted to earlier travellers, in particular Ibn Jubayr, for accounts of certain regions, and doubts have been raised about whether some journeys, including his visit to the Bulghars, were undertaken at all. The loss of his original notes to pirates in the Indian Ocrean forced him to rely on his memory for a large part of his account. Despite this, his unpretentious but often vivid narrative has an obvious immediacy and appeal to modern readers, not least for its being a vivid reminder of the extent to which the medieval Islamic world formed a unified entity, allowing extensive freedom of travel to anyone with the necessary means and nerve to undertake it. As such, it is fitting that it should have provided the inspiration for a modern 'classic' of travel literature, Tim Mackintosh-Smith's *Travels with a Tangerine*.

References

Gibb and Beckingham (1994), Mackintosh-Smith (2001, 2002).

PAUL STARKEY

IBN GABIROL

Solomon b. Judah Ibn Gabirol, a Jewish poet and philosopher, lived in Islamic Spain. He is considered to be the second Jewish Neoplatonist after Isaac Israeli (d. AD 932/55) and is one of the greatest Jewish philosophers in Spain. He was born in Malaga AD 1021 and lived in Saragossa where he also received his religious and philosophical education.

He had founded the Jewish Spanish school of philosophy, but was mainly known in the Jewish community for his biblical poems. His greatest work is the Hebrew poem of *Kater Malkhut* (*The Crown of the Kingdom*). Though this work is considered a book of prayer, it contains a great number of philosophical concepts and has great affinity to his famous philosophical work *Fons vitae*. The latter exists only in a Latin fragment which was originally written in Arabic and for a long time was thought to have been written by a Muslim or a Christian. Only in 1846 its original author was discovered by the French Jewish scholar Solom Munk. It is a systematic philosophical work, undoubtedly Neoplatonist, but, nevertheless, demonstrates originality. He argues that matter and form emanate directly from God and that creation, as an act of the divine will, should not represent duality in the Godhead. In addition, the divine will is presented as a mediator and a connecting point between God and the world. The Divine will here could be compared with the Christian *logos*. This is an attempt to change the fatalism of Neoplatonism into a voluntary system.

Ibn Gabirol died in Valencia around 1054 and AD 1058.

References

Nasr and Leaman (1996: I, 712–18).

MAHA EL-KAISY FRIEMUTH

IBN HAJAR AL-'ASQALANI, AHMAD B. 'ALI (AD 1372–1449)

Egyptian biographer, historian and *hadith* scholar. Born in Cairo into a well-to-do merchant family, he was orphaned as a child. By the age of eleven, however, he had learned the Qur'an by heart, and at about the age of twenty, decided to specialise in *hadith* studies. He spent some time travelling in Yemen, Palestine and Syria, collecting *hadith* and pursuing his studies, before embarking on a career as a teacher, preacher, *mufti*, librarian and judge. A prolific writer, his most famous single work, *al-Durar al-Kamina fi A'yan al-mi'a al-Thamina*, contains over 5,000 biographical notices of eminent persons who died during the eighth century of the *hijra* and represents probably the first example of a 'centennial' biographical dictionary of this sort. Among his other

works, which continue to be of value for present-day historians, *al-Isaba fi Tamyiz al-Sahaba* deals with the Companions of the Prophet and is noteworthy as an example of a comparatively late scholar returning to the original sources in order to verify his information. His other writings include *Fath al-Bari*, a commentary on the *Sahih* of al-Bukhari, *Tahdhib al-Tahdhib*, and *Inba' al-Ghumr bi-Anba' al-Umr*. The details of his life are known to us through two biographies compiled by his student al-Sakhawi (1427–97).

Though many of Ibn Hajar al-Asqalani's works are, by their very nature, somewhat mechanical in approach, involving above all the faithful reproduction of data gathered by previous scholars, the sheer range and volume of material that his works encompass are a tribute to the author's extraordinary industry, and have ensured that his works remain indispensable for contemporary scholars.

References

al-Durar al-Kamina (1929–31), Al-Isaba fi Tamyiz al-Sahaba (1905–7), Auchterlonie (1987), Gibb and Bosworth (1960–2003: III), Rosenthal (1952).

PAUL STARKEY

IBN HAWQAL, ABU AL-QASIM MUHAMMAD IBN 'ALI AL-NASIBI (*fl.* AD 943–88).

Geographer and traveller, a member of the so-called 'classical', or 'Balkhi', school of Arabic geographical literature. A successor to al-Istakhri, little is known of his life, other than sparse autobiographical information contained in his work *Kitab Surat al-Ard wa-Sifat Ashkaliha wa-Miqdariha fi al-tul wa'l-'ard* (also known as known as *al-Masalik wa'l-Mamalik*), which appeared in successive versions between about AD 967 and 988. Ibn Hawqal was born in Mesopotamia and probably spent his early years there before beginning, in AD 943, a series of journeys that took him to most parts of the Islamic world, including North Africa, Spain, Sicily, Egypt, Persia and Transoxania. Rumoured to have been a Fatimid secret agent, and certainly in sympathy with the movement, Ibn Hawqal met al-Istakhri as a young man, and his work is highly dependent on al-Istakhri's *Kitab Mamalik wa'l-Masalik* for much of its content. Although parts of Ibn Hawqal's work are little more than a stylistically improved rewriting of his predecessor's work, however, his book also contains new material gleaned during his own travels, and his information on the Sahara in particular appears to be quite new. Ibn Hawqal's work is especially notable for the interest that the author shows in current economic conditions in the areas that he visited. Although there is some indication that he originally conceived it as merely a commentary on a series of maps, the work illustrates the increasing importance attached to the text as a work in its own right by al-Istakhri's successors.

In addition to the *Kitab Surat al-Ard*, Ibn Hawqal is also credited with another geographical work on Sicily, which has not survived.

References

Kramers (1938–9), Miquel (1967–88), Young *et al.* (1990: 301–27).

PAUL STARKEY

IBN HAZM, ABU MUHAMMAD 'ALI B. AHMAD B. SA'ID
(AD 994–1064)

Zahiri theologian, historian, poet and *wazir*. He was born in Cordova in AD 994, his father being the *wazir* of the Umayyad

Caliph al-Mansur and of his son, al-Muzaffar of Andalusia. The political instability of this time and the attack of the Berbers on Cordova led to the death of Ibn Hazm's father (AD 1013). Ibn Hazm's loyalty and support towards the royal Umayyad family led to his expulsion from Cordova after the destruction of his family's house. He was twice imprisoned and eventually when the Umayyads returned to Cordova he was also appointed twice as *wazir* in AD 1022 and 1027. He decided in the end to withdraw from politics and devote his time to his writings.

Ibn Hazm received an excellent education from the best scholars of Cordova in the fields of grammar, lexicography, theology, law, rhetoric and philosophy. He left numerous works in many fields, mainly theology, literature, logic, ethics and history. In his *Kitab al-Shirka*, he followed Ibn Hanbal, calling for a return to the literal meaning of the Qur'an and *hadith* as the only source for belief. In *Kitab al-Milla* he rejected the use of analogy *qiyas* and allowed the use of consensus *ijma'*, but only in cases where there was no clear text. He also rejected *ta'wil* as a method for interpreting obscure verses of the Qur'an. However, his most influential theories were in the field of linguistics. He believed that language ought to be clear and the meaning of the words should lead to what the words signify. He rejected all theories which explain syntax by hidden meanings, in his opinion, one should not find alternatives to the literal sense by hidden meanings and symbols of one's own, but rather should make use of the actual meaning of the words. Thus the psychological intention of the speaker or the listener should not interfere with the meaning of the speech. Hence, God's usage of language must be understood in this light and it too should be interpreted literally. However, this did not prevent him from studying Aristotelian logic. In his *Kitab al-Taqrib* he considers logic as a way to explain our capacity for understanding, created by God in all humans. Some Muslim scholars, however, claim that Ibn Hazm did not really understand the philosophical meaning behind Aristotle's logic.

After a long active life, politically and intellectually, Ibn Hazm died in Manta Lisham in AD 1064.

References

Gibb and Bosworth (1960–2003: III, 790–9).

MAHA EL-KAISY FRIEMUTH

IBN JUBAYR AL-KINANI, MUHAMMAD IBN AHMAD (AD 1145–1217)

Medieval Andalusian traveller and travel writer. Born in Valencia, Ibn Jubayr served for a period as Secretary to the Governor of Granada. His first journey, recorded in his memoirs and apparently undertaken as expiation for the sin of drinking wine, lasted from 1183 to 1185, during which time he visited Alexandria, Mecca (where he stayed for nearly a year), Iraq and Syria before returning to Granada. His journey included a narrow escape from shipwreck in the Straits of Messina. He later visited the East again twice, though without recording his journeys, and died in Alexandria. A primary purpose of compiling his travel account (*Rihla*) was to give guidance to future travellers making the pilgrimage to Mecca, and the account of his travels includes a full and valuable account of the pilgrimage ceremonies. Though marred at times by an excessively ornate style (including some use of rhymed prose), the work is notable for its vigorous descriptions of the author's experiences, including his voyages across the Mediterranean and some memorable encoun-

ters with customs officials. As such, it has remained to this day a valuable source of historical information on political and social conditions in the Middle East at the time.

Ibn Jubayr's *Rihla* may be accounted the first in a line of travel narratives, especially popular in Andalusia and North Africa, that while taking as their starting point a pilgrimage to Mecca and the Holy Places, at the same time allowed the author scope for relating other experiences and for the expression of his own attitudes and views. One of the most readable of medieval Arabic travel books, it became widely known, not only in the Islamic West – where it proved a model and useful source of information for later authors, including his better known successor Ibn Battuta and Ibn Battuta's editor Ibn Juzayy – but also in the East, through the extracts inserted into the standard commentary on the *maqamat* of al-Hariri by his own student al-Sharishi.

References

Broadhurst (1952).

PAUL STARKEY

IBN KATHIR, 'IMAD AL-DIN ISMA'IL IBN 'UMAR (AD 1300–73)

Jurist, exegete. Born in Basra in AD 1300, he moved to Damascus when he was six, where he studied with some of the most famous scholars of his time including the Hanbali theologian, jurist and reformer Ibn Taymiyya (d. AD 1328). Ibn Kathir became known as a scholar of law and a teacher of *hadith* as well as being praised as one of the most respected preachers and lecturers in Damascus. He died in AD 1373. His major work, a commentary on the Qur'an entitled simply *Tafsir al-Qur'an*, provides a synopsis of earlier material in a readily accessible form, a factor which gave the work much popularity in subsequent generations. His reliance is totally upon *hadith* material; the era of Ibn Kathir, in fact, marks the triumph of traditionalism over the powers of rationalism. Ibn Kathir frequently structures his commentary around extracts from the classical books of *hadith*, citing those reports relevant to the passage in question. In doing so, the tradition of *tafsir* was being transformed, with the significance of the disciplines of grammar, law and theology being downplayed.

References

Calder (1993: 101–40).

ANDREW RIPPIN

IBN KHALLIKAN, AHMAD IBN MUHAMMAD (AD 1211–82)

Arabic biographer, best known for his popular and invaluable biographical dictionary *Wafayat al-a'yan wa-anba' abna' al-Zaman*, which contains biographies of some 855 eminent Muslims whose date of death the author could ascertain, arranged in alphabetical order. Born in Irbil to a Kurdish family that claimed descent from the Barmakids, Ibn Khallikan studied with scholars in Irbil, Mosul, Damascus, Aleppo and Egypt, before embarking on a legal career that alternated between Egypt and Syria. He was appointed deputy *qadi al-qudat* in Egypt in AD 1247, but in 1261 moved to Syria, where he stayed for ten years as *qadi al-qudat* until his dismissal in AD 1271. Following further service in Egypt, he returned to Syria as *qadi* in AD 1277, where he remained until his death.

Ibn Khallikan's *Wafayat* intentionally omits groups of people on whom information was already widely available elsewhere, including the Companions of the Prophet, second generation 'trans-mitters', and the Islamic caliphs. It has been widely admired not only in the Arab world but also in the West, for its combination of accurate information (particularly on Ibn Khallikan's contemporaries), revealing anecdotes, and the author's ability to sum up the essence of a person's character in no more than a few words Described by Ibn Taghribirdi as the 'acme of excellence', it is also valuable for its quotations from earlier sources that are now lost or as yet unpublished.

References

Auchterlonie (1987), McGuckin de Slane (1842–71), *Wafayat al-a'yan* (1968–72).

PAUL STARKEY

IBN KHURRADADHBIH, 'UBAYDALLAH IBN 'ABDALLAH (AD 820 or 825?–911?).

Born into a well-connected Persian family, and a Zoroastrian before his conversion to Islam, Ibn Khurradadhbih held the post of *Sahib al-Bari wa-al-Khabar* and occupied a conspicuous position at the court of the Caliph al-Mu'tamid. He is known to have written on a variety of topics, including history, genealogy, *nudama'* (boon companions), food, drink and music, but many of the works attributed to him by Ibn al-Nadim are now lost. His most famous surviving work, his *Kitab al-Masalik wa-al-Mamalik*, represents one of the earliest surviving contributions to the Arabic geographical tradition and was used as a model by many later geographers. Probably intended, at least in part, to provide practical information for members of the state postal and intelligence services, it represents the first surviving example of its genre, combining materials from classical sources, mainly Ptolemy

257

(whom he may have translated into Arabic), with an organisational structure reflecting the Persian tradition. Ibn Khurradadhbih's world is divided into four main regions corresponding roughly to the points of the compass – *mashriq*, *maghrib*, *jarbi* (north) and *tayman* (south) – to which he adds a fifth, the Sawad of Iraq, from which all the others radiate, and it is with this region, centred on Baghdad, that he begins his book. Although much of his account is a mundane collection of itineraries and other administrative information, he frequently enlivens it by the insertion of historical or other anecdotes or of snippets of poetry, and the work concludes with a collection of supplementary information on regions as diverse as Sicily and Scandinavia. Although clearly important as the first example of its genre to have survived until modern times, the authenticity of the surviving version of Ibn Khallikan's work and the precise date of its composition have been the subject of some controversy.

Also surviving by Ibn Khurradadhbih is a treatise on music, *Kitab al-Lahw wa-al-Malahi*. The work uses a largely Persian technical vocabulary and reflects the concerns of practicing musicians rather than theorists.

References

de Goeje (1889), Miquel (1967–88).

PAUL STARKEY

IBN MAJA, ABU 'ABDULLAH MUHAMMAD IBN YAZID (d. AD 887)

Author of the *hadith* collection, *Kitab al-Sunan*, the final canonical collection of traditions. Born in Qazwin, he travelled widely through Iran, Iraq, Syria and Egypt in search of authentic *hadith* reports, of which he compiled about 4,000 into a book of some 150 chapters. While the book did not receive unanimous assent by all Muslims, it did gain its status as one of the six respected books of *hadith* by the eleventh century AD.

References

Siddiqi (1993: 69).

ANDREW RIPPIN

IBN MAJID, SHIHAB AL-DIN AHMAD (*c.* 1436-*c.* 1500)

Arab navigator, probably born in Oman, and author of some forty works on navigation and related topics. Little is known of the life of the author himself, who by his own account spent some fifty years at sea; it appears, however, that he came from a family that had already distinguished themselves as Red Sea navigators. By around AD 1000, a number of navigational works had begun to be compiled by Arab authors, and around AD 1100 a group of authors known as the 'Three Lions' (Muhammad ibn Shadhan, Sahl ibn Abban and Layth ibn Kahlan) compiled navigational works on which Ibn Majid appears to have drawn for his own work; little is known of how Ibn Majid's work relates to these sources, however, as the originals are no longer extant.

The most important of Ibn Majid's works are his *Hawiyat al-Ikhtisar fi usul 'Ilm al-Bihar*, composed in the *rajaz* metre, and *Fawa'id fi usul 'Ilm al-Bahr wa'l-Qawa'id*, written in prose. The topics covered by these two works, which to some extent overlap, include, *inter alia*, the lunar mansions, compass rhumbs, the sea routes of the Indian Ocean, routes along the coast of India to Sumatra, China and Taiwan, the coastal regions of Asia and Africa, important islands, latitudes, and navigational seasons and monsoons. Among his other works, many of which he composed in verse, are a number dealing with aspects of navigational astronomy. Ibn Majid was the first Arab navigator to extend the description of the east African coast southwards beyond Sofala. His name apparently remained known to navigators in the Indian Ocean until the nineteenth century and, although sometimes rather haphazard in terms of their organisation, his works, with their mixture of theoretical and practical information, remain of considerable value to the scholar.

Ibn Majid's career coincided with the arrival of Portuguese navigators in the Indian Ocean via the Cape of Good Hope, paving the way for a new era in European exploration and colonisation of India and the eastern Islamic world. Ibn Majid was certainly aware of the activities and importance of the Portuguese, but the claim, originally put forward by Gabriel Ferrand, that Vasco da Gama relied on Ibn Majid to guide him from Malindi to Calicut is almost certainly false.

References

Ferrand (1921), Tibbetts (1971).

PAUL STARKEY

IBN MASARRA, MUHAMMAD IBN 'ABDALLAH (AD 833–931)

Andalusian philosopher and mystic, born in Cordova. He lived at a difficult time under the rule of the traditional *Maliki Fuqaha'*. His father was a Mu'tazilite and was persecuted for his teaching of their doctrines. Ibn Masarra was one of his father's students, receiving his theological and ascetic education from him. After his father died in Mecca AD 899, Ibn Masarra was accused of heterodoxy by a famous *faqih*, Ahmad b. Khalid, who had written a short work denouncing Ibn Masarra's doctrines. Therefore he

left for the east and remained there for some time, probably in Mecca. Ibn Masarra returned home probably around AD 912 when 'Abd al-Rahman III had introduced a more tolerant policy. There he led a peaceful ascetic life with his disciples.

The two most important works of Ibn Masarra, *The Book of Letters* and *The Book of Enlightenment* are unfortunately lost and known to us only through their titles. The Spanish Arabist Miguel Asyn Palacios collected information about him from the writings of Ibn 'Arabi, Ibn Hazm, Sa'id Toledo, al-Shahristani, Ibn Abi Usaybi'a and Ibn Al-Qifti. It seems that his thought had great affinity with the teaching of Pseudo-Empedocles, which is probably of Neoplatonic origin. The main feature of this teaching is the concept of the unity of God's attributes and the human soul's unity with God as the final goal of human intellect. Samuel Stern, however, considers this link with Pseudo-Empedocles to have no real basis but to depend merely on a report from Sa'id Toledo's *Tabaqat al-Umam* which relies on a saying of al-'Amiri that Empedocles influenced all *batini* philosophers and mystics. Goodman, however, argues that one can trace in the thought of Ibn Masarra the main line of PseudoEmpedocles' teaching on creation, the position of the human soul as a link between God and the material world and the idea that the soul receives the necessary knowledge of God, which is summed up in the concept that knowing yourself means knowing your God.

According to Asyn Palacios, the mystic thought of Ibn Masarra influenced Jewish and Christian scholars. Among Muslim mystics, he is considered to have influenced Ibn al-'Arabi and Ibn al-'Arif. Ibn Masarra led a peaceful ascetic life in the mountains near Cordova, where he died in October AD 931.

MAHA EL-KAISY FRIEMUTH

259

IBN MISKAWAYH, ABU 'ALI AHMAD MUHAMMAD B. YA'QUB (AD 936–1030)

Historian, philosopher, physician and librarian. He was born in AD 936 in Rayy. It was said that he was a Zoroastrian convert to Islam, but Kraemer considers that all Miskawayh's family previously converted to Islam. Khwansari considers him, however, to be a Shi'ite Imam but his Shi'ism can probably best be compared with that of the Sincere Brethren (Ikhwan al-Safa'). He served as librarian in the court of many Buyid princes: Rukn al-Dawla, Mu'ayd al-Dawla and 'Adud al-Dawla. He was one of al-Sijistani's circle and a member in Ibn 'Adi's philosophical school in Baghdad.

Miskawayh's works mainly express a humanistic standpoint. He considers that humans should be active members of society and not isolated individuals. His great historical work is *Tajarib al-Umam* in which he gives copious historical details. This work records the experience of the nation from a secular perspective. He sees it as a book which lets us learn from the experience of our wise forefathers and therefore he omits all miraculous stories because they do not teach human behaviour. For the same reason he also omits the period of pre-Islamic history from his work. However, his greatest work, known as *Tahdhib al-Akhlaq,* was in the field of ethics. In this work he considers that humans are sociable by nature and need to live in a society. His theories on ethics are said to have influenced al-Ghazali in his work *Mizan al-'Amal* and also the teaching of Muhammad 'Abdu. Miskawayh died on 16 February 1030 in Isfhan.

References

Kraemer (1992: 223–33).

MAHA EL-KAISY FRIEMUTH

IBN QAYYIM AL-JAWZIYYA (AD 1292–1350)

Theologian and legal scholar of the Hanbali school. Born in Damascus, he became the most famous follower of Ibn Taymiyya, whose ideas he absorbed and then helped to disseminate. He was less confrontational in style than his teacher, however, and so although he was imprisoned for two years, from 1326 to 1328, at the same time as Ibn Taymiyya, he was released when his master died. H. Laoust described him as 'much less of a polemicist than his master and much more a preacher', so that although he was concerned about most of the same issues he campaigned against them with much less animus. In particular he was less antagonistic towards Sufism. A recent work has also made more widely known his expertise in the field of medicine.

References

Johnstone (1998), Watt (1985: Chapter 18).

HUGH GODDARD

IBN QUDAMA (AD 1147–1223)

A scholar of the Hanbali school, who was critical of the whole tradition of *kalam* (rational theology) in Islam. He was born near Jerusalem, and as a result of the disruption caused by the crusaders' conquest of that city he and his family moved when he was about ten to Damascus, where he studied Qur'an and *hadith*. He visited Baghdad on several occasions, and also Mecca, and he took part in the expedition led by Saladin to reconquer Jerusalem in 1187, but he spent most of his life in Damascus, and it was there that he died. He wrote a number of works on jurisprudence, and in his *Tahrim al-Nazar fi Kutub Ahl al-Kalam* (*Prohibition of the Study of the Books of the Theologians*) he condemns not only the Mu'tazila but also the theologians of the Ash'ari school.

References

Makdisi (1962).

HUGH GODDARD

IBN QUTAYBA, 'ABDALLAH IBN MUSLIM (AD 828–89)

'Abbasid literary critic and religious scholar. Born in Kufa to an Arabised Persian family, Ibn Qutayba served as a *qadi* in Persia for some twenty years, before moving in AD 871 to Baghdad, where he later died. His writings covered a wide range of subjects on both religious and secular subjects, and are an important source of information on early Arabic poets and poetry in particular. A passage from his work *al-Shi'r wa'l-Shu'ara'* is quoted frequently as the classic description of the traditional Arabic *qasida* (ode).

His non-religious works include *Adab al-Katib*, a handbook for secretaries laying much emphasis on correct grammatical and linguistic usage, *'Uyun al-Akhbar*, an anthology of prose and poetry, arranged by subject, which incorporates material of the 'Mirror for Princes' type, *al-Ma'arif*, a handbook of history, *Kitab Ma'ani al-Shi'r*, on the motifs of early Arabic poetry, and *al-Shi'r wa'l-Shu'ara'*, to which we have already referred, an anthology arranged on a largely chronological basis. The last named work represents an important source of information on both the early poets and the *muhdathun*, and is particularly interesting for Ibn Qutayba's rejection of traditional arguments in favour of the supremacy of the pre-Islamic poets over their later counterparts.

Among Ibn Qutayba's contributions to Islamic theology are his *Ta'wil Mushkil al-Qur'an*, a treatise on Qur'anic rhetoric and the doctrine of *i'jaz*, and the important *Ta'wil Mukhtalif al-hadith*, in which he sets out his religious and political ideas. From these and other works, it appears that he was a strong supporter of the efforts of al-Mutawakkil to restore the traditional form of Sunnism following the abandonment of the Mu'tazilite ideology.

Ibn Qutayba occupies an important chronological position in the history of the development of Arabic prose writing after Ibn al-Muqaffa' and al-Jahiz. His style is generally straightforward and free of the artifice that characterised the writings of many of his contemporaries. As a grammarian, he has often been held to have created a 'synthesis' between the rival schools of Kufa and Basra, but there is little historical justification for this view.

References

Gaudefroy-Demombynes (1947), Lecomte (1965).

PAUL STARKEY

IBN RUSHD, ABU AL-WALID IBN AHMAD (AVERROES) (AD 1126–98)

Ibn Rushd (Averroes), Abu al-Walid Ibn Ahmad, the leading philosopher of Islamic Spain, al-Andalus, was also a renowned Islamic lawyer and an influential physician. In addition to his numerous philosophical works, his writings include important works in both law and medicine. He was well grounded in the Islamic religious sciences including Islamic theology (*kalam*), of which he was critical, and was deemed an authority on Arabic poetry.

The most Aristotelian of the Islamic philosophers, Ibn Rushd was born in Cordova in AD 1126, the son and grandson of distinguished Cordovan judges. In 1169, Ibn Tufayl introduced him to the genuinely philosophical ruler of the Almohads, Abu Ya'qub Yusuf (r. AD 1163–84), who was seeking someone to write commentaries on Aristotle. For this task, Ibn Tufayl, who had been asked to do so but declined, recommended Ibn Rushd. Ibn Rushd's first official duties, however, were legal. In AD 1169 he was appointed judge in Seville and in AD 1171 judge of Cordova. In AD 1182, he succeeded Ibn Tufayl as physician in the Almohad court, serving its ruler Abu Ya'qub until the latter's death in AD 1184. He continued to serve Abu Ya'qub's son, al-Mansur from 1184 until AD 1195, when he fell out of favour, was exiled and his books burnt. It appears that public pressure from religious conservative scholars played a role in this. Shortly thereafter, however, Ibn Rushd was reinstated. He continued to serve the Almohads until his death in AD 1198.

For the historian of Western philosophy, Ibn Rushd is best known for his commentaries on Aristotle. These commentaries in their Latin versions conditioned the development of Aristotelianism in both medieval Europe and renaissance Italy. His commentaries included both criticisms of earlier Aristotelian commentators and expansions on Aristotle that often reveal Ibn Rushd's original insights. He also wrote a commentary on Plato's *Republic* (whether he had access to a translation of the original Greek or was simply commenting on a translation of a prosaic summary of this work's political themes is not clear). He also wrote commentaries on Porphyry's *Isagoge*, on one the treatises by Alexander of Aphrodisias on the intellect, short commentaries on some of Galen's medical treatises, and a short commentary on Ptolemy's *Almajest*. Medieval Arabic sources mention treatises Ibn Rushd devoted to criticisms of aspects of the thought of al-Farabi (Alfarabi) and Ibn Sina (Avicenna). These are not extant.

In the Islamic world, it is Ibn Rushd's works dealing in one way or another with his defence of philosophy that have left their mark. They also reveal quite pointedly his individual thought. These include a trilogy consisting of an epistle on divine knowledge, followed respectively by *Fasl al-Maqhl* (*The Decisive Treatise*) and *Kitab al-Kashf 'an Manahij al-Adilla fi 'Aqa'id al-Milla* (*Exposition of the Methods of Proofs Regarding the Beliefs of the [Islamic] Religion*). They also include his large work, *Tahafut al-Tahafut* (*The Incoherence of 'The Incoherence'*), a detailed reply to Ghazali's *Tahafut al-Falasifa* (*The Incoherence of the Philosophers*) that quotes almost all of the latter work, critically commenting on it paragraph by paragraph.

In his *Tahafut*, Ghazali did not merely offer a logical critique of the philosophical systems of al-Farabi and Ibn Sina: he condemned them as infidels for their doctrine of an eternal world, and in the case of Ibn Sina, for his theory that God knows particulars only 'in a universal way', and his denial of bodily resurrection that affirms that only the human immaterial soul is immortal. The charge of infidelity is a legal charge. In the trilogy, particularly the *Fasl*, Ibn Rushd addresses himself to answering this charge. Underlying his reply are certain doctrines enunciated by al-Farabi, namely, that religion is a symbolic representation of philosophy, does not contradict it, but is its expression in the language the non-philosopher majority of mankind can understand, and that only the philosophers are allowed to interpret it philosophically.

Ibn Rushd begins his *Fasl* by raising the broad question, namely, whether the study of philosophy is allowed, prohibited, recommended or obligated by Islamic law. Basing himself on certain Qur'anic utterances, he concludes that the study of philosophy is obligatory, but only for those capable of it. Turning to Ghazali's charge of infidelity leveled at the Islamic philosophers, Ibn Rushd points out that there can be no legal judgmental consensus (*ijma'*) on such theoretical matters, consensus pertaining only to the legal aspects of human practical conduct.

Humanity, Ibn Rushd then argues, divides into three classes: the demonstrative, confined to the few, namely, the philosophers, the dialectical, confined to a larger group, namely, the theologians, and the rhetorical, embracing the majority. Scriptural verses also divide into three classes. The first consist of verses whose meaning is understood in the same way by philosophers, theologians and the masses. These must be accepted literally. A second class of texts are by nature abstruse and should be understood by the demonstrative method, but only by those qualified to do so. Then there is a third class of texts whose classification in terms of the other two is not certain. Some interpret them metaphorically, some take them literally. Scholars who err either in taking them metaphorically, or err in the metaphorical interpretations they offer, should not be condemned as infidels. Such errors are permissible.

Turning to the first of the three doctrines condemned by Ghazali as irreligious, that of the world's eternity, Ibn Rushd tries to show that the difference between the Ash'arite theologians (as represented by Ghazali) and the philosophers is not that great to warrant such a condemnation He also points out that the doctrine of creation *ex nihilo* is not mentioned in the Qur'an. As for the doctrine that God does not know particulars, its condemnation is based on a misunderstanding of the peripatetics who only deny that God knows particulars as humans do. With humans it is the particular which is the cause of this knowledge, with God, it is divine knowledge that is the cause of the existence of particulars.

In both *Fasl* and *Kashf*, Ibn Rushd turns to the question of the hereafter. The first move in his defence of the philosophers is to maintain that the Qur'anic texts that speak of the hereafter belong to the class where the question of whether or not they are to be taken literally is not certain. Hence, any error in this regard, is permissible. In *Kashf,* he maintains that all religions agree that there is a resurrection. These religions only differ on its nature, though, in reality, they differ not so much regarding the nature of its existence as they do regarding the observable things used to symbolise this unseen state. While belief in the resurrection is obligatory on all Muslims, members of each class, demonstrative, dialectical and rhetorical, must interpret the texts enunciating it according to where their reflections lead them. Such interpretations would then be commensurate with the individual's intellectual capacity.

In this discussion Ibn Rushd seems to affirm a doctrine of individual immortality. It is however difficult to see how such an affirmation could be consistent with his theory of the intellect, a theory he formulates in the context of his commentaries on Aristotle's *De Anima.* One encounters some variation and some hesitation in his formulations of the theory. Still, one can perhaps indicate what seem to be some of its essentials:

The human soul receives images from the senses. Its theoretical rational faculty then abstracts their form. Although the abstracted form differs from the form that exists externally in matter, it resembles it in that it is also generable and corruptible. Just as in the Aristotelian scheme of things the external form cannot exist independently of the particular, similarly, although perceived by the mind in abstraction from the material images, the form cannot exist independently of them. In its ontological status in the soul as a generable and corruptible entity, it must have an aspect that takes the part of form, a higher form, and an aspect that takes the part of matter. That which takes the part of the higher form is the agent that moves the abstracted form from potency into actuality. This is the active intellect, an autonomous, ever existing actual entity, external to the soul. It becomes individuated only when it is actualising the rational faculty (in the way light is individuated by the objects when it illuminates them). Regarding the material part of the generable and corruptible form, in one place Ibn Rushd suggests that it is a disposition that requires a subject. Then taking his cue from Aristotle, he suggests that this subject is something analogous to prime matter, potentially receptive of all forms. It does not belong to any one individual soul. Akin to prime matter, without form it has no existence.

Turning to Ibn Rushd's *Incoherence*, it is a large, complex work, very rich in argument. Something of its ethos can perhaps be best captured if one considers its answer to Ghazali's critique of causality. Ghazali had argued that in the natural realm a necessary causal connection between what is habitually believed to be causes and effects can be proved neither logically nor empirically. Logically, cause and effect being two distinct things, neither the affirmation nor negation of the one entails the affirmation or negation of the other, hence the existence or nonexistence of the one does not necessitated the existence or nonexistence of the other. Observation only shows concomitance between natural events, not any necessary causal connection. We see the cotton burn with its contacting the fire, not its burning by the fire.

This, Ibn Rushd maintains is sophistry. One cannot deny efficient causes observed in sensible things. It should be noted here that Ibn Rushd does not address himself to the question of whether we have empirical knowledge the necessity of

causal connection. As he proceeds, however, he makes his case stronger. He insists that causal action is part of the definition of a thing, so that if one denies it, one denies the differentiation between things. Again, he asks: is it possible for the contact between cotton and fire to take place without the cotton burning? Only if there is a natural impediment, he answers. This, however, he continues, does not deprives the fire of its property of causing conflagration. In other words, fire to be fire, must be burning something. In an earlier discussion (the third), Ghazali had argued that action cannot be attributed to inanimate things and that while to use a verb of action such as 'to burn' when applied to fire, is correct Arabic usage, it is only correct 'metaphorical' usage. To which Ibn Rushd answers laconically that when someone is killed by accidentally falling in a fire, no one would say that that person was burnt 'metaphorically'.

Ibn Rushd also asks how can Ghazali and the Ash'arites maintain the principle that every event must have a cause (the principle on which their proof for God's existence is based) when they maintain that real causes are not observed in nature? Moreover, he holds that to deny natural causes is the denial of demonstrative science. This means that there is no necessary knowledge. It follows, then, that if there is no necessary knowledge, the denial of necessary knowledge itself cannot constitute necessary knowledge. He also questions the Ash'arite view that the uniformity of nature is the result of habit. Is this God's habit? But 'habit' is a disposition acquired by living creatures. To attribute it to God is to deny him perfection. Could it then be the habit of inanimate things? But this would be a misuse of language, as inanimate things possess qualities and natures. If this is what the theologians mean by habit, they would be tacitly admitting that things have natures that prescribe their orderly activity. And if by habit they mean our habit of discerning the natural order, then this is what is meant by reason.

Whether or not in such comments Ibn Rushd fully answers Ghazali's critique of natural causality, he certainly indicates relevant factors that cannot be ignored in examining this issue. In this he blunts the edge of some of Ghazali's arguments. Throughout his *Incoherence,* Ibn Rushd strives to clarify issues, offering comprehensive rational analyses. Although mainly directed against Ghazali, it is also critical of Ibn Sina. Its perspective is Aristotelian, a tone of rational sobriety pervades it.

References

Ahwani (1950), Black (1999), Bouyges (1930, 1938–52), Butterworth (1985), Davidson (1992), Druart (1994: 35–57), Endress (1995: 9–49), Fakhry (2001), Hourani (1961), Ibn Rushd (1964, 1974, 1986), Ivry (1966: 76–85; 1994), Kogan (1985), Najjar (2001), Taylor (1998: 507–23), Van Den Bergh (1954).

MICHAEL E. MARMURA

IBN RUSTIH, ABU 'ALI AHMAD IBN 'UMAR
(*fl.* AD 903)

Persian geographer. Born in Isfahan, Ibn Rustih was the author of a major work of geography, *Kitab al-A'laq al-Nafisa,* of which only an incomplete version of its seventh part now survives; the value and influence of the complete work can accordingly only be guessed at. The surviving part of his work includes a discussion of Greek, Indian and Arab cosmological theory, his views on which he justifies through quotations from the Qur'an; he then moves on to a description of the Holy Cities of Mecca and Medina. This juxtaposition of topics has led commentators to suggest that the author was a supporter of the Shu'ubiyya, a view that would certainly be compatible with his

Persian origins; his interest in non-Arab and non-Muslim peoples such as the Khazar, Bulghars and Rus may also be relevant in this connection.

In terms of its arrangement, Ibn Rustih's work belongs to the 'Iraqi' rather than the 'Balkhi' school, employing a system of seven *aqalim* derived from the Greek geographers; among the Arabic sources that he almost certainly consulted was the *Kitab al-Masalik wa-al-Mamalik* of Ibn Khurradadhbih.

References

Miquel (1967).

PAUL STARKEY

IBN SAB'IN, 'ABD AL-HAQQ
(AD 1217–69)

Peripatetic philosopher and Sufi. He called himself Ibn Dara. *Dara* here means a circle or ring which is said to signify the number zero and according to some methods of calculation it corresponds to the figure seventy (*sab'in*). Ibn Sab'in's life was full of misfortune and suffering, Massignon considers his life to have consisted of quarrels, controversies and persecution. He was born in Murcia in AD 1217, where he also studied philosophy, medicine, alchemy and Andalusian Sufism, which was influenced by the school of Ibn Masarra. However, his Sufi doctrines were suspect because of his belief of God as the entire reality of all existing things, which implies a pantheistic tendency. Therefore, he was compelled to leave his native land and in around the AD 1246 he settled somewhere in Ceuta. But soon he had to move again to Badis and then to Bougie. There he met al-Shushtari, who became his faithful disciple and defender. He moved again to Tunis where he suffered hardship and persecution by traditional *'ulama'.* Around AD 1250 he left for Cairo, where for some time he was left in peace. After a while the Mamluk Baybars I became displeased by his teaching and he was expelled from the country. Finally, he left for Mecca where he remained until his death in AD 1269.

In Mecca he composed most of his works, the most important of which are *The Escape of the Gnostic*, and *Mysteries of Oriental Wisdom*. In both works he demonstrates his concept of pantheism, arguing that the categories of Aristotelian logic are only illusion and in fact they represent one and the same reality. In addition, our soul and rational intellect are only a reflection of the divine intellect and not independent phenomena. Ibn Sab'in was also critical of other Sufi philosophers such as Ibn 'Arabi and Ibn al-Farid. He founded a group which was called Sab'iniyyia, attacked by Ibn Taymiyyia in *The Book of Alexandrian Questions*.

References

Ibn Sab'in (1978).

MAHA EL-KAISY FRIEMUTH

IBN SA'D, ABU 'ABDALLAH MUHAMMAD (*c.* AD 784–845)

Religious scholar and compiler of the important biographical dictionary *Kitab al-Tabaqat al-Kabir*. Ibn Sa'd served in Baghdad as secretary to the historian al-Waqidi, who had himself compiled a biographical dictionary entitled *Kitab al-Tabaqat*, now lost; Ibn Sa'd drew heavily on this work for his own *Tabaqat*, as well as on the work of Ibn al-Kalbi, with whom he had also studied.

Ibn Sa'd's compilation, which was intended primarily as an aid to the study of the *hadith*, begins with the Prophet Muhammad himself, following which he goes on to give accounts of some 4,000 other eminent personalities who had played a part as narrators or trans-mitters of tradition. His entries are arranged partly on a geographical basis, partly on the basis of their stages of remove (*tabaqa*) from the Prophet himself – an arrangement that was subsequently adopted by many other compilers of biographical information in different fields; the information provided is fuller for the earlier period than for personalities nearer to Ibn Sa'd's own time. Ibn Sa'd's compilation was widely used by later medieval authors and it remains to this day an important source of information on personalities in early Islam.

References

Duri (1983), Khalidi (1994).

PAUL STARKEY

IBN SINA, ABU 'ALI AL-HUSAYN (AVICENNA) (AD 980–1037)

Better known in Europe by the Latinised name Avicenna, probably the most significant philosopher in the Islamic tradition and arguably the most influential philosopher of the pre-modern era. Born in Afshana near Bukhara in central Asia in about AD 980, he is best known as a polymath, a physician whose major work the *Canon* (*al-Qanun fi'l-tibb*) continued to be taught as a medical textbook in Europe and in the Islamic world until the early modern period, and as a philosopher whose major *summa* the *Cure* (*al-Shifa'*) had a decisive impact upon European scholasticism and especially upon Thomas Aquinas (d. AD 1274). A precocious scholar who may have been born into an Isma'ili family, he claims to have mastered all the sciences by the age of eighteen including Hanafi jurisprudence (*fiqh*) in Bukhara and entered into the service of the Samanid court of Nuh ibn Mansur (r. AD 976–97) as a physician. But it seems that the excellent library of the physicians at the Samanid court assisted Ibn Sina in his self-education. An itinerant scholar following the vagaries of patronage in central Asia and Iran in the late tenth and early eleventh centuries with the Samanids, Qarakhanids and Buyids, he was fond of luxury, had a fiery temper not being able to suffer fools no matter how 'eminent', and died as a result of an excess of wine and sex in 1037 in Hamadan in Iran. Sources on his life range from his 'autobiography' written at the behest of his disciple 'Abd al-Wahid Juzjani, his private correspondence including the collection of philosophical epistles exchanged with his disciples and known as *al-Mubahathat* (*The Discussions*) to legends and doxographical views embedded in the 'histories of philosophy' of medieval Islam.

Ibn Sina wrote three 'encyclopaedias' of philosophy. The first of these is *al-Shifa'* (*The Cure*), a work modelled on the corpus of the 'philosopher', viz. Aristotle, that covers the natural sciences, logic, philosophy and theology. It was this work that through its Latin translation had a considerable impact on scholasticism. The other two encyclopaedias were written later for his patron the Buyid prince 'Ala' al-Dawla in Isfahan. The first, significantly in Persian, entitled *Danishnama-yi 'Ala'i* (*The Book of Knowledge for 'Ala' al-Dawla*) is an introductory text designed for the layman and closely follows his own Arabic epitome of *The Cure*, namely *al-Najat* (*The Salvation*). The second, whose dating and interpretation have inspired debates for centuries, is *al-Isharat wa'l-Tanbihat* (*Pointers and Reminders*), a work that does not present completed proofs for arguments and reflects his mature thinking on a variety of logical and metaphysical issues. A further work entitled *al-Insaf* (*The Judgement*) which purports to represent a philosophical position that is radical and transcends Aristotelianising Neoplatonism is unfor-

tunately not extant and debates about its contents are rather like the arguments that one encounters concerning Plato's esoteric or unwritten doctrines.

Logic is a critical aspect of and propaedeutic to Avicennan philosophy. His logical works follow the curriculum of late Neoplatonism and comprise nine books, beginning with his version of Porphyry's *Isagoge* followed by his understanding and modification of the Aristotelian *Organon* that critically in the Arabic tradition included the *Poetics* and the *Rhetoric*. His views on logic represent a significant metaphysical approach and it could be argued generally that metaphysical concerns lead Ibn Sina's arguments in a range of philosophical and non-philosophical subjects. For example, he argues in *The Cure* that both logic and metaphysics share a concern with the study of secondary intelligibles (*ma'qulat thaniyya*), abstract concepts such as existence and time that are derived from primary concepts such as humanity and animality. Logic is the standard by which mental concepts, or the mental 'existence' that corresponds to things that occur in extramental reality, can be judged and hence has both implications for what exists outside of the mind and how one may articulate those concepts through language.

Ibn Sina is well known as the author of one of the most important and influential proofs for the existence of God, a good example of a philosopher's intellect deployed for a theological purpose, a common feature of much medieval philosophy. The argument runs as follows. There is existence, or rather our phenomenal experience of the world confirms that things exist, and that their existence is non-necessary because we notice that things come into existence and pass out of it. Contingent existence cannot arise unless it is made necessary by a cause. A causal chain in reality must culminate in one un-caused cause because one cannot posit an actual infinite regress of causes (a basic axiom of Aristotelian science). Therefore, the chain of contingent existents must culminate in and find its causal principle in a sole self-subsistent existent that is Necessary. This, of course, is the same as the God of religion. An important corollary of this argument is Ibn Sina's famous distinction between existence and essence in contingents, between the fact that something exists and what it is, a distinction that is arguably latent in Aristotle although the roots of Ibn Sina's doctrine are best understood in classical Islamic theology or *kalam*. Existents in this world exist as something, whether human, animal or inanimate object, they are 'dressed' in the form of some essence that is a bundle of properties that describes them as composites. In contrast, God is absolutely simple, and cannot be divided into a bundle of distinct ontological properties that would violate his unity. Contingents, as a mark of their contingency, are conceptual and ontological composites at the first level of existence and essence and at the second level of properties both essential and accidental that are true of particular contingents. Contingent things in this world come to be as mentally distinct composites of existence and essence bestowed by the Necessary. Later arguments raged concerning whether the distinction was mental or 'real', whether the proof is ontological or cosmological. The clearest problem with Ibn Sina's proofs lies in the famous Kantian objection to ontological arguments: is existence meaningful in itself? Further, Cantor's solution to the problem of infinity may also be seen as a setback to the argument from the impossibility of actual infinites.

The second most influential idea of Ibn Sina is his theory of the knowledge. The human intellect at birth is rather like a *tabula rasa*, a pure potentiality that is actualised through education and comes to know. Knowledge is attained through empirical familiarity with objects in this world from which one abstracts universal concepts. It is developed through a syllogistic method of reasoning, observations lead to prepositional statements, which when compounded lead to further abstract concepts. But the question arises: how can we verify if a proposition is true? How do we know that an experience of ours is veridical? There are two methods to achieve this: first, the standards of formal inference of arguments – is the argument logically sound, second, and most importantly, there is a transcendent intellect in which all the essences of things and all knowledge resides. This intellect, known as the active intellect, illuminates the human intellect through conjunction and bestows upon the human intellect true knowledge of things. Conjunction, however, is episodic and only occurs to human intellects that have become actualised and adequately trained. The active intellect also intervenes in the assessment of sound inferences through Ibn Sina's theory of intuition. A syllogistic inference draws a conclusion from two prepositional premises through their connection or their middle term. Sometimes, it is rather difficult to see what the middle term is, thus when someone reflecting upon an inferential problem suddenly hits upon the middle term, and thus understands the correct result, they are helped through intuition inspired by the active intellect. There are various objections that can be raised against this theory, especially because it is predicated upon a cosmology widely refuted in the post-Copernican world.

Ibn Sina's epistemology is predicated upon a theory of soul that is independent of the body and capable of abstraction. This proof for the self in many ways prefigures the Cartesian *cogito* and the modern philosophical notion of the self by some 600 years. It is the so-called 'flying man' argument or thought experiment found at the beginning of his *Fi'l-Nafs/De anima* (*Treatise on the Soul*). If a person were created in a perfect state, but blind and suspended in the air but unable to perceive anything through his senses, would he be able to affirm the existence of his self? Suspended in such a state, he cannot affirm the existence of his body because he is not empirically aware of it, thus the argument may be seen as affirming the independence of the soul from the body, a form of dualism. But in that state he cannot doubt that his self exists because there is a subject that is thinking, thus the argument can be seen as an affirmation of the self-awareness of the soul and its substantiality. This argument does raise an objection, which may also be levelled at Descartes: how do we know that the knowing subject is the self?

Ibn Sina's other contributions lie in the fields of medicine, the natural sciences, musical theory and mathematics. In the Islamic sciences, he wrote a series of short commentaries on selected Qur'anic verses and chapters that reveal a trained philosopher's hermeneutical method and attempt to come to terms with revelation. He also wrote some literary allegories about whose philosophical value recent scholarship is vehemently at odds.

Ibn Sina's major achievement was to propound a philosophically defensive system rooted in the theological fact of Islam and its success can be gauged by the recourse to Avicennan ideas found in the subsequent history of philosophical theology in Islam. In the Latin West, his metaphysics and theory of the soul had a profound influence on scholastic arguments and as in the Islamic East, was the basis for debate and argument. Just two generations after him, al-Ghazali (d. AD 1111) and al-Shahrastani (d. AD

1153) in their attacks testify to the fact that no serious Muslim thinker could ignore him as they regarded him as the representative of philosophy in Islam. In the later Iranian tradition, Ibn Sina's thought was critically distilled with mystical insight and he became known as a mystical thinker, a view much disputed in more recent scholarship. Nevertheless the major works of Ibn Sina, whether *The Cure* or *Pointers* became the basis for the philosophical curriculum in the *madrasa*. While our current views on cosmology, the nature of the self and knowledge raise distinct problems for Avicennan ideas, they do not address the important issue of why his thought remained so influential for such a long period of time.

References

Corbin (1961), Gohlman (1974), Goodman (1992), Gutas (1988), Hasse (2000), Ibn Sina (1954, 1972, 2000, 2004), Janssens (1991–9), Janssens and De Smet (2002), Michot (1986), Rahman (1952), Reisman (2002), Reisman and Al-Rahim, (2003), Street (2004), Wisnovsky (2001, 2003).

SAJJAD H. RIZVI

IBN TAGHRIBIRDI, ABU AL-MAHASIN YUSUF
(*c.* 1410–70)

Egyptian historian, born in Cairo, the son of a Mamluk officer originally from Anatolia who had risen in rank to become Commander-in-Chief of the Egyptian army. Ibn Taghribirdi himself saw active service in Sultan Barsbay's Syrian campaign of 1432.

In addition to the traditional Islamic disciplines, Ibn Taghribirdi studied music, Turkish and Persian. His connections at the Mamluk court gave him access to privileged information, which he used in his writings. His most important works are:

1. a biographical dictionary entitled *al-Manhal al-Safi wa'l-Mustawfi Ba'd al-Wafi*;
2. a history of Egypt in the traditional chronicle style entitled *al-Nujum al-Zahira fi Muluk Misr wa'l-Qahira*;
3. a contemporary chronicle entitled *Hawadith al-Duhur fi Mudiyy al-Ayyam wa'l-Shuhur*.

The first of these three works, *al-Manhal al-Safi*, continues a tradition of biographical dictionaries commenced by Ibn Khallikan's *Wafayat al-A'yan wa-Anba' Abna' al-Zaman*, and contains information about the careers of rulers and scholars from 1258 to 1451. The second work, *al-Nujum*, covers the period 641–1467, and also continues the series of biographies commenced in *al-Manhal*. The third work, *Hawadith al-Duhur*, covers events in the writer's lifetime between 1441 and 1469. Following the deaths of al-Maqrizi in 1441 and of al-'Ayni in 1451, Ibn Taghribirdi had assumed the position of the leading historian of contemporary Egypt, and his work represents a continuation of al-Maqrizi's *al-Suluk li-Ma'rifat Duwal al-Muluk*.

In addition to the historical works for which he is best known, Ibn Taghribirdi also wrote on music and poetry.

References

Humphreys (1991), Popper (1954–60).

PAUL STARKEY

IBN TAYMIYYA
(AD 1263–1328)

Important thinker of the Hanbali school, whose ideas were hugely influential on modern revivalist movements in Islam such as those of Muhammad ibn 'Abd al-Wahhab. He was born in Harran in Syria, and was educated in Damascus in the fields of law and theology. When he became a teacher himself, however, he taught the exegesis of the Qur'an. A crucial turning-point in his life came in AD 1292 when, during the pilgrimage to Mecca, he became aware of a number of practices, such as visiting the tomb of Muhammad, which were new, and which he became convinced were unlawful innovations. For the rest of his life, therefore, he devoted himself to the task of seeking to purify Islamic practice, and he entered into controversy with those who were responsible for this state of affairs, including philosophers, theologians, Shi'is, Sufis who countenanced the possibility of human beings being united with God, and Christians, all of whom he attacked with both his tongue and his pen. He was imprisoned on five occasions during the last years of his life, and it was there that he died in AD 1328, having been deprived even of paper and ink as a desperate measure by the authorities to prevent the dissemination of his views. The positive points in his opinions included strict monotheism, with no possibility of intermediaries between God and human beings, the authority of only the Qur'an and the *hadith*, and not the consensus (*ijma'*) of the community, and the obligation of legitimate Islamic rulers to enforce Islamic law (the *shari'a*).

References

Hallaq (1993), Khan (1983), Lambton (1981: Chapter 9), Makari (1983), Memon (1976), Michel (1984), Sivan (1990).

HUGH GODDARD

IBN TUFAYL, ABU BAKR (ABUBACER) (AD 1105–85)

Known in the medieval Latin world as Abubacer. Physician, astronomer and an eminent philosopher of Arab Spain (al-Andalus), born in AD 1105 near Granada and died in AD 1185. He acted as physician and *wazir* to the Almohad ruler, Abu Ya'qub Yusuf (AD 1163–84) and also to his son al-Mansur. Ibn Tufayl's fame rests on the one work of his that has survived, the literary masterpiece and philosophical novella, *Hayy Ibn Yaqzan*.

The work is written in the form of an answer to a friend who asked Ibn Tufayl to reveal to him the secrets of Ibn Sina's mystical philosophy. As the mystical experience is ineffable, Ibn Tufayl states, in effect, that he can only suggest the sort of thing its pursuit involves by telling a story. The 'mystical' thought of Ibn Sina embedded in the story derives largely from certain sections of the latter's work, the *Isharat wa al-Tanbihat*. Before indulging in his narrative, Ibn Tufayl begins with a summary of the introduction of philosophy to al-Andalus, in which he levels some criticisms of al-Farabi, al-Ghazali and Ibn Bajja (Avempace).

The title of the story takes its name from that of its hero Hayy Ibn Yaqzan, literally, 'The Living Son of the Awake'. In a tropical island, perfect in climate and inhabited only by non-ferocious beasts, an infant boy is found. The author gives two possible accounts of his being in this island. The first is that as a result of the island's perfect clime, the child was spontaneously generated. The second is that on another island, the sister of its ruling tyrant, having secretly married against her brother's will, gave birth to the infant. Fearing his destruction by her brother, she places him in a well-sealed box and resigning his fate to divine mercy, she puts the box in the sea, the tide bringing it to an island.

The infant is discovered by a roe deer that had lost its young. The deer suckles the baby and rears him. The boy learns to clothe and arm himself, competing with the other animals for food. The only language he knows is the sound made by the deer. As his mother, the roe deer

ages and weakens, he takes care of her. She eventually dies, her death marking a turning point in Hayy's life. At first he seeks a mechanical explanation for her death, dissects her seeking to remove the impediment that caused her dysfunction, hoping to bring her back to life. In this he fails and he realises that his real mother was not the physical deer but the spirit that animated her body, now separated and gone.

With his mother's death, Hayy's self-education takes a reflective and philosophical turn. He examines nature, becomes aware of unity and plurality, the particularity of things and their universal natures. He discovers the principle that every event must have a cause. His reflections lead him to the conclusion that there must be a first cause, the source and creator of all other existents. His thoughts now are totally directed to this first cause, God. Through contemplation, ascetic self-discipline, he attains direct vision of God. He at first falls into the error of identifying his own essence with that of God, but divine grace leads him away from this mistake. His visions of God, at first a few glimmerings become with his constant meditations, more frequent and easier to attain. In this intellectual and spiritual vision he sees at one glance the entire emanative cosmic system and the unity of all things.

A community, in a nearby island, had been converted to a monotheistic religion revealed to the ancient prophets. This religion – and here al-Farabi's theory of prophethood is in effect adopted – represents philosophical truth in symbolic form. Two friends, Salaman and Absal, both strict adherers of the religious law differed in attitude. Salaman was a literalist. Absal wanted to probe the hidden meaning of the revealed world. Finding none in the island having a similar disposition, he goes to Hayy's island (thinking it uninhabited), to lead an ascetic life of contemplation. There he encounters Hayy. He teaches Hayy language and discovers that Hayy through self-education has attained the highest truths of which Absal's religion was but an imaged copy. On his part Hayy finds nothing in Absal's religion to contradict what he has experienced.

With a strong desire to teach the people of Absal's island the inner meaning of their religion, Hayy and Absal wave to a ship that takes them to Absal's community. Hayy is well received, but as soon as he tries to indicate to the community the inner meaning of their scripture, he encounters silent resentment and realises that they are incapable of such knowledge. Adjuring them to disregard everything he said and to continue to believe the scriptures in their literal sense, he and Absal return to their island, leading the life of ascetic mystics to the end of their days.

This tale has been variously interpreted. But there are elements of Al-Farabi's religious and political philosophy that are evident: religion is the imaged symbolic form of philosophy expressed in the language the non-philosopher can understand, its inner meaning should be confined only to those capable of understanding it, there is no real conflict between philosophy and religion as both represent two different levels of comprehending the same truth.

References

Gautier (1936), Goodman (1972), Hawi (1974), Hourani (1956: 40–6), Marmura (2004: 409–25).

MICHAEL E. MARMURA

IBN TUMART (*c.* AD 1070–1130)

Self-proclaimed *al-mahdi* ('guided one' or deliverer) who made a considerable impact on the western end of the Islamic world. He was born in Morocco, and after a year of study in Cordoba about AD 1106 he travelled to Egypt, Arabia and Iraq, where he seems to have developed a vision of Islamic reform in the West. When he returned, therefore, around AD 1117, he began to preach the importance of the proper observation of Islamic practice, a message which provoked considerable opposition in some places. He did win some support, however, and a meeting with one supporter, 'Abd al-Mu'min, proved particularly significant for the future. In AD 1121, after a period of meditation in a cave, he proclaimed himself the *mahdi* and was at once recognised as such by ten followers. During the remaining years of his life he established control over a small area in the south of Morocco, but after his death, under the leadership of 'Abd al-Mu'min, the Almohad state (literally '*al-muwahiddun*', strict upholders of the unity of God) seized control of the whole of Muslim North Africa and Spain. The main distinctive feature of Ibn Tumart's thought was his strict monotheism, which led him to describe his opponents as anthropomorphists, against whom *jihad* (military struggle) was therefore legitimate.

References

Abun-Nasr (1987: 87–103), Macdonald (1903: Part III, Chapter 5), Watt (1985: Chapter 15).

HUGH GODDARD

IBN YUNUS, MATTA

Ibn al-Nadim calls this Christian logician Abu Bishr Matta Ibn Yunus, he lived in Baghdad and was a member of the Farabian school. He was considered the best logician of his time and the master of al-Sijistani and Ibn 'Adi. He translated many books from Syriac into Arabic and wrote commentaries on most of Aristotle's works on logic.

Abu Hayyan al-Tawhidi reports in his *Kitab al-Imta'* a famous debate between Matta Ibn Yunas and the well-known philologist Abu Sa'id al-Sirafi which took place in Baghdad in AD 932. Matta argued here that logic is superior to the study of grammar and languages because it conveys the framework of ideas needed to present a sound argument and, therefore, it emphasises the meanings rather than the positions of words. As a result, logic is an inquiry into intelligible notions which are the same for all men and nations, while grammar is tied to a certain language system belonging to one particular nation. However, according to Abu Hayyan's report, the outcome of this debate was a victory of grammar and al-Sirafi over the logic of Matta Ibn Yunus.

References

Kraemer (1992: 110–12).

MAHA EL-KAISY FRIEMUTH

IBRAHIM

Abraham, and as such the father of Ishmael/Isma'il, who is the 'father of the Arabs' and Isaac/Ishaq, the 'father of the Jews'. Ibrahim is accepted as one of the prophets in Islam. He and Isma'il are believed to have built the Ka'ba.

References

Waines (1995: 13–14, 92).

See also: **Hagar; Isma'il, Son of Ibrahim;** *nabi*

ANDREW J. NEWMAN

IBRAHIM B. AL-MAHDI
(AD 817–39)

In the widespread turmoil caused by the power struggle between al-Amin and al-Ma'mun, their uncle Ibrahim b. al-Mahdi was proclaimed as a rival 'Abbasid caliph in Baghdad. His reign, not generally recognised outside the capital, was brought to an abrupt end with the arrival in AD 819 of al-Ma'mun. Ibrahim went into hiding and died in AD 839.

References

Hodgson (1974: 475), Le Strange (1924: 28, 42, 92, 143, 222, 226), Shaban (1971: 45), al-Tabari (1985–95: XXXII, see index; XXXI, 179–248 *passim*), .

RONALD PAUL BUCKLEY

IBRAHIM B. AL-WALID
(d. AD 750)

Ibrahim succeeded his brother Yazid b. al-Walid as Marwanid (Umayyad) caliph but his authority was not generally recognised outside southern Syria. Shortly after Ibrahim's accession, the Governor of Armenia, Marwan b. Muhammad, entered Syria and defeated his forces (November AD 744). Marwan was acknowledged as caliph and Ibrahim subsequently gave him his oath of allegiance and was granted amnesty. He died in AD 750.

References

Gibb and Bosworth (1960–2003: III: 990–1), Muir (1915: 409–10), al-Tabari (1985–95: XXVI, 193–257 *passim*), Wellhausen (1963: 369, 374, 376, 378, 384).

RONALD PAUL BUCKLEY

IBRAHIM, SULTAN
(r. 1640–48)

Ottoman sultan, son of Ahmed I. During the first years of Ibrahim's reign, the Grand Vizier Mustafa Pasha worked to stabilise the Empire's finances and administration. In 1644, a palace faction secured Mustafa Pasha's execution and seized power. The attack on Crete which began in 1645 created a further crisis when, in 1646 and 1647, the Venetian fleet blockaded the Dardanelles. In the meantime, the Sultan's mental condition deteriorated. His irresponsibility and reckless spending led, despite his mother Kosem's protests, to his deposition and execution in 1648. His major service to the Ottoman Empire was to restock the dynasty with male offspring.

References

Imber (2002: 83–5), Mantran (1989a: 237–8).
COLIN IMBER

'ID

Lexically, it is derived from the root designating the frequent occurrence or return of an object or incident. It refers to any festival or holiday which occurs regularly. In the Muslim calendar, there are two celebrations: the sacrifice festival *'Id al-adha* which occurs during the time of pilgrimage to Mecca and *'Id al-fitr* which marks the end of fasting during the month of *Ramadan*.
MAWIL IZZI DIEN

'ID AL-ADHA

See: **Feast of the Sacrifice**

'ID AL-FITR

See: **Breaking of the Fast**

'IDDA

The Arabic word *'idda* (number) is used for the period of waiting prescribed in Islamic law during which newly widowed and recently divorced women are prevented from entering into a new contract of marriage. The Qur'anic authority for the different prescriptions is found in Q.2:228 and Q.234. In the case of a divorced woman, the time of waiting is three menstrual periods. For non-menstruating women or those past the age of menstruation the time is three months (Q.65:4). This is intended to provide sufficient time to ascertain whether or not there is an unborn child of the dissolved marriage. In the case of a widow the *'idda* is four months and ten days. The longer period of waiting in this case provides additional time for mourning. In either case, however, an unborn child is taken to term before another marriage. This establishes paternity and ensures that provision is made by the former husband, or from the estate of the deceased husband, for the welfare of mother and child.

References

Bouhdiba (1985: 14–18, 30–42), Momen (1985: 8, 182–3), Omran (1992: 15–26).

See also: **divorce**
EDWARD D. A. HULMES

IDOL WORSHIP

A passage in the Qur'an (Q.5:92) clearly condemns the worship of idols as Satan's handiwork as a reaction to the reputed 360 images set up in the Ka'ba at Mecca. This polytheistic pantheon was international as it was representative of the many traders who came to pre-Islamic Arabia. The principal deities were Hubal, god of the moon, the goddesses – al-Uzza, al-Lat, Manat and Wuda who all had their own temples. Idol worship consisted mainly of pilgrimage during the seasonal communal fairs accompanied by processions, singing and dancing and sacrifices. After the conquest of Mecca in AD 629 the Prophet entered the Ka'ba and ordered the destruction of all the images.

References

Endress (1988).

JENNIFER SCARCE

IDRIS

A Qur'anic reference (21:85) to the biblical Enoch.

ANDREW J. NEWMAN

AL-IDRISI, MUHAMMAD IBN MUHAMMAD
(AD 1100–*c.* 1162)

Arab geographer. Born in Ceuta (North Africa), al-Idrisi studied in Cordoba but spent most of his life in Palermo in Sicily, where he enjoyed the patronage of the Norman King Roger II. Although, by his own account, he had travelled a great deal in Spain and North Africa, few details of his life are known, probably because many of his fellow Muslims regarded his career at the court of a Christian king with distrust. Al-Idrisi's best-known work, *Nuzhat al-Mushtaq fi Ikhtiraq al-Afaq*, also known as the *Kitab Rujar* or *al-Kitab al-Rujari*, after his patron, was completed in 1154. This work, of which a number of abridged versions are also extant, made use of Ptolemy as well as of earlier Arab geographers such as al-Bakri, but it is perhaps most notable for the series of rectangular maps that accompany it, based on the astronomical clime system and clearly deriving from the Ptolemaic–Khwarazmi tradition (though his first map is circular and appears to be derived from the al-Istakhri–Ibn Hawqal maps); in al-Idrisi's system, the world is divided into seven climes, each of which was further subdivided into ten sections. Al-Idrisi is said to have later compiled another geographical work entitled *Rawd al-Nas wa-Nuzhat al-Nafs*, though the precise relationship between this and his major work is so far unclear. He also made a major contribution to the study of medicinal botany through his work *Kitab al-Jami' li-Sifat Ashtat al-Nabatat*, which is notable for the synonyms that the author provides for the names of drugs in different languages.

Al-Idrisi's work is probably the best known of all the Arab geographers to Europeans, largely on account of the early publication in Rome of a printed version of his work in 1592, and of a Latin translation in Paris in 1619. Despite the obvious fascination of his work, however, al-Idrisi gives little indication of any very profound geographical or astronomical understanding, and his work is probably best treated with some caution.

References

Bombaci *et al.* (1978), Kratchkovsky (1960–1: 1–72), Miller (1926–7), Oman (1961: 25–61).

PAUL STARKEY

IDRISIDS (AD 789–985)

A descendant of the Caliph 'Ali, Idris, took refuge in the Far Maghrib from 'Abbasid persecution, and introduced, for the first time into the Muslim West, Shi'ism, albeit in an attenuated form, until they were superseded by the much more aggressively Shi'ite radical movement of the Fatimids. The Idrisid capital at Fez became the home of the privileged religious and social elite of the Sharifs (pl. *Shurafa'*, colloquial form, *Shorfa* 'Noble ones'), descendants of the Prophet's grandsons, above all of Hasan, who have played a leading role in Moroccan life up to the present day.

References

Bosworth (1996: No. 8), Gibb and Bosworth (1960–2003), Terrasse (1949–50: I, 107–34).

C. E. BOSWORTH

IHRAM

See: **ritual prayer and worship (al-salat)**

IHSAN

'Excellence', 'virtue', referring to the performance of good deeds. The third of the distinctive aspects of Islam, including belief (*iman*) and practice/submission (*islam*).

References

Waines (1995: 104, 131–2).

See also: **faith and action; *iman*; *islam***

ANDREW J. NEWMAN

IHYA' 'ULUM AL-DIN

This is the greatest and best-known work of the theologian and mystic Abu Hamid Muhammad b. Muhammad al-Ghazali (AD 1058–1111). It is widely regarded as one of the most complete compendiums of Muslim thought and practice ever written, and is among the most influential books in the history of Islam. As its title indicates, it is a sustained attempt to put vigour and liveliness back into Muslim religious discourse, and for that reason it is commonly known in English as *The Revival of the Religious Sciences.*

Al-Ghazali composed the *Ihya'* in the years following his resignation from his professorship at the Nizamiyya college in Baghdad in AD 1095, possibly between 1095 and AD 1102. In these years he wandered in Syria, Palestine and maybe Egypt, and also performed the pilgrimage to Mecca. It was a tumultuous period of his life, when he was coming to terms with the realisation that the intellectual disciplines he had previously mastered did not yield certainty, *yaqin*, in belief, but that experience or 'tasting', *dhawq*, was a more reliable means of knowing God and approaching closer to him. The *Ihya'* is the fruit of his reordered thinking at this time.

These changes in al-Ghazali's intellectual and spiritual orientation are reflected in the approach he adopts in the work. Far from being an apologetic exposition of the main points of doctrine that had been disputed among theologians for centuries, in the style, for example, of earlier Ash'ari and Mu'tazili treatises, it is a guide to practical holiness. While it begins with epistemological and theological discussions similar to those in works of systematic theology, it builds upon them explanations of how to make the teachings of Islam a personal possession, and even more how to look on life *sub specie aeternitatis*.

The *Ihya'* also differs from many extant earlier treatises in having a readily accessible structure. It is divided into four 'quarters', *arba'*, which are further divided into expositions, *bayan*, and so on. The clarity of its structure has frequently been remarked upon, even though some of the separate elements were very probably not written in the order in which they appear.

The first quarter of the *Ihya'*, on acts of worship, *'ibadat*, is concerned with basic questions of knowledge and the being and character of God, and then with the five major observances of Islam, the recitation of the Qur'an and forms of prayer. The second quarter, on the customary actions of life, *'adat*, is concerned with such matters as eating, marriage, earning a wage, friendship, travelling, enjoining good and forbidding bad, and the example of the Prophet. The third quarter, on the ways to perdition, *muhlikat*, leads on from these two by expounding the nature of humankind and counselling against the vices and sins that can seize the individual and lead to damnation. And finally the fourth quarter, on the ways to salvation, *munjiyyat*, sets out the qualities of character that lead to eternal reward. Together, these four quarters give abundant teaching about correct beliefs and practices, together with guidance about the life that builds upon these to make them not so much ends in themselves as means towards deeper awareness of the divine.

The full character of the *Ihya'* cannot be appreciated from a simple enumeration of its parts. For each of its books and divisions contains a wide range of material, including readings from the Qur'an and *hadith* (many of which were rejected as spurious by later authors), exegetical expositions, stories from the life of the Prophet and the Companions, legal discussions, rational arguments, and sayings from wise men and mystics. All these are employed to make clear that the true Muslim life goes beyond intellectual awareness of the teachings of Islam or perfunctory compliance with what they require to insight into the purpose they serve and spiritual growth in observing them. This is the experience, *dhawq*, that al-Ghazali had come to realise was the true source of certainty, and it characterises the *Ihya'* from its very beginning, where al-Ghazali castigates scholars who have abandoned their duty of guiding people in the life of true faith, to its end where in the fortieth book, *The Remembrance of Death and the Afterlife*, he emphasises the need to recognise the impending reality of death and to live life accordingly. It shows that the *Ihya'* is as much a Sufi work as it is a work of *kalam* or *fiqh*.

This attempt by al-Ghazali to demonstrate the deeper values of the major teachings and observances of Islam had the wider effect of legitimising moderate Sufism in the eyes of Muslims by demonstrating that it was not only compatible with theological and legal prescriptions, but actually upheld them. Thus it showed a way by which the intellectual sciences and spiritual practices that threatened to diverge into contradictory forms of Islam in al-Ghazali's time could be recombined. But whether it achieved this purpose in the long run is open to question, because it has frequently been seen as an influence to otherworldly preoccupations and the concomitant of political quietism.

The *Ihya'* was evidently popular within al-Ghazali's own lifetime, as he made a number of epitomes of it, including the Persian *Kitab al-Arba'in fi Usul al-Din* and the *Kimiya' al-Sa'ada*, the latter expressly intended for a more popular audience. These shorter works are not, however, simple abridgements of the *Ihya'*; while they follow its main outline they contain discussions on some matters that show al-Ghazali came to new understandings after he had finished his major work. But he also encountered criticisms of the work, and composed the *Imla' 'ala Ishkalat al-Ihya'* in its defence.

Despite its importance in the Islamic world, no critical edition of the *Ihya'* has so far been made. There is an English translation by Faslul-Karim (1978–9), though this is far from satisfactory, and there is a French synopsis by Bousquet (1955). Over half of the forty individual books have been translated into English, French and German, some in well-annotated, readable editions. The full weight of the *Ihya'* in the history of Islamic intellectual and spiritual development, and its place in debates between pietists and political activists has yet to be analysed thoroughly.

DAVID THOMAS

IJARA

The use and enjoyment of property for a time, including hire, rental and lease.

References

Coulson (1964: 111), Izzi Dien (1997).

MAWIL IZZI DIEN

IJAZA

'Permission', 'licence'. An actual, or notional, authorisation from a teacher to his student allowing him to teach specified subject matter based on study thereof with the teacher in question.

References

Waines (1995: 283).

ANDREW J. NEWMAN

IJMA'

The unanimous consensus of the learned scholars (*mujtahidun*). *Ijma'* is the collective opinion, while *ijtihad* is the deduction made by a single learned scholar *mujtahid*. Technically, the word means the 'agreement' of the knowledgeable Muslims after the death of the Prophet. The concept seems to have been created to estabilish a legal device to assist in interpreting Islamic law as well as a political solution to maintain the unity of Muslims after the death of the Prophet. Despite that *Ijma'* was seen by many Muslim lawyers to be 'almost divine' in its authority. However, the fact remains that, apart from the Qur'an and Sunna, all other sources of Islamic law are generally referred to as secondary sources. In practice, to achieve a "total agreement" of all Muslim scholars could prove difficult without the existence of an official authority. Perhaps the best alternative to a full *Ijma'* would be the employment of the tacit or silent *Ijma'*, which takes place when a scholar pronunces an opinion on a certain legal matter and this remains uncontested. The legal value of such 'agreement' would be nothing more than that of *ijtihad*. However in the modern world of Islam, silent *Ijma'* seems to be the way for the future application of Sunni Islamic law.

References

Coulson (1964: 59, 78), Izzi Dien (1997: 46–9, 167–78).

MAWIL IZZI DIEN

IJTIHAD

See: **abortion**

IKHSHIDIDS (AD 935–69)

A Turkish governor of Egypt, Muhammad b. Tughj, adopted the ancient Iranian title, used in central Asia, of Ikhshid, and ruled in Egypt and southern Syria autonomously of the caliphate. His sons, however, proved weaklings and were under the tutelage of the real ruler of Egypt, the black slave eunuch Kafur, who in the end assumed power himself. Kafur was a liberal patron of Arabic culture, with the poet al-Mutanabbi at his court for a time.

References

Bosworth (1996: No. 26), Gibb and Bosworth (1960–2003), Bianquis (1998: I, 112–19).

See also: **Hamdanids**

C. E. BOSWORTH

IKHWAN AL-SAFA'

The philosophy of the group of Arab philosophers of the tenth or eleventh century AD known as the Ikhwan al-Safa' (Brethren of Purity) is a curious but fascinating mixture of the Qur'anic, the Aristotelian and the Neoplatonic. The group wrote fifty-two epistles, which are encyclopedic in range, covering matters as diverse as arithmetic, theology, magic and embryology. Their numerology owes a debt to Pythagoras, their metaphysics are Aristotelian and Neoplatonic and they incorporate also a few Platonic notions into their philosophy. The latter, however, is more than a mere synthesis of elements from Greek philosophy, for it is underpinned by a considerable Qur'anic substratum. There are profound links between the epistemology and the soteriology (doctrine of salvation) of the Ikhwan, and it would not be an exaggeration to say that the former feeds the latter. In the history of Islamic philosophy the Ikhwan illustrate a group where the Aristotelian and the Neoplatonic clash head-on and where no attempt is made to reconcile competing and contradictory notions of God, whom the Epistles treat in both Qur'anic and Neoplatonic fashion. The final goal of the Ikhwan is salvation, their Brotherhood is the ship of that salvation, and they foster a spirit of asceticism and good living accompanied by 'actual knowledge' as aids to that longed-for salvation.

The Arabic name Ikhwan al-Safa' has been translated as both 'Brethren of Purity' and 'Brethren of Sincerity'. Both are possible, though the former is probably to be preferred because of the emphasis throughout the group's writings on the concept of purity achieved via a life of asceticism and virtuous living.

Little firm information is available about their exact identities, their lives and the precise time during which they flourished. Most scholars agree, however, that they lived in Basra in the tenth or eleventh century AD; beyond that there has been much diverse speculation. Their own thought and philosophy is enshrined in fifty-two epistles (rasa'il) of varying lengths which are encyclopedic in their scope and cover a vast number of topics. Formally, these epistles divide into four major sections: the first fourteen deal with the mathematical sciences, the next seventeen are on the natural sciences, a further ten deal with the psychological and rational sciences and the final eleven come under the heading of theological sciences. It should be noted that the Ikhwan's usage of these divisions is much broader in range than might be expected at first sight. For example, the last of the epistles grouped under the heading 'theological sciences' deals with magic and related subjects. What may broadly be said to link all the epistles, however, is a mixed Aristotelian and Neoplatonic substratum, though it must be stressed here that the epistles of the Ikhwan al-Safa' are more than just a synthesis of Aristotelian and dominant Neoplatonic themes. The incorporation by the Ikhwan of syncretic philosophical and theological themes, motifs, elements and doctrines in their writings was done with a particular soteriological purpose. Their eclectic borrowing was done with a view to bolstering the doctrine of purity which their name so neatly reflects.

The metaphysics of the Ikhwan al-Safa' are built upon those of Aristotle and Plotinus, though it must be emphasised that it is a Middle Eastern version of Aristotelianism and Neoplatonism which we encounter when we read the rasa'il of the Ikhwan. In the first place, their terminology is infused with such terms as matter and form, substance and accidents, the four causes and potentiality and actuality. Their usage of such terms, however, does not always adhere to the classical Aristotelian paradigm or usage. The development of terminology is often in a Neoplatonic direction. For example, the Ikhwan held in one place that substance was something which was self-existent and capable of receiving attributes. We recognise here a description akin to Aristotle's usage of the word 'substance' in the Metaphysics. But elsewhere, confusingly, form is divided into two kinds, constituting and completing; constituting forms are called substances and completing forms are called accidents. Similarly, the Ikhwan adopted a fourfold terminology of causes – material, formal, efficient and final – but the shades of astrology and Neoplatonism hang heavily over at least two of the examples of these four causes which they provide. They say that the material cause of plants is the four elements of fire, air, water and earth, and that their final cause is to provide food for animals: both of these ideas are recognisably Aristotelian in their orientation, but the Ikhwan then go on to suggest that the efficient cause of plants is the power of the universal soul and that their formal cause has complicated astral elements.

It is, however, the Neoplatonic elements which dominate the articulation of all thought in the writings of the Ikhwan al-Safa' and their metaphysics are no exception. The latter are imbued in particular with the Neoplatonic concepts of emanation and hierarchy. By contrast with the simple triad of Plotinus, which comprised the three hypostases of the One or the Good, intellect and soul, with the lower eternally emanating from the higher entity, the Ikhwan elaborated this into an emanationist hierarchy of nine 'members', hypostases or levels of being, as follows: the Creator, the Intellect, the Soul, Prime Matter, Nature, the Absolute Body, the Sphere, the Four Elements and the Beings of this world in the three divisions of mineral, plant and animal. In such a hierarchical profusion we can perhaps see the ghosts of Iamblichus and Proclus, who also multiplied the hypostases about which they wrote. It is noteworthy that for the Ikhwan, and in contrast to the view of Plotinus, matter becomes a full part of the emanationist hierarchy and is regarded in a positive light. Further, and this time in a very Neoplatonic way, God in the Ikhwan's scheme entrusts the movement of the world and the spheres to the universal soul, and it is the latter which channels God's gifts finally into matter itself.

The Neoplatonic dimensions of the thought of the Ikhwan have profound implications for their view of God. The picture which they present of the deity in their epistles is a confused and ultimately contradictory one. No attempt is made to reconcile what is in fact irreconcilable. On the one hand, the Ikhwan present a God at the top of a complex emanationist hierarchy who is unknowable in the classic Neoplatonic sense. On the other hand, the Ikhwan present a Qur'anic God who is a guide and a help, and who is invoked at the end of many of the epistles as one who will grant success in correct action and show his people the path of righteousness. The majority of epistles also invoke God with the traditional Islamic *basmala*, 'In the name of God, the Merciful, the Compassionate'. However, God's power, as noted previously, seems to be 'shared' in some way when it is exercised via the universal soul. To what extent, one may reasonably ask, does that compromise the traditional Islamic view of God? Further, to what extent do the recognisably Islamic features in the Ikhwan's portrait of God prevent that deity being considered as a total mirror of Plotinus' One?

The metaphysics of the Ikhwan al-Safa' must therefore be regarded as *sui generis*. Their mixing of Aristotelian and Neoplatonic elements had profound implications both for their theology and the coherence of the philosophy. Contradictions abound, and if reasons be sought for this, it is worth remembering one theory, promulgated by A. L. Tibawi (1955), that the epistles are akin to the minutes taken during the deliberations of a learned society, meeting on many occasions over a period of years. This would account for both contradiction and repetition. We know from the epistles themselves that the authors urged their brothers to meet specially at set times, in closed sessions.

Thus far in this article, nothing has been said about the impact of Platonic thought on the epistles of the Ikhwan.

This is because the Brethren revere the Platonic *hero* rather more than they revere purely Platonic *philosophy*. Socrates is admired as a great and wise philosopher who knew how to meet death bravely. However, some Platonic imagery does permeate the epistles. The most notable image is that of the body constituting a prison for the soul. The Ikhwan indeed compare the soul in the body to the state of a man imprisoned inside a lavatory: the body's blemishes and sins are like the filth in the lavatory. It is clear that the Ikhwan were familiar with Plato's doctrine of Forms or *ideai*, since they quote a speaker saying that the different types of animal in the world simply mirror those in the world of the spheres and the heavens. However, this is not a doctrine for which the Ikhwan seem to have had much use, for they neither discuss nor elaborate upon it.

It is, therefore, unsurprising that the Ikhwan's epistemology differs quite radically from that of Plato. The latter looked forward to a state of real knowledge achieved when the soul was separated from the body, but in the soteriology and epistemology of the Ikhwan, one could gain some knowledge of the divine in this world to help one reach Paradise. Indeed, they present their epistles to the world as a body of just such knowledge. For them, learning was much more than mere recollection or reminiscence. They held that the soul was 'potentially knowledgeable' and, with instruction, could become 'actually knowledgeable'. That instruction should be via the senses, the intellect and logical deduction, and they stressed that we could know nothing without the senses. This is indeed a far cry from Plato's well-known suspicion of evidence or knowledge gleaned via the senses, and his overwhelming exaltation of the intellect.

The mass of information – philosophical, theological and other – adumbrated in such an encyclopedic manner in the epistles of the Ikhwan al-Safa' is probably incomprehensible as a totality unless one bears in mind the driving force which lies at the heart of the epistles themselves. The Ikhwan did not compile the epistles from a pure love of knowledge and for no other reason. The magpie eclecticism with which they surveyed and utilised elements from the philosophies of Pythagoras, Plato, Aristotle and Plotinus, and religions such as Christianity, Judaism and Hinduism, was not an early attempt at ecumenism or interfaith dialogue. Their accumulation of knowledge was ordered towards the sublime goal of salvation. To use their own image, they perceived their Brotherhood, to which they invited others, as a 'Ship of Salvation' that would float free from the sea of matter; the Ikhwan, with their doctrines of mutual cooperation, asceticism and righteous living, would reach the gates of Paradise in its care.

What, then, did it mean for the Ikhwan al-Safa' to 'do philosophy'? It did not mean to throw off the religious constraints of the Qur'an and to become pure rationalists. Though they often use the Qur'an as a cloak to disguise their Neoplatonism, one cannot ignore the massive Qur'anic substratum elsewhere in their writings, which has no such intent. 'Doing philosophy' did not mean either the uncritical acceptance of the data from a variety of sources such as Pythagoras, Plato and Aristotle, not to mention Plotinus, even though they were profoundly influenced by at least three of these four ancient masters and it is no misnomer to describe the Ikhwan as 'Muslim Neoplatonists'. Philosophy, for the Ikhwan, was still the handmaiden of a precise theological goal: salvation for the soul. Their eclecticism and tolerance provided them with a unique methodology for the achievement of that goal. Thus they searched out the texts of other creeds and the philosophies of non-Muslim sages in search of materials which might bolster their own ethics of purity and asceticism. Their intellectual heroes were Socrates and Jesus as well as Muhammad. Above all, knowledge and philosophy were always soteriological tools and never ends in themselves.

References

Diwald (1975), Goodman (1978), Ikhwan al-Safa' (1957), Marquet (1975), Nasr (1978), Netton (1991, 1996: 222–30), Tibawi (1955).

IAN RICHARD NETTON

Reprinted from the *Routledge Encyclopedia of Philosophy*, Edward Craig (ed.), Vol. IV, pp. 685–8.

ILHAD

'Heresy', 'apostasy', 'deviation'. The term appears several times in the Qu'ran (Q.7:180, Q.41:40, and Q.22:25) and in early Islamic history was used to refer to those who deserted the *umma* or rebelled against the caliph but later described those who rejected religion per se. The Isma'ili Shi'a were also referred to as heretics.

References

Gibb and Bosworth (1960–2003).

ANDREW J. NEWMAN

IL-KHANIDS (AD 1256–1353)

These Mongol rulers (lit. 'territorial, i.e. subordinate, Khans') were a branch of the Mongol ruling family. The founder Hulegu, grandson of Chingiz Khan, was given the task of consolidating Mongol power in western Asia, above all, in Iran and Iraq, although Il-Khanid attempts to penetrate to Syria and beyond were halted by the Mamluks. The Il-Khanids became after a while Sunni Muslims, and under them, Iran enjoyed a period of economic and social revival, with their courts as centres for the cultivation of literature and the natural sciences, and distinctive styles of architecture and ceramics emerged. The Il-Khanate eventually fell apart, leaving the field free for Timur to reconstitute an empire of his own.

References

Bosworth (1996: No. 133), Gibb and Bosworth (1960–2003), Grousset (1970: 347–91), Morgan (1986), Spuler (1955).

C. E. BOSWORTH

ILTIFAT

A stylistic feature or literary figure of the Qur'an which categorises disruptions in the narrative voice or in the audience addressed in the text. Classified as one of the subtleties of the Arabic text, exegetes and rhetoricians compiled lists of the occurrences, collecting some fifty examples. The figure is defined as 'the change of speech from one mode to another, for the sake of freshness and variety for the listener, to renew his interest, and to keep his mind from boredom and frustration, through having the one mode continuously at his ear' (al-Zarkashi, quoted in Abdel Haleem, 1999: 186–7). A common example is Q.35:9, 'God is He that looses the winds that stir up cloud, then We drive it to a dead land' with the shift in referring to God from the third person to the first person. This is paralleled in both the change in reference and in the content of the text itself in Q.6:99. This switch can also occur in the way people are addressed in a verse, as Q.47:22–23 shows in its move from second-person to third-person address: 'If you turned away, would you then haply work corruption in the land and break your bonds of kin? Those are they whom God has cursed'. Other shifts (frequently hidden in English translation) involve a change from a singular to plural 'You' as subject or addressee. Changes in verb tense, case marker and using a noun in place of a pronoun are also sometimes included in this classification.

References

Abdel Haleem (1999: Chapter 13).

ANDREW RIPPIN

ILYAS, MUHAMMAD (1885–1944)

The founder of probably the most influential, in numerical terms, Islamic revivalist movement of the twentieth century. Muhammad Ilyas was trained at the main Sunni institution of learning in South Asia, the Deoband Seminary, and as a young man he became concerned about both the persistence of pre-Islamic (Hindu) practices among many of the rural Muslims of north India and the failure of the traditional Islamic schools, to address, yet alone resolve, this issue. From his base at Nizamuddin in Delhi he therefore began to send out Muslim teachers to educate Muslims in the proper practice of their faith in the context of their own communities. The group he established to further this approach, the Tablighi Jama'at (Preaching Movement) has become hugely influential across the Muslim world and among diaspora communities, and its annual conferences in Pakistan have an attendance of over one million people. The message spread involves six simple points: knowing and reciting the Islamic declaration of faith; saying *salat* (prayers) correctly; learning basic Islamic knowledge and performing *dhikr* (mentioning the names of God), if possible communally; paying respect and being polite to fellow Muslims; practising honesty and sincerity (*ikhlas*); and spending time away from worldly pursuits in order to undertake preaching tours to spread this message. It is this last practice that explains the enormous success of the movement, and the Sufi elements of its practice, together with its avoidance of political argument, have made it hugely influential as an example of what is sometimes called 'Islam from below'.

References

Haq (1972), Metcalf (1994: 706–25), Nadwi (1983), Sikand (2002).

HUGH GODDARD

'IMAD AL-DAWLA, 'ALI B. BUYA (r. AD 932–49)

Eldest of the three Buyid brothers who founded the dynasty of that name in Persian and Iraq. Originally in the service of another Daylami commander Mardavij, already before the latter's death in AD 935, 'Ali had secured control of Fars and central Persia from the 'Abbasid caliph's governors. He then sent his brother al-Hasan (the future Rukn al-Dawla) to occupy Ray, and the third brother Ahmad (the future Mu'izz al-Dawla) to Khuzistan and Kirman, with the latter eventually occupying Baghdad and inaugurating a period of tutelage by Shi'ites over the Sunni 'Abbasid caliphs. It was at this point that the brothers assumed the honorific titles by which they are best known. 'Imad al-Dawla's dominions were inherited by his nephew 'Adud al-Dawla, the greatest ruler of the dynasty, under whom the Buyid lands were to reach their greatest extent.

References

Busse (1969: 17–38; 1975: 253–62), Gibb and Bosworth (1960–2003).

C. E. BOSWORTH

IMAGINATION

The Muslim philosophers, following Aristotle, consider imagination as a faculty in the intellect which enables us to create images from sensible perceptions and presents them to the mind. The first stage of thinking is divided into two steps: first, when the intellect receives sensible information through the different senses, and second, when the intellect abstracts different concepts from this sensible information. Ibn Sina explains that the role of the imagination is mainly concentrated in the first step of thinking. In this stage the mind receives information from the material world through the different senses. This sensible information will be transformed by the faculty which is called imagination into images which the mind is able to possess. At this stage, the mind is perceiving through the images of things as they appear in the mind. This is a direct and simple stage of thinking. These images, however, would in some cases be abstracted by other powers in the mind which belong to what philosophers call the theoretical intellect. However, Ibn Sina and Ibn Rushd mention a stronger form of imagination which they call the prophetic imagination. This kind of imagination is only restricted to some chosen individuals with a strong imaginative faculty which is able to receive images, not from the material world but from the divine. The difference between this kind of knowledge and philosophical knowledge is that this prophetic knowledge is given in figurative language and symbolic images. The aim of this kind of knowledge is to guide the masses and give them a symbolic and general idea about God and the divine world. Thus imagination is mainly the faculty which explains and simplifies knowledge through symbols and images.

References

Davidson (1992), Gutas (1988: 157–80).

Maha El-Kaisy Friemuth

IMAM

The word is associated with the Arabic preposition *amama*, meaning 'in front of'. This meaning develops in ways that suggest precedence, leadership and authority. A person known as an imam exercises this leadership among his local co-religionists. In some cases the personal authority and influence of an imam is acknowledged much more widely, however. At the local level the imam is chosen to serve in the mosque as leader and model during the five daily times of public prayer and worship because his exemplary life as a Muslim marks him out as someone who is thus *entitled* to undertake such a leadership role on behalf of the community. To do this he stands literally 'in front' of the group of worshippers in a mosque, directing the course and the tempo of the successive stages of the prayer ritual. He and all the worshippers lined up behind him face Mecca and unite in the prescribed orderly ritual. (A woman may on occasions lead public prayer and worship for the female members of her household.) The role of an imam is not limited to the coordination of public prayer. He is involved in all the rites of passage which feature in the lives of Muslims, from the naming of a child, to performing the marriage ceremony and finally to conducting the funeral ceremony and committing the body of the deceased to the grave. Muslims often claim that in Islam there is no ordained 'clergy' such as is to be found in Christianity, for instance. Trained imams, however, are frequently appointed to direct the work of local Islamic communities. It is true, however, that in the absence of such an exemplary, trained and salaried official, any well-regarded male member of the community may act as imam for the purpose of leading public prayer.

The word carries a different, or rather, an additional meaning for Shi'i Muslims, who regard their imams not just as individuals whose lives uniquely exemplify the life of a faithful Muslims, but also as those whose intercession may fervently be sought in order that the petitioner may not finally fail to be saved. Some of these venerated figures are credited with supernatural knowledge and superhuman wisdom. It is not an exaggeration to say that in some cases these figures hold a position in the lives of those who revere them not too different from that occupied by the Prophet Muhammad. The figures of 'Ali ibn Abi Talib, the fourth of the Rightly Guided Caliphs, and his descendants occupy a central position in Shi'i piety as unique intercessors and spiritual directors of the faithful. In this function the imam assumes an almost intermediary role between the Creator and the created human being. In so doing the imam begins to exert a temporal, civil power in such a way as to challenge the legitimacy of the civil authority. Cases have been known in which those who have challenged the authority of the imam have been described as usurpers. The doctrine of the 'Hidden Imam' is a distinctive feature of 'Twelver Imam' Shi'ism. The belief that in this special sense there can be only one Imam at a time is common among Shi'i Muslims. In general terms the title of Imam implies that its bearer is a 'model' for other Muslims to follow. In this honorific sense, the title was bestowed on the leaders of the founders of the different Schools (madhahib) of Islamic jurisprudence (fiqh). Other notable figures in the history of Islam, such as Abu Hamid Muhammad al-Ghazali, have also been awarded this honorific title.

See also: Isma'ilism/Batinism (al-Isma'i-liyya/al-Batiniyya); Muhammad al-Mahdi; Shi'ism

Edward D. A. Hulmes

IMAMA

Imamate, the term given to the doctrine of leadership in Islam. This is conceived of in a broad fashion, including both leadership in prayer and politico-religious authority. This article concentrates on the latter. Who should be the leader of the Muslims? How should they be selected? What role is to be performed once confirmed in office? These questions have led to the most explicit sectarian divisions within Islam, and many Muslims trace the origins of the dispute to the life of the Prophet Muhammad. Did Muhammad designate a particular person to be leader of the Muslims? Did he outline a procedure whereby such a person might be selected? Did he describe certain qualities which the leader of the Muslims should have? Muslims have taken a number of different positions on these issues, and have developed these positions into established theological and legal traditions. The main groups are the Sunnis, the Kharijites and the Shi'a. The last of these, the Shi'a, are themselves divided into various subgroups – this article will concentrate here on the differences in the theory of imama and not on the historical events that are purported to have lead to the divisions within the Shi'a (for these, see the article Shi'a).

The leader of the Muslims is called the caliph (khalifa) or imam. Generally speaking, the former term is used more in historical texts, whilst the latter is the more common term in theological and legal texts. An issue which faced the Muslim community when the Prophet died in AD 632 was his successor. Many argued that the Prophet Muhammad had designated someone to succeed him as leader; they differed, however, over the identity of that successor. A number of possible candidates were considered, but two were, by far, the front runners. Some argued that the Prophet had designated his companion Abu Bakr. The designation of Abu Bakr to lead prayers when the Prophet was unwell, was, in their eyes, evidence of the Prophet's preference for Abu Bakr. Leading prayers was a symbolic responsibility in the Muslim community, designating not merely knowledge of the ritual requirements of prayer, but also religious and political authority over the community. Others argued that the Prophet had in fact designated his cousin and son-in-law 'Ali. Their evidence for this was that the Prophet had described 'Ali in terms that implied his leadership on a number of occasions. The Prophet is reported as saying 'I am the city of knowledge and 'Ali is its gate'. In the famous 'event of Ghadir Khumm', the Prophet says 'Whoever takes me as his patron, takes 'Ali as his patron also'. It is important to recognise here that the two parties, supporting Abu Bakr and 'Ali, were not arguing over how the rightful leader comes to be known. The procedure is agreed by both parties: the leader is designated by the Prophet, and presumably a leader designated by the Prophet can himself, in turn, designate his successor. Their dispute was merely over the identity of the designated person.

Others argued that a leader should be selected on the basis of set criteria, that is, those who argued that the Prophet had designated a successor were reading too much into the evidence. Instead, the Prophet outlined the qualities of a leader of the Muslims. These are listed in various theological and legal works, and the scholars are far from unanimous on the content of this list. Excellence (*fadl*) is one such criterion which was widely supported. That only the 'best' (*al-afdal*, or 'most excellent') of the Muslims should

be imam was a view held by the followers of Ahmad b. Hanbal (d. AD 855) and ultimately the great Sunni theologian Abu'l-Hasan al-Ash'ari (d. AD 935–6). According to some sources Abu Hanifa (d. AD 767) held this view also. The *shafi'is* disagreed: the imam need not be the 'best', in the sense of the most pious or religiously observant. For them, the main aim was to preserve the unity of the community and if appointing the 'best' might lead to division, a less pious, less observant person might become caliph. For *shafi'i*s, the 'best' may not necessarily be the most appropriate.

If the 'best' Muslim was to be imam (as Ibn Hanbal and al-Ash'ari argued), then what were the constituent elements of this excellence? Did *fadl* apply to religious dedication only, or did it also include knowledge of the law? What of military skill and diplomatic abilities? Should these be included in the criterion of excellence? That he be a Muslim was universally accepted, but what kind of Muslim qualifies as imam of the community? The dispute amongst the various Sunni groups was extensive and demonstrates that a generally agreed Sunni position was not established until quite late on in the classical period. If military skill and diplomatic abilities were included in the definition of excellence, then this comes very close to the *shafi'i* position that the most appropriate imam is the person who can most effectively maintain unity, prevent discord, and sustain the integrity of the Muslim community.

Another criterion (or qualification) for the imam was that he be of the same tribe as the Prophet Muhammad (that is, the Quraysh tribe). The rationale for the inclusion of this quality is not obvious. It was, almost certainly, a remnant of the Arab custom of transferring the leadership of the tribe to the most worthy male, rather than following a system of strict primogeniture. It is, however, difficult to justify the prerogative of one tribe over all other lines of descent on purely rational grounds, and ultimately later writers justified it on the basis of revelation (principally prophetic precedent). There were those who rejected the stipulation of Quraysh descent for the imam: these included the Kharijites (and a few early Mu'tazilis), they saw no reason to prefer one tribe over another: the best of the Muslims could come from any ethnic group. Some Kharijites even considered women possible contenders for the imamate, though this was not the commonly held Kharijite view.

If the imam qualified for the position on the basis of his personal qualities, then how was the community to know who was the imam? Those who supported the selection of the imam on the basis of personal qualities differed over how these qualities might be recognised within the community: by what procedure does one know that an individual is the rightful imam? Most argued that the imam must be selected by the 'those who loose and bind' (*ahl al-hall wa'l-'aqd*), a group of selectors who represent either the wishes, or (more commonly) the best interests, of the people. Some modern Muslims have attempted to discern democracy within this structure. Who are the *ahl al-hall wa'l-'aqd*? Here, once more, there is dispute. Some, like al-Ash'ari, was famous for arguing that a single elector can establish the right of a candidate for the imamate. Others argued in less specific terms for a wider conception of representation. Some argued that the designation of the current imam of his successor was, at one step removed, the workings of the *ahl al-hall wa'l-'aqd*, because they had selected the first imam as the most appropriate to make political decisions. One such political decision was who should lead the community after the current imam's death. Hence designation

of the reigning imam was a legitimate means of coming to know the identity of the next imam. Such argumentation was clearly intended to justify the variety of designation/election/selection mechanisms found during the *rashidun* period: Abu Bakr was selected by the gathering at Saqifa; 'Umar was designated by Abu Bakr; 'Uthman was selected by a *shura* appointed by 'Umar; 'Ali was invited to be caliph, ostensibly by those who had opposed 'Uthman. Which one of these different procedures was the correct procedure for selecting the imam? There does not appear to be a strong conception in the classical Sunni literature of a vote, or election as such – rather the best candidate (*al-afdal*) will inevitably emerge from the discussions of the *ahl al-hall wa'l-'aqd*. The selection of a candidate by the *ahl al-hall wa'l-'aqd* can be distinguished from the procedure known as the *bay'a* (the swearing of allegiance). This is formally a contract between the selectors (or in some theories, the community more generally) and the person selected to be imam. It is best considered as the formalisation of the investiture. The established Sunni position was that the imam could be decided by designation by the previous imam (which was to become the common procedure in Muslim history) or by the selection of the *ahl al-hall wa'l-'aqd*.

The Shi'i groups had argued that the Prophet had designated his cousin and son-in-law 'Ali as the leader of the Muslims after his death. For Shi'i groups this was not a simple selection of the best candidate by the Prophet, but a stipulation that 'Ali and his descendants should be the imams of the Muslim community. Who qualified as a descendant of 'Ali? This was disputed amongst the Shi'i groups. The later, established Shi'i traditions argued that only his descendants through his marriage to the Prophet's daughter Fatima were eligible. Some earlier Shi'a argued that any descendent of 'Ali might qualify, the best example of such a view is that held by the followers of al-Mukhtar who rebelled against the Umayyad caliphate in AD 685. He declared Muhammad Ibn Hanafiyya ('Ali's son by Khalwa of the Banu Hanifa) to be the imam. Ibn Hanafiyya was not a descendant of the Prophet (but merely a descendant of 'Ali); he was not born of Fatima, the Prophet's daughter. Such a view privileges 'Ali's descent over prophetic descent, and the groups which developed out of al-Mukhtar's uprising were famous for their 'extreme' (*ghali*, pl. *ghulat*) views on the status of 'Ali. Their view was, however, marginalised as later developments confirmed that only 'Fatimid' descendants could be considered for the imamate.

Of the various Shi'i groups, the supporters of Zayd b. 'Ali's revolt in AD 740, devised a system closest to the Sunni position on the imamate. Zayd was a great-grandson of 'Ali and as such claimed the imamate for himself. His rebellion was unsuccessful, but his followers and their successors eventually devised one of the long-standing Shi'i groups, namely the Zaydiyya. The Zaydiyya declared that any member of the 'people of the house' (*ahl al-bayt*) of the Prophet Muhammad could rise up against the illegitimate political powers who claimed the imamate, and establish himself as imam. The qualifications of this person to the imamate were not dissimilar to those discussed by Sunni authors – he must be pious, learned and be able to command sufficient military support to establish himself in political control. Such a member of the *ahl al-bayt* was worthy of support by the individual believer's support. In some respects, the qualities of a Zaydi imam were similar to those proposed by Sunni thinkers, except they added the stipulation that he should be a descendant of the sons of Fatima, al-Hasan and al-Husayn, and not the

broader stipulation that he be of Quraysh descent.

More radically different views of the imam can be found in the two other main Shi'i groups – the Isma'ilis and the Twelvers (Ithna'ashariyya). Both Isma'ilis and Twelvers argue that after the Prophet Muhammad, there is a series of imam*s* from 'Ali's descendants, beginning with his two sons al-Hasan and al-Husayn, and following the line of descent from the latter. However, both the role and identity of the imam is conceived of differently by each tradition.

The Twelvers consider the current imam responsible for designating his successor imam in a procedure termed *nass*. Each of their imam*s* designated their successor through *nass*, as 'Ali, the first imam, had been designated by the Prophet Muhammad. This designation cannot be questioned because the imam is viewed as inheriting the Prophet's quality of sinlessness. Imam*s*, for the Twelvers, are similar to prophets in that their actions are a guide for believers. They differ from prophets in that they do not bring a revelation. For the Twelvers, the imam does not have to have political power to be imam. His legitimacy does not depend on his recognition as imam by the community since legitimacy comes from God, not any representative body of the people, or the scholars, or the *ahl al-hall wa'l-'aqd*. This will inevitably lead to instances where the community oppresses the imam since they have failed, through human disobedience, to recognise his rightful position as leader. In such circumstances, when the imam faces persecution, he may perform *taqiyya* – that is, he may appear to accept the rule of an illegitimate usurper of the imamate, but he is, in fact pretending to accept this oppressive rule. The Shi'a as a community and as individuals can perform *taqiyya*, if required. At other times the oppression may become so intolerable for the imam that he goes into hiding (*ghayba*). Most of these beliefs are outlined in Twelver books of *hadith* (often called *akhbar*) in reports attributed to the sixth imam Ja'far al-Sadiq (d. AD 765). The *ghayba*, Twelvers believe, happened in AD 874 when the twelfth imam disappeared. It is from this event that the Twelvers were given their name. The imam's period of concealment (*ghayba*) has lasted to this day, and his reappearance is viewed within Twelver theology as a messianic *parousia*, at which time a rule of justice will come about on earth. For this reason the twelfth imam is given the Muslim messianic title *al-mahdi* by Twelver Shi'is.

The Isma'ilis adopted some, though not all, of the characteristics of the imam found in Twelver Shi'i belief. In historical terms they differ from the Twelvers in that after Ja'far al-Sadiq, they trace their line of imams through Ja'far's older son Isma'il. The Twelvers consider Isma'il to have predeceased Ja'far, and hence he is ineligible for the imamate. Some Isma'ilis considered him to have gone into hiding and not died, though most considered the imamate to have passed to his son, Muhammad b. Isma'il. This is where the line of Isma'ili imam*s* differs from that of the Twelvers. However, their conception of imamate differs also. For Isma'ilis, the imam is sinless and infallible, as he is for the Twelvers. However, the imam was considered part of a cyclical view of time in which the series of prophet–executor (*wasi*)–seven imam*s* is repeated in human history. The last imam was to be the Prophet of the next era, and so on until the end of time. Muhammad was, of course, the Prophet. 'Ali was the *wasi*, and the seven imam*s*, ending with Muhammad b. Isma'il as the prophet of the next era. For Isma'ilis then, 'Ali was not the first imam: he was the executor (*wasi*). The first imam was al-Hasan. Muhammad b. Isma'il, however, had gone into a period of concealment (*satr*)

and would return as the Prophet of the next cycle in due course. Muhammad b. Isma'il was represented by a series of 'missionaries' (*da'is*) who were based in Salamiyya in Syria. When, in the late tenth century AD, one of these missionaries, 'Abdallah, claimed the imamate for himself, this split the Isma'ilis. 'Abdallah (or 'Ubaydallah as he was known in non-Isma'ili sources) went on to found the Fatimid dynasty which ruled over North Africa and Egypt until AD 1171. The imamate was lodged in the position of the Fatimid caliph and the earlier conception of the hidden Muhammad b. Isma'il was eventually played down. Instead the Fatimid caliphs were presented as descendants of Muhammad b. Isma'il who had been called to re-establish the imamate after a period when it had lapsed. All the contemporary branches of the Isma'ilis trace their origins to the Fatimid line of caliphs – their differences lie in the various succession disputes during and after the Fatimid caliphate. Of course, the Isma'ili dogma of the imam as potential prophet, and the Fatimid panegyrics concerning their caliph imam, lead to a potential for the deification of the imam amongst the more extreme followers. This occurred most obviously in the Druze movement which considered the Caliph al-Hakim (r. AD 996–1021) to be a manifestation of God. Isma'ili thought was also particularly receptive to Neoplatonic ideas in which aspects of the imam's character or function are seen as emanations of the Godhead. Such philosophical conceptions of the imamate were also present in the Twelver tradition, and there was much interaction between the Isma'ili and Twelver traditions in the area of philosophical theology.

Weber outlined a number of different conceptions of leadership, and within the Muslim discussions of the imamate one sees Weber's typology exemplified. The Sunni conception of an imam from the Quraysh tribe, whose role it is to govern the Muslim community rather like an old Arab tribal chief, reflects Weber's traditional model of leadership. The Kharijite view, which rejects any prerogative for the Quraysh tribe and attempts to view the imam as a servant of the community who can be removed if found to err from the true path is, perhaps, closest to Weber's legal–rational model. Finally, the Shi'a, particularly the Twelvers and the Isma'ilis, have constructed theories of the imamate where the imam is blessed with special powers and knowledge and has a particular relationship with God, which is unavailable to the ordinary believer. Here the imam is law-giver and lord, and can most aptly be associated with Weber's charismatic model of leadership. The issues of who is to lead the community, what sort of leader he might be, and how he is chosen are central to the direction and survival of any religious community. The centrality of these questions makes schismatic tendencies inevitable, and these can be seen in the history of the Muslim divisions between the Sunnis, the Shi'a and the Kharijites.

References

Amir-Moezzi (1994), Crone and Hinds (1986), Madelung (1996), Watt (1973).

ROBERT GLEAVE

IMAN

The Arabic root of this word, which means 'faith', suggests peace of mind, security, the absence of fear. In relation to Islam *iman* is used to express a disposition of the heart and mind, echoing the words of the Prophet Muhammad in which he defined *iman* as 'a confession with the tongue, a verification with the heart, and an act with the body'. More specifically, *iman* has come to refer to the major aspects of religious belief in Islam, namely: belief in God (Allah), belief in the angels of God, belief in the holy books revealed by God at different times and in different places, culminating in the Qur'an, belief in all the prophets of God, belief in the day of judgement, belief in predestination. By accepting these articles of faith a Muslim is 'rendered secure' in the profession and the practice of what God has revealed. The 'religion' (*din*) of Islam is divided into three related parts, *'ibadat* (the religious duties of a Muslim), *iman* (the faith of a Muslim, as defined previously), and *ihsan* (the practice of a virtuous life in accordance with Islamic principles).

References

Hitti (1973: 128–30), Tritton (1968: 36–57).

EDWARD D. A. HULMES

IMPERIALISM

The rule of an emperor or empire, in which areas are dominated by a metropolitan centre. Imperialism has been associated with colonialism, although other techniques of political, cultural and economic domination may be used. The passing of European colonial rule in the Middle East did not see an end to imperial relationships between Western and Middle Eastern countries. Following the Suez crisis in 1956, the USA superseded Britain and France as the principal imperial power in the Middle East. The USA developed a system of regional pre-eminence based on its political values, its military and economic power, and its relationships with subordinate allies.

References

Ayubi (1995: 86–134), Bill and Springborg (1994: 341–73, 384–99), Fernandez-Armesto

(1995: 188–91, 214–24), Hourani (1991: 265–372, 419–28).

SIMON W. MURDEN

IMRU' AL-QAYS IBN HUJR (d. *c.* AD 550)

Pre-Islamic poet and author of one of the *mu'allaqat*, died *c.* AD 550. Despite his reputation as one of the best known pre-Islamic poets, the details of Imru' al-Qays's life are obscure and the sources contradictory. The most usual version describes him as living at the court of Hujr, the last king of the Kinda, of whom he was the youngest son; of being expelled from his father's house, and of living the life of an outcast in the desert, indulging himself in the pleasures of hunting, drinking, song and sex. When his father was killed in an uprising, he devoted his life to avenging his death, and to this end is said to have reached the court of the Emperor Justinian. He allegedly died from putting on a poisoned robe sent to him as a punishment for seducing the Emperor's daughter and died near Ankara about the middle of the sixth century AD.

The most reliable edition of Imru' al-Qays's *Diwan*, that of al-Sukkari, contains sixty-eight poems, of which thirty-one are in the form of the *qit'a*, twenty-one in the form of the *qasida*, and the rest fragments. The authenticity of many (probably the majority) of these poems is, however, doubtful. The poet's reputation rests essentially on his *mu'allaqa*, chronologically the first of the celebrated collection of pre-Islamic odes and also, in the opinion of many critics, the finest. He has sometimes been credited with inventing the 'deserted encampment' motif that forms an essential part of the *nasib*, and the first line of his *mu'allaqa* (*qifa nabki min dhikra habibin wa-manzili* ...) has some claim to be among the best-known lines of pre-Islamic poetry. It is followed by a sequence of themes that deviates somewhat from the conventional one, involving past love affairs, a description of the poet's horse, a hunting scene, a banquet and a particularly vigorous description of a thunderstorm among the hills of Najd.

Imru' al-Qays's pre-eminence as a poet was acknowledged by the Prophet Muhammad, who is said to have described him as 'the most poetical of the poets, and their leader into hellfire'.

References

Abu Deeb (1969: 3–69), Arberry (1957), Haydar (1977: 227–61; 1978: 51–82), Stetkevych (1993a; 1993b: 241–85).

PAUL STARKEY

AL-INJIL

'The Gospels' which, as with the five Old Testament books of Moses and the Psalms, are accepted as divinely revealed (e.g., Q.3:3).

See also: '*Isa*; *al-Tawrat*; *al-Zabur*

ANDREW J. NEWMAN

AL-INSAN AL-KAMIL

'The perfect man' is the individual who maintains the link between God and creation and acts for the believers as a perfect mirror of the divine. Many Sufis discussed the perfect man including Ibn al-'Arabi and 'Abd al-Karim al-Jili who argued that there must always be a perfect man in the world at any one time for existence to continue, as God's generosity requires that such an individual be present to make God known to the creatures.

References

Takeshita (1987).

LLOYD RIDGEON

INSPIRATION (*WAHY*)

Explicit philosophical discussion of *wahy* is not extensive. An important issue is the relative status and possible harmonisation of knowledge gained through philosophy and *wahy*. For al-Kindi, *wahy* ultimately takes precedence, although there is no conflict between the two types of knowledge. However, al-Kindi also seems to emphasise as distinctive the telling and succinct power of expression of *wahy*, implying that this, rather than its content, is what sets it apart from philosophical reasoning. *Wahy* is also seen by the Ikhwan al-Safa' as what the intellect cannot grasp by conventional learning.

Wahy need not be confined to scriptural prophets, but is available to other righteous people. This view is sometimes used, as by the Ikhwan al-Safa' and Ibn Sina, to buttress their own claims to receive *wahy*. For the Ikhwan reception of *wahy* is the highest spiritual state. The Ikhwan note that receiving *wahy* might entail dream visions, a rarer waking vision, or hearing a sound or speech without seeing anything. They understand the vision that the recipient of *wahy* might perceive as the formation of images by the soul, in accordance with their psychological theories, resembling those of al-Farabi.

Wahy is given only limited attention by al-Farabi, who describes it simply as what our intellects cannot grasp. Within the works of Ibn Sina, the fullest description occurs in *Fi Ithbat al-Nubuwwat* (*On the Proof of Prophecies*). *Wahy* is described here as the emanation from the universal intellect, a description also given by the Ikhwan (prophecy). It thus involves the reception of forms flowing from the active intellect, forms made particular by the particularity of the recipient. Ibn Sina stresses in his theories of prophecy the role of human preparedness and endowment in ways frequently overshadowing the revelatory role of God. *Wahy* is constantly available to the suitable candidate, the emphasis thus falling on questions of human suitability rather than divine initiative.

For Ibn Rushd, the attempt to integrate the knowledge gained through philosophy and *wahy* is paramount. Rejecting the emanationist understanding of inspiration offered by Ibn Sina, he treats *wahy* as part of the discussion of God's attribute of speech, describing it as either the creation of meaning in the soul or the disclosure of meaning to it. *Wahy* is also a multi-level phenomenon, incorporating demonstrative, dialectical and rhetorical proofs so as to impact all levels of society. In this it contrasts with philosophy, the practice and privilege of the few. Further, for Ibn Rushd, *wahy*, not miracles, constitutes the proof of prophethood.

References

Brewster (1975: 154–62), Ibn Rushd (1998: 131–3, 185; 2001: 48–9, 105), Ibn Sina (1968; 1972: 112–21), Rosenthal (1953: 246–78).

MARIN WHITTINGHAM

INTEGRATION VERSUS ASSIMILATION

In the contemporary encounter with the West and modernity dating from the early nineteenth century, the strategies adopted by most Muslim secular intellectuals and Muslim political establishments generally initially involved efforts to incorporate or emulate certain Western institutions and lifestyles. In the Ottoman Empire these extended to such local rulers as Egypt's Muhammad 'Ali (1805–49) and, later in the century, the Young Ottomans. In Iran, the Qajar shahs also undertook efforts to reorganise central political institutions along seemingly Western lines. In the twentieth century Ataturk (1923–38), who disestablished Islam in Turkey, and Reza Pahlavi (1925–41), in Iran, for example, continued such efforts, even if each followed independent foreign policies. Preoccupation with 'socialist', if pan-Arab, politics in the 1950s and 1960s bespoke a similar interest in integrating into the modern world system, and achieving Western standards of living, by pursuing non-aligned and independent foreign and domestic policies.

The elitism of this socialist discourse coupled, especially, with the political failures of the 1960s and 1970s discredited socialist policies and encouraged a new generation of intellectuals in their search for an indigenous, if similarly independent, discourse. Islamist discourse, whose appearance can be dated to the 1980s, increasingly rejected the assimilation of Western lifestyles and institutions let alone the goal of integration into, and accommodation with, modernity.

Distinctly separatist and puritanical responses to modernity include Wahabism, dating to the eighteenth century AD and established in Saudi Arabia in the early twentieth century. More recent manifestations include such movements as the Egypt-based al-Takfir wa'l-Hijra, which organised the assassination of Anwar Sadat in 1981, and Salafism. The latter is at the intellectual core of various activist anti-Western Islamist movements, the more extreme of which includes al-Qa'ida and Algeria-based Islamist movements which have decried association, and promoted overt confrontation, with manifestations of the Western experience. Although minority trends within contemporary Islam, to the extent that such emotionally charged political issues as the situation of the Palestinians remain unsettled the especially anti-US dimension of such movements' anti-Western discourse will continue to attract widespread, if only indirect, sympathy.

References

Hourani (1991: esp. 265–6, 416–17).

See also: **freedom; Marxism and Islam; materialism; modernity;** *salaf*; **socialism**

ANDREW J. NEWMAN

INTIFADA, PALESTINIAN

The uprising of Palestinians against the Israeli occupation of the West Bank and Gaza. Spontaneous disturbances in late 1987 were quickly organised by the PLO and Hamas. The uprising took the form of stone-throwing against Israeli soldiers, attacks on Israeli settlers, and strikes and economic boycotts. Israel's response killed many hundreds, and in turn Islamic militants increasingly adopted the tactic of suicide bombings. The uprising encouraged the Israeli Prime Minister, Yitzhak Rabin, to embark on the Oslo Peace Process after 1993. The conflict subsided, but growing frustrations saw another upsurge from the late 1990s. When the Likud Party leader, Ariel Sharon, made a visit to Jerusalem's Al-Aqsa mosque on 28 September 2000, the violence escalated.

References

Bill and Springborg (1994: 352–6), Sharoni and Abu-Nimer (2000: 187–96), Usher (1997: 339–54).

SIMON W. MURDEN

IQBAL, MUHAMMAD (1875–1938)

The most sophisticated Muslim intellectual in South Asia in the first half of the twentieth century. Born in Sialkot (in what is now Pakistan) Iqbal studied in Cambridge, Heidelberg and Munich, where he completed his doctorate in 1908 under the title *The Development of Metaphysics in Persia*. This reflected his interests in both philosophy and literature, especially poetry, and he later came to be regarded as the greatest Urdu poet of the twentieth century. In theology he followed in the reformist tradition of Sayyid Ahmad Khan, advocating the reformulation of traditional Islamic teachings, most notably in his lectures on *The Reconstruction of Religious Thought in Islam*, which have been described as 'speculative modernism' (M. Ruthven). By profession he was a lawyer and in the debates between the two world wars about how British India should develop after independence from Britain at some future date he became a vigorous supporter of the idea of a separate state for Muslims, to be called Pakistan, which he envisaged as being both a democratic and a socialist state.

References

Iqbal (1934), Malik (1971), Raschid (1986), Schimmel (1963).

HUGH GODDARD

IQRAR

Acknowledgement, confession. A theological term used for the confession of a sin. In legal terms it refers to the recognition of legal status or statement such as the admission of guilt.

References

Ibn Manzur (n.d.).

MAWIL IZZI DIEN

IRANIAN REVOLUTION

The 1979 Iranian Revolution, or *Inqilab-i Islami* ('the Islamic Revolution') as it is known in Iran, represents the greatest success of revolutionary Islamist ideas in the twentieth century. The idea that a revolution is necessary to sweep away a defunct or unethical regime emerged in European intellectual circles reflecting on the success of the French Revolution of 1789; the necessity of a revolution was later radicalised by the Marxist tradition and supposedly epitomised in the Russian Revolution of 1917. In the twentieth century, Muslim thinkers, unimpressed by colonial occupation (and the secular leftist ideologies adopted by many of the independent Muslim states) began to devise a notion of a specifically Islamic revolution, whereby the 'un-Islamic' political systems that dominated the Muslim world might be removed and replaced with a revolutionary Islamic alternative. In Sunni discussions, the thought of Mawdudi and Sayyid Qutb were particularly influential. In the Shi'i world, during the 1950s and 1960s, similar ideas began to emerge through the work of Iranian intellectuals. Clerics such as Ruhallah Khumayni and Murtada Mutahhari, and laypeople such as 'Ali Shari'ati and Mahdi Bazargan clearly envisaged a total upheaval of the current political system, which was viewed as irredeemable and beyond reform (though they differed in their visions of the appropriate Islamic replacement). Their ideas inevitably brought them into conflict with the monarchical regime of Muhammad Rida Pahlavi, the Shah of Iran, and these ideologues and their followers began to form a substantial Islamist opposition movement to the Shah's rule. The Islamists, with their different programmes, were not the only opposition force: the Shah faced opposition from secular leftists (such as the National Front) and radical communists (the Tudeh Party). However, they appear to have had some advantages over these other groups which eventually permitted the 1979 revolution to adopt an 'Islamic' character. First, socialism and Marxism were, despite the efforts of these groups, seen as foreign ideologies by Iranians, and one of the mainstays of the opposition's appeal was a rejection of the Shah's westernisation policy and the secularisation of Iranian society. The Islamist ideologues were keen to demonstrate that their ideas were rooted in the Iranian Shi'i Muslim tradition and, hence, were an expression of Iranian identity. Second, the network of religious institutions across the country (seminars, schools, mosques, charitable foundations) enabled Islamist ideas to be disseminated in Iranian society with greater success than the secular alternatives. This was particularly true for the scholars (*'ulama'*), but lay Islamist ideologues also utilised traditional institutional models, exemplified in the establishment of the Husayniyyah-yi Irshad in Tehran. Third, the Shah and his foreign allies (principally the USA) were most concerned with the threat of communism and the threatened influence of the Soviet Union in Iran. This policy had two important effects. First, the Shah expended much energy attempting to root out the Tudeh Party and the National Front. Second, the regime's success in suppressing leftist opposition, gave oppositional space to the Islamists.

These advantages came to the fore in the 1970s because of the Shah's foreign policies of alliance with Western powers and Israel, a worsening economic situation and the establishment of an effective one-party state in March 1975. The events leading up to the Revolution in 1979 are well documented in a number of excellent Western language accounts. In brief, demonstrations against the Shah's policies began in 1978, when the clerical leader Ayatallah Ruhallah Khumayni was pilloried in the state-controlled press. Khumayni had been expelled from Iran in 1963 following protests against the Shah's modernisation plan (the so-called 'White Revolution'). From his exile first in Turkey, then in Najaf (in southern Iraq) and eventually in Paris, Khumayni had denounced the Shah in vitriolic terms and a large number of seminary students (*tullab*) had become devotees of his ideas. When he was openly insulted by the state-controlled press, the *tullab* embarked on a series of demonstrations at forty-day intervals. As Khumayni's supporters were wounded or killed in one demonstration, the traditional Shi'i mourning ceremony forty days later provoked another demonstration. This cycle continued for sometime, and Khumayni called for the violent overthrow of the 'Shah's despotic regime'. Despite the Shah's attempts at both repression and concession to the opposition forces, it became increasingly clear he was unable to maintain control. He prevaricated over the use of overwhelming force against the demonstrations, resulting in a haemorrhage of support in the previously loyal army. He eventually left Iran on 16 January 1979, Khumayni returned from Paris to a hero's welcome on 1 February. Khumayni's exile had, ironically, made him the natural leader for the revolutionary movement. In Iraq and Paris he was able to speak and publish more freely than his contemporaries in Iran. He stood apart from rival opposition figures in his uncompromising call for the Shah to leave. Some were drawn into the attempts at compromise in the final months of the Pahlavi regime, and this weakened their popular appeal. Others had first-hand experience of Pahlavi repression and, hence, moderated their rhetoric or kept silent.

Khumayni came to power and began to implement the Islamic revolutionary ideology developed over the past decade or more. He proposed a revival of the Shi'i legal doctrine of *wilayat al-faqih* ('the guardianship of the jurist', in Persian, *velayat-i faqih*). This doctrine placed aspects of temporal control of the Shi'i community in the hands of the 'jurist' (*faqih*, a scholar). In the past, the doctrine of *wilayat al-faqih* had been employed to provide guardianship for orphans and other dispossessed persons. It had also been used in Shi'i legal texts to refer to the delegation of some of the powers of the imam (who according to Twelver Shi'i belief was now in hiding) to the jurist. Khumayni expanded the role of the jurist to include not merely matters of religious import, but also political issues. The jurist was, under Khumayni's theory, to be the supreme interpreter and enforcer of the *shari'a*, and hence the one who controls the workings of society until the return of the imam. Khumayni argued that if a scholar-jurist was able to establish himself in power it was obligatory on all other jurists to support and follow him, even if he was not actually the most senior and learned of the scholarly class (*'ulama'*). This development was, paradoxically, both innovative and traditional. It was innovative in that it expanded the remit of the scholar-jurist to include political matters, it was traditional in that it employed an established (though perhaps neglected) element of Shi'i jurisprudence. In the internal battles between elements of the revolutionary movement which emerged after the overthrow of the Shah, Khumayni managed to control the drafting and implementation of the new constitution of the Islamic Republic of Iran, such that the doctrine of *wilayat al-faqih* was enshrined as the ruling principle of governance.

The constitution of the Islamic republic, which was accepted by popular vote in 1979, is a strange document which includes not only Khumayni's doctrine of the supreme authority of the jurist, but also elements of popular election (in the form of the *majlis* or parliament). The document, to an extent, reflects the competing elements of the revolutionary movement. Madhi Bazargan (a long-time Islamic activist who had been imprisoned by the Shah's regime) and Ayatallah Taliqani (a cleric with reformist leanings) both argued that a solidly democratic constitution was the most effective way of preserving the Islamic nature of both the Revolution and Iranian society gen-

erally. On the other hand, the Mujahidin-i Khalq styled themselves as 'Islamic Marxists', with the call 'Marxism is our ideology, Islam is our creed'. Using the rhetoric of revolution and a classless society, they had established a network of cells across Iran during the 1960s, and played an important role in the revolutionary movement. Whilst not directly linked to the Mujahidin, the sociologist 'Ali Shari'ati (who died in 1977, a year and a half before the revolution) was also an important figure. He did not found a political party, but did provide a large section of the middle classes with a relatively sophisticated Islamic ideology through which they could channel their criticism of the Shah. Indeed, Shari'ati, it could be said, was crucial to the success of the Revolution, since it was only when the middle classes began to oppose the Shah that the Pahlavi regime began to crumble. Without Shari'ati's teaching, preaching and publishing, they may not have agreed to such a prominent role for Islam in the new post-shah political order.

In the end, however, it was Khumayni's version of revolutionary Islam which was implemented politically, and it was Khumayni who succeeded in establishing himself as the 'just jurist' who oversaw the whole political process. The reasons for Khumayni's success over the other Islamicist groups lie in his personal charisma, his refusal to compromise with the Shah, and his skilful manipulation of the media from exile. His face was the best known of the clerics, and his fiery speeches were heard in Iran through tape cassettes smuggled into Iran and distributed around the country. He established a loyal band of supporters in Iran who prepared the way for his acceptance as leader on his return. In short, Khumayni was better organised than any other Islamist revolutionary figure and, hence, his well-prepared and comprehensive ideology of *wilayat al-faqih* was the natural ideological mainstay of the Revolution.

Khumayni's leadership was tested regularly during the 1980s. The popularly elected President Bani Sadr was deposed and publicly disgraced in 1981. The Mujahidin activitists posed too great a threat and were suppressed in the early 1980s. In 1988, the cleric who had been officially designated as Khumayni's successor as 'jurist', Ayatallah Muntaziri was publically criticised for promoting a more 'liberal' version of *wilayat al-faqih*. These threats to his leadership, combined with the war with Iraq from 1980 to 1989, were repelled and Khumayni's ability to withstand such challenges demonstrated his almost absolute control of the political process. He died in 1989, and Ayatallah Khameneh'i assumed the position of Rahbar-i Inqilab (Leader of the Revolution). Khameneh'i will hold this position for life, though the powerbase he has inherited from Khumayni has come under serious threat from the office of the President. Under the constitution, the list of candidates for the presidency must be passed by the Supreme Guardian Council (a body made up, in the main, of clerics who have been generally sympathetic to Khumayni's vision of an Islamic state). In 1997, a cleric with impeccable *'ulama'* credentials, Muhammad Khatami, was included on the ballot paper and won by an impressive margin. Khatami has attempted to implement a series of political reforms which include reducing the censorship of the press, greater openness in government and the creation of an effective civil society in Iran. He has had some success, but the factional state of Iranian politics has hindered his progress. In particular supporters of Khameneh'i have blocked important reforms, and frustration with Khatami's lack of progress has lead to street protests, lead by university students. The outcome of the current (early part of the new millennium)

tension is difficult to predict, though it seems clear that the end of the term of Khameneh'i's office (which can only occur on the occasion of his death) will mark a turning point in the development of the religious nature of the Islamic republic.

The Revolution has not prompted a series of Islamist political successes in the Muslim world. The conditions which brought Khumayni to power were obviously particular to Iran. Other Arab leaders were (and still are) not as overtly pro-Western as the Shah. In addition, Khumayni's ideology is specifically Shi'i, and does not transport well into a Sunni milieu. The general Arab support for Iraq's war with Iran also dampened the possibility of popular, Iranian-style, Islamic revolutions. Even amongst Shi'i communities in Iraq, Lebanon and the Indian subcontinent, the dominant political discourse is not Khumaynist.

The Revolution, however, has raised a number of important questions about the role of religion in modern society. It seems clear that any sociological approach which posits the increasing secularisation of modernising societies is inadequate to explain the Iranian case. Here the Shah's programme had many of the hallmarks of a modernising process (greater roles for women in public life, alliances with modernising Western countries, a defence of capitalism against the communist threat), though his rule fell to a movement which was predominantly religious in character. Modernisation does not inevitably mean secularisation and the marginalisation (and privatisation) of religion. Further, the 'rationalisation' process, in which ideas are supposed to become more important than personalities in modern religion, is also challenged: the Iranian Revolution took its religious course in large part because of the force of Khumayni's personality. Finally, the Revolution demonstrated to the Western world that Islamic ideology could become an effective vehicle for anti-Western protest, and that the security of Western interests in the Middle East and elsewhere depends on coming to terms with the permanence of the 'Islamic factor' in the politics of the Muslim world.

References

Abrahamian (1982), Arjomand (1988), Dabashi (1993), Fischer (1980).

ROBERT GLEAVE

IRAN–IRAQ WAR

After the 1979 Iranian Revolution in which the Pahlavi Dynasty was overthrown and an Islamic Republic formed, Iraq attacked ten civilian and military targets on Iranian soil in September 1980. Iraqi troops also invaded Iranian territory along the border. There ensued a bitter, bloody war between the two countries which lasted until a UN-sponsored ceasefire, agreed first by Iraq in July 1987 (on condition that Iran also accepted it) and eventually by Iran in July 1988. The Iraqi regime, led by Saddam Husayn, argued that Iran had carried out attacks against Iraq, including an attempt on the Deputy Prime Minister's life, and had sponsored an insurgent terrorist opposition group in Iraq, al-Da'wa. The Iranian regime refuted these claims, arguing that the Iraqi attack was unprovoked and that Iraq was primarily interested in securing access to the Shatt al-'Arab waterway which formed the border between the two countries. Undoubtedly, the Iraqis were concerned with the Shatt al-'Arab, but they were also concerned about the exportation of the Iranian 'Islamic revolution' lead by the Shi'i cleric Ayatallah Khumayni to their own (majority Shi'i) population. Khumayni's vision of a state, run according to the rules of the *shari'a*, worried the secular Ba'thists of Iraq. Iran, in contrast, was keen to see an activa-tion of Islamic resistance outside of its borders, since the establishment of an 'Islamic bloc' would bolster its standing on the world stage, even if Iran's Islamic colleagues were Sunni rather than Shi'i.

At first, Iraq achieved some military success, taking advantage of the disputes within the Islamic Republic between the non-clerical president Bani Sadr and Khumayni's activists. In September 1981, following a reorganisation of the military command in Iran, the Iranian forces embarked on a series of successful counterattack measures, including the famous *Fath Mubin* ('Clear Victory') attack in the Shush area, in which waves of Iranian soldiers were sent out on martyrdom missions against the Iraqi enemy. Though they killed large numbers of Iranian troops, the Iraqis were forced back to the border. Similar tactics were tried throughout the Khuzistan province. In June 1982, Saddam Husayn sued for peace as his forces had been forced back. The Iranians, now encouraged by their victories demanded more from the negotiations than the Iraqi president was willing to give. The war continued and in July 1982, Iranian troops moved towards the Iraqi port city of Basra. Though unable to take Basra, Iran continued its policy of attacking Iraqis on Iraqi soil. The inevitable retaliation heightened the ferocity of the war with ground and air campaigns from both sides continuing into 1983. In early 1983, the war began to be played out in the Persian Gulf, as Iraqi forces attacked Iranian oil interests in the Gulf, and Iran retaliated in like fashion. The war continued with Iraqi campaign following Iranian operation, with little discernable victor in sight. In October 1983, US warships moved into the area to protect American allies, their interests and the international shipping lanes. US armed forces were to clash with Iranian gunboats and navy vessels throughout the remaining period of the war. Some of the more important events of the ensuing conflict included the 1984 attacks by both Iraq and Iran on tankers in the Gulf which had a serious affect on oil supply from the area; in 1985, attacks on civilian targets, which had stopped in 1984, were resumed by the Iraqis; in 1986, the Iran–Contra story broke in the world media, in which the USA was selling arms to Iran, through the good agency of Israel; in 1987, the Iraqis recaptured the Fa'u peninsula on the Gulf coast, forcing Iranians back across the Shatt al-'Arab; in July 1988, a missile from the USS *Vicennes* downed an Iranian passenger plane, killing 290 civilians. By this time, it was clear that a stalemate had emerged between Iraq and Iran, and the United Nations was beginning to make a determined effort to achieve a lasting and permanent ceasefire. The UN secretary, Pérez de Cuéllar, made numerous diplomatic visits to Baghdad and Tehran, and a ceasefire was only concluded in July 1988. Khumayni said accepting peace with Saddam was like 'drinking poison', though for the sake of the Islamic Republic he was willing to do so.

The war was, in many respects, unconnected with religion. Instead geopolitics and economics seemed to be the major spur for military action on both sides. However, the war does raise some interesting questions regarding the use of religion in warfare, and the use of war for religious purposes. Most Western commentators and governments viewed the war as between a secular, modernising dictatorship (Iraq) and a medieval-style religious oligarchy (Iran), and in choosing between these two, decided to support the former. Some commentators attempted to link the Iraqi and Iranian sides to the Sunni–Shi'i division in Islam, though this ignores the fact that most of the foot soldiers of the Iraqi army were Shi'i. More interesting is the use of religion by both sides to support the war. Both the Iranians and the Iraqis described the war as a *jihad*, though, of course, the classical regulations for a *jihad* are difficult to apply to the context of a modern war between two Muslim nations. More potent was the call, on both sides, for martyrdom (*shahada*) and self-sacrifice: two essential elements of the forces' morale in a long and (seemingly) pointless war. The Iranians in particular utilised examples from the life of the Prophet Muhammad and his dealing with his enemies to justify every diplomatic, political and military manoeuvre of the war. The operations against Iraq were given religious names such as 'Karbala'' (the site of the battle of Imam Husayn in AD 680) or 'Muslim Ibn 'Aqil' (Imam Husayn's cousin who was martyred in Kufa whilst trying to rally support for Husayn). Similarly the truce, when signed, was compared to the treaty of al-Hudaybiya in AD 628, when the Prophet Muhammad made peace with his sworn enemies, the Meccans. In line with the required political (and religious) rhetoric of these two countries, neither would accept responsibility as the aggressor after the war, and both considered themselves to have been the victors at the war's end.

References

Gieling (1999), King (1987).

ROBERT GLEAVE

IRJA'

The notion that faith alone is equated with belief, not actions (Q.9:106), such that judgement on the latter is suspended in this world.

References

Watt (1973: 123–4, 126).

ANDREW J. NEWMAN

IRRIGATION (*AL-SIQAYA*)

Strenuous efforts have been made since ancient times in the Near and Middle East to conserve water, and then to distribute it for human needs, animal husbandry, horticulture and agriculture. For thousands of years the annual inundation of the surrounding land by the White and Blue Nile river systems sustained the life of the peoples of parts of northeastern Africa. The floodwater submerged large strips of land on either side of the river's course. It was then diverted further into local irrigation channels by traditional farming methods, which included the retention of floodwater in fields by means of bunds (dykes). The reliability of this annual inundation made the cultivation of crops possible even in the midst of the desert areas of the Sudan and Egypt where subsistence farming provided the only means of support for small communities. A supply of irrigation water promotes the fertility of the soil. Too much irrigation water leads to waterlogging and crop failure. Close attention has to be paid to drainage, whether the irrigation system in use is ancient or modern. The completion of the High Dam at Aswan in Egypt and the Kenana irrigation canal in the Sudan has made the conservation and the distribution of Nile floodwater easier for the authorities to supervise and control. Water from the dam built in 1000 BC at Ma'rib in the Yemen helped to irrigate a part of *Arabia Felix* already famed for its fertility. Ancient canals (*qanawat*), some of which remain in use in places in Afghanistan, Iran and the Gulf States, brought subterranean water to local communities. These ancient engineering works link up wells in which groundwater is trapped. The fearsome deserts of Arabia are said to conceal vast supplies of underground water, yet to be exploited. Further north in Mesopotamia the land 'between the two rivers' (the Tigris and Euphrates) was already known in the ancient world as the Fertile Crescent. Syria, Turkey and (until the recent conflict) Iraq have collaborated in the construction of irrigation schemes in this area. The introduction of modern irrigation techniques in the Near and Middle East is expensive, however. In parts of Arabia, Kuwait and Iraq, for instance, desalination plants are being constructed to convert salt water in the marshy river deltas and from the sea itself for irrigation purposes.

References

Mostyn and Hourani (1988: 97–9), Schacht and Bosworth (1979: 211–14).

See also: **agriculture (*al-filaha*, *al-zira'a*); gardens, Islamic; Nile, the river**

EDWARD D. A. HULMES

'ISA

'Jesus', also called 'the word of Allah' in the Qur'an (Q.4:171), the spirit of Allah (Q.4:171) and the messiah (Q.3:45, Q.4:171) and acknowledged also as a 'messenger' and 'prophet' (e.g., Q.4:163). His virgin birth is acknowledged (Q.3:47, Q.19:20). Jesus only appeared to die on the cross (Q.4:157), however, and both his trinitarian nature and his filial relationship to Allah are also rejected (Q.4:116, Q.5:116, Q.19:35). He performed miracles but only 'by Allah's leave' (Q.3:49).

See also: **rasul**

ANDREW J. NEWMAN

ISAAC

See: **Ishaq**

ISAWA

The Isawa were the descendants of the followers of Ibrahim, the Kano court *mallam* (Islamic teacher), who was active in the city in the middle years of the nineteenth century. They were Muslims, but their beliefs focused less on the Prophet Muhammad than on the Prophet 'Isa (Jesus), about whom the Qur'an has much to say (cf. Q.16, *Maryam*). 'Isa is one of the six major 'Messengers' (*rasul*) of God in Islam. For details about the Isawa there are few reliable historical sources. An account of their origins, beliefs and religious practices was compiled in the first half of the twentieth century by Dr W. R. S. Miller, who worked among the Isawa for a short period in Nigeria during the First World War. When Miller came across them, they were living in eschatological expectation of the imminent arrival of a white disciple of Jesus, who would deepen their understanding of Qur'anic teaching about 'Isa. Not surprisingly, perhaps, it was Miller who was thought to be the anticipated white teacher.

Mallam Ibrahim was a recognised Islamic scholar at the court of the Emir of Kano, Muhammad Bello, but the presence in northern Nigeria of a group of Muslims who appeared to have syncretistic beliefs made for tensions between them and more traditional Muslims. On a visit to Cairo Ibrahim had discovered a copy of the New Testament in Arabic. He began to compare the accounts of Jesus given there with what the Qur'an states about the Prophet 'Isa, using such title as *al-masih 'Isa* (Christ Jesus), *rasul* ('messanger' [of God]), *kalimatuhu* (His word), *wa-ruhun minhu* (His spirit), and *wajihan* (one worthy of regard). From his comparative studies, Ibrahim concluded that the traditional position with regard to 'Jesus' was defective. He was accused of heresy but refused to recant. Given a day in which to repeat the Islamic creed and to perform *salat*, he refused to do either. In consequence, he was brutally executed in the marketplace in Kano for apostasy, suffering an agonising death as a pointed stake was pushed from his anus to his throat. Whilst dying he counselled his followers to seek refuge outside the borders of Bauchi, Kano and Zazzau (Zaria), where they would receive a revelation about the true religion with God. Many were hunted down and killed. Others held to a belief in the second coming of 'Isa. Under the leadership of Yahayya in Turuwa they continued to resist the charge that they had abandoned Islam.

Miller took a great interest in this community, which appeared to be based upon a set of beliefs that could never be either fully Islamic or fully Christian. The Isawas were too few in number ever to have made an impact on the development of Islam or Christianity in West Africa. Their emergence and ultimate decline furnished a historical oddity rather than a blueprint for future dialogue between Muslims and Christians. Miller stated that the Isawas held to 'all the Moslem ritual', but in the light of the 'slight deviations' from Islamic tradition, which he enumerated in a report for the Resident of Zaria, it is clear that they did not. He did this in order to gain the Resident's approval for the establishment of an Isawa community at Gimi. He no doubt felt that this would provide an unique opportunity for Christian evangelism, but his concern for the Isawa survivors was genuine. Approval was given and the community was established in 1914. Miller's report to the Resident contained the following points about the Isawas.

1. They adhere strictly to a belief in the absolute unity of God.
2. They reject the notion that there was anything 'unusual' about Muhammad, refusing to retain the second part of the Islamic creed which runs, 'and Muhammad is uniquely the Messenger of God'.
3. They reject Islamic traditions, insisting on the authority of the

Qur'an and the Christian Scriptures alone.

4. They declare that Jesus Christ is the 'Word' and 'Spirit' of God, and that he alone is the saviour of the world, 'Muhammad never having announced himself as such'.

5. They refuse to carry out normal Islamic ritual, declining to turn to face Mecca in prayer. Fasting can be observed at any time and not just during the month of Ramadan.

6. The smoking of tobacco and the chewing of the *kola* nut is forbidden.

7. They place great emphasis on the Resurrection, holding that Christ alone has power to raise the dead.

Within a few months 120 men, women and children were at work constructing houses and a church at Gimi. The site had been donated by the Emir. Members of the community worked on the land. For two years the community prospered. Then the rains failed for two successive seasons. Famine and malnutrition ensued. Miller, who had taken the initiative in the project, had not been informed about the history of the place. Close by the village was a river used for drinking water as well as bathing. Many fell ill and died from a disease, said to be the work of demons, which had ended previous attempts to live in the area. Miller eventually diagnosed the mysterious disease as *trypanosomiasis*, 'sleeping sickness', but not before painful degradation had reduced the community almost to the point of extinction. Miller took responsibility for this débâcle and it troubled him for the rest of his life. Of the few surviving members of the Gimi community some of the children, who had been away for a time at school in Zaria, moved to other Muslim provinces. More traditional Muslims looked on the demise of the Isawa as God's justifiable punishment for heresy. The heretics, in other words, had suffered the fate that awaits all apostates from Islam.

References

Hulmes (1988: 233–46), Linden (1974).

See also: **Miller, Dr Walter R. S.**

EDWARD D. A. HULMES

ISFAHAN

A city located on the 'life-giving' river Zayande in west-central Iran, some 200 miles (320 kilometres) south of Tehran. It is Iran's third largest city. Captured by the Arabs in AD 642, it became the capital of the Saljuq Turks in the eleventh century AD. Four centuries later it was the capital of Iran's Safavid dynasty. It became the capital of Shah 'Abbas I ('the Great') in 1598, who rebuilt and enlarged it. In this period the city began to emerge as one of the most impressive in the Islamic world, with many mosques, tombs, palaces and Islamic schools (*madrasas*) for the study of the Islamic sciences. Twelver Shi'ism flourished in the city. The Israqi ('illuminationist') 'School of Isfahan' developed philosophical teology (*al-Hikmat al-Ilaiya*) on rational and intuitive principles. Among the architectural glories of Isfahan are the Grand (Royal) Mosque (*Masjid-i Sa*) and the *Masjid-i Sayk Lutf-alla*. The Royal Square (*Maydan-i Sa*) is located in the centre of the city, with mosques and palaces at the south end and the maze of the bazaar to the north. After it was captured and sacked by Afghans in 1722 the city fell into decline. During the reign of Reza Shah Pahlavi (1925–41) repair and reconstruction work was carried out extensively in Isfahan. The refining of petroleum oil and the manufacture of steel were expanded. Traditional crafts such as the making of carpets, rugs, textiles and tiles continue to flourish. The University of Isfahan was founded in 1936.

References

Arberry (1953: *passim*), Momen (1985: 112–13 and *passim*).

EDWARD D. A. HULMES

AL-ISFAHANI, ABU AL-FARAJ (897–*c.* AD 962)

Arab historian, musicologist, poet and prose writer. Born in Isfahan, he studied in Baghdad, where he spent the majority of his life and where he died. Abu al-Faraj worked as a civil servant and occupied a respected position at the Buyid court of Mu'izz al-Dawla, though there is little evidence for his alleged association with the court of the Hamdanid prince Sayf al-Dawla at Aleppo.

Abu al-Faraj's fame depends on his monumental *Kitab al-Aghani*, a collection of information about poets, musicians and singers, and about their poems and songs, from pre-Islamic times until the end of the third century of Islam. The work, which is essentially a compilation, runs to several thousand pages, but was left unfinished by the author. The starting point for its composition was to provide an account of the hundred best songs chosen for the caliph Harun al-Rashid by a group of musicians including the famous Ibrahim al-Mawsili, but this section occupies only about a third of the total work – the remainder being taken up with accounts of the caliphs and their descendants and with information on other songs and singers selected by the author himself. In addition to the basic information provided about the poets' and musicians' lives, the work provides details of many aspects of court and social life under the Umayyads and early 'Abbasids, and is rich in quotations from the works of earlier writers, many of which have now been lost; as such, it has continued to represent a treasure trove for literary historians of the period. Although, like many works of medieval Arabic *adab*, Abu al-Faraj's composition suffers from a tendency to digression, recurrent themes such as the permissibility of listening to music give the work a semblance of unity.

In addition to the *Kitab al-Aghani* for which he is renowned, Abu al-Faraj also composed a biographical work on the descendants of Abu Talib entitled *Maqatil al-Talibiyyin wa-Akhbaruhum*; an account of slave-girl poetesses entitled *al-Ima' al-Shawa'ir*, and a work on the condition of strangers entitled *Adab al-Ghuraba'*. A number of other works attributed to the author are now lost.

References

Kilpatrick (2002), Sawa (1989).

PAUL STARKEY

ISHAQ

The other son of Abraham/Ibrahim and held to be the 'father of the Jews' as Ishmael/Isma'il, Ibrahim's son by Hagar, is regarded as the 'father of the Arabs'.

See also: **Hagar; Ibrahim; Isma'il, son of Ibrahim,** *nabi*

ANDREW J. NEWMAN

ISHMAEL

See: **Isma'il, son of Ibrahim**

ISHRAQ

Arabic term for 'illumination', the poetic nom de plume of the Safavid philosopher Mir Damad and the name of the philosophical tradition founded by Shihab al-Din Suhrawardi. The illuminationist (*ishraqi*) tradition built upon his critique of Aristotelianism and advocated a more Neoplatonic method that considered philosophy to be more than just a rational inquiry. But the systematic aspects of illuminationism as expressed in commentaries on Suhrawardi's should not be neglected in favour of an emphasis on the 'mystical' and 'theosophical'. This tradition has dominated the history of philosophy in the Islamic East and inspired the creativity of later Islamic philosophy. Practitioners have fluctuated between the poles of reason and intuition, with the best thinkers in the tradition holding a mean.

The first major *ishraqi* thinker was Shams al-Din Muhammad Shahrazuri (d. after AD 1288), the first commentator on Suhrawardi's *Hikmat al-Ishraq* (*Philosophy of Illumination*). He wrote an illuminationist history of philosophy *Nuzhat al-Arwah* (*Comfort of Souls*) that in keeping with the holistic outlook of *ishraqi* philosophy combines a Greek genealogy of philosophy with a hermetic, Egyptian and Persian provenance. It was extremely influential in the Safavid period and the model for a later *ishraqi* history *Mahbub al-qulub* (*Beloved to the Hearts*) of Qutb al-Din Ashkiwari Lahiji (d. *c.* 1680). Shahrazuri also wrote an independent encyclopaedia *al-Shajara al-Ilahiyya* (*The Divine Tree*), which remains, like most *ishraqi* works, unedited. This text is divided into five treatises. The first on method and the division of the sciences reveals this text to be a unique composition in Islamic philosophy as it prefaces the logical section with the rather modern question of method. The second treatise on logic includes the peripatetic approach, fragments of Stoic logic, Suhrawardi's reform of logic and an extensive commentary on a key text on semantics, the *Isagoge* of Athir al-Din al-Abhari (d. AD 1264). The third treatise is on ethics, both private and public and statecraft and combines the Platonic tradition of al-Farabi's politics with *ishraqi* political theory and the work of Nasir al-Din al-Tusi. The fourth treatise on

physics summarises salient features of Avicenna's natural philosophy. The final treatise on metaphysics is the critical illuminationist culmination of the text. It upholds essentialism, the ontological status of the imaginal realm, the Platonic world of Forms, and the hierarchy of lights. One notices in Shahrazuri's work a trend that reappears continuously: an attempt at combining Avicennan doctrines with *ishraqi* ones in the desire to create a new philosophical synthesis, an endeavour that culminates in the work of the Safavid philosophers Mir Damad and his son-in-law Sayyid Ahmad 'Alawi (d. 1651), who wrote an *ishraqi* commentary on Avicenna entitled *Miftah al-Shifa'* (*Key to the Cure*).

The Jewish philosopher Sa'd ibn Mansur ibn Kammuna (d. AD 1284) was perhaps the most creative *ishraqi* thinker. He wrote a commentary on *al-Talwihat* (*Intimations*), Suhrawardi's key critique of Aristotelianism, as well as an independent work of great subtlety entitled *al-Jadid fi'l-Hikma* (*The New Philosophy*) or *al-Kashif* (*The Revealer*). Ibn Kammuna continued Suhrawardi's project in a rationalist direction and also wrote one of earliest *ishraqi* commentaries on Avicenna's *al-Isharat wa'l-Tanbihat*. Of particular doctrinal interest is his discussion of the nature of divine knowledge and his famous critique of the Avicennan proof for the existence of God as the Necessary Being which became known in the subsequent history of philosophical theology in Islam as Ibn Kammuna's objection (*shubhat Ibn Kammuna*).

The most famous *ishraqi* philosopher was Qutb al-Din Shirazi (d. AD 1311), a scientist trained at Maragha and possibly a Sufi who attempted to reconcile *ishraq* with the monistic tendencies of the metaphysics of the school of Ibn 'Arabi. His major encyclopaedia *Durrat al-Taj* (*The Glittering Crown*) was never edited fully. His commentary on *Philosophy of Illu-*

mination was also the most influential understanding and explanation of Suhrawardi's text. He made knowledge by presence the key doctrine of his psychology and epistemology and was also known to have accepted the possibility of metempsychosis in contra-distinction to most other Islamic philosophers.

The first Persian commentary on *Philosophy of Illumination* was the *Anvariyya* (*Treatise of Lights*) written by a sixteenth-century Sufi and philosopher in India, Muhammad Sharif Nizam al-Din Haravi. Composed in 1600, it includes a Persian translation of the text, comparisons with Sufi metaphysics, and interestingly engages *ishraq* with the philosophy of Advaita Vedanta, a project that was widely followed in seventeenth-century India especially in the salon of Mulli Muhammad Shafi'i Yazdi known as Danishmand Khan (d. 1670), the financial controller of the military in the reign of Awrangzeb.

Other illuminationists included: Ibn Abi Jumhur al-Ahsi'i (d. 1501), a Shi'i theologian whose work *al-Mujli* (*The Brilliant*) attempted a wide-ranging synthesis of Sufi metaphysics of Ibn 'Arabi, *ishraq* based on copious citations of Shahrazuri's *Divine Tree*, Avicennan philosophy and esoteric Shi'ism, that prefigures the system of Mulla Sadra; Jalal al-Din Davani (d. 1501), a philosopher of Shiraz who wrote an influential commentary on *Temples of Light* that was popular in Iran and India; his student Mahmud Nayrizi who emigrated to India and was the teacher of the famed Iranian *ishraqi* philosopher at the court of Akbar, Fathullah Shirazi (d. 1589); Ghiyath al-Din Mansur Dashtaki (d. 1541), another Shirazi philosopher and courtier; and Mir Damad (d. 1631), a most difficult philosopher of the time of Shah 'Abbas whose essentialism was the cornerstone of his metaphysics and his famed proof for the

creation of the world in the intermediate temporal realm of perpetuity (*huduth dahri*).

Apart from Haravi and Fathullah Shirazi, other prominent Iranian illuminationists in India included the Sufi and poet Muhammad Dihdar Sharazi (d. 1607), the Shi'i theologian Qadi Nurullah Shustari (d. 1610), the Zoroastrian priest Azar Kayvan, and the itinerant philosopher and mystic Mir Findiriski (d. *c.* 1631), a close associate of Mir Damad. *The Temples of Light* was an extremely influential work and Indian Islamic philosophers produced many commentaries upon it. *Ishraq* played a role in the political philosophy of Abu'l-Fazl (d. 1602) in the *Akbarnama* and *A'in-i Akbari*, portraying the Mughal Emperor Akbar (d. 1605) as a divine light determined to be a superior being by the Light of Lights and hence possessing the right to rule India. *Ishraq* also found its way into Indian Sufi texts. The influential *Hawd al-hayat* (*Pool of Life*), a Sufi 'yogic' text penned by the Shattari Sufi Shaykh Muhammad Ghawth Gwaliyarii (d. 1563) reveals the imprint of illuminationist ideas.

References

Corbin (1972: II), Hadot (1995), Haeri Yazdi (1992), Kuspinar (1996), Nasr and Leaman (1996: I, 465–96), Perlmann (1967–71), Rizvi (1975), Schmidtke (2000), Walbridge (1992).

SAJJAD H. RIZVI

ISLAM

'Submission', 'peace'. The third major Semitic faith itself as revealed from Allah via the Prophet Muhammad (d. AD 632) beginning AD 610 and named as such in Q.5:3. Islam accepts those named as such in the Old Testament, and others, including Jesus, as its own prophets. Also a reference to one of the three key aspects of the faith itself, along with *ihsan* and *iman*.

References

Waines (1995: 13–14, 103–4).

See also: **ihsan**; **iman**; 'Isa

ANDREW J. NEWMAN

ISLAM AND AFRICAN TRADITIONAL RELIGION

Islam, like Christianity, entered the continent of Africa as a monotheistic faith and a coherent system of religious belief and social organisation, which is based upon the acknowledgement of divine authority and power over the created order. The peoples of Africa were not without their own ancient belief systems, however, in which supernatural power and authority were recognised in the social and religious practices of what may conveniently be termed African traditional religion (ATR). The phrase 'African traditional religion' remains a useful umbrella term for those ancient but still resilient beliefs, which are held in widely separated tribal communities. ATR is not an institutional religion in the Western sense. Its adherents are not united across widely dispersed areas of the continent in a common set of religious beliefs, practices and social conventions. This said, it is also clear that many of these beliefs, practices and conventions have long since leapt across tribal boundaries. For the purposes of this entry it will be sufficient to raise questions about the developing relationships between those who eventually adopted Islam or Christianity (and who sought to commend one or the other of these essentially missionary systems of belief to their African neighbours) and those who continued to hold the ancient traditional African beliefs. Questions arise about the tensions in local African communities between the adherents of these distinct and even conflicting religious systems, each of which offers an independently coherent way of life in Africa. Of particular interest is the incidence of religious syncretism, by which the integrity of different belief systems appears to be compromised by local attempts to conflate them.

Many local deities are worshipped in African tribal communities, although belief in a Supreme God, who presides over the created universe, is widespread. Spirit forces influence the daily life of individuals and communities, sometimes benignly, sometimes less so. Because of this there is need for an intermediary, a shaman, one who can act as a mediator between the world of spirits and the world of human intercourse. Priests, whose office and authority are often hereditary, possess the sacred knowledge and magical powers which enable them to conduct appropriate religious ceremonies and rites of passage, in order to preside over worship, to appease offended deities, to make the necessary sacrifices, and to read the signs of the times for the benefit of the community they serve. John Mbiti has noted that ATR provides its followers with a sense of community and security. From this they derive a knowledge of their identity in communal rather than individual terms. Africans are, naturally, reluctant to abandon their ancient religious beliefs and customs when conversion to Islam or Christianity involves them with radical discontinuities. For this reason it often happens that traditional religious beliefs and customs continue after conversion to another religion does take place. Conversion to another religion always carries a risk that the old sense of security and community might be lost.

In African tribal communities every aspect of life is believed to be linked to the spiritual realm. The relationship between what is seen in this world and what is for the most part hidden beyond present experience is accepted so naturally that it can be difficult to find a word or phrase in some African languages which translates the word *religion* as it tends to be understood today in Western secular societies. Despite the dramatic social, political, and economic changes that have occurred in Africa in recent times, especially since the ending of European colonial rule, ATR continues to exercise a stabilising influence on community life in many parts of the continent. In the case of Islam it is pertinent to ask if Muslims have been more successful than Christians (for instance) in accommodating their beliefs and social organisation to those traditionally held by non-Muslim Africans. As in Islam, the Supreme Being is known in ATR by different names: 'the Wise One', 'He who is everywhere', 'He who sees and knows all', 'the Discerner of hearts', who 'sees both the inside and the outside of Man', 'He who roars so that all nations are struck with terror', 'the Owner of the Sky', 'the Unexplainable', 'He who is of Himself' (self-existent). The Supreme Being is neither a child nor an old man. He has neither wife nor children. He is the same today as He was yesterday. He has pity for his creatures and delivers them from danger, illness, pestilence, war. He answers their prayers for the fertility of the women, the cattle and the soil. He makes the seasons to follow in regular sequence so that the crops needed for food grow under the sun and rain. Disasters may be seen as punishment for human wickedness and disobedience. In ATR the sanctions of ancient religious beliefs regulate and help to preserve the organic unity of community life. It has been asserted that European ('Christian') ideas, introduced into West Africa by expatriates, threaten that indigenous stability by introducing individualism, ruthless competition, poverty, crimin-

ality, and a religion that militates against established beliefs and customs. By way of contrast, an African society is grounded in the common interest and sustained by cooperative effort. Everyone is provided with a home, a share of the available food and drink, and the other necessities of life. It has been argued (notably by E. W. Blyden) that the influence of Muslim teachers in West Africa has been demonstrably more salutary than that of Christian missionaries. His analysis is provocative but it still focuses attention on the developing relationship between Islam and ATR. Does Islam enable converts to retain their own cultural values and traditions without compromising their new beliefs? Does Christianity in contrast tend to disparage African beliefs and customs? Does Islam help to unify Africans and to conserve the best features of traditional religion? Is Christianity an alien disrupting influence? A case in point is polygamy. Christians condemn the practice. Islam presents the ideal of monogamy whilst (it may be thought) allowing for human need and fallibility. In the context of the rich diversity of West African life Blyden held that Islam had displaced or unsettled nothing as good as itself. It had established a vast total abstinence society throughout Central Africa. It had been a unifying factor, binding tribes together in one strong religious fraternity. It had fostered egalitarianism and industry. It had been responsible for such scholarship and learning as was to be found in West Africa.

References

Achebe (1964), Gray *et al.* (1978: 103–4, 334–53), Idowu (1962), Mbiti (1975).

See also: **'beautiful names of God'; Blyden, Edward Wilmot; Crowther, Samuel Ajayi**
EDWARD D. A. HULMES

ISLAM AND CHRISTIANITY IN WEST AFRICA

Christianity has a long history in Africa, going right back to New Testament times, to the Flight of the Holy Family into Egypt during the days of Herod and to the establishment of Christian communities in Ethiopia (Abyssinia). Christianity arrived in West Africa much later, however. The achievements of European and African Christians on the West African coast from the fifteenth to the eighteenth centuries is not easy to assess. Portuguese, Italian and German missionaries laboured to spread the Christian Gospel and to understand African beliefs, customs and ways of life. In the early sixteenth century the Oba of Benin sent an ambassador to Lisbon. The King of Portugal responded by sending Catholic missionaries to Benin. The earlier Catholic missions in Benin and Warri failed initially because of the stability of ancient African religious and cultural traditions. Another factor for the apparent failure was the fact that the European was unable to resist the deadly effects of tropical diseases in what was justifiably called 'the white man's grave'. A further inhibiting factor was the growing support given to the slave trade by nations that described themselves as Christian. A balanced account of the origins and development of the African slave trade will include mention of the groups of Muslims who brought non-Islamic slaves from the interior to the coast for the European slave-traders to transport by sea to the New World. The work of the Catholic Church throughout West Africa has continued to the present day. Protestant Christian missionaries began to arrive on the West African coast towards the end of the eighteenth century. The decision of Christian missionary groups to refrain from 'competition' in the same geographical areas did not entirely remove the impression that they were working for different ends and with far from complementary objectives. The abortive first Niger Expedition of 1841, undertaken by the Church Missionary Society (CMS), included S. A. Crowther. The expedition was a reconnaissance, intended to locate suitable places in the Niger area at which Anglican missions in Nigeria might be established. The Wesleyan Missionary Society, a committee of the English Methodist Conference, established a mission station at Badagry in Nigeria in 1842. The Foreign Mission Committee of the United Presbyterian Church of Scotland started a mission in Calabar in the south-eastern part of Nigeria in 1846 under the leadership of Hope Waddell. The Foreign Mission Board of the Southern Baptists Convention of the USA sent missionaries to Ijaye in 1853. The American Presbyterians had already assisted freed black American slaves to return to Liberia. One of their more prominent protégés was E. W. Blyden. The Société des Missions Africaines (SMA) brought Catholic missionaries to the scene in 1867. The Holy Ghost Fathers (the Spiritans) arrived in the eastern part of Nigeria to work among the Ibos in 1884. Today the Christian churches in West Africa are led by Africans.

Renewed by missionary zeal in the nineteenth century, both Christianity and Islam began to expand and to present a vigorous challenge to the animism which for centuries had guided the lives of the indigenous peoples of the region. They also presented a challenge to each other. Islam appeared to be in a better position to speak for indigenous African tradition and culture than Christianity. In the first place Islam did not suffer from the disadvantage of being identified as a culturally alien religion like Christianity. The latter had been brought into West Africa by Europeans, many (if not most) of whom had other reasons – chiefly economic – for exploiting the local populations. Further the Europeans, whether administrators, merchant venturers, or missionaries, were supported by British naval and military presence. By contrast the spread of Islam throughout West Africa had been a largely peaceful process, despite the occasional eruption of warring *jihad*. Some have taken the view that Christianity, unlike Islam, subjected the African to a position of cultural dependency and deprivation, and that even today Christianity has too 'white' a colouring. It has been suggested that there is another important difference between Islam and Christianity in the way in which the former threatens the traditional integrity and cohesion of Africa tribal societies less than the latter. Islam, in other words, is more easily assimilated, inculturated, to and in African society than Christianity, which preaches radically different ethical as well as theological norms.

References

Ajayi (1977), Ayandele (1966), Blyden (1967), Gray *et al.* (1978: 319–20), Sanneh (1983: 210–41), Trimingham (1962).

See also: **Crowther, Samuel Ajayi**

Edward D. A. Hulmes

ISLAM AND INDIAN RELIGIONS

Although Muslim armies conquered the Indian subcontinent early in Islamic history, in AD 711–12, formal caliphal authority over the region quickly lapsed until the twelfth century when Muslim armies conquered some northern areas, including Delhi, which commenced a retaking of the entire region. For the most part, however, the subcontinent was Islamised primarily by Sufis beginning in the fourteenth century. The latter's doctrines and practices, as they often incorporated those of existing Indian religious doctrines, such as pantheism, Hindu mysticism and yogic practices and emphasised the interiorisation of spirituality over conformity to the externals of Islamic doctrine and, especially, practice, generated opposition among traditional Muslim clerics. At Akbar's accession in the mid-sixteenth century, the Sufism of Ibn al-'Arabi (AD 1165–1240) was influential. Akbar's concessions to pantheism especially generated concern among the traditionalists. The rise of the Naqshbandi Sufism of Ahmad Sirhindi (d. 1624) and his students was predicated on a re-focus on *hadith* and the *shari'a*. Sirhindi attacked Akbar's experimentalism with Hindu, Jain and Buddhist ideas and attracted such support that Akbar's successors disassociated themselves from his religious policies. Nevertheless, Indian pantheism remained sufficiently attractive that by the eighteenth-century Indian Muslim scholars were actively seeking compromises between their tradition and traditional Indian spiritualism especially as mediated through Sufism. Shah Wali Allah (d. 1763), his sons and followers, although fiercely opposed to idolatry, nevertheless admitted the necessity of the law's mediation with local conditions, and permitted a reconciliation between aspects of indigenous Deobandi tradition and pantheism. Their teaching and their translations of basic Islamic texts into Persian and Urdu bridged the gulf between mysticism and tradition, facilitated the popularisation of the faith and engendered a widespread, popular, religious revival first on a regional and then international level. This eclecticism was, however, further changed by both the early nineteenth century arrival of Wahhabi tradition and Westernism generally and Christianity in particular. In the late nineteenth century, these ideas in turn fused into Ahmadi Islam, whose founder, claiming association with both Jesus and Krishna, proclaimed himself the *mahdi* who had returned to earth. There is no doubt that Islam's monotheism also facilitated both the rise of Sikhism and of an increasingly monotheistic Hindu discourse, a greater universalism in Hindu doctrine and practice and efforts at pro-selytisation, as well as some disaffection among Hindus with the caste system. In reality, none of India's 'original' religions or more recent arrivals has remained unchanged, in doctrine or practice, for its interactions with the others.

References

Schimmel (1980).

See also: **pantheism**

ANDREW J. NEWMAN

ISLAMIC ARISTOTELIANISM

Islamic Aristotelianism is a label that picks out a number of related philosophical movements that flowered at different times and places through the Islamic world.

The Christians studying philosophy in the realms conquered by the invading Muslim armies took Aristotle to be the greatest philosopher of all time. These scholars were not, on the whole, working with the Aristotelian corpus but with texts in Syriac descended from sixth-century Alexandrian summaries. It was not until after the 'Abbasids came to power in AD 750 that efforts were made to translate each of the books of the Aristotelian corpus into Arabic, efforts which went on with increasingly precise results over the next two and a half centuries. By the end of the tenth century AD, nearly the whole corpus had been translated, along with a great many commentaries of the peripatetic schools of late antiquity.

The celebrated al-Kindi (d. *c.* AD 866) carried on the intensely pious homage paid to Aristotle throughout the early period, but no systematic philosophical work based on the Aristotelian texts and deploying Aristotelian methods and principles was carried out. Al-Kindi's Aristotelianism lay more in establishing a programme for acquiring texts, some genuinely Aristotelian, others, like the *Theology of Aristotle*, in fact Neoplatonic. Still, his translation circle, and even more that of his contemporary, Hunayn ibn Ishaq (d. AD 873), contributed importantly to the number of Aristotelian texts available in Arabic.

It was not until Abu Nasr al-Farabi (d. AD 950) and his senior colleague Abu Bishr Matta (d. AD 940) began working to revive a textual study of the Aristotelian corpus in Baghdad in the early tenth century that a tradition arose which may be termed Aristotelian in the strictest sense. It depended upon and motivated the completion of an Arabic rendition of the corpus, and the translation from Greek into Arabic of a number of respected commentaries. Al-Farabi wrote a fascinating little text, *On the Appearance of Philosophy*, which told how the Alexandrian school (where, as far his tradition was concerned, Aristotle had died) transferred to Baghdad. According to this account, only one teacher with direct links to the tradition had been left; he taught two students, who in turn taught al-Farabi and Abu Bishr. The account is tendentious and ahistorical but serves to show that al-Farabi and Abu Bishr wanted to claim a direct link to Alexandrian Aristotelianism, a tradition which had nearly died out. Their textual Aristotelianism had a lasting influence on later Aristotelians.

Thirty years after al-Farabi had died, while the Baghdad school carried on his and Abu Bishr's work, the most influential philosopher in Islamic history was born in Bukhara: Ibn Sina (d. 1037). Ibn Sina always saw himself as a peripatetic whose philosophical work was an extension and repair of Aristotle's work, a repair he was entitled to make by virtue of his Intuition. He saw philosophy as a cumulative project, carried out over time by a number of philosophers. He did not claim for himself any direct link to a peripatetic tradition, he could do without such a link by virtue of, once again, his Intuition. But in the cumulative project to which Ibn Sina belonged, Aristotle had come closest to the truth, and his work should be the starting point. Ibn Sina said of the peripatetic tradition that:

> we acknowledge the merit of the most excellent of their predecessors [Aristotle] in being awake to that concerning which his masters and teachers were in deep sleep, in distinguishing the parts of the sciences one from another and in classifying them better than they, in perceiving the truth in many things ... This is the utmost that can be accomplished by a person who is first to try his hand at separating what lay confused and restoring what lay impaired, and it behoves his successors to gather the loose ends he left, and repair any breach they find in what he constructed ... But his successors were unable to free themselves of the imperfections of what they inherited from him, and they spent their lives in efforts to understand what he had accomplished best and in partisan adherence to some defective theories he originated.
>
> (Quoted in Gutas 1988: 45)

Ibn Sina attacked the Baghdad peripatetics as faulty Aristotelians for precisely these reasons, though he explicitly exempted al-Farabi from his attack, referring to him as 'the second teacher' (after Aristotle himself).

Ibn Sina abandoned textual study of Aristotle fairly early in his career, dealing rather with individual philosophical problems in an order which sometimes differed from the ordering of the Aristotelian corpus. He read his Aristotle through the eyes of later Neoplatonising commentators like Ammonius; further, he made Aristotle speak to the concerns of contemporary Muslim theology. The synthesis he came to may be called Avicennan Aristotelianism.

In the late tenth century a number of alumni of the Baghdad school went to Spain, establishing there a school implementing the methods and pursuing the goals of the Baghdad peripatetics. The school produced a few notable Aristotelians, but without doubt the greatest of the textual Aristotelians in the Islamic world was Ibn Rushd (d. AD 1198), one of the last in the Spanish line of Baghdad peripatetics. His project was to recover a true reading of the texts, now problematised by the massively popular Avicennan reading, but not even truly recovered by the people in his school who had gone before him: 'One of the worst things a scholar can do is to deviate from Aristotle's teaching and follow a path other than Aristotle's – this is what happened to al-Farabi in his logical texts, and to Avicenna in the physical and metaphysical sciences' (Averroes 1983: 175).

The Averroist reading had real impact on Jewish and Christian scholars of the Middle Ages, but had virtually no impact on Muslim writers until the seventeenth-century Isfahan school of philosophy, which also had an interest in textual Aristotelianism.

Much work remains to be done in charting the later fortunes of Arab Aristotelianism, which is unfortunate because it is undoubtedly the most interesting historical period of the movement. Post-Averroist Aristotelianism in the western regions of Islam continued to attempt literalist readings of the corpus for some years into the thirteenth century, but their efforts were soon swamped by the rise of Avicennan Aristotelianism, which became the standard form of Aristotelian philosophy in Arabic. The term *mashsha'un* (peripatetics) was used to refer to these post-Avicennan philosophers, and it is they who are the continuing representatives of one line of Aristotelianism down to the present day.

But there are other, more diffuse Aristotelianisms in Islam. Two groups read Ibn Sina's works closely, disagreeing with much of what he had written, but taking up what they thought promising or successful. These scholars, *ishraqi* philosophers on the one hand, and theologians on the other hand, do not represent Avicennan Aristotelianism, but they have explored and extended its component concepts and systems.

References

Averroes (1983), Corbin (1993), Gutas (1988: 159–76; 1999: 155–93), Peters (1968), Wisnovsky (2003).

TONY STREET

ISLAMIC BANKING

Islam formally prohibits the collection of usury/profit or interest (*riba*) from the loan of money or goods (Q.2:278). Although in the past individuals and banking institutions in Muslim countries have often given interest on deposits and received interest on loans, in recent decades a new wave of Islamic banks have appeared in the Middle East and there has also been a revival of concern for avoiding interest charges and payments and with other rudiments of a distinctly Islamic economic system.

References

Sadowski (1991: 229–32, 237–48).

ANDREW J. NEWMAN

ISLAMIC CIVILISATION

Deriving from Marshall Hodgson (d. 1968), the social and cultural complex stretching from North Africa as far east as the Pacific which is historically associated with Islam and Muslims both by Muslims and non-Muslims of this region.

References

Hodgson (1974: esp. 3–99).

ANDREW J. NEWMAN

ISLAMIC/ARABIC LOGIC

By the middle of the tenth century AD, the Arabic term *mantiq* had come to signify the Aristotelian tradition of logic to the exclusion of other traditions of distinguishing good from bad arguments. By that time, the whole of the *Organon* was available in Arabic translation, along with many commentaries, and many short introductions to logic on the whole like those of the later Alexandrian school. The two and a half centuries of translation (roughly, AD 750–1000) had seen an active assimilation of the Greek discipline into an Arabo-Islamic linguistic and cultural context.

The first really great logician writing in Arabic was working through – and making possible – the successful completion of this first period of assimilation: Abu Nasr al-Farabi (d. AD 950). It seems that al-Farabi's interests shifted as time went by, and it is not clear that all the things he was doing in logic cohere or are even mutually consistent. In any event, al-Farabi was concerned at one point in his life with showing that logic should find a place among the Islamic sciences, along with *fiqh* (jurisprudence), *kalam* (dialectical theology), and *nahw* (grammar); these Islamic sciences were acquiring their classical formulation during his lifetime. In fact, al-Farabi's senior colleague, Abu Bishr Matta (d. AD 940), had faced humiliation at the hands of a grammarian who was questioning precisely the utility of an independent science of logic. To this end al-Farabi wrote works which showed the antiquity of logic (*Kitab al-Huruf*), the lucidity of its technical terms (*al-Alfaz al-Musta'mala fi 'l-Mantiq*), and its complementarity with and utility for the other Islamic sciences (*al-Qiyas al-Saghir*).

Later scholars were to take up this Farabian task and bring it to a successful conclusion, among others Ibn Hazm (d. AD 1064), a Zahirite jurist in Spain, and Abu Hamid al-Ghazali (d. AD 1111), an extremely influential *shafi'ite* jurist in Iraq. Ghazali went so far as to preface his last great juridical *summa*, *The Distillation of the Principles of Jurisprudence*, with a treatise on logic, claiming that no one could truly cope with juristic reasoning without some knowledge of logic. From this point on (that is, from the early AD 1100s), logic was widely accepted as a part of the studies used to form a religious scholar. That said, other, more fideistic Muslim scholars continued to resist logic, and the following *fatwa* by Ibn Salah (d. AD 1245) is representative:

As far as logic is concerned, it is a means of access to philosophy. Now the access to something bad is also bad. Preoccupation with the study and teaching of logic has not been permitted by the law-giver ... The use of the terminology of logic in the investigation of religious law is despicable and one of the recently introduced follies ...

(Quoted in Goldziher 1981: 205)

For the most part, however, fideistic Muslims mainly condemned logic, at least formal logic, as merely laughable and boring (this from Ibn Taymiyya, d. 1328):

The validity of the form of the syllogism is irrefutable ... But it must be maintained that the numerous figures they have elaborated and the conditions they have stipulated for their validity are useless, tedious, and prolix. These resemble the flesh of a camel found on the summit of a mountain, the mountain is not easy to climb, nor the flesh plump enough to make it worth the hauling.

(Hallaq 1993: 141)

The second task al-Farabi undertook is one which mattered more and more for him as time went by. Al-Farabi realised that the short treatises on logic adopted from the Syriac Christians misrepresented in serious ways the logic that Aristotle had set out in his original texts, and al-Farabi wanted to recover this true, textual Aristotelian doctrine. They had, moreover, ignored many important parts of logic. Al-Farabi wrote close exegeses of the whole of the Organon, and began to explore a series of stratagems for making sense of the apparent inconsistencies in Aristotle's texts.

Ibn Sina (d. AD 1037), the most influential logician in the history of Islam, followed an entirely different approach to Aristotle's texts. Ibn Sina, by virtue of his doctrine of Intuition, considered himself in a position to judge and correct the philosophers who had gone before him, even Aristotle. This he did with, among other things, the Aristotelian modal syllogistic, of which he said: 'You should realise that most of what Aristotle's writings have to say about the modal mixes are tests, and are not genuine opinions – this will become obvious to you in a number of places' (Ibn Sina 1964: 204).

Ibn Sina then presented the system he thought Aristotle's writings should have been presenting. The difference between the Avicennan and the Farabian approaches to Aristotle's logic is that, whereas al-Farabi thought that with sufficient attention one could find a coherent system in Aristotle, Ibn Sina thought that he already had that system and used it to identify and clarify obscure parts of the text.

The history of logic in the realms of Islam after Ibn Sina is the history of the gradual conquest of the Avicennan system over the Farabian, which was studied in Baghdad down to sometime in the twelfth century, and in Spain until the early thirteenth century AD. The last of the great Farabian logicians was Ibn Rushd (d. AD 1198), who used Farabian distinctions with increasing subtlety to emerge with one of the most influential interpretations of Aristotle ever produced. It took him a number of attempts to achieve his best interpretation, but he said at one point of his efforts, when considering earlier attempts to make sense of the Aristotelian textual problems:

> These are all the doubts in this matter. They kept occurring to us even when we used to go along in this matter with our colleagues, in interpretations by virtue of which no solution to these doubts is clear. This has led me now – given my high opinion of Aristotle, and my belief that his theorisation is better than that of all other people – to scrutinise this question seriously and with great effort.
>
> (Averroes 1983: 181)

The other scholar to whom Ibn Rushd made constant reference was Ibn Sina, who had problematised the Aristotelian system in important ways and thereby determined the points in the system on which Ibn Rushd had to dwell longest. But no one really followed the insights of Ibn Rushd except for Jews and Christians in the Latin West, and by the end of the thirteenth century, Avicennan logic was all that mattered in the Islamic world.

One of the most neglected areas of Islamic studies is analysing the works of the philosophers writing under the influence of Ibn Sina. From a strictly formal point of view, these writers were probably the best logicians writing in Arabic. They responded to the Avicennan system by repairing and extending it in interesting ways. How long they went on doing so is a matter of debate: whether or not there was in any sense a demise of logic in the Arab world similar to the demise of medieval logic in the West is a question which at this stage we cannot answer.

References

Averroes (1983), Goldziher (1981), Gutas (1988: 159–76), Hallaq (1993), Lagerlund (2000), Lameer (1994).

TONY STREET

ISMA'IL IBN JA'FAR AL-SADIQ (d. AD 760)

Ja'far al-Sadiq had originally designated his eldest son, Isma'il, as his successor, but preferred the younger son, Musa al-Kazim, after learning of Isma'il's alleged excessive drinking habits. The accession of Musa as the seventh of the visible Shi'i Twelver Imams was generally accepted, but there were those who objected on the grounds that the infallibility of a designated imam is not prejudiced by a predilection for wine. Those who took this view remained loyal to Isma'il who, although he died in AD 760, some five years before the death of his father, was considered by the Seveners to be the legitimate seventh and Hidden Imam, al-mahdi ('the rightly guided one'). They were also known as Isma'ilis. This dispute about the imamate led to the division in Shi'i Islam between Sevener and Twelver (Ithna 'Ashari) believers. The latter accepted Musa al-Kazim as the seventh in line, followed by five more. The Twelver line ended with Muhammad al-Muntazar, whose 'disappearance' in AD 878 led to his designation as *al-mahdi*.

References

Hitti (1973: 439–43), Momen (1985: 34, 39–41, 165–6).

See also: **Fatimids, Isma'ilis/Batinism (al-Isma'iliyya/al-Batiniyya); Ja'far al-Sadiq, Muhammad al-Mahdi, Shi'ism.**

EDWARD D. A. HULMES

ISMA'IL, SON OF IBRAHIM

The son of Ibrahim by Hagar and held to be 'the father of the Arabs', including the Prophet himself, as Ibrahim's other son Isaac/Ishaq was that of the Jews. Muslims believe that Ibrahim later visited Isma'il and together they built the Ka'ba.

References

Hourani (1991: 150), Waines (1995: 13–14, 92).

See also: **Hagar, Ibrahim**

ANDREW J. NEWMAN

ISMA'ILISM/BATINISM (AL-ISMA'ILIYYA/ AL-BATINIYYA)

The Isma'ilis are an Islamic sect with their origins in Shi'ite doctrine. In many ways they are similar to the Twelver Shi'ite denomination in the sense that they conform to the general doctrines of the infallibility of their imam*s*, occultation/concealment (*ghayba*) and the messianic concept of *al-mahdi*. However they depart from mainstream Shi'ism in that they believe that the true successor of the sixth imam, Ja'far al-Sadiq (d. AD 765) was his elder son Isma'il (d. AD 760) and not Musa al-Kazim (d. AD 799), as the Twelvers believe. In the study of Islam and the Qur'an in particular, they believe that each exterior reality (*zahir*) has an esoteric internal aspect (*batin*) and vice versa, as well as each element of revelation (*tanzil*) having a hermeneutic and esoteric exegesis (*ta'wil*). In addition, Neoplatonism, astrological beliefs and superstitious ideas concerning the mystical meanings of numbers, particularly the number 7, also play a part in their doctrine. As such, the Isma'ilis believe Muhammad b. Isma'il to be the seventh 'executor' of the Prophet Muhammad and therefore, also a prophet, it is also for this reason that the Isma'ilis are also known as the Seveners (*al-sab'iyya*) in contrast to the Twelver Imamites. It is also worth mentioning that the Isma'ilis established their own state, commonly known as the Fatimid caliphate, which in its day rivalled that of the 'Abbasids. However, this power did not last long before schisms set in and the Isma'ilis have given rise to a number of others sects including the Qaramita, Musta'lians, Nizaris, Agha Khanis and Druzes. Today, Isma'ilis can be found in various parts of the world including the Middle East, Indian Subcontinent, East Africa, the USA and UK.

References

Daftary (1998: 50–8, 63–8), Hanafi (1980: 52–7), Netton (1997: 127–8), Tabataba'i (n.d.: 78–83).

See also: **Ithna'asharism (al-Ithna'ashariyya); Shi'ism; Sunnism**

GAVIN PICKEN

ISNAD, SANAD

The 'support' or chain of transmission which serves to authenticate the transmission of a *hadith* report. A typical report reads as follows (from al-Bukhari, *al-Sahih, Kitab al-Zakat*):

'Ali ibn al-Ja'd told us that Shuhba informed him saying that Mahbad ibn

Khalid said he heard Haritha ibn Wahb al-Khuza'i saying that he heard the Prophet saying, 'Give charity! A time will come when people will walk around with their charity and someone to whom it is offered will say, "If you had come yesterday, I would have taken it from you. Today, however, I have no need of it"'.

The *isnad* is expressed through the words of the author/compiler of the *hadith* collection, the 'us' in the first part of the above report. The path of transmission is then traced by using a variety of terms which are sometimes argued to suggest different modes of transmission; whether somebody 'was told', 'heard' or 'received on the authority of' is indicated by the use of different words. The rigorousness with which such differentiations were applied historically, however, is open to question.

Muslims paid a good deal of attention to the qualities of the *isnad*, using it to differentiate reliable and authentic reports from those less trustworthy.

References

Calder *et al.* (2003: 3.2).

See also: **Hadith, Technical Terminology of**
ANDREW RIPPIN

ISRA'

The 'Night Journey' from Mecca to Jerusalem experienced by the Prophet Muhammad, some time before the *hijra*, and referred to in Q.17:1–2. There, it is argued, he prayed with others of the prophets at the site of the ruined Temple and then ascended into Heaven itself and received certain commands from Allah. The Dome of the Rock, built in AD 691, stands over the site from which the ascension took place, with the al-Aqsa mosque nearby.

References

Waines (1995: 22–3).

See also: **al-Masjid al-Aqsa,** *mi'raj*
ANDREW J. NEWMAN

ISRAFIL

One of the four great angels, who will blow his trumpet at the end of time and thereby shatter all forms and creation.

References

Waines (1995: 130).

See also: **angels**
ANDREW J. NEWMAN

AL-ISTAKHRI, IBRAHIM IBN MUHAMMAD (d. *c.* AD 961)

Arab geographer, probably of Persian origin, who lived for a time in Baghdad. A member of the so-called 'Classical', or 'Balkhi' school of geographers writing in Arabic, few details are known of his life, and there is no agreement even on the extent of his own travels. His *Kitab al-Mamalik wa-al-Masalik* draws heavily on a book by Abu Zayd Ahmad al-Balkhi (died *c.* AD 934), now lost, to the extent that it is now impossible to evaluate the respective contribution of the two authors to the growth of the Islamic geographical tradition. It seems likely, however, that al-Balkhi's book was essentially a collection of maps, accompanied by a commentary, arranged according to twenty geographical divisions of the then Islamic world, and that this arrangement was taken over by al-Istakhri, who extended al-Balkhi's commentary, modifying it to reflect his own priorities and the perceived importance of the eastern regions of the Islamic world, particularly Persia, both men's work is based on a division of the world based on political regions (the *keshvars* of the Iranian tradition) rather than on the Ptolemean concept of 'climes'.

Al-Istakhri's work, which begins with a description of Arabia and describes the Islamic world from North Africa to India, was criticised by later authors, but was nonetheless extensively used by the later geographers of the 'Balkhi' school, including Ibn Hawqal, whom he is known to have met, and al-Muqaddasi.

References

de Goeje (1870), Miquel (1967–80).

PAUL STARKEY

ISTANBUL

Capital of the Ottoman Empire as Constantinople (AD 1453–1923), ancient Byzantium, and also called Qu(n)staniyya and many other honorific titles, now largest conurbation in Turkey and of great historical importance. Strictly, (I)Stamboul is a walled city on seven hills, between the Golden Horn, Sea of Marmara and the Wall of Theodosius.

Founded as a Greek colony (*c.* eighth century BC), part of the Persian Empire (512 BC) and later ruled by Alexander the Great. A free city under the Roman Republic, it became the ecclesiastical centre of Christendom under Constantine the Great (AD 324–37). The city was periodically besieged by Arabs, Persians, Bulgars and Russians (sixth to thirteenth centuries), then captured by Crusaders (AD 1203) until it was returned to Greeks (AD 1261) but was besieged by Mehmed II (1451–81) who declared Istanbul his capital (30 May 1453). The Ottoman Empire flourished from Istanbul until 1923 when the capital of the Turkish Republic moved to Ankara. Constantinople was renamed Istanbul in 1930.

In 1453 Aya Sofya became Mehmed II's Great Mosque. Other Byzantine churches were converted into mosques. Many Greek residents embraced Islam. People were compulsorily transferred from conquered cities in Rumeli, Armenia, Greece and Anatolia. According to the 1477 census, 60 per cent of Istanbul's inhabitants were Muslim, 21.5 per cent Greek Orthodox and 11 per cent Jews. Moriscos from al-Andalus stirred up anti-Christian feeling in Istanbul after 1570. Significantly, Ottoman Istanbul was to become a sacred Muslim city in character, with its traditional way of life orientated around the Great Mosque, where the ruler joined communal prayers and received petitions. In official documents the city was called 'the city full of Muslims', with its merchant class, craftsmen and military administrators. Yet the Islamic ideal of tolerance meant that non-Muslim and Muslim worked and lived alongside in this cosmopolitan city and all could consult a *qadi*. Religious buildings reinforced Istanbul's sacred status. The buildings that established the socio-economic life of Istanbul (markets, *khans*, caravanserai, harbour-quays, hospitals, workshops, bath, water supply, public welfare) began as *waqfs* of the Great Mosque and of elaborate *waqf*-complexes. Mehmed II developed Saray Burnu, building Topkapi Sarayi and Fatih Camii (1463–71) with appurtenances. To encourage settlement and prosperity, his pashas were each instructed (1459) to build an eponymous district (*nahiye*) based on a single nucleus around a complex (market, mosques [*mesjid* and *jami*], hospital, library, school, hospice, etc.) in various quarters (Mahmud Pasha, Murad Pasha, Davud Pasha, etc.), each complex endowed by *waqfs*. State regulations controlled building styles, cleanliness and street planning, and prescribed non-Muslim activities.

By the sixteenth century, old quarters were densely populated. More *meshids* and *jamis* built, notably complexes built between 1540 and 1588 for Sultan Suleyman the Magnificent (1520–66) by architect Sinan, including Suleymaniyye and the Kara Ahmet Pasa complex (1554) in Topkapi. In 1609 Sultan Ahmet I (1603–17) founded the Blue Mosque, one of two supreme imperial mosques of Istanbul.

Population increase within the city walls from the sixteenth century onwards led to overcrowding, increase in crime and water shortages. Many characters were attracted by charitable foundations and hospices: beggars, dervishes, mystics and bigoted preachers thrived. Regulations were rarely observed and the wooden houses in narrow streets were subject to fire damage and looting by Janissaries. Mosque complexes continued to be built in eighteenth century (Kosem Valide Sultan, Nur-I 'Othmaniyye complex, 1748–56), but there was a decline in investment in hospitals and hospices, with more spent on libraries and fountains. The Topkapi Palace houses important collections of manuscripts. In the twenty-first century, the tradition of scholarship continues in its universities (Istanbul, Marmara, Minar Sinan, Yildiz, Bosphorus), museums, archives and libraries. Istanbul, extending well beyond the original walled city, continues to be prosperous and is a focus for economic migration from Anatolia and Eastern Turkey.

References

Crane (2000), Mansel (1997), Raudvere (2002), White (2002).

JANET STARKEY

ITHNA'ASHARISM (AL-ITHNA'ASHARIYYA)

This is by far the largest Shi'ite denomination in term of numbers and they conform to the general nature of Shi'ite doctrine in terms of their belief in the infallibility of their imams (*'isma*), occultation/concealment (*ghayba*) and the messianic concept of *al-mahdi*. Their name al-Ithna'ashariyya literally means 'twelvers' in Arabic and is an indication of their belief in the twelve infallible imam*s*, which has caused them to also be known as Imamites (*al*-Imam*iyya*) and which in turn distinguishes them from the remainder of the Shi'ite subsects. As such, they believe that the 'Imamological' lineage continues after 'Ali (d. AD 661) and continues until the sixth imam, Ja'far al-Sadiq (d. AD 765), where they differ from the Isma'ilis in that the 'Twelvers' believe that the true successor of Ja'far was Musa al-Kazim (d. AD 799) and not his elder son Isma'il (d. AD 760). This 'lineage' continues until the twelfth imam Muhammad b. al-Hasan al-'Askari, who reportedly went voluntarily into concealment/occultation (*ghayba*), as such was no longer subject to mortality and will return as *al-mahdi* to right all wrongs. As with other major Shi'ite thought and practice the 'Twelvers' practice dissimulation (*taqiyya*), temporary marriage (*mut'a*), and have a unique jurisprudential (*fiqh*) system known as the Ja'fari school (*al-Madhhab al-Ja'fariyya*) affiliated with the sixth imam Ja'far al-Sadiq (d. AD 765). It is also worth mentioning that this form of Shi'ism was rather obscure until the advent of the Safavids, who adopted it as their state religion at the beginning of the sixteenth century and, hence, it flourished in Persia under their patronage. This situation has remained up to the present day until the Iranian revolution, when a new theocratic state was formed under the direction of Ayatallah Khumayni, was been instrumental in the revival of Ithna'asharism.

References

Hanafi (1980: 46–57), al-Johani (1999: 51–7), Netton (1997: 131), Tabataba'i (n.d.: 82–4, 173–217).

See also: **Shi'ism; Sunnism**

GAVIN PICKEN

IWAN

The *iwan* is one of the most versatile units in Islamic architecture particularly in Iran and central Asia. It is a vaulted or flat-roofed hall open on one side and closed on the other three. Although its origin has been traced to pre-Islamic Parthian and Sassanian palaces the form was fully absorbed by the twelfth century AD into the classic plan of an open court with an *iwan* centred on each side. Both the Friday Mosque of the tenth to thirteenth centuries and the Royal Mosque of Shah Abbas I (1587–1628) built between 1613 and 1630 in Isfahan, though very different in their scale and interpretation, are firmly based on this plan. The *iwan* also feature in secular buildings such as palaces and caravansarais.

References

Grabar (1990).

JENNIFER SCARCE

'IZRA'IL

One of the four great angels, and the Angel of Death referred to in Q.32:11.

See also:**angels**

ANDREW J. NEWMAN

J

AL-JABARTI, 'ABD AL-RAHMAN IBN HASAN (1753–1825)

Egyptian historian. Al-Jabarti was born into a religious and learned family in Egypt. After a traditional education he developed into a historian of Egypt. His main work is *'Aja'ib al-athar fi al-tarajim wal-akhbar*, a history of Egypt that covers the years 1688–1821. This is a partly traditional work containing biographical entries but it also has narrative sections. He wrote it in its final form in three volumes in 1805–6 and added a fourth volume for the years 1806–21 in which he attacked the regime of Muhammad 'Ali in Egypt. Publication of the book was banned and it was only in 1878 that the section dealing with the French occupation appeared. Soon after, the whole chronicle was published. Al-Jabarti's work provides a general and accurate picture of Egyptian history during the period and is the best source for the French occupation. He is writing as an insider looking at the effects of a foreign occupation on local society. He deplores the disturbing effects the French have while at the same time admiring several aspects of French civilisation.

References

Ayalon (1960).

DEREK HOPWOOD

JABIR IBN HAYYAN

Ibn al-Nadim mentions his name in *al-Fihirst* as Abu 'Abdallah al-Kufi al-Sufi. He is a representative of early Arabic alchemy. In the many works attributed to him, he is considered to be a student and the holder of the knowledge of Imam Ja'far al-Sadiq, father of Imam Isma'il of the Isma'ili Shi'ite sect. Jabir seems from Ibn al-Nadim's report to be a legendary character, who figures in many Shi'ite stories. However, Corbin mentions that the alchemist Aydamur al-Jildaki states that there was an alchemist called Jabir Ibn Hayyan, a follower of the sixth Imam and that he died in Tus in Khurasan in the year AD 815.

About 3,000 treatises are attributed to him. They are held to be encyclopaedias of all sorts of knowledge. Paul Kraus has studied them carefully and has come to the conclusion that they must have been written by different authors and that this process centres upon a primary work which was presumably started around ninth or tenth century and cannot be dated to the eighth century. However, Corbin does not rule out the possibility that this early central work could have received its subject-matter from an earlier source (eg. from Jabir's work).

The most important subject of the Jabirian corpus is his study on the science of the Balances. It concerns the relationships that exist between the manifest and the hidden in the body. The theme of *al-zahir* and *al-batin* (the exoteric and the esoteric) is one of the important themes in Isma'ili philosophy which flourished in the ninth and tenth century. Jabir also devoted a treatise entitled *The Book of the Glorious One* (*Kitab al-Majid*) to the Balance of the Letters. Here he elucidates three important letters: *'ayn, mim* and *sin*. *'ayn* symbolises the Imam 'Ali, the Silent One, *mim* symbolises the Prophet, *al-natiq*, the enunciator and *sin* symbolises the Hidden Imam.

References

Corbin (1986).

MAHA EL-KAISY FRIEMUTH

JABR

'Compulsion', 'determinism', as it relates to predestination, the notion that man has no free will independent of the Divine.

References

Watt (1973: 33, 148).

See also: **free will and predestination**

ANDREW J. NEWMAN

JACOB

See: **Ya'qub**

JA'FAR AL-SADIQ
(*c.* AD 700–65)

Known as *al-Sadiq* (the truthful one), he was the sixth in the line of Shi'i Twelver Imams. He was born *c.* AD 700, the eldest son of the fifth imam, Muhammad al-Baqir. During his lifetime he gained a reputation for learning and piety. He contributed to the collections of *hadith* and wrote a commentary on the Qur'an. He was revered as a teacher, whose pupils included the founders of two of the schools of Islamic jurisprudence (*fiqh*), Abu Hanifa and Malik ibn Anas. Both men are reported to have been members of his academic circle. Political turbulence marked his years as Imam. Under the Umayyads he enjoyed a relatively undisturbed existence in Medina. After the accession of the 'Abbasids attempts were made on his life. Called to Kufa to give an account of himself, he was sometimes kept in prison. Ja'far died, reportedly by poisoning at the hands of the second 'Abbasid caliph, al-Mansur, in AD 765.

References

Hourani (1991: 36, 40, 184), Momen (1985: 38–9).

See also: **Isma'il ibn Ja'far al-Sadiq; Muhammad al-Mahdi; Shi'ism**

EDWARD D. A. HULMES

JAHANGIR B. AKBAR
(r. 1605–27)

Mughal emperor, who in general continued his father's policies but who could not be unaffected by a revival of the influence of the traditionalist *'ulama'* who had been so condemnatory of his father's policies. Hence, there were bursts of intolerance against the Shi'ites, and stern measures against the Sikh *guru* Arjun, which laid the foundations for the strong hostility of the Sikhs to the Muslims which later contributed substantially to the decline of the Mughals. However, Jahangir regarded the Naqshbandi adherent and religious revivalist Ahmad Sirhindi as a pious fraud, and briefly imprisoned him. The Mughal Empire flourished under his just and benevolent rule; he was the best educated and most cultivated of his house, a great builder and layer-out of gardens, lover of nature and patron of miniature painting, whilst his own memoirs written in Persian, *Tuzuk*, are the equal of Babur's autobiography in literary style and historical interest.

References

Gibb and Bosworth (1960–2003), Richards (1993: 94–118).

C. E. BOSWORTH

JAHILIYYA

The abstract noun *al-jahiliya*, and its adjectival form *jahili*, are used by early Muslim writers to refer to the time before Islam came to the Arabian peninsula. However, it is more than merely an item of descriptive terminology: it is part of the religious message of Islam in which the time before Islam is contrasted (unfavourably) with the Islamic period. *Al-jahiliya* is normally translated as 'ignorance' (or more mildly, 'unawareness'). The time of the Jahiliyya was the time when the Arabs were ignorant or unaware of Allah's message of Islam. This period of ignorance came to an end with the beginning of Muhammad's prophetic mission in AD 610.

The term is used in the Qur'an four times. At Q.3:154, 'suspicions of the Jahiliyya' (*zann al-Jahiliyya*) disrupted the sleep of the hypocrites amongst the Muslim army. The reference is normally thought to refer to the hypocrites during the battle of Uhud. At Q.5:50, the 'judgement of the Jahiliyya' is mentioned as part of a rhetorical statement meaning 'Do you really wish to return to the judgement of the Jahiliyya?'. Q.33:33, in a statement addressed to the Prophet's wives, God pleas with them to stay at home and 'not to dress up as one did during the Jahiliyya' (*la tabarrijna tabarruj al-Jahiliyya*). Q.48:26 refers to the unbelievers who take on, in their hearts 'the zeal of the Jahiliyya' (*hamiyyat al-Jahiliyya*). These references presume knowledge on the reader's part of what is meant by the term Jahiliyya, and no explicit indication of its meaning is found in the Qur'an.

The ambiguous Qur'anic usage of Jahiliyya contrasts with the almost uniformly negative use of the term in *hadith* literature, where a standard *hadith* structure is often used: 'He who dies without doing "such and such", dies the death of the Jahiliyya'. The 'such and such' inserted can include 'dying without knowing an imam', 'dying separated from the rest of the Muslim community' and 'dying in battle supporting the blind' (probably meaning the morally blind).

The Jahiliyya, from the perspective of developed Muslim theology and law, was a period of unrelenting barbarism, only occasionally salvaged by the appearance of prophets (such as

Abraham, Shu'ayb, Hud and Salih), and the presence of 'devout monotheists' (*hunafa'*). Muslim writers often use the contrast between *jahiliyya* and *islam* to demonstrate the superiority of a Muslim belief or practice. The worship of idols is a practice associated with the Jahiliyya, Islam came to reform this heathen practice. More recently, Muslim writers have contrasted the treatment of women during the Jahiliyya (as chattels with no legal recognition) with the recognition they received during the early Muslim period. The Jahiliyya serves as a useful 'antithesis' to Islam, and a common rhetorical device whereby the glory of 'Islam' might be disassociated with the un-Islamic, barbaric past.

On occasions, elements of Jahili Arab culture are referred to without this pervasive opprobrium. This normally occurs in so-called 'profane' literature, such as poetry and studies of language. The famous poets of the Jahili Arabia are often cited as examples of the use of this or that obscure word. Poets such as al-Musayyab, Imru' al-Qays b. Hujr and Ibn Kami'a are cited in early sources as examples of the excellence of the Arabic language. However, the excellence of Jahili poetry is never allowed to compromise the perfection of the Arabic within the Qur'an. The Qur'an itself challenges the Jahili poets to 'produce a verse like' the Qur'an. The impossibility of the poets reproducing verses of the quality of those found in the sacred book of the Muslims forms part of that 'superiority polemic'. Jahili poetry was on occasions used to elucidate obscure and difficult Qur'anic expressions. These have been the principal uses of the concepts of *jahiliyya* and *jahili* in Muslim literature until the modern period. The extent to which the depictions of pre-Islamic society found in early Muslim literature might prove useful for the study of pre-Islamic Arabian culture has

been debated by Islamicists. Bravmann, and more recently Watt, use these early accounts in their presentations of the emergence of Islam. Wansborough, Hawting and Crone have, in different ways, cast doubts on the historical accuracy of the depictions of Jahili society.

In the modern period, the term Jahili has entered into the political lexicon. The eighteenth-century reformer Muhammad b. 'Abd al-Wahhab (d. 1792) had listed those elements of the Jahiliyya which he believed to be anathema to true Islam. This list included the worship of the pious dead and pleading to the dead for their intercession. By this, Muhammad b. 'Abd al-Wahhab loosened the concept of Jahiliyya away from a specific time period, and began to use it as a polemic device, whereby the contemporary 'unorthodox' practices might be condemned. The twentieth-century Egyptian activist Sayyid Qutb further abstracted the concept from any historical reference. Jahiliyya became, for Qutb, a reference to any society which failed to heed and conform to (his version of) the 'law of Islam'. Hence Western societies were unavoidably Jahili, as were many societies which claimed to be Muslim. A mere majority of citizens in a country being Muslim, or the leaders proclaiming themselves Muslim, was for Qutb insufficient. Government and society must actively implement Islam on its citizens to avoid being declared Jahili. Since, according to Qutb, the aim of the Prophet's mission was to eliminate the Jahiliyya (by force if necessary), true Muslims have the right, when fulfilling their duty to Islamise human society, to use force (such as paramilitary activity, often labelled 'terrorist' by opponents). Jahiliyya has, then, in the modern period, become an important part of Muslim political rhetoric.

References

Bamyeh (1999), Bravmann (1972), Gibb (1962), Hawting (1999), Kister (1980), Wansbrough (1977).

ROBERT GLEAVE

AL-JAHIM

'The burning'. That rank of Hell to which idolaters are consigned in the Qur'an (Q.5:10, Q.9:113, Q.22:51).

See also: **al-Nar; Sirat al-Jahim**

ANDREW J. NEWMAN

AL-JAHIZ, 'AMR IBN BAHR (*c.* AD 776/7–868/9).

'Abbasid prose writer, usually regarded as the leading exponent of medieval Arabic *adab* literature, which combined entertainment with an educative function. Born in Basra to a family of humble origins, his grandfather was probably an east African slave. Al-Jahiz (a nickname, meaning 'goggle-eyed', a reference to his alleged ugliness) received his early education in Basra, but moved to Baghdad in about AD 817, having attracted the attention of the caliph al-Ma'mun with a work on the imamate. He then spent a number of years in Baghdad, where he produced a large number of works on various topics under the patronage of officials including the vizier Ibn al-Zayyat and the chief *qadi* and Mu'tazilite spokesman Ahmad ibn Abi Du'ad. He returned to Basra for the last years of his life.

Al-Jahiz's prodigious output includes nearly 200 titles, of which around seventy-five survive in whole or in part. They embrace a multitude of themes and subject matter and range from short epistles to large-scale works in several volumes. Many reflect the theological and religious controversies of the day, in particular the arguments propounded by the 'rationalist' theological school of the Mu'tazilites. Among his most significant works are: (a) *Kitab al-Hayawanat*, a monumental work in seven volumes, comprising a collection of instructive and entertaining information about animals, with the purpose, it has been argued, of demonstrating man's unique status as a creature of free will; (b) *Kitab al-Bayan wa'l-Tabyin*, a popular treatise on rhetoric; (c) *Kitab al-Bukhala'*, his celebrated work on misers and mendicants; and (d) *Risalat al-Qiyan*, on singing girls. Literary value aside, many of his works are of interest for their reflection of social conditions not only in contemporary 'Abbasid society but also in preceding periods – *Risalat al-Qiyan*, with its fascinating observations on music, singing girls and relations between the sexes, being a particular case in point.

Al-Jahiz's style reflects his own omnivorous intellect, with a tendency to pile phrase upon phrase and to proceed by a process of 'train of thought' rather than strict logic. His language at times gives hints of colloquial Arabic constructions, and though his prose is marked by the parallelism characteristic of the *adab* genre, he generally avoids the more complex type of rhyming prose (*saj'*) employed by many other writers.

Though too much of an individualist to found a 'school', al-Jahiz nonetheless attracted numerous admirers among later writers and his reputation as the leading exponent of *adab* literature of the 'Abbasid period has survived until the present day.

References

Ashtiani *et al.* (1990: 78–95), Beeston (1980), Pellat (1953).

PAUL STARKEY

JAHM IBN SAFWAN
(d. AD 746)

One of the most significant theological thinkers at the end of the Umayyad period. He lived in Khurasan, at the eastern end of the Islamic world and was the intellectual force behind a rebellion against Umayyad rule in that part of the world. As a result of this he was captured and executed, for a combination of rebellion and unbelief. His theology stressed the absolute unity of God, so that God has no attributes, and the Qur'an has not always existed but is rather created, that human beings may have the impression of free will but ultimately all human actions are created by God, and that ultimately God alone exists, so that at the end of the world heaven and hell will cease to exist and, as before creation, only God will continue to exist. Qur'anic references to God's attributes and to heaven and hell, in his view, therefore needed to be interpreted allegorically.

References

Caspar (1998: Chapter 6), Watt (1998: Chapter 5).

HUGH GODDARD

JAHMISM (AL-JAHMIYYA)

An early theological school attributed to its founder Jahm b. Safwan (d. AD 746). The Jahmites were pure Jabrites (al-Jabriyya) believing in the concept of *jabr*, meaning that the human being has no actions of his own, doesn't have the ability to act on his own and that human 'actions' therefore, are only a metaphor for the actions of Allah. He concluded this from another principle which he held: that Allah can have no attribute, which also simultaneously exists in His creation and consequently, he denied that Allah is 'living' (*hayy*) and 'has knowledge' (*'Alim*), whereas he would confirm that Allah has 'ability' (*qadir*), acts (*fa'il*) and creates (*khaliq*). He also believed in the 'created' Qur'an, that Paradise and Hell were not eternal and that faith (*iman*) was a matter of the knowledge (*ma'rifa*) of Allah alone with no external manifestation as such (cf. Sunnism). The Jahmites (al-Jahmiyya) influenced others in the classical period but no longer exist in the modern era as an independent theological school.

References

al-Johani (1999: 1040–1), Netton (1997: 132–3), al-Shahrastani (2002: 67–9), Watt (2002: 143–8).

GAVIN PICKEN

JALALAYN

Jalalayn, 'the two Jalals', refers to the commentary on the Qur'an written by Jalal al-Din al-Mahalli (d. 1459) which was completed by Jalal al-Din al-Suyuti (d. 1505). The work focuses upon grammatical issues, which are presented succinctly in a manner appropriate to those who have a solid training in the subtleties of the Arabic language. Al-Suyuti also complied another work of exegesis, *al-Durr al-Manthur fi'l-Tafsir bi'l-Ma'thur*, (*Scattered Pearls in the Interpretation of the Qur'an by Tradition*), which is a vast compendium of older sources brought together complete with abbreviated *isnad*s in order to provide an overview of opinion. This latter work is more in keeping, in fact, with the overall character of al-Suyuti's work. He was a polymath whose compilations on many subjects clearly aimed to compile a sum of useful knowledge as it had been transmitted from the past. Much of the same material finds itself repeated in multiple works all by al-Suyuti, the apparent vast number of his books is exaggerated by the tendency also to create separate works on individual subjects which are also found in his larger compendia. He is also the author of the classic work on the Qur'anic 'sciences', *al-Itqan fi 'Ulum al-Qur'an*. Al-Mahalli, in contrast, was a significant scholar of his era who taught law and was respected for his knowledge of grammar, logic and theology. His legacy has perhaps been downplayed because of the significance of his student, al-Suyuti.

References

Gibb and Bosworth (1960–2003: IX, 913–16).

ANDREW RIPPIN

JAMI, 'ABD AL-RAHMAN (d. 1492)

A Naqshibandi Sufi who resided mainly in Herat, 'Abd al-Rahman Jami (1414–92) wrote many works in Persian and Arabic but is celebrated for presenting Ibn al-'Arabi's thought in a more comprehensible form in his *Risala fi'l-wujud*, and for his biography of Sufi mystics in *Nafahat al-uns*.

References

Heer (1979a, 1979b).

LLOYD RIDGEON

JAMI'AH

See: **mosque**

JANISSERIES

The Janisseries were the soldiers of the Ottoman Empire who were recruited mainly from the Balkans. They regarded Hajji Bektash their patron saint, and therefore the links with the Bektashiyya Sufi order were strong. The Janisseries were disbanded in 1826.

References

Goodwin (1994).

LLOYD RIDGEON

AL-JANNA

See: **Heaven**

JASAD

Body. According to Muslim theologians, divisible into parts, the smallest of which is called an atom, *jawhar*. The functioning of this *jasad* rests on the inherence of different accidents, *a'rad*, which initiate its activity. The atom and accidents can only exist together and therefore, their resurrection must include both *jasad* and soul. The Sufis, however, see *jasad* as a contrast to the soul, the weakness of which prevents people from recognising the reality of this world. It disturbs the soul from its true role, which is to meditate and attain the truth about God. The Muslim philosophers, too, consider the powers of the body as disturbing to the intellect, the highest power of the soul. The body, with its appetitive faculties, is the greatest obstacle to attaining knowledge and philosophy. Thus, a philosopher is one who is able to control the powers of his body and direct them towards the faculty of the theoretical intellect, the part of the intellect which is able to reach the highest knowledge. Therefore, for the Arab philosophers and for the Sufis, the nature of the afterlife can only be spiritual, because the deepest value of earthly life is to be able to reject the pleasure of the body and to purify the soul in order to enjoy the eternal world. Thus, humanity, in this view, is moving from the material to the spiritual, which is the nature of the divine world.

References

Arberry (1966), Leaman (1999).

MAHA EL-KAISY FRIEMUTH

JAWHAR

Substance. A concept which is used by the Muslim philosophers to signify the essence of a thing that differentiates it from others, while for the Muslim theologians, *Mutakallimin,* it means the atom, the smallest part of the body. Many theologians have referred to the atom also as a substance. The Mu'tazilite theologians, such as 'Abd al-Jabbar, agree with the Muslim philosophers in using the word *jawhar*, substance, to refer to the element of permanence, which relates things to their species and genus. Accidents, in contrast, exist only in a substance or atom and express the elements of change in it. This means that the changes which happen remain among the permanent features of the *jawhar*, substance. Though some accidents do not affect the body for long, the basic features of the body always stay the same. Thus *jawhar* here is used to refer to the atom or the body but at the same time it refers to the permanent element which keeps the body in the same state despite the changes which take place.

References

Peters (1976).

See also: **essence**

MAHA EL-KAISY FRIEMUTH

JENNÉ (DJENNÉ)

See: **Timbuktu**

JERUSALEM

Sacred to Islam, Judaism and Christianity. There are some 300 references to Jerusalem in the Bible of which around 75 per cent are found in the Hebrew of the Old Testament. For Islam, the city is of fundamental importance in relation to: the mission of the Prophet Muhammad; the early history of Islam; the relationship between Christianity and Islam from the arrival of Islam in Palestine until the present day; relations between Islam and Judaism; and how Muslims view their relations with the non-Muslim world in the changed atmosphere following the emergence of al-Qa'ida and of Usama bin Ladin.

Al-Quds is not mentioned by name in the Qur'an. Nonetheless, the reference in Q.17:1 to 'the furthermost mosque' (*al-Masjid al-Aqsa*) is usually understood as referring to Jerusalem. This reference itself explains the unique significance of Jerusalem for Muslims because the chapter in which it comes is entitled '*al-isra*", that is to say, the miraculous Night Journey of the Prophet Muhammad from Mecca to Jerusalem.

Related to the Night Journey is the miraculous ascent of the Prophet Muhammad to heaven (*al-mi'raj*). In Muslim belief, Muhammad ascended from what is now the Dome of the Rock to the seventh heaven where he came before the throne of Allah. This visit is commemorated on the night of 27 Rajab by readings and prayers similar to those marking the Prophet's birthday.

Jerusalem has a double significance in relation to prayer. On the return from the miraculous ascent to heaven, the Prophet is said to have received directives from Allah that defined the duty of prayer as being obligatory five times daily. In addition, the direction of prayer for Muslims was, initially, not towards Mecca but towards Jerusalem.

It is normally accepted that the subsequent change of the direction of prayer towards the Ka'ba in Mecca occurred soon after the *hijra* (Q.2:142–3).

Following the death of the Prophet, the Caliph 'Umar is said to have taken the surrender of the city from the Byzantines. One of the hills of Jerusalem, Mount Scopus, commemorates the story of his arrival (usually placed in either 637 or AD 638) since on this elevated point he is said to have exclaimed 'Allahu Akbar'. From this comes its Arabic name, 'Jabal Al-Mukabbir'.

Jerusalem is also of significance in relation to the *hajj*. Before Israel's occupation of Jerusalem in 1967, many Muslims would begin their pilgrimage by prayer at the Al-Aqsa Mosque. Numerous *hadiths* proclaim the benefits of prayer there: 'It is the land of the ingathering and aggregation, go to it and worship in it for one act of worship there is like a thousand acts of worship elsewhere'; 'Whoever goes on pilgrimage to the Jerusalem sanctuary and worships there for one and the same year shall be forgiven all his sins'.

When the caliphate became established in Damascus, Jerusalem was the site chosen for the first great purely Islamic buildings, during the time of the Caliph Abd al-Malik and of his son, Al-Walid (AD 685–715). The Holy Sanctuary (Al-Haram al-Sharif) was laid out in magnificent style, including the Dome of the Rock and the Al-Aqsa Mosque. The location coincides almost exactly with a site especially holy to Jews, the Temple Mount.

The founders of the Sanctuary found it perfectly natural to use Byzantine craftsmen in embellishing their structures. The Dome of the Rock in particular demonstrates the meeting point between Byzantine art and the nascent art of Islam, with a notable absence of representation of human or animal form.

Confrontation between Christianity and Islam found its most violent expression over Jerusalem. It was the fear that Jerusalem would be lost following the Byzantines' defeat at Manzikert in AD 1071 that led to the call for the First Crusade. Following the capture of Jerusalem by the crusaders in 1099, the Knights Templar had their headquarters in the Al-Aqsa Mosque. Until the taking of Constantinople by the Ottoman Turks in 1453 Jerusalem never ceased to occupy the mind of Christian Europe. Indeed, in the sixteenth century, the Emperor Charles V went on crusade to Tunis and Algiers with a view to regaining Jerusalem.

A different perspective on the significance of Jerusalem came to be of dominant importance with the growth of Zionist aspirations among both Christians and Jews, especially in the late nineteenth and early twentieth centuries (2 Sam. 5:7, Jerusalem is 'the stronghold of Zion').

Eventually, the joining of political and strategic considerations to sympathy for Jewish Zionists led to the promulgation of the Balfour Declaration in 1917. When this was incorporated in the League of Nations Mandate granted to Britain in 1922, the process began that led to the creation of the State of Israel in 1948. Israel proclaims Jerusalem to be its eternal and undivided capital.

Jerusalem in the 1970s assumed the greatest significance as the symbolic representation of the aspirations of Muslims. King Faysal b. Abd al-Aziz (assassinated 1975), in promoting the Islamic Conference, used the image of prayer to represent the aspiration of all Muslims to pray freely at al-Aqsa Mosque.

In late September 2000, Ariel Sharon, later to be Prime Minister of Israel, chose to visit the Haram with a considerable escort. When Palestinians protested, disturbances broke out and many Palestinians were killed by Israeli forces on succeeding days. In the following months violence escalated in the Palestinian territories and Israel attacked by land, sea and air.

On 11 September 2001, hijacked aircraft were used to attack targets in the USA. Usama bin Laden, in justifying these attacks, said that Americans would never be able to rest secure until there was freedom for Palestine, including Jerusalem.

References

Asali (1989), Cresswell (1932/40), Hamilton (1949), Richmond (1924).

LESLIE MCLOUGHLIN

JESUS

See: 'Isa

JEWS AND ISLAM

The position of Jews within the Islamic belief system should be distinguished from their position with the various Muslim empires and states. The Qur'an speaks of the 'the Children of Israel' (Banu Isra'il) as the nation to whom God sent the prophets of the past, and who, like most nations of the past, failed to recognise God's messengers, and were punished. It seems that the term Banu Isra'il refers at times to the Jews of the past (in the rarefied world of salvation history), and to the Jews contemporary to the collation of the Qur'an. The more common term for Jews (certainly in works of heresiography, history, theology and law) is *Yahud*, and this is also found in the Qur'an. This term is only used to describe the Jews of the time in the Qur'an. Medieval scholars might cite Qur'an or *hadith* references to the Banu Isra'il to illustrate a point concerning their contemporary Jews, but they would invariably refer to the Jews and Judaism using the terms *Yahud, Yahudii* and *Yahudiyya*.

In Muslim salvation history, the Jews are the community most favoured by God with visitations from his messengers. The Jewish/Hebrew prophets are mentioned extensively in the Qur'an, indeed the similarity of the Qur'anic narratives with the Jewish tradition when relating the actions of Abraham or Moses, for example, is clear. The Qur'an is informed by Jewish tradition, though it is not necessarily informed about Judaism more generally. The assertion that the Jews consider the Prophet Ezra ('Uzayr in the Qur'an) the 'son of God' in Q.9:30 perhaps derives from unorthodox Jewish sects combined with an attempt to condemn Jewish belief in the same terms as Christian beliefs concerning Jesus. Muslim commentators on the Qur'an utilised Jewish stories in their explanation and contextualisation of Qur'anic references to Hebrew prophets with stories of Jewish or Christian origin (termed 'Isra'iliyyat'). The term came to mean not merely Jewish or Christian stories, but also other fables often considered spurious by the *mufassirun*.

In terms of Islamic law, the Jews form a protected community (*ahl al-dhimma*) under Muslim rule, permitted to follow their own religion on provision of a 'head-tax' (*jizya*). This status distinguishes Jews and Christians (the 'people of the Book', *ahl al-kitab*) from other religious communities who are normally classed as *mushrikun*, or *kafirun*, the latter, strictly speaking, being not permitted to live within the 'abode of Islam'. This protected status is contingent on them abiding by the regulations imposed by the Muslim caliph, which in the literature of *fiqh*, included the prohibition on proselytising amongst the Muslims and restrictions on the construction of places of worship. In purity laws, there were debates concerning whether or not physical contact with Jews (like other nonMuslims) gave rise to a breach of the purity state (*tahara*), and there is mention of whether it is permitted to say 'Peace be with you' (*al-salam 'alaykum*) to Jews or Christians.

In Muslim theology, the Jews were viewed as one of the previous communities of God who, like the Christians, have subjected the teachings of their prophets to *tahrif* (alteration). Whilst the Torah is a revelatory book in origin, it has lost its authoritative status through corruption (intentional or otherwise) by the Jews. In this, once again, they share a characteristic with the Christians. There are *hadith* from the Prophet Muhammad which distinguish between the Jews and the Christians (the latter being more devout and closer to the Muslims), but in Muslim literature generally, the two communities share similar status, and similar fates in the afterlife. Specific anti-Jewish polemic (what might be termed anti-Semitism in a modern context) by Muslims was not so common. The characterisations of Jews as greedy, mean and dishonest were not prevalent elements of medieval Arabic literature. Such characterisations have appeared in modern Muslim literature, but this probably reflects the influence of Western European anti-Semitic stereotypes. Further, the Christian epithet of Jews as 'Christ-killers' was almost unknown amongst Muslims, since traditional Muslim theology did not recognise the death of Christ on the cross in the first place.

Exactly how these theoretical statements were realised in Muslim history is more difficult to establish. Important collections of Jewish documents, such as the Cairo Geniza unearthed in the late nineteenth century, give a portrayal of Jewish life under Muslim rule through time. The Jewish community described in the Geniza documents faced social pressures and often found it difficult to maintain the Jewish character of their community under Muslim dominance. However, there is ample evidence from elsewhere within the Muslim world of Jews participating in intellectual life and contributing to the development of the Islamic sciences. Jewish thinkers (writing in Arabic, or having their works translated into Arabic) were read and studied by Muslim scholars, and Jewish thought in Muslim lands was influenced by Muslim theological and philosophical developments. A well-known example of this phenomenon was Ibn Maymun (Moses Maimonides, d. AD 1204).

In the modern period, the establishment of the State of Israel in 1948 radically changed the attitude of many Muslims towards Jews. The injustice perceived to have been perpetrated by the newly established state against Palestinian Arabs, and the subsequent wars between Israel and her neighbours, has given rise to crude anti-Semitism (exemplified, for example, in newspaper cartoons) within Arab political rhetoric. Jews living in Muslim countries began to emigrate to Israel and the West to escape persecution from both individual Muslims and Arab governments. The trend has meant that the Jewish communities living under Muslim rule have been gradually reducing in number, and Arab society has lost an important part of its cultural capital. The inclusion of references to the spurious *Protocols of the Elders of Zion* in the footnotes of the writings of respected Muslim thinkers, such as Sayyid Qutb is but one indication of the paucity of serious modern Muslim discussion concerning the relationship between Islam and Judaism, and the position of Jews within an Islamic state.

References

Goitein (1967–93), Lewis (1984), Reif (2000), Wassertrom (1995).

ROBERT GLEAVE

JIBRIL

Or Jibra'il. Gabriel, one of the four great angels, and the Angel of Revelation.

References

Waines (1995).

See also: **angels**

ANDREW J. NEWMAN

JIDDAH

Also spelt Djudda, Jidda, Jeddah, Judda, once a modest Red Sea port on the Tihama plain of Makka Province (*mintaqa*), in central al-Hijaz, and now one of Saudi Arabia's most important cosmopolitan metropolises, located on trade and pilgrimage routes from Africa, the Mediterranean and the Indian Ocean, and gateway to Makka, 43.5 miles (70 kilometres) inland. The name probably derives from *jidda* (grandmother), as it is the supposed site of Eve's tomb, which was levelled in 1928 in deference to Wahhabi dislike of superstition. Though Jiddah existed in pre-Islamic times, it was established as the port for Muslim pilgrims in AD 646 by Caliph 'Uthman b. 'Affan (AD 644–56). There are no early Islamic buildings intact though two mosques were attributed to the second caliph 'Umar al-Khattab, and one to the Prophet, according to Nasir-e Khusraw (AD 1050).

By the tenth century, Jiddah was a fortified commercial centre, according to Ibn Hawqal and al-Maqdisi, trading with Egypt and the Yemen, with marvellous palaces and *khans* built by its Persian merchants, according to Ibn al-Mujawir in AD 1219 and al-Tujaybi in 1297. It was governed by a Makkan *sharif* who levied taxes on pilgrims and customs on goods into al-Hijaz: Saladin later abolished taxes on pilgrims, according to Ibn Jubayr who described the town in 1183.

After 1425 the Mamluks of Egypt controls Jiddah's prosperity, despite threats from the Portuguese especially 1516–17. Ottoman pashas enhanced its transit role from 1517 to the seventeenth century. It was ruled by the *sharifi* Hasanids in the seventeenth and eighteenth centuries, and from the late eighteenth century Ottoman control was challenged by the Wahhabis until 1813, when Muhammad 'Ali Pasha restored nominal Ottoman control. From 1840 it was self-governing under a *wali*; Turkish troops surrendered Jiddah to British naval forces in 1916. It was incorporated into the Kingdom of the Hijaz until 1925, when *sharifi* forces submitted to Al Sa'ud. The British recognised Sa'udi sovereignty over al-Hijaz and Najd through the Treaty of Jiddah (1927). Jiddah became part of Saudi Arabia from 1932 attracting Bukharis, Yamanis, Hadramis, Harb, Europeans and Sudanese. Its town wall was demolished in 1947 after which the city expanded rapidly as Sa'udi's diplomatic capital, its wealth additionally based on oil revenues. Two 'pilgrim towns' were built after 1950, modern highways link the port with the Islamic holy cities, whilst the King 'Abd al 'Aziz International Airport (opened 1981) is now the entry point for most Muslim pilgrims.

References

Burckhardt (1968: 9–11), King (1998: 32–51), Pesce (1974), Searight (2005: 109–116).

JANET STARKEY

JIHAD

The Arabic root from which the word *jihad* is derived carries the meaning of personal effort, of striving to the uttermost of one's ability, in response to the call of God to engage in the unremitting struggle against unbelievers and unbelief. At the same time it has to be recognised that war (Holy War) against unbelievers is sanctioned in the Qur'an. It is in this latter sense that the word *jihad* is commonly understood in the non-Islamic world. Muslims, however, insist that to think of *jihad* exclusively in these terms is to misinterpret a fundamentally *spiritual* Islamic concept. 'The holy war has ten parts: one is fighting the enemy of Islam, nine are fighting the self'. This gives rise to the two senses in which *jihad* is to be understood by Muslims. *The Greater Jihad* is that which involves every member of the Islamic community in the continuing struggle against any kind of infidelity to Islam. It calls for strenuous *personal* efforts to proclaim the message of Islam throughout the world. *The Lesser Jihad* is that which, though important on specific occasions involves armed struggle against those who traduce Islam or refuse to accept it. The two related meanings of *jihad* are illustrated in several passages in the Qur'an, for example in Q.2:190–4, Q.4:89, Q.9:20, 81, Q.22:78. Muslims, namely, those who lose their lives in the struggle against unbelievers 'in the Way of God' are known as *shuhada'* – martyrs (sing. *shahid*). In recent years, this honorific title has been accorded to those described as *mujahidin*, who have died in the armed struggle against the designated enemies of Islam in the Middle East and elsewhere, either in battle or as suicide bombers. They die believing that as martyrs they will go straight to Heaven and live in the presence of God, who rewards them for their fidelity and their sacrifice (Q.3:157–8). Not surprisingly, these *muja-hidin*, 'those who struggle to the utmost' in the service of Islam, are described as 'freedom fighters' or as 'terrorists', depending on the observer's point of view.

References

Ali (1968: 444 n.1270), Brown and Palmer (1987: 159–65), Momen (1985: 8, 180).

EDWARD D. A. HULMES

AL-JILANI, 'ABD AL-QADIR (d. AD 1166)

A Hanbali Sufi, born in Iran but active in his hospice in Baghdad, al-Jilani is considered the founder of the Qadiriyya Sufi order which came in to existence after his death. He espoused a 'sober' variety of Sufism that drew inspiration from Ibn al-Hanbal, and in which jurisprudence and mysticism complemented each other. He had forty-nine children and many disciples.

References

Al-Jilani (n.d.).

LLOYD RIDGEON

AL-JILI, 'ABD AL-KARIM (d. 1428)

A mystic who discussed the idea of the perfect man in his book *al-Insan al-kamil*, al-Jili continued the analysis of the various levels of existence, or divine manifestation, that had been elaborated by Ibn al-'Arabi.

References

Nicholson (1921).

LLOYD RIDGEON

JINAZA

See: **death and burial**

JINN

Beings created out of 'smokeless fire' (Q.55:15), where man was created from clay. Some were said to have accepted the revelation of the Prophet Muhammad. Also, the title of Q.72.

References

Rahman (1979: 34).

See also: **nubuwwa, tibb nabawi**

ANDREW J. NEWMAN

JINNAH, MUHAMMAD 'ALI (1876–1948)

First President of Pakistan, born in Karachi. Jinnah's father was an Isma'ili from the prosperous business Khoja community from Kathiawar. Educated in Karachi at the Sindh Madrasa al-Islam, then at the Mission School, Jinnah began studying in England in 1892; he qualified as a barrister and was called to the Bar in 1897. On his return from England he started a legal practice in India, then began a political career in 1906 as Private Secretary to the President of the All India Congress, which was emerging as the leading party for independence from Britain. In 1910 he was elected to the Imperial Legislative Council, where he supported Muslim interests, including the Waqf Validating Bill.

As early as 1913, Jinnah had joined the All India Muslim League. Through his efforts, the League and Congress Party formed the Lucknow Pact (1916), in which for the first time Congress recognised Muslim demands for a separate electorate. A charismatic and diplomatic national leader, Jinnah initially advocated Hindu–Muslim unity, but by 1929 he had abandoned the Indian National Congress to focus on an independent Muslim state. In 1934, having been elected President of the All India Muslim League, he called a meeting of its council to begin its transformation from a group of rich landlords and middle-class representatives to a League that represented the whole Muslim community of India.

After the collapse of hopes of Hindu–Muslim unity, Jinnah proposed an independent state for the Muslims of India in the Lahore Resolution (23 March 1940). A skilled negotiator who believed in non-violence and who based his struggle for the freedom of India and of the Muslims on constitutional lines (with landslide victories for the Muslim League in the 1945–6 elections), Jinnah was determined to realise his dream of a Muslim state of Pakistan through his scheme of partition. He united Indian Muslims under the Muslim League and stimulated their sense of nationhood. As its first governor general, he founded the Muslim state of Pakistan on 14 August 1947, despite civil strife, an unstable economy and millions of displaced refugees.

Jinnah acquired a reputation in his own lifetime as an honest, shrewd, focused and, at times, reticent leader, who never exceeded his powers as President of Pakistan, and was given the title Quaid-i-Azam (Supreme Leader) by the Muslims of India.

References

Bat (1998), Samad (1995).

PAUL STARKEY

JIZYA

This was the per-capita tax formerly paid by non-Muslims when living under the aegis of Islam. It was introduced by the Prophet Muhammad in the year AD 630–1. It required non-Muslim adult males to pay a form of poll tax on behalf of themselves and their families in order to enjoy the benefits of protected, 'client', status in an Islamic society. In that year, 'the year of delegations', *sanat al-wufud*, representatives of other tribal groups arrived in Madina to offer allegiance to Muhammad as leader of the Islamic community. Peace treaties were concluded with them. In return for the payment of 'compensation', *jizya*, individuals and groups were granted client status under the protection of Muslims. These non-Muslims became known as *ahl al-dhimma*, 'people under a covenant of protection'. For the most part they were also *ahl al-kitab*, 'people of the Book', who belonged to Judaism or Christianity, religions acknowledged along with Islam as being divinely revealed. With the growth and spread of Islam, pagans and other believers were brought under Islamic hegemony. Originally obliged to convert to Islam or to accept death, they were subsequently accommodated on the same terms as the people of the Book. The word *jizya* appears once in the Qur'an (Q.9:29), where it is given neither monetary value nor legal definition. The minimum annual payment was set at one *dinar*. According to Abu Hanifa (d. AD 798), children, females, monks, hermits, the poor and the infirm, were not required to pay the tax, although in practice it seldom amounted to much. Later it was levied by the Ottomans as a form of scutage, payable by non-Muslim subjects to secure exemption from military service. It was the readiness to pay the poll tax, however, which expressed a willingness on the part of those who did not accept Islam to abide by Islamic ideals and to refrain from impeding its progress. This, in theory at least, left non-Muslims free to live according to their own consciences, customs, and beliefs. They were not required to pay the obligatory poor tax (*zakat*) levied annually on Muslims. In recent times the level of tolerance extended to non-Muslims dwelling in some Islamic countries has been significantly restricted.

References

Hitti (1973: 119, 171, 320, 510).

See also: **kharaj**

EDWARD D. A. HULMES

JOB

See: **Ayyub**

JOHN

See: **Yahya (John the Baptist)**

JONAH

See: **Yunus**

JOSEPH

See: **Yusuf**

JUDGEMENT ON THE *YAWM AL-QIYAMA*

The Qur'an describes the day (Q.35:10, Q.70:5–44, Q.73:17–18, Q.75:6–12, 22–30, 99, Q.73:14, Q.82:17–19) as that whereon men are judged according to their deeds and belief and condemned to Heaven or Hell.

References

Waines (1995: 130).

See also: **'Isa; scales, judgement with; shafa'a; yawm al-qiyama**

ANDREW J. NEWMAN

AL-JUNAYD, ABU'L-QASIM MUHAMMAD (d. AD 910)

Recognised as one of the most influential of all Sufis. Residing mostly in Baghdad, he discussed mystical experience, namely annihilation of the individual's creaturely nature (*fana'*) and subsistence in the divine (*baqa'*). Yet the state of subsistence did not imply identity with the divine. His form of Sufism has often been considered 'sober' as opposed to the intoxicated variety. He was the spiritual guide of many famous Sufis, including Hallaj.

References

Abdel-Kader (1976).

LLOYD RIDGEON

JUNDISHAPUR

Also called Gondeshabur, Djundaysabur and, in Syrian, Beth-Lapat. The Sasanid Emperor Shapur I (AD 241–72) established the Academy of Jundishapur in a city (now the ruins of Shahabad near Ahwaz) in Khuzistan, south-west Iran, as a centre of learning to rival Antioch. Shapur nicknamed it Vehaz-Andrevi Shapur ('Shapur is better than Antioch')! Under the influence of his wife, Christian daughter of a Roman emperor, he aimed to integrate Sanskrit, Hebrew, Syriac and Greek knowledge into Persian and Arabic. Nestorians fled Edessa for Jundishapur under Shapur II in AD 489, bringing their heritage of Greek learning, particularly of medicine. By AD 529, Greek philosophers from Plato's Academy in Athens brought with them works of Aristotle, Plato, Euclid and Ptolemy, whilst Indian scholars contributed moral philosophy, mathematics with Hindi numerals, astronomy, and Sanskrit. Nestorian Christian Syriac-speaking scholars of Greek, Arabic and Pahlavi-speaking Muslim scholars

of Syriac translated Greek scientific, philosophical and medical texts, such as Hippocrates and Galen, into Syriac or Pahlavi. Jundishapur reached a peak as a centre of learning under Khusraw Anushirwan (AD 531–79).

Conquered by Muslims (AD 636) and by Abu Musa al-Ash'ari (AD 738), the Academy continued to flourish until the eleventh century. Its medical school, managed by Syrian Christians, treated illness by rational scientific methods. Notable Muslim scholars included, according to legend, the physician, Harith ibn Kalada, a contemporary of the Prophet. Hunayn ibn Ishaq, a foremost translator of medical and other texts in the 'House of Wisdom' in Baghdad studied medicine in Jundishapur. In AD 787 Jurjis Bukhtyishu was appointed Court Physician in Baghdad, whilst the 'Abbasid caliph Harun al-Rashid (d. AD 833) used the Academy as a model for his own hospital in Baghdad and employed physicians from the Masawayh family from Jundishapur. The Caliph al-Mamun (AD 813–33) transformed the caliphal library in Baghdad into the House of Wisdom in AD 830 along lines established at Jundishapur.

References

Brody (1955), Montgomery (2000), Nagamia (1998).

JANET STARKEY

AL-JUWAYNI, IMAM AL-HARAMAYN (AD 1028–85)

An important thinker of the Ash'ari school of Islamic theology, who is also significant as the teacher of al-Ghazali. He was born in Nishapur in Iran, and after studying and teaching there he spent four years in Mecca and Medina, which was the origin of his honorific title 'Imam of the Two Holy Places'. He was able to return to his hometown afterwards, however, and he taught there until his death. His works, especially *Kitab al-Irshad* (*The Book of Guidance*), demonstrate a somewhat greater openness to philosophy than was evident in the work of earlier Ash'ari theologians such as al-Baqillani, and a significant part of his legacy is the encouragement which he gave to his pupil al-Ghazali to study philosophy. In his political thought he adapted to the realities of power in his day, and gave more authority to the sultan (the de-facto military ruler) than had been suggested by al-Mawardi.

References

Lambton (1981: Chapter 7), Walker (2000), Watt (1985: Chapter 12).

HUGH GODDARD

K

KA'BA

The large cube of stone covered in a black cloth at the centre of Mecca's Grand Mosque, in which stands the Black Stone. Muslims pray toward the Ka'ba, as the site dedicated to the worship of Allah. The Ka'ba is surrounded by a precinct called the *haram* which, in fact, encompasses the city itself and which non-Muslims may not enter and in which the taking of life is forbidden. Tradition has it that Adam built the Ka'ba but beginning with the early caliphs its precincts were considerably enlarged and its structure greatly embellished.

References

Hourani (1991: 150), Waines (1995).

See also: **Adam.**

ANDREW J. NEWMAN

KABUL

National capital in eastern Afghanistan. On the Kabul River at 5,900 feet (1,800 metres) between the Asmai and Shir Dawaza mountains, Kabul controls routes across the Hindu Kush and south to India. The people are mainly Dari-speaking, with a large percentage of Pashtuns.

Kabul is mentioned in the Indian *Rigveda* (*c.* 1500 BC) and Buddhism flourished in Kabul valley which was also influenced by the Hindu Gandhara kingdom. During Mu'awiya's caliphate the governors of Sistan raided Kabul for slaves. The Governor of Khurasan sent expeditions to encourage Islam in Kabul, as did forces under al-Ma'mun in AD 795, but it was the Saffarids of Sistan who reinforced Islam around AD 870, followed by Islamisation by the Ghaznawids in the tenth century AD, when Kabul was an army depot for elephants and a prosperous commercial centre with a mixed Muslim and Indian population. Ibn Battuta described it as a village (AD 1333). In 1504 Babur (d. 1530) arrived from Transoxania and made Kabul his capital, where he established gardens and is buried. Kabul remained under Mughal control until 1738 when it was conquered by Nadir Shah of Iran, then by Ahmad Shah Durrani of Qandahar. The Durrani Empire made Kabul its capital from 1776. British forces were massacred there in 1842. When the Soviet Union invaded Afghanistan in 1979, Kabul disintegrated during guerrilla activity until the Soviets were replaced by the Taliban. The Taliban were overthrown with the help of American forces in 2002.

References

Griffin (2003), Rasanayagam (2003), Roy (1990).

JANET STARKEY

KAFFARA

Kaffara is derived from the same root as *kufr* or turning into infidelity. However, it seems to have the reverse action of turning something wrong into something correct In Islamic law it designates atonement or expiation. It usually consists of releasing a slave, fasting a number of days, or else feeding and clothing a certain number of poor people.

References

Ibn Manzur (n.d.).

MAWIL IZZI DIEN

AL-KAFI

This collection of *hadiths* from the Prophet Muhammad and the Twelve Imams is the earliest of the four authoritative Shi'i collections, and is often regarded as the most reliable. It was compiled by Abu Ja'far Muhammad b. Ya'qub b. Ishaq al-Kulini, or al-Kulayni (d. 939–40 or AD 940–1), who according to later reports spent twenty

years working on it. He completed it in Baghdad, where he spent the latter years of his life. This would have been during the Lesser Occultation of the Twelfth Imam, when he continued to communicate with his followers through his four agents, the *abwab*, the last of whom died in AD 941, and almost within living memory of the last imams themselves.

The *Kafi fi 'Ilm al-Din* (*The Sufficient concerning Knowledge of Religion*) is divided into two parts and arranged into thirty-one books, *kutub*, starting with the priority of knowledge and the oneness of God, and moving through the various topics of theology, the principle observances of Islam and questions of law and livelihood, to issues of inheritance and oaths. The two overall parts, *usul*, the fundamentals of religion (eight books), and *furu'*, the branches of practice (twenty-six books), are supplemented by a further part entitled *al-Rawda* (*The Garden*), which contains miscellaneous letters and speeches of imams, and prayers and *hadiths* in praise of the Prophet's family and their supporters.

In respect of its overall structure, the *Kafi* is not dissimilar from many other books of *hadith*. In fact, its organisation of sayings according to subject matter, allowing easy access to their theological and practical teachings, suggests direct comparison with the Sunni compilations of al-Bukhari and Muslim. But its distinctive features are, of course, the inclusion of *hadiths* from the imams as well as the Prophet, and also books and sections devoted to specifically Shi'i matters. Thus, among the first books on the fundamentals of religion is a section on the history of the imams, *abwab al-tarikh*, and later there are sections on *ziyarat*, visits to Shi'i holy places, including the mosque of Ghadir Khumm where Shi'is believe the Prophet designated 'Ali as his successor, and on *mut'a*, the distinctive form of temporary marriage. These sections make explicit the importance of the imams and the authority of their examples and teachings.

Al-Kulini explains his intention in making this compilation in the introduction (a feature in which the *Kafi* can be compared to the *sahih* of Muslim b. Hajjaj), where after emphasising the importance of the imams, he argues that everyone must have a guide who will dispel their ignorance, viz., this book, which will present the teachings of the imams. Referring to the method he has employed in the compilation, he briefly explains that he has preferred to leave contradictory sayings to the judgement of the imams themselves and simply to accept *hadiths* on the basis that 'Whatever you have accepted in the principle of obeying, *al-taslim*, is sufficient for you'. Thus, he selects *hadiths* that are most apposite to the purposes of each chapter, and lists them in order of the most to the least relevant.

The *Kafi* was not immediately accorded any special status among Shi'is, and al-Kulini was not remembered for anything significant. But in the early eleventh century AD Shi'i authors began to show awareness of its merits, and it was gradually admitted to its position of pre-eminence. In Safavid Persia its authority was secured, and a succession of commentaries, studies and translations were composed on it. Its central importance for Shi'i Muslims remains undiminished.

There are numerous editions of the *Kafi*. An English translation based on the Tehran 1955–8 edition begun in Tehran in 1978 is in progress.

DAVID THOMAS

KAFUR

A well in Paradise.

ANDREW J. NEWMAN

AL-KALABADHI (d. 990 or AD 994)

The Sufi author of *Kitab al-ta'arruf li-madhhab ahl-al-tasawwuf* (*Introduction to the School of the Sufis*) in which an 'orthodox' interpretation of Sufism is offered, including an explanation of Sufi stations, Sufi terms, and mystical experience. He states that some Sufis have divulged secrets to the public, which has caused some problems (a reference perhaps to Hallaj, and Sufis of a similar nature).

References

Arberry (1935).

LLOYD RIDGEON

KALAM AND THE *MUTAKALLIMUN*

'Speech' and the term used to refer to Islamic scholastic theology, theologians being called *mutakallimun*. Following the death of the prophet in AD 632, the community sought to preserve the established body of precedents as the basis for the formulation of legal decisions. The expansion of the realm of Islam, however, and the requirement for formulating decisions on an ever widening range of issues, for which there were apparently no available precedents, coupled with continuing Shi'i challenges to the legitimacy of Umayyad and 'Abbasid rule, encouraged the collection of a wide body of prophetic traditions. Hence the term 'traditionalist' being applied to, those who collected, and sought primary recourse to these texts in the jurisprudential process. Philosophical, or rationalist, approaches to the law, based on subjecting the revealed texts to argument and reasoning or even the formulation of decisions based entirely on recourse to reason without reference to the Islamic revelation, promised a middle position between the claims of the Umayyads and certain Shi'i elements. In the early ninth century the 'Abbasids accepted elements of Mu'tazilite discourse, especially the createdness of the Qur'an and free will, the latter in opposition to traditionalist arguments for predestination which lent legitimacy to Umayyad rule, to bolster their own authority. Although al-Ash'ari eventually abandoned his early philosophical leanings and rationalist discourse for the traditionalism of Ahmad ibn Hanbal, he applied aspects of Mu'tazilite argumentation while acknowledging the ultimate transcendence of the Divine. His discourse was initially opposed by the Sunni Saljuqs but, as the ideological battle with the Shi'i Fatimids intensified, Ash'arism became the preferred theological discourse among Sunni theologians and the basis of opposition to forms of philosophical reasoning.

References

Fakhry (1983), Rahman (1979: 85–6), Watt (1973).

See also: *'adl*; **anthropomorphism; attributes of God;** *bila kayfa*; **free will and predestination;** *mihna*

ANDREW J. NEWMAN

AL-KALAM, 'ILM

Islamic scholastic theology, in distinction to that tradition which emphasised recourse only to the revealed and literally accepted texts of the faith.

References

Rahman (1979: 85–99).

See also: **kalam and the** *mutakallimun*

ANDREW J. NEWMAN

KALILA WA DIMNA

The collection of animal fables that features the two jackals Kalila and Dimna is among the most popular in Arabic or any other literature. It was translated in the eighth century by the Persian convert to Islam 'Abdallah Ibn al-Muqaffa' (d. *c.* AD 756), and quickly became a staple of storytelling and reading. The fables were, in fact, retold so frequently that it is no longer possible to identify the original core with any great certainty, nor even to restore the translator's original Arabic wording or style. Even so, Ibn al-Muqaffa' is recognised as the main channel through which the collection became the cherished possession of the Islamic world, from where it was introduced to audiences further afield.

These stories of the two jackal brothers originated in India sometime before AD 300. Their first author is unknown, though they were attributed to a sage named Bidpai. In the sixth century, and before AD 570 they were translated from Sanskrit into Pahlavi for the Sasanian king Khusraw I, Anushirwan (AD 531–79), by his physician Burzoe. And it is this version, which slightly expanded the Sanskrit original with stories drawn from other Indian sources, that Ibn al-Muqaffa' translated into Arabic. The latter, in turn, made his own additions.

Since it is not possible to trace back the evolution of this Arabic work much before the thirteenth century, when the earliest extant manuscripts of it were copied, it is difficult to recover this original translation of Ibn al-Muqaffa' with any certainty (though surviving translations from his work into other languages which predate these direct sources offer some help in this). The huge discrepancies between the manuscripts indicate that later authors felt at liberty not only to remove stories from the original or add to it, but also to change its wording at will. Even so, it seems clear that Ibn al-Muqaffaʻ followed his Pahlavi source in presenting a number of frame stories into which are inserted substories and even sub-substories. He prefaced these with his own introduction, which he made to resemble his source by including his own substories, and also with an account of how the physician Burzoe obtained the stories from India in the first place.

This introduction contains praise for the fables as sources of wisdom and instruction, and advises that they must be read thoroughly and also reflected upon if they are not to remain like nuts in their shells. A further hint of their deeper significance follows after the account of Burzoe's journey to India in the third preparatory chapter. Here, Burzoe speaks for himself about his inquiries into forms of religion and the disappointment these brought him, resulting in his decision to live a life of asceticism and preparation for what may come without confessing any faith. The various religions, he bitterly observes, are made up of those born into them, those forced into them, and those who gain material profit from them. In other words, any person capable of reflection must remain sceptical and look to his own resources for self-improvement and reassurance about the ills of life.

This remarkable passage may be one of the main additions which Ibn al-Muqaffaʻ made in his translation. If so, it attests to his dangerously independent spirit, and points to the significance of what he has already said about the deeper purpose of the tales. They provide for the religious sceptic guidance that is founded on no higher authority than their power to evoke assent by unaided reason. This suggests a form of atheistic humanism. However, one should admit a note of caution, since there is no clear indication that this rejection of confessional surrender came from Ibn al-Muqaffaʻ, or is Islamic in any obvious way, so it may have been present in his source.

The tales that form the main body of *Kalila wa Dimna* were probably organised into the ten frame stories of the Pahlavi original, together with four others, two of which can be traced to identifiable Indian sources. It is possible that Ibn al-Muqaffaʻ added a substantial part of the conclusion of the first of these stories, 'The Lion and the Ox', in which the jackal Dimna is tried and punished for his treachery.

Each of these frame stories is introduced by an Indian king requesting Bidpai the sage to tell him a story that contains a particular moral or political lesson, about such matters as a liar turning two friends into enemies, securing and maintaining friendship, action without prior reflection, and so on. In each case the philosopher gives his lesson through stories which themselves contain all the substories that give the book its charm, telling of animals that act out the intended lesson and leaving the significance unspoken. The tales operate on a number of levels, offering both delight in the multitude of creatures that combine their typical animal traits with human characteristics (an anticipation of Chaucer), and also the satisfaction of deriving a moral for oneself. It is not surprising that they were retold so frequently and remoulded in the process, nor that they provided one of the most fertile sources for illustrators in many parts of the Islamic world.

Editions of *Kalila wa Dimna* are frequently affected by editorial partiality. Those of Cheikho (1905), and Husayn and ʻAzzam (1941), are based upon the soundest principles. Miquel (1957) offers a complete French translation of the latter. In English, Atil (1981) and Wood (1980) retell selected tales.

DAVID THOMAS

KANEM-BORNO, ISLAM IN

Kanem-Borno was one of the most powerful and enduring empires in the central Sudan. The kingdom of Kanem lay to the east of Lake Chad, that of Borno lay to the west and south. The territories of the former empire of Kanem-Borno are now part of the Republics of Chad, Niger and the north-western regions of the Republic of Nigeria. Tradition holds that Kanem was founded by the Arab, Sayf ibn dhi Yazan, who gained control of a group of Negro nomads called the Magumi. He founded a dynasty that was to rule Kanem-Borno until 1846, thus making it one of the longest lasting dynasties in world history. The dynasty was known as the Sefawa after his first name. In the ninth century AD the Sefawa migrated to Kanem from the Sahara. The empire of Kanem-Borno developed independently of the empires of Ghana and Mali. One of the reasons for this was probably the relatively isolated position of the original homeland of Kanem, which was separated from the lands to the south and west by barren desert. By the eleventh century AD, Sefawa rulers had embraced Islam and had begun to extend their control to neighbouring Borno. The rulers of Kanem were forced to move their capital (Birni Gazargamo) into Borno in the late fourteenth century after attacks by the *Bulalas*. Borno gradually emerged as the centre of a reinvigorated political entity, with Kanem as a protectorate. Originally the people were nomads, with no fixed capital or towns. The state was a confederation of nomads loosely brought together under an acknowledged ruling group. By the late twelfth century AD, Islam had become the state religion. By the middle of the thirteenth century a hostel had been built in Cairo for students from Kanem. The developing political system was essentially feudal, with a complicated and hierarchical administration at the head of which was the *mai*, the ruling king, whose claims to divinity were acknowledged. From the fifteenth century, the influence of Kanem-Borno extended north to Fezzan in Libya, west into Hausaland, and to Bagirmi in east. The empire reached its apogee under Mai Idris Alawma during the sixteenth century. In its heyday it grew prosperous and powerful on the basis of the trans-Saharan trade. The wealth of Borno came principally from the export of African slaves. The empire of Kanem-Borno was constantly challenged by internal and external threats, the most significant of which was the *jihad* (1804–11) of the Fulani scholar and mystic, Shehu Usuman dan Fodio. In 1808, the empire's capital was destroyed; the ancient dynasty of the Sefawa deposed. Borno was subdued by warlord Rabbeh in 1893. He was killed by French troops in 1900. From 1901, as part of the continuing and aptly named 'scramble for Africa', the lands of the former empire were absorbed in the British, French and German colonies which were to become the states of Niger, Cameroon and Nigeria. In the case of the latter, the surviving emirates recognised by the British in their policy of indirect rule now form Borno state in the north-western parts of modern Nigeria.

References

Cohen (1967), Davidson (1977: 97–105), Hiskett (1994: 92–3).

See also: **Fodio, Shehu Usuman dan; *jihad*; slavery and the slave trade in West Africa.**

EDWARD D. A. HULMES

KARACHI

Former national capital of the Islamic Republic of Pakistan and its largest commercial and banking centre, capital of Sind Province, southern Pakistan, its largest seaport on the Arabian Sea near the Indus River Delta, and outlet for landlocked Afghanistan. Built by Sir Charles Napier to serve the Indus River Valley and the Pundhab from 1843 and improved in 1854 and 1873, based on a Sind fishing village from 1725. The *amir* of Talpur seized Karachi from the Khan of Kalat in 1795. After 1861, a railway connected the city with Kotri and in 1878 with the Pandhab. Over 50 per cent are Muslim migrants from India, and the city expanding tenfold 1947–72. Cultural and social activities are essentially Muslim in character.

References

Schubel (1993).

JANET STARKEY

KARBALA', BATTLE OF

The brief encounter at Karbala', some 25 miles (40 kilometres) to the northwest of Kufa in Iraq, took place on 10 Muharram AD 681. It was fought out between a force of 14,000 men, sent by the Umayyad Caliph Yazid I, and a small number of people, including members of his family, led by al-Husayn, the grandson of the Prophet Muhammad. al-Husayn's party was neither prepared for, nor looking for, a military confrontation. He was on his way to Kufa in response to an appeal from the Iraqis there that he should act swiftly to succeed the Caliph Mu'awiya, who had died a year earlier. Refusing to accept a demand that he accept the legitimacy of Yazid's succession in the caliphate, and refusing to surrender, al-Husayn was killed. After taking thirty wounds from swords, lances and arrows, he fell and was trampled under the feet of enemy horses. He had attempted to negotiate a withdrawal for the members of his small group but this was refused. Nor were they allowed access to water. Almost all his company perished in the conflict. His body was decapitated. The head was sent to Yazid in Damascus, but given back to al-Husayn's sister, who returned it to Karbala'. There it was reunited with the rest of the body and placed in the shrine that continues to attract Muslim pilgrims, who honour al-Husayn as 'lord of the [Shi'i] martyrs'. For Shi'i Muslims the words 'The Day of Karbala' (*yawm Karbala'*) became a battle cry that announced vengeance on the enemies of al-Husayn.

References

Hitti (1973: 190–1), Momen (1985: 35, 118).

See also: **al-Hasan, ibn 'Ali ibn Abi Talib; al-Husayn, ibn 'Ali ibn Abi Talib; Mu'awiya b. Abi Sufyan;, Shi'ism**

EDWARD D. A. HULMES

KASB/IKTISAB

'Earning profit', in the positive material sense but also in the sense of any good or evil a person obtains as a result of his actions. Also a term used by al-Ash'ari in discussing the omnipotence of Allah and free will, whereby man 'acquires' voluntary acts from Allah for which acts, therefore, man is accountable, as opposed to such involuntary acts as shivering from the cold, also 'acquired' from Allah.

References

Waines (1995: 121–4).

ANDREW J. NEWMAN]

KATIB ÇELEBI (MUSTAFA B. 'ABDULLAH OR HACI HALIFA) (1609–57)

Turkish officer, scholar and writer. Born in Constantinople (Istanbul). Katib Çelebi's early career was spent as an army officer but on receiving an inheritance he abandoned his original profession to devote himself to study and writing. Among the most prolific authors of the Ottoman Empire in the seventeenth century, he produced works in both Turkish and Arabic on history, geography, astronomy, theology and law, as well as some inferior poetry. A serious and even-tempered man, he seems to have had little time for humour or exaggeration, and the simple, straightforward prose style of his works reflects this temperament.

Among his most important works, which are still consulted today for the valuable information they contain, are:

1. a bibliographical dictionary of Ottoman literature entitled *Kashf al-Zunun 'an Asami al-Kutub wa'l-Funun*, written in Arabic this work lists some 14,500 titles in alphabetical order and is particularly valuable for its inclusion of long extracts from works that have not otherwise survived;
2. an incomplete cosmography in Turkish entitled *Cihannuma:* this work exists in two versions, the second being based partly on writers in Latin, including Mercator and Hondius, whose *Atlas of Asia Minor* (1621) Katib Çelebi translated into Turkish;
3. a biographical dictionary of famous men, arranged alphabetically in Arabic, *Sullam al-Wusul ila Tabaqat al-Fuhul*;
4. a history of the Ottoman navy to 1656 in Turkish entitled *Tuhfat ul-Kibar fi Asfar ul-bihar*.

References

Lewis (1957), Mitchell (1831).

PAUL STARKEY

AL-KAWTHAR

Name of Q.108, referring also to a pool into which the rivers of Paradise empty, or those rivers themselves.

ANDREW J. NEWMAN

KHADIJAH

The Prophet Muhammad's first wife, Khadijah, was born into the Qurashi family of 'Abd al-'Uzza. She was already twice widowed and independently affluent when she met Muhammad, whom she took into her service. Her commercial interests involved her in the lucrative caravan trade, which brought goods from the southern regions of the Arabian Peninsula northward through Mecca and thence to Syria. Goods from the Fertile Crescent were transported southwards on the return journey. It was not long before she noticed the reliability of her new employee, Muhammad, whose integrity was to earn him the title of *al-Amin* (the Trustworthy One). In *c.* AD 595, after having proved himself when put in charge of a shipment of Khadija's merchandise, he accepted her proposal of marriage. Tradition maintains that at the time of the marriage she was forty years old and his senior by fifteen years. Until she died in AD 619, she was Muhammad's only wife. She bore him at least two sons, who died in infancy, and four daughters, Umm Kulthum, Ruqayya, Zaynab and Fatima. The best-known daughter was Fatima, who married Muhammad's cousin, 'Ali ibn Abi-Talib, the man regarded by Shi'i Muslims as Muhammad's divinely appointed successor (*khalifa*). Muhammad's marriage to

Khadija brought him not only domestic happiness but an improved social position and financial security. More importantly, perhaps, was the support she gave when he began his mission as the Messenger of God in the year AD 610. From the outset he was opposed in Mecca by those who saw in the message of Islam a threat to their vested commercial interests. Throughout this difficult period Khadija offered him the support and encouragement to persist in his vocation. She was the first of the small number who accepted Islam in Mecca before the *hijra*. She died in AD 619. The Prophet felt her loss keenly. The year of her death is known as 'the Year of Sadness', the year in which his uncle and protector Abu Talib also died.

See also: **Muhammad ibn 'Abdallah, the Prophet of Islam; wives of the Prophet Muhammad**

EDWARD D. A. HULMES

KHALWA

Meaning retreat and seclusion, *khalwa* came to be a practice of the Sufis in which the temptations of communal living were abandoned for set periods of time for spiritual devotion and asceticism. In the Persian Sufi tradition, a common form of *khalwa* was *chilla*, or periods of forty days for prayers, spiritual contemplation, *dhikr*, and similar practices.

References

Elias (1995: 119–24), Waley (1993: 519–22).

LLOYD RIDGEON

KHAMR

Khamr is an Arabic term designating the offence of imbibing alcohol, the latter being perceived as a mind-altering substance that has the potential to create or exacerbate social disorder. Even the drinking of a small quantity of alcohol is a punishable offence if proven. The usual conditions apply before the offender is liable to punishment, i.e., sane, of mature age and Muslim, but he/she must also have consumed the alcohol from personal choice and must be aware that it is prohibited (as in the case of a recent convert to Islam). Punishment is also waived if it has been taken as medication in the event of there being no alternative. The punishment for the proven offence of *khamr* consumption is eighty lashes, although some adherents to the *shafi'i* school lower this to fourty. The lashes may be administered with minor instruments such as date palm leaves, shoes and even the hem of a dress.

References

al-Zuhayli (1985: VI, 148, 155, 195).

See also: **alcohol**

MAWIL IZZI DIEN

KHANAQAH

The *khanaqah* is the building used by Sufis for their devotional activities. Some *khanaqahs* were big enough to accommodate aspiring Sufis while also providing soup-kitchens and other facilities required for communal living. It appears that the first type of *khanaqah* appeared in the ninth century in Khurasan, but the institution spread rapidly throughout the Islamic world.

References

Kiyani (1969), Nizami (1957).

LLOYD RIDGEON

AL-KHANDAQ, BATTLE OF

The Battle of the Trench (*al-khandaq*), is so named because of the tactics employed by the Prophet Muhammad in the defence of Medina in AD 627 against the 'Confederates' (*al-ahzab*), i.e., the Meccans, who were aided by Bedouin and Abyssinian mercenaries. To the surprise and discomfiture of his enemies he had a protective trench dug round Medina. The attackers withdrew after a month's siege, during which twenty men fell on both sides. Muhammad then accused the Medinan Jews of the Banu Qurayza of siding with the confederates. The tribe was expelled from the city after 600 of their men had been put to death. Their women and children were sold as slaves.

References

Q.33:9–27.

See also: **al-Hudaybiyya, Treaty of; Khaybar**

EDWARD D. A. HULMES

KHARAJ

The word is used in Islamic law of the land-tax imposed on non-Muslims living in an Islamic state. As distinct from the *jizya* (poll tax) the *kharaj* was raised on 'the yield of the fields' as a tax on landed property. This tribute paid in kind from the harvests reaped in lands that had recently become parts of an expanding Islamic empire was an essential contribution to the economy of the growing state.

References

Hitti (1973: 170–1, 320, 510).

See also: *jizya*

EDWARD D. A. HULMES

KHARIJISM (AL-KHAWARIJ)

One of the earliest Islamic sects, whose name al-Khawarij (sing. *Khariji*) means

literally 'to go out' and in the specific sense, to secede and oppose a legitimate imam. The imam in question in this case was the fourth caliph 'Ali b. Abu Talib who resorted to arbitration with Mu'awiya b. Abi Sufyan in the Battle of Siffin in AD 657, which caused a section of his troops to record their opposition vocally with the statement *la hukma illa li-llah* (judgement is Allah's alone). These dissenters joined forces with others at Kufa and consequently made their base at Nahrawan, where 'Ali engaged them and killed the vast majority of them, including their leader 'Abdullah b. Wahb al-Rasibi in AD 658. They sought revenge however and hatched a plot to kill 'Ali, which they executed in the mosque at Kufa, where the Caliph was assassinated by 'Abd al-Rahman b. al-Muljam al-Muradi, whose family members had been killed at Nahrawan. This political splinter group not surprisingly became a puritanical, extremist religious sect, who had little in the way of a uniform doctrine but whose basic principle was that whoever committed a major sin (*murtakib al-kabira*) has become an apostate (*murtadd*) and therefore must be killed, with his wives and children and if he is a caliph or imam, his caliphate/imamate should also be seized. Not satisfied with this, such a person would also be confined to Hell forever in the hereafter. On this basis they consider certain prophetic Companions, such as 'Amr b. al-'As and Abu Musa al-Ash'ari to be disbelievers because of their participation in the arbitration at Siffin, as well as rejecting the caliphates of 'Uthman and 'Ali. As a consequence of this they also reject *hadith* literature, which is narrated by such companions. Their emphasis is very much on the Qur'an, but despite this they have adopted the theological views of a number of other sects including those of the Jahmites and Mu'tazilites. The Kharijites are almost extinct in the current period except for a moderate subsect termed the 'Ibadites and some extremist Muslim groups who adopt a similar puritanical approach.

References

Hanafi (1980: 59–62), al-Johani (1999: 1053–4), Netton (1997: 145–6), Watt (1997: 1–13; 2002: 9–37).

GAVIN PICKEN

KHARTOUM (AL-KHURTUM)

Capital city of the Republic of Sudan situated on the Nile just south of the confluence of the Blue and White Niles. At the time of the Turco-Egyptian invasion in 1821 it was only a village when it was chosen to be the capital of the newly conquered territory. It developed into a flourishing town with a mixed population including European traders, missionaries and consuls. It fell to the Mahdist forces in 1885 when the Anglo-Egyptian garrison (which included General Gordon) was massacred. During the Mahdist period Khartoum was abandoned and the capital moved across the river to Omdurman. It was retaken in 1898 by General Kitchener who began the town's reconstruction as the capital of the Anglo-Egyptian Sudan. The grid pattern of the tree-lined streets was based on the lines of the Union flag. It became the administrative centre and place of residence for the Europeans. A bridge joins it to north Khartoum and to Omdurman. It is a centre for trade from the river and from the Jazira, the irrigated area to the south. There are a few manufacturing industries and it is the home of Khartoum University (formerly Gordon College). The development of the modern city has been hampered by the prolonged civil war, the influx of refugees, poverty and the creaking infrastructure.

References

Walkley (1935–6).

DEREK HOPWOOD

KHAYBAR

Towards the end of his decade in Medina, the Prophet Muhammad launched a series of successful attacks against neighbouring tribes, increasing his reputation as both military and spiritual leader of the Islamic community. In AD 628 he attacked a series of fortified oasis settlements of Jews at Khaybar, to the north of Medina. The Jews surrendered with all their possessions and paid tribute after being promised that their lives would be spared. In consequence they became effectively tenants of the lands on which they lived and *dhimmis* of their new protectors. Muhammad's attempts to bring Jews, Christians and Muslims together under his leadership and the banner of Islam were effectively at an end.

See also: **al-Hudaybiyya, Treaty of; al-Khandaq, Battle of**

EDWARD D. A. HULMES

KHAYYAM, 'UMAR
(AD 1048–1131)

Noted in the West as a poet (after Edward Fitzgerald's translations in the nineteenth century), 'Umar Khayyam is also recognised in his homeland of Iran as a mathematician, philosopher and astronomer. As a poet he is celebrated for his Persian quatrains, the messages of which have been interpreted as materialist, fatalist and Sufi.

References

Avery and Heath-Stubbs (1989).

LLOYD RIDGEON

AL-KHIDR (AL-KHADIR)

Literally, 'the green one', not mentioned by name in the Qur'an but said to be referred to in Q.18:64 in the story of Moses. Presented as an episode in the life of Moses, the encounter with the mysterious and unidentified servant of God – glossed by the later exegetical tradition as al-Khidr – has been a popular and evocative source of Muslim speculation. The mysterious servant is described as the recipient of God's mercy who had been taught part of His secret knowledge. He guides Moses through events that are incomprehensible to the prophet, all the while encouraging him to be patient. Three episodes occur in which al-Khidr sinks a ship, kills a young man, and repairs a wall for undeserving people. Moses is appalled but al-Khidr, just prior to leaving Moses, explains his reason for his actions, each of which is destined to bring good out of an apparent evil. Al-Khidr's insight, as compared to Moses' failure to comprehend his situation, is used as a representation of spiritual knowledge (the 'inner', *batin*, realm) and ignorance (the 'outer', *zahir*, dimension) especially in Sufi circles.

References

Jung (1959: 69–81).

ANDREW RIPPIN

KHITAN

See: **circumcision**

KHUMAYNI, IMAM RUHALLAH (?1900–89)

Iranian spiritual leader. Born the son of a religious scholar, Sayyid Mostafa, who died six months after Khumayni's birth, he was brought up first by his mother and aunt and then by an elder brother after their death. With him he memorised the Qur'an and learned the principles of the Shi'i branch of Islam. He then left home to study law and in the 1920s moved to the holy city of Qom with his teacher to continue his studies. He rose from pupil to *ayatallah* – the rank of a leading Shi'i scholar. His teachings, which included mysticism, attracted a growing number of followers and students. He also began openly to criticise the policies of the Iranian ruler, the Shah, which he believed violated Islamic tradition. In the 1960s the Shah had introduced the White Revolution that included equal rights for women and secular education. From Qom Khumayni bitterly attacked these new proposals and in 1962 he was arrested. This turned him into a national hero. Although released he refused to keep silent and was arrested a second time the following year. Fearing his influence the Shah exiled him, and he settled in Iraq in one of the Shi'a holy cities – Najaf. There he enunciated his doctrine of Vilayat-i Faqih – the rule of the jurist – that called for the clergy to rule in Iran. He spread this doctrine through his network of student followers and the Shi'a clergy also played an important role inside Iran in mobilising opposition to the Shah. He moved to Paris in 1978 from where he stepped up his message to overthrow him.

The Shah was finally ousted in 1979 and Khumayni made a triumphant return. He could now put his ideas into practice. A new constitution was promulgated declaring an Islamic republic of which he was named imam/spiritual leader for life. The Shi'a clergy were given important positions in government but he himself did not take part in the actual governance of the country. In fact, he criticised them for their disagreements that threatened the unity of the state. He called on them to leave politics to the Government. The prolonged war against Iraq (1980–8) distracted attention from these disputes. Saddam Husayn of Iraq believed the clerical regime would put up little resistance to his invasion, but the Iranians fought determinedly while facing great casualties. Khumayni finally accepted the bitter cup of a cease fire because of mounting losses. Quarrelling now returned and at the same time his health deteriorated and, fearing for the revolution, he issued a number of edicts that strengthened the power of the president and of parliament. He died in June 1989 amid great national mourning. Despite all the problems, he left a firmly established Islamic state behind him.

DEREK HOPWOOD

KHUTBA

The word, meaning 'public address', is used specifically with reference to the sermon delivered in the mosque on Fridays by the *khatib* (preacher) before the congregational prayer and worship (*salat al-jum'a*). The sermon is delivered from a pulpit or dais, following the example of the Prophet Muhammad, who began the practice in Medina. A *khutba* should include some elements prescribed in Islamic law. It should open with 'Praise be to God!' (the *hamdala*). The twin parts of the profession of faith are repeated, blessings are invoked on Muhammad, and the unity (*tawhid*) of God is reaffirmed. The sermon usually contains an exhortation to live more faithfully according to the principles and precepts of Islam. Spiritual encouragement is also a characteristic feature. The integral relationship between every aspect of life in Islam blurs the Western distinction between religion and politics, between church and state. This means that these sermons sometimes assume an overtly political nature. In Islamic countries the *khutba* often concludes with the invocation of blessings on political rulers and leaders.

EDWARD D. A. HULMES

AL-KHUWARAZMI, ABU JA'FAR MUHAMMAD IBN MUSA (*c.* 800–850)

Arab geographer, astronomer and mathematician. One of the most important figures in the early history of Arab science, little is known of al-Khuwarazmi's life, beyond the fact of his attachment to the famous Bayt al-Hikma in Baghdad under the patronage of the Caliph al-Ma'mun. His name, however, suggests that he came from the eastern part of the Islamic world.

Al-Khuwarazmi's importance lies in his contribution to the medieval Arab scientific tradition in at least two fields. As a geographer, his *Surat al-Ard* is closely based on Ptolemy's *Geographia* (the question of whether a direct Arabic translation of the Greek work ever existed is so far unresolved), though he has rearranged the material according to the 'longest day clime' system, frequently used by later Arabs, with separate lists for towns, rivers, mountains, etc. The essential feature of this system was the division of the known inhabited world into strips parallel with the Equator defined by values for the length of the longest day. Coincidentally or not, this system places Iraq in the middle clime, that is, at the centre of the civilised world.

Of equal, if not greater, importance for the subsequent development of science was al-Khuwarazmi's work in the field of mathematics. Not only did he produce the first work in Arabic on arithmetic as such, he also produced the first work on algebra and geometry, and was instrumental in consolidating the use of 'Indian' numerals and the idea of the decimal place. A Latin version of his treatise on Hindu numerical reckoning, *Algoritmi de numero indorum* (hence our 'algorithm'), has ensured the survival of his name in the Western tradition. Another book, *Kitab al-Mukhtasar fi Hisab al-Jabr wa al-Muqabala*, quickly became known in the West through translations into Latin by Robert of Ketton and Gerard of Cremona. Al-Khuwarazmi was also the first author of Arabic books of astronomical tables based on trigonometrical principles, though his *Zij al-Sindhind* survives today only in Latin translation.

Apart from its intrinsic importance in the development of medieval Arab science, al-Khuwarazmi's work is of particular interest for its attempt to harmonise the twin heritages of the Greek and Indian scientific traditions.

References

Rashed (1996: II, 349–55), Rosenfeld (1983), Young *et al.*. (1990: 301–27).

PAUL STARKEY

AL-KINDI (d. *c.* AD 870)

The first of a line of Islamic philosophers who were also physicians and scientists, was born in the city of Kufa, where his father was Governor. Little is known about his philosophical and scientific education. He was, however, closely associated with the Syriac-speaking Christian scholars who were translating Greek science and philosophy to Arabic. The 'Abbasid caliphs, la-Ma'mun (d. AD 833), al-Mu'tasim (d. AD 842) and al-Wathiq (d. AD 847) were his patrons and he acted as tutor to one of al-Mu'tasim's sons. For reasons not fully known he fell momentarily out of favour with the Caliph al-Mutawakkil (d. AD 861).

One medieval Arabic source mentions some 240 scientific and philosophical treatises that he wrote. Only a few of his treatises have survived. The philosophical treatise that have survived include one on definitions that marks an important step in the development of an Arabic philosophical vocabulary. They also show how the conceptual framework of his philosophy derives from Aristotle, Plato, and the Neoplatonists. The end result, however, remains other than the sum of its parts. His philosophy remains distinctively 'Kindian'. This is perhaps best seen in the longest of his surviving philosophical treatises, *On First Philosophy.*

Divided into four parts, in the first introductory part he defends and recommends the study of philosophy, which he defines as 'knowledge of things in their true natures to the extent of man's ability'. The noblest philosophy is First Philosophy, namely, 'knowledge of the First Truth who is the cause of every truth'. He then writes, 'we must not be ashamed of deeming truth good and acquiring truth from wherever it comes, even if it comes from races remote and nations different from us'. In this introduction, he singles out Aristotle as the foremost philosopher. He also indicates that knowledge of the things in their true nature entails 'knowledge of divinity, unity, virtue and total knowledge of everything beneficial and the way to it'.

The second part is a lengthy sustained argument for the creation of the world *ex nihilo,* at a finite moment in the past from the present. He first argues for the finitude of the body of the universe. If we suppose it to be infinite, then in principle we can remove a finite part of it. What remains would still be infinite, but an infinite less than the infinite from which the finite part has been removed. This means for al-Kindi that we would have unequal infinities, a contradiction. He then argues that body cannot exist without being in motion. He tries to show that both time and motion must be finite. Implicit here is the doctrine that time and motion are created with the world. Creation does not mean that a static world existed and then at one moment in time was 'given a push', so to speak, which started it moving. For al-Kindi, there can be no static body.

The third and fourth parts are devoted to analyses of the nature of oneness, leading to a demonstration that there must be only one being who is absolutely one, utterly devoid of plurality. This for al-Kindi is the True One – al-Kindi does not use the term 'God', but clearly, the True One refers to God. The demonstration rests on a consideration of the pluralities that abound in the world. These consist of unities. These unities, he then argues, do not exist in pluralities essentially. Al-Kindi then posits a premise, namely, that whatever exists in one thing accidentally, must exist in another essentially. Thus if C exists accidentally in B, it must exist essentially in A. Moreover, its essential existence in A is the cause of its accidental existence in B. He then tries to show that the unity that is essential, that is the source of the accidental unities without which the pluralities in the world cannot exist, must belong to a being who is utterly one, the True One. It is unity, though accidental in things, that gives created things their identifiable existence. This unity, al-Kindi states, is an emanation, *fayd,* from the True One, adding that the one who bestows unity, is the giver of existence. (It should be noted that the term *fayd* is used only once in this treatise.)

The other shorter treatises also reveal his individuality. They also anticipate views that were more fully developed by subsequent philosophers. This is seen when he tells us that prophetic knowledge is received instantaneously, without exertion, probing or the devices of mathematics. This anticipates Ibn Sina's far more developed argument for the possibility of the highest form of prophecy, the intellectual, which rests on the concept of intuition. Kindi's statement on prophethood brings us to another aspect of his philosophy, namely its being in harmony with accepted Islamic beliefs. We see this in his insistence on creation *ex nihilo.* In other treatises he expresses his adherence to the doctrine of bodily resurrection, also his belief in the inimitability of the Qur'an in terms of its literary excellence.

While his thought is in harmony with accepted Islamic beliefs, in spirit it remains highly philosophical. As expected, this is seen in his specialised philosophical treatises. But it is also seen and immediately sensed in his more popular writings – in his many maxims and in his treatise, *The Epistle of Ya'qub Ibn Ishaq al-Kindi on the Device for Dispelling Sorrows,* where he tries to show that sorrows are dispelled when philosophical, none worldly concerns, are pursued.

Al-Kindi opened the door for the entry of philosophy into the Islamic world. He was certainly Islam's first metaphysician. Although it cannot be said that he left a school, he had followers such as al-Sarakhsi (d. AD 899) and al-'Amiri (d. AD 992).

References

Atiya (1966), Ivry (1974), Jayyusi-Lehn (2002: 137–51), Jolivet (1971), Marmura and Rist (1963).

MICHAEL E. MARMURA

AL-KIRMANI, HAMID AL-DIN ABU'L-HASAN AHMAD IBN 'ABDALLAH

Isma'ili missionary, defender of his imam and philosopher at the time of the

Fatimid imam-caliph al-Hakim bi-Amrallah (r. 996–1021). He was one of the first eastern Iranian Isma'ili missionaries to take up residence in Cairo, the Fatimid capital. Because of his debating and disputational activities in Iraq on behalf of the Isma'ili cause recorded in his non-extant work *al-Majalis al-Baghdadiyya wa'l-Basriyya*, he was given the honorific *hujjat al-'iraqayn* (The 'proof' of the Isma'ili cause for Iraq and Western Iran). His systematic scientific and philosophical contributions make him a true rival of his contemporary Ibn Sina, as he was always more than an apologist for the Fatimids. When called upon, he did defend the normative, ordinary imamate of al-Hakim at a tense moment when some were advocating his divinity (a group that later became the Druze). Asked either by the head of the mission or the Imam himself, he wrote a treatise in AD 1015 entitled *Mabasim al-Bisharat* (*Smiles of Glad Tidings*) affirming that the divinity of al-Hakim was incompatible with the Isma'ili theological insistence upon the utter transcendence of God. He also wrote *al-Risala al-Wa'iza fi Nafy Ithbat Uluhiyyat al-Hakim* (*The Treatise that Preaches the Refutation of the Doctrine of al-Hakim's Divinity*) in AD 1017 in this cause. After the controversy, he apparently returned to Iraq to finish writing and died sometime after AD 1021, the date of the completion of his main work *Rahat al-'aql* (*Comfort of the Intellect*). It is unclear if he was aware of the disputes and dissension in the Fatimid capital in his absence after his departure.

Al-Kirmani's pen was prolifically wielded in polemics favouring the Fatimids, especially when in residence in Cairo. These included accounts of his disputations, a refutation of al-Jahiz's *al-Risala al-'Uthmaniyya* entitled *Ma'asim al-Huda* (*Protecting Links to Guidance*),

al-Maqayis (*Arguments*), which was an attack on extremists who held among other views the validity of metempsychosis, a refutation of the Caspian Zaydi imam al-Mu'ayyad bi-llah (d. AD 1020) entitled *al-Kafiya* (*The Sufficient Treatise*), and *Tanbih al-Hadi* (*Reminder to the Guide*), an Isma'ili heresiography. Two other significant doctrinal works were *al-Risala al-Durriya* (*The Brilliant Treatise*) on the key Islamic doctrine of *tawhid*, and *Kitab al-Riyad* (*The Meadow*), a complex and obscure adjudication between Abu Ya'qub al-Sijistani and Abu Hatim al-Razi on aspects of philosophy and theology.

His major work *Comfort of the Intellect* is a systematic work of philosophy that includes a Neoplatonic cosmology akin to other Islamic philosophers (but quite unlike other Isma'ili thinkers) and proffers a philosophical consolation and path of the intellect that is in harmony with the divine revelation and the teachings of the imam*s*. He uses the (Neo)Platonic allegory of the city of gnostic knowledge with chapters styled ramparts (*aswar*) and sections called pathways (*mashari'*). The seeker would have to travel across the fifty-six pathways and the seven ramparts of the city to arrive at full intellectual knowledge of the cosmos. The first rampart prepares the seeker for the journey of the soul. The second discusses the nature of God and insists apophatically upon the inapplicability of the term 'existence' to God. God is described in the manner of the *via negativa*. The third rampart examines the incipience of creation through the primordial pen, a Qur'anic concept associated with the Neoplatonic *nous*. The fourth rampart describes the procession of being through the scheme of emanation. The fifth discusses constituents of the cosmos and their homology with sacred letters writ large. The sixth rampart follows the homology between the celestial spheres and the earth and their constituent substances and elements. The final rampart focuses on the phenomenal world and the journey of the rational soul within it and its culmination in the Resurrection. The cosmological and human hierarchies are seen as homologous: the human soul is a microcosm of this universal design, and the four levels of the cosmos, namely the realms of divine nature, nature, religion and the primordial, are aspects of a macrocosmic design. In its systematics, al-Kirmani's work reveals the strong imprint of classical Islamic Neoplatonism. The world arises from an emanative scheme of ten intellects issuing from the divine principle. He rehearses the Aristotelian proof of a creator as the Unmoved Mover who causes the cosmos, a form of cosmological argument. These arguments became commonplace in Islamic philosophy but were unusual in an Isma'ili setting, a tradition that was at times hostile to the Graeco-Arabic tradition of philosophy. However, in keeping with the apophatic nature of the Isma'ili doctrine of God, the creator is placed outside of the emanative scheme so as to avoid implicating him in any analogous 'space' with the creation. The content of this philosophy is a training of the soul. The believer has an obligation to acquire knowledge, which for al-Kirmani is not confined to religious duties but includes metaphysical and cosmological understanding.

Legacy, though important in his time and in the Tayyibi tradition that has especially embraced the esoteric doctrine of some of his works, al-Kirmani was somewhat of a maverick in the Isma'ili tradition. His systematic engagement with the *falsafa* tradition and the emanationist Neoplatonism cosmology common to al-Farabi and Ibn Sina was not widely accepted in later Isma'ili thought. His concomitant intellectualism may have also posed problems. However, because he embraced the main Neoplatonic trends of Islamic philosophy, he was approvingly cited by later philosophers such as Mulla Sadra for some of his subtle disquisitions on the nature of the soul and intellect.

References

De Smet (1995), Haji (1999), Peterson (1990), Walker (1999).

SAJJAD H. RIZVI

KITAB AL-AGHANI

This collection of poems from early 'Abbasid times, together with accounts of their authors and the circumstances of their composition and musical performance, is the major work of Abu 'l-Faraj 'Ali b. al-Husayn b. Muhammad al-Qurayshi al-Isbahani (897–c. AD 972), a friend and companion of leading officials of the Buyid court, and himself a Shi'ite although he traced his descent from the Umayyads (he is also known by the Persian form of his name, al-Isfahani, or simply as Abu 'l-Faraj). Thanks to the wealth of biographical and cultural comments it contains, *The Book of Songs* is an encyclopaedic conspectus of life in 'Abbasid times and earlier, and offers valuable glimpses into the more secular pursuits of the cultured elite. By al-Isbahani's own account, it took him fifty years to compose, and he never finally completed it.

The *Kitab al-Aghani* begins with a collection of the hundred best songs that had been chosen for the Caliph Harun al-Rashid (AD 786–809) by the musicians Ibrahim al-Mawsili, Isma'il b. Jami' and Fulayh b. al-'Awra', and revised later for al-Wathiq (AD 842–7) by Ishaq b. Ibrahim al-Mawsili. In each instance al-Isbahani gives biographical details about the poet, and also identifies the composer of the melody to which his words were set, often quoting at length passages from the poet's other verses and adding background colour from his times and earlier.

This selection is, however, only part of al-Isbahani's total work. He continues with notices on caliphs and members of their families who were poets, and then with poets he himself has chosen. This makes up by far the longest part of the work.

While it is structured on individual poets and their best-known verses, the *Kitab al-Aghani* adds such copious amounts of information about 'Abbasid, Umayyad and also pre-Islamic times, together with long passages of poetry, that it can be considered a virtual social history of Islam in its first three centuries. It is, however, first and foremost a literary work, and as such is the foremost example of the book of songs genre.

The best edition of the *Kitab al-Aghani* is that published in Cairo, 1927–74, 24 vols. Guidi (1895–1900) provides useful indexes of poets, etc., that can be used in conjunction with this edition (the *Tables* are based on the earlier Bulaq edition, but the page numbers from this are given in the margin of the Cairo edition).

References

Kilpatrick (2003).

DAVID THOMAS

KITAB AL-HIYAL (BOOK OF INGENIOUS DEVICES)

The three sons of Musa Ibn Shakir – Muhammad, Ahmad and al-Hasan – referred to collectively as the Banu Musa, were among the leading patrons of scientific advancement in ninth-century Baghdad. Al-Nadim says in the *Fihrist* that they were interested in geometry, mechanics, dynamics, music and astronomy, and also that in order to study scientific works from classical times they employed the services of a team of translators, among whom were the illustrious Hunayn Ibn Ishaq and Thabit Ibn Qurra. The *Kitab al-Hiyal* (*The Book of Ingenious Devices*) is one of the major surviving works ascribed to them, and an important witness of technological attainment in their time.

There is no clear indication of the date of this work. But since the Banu Musa as children were wards of the Caliph al-Ma'mun (d. AD 833), and Muhammad the oldest of them died in AD 872–3, it would presumably have been composed in the second quarter of the century. The middle brother Ahmad was probably mainly responsible, since only his name is mentioned in the body of the text after the initial ascription to all three, and he alone is credited with the work by later medieval authors. He, rather than Muhammad or al-Hasan, was also remembered for his unrivalled skill in constructing ingenious devices.

The *Kitab al-Hiyal* as it can now be reconstructed from the three main surviving manuscripts contained descriptions for the construction and use of probably 100 devices of various kinds. These range from beakers, pitchers and jars that deliver measures of liquids in surprising ways and flasks that dispense both water and wine, to self-replenishing troughs and basins, fountains discharging in different sequences, lamps with automatic wicks, and an underwater grab. Each of the devices is described in detail, with an accompanying diagram, and in addition to the manner of construction, instructions for operating it are also given.

A characteristic feature of nearly all the curious devices described is that they are intended for personal use. The pitchers dispensing measured quantities of wine or quantities of wine and water, or refusing to dispense expected measures, can be imagined as gadgets built to amuse or mystify guests at a party, while fountains with varied displays would be part of grander entertainments. Even the underwater grab, Model 100, is designed for personal use: 'a machine with which the person can extract jewels from the sea if he drops them, and with which things that fall into wells or are submerged in rivers, seas and so on, may be extracted'. Any notion that this device could be constructed on a scale large enough for industrial dredging purposes is absent.

In consequence, it would be easy to judge the *Kitab al-Hiyal* as a work written to please the idle rich, who were already acquainted with such amusements as water clocks, automata and mechanical toys. But it is important to note the mechanical principles according to which the devices are built, and also not to underestimate the technological sophistication that is presupposed in their invention and construction. Although these are not demonstrated, they can be deduced from almost every one of the descriptions, and include such features as small variations in pressure of liquid flow to ensure appropriate different chambers within vessels are filled, and the conical valve, which is known previously only in Archimedes. The manner in which they are employed in the construction of these devices points to the much wider context in which they could have been applied for practical purposes.

The *Kitab al-Hiyal* is thus a document of some social significance, because it witnesses to the degree of mechanical knowledge and understanding of early 'Abbasid times. Much of this was, of course, inherited from earlier ages, and particularly from the Greek masters of mathematics and engineering Philo of Byzantium and Hero of Alexandria, some of whose constructions closely parallel those of the Banu Musa, making it difficult to gauge the degree of originality present in the *Kitab al-Hiyal*. Nevertheless, the book was held in esteem for centuries after it was written: as late as the fourteenth century AD Ibn Khaldun hails it as mentioning 'every astonishing, remarkable and nice mechanical contrivance', and it was judged a key contribution to mechanics within Islam. It has been suggested (though with some reservation in the present state of incomplete knowledge about channels of transmission) that some of the book's ideas, and particularly the conical valves which it incorporates into a number of its devices, may have been influential upon early European scientific advances. Whether or not this is the case, the *Kitab al-Hiyal* compels admiration as a work of empirical inventiveness that bases ingenious mechanical masterpieces on unfailingly sound principles of engineering.

There is no edition of the *Kitab al-Hiyal*, though the translation of Hill (1979) goes far in making good this lack.

References

Hill (1993, Chapter 7).

DAVID THOMAS

KITAB AL-SUNAN AL-KUBRA

This compilation of *hadiths* (*The Greater Book of Traditions*) is one of the best-known works of the *muhaddith* Abu 'Abd al-Rahman Ahmad b. 'Ali b. Shu'ayb al-Nasa'i (AD 830–915), who travelled widely and finally settled in Damascus, where he died after ill treatment by a mob. Its title distinguishes it from its author's *Kitab al-Sunan al-Sughra*, known also as *Al-Mujtaba* (*The Selection*), which is a distillation of the *sahih* traditions contained in it and one of the *Kutub al-Sitta*, the collections of *hadiths*. The longer and shorter works were not always distinguished in transmission.

Like the other collections, al-Nasa'i's *Sunan* is a *musannaf* work, assembling *hadiths* according to theme. It comprises fifty-one books, which cover areas similar to the other *sunan* works, from cleanliness and prayer, through the accepted observances and practices, to the behaviour of judges, taking refuge in God, and beverages. Some of the subjects included do not appear in other collections.

The compilation is characterised by the great care taken over variant forms of the *hadiths*. Whereas the contemporary *muhaddiths* Abu Da'ud and al-Tirmidhi refer to these in notes added to the main version of a *hadith*, al-Nasa'i quotes all the variants in full, and has sometimes been criticised as overscrupulous.

The *Sunan* was accepted as authoritative at an early date, and for some scholars was equal to Muslim's *Sahih*. It has been the subject of numerous commentaries.

The *Sunan al-Kubra* and *Sunan al-Sughra* have been published often. A recent edition of the former is edited by al-Bandari and Hasan (1991). The latter has been published together with al-Suyuti's commentary upon it, most recently in Beirut (1988).

References

Robson (1956: 38–59).

DAVID THOMAS

KITAB AL-SUNAN OF AL-SIJISTANI

This collection of *hadiths*, one of the Sunni *Kutub al-Sitta*, is the major work of Abu Da'ud Sulayman b. al-Ash'ath al-Sijistani (AD 817–89). He originated in Khurasan (his birthplace has sometimes been thought to be the village of Sijistana near Basra, but is much more likely the town of Sijistan in the eastern part of the Islamic empire), but studied and taught mainly in Basra, where he died.

It is said that Abu Da'ud was engaged in this compilation for twenty years, and that from 500,000 traditions he selected 4,800. Like the other five compilations, it is a *musannaf* collection, dividing the traditions according to theme. It comprises forty books, beginning with cleanliness and prayer and ranging through the observances and practicalities of the religious life to the importance of following the example and manners of the Prophet. It is regarded as including details about ritual and legal thinking that other collections do not and, like the other *sunan* works (as distinct from the two *sahih* to concentrate on these matters rather than theology.

Alongside *sahih* traditions, the *Sunan* admits others of less sound provenance, about which Abu Da'ud frequently expresses an opinion. In fact, a distinguishing feature of the collection is the notes from Abu Da'ud often added to *hadiths* as comments on the transmitters and their reliability or on the situation in which the Prophet uttered a particular statement or the variant forms in which it was transmitted. His readiness to accept these latter traditions has led to his work being generally ranked below the two *Sahihs* of al-Bukhari and Muslim, but it is conventionally regarded as the most important of the four *sunan* works. Its authority as a source of *hadiths* was agreed early; Abu Sulayman Ahmad b. Muhammad al-Khattabi (d. *c.* AD 998) wrote a commentary on it, the *Ma'alim al-Sunan*, in the tenth century.

The *Kitab al-Sunan* has been published often. A reliable edition is Al-Khalidi (1996).

DAVID THOMAS

KITAB AL-SUNAN (IBN MAJA)

This compilation of *hadiths*, one of the Sunni *Kutub al-Sitta*, is the work of Abu 'Abdallah Muhammad b. Yazid Ibn Maja (824/AD 5–87), who was born and died in Qazwin, south of the Caspian Sea. Like other *muhaddith*s before and after, he travelled widely in search of traditions.

The *Kitab al-Sunan* comprises 4,341 *hadiths* in thirty-seven books, each divided into chapters. These cover the same range of ritual and practical observances as other *sunan* works (cleanliness, prayer and other pillars, marriage, divorce, food, drink, trade and manners), and concluding with *fitan*, which embraces the tribulations of this world and the judgement, and *zuhd*, which ends with descriptions of the fire and the garden. There is also an Introduction, in which matters of belief, the excellences of the Rightly Guided Caliphs and leading Companions, early heresies, and the virtue of gaining religious knowledge are detailed.

Ibn Maja's *Sunan* has generally been regarded as the least authoritative of the *Kutub al-Sitta*. Scholars began to place it with the other five from the early twelfth century, but even in the fourteenth century Ibn Khaldun did not recognise it. This is largely because it was thought to contain weak traditions that do not appear in the other recognised collections elsewhere, including praise for individual tribes and towns, among them Ibn Maja's native Qazwin (No. 2780 in the edition cited below). It has been computed that of the 4,341 *hadiths* included, 1,339 do not appear in the other recognised collections, of which some 712 are either *da'if*, weak or *munkar*, unacknowledged.

References

'Abd al-Baqi (1995).

DAVID THOMAS

KNOWLEDGE

A reference to the importance of *'ilm* (knowledge) to Islam. A famous *hadith* whose authenticity has been challenged quotes the Prophet as enjoining believers to 'seek knowledge even as far as China', however the *hadith* 'Seeking knowledge is an obligation upon every Muslim' is widely accepted.

References

Waines (1995: 36–40, 288).

See also: **rihla fi talab al-'ilm.**

ANDREW J. NEWMAN

KONYA

The city, built up on one of the oldest settlements in the world, is located on the south-west fringes of the Central Anatolian Plateau in Turkey, north of the Taurus mountains. Legend has it that Konya was the first city to emerge after the Great Flood, which is mentioned in ancient Mesopotamian as well as biblical records. Beginning in the third century BC Konya became an autonomous Greek city. In Roman times it was part of the province of Galatia and known as Iconium, a name which has been linked etymologically with the Greek word *eikon*. Later, in the fourth century AD, it was the capital of the province of Lycaonia. Towards the end of the eleventh century AD the Saljuq Sultans of Rum made it their capital. It was renamed Konya in the thirteenth century AD. Under the rule of this dynasty the city became famed for its art treasures, its Islamic schools, its museums and buildings. During the Ottoman period the city fell into decline, but the construction of the railway link between Istanbul and Baghdad at the end of the nineteenth century helped to revive its fortunes as a commercial centre. Konya has long been famed for its carpets and rugs. The Islamic poet and mystic, Jalal al-Din al-Rumi (AD 1207–73) was invited to live in Konya. He died there. He founded the Mevlevi (Mawlawiyya) order of Islamic mystics, often referred to in the West as 'the Whirling Dervishes'. His poetic work, the *Mathnawi*, is a compilation of mystical stories and discourses. His tomb, a place of pilgrimage for Muslims, is in Konya. The church of Amphilochius is one of several Christian sites in the city. Selcuk University was founded in the city in 1975.

References

Nicholson (1953: 298, 393, 404), Schacht and Bosworth (1979: 196, 264).

EDWARD D. A. HULMES

AL-KUFA

In Iraq, on the Hindiyah branch of the middle Euphrates, *c.* 7 miles (11 kilometres) north-east of al-Najaf is the site of one of the earliest Arab mosques. Three phases can be distinguished: political (before 150), cultural (150–250) and Shi'ite (150–250). Populated by South Arabians and Persians, Kufa was the seat of the governor of Iraq and sometimes shared this position with its sister city, Basra.

In AD 638 Muslims under caliph 'Umar I (r. AD 638–43) founded a multi-tribal garrison town as a semi-nomadic encampment (*hira*) and a base for Islamic expansion into Persia, on a previously unoccupied site near al-Hira, capital of the Lakhmids, Sasanid vassals. Many of the early immigrants were Yamani city dwellers. The original Friday mosque (AD 638) was built by General Sa'd ibn Abi 'l-Waqqas. As in Basra and Fustat, it was austere with a square enclosure surrounded by ditches rather than walls, with a covered 200-cubit south colonnade (*zulla*) forming the sanctuary. Sa'd also built the earliest Islamic government house (*dar al-imara*) against the *qibla* wall of the mosque, later destroyed by 'Umar I as being unacceptably grandiose and a threat to his authority.

Kufa supported 'Ali against 'Uthman (AD 654–6), which gave Kufa its lasting Shi'i inheritance. In AD 656–7, 'Ali moved his capital to Kufa from Medina and was assassinated in the mosque (AD 661), which became a Shi'ite shrine. Under the 'Abbasids, Shi'ism as a faith gained ground and flourished especially in Baghdad and Qumm.

According to Tabari (I: 2492, II: 8–15), Ziyad ibn Abihi (d. AD 673), Governor of Basra, rebuilt the mosque (AD 665–70) on grander scale in Perso-Iraqi tradition using non-Muslim Persian builders, for he recognised its political and social importance as place of assembly; he led Friday prayers himself. Marble columns were brought from Jabal Ahwaz, the drums being linked by iron rods. Nearby Ziyad also rebuilt the official residence (*dar al-imara*) in Sasanian style and it remained the administrative headquarters for Mesopotamia and Kufa province for about 150 years. According to Tabari (d. AD 923), Ziyad's Syrian troops used the mosque as a military base against the rebels.

In AD 683, Kufa recognised 'Abd Allah ibn al-Zubayr as caliph during the civil war following the death of the

Caliph Yazid I. In AD 684, 'the penitents' advanced from Kufa but were defeated by the Umayyad army on the Syrian border. Shortly after this, al-Mansur dominated Kufa in the name of Muhammad ibn al-Hanafiyya, another son of 'Ali, but in AD 685 Kufa violently opposed al-Mukhtar's Shi'i doctrine. Khariji assaults on the turbulent city continued, especially between AD 695 and 745.

Under the governorship of Khalid al-Kasri (AD 723–37) the town was planned with a monumental centre with markets and fortress, tribal dwelling areas (*khitat*) and cemeteries (*jabbanat*), privileged residential lots given as favours to the Companions, avenues, small clan or quarter mosques and bathhouses. Kufa was unsettled after the death of Husayn in Karbala', when he was *en route* for Kufa, an event that ultimately led to the fall of the Umayyad dynasty in AD 750 and the end of a purely Arab period.

Kufa was Iranised (AD 750–63) with an influx of Khurasanian soldiers. Abu al-'Abbas al-Saffah (r. AD 749–54) was proclaimed the first 'Abbasid caliph in Kufa, after which they made Kufa their administrative capital until Baghdad was founded (AD 762–3) by the second caliph al-Mansur, after which Kufa though fortified by him, lost much of its cultural importance. Baghdad was designed using building expertise from Kufa and its concentric design included the Kufa Gate, which faced Mecca. Lively cultural exchange continued between Baghdad and Kufa. Al-Mansur made his nominated successor 'Isa ibn Musa Governor of Kufa.

There was a vast marketplace (*kunasa*) in Kufa. It was a focus for caravans and auditorium for Islamic traditions, anecdotes (*akhbar*) and genealogies, poetry and storytelling. There were many scholars in Kufa including Ibn al-Kalbi (d.

AD 819), the *qadi* al-Sha'bi (d. 721), Abu Yusuf (d. 798), Ibn Mas'ud and his disciples, and doctrinal creeds (*fiqh akhbar*) of theologian Abu Hanifa (AD 699–767), for *fiqh* of Kufa preceded *hadith*. The Sunni Hanafi law school developed in Kufa (ninth century AD), based on systematic justification of legal rules. Like Basra, Baghdad and Najaf, Kufa was an important centre for the study of Arab culture, philology, literary criticism (*naqd*) and *belles lettres* (*adab*). The school of grammar emphasised spoken Arabic whilst the Kufic was used by earliest Muslims to write the Qur'an.

At the end of the ninth century AD, Isma'ilis caused disruption to Kufa which became provincialised and decadent by the tenth century. The city was sacked by Qarmatians betweens 905 and AD 927 and never recovered. Najaf or Mashhad 'Ali became centres of Shi'i pilgrimage, replacing Kufa which was ruined by Bedouin Banu Asad, the Tayyi' and Shammar. Ibn Jubayr saw the mosque in AD 1184, describing its vast *apadana*, and as a deserted ruined city overgrown with orchards. Ibn Battuta (fourteenth century), described Kufa as almost deserted, the Niebuhr found the mosque in a ruined state (1765) as did Massignon (1908, 1934), yet remains still existed in 1965.

References

Creswell (1989: 9–10, 261–4), al-Deihani (1993), Hillenbrand (1994: 62, 67–8, 391–2, 393, 409), Meisami and Starkey (1998: I, 78; I, 340–1), Watt (1968: 43).

JANET STARKEY

KUFR

'Unbelief', by implication an active effort to deny the existence of the Divine and His mercy.

References

Waines (1995).

ANDREW J. NEWMAN

KURDISTAN

Traditional mountainous region of the Kurds in parts of eastern Turkey, Iran, Iraq, north Syria and Armenia. Kurdish is a west Iranian language related to Fars and Pashtu. Kurdistan was traditionally occupied by nomad and peasants. It is watered by the Aras, Kizil Uzun, Euphrates and Tigris, with Lake Van. Occupied from Palaeolithic times, Kurdistan has never enjoyed political unity though it is strategically important. Kurds have played an important part in the history of Islam, with both Sunni following the *Shafi'i* law school and Shi'i, Sufi orders (Qadiriyya, Naqshbandiyya, Qadiri) and heretical sects.

At time of the Arab conquest (seventh century), *Kurd* (pl. *Akrad*) was applied to Iranicised tribes, plus some autochthonous Semites and Armenians. Islamic frontiers were enlarged with the help of political and military Kurdish leaders. There was a succession of Kurdish dynasties in parts of the region (sixth to tenth century AD), such as the Hasanwaihids of Dinavar in the Kermanshah region (AD 959–1015), the Shaddadids of Arran, the Rawwadids of Tabriz and Azerbayjan, and the Marwanids of Diyarbakr (AD 983–1085). 'Kurdistan' dates from the time of Sultan Sanjar (d. AD 1157). From the sixth century to the thirteenth century there were major Kurdish population movements with wars between Ottomans and Safawids, and large Kurdish families divided towns among themselves. From the twelfth century Sufis prospered in Kurdistan and membership of a mystical *tariqa* is still common in rural areas.

Ayyub, a Rawadi Hadhbani Kurd, was Saladin's uncle (d. AD 1193), the founder of the Ayyubid dynasty. The Ayyubids destroyed the Fatimid caliphate in Egypt (AD 1171) and unified Islamic enthusiasm against Latin control of Jerusalem (AD 1187). Ayyubid Kurds were Sunni dedicated to militarily overthrow political Shi'ism and reinstate traditional Islam, partly by encouraging scholarship in Arabic, theology and law, through private and state-sponsored *madrasas*. They built mosques, schools, hospitals and fountains. Kurdish theologians taught in al-Azhar in Cairo and in Constantinople. Sufism, through its association with craft guilds, remained an active socio-religious influence alongside rejuvenated traditional Islamic practice. The northern Ayyubids were defeated by Mongols (AD 1258–60). Only the Kurdish principality of Diyarbakr survived Timurid attacks (1394, 1401).

Several Kurdish principalities existed until the end of the nineteenth century in Turkey (Bohtan, Hakkara, Bahdinan, Sulaymaniyya, Soran, Baban) and Persia (Mukri, Ardalan) and the great tribes still exist. Only Iran recognises its Kurdish region, Kordestan. The 1908 Revolution drew Kurds into politics, and over the centuries Kurdish Sufi leaders preached social revolution. In 1914–18 the idea of an autonomous Kurdistan was suggested by Western powers. Kurdish nationalist movements with their own societies, newspapers, web sites and television channels disrupt Turkey. The recognistion of Kurdish, banned in Turkey in the late twentieth century, has just been accepted as a prerequisite for Turkey's admission into the EU. After 1991, many Kurds fled to Europe and Canada from Iraq and Turkey. Iraq's Kurdish area was semi-autonomous after 1991, and has now 'an anomalous position under the

Coalition (2003–4), although the kurdish parties are integral to the new Iraqi constitution (2006).

References

Bosworth (1967: 61, 88–9), Bruinessen (2000), Ivanov (1953).

JANET STARKEY

KURSI

The *kursi* is a folding portable bookstand on which the Qur'an is placed in both mosque and mausoleum for readings and recitations. Two rectangular wooden panels are interlocked and hinged to form a saltire shape when the bookstand is open. Surfaces were decorated with inscriptions from the Qur'an in various styles of calligraphy, intricate scrollwork motifs, radial geometric panels either carved in relief or strikingly inlaid in ebony, ivory and silver as in some Ottoman Turkish examples. A *kursi* offered as a pious donation could also be inscribed with the donor's name and date.

References

Roxburgh (2005).

JENNIFER SCARCE

KUTTAB

The *kuttab* is the traditional elementary school where Muslim children learnt to read and write and to memorise the complete text of the Qur'an in Arabic. Children attended the *kuttab* between the ages of five and ten for about two to five years depending on their ability to assimilate the Qur'an. The structure and location of a *kuttab* was flexible ranging from a modest local schoolroom to the mosque where the teacher would sit against a pillar near the *qibla* and gather

his pupils informally around him. Attendance at a *kuttab* completed a child's education unless he progressed to the more specialised curriculum of a *madrasa*. Today attendance at a *kuttab* is regarded as a pre- or post-school activity.

References

Lane (1908), Lewis (1971: 96–7).

JENNIFER SCARCE

AL-KUTUB AL-SITTA

Among the many collections of the sayings and actions of the Prophet, preeminence is given to the *Kutub al-Sitta* (*The Six Books*), as the most complete and authoritative source of his *sunna*. For Sunni Muslims, they are second only to the Qur'an as a source of the fundamental teachings of Islam. They were made in the latter part of the ninth century and were gradually accorded their unsurpassed recognition over the following centuries.

In chronological order of the deaths of their compilers, the six works are: the *Jami' al-Sahih* of Abu 'Abdallah Muhammad b. Isma'il al-Bukhari (d. AD 870), the *Jami' al-Sahih* of Abu al-Husayn Muslim b. al-Hajjaj (d. AD 875), the *Kitab al-Sunan* of Muhammad b. Yazid Ibn Maja (d. AD 887), the *Kitab al-Sunan* of Abu Da'ud Sulayman al-Sijistani (d. AD 889), the *Jami' al-Sahih* of Abu 'Isa Muhammad b. 'Isa al-Tirmidhi (d. AD 892), and the *Kitab al-Sunan* of Abu 'Abd al-Rahman Ahmad al-Nasa'i (d. AD 915). Among these, the *Sahih*s of al-Bukhari and Muslim are regarded as unrivalled in their soundness.

All these six are *musannaf* collections, since their organising principle is to categorise their *hadiths* by theme, in contrast to the *musnad* collections which categorise them according to the name of the first transmitter from the Prophet. Their authors all divide their contents into books: al-Bukhari into ninety-seven, by far the largest; Muslim into fifty-four; Ibn Maja into thirty-seven; Abu Da'ud into forty; al-Tirmidhi into forty-six; and al-Nasa'i into fifty-one. And all except Muslim subdivide these books into chapters. Since these divisions are attempts to impose systematisation on words and actions that were recalled from diverse situations in the life of the early community, they contain widely varying numbers of *hadiths*, according to the relationship between what a *hadith* contains and the theme of the division.

The two collections of al-Bukhari and Muslim were very quickly acknowledged as reliable, and those of Abu Da'ud, al-Tirmidhi and al-Nasa'i were recognised within a few centuries. But Ibn Maja's *Sunan* was only included with the other five much later. This is largely explained by the different approaches adopted by the collectors. Al-Bukhari and Muslim admit only *sahih hadiths*, those that according to the criteria they set were certainly, or almost certainly, traceable back to the Prophet himself. On the other hand, the collectors of the *sunan* works admit *hadiths* of less reliable derivations – by al-Tirmidhi they are categorised from *sahih*, 'sound', to *munkar*, 'unacknowledged' – and Ibn Maja was regarded as having allowed *hadiths* of unattested origin and from people suspected of lying.

As sources of information about the Prophet's teachings and lived example, the six books were studied and discussed by Muslims from an early stage, both regarding the reliability of their *hadiths*, and the actual teachings they contain, as well as the advantages of one over others. For Sunnis they come second only to the Qur'an as inspirations of faith, and form the indispensable basis of legal, theological and spiritual reflection, as well as repositories of sayings that can be applied to all the diverse experiences of everyday life.

DAVID THOMAS

L

LANE, EDWARD WILLIAM (1801–76)

British scholar and lexicographer. Lane was born in Hereford and educated at Cambridge University where he showed an aptitude for Eastern Studies. He suffered from ill health and decided that living in Egypt might help him recover. In 1825, he left for Alexandria and on arrival in Cairo he decided to devote his time to sketching antiquities and to writing a description of Egypt, inspired by the numerous other scholars who were already there. He travelled widely through the country sketching and writing and eventually in 1836 published his classic account of contemporary Egyptian in two volumes – *Manners and Customs of the Modern Egyptians*. It was an immediate best-seller and has remained the standard work of its kind, the first sociological study of a Middle Eastern society. He lived amongst the people and observed and reported on them sympathetically. It was naturally of its time and has been criticised (by Edward Said in particular) for its 'orientalist' attitudes.

Lane returned to Cairo in 1842 where he developed a new interest in lexicography and determined to compile a comprehensive Arabic–English dictionary based on classical Arabic sources. He spent the rest of his life devoted to this great undertaking. In 1849 he was back in England with his dictionary materials. For more than twenty-five years he laboured on his project and by his death he had published many parts but it remained incomplete. It was partly finished by his nephew Stanley Lane-Poole. It remains a monument of Arabic lexicography.

References

Ahmed (1978).

DEREK HOPWOOD

LAS NAVAS DE TOLOSA, BATTLE OF

Fought between the Berber-led Almohad Empire and the combined Christian forces of Leon, Castile, Navarre and

Aragon. The Christians attacked the massive Muslim army of Muhammad bin Ya'qub on the plains north of Jaen on 16 July AD 1212. In a battle that ebbed and flowed, the decisive moment came with the failure of an all-out Muslim charge. The Almohads retreated to their Moroccan heartland, leaving the remaining Muslim states vulnerable. Christians retook Cordova in AD 1236, Valencia in AD 1238 and Seville in AD 1248, leaving only Granada as the last Islamic state in Spain.

References

Lapidus (1999: 367, 384), Sweetman (1984: 99–100).

SIMON W. MURDEN

AL-LAT

The names of the three principal goddesses ('the daughters of Allah'), who were worshipped among many other deities in pre-Islamic Arabia, appear in Q.53:19–20 *al-Najm,* the Star. They are al-Lat (the goddess), al-'Uzza (Venus, the morning star) and Manah (goddess of destiny). The message of Islam, fearlessly proclaimed by Muhammad, was that God (Allah) is One and that He has neither daughters nor sons. Pagan belief held that these goddesses represented female attributes of God, al-Lat was visualised in human form. Pilgrims went to worship and sacrifice at her sanctuary in al-Ta'if to the south of Mecca. Al-'Uzza was associated with the spirit of a sacred tree, Manat with a sacred white stone. Controversy over the so-called 'Satanic Verses' arose early in Islam after the Prophet Muhammad is alleged to have claimed to have received a revelation reading, 'these [the goddesses] are the exalted ones, whose intercession is

hoped for'. These words were subsequently 'abrogated', leaving Q.53:19–20 as it now stands.

See also: **pre-Islamic Arabia**

EDWARD D. A. HULMES

AL-LAWH AL-MAHFUZ

'The preserved tablet', on which the Qur'an was said to have been written (Q.85:21–2) but traditionally in a metaphysical, and pre-existential sense.

References

Amir-Moezzi (1994: 96).

ANDREW J. NEWMAN

LAW, ISLAMIC

See: *shari'a*

LAWRENCE, THOMAS EDWARD (1888–1935)

British soldier and author. Lawrence was born in Wales, the illegitimate son of an Irish aristocrat and was educated at school and university in Oxford. After graduation he was attracted to the Middle East and in 1910 joined an archaeological expedition to the Hittite city of Carchemish with the famous British archaeologist Leonard Woolley. He later travelled in the Sinai desert, which he helped to map, earning from some the accusation that he was acting as a spy. He also learned Arabic although how well is disputed. He was in the Middle East when the First World War began and joined British military intelligence in Cairo. He helped to produce the *Arab Bulletin,* a publication that attempted to distil British knowledge about the Arab world. He soon became known for his unorthodox approach to military life, discipline and dress, but appreciated for his intelligence. The British in Cairo were at the time pondering the wisdom of supporting the Arabs of the Hejaz in a rising against the Ottoman army. Lawrence was sent to join Faysal, the son of the Hashimite leader Husayn in the Hejaz and quickly developed a relationship of trust with him. He was convinced that Britain should support the Arabs and offer them some form of independence after the war. He persuaded the British in the shape of General Allenby that he should be allowed a fairly free hand in helping to organise the Arab revolt. He became military adviser to the Arab forces, unified them and led them in various guerrilla attacks particularly those against the Hejaz railway that was used to transport Ottoman troops. By a daring move across the desert planned by Lawrence the Arabs forces captured Aqaba in the north (now in Jordan) and thus weakened the Ottoman presence in the area. It was at this period that Lawrence claimed he was captured by the Turks and subjected to degrading treatment at the hands of the local Ottoman commander. This experience, he said, irrevocably ruined his life. Lawrence, however, had an active imagination, and no one has ever been quite sure whether the incident actually took place.

He continued to help to direct the revolt, although he felt he was now betraying the Arabs as he had learned that the French and the British had concluded the Sykes–Picot Agreement which seemed to him to subject the Arabs to foreign authority rather than give them the full independence they believed they had been promised. Lawrence and Faysal reached Damascus together in the wake of the retreating Turks but he soon left the area disillusioned. He agreed to accompany Faysal to the Paris Peace Conference to put the case for Arab independence but there

they were no match for the policies and statesmen of the British and French. Lawrence's exploits in the desert were publicised at home by the American journalist, Lowell Thomas, and he thus gained the soubriquet 'Lawrence of Arabia', becoming perhaps the most famous Briton of his time. Oddly dissatisfied with his role and fame, he retired to write his memoirs of the revolt, *Seven Pillars of Wisdom* – a best-selling literary mixture of fact and imagination.

From 1921 to 1922 Lawrence was attached to the Middle East Division of the Colonial Office and helped Churchill and others to settle the future of the Middle East under the British in an attempt to repay the Arabs partially for their role in the war. In an effort to escape further notoriety he joined the RAF under the name of Ross. When discovered by the press, he joined the army as T. E. Shaw in 1923 and the airforce again from 1925 until 1935. He was killed shortly after in a motorcycle accident.

References

Asher (1998), Wilson (1990).

DEREK HOPWOOD

LAYLAT AL-ISRA' WA'L-MI'RAJ

See: **Night Journey, The**

LAYLAT AL-QADR

'The Night of Destiny' on which, in AD 610, the entire Qur'an is held to have been sent to Muhammad's soul, and said to be 27 Ramadan. See Q.97.

References

Waines (1995: 91, 284).

ANDREW J. NEWMAN

LEAGUE OF ARAB STATES

The organisation of Arab states established in 1945, operating under a charter and serviced by a headquarters in Cairo. By 1990, it had twenty-one members. It has been an important Arab forum, with its members linked by wide-ranging agreements and regular summits and ministerial meetings, but the organisation rarely fulfilled its potential. When Egypt made a separate peace with Israeli in March 1979, it was suspended from the League and the headquarters moved to Tunis. Egypt's status was restored in March 1989, but in 1990–1 the organisation failed to deal with Iraq's invasion of Kuwait.

References

Bill and Springborg (1994: 357–8), Owen (2000: 68, 73), The official website of the League of Arab States: http://www.arableagueonline.org/arableague.

SIMON W. MURDEN

LEBANESE CIVIL WAR (1975–91)

Fought between the militias of Lebanon's sectarian groups with the participation of Israeli, Syrian and Palestinian forces. Following independence in 1945, Christian, Muslim and Druze all worked within a political system that divided up powers according to confessional group, with Maronite Christians being the most important. By the 1970s, the system was beleaguered by demographic changes and external influences, especially the arrival of large numbers of armed Palestinians. On 13 April 1975, Maronite militiamen attacked the Palestinians. The subsequent fighting pitted the leftist forces of the Lebanese National Movement (LNM) and the Palestinian Liberation Organization (PLO) against the Lebanese Front. LNM–PLO forces proved

superior. Fearing defeat, the Maronite President appealed for Syrian intervention, which came in June 1976. The Israeli invasions of 1978 and 1982 added to the complexity. Some Christians allied themselves to Israel, while Sh'ia Muslims grew into an important new power by forming the Amal and Hizballah militias. The influence of the PLO was significantly reduced after 1982, but the country descended into chaos until the Syrian army again restored order. On 13 October 1990, the Maronite forces of Michel Aoun were crushed, opening the way to a peace process. Following negotiations between Lebanese parliamentarians in Ta'if, Saudi Arabia, Syria presided over a peace process which increased Muslim influence.

References

Hourani (1991: 429–33), Norton (1991: 457–73).

SIMON W. MURDEN

LEO AFRICANUS (HASAN IBN MUHAMMAD AL-WAZZAN AL-ZIYATI) (1485–1554)

Traveller, writer and intellectual. Born in Granada, but expelled by the Christian conquest of 1492, he was educated in Fez and travelled widely in Africa on diplomatic and trading missions. He was captured by Christian buccaneers in 1517 and given to Pope Leo X as a slave, but was soon freed and converted to Christianity. Taking the name Giovanni Leone, he became a scholar and teacher of Latin and Arabic, and wrote about his travels in *Descrittione dell' Africa*. He eventually returned to North Africa probably to live as a Muslim.

References

Masonen (2002: 115–43).

SIMON W. MURDEN

LIBER DE CAUSIS

A Greek work which is known to the Arabs under the name of *Pure Goodness* (*al-Khayr al-Mahd*). This work was attributed to Aristotle and translated probably from Arabic to Latin. It was known in its Latin version with the title *Liber Bonitatis Purae* and also as *Liber de Causis*. The problems surrounding its authorship have been known to the West since the thirteenth century when Albertus Magnus in AD 1206 attributed it to a Jewish scholar called Ibn Dawud who was supposed to have compiled it from the sayings of Aristotle, Avecnna, al-Ghazali and al-Farabi. However, Thomas Aquinas, who was a contemporary Albertus Magnus, recognised in AD 1224 that the book which the latter mentions must have been taken from Proclus' *Elements of Theology*. This shows that the book, in fact, contains Neoplatonic thought and is by no means Aristotelian. Whether this book was translated into Arabic and whether the Arabs were responsible for the problems of its authorship is not yet determined. Badawi argues that the book was known to the Arabs before al-Farabi and Ibn Sina (who refer in some of their works to God as the first or pure Goodness) with the title *The First Goodness, al-Khayr al-Awwal*. He depends on the reference of Ibn al-Nadim for a book with the title *The First Goodness,* which he attributes to Proclus. Fakhry also mentions an earlier reference to this work in *Siwan al-Hikma* of al-Sijistani, he is referring here to a work attributed to Proclus entitled *Niskus Minor* or *The Pure Goodness*.

References

Badawi (1977), Fakhry (1983: 19–31).

MAHA EL-KAISY FRIEMUTH

LIBERIA, ISLAM IN

Liberia (the name means 'land of freedom') is a republic situated on the west coast of Africa. The region it now occupies was once the home of the Mande, the Kru and other Melle-speaking communities, who were already in process of establishing closer political, social and economic relationships before the Portuguese merchant venturers and colonialist administrators arrived in the fifteenth century. Isolated by the surrounding forests and mountains from the expansionist designs and the influence of the empires of Ghana, Mali and Songhay, the region saw the emergence of several small, widely scattered small states, which found ways of working together for the purposes of trade and mutual defence. As in other parts of the savannah and the tropical forest lands of West Africa, migration made for a population on the move. Among those who came and stayed were Muslims from the empires of the savannah to the west, north and east, and from the central deserts still further north. 'The impact of Islam was sufficiently great to have led to the invention of an indigenous alphabet among the Vai, a subgroup of the Mande, in the early decades of the nineteenth century' (Bowen Jones 1978: 309). Of the many tribes within the borders of Liberia the Vai and Mandingo are largely Muslim.

The modern republic of Liberia is bordered to the west by Sierra Leone, by Guinea to the north-west, and by Ivory Coast to the east. It was founded in 1821 by the American Colonisation Society and became a fully independent colony in 1847 after pressure was brought to bear by the British. The principal aim of the American Colonisation Society was humanitarian in that it sought to persuade former black slaves and their dependants to return to a place on the west coast of Africa, where they could be truly free after being oppressed, in particular, on the plantations in the southern states of the USA. The capital of Liberia, its chief port and main commercial centre is Monrovia. The Constitution of Liberia is modelled on that of the USA. The President is elected initially for an eight-year term. In the recent disturbances in Liberia, especially in the capital, Monrovia, and during the final days of the presidency of Charles Taylor (August 2003), repeated attempts were made to press the USA to intervene militarily to end the civil war. These appeals were made not only by the people of Liberia but also by leaders in other countries in the world community on the grounds that the USA has a special responsibility in that region, having been instrumental in establishing Liberia in the early years of the nineteenth century.

The first settlers to return to Liberia from the USA were called Americo-Liberians. One of them was the black scholar Edward Wilmot Blyden, who was to gain international recognition as a passionate advocate of the right of Negroes (his word) to live in freedom from slavery in America and from the continuing burden of European colonial dependency in Africa. Working in and from Liberia, he travelled extensively, lecturing and writing prolifically about what he observed. One late example of his concern for his adopted homeland is provided by his essay 'The Future of Liberia', which was published in the *Liberia Bulletin* (no. 26), in February 1905. Blyden's listeners and readers in the USA and in Europe were informed about the quality and depth of Islamic learning and culture in that part of West Africa. To his intense disappointment, he was unable to persuade large numbers of American blacks to return to Africa. Fewer and fewer chose to return after the end of the American Civil War in 1865.

It is fair to say that the ending of the African slave trade and the establishment of both Sierra Leone and Liberia in West Africa as havens for liberated African slaves owed much to the impetus of Christian campaigners. In both Sierra Leone and Liberia it is not surprising, therefore, to discover that new Christian missions were established at an early date. The influence of that missionary activity has tended to obscure the continuing resilience of Islamic life and culture in the region.

References

Davidson (1977: 252–60), Earthy (1955), Hulmes (1990: 44–65).

See also: **slavery and the slave trade in West Africa; Blyden, Edward Wilmot**
EDWARD D. A. HULMES

LIGHT VERSE

Q.24:35. An image-complex related to the vision of God, used as a focus of speculation and devotion to the divine being. The verse reads:

> God is the light of the heavens and the earth. The parable of His light is as if there were a niche and within it a lamp. The lamp enclosed in glass, the glass as it were a brilliant star. Lit from a blessed tree, an olive, neither of the east nor of the west, whose oil is well-nigh luminous, though fire barely touched it. Light upon light! God guides whom He will to His light: God sets forth parables for people: and God knows all things.

References

Yusuf Ali (1968: 907–8).
ANDREW RIPPIN

LOT

See: **Lut**

LUQMAN

A pre-Islamic prophet mentioned in Q.31:12, the *sura* being named after him. Described as a man of wisdom, Luqman has been identified as a pre-Islamic sage and developed into a sayer of proverbs, some of which are similar to the aphorisms attributed to Ahiqar of Near Eastern wisdom literature. According to Q.31:13–19, he offered the wisdom to his son of the knowledge and power of the one God. The exegetical tradition continued this pattern of the Islamicisation of pre-Islamic knowledge, fitting Luqman into the model of the other prophets but with special emphasis on his wisdom. Luqman becomes a writer of tales in the style of Aesop.

References

Gibb and Bosworth (1960–2003: V, 811).

ANDREW RIPPIN

LUT

The prophet Lot who attempted to warn his people of Allah's imminent punishment, and whose household, except for his wife, were saved. See Q.11:70–1.

See also: **rasul**

ANDREW J. NEWMAN

M

AL-MA'MUN, 'ABDALLAH B. AL-RASHID, ABU JA'FAR
(AD 813–33)

The struggle for power between the 'Abbasid caliph al-Rashid's sons al-Amin and al-Ma'mun was decided in al-Ma'mun's favour with the killing of al-Amin and the taking of Baghdad (AD 813). The temporary lapse of central authority led to general unrest, and al-Ma'mun subsequently faced a number of threats including widespread revolts in Egypt and a serious Shi'ite insurrection in Iraq in AD 815. Nevertheless, al-Ma'mun managed to assert his authority and the prosperity of the 'Abbasid caliphate was continued during his reign.

In addition to military control, al-Ma'mun wanted to tighten the religious basis of the empire. He thus gave official state recognition to the theological positions of the Mu'tazilites and allowed them to practise a kind of inquisition (*mihna*) under which those not espousing their view regarding the creation of the Qur'an were persecuted. Al-Ma'mun's nomination of 'Ali b. Musa al-Rida ('the chosen one'), a descendant of 'Ali b. Abi Talib, as his successor was perhaps an attempt to reconcile those of Shi'ite sympathy. Al-Rida, however, died before the Caliph and was replaced by al-Ma'mun's brother Muhammad b. al-Rashid, the future al-Mu'tasim.

References

Hodgson (1974: 299–300, 475–9), Kennedy (1981: 135–40, 154–62, 164–76; 1996: 148–57), Muir (1915: 495–511), Shaban (1971: 41–5, 52–61), al-Tabari (1985–95: XXXI, see index; XXXII, see index).

RONALD PAUL BUCKLEY

AL-MA'ARRI, ABU AL-'ALA'
(AD 973–1058)

Syrian poet and prose writer. Blinded by smallpox at an early age, al-Ma'arri studied in his home town of Ma'arrat al-Nu'man and in Aleppo before travelling to Baghdad, but he apparently found literary life in the city uncongenial and, prompted partly by his mother's illness, returned to Ma'arrat al-Nu'man in 1010 where he led a secluded life until his death. He described himself as 'doubly imprisoned' by his blindness and seclusion, and although he received many students, he continued to lead a life of extreme asceticism, sleeping on his prayer-mat and never marrying.

Al-Ma'arri's output, which is characterised by an attitude of pessimism and misanthropy, can hardly be understood without reference to his disability. It nonetheless represents one of the most important contributions to the literature of the 'Abbasid period, remarkable not only for the author's linguistic prowess and technical accomplishment but also for its freshness and unconventionality. Not all of the works attributed to him by later biographers have survived. Of those that do, his first collection of poetry, *Saqt al-Zand*, is remarkable for its inclusion of a number of poems devoted to a description of different types of armour. His second collection, *Luzum ma la Yalzam* or *al-Luzumiyyat*, is characterised not only by a highly ornate style but also by the use of a double rhyme scheme instead of the conventional Arabic system of monorhyme; in addition to its technical interest, the work quickly attracted attention for the author's views expressed therein, some of which were held to be incompatible with Islam. Al-Ma'arri's reputation as a heretic or freethinker was later given a further boost when he was accused of trying to surpass the Qur'an in a work entitled *al-Fusul wa al-Ghayat*.

Of al-Ma'arri's prose works, the most significant is *Risalat al-Ghufran*, composed about AD 1033, which describes the visits of the scholar Ibn al-Qarih to Heaven and Hell, where he converses with scholars and poets from previous ages; this work, a vivid and unique expression of an artistic vision, has been frequently discussed in the West as a precursor to Dante's *Divine Comedy*. An earlier, recently rediscovered work, *al-Sahil wa al-Shahij*, composed around AD 1019, contains a discussion of contemporary political events between a horse and a mule and provides direct evidence of the author's keen interest in contemporary society, despite his reclusive lifestyle.

References

Ashtiany *et al.* (1990: 328–38), Cachia (1970: 129–36), Nicholson (1900–2), Sperl (1989).

PAUL STARKEY

MADRASA

The *madrasa* (a place of study) is a residential institute for higher education open to students who had completed the curriculum of the primary *kuttab* school with memorisation of the Qur'an. Courses taught included further study of the Qur'an, the *hadith*, logic, jurisprudence, Arabic grammar and rhetoric, and the natural sciences of mathematics and medicine. The *madrasa*, which had developed into a distinct institution by the eleventh century AD, relied on various sources of funding – state endowments, charitable donations from private individuals, trade and craft guilds. Providing the *madrasa* offered space for teaching and prayer and accommodation for staff and students, there was scope for architectural variation. The *madrasas* of fourteenth-century Fez, for example, are compact, based on a standard plan of an enclosed courtyard with pool, within two storeys, the lower one with a prayer hall and lecture spaces, the upper one concealing a rabbit warren of students' rooms. The internal façades are covered with glazed tile mosaic, carved wood and moulded stucco in intricate designs. In contrast the *madrasas* attached to the great mosque complexes of Istanbul and Edirne are austere courtyards enclosed within domed colonnades of grey stone.

References

Makdisi (1981), Peretic (1912).

JENNIFER SCARCE

MAFATIH AL-'ULUM

This handbook of the major branches of knowledge that a properly educated Muslim might be expected to know about was composed by the little-known Abu 'Abdallah Muhammad b. Ahmad al-Katib al-Khuwarazmi (not the same as the great mathematician Muhammad b. Musa 'l-Khuwarazmi, who lived in the early ninth century AD). It is dedicated to Abu 'l-Hasan 'Ubaydallah al-'Utbi, who was Vizier to the Samanid ruler Nuh II Ibn Mansur (AD 976–97), and so it must have been written in the latter tenth century in Bukhara or some adjacent area of the north-eastern Islamic empire.

The *Mafatih al-'Ulum*, 'The Keys of the Sciences', is intended as a ready guide, primarily for the secretaries, *kuttab*, of which al-Khuwarazmi was himself one, whose work required them to be acquainted with the many disciplines and accompanying terminologies that were recognised in the Islamic world. This was an indispensable part of the *adab*, 'polite accomplishment', that any secretary who wished to advance in his profession of composing letters for his employer must have. In particular, al-Khuwarazmi says that he has included all the conventional and technical terms used by the various experts which the books that are restricted to grammar

omit, and consequently fail those who are seeking fuller accomplishment.

Far from being a reasoned exposition of the relationship between the branches of knowledge, such as the philosopher al-Farabi's slightly earlier *Ihsa' al-'Ulum* (*Ennumeration of the Sciences*), the *Mafatih al-'Ulum* accepts without discussion the conventional classification of its time. It is organised into two main discourses, *maqalatan*, one on the sacred sciences, *'ulum al-shari'a*, and the related Arab sciences, and the other on the foreign sciences, *'ulum al-'ajam*, of Greek and other origins. Within each there is a clear subdivision into chapters, *abwab*, and sections, *fusul*. Al-Khuwarazmi lists the main divisions of the work at the outset, thus making it a handbook which any busy professional could consult with reasonable ease.

The first discourse comprises six chapters with fifty-two sections. These chapters are on: legal thinking, *fiqh*, theology, *kalam*, grammar, *nahw*, writing, *kitab*, poetry and prosody, *shi'r wa'l-'arud*, and history, *akhbar*. The second discourse comprises nine chapters in forty-one sections on: philosophy, logic, medicine, arithmetic, geometry, astronomy, music, ingenious mechanical devices and alchemy. This two-part list, which follows the accepted Muslim division of the contemporary disciplines, provides a revealing insight into the extent and limitations of knowledge as these were recognised in the tenth-century AD Islamic world. Clearly, the Qur'an-based and Arab sciences of the earliest times had developed into substantial subjects worthy of study, while the Hellenistic and eastern sciences had realistically been acknowledged as important and necessary aspects of Muslim intellectual and practical life.

The sections into which these chapters are divided reveal further the extent of knowledge expected from the fully educated individual, and also indicate how the many intellectual pursuits were thought to be related at the time al-Khuwarazmi wrote. The wealth of the detailed terminology they contain is also informative about the contemporary understanding of the main activities thought appropriate within each. An instructive example is given in Chapter 2 of the first division, on *kalam*.

This chapter contains seven sections, the first on the agreed terms used by theological practitioners, among whom the Mu'tazila are mentioned as leading exponents of the discipline, the next five on the groups within Islam and among the major religions and sects of the day, and the last on the subjects of theological discourse. Section three is on the subdivisions among the Christians and their conventional terminology. Here are listed the three denominations of Melkites, Nestorians and Jacobites, each owing their origin to an individual founder (the name Melkite being said to have come from a certain individual named Malka', rather that the more usual Muslim derivation from the Roman emperor or 'king', *malik*). And then the key terms *uqnum*, hypostasis; *ittihad*, uniting of divine and human in Jesus Christ; *nasut*, human nature; *lahut*, divine nature; and finally *haykal*, sanctuary, 'the home of images, in which are found images of the prophets, peace be upon them, and images of the kings', are listed and briefly defined.

This summary is almost brutal in its brevity, and might lead one to suppose that for general purposes Christianity was of little importance in al-Khuwarazmi's world, and its origins and beliefs of little interest and maybe somewhat vague. Furthermore, the contents of the chapter as a whole suggest that the role of *kalam* was largely regarded as being to defend Islam against heretics and opponents, which is narrowed down greatly from its expansive vigour of a century earlier.

Here and throughout the *Mafatih al-'Ulum* can be seen al-Khuwarazmi's genius for simplification and clarification, which could guide busy scribes to key concepts and vocabulary items divested of complications and unnecessary details. This striking characteristic of the work makes it an often fascinating witness to the elements of learning that for the generally educated were considered essential, and hence to the aspects of knowledge that were regarded as important. It is thus valuable as a social document, and also because it reveals the assumption discernible in many branches of Islamic learning in the tenth century that knowledge comprised a finite body that could be encompassed and categorised. The same assumption lies beneath the composition of heresiographical works in religion, in the construction of philosophical systems of cosmology, in treatises on political theory and legal teachings, and in many other aspects of Islamic intellectual life.

The *Mafatih al-'Ulum* has been printed a number of times, the edition by van Vloten (1895–1968), being widely regarded as the standard text. It has not been translated in its entirety, though many of its individual parts have been translated into German or English, references are given in the article 'Al-Khuwarazmi'.

References

Bosworth (1963: 97–111), Van Vloten (1895).

DAVID THOMAS

AL-MAGHAZI

The work bearing this title presents one of the earliest records of the military campaigns (*maghazi*) of the Prophet Muhammad. It was prepared by Musa ibn 'Uqba (died AD 758) and revised in AD 1387 by Ibn Qadi Shuhba.

MAGHRIB

Arabic for '[the land of] the sunset', hence 'the West', is used for the western part of the Muslim world, especially North Africa from the Atlas Mountains to the coastal plains, an area where the Berbers were established before 1200 BC. The southern slopes fade into the desert of the Sahara to the south. The Africa Minor of classical times, it periodically included Moorish Spain and is divided into Tripolitania and Cyrenaica (Libya), East Maghrib, Tunisia (Ifriqiya) and Far Maghrib (Morocco). The Maghrib includes Morocco, Algeria, Libya, and Tunisia and sometimes Mauritania and Western Sahara.

The first wave of Muslim invaders defeated the Byzantine Prefect Gregory at Sbeitla in AD 647 and according to tradition 'Uqba b. Naf'i led the Umayyad invasion of the Maghribi coastal plains reaching the Atlantic c. AD 670. He founded al-Qayrawan as his capital, building the first mosque in North Africa there: it was to become the fourth most holy Islamic centre after Mecca, Medina and Jerusalem. In AD 703–11, a second Umayyad leader, Musa b. Nusayr, conquered Ifriqiya, converted the Berbers who with the Arabs invaded Spain. In reaction to the Arabs, Berbers aligned themselves as Kharjirites in Ifriqiya. Adherence to Islam was patchy until the arrival of Idris b. 'Abdallah, a descendant of the Prophet, who had escaped from 'Abbasid Egypt. Idris I (r. AD 788–91) was proclaimed ruler by Muslim Berbers in Volubilis but assassinated by an agent of Harun al-Rashid, the 'Abbasid caliph in Baghdad. Idris I, patron saint of Morocco, was buried in Moulay Idris, the city he founded and it is still one of the greatest Islamic shrines. His son, Moulay Idris II (r. AD 804–28), a dedicated Muslim *sharif* and a charismatic leader who united warring tribes through allegiance to Islam, established Fez as his capital and became its patron saint. Fez attracted 'refugees' from Cordoba (AD 818) and al-Qayrawan (AD 825) to become the most advanced centre of Muslim culture in the eastern Maghrib by AD 859.

In Ifriqiya, Ibraham b. Aghlab left Baghdad in the ninth century AD to found the Sunni Aghlabid dynasty that brought an era of Islamic consolidation with new mosques at al-Qayrawan, Sousse, Tunis and Sfax, and *ribats* and waterworks in Ifriqiya. In AD 909 the Aghlabids were conquered by Shi'i Fatimids in Ifriqiya. Their leader, 'Ubaydallah, declared himself *mahdi* and built a new capital, Mahdia. The Fatimids moved their capital from al-Qayrawan to Cairo (AD 969) and left Ifriqiya to be ruled by the Zirids, until AD 1046 when the Zirids transferred allegiance to the Sunni caliph in Baghdad. Fatimid reaction from Cairo was swift with an orgy of destruction by their agents, the Banu Hilal.

From the ninth century AD, most Maghribi scholars adhered to the Sunni Maliki school of law; including Darras ibn Isma'il (d. AD 968) from Fez who wrote a critique on Maliki law; Ibn Abi Zayd al-Qayraqani of Ifriqiya (d. AD 996) produced an authority of Miki *fiqh*; and Abu 'Imran al-Fasi (d. AD 430–1039) developed theological ideology for the Malikites. Isma'ili teaching also influenced scholars such as the esoteric Ibn Hani' al-Andalusi (d. AD 973), court poet of the Banu Hamdun, rulers of Masila in Ifriqiya (Tunis). The rounded Maghribi script with exaggerated extension of horizontal elements and final open curves below the register was the early script used by Muslims of the

Maghrib and is still used in northern Africa from Morocco to Tripoli.

In the eleventh century AD the Maghrib developed from an Islamic frontier ruled by feudal warlords to an area with major Muslim administrative and cultural centres. From the Sahara, the Sanhaja Berber nomads established the Almoravid empire (*al-murabitun*) in the Maghrib (AD 1056–1147), based on wealth in gold from Niger and salt from Sijilmassa. Their leader, Yusuf b. Tashfin (AD 1062–1107), founded Marrakesh, building a mosque there in AD 1062 where the Kutubiyya now stands, then conquered Fez. By AD 1086 his empire extended from Algiers to Andalusia. He imposed strict traditional Islam and converted West African and Berber communities, for whom Islam was made accessible through *marabouts*. His son, 'Ali (AD 1107–44) embellished Marrakesh but was otherwise ineffectual, though pious and, in turn, the Almoravids were seen as infidels.

Islam was reflected in medieval poetry and prose focused on theology and jurisprudence. The chief centres of learning included al-Qayrawan (the capital of the Zirid rulers of Ifriqiya) and Fez, and later Marrakesh, Tlemcen and Bougie. Qayrawani scholars included Abu al-'Arab Muhammad (d. AD 945) expert on *'ulama'*, poet and historian Ibn Raqiq (d. after AD 1027), physician and historian Ibn al-Jazzar (d. AD 1005), Ibn 'Arafa (d. 1401) expert in Maliki jurisprudence, the poet Ibn Sharaf (*c.* AD 1000–1067) patronised by al-Mu'izz ibn Badis, ruler of Qayrawan, and the encyclopaedist, Ibn al-Rashiq (AD 1000–1063/71) who was court poet to the Zirid ruler al-Mu'izz. Maghribi scientists included Ibn Juljul, Ibn al-Salt and the twelfth-century pharmacologist, al-Ghafiqi, whose *Book of Simple Drugs* describes proprieties of plants known in the Muslim world.

The Almohads, Masmouda Berbers, under the powerful and pious orator Muhammad Ibn Tumart (d. AD 1133) a descendant of 'Ali, the Prophet's son-in-law, established their empire (AD 1130–1269) which extended to Tripolitania. Called *mahdi* by his followers, he founded a doctrine of absolute unity with God (*al-muwahhidun*) that was to control the Maghrib for almost a century. He was succeeded by an Algerian potter, 'Abd al-Mu'min (AD 1133–63) who controlled a vast empire from Spain to Ifriqiya. His grandson, Ya'qub al Mansur (AD 1184–99), is remembered as a builder of mosques, especially the Kutubiyya in Marrakesh, and the unfinished Mosque al-Hasan ('the beautiful') in Rabat, a city he founded. Ya'qub al-Mansur also built the first large hospital in the Maghrib in Marrakesh attracting doctors such as Ibn Tufayl (*c.* AD 1110–85) who was Chief Physician and probably Prime Minister under Yusuf (d. AD 1184) and Qadi Ibn Rushd (1126–98). In Ifriqiya, the independent Hafsid dynasty made Tunis their capital in the early thirteenth century, helping Muslims persecuted by the Christian Spain, resisting Crusaders (AD 1270). Al-Mustansir (AD 1249–77) became the leading monarch in the Islamic world, based on proceeds of expanding trade and piracy. The Almoravid and Almohad eras are remembered as the golden age of Islamic civilisation.

From the late thirteenth century charismatic Sufi leaders and saints formed foci of veneration in particular cities. A reformed Maliki tradition continued to be important alongside Sufism and speculative theology. The absolute disarray of the Almohads from AD 1213 led to the Marinid dynasty, that advocated traditional Islam and developed *madrasa* including the Bu Inaniyya, built by Sultan Abu Inan (AD 1351–8) in Fez.

Christian re-expansion from mainland Spain drove Muslims to the Maghrib (AD 1009–1260). The cultural prestige of Fez was enhanced after ancient Arab manuscripts were returned from Spain (AD 1268). Yet this time of violence was also one of brilliant intellectual thought by Jews and Christians as well as Muslims working in a cosmopolitan society. The Marinids encouraged scholars, including the historian Ibn 'Idhari (d. AD 1312) an official from Fez, and Ibn Battuta (d. 1368 or AD 1377) born in Tangiers who travelled 75,000 miles (121,000 kilometres). The distinguished Muslim jurist and statesman Ibn Khaldun (AD 1332–1406) was born in Tunis and patronised in the courts of Fez, Granada, and Cairo. His al-Muqaddima sets out historical principles, centuries ahead of his time. There was a tradition of biographies/histories of local dynasties and cities and many historians also wrote on a wide range of topics, including religious morals and law, such as the Sufi Ibn Marzuq (AD 1310–79), from Tlemcen who became secretary to the Marinid Sultan Abu al-Hasan (AD 1331–51). The Marinids also introduced Islamic codes of conduct while their eye for architectural beauty was outstanding.

After the Christian conquest of Granada in 1492 the Maghrib was increasingly in political and intellectual contact with Europe: Portuguese and Spanish Christian merchants moved into the Maghrib. Under Muhammad al-Mahdi (1554–7), the Sa'dians, descendants of the Prophet who came to Wadi Dar'a from Arabia in the fourteenth century, moved north and south to Timbuktu to re-establish the observance of Islam and throw out Christian invaders. Again they enriched palaces, mausolea and mosques, including the Qayrawiyyri in Marrakesh.

The Alouites, also descended from the Prophet, still rule Morocco and the king is also its religious leader. In 1666, the first Alouite king, Mawlay al-Rashid (1664–72), was invited to rule Fez by its townspeople. He revived the life of its mosques, but his brother, Mawlay Isma'il (r. 1672–1727) was one of the cruelest rulers of Morocco. After the capture of Constantinople by the Ottoman Turks in 1453, Qahir al-Din (Barbarossa) secured Ottoman support against Spanish naval raids. By 1529 he had taken Algiers, and in 1534 expelled the Hafsids from Tunis and Kairoun. By 1536 the Ottomans established effective control, but wars against Spain continued until 1574 when Tunis, Tripoli and Algiers were made regencies of the Ottoman Empire until the eighteenth century when wars within the Maghrib hastened disintegration of Ottoman control. In the early eighteenth century the Karmanli dynasty ruled for about 120 years, until the Ottomans resumed control.

European interest in the region revived so by 1830 France had annexed Algeria and attacked Tunisia in 1836. The Sanusiyya order was established in 1837 and became very influential in political life, especially in Libya. Britain, Italy, Germany, Spain and France fought over control of North Africa. Eventually French protectorates were established in Tunisia (1881–1956), Algeria (c. 1830–1962) and Morocco (1912–56), whilst Libya was colonised by the Italians from 1911, then ruled by a Sanusi monarch from 1951. Following independence, Bourguiba in Tunisia audaciously downgraded the Zaytuna University to a theological faculty and tried to end the tradition of the Ramadan fast. Morocco has hosted the Islamic Conference Organisation as part of its official responsibilities. Late twentieth-century reaction to Francophone influences have meant an upsurge in radical Islam especially in cities, notably the Algerian Front Islamique du Salut, and the puritanical Muslim regime in Libya under Gaddafi (1969–), alongside traditional and Sufi practices. All Muslims in Morocco are Sunnis, following the Maliki school. Yet in rural areas Islam continues to revolve around *marabouts*, pilgrimage festivals and the local mosque. Religious brotherhoods include the Tijaniyya, Darqawa, Tayyibiyya-Tuhama, Katiyya, etc., and the cult of saints, some of them *sharifs*, is highly developed.

References

Brett (1999), Gibb (1971), Golliday (1988), Maxwell (1966), Meisami and Starkey (1998: II, 484–8), Powers (2002).

JANET STARKEY

MAGIC AND TALISMANS

In the context of religious belief and practice, the word 'magic' refers to a ritual act, or acts, which are believed to enlist the power of transcendent forces in order to influence the course of nature. In the Islamic world, magic is variously described as 'lawful' or 'unlawful', as 'white magic' (*al-sihr al-abyad*) or as 'black magic' (*al-sihr al-aswad*). An example of 'lawful magic' (*sihr halal*) is the effect of Arabic on the hearer, especially the Arabic of the Qur'an. The Holy Book is the greatest miracle in Islam. It is the supreme example of that which is lawful, because it comes from God. Its last two chapters are quoted by Muslims who seek to turn away, seeking refuge, from anything that does not have divine sanction. Unlawful magic is that which is worked by the collusion of men with malevolent *jinn* and *ifrits* (*'afarit*, demons). The mysterious power of magic is associated in Islam with the various orders of created spirits, some beneficent, some malevolent, known as

jinn. Lower than the angels (*al-mala'ik*), the *jinn* have the power to assume human or animal form and to interfere in the lives of mortals. Their status in Islam is the subject of Q.72. In pre-Islamic Arabia, the magician (*al-sahhar*), the soothsayer (*al-'arraf*) and the poet (*al-sha'ir*) were considered to possess esoteric supernatural knowledge and to be under the influence of the *jinn*. Sorcery is forbidden in Islam. The use of amulets and talismans is common among the Muslims of North and West Africa. Ancient incantations, or quotations from the Qur'an, are often sown into a leather pouch, which is then worn round the neck or attached to the body to protect the wearer against evil forces. Magic is neither to be taught not learned except under certain conditions. The fact that these conditions are not precisely stated makes Islamic attitudes to magic in the modern world somewhat ambivalent. Though still popularly held by many people, the belief that magical and astrological principles are useful for understanding and interpreting the universe is not easily reconciled with a monotheistic religion such as Islam.

References

Schacht and Bosworth (1979: 381, 438, 442–3), Tritton (1968: 147–9).

See also: **alchemy (*al-kimiya'*); astrology (*'ilm al-falak, 'ilm al-nujum*); pre-Islamic Arabia**

EDWARD D. A. HULMES

MAHDI

'The guided one', whom many Muslims believe is from the family of the Prophet and who will return before the Day of Judgement. Though the term probably originated in the late seventh century AD, among followers of Muhammad b. al-Hanafiyya, it became especially identified with the Twelfth Imam, whose followers identify him as the *mahdi*. The term has been appropriated for, and by, a number of figures in Islamic history.

References

Waines (1995: 164–9, 185, 285).

See also: **ghayba**

ANDREW J. NEWMAN

AL-MAHDI, MUHAMMAD B. AL-MANSUR, ABU 'ABDALLAH (AD 775–85)

The 'Abbasid caliph al-Mahdi inherited a comparatively peaceful empire from his father al-Mansur. During his ten-year rule, al-Mahdi largely continued the policies adopted by his predecessor. He did, however, attempt to reconcile the Shi'ites to 'Abbasid rule by, for example, granting estates and positions at court to members of the 'Alid family. Al-Mahdi is perhaps chiefly remembered for his religious persecution of the Manicheans (*zanadiqa*) whose beliefs were attracting many Muslims including some in his own court. He was succeeded by his eldest son Musa al-Hadi.

References

Kennedy (1996: 137–40; 1981: 96–108), Shaban (1971: 21–6), al-Tabari (1985–95: XXVIII, 69–98 *passim*, 220–78 *passim*; XXIX, see index).

RONALD PAUL BUCKLEY

MAHDISM (SUDAN)

The term for an Islamic saviour figure used by Muhammad Ahmad Ibn Al-Sayyid 'Abdallah (1844–85). In the 1860–70s, he developed mystical beliefs within the Sammaniyah brotherhood and gained a following. He declared himself the *mahdi* (the Rightly Guided

One) in 1881, and initiated a *jihad* to expel Anglo-Egyptian influence. The high point of his *jihad* came with the fall of Khartoum on 26 January 1885, in which Maj.-Gen. Charles Gordan was killed. The Mahdi's realm ranged from the Red Sea to central Africa, but he died in June 1885. His followers were eventually subdued by forces led by General Sir Herbert Kitchener at the Battle of Omdurman on 2 September 1898.

References

Lapidus (1999: 854–9), Perret (1996: 98, 155, 225).

SIMON W. MURDEN

MAHFOUZ, NAGUIB (1911–2006)

Egyptian writer. The Arab world's greatest novelist, he was born in Cairo and has spent all his life in that city. His work has been deeply influenced by Cairene society and Egyptian history. His father was a minor government official who sent his son to secular state schools. He also studied philosophy for a time at Cairo University but started writing before completing his degree. Like other Egyptian authors, he earned his living in government service until his retirement in 1971.

During his long life he has written dozens of works, mostly novels and some short stories, often very controversial, arousing the anger of secular governments and Muslim opponents alike. He was awarded the Nobel Prize for Literature in 1988. He was badly wounded in 1994 by two Muslim militants who attempted to assassinate him because of his well-known views.

He has brought the Arabic novel to a high level of achievement, sometimes boldly experimental in form, often allegorical in the attempt to criticise policy

and beliefs in a highly censored environment. He has shown a deep commitment to social and political ideologies
and is a thinker of integrity and depth.

His best-known works are *The Cairo
Trilogy*, an impressive Dickensian-like
portrayal of generations of life in lower
middle-class Cairo. His most controversial is *Awlad haratna* (*Children of our
Quarter*, translated as *Children of Gebe-
laawi*), a wide-ranging allegory of the role
of religion and science in human society.

References

El-Enany (1993), Somekh (1973).

DEREK HOPWOOD

MAHMUD I (r. 1730–54)

Ottoman Sultan, son of Mustafa II. On
his accession Mahmud suppressed the
rebellion of Patrona Halil that had
forced Ahmed III's abdication. Shortly
afterwards, the rise of Nadir Shah in
Iran and the Russian seizure of Azov in
1736 led to Ottoman withdrawal from
territories in Iran conquered in the
1720s, and peace with Nadir Shah. In
the same year, Mahmud declared war
on Russia, which formed an anti-
Ottoman alliance with Austria. The war
ended in 1739, with the treaty of
Belgrade restoring the territories lost by
the treaty of Passarowitz. A second war
with Nadir Shah ended in 1746 with a
treaty re-establishing the borders fixed
in 1555. A period of peace followed.

References

Mantran (1989b: 277–9).

COLIN IMBER

MAHMUD II (r. 1808–39)

Ottoman Sultan, son of 'Abdul-hamid I.
Mahmud came to the throne as a result
of Bayraktar Mustafa Pasha's counter-
coup to restore Selim III and the assassination of Selim. Shortly afterwards,
Bayraktar Mustafa lost his life in a
Janissary rebellion. His death returned
political authority to Mahmud, who
attempted to reform the Empire's military and administrative structure. In
1826, he destroyed the Janissary corps
during a rebellion opposing his efforts
to form a new army. In the provinces
he replaced powerful notables with
nominated governors, in 1822 finally
defeating Tepedelenli Ali Pasha. He
reorganised the central government into
ministries. He carried out his reforms in
the face of constant crises. The Treaty of
Tilsit with France in 1807 allowed the
Russians to declare war in 1810, and to
encourage Serbian efforts to win independence. In 1829 Serbia acquired the
status of automous province. Meanwhile, insurrection in Greece led to the
intervention of Britain, France and
Russia. In 1827, a Franco-British fleet
destroyed the Ottoman fleet at Navar-
ino. In 1828 Russia declared war and,
by 1829, had advanced as far as Edirne.
The London Conference of Britain and
France prevented Russia dismembering
Ottoman provinces in the Balkans. In
the same year, Greece achieved independence and France occupied Algiers.
Meanwhile, the quasi-independent Governor of Egypt, Muhammad 'Ali sought
the governorship of Syria as compensation for the assistance he had provided
Mahmud during the Greek war. When
Mahmud refused, he occupied Syria and
Palestine and invaded Anatolia. By 1833
he had reached Kutahya. French and
British intervention and a Russian pre-
sence on the Bosphorus resulted in the
treaty of Kutahya granting Muhammad
'Ali the governorships of Egypt and
Crete, and his son Ibrahim the gover-
norship of Syria, Cilicia and the Hijaz.
In 1839, Mahmud sent an army against

Ibrahim in Syria. It suffered a defeat at Nisibin, while Mahmud's fleet capitulated at Alexandria. Mahmud died in the aftermath of these events.

References

Mantran (1989c: 434–45).

COLIN IMBER

MAHR (BRIDE PRICE)

See: **marriage**

MAIMONIDES (1135–)

Moses b. Maimon, known as Maimonides, a Jewish philosopher who lived in Islamic Spain and was greatly influenced by Islamic philosophy and thought. He was born in Cordoba in 1135, the son of a rabbi and judge in the Jewish community. The Jewish community adopted Arabic as their intellectual language and read Arabic literature and philosophy. But, because of the political instability of the time, his family lived for some time in Fez AD 1148–60 and then went to Egypt. In AD 1185 Maimonides was appointed as physician to the Vizier of Salah al-Din al-Ayyubi. He also became the Chief Rabbi of the Jewish community in Egypt.

Maimonides followed the Islamic philosophy of the western half of the empire, following Ibn Rushd and Ibn Bajja. He was also a faithful follower of the Aristotelian school and opposed Neoplatonism as it was studied among the eastern Muslim philosophers. His main conviction was that the search for the truth lies in a thorough application of strictly rational demonstrative methods. In his famous book *The Guide* he, like Ibn Rushd, attempts to refute al-Ghazali's argument against the ability of philosophy to reach the truth about God and the origin of the world through demonstrative theory. He argues that al-Ghazali and the Ash'arite arguments are far from the demonstrative, but rather dialectic in style. Finally, Maimonides also wrote works to do with the Jewish religion such as *The Commentary on the Mishnah* (in Arabic) and *The Mishnah Torah* (in Hebrew).

References

Nasr and Leaman (1996: I, 725–39).

MAHA EL-KAISY FRIEMUTH

MA'IN

Ancient South Arabian kingdom (fourth to second century BC), possibly conquered by the Sabaeans. The Minaeans were peaceful merchants engaged in the aromatics trade from democratic city states, including Qarnaw (Khirbet Ma'in), Yathil (Barakish) and Dedan (al 'Ula in northern Hijaz). Others possessed palm groves and cattle, according to Pliny, but little else is known of the Minaeans. Their trading monopoly disintegrated (first century AD), taken over by the Nabateans and North Arabians. The region came under Muslim influence (seventh century AD). In the sixteenth century it became part of the Ottoman Empire and came under the suzerainty of the imam*s* of Yemen.

References

Schippmann (2001), Simpson (2002).

JANET STARKEY

MAJAZ

Figural or idiomatic language. While the term appears to have undergone a semantic development in early Islamic times among grammarians, literary critics and jurists, its evolved sense in hermeneutics is that sense of language which is opposed to the *haqiqa*, the 'actual', 'literal', or 'real' sense of language (but also the 'non-idiomatic' on occasion). The existence of figural language was a topic of great debate in medieval Muslim intellectual circles. To be able to determine whether the Qur'an meant what it appeared to say in every instance was, of course, of tremendous significance. Did God really have a hand as in Q.3:73? Can one really 'ask' a town (rather than its inhabitants) as in Q.12:82? The dichotomy between the figural and the literal was probably first developed by the Mu'tazila in their dealing with anthropomorphism.

References

Heinrichs (1984: 111–40).

ANDREW RIPPIN

MAJLIS

'A gathering', also assembly, parliament.

See also: **nass**; **shura**.

ANDREW J. NEWMAN

MAJUS (ZOROASTRIANISM)

Zoroastrians (called *majus* in Arabic texts) trace the beginnings of their faith to the teachings of Zoroaster, an Iranian 'prophet' who lived and taught in the sixth century BC according to traditional sources (this time scale has been re-evaluated by Western scholars, who consider Zoroaster to have been active sometime between 1400 BC and 1200). The doctrines of Zoroastrianism, like any significant religious tradition, have been in flux throughout the history of the faith. This flux is reflected in the evaluations of Zoroastrianism by those of other faiths. With respect to Islam, Muslim writers, and the Qur'an itself, display an uncertainty about the status of Zoroastrians within the divine plan. Are Zoroastrians 'people of the Book' (*ahl al-kitab*) or pure 'unbelievers' (*kuffar* or *mushrikun*)? The most obvious Qur'anic reference to the *majus* is Q.22:17 'Those who believe, who are Jews, who are Sabeans, Christians, the *majus* and those who associate [other gods with God] – indeed God will distinguish between them on the day of Judgement: God is the witness of all things'. Christians and Jews are normally counted as 'people of the Book' without any dispute, since God afforded them a revelation before the time of the Prophet Muhammad. This status gains Christians and Jews certain accepted status both within the 'ideal' Muslim society, and also within the story of God's relations with the world. To qualify as a 'people of the Book', Zoroastrians required a scripture which was recognised as having divine origins. For those who argue that Zoroastrians are 'people of the Book', this scripture is to be found in the Avesta. The Avesta, as it exists today, is a collection of devotional religious literature (hymns, prayers and liturgies), divided into twenty-one books (*nasks*). The prophet Zoroaster is traditionally considered to have written only the section called 'the *Gathas*' (a series of seventeen hymns). The rest of the Avesta has no named authors. The collection reached its final form during the Sasanid period, and many copies of the Avesta, written in the sacred language known simply as 'Avestan', have an accompanying translation (or more accurately interpretation) in Pahlavi, the language of the Sasanid Empire. This translation/interpretation is called the 'Zand'. Much of the contents of the Avesta were lost during the Muslim (and later Mongol) invasions of Iran. Whether the collection known as the Avesta (perhaps together with the Zand) qualifies as a sacred 'book' is a matter of dispute amongst Muslim writers.

The dispute centres around certain doctrines presented in the Avesta and elaborated by subsequent Zoroastrian tradition. For example, the Avesta certainly contains an embedded dualistic view of the world, whereby there are two eternal powers, one good and the other evil. Whether this duality in the divine powers precludes the admission of Zoroastrians into the fold of monotheism is the crucial issue. Scholars, both within the Zoroastrian tradition and outside it have argued over whether Zoroaster's teachings, presented in various formats within the Avesta, were monotheist, dualist or polytheist.

Within ancient (pre-Sasanid) Zoroastrianism, there were two major strands of belief: the 'orthodox' Mazdaean (that is the strand which became accepted as presenting the central Zoroastrian tenets) and the Zurvanites. The former maintained an ancient commitment to dualism: the idea of the world being the battleground between two forces: the eternal God Ahura Mazda (known as Ohrmazd, Yazdan or Hurmuz in other Persian texts), and his adversary, the evil Angra Mainyu (also called Ahriman). Ahura Mazda created the world in order to do battle with his adversary. This creative power was exercised through subsidiaries beings – the 'Holy Spirit', Spenta Mainyu, and the six 'Holy Immortals', Amesha Spentas. With these seven beings each occupying one level of the seven-tiered heaven, Ahura Mazda also calls on various 'lesser Immortals' (*yazatas*) who function in a manner similar to the *jinn* of the Qur'an and Muslim tradition. The evil Angra Mainyu also has a pantheon of evil spirits on whom he calls to fight his cause. Whilst the structure of the cosmology seems highly pantheistic, it appears that only the two Gods, Ahura Mazda and Angra Mainyu are eternal. The other divine beings are expendable, and many do indeed die in the course of the battle between good and evil. The apocalyptic of the Zoroastrians includes the idea of a world saviour (the Saoshyant) who will bring about the final battle between the forces, the Good will ultimately be victorious. The victory, and ultimate superiority of the Good, is part of the claim made by some Zoroastrians that they are ultimately monotheists. In the midst of the cosmic battle, human beings are created as potential warriors for Ahura Mazda, though they have the choice to reject this and side with evil.

The Zurvanites, who emerged in the fifth century BC, were more explicitly monotheist. They argued that there was one God, Zurvan ('Time') who was responsible for both Ahura Mazda and Angra Mainyu. The Orthodox objected to this attempted monotheism, since it postulated a common origin for good and evil, though the division between the two camps was not so strict. Zurvan was, for many, so remote as to be unworthy of worship – only Ahura Mazda was worthy of such veneration. The methods of Zoroastrian worship also caused some Muslim writers alarm since the Zoroastrians worship Ahura Mazda through fire. Sacred flames are kept alight permanently as symbols of Ahura Mazda's power. For some Muslim writers this was unacceptably close to idolatry, and some called the Zoroastrians 'Fire-worshipers', an accusation educated Zoroastrians vigorously denied.

Whilst the monotheistic and dualistic tendencies were clearly in conflict, the establishment of Zoroastrianism as the state religion, first during the Achaemenid period of Cyrus the Great and his successors, and then again during the Sasanid period, lead to other tensions. Established Zoroastrianism (that is, the priestly interpretation of the 'Magi' or Magian Zoroastrianism) had a strict conception of the division between its priesthood and its laity, together with a stratified conception of society from the imperial classes to the common folk. It faced challenges from both mystical and egalitarian trends during the Sasanid periods. The first, gnostic emphasis, was found in the teachings of Manu, later formalised into the separate religion of Manichaeism, the second is most obvious in Mazdakism. Manichaeism was strictly dualist, and controversial since Mani did not appear to express a preference for the good or evil divine figures in his cosmology. Mazdakism was a radical egalitarian doctrine which did not recognise stratification on the basis of wealth or nobility. The later Sasanid king Kavad was said to favour Mazdakism, and a number of movements of the early Islamic period were said to be Mazdaki in character.

The Sasanid Empire fell to the Arab Muslim armies in the seventh century AD. The decisive battles were at al-Qadisiyya in AD 636 and Nihavand in AD 642. *Majus* now found themselves living under the rule of the Muslims, and whilst there is no clear evidence of immediate mass conversions to Islam, it is clear that the Sasanid bureaucrats were willing to work for their new Muslim lords in an administrative capacity. Eventually, many converted to Islam and, coming as they did from a milieu of developed literacy, supplied Islam with some of its earliest literary luminaries and religious experts. The Zoroastrian hierarchy had to survive without state-sponsorship, and in a hostile religious environment. Inevitably, some Zoroastrians left Iran in search of greater religious freedom, settling in AD 936 in Gujarat on the west Indian coast. There they established a thriving Zoroastrian community (known as the Parsis) which remains vibrant until today, particularly in Mumbai (formerly known as Bombay) and the Surat coast. Other Zoroastrians stayed in Iran, and kept the faith alive within a more monocultural Muslim context. The 'Irani' Zoroastrians (as they were known) congregated in Kerman and Yazd (where the oldest surviving 'eternal fire' is to be found today). Whilst the Parsi and Irani Zoroastrian communities developed in different theological and social directions, the relations between the two branches have, on the whole, been very good. There seems to have been very little development in the theological tenets of Zoroastrianism in either community between the arrival of Islam and the onset of modernity. What shifts there were, were probably the result of Muslim influence on Zoroastrianism. The conception of Zoroaster as a prophet, with his revelatory scripture was probably a reflection of the need to be considered *ahl al-kitab*. Killing animals for food involved mentioning the name of Yazdan, a practice adopted from Muslim ritual slaughter.

Whatever the Muslim theological difficulties in classifying *majus* as *ahl al-kitab*, the administrative structure seems to have considered them to be 'people of the Book' from an early stage. The demands of paying the *jizya* (the tribute offered by conquered 'people of book' to the conquering Muslim forces) were imposed quite early on the Zoroastrian community. Indeed according to one report the Prophet Muhammad himself demanded the *jizya* from Zoroastrians, though this report is probably part of a polemic between those who considered the *majus* unbelievers and those who considered them *ahl al-kitab*. There appears to have been very little interference with the cultic aspects of Zoroastrian practice in early Islam, though there were isolated instances of persecution.

In the Muslim era, one reads of occasional Zoroastrian-inspired uprising in Iran and elsewhere. For example, the revolt in Nishapur (AD 766–9) lead by Bihafarid was put down by the famous Shi'i warrior Abu Muslim. Bihafarid, according to the heresiographers, claimed the position of Zoroaster as prophet, bringing a new book and abolishing a number of traditional Zoroastrian practices. The Zoroastrian priests (*mabadan*) were active in encouraging Abu Muslim to suppress this heretical revolt. This indicates their continued local power despite having lost the status as the representatives of the state religion. The division into 'orthodox' Zoroastrians and various anti-priestly trends within the community is mentioned in a number of subsequent Muslim *firaq* works.

The Parsi community was more active, operating as one amongst many different religious communities. Fire temples were established in Surat, and continue to function as places of worship today, though the religious authority seems to have remained with the priests in Yazd and Kerman. The *fatwa*-like question-and-answer documents known as the *rivayats* were written between the fifteenth and eighteenth centuries. They demonstrate both the conservative nature of Zoroastrian doctrine during the period, and the power of the Irani priests, since it was their answers which were considered authoritative in India.

The nineteenth century began to see change in Zoroastrian doctrines. The polytheism implicit in the Avesta (the various *yazatas* and the Amesha Spentas) was interpreted metaphorically (as referring to intermediate intelligences between man and God) by some priests, and the Zurvanite heresy, with its convenient monotheism, was resurgent. Some Parsi Zoroastrians called for an abolition of all the traditional rituals since Zoroaster, they claimed, had preached a simple monotheism which demanded no ritual observance. This was greeted by others as dangerous, and they asserted the esoteric value of rituals as a means of 'spiritual satisfaction' – thereby preserving the traditional practices. The debate continues to the present day amongst the Zoroastrian community, now dispersed like other Iranian and India communities. The Parsis were, occasionally, targeted by evangelicals from the Christian churches who used elements within the Zoroastrian tradition to demonstrate the role of Christ as the Parsi saviour. The movement to return to the 'original' Zoroastrianism of Zoroaster, and remove the obsolete rituals which had been introduced in the intervening years, demonstrates that Zoroastrianism was not immune to standard religious reaction to the threat of modernism: a return to the sources replaces a reliance on traditional methods of interpretation. This desire to preserve original Zoroastrianism was a factor in the foundation of the 'Amelioration Society' by the Zoroastrian Hataria in 1854. Through the society, he aimed to preserve Zoroastrianism in the land of its origin, as he had become worried by the decline in the numbers and religiosity of Zoroastrians in Iran.

In Iran today remnant communities of Majus (or Zartushtiyan as they are known in modern Persian) continue to be active in Yazd, Kerman and Tehran. The community, which used to be primarily rural has become urbanised, and as is common with rural–urban migration, the established authority structures have broken down. Priests whose position had been based around the maintenance of village life, were unable to retain this position in the context of city life. Today they are a recognised minority within the Islamic Republic of Iran, though this does not necessarily prevent instances of discrimination in public life.

References

Boyce (1975), Hinnells (1981), Zaehner (1955).

ROBERT GLEAVE

MALI, ISLAMIC EMPIRE OF

The medieval empire of Mali attained the peak of its power and prestige in the early years of the fourteenth century during the reign of Mansu Musa, who ruled from AD 1312–37. Islam was established at the royal court. Mali was already one of Africa's chief suppliers of gold. In AD 1324 he made the pilgrimage to Mecca (*hajj*), and visited Cairo, taking with him generous gifts of gold. Included as further gifts in his entourage were large numbers of African slaves. Such was the munificence of his gifts of gold that the precious metal was devalued in Egypt in consequence. The trade in African slaves also brought the empire prosperity as well as notoriety. Timbuktu and Jenné became important centres of trade, Islamic learning and culture. The decline of Mali began in fifteenth century as a result of internal weaknesses, disputes about the succession of its rulers, civil unrest, and the growing opposition of tribute paying states. Sporadic attacks and incursions by groups such as the Tuareg accelerated the decline of the empire. The Mali empire was followed by the Songhay empire of Gao which rose to power in the late fifteenth century. At that time Songhay under *Sunni 'Ali* ('the Great') took Timbuktu and Jenné. Songhay began to replace Mali as most important power in western Sudan. At its height Mali was one of the largest empires in West Africa. Its Islamic rulers controlled a vast network of trade routes, which linked the remote parts of the Sahara desert with the lands of the savannah, the tropical forest, the West African coast and the North African littoral. Mali was acknowledged to be an important empire by other states in North Africa. Ambassadors were exchanged with Morocco and Egypt. Islam continued to act as a supranational unifying force throughout the western Sudan. Without an official professional clergy, Islam was carried throughout the empire by teachers and traders who moved freely along the trade routes, assuming as individual Muslims the responsibility for transmitting the ideals of Islamic belief, learning and culture to those with whom they came in contact.

References

Davidson (1977: 46–54), Levtzion (1973, 1977: 123–4).

EDWARD D. A. HULMES

MALIK

The angel who is gate-keeper of hell (Q.43:77).

ANDREW J. NEWMAN

MALIK B. ANAS

The eponym of the fourth school of Islamic law was born in the year AD 911/12, his actual age at death being uncertain as there have been conflicting reports, some putting him at eighty-seven and others at ninety years old. His father was not regarded as a reporter of *hadith*, but he is known to have narrated one reported by Malik. In fact, Malik's father was an arrowsmith and familiarity with this craft in his formative years may well have been instrumental in developing the son's precise and systematic approach. Malik's great grandfather was one of the Prophet's Companions.

One interesting incident occurred in the life of young Malik when he and his brother were asked the solution to a theological question by their father. His brother answered, but Malik did not and their father turned to his silent son and observed, 'you were too busy playing with your pigeons'. This incident may have represented a turning point for Malik, who went on to dedicate himself to acquiring and practising the knowledge of Islamic law and theology.

Malik was raised in the influential environment of Medina, the town to which the Prophet had emigrated and established the first Islamic state. Many Muslim scholars and theologians were of the opinion that the true knowledge and legacy of Islam could only be acquired from living in Medina, a view endorsed by the tradition of the prophet who stated, 'the Islamic faith will be sheltered by Medina'. Shafi'i is reported to have maintained that, 'the principles of the people of Medina leave little doubt as to their correctness'. Malik was really a Medinan scholar in every sense, particularly in his interpretation of Islam through the practice of the people of Medina which represents the prophetic living model of an Islamic town. He is reported to have matured in his academic life around AD 747, a time when he began issuing *fatwas* to the public.

Ibn Shihab al-Zuhri was perhaps one of Malik's most influential teachers: being one of the earliest documenters of *hadith*, a position Zuhri undertook reluctantly following a command from the Caliph 'Umar 'Abd al-'Aziz. Malik's own method of documentation focused on the strength of the chain of narration right back to the Prophet himself and doubtless this attention to detail has been extremely valuable in providing reliable data for Islamic law and theol-

ogy. However, one might also question the validity of not resorting to the narrations of weak traditions, as some of the traditions may still have possessed some important details that have been omitted because of the apparent unreliability of one or two narrators. Indeed, this has been a problem in Islamic law that has been solved by some scholars who have either referred to weak *hadith* or utilised analogy.

Malik's renowned work, the *Muwatta'*, illustrates his powers of documentation. This book contains details of the prophetic tradition that were gleaned from the most reliable of sources. Perhaps his insistence on taking only the straight and precise narrations reflects the skill of the arrowsmith, a craft that brooked no deviation or tolerance of error. The title, *Muwatta'*, signifies simplification and accessibility, attributes that Malik intended for his work. His aim had been to select the most authentic traditions of the Prophet and actions of the people of Medina and document them in an easily understood manner for the lay reader. He worked on the *Muwatta'* for quite a few years and it was not completed until AD 775 when Malik was approximately sixty-six years old. It is viewed as one of the pioneering compilations that combined both the traditions of the Prophet and the statements of his companions with Malik's own individual legal flavour. The *Muwatta'* also presents a cohesive text for previously scattered narrations that had the potential for being lost, misconstrued or altered. It is true that some scholars preceded Malik in textually compiling the prophetic tradition, such as 'Abd al-Malik b. Jurayj, Sa'id b. Abu Aruba, 'Abd al-'Aziz Abi Salama and Abu Bakr b. Muhammad. Even Abu Hanifa is reported to have worked on such a compilation, but none produced such a volume as the *Muwatta'*. One of the main differences between the

Muwatta' and Bukhari's 'correct' collection lies in the fact that Malik included what scholars refer to as the disconnected tradition *munqati'*, this being defined as a statement made by someone from the second generation after the Companions of the Prophet, such as the generation of Malik himself who wrote about 'Umar.

The *Muwatta'* was placed as the third most authentic work after those of Bukhari and Muslim; however, it is important to observe at this point that Malik is considered to be more authentic when judged according to his time. The prevailing narration methodologies for Bukhari and Muslim were much more stringent and restricted. Due to Malik's confidence and profound knowledge, he was able to include *hadiths* on the basis of his own intuition, whereas the other two scholars adhered to their set methodology.

One of the debatable issues surrounding the *Muwatta'* relates to the scribe, Habib b. Ibrahim, who actually assisted Malik by writing down the words of Malik whilst he was teaching. His personal integrity was called into question and Ibn Hanbal described him as unauthentic, while some other scholars referred to Habib as a weak narrator. However, Malik did check what he had written before passing the material to his students. Both Abu Dawud and Ibn Hibban accused Habib of narrating falsehoods, but such a statement should be taken in context, as narrators of *hadith* would describe others as 'liars' solely to indicate possible incorrectness of content and not the moral intention of the narrator. Nevertheless, this does pose a dilemma as to the ultimate authenticity of the *Muwatta'* at least from the point of view of its composition. Malik has been further criticised for the making of some grammatical mistakes in his spoken Arabic. The famous philosopher Al-Asma'i stated, 'I never respected any scholar as I did Malik, but when I heard him making oral errors, my respect for him was diluted'. Could this weakness be ascribed to the fact that he was only narrating the traditions he had heard from others and he was loath to alter such traditions, even if they were grammatically incorrect due to the fault of the narrator? Malik was a documenter not an editor and it is perhaps unwarranted to undermine his work on such a basis. This might also answer a few more questions that have been raised in relation to the *Muwatta'*. The narration about the breast-feeding of adult males is one example here, where the language used appears inappropriate and the actual meaning is unclear. It is feasible that individuals who may not have fully grasped the context of the *hadith* originally narrated it in a colloquial style. Furthermore, the apparent weakness of Malik's style in the *Muwatta'* could be explained by the author's original intention that the narrations should be accessible to the general public and his use of simple language was a deliberate attempt to ensure that everyone was able to understand.

References

al-Diqr (1988), Coulson (1964: 43–7), Izzi Dien (2004: 16–22).

MAWIL IZZI DIEN

MALIKI MADHHAB

See: **Malik B. Anas**

MAMLUKS (1250–1517)

Turkish commanders (*mamluks*, lit. 'military slaves') seized power in Cairo and Damascus from their Ayyubid masters and built up a powerful state, with its ruling stratum continuously replenished by Turkish slaves from south Russia and then by Circassians from the Caucasus, which endured for over two centuries. The Mamluks acquired great contemporary kudos in religious circles from their strict Sunni tradition and their encouragement and patronage of the dervish orders. Above all, they defended the borders of Islam by repelling Hulegu's Mongols from Palestine and a second Mongol attack on Syria forty years later, and by reducing the last footholds of the Frankish Crusaders on the Syro-Palestinian littoral. However, the last Mamluks came up against the Ottomans, who invaded Syria in 1516 and ended their rule in Egypt during the next year, although the Mamluks survived as a military aristocracy within the society of Ottoman Egypt until the early nineteenth century.

References

Bosworth (1996: No. 31), Garcin (1998), Gibb and Bosworth (1960–2003), Holt (1986: 82–166, 178–206), Irwin (1986), Northrup (1998).

C. E. BOSWORTH

MANAH (MANAT)

See: **al-Lat**

AL-MANSUR, 'ABDALLAH B. MUHAMMAD, ABU JA'FAR (AD 754–75)

al-Mansur succeeded his brother al-Saffah to become the Second Caliph of the 'Abbasid dynasty. He was one of the greatest of the 'Abbasid caliphs and under his reign the new regime was consolidated. In his first years in office, however, he had to overcome a number of threats to the unity of the empire, these including his uncle 'Abdallah b. 'Ali who made his own bid for the caliphate, the Shi'ite revolts of Ibrahim and

his brother Muhammad b. 'Abdallah in the Hijaz and Basra in AD 762 and serious disturbances in Khurasan. Significantly, al-Mansur had Abu Muslim, who commanded the loyalty of the Khurasanian army, executed, thus ensuring their undivided allegiance.

Al-Mansur was responsible for the construction of Baghdad (begun in AD 762), his new capital, on the banks of the Tigris. In Baghdad, and with the Khurasanian army as the base of his power, he began the establishment of a highly centralised government apparatus and an efficient bureaucracy to supervise the empire. Nevertheless, al-Mansur introduced no great innovations in government, being content largely to follow in the footsteps of the Marwanid caliphs whom the 'Abbasids had ousted. The Umayyad regime had, however, ruled a largely Arab empire, whereas the 'Abbasids ruled a Muslim empire only partly composed of Arabs. This was reflected in the membership of the political elite, which was increasingly composed of non-Arabs.

All subsequent 'Abbasid caliphs were al-Mansur's lineal descendants. He was succeeded by his son Muhammad b. al-Mansur, to whom he gave the title *al-mahdi* (the Rightly Guided One), a term used by the Shi'a for their expected restorer of Islamic justice.

References

Hitti (1970: 290–5), Hodgson (1974: 284–9), Kennedy (1981: 57–96; 1996: 128–37), Le Strange (1924: 4, 5, 9, 24, 38, 41, 65, 77, 102, 237, 303), Muir (1915: 446–66), Shaban (1971: 6–19), al-Tabari (1985–95: XXVII, 149–212 *passim*; XXIX, 3–157 *passim*).

RONALD PAUL BUCKLEY

MAQAMAT

A *maqam* is a spiritual station in which the Sufi has acquired knowledge of the divine through his own effort. Sufis described many stations in their journeys to God, such as the station of fear of God, hope, expansion and contraction.

References

Schimmel (1975: 109–30).

LLOYD RIDGEON

AL-MAQQARI, SHIHAB AL-DIN AHMAD IBN MUHAMMAD (*c.* 1577–1632)

North African historian and biographer. Born into a scholarly family in Tilimsan (Tlemcen), in what is now Algeria, al-Maqqari lived most of his life in Morocco, serving as Imam and Mufti at the Qarawiyyin mosque in Fez between 1613 and 1617. From there, he travelled east, visiting Cairo, Jerusalem, Damascus and the Holy Places of Mecca and Medina, where he gained a reputation as a talented teacher. He died in Cairo, after being taken ill as he prepared to set out for Damascus, where he had intended to settle permanently.

Al-Maqqari's most important work is his historical account of al-Andalus entitled *Nafh al-Tib min Ghusn al-Andalus al-Ratib*. This work, one of our most valuable sources for the history of Islamic Spain, falls into two distinct parts. The first of these provides valuable information not only on the geography and history of the country itself, but also on its literary history and previous generations of scholars. The second part is devoted to a biography of the scholar and courtier Lisan al-Din Ibn al-Khatib (AD 1313–75), who had served as Vizier to Muhammad V in Nasrid Granada. It also includes biographies of Ibn al-Khatib's ancestors and teachers, and a list of Ibn al-Khatib's works.

Among al-Maqqari's numerous other works, not all of which have survived, are a biographical work, *Rawdat al-as al-'Atirat al-Anfas fi dhikr man Laqituhu min A'lam al-Hadratayn Marrakush wa-Fas*, containing an account of many North African scholars, and a biography of the *qadi* 'Iyad (AD 1083–1149) entitled *Azhar al-Riyad fi Akhbar 'Iyad*, written while al-Maqqari was in Fez. Like the author's other writings, the importance of the latter work derives not only from the intrinsic value of the information contained in it but also from its inclusion of many quotations from older historical and literary works now lost. Among al-Maqqari's writings that have not survived is a commentary on the *Muqaddima* of Ibn Khaldun.

References

de Gayangos (1840–3).

PAUL STARKEY

MARABOUT

The word *marabout* is derived from the Arabic *murabit* – a resident of the *ribat* (a Sufi lodge) and was used commonly in North Africa.

LLOYD RIDGEON

MARCO POLO (AD 1254–1324)

Venetian merchant and traveller. In AD 1271, Marco Polo embarked on a family trading expedition which was to reach the court of Kublai Khan in China by AD 1275. During his seventeen-year stay, he claimed to have become adviser and emissary of the Emperor. In AD 1292, he accompanied a Mongol princess to Persia by sea, and then returned to Venice. He was later captured by Genoese traders, and during his confinement compiled the account of his journey, *Il Milione*. It became a key source on the geography and culture of the Orient.

References

Maraini (1976: 757–60), Polo (1968: 33–57, 252–66).

SIMON W. MURDEN

MARINIDS (1217–1468)

This Berber dynasty arose in Morocco out of the decline of the Almohads, establishing their capital at Fez, reconstituting the Almohad empire, aiding the Nasrids of Granada and trying, unsuccessfully, to recover the lost Muslim territory in Spain. Latterly, the shores of Morocco came under Portuguese and Spanish attack, and as their power weakened, they were replaced in Morocco by the Wattasids and in the eastern Maghrib by the Hafsids. Warfare against the Christians stimulated a spirit of religious fervour and *jihad* within North Africa, there was a revivified Malikism and a great surge of popular Sufism, seen in the growth of dervish orders and the emergence of the characteristic feature of Maghribi Islam, maraboutism, the intense veneration of Sufi saints and holy men.

References

Bosworth (1996: No. 16), Gibb and Bosworth (1960–2003), Terrasse (1949–50: II, 3–104).

C. E. BOSWORTH

MARJ RAHIT, BATTLE OF (AD 684)

After the Prophet's death and the period of the Rightly Guided Caliphs (*rashidun*), the Banu Umayya ruled the emerging Muslim empire from their capital, Damascus. The Umayyads were not, however, immune to internal disputes, particularly regarding issues of caliphal succession. One such dispute occurred on the death of the third Umayyad caliph, Mu'awiya II (r. for less than one year, AD 683). The dispute was played out militarily at the battle of Marj Rahit, a plain near to Damascus (there is scholarly dispute about the exact location of Marj Rahit).

Ibn al-Zubayr was the son of the Prophet's companion, al-Zubayr, who had rebelled against the caliphate of 'Ali and been defeated in 'the Battle of the Camel' in AD 656. Ibn al-Zubayr therefore had a certain authority derived from his lineage, and more importantly, he had succeeded in constructing an alternative to the Umayyad caliphate, based in the Arabian peninsula (particularly in Mecca and Medina). His control of these two holy cities was such that in AD 683, on the death of Yazid, he declared himself the 'commander of the faithful' (*amir al-mu'minin*). Mu'awiya II had tried unsuccessfully to quell Ibn al-Zubayr's rebellion, and the battle between the Umayyads and Ibn al-Zubayr's forces is normally called the second *fitna* (civil war). Mu'awiya II's death later in AD 683 left the Umayyads with no clear successor. A faction of the Umayyad military forces, called the Qays, supported Ibn al-Zubayr. Their bitter rivals, the Kalb, supported another Umayyad (but not from the line of Mu'awiya II) Marwan b. al-Hakam. The dispute between the Qays and the Kalb is considered by some authors as originating in geographical origin (Qays from northern Arabia, Kalb from the south), and by others, as based on tribal ancestry (Qays trace their lineage to the pre-Islamic figure of Qays 'Aylan, Kalb trace their ancestry to Kalb b. Wabara). On Mu'awiya II's death, the two factions rallied around the two possible successors. Ibn al-Zubayr sent out his forces under the leadership of a Qaysi, al-Dahhak b. al-Qays. In his role as the new 'caliph' Ibn al-Zubayr had appointed al-Dahhak as Governor of

Damascus. Al-Dahhak was, then, simply moving to take up his new position. Marwan gathered his troops and first encountered al-Dahhak at Marj al-Suffar, another plain area close to Damascus. This was merely a skirmish, and the major battle between the two forces took place on the first day of Muharram (18 August 684) at Marj Rahit. Marwan's forces, under the leadership of his general 'Abbad b. Ziyad, were outnumbered by those of al-Dahhak, and yet they were victorious. Al-Dahhak was beheaded in battle, and the Qays scattered. Ibn al-Zubayr's rival caliphate was to fall later in AD 692, the Umayyad general al-Hajjaj laid siege to Mecca, killing Ibn al-Zubayr and recapturing the holy city for the Umayyads. The battle of Marj Rahit was, in some ways, the decisive (though not final) defeat for Ibn al-Zubayr. It was an opportunity to take control of the Muslim empire and defeat the Umayyad forces – an opportunity his supporters failed to take and which ultimately lead to his power being restricted to the Arabian peninsula.

The differences between Ibn al-Zubayr and the Umayyads ultimately rest on conflicting ideas of the qualifications of leadership in early Islam. The Umayyads had taken power, partly through the prestige of their Arab (pre-Islamic) lineage, partly through the cry of the injustice perpetrated against the caliph 'Uthman, and partly through military force and cunning. Ibn al-Zubayr's claim was based on his father's early conversion to Islam, and, hence, his conception of leadership was an amalgam of Arab notions of the inheritance by the son of the father's laudatory characteristics, with a notion of the precedence of those family lines which first converted to the cause of the Prophet. At Marj Rahit, the former was victorious over the latter.

References

Donner (1981: 24–126), Hawting (1986), al-Tabari (1879–1901: II, 470–86).

ROBERT GLEAVE

MARJI' AL-TAQLID

'The source of emulation'. In Twelver Shi'ism, an authority of such high ranking that he can issue unprecedented decisions in matters of law and theology.

References

Momen (1985).

See also: **ayatallah**; **Hujjat al-Islam**; **mujtahid**

ANDREW J. NEWMAN

MARRIAGE

In Islam, marriage is a civil contract between a man and a woman, who express their mutual agreement to live together according to Islamic law. It is a matter of family honour on both sides that a bride enter the marriage state as a virgin. Marriage is considered to be the 'stronghold' (*hisn*) of chastity (cf. Q.4:24). In accepting the dowry (*mahr*), which is paid to her by the bridegroom, the bride effectively consents to the union. She cannot be compelled to marry against her express wish, although her silence has been interpreted historically as consent. In many Islamic communities today, 'arranged marriages' are common. The rights of parents to arrange a marriage for a daughter to someone in a distant Islamic community, whom she has not met, are being increasingly challenged by Muslim women (in some cases, no more than young girls), especially in Europe. A Muslim husband's demand to exercise his conjugal rights over his wife is also under question in the modern world.

The marriage ceremony is usually conducted in the presence of witnesses by a local imam, either in a mosque or at the home of the bride or the bridegroom. A Muslim man may marry a non-Muslim woman, in which case the children of the marriage are to be brought up as Muslims. The marriage of a Muslim woman to a non-Muslim man is widely discouraged and actually forbidden. After the marriage vows are exchanged, God is invoked as 'the best of witnesses' to bless a union 'of love, mercy, peace, faithfulness, and cooperation'. The marriage contract is signed by both partners, by two adult witnesses, and by the officiating imam. The celebrations that follow the marriage may continue for several days according to local custom.

The fourth chapter of the Qur'an (*Surat al-Nisa'*), as its title indicates, deals with the rights and duties of women in an Islamic community. Q.4:1–14 are concerned with family relationships and with marriage, inheritance, and the welfare of orphans. Q.4:3 is often quoted as sanctioning polygamy in Islam, although the added proviso is variously, if not ambiguously, interpreted: 'marry the women whom you choose, two, three, or four, but if you fear that you may not be able to treat them equitably, then only one'. In the case of remarriage after divorce, the requirements of Islamic law are explicit. If either partner of an Islamic marriage apostatises from Islam, the marriage is thereby annulled and no formal pronouncement of divorce is required.

References

Bouhdiba (1985: 14–18, 30–42), Omran (1992: 15–26).

See also: **divorce**

EDWARD D. A. HULMES

MARV

Known as Great Merv, in Persia as Mouru and as Marw al-Shahidjan or 'Royal Merv, Marv is a Transoxianian city in historic Khurasan, near Mary, in a fertile but unhealthy oasis on the river Murghab south of the Karakum Desert, Turkmenistan, on the silk road and on a political junction between Central Asia and Iran. The garrison for three Iranian empires, as famous, in its time, as Baghdad, Cairo and Damascus. Several sites of different periods lie side by side: Gavur-Qa'la ('unbelievers' town', Sasanid and early Muslim), Sultan Qal'a (eighth to thirteenth centuries AD) destroyed by Mongols AD 1221 'Abd Allah-Khan-Qal'a (fifteenth century).

The earliest city, now a fortified citadel, was probably founded by Cyrus the Great (559–530 BC) when the city was seat of a *satrapy* of the Persian Achaemenid empire that stretched from Central Asia to Turkey, and India to Egypt. Alexander the Great incorporated Marv into the Seleucid empire (312–175 BC). Marv became a vast walled city, Antiochia Margiana, under Antiochus I (281–261 BC) and as Gavur-Qa'la flourished under the Greeks, the Parthians (247 BC–AD 224) and Sasanids (*c.* AD 224–651) with a substantial Christian population. The last Sasanian ruler, Yazdgard III, was murdered near Marv (AD 651), when the Sasanians were overthrown by Arab Muslims. They established Marv as capital of Khurasan, as a base to expand Islam into Central Asia and China.

In AD 747 Umayyad forces were expelled by the revolutionary leader, Abu Muslim, who built his palace (*dar al-imari*) and a mosque (Istakhri 1:259, 11.4–9) to reflect the secular political power of the 'Abbasids entwined with religious authority. The greatest site was the Islamic city, Sultan-Qa'la, a major Islamic centre (AD 813), when Caliph al-Ma'mun lived temporary in Marv.

From the eighth to the thirteenth centuries AD, rich merchants, craftsmen in specific quarters, markets and a hierarchy of officials flourished in the city. A feudal system prospered in the oasis, developing agricultural innovations, cultivating the silkworm, exporting silk and cotton textiles as one of the great emporiums on major caravan routes, and manufacturing steel by the ninth century AD.

Between the eleventh and thirteenth centuries AD, authority was based on family allegiances to local princes in a hierarchy to the caliph. Capital of the eastern Saljuq Empire (AD 1037–1157), with a central walled city (*sharistan*), citadel (*arq*), central square (*maydan*), markets, *madrasas*, Friday Mosque and smaller mosques in the suburbs (*rabah*). Marv reached its zenith under Sultan Sanjar (r. AD 1118–57). The huge Saljuq Sultan Sanjar's mausoleum complex (*c.* AD 1152), the first dated example of a mosque-mausoleum, still dominates the city. Rivalling Baghdad, Cairo and Damascus, it was a city of fabulous palaces, silk workshops gardens and orchards. A fortified citadel was built in the Sultan-Qal'a (1.5 square miles; 4 square kilometres), which contained the *Arg* or Shahriyar palace. Privately funded *madrasas* specialising in Islamic law (*madhhab*s) were founded by early Saljuqs. Many scholars, including the Persian astronomer-poet 'Umar Khayyam, were attracted by its fabled libraries as a major centre of Islamic learning under the 'Abbasids. The city was later pillaged by Ghuzz Turkmen tribesmen, Khwarazmshahs and the Ghurids of northern Afghanistan, and by AD 1221 Marv was destroyed by three waves of attacks by Mongols who killed *c.* 1.3 million, according to Juwayni.

The 'Abdallah-Khan-Qal'a, rebuilt by Shah Rukh (1409) was smaller and less prosperous. Under continual attack by Uzbeks and Tekke Turkmen, by the eighteenth century Marv was deserted, replaced by Bairam Ali. Marv was occupied by Russians (1884), dams rebuilt and the railway developed. Marv fell into obscurity in the early twentieth-century but is now a World Heritage Site.

References

Durrani (2004: 18–30), Herrmann and Kennedy (1999), Herrmann *et al.* (2002), Sachs (1970).

JANET STARKEY

MARWA

See: *al-Hajj*

MARWAN B. AL-HAKAM
(AD 684–5)

Marwan I was the founder of the Marwanid line within the Umayyad dynasty. The death of his predecessor Mu'awiya b. Yazid (AD 684) resulted in a serious crisis for the regime. Important provinces within the empire were no longer totally under the control of the Umayyads and some Syrians, including the Qays tribesmen and leading members of the Umayyad family, were prepared to acknowledge the rule of 'Abdallah b. al-Zubayr in the Hijaz. Marwan, a cousin of Mu'awiya b. Abi Sufyan, was eventually acknowledged as Caliph by the Syrians after the battle of Marj Rahit in which Marwan's Kalb supporters defeated the Qays. In Marwan's nine-month rule he also managed to establish his authority over Egypt, but the final subjugation of Ibn al-Zubayr was left to his son and successor 'Abd al-Malik b. Marwan.

References

Hitti (1970: 192–3), Hodgson (1974: 221), Kennedy (1996: 91–3), Shaban (1971: 93), al-Tabari (1985–95: XX, 47–69, 159, 160–2).

RONALD PAUL BUCKLEY

MARWAN B. MUHAMMAD (AD 744–50)

Marwan II was the last of the Marwanid (Umayyad) caliphs. Marwan, a general on the Byzantine front and the strongest military commander in the empire, styled himself as avenger of the murdered al-Walid b. Yazid (AD 744). When al-Walid's successor Yazid b. al-Walid died, Marwan and his troops crossed the Euphrates, occupied Damascus and deposed the newly elected caliph Ibrahim. Although Marwan proclaimed himself as ruler, his claim was one among several and it took him three years to establish his authority. However, an even greater danger was emerging, not in Iraq but in the relatively distant Khurasan. This was eventually to lead to the overthrow of the Marwanids and the installation of a new dynasty, the 'Abbasids. In October AD 749 the Khurasanian forces entered Kufa and Abu al-'Abbas al-Saffah was acknowledged as the new *amir al-mu'minin* ('commander of the faithful'). Marwan led the Syrian army across the Tigris and engaged the Khurasanians on the banks of the Great Zab, a tributary of the Tigris. The decisive defeat (February AD 750) suffered by the Syrians marked the end of further resistance to the advancing Khurasanian army and Syria itself was soon to capitulate. Marwan retreated to his capital Harran, but receiving no support he fled to Egypt where he was eventually captured and killed (August AD 750).

References

Hodgson (1974: 272–4), Kennedy (1996: 114–16), Shaban (1971: 160–4), al-Tabari (1985–95: XXVII).

RONALD PAUL BUCKLEY

MARXISM AND ISLAM

Given its position as the established, markedly anti-Western and anti-capitalist, ideology of the former USSR and mainland China, aspects of Marxist thought, including its emphasis on classes, became increasingly popular in the Islamic world, especially the Middle East as the European imperial powers moved to reassert their authority in the latter at the end of the Second World War or these were replaced as such by the USA. In the 1950s and 1960s, intellectual and practical alliances with Marxism and Marxists promised both a theoretical and practical alternative to the overtly Western and 'capitalist' path to modernism supported by Western-backed rulers as 'Islamic' alternatives', associated with the nineteenth-century failure to resist the encroachment of the West, seemed less palatable. For Arabs, the aftermath of the 1957 Suez War and the 1967 Arab–Israeli War, and Israel's expulsion of Palestinians only emphasised the complicity of the Western powers, especially the USA, in the region's backwardness. In Iran, US support for the Shah through the 1953 coup against Prime Minister Mosaddeq and the 1963 anti-Shah riots lent especial urgency to the need to elaborate a distinctly alternative anti-Western/anti-capitalist discourse and strategies. The discourses of the many political parties and ideologues which appeared in the region during the Cold War ran the gamut between rigid Stalinist formalism to efforts to blend aspects of Marxist analysis with aspects of Islamic discourse, the latter especially in recognition of the continuing influence of Islam among the less-educated 'masses'. The proponents of these discourses generally retained Lenin's emphasis on 'the party' as the 'vanguard' of any and intellectual and political activity and struggle. However, especially since most of the region's 'Marxists' were in fact drawn from a narrow, secularised socio-economic elite, their discourse failed to gain any 'mass' appeal. These movements' consistent failure to attract non-elite support facilitated moves to isolate them by their respective state institutions. In the process, as in the case of Egypt under Anwar Sadat, the latter often promoted as political/ideological alternatives newer Islamic political parties whose discourse, directed to the same audience, incorporated appeals to modernity but on a distinctly Islamic axis. The latter discourse was increasingly popular, especially in the face of the combination of the continued secularist and pro-Western tendencies of the region's governments and their failure to 'modernise' their societies internally sufficiently to counter Western, and especially American, political, economic and cultural influence domestically and in the face of such continued external issues as the situation of the Palestinians.

References

Ayubi (1993), Kerr (1971), Munson (1988).

See also: **materialism; modernity; secularism; socialism**

ANDREW J. NEWMAN

MARYAM

The mother of Jesus. The Qur'an treats Jesus's early life, especially Mary and Jesus's birth, extensively. Mary's father was 'Imran and her mother took a vow to offer her child to the service of God. Zechariah, the father of John the Baptist, looks after Mary in the temple. Angels tell Mary that she has been chosen to bear Jesus, whose name is al-Masih, 'Messiah'. Mary is impregnated by the breath of the angel Jibril. After experiencing childbirth accompanied by several miracles, Mary is accused by the townsfolk of having acted immorally, but Jesus speaks from the cradle to

defend her. Throughout the Qur'an, Jesus is called 'son of Mary'.

References

Calder *et al.* (2003: §4.1), Stowasser (1994: Chapter 7).

ANDREW RIPPIN

MASABIH AL-SUNNA

This aptly entitled collection of *hadiths*, 'Lamps of the Sunna', is a codification of the most reliable traditions of the Prophet intended for practical use. It is the best-known work of Abu Muhammad al-Husayn b. Mas'ud al-Farra' (or Ibn al-Farra') al-Baghawi (d. 1122 or AD 1117), who was known as Muhyi 'l-Sunna, 'Reviver of the Sunna', and Rukn al-Din, 'Support of Religion', for his work on traditions.

The significant feature of the *Masabih al-Sunna* is that it groups together *hadiths* from earlier collections according to their reliability. It follows the principle of the *musannaf* works by presenting *hadiths* on a common theme, but builds upon these by codifying individual sayings into *sahih* (sound) and *hasan* (good). Thus, a typical chapter of the work comprises two sections, one presenting *hadiths* on the appropriate topic from the collections of al-Bukhari and Muslim, and the other *hadiths* from other sources, such as the *sunan* works of Abu Da'ud, al-Tirmidhi, al-Nasa'i and Ibn Maja, the *Musnad* of Ahmad Ibn Hanbal, and works of other recognised *muhaddith*s.

The *Masabih* assumes the reliability of the categorisations of individual *hadiths* that were established in the major compilations of the ninth century AD and earlier. Thus it accepts that the *hadiths* contained in the collections of al-Bukhari and Muslim are all *sahih*, and that the recognition given by other compilers is dependable. Its value can be seen to lie in its character as a codification of these earlier collections, rather than a work of primary *hadith* scholarship. This is implicitly acknowledged in its omission of both the *isnad* chains which are the crucial feature of the canonical collections, with the name of the Companion who transmitted a tradition from the Prophet normally sufficing, and also of the collections from which *hadiths* are taken. In the first section of each chapter, which comprises traditions from the two *Sahih* works, this might not present a problem, but in the second section, where traditions from a range of sources are gathered, it might be less easy to trace them. Here, however, al-Baghawi does offer a little help by commenting briefly on whether a *hadith* is *gharib*, *mursal* or *munqati'*, all of which for him are *hasan*.

This practical collection contains about 4,500 *hadiths*, nearly half of which come from either al-Bukhari or Muslim or both. Its popularity and usefulness are attested by the commentaries that were written on it. However, it was often known in later times in the revision made by Wali 'l-Din al-Tabrizi, the *Mishkat al-Masabih*. The *Masabih al-Sunna* has been published a number of times, though no scholarly edition has been made.

DAVID THOMAS

MASJID

See: mosque

AL-MASJID AL-AQSA

'The farthest mosque', the Qur'anic reference (Q.17:1) to Jerusalem's Temple Mount and the Temple of Solomon. The golden-domed mosque of this name dates from the seventh century AD.

See also: **isra'**

ANDREW J. NEWMAN

MATERIALISM

To the extent that materialist philosophy considers aspects of spiritual and religious life and meaning an element of phenomenological superstructure, it is formally incompatible with the fundamental beliefs of Islam, as well as the other 'revealed' religions. Nevertheless certain aspects of materialist thought, particularly the Marxist emphasis on class analysis, if not the inexorably and predetermined course and outcome of Marx's class struggle, have been important vehicles in contemporary secular politics and political thought in the Islamic world.

References

Abrahamian (1989).

See also: **free will and predestination; Marxism and Islam; socialism**

ANDREW J. NEWMAN

MATHEMATICS

As Islam progressed from Arabia to Spain in the west and China in the east in the years following the death of the Prophet Muhammad in AD 632, Muslims proved themselves adept in developing as well as assimilating the scientific discoveries made in the ancient civilisations of Mesopotamia and Asia. Mathematical treatises were among the many Greek and Indian texts to be translated into Arabic in institutions such as the Bayt al-Hikma (House of Wisdom) in Baghdad. A circle or a dot had been used as a symbol for 'zero' by Babylonian, Maya and Hindu mathematicians for centuries before Arab mathematicians began to use the word *sifr* as a translation of the Sanskrit term *sunya* ('void'). The English words 'cipher' and 'zero' are both derived from the Arabic word *sifr*. In addition to his compilation of astronomical tables, the best-known and most influential Muslim mathematician, al-Khwarizmi (AD 780–850), wrote works on arithmetic and algebra that were used as standard textbooks in Europe as late as the sixteenth century. Muslims continued to contribute to the theory of numbers and the solving of equations. European merchants continued to use sources originally written in Arabic to conduct their arithmetical transactions.

References

Hitti (1973: 363–407, 574), Schacht and Bosworth (1979: 461–89).

See also: **astrolabe (*al-asturlab*)**; **astronomy (*'ilm al-falak*, *'ilm al-nujum*)**; *Banu Musa*; **Ptolemy (Claudius Ptolomaeus)**

EDWARD D. A. HULMES

MATN

The actual information in the text of a *hadith* report in contrast to its chain of transmission. It is from this material that support was sought for a point of law. While the wording of such reports is, of course, important, significant variation in the wording of similar reports led to a general consensus that most reports were transmitted by the sense rather than the literal wording. The *matn* of a tradition was also used as a criterion by which to judge the acceptability of a report. Those reports which contained material that was in conflict with the Qur'an or *mutawatir* traditions, for example, were to be declared forged.

References

Gibb and Bosworth (1960–2003: VI, 843).

ANDREW RIPPIN

MATTER AND FORM

Most Arab and Muslim philosophers adopt the Aristotelian concept of matter and form in their perception of the nature of things. The Aristotelian theory is that every material existent thing must be a composite of matter and form, the matter is its material basis, while the form is the element which shapes it and initiates power and activity in everything. Matter is also considered the potential of existence, while form is the factor that actualises matter and brings it into existence. Thus, every material existent has a duality in its essence. However, some philosophers, such as Ibn Sina, though they accepted this duality, raised the problem of how the composite of matter and form can come into existence. For if the form has the ability to bring matter into existence, it is then in itself a kind of necessary existence (or a God). Therefore the duality in all things is not that of matter and form but of essence and existence, because of the composite essence: matter and form need a third element in order to come to be. Ibn Rushd, for his part, does not accept the theory of the third element of existence but rather believes, like Aristotle, that all beings and things continue to exist by the power of the natural law which is attributed to form in its relation to matter.

References

Ibn Sina (1960).

MAHA EL-KAISY FRIEMUTH

AL-MATURIDI (*c.* AD 870–944)

The founding figure of one of the two great schools of thought in Islamic theology, the other being that of al-Ash'ari. Al-Maturidi was born in what is now Samarkand, in Uzbekistan, and it is in the eastern regions of the Islamic world that his school has been most influential, with the Ash'ari school being more dominant in the central and western regions. Generally speaking al-Maturidi's views adopt a position somewhere in between those of the Mu'tazila on the one hand and the followers of al-Ash'ari on the other so that, for example, al-Maturidi allows a greater possibility of human beings coming to a knowledge of God through the use of reason, even without revelation, and a greater element of human responsibility for human actions, even if in some respects they remain acts of God. His greater openness to the use of human reason has caused his views to be of considerable interest to modern Islamic thinkers who wish to emphasise the importance of human reason and responsibility but without running the risk of being accused of reviving the views of the Mu'tazila.

References

Caspar (1994: Chapter 8), Watt (1998: Chapter 10), Williams (1994: 145–51).

HUGH GODDARD

MATURIDISM (AL-MATURIDIYYA)

A school of scholastic theology (*'ilm al-kalam*) belonging to the Sunni denomination attributed to its founder Abu Mansur Muhammad al-Maturidi (d. AD 944) and often mentioned in comparison with that of al-Ash'ari, who was his contemporary. Little is known about al-Maturidi's life, but he did leave a substantial number of works, displaying his thought on Islamic doctrine and creed, which seem to incline to the views of the Jahmites. His thought was developed by a number of scholars in the Samarkand region, where it first received recognition and continued to progress until it

flourished under the patronage of the Ottoman sultans, who promoted it along with the Hanafite school of law, to which al-Maturidi also belonged. The al-Maturidi methodology seemingly treads a middle path between the Ash'arite and Mu'tazilite positions, with a strong emphasis on the intellect (*al-'aql*) and consequently an esoteric interpretation (*ta'wil*) of the divine attributes (*al-sifat*). In addition, they differ from their Sunni co-religionists by stating that faith (*iman*) is belief in the heart only, i.e., is either present or not and hence, neither increases nor decreases – a view proposed by the Muji'ites. The al-Maturidi school has maintained its presence in the regions formerly ruled by the Ottoman caliphate and is still taught in certain institutions, such as that of the Deobandis in India.

References

al-Johani (1999: 95–106), Netton (1997: 166), Watt (1948: 6–10, 154–60; 1997: 67–8, 104–5, 138, 141; 2002: 312–18).

GAVIN PICKEN

AL-MAWARDI, AHMAD IBN MUHAMMAD (AD 974–1058)

*Shafi'i*te scholar and jurist. Born in Basra, he studied there and in Baghdad and served as *qadi* in a number of cities, before being appointed to that position in Baghdad itself, where he died. While in Baghdad, he played an important diplomatic role under the caliphs al-Qadir (r. AD 991–1031) and al-Qa'im bi-Amr Allah (r. AD 1031–75) in the 'Abbasid caliphate's relations with the rising powers of the Seljuks and Buyids (Buwayhids).

In addition to the works of political and social theory for which he is best known, al-Mawardi's writings include works in the Islamic religious tradition, as well as some philological works, not all of which survive. In the field of political science, his most important work is his *Kitab al-Ahkam al-Sultaniyya*, a work on public law in which he sets out a theory of the caliphate, including such matters as the means by which a caliph is appointed to office, and his qualifications and duties; in this connection, the author laid considerable stress on the intellectual and moral qualities required both of the caliph himself and of those appointing him. Other sections of the work deal with topics such as taxes, the division of plunder, the revival of waste land through cultivation and irrigation, the organisation of the state *diwans*, and problems arising from the *iqta'* system of land grants and tenure. In a similar field, al-Mawardi is also the author of a work in the 'Mirror for Princes' tradition, entitled *Nasihat al-Muluk*, while another work, *Qawanin al-Wizara*, deals with the moral and intellectual qualities required of a vizier.

In the religious field, al-Mawardi's *Kitab al-Hawi al-Kabir fi'l-Furu'* provides an account of the *shafi'i*te legal system, while his widely read *Kitab Adab al-Dunya wa-'l-din* deals with ethical issues.

References

Gibb (1962: 151–65), Khan (1983), Rosenthal (1958).

PAUL STARKEY

MAWAT

See: **ahkam al-aradi (land law)**

MAWDUDI, ABU'L-A'LA (1904–79)

One of the most important leaders of the Islamic revival in the twentieth century.

Mawdudi was born in Hyderabad in south India, and after a number of years of traditional Islamic education he was forced to withdraw from further formal study as a result of the death of his father. He continued to read widely, however, and during the 1920s he began to write broadly on a number of themes concerning Islam, including the Qur'an, and the position of Muslims within Indian society. In the 1930s he opposed the movement for the creation of Pakistan as a separate state for Muslims following independence from Britain, arguing that the new state would be based on nationalism rather than Islam. In 1941 he founded a movement to disseminate his ideas, the Jama'at-i Islami (literally 'Islamic Group'), with the idea that its members would serve as the vanguard for the transformation of the Islamic community through its adoption and proper practice of the ideology of Islam. In 1947, when the new state of Pakistan was created, Mawdudi elected to migrate to it, though branches of the Jama'at-i Islami were established in both India and Pakistan, and for the remaining years of his life Mawdudi sought to transform Pakistan into a truly Islamic state. He came to enjoy huge influence across the whole of the Islamic world as a result of his prolific writings, which were translated into Arabic and many other languages, and he has been described by R. Nasr as 'the foremost revivalist thinker of his time'. The view of Islamisation which he represents, a kind of 'Islam from above' is in sharp contrast, however, to that adopted by Muhammad Ilyas.

References

Ahmad and Ansari (1980), Mawdudi (1955), Nasr (1996, 1994).

HUGH GODDARD

MAWLAWIYYA/ MEVLEVIYYA

The Sufis of this order trace their origins to Jalal al-Din Rumi (d. 1273). The Mawlawiyya has been confined in the main to Anatolia, and is celebrated for its *sama'* during which Rumi's verses are sung while the Sufis spin around in ritual devotion to God. These Sufis have been called the 'whirling dervishes'. The order was outlawed in 1925 when Ataturk banned all Sufi activity in Turkey.

References

Chittick (1991).

LLOYD RIDGEON

MAWLID (MILAD) AL-NABI

The phrase means 'Birthday of the Prophet' (Muhammad). He was born on 12 Rabi' al-Awwal, most probably in the year AD 570. It was not until several centuries later, however, that the celebration of his birthday as a public holiday was organised according to local custom. By the end of the eighth century AD after the *hijra* celebrations in honour of the Prophet, his birthday and his birthplace (a humble dwelling in the *suq al-layl* in Mecca) had been introduced in Morocco and Egypt. In the time of the Fatimid caliphs in Cairo, the occasion of the Prophet's birthday was already a day for popular celebrations. Processions and eulogies of the Prophet mark the day. His readiness to give away his goats-hair cloaks as a mark of charity or favour prompted a tradition that is often recalled on this day by the recitation of a poem specially composed for the occasion. The best known, perhaps, is that of *al-Busiri*, called *al-Burda* (*The Mantle*).

EDWARD D. A. HULMES

MAYSIR

See: **gambling**

MEANING

The word *ma'na* can be translated to mean a qualifier which brings a thing to act in a certain way after being at rest. The Muslim theologians used this term interchangeably with attribute or accident, but in such a way as to mean a qualifier which qualifies a thing by a certain attribute. At an early stage, however, Mu'ammer, an early Mu'tazilite theologian from the Baghdadi school, had formed a theory known as the theory of *ma'ani*. As reflected in the Aristotelian theory of potentiality and actuality, it explains the movement of a thing from being a possible existence to an existence in actuality. Mu'ammer considers that the movement of a thing from potentiality to actuality is due to a *ma'na* which qualifies its movement. But this *ma'na* in itself is also qualified by another *ma'na* or an infinite series of *ma'ani*. This theory acknowledges both the Aristotelian theory of potentiality and actuality and the accidents of the atomism theory. Since Mu'ammer, like other Muslim atomists, believes that the atoms and the accidents are created by God, his concern here is not how a thing comes into existence from its potential stage but mainly how it moves. This movement of a thing is not due to its nature, according to Aristotle, but is qualified by the existence of certain qualifier which Mu'ammer calls *ma'na*. *Ma'na* qualifies a thing to receive a certain quality or accident, in this case, the quality is movement. Thus, instead of explaining the movement of a thing as an accident which comes to inhere in it, following the atomists, he considers that this accident can only inhere in the thing when there exists a *ma'na* which qualifies the accident (movement) to inhere in the thing. This *ma'na* exists within the thing and appears at a certain moment to qualify a certain accident. Thus the thing in itself contains a series of infinite *ma'ani* which are able to qualify unlimited accidents. Wolfson points out that many Muslim theologians such as Ibn Hazm and al-Baghdadi criticised this theory because it permitted the existence of infinite *ma'ani* in things, basing their arguments on verses such as: 'He (God) counted everything in number' (Q.72:28) or 'with Him everything is in measure' (Q.13:9) which means that everything except God is finite.

References

Wolfson (1976: 147–67).

MAHA EL-KAISY FRIEMUTH

MECCA

The oasis city of Mecca is located near to the eastern shore of the Red Sea in the mountainous region of western Saudi Arabia. Access to Mecca and the other holy sites of Islam in Arabia is forbidden to non-Muslims. Residence in the city is permitted only to Muslims, amongst whom are to be found individuals and groups from every part of the Islamic world. The growing population numbers in excess of half a million. Mecca is situated approximately halfway along the ancient camel-caravan trade route that led from the southern tip of the *jazirat al-'arab*, 'the Island of the Arabs'. That south-western region was known to Latin geographers as *Arabia Felix* for its comparative fertility and for the developed civilisations. The caravans carried northwards spices, silks and other exotic items from India and China for sale in the markets of Mesopotamia. On the return journey the caravans carried oils, cereals, brass and copper artefacts and other tradable goods south. The round trip sometimes took as much as two years to make. By the time of Ptolemy (the second-century AD Greek astronomer and geographer, who called the city *Macoraba*), Mecca was already an ancient commercial centre and a place where the followers of numerous idolatrous sects in pre-Islamic Arabia gathered at specified times of the year for the pilgrimage to the Ka'ba.

Mecca lies in a narrow, comparatively sheltered, valley among the rocky hills of the Hejaz (*al-hijaz*), 'the barrier', which runs northwards parallel to the Red Sea as far as the Gulf of Aqaba (*al-'aqaba*). This barrier separates the long narrow coastal strip along the Red Sea from the fearsome interior deserts of *al-Nafud*, and *al-Rub' al-Khali* (the empty quarter) to the east and the south-east of Arabia. Mecca is not only the most important city in the Hejaz, but also the holiest city in the Islamic world and the most important focus on earth for Islamic worship, devotion and pilgrimage. It is the place to which devout Muslims throughout the world turn before performing *al-salat* (ritual prayer and worship). The cities of Mecca and Medina are known to Muslims as *al-haramayn* 'the two Holy Places', *al-Quds*, Jerusalem, is known to Muslims as *thalith al-haramayn*, 'the third Holy Place'. Despite the pre-eminence of Mecca as a sacred place, it is not the capital city of Saudi Arabia. The capital of the kingdom is Riyadh (*al-Riyad*), located some 500 miles (800 kilometres) to the north-east of Mecca. Riyadh, with its network of transportation links is the commercial and educational hub of the kingdom. Jidda is situated on the Red Sea coast some 45 miles (70 kilometres) miles due west of Mecca. Apart from its importance as a commercial and diplomatic centre it is the principal entry point for Muslim pilgrims arriving either by sea or by air to visit the holy places.

In the centre of Mecca stands the Great Mosque (*al-haram al-sharif*), in the courtyard of which is the Ka'ba, the cubic structure, which is the focal point of Islamic devotion to God. The Black Stone (*al-hajr al-aswad*) is secured in the south-eastern corner of this cube-shaped sacred shrine. The stone is believed by Muslims to have been given by the Angel Jibril to Ibrahim and his son Isma'il, who were engaged in rebuilding the ruined Ka'ba. Close by *the Ka'ba* is the well of *zamzam*, the sacred well of Mecca, sometimes known as the well of Isma'il. According to Islamic tradition, the well is associated with the efforts of Hagar, the wife of Ibrahim, to find water for her infant son, Isma'il, when she was searching for water in the desert to give to her son. She and the child had been expelled from Ibrahim's household because of the jealousy of Sara, his first wife.

Muhammad was born in Mecca *c*. AD 570 into the tribe of the Quraysh of the clan of Hashim. His career and mission are considered in other entries in this volume but brief mention of his association with the city of his birth may be made here. After his call to be the Messenger (*rasul*) of Allah, whilst meditating in the hills above Mecca in the year AD 610, his mission in the city lasted for little more than a decade. Increasing hostility from the people of Mecca, both to him and his mission, led to his decision to move with a few Muslim companions from Mecca to Yathrib (Medina) in the year AD 621/2. This event, known throughout the Islamic world as the *hijra*, meant a radical change of life for him and his supporters. In AD 639 the Caliph 'Umar (AD 634–44) decreed that the *hijra* should mark the official start of the Muslim era, i.e., the year 1 AH (*anno hejirae*). Having established the Islamic commu-

nity (*al-umma*) in the city of his adoption, Muhammad eventually returned to Mecca, recapturing it shortly before his death in AD 632. The Ka'ba and its environs were purged of idolatry, rededicated to the worship of the One God (Allah), and established henceforward as the centre of Islamic devotion and pilgrimage.

In the days of Muhammad, the city was a thriving commercial centre, which provided lucrative business for traders and brokers, among whom the members of the Prophet's own tribe were prominent. Muhammad devoted himself during the early days of his ministry in the city to a campaign in which the existing religious beliefs and social mores of this fellow citizens were challenged in the name of Islam. The strictly commercial importance of the city declined as its sanctity increased, although the local manufacture of utensils, furniture and textiles continues. Its financial viability is guaranteed principally by the income generated during the annual pilgrimage and by the munificence of Islamic rulers and benefactors. As the number of pilgrims undertaking the *hajj* or the *'umra* grew, however, the influx of large numbers of pilgrims faced the local population and the national authorities with considerable logistical problems. The adequate provision of accommodation, food and drink, health services, protection, not to mention control of entry to the holy site and the supervision of the various stages of the pilgrimage, called increasingly for preliminary organisation. In 2003, for instance, provision had to be made for the welfare of some 2 million Muslim pilgrims. Over the centuries, Mecca felt the influence of the Umayyads, the 'Abbasids, the Egyptian Mamluks, the Ottoman Turks, the Wahhabis, and ultimately the Saudis after the Kingdom of Saudi Arabia was established in 1932. In recent years, the city has seen many changes. The areas around the central Holy Places have been cleared. The mosque has been enlarged. Many of the old two- or three-story dwellings made of rock remain. Modern buildings are constructed of concrete. Some parts of the city contain houses of inferior quality, which serve the needs of the poorer inhabitants, amongst whom are to be numbered the less affluent pilgrims who stay in Mecca after the pilgrimage is completed.

References

Abdul-Rauf (1978: 578–607), Burton (2004: 1855–56), Watt (1953).

See also: **calendar, Islamic (*al-taqwim al-islami, al-hijri*); al-Hajj; hijra; Medina; Muhammad ibn 'Abdallah, the Prophet of Islam; ritual prayer and worship (*al-salat*); 'umra.**

EDWARD D. A. HULMES

MECCAN AND MEDINAN REVELATIONS

Muslim tradition early on separated the Qur'an into two sections. The first comprised *suras* revealed prior to the *hijra* to Medina (most were thus revealed in Mecca but some were promulgated outside the town) and termed the Meccan *suras*. The second comprised *suras* revealed after the *hijra* and were termed the Medinan *suras* (even though some where, in fact, revealed in Meccca after the town was taken over by the Muslims). Lists of *sura*-ordering according to the sequence of revelation were established early on, separating the chapters into these two divisions. The extent to which this separation was done systematically is not clear, the appeal was often to historical memory rather than specific information. Some importance is placed on certain characteristics of the Meccan sections which serve to distinguish those

sections along with the information provided by the 'occasion of revelation' (*asbab al-nuzul*) material. For example, some authorities report that every verse which contains the phrase 'O people' was revealed in Mecca, while those that start 'O believers' were revealed in Medina. That means, it is explained, that 'O people' is addressed to the people of Mecca, while 'O believers' is addressed to the people of Medina.

In general terms, it was also recognised that the Meccan *suras* were those that emphasised the need to build faith and community and which counsel the need to maintain patience in the face of adversity. The Medinan *suras* were those that counselled activism and promulgated law; it was also recognised that they tended to consist of longer verses.

In creating the classification system, Muslims worked on the basis of entire *suras* while recognising that an individual *sura* might have verses from both contexts. The beginning verses of a *sura* determined its classification. Significant disagreement occurred over some *suras* and their classification, the most obvious being *Surat al-Fatiha* (Q.1), the classification of which was uncertain. In Western scholarship on the Qur'an there has been a general tendency to refine the criteria and the analysis of the composition of the *suras* more finely than Muslim tradition allowed. Thus, dating is spoken of as applying to groups of verses rather than entire *suras* (this tendency has been taken to its extreme in the work of Richard Bell) and the Meccan period is generally divided into three parts: early, middle and late, using thematic and stylistic criteria to separate the subgroupings.

References

Gibb and Bosworth (1960–2003: V, 402–4, 414–19).

ANDREW RIPPIN

MEDICINE AND PHARMACOLOGY

In the Middle Ages, the identification of healing remedies, the preparation of drugs and the isolation of poisons and anti-toxins helped to make the study and practice of pharmacology a bridge between alchemy and medicine. The extensive literature of pharmacology in Arabic indicates the importance attached to the subject by Muslims, who also made significant contributions to the development of medical theory and practice. Perhaps the best known of their manuals on medicine is the *Firdaws al-Hikma* (*The Paradise of Wisdom*), compiled in the ninth century AD by 'Ali b. Rabban al-Tabari. His contemporary Hunayn b. Ishaq wrote on ophthalmology. Among the contributions to medical knowledge made by the Persian polymath and physician Rhazes of Baghdad (al-Razi, AD 865–925) was his work on distinguishing smallpox from measles. The Persian Islamic scholar Ibn Sina (AD 980–1037), and the Spanish-Arab Islamic scholar Ibn Rushd (AD 1126–98) also wrote works on medicine which questioned some of the received wisdom of the ancient writers Hippocrates and Galen. In the field of diagnosis Ibn al-Khatib of Granada drew attention to the fact that disease is spread by contagion, an observation that was not generally accepted during the fourteenth century AD when the Black Death was raging in Europe, The surgeon al-Zahrawi (d. AD 1013) compiled a treatise on surgery, the title of which will appeal to most students, whatever their chosen discipline: *al-Tasrif li-Man 'Ajaz 'an al-Ta'alif* (*A Help to Anyone who Finds Long Treatises Difficult*).

References

Browne (1921), Hitti (1973: 574–9), Schacht and Bosworth (1979: 445–59).

See also: alchemy (*al-kimiya'*); astrology (*'ilm al-fatlak, 'ilm al-nujum*); Galen (*Jalinus*, Claudius Galenis); Hippocrates (*Buqrat*)

EDWARD D. A. HULMES

MEDICINE, GREEK

Greek medicine was the basis of scientific/medical works that influenced early and medieval Christian Europe and the Islamic Middle East. All the scientists and physicians of the period concentrated mainly on translating or slightly adding to the theoretical medical knowledge of the Greeks. Their medical practices flourished in the Greek schools which were established in the Byzantine and Persian empires. The most famous schools were in Alexandria and Jundishapur.

The most important works taught in these schools and translated first into Syriac and then into Arabic are the following: the *Materia Medica* by Rufus of Ephesus, the surgical chapters of the Greek encyclopaedia by Paul of Angina working in Alexandria and, most influential of all, the medical writings of Galen. Thus, Greek medical works had a dominant influence on the Islamic world in medieval medicine.

References

Gibb and Bosworth (1960–2003: X, 452–60).

MAHA EL-KAISY FRIEMUTH

MEDICINE, ISLAMIC

The earliest form of Islamic medicine is called *al-Tibb al-Nabawi*, it is a pre-Islamic medical tradition which mainly depended on using plants as remedies. The main source of this kind of medicine is known to us through some early *hadiths*. There is a story of a physician with the name al-Harith b. Kalada who is said to have studied in the Jundishapur school in Persia and was the physician of the prophet. This kind of simple medicine was influenced by magic and later on by some Greek ideas which flourished in the Persian and Roman empires before Islam. Umayyad and 'Abbasid rulers at first used Nestorian Christian physicians, but with the flourishing of Arabic translations of Greek medical and philosophical texts, Arab physicians gained access to Hellenistic medicine. Four important Arabic medical encyclopaedic works became the basis of Islamic–Greek medicine in the tenth and eleventh centuries: two of these works were written by Abu Bakr al-Razi: *Kitab al-Mansuri fi al-Tibb* and *Kitab al-Hawi*. The other two works are: *Kitab Kamil al-Sina'a al-Tibbiyya* written by 'Ali b. al-'Abbas al-Majusi with the aim of filling the gaps in *Kitab al-Hawi*. The last and most important work of this period is the famous *Kitab al-Qanun fi al-Tibb* composed by Ibn Sina. The earliest hospital in the Islamic world was established in the time of the 'Abbasid caliph Harun al-Rashid. However, the most important hospital was built under 'Adud al-Dawla in AD 982 in Baghdad. Hospitals in Damascus and Cairo followed in the eleventh and twelfth century. Physicians of this period were granted a license, *Ijaza,* following the completion of their medical education. Arab physicians made great contributions to the medical knowledge inherited from the Greeks, mainly in the fields of pharmacology.

References

Gibb and Bosworth (1960–2003: X, 452–60), Ullmann (1978).

MAHA EL-KAISY FRIEMUTH

MEDINA

An oasis city situated in the Hejaz region of western Saudi Arabia, *c.* 100 miles (160 kilometres) to the east of the Red Sea coast and *c.* 280 miles (450 kilometres) north-east of Mecca. From pre-Islamic times it was known for its small-scale industries producing agricultural implements, metalwork, armour and jewellery. More recently, the manufacture of pottery, tiles and bricks, furniture and the servicing and repair of motor vehicles have provided opportunities for employment. The economy is supplemented for the growing population (now approaching 750,000) by income derived from farming and the provisions made for the accommodation of Muslim pilgrims. A relatively plentiful supply of water in the subsoil is increased by the winter rainfall that produces seasonal torrents of water coursing through the *wadis*. This facilitates the growing of crops such as cereals, fruit, dates and vegetables. The city's date palms produce fruit that is world famous for its quality. These dates are processed locally and widely exported. Water supplies, originally provided by draw wells, have been controlled since the early years of the twentieth century by irrigation pumps. Work on the rail link between Medina and Damascus was started by the Turks in 1908 and completed a few years later. The railroad was intended to strengthen the Ottoman Empire and to ensure Turkish control over the route travelled by pilgrims on their way to and from Mecca for the *hajj*. It was put out of commission by the *sharif* of Mecca Husayn ibn 'Ali, who was helped by the British officer, Lawrence of Arabia (T. E. Lawrence, 1888–1935). Plans for its reconstruction and maintenance of the railroad have often been considered since. The city has good road links to the north through the Hejaz into Jordan. A road to the west connects the city to its Red Sea port, Yanbu' al-Bahr. Roads to the south lead to Mecca and

Jidda. The nearby airport of al-Jiladayn provides passengers and freight services to other centres in the Arabian peninsula and further afield to Egypt, Syria and Jordan.

Medina, formerly known as Yathrib, is considered by Muslims to be the second most important city in the world after Mecca. As in the case of Mecca, non-Muslims are denied entry into Medina, which took its new name from a number of Arabic epithets applied to the place where the Prophet (Muhammad) made his home: *madinat al-nabi,* 'city of the Prophet'; *madinat rasul Allah*, 'city of the Messenger (or Apostle) of God'; *al-madina al-munawwara*, 'the luminous city'. When he and his Muslim companions were obliged to leave Mecca because of the persecution they suffered there at the hands of unbelieving Meccans in AD 621/2, the year of the *hijra*, they 'emigrated' to the ancient city of Yathrib. They went at the invitation of a group of the city's representatives, who were in search of a leader who might succeed in uniting the clan factions in Yathrib. In honour of the Prophet's arrival the place was given its new name, Medina. The city is also known as *dar al-hijra* 'the house of the emigration'. For the next decade, AD 622–32, Muhammad succeeded in defending the city against its Meccan enemies, in establishing the *umma* as the exemplary community for the regulation of Islamic society, and as a base for his efforts to convert the peoples of Arabia to Islam. The 'Constitution of Medina' was the document which regulated relationships between the various clans in the city and the Prophet Muhammad. The Constitution guaranteed parity of esteem between those who had 'emigrated' (*al-muhajirun*) from Mecca to Yathrib as Companions of the Prophet and those who became 'helpers' (*al-ansar*) of the Prophet in Medina. It also set out the initial agreement between the Medinan Muslims and the Jews, which lasted for only a few years until the latter refused to accept Muhammad as leader and declined to accept Islam. In consequence, Jews were no longer tolerated in the city. They were ultimately to be driven out of their settlements in the Hejaz. Christians (Melkites) as well as Jews had settled in the cities of the Hejaz.

The tomb of Muhammad in the city's chief mosque is visited by Muslim pilgrims, many of whom take the opportunity of visiting Medina after making the *hajj* to Mecca. The tombs of the first two of the four Rightly Guided Caliphs, Abu Bakr and 'Umar ibn al-Khattab, and of Muhammad's daughter Fatima are located in Medina. The early history of Yathrib is obscure. From pre-Christian times Jews had settled there, as in Mecca, but their numbers were increased after the Roman emperor Hadrian expelled them from Palestine in the first century AD. After the death of the Fourth Rightly Guided Caliph, 'Ali ibn Abi Talib, in AD 661 and the rise of the Umayyads, the capital of the caliphate was transferred to Damascus. Twenty years later, the city was sacked on the orders of the Caliph. The political importance of Medina then began to decline as the city came under the control of local governors appointed from Damascus. From time to time, *sharifs* of Mecca made incursions. In 1517, the city fell to the Ottoman Turks after their conquest of Egypt. Their control eventually weakened and for a few years in the early nineteenth century the reforming zeal and the strictly unitarian convictions of Islamic puritans known as the Wahhabis prevailed in Medina as elsewhere in the region. In 1812 the Turks under Muhammad 'Ali retook the city. They remained in effective control until the Islamic revival under Ibn Su'ud a century later. Husayn ibn 'Ali, who had been responsible for the construction of the Hijaz railway, rebelled against Turkish hegemony but soon came into conflict with Ibn Su'ud, as a result of which the city passed into the control of the Su'ud dynasty in 1925. The importance of Medina as a centre of Islamic devotion remains. The reputation of the centres of learning and legal studies in Medina, the size of their endowments, the reputation of their teachers, the provision made for less affluent students, and of the value of the honours the qualifications earned by successful graduates, all continue to attract students as well as pilgrims from many parts of the world.

References

Burton (2004), Watt (1956).

See also: ***al-Hajj***; **Mecca; Muhammad ibn 'Abdallah, the Prophet of Islam; pre-Islamic Arabia**

EDWARD D. A. HULMES

MEDITERRANEAN

Intercontinental salty sea, 2,000 miles (3,218 kilometres) long, between Europe, Egypt, the Levant, Turkey, the Balkans and North Africa. Major land and sea routes connect the predominantly Muslim eastern Mediterranean with mainly Christian western Europe. It is a nervous white sea (Akdeniz, Bahr al-Abyad), dominated by winds rather than currents. Its livelihood is based traditionally on the cultivation of the live and to the south the region is bounded by deserts and date cultivation as Brandel identified. Around its shores live Christians including Copts, Muslims, Jews and Druze, and previously pagans, Zoroastrians and Baha'is. The great cosmopolitan Mediterranean cities (Alexandria, Venice, Marseilles, Tunis, Istanbul) with their commercial prosperity and progressive atmosphere may have more in common with each other than they have with their rural hinterlands. They are cities where multiracial communities cohere, though those in the south and east (Alexandria, Algiers, Tel Aviv) are increasingly monoglot. The Grand Tour embraced the Mediterranean, which continues to attract tourists to a kind of Eden, to worship the sun, ancestors or imperial ruins. It also has ethnic strife, terrorism and militant tribalism, prosperity and poverty, gangsters and gardens and several wars in progress.

The Mediterranean has been the arena for friction between Christian and Muslim communities since AD 476 when Muslim Arabs moved into North Africa. Islamicised Arabs struck a fatal blow to the fulcrum around which empires (Ancient Egyptian, Hittite, Aegean, Roman, and Byzantine) had flourished, the basis of later laws, art and culture. Beyond these empires lay the uncivilised world, chaos and darkness. By the ninth century, the Church had lost control of its strategic coastline for Arabs had invaded Crete, Sicily, southern Italy, Spain (AD 711) and southern Gaul. Repulsed at Poitiers (AD 732), they continued to raid southern France, especially Provence. Muslim traders frequented the Dalmatian coast. By the eleventh century, Christians had begun to conquer Spain and Sicily and controlled al-Andalus by thirteenth century. With Islam the dominant religion in the south and east the Mediterranean changed for Christian Europe. The sea's focal role for communication of culture became a mental barrier wilfully reinforced by myths, errors and ignorance. Hostility produced an anti-Islamic polemic in which Christian Europe stereotyped Islamic lands as dangerous and Muslims as monstrous. Muslims became alien, cruel, self-indulgent villains in contrast to self-sacrificing, virtuous Christian heroes in the propaganda of medieval European literature (see *Piers Plowman*, Saracens in the *Song of Roland*, etc.). In AD 1095, the First Crusade was launched to wrest the Holy Land from the Muslims and decades of confusion ensued, culminating in the sack of Constantinople (AD 1204) by Crusaders during the Fourth Crusade.

The propaganda myths were powerful and led to many conflict, yet Christians and Muslims often tolerated and collaborated with each other. Muslims emphasised the local rule and accepted a pluralistic society including Muslims, Jews and Christians. Many of the finest Islamic writers flourished in countries around the Mediterranean and through them classical scholarship was reintroduced to Europe through translation of Arabic texts, in Toledo and Palermo, for example. Arab historians and geographers, such as Ibn Jubayr (AD 1145–1217), provided a valuable source on the medieval Mediterranean.

The history of Islam in the Mediterranean is closely bound up with the expansion of the Ottoman Empire (1453–1923), which dominated the eastern Mediterranean and North Africa. Islamisation of the Balkans occurred under Turkish rule, by AD 1509 many Orthodox Christians had converted in Herzegovina.

With the development of sea routes to India via the Cape of Good Hope, the Mediterranean Basin declined in relative influence. In the eighteenth and nineteenth centuries the British and French dominated the region, especially after the opening of the Suez Canal in 1869. East–West tensions continued with the expansion of colonial empires of Italy, France and Britain (until the 1950s). As part of the dynamic of dependency, collaborators of imperialists saw Europe as advanced. Europeans wrote arrogantly of the inferiority of Islam. In opposition, Muslim pioneers of Islamic modernism including al-Afghani and Muhammad 'Abduh (1849–1905) tried to demythologise Islam and reminded the West that it only improved itself by borrowing from Muslim scholarship. In contrast, Taha Husayn (1889–1973) argued that Egyptian culture was essentially Mediterranean rather than Oriental, seeing modernisation as revival rather a European imposition.

As colonial domination of Muslim states unravelled through associated conflicts, especially in North Africa, so scholars have continued to reassess the paradoxes of the Mediterranean as a cultural region. Islam continues to flourish in the eastern Mediterranean and North Africa often as the state religion (e.g., Libya), Islam is also the second religion in France and Spain. Expansion of Muslim communities in southern France, Italy, and Spain is inherited from colonial eras of the nineteenth and twentieth centuries and also reflects issues of economic migration (Turks working in Germany car industry, for example), political asylum seekers (from Kurdistan, central Asia, Iraq, etc.). The independence of Algeria was proclaimed in 1962, yet many Maghribis have migrated to France. Areas of friction with non-Islamic groups are often an outcome of the disintegration of the Ottoman Empire (the Balkans and Cyprus, for example), and the impact of two world wars (Palestine and Israel). The Mediterranean continues to be a sea of contact and sometimes conflict between and within Islam, Judaism and Christianity. An additional non-Mediterranean element needs to be critically assessed: the USA gained military and naval power in the region after the Second World War. Algeria and Egypt are under threat from local

Islamic fundamentalists and some political groups are causing instability around the Basin.

References

Braudel (1975), Broadhurst (1952), Clancy-Smith (2001), Meisami and Starkey (1998: I, 340).

JANET STARKEY

MEHMED I (r. 1413–21)

Ottoman Sultan, son of Bayezid I. In 1413, by defeating his brother Musa he reunited all Ottoman territory under his rule. In 1416, he overcame an invasion by his brother Mustafa, who had disappeared, perhaps as Timur's captive, after the battle of Ankara. In the same year he suppressed a rebellion in western Anatolia, and another in the Dobrudzha led by a follower of Musa, Sheykh Bedreddin. In the same year, too, the Venetians destroyed his fleet. Despite these setbacks, in 1417–18 he conquered some new territory in southern Albania.

References

Imber (1990: 55–90).

COLIN IMBER

MEHMED II, 'THE CONQUEROR' (r. 1451–81)

Ottoman Sultan, son of Murad II. Mehmed first ascended the throne in 1443, following his father's abdication after the Hungarian invasion of 1443. During the autumn of 1444 he remained in Edirne while his father encountered the Hungarians at Varna. The Grand Vizier Halil Candarlı removed him from the throne following a Janissary rebellion and a fire in Edirne in 1446.

Mehmed's second reign began in 1451. His conquest of Constantinople in 1453 inaugurated a career of continuous warfare. By 1460 he had removed the independent Byzantine rulers from the Peloponnesos and from Trabzon. He began his assault on the Genoese colonies with the occupation of Pera in 1453. Enez and Phokaia followed, and Lesbos in 1462. In 1459, he expelled the Genoese from Amasra, and in 1475 from Caffa in the Crimea. The same campaign established his suzerainty over the Crimean Khanate. In the Balkans he failed to capture Belgrade in 1456, but his conquest of Serbia between 1455 and 1458, his defeat of Vlad the Impaler of Wallachia in 1462, and conquest of Bosnia in 1463 gave him an extended frontier with Hungary, leading to intermittent hostilities. Hungary found an ally in Venice which, facing Ottoman pressure in the Peloponnesos, declared war in 1463. The alliance proved ineffective. In 1470, Venice lost Negroponte (Evvoia), leading her once again to seek an ally. Mehmed's annexation in 1468–9 of Karaman had brought him into conflict with Uzun Hasan, the Akkoyunlu ruler of Iran, Iraq and eastern Anatolia. Venice and Uzun Hasan formed an alliance which ended in 1473 when Mehmed routed Uzun Hasan near Bayburt. His assault on the Venetian strongholds in Albania in 1478 persuaded Venice to seek peace. A treaty in 1479 ended the war. In the same year Mehmed occupied Cephalonia, Levkas and Zante as a preliminary to the capture of Otranto on the Italian mainland in 1480. In the same year his fleet and army made an unsuccessful assault on Rhodes. Mehmed died in 1481 at the outset of a campaign towards the east.

References

Babinger (1978), Imber (1990: 145–253), Vatin (1989).

COLIN IMBER

MEHMED III (r. 1595–1603)

Ottoman Sultan, son of Murad III. On his accession, Mehmed executed his nineteen brothers. It was public outrage at this act that led to the abandonment of royal fratricide. Mehmed succeeded at a time of crisis in the war with Austria. At the urging of the Grand Vizier and others, he accompanied the army to Hungary in 1596 and was present at the victories of Eger and Mezo-Keresztes. However, he refused to accompany subsequent campaigns. His reign also saw the beginning of large scale rebellions in Anatolia and, in the year of his death, Shah Abbas I's recapture of Tabriz.

References

Bacqué-Grammont (1989: 157–8), Imber (2002: 67–73).

COLIN IMBER

MEHMED IV (r. 1648–87)

Ottoman Sultan, son of Ibrahim. Mehmed succeeded at the age of seven, with his mother Turhan Sultan as regent. Financial and political crises and the Venetian blockade of the Dardanelles in 1656 persuaded Turhan to nominate Mehmed Koprulu as Grand Vizier with absolute power. He died in 1661 having reopened the Dardanelles and restored the Treasury. His son Fazil Ahmed Pasha succeeded. In a war with Austria between 1662 and 1664, the Ottomans acquired Nove Zamky, despite a defeat at St Gotthard. In 1669 Fazil Ahmed completed the conquest of Crete. War continued with the capture of Kameniec in the Polish Ukraine in 1672. In the 1670s Fazil Ahmed began a series of legal reforms. Fazil Ahmed's successor in 1676, his protégé Kara Mustafa Pasha, was less successful in his wars with Russia in the Ukraine. His decision in 1682 to support Imre Tokoly

as King in Austrian-ruled Hungary led to war with Austria and the failed siege of Vienna in 1683. The siege led to the formation of the Holy League of Austria, Poland, Russia, Venice and the Papacy. In 1686 the Austrians occupied Buda. In 1687, the Venetians occupied Athens and the Peloponnesos. These disasters led to the decision to depose Mehmed IV.

References

Mantran (1989: 238–48).

COLIN IMBER

MEHMED V, RESAD (r. 1909–18)

Ottoman Sultan, son of 'Abdul-Mecid. He succeeded to the throne following the deposition of 'Abdul-Hamid. His accession saw the reinstatement of the 1876 Constitution and the restoration of the Parliament. Effective power remained, however, with the Committee of Union and Progress (CUP) who had engineered the coup which brought him to the throne. The CUP also enjoyed a large majority in the Parliament. The CUP government could not prevent the dismemberment of the Empire. In 1911, Italy occupied Tripolitania and the Dodecanese, at a time when full-scale rebellion in Albania diverted the Empire's resources. In October 1912, a coalition of Balkan states declared war: by November, the Bulgarians had reached the last line of defence before Istanbul. In January 1913, a coup led by the leading Unionist, Enver Pasha, again gave the CUP control of the Government, which they had lost six months previously. During 1913, the second Balkan war, fought between the Balkan states over the spoils of their previous victory, and Enver Pasha's reconquest of Edirne regained some territory for the Empire. The Turco-Bulgarian treaty of September 1913 awarded territory to the east of the Maritsa river to the Ottoman Empire. In November 1914, at the urging of Enver Pasha in particular, the Ottoman Empire entered the First World War as an ally of the Central Powers. Despite victories over the British at the Dardanelles in 1915 and at Kut in 1916, the Ottomans ceded territory on all fronts. By 1917, the Russians had occupied Erzurum and much of north-eastern Anatolia, the British had advanced into Iraq, and in December, occupied Jerusalem. In 1917–18, the revolution in Russia allowed Ottoman forces to reoccupy Kars and Ardahan lost to Russia in 1877. By mid-1918, however, when Resad died, it was clear that the war was lost.

References

Ahmad (1969), Dumont and Georgeon (1989: 577–636).

COLIN IMBER

MEHMED VI, VAHIDEDDIN (r. 1918–22)

Ottoman Sultan, son of 'Abdul-Mecid. He came to the throne at the end of the First World War. After his accession, British advances in Syria and Iraq, the French landings in Thessaloniki and Beirut, and the collapse of the Central Powers made Ottoman defeat inevitable. With the Greek invasion of 1919, the Allied occupation of former Ottoman territories, and their partition at the Treaties of Mudros in October, 1918 and Sèvres in August 1920, the Ottoman Empire effectively ceased to exist. It was the nationalist Mustafa Kemal who, despite rebellions in favour of the monarchy, led the resistance to the Greeks and the Allied occupiers. The armistice

at Mudanya in October 1920 forced the allies to recognise the victory of the Kemalists. In November, the Grand National Assembly in Ankara voted for the abolition of the monarchy, marking the formal ending of the Ottoman Empire, and the establishment of the Turkish Republic on a portion of old Ottoman territory.

References

Dumont and Georgeon (1989: 636–47).

COLIN IMBER

MESOPOTAMIA

From the Greek 'land between the Rivers', Mesopotamia is the area between the Tigris and the Eurphrates, especially Baghdad north to the Anti-Taurus mountains and south to the Arabian Gulf including the Zagros mountains to the east and the Arabian Plateau and desert to the west, now known as Iraq. 'Al-Jazira' is used by Arab geographers for the northern part between Tigris and Eurphrates. Earliest human civilisations flourished in the region from 10,000 BC with evidence of the earliest known irrigation systems, pottery, trading networks, clay bricks and religious cults. By the fourth millennium BC, one saw the earliest cities (Eridu, Kish, Uruk, Isin, Lagash, Ur) of the Sumarians and cuniform writing was invented. Sumerian deities were localised, focusing on the fertility of the community. Empires included the Akkadian (c. 2112–2004 BC), Assyrian, Babylonian and Parthian (247 BC–AD 224) and it was then ruled by Romans and Byzantines.

The area was of great importance historically as it was on caravan routes between Iraq and Anatolia, on the Fertile Cresent. It was an immense cultivated area with a wide range of agricultural and industrial products mentioned by al-Muaddasi and Ibn Hawqal (L. AD 943-88).

Mesopotamia was conquered by Arabs (AD 637) and administered from Kufa but was an area of battle between Syrians and Iraqi Shi'is in the Umayyad period. It did not submit easily to 'Abbasid rule, rebellions finally being subdued under al-Mu'tadid, when Mesopotamia virtually became (caliph from AD 892) an autonomous principality. The area provided poets and scholars, especially grammarians, who flourished in Baghdad under enlightened patrons. Shi'is developed politico-religious poetry.

The Saljuqs captured Baghdad in AD 1055. During Saljiq domination the Nizamiyya collapse of Sunni religious science was founded. Its most respected teacher and Sunni intelllectual was al-Ghazzali (AD 1058–1111). The Sunni Ayyubids dominated under Saladin. Small Shi'ite dynasties squabbled under the Sunni caliphate (eleventh and thirteenth centuries). Eastern Mesopotamia (1225–1250s) became a great centre for construction, textiles and metalwork, especially in Mosul. From the Mongol conquest (AD 1258) and the Ottoman conquest (1534) there was a series of dynasties and Mesopotamia declined economically.

From the early sixteenth to early nineteenth century, eastern Mesopotamia became, piecemeal, part of the Ottoman Empire, a frontier bastion gainst Persia, Kurds and Arabs. In contrast, the western Fertile Crescent was peaceful from 1516. Mesopotamia attracted little European attention though Basra was a base for the East India Company from 1763. Administrative reorganisation occurred throughout the nineteenth-century Ottoman territories. By 1918 Britain occupied Iraq after the Mudros Armistice between Turkey and the Allies. Poor adminis-

trative management led to demands for a Muslim Arab state in the country under the British Mandate (1920) with tribal insurrections in the Middle Euphrates, especially at al-Najaf and Karbala'. Faysal (d. 1933), the second son of Sharif Husayn of Mecca, was established as constitutional monarch of Iraq through a referendum (1921). The area has suffered under the despotism of the secular regime of the Ba'athists and Saddam Husayn who suppressed the Shi'i population. Recent conflict with Coalition forces (2003–) has exposed fissures between Sunni and Shi'i communities in the region. Yet Sufi orders continue to worship under and shrines such as al-Najaf and Karbala' continue to be important sites of Shi'ite pilgrimage.

References

Creswell (1989), Robinson (2000).

JANET STARKEY

MESSENGERS

Rasul, one of two classes of prophets in Islam who, usually, is a bearer of a new religion or major new revelation within an existing religion. All peoples are held to have been sent a *rasul* (Q.10:47–8).

See also: **nabi**; **nubuwwa**; **rasul**

ANDREW J. NEWMAN

MESSIANISM/ MILLENARIANISM

Whilst Sunni theology does include a messianic element, it is in Shi'i thought that Muslim messianism is most clearly displayed. In both Sunni and Shi'i Islam, the messiah is termed *al-mahdi*, and has been applied to different figures in Muslim history. In Sunni Islam, the *mahdi* is seen as the one who will restore God's rule on earth after a period when humankind has gone astray. In this sense, the *mahdi* has much in common with the Judeo-Christian concept of the messiah. The Arabic term *al-masih*, which corresponds to the most literal meaning of messiah ('the anointed one'), was taken from Aramaic, appears in the Qur'an (e.g Q.3:40 'al-Masih, Jesus, son of Mary'), and appears to be a title accorded to Jesus. Jesus is accorded some messianic status in Sunni Islam, being the prophet who will return at the end of time. According to these theologians, he will establish a reign of justice in anticipation of God's last judgement. The Qur'an itself is less than clear on these matters, and, hence, apocalyptic theology has been unconstrained by scriptural diktat – the result is that the *masih*, Jesus, is sometimes seen as separate from the *mahdi* by Sunnis, and at other times as identical with him.

In Shi'i Islam, where the oppression of the majority Sunni community has been keenly felt, the desire for a messianic figure has been reflected in a detailed set of theological doctrines and dogmas. For them, the *mahdi* is a member of the *ahl al-bayt* (the descendants of the Prophet Muhammad) who will rise up (*qa'im*) at some future time in order to restore God's rule after the tyranny of ungodly rule. In Twelver Shi'ism, the idea of the Hidden Imam who has concealed himself from view in order to avoid persecution (that is, the doctrine of *ghayba*) is accompanied by the belief in the return (or more accurately the reappearance) of that person as a precursor to the end times. The doctrine itself took some time to stabilise, with the belief in the concealment (*satr*) of a number of the Twelve Imams being held by the Imamiyya before the emergence of specifically Twelver doctrine. In Isma'ili Shi'i history, one also finds the use of the messianic *mahdi* motif being used for the Fatimid caliph named al-

Mahdi, though since the end times did not come after his death, the Isma'ili thinkers separated the concepts of *mahdi* from *qa'im*, the latter being reserved for the messiah. Amongst later (non-Nizari) Isma'ili traditions, the Imam is believed to have disappeared, though there is no significant emphasis on his messianic reappearance – instead the community is lead by *da'is*.

The messianic emphasis is, sometimes, conjoined with millenarianism in Islam. That is, the *mahdi* figure is thought to be about to appear and rule for a divinely designated period of time (nominally, 1,000 years). Shi'i Islam, once again, is the most fertile ground for such movements. Shah Isma'il, when he instituted the Safavid dynasty in Iran (1501), was seen as a millennial figure by his supporters, the Qizilbash. Similarly, Shi'i insurgents during the Safavid period (such as the members of the Nuqtavi movement) envisaged some sort of millennial appearance of a messianic figure. Most famously, the Babi movement in Iran under the Qajars (the Safavids' successors), saw their founder, Sayyid 'Ali Muhammad 'the Bab', as inaugurating a new religion for a new era which was associated with the 1,000-year anniversary of the concealment of the Twelfth Imam of Imami Shi'ism. In Sunni Islam, there have also been examples of millenarian movements. In the modern period the Ahmadiyya, a Pakistani movement based around the teaching of Ghulam Ahmad, provide the most pertinent example. Ghulam Ahmad (d. 1908) claimed to have received revelations from God confirming that he was the messiah and the *mahdi*.

For established Islamic scholars, the need to suppress messianic and millenarian movements is undoubtedly linked to the disruption they cause to the stable hierarchy of authority they have sought to institute. Charismatic figures, in the Weberian sense, disrupt the routinised authority of the *'ulama'* and destabilise their power base. For this reason, the messianic/millenarian movements mentioned above (and many others not mentioned here) have usually been ostracised by the Muslim religious establishment and subjected to *takfir* (excommunication).

References

Amir-Moezzi (1994), Freidmann (1989), Nasr *et al.* (1988), Sachedina (1981).

ROBERT GLEAVE

MIHNA

Referring to the 'inquisition' authorised in AD 827 by the 'Abbasid caliph al-Ma'mun against those, such as Ahmad ibn Hanbal, who believed in the uncreatedness of the Qur'an.

References

Watt (1973: 178–9).

See also: **attributes of God;** *kalam* **and the** *mutakallimun*

ANDREW J. NEWMAN

MIHRAB

The *qibla* wall is identified by a *mihrab*, a centrally placed pointed niche where the prayer leader stands. The earliest example of a *mihrab* is in the mosque of the Prophet at Medina installed during the rebuilding of AD 706. A *mihrab* is a focal point for brilliant decoration in moulded and carved stucco, inlaid stone mosaic and polychrome glazed tilework employing the full Islamic decorative repertoire of geometrical motifs, interlaced foliage and many forms of Arabic calligraphy for quotations from the Qur'an and inscriptions recording the

donor's name and date. A large mosque may also have several *mihrabs* both along the *qibla* wall and also externally to guide an overflow of worshippers.

References

Serjeant (1939).

JENNIFER SCARCE

MIKHA'IL

'Michael', one of the four great angels.

See also: **angels**

ANDREW J. NEWMAN

AL-MILAL WA'L-NIHAL

This is the best known work of Abu 'l-Fath Muhammad b. 'Abd al-Karim al-Shahrastani (*c.* AD 1086/7–1153), and the most comprehensive heresiographical work written in the classical Islamic world. It brings together the beliefs and teachings of a host of sects and groups from within the Muslim world and outside, and seeks to put them into relation with one another by arranging them in a strict hierarchical order. This makes it an invaluable source of information about the range of religious and philosophical attitudes known in the early Islamic world, and about how Muslims thought they were connected.

The breadth of al-Shahrastani's conception is concisely expressed in the title of the work. This employs terms familiar from the heresiographical tradition, but from the evidence of the contents of the work appears to use them to designate on the one hand communities which possess revealed religions, *milal*, and on the other groups and movements with beliefs of human origin, *nihal*. So it encompasses what might be termed heavenly and earthly perceptions of reality. While translations of this title as *Book of Religions and Philosophical Sects* and *Livre des religions et des sectes* preserve its succinctness, they do not preserve the full comprehensiveness suggested by these two names.

Internal evidence indicates that al-Shahrastani was engaged in writing the *Milal* in AD 1127–8. Although he is generally silent about his sources, comparison with other works where this is possible shows that in the main he made new compilations from existing works rather than researching into beliefs and opinions for himself. He intimates at the outset that his intention is to bring together the different beliefs known in the world as an example for anyone who wishes to learn from them. While he acknowledges in his first introduction that only the sect that follows the Prophet will be saved, he declares in his second introduction that he will present the doctrine of each group just as he finds it 'in their books', without unduly building them up or breaking them down, not distinguishing the correct from the incorrect in what they contain or singling out the true from the false. Thus, he shows himself as interested in exploring and presenting the divine beliefs and opinions as in deciding which of them may be right. His objectivity is made clear in a comment at the end of his five introductions, where he points out that the followers of opinion can be discoverers of truth while the recipients of revelation can be unthinking conformists, *muqallidun*, and that both can establish workable rules for society.

The *Milal* begins with these five separate introductions, in which al-Shahrastani discusses in turn the divisions of peoples throughout the world, the divisions of sects within Islam, the origins of differences and disputes throughout the world, the origins of these within Islam, and the ordering of this work itself. And then, recalling the title of the work, he adopts a major two-part division into Islamic and other beliefs who possess a revealed scripture or something like it, and those who do not have a scripture but follow opinions. As D. Gimaret has shown (Gimaret and Monnot 1986: 14–30), the divisions and subdivisions of the *Milal* then follow a strict logical order of rank, signalled by brief though clear headings.

The first main division of the *Milal* is of those who profess religious affiliations and communities, *arbab al-diyanat wa'l-milal*, comprising the two subdivisions of Muslims and those who are outside 'the Hanifite community'. In his first introduction, al-Shahrastani quotes the *hadith* which refers to seventy-one sects of Jews, seventy-two of Christians and seventy-three of Muslims (and adds seventy sects of Mazdeaens), but he does not by any means follow it here (unlike, for example, al-Baghdadi in the *Farq bayn al-Firaq* with regard to Muslim sects).

He divides the Muslims into the *Ahl al-usul* and the *Ahl al-furu'*, ranking under the former the three major groups of Mu'tazila, Jabriyya and Sifatiyya, the Khawarij and Murji'a, and the Shi'a, and under the latter the groups which hold conflicting legal interpretations and judgements. Under each of these headings, he further groups individual sects and subsects as these were identified and occasionally concretised into distinct entities by predecessors, briefly stating their origins and characteristic teachings. It is noteworthy that he largely dwells on sects from two or even three centuries before his own time, of which many had long disappeared, and shows only intermittent interest in pursuing their development to the present.

In the second subdivision of these religious communities, al-Shahrastani

415

groups the people of the Book, the Jews and Christians, and those with something resembling a book, *lahu shubha kitab*, the Majus, the dualists and the Manichaeans. Then, under each of these he ranks subgroups and outlines their main characteristics. Among the Jews he describes only four subgroups, and among the Christians only three, the major denominations of Melkites, Nestorians and Jacobites, and contents himself with brief remarks about a few of the remaining seventy-one and seventy-two sects into which he says the two faiths further divided. It is intriguing to note here how, at the mercy of his sources presumably, al-Shahrastani mixes some accuracy of detail, for example in his presentation of Christian Christological models, with inaccuracy, making the Melkites ('the king's men', *al-Malkaniyya*) the followers of a certain Malka, and the fifth-century bishop Nestorius a contemporary of the ninth-century Caliph al-Ma'mun.

The second main division of the *Milal* is of those who follow opinions and sects, *Ahl al-Ahwa' wa'l-Nihal*. These comprise the three subdivisions of Sabians, philosophers and pre-Islamic Arabs and Indians, which are further divided into groups and in the case of the philosophers into individual thinkers. He identifies three groups of Sabians, those who believe in spiritual forces, *ashab al-ruhaniyyat*, those who believe in astral deities and representations, *ashab al-hayakil wa'l-ashkas*, and the people of Harran. Following his usual method, al-Shahrastani sketches the main outline of their beliefs and offers some critical explanation of how these originated and what they mean.

Turning to the philosophers, he discusses the doctrines of major thinkers of the ancient and Islamic worlds, first the Seven Sages from Thales to Plato, then the original philosophers, the later philosophers, comprising Aristotle and his successors, and, fourth, the modern Islamic philosophers, *al-muta'akhkhirun min falasifat al-Islam* who, after a simple list of names, are represented solely by Ibn Sina. His ideas are summarised and discussed at exhaustive length, showing the fascination, if not unqualified attraction, they held for al-Shahrastani.

In the third subdivision al-Shahrastani surveys the pre-Islamic Arabs, giving their beliefs and practices in general, and then dividing them into the groups which he describes as *mu'attila* and *muhassila naw' tahsil*, those without any apprehension of true religion and those with some. Then, finally he surveys the opinions of the Indians, whom he divides into the five groups of Brahmins, *Barahima*, those who believe in spiritual forces, *ashab al-ruhaniyyat*, worshippers of celestial objects, idolaters, and wise men. Each of these is further subdivided, with interestingly the Buddhists being included with the Brahmins.

Clearly, the *Milal* is an ambitious and wide-ranging work. Throughout, it preserves its dual character of being both a hierarchical ordering of religions and opinions, with Islam naturally supreme and those remotest from it the most erroneous, and also an even-handed presentation of the doctrines of the peoples of the world, at once a vindication of Islam and an encyclopaedia of religious beliefs and opinions. It remains the most comprehensive work of its kind by a Muslim.

The most reliable editions of the *Kitab al-Milal wa'l-Nihal* are Cureton (1842–6) and Badran (1951 and 1955). The two-volume French translations Gimaret and Monnot (1986) and Jolivet and Monnot (1993) are copiously annotated. Kazi and Flynn (1984) is an English translation of part of the first major division of the work.

DAVID THOMAS

MILLER, DR WALTER R. S. (1872–1952)

The name of the Christian missionary, Dr Walter Miller, appears in this volume by virtue of his efforts over the first half of the twentieth century to promote the welfare of Muslims in northern Nigeria, to understand the distinctive aspects of African Islam that guided their way of life, and to share his knowledge and insights with his co-religionists. His obituary, published in the London *Times* on 27 August 1952, included the following summary of a remarkable career:

> A team of young missionaries led by Bishop Tugwell set out from Lagos 52 years ago on a trek of 700 miles. After three months of hardship they reached their destination the city of Kano, in the heart of the Muslim emirates of northern Nigeria. They were refused admittance and withdrew to Zaria, where one of the members of the team, a young doctor who had recently qualified at St Bartholomew's Hospital, succeeded in establishing an outpost of Christendom. At first the prejudice against this Christian missionary was so great that it proved quite impossible for him to engage in medical work, so Dr Miller turned his attention to educational activities and built up a boys' school that soon became known far and wide. From this school came the first of the Hausa people who were qualified to hold responsible positions in Government service.

Miller was born in Honiton, Devon in 1872. He died in Nigeria in 1952 at the age of eighty. Eight years after his death Nigeria became an independent state. He was primarily a medical doctor, serving the Church Missionary Society (CMS). His independent opinions and his increasingly unorthodox Anglican theology led to disagreements with the church authorities. Trinitarian theology and institutional Christianity lost their attraction for him as he considered the Islamic concept of *tawhid*, the unity and the unifying power of the One God. Social action, especially in the form of preventative health measures and modern medical treatment, was the key to his interpretation of Christian mission among Muslims. He was quick to point out the consequences of a missionary strategy that could only serve to isolate converts to Christianity, leaving them ostracised and without support in an Islamic society. In this, he led by example, assuming personal responsibility for providing a home and education for some of the Africans who converted from Islam.

Fluent in the Hausa language, he translated the Bible into that tongue in 1931. It was published by the British and Foreign Bible Society a year later. In 1935, feeling that his work was done, he resigned from the CMS and returned to England. Unable to settle in retirement, he returned in a private capacity to Nigeria in 1939, to live in a house on the Jos Plateau. He taught Hausa to British troops during the Second World War. To the end of his life he believed that Christianity was the true Islam, in that it affirmed the unity of God and the exemplary obedience of Jesus 'the Christ', without the stultifying influence of the fatalism associated with Islamic belief, a fatalism that he believed could only militate against medical efforts to tackle disease and deprivation. This was the reason why he was at pains to understand and support the Islamic community known as the Isawa. In their attempts to follow 'Jesus' ('Isa) he felt that they were already, as he put it, 'half way to Christ'. Their existence and demise at Gimi near Zaria in the early years of the twentieth century (considered in a separate entry on the Isawa) brought him frustration and anguish. As a notable pioneer in the field of Christian–Muslim dialogue he has a place in the history of Islam in West Africa.

References

Hulmes (1988: 233–46), Miller (1936).

EDWARD D. A. HULMES

MINARET

The minaret (from Arabic, *manara* 'lighthouse') is the tower of a mosque from which the *mu'ezzin* calls the faithful to prayer. This traditional definition of function is controversial as a minaret is not strictly necessary. The call to prayer can easily be made from the roof of the mosque or of any high building. During the Prophet Muhammad's lifetime, prayer was announced from the roof of his house, while the early mosques at Medina have raised platforms for the same purpose. Various models have been proposed for the origin of the minaret – Zoroastrian fire towers, Roman watch towers, coastal lighthouses, church towers – but the question remains open. Minarets in this context are also found as prominent free-standing buildings where they may have functioned as watchtowers or as commemorative monuments. In terms of structure and ornament the minaret is ideal for experiment in form, material and decorative technique. The Great Mosque at Samarra of the ninth century AD is dominated by a huge conical brick minaret ascended by a spiral ramp. The mosques of Mamluk Cairo of the thirteenth to fifteenth centuries usually have a single tall minaret of finely dressed stone punctuated by one or two ascending balconies decorated with carved stalactite motifs or geometrical fretwork. In North Africa the minarets of Morocco and Tunisia of the twelfth century are massive stone structures of square section with inter-laced decoration picked out in sharp relief in brick. Possibly the most dramatic use of the minaret is seen in Ottoman Turkish architecture from the fifteenth century onwards where tall stone sharply pointed columns are placed at the corners of mosques to balance the multiple domes and semi-domes.

References

Bloom (1989).

JENNIFER SCARCE

MINBAR

The *minbar* or pulpit usually made of carved wood is located at the *qibla* wall of a mosque to the right of the *mihrab*. It is a piece of furniture consisting of a staircase that ascends to a small platform usually covered with a pointed roof. A *minbar* is necessary in large mosques for the preacher to give the Friday sermon and make announcements. As yet the earliest identified *minbar* is a beautiful example of teakwood carved with panels of interlaced geometrical and foliage designs in the Great Mosque of Qairawan in Tunisia, which was rebuilt in 1862. A *minbar* was also portable, the Umayyad Caliph Mu'awiya I (AD 661–80) took his personal *minbar* on his travels.

References

Scarce *et al.* (1976: 273–4).

JENNIFER SCARCE

MIR DAMAD (SAYYID MUHAMMAD BAQIR IBN SHAMS AL-DIN MUHAMMAD AL-HUSAYNI AL-ASTARABADI) (d. 1631)

One of the most subtle and difficult Shi'i thinkers of the Safavid period. An illuminationist philosopher (as evidenced by his choice of his poetic nom-de-plume Ishraq), known for his novel solution to the problem of time and creation, he also contributed to the study of Shi'i tradition and had an important role in popularising the collection of supplications known as *al-Sahifa al-Sajjadiyya* (or *al-Kamila*) attributed to the fourth Shi'i Imam 'Ali ibn al-Husayn Zayn al-'Abidin (d. AD 714). Henry Corbin considered him to be a key figure of the philosophical 'school of Isfahan'. Born in Astarabad in 1562 but raised in the holy city of Mashhad, little is known about his early life except that he studied philosophy with Fakhr al-Din Sammaki, a illuminationist philosopher of Shiraz, and jurisprudence and the science of tradition (*hadith*) with Shaykh al-Husayn ibn 'Abd al-Samad (d. 1576), Sayyid al-Husayn al-Karaki (d. 1593) and his own uncle 'Abd al-'Ali al-Karaki (d. 1585). Popularly known as *Mu'allim-i Thalith* (Third Teacher) after Aristotle and al-Farabi and *Sayyid al-afadil* (Master of Scholars) because of his famed knowledge and wisdom, Mir Damad belonged to a powerful family of Persian *sayyids* from Astarabad and was a close confidant of Shah 'Abbas I. He moved to Qazvin, the Safavid capital under Shah Tahmasp (d. 1576), where he met Shaykh Baha' al-Din al-'Amili (d. 1621), the jurist and architect who became a great friend, and perhaps his most famous student, Mulla Sadra Shirazi (d. 1641). He moved with the court to Isfahan and was a renowned figure among the intellectuals of his time. The court *munshi* of Shah 'Abbas, Iskandar Beg wrote of him in 1616, 'today he lives in the capital Isfahan and I hope that his most gracious being will continue to adorn the garden of time for years to come allowing seekers of knowledge to be graced by the illuminating rays of

his solar mind'. A prominent jurist who upheld the views of his maternal grandfather the Arab Shaykh 'Ali al-Karaki (d. 1534) on the authority of the *mujtahid*, he in turn became *Shaykh al-Islam* of Isfahan, conducting the coronation of Shah Safi in 1629. He died and was buried in Najaf in 1631, whilst accompanying the Shah on a pilgrimage to the Shi'i holy sites in Iraq.

Mir Damad wrote over sixty major works on the scriptural and intellectual sciences, and commentaries on the works of Ibn Sina and Suhrawardi. The latter are notoriously difficult, written in obscure and at times cryptic Arabic. Popular anecdotes in the biographical literature contain jokes suggesting that even God has difficulty understanding him. He authored *al-Rawashih al-Samawiyya* (*Heavenly Percolations*) on the main Twelver Shi'i collection of tradition, *al-Kafi*, laying out his hermeneutics, juristic method and commentary on the text. A key juridical work is *al-Ithna'ashariyya* (*The Duodecade*) that discusses twelve key issues in jurisprudence and Shi'i positive law. *Al-Sirat al-Mustaqim* (*The Straight Path*) and *al-Ufuq al-Mubin* (*The Clear Horizon*) are his main works in philosophical theology that were later popular in India and many manuscripts may be found in Indian libraries and collections. *Nibras al-Diya'* (*Lamp of Illumination*) on the Shi'i doctrine of *bada'* (the notion that God 'seems' to change his mind to accommodate historical contingency) is an attempt at defending the doctrine against Nasir al-Din al-Tusi's denial of its existence, but is appended with an astounding idiosyncratic discussion of letters and their symbolism. He argues that *bada'* lexically means the appearance of a view that did not exist previously. Such a notion cannot arise with respect to divine knowledge, volition or determination. However, it may come about in our perception of the divine will. He explains the notion by drawing the analogy with the divine law, which changes and is abrogated in each successive dispensation. Similarly, there is an ontological dispensation that changes but appears to us as if God has changed his mind. *Jadhavat* (*Embers*) is a Persian treatise written for Shah 'Abbas on the mysterious letters that preface some chapters of the Qur'an and includes a mystical exegesis of Moses' epiphany on Mount Sinai. It contains a striking illuminationist cosmology and hierarchy of lights emanating from the Light of Lights. *Taqwim al-Iman* (*Strengthening of Faith*) is a major summa of philosophical theology, and has been published with an insightful commentary by his student and son-in-law Sayyid Ahmad 'Alawi (d. 1651) entitled *Kashf al-Haqa'iq* (*Uncovering the Realities*). The work is divided into five chapters. The first chapter establishes the principles of philosophical inquiry and focuses on the nature of metaphysics. It includes a primary discussion of modalities and types of argumentation for the existence of something. The second chapter furthers discussion of argumentation and relates the semantics of existence with the hierarchy of being. The third chapter sets out a proof for the existence of God as necessity and describes his relationship with the world, the Aristotelian categories and other key ontological concepts. The fourth chapter continues the discussion *via negativa* and includes a key section on the incipience of the cosmos. The final chapter deals with Mir Damad's epistemology. Throughout the work, one notices a critical engagement and critique of the metaphysics of Ibn Sina.

His major philosophical treatise is *al-Qabasat* (*Burning Embers*), a work that attempts to solve the age-old problem of time and creation. Sayyid Ahmad 'Alawi wrote a useful commentary on it. In his introduction, he states that he was asked by one of his students to pen a treatise establishing a philosophical proof for God's singularity as an eternal being and the process by which he brings the cosmos into being through *ibda'* (creating something from nothing) and *takwin* (engendering in the world of generation and corruption). The purpose of the text is, thus, to explain the nature of the incipience of the cosmos (*huduth al-'alam*). The work is divided into ten embers or chapters. The first sets the 'Avicennan scene' by describing his views on the nature of the cosmos's logical posteriority to God (*huduth dhati*) and Ibn Sina's three modalities of time: *zaman* (time) which describes the relationship between mutable entities), *dahr* (perpetuity) that locates the relationship between mutable and immutable entities and *sarmad* (eternity), the sole ontological plane of the divine and the relationship of immutability. The remaining chapters demonstrate that all relationships of prior and posterior, between existents and essences entail the priority of the divine. Chapter 2 discusses modes of priority. Chapter 3 sets forth his ontology of existence and the precedence of essences that expresses his essentialism. The fourth chapter introduces scriptural arguments for his contention that only God is eternal. The fifth chapter introduces an essentialist natural philosophy. The following chapter criticises Aristotelian positions on the connection between time and physical motion, and modifies the famous argument of Philoponus against Aristotle using the impossibility of an actual infinite numerical sequence to prove that the cosmos must have a beginning. In the seventh chapter, he deals with objections to his views. The eighth chapter discusses divine power and its connection to the question of the incipience of the cosmos. The penultimate chapter examines the chain of intellectual substances emanating from God. The final chapter relates the question of creation to divine will and determination. The central doctrine of the work is perpetual incipience (*huduth dahri*). The traditional debate between theologians and philosophers had pitted temporal incipience (*huduth zamani* or the idea that God had created the world in time) against the notion of essential incipience (*hudath dhati* that reduced the world's posteriority of God to a logical consequence of contingency following necessity). Mir Damad argues that both positions are inadequate. Temporal incipience begs the question of the world being created in a time after a time (the lapse between God's 'time' and the world's 'time'). Essential incipience is reductionist and seems to rob God of agency to create volitionally. He sought to find the middle path, a reconciliation with scripture that seemed to suggest that God was a willing creator, whilst avoiding the problems entailed by a timeless God acting in time. He felt that the best solution was to locate creation outside of both time and eternity in the intermediate ontological plane of perpetuity (*dahr*) which described the relationship between an immutable and timeless God and a mutable and timed world.

Apart from the difficulty of his prose style, Mir Damad was known for the independence and creativity of his thought. He did not simply follow a school line whether Avicennan or illuminationist. Apart from his unique views on time and creation, he reduced the Aristotelian categories to two main divisions of substance and accident, continuing Suhrawardi's reform of category theory. On the issue of the existence–essence distinction in contingents, he remained a committed essentialist, like most other illuminationists. His theory of causality

retained a Shi'i adherence to freewill by distinguishing between the cause (*fa'il*) and the agent (*ja'il*) of an action or event. Agency is exclusive to God the Creator but causality is open to all existents.

However, despite holding some unique and interesting philosophical doctrines, Mir Damad lost the battle for influence to his student Mulla Sadra. The notion of perpetual incipience was discarded, and his essentialism made obsolete. Later thinkers whilst appealing to the illuminationist elements in his thought, neglected his other philosophical contributions. In more recent times, his juridical views have undergone a revival, but the publication of many of his works in the last two decades is unlikely to revive a serious fresh engagement with his thought that is considered 'odd' and dated.

References

Ashtiyani (1974: I), Corbin (1972: IV: 9–53), Hadi (1984), Iskandar Beg (1971), Mir Damad (1977), Musavi-Bihbahani (1998), Nasr and Leaman (1996: I, 597–634), Rahman (1980: 139–51).

SAJJAD H. RIZVI

MIRACLES

The question of miracles was one of al-Ghazali's topics in attacking the concept of causality proposed by Ibn Sina and al-Farabi in *Tahafut al-Falasifa*. The philosophers believed that the world consists of a series of causes and effects which go back to the First Cause (God). This First Cause, however, set the first impulses and let the power of natural laws govern the cosmic system. Thus, there is for every effect a logical direct cause. In this system, al-Ghazali insists, there is no room for miracles or the reversal of normal events. Miracles can only be caused by a willing Agent who, as He started the existence of things in a certain manner, would be able to reverse them. Thus, al-Ghazali asks here why God cannot reverse the motion of the sun and let it rise in the west and set in the east if He wants, what are the logical arguments against this possibility? This, for al-Ghazali, was an introduction to an attack on a system of causality by philosophers which does not allow the existence of the miracles of the prophets and saints. If God is the real *sani'*, creator, al-Ghazali argues, and the First Cause of the world, then His knowledge and His divine will can provide miracles for different chosen individuals when these miracles are part of His revealed message to the people. Thus, the religious causality which presents God as the sole or the willing agent for all events is the basis for theologians to accept the notion of miracles, however, this same reasoning presents a problem to philosophers in acknowledging the existence of miracles.

References

al-Ghazali (2000).

MAHA EL-KAISY FRIEMUTH

MI'RAJ

'The Ascent', a reference to the ascent to Heaven undertaken by Muhammad on the occasion of the *Isra'* (Night Journey) from Mecca to Jerusalem.

References

Waines (1995: 22–3).

See also: **isra'**

ANDREW J. NEWMAN

MISBAHA, SUBHA

These are the Arabic words for the Islamic rosary. The words come from a derived form of a root that suggests giving praise and glory to God, as in the expression *subhan Allah,* 'Praise God!' As an aid to devotion, meditation and prayer, *misbaha* assists Muslims to focus on the 'beautiful names', *al-asma' al-husna,* or 'attributes' of God. It is said that Sufi mystics encouraged the practice of using an Islamic rosary. The practice is discouraged as an innovation (*bid'a*) by more puritanical Muslims. Each of the ninety-nine 'names' or 'attributes' of God may be committed to memory and then recited at will as a kind of supererogatory prayer, using the beads of the rosary as counters. A *misbaha* may consist of a string of ninety-nine beads, or a string containing thirty-three beads that can be 'told' three times to complete the devotion. Usually fashioned from wood, bone or stone, the beads of a *misbaha* are normally supplemented by a more prominent vertical piece on the string, which signifies the oneness and unity of God. The Islamic rosary is not to be confused with the so-called 'worry-beads', which are often to be seen in Islamic countries as elsewhere.

See also: **beautiful names of God; ritual prayer and worship (*al-salat*)**

EDWARD D. A. HULMES

MISHKAT AL-MASABIH

This popular *hadith* collection is the work of Wali al-Din Muhammad b. 'Abdallah al-Khatib al-Tibrizi (fl. AD 1337). It is a revision of Abu Muhammad al-Husayn al-Baghawi's *Masabih al-Sunna* (*Lamps of the Sunna*), and its title, which can be translated as 'The Niche of the 'Lamps'' (cf. Q.24:35), indicates its purpose as to boost the illumination shed by the earlier collection.

Al-Baghawi's earlier work brings together *hadiths* from the *Kutub al-Sitta* and other respected sources under thematic headings as a guide to reliable prophetic teachings about given topics. It aids readers by grouping in each chapter first the *hadiths* from the *Sahih* works of al-Bukhari and Muslim, and then *hadiths* from other collections which cast further light on a particular topic.

Al-Tibrizi's *Mishkat al-Masabih* adds further details to this codification of traditions, by naming the compilation from which each is taken, by frequently remarking on the reliability of a tradition when it comes from a source other than the two *Sahihs*, and by adding to each chapter a third section containing further traditions from the Prophet, Companions or Followers on the topic under examination. It thus increases the reliability of the *Masabih*, and makes good the omissions for which al-Baghawi had been criticised, 'even though his transmission, he being a reliable authority, is equivalent to an *isnad*', as al-Tibrizi declares in his Introduction.

It is estimated that the *Mishkat* contains 5,945 *hadiths*, 1,511 more than the *Masabih*. These are grouped in twenty-six books, divided into chapters, which cover the same range of ritual and legal topics as the *sunan* compilations, beginning with the pillars and proceeding through marriage, foodstuffs, clothing, business, civil and military matters, to the concluding book on *Fitan*, in which are mentioned all the trials of this life and the life to come, together with the charismatic character of the life of the Prophet and early Muslim community.

The *Mishkat al-Masabih* attracted commentaries in the centuries after it was written, and it is often published together with one or other of these. It is available in a number of English translations, among them Robson (1963–5).

DAVID THOMAS

MODERNITY

Prior to the nineteenth century, the long history of cultural, as well as socio-economic and political, interaction and exchange between the West and the Islamic world were based on a relatively equal non-subordinate economic, political and military relationship. As well as a political response, the advent of Western imperialism, coupled with Western scientific and technological advances, also generated a new intellectual discourse among and between Muslims. Such scholars as the Iranian Jamal al-Din Afghani (d. 1897), the Egyptian Muhammad 'Abduh (d. 1905) and the latter's student the Syrian Rashid Rida (d. 1935) endeavoured to establish the inherent compatibility of the faith with such apparently exclusively Western concepts as reason, progress and social solidarity. Arab and Turkish nationalist thought, however, increasingly stressed the link between Western advances and secularism. The Egyptian Taha Husayn (d. 1973), for example, rooted the response to the West in Egyptian and Arab heritage. As socialist polemic dominated Arab political discourse in the 1950s and 1960s, the Muslim Brothers, based in Egypt and Syria, and the former including the Egyptian cleric Sayyid Quyb (executed in 1966), addressed the compatibility of social justice from an Islamic axis. In Iran 'Ali Shari'ati (d. 1977) and the Ayatallah Khumayni (d. 1989), the latter exiled from Iran from 1964, were among those working to effect a revitalisation of Shi'ism and Iranian society in the face of Western challenges. Such Westernised Muslim scholars as the Pakistani Fazlur Rahman (d. 1988) also participated in such processes. The 1979 establishment of an Islamic Republic in Iran heralded a new confidence among Muslim intellectuals even, in the person of 'Abdurrahman Wahid, as far afield as Indonesia as to the possibility of establishing a distinctly positive Muslim response to the West and modernity.

References

Hourani (1970, 1991), Keddie (1981).

See also: **socialism**

ANDREW J. NEWMAN

MONGOL INVASIONS

The Mongols, a tribe from the Asian steppe grassland, were a nomadic people who in the thirteenth century, under the leadership of Chingiz Khan, established an empire enormous by any standards. The Mongol empire stretched from the edge of Europe (modern-day Hungary) to the Far East (Korea), incorporating different cultures and influences along the way and can hardly be considered a homogeneous entity. Its unifying factor was the rulership of the many descendants of Chingiz himself. The Mongol victories in Asia, north of the Chinese wall need not concern us here. The decisive moment for the Muslim world came in AD 1215 when Chingiz received an ambassador from Sultan Muhammad, the Muslim ruler of Khwarazm, the area around the Amu Daryu river, forming part of modern-day Uzbekistan. Chingiz Khan's expansion of his Mongol area had led him to have a common border with Sultan Muhammad's kingdom. Sometime, between one and three years after this first contact, the two powers went to war. In itself this skirmish was insignificant, but set the scene for increasing hostilities between the two following the execution of 450 merchants from Mongol territory at Utrar on the border of Khwarazm and Chingiz's lands. Chingiz, angered by this act of barbarism, demanded reparation but his ambassadors were either killed or insulted. Chingiz's army besieged Utrar, and went on to the greater prizes of Bukhara and Samarkand. The Mongol army was an excellent fighting unit. Chingiz appointed his sons as generals, and they served him with an impressive dedication. As the Khwarazmshah dynasty of Sultan Muhammad collapsed, Chingiz sent out his army, whilst he stayed in central Asia. The Mongols continued to threaten the central Islamic lands, pressing on into Azerbaijan and the Caucasus, eventually reaching the Crimea. They returned along the Caspian Sea shore to rejoin Chingiz. In AD 1220, his forces captured Balkh, and one of his sons Toluy captured Khurasan, sacking the cities of Harat (modern-day Herat) and Nishapur. Muslim writers describe the viciousness and violence with which the Mongols conducted their campaign. Hundreds of thousands were killed in the most brutal fashion, since 'mercy was an unknown virtue' in the Mongol moral lexicon. Chingiz himself returned to Mongolia, leaving behind his many descendants, and a developing, sophisticated bureaucratic system, to maintain his empire in the Muslim world. He died in AD 1227.

Amongst those who continued his work was his grandson Hulegu Khan. Hulegu, son of Toluy, was sent to quell the annoying Isma'ili warriors, who were proving stubborn and resistant to Mongol domination of Iran. During AD 1256, Hulegu's army wiped out most of the Nizari Isma'ili fortresses, including the castle at Alamut, north of Qazwin. He continued to expand the area under Mongol control, and marched on towards the seat of the 'Abbasid caliphate, Baghdad. The 'Abbasid caliphate was already a poor reflection of its previous glory. Internal strife within the Muslim empire had left the Caliph as a weak, almost titular, emperor, and his army was no match for the organised Mongol forces. Baghdad fell in January AD 1258, and Hulegu had the last 'Abbasid Caliph, al-Musta'sim, executed.

Hulegu continued his power grab. He captured Aleppo and Damascus, and was about to attack Egypt when he heard of the death of the Fourth Khan, Mongke, grandson of Chingiz. Hulagu turned back for Persia, leaving behind a meagre force which was defeated in the battle of 'Ayn Jalut in AD 1260. The Mamluk sultans of Egypt, who ruled under the supposed authority of newly 'discovered' descendants of the 'Abbasids, successfully protected the western part of the empire from the heathen Mongols.

Hulegu returned to Persia, establishing the Il-Khanid ('the lesser Khan') dynasty, so called because he ruled in the name of the Great Khan of Mongolia, an office which Qubilai Khan (Kublai Khan, visited by Marco Polo, d. 1294), the brother of Monke, had adopted. Hulegu continued to rule his multiethnic, multireligious population on the Mongol model. Religion did not seem to be of much importance to him. He is reported to have favoured the Christians, but he is also famous for the construction of Buddhist temples. He died in 1265 and was supposedly buried on an island in Lake Urumia. His descendants ruled in Mongol Khan fashion until Ghazan Khan, Hulegu's great-grandson and the Seventh Il-Khan of Persia, converted to Islam. Ghazan was supposedly persuaded to convert to Islam by his Muslim general Nawruz. Through Ghazan's efforts the Il-Khans ruled Iran with Islam as the state religion. He broke away from loyalty to the great Mongol Khanate in Peking, presumably feeling freed by the death of Qubilai one year before he came to power. From then on the Mongol Il-Khans ruled as Muslims.

The Mongol invasions are portrayed as disastrous for Muslim civilisation. Infidels conquered a large section of the 'House of Islam', abolished the caliphate, killed the Caliph and brought with them infidel religions, which they permitted to flourish within the Muslim world. What is more, they destroyed the institutions of Muslim learning, and the scholars were bereft of the crucial royal patronage necessary to maintain religious learning. Many modern Muslim reformers, amongst the Jamal al-Din al-Afghani, have argued that the Mongol destruction set back Muslim civilisation to such an extent that they had not recovered when faced with the European threat in the eighteenth century. Muslims were so backward that the Europeans were able to conquer the lands of Islam with ease.

Whatever the polemic nature of the criticism of the Mongols by both contemporary and later Muslim writers, it is clear that before they settled as rulers, they did employ brutal techniques in their campaigns. Yet, they were also an effective and formidable fighting force, and for this a sophisticated military infrastructure is required. They operated entirely as cavalrymen, in multiple fighting units of ten (*tumans*), linking together to make 100 men. These 100 then operated with others to make 1,000, and then with others to make 10,000. This, supposedly, created a tribal feeling within the fighting units, making them highly mobile, and staunchly loyal to their fellow *tuman* members and, hence, effective against their foes.

The Mongol legal system was, according to historians, well developed, based upon the Great Yasa of Chingiz Khan (though its effect has, according to some been exaggerated). They also employed a taxation system which naturally benefited the Mongol rulers at the expense of the conquered population. They were, however, flexible in their adoption of local administrative systems. Perhaps the most impressive element of their infrastructure was the communications system. The Yam, as it was called, was a network of post stations, one day's travel apart. Royal decrees, military orders and the like could be quickly posted from one part of the Empire to another, and most importantly from the great Khan to his underlings. The subsequent postal systems of the Muslim empires were probably influenced by the Mongol model. In all, then, the Mongol invasions were certainly a destructive whirlwind which caught the rather lackadaisical Muslim empire off guard. Internal disputes always aid an external foe, and the 'Abbasid caliphate was no exception. However, the harsh judgement of both contemporary and later Muslim writers should not prevent contemporary historians from being impressed with the scale of Mongol military success, and from recognising the legacy of their infrastructure, from which subsequent Muslim empires undoubtedly benefited.

References

Boyle (1977), Morgan (1986a, 1986b).

ROBERT GLEAVE

MONGOLS

The Mongols burst out of their homeland around Lake Baikal in Siberia in the early thirteenth century, invading China and then the Islamic lands of central Asia and Iran, leaving a trail of destruction and sacking Baghdad itself in 1258. The Great Khans eventually established themselves in China as the Yuan dynasty, but subordinate branches established themselves in the Islamic lands, including the Il-Khans in Persia and Iraq and the Chaghatayids in Transoxania and eastern Turkestan (AD 1227–1363), whilst the so-called 'Golden Horde' (AD 1227–1502) controlled the

south Russian steppes, from there leading raids into central Europe. The Mongols in the Islamic lands gradually abandoned their native animist or Buddhist beliefs for Islam, with their power stretching right across Asia, a movement of ideas and cultural and artistic traditions from distant China was now possible in the Persian world.

References

Bosworth (1996: 243–5, and Nos. 131–4), Gibb and Bosworth (1960–2003), Grousset (1970: 189–391), Morgan (1986).

C. E. BOSWORTH

MONTHS, ISLAMIC

In the lunar year of the Islamic calendar, six months of thirty days alternate with six months of twenty-nine days, making a total of 354 days. The twelve lunar (synodic) months are:

1. Muharram, 'the sacred month'.
2. Safar, 'the empty, void, month'.
3. Rabi' al-Awwal, 'the first Spring'.
4. Rabi' al-Thani, 'the second Spring'.
5. Jumada al-Ula, 'the first month of dryness, hardness'.
6. Jumada al-Akhira, 'the last month of dryness, hardness'.
7. Rajab, 'the awesome month'.
8. Sha'ban, 'the month of dispersion'.
9. Ramadan, 'the month of fasting'.
10. Shawwal, 'the month of departure'.
11. Dhu'l-Qa'da, 'the month of repose'.
12. Dhu'l-Hijja, 'the month of pilgrimage' (to Mecca).

See also: **calendar, Islamic (*al-taqwim al-islami, al-hijri*)**

EDWARD D. A. HULMES

MOON, SPLITTING OF THE

Spoken of in Q.54:1–2 ('The hour has drawn near, the moon is split, yet if they see a sign they turn away and say, "this is continuous magic'"), sometimes understood as a miracle of Muhammad. A story is told that Muhammad stood on the hill called Abu Qubays in Mecca overlooking the Ka'ba (near Safa, now home of the mosque of Bilal). The moon split in two and then moved around the Ka'ba. The event was rejected by the unbelievers as sorcery, a charge reflected in the polemic of the Qur'an. Some Muslims deny this miracle-working of Muhammad and see the reference being to events connected to the Day of Judgement. Reference is found in works of *hadith* to this event, for example in al-Bukhari, *al-Sahih, Kitab al-Tafsir* (60) in his presentation of reports related to Q.54. Ibn 'Abbas is reported to have said, 'The moon was split during the lifetime of the Prophet' and Anas said, 'The people of Mecca asked the Prophet to show them a miracle. So he showed them the miracle of the splitting of the moon'.

References

Bukhari (1974: VI, 364–6).

ANDREW RIPPIN

MOSAIC

A technique where small pieces of coloured stone, ceramic and glass are arranged into patterns to cover a floor, wall, dome or column to form a decorative and durable surface. Adapted from Roman and Byzantine models the earliest mosaics in Islam are located in the Dome of the Rock of AD 692 where they adorn the arcades and drum of the dome with a display of jeweled vases, acanthus and vine scrolls worked in green, blue, mother of pearl and gold pieces all linked by a continuous band of Qur'anic quotations in angular Kufic calligraphy. A comparable richness is

seen in the mosaics of the Great Mosque at Damascus built by Caliph Walid I (AD 705–15) which extend across the west wall. Here a panoramic landscape of pavilions and palaces among huge flowering trees is worked in green and blue against gold. This fine multimedia technique from the eleventh century onwards is replaced by glazed polychrome ceramic tile mosaic in Iran, central Asia, Morocco and Turkey.

References

Grabar (1968).

JENNIFER SCARCE

MOSES

See: **Musa**

MOSQUE

The mosque (from Arabic *masjid* 'place of prostrations') is the most important building in both religious worship and architecture in Islam. The great cities of the Islamic world – Cairo, Damascus, Fez, Isfahan, Istanbul, Jerusalem – are justly famous for the scale, form and ornament of the mosques which their rulers, wealthy citizens, neighbourhood communities, religious and commercial guilds have commissioned. Yet such magnificence is misleading as the basic rituals of Islam are simple, requiring only a space for prayer, which can be observed anywhere providing the worshipper faces towards Mecca. The Prophet Muhammad left no instructions about specific places of worship and indeed the earliest mosque has been identified with his house in Medina, a modest structure of sun-dried brick with palm-thatched colonnades enclosing a courtyard. As the Muslim community expanded, however, religious practices became increasingly codified requiring attendance at noon prayer and a sermon on Fridays. Once the basic requirements of a congregational mosque have been satisfied – a space for worshippers, a *mihrab* niche to indicate the *qibla* or direction of prayer, a *minbar* or pulpit for the Friday sermon and a platform for the call to prayer there was considerable flexibility. Three classic types evolved:

1. The Arab mosque of square or rectangular plan with an open colonnaded court and a hall of multiple rows of columns on the qibla side mainly built in Iraq, Syria, Egypt and North Africa. The proportions varied from the spacious courtyard of the ninth century mosque at Samarra to the excessively deep columned hall concealed beneath pointed roofs of green glazed tiles of the Qarawiyin mosque of the ninth to the twelfth century AD date at Fez.

2. The closed mosque. Here the main feature is a domed hall on the *qibla* side to accommodate the worshippers and shield them from severe weather conditions. Examples are mainly found in Turkey in the stone architecture of Seljuk mosques in Konya and Kayseri of the twelfth–thirteenth century date and of the Ottoman imperial mosques of Istanbul and Edirne built from the fifteenth century onwards.

3. The open-court mosque typical of Iran and central Asia, based on a large square or rectangular courtyard with an open vaulted hall (*iwan*) in the centre of each side. Beyond this framework the mosque can be extended indefinitely with domed halls, courts and passages. Outstanding examples in Iran include the Friday mosque of tenth–thirteenth century date and the royal mosque of Shah Abbas I built between 1613 and 1630, both in Isfahan.

References

Frishman and Khan (1994), Hillenbrand (1994: 31–128).

JENNIFER SCARCE

MOSUL

The third city of Iraq in the north of the country on the west bank of the river Tigris opposite the ancient city of Nineveh. It is not certain whether Mosul existed in antiquity but it was the seat of a Christian metropolitan together with Nineveh. The latter city fell in AD 641 to the Arabs who then crossed the river and settled in Mosul. It was and remained a provincial town fought over by various dynasties. By AD 1127 the town was almost in ruins when the Zangids rebuilt it and added splendid buildings, fortifications and gardens. It was spared by Tamerlane and became part of the Ottoman Empire in 1535. It was for long attached to the Turkish province of Diyarbekir. It suffered from neglect and European travellers commented unfavourably on its condition often caused by the numerous feuds that took place there. In 1879 Mosul was made chief town of the *wilaya* of Mosul, although its importance had lessened because its trade was diverted through the Suez Canal and because of the growth of Basra as a port.

The British occupied Mosul after the end of the First World War and attached it to the new state of Iraq. It developed as an industrial centre with oil fields nearby but as a city remained inferior to Baghdad and Basra.

References

Michell (1995).

DEREK HOPWOOD

MOVEMENT AND MOTION

The Arab philosophers, following the Greeks, studied the movement of bodies under the name of physics and also in their study of metaphysics. Movement is the transformation of a material object from one point to another. It is related to material things and it signifies the quality of being mobile (able to move). In the Aristotelian theory of matter and form, the form is the element which gives power and initiates activity in matter, this actuality is based on the movement which inheres in material things which are capable of existence. Thus, motion is a natural power that inheres in things and denote their actual existence and their capacity to change by which the material world evolves. However, there are two kinds of motion: circular motion and upward-downward motion. The former is the motion of the celestial spheres and is considered the most perfect motion because it does not involve change, having neither beginning nor end, and is considered eternal, the latter is the movement of things in the earthly world and it signifies a starting and an end point for every material thing. Therefore, in the Aristotelian tradition, movement is a universal concept which indicates the point of existence and the transformation from potentiality to actuality. For the Muslim theologian, in contrast, movement is an accident, *'arad*, which is created by God in the atom and causes its motion towards other atoms and therefore causes the existence of things.

References

Ibn Sina (1960).

See also: **time and eternity**

MAHA EL-KAISY FRIEMUTH

MU'AWIYA B. ABI SUFYAN
(AD 661–80)

Mu'awiya I was the founder of the Umayyad dynasty, with its capital in Damascus, the first dynasty in the history of Islam. Under Mu'awiya, the unity amongst Muslims which had been destroyed following the murder of 'Uthman b. 'Affan (AD 656) and the subsequent *fitna* for control of the Muslim community was largely restored and the credibility of the caliphate was ensured.

After the murder of 'Uthman, his cousin and governor of Syria Mu'awiya refused to give allegiance to the new caliph 'Ali b. Abi Talib. The two sides with their supporters eventually met at the Battle of Siffin (AD 657) but the resulting arbitration only served to alienate a large number of 'Ali's followers and to weaken his position as Caliph. Mu'awiya was formally proclaimed Caliph in Jerusalem in AD 660 but was not at first acknowledged as such outside Syria. With 'Ali's assassination (AD 661) and the subsequent abdication of 'Ali's son al-Hasan, Mu'awiya soon received general recognition throughout the Empire. He ruled more like an Arab chief than an autocrat, operating through a process of compromise and mutual agreement with those who had authority in the provinces and supporting those who were ready to support him.

In Mu'awiya's nomination of his son Yazid as his successor and his persuading the Muslim community to accept this, the hereditary principle was introduced into caliphal succession. This was subsequently never to be completely abandoned.

References

Hitti (1970: 178–86), Hodgson (1974: I, 217–19), Kennedy (1996: 82–9), Shaban (1971: 79–91), al-Tabari (1985–95: XVIII, see index).

RONALD PAUL BUCKLEY

MU'AWIYA B. YAZID
(AD 683–4)

Mu'awiya II, the third Umayyad caliph, was the son and successor of Yazid b. Mu'awiya. His rule was not universally recognised, all provinces of the Islamic empire apart from Syria acknowledging the caliphate of 'Abdallah b. al-Zubayr in the Hijaz. Mu'awiya ruled for only three months before he died leaving no designated heir. His death marked the end of the Sufyanid branch of the dynasty.

References

Hitti (1970: 192, 281), Shaban (1971: 92), al-Tabari (1985–95: XX, 1–6, 48–9, 160).

RONALD PAUL BUCKLEY

MUFTI

A religious legal scholar who expounds the law. He assists the qadi or judge and supplies him with *fatwas*. He must be learned in the Qur'an, *hadith* and in Muslim works of law.

References

al Dhahabi (n.d.: 88).

MAWIL IZZI DIEN

MUGHALS (1526–1858)

This dynasty, whose name echoes their Turco-Mongol ethnic origin, were the greatest Muslim dynasty ever to hold power in the Indian subcontinent. The greatest emperor of the line, Akbar, built up an extensive empire, whose subjects remained, however, in majority Hindu. A splendid Indo-Muslim culture evolved, whose architectural monuments are visible in the Red Fort at Delhi and the Taj Mahal at Agra. Under Awrangzib, the Empire reached its greatest territorial extent, but in the eighteenth century, the Empire was beset by aggressive, anti-Muslim peoples such as the Marathas and Sikhs and by the encroachment of British colonial power. It was reduced merely to territory around Delhi and in the aftermath of the Indian Mutiny (1857–8), the last faineant emperor was deposed and the British Government of India took over the subcontinent.

References

Bosworth (1996: No. 175), Gibb and Bosworth (1960–2003), Richards (1993).

C. E. BOSWORTH

AL-MUGHNI

This is a major compendium of Hanbalite law, written by Muwaffaq al-Din Muhammad 'Abdallah b. Ahmad Ibn Qudama (AD 1147–1223), the leading Hanbali jurist of his day and fierce opponent of speculative theology (for which he has been compared with the early Christian writer Tertullian).

The *Mughni* is based upon the *Mukhtasar fi 'l-fiqh* of Abu 'l-Qasim 'Umar b. al-Husayn b. Abdallah al-Khiraqi (d. AD 945), a student of the two sons of Ahmad Ibn Hanbal himself. This was regarded by Hanbalis as an important source of the Imam's legal pronouncements, and at least one commentary had been written upon it before Ibn Qudama's time, by the leading scholar Abu Ya'la Muhammad b. Husayn al-Farra' (d. AD 1065). Ibn Qudama was evidently working in an established Hanbali tradition.

Following the structure of the *Mukhtasar*, the *Mughni* is divided into a series of books devoted to the main topics of *fiqh*. These include: cleanliness and ablution, prayer and other pillars, marriage, divorce, hunting, fighting, faith, pledges, reparation and oaths. Each book comprises a series of questions raised by al-Khiraqi in the *Mukhtasar*, and Ibn Qudama's own views. These he usually sets out under a number of specific points that he sees deriving from the question. In all, there are 8,880 separate opinions, either on the original question or on the points which Ibn Qudama sees arising from it. He examines each issue in minute detail, often weighing earlier opinions from Hanbalis and others in the process. It is these considered arguments and judgements, rigorously established on the precedents of earlier masters, or sometimes Ibn Hanbal or the Prophet himself, that give the *Mughni* its value as a compendium of Hanbali jurisprudence, and make it an invaluable repository of legal thinking from the early Middle Ages.

The *Mughni* has appeared in a number of editions. The Beirut, 1985, edition is systematically laid out and complemented by full indexes.

DAVID THOMAS

AL-MUHAJIRUN

The name (meaning 'the Emigrants') was given to the Muslims who, having supported the Prophet Muhammad from the beginning of his mission in Mecca, 'emigrated' during and after the *hijra* to Medina to assist him in establishing the Islamic community (*umma*) there. Many of the *Muhajirun* fought alongside the Prophet in the victory gained at Badr. After their initial disagreements in Medina the 'Supporters' (*al-Ansar*) and the 'Emigrants' joined together to form the 'Companions' (*al-Sahaba*). The name *al-Muhajirun* was later given to those who migrated to the distant parts of the Islamic empire in order to take part in *jihad* for the protection and expansion of Islamic interests.

References

Hitti (1973: 116, 140), Momen (1985: 6, 18, 26).

See also: **al-Ansar**; **Mecca**; **Medina**

EDWARD D. A. HULMES

MUHAMMAD AL BAQIR (ABU JA'FAR MUHAMMAD IBN 'ALI) (676–731)

The fifth of the Twelve Shi'i Imams. For his erudition and his capacity for 'opening up' his knowledge, he was called *al-baqir,* literally, 'the splitter up'. He was born AD 676, the son of the Fourth Imam, 'Ali Zayn al-'Abidin. Muhammad's more politically outspoken half-brother, Zayd, who expressed support for what had been achieved during the Rightly Guided Caliphates of Abu Bakr and 'Umar ibn al-Khattab, pressed his own claims to the succession. Muhammad countered this by appealing to the doctrine of divine ordinance (*al-nass*), according to which it is an incumbent imam who designates his successor. It was the party of the Fourth of the Rightly Guided Caliphs, 'Ali ibn Abi Talib, which was known originally as *ahl al-nass wa'l-ta'yin,* 'the people of divine ordinance and designation'. Muhammad al-Baqir widened Shi'i understanding of the nature and function of a prophet and an imam in the divine economy, tracing their offices to the beginning of creation and insisting that for as long as one of either remained on earth, 'God withholds his chastisement from the World'. He died *c.* AD 731, reputedly at the hands of a poisoner, and was buried as a martyr in Medina.

References

Momen (1985: 34–8, 147–8, 153).

See also: **Twelver Imams; Shi'ism**

EDWARD D. A. HULMES

MUHAMMAD OR AHMAD

See: **Muhammad ibn 'Abdallah, the Prophet of Islam**

MUHAMMAD 'ALI (1769–1849)

Ruler of Egypt. He was born in Macedonia, his father an Ottoman soldier of Albanian origin. He early enlisted in the local force of irregulars and in 1801 was ordered to join the Ottoman troops in Egypt who were attempting to restore order after the disruption of the French occupation. It was a period of uncertain authority and with great skill he worked his way to the top and seized power. The Ottomans reluctantly appointed him Governor General. He then set about eliminating all challenges to his position, most notoriously massacring the leading Mamluks (who had held semi-independent power) at a gathering in the citadel in 1811.

Once in undisputed power Muhammad 'Ali, with strong modernising tendencies began to introduce a tightly controlled centralised economic system which included control over the land. He created a loyal elite, a strong army and navy, a solid economic base and an effective administration. He had lands surveyed and registered and introduced state monopolies, particularly in cotton. He also attempted to create local industries. He was keen to improve education and technical skills and established sev-

eral professional schools and began the practice of sending students to study in Europe.

He had equally great ambitions abroad and sent his sons on military expeditions. In 1811 he was asked by the Ottomans to put down the Wahhabi movement in Arabia. He conquered large parts of the Sudan in 1820–2 and sent his son Ibrahim Pasha to occupy Palestine and Syria in 1832.

He later had to face difficulties though. His industries largely failed due to lack of resources and expertise and international competition. The cotton crisis of 1836–7 brought down prices and caused his economic policies to falter. Abroad, his imperial ambitions largely foundered on Ottoman and European opposition. He was forced to withdraw from Syria but in return was granted the hereditary rulership of Egypt. By the late 1840s he was growing incapable of ruling and ceded power in 1848 to his stepson Ibrahim. He was a great man who founded a ruling dynasty and who laid the foundations for the modernisation of his adopted country.

References

Dodwell (1931), Marsot (1986).

DEREK HOPWOOD

MUHAMMAD 'ALI'S HOUSE (1805–1953)

Muhammad 'Ali was a commander from Macedonia in the Ottoman Turkish army sent out to dislodge the French occupiers of Egypt. He stayed on as Governor till his death in 1848, active in improving the Egyptian economy and encouraging Western scientific and technical inventions which might modernise the society and economy and thereby fend off European political encroachment. His successors, however, got heavily in debt to European creditors, and from 1882 to 1922 Egypt was under a British protectorate. The line lasted, increasingly out of touch with nationalist feeling in Egypt, till the military *coup d'état* of 1952–3.

References

Bosworth (1996: No. 34), Fahmy (1998), Gibb and Bosworth (1960–2003), Holt (1966: 176–230, 293–8), Hunter (1998), Vatikiotis (1980).

C. E. BOSWORTH

MUHAMMAD AL-JAWAD

See: **Muhammad al-Taqi**

MUHAMMAD AL-MAHDI

Abu'l-Qasim Muhammad ibn Hasan is named as the last of the Twelve Shi'i Imams. Following the death of the Eleventh Imam, Hasan al-'Askari, considerable uncertainty and disagreement about the succession arose among Shi'i Muslims, who were divided in consequence by factional interest and sectarian enmities. Had al-'Askari died, or gone into occultation? Did his disappearance signal the end of the visible imamate? Was there a son designated to succeed him? The confusion was not ended by the nomination of Muhammad (ibn Hasan), his putative son, who was believed by many to have gone into occultation in any case. Two of the honorific titles accorded to him by those who accepted that he was the son of al-'Askari indicate that among Twelver Shi'is Muhammad had become the Hidden Imam, the *mahdi*, 'the Rightly Guided One', who would one day reappear to bring justice into an unjust world. Muhammad was also known as *al-Muntazar*, 'the Expected One', for the same reason.

References

Momen (1985: 45, 59–60, 73, 161–2).

EDWARD D. A. HULMES

MUHAMMAD AL-TAQI

Abu Ja'far Muhammad ibn 'Ali, the Ninth of the Twelver Shi'i Imams, was born in Medina in AD 810. He became known as *al-Taqi* ('the God-fearing) and *al-Jawad* ('the Generous'). Whilst still only seven years old he succeeded his father, the Eighth Imam, 'Ali al-Rida. Not surprisingly, there were those who considered that he was too young to succeed to the imamate. Stories about his precocity were circulated in his defence, and some pointed out that the Prophet 'Isa (Jesus) was even younger when he spoke from the cradle to identify himself and his divinely appointed mission (cf. Q.19:16–17). Muhammad al-Taqi was renowned for his public defence of Islamic tradition. He died in Baghdad in AD 835, another of the Twelver Imams reputed to have been poisoned, in this case by his apparently disaffected wife, Umm al-Fadl, daughter of the Caliph Ma'mun. He is buried in the Qurashi cemetery in the city.

References

Momen (1985: 42–3).

EDWARD D. A. HULMES

MUHAMMAD B. QALAWUN, SAYF AL-DIN

Called al-Malik al-Nasir (r. three times between 1293 and AD 1341). Mamluk sultan in Egypt and Syria of the Bahri line and son of Sultan Qalawun al-Alfi (r. AD 1279–90). Unusually amongst Mamluk rulers, his reign was not filled with warfare, once the island of Arwad off the Syrian coast had been captured from the Franks in AD 1302 and the

Mongols finally repelled from Syria in AD 1303, hence his largely peaceful reign and achievements as a successful ruler, the second of the short-lived line of Qalawunid hereditary sultans, were not based on military prowess. Notable were his attempts to strengthen the financial basis of the State by cadastral surveys for taxation and the redistribution of land grants, and the cultivation of external trade through the Red Sea in the hands of the Karimi merchants. His reign was one of intense religiosity, involving a plethora of competing Sufi orders, provoking a reaction from intransigent rigorists like Ibn Taymiyya, and bouts of intense persecution of Christians and Jews, groups that were prominent as officials of the administration.

References

Gibb and Bosworth (1960–2003), Holt (1986: 107–20), Irwin (1986: 85–124), Northrup (1998: 152–3).

C. E. BOSWORTH

MUHAMMAD B. SUʻUD
(d. 1765)

Founder of the first Suʻudi state in eastern Arabia. A member of the ʻAnaza Bedouin tribe, he succeeded to the base which his father had in 1724 or 1727 taken over at Dirʻiyya merely as one of several petty shaykhdoms jockeying for power in Najd. But espousal of the cause of the puritanical religious reformer Muhammad b. ʻAbd al-Wahhab provided a special impetus to his efforts, and from 1745 till his death he was engaged in an indecisive series of struggles with rivals such as the *amirs* of Riyad and of Najran in south-western Arabia, which nevertheless provided a basis for his son ʻAbd al-ʻAziz further to consolidate Suʻudi power.

References

Gibb and Bosworth (1960–2003), Vassiliev (1998: 60–2, 83–5).

See also: **Wahhabis**

C. E. BOSWORTH

MUHAMMAD B. TUGHLUQ
(r. AD 1325–51)

The second ruler of the Tughluqid line of Delhi sultans, under whom the sultanate dominions reached their greatest extent. He annexed territory in the Deccan, founding there in AD 1327 a second capital, Dawlatabad or Deogiri, as a base for controlling this, and he fought off a Chaghatayid Mongol attack on north-western India, after which generally friendly relations with the Mongols were maintained. But he was later beset by rebellions, losing Bengal to the Ilyasid sultans, Madura or Maʻbar in the extreme south, and then virtually the whole of the Deccan passed to the Bahmanid line of sultans, so that by Muhammad's death, he controlled no territory south of the Vindhya Mountains. The Moroccan traveller Ibn Battuta arrived in Delhi in AD 1333 and stayed there nine years, functioning as Maliki Grand Qadi of Delhi, so that his account of this phase of his life is a major source for Tughluqid social and religious history. He characterised the sultan as severe and bloodthirsty but also as a pious and rigorist Muslim.

References

Gibb and Bosworth (1960–2003), Jackson (1999: 255–77).

C. E. BOSWORTH

MUHAMMAD B. TUMART
(d. AD 1130)

Masmuda Berber scholar who became the spiritual founder of the Almohad dynasty of North Africa. He studied in the Muslim East, and on return to the Maghrib in *c.* AD 1116, built himself up as the *mahdi* or 'Divinely Guided One' who would revive Islam in the Maghrib and purge it of un-Islamic accretions, placing special stress on the spiritual unity of God, *tawhid,* as opposed to the anthropomorphism of which he accused the Almoravids, and conspicuously modelling himself on the Prophet Muhammad. He composed various treatises in Berber for the religious education of his followers, but also stressed the importance of learning Arabic for reading the sacred texts directly. After Ibn Tumart's death, it was his lieutenant 'Abd al-Mu'min who built up the Almohad movement as a great military-religious power in North Africa and Spain.

References

Gibb and Bosworth (1960–2003), Huici Miranda (1956–7), Le Tourneau (1969), Norris (1982: 157–83).

C. E. BOSWORTH

MUHAMMAD IBN 'ABDALLAH, THE PROPHET OF ISLAM (*c.* AD 570–632)

Islamic tradition affirms that Muhammad ibn 'Abdallah, the Prophet of Islam and the Messenger of God, was born in Mecca in *c.* AD 570. Also in the same year another remarkable event occurred in Mecca. An attack was launched on the Ka'ba by Abraha, the Abyssinian viceroy of the Yemen, who used elephants in his attacking force (cf. Q.105:1–5). The attack failed. The city was spared.

Tradition places both these auspicious events, the birth of the Prophet and the saving of the Ka'ba with the deliverance of the inhabitants of Mecca from foreign attack in 'the Year of the Elephant'

(*'am al-fil*). Muhammad was the posthumous son of 'Abdallah ibn 'Abd al-Muttalib. Little is known about Amina, the mother of Muhammad. She belonged to the clan of Zuhra and is reported to have had family connections with Yathrib (Medina), the place to which Muhammad moved in AD 622. Amina died when the boy was six years old. As a result of this second bereavement, Muhammad grew up in comparatively penurious circumstances (cf. Q.93:6–8). He was taken into the household of his paternal grandfather, 'Abd al-Muttalib, who was head of the prestigious clan of Hashim and a leading figure in Meccan society. After the death of his father, a wet nurse from a nomadic tribe weaned the boy Muhammad. He is said to have spent time living in the desert country near Mecca, learning about the high culture of the Bedouin way of life. On the death of 'Abd al-Muttalib, the duty of safeguarding the interests of the young man passed to Muhammad's paternal uncle, Abu Talib, whose protection and patronage enabled the Prophet to withstand opposition in Mecca when his mission began. This link with more affluent members of his own tribe, the Quraysh, afforded Muhammad the kind of personal security in the face of persecution he might otherwise have lacked in furthering his mission in Mecca.

The name Muhammad may be translated as 'the highly praised one'. It continues to be the name most frequently given to a male child by Muslim parents. When referring to, or speaking of, the name of the Prophet, Muslims habitually observe the Qur'anic injunction (Q.33:56) and say: *salla allahu 'alayhi wa sallam,* 'God bless him and grant him salvation'. These words serve to express recognition of Muhammad, not only as the leader of the embryonic Islamic community, the *umma,* in his native city and later in Medina, but also as the Muslim whose example of submission to the revealed will of God has inspired all followers of Islam to the present day. In the Qur'an, as well as having an entire chapter named after him, his name is mentioned in Q.3:144, Q.33:40, Q.48:29. The emphatic variant *Ahmad* appears in Q.61:6. Other names and titles are used by Muslims to honour the Prophet. These include: *al-Amin* (the Trustworthy One), *habib Allah* (the Beloved of God), *khatim al-anbiya'* (the Seal of the Prophets). Of these titles, the one to which particular significance is attached by Muslims is *khatim al-anbiya'*. As 'the Seal of the Prophets', Muhammad is believed to be the last of the line of special messengers (*rusul*) to be sent by God with the unique message of Islam for mankind.

Muhammad's paternal uncle, Abu Talib, is said to have taken him on caravan journeys to Syria. On a journey to Syria, when he was twelve years old, he is reputed to have met a Christian monk called Bahira, who lived in a cell near Busra, and identified various indications of prophethood. There is a wealth of narration about Muhammad's character and achievements. At the age of twenty-five he married a wealthy widow, Khadija, who was his senior by some fifteen years. Noting his reliability and integrity (*al-Amin*, 'the Trustworthy'), she had employed him occasionally on her caravan expeditions north and south from Mecca. Marriage to Khadija relieved his economic necessity and allowed him to withdraw from society and continue to practice the life of meditation that he increasingly desired.

Growing dissatisfaction with the life of society in Mecca, and especially with the religious beliefs of his contemporaries, led Muhammad to withdraw frequently to a cave (*ghar*) on Mount Hira' above Mecca. It was whilst he was meditating there on one occasion in AD 610 that the first verses (*ayat*) of the Qur'an were revealed to him. This first revelation (introduced by the Arabic imperative *iqra'*, meaning 'recite' or 'read!') appears as the ninety-sixth *sura* in the sequence of 114 that constitute the complete Qur'an, i.e., 'that which is to be read aloud'. Tradition maintains that he was 'unlettered' or 'unlearned' (*ummi*). The significance of the term for Muslims, however, is that his 'illiteracy' confirms the divine favour that enabled him to 'recite' what he could not otherwise have read, when the words of the Qur'anic revelations were repeated to him through the mediation of the Angel Jibril. Further, the miracle of the incomparably beautiful language in which the message of Islam is expressed is only to be understood as an act of divine intervention, given the fact that the human recipient, Muhammad, is described as *ummi*. These revelations, preserved in the memories of Muhammad's followers and collected on whatever material was to hand by those who first heard the Prophet uttering them, were progressively revealed to him between the years 610 and AD 632 in Mecca and Medina. After his death, they were gathered together to form the final authorised text of the Qur'an.

On leaving the cave, Muhammad returned to Mecca, where the Ka'ba, a sacred structure housing the multiplicity of deities worshipped by visiting pilgrims, presented a challenge to the Islamic monotheism he had just been called to proclaim. From all accounts, Khadija was the first person to accept his mission. She remained his most loyal supporter and his only wife, until her death in AD 619, the 'Year of Sadness', the year in which Abu Talib also died. She bore him two sons, neither of whom survived infancy, and four daughters, Umm Kulthum, Ruqayya, Zaynab and

Fatima. The loss of male descendants was a tragedy that gave Muhammad's opponents in Mecca an opportunity for making a tasteless jibe. There were a few other converts whilst he remained in Mecca. Abu Bakr al-Siddiq, whose young daughter 'A'isha he was to take as his wife was one of them. Abu Bakr was to be the first of the Rightly Guided (al-Rashidun) Caliphs. 'Umar ibn al-Khattab, who was to be the Second Caliph, also accepted Islam as well as 'Uthman who became the third Caliph. Muhammad's cousin and future son-in-law, 'Ali ibn Abi Talib, the Fourth Caliph, was another convert. Abu Talib continued to use his influence to protect the Prophet, but he never became a Muslim. Opposition to the Prophet's mission came chiefly from those in Mecca who had most to gain from their commercial interests, which included providing for the pilgrims who came to Mecca in order to worship the gods and goddesses housed in the Ka'ba. The message of Islam threatened this lucrative business. Among the leaders of this opposition was Abu Sufyan. More converts came from the ranks of the poor and disadvantaged. The persecution of Muslims increased. In AD 615 a number of them (including 'Uthman ibn 'Affan, later to be the Third Caliph) were sent from Mecca to seek refuge in Christian Abyssinia. Bereft of many of his followers, and still harassed by detractors, Muhammad continued his mission. The Qur'an (Q.17:1, Q.53:1–18) refers to the mysterious events of his Night Journey (isra') from the Ka'ba to Jerusalem (al-Quds) astride al-Buraq (a white animal larger than a donkey but smaller than a mule), and his Ascent into Heaven (mi'raj), which are traditionally said to have taken place in AD 619. As already noted, this year, 'the Year of Sadness', was the year in which both Khadija and Abu Talib died. The death of the latter deprived the Prophet of his protector in Mecca. Within a few months of these personal losses, a small group of men who lived in Yathrib, a town situated some 280 miles (450 kilometres) northeast of Mecca, approached Muhammad. His reputation had already reached the place, where the enmity of different tribes was making social relationships fragile. Hoping for an outside mediator, and knowing of his difficulties in Mecca, the members of another deputation returned and invited him to leave Mecca for Yathrib, soon to be renamed madinat al-Nabi ('City of the Prophet', Medina) in honour of his arrival there. The move, al-hijra, was made in AD 621/2. It was made clandestinely (cf. Q.9:40) by Muhammad and Abu Bakr al-Siddiq, after 200 of his followers, subsequently known as the Emigrants (al-Muhajirun), had already emigrated there. The event was to mark the start of the Islamic era.

The Prophet entered his new domain with appropriate simplicity and modesty. He alighted from his camel and followed it to the place where it stopped. He then bought the place, reputedly from two orphan boys. His dwelling was erected there. Adjacent was a small sanctuary in which prayers could be said. A simple mosque was built on the site. After his death, the site was used to erect the famous Mosque of the Prophet. Having arrived in Medina, Muhammad was welcomed not only by the 'Emigrants' but by the 'Supporters' (al-Ansar), i.e., the inhabitants of the city who had also embraced Islam. Apart from reconciling the conflicting interests of other factions in the city, the Prophet was soon faced with the task of reconciling the members of these two groups of ostensible supporters. His years as a somewhat isolated 'warner' (nadhir), prophetic seer and apocalyptic visionary in Mecca had ended. His task was now to establish the Islamic community (*umma*), to give it leadership and organisation. He also had to defend it from its enemies, notably in Mecca. The shift in emphasis is reflected in the contents of the Qur'anic *suras* revealed in Mecca and Medina. The former are characterised by short, visionary, polemical utterances about the need for submitting to the revealed will of God, and about the penalties for unbelief and apostasy. The latter are longer and concerned with the regulation of an Islamic society that required laws, direction, leadership and defence. Among the groups with whom Muhammad had to deal were many individuals whose temperaments were too lively to allow for inaction. He harnessed their vigour and used it in the consolidation of the Islamic community and in the promulgation of Islam. It does not appear that in the first instance he intended to set up a new religion. His aim was rather to re-establish and to 'perfect' an old one (cf. Q.5:3). To begin with he sought acceptance with the people of the Book (*ahl al-kitab*), Jews and Christians in Medina, on the grounds that they, too, were recipients of a revealed scripture from the one true God. It became clear that neither Jews nor Christians were inclined to see Islam as the correction and fulfilment of their own religions. Rejected by them in this way, he began to see them as enemies of the true faith, enemies who were potentially more dangerous because they persisted in distorting the scriptural message, the 'Book', which they had once been given, and which was now being offered to them again in the form of the Qur'anic revelations.

The Islamic community in Medina could not survive on newly acquired religious fervour. The commercial dominance of the Quraysh in Mecca confirmed Muhammad's decision to attack a caravan returning from Syria to Mecca in AD 624 and to do so during one of the

months when, by long-established tradition, there was a cessation of armed hostility; this brought him into conflict with the Meccans. The leader of this caravan was Abu Sufyan, who sent for assistance when he heard of Muhammad's decision to attack. The battle that ensued that year in the month of Ramadan resulted in a victory for Muhammad. His force of some 300 men took on and defeated a force of some 1,000 Meccans. The victory, despite the odds, confirmed the Prophet's standing as the Messenger of God and stilled the criticism of his leadership. A year later, at Uhud, he was less successful. The battle, during which he sustained a wound, was indecisive and costly. There followed further armed conflicts, the Battle of the Ditch (al-Khandaq) in AD 627 and at Khaybar in AD 628, in which the Muslims were successful. These and other engagements (described in separate entries) have acquired a symbolic significance for Muslims, who interpret the lessons to be drawn from them as applicable in every aspect of human endeavour. The principles are clear. Success is assured, whenever (as at Badr) belief in God is upheld, discipline is maintained, and the Prophet's orders followed. Whenever (as at Uhud) contentiousness, indiscipline and disobedience compromise the principles of Islam, God's favour is withdrawn and failure is inevitable.

After his break with the Jewish tribes, who declined to accept him as Prophet, Muhammad turned his attention to the subjection of neighbouring tribes. He gained a diplomatic victory in AD 628 by concluding the treaty, or peace of al-Hudaybiyya. Khaybar was sacked later in the same year. By this time his reputation was acknowledged throughout the region. Friday, not the Jewish Sabbath or the Christian Sunday, became the day on which public communal worship and prayer was to be conducted in mosques. The characteristic Call (*adhan*) from the minaret, rather than the sounding of bells and gongs, summoned Muslims to prayer. Non-Muslims were forbidden access to the holy places in Mecca (cf. Q.9:28ff, Q.9:17–18). In AD 629 Muhammad returned to Mecca, to perform the *'umra*, to pass seven times round the Ka'ba in a demonstration of Islamic devotion and to kiss the Black Stone. On his orders, the Ka'ba was cleansed of the reputedly 360 idols it housed, during which process he was heard to exclaim, 'Truth has come and falsehood has vanished', and to call out repeatedly, 'God is Greater!' (*Allahu akbar*). In the same year, an expedition was sent to Tabuk to the north on the Syrian border. Treaties were concluded with nearby tribal groups in return for the payment of tax. The following year, AD 630/1 is known as 'the Year of Delegations' (*sanat al-wufud*). It was a time when delegations from near and distant parts came to offer allegiance to the Prophet of Islam and to agree to pay tribute. A year later Muhammad returned to Mecca to make the 'Farewell Pilgrimage'. Tradition includes the following exhortation made to his followers in his last sermon on that occasion: 'Know that every Muslim is a brother to every other Muslim and that you belong to one brotherhood. For this reason it is not lawful for any of you to take for himself that which belongs to his brother, unless it is given willingly'. On his return to Medina he fell ill with a fever. There are traditions that record how a Jewess in Khaybar had taken revenge on Muhammad by administering poison to him. Thus weakened by the accumulative effects of poison, relentless labour, and fever, he lingered for a few days, then rose to perform the prayers in the mosque and died later in the day, 8 June, AD 632.

As prophet, teacher, lawgiver, judge, statesman, diplomat and military commander, Muhammad remains an exemplary figure for Muslims. In immediate practical terms, however, his death precipitated a crisis that has never been fully resolved. He left no clear instructions about who was to succeed him. From the outset, therefore, the leadership of the Islamic community became a contentious issue for Muslims. The divisions in the household of Islam began effectively with the election of the first of the Rightly Guided (*al-Rashidun*) Caliphs. Despite this, Muhammad's achievements in so many fields are evident from the growth and development of Islam in the short period from his Call in 610 until his death in AD 632. The monotheistic belief, religious duties, ethics and social organisation of Islam displaced those of a widespread polytheistic paganism. He laid the foundation for the Islamic community and prepared the way for the rapid spread of Islam far beyond the borders of Arabia within a century of his death. In the process he succeeded in uniting the disparate peoples of 'the Island of the Arabs' under the banner of Islam.

References

Guillaume (1955), Watt (1953, 1956).

See also: **Mecca; Medina; Night Journey, The; Qur'an;** *umma*; **Shi'ism; Sunnism; wives of the Prophet Muhammad**

EDWARD D. A. HULMES

MUHASABA

This term denotes the Sufi examination of the soul, which became an important element in the thought of Sufism in its formative period in the ninth century. By the thirteenth century AD Sufis were at pains to determine the origin for any action or thought, namely whether a thought was inspired by God, an angel, the human ego, or by Satan. Thereby Sufis believed that they would know how to respond to any thought and which course of action would be the most felicitous.

References

Waley (1993: 538–41).

LLOYD RIDGEON

AL-MUHASIBI, ABU 'ABDULLAH AL-HARITH B. ASAD (*c.* AD 782–857)

One of the most influential scholars within the field of Islamic mysticism. Born in Basra around AD 782. His early life in this city is particularly vague but it appears that he was born into a relatively wealthy family and thus, we may assume that he benefited from a thorough education, which was common during this period. In addition, the name 'Anazi, with which he is often associated, appears to indicate his Arab origins, being linked with the Arabian tribe of 'Anaza. It is also worth mentioning that his cognomen of al-Muhasibi – meaning 'the one who takes his soul to account' – was attributed to him due to the fact that he continuously performed this act of spiritual purification, or alternatively because he would never utter a word until he had first 'examined it' to assess its benefit. The young al-Muhasibi moved with his family to the capital Baghdad and it is here that a further tapestry of anecdotal narrations begins to colour his life. His religious fervour and commitment are illustrated in two related stories regarding his father, where he first demands that his father divorce his mother in public at one of the city's gates (*bab al-*

taq), due to his erroneous religious views. Similarly, upon his father's death we find him refuse a substantial inheritance of 30,000 *dinars*, despite his apparent poverty, once again on the basis of his father's unorthodox beliefs and due to the prophetic narration that forbids inheritance between practitioners of Islam and those of other religions. It is not clear if al-Muhasibi married at this or any other stage of his life, nor do we know if he was engaged in any formal employment but it does appear that he may have written letters for the public for which he may have been reimbursed. His undoubted writing talent was put to a different use however as his student al-Junayd (d. AD 910) asserts,

> He (al-Muhasibi) would say, 'ask me', to which I would reply, 'I have no question to ask', and he would repeat, 'ask me about what occurs in your soul', and questions would crowd in on me such that I would ask him and he would answer me immediately and then return home, writing them as books.

This unique and very hands-on approach supplied al-Muhasibi with the basis for his essential works on moral psychology for which he became renowned. According to al-Subki (d. AD 1370) he was a prolific writer, authoring over 200 works but unfortunately, only thirty-four can be identified and of these only twenty-seven remain extant. Among these existing works there are a variety of subject matters that al-Muhasibi deals with, for example, in works like *Fahm al-Qur'an* (*Comprehending the Qur'an*), he exhibits his theological training by refuting 'erroneous' and 'unorthodox' views employing a dialectic method. This type of work not only displays his knowledge of the various sectarian positions held by such groups as the Mu'tazilites and the Shi'ites, common to his era but also his knowledge of their scholastic theological vernacular, which he employs to his own advantage in defending the 'orthodox' position. This particular work is also interesting in the sense that it also demonstrates al-Muhasibi's familiarity with Qur'anic exegesis (*tafsir*) and his proficiency regarding its methodology. In addition, al-Muhasibi is considered to be of the al-Shafi'i school in juristic matters, as he is commonly held to have been one of al-Shafi'i's students. However, in works like *Fahm al-Salat* (*Comprehending the Ritual Prayer*) he exhibits his skill as a jurist, not only quoting evidences directly but also deriving rulings from the source texts, which not only demonstrates his knowledge of jurisprudence (*fiqh*) but also of its principles (*usul*), causing some contemporary scholars to credit him with the faculty of *ijtihad*. Similarly, his works also exhibit numerous prophetic narrations, which is not unusual in itself but is made significant by the fact that they are accompanied by his own, personal chains of transmission from scholars of this discipline, denoting his knowledge of this field also.

Although al-Muhasibi was known for his skills in many spheres of learning, as displayed here, including the Qur'an, prophetic narration (*hadith*) and scholastic theology (*kalam*), it is for his mastery in the field of Islamic spirituality that he is remembered. His writing ability is witnessed again here where we see him utilise a variety of literary devices to achieve his goal, most of his treatises take the form of a spiritual master instructing and answering the queries raised by his student – a clear indication of his pedagogical skill. Alternatively, his own quest for spiritual purity becomes apparent in other styles

of writing, which appear as a series of pious sermons on ascetical themes and often seem autobiographical in nature. The aforementioned styles are employed in a variety of books, treatise and epistles, which form the basis of his teaching. One of the most striking of these works is *Kitab al-Tawahhum* (*The Book of Imagination*), primarily an eschatological work. It charts the spiritual journey of the human being after death, 'imagining' the state of the soul at each stage. This small treatise is one of the most lucid and emotive of al-Muhasibi's works demonstrating not only his literary ability but also his power of imagination, which are employed efficiently to effect a change in the reader. Similarly, in what is regarded by many as his *magnum opus*, *Kitab al-Ri'aya li Huquq Allah* (*The Book of Observance of the Rights of God*), al-Muhasibi once again displays his ability as a physician of human, moral psychology. In this work and others such as *Kitab al-Wasaya* (*The Book of Counsels*), *Adab al-Nufus* (*Etiquettes of the Souls*), *Sharh al-Ma'rifa wa Badhl al-Nasiha* (*The Exposition of Gnosis and the of Provision of* Advice) and *Kitab Bad' Man Anaba ila Allah* (*The Beginning for the One Who Returns to God*), he presents his methods for achieving positive spiritual excellence via inner concentration, spiritual introspection and self-examination. He was not merely an ascetic – although he was known for his renunciation of the world – but for al-Muhasibi, an inward asceticism of the heart, was also vitally important. To this effect, his goal is not divine union or incarnation like that of the 'ecstatic' Sufis but rather, an evacuation of all falsehood from the inner sanctuary of the soul, to allow it to be purified and consequently elevated, by attaining closeness to God. As such, al-Muhasibi demonstrates a profound knowledge of human nature and its weaknesses that predates Freud by a millennium, albeit in a religious context and reveals 'the discerning wisdom and inspired insight of a true spiritual director and shepherd of souls'.

This rich period into which al-Muhasibi was born and lived was the 'golden age' in the development of what would become known as Sufism and culminated in what was later referred to as being the 'Baghdadi School'. Due to its heavy emphasis on extreme asceticism and its strong moral teaching, the Baghdadi School was often termed the 'sober (*sahw*) school' of Sufism and was said to be exemplified by al-Junayd (d. AD 910), who, as mentioned earlier, was a student of al-Muhasibi and as such al-Muhasibi was not only a major figure of this 'school' but was also one of the major contributors to its thought and teaching. This 'school' had amongst it ranks, in addition to al-Muhasibi, some of the most famous names to be found in Sufi history and was to have arguably the greatest influence on future generations. His unique and personal approach to spirituality is also tangible at an individual level and can be seen in the works of the likes of Abu Talib al-Makki (d. AD 996), al-Ghazali (d. AD 1111), Ibn al-Qayyim al-Jawziyya (d. AD 1350) and Ibn Abbad of Ronda (d. AD 1390).

Regardless of his favourable notoriety he was not without criticism, being persecuted by the imam Ahmad b. Hanbal (d. AD 856) for his 'unorthodox' views. The nature of the dispute with Ahmad is vague but a variety of theories exist for the exact reasons for his disapproval. The issue is compounded by the fact that Ahmad reportedly praised al-Muhasibi and consequently disparaged him in the very same breath, advising the person with whom he was speaking to avoid his company. This raised the question as to what exactly was Ahmad's objection to al-Muhasibi. The first suggestion is that he considered al-Muhasibi's methodology of self-purification too extreme and perhaps considered it to be an innovated devotional style. However, as we have seen, al-Muhasibi was not only a scholar grounded in a variety of fields of knowledge but on reading his works we find his teachings steeped in quotations from the Qur'an and *sunna* as well as from the earliest generations, indicating not only the authenticity of his thought but also its 'orthodoxy'. Similarly, Ahmad is also said to have objected to al-Muhasibi on the basis of him using weak (*da'if*) *hadith*, this to some extent is true but it should also be noted that al-Muhasibi rarely does this without first establishing his ideas by utilising authentic texts from either the Qur'an or the *sunna* – a practice which is known and accepted by *hadith* scholars, albeit with some prerequisites. The last and perhaps most likely reason for Ahmad's disapproval of al-Muhasibi is that he used a dialectic method, similar to that used by the Mu'tazilites, in his attempts to defend the 'orthodox' position from the onslaught of the aforementioned sect – a methodology to which Ahmad was vehemently opposed. This was felt by al-Muhasibi to be the most efficient way of dealing with 'deviant' sects, i.e. by defeating them with their own methodological principles and terminological vernacular. This of course became a trend that flourished later under Abu 'l-Hasan al-Ash'ari (d. AD 935–6) and this theological 'school', i.e. the Ash'arite 'school' proved to be the defender of 'orthodoxy' against the onslaught of rationalism.

Nevertheless, whatever the true nature of Ahmad's dispute with al-Muhasibi it resulted in him fleeing Baghdad, presumably under threat of harm from the Hanbalites, resulting in a period of self imposed exile in Kufa. He appears to have 'repented' from what he was accused of, which was apparently rejected by Ahmad and as a result only four people are reported to have prayed the funeral prayer for him when he died in AD 857. Quite regrettably, this vilification did not end with the death of Ahmad but indeed, continued with his subsequent followers from the Hanbalites such as Abu Zur'a al-Razi (d. AD 878), Ibn al-Jawzi (d. AD 910) and 'Abd al-Rahim 'Iraqi (d. 1403).

Despite this, the significance of al-Muhasibi as a writer is clearly established, not only was he the first to write in depth on spiritual matters but he was also the first to treat the human soul in so much detail; indeed, his are the earliest works to reach us on this topic. What is also apparent is that this was not the only field with which al-Muhasibi was familiar with, but in fact he was well acquainted with a variety of Islamic fields of learning, including the views of those before him and those of his own contemporaries. In addition, al-Muhasibi clearly reflected the society in which he lived as he not only discussed the issues which concerned the scholarly elite but also debated the opinions of the various sects present at the time. In addition, he paid great attention to the spiritual welfare of his community, choosing not the quietist life of the ascetic but rather to interact with his society at large, to bring about change at a personal, spiritual level.

Perhaps it is fitting to end with a quote from the most famous of the later Hanbalite scholars, who did appreciate the value al-Muhasibi's teaching, the celebrated *shaykh al-Islam* Ahmad b. 'Abd al-Halim Ibn Taymiyya, who said, 'He possessed knowledge, virtue, asceticism and discourse regarding the spiritual realities (*al-haqa'iq*), which was proverbial'.

References

Arberry (1990: 46–52), Knysh (1999: 45–52), Mahmud (1973: 31–103), Al-Muhasibi (1982: 9–192), Picken (2005: 141–250), al-Shami (1999: 7–19), Smith (1935: 1–59), 'Uwayda (1994: 7–49), Van Ess (1961: 1–30).

GAVIN PICKEN

MUHKAMAT AND *MUTASHABIHAT*

The 'clear' and the 'ambiguous' verses of the Qur'an, a hermeneutical category derived from Q.3:7:

> It is He who has sent down upon you the book, wherein are the *muhkamat* verses that are the essence of the book, and others, *mutashabihat*. As for those in whose hearts is swerving, they follow the *mutashabihat*, desiring dissension, and desiring its interpretation (*ta'wil*) and none knows its interpretation save only God and those firmly rooted in knowledge who say, 'We believe in it, all is from our Lord'.

The verse itself provoked a good deal of controversy which becomes reflected in the wide variety of interpretations which are put forth for these two terms. The *muhkamat* can be verses of which knowledge was desired (concerning legal provisions and the promise and the threat of the afterlife), verses with only one dimension, or verses which require no further explanation. The *mutashabihat* are those verses whose meaning is known to God alone (such as the nature of the resurrection, the judgement day and the life after death), those that have more than one dimension, or those that require further explanation.

References

Wild (2003: 422–36).

ANDREW RIPPIN

AL-MUHTADI, MUHAMMAD B. AL-WATHIQ, ABU ISHAQ (AD 869–70)

The 'Abbasid caliph al-Muhtadi was chosen by the Turkish military leaders to replace al-Mu'tazz whom they had assassinated. Al-Muhtadi's attempts to restore some dignity and independence to the caliphate and to maintain order among the troops on which his survival depended met with little success and after a rule of only eleven months he also was killed. The Turkish generals in Samarra chose as his successor Ahmad b. al-Mutawakkil al-Mu'tamid, a development which marked a temporary halt to the chaos which had beset the 'Abbasid caliphate for the previous ten years.

References

Kennedy (1996: 174–5), Muir (1915: 539–43), Shaban (1971: 85–7), al-Tabari (1985–95: XXXVI, 1–108 *passim*).

RONALD PAUL BUCKLEY

MU'IZZ, MA'ADD AL-B. AL-MANSUR (r. AD 953–75)

Fourth Caliph of the Fatimid dynasty. The greater part of his reign was taken up with maintaining the impetus of the Isma'ili *da'wa* in the Maghrib from his brilliant court at al-Mahdiyya, combatting the Sunni Umayyads of Spain and the Christian Byzantines in Sicily and the Mediterranean, and denouncing the alliance of these latter two powers as sacrilegious. It was the dream of his family that the 'Abbasid usurpers of the caliphate and imamate should be overthrown and the true descendants of 'Ali and Fatima, the Fatimids, given their rightful place as spiritual and temporal leaders of the Islamic world. The conquest of the lands further east was thus

an all-dominating aim, and al-Mu'izz's last years were concerned with organising the conquest of Egypt from the last Ikhshidids, and in AD 969 his general Jawhar entered Old Cairo, making al-Mu'izz the most powerful monarch of the Islamic world, although he was unable to make further headway in Syria against the rival branch of radical Shi'ites there, the Carmathians.

References

Dachraoui (1981: 219–75, Gibb and Bosworth (1960–2003).

C. E. BOSWORTH

MUJADDID

'Renewer', a term given to, and assumed, by prominent religious scholars and leaders in accordance with the well-known prophetic *hadith* that 'at the beginning of every hundred years Allah will send a renewer for my community'.

References

Waines (1995: 191, 210, 252, 286).

ANDREW J. NEWMAN

MUJAHID

See: **jihad**

MUJTAHID

'One who strives', referring to a cleric permitted to exercise *ijtihad* (independent legal reasoning) and thereby issue an original legal ruling (*fatwa*) absent precedent in the revealed texts of the faith. Among Sunnis it is often accepted that the 'gate of *ijtihad*' was closed in the later medieval period, with the term '*mujtahidun*' generally referring to the founders of four eponymously named Sunni schools of law and their immediate followers. As that 'gate' was closing for Sunnis, however, Twelver Shi'i scholars were evolving a system of jurisprudential methodology which, by the early nineteenth century, was predicated on recourse to the Qur'an, the traditions of the Prophet and the Imams, consensus and *ijtihad*, and whose adherents were known as Usulis. Twelver Shi'ism became Iran's established faith during the Safavid period (1501–1722), and by the dynasty's second century Usuli scholars formally presented the *mujtahid*, or *faqih*, as the 'deputy' of the Hidden Imam authorised during the latter's absence to issue rulings on matters of doctrine and practice, for example, as well as lead the Friday congregational prayer and collect and distribute the Shi'i *khums* (fifth) tax. Individual believers were held to be obliged to follow the rulings of a living *mujtahid* who achieved his, or her, standing as such by peer recognition. Usulis also claimed the right to interact with the established, but implicitly illegitimate, political institution on the grounds of protecting believers' welfare and interests. The Akhbari school opposed the development of *ijtihad* and the evolution of the *mujtahid*'s authority, arguing the sole sources of the law were the Qur'an and the traditions of the Prophet and, especially, the Imams. Following the fall of the Safavid dynasty, the disestablishment of the faith in Iran and the relocation of the senior Twelver religious leaders to Iraq's Shi'i shrine cities, Najaf and Kerbala, the Usuli school triumphed over Akhbaris. Subsequent developments in Usuli discourse in the nineteenth and twentieth century owed for the evolution of such concepts as *marja' al-taqlid* (the source of emulation) and the differentiation of senior *mujtahidun* as *hujjat al-islam* and *ayatallah*, and, in the mid-twentieth century, the principle of rule

by an expert in jurisprudence as the representative of the absent Imam, embodied in the term *vilayat-i faqih* (deputyship of the *faqih*) as delineated by the Ayatallah Khumayni (d. 1989), the system of government established in Iran's Islamic Republic following the fall of the last shah, Muhammad Reza Pahlavi, in 1978.

References

Cole (2002), Momen (1985).

See also: **ayatallah**; **Hujjat al-Islam**; **Marji' al-taqlid**

ANDREW J. NEWMAN

AL-MUKHTAR IBN ABI 'UBAYD AL-THAQAFI (*c.* 622–87)

Shi'ite Muslim leader born in al-Ta'if, and instigator of a pro-'Ali revolt in opposition to the ruling Umayyad dynasty. Al-Mukhtar came from a distinguished family that had already played a part in the conquest and administration of Iraq. His call for rebellion in AD 685 to avenge the blood of Husayn was made in the name of a possibly reluctant Muhammad ibn al-Hanafiyya, a son of 'Ali, the Fourth Caliph, by a woman of the Hanifa tribe. Al-Mukhtar's appeal was addressed mainly to the Arab tribesmen of Iraq, many of whom had Shi'ite sentiments, though he is also said to have numbered some 2,500 non-Arab, mainly Persian converts, the *mawali*, among his supporters. As part of his appeal, al-Mukhtar preached the imminent arrival of a *mahdi*, or saviour, who would restore equality among Arab and non-Arab Muslims. For a time, Mukhtar's propaganda was successful: he succeeded in expelling his rival Ibn al-Zubayr's governor of Kufa, and in

August AD 686, his troops defeated an Umayyad army on the banks of the Khazir river. His success, however, was short-lived: the *ashraf* (clan leaders) who had at first rallied to al-Mukhtar soon deserted him again for his rival Ibn al-Zubayr, and after regrouping at Basra, they marched back to Kufa, where in AD 687 they defeated al-Mukhtar's army, killing him together with some 200 of his supporters.

Al-Mukhtar's rebellion itself was a short-lived and unsuccessful affair – no more than the actions of an opportunist taking advantage of a confused political situation. His message of the equality of Arab and non-Arab Muslims and of the coming of the *mahdi*, however, arguably paved the way for later Shi'ite movements in the region, and his revolt accordingly acquired historical significance as a harbinger of things to come.

References

Gibb and Bosworth (1960–2003), Shaban (1971: 94–6).

PAUL STARKEY

AL-MUKTAFI 'ALI B. AL-MU'TADID, ABU MUHAMMAD (AD 902–8)

al-Muktafi acceded to the 'Abbasid caliphate in Iraq after his father al-Mu'tadid. The restoration of the power and dignity of the caliphal office begun under al-Mu'tamid reached its high point with al-Muktafi. His six-and-a-half-year reign witnessed the defeat of the Qaramita (Carmathians) who threatened the integrity of Syria. The Tulunid dynasty was also overthrown thus bringing the important provinces of Egypt and Syria once again under 'Abbasid control. On al-Muktafi's death, the army was an effective and loyal force, Egypt and Syria had been

regained and the treasury was full. He was succeeded by his brother Ja'far b. al-Mu'tadid al-Muqtadir.

References

Bowen (1928: see index), Kennedy (1996: 186–7), Le Strange (1924: 195, 252–4, 260), Muir (1915: 554–6), Shaban (1971: 135–7), al-Tabari (1985–95: XXXVIII, 103–85 *passim*).

RONALD PAUL BUCKLEY

MULUK AL-TAWA'IF

The collapse of the Umayyad caliphate in Spain allowed a welter of local princes (the 'Party Kings') to emerge, some of these being Arabs, some Berbers and some Saqlabis of northern European slave origin. This relaxation of Muslim power allowed the Christian kingdoms of northern Spain to begin the *Reconquista* and liberate the Christian population under Muslim rule (the Mozarabs), a process only briefly halted by the Almohads, who crossed over from Morocco in AD 1086 and swept away the 'Party Kings'. Despite political fragmentation, their age had been one of cultural brilliance, above all, for Arabic literature.

References

Bosworth (1996: No. 5), Gibb and Bosworth (1960–2003), Makki (1992: 49–60), Wasserstein (1985).

C. E. BOSWORTH

MU'MININ

'The believers', title of Q.23.

See also: **amir al-Mu'minin**

ANDREW J. NEWMAN

MUNAFIQUN

The 'hypocrites', title of Q.63 and referring to a group in Medina who professed support for Muhammad but actually supported the Meccans and, hence, withdrew their forces from the Muslim armies just before the battle of Uhud, in AD 625, three years after the *hijra*.

References

Gibb and Bosworth (1960–2003), Rahman (1979: 22).

See also: **nifaq**

ANDREW J. NEWMAN

MUNKAR AND NAKIR

The two angels who judge the dead as believers or unbelievers, based on their affirmation of the Prophet's mission.

References

Waines (1995: 129).

ANDREW J. NEWMAN

AL-MUNQIDH MIN AL-DALAL

Written by one of the greatest Muslim minds, Abu Hamid Muhammad b. Muhammad al-Ghazali (AD 1058–1111), this is among the most original works that have survived from the classical period of Islam, the closest Islamic equivalent to a spiritual autobiography and often compared with St Augustine's *Confessions* and John Henry Newman's *Apologia pro vita sua*. For this reason it has been entitled *The Confessions of al-Ghazali*, though it is commonly translated as *Deliverance from Error*. An exact translation would be *The Deliverer from Error*.

The *Munqidh* is among al-Ghazali's later works. This is evident from references he makes in it to a number of his earlier works, including the *Tahafut al-Falasifa* and *Ihya' 'Ulum al-Din*, and from the explicit mention of his return

to Nishapur in AD 1105–6 after his years of wandering. The years AD 1107–9 are most likely.

Unusually in works from this time, the *Munqidh* is written in the first person. It is presented in large part as al-Ghazali's journey from the fervent search for intellectual truth of his early years to the certitude of mystical experience and awareness of prophetic truthfulness that he increasingly embraced in the years after he relinquished his teaching post in AD 1095. He tells how he began by resolving to dismiss everything except 'that knowledge in which the object is disclosed in such a fashion that no doubt remains along with it'. He quickly realised that this could only be found either through what his senses told him or by necessary truths. But his senses proved false, and necessary truths could only be proved more genuine than, say, dreams by recourse to the primary forms of knowledge that al-Ghazali had ruled inadmissible. So he found himself in an intellectual quandary, which led him into a two-month period of scepticism from which he was released not by his own rational faculties 'but by a light which God most high cast into my breast'.

Having recovered through this mysterious divine intervention, on which he does not expand, al-Ghazali relates how he then set about investigating the four groups of 'seekers' whom he thought together or singly must have access to the truth. These were the *Mutakallimun*, the apologetic theologians; the *Batiniyya*, the 'Interiorists', the name he gives to the Isma'ilis who attribute all authority to their imam; the *Falasifa*, the Greek-influenced philosophers who trust in logic; and the Sufis, the mystics who claim to have illuminative insight. He finds that the first three of these groups do not help at all, since either their intentions do not conduce towards the discovery of truth or their methods are seriously flawed. Then, in the most important part of the *Munqidh*, when he turns to the Sufis al-Ghazali describes how he realises the difference between knowing about something and actually experiencing it. His desire for this 'tasting', *dhawq*, of religious truth led him to see 'that this was only to be achieved by turning away from wealth and position and fleeing from all time-consuming entanglements'. After a period of indecision when he hesitated to do what he knew was right, his resolve was sealed by physical incapacity – 'my tongue would not utter a single word nor could I accomplish anything at all' – and he left his post in Baghdad for a life of wandering to holy places in Damascus, Jerusalem, Mecca and Medina. In the course of this he came to appreciate that *dhawq*, immediate experience, and *iman*, faith in what is accepted from others, ranked alongside *'ilm*, verification by proof, and he comprehended that knowledge is wider than rational intellection.

He goes on to describe a further stage entailed by his mystical experience, which is the perception of the truth of revelation, and this main personal argument of the *Munqidh* now climaxes in recognising the role of the prophets as channels of revelation, again through the immediate experience that brings personal conviction of the truth of their teaching.

Al-Ghazali concludes by describing how, with his newly acquired realisation, he questioned exponents of the four groups he has previously examined but he felt unable to challenge them until, he says, God willed that he should be summoned back to public teaching, and he realised that he himself might be the *mujaddid*, the 'renewer' for the sixth/twelfth century. He thus engages with the exponents of the groups, demonstrates their errors, and shows that only the Prophet gives knowledge that leads

to healing and 'increases a man's reverence and fear and hope'. At this point the *Munqidh* concludes.

The typical clarity of structure and argument that this shares with al-Ghazali's other works gives the *Munqidh* a certain schematic quality, and has raised doubts about its autobiographical pretensions. At one extreme it has been characterised as an almost entirely fictionalised exercise in self-promotion, intended to present al-Ghazali as the reformer of the age. But such a view seems to go too far in suggesting he suppressed or invented facts, for behind the story of his own emergence into spiritual truth and his proof of the errors of others there is a uniting chain of autobiographical details that have the mark of unpretentious sincerity. But maybe it is wrong to look for unadorned biographical detail from an author working in a literary context where the convention supported impersonality, and from a work that is intended as much to expose and refute the major spiritual errors of the day as to plot the author's personal escape.

The *Munqidh* is available in a number of editions, though there is no critical edition based on all the known manuscripts. It has been translated into many European languages, and among the English translations those of Watt (1994) from which the quotations above have been taken, and McCarthy (1980) (which incorporates readings from a very early MS of the work), are generally considered to be the best.

DAVID THOMAS

AL-MUNTASIR, MUHAMMAD B. AL-MUTAWAKKIL, ABU JA'FAR (AD 861–2)

After the assassination of al-Mutawakkil, his eldest son Muhammad was installed as 'Abbasid caliph with the title al-Muntasir. Al-Muntasir restored the Turkish military leaders to their former position after his father's attempts to limit their influence. He also attempted to reconcile the Shi'ites to 'Abbasid rule by returning to the 'Alid family their confiscated estates and permitting pilgrimages to their graves and shrines. Al-Muntasir died after a reign of only six months and was succeeded by his cousin Ahmad b. Muhammad al-Musta'in.

References

Kennedy (1996: 170–1, 172–3), Muir (1915: 531), al-Tabari (1985–95: XXXIV, 195–224 *passim*).

RONALD PAUL BUCKLEY

AL-MUQADDASI, MUHAMMAD IBN AHMAD (after 940–no earlier than AD 990)

Born in Jerusalem to a family of master builders, al-Muqaddasi (also known as al-Bashshari) was a travelling merchant by profession and, like his predecessor Ibn Hawqal, possibly also an Isma'ili agent. Few further details of his circumstances are known, though by his own account his itinerant life was an adventurous one.

Al-Muqaddasi's highly original geographical work, *Ahsan al-Taqasim fi Ma'rifat Aqalim*, completed about AD 990, represents the culmination of the so-called 'Classical', or 'Balkhi' school of Arab geographers. The work builds on the foundations of the other members of the school, al-Balkhi, al-Istakhri and Ibn Hawqal, but is both less conventional and more structured than those of his predecessors. What sets his work apart from that of his predecessors even more than his methodical approach, however, is his obvious enjoyment in seeing things for himself. His work abounds with descriptions of the physical features, economic conditions and social customs of the various regions of the Islamic world – to which may be added an eye for architecture that no doubt had its origins in his family background.

Al-Muqaddasi's professed intention was to turn geography into a noble science, useful for princes and viziers as well as for merchants and the cultivated man (*adib*). His descriptions of each of the fourteen *aqalim* of the Islamic world – six Arab, eight non-Arab – follow a fixed pattern: in his scheme, there is a parallelism between the two groups of provinces, each province has a metropolis (*misr*) at its heart, and together they are united in what he terms the *mamlakat al-Islam*. Although, as for his predecessors, the unity of the *mamlaka* is symbolised by Baghdad, he also appears conscious of that city's imminent decline.

Although some manuscripts of *Ahsan al-Taqasim* are accompanied by versions of al-Istakhri's maps, al-Muqaddasi himself makes no mention of them.

References

Collins (1994), de Goeje (1906), Miquel (1967).

PAUL STARKEY

MUQADDIMA

This work, 'The Prolegomenon', is the introduction to the *Kitab al-'Ibar* (*The Book of Examples*), written by the great Maghribi historian Wali 'l-Din 'Abd al-Rahman b. Muhammad Ibn Khaldun (AD 1332–1406). It is widely regarded as the greatest Arab historical writing and is ranked among the pivotal analyses of human civilisation. It has attracted for its author the title of inventor of the science of history.

Ibn Khaldun led a hectic life of public service in the courts of North African and Andalusian rulers, experiencing regular success and failure. In AD 1375 he was forced to leave Spain, and took refuge in the mountains east of Tlemcen in present-day Algeria. Here, between 1375 and AD 1379 he wrote the first draft of the *Muqaddima*, as well as sections of the *Kitab al-'Ibar*; he continued to redraft it for the rest of his life.

The *Kitab al-'Ibar* is a universal history of a traditional kind with few features to distinguish it from many other works in the genre, except that it provides important information about North African and Andalusian history with clarity and conciseness. By contrast, however, the *Muqaddima* stands out as an examination of and prescription for historical writing that transcends anything known before and foreshadows disciplines that developed centuries afterwards, including the philosophy of history, sociology and economic history.

In the *Muqaddima*, which comprises the general introduction to the *Kitab al-'Ibar* together with Book I, Ibn Khaldun offers an analysis of historical writing and of the nature of civilisation. In the general introduction, which sets the tone for the rest of the *Muqaddima*, he begins by expressing unease with the static approach he has noted in historical works he has seen, and baulks at anachronistic comparisons between different periods in history based on uncritical analyses of changing historical conditions. He also rejects sensationalistic gossip intended only to titillate, and prejudiced judgements arising from personal dislike. It is the facts themselves of any situation or period that must be paramount, and the writing of history should therefore arise from them. This is why it can be described as the science of civilisation, *'ilm al-'umran*.

Book I comprises six chapters. Chapter 1 is concerned with human civilisation is general and examines the factors that influence it, including geography, climate (which affects skin colour and character), availability of food, and the chosen individuals through whom divine knowledge about the nature of the world is transmitted. Chapter 2 then examines desert society and the primitive forms of social coherence and authority to be found in it, leading to observations about the need for charismatic leadership as a uniting factor. Chapter 3 continues from this to inquire into forms of government, and the reasons why the strength of dynasties has a natural span leading to institutional ossification and decay. Chapter 4 focuses on the character of the city as the product of dynastic government and the repository of the great monuments of kingly aspirations. Then Chapter 5 examines the diversity of trades and means of livelihood in the city, leading to the need for intellectual endeavour. This is continued in Chapter 6, where the life of the mind is discussed, leading into the variety of intellectual disciplines and religious sciences. This chapter concludes with a discourse on the origins and achievements of the Arabic language.

A bare outline cannot convey the wealth of detail contained in the *Muqaddima*, about Islamic history and culture, the contemporary Maghrib, poetry, grammar, urban life and trades, and in addition Ibn Khaldun's frank judgements about his own and earlier societies. But an outline does show the unity of the work, and its author's conception of how civilisation comes into being and is maintained through economic and social forces. It is this feature that gives the *Muqaddima* its importance. For in identifying the mechanisms of civilised life, Ibn Khaldun moves historical writing from the practice of chronicling information or constraining it into preconceived frameworks to an analytical procedure in which observation of the raw facts leads to inferential speculation about the processes of which they are part.

In dispensing with uncontextualised assertions about the progression of events and advocating a new approach based on the facts as they can be seen, he was fully aware of what he was doing, as he says in his concluding remark, 'A person who creates a new discipline does not have the task of enumerating (all) the (individual) problems connected with it'. But his innovative approach to history remained disregarded for centuries after his time. Its full stature was realised only relatively recently, when the singular achievement that it is was identified and Ibn Khaldun seen as a lone genius who anticipated methods and distinct disciplines that have now become integral parts of the recording and interpretation of historical events.

Among the available editions of the *Muqaddima*, that in al-Hurini (1858) is often reproduced. There is a full English translation by Rosenthal (1958). There are many studies of the *Muqaddima*, among which may be noted Mahdi (1957) and Al-Azmeh (1982).

DAVID THOMAS

MUQARNAS

Muqarnas is a decorative system of honeycomb or stalactite vaulting made up of small intersecting niches based on the application of geometric principles. It is the most distinctive, versatile and universal means of ornament in Islamic architecture, widely used from the twelfth century onwards to line vaults, border colonnades and entrances, outline and emphasise features such as column capitals and minaret balconies.

Muqarnas stalactites are made in a range of materials – carved stone and wood, brick, polychrome mosaic and painted tilework, moulded stucco. Excellent examples of *muqarnas* are seen in stone at the entrance of the Sultan Hassan mosque in Cairo of AD 1356, in tile mosaic in the Royal Mosque of Isfahan of 1603–30, and most flamboyantly in carved stucco lining the dome of the Hall of the Two Sisters of the Alhambra *c*. AD 1380.

References

Behrens-Abouseif (: VII, 501–6), El-Said and Parman (1976), Rosintal (1928).

JENNIFER SCARCE

AL-MUQTADI, 'ABDALLAH B. MUHAMMAD, ABU'L-QASIM (AD 1075–94)

al-Muqtadi succeeded his grandfather al-Qa'im as 'Abbasid caliph in Baghdad. With the arrival of Tughril Beg (AD 1055) the caliphate fell under the tutelage of the Saljuqs who became effective rulers of the empire. When in AD 1091–2 Malikshah made Baghdad his capital, the caliph became more than ever a puppet in the hands of his Saljuq masters. He was still the spiritual head of the Sunni Muslim community but control of financial and civil affairs lay firmly in the hands of the Sultan. In what was common policy among the Saljuqs, Malikshah had al-Muqtadi marry his daughter (AD 1087), hoping in this way to combine the caliphate and the sultanate in the male offspring. Malikshah subsequently tried to depose al-Muqtadi and replace him with his grandson, at the time only five years old, but the attempt failed when Malikshah died a couple of months later. The infant son, Abu Fadl Ja'far, also passed away shortly afterwards. Al-Muqtadi was succeeded by his son Ahmad b. al-Muqtadi al-Mustazhir.

References

Boyle (1968: V, 99–102, 212–13, 250), Gibb and Bosworth (1960–2003: VII: 540–1), Hitti (1970: 476–7), Ibn al-Jawzi (1938:VIII, 291–5; IX: 84), Ibn al-Tiqtaqa (1860: 342–6), Le Strange (1924: 283, 292, 293, 326).

RONALD PAUL BUCKLEY

AL-MUQTADIR, JA'FAR B. AL-MU'TADID, ABU'L-FASL (AD 908–32)

The 'Abbasid caliph al-Muqtadir succeeded his brother al-Muktafi. The revival of the caliphate which had reached its climax under al-Muktafi witnessed a sharp reversal under the new caliph. Indeed, al-Muqtadir's long term in office represents a particularly low point in the history of the caliphate in Iraq. The good relations that had existed between the previous three caliphs and the Turkish military were lost thus opening the way for discord and mutiny. Internal rivalries within the civil administration were permitted to surface and the regime was beset with severe financial difficulties. During al-Muqtadir's reign two attempts were made to depose him. The first occurred just four months after he acceded to the caliphate and was organised by some leading bureaucrats and military leaders. This resulted in the installation of 'Abdallah b. al-Mu'tazz as caliph for one day. Following this, a military coup in AD 929 led to the deposition of al-Muqtadir and the inauguration of his brother Muhammad b. al-Mu'tadid al-Qahir. A mutiny in the army a few days later, however, led to the reinstatement of al-Muqtadir. Al-Muqtadir was eventually killed in an encounter with Mu'nis al-Muzaffar, a military commander in

Baghdad. He was replaced, once again, by Muhammad al-Qahir.

References

Bowen (1928: see index), Kennedy (1996: 187–95), Le Strange (1924: 115, 120, 154, 195, 206, 231, 255–7, 323), Muir (1915: 565–8), Shaban (1971: 137–56), al-Tabari (1985–95: XXXVIII, 187–207 *passim*).

RONALD PAUL BUCKLEY

AL-MUQTAFI, MUHAMMAD B. AL-MUSTAZHIR, ABU 'ABDALLAH (AD 1136–60)

The 'Abbasid caliph al-Muqtafi, a son of al-Mustazhir, succeeded his uncle al-Rashid. Two centuries of Buyid and Saljuq rule in Baghdad had resulted in the caliphate playing the purely religious role of spiritual head of Sunni Islam, while governmental and military affairs were firmly in the hands of the *amir* or sultan. As was the case regarding his immediate predecessors, al-Mustarshid and al-Rashid, however, factionalism and rivalries among the Saljuqs enabled al-Muqtafi to restore some of the former independence of the caliphate and his personal army extended his authority over all central and lower Iraq, thus establishing a caliphal state. Al-Muqtafi was succeeded by his son Yusuf b. al-Muqtafi al-Mustanjid.

References

Boyle (1968: 127–8, 167–8, 175), Gibb and Bosworth (1960–2003: VII, 534–5), Ibn al-Jawzi (1938: X, 60–2), Ibn al-Tiqtaqa (1860: 357–63), Le Strange (1924: 260, 273, 294, 328–30), Muir (1915: 554–6).

RONALD PAUL BUCKLEY

MURAD I (r. AD 1362–89)

Ottoman ruler, son of Orhan. His reign began, probably, with a fratricidal war.

Despite the temporary loss of Gallipoli in AD 1366 and, with it, control of the Dardanelles, Murad conquered Adrianople in 1369(?) and with his defeat of the Serbian lords of Macedonia in AD 1371 expanded his territory into Thrace and Macedonia, occupying Serrai in AD 1383 and Thessaloniki in AD 1387. His marriage to a Bulgarian princess gave him suzerainty over Bulgaria. In Anatolia Murad acquired the principalities of Germiyan and Hamid in the 1370s. The conquest of Sofia in AD 1385 and Nis in AD 1386, gave him access to Serbia. His first incursion ended with defeat at Plocnik in AD 1386, his second with his death at the Battle of Kosovo in AD 1389.

References

Imber (1990: 26–36), Reinert (1993).

COLIN IMBER

MURAD II (r. 1421–51)

Ottoman Sultan, son of Mehmed I. After defeating his uncle Mustafa, in 1422 he besieged Constantinople as a reprisal against the Byzantine Emperor for releasing Mustafa from captivity. He ended the siege in order to confront a brother who challenged his rule. During the 1420s, Murad annexed the principalities of western Anatolia that had regained their independence after 1402. In 1430 he captured Thessaloniki which had reverted to the Byzantines in 1403, and occupied Ioannina. Following his marriage in 1435 to Mara, the daughter of the Despot, his forces overran Serbia. In 1440 he unsuccessfully besieged Belgrade. These campaigns inspired the formation of a crusading coalition of Hungary, Byzantium, and the emir of Karaman, with the Pope, Venice and Burgundy who were to provide ships to block the Straits. Murad defeated the crusaders at the Zlatitsa Pass in the winter of 1443, and a second crusader army at Varna in 1444. After this victory Murad subdued his rebellious vassals in the Peloponnesos, and defeated a Hungarian attack at Kosovo Polje in 1448.

References

Imber (1990: 91–143), Flemming (1994).

COLIN IMBER

MURAD III (r. 1574–95)

Ottoman Sultan, son of Selim II. On succeeding to the throne, Murad executed Selim II's four infant sons. He retained the services of his father's Grand Vizier, Sokollu Mehmed Pasha until his assassination in 1578. With his death, the war party around the Sultan opened hostilities with Iran, which Sokollu had opposed. The war concluded in 1590, with the annexation of territory in the Caucasus and Azerbaijan. In 1593, despite opposition, the Grand Vizier Koca Sinan Pasha successfully argued for war against Austria. Murad died at a time of severe Ottoman setbacks in the war.

References

Bacqué-Grammont (1989: 155–7), Imber (2002: 63–7).

COLIN IMBER

MURAD IV (1623–40)

Ottoman Sultan, son of Ahmed I. Succeeded to the throne at the age of twelve, with political power resting with his mother Kosem. The Empire's crises contined during the 1620s. The rebel governor of Erzurum, Abaza Mehmed Pasha did not surrender until 1628, and attempts to recapture Baghdad in 1626

453

and 1630 failed. Rebellious troops and extremist preachers in the capital threatened Murad's throne. With the restoration of order, in 1635 Murad led an army that conquered Erivan. In 1638–9 he recaptured Baghdad. Fearing their treachery, he executed three of his brothers during the Erivan and Baghdad campaigns.

References

Imber (2002: 79–82), Mantran (1989a: 234–6).

COLIN IMBER

MURAD V (r. 1876)

Ottoman Sultan, son of 'Abdul-Mecid. He came to the throne following the deposition of 'Abdul-'Aziz. He was removed three months later, following a nervous breakdown.

References

Dumont (1989: 515).

COLIN IMBER

MURAQABA

This term denoted for Sufis attention to contemplation and meditation that is necessary in the path. It is a form of intense concentration on the object (i.e. God).

References

Waley (1993: 535–8).

LLOYD RIDGEON

MURJI'ISM (AL-MURJI'A)

An early theological school which proposed the concept of '*irja*', which is a word used with two meanings: first, with the meaning of 'delay' or 'postponement' (*ta'khir*), in the sense that they believed in postponing the judgement upon a person regarding his faith until the Day of Judgement, where Allah will then judge him accordingly. Second, with the meaning of 'giving hope' ('*ita' al-raja*'), in the sense that they believed intrinsically in the mercy of Allah to forgive any sin, to the extent that they would say, 'No sin can harm faith and no righteous action avails disbelief'. To this extent the Murji'ites were the exact opposite of the Kharijites and it is useful to compare the two when discussing these two sects. As such the Murji'ites do not exclude anyone from the fold of Islam despite having committed major sins and even if he is a caliph/imam, this does not justify his removal. In addition to this extremely tolerant approach they also stated that faith (*iman*) is belief in the heart only, i.e., is either present or not and hence, neither increases nor decreases and as such there is no great emphasis on actions. It is also worth noting that Abu Hanifa (*c.* AD 699–767), the renowned jurist, was affiliated with this school, which may have affected other schools such as Maturidites at a later date. The Murji'ites influenced others in the classical period but no longer exist in the modern era as an independent theological school but their views may still be found as separate entities in the literature concerning Islam.

References

Hanafi (1980: 57–9), al-Johani (1999: 1143–5), Netton (1997: 181), al-Shahrastani (2002: 110), Watt (1948: 40–8; 1997: 23).

GAVIN PICKEN

MURSHID

The *murshid* is the spiritual guide of Sufi novices. (Other terms for the *murshid* include *shaykh* and *pir*). The *murshid* is to be obeyed by the disciple, as it is believed that the *murshid* himself has followed the Sufi path and thus knows the correct method of progression. Those who have enjoyed 'unveilings' but who have not followed the path are considered unfit to train others.

References

Jahanbakhsh (1998: 129–47).

LLOYD RIDGEON

AL-MURTADA, 'ABDALLAH B. AL-MU'TAZZ (AD 908)

Less than four months into the troubled reign of the 'Abbasid caliph al-Muqtadir (r. AD 908–32), an attempt to depose him in favour of 'Abdallah b. al-Mu'tazz, a son of al-Mutawakkil, was orchestrated by commanders in the military establishment along with some leading bureaucrats. The coup was initially successful and 'Abdallah was installed as Caliph with the honorary title *al-Murtada*. One day later, a counter-coup resulted in the removal of al-Murtada and the reinstatement of al-Muqtadir.

References

Bowen (1928: 79–190 *passim*), Ibn al-Jawzi (1938: VI, 84–8), Kennedy (1996: 188, 193), Shaban (1971: 137).

RONALD PAUL BUCKLEY

MURU'A

In pre-Islamic Arabia *muru'a* ('manliness') was considered to be a supreme virtue. The demonstration of courage by their menfolk in taking vengeance when the need for it arose was demanded by women as proof of manhood. The prosecution of vendetta over the course of generations was not eliminated by the coming of Islam, but its incidence was reduced over time. The virtue of manliness was enculturated and admired for less bloodthirsty reasons in Islamic communities.

References

Hitti (1973: 25, 95, 253, 335).

EDWARD D. A. HULMES

MURUJ AL-DHAHAB

This is the best-known work of Abu 'l-Hasan 'Ali b. al-Husayn al-Mas'udi (*c.* AD 893–956), and is widely regarded as one of the fullest historical works written in the early Islamic period. As late as the fourteenth century, Ibn Khaldun in the *Muqaddima* noted the qualities that to many made it 'the basic reference work for historians, their principal source for verifying historical information'. And he himself held it in high regard, despite noting a number of inaccuracies.

Al-Mas'udi composed the *Muruj* in AD 943 while he was living in Egypt. He made a revision in AD 947 and again shortly before his death in AD 956 (this latter text has not survived). This was after a life of many travels which he refers to in the work, from his native Baghdad to Persia, India and maybe further east, the southern Caucasus and Caspian Sea, Syria, Palestine, Arabia, Egypt and the east African coast. He incorporated all the knowledge he obtained into this extensive work, which he entitled *Muruj al-Dhahab wa Ma'adin al-Jawhar*, 'Meadows of Gold and Mines of Precious Stones' (see Khalidi 1975: 2, n2 for a defence of the meaning of the title as 'meadows of gold').

In essence, the *Muruj* traces the history of the world from the creation to the reign of the 'Abbasid Caliph al-Muti' li-llah. It comprises 132 chapters, sixty-nine on the period up to the coming of the Prophet Muhammad, and the remainder tracing the Prophet's life and the succeeding caliphates. Al-Mas'udi explains his intention in the first chapter as being to abridge two even longer histories he had previously written and to add further facts, as well as to make up deficiencies in previous writing of this kind. He has given his work this title because 'it reproduces the striking parts and principal passages of our earlier works'.

The two parts of the work differ noticeably in character. In the chapters concerned with pre-Islamic history a wide diversity of subjects is treated, geographical, scientific and cultural as well as strictly historical. Here al-Mas'udi displays the fruits of his travel and of his reading in the authors he lists at the beginning. Then, in the chapters concerned with the history of Islam, the focus narrows to the Prophet himself followed by the chronological order of caliphs who succeeded him. There is still diversity and richness in the narrative, but the subject matter remains for the most part fixed on the Islamic world.

This narrowing of focus in the *Muruj* discloses al-Mas'udi's deeper intention, which was to discern in the vagaries of world history a pattern that led through the ages and successive kingdoms to the coming of Muhammad and the triumph of the state built on the teachings he delivered. This state was the embodiment of all that had preceded it. But al-Mas'udi was fully aware that factors such as environment and human capability play a part in influencing events as well as divine intention, and he acknowledges the effects these can have on the rise and fall of nations and dynasties. His work may thus be seen as a signal attempt to make sense of the stream of events and to apply methodological principles in studying them.

This being said, it cannot be denied that the *Muruj al-Dhahab* may be read for enjoyment as well as instruction about the direction of history. In this sense it fits into the genre of *adab*, the cultivated literature that was intended to delight and entertain. Its numerous digressions and enumerations of strange and exotic facts could well explain why, apart from the *Kitab al-Tanbih wa'l-Ishraf*, it is the only surviving example of al-Mas'udi's whole oeuvre.

The standard edition of the *Muruj al-Dhahab* is by Barbier de Meynard and Pavet de Courteille (1861–77), together with a French translation. This was revised by Pellat (1966–74). There is a partial English translation by Lunde and Stone (1989).

References

Khalidi (1975), Shboul (1979).

DAVID THOMAS

MUSA

A reference to 'Moses', who is called a *rasul* in Islam, as he brought a new revelation (the Mosaic law) (Q.87:18–19), not a *nabi*. Moses' story is recounted in detail in the Qur'an, but he is also often associated with the exoteric law, as witness his encounter with al-Khidr (Q.18:61f), a figure identified with transcendent knowledge. See Q.28:15.

See also: **Harun;** *nabi*; *rasul*

ANDREW J. NEWMAN

MUSA AL-KAZIM (ABU'L-HASAN MUSA IBN JA'FAR)

The Seventh of the Shi'i Twelver Imams. His mother, a slave called Hamida, gave birth to him whilst journeying between Mecca and Medina, *c.* AD 745. The death of his father, the Sixth Imam

Ja'far al-Sadiq, occasioned a dispute about succession to the imamate. It was expected that Ja'far's eldest son, Isma'il, would succeed, but Ja'far was persuaded to prefer Musa after learning of Isma'il's profligate lifestyle. In the event, Isma'il predeceased his father, but Musa's succession was disputed throughout his tenure of office. The 'Abbasid caliphs were particularly hostile to him. Musa was arrested in AD 793, sent to Basra and thence to Baghdad, where he was imprisoned and murdered by poisoning in AD 799. Rumours began to circulate that he would be the last of the line of visible Imams, that he had not died, and that he would one day return as *al-mahdi*, 'the Guided One'. A shrine in Baghdad was erected to honour *al-Khazimayn*, i.e., the two Khazims (the Seventh Imam and his grandson, Muhmmmad al-Taqi, the Ninth Imam).

References

Momen (1985: 39–41).

See also: **Isma'il ibn Ja'far al-Sadiq; Isma'ilism/Batinism (al-Isma'iliyya/al-Batiniyya); Muhammad al-Taqi**

EDWARD D. A. HULMES

MUSA, PRINCE (r. 1411–13)

Ottoman prince, son of Bayezid I. After the battle of Ankara in 1402, he came into the captivity of his brother Mehmed I. In 1409, Mehmed released him to confront their brother Suleyman in Rumelia. After the defeat of Suleyman in 1411, he ruled independently in Rumelia until his defeat by Mehmed in 1413.

References

Imber (1990: 55–73).

COLIN IMBER

MUSA SHAKIR, SONS OF

See: *Banu Musa*

MUSAYLIMA

The name *musaylima*, a derisive diminutive in Arabic, refers to a prophet who led the Banu Hanifa in central Arabia against the forces of Abu Bakr during the *ridda* ('apostasy' or 'secession') wars in AD 632–4. Musaylima and his army of some 40,000 men provided stubborn resistance to the Muslim forces until he was defeated by a force under the command of Khalid ibn al-Walid.

References

Hitti (1973: 140–2).

EDWARD D. A. HULMES

MUSHRIKUN

'Those who associate', a term for idolaters or pagans.

References

Waines (1995: 105).

See also: *shirk*

ANDREW J. NEWMAN

MUSLIM

'One who has surrendered' to Allah and His will.

References

Waines (1995: 13–14, 103–4).

ANDREW J. NEWMAN

MUSLIM IBN AL-HAJJAJ
(AD 817/21–75)

Collector of *hadith*. Born in Nishapur, Muslim travelled widely throughout the

Islamic world in search of traditions related from Muhammad. It is said that he heard a total of 300,000 of these, of which he selected some 3,000 and compiled them into a book known as *al-Jami' al-Sahih*, 'The Reliable Collection [of *hadith*]' or simply *al-Sahih*, 'The Reliable [*hadith*]'. This work, along with that of al-Bukhari by the same name, became accepted as the most reliable collection of prophetic traditions by the Sunni community. Organised by legal topic, Muslim's work contains fifty-two books covering all the major aspects of Islamic law, the life of Muhammad, theology, eschatology and exegesis. Numerous commentaries on the work exist.

References

Juynboll (1984: 263–302), Siddiqui (1976).

ANDREW RIPPIN

MUSLIM LEAGUE

The All India Muslim League (ML) was founded in Dhaka in 1906 to articulate the concerns of an Indian Muslim elite about the future prospects of living under a Hindu majority. As direct British control increased over India during the nineteenth century, the balance of power between the Hindu majority and Muslim minority (which made up around one-quarter of the population) had begun to shift. While traditionalist nineteenth century movements such as Deobandism tended to emphasise that the survival of Islam under non-Muslim rule depended mainly upon religious reform, others including the modernist, Sayyid Ahmad Khan (1817–98), were responsible for the birth of what might be called 'Muslim identity politics'. Well known for establishing the Anglo-Oriental College at Aligarh in 1877, Khan also advised Muslims not to join the Indian National Congress (INC) when it was established in 1885. Indeed, he is credited with originating the so-called 'two-nation theory', which suggested that India comprised two distinct 'peoples', 'Hindus' and 'Muslims'. Against this context, Robinson reports that Khan established the All-India Muslim Educational Conference in 1886, drawing together Muslim elites from across the subcontinent for the first time. Both the Conference and Aligarh, then, were instrumental in the emergence of the ML, providing much of its main support along with the landed and government service classes.

ML demands for the right to separate Muslim electorates and representation in new legislative councils were first acknowledged by the British Viceroy, Lord Minto, in 1909. Religious differences had played an important part in the way that the British imagined Indian society, so, as well as Muslim elites, the colonial authorities played a key role in legitimating the idea of 'Muslims' as a distinctive political category. During and immediately after the First World War, however, the ML attempted to make common cause with the INC in their pursuit of 'self-rule'. As Robinson again suggests, ML supporters were increasingly young professionals, lawyers and newspaper editors and one of these, Muhammad 'Ali Jinnah (1876–1948), did much to advance the cause of Hindu-Muslim unity. Indeed, Jinnah had seemed destined for the INC leadership until Gandhi returned from South Africa with a more radical agenda. However, into the 1920s, and as the INC supported *khilafat* movement collapsed, Hindu nationalism and communal violence grew amid fears that the INC was championing the Muslim cause. This new climate tended to inhibit compromise and it became clear that the INC were not convinced that the

ML's demands were equitable. Jinnah had hoped for a Muslim province in Sindh, political reforms in North-West Frontier Province (NWFP) and Baluchistan, as well as proportional representation for Muslims in Punjab and Bengal, with 30 per cent of seats in the central legislature of India reserved for Muslims.

While Hindus increasingly found a voice in Gandhi, Muslims were disunited and the ML in a state of disarray. Ahmed reports that its total membership in 1926 had been just over one thousand. It was against this context that the first calls for a separate Muslim homeland began to emerge. This was reflected, for example, in the 1930 presidential address of Muhammad Iqbal (1877–1938), the leading intellectual of twentieth century South Asian Islam. Speaking to the annual meeting of the ML in Allahabad, he expounded the idea of a single, amalgamated and self-governing north-west Indian Muslim state based upon Islamic principles. However, Iqbal did not speak either of a Muslim 'nation' or of 'Pakistan' (in Urdu, 'pure' (*pak*) 'land' (*stan*)). Rather, this name was actually coined by Chaudhri Rahmat 'Ali, a Cambridge University student and his friends, who, inspired by Iqbal, suggested a ten state Muslim federation in India. The biggest of these would be given a name derived from the first letters of Punjab, Afghanistan (i.e. NWFP), Kashmir and Sindh, as well as the '*stan*' in Baluchistan. Initially Iqbal's ideas were rejected out of hand for they resolved only the predicaments of a fraction of India's Muslims and especially those in northern provinces such as Punjab. Indeed, while they agreed with the ML that Muslims must maintain their separate identity, the Deobandi '*ulama*' tended to argue that religion was no basis for the division of India, the ML was seen as Western-influenced and secularist. It was against this context that, having withdrawn from India in 1930, Jinnah was eventually persuaded to return from a law practice and failed political career in London to lead the ML as President once more.

With little time to organise for the first general elections of 1937, the ML under Jinnah secured only 4.6 per cent of the total Muslim vote. The INC won a majority of the provincial contests and refused to admit any ML representatives into its cabinets. At this point the ML was still not a major player in Indian politics. However, its fortunes began to change in 1939 when the INC resigned power in protest at Britain's declaration of war against Germany on India's behalf. The British were especially keen for Muslims to support the war because around 50 per cent of the Indian army was Muslim and the ML was the only credible 'All India' Muslim party. Thereafter, Jinnah was increasingly seen as the 'sole spokesmen' of Indian Muslims and while the INC leadership spent most of the Second World War in jail the ML supported the war effort. In March 1940 the so-called 'Lahore resolution' was made, arguing that Indian Muslims were a 'nation' not a 'minority' and demanding a separate Muslim homeland. No precise geographical boundaries were delineated and there was still no mention of 'Pakistan' or 'partition'. Indeed, it was not clear whether the Muslim states were to be located within or without a federal India. Nevertheless, under the leadership of Jinnah, the idea of a Muslim homeland became the ML's main goal. This, despite the fact that subcontinental Muslims did not share a common language, culture, or territory, and were divided by various theological sects. As Jalal insists, there was also a conflict of interests between Muslims in 'majority-Muslim' and Muslims in 'minority-Muslim' provinces. The ML's leadership and main constituency at this point was based in minority provinces such as Uttar Pradesh (UP) rather than majority provinces such as Bengal and Punjab which were more indifferent to the idea of a separate Muslim homeland. For those in minority provinces it was thought that the creation of such a homeland was the only way to secure adequate protection at independence. Robinson reports that scholars and Sufis from UP toured schools and shrines in the majority provinces to mobilise support, as did students from Aligarh.

In 1944 the ML claimed a membership of 4.5 million and gathered 75 per cent of Muslim votes in central and provincial elections. However, it formed governments only in Bengal and Sindh. Nevertheless, by 1946, it had won 90 per cent of Muslim seats at the general elections. Overseeing a huge shift from elite to mass politics, Jinnah had sold the idea of 'Pakistan' as a place where religious and civil rights could be safeguarded to ordinary Muslims. In order to resolve the question of independence, a delegation was sent from Britain to India by the new Labour government. Three tiers of government were proposed – 'provincial', 'federal' (i.e. 'Pakistani' and 'Hindustani') as well as 'central' where representatives of the two federal governments would deal with matters of common concern such as defence and foreign policy on an equal basis. Within such a power-sharing confederacy, the ML envisioned that 'Pakistan' would include an undivided Punjab and Bengal with the non-Muslim presence there safeguarding the interests of minorities on both sides of the proposed borders. However, the INC was prepared neither to share power with the ML at 'all India' level

nor accommodate the idea of Muslim majority provinces. With civil disorder threatening, Britain sent Mountbatten to India in 1947 to enforce a settlement and it soon became clear to him that power would have to be transferred to two governments. The INC was easily persuaded of the need for 'Partition' as it would produce a strong central government in India but for the ML it meant a failure of its stated aim to protect the interests of all subcontinental Muslims. With one third 'left behind' in India, as Jinnah himself put it, the Pakistan that emerged was 'truncated' and 'moth-eaten'. However, it was one of the largest Muslim nations in the world.

In 1947 the ML became the major political party of Pakistan ruling intermittently until 1958 and then again for short periods in the 1960s, 1980s and 1990s. However, Partition was an extremely painful and bloody process and, with an unequal share of resources, not for the last time, Pakistan went to war with India over the disputed territory of Kashmir in 1948. In that same year Jinnah, the Qaid-i A'zam (the Great Leader), died from lung cancer leaving the country to an ongoing struggle between Muslim nationalists, who maintain that Pakistan should be a secular democracy, and religious traditionalists and Islamists, who argue that it should be an Islamic state with Islamic institutions and shari'a. After Jinnah's death, the ML and its branches became involved in power struggles and corruption. The party did not possess the same grassroots in Pakistan as the INC in India, for many of its leaders were the so-called 'muhajirs' (migrants) whose power bases lay over the border in Muslim-minority areas. Political instability in Pakistan eventually led to the first of a number of military takeovers which have continued to this day.

During the rule of General Ayub (r. 1958–62), the party was reformed with two factions emerging, one associated with the General and another opposed to him. Since then a number of parties have used the name 'Pakistan Muslim League' but despite certain continuities they have little real connection now to the original.

References

Ahmed (1997), Jalal (1994), Robinson (1997).

See also: **Deobandism.**

SEÁN McLOUGHLIN

MUSLIM WORLD LEAGUE

Founded in Saudi Arabia during 1962, the Muslim World League (Rabitat al-'Alam al-Islami) is a transnational cultural, welfare and *da'wa* (propagation) organisation that has sought to export Wahhabism on a global scale. The League first emerged as part of Saudi Arabia's 'pan-Islamic' attempt to counteract communism and especially the pan-Arab nationalism and socialism of revolutionaries such as General Jamal Nasser's of Egypt (r. 1956–70). Into the 1970s, oil wealth accelerated the League's attempts at international Islamic cooperation, with a World Council of Mosques established in 1975 and the Islamic Fiqh Academy in 1976. The 'Islamic' Revolution of 1979, which saw Iran emerge as a rival to the Saudis in terms of putative worldwide Islamic 'leadership', provided a further spur to such 'coordinating' activity.

The League's privileged access to Saudi funds has facilitated close cooperation between Wahhabism and international Salafi and Islamist movements such as al-Ikhwan al-Muslimun and Jama'at-i Islami. Indeed, under the leadership of the Wahhabi Grand Mufti of Saudi Arabia, representatives of both these movements were among the twenty-one scholars and intellectuals who came together as founding members of the League's council. At different times, Saudi patronage of a wide range of projects and causes, from the International Islamic University in Islamabad to the Afghan *mujahidin*, has been important in reinforcing such ties. However, this has not always been enough to silence Islamists' criticism of the regime, as was illustrated by their protests at Saudi cooperation with America during the Gulf War of 1990–1.

Today the League has branches worldwide, from Buenos Aires to Kuala Lumpur. Its main activities comprise the training of religious functionaries and *du'at* (missionaries), the building of mosques, schools, libraries, hospitals and clinics, as well as the distribution of copies of the Qur'an, journals and other religious literature. The stated aim of the League is to 'unify' Muslims and 'defend' Islam in the face of 'false' representations made in the Western media. On the World Wide Web, it is widely reported that the League has acted as a non-governmental observer at the United Nations Economic and Social Council; it is also a member of UNESCO and UNICEF. Like many other Islamic organisations post 9/11, however, the activities of some of the League's membership have come under intense scrutiny, especially from the US Government.

SEÁN McLOUGHLIN

MUSNAD

This is the best-known work of the early 'Abbasid theologian and jurist Ahmad Ibn Hanbal (AD 780–855), who is remembered for his stand against the Mu'tazili-influenced enforcers of the doctrine that the Qur'an was created and, even more important, as the founder of one of the four Sunni law schools. It is among the largest collections of *hadith* known, and the most celebrated example of the *musnad* form of *hadith* collections.

Musnad collections, the earliest type of systematic compilations of *hadith*, have their contents arranged according to the Companion who heads the line of transmitters from the Prophet. This is unlike the *musannaf* type, of which the *Sahihs* of al-Bukhari and Muslim are primary examples, in which the contents are arranged according to their subject matter. Hence the name, *musnad* denotes its 'leaning' or resting on the authority first known to have transmitted it.

Ibn Hanbal's *Musnad* is not the earliest example of this form of compilation, those of Abu Dawud al-Tayalisi (d. AD 819) and al-Shafi'i (d. AD 820), with whom Ibn Hanbal studied, certainly predate it. Precise information about the circumstances of its composition is lacking, but Ibn Hanbal must surely have been preoccupied with it for much of his life. According to the biographical report about him given by al-Subki, he asked his son to remove a questionable *hadith* when he was on his deathbed, suggesting that he was revising it in his latter years and died without completing it. This son, 'Abdallah (d. AD 903), in fact brought together the unfinished *Musnad*, and it now survives in the edition that he made, in which his father's work is supplemented by his own and later additions.

As far as can be seen, Ibn Hanbal did not explain his intentions in writing, nor did he compose an introduction to the *Musnad*. It begins abruptly with the Prophet's closest friend Abu Bakr al-Siddiq, from whom eighty-two *hadiths* are transmitted, and then moves through the Companions in order, beginning with the four Rightly Guided Caliphs

and the remainder of the ten Blessed Companions, and continuing with those who were closest to the Prophet including al-Hasan, al-Husayn and 'Abdallah Ibn 'Umar, from whom over 2,000 *hadiths* are reported, and concluding with Abu Hurayra, from whom nearly 4,000 *hadiths* are listed, Jabir Ibn 'Abdallah and Anas Ibn Malik. According to the numbering in the 1993 Beirut edition of the *Musnad*, this amounts to a massive 15,305 traditions attributed to individual Companions of the Prophet.

These prominent individuals, thirty-two in all, are followed by groups of authorities, including the Wives of the Prophet and other prominent women, among whom 'A'isha comes first with more than 2,400 *hadiths* transmitted in her name. There are also many anonymous transmitters who contribute thousands more *hadiths*, and in all well over 27,500 are collected together in the *Musnad* as a whole.

This prodigious achievement evoked admiration from an early stage. About a century and a half after Ibn Hanbal's death, al-Nadim in the *Fihrist* displayed exaggerated esteem typical of many when he computed the number of *hadiths* in the *Musnad* at the vague though redolent number of 'more than forty thousand'. But impressive though the work is in volume, its usefulness has always been thought rather restricted, since without knowing the first-generation authority from whom a tradition is transmitted it is impossible to find it. This greatly limits its usefulness. Compared with the great works from the succeeding generation, the *Musnad* has been subject to extensive criticism for its lack of rigour in testing the authenticity of traditions, and also for admitting material that was considered extraneous. But Ibn Hanbal's concern may well have been to compile all the traditions that had been and could be attributed to the Prophet, so that in the face of the contemporary challenge from rationalist thinkers more traditionally minded Muslims would have a means of defence. The primary necessity would have been to collect the attributable *hadiths* rather than sift out what could only be attributed with certainty.

Due in part to Ibn Hanbal's saintly reputation, the *Musnad* was regarded with reverence in the centuries following his death. It was commented upon and adapted in many later works, and abridgements of it proved popular. As might be expected, it was also reordered according to *musannaf* principles, and its contents compared with those of the *Kutub al-Sitta*. But it never rivalled these compilations, and in later times it remained comparatively unstudied.

The first full edition of the *Musnad* edited by Ghamrawi (1896) has been republished in a clearer layout with *hadiths* numbered, by 'Abd al-Baqi (1993). The edition by Shakir (1954) is accompanied by extensive commentaries and indexes.

DAVID THOMAS

AL-MUSTADI, AL-HASAN B. AL-MUSTANJID, ABU MUHAMMAD (AD 1170–80)

The 'Abbasid caliph al-Mustadi succeeded his father al-Mustanjid under the Saljuqs in Baghdad. His reign was of little historical significance. By AD 1171, a few months after al-Mustadi's accession, Salah al-Din (Saladin) had put an end to the rival Fatimid dynasty and al-Mustadi's name replaced that of the Fatimid caliph in the Friday sermon in Egypt and Syria. Thus, the at least nominal authority of the 'Abbasid caliphs was once again recognised in these areas. Al-Mustadi was succeeded by his son Ahmad b. al-Mustadi al-Nasir.

References

Gibb and Bosworth (1960–2003: VII, 707), Ibn al-Jawzi (1938: X, 232–5), Ibn al-Tiqtaqa (1860: 366–70), Le Strange (1924: 260, 280), Muir (1915: 586).

RONALD PAUL BUCKLEY

AL-MUSTA'IN, 'ABBAS (OR YA'QUB) B. AL-MUTAWAKKIL, ABU'L-FADL (AD 1406–14)

al-Musta'in acceded to the 'Abbasid caliphate in Cairo after his father al-Mutawakkil I, the first of five brothers to hold the office. During al-Musta'in's reign the Sultan al-Nasir Faraj headed a military expedition to fight rebel Syrian *amirs* led by Shaykh al-Mahmudi and Nawruz al-Hafizi. The Caliph, who had accompanied Faraj's forces, was subsequently captured and in order to act as a figurehead around which the divided rebel camp could unite in their attempt to overthrow Faraj was elected as sultan (1412). Al-Musta'in then formally deposed Faraj and the Mamluk state was partitioned between Shaykh al-Mahmudi and Nawruz. Al-Musta'in returned to Cairo with Shaykh al-Mahmudi who was to rule Egypt as nominal sultan, but Shaykh al-Mahmudi quickly stripped al-Musta'in of his title of Sultan and his role as Caliph and imprisoned him first in the Citadel in Cairo (until 1417) and then in Alexandria where he died of plague (1430). Another son of al-Mutawakkil was chosen to replace him, Dawud b. al-Mutawakkil al-Mu'tadid II.

References

Gibb and Bosworth (1960–2003: VII, 723), Holt (1984: 506–7), Ibn Iyas (1975: I, 745, 746, 747, 761, 793, 816–28 *passim*; II: 3–12 *passim*, 74, 130), Petry (1998: 291–2, 303), Salim (1965: 33–5), al-Suyuti (1969: 505–8).

RONALD PAUL BUCKLEY

AL-MUSTA'IN, AHMAD B. MUHAMMAD, ABU'L-'ABBAS (AD 862–6)

After the death of al-Muntasir, his cousin al-Musta'in was installed as 'Abbasid caliph by the Turkish military leaders who were in effective control of the Government. In a power struggle between the largely Turkish Samarra army and the rival army of the *shakiriyya*, recruited by al-Mutawakkil and with which al-Musta'in had allied himself, al-Musta'in was deposed and exiled to Wasit. He was eventually murdered by order of the man chosen by the Turks to replace him, Muhammad b. al-Mutawakkil al-Mu'tazz.

References

Kennedy (1996: 173–4), Muir (1915: 531–5), Shaban (1971: 80, 82, 84), al-Tabari (1985–95: XXXV, see index).

RONALD PAUL BUCKLEY

MUSTA'LIANS (AL-MUSTA'LIYYA)

A subsect of the Shi'ite Isma'ili grouping who were named as such due to their support of Abu 'l-Qasim Ahmad (AD 1094–1101). After the death of the Fatimid ruler al-Mustansir (AD 1036–94) a dispute broke out when his elder son Abu Mansur Nizar, who was named as successor by his father, was passed over by the powerful vizier al-Afdal. Thus, Abu 'l-Qasim Ahmad, Nizar's much younger half brother was crowned Caliph with the title of al-Musta'li bi-llah. Consequently, Nizar disputed this claim but was captured, imprisoned and eventually killed by al-Afdal. The until-then-unified Fatimid caliphate was never to recover from this incident and, as a result, those who supported al-Musta'li bi-llah were known as Musta'lians (al-

Musta'liyya), whereas the supporters of Nizar were known as Nizaris (al-Nizariyya). Musta'lian Isma'ilism lasted only a few years in power but exists today in a transformed version in the Bohora subsect.

References

Daftary (1998: 106–14, 185–93), al-Johani (1999: 383–6), Netton (1997: 183), Tabataba'i (n.d.: 81–3).

GAVIN PICKEN

AL-MUSTA'SIM, 'ABDALLAH B. AL-MUSTANSIR, ABU AHMAD (AD 1242–58)

The last of the 'Abbasid caliphs in Baghdad, al-Musta'sim was the son and successor of al-Mustansir. During his reign, Huleku left Mongolia at the head of a second wave of Mongol conquests with the intention of destroying both the Isma'ilis and the caliphate. After an exchange of messages in which al-Musta'sim refused to present himself, Huleku entered Baghdad (AD 1258), plundered the city and massacred most of its inhabitants including the Caliph. Thus ended the longest-lived and most celebrated dynasty in Islam. From one perspective, the Mongol conquest did little more than remove an institution that was already largely moribund, the caliphs having forfeited almost all their authority to sultans in the capital and the provinces. But the caliphate's loss of secular power was compensated by an increase in its religious significance and it played an essential role as symbol of the unity of the Sunni Muslim community. Indeed, the collapse of the caliphate had a profound psychological effect on the Sunnis and historians refer to the event as a major disaster. Even the Mongols, who entertained similar ideas regarding the sacred nature of the sovereign, were loath to spill al-Musta'sim's blood for fear of divine retribution. Thus, the Caliph is reported to have been rolled in a carpet and trampled or kicked to death.

References

Boyle (1968: 346–9), Hitti (1970: 486–7), Ibn al-Tiqtaqa (1860: 382–90), Le Strange (1924: 273, 293, 342, 343), Muir (1915: 590–1).

RONALD PAUL BUCKLEY

AL-MUSTA'SIM, ZAKARIYYA' B. AL-WATHIQ I, ABU YAHYA (r. AD 1377 and AD 1386–9)

When the 'Abbasid Caliph al-Mutawakkil I was deposed by Sultan Ayanbak al-Dubri, Zakariyya' was installed as his replacement with the honorific al-Musta'sim (AD 1377). He remained caliph for some two to three weeks before al-Mutawakkil was reinstated. Al-Mutawakkil was subsequently again deposed by the sultan Barquq who chose al-Wathiq II to replace him. Al-Wathiq II remained as caliph until his death in AD 1386 when al-Musta'sim was once more reinstated. He reigned until AD 1389 at which time Barquq seems to have regretted his former actions and reinstated al-Mutawakkil, thus deposing al-Musta'sim for the second time. He died a couple of years later. As with the majority of the 'shadow' caliphs under the Mamluks, al-Musta'sim's periods in office were of little historical significance.

References

Ibn Iyas (1975: I, 205, 206, 333, 377, 378, 466, 550, 745), Salim (1965: 32–3), al-Suyuti (1969: 505).

RONALD PAUL BUCKLEY

MUSTAFA I (r. 1617–18, 1622–3)

Ottoman sultan, son of Mehmed III. As Mustafa was mentally disturbed, the faction that had brought him to power deposed him after less than a year. His second reign followed when the Janissaries murdered Osman II and reinstated him on the throne. During his second reign, Shah 'Abbas I captured Baghdad, and Abaza Mehmed Pasha rebelled in Erzurum.

References

Imber (2002: 77–9), Mantran (1989a: 233–4).

COLIN IMBER

MUSTAFA II (r. 1695–1703)

Ottoman sultan, son of Mehmed IV. Following his accession the Ottomans retook Chios from the Venetians, but in 1696, the Russians took Azov in the Crimea. In 1697 Mustafa and his Grand Vizier Elmas Mehmed Pasha took the field against the Austrians, but suffered defeat at Zenta. This persuaded him to open peace negotiations which concluded with the treaty of Carlowitz in 1699, ceding Hungary and Transylvania to Austria, Podolia and the western Ukraine to Poland, Azov and part of Ukraine to Russia, and Athens, the Peloponnesos and parts of Dalmatia to Venice. In the aftermath of Carlowitz, Mustafa undertook reforms in the tax system. However, his cut in Janissary numbers provoked a rebellion which led to his abdication in 1703.

References

Mantran (1989a: 249, 272), Quataert (2000: 43).

COLIN IMBER

MUSTAFA III (r. 1757–74)

Ottoman sultan, son of Ahmed III. The first part of Mustafa's reign was a period of peace, allowing the Grand Vizier to introduce military and other reforms. This period came to an end with the decision in 1768 to respond to the Polish call for assistance against Russia. In 1768–9, the Russians occupied Moldavia and Wallachia. In 1770, the Russian Baltic fleet entered the Mediterranean and destroyed the Ottoman fleet at Cesme. On land the Russians occupied the Crimea and the Dobrudzha. In 1772, after peace negotiations failed, they entered Bulgaria. The Sultan died before hostilities ended.

References

Mantran (1989b: 268–70, 279).

COLIN IMBER

MUSTAFA IV (r. 1807–8)

Ottoman sultan, son of 'Abdul-Hamid I. Mustafa came the throne after the abdication of Selim III. Selim's supporters, under the leadership of the lord of Ruschuk, Bayraktar Mustafa, attempted to restore Selim. On Selim's assassination, Bayraktar proclaimed Prince Mahmud Sultan.

References

Mantran (1989c: 432–4).

COLIN IMBER

AL-MUSTAKFI I, SULAYMAN B. AL-HAKIM, ABU RABI'A (AD 1302–40)

Al-Mustakfi I succeeded al-Hakim I as 'Abbasid caliph in Cairo under the Mamluks. The 'Abbasids were 'shadow' caliphs and merely the nominal holders of sovereignty. With few exceptions, al-Mustakfi and his successors wielded no authority, their secular powers being appropriated by the Sultan who was elected by the Mamluks. The role of the caliphs was generally limited to ceremonial occasions, mainly the inauguration of the new sultan where the caliph formally legitimised his rule and conferred on him a diploma of investiture. The caliphate did, however, remain a symbol of the Sunni Muslim community and deference to the caliph was viewed as a kind of religious duty. Al-Mustakfi was imprisoned twice by the Mamluk Sultan and was finally exiled to Qus where he died in AD 1340. While in exile, he designated his son Ahmad b. al-Mustakfi to succeed him, but the Mamluk sultan al-Nasir installed instead a cousin of al-Mustakfi, Ibrahim b. Muhammad al-Wathiq.

References

Ibn Iyas (1975: 410, 413, 423, 431, 472, 474), Salim (1965: 25–6), al-Suyuti (1969: 484–7).

RONALD PAUL BUCKLEY

AL-MUSTAKFI II, SULAYMAN B. AL-MUTAWAKKIL I, ABU RABI'A (AD 1441–51)

Al-Mustakfi II succeeded his brother al-Mu'tadid II as 'Abbasid caliph in Cairo under the Mamluks and was the third son of al-Mutawakkil I to hold the office. As with most of the 'Abbasid 'shadow' caliphs, al-Mustakfi's reign was of no historical importance. The Mamluk sultans showed the caliphate formal deference but in practical terms it remained a mere symbol of Mamluk legitimacy. Al-Mustakfi was succeeded by his brother Hamza b. al-Mutawakkil al-Qa'im.

References

Ibn Iyas (1975: II, 230, 282, 287, 288), Salim (1965: 36–7), al-Suyuti (1969: 511–13).

RONALD PAUL BUCKLEY

AL-MUSTAKFI, 'ABDALLAH B. AL-MUKTAFI, ABU'L-QASIM (AD 944–6)

The 'Abbasid caliph al-Mustakfi was appointed by the Turkish *amir al-umara'* as successor to his deposed predecessor and cousin al-Muttaqi. Al-Mustakfi's reign is notable for having witnessed the arrival of Ahmad b. Buya, the future Mu'izz al-Dawla, and the beginning of the Buyid amirate in Baghdad (AD 945). While the Buyids did not wish to abolish the institution of the caliphate, nevertheless the role of subsequent 'Abbasid caliphs was largely reduced to legitimising the Buyid rulers and giving *post facto* formal sanction to their government policies. Al-Mustakfi was soon deposed and replaced with al-Fadl b. al-Muqtadir al-Muti'. He died in captivity in AD 949.

References

Bowen (1928: 385–92 *passim*), Ibn al-Jawzi (1938: VI, 339), Ibn al-Tiqtaqa (1860: 334–6), Kennedy (1996: 198, 217, 218), Le Strange (1924: 118, 231), Muir (1915: 574–5).

RONALD PAUL BUCKLEY

AL-MUSTAMSIK, YA'QUB B. AL-MUTAWAKKIL II, ABU'L-SABR (r. AD 1497–1508 and 1516–17)

al-Mustamsik succeeded his father al-Mutawakkil II as 'Abbasid caliph in Cairo. Under the Mamluks, the caliphate still functioned as symbol of the Sunni Muslim community and had a ceremonial role in the investiture of the new sultan, but it possessed no secular authority. Thus, al-Mustamsik's reign, like that of the majority of those who held the office, was of no historical significance. As a result of internal rivalries among the Mamluks, al-Mustamsik was deposed (1508) and replaced with his son al-Mutawakkil III. In 1516, al-Mutawakkil III accompanied the sultan Qansuh al-Ghawri on a military expedition to Syria to fight the Ottoman sultan Selim I at Marj Dabiq. During the battle (24 August 1516), al-Ghawri fell from his horse and died, while al-Mutawakkil III was taken prisoner. Al-Mustamsik replaced his son in the ceremonial duties of the caliphate but was, obliged to give up the office when al-Mutawakkil III eventually returned to Egypt with the Ottomans (1517). He died in 1521.

References

Ibn Iyas (1975: III, 378–444 *passim*; IV, see index; V, 64, 104, 105, 110, 192, 360, 389, 390), Salim (1965: 41–3).

RONALD PAUL BUCKLEY

AL-MUSTANJID, YUSUF B. AL-MUQTAFI, ABU'L-MUZAFFAR (AD 1160–70)

The 'Abbasid caliph al-Mustanjid was the son and successor of al-Muqtafi. Since the arrival of the Saljuqs in Baghdad (AD 1055) the caliphate had been under the tutelage of the sultans. The reign of al-Mustanjid was a continuation of that of his predecessors in that he and his court officials persisted in the attempts to restore control over Iraq and to reassert the independence of the caliph. Al-Mustanjid was eventually murdered by 'Adud al-Din, a senior Saljuq official, as a result of rivalries between 'Adud and al-Mustanjid's *wazir* Ibn al-Baladi. He was replaced with his son al-Hasan b. al-Mustanjid al-Mustadi.

References

Gibb and Bosworth (1960–2003: VII, 726–7), Ibn al-Jawzi (1938: X, 192–4), Ibn al-Tiqtaqa (1860: 363–6), Muir (1915: 586).

RONALD PAUL BUCKLEY

AL-MUSTANJID, YUSUF B. AL-MUTAWAKKIL I, ABU'L-MAHASIN (AD 1455–79)

al-Mustanjid was the fifth son of al-Mutawakkil I to become 'Abbasid 'shadow' caliph in Cairo under the Mamluk sultans. He succeeded his brother al-Qa'im. When Khushqadam seized the sultanate in 1461, al-Mustanjid was imprisoned in the citadel in Cairo where he remained incarcerated until his death. He left no male descendants and was succeeded by his nephew 'Abd al-'Aziz b. al-Musta'in, the future al-Mutawakkil II.

References

Gibb and Bosworth (1960–2003: VII, 727), Ibn Iyas (1975: II, 328, 329, 369, 371, 378, 457; III, 4, 13, 65, 75, 125, 134, 151, 152), Salim (1965: II, 38–9), al-Suyuti (1969: 513–14).

RONALD PAUL BUCKLEY

AL-MUSTANSIR, AHMAD B. AL-ZAHIR, ABU'L-QASIM (AD 1261)

al-Mustansir, an uncle of the last 'Abbasid caliph in Baghdad, al-Musta'in, was the first of the 'Abbasid caliphs in Mamluk Egypt. In AD 1258 the Mongols led by Huleku entered Baghdad, plundered the city and slaughtered most of its inhabitants including the reigning caliph. Ahmad had been able to escape the massacre of his family and made his way to Cairo. A few days after his arrival, and when his genealogy had been examined and declared authentic by the chief *qadi*, he was installed as caliph by the Mamluk sultan al-Zahir Baybars (9 June 1261) with the honorific 'al-Mustansir', the same title as his brother al-Mansur who had been caliph in Baghdad (r. AD 1226–42). In return, the new caliph was obliged to legitimise Baybars' rule by formally investing him with the office of sultan and delegating to him his leader-

ship over the Islamic territories. It was indeed the Mamluk sultan who held the reigns of power, the caliphate still bearing the name but with none of its authority. Less than six months after becoming caliph, an ill-conceived attempt by al-Mustansir to retake Baghdad came to an abrupt end when he was killed in an encounter with Mongol forces en route. He was succeeded by another member of the 'Abbasid family, Ahmad b. al-Hasan al-Hakim.

References

Arnold (1924: 90–5), Ayalon (1960: 41–59), Ibn Iyas (1975: I, 312–19, 426, 431), Petry (1998: I, 255), Salim (1965: II, 22–3), al-Suyuti (1969: 477–8).

RONALD PAUL BUCKLEY

AL-MUSTANSIR, AL-MANSUR B. AL-ZAHIR, ABU JA'FAR (AD 1226–42)

al-Mustansir was the son and successor of the 'Abbasid caliph al-Zahir. Very little information exists regarding al-Mustansir and it is difficult to learn of his activities or assess his significance. One of the most notable events during his reign was his founding of the college of the Mustansiriyya in Baghdad, one of the first universities in the world. During al-Mustansir's reign Jenghiz Khan, the leader of the Mongol hordes, died. A brief hiatus ensued, but the westwards advance was soon resumed under Huleku, a grandson of Jenghiz. Al-Mustansir was succeeded by his son 'Abdallah b. al-Mustansir al-Musta'sim.

References

Gibb and Bosworth (1960–2003: VII, 7127–9), Ibn al-Tiqtaqa (1860: 380–2), Le Strange (1924: 266–7, 278, 299, 337, 346), Muir (1915: 589).

RONALD PAUL BUCKLEY

AL-MUSTANSIR, MA'ADD B. 'ALI (r. AD 1036–94)

Fatimid caliph in Egypt, in whose time the empire reached its zenith of power and splendour but whose personal power was circumscribed by successive viziers and commanders. The original heartland of the Fatimid *da'wa*, North Africa, fell away in 1051 under the Zirid governors, who now acknowledged the 'Abbasids as their suzerains, Fatimid commanders had to fight to retain the possessions in southern Syria against the incoming Saljuqs, and overlordship of the Holy Places in Arabia was lost after AD 1081. However, a peak of political might was reached when in AD 1059 the *khutba* in Baghdad itself was briefly made for the Fatimids by a Turkish commander there. Extensive Isma'ili propaganda was meanwhile being carried out in Yemen, where the Sulayhid rulers became vassals of the Fatimids, at the Buyid court in Iran and in Khurasan, under such outstanding missionaries as al-Mu'ayyad fi 'l-Din Shirazi. It was only after al-Mustansir's death that the serious split in Isma'ilism took place between the majority, followers of al-Mustansir's son al-Musta'li, and the minority who regarded the dead caliph's eldest son, Nizari, as unjustly excluded from succession.

References

Gibb and Bosworth (1960–2003), Sanders (1998: 152–3).

C. E. BOSWORTH

AL-MUSTARSHID, AL-FADL B. AL-MUSTAZHIR, ABU MANSUR (AD 1118–35)

al-Mustarshid succeeded his father al-Mustazhir as 'Abbasid caliph under the Saljuqs. The rivalries and factionalism within the Saljuq state which occurred after the death of the sultan Malikshah (AD 1118) and later Mahmud (AD 1131) enabled al-Mustarshid to reassert some of the authority of the caliphate. He thus became the first 'Abbasid caliph under Saljuq tutelage to raise and lead an army and was involved in military actions to remove them from Iraq. When al-Mustarshid marched into western Persia to fight Mas'ud b. Muhammad, a brother of Sultan Mahmud, who was claiming the sultanate, his forces were defeated and he was taken prisoner. Al-Mustarshid was later killed in Adherbayjan while still in captivity and was succeeded by his son al-Mansur b. al-Mustarshid al-Rashid.

References

Boyle (1968: V, 121–2, 127–8), Gibb and Bosworth (1960–2003: VII, 733–5), Ibn al-Jawzi (1938: IX, 197–9), Ibn al-Tiqtaqa (1860: 348–55), Le Strange (1924: 259, 275), Muir (1915: 583–4).

RONALD PAUL BUCKLEY

AL-MUSTAZHIR, AHMAD B. AL-MUQTADI, ABU'L-'ABBAS (AD 1094–1118)

The 'Abbasid caliph al-Mustazhir was the son and successor of al-Muqtadi. Before al-Mustazhir assumed office the crusades were already raging in Syria-Palestine and his reign witnessed the fall of Jerusalem (AD 1099). This event, and indeed the crusades in general, however, had little effect on the Caliph. His reign was not peaceful and he had troubles nearer to home to occupy him. The deaths of the sultans Nizam al-Mulk and Malikshah had considerably weakened the Saljuq state which was now embroiled in factionalism and open hostilities. Al-Mustazhir was inevitably drawn into these conflicts since the various aspirants to the Saljuq sultanate looked to him for formal support for their claims. He was succeeded by his son al-Fadl b. al-Mustazhir al-Mustarshid.

References

Boyle (1968: V, 106, 107–8, 116, 248, 255, 292), Gibb and Bosworth (1960–2003: VII, 755–6), Ibn al-Jawzi (1938: IX, 81–3), Ibn al-Tiqtaqa (1860: 346–8), Le Strange (1924: 272–3, 279), Muir (1915: 582–3).

RONALD PAUL BUCKLEY

MUT'A

The word is used for a temporary marriage (*nikah al-muwaqqat*), sometimes known as a 'marriage of pleasure', which is terminated by the partners after the specified period agreed between them. The arrangement is neither universally recognised nor tolerated in Islamic communities. Forbidden among Sunni Muslims, who consider that it encourages prostitution, *mut'a* is permitted among some Shi'i groups, although not (for example) by Zaydis. A temporary marriage, with its predetermined financial agreement, may be fixed for a period of a few hours or for a much longer term. Some Shi'is maintain that the practice was permitted during the lifetime of the Prophet Muhammad, though forbidden by the second of the Rightly Guided Caliphs, 'Umar (Caliph from AD 634–44). Others claim that the words of Q.4:24 may be interpreted to sanction temporary marriage.

References

Bouhdiba (1985: 14–18, 19–22, 30–42), Momen (1985: 182–3, 338n), Omran (1992: 15–26, 40–58).

See also: **marriage; divorce**

EDWARD D. A. HULMES

AL-MU'TADID I, ABU BAKR B. AL-MUSTAKFI I, ABU'L-FATH (AD 1352–62)

al-Mu'tadid I acceded to the 'Abbasid caliphate in Cairo after his brother al-Hakim II. Although the existence of the Sunni caliphate in Egypt gave the Mamluks a prestige not possessed by other rulers in the Islamic world, as with most of the 'Abbasid 'shadow' caliphs al-Mu'tadid had no secular authority and his ten-year reign was of no historical significance. He designated his son Muhammad b. al-Mu'tadid, the future al-Mutawakkil I, to succeed him.

References

Ibn Iyas (1975: I, 549, 553, 582, 587), Salim (1965: II, 28–9), al-Suyuti (1969: 500–1).

RONALD PAUL BUCKLEY

AL-MU'TADID II, DAWUD B. AL-MUTAWAKKIL I, ABU'L-FATH (AD 1414–41)

Al-Mu'tadid II was the second son of al-Mutawakkil I to be chosen as 'Abbasid caliph in Cairo under the Mamluks. He replaced his deposed brother al-Musta'sim. His period in office consisted largely of ceremonial duties and was of no historical importance. He was succeeded by another brother, Sulayman b. al-Mutawakkil al-Mustakfi II.

References

Ibn Iyas (1975: I, 745; II, 11–15 *passim*, 63, 66, 67, 79, 191–9 *passim*, 230, 238), Salim (1965: II, 35–6), al-Suyuti (1969: 509).

RONALD PAUL BUCKLEY

AL-MU'TADID, AHMAD B. AL-MUWAFFAQ, ABU'L-'ABBAS (AD 892–902)

Al-Mu'tadid succeeded al-Mu'tamid as 'Abbasid caliph in Iraq. Like his father al-Muwaffaq, al-Mu'tadid fostered good relations with the Turkish army, which remained loyal to him and formed the main instrument of government policy. He personally took part in campaigns and devoted himself to military activities more than any 'Abbasid caliph. Al-Mu'tadid was, moreover, a capable and effective ruler who managed to maintain the integrity of the state through diplomacy, compromise and, when necessary, force.

al-Mu'tadid's reign witnessed the final restoration of Baghdad as the capital of the empire, this having been Samarra for the previous fifty-years under his predecessors. Despite the change of capital, however, the military control of government begun under al-Mu'tasim was to remain a constant threat to the caliphate.

References

Kennedy (1996: 178–86), Le Strange (1924: 248–53), Shaban (1971: II, 113–26), al-Tabari (1985–95: XXXVIII, 1–101 passim).

RONALD PAUL BUCKLEY

AL-MU'TAMID, AHMAD B. AL-MUTAWAKKIL, ABU'L-'ABBAS (AD 870–92)

al-Mu'tamid was the third son of al-Mutawakkil to accede to the 'Abbasid caliphate in Iraq. During al-Mu'tamid's reign his brother Abu Ahmad, who had developed strong ties with the military establishment, was given authority over the troops in Samarra. In acknowledgment of his status, Abu Ahmad was awarded the honorary title al-Muwaffaq ('he who is successful with the help of God'). He was to emerge as effective ruler while his brother remained caliph in name only. Al-Muwaffaq was responsible for reasserting the authority of central government and for dealing with a number of serious regional uprisings including, most notably, the revolt of the Zanj in southern Iraq (AD 869–83).

Largely due to al-Muwaffaq, the twenty-two year reign of al-Mu'tamid was relatively peaceful and free of the murders and depositions which had been the fate of previous caliphs. Al-Muwaffaq died in AD 891 and his position was immediately taken by his son Ahmad who assumed the title al-Mu'tadid. When al-Mu'tamid died a year later al-Mu'tadid was acknowledged as caliph.

References

Bowen (1928: see index), Kennedy (1996: 175–81), Muir (1915: 544–52), Shaban (1971: II, 87, 92, 113), al-Tabari (1985–95: XXXVI, 115–99 passim; XXXVII: 51, 88–97, 114, 144, 166–7, 178).

RONALD PAUL BUCKLEY

AL-MU'TASIM, MUHAMMAD B. AL-RASHID, ABU ISHAQ (AD 833–42)

The 'Abbasid caliph al-Mu'tasim was the brother and successor of al-Ma'mun. Al-Mu'tasim's reign witnessed the beginning of a profound change within the 'Abbasid regime. During his brother's caliphate, al-Mu'tasim had already begun to acquire a private army composed largely of slaves sent to him from Turkestan. This new cohesive force formed the power base of al-Mu'tasim's rule and reduced his dependence on the Khurasanian army, the previous mainstay of the regime. Since, however, the military elite was not drawn from the traditional recruiting grounds of Khurasan, Iraq and Syria and had a different origin, language and customs from the majority of Muslims they were largely divorced from the rest of society. This in turn served further to alienate the Caliph from his subjects.

Partly as a result of riots between al-Mu'tasim's troops and the citizens of Baghdad and partly to house his new military elite, al-Mu'tasim left Baghdad and constructed a new capital at Samarra. He was succeeded by his son Harun b. al-Mu'tasim al-Wathiq.

References

Hodgson (1974: I, 481–3), Kennedy (1996: 158–62, 165–8), Muir (1915: 512–19), Shaban (1971: II, 61–9), al-Tabari (1985–95: XXX, see index).

RONALD PAUL BUCKLEY

MU'TAZILISM (AL-MU'TAZILA)

A school of scholastic theology (*'ilm al-kalam*) whose origins are obscure but seems to have been influenced by the other tendencies of the period including Murji'ism, Qadarism and Kharijism. The earliest scholars of this tendency seemingly came from Basra and the circle of al-Hasan al-Basri (AD 642–728). However, Mu'tazilism in its true form took shape when it began employing Greek philosophy and Aristotelian logic under the auspices of Abu Hudhayl Hamdan al-'Allaf (AD 753–841) and Bishr b. Mu'tamir (d. AD 841), in Basra and Baghdad respectively. Both these theologians had influence in the 'Abbasid court, which was probably due to the ability of the Mu'tazilite method to refute other religious positions in court debates. As for the doctrine of the Mu'tazilites, it revolves around five basic principles (*usul*: first, Divine Unity (*al-tawhid*), by which they mean that Allah is incomparable and unique – a view common to Sunni belief, but they employ it to mean that the Divine attributes (*al-sifat*) are not a distinct quality, as this would indicate multiplicity but are in fact identical with His essence and

as such they deny their true nature to a large extent. Due to this, they believe that the Qur'an is created as it is considered the 'work' of Allah and not His speech, which also dictates that the Qur'an in their view is not eternal, as this would also indicate duality. This particular position is a view for which the Mu'tazilites became famous, as it was adopted as the state belief and consequently, the 'inquisition' (*al-mihna*) was enforced during the reign of al-Ma'mun (AD 786–833) and lasted for thirteen years. In addition, the Beatific Vision in the hereafter is also rejected by the Mu'tazilites, as they say this would indicate 'shape, form and direction', which are purely human qualities. Second, justice (*al-'adl*), in the sense that Allah is just to His creation and does only that which is in their interests. As such they deny that any evil action can be attributed to Him and that human beings themselves create and determine such actions. Also, based on the principle of Divine justice they reject the concept of intercession on the Day of Judgement, since Allah is ultimately fair every human being will be dealt with justly and hence will not be in need of anyone's intercession. Third, 'the promise of reward and threat of punishment' (*al-wa'd wa al-wa'id*), which essentially means that the righteous will be rewarded with good, whereas the sinful will be rewarded with torment, a further subtle argument is progressed here – that this is due purely the fact that each group will be recompensed due to them deserving it (*al-istihqaq*) and not due the actual promise of Allah. Similarly, a person who commits a major sin (*murtakib al-kabira*) will not be forgiven unless they repent. Fourth, the 'intermediate state' (*al-manzila bayna manzilatayn*), which means that a person who commits a major sin (*murtakib al-kabira*) is neither a believer (*mu'min*) nor a disbeliever (*kafir*) and is in an 'intermediate state' between belief and disbelief, which they term reprobate (*fasiq*). Finally, 'enjoining the good and forbidding the evil' (*al-amr bi 'l-Ma'ruf wa nahy 'an al-munkar*), which means that this process is a duty by whatever means are appropriate, i.e., via debate, knowledge or the sword, to propagate Islam. It also implies however that it is permissible to oppose the caliph if he strays from the truth and that these methods may be employed to vindicate their position against those who oppose their views. Due to these principles the Mu'tazilites were also known as 'the people of Divine unity and justice' (*ahl al-'adl wa 'l-tawhid*), Qadarites (al-Qadariyya) and the 'harbingers of doom' (*al-wa'idiyya*). The views of the Mu'tazilites remain today within a number of sects including the Shi'ites and the 'Ibadites and in the modern era those who approach Islam from a similar rationalistic view are often termed 'neo-Mu'tazilites' (*al-Mu'tazila al-jadida*).

References

Hanafi (1980: 63–76), al-Johani (1999: 64–75), Netton (1997: 185–6), al-Shahrastani (2002: 39–40), Watt (1948: 61–88, 1997: 46–55, 2002: 209–50).

GAVIN PICKEN

MUTAWATIR

'Widespread' or 'universal' transmission. A part of the technical terminology of *hadith* transmission that has particular application in relationship to the Qur'an. When transmission of a report is found among multiple transmitters then it may be designated as *mutawatir*, the term is applied whether the transmission is of the actual wording or only of the sense of the tradition. There is no absolute agreement as to how many transmitters are required to bring a

report to this status but the principle is such that it suggests that the possibility of forgery is not feasible given such widespread transmission. The term has a particular application within theological epistemological discussions, providing a source of knowledge differentiated from sense data and reason.

References

Gibb and Bosworth (1960–2003: VII, 781).

ANDREW RIPPIN

AL-MUTI', AL-FADL B. AL-MUQTADIR, ABU'L-QASIM (AD 946–74)

Shortly after the arrival of the Buyids in Baghdad (AD 945), the Buyid *amir* Mu'izz al-Dawla deposed the current 'Abbasid caliph al-Mustakfi and chose al-Muti' to replace him. The power and dignity of the 'Abbasid caliphate reached a particularly low point during the reign of al-Muti', the Caliph being reduced to a mere puppet in the hands of the Buyid *amirs* and serving merely to give formal sanction to their rule. Al-Muti' was eventually deposed and was succeeded by his son 'Abd al-Karim b. al-Muti' al-Ta'i'.

References

Bowen (1928: 392–3, 395, 397), Gibb and Bosworth (1960–2003: VII, 799), Ibn al-Jawzi (1938: VI, 343–5; VII, 66–8, 79), Ibn al-Tiqtaqa (1860: 336), Kennedy (1996: 218, 241), Muir (1915: 578–9).

RONALD PAUL BUCKLEY

AL-MUTTAQI, IBRAHIM B. AL-MUQTADIR, ABU ISHAQ (AD 940–4)

al-Muttaqi was chosen by the Turkish *amir al-umara'* to succeed his brother the 'Abbasid caliph al-Radi. During al-Radi's reign, control of all civil and military affairs had devolved to the *amir al-umara'*, thus divorcing the caliph from his administrative duties. In addition, the *amir al-umara'* had removed the military power of the dynasty by disbanding the army of Baghdad and had done away with the office of *wazir* and the various administrative bureaux (*diwan*s). Al-Muttaqi endeavoured to restore some authority to the caliphate by, for example, attempting to abolish the post of the *amir al-umara'* and reinstate that of the *wazir*. He was, however, ultimately unsuccessful and was deposed and replaced with 'Abdallah b. al-Muktafi al-Mustakfi. Al-Muttaqi died in AD 968.

References

Bowen (1928: 364–85), Ibn al-Jawzi (1938: VI, 316–19), Ibn al-Tiqtaqa (1860: 332–4), Kennedy (1996: 198), Le Strange (1924: 156), Muir (1915: 572–4).

RONALD PAUL BUCKLEY

MUWATTA'

This is the best-known work of Malik Ibn Anas (d. AD 796 aged about eighty-five), and the foundation text of the Maliki law-school that was named after him. It is possibly the earliest legal formulation that has survived in Islam, and is also one of the earliest known collections of *hadith*. Among Malikis, its authority is indisputable, and many Muslims (including the Caliph al-Mansur, according to a late and not entirely trustworthy report) have wanted to accord it canonical status. While it does not occupy the same position in many estimations as the *Kutub al-Sitta*, it is universally valued as both a *hadith* collection and a register of the legal teaching approved and practised among early

legal experts in Medina, where Malik lived and died.

The *Kitab al-Muwatta'* was passed down in a number of different recensions, as many as thirty according to one report. The main reason given to account for this is that Malik used the text for teaching over a period of maybe thirty years, and inevitably made changes in it in this time. Of the recensions presently available, the best known is that of Yahya b. Yahya 'l-Laythi (d. AD 848–9), which probably represents almost the final product of Malik's editorial work, since Yahya studied under the Imam in the last year of his life. Most of the other recensions resemble this closely, though that of Muhammad b. al-Hasan al-Shaybani (d. AD 805), which is also well known, differs noticeably in many places.

The meaning of the title *Al-Muwatta'* has been explained as the book that smoothes, *yuwatti'u*, the way for the reader and makes knowledge easy, or as the book over which Malik's contemporary scholars agreed, *wata'u*. It is often translated into English as 'The Well-Trodden Path', signifying the way that has been made easy to follow by Malik and his predecessors, and also the way that is acknowledged and agreed. This 'way' is the legal and ritual teachings of Islam as accepted among the people of Medina in Malik's own time. It has been pointed out that Malik had two intentions in writing: to set down the essentials of the faith in order to save it from being lost, and more subtly to situate *hadiths* in the context of Medinan practice in order to show how they had been incorporated into Muslim life, and so to prevent them being used in isolation for purposes they had not been intended to serve. It is in demonstrating how the first generation's teachings were put into practice by those who followed them that the distinctive significance of the *Muwatta'* lies.

The work brings together the sayings from these first generations of Islam under recognisable headings, beginning with prayer and other Pillars, and continuing with such subjects as marriage, divorce, business transactions, legal judgements, and wills. Within each book subjects are divided into chapters, which each usually contain *hadiths*, first from the Prophet, then from his Companions, and finally from Malik himself relating the views or practices of his own time, or occasionally his own opinions. In all, the work comprises 703 chapters in forty-five books, 1955 individual *hadiths*.

The character of the *Muwatta'* can be exemplified from the opening chapters of the book on Prayer in Congregation. Here Malik begins by quoting *hadiths* from the Prophet on the superiority of congregational over individual prayer, together with a *hadith* from his secretary Zayd Ibn Thabit to the same effect. He goes on to quote the Prophet extolling the virtues of the *'isha* and *subh* prayers, together with remarks from 'Uthman Ibn al-'Affan about them. And then he quotes the Prophet on the virtues of praying behind the imam rather than individually, followed by comments from Followers of the Companions about performing prayers which have already been completed a second time behind the imam. Lastly he gives his own comment: 'I do not see any harm in someone who has already prayed in his home praying with the imam, except for *maghrib*, because if he repeats it he makes it even' (i.e. the total number of *raka'at* becomes even). Here, his own words provide a closing commentary that both sums up the teaching about repeated prayers, and provides a logical reason why some can be repeated in congregation but others cannot. In this respect, it has the force of a justification and even a form of rational exegesis that completes the previous contributions.

The *Muwatta'* is characterised by frequent approbatory and elucidatory comments from Malik on earlier views, and also by his constant references to the practice of Medina as authority. He does not always deem it necessary to discover a prophetic *hadith* in order to know what is orthodox practice, because the consensual agreement of the community, in which the custom of the Prophet and his Companions must be assumed to be enshrined, is sufficient. This shows how the *Muwatta'* is both a compilation of *hadith* and an embryonic codification of legal teachings.

The *Muwatta'* in the recension of Yahya b. Yahya al-Laythi has been published many times; a serviceable edition is that of 'Amrush (1984). There is an English translation by Bewley (1989) (a revision of her 1982 joint translation). Dutton (2002) contains an extensive analysis of the work.

DAVID THOMAS

N

NABI

The second of two classes of prophets in Islam who brings a message related to an existing faith, including both warnings but also good news. Ayyub, Da'ud, Harun, Ibrahim, Ishaq and Sulayman are called *nabi*. Muhammad himself is called both a *nabi* and a *rasul*; however every *nabi* is not a *rasul*. See Q.19.

See also: **messengers;** *nubuwwa*; **prophets;** *rasul*

ANDREW J. NEWMAN

NABIDH

See: **alcohol**

NAFS AND RUH

Nafs and *ruh* are the terms by which the Qur'an refers to the human soul and to the angels. *Nafs* can be understood as the human soul or denoting the different stages through which the human soul moves from a lower spiritual life to a higher level, attaining happiness. The Qur'an mentions three levels of *nafs*: *al-'ammara bi 'l-su'*, commanding to evil (Q.13:53), *al-lawwama*, self-reproaching which recognises evil and asking for God's guidance (Q.75:2), and *al-mutma'inna*, the tranquil soul which has achieved peace with God (Q.82:27). Ibn Sina, whom we can consider the first Muslim thinker to have written a systematic psychology, distinguished, in Aristotelian style, three kinds of *nafs*: one which is connected to bodily growth and desires, another which cares for emotions and figurative understanding of the world in simple images, and a third which raises the human intellect to perceive the divine world in its abstract form.

The term *ruh*, however, has more esoteric feature. The Qur'an speaks of *ruh* in connection with the creation of Adam as a breath from God's spirit *ruh* (Q.15:29) and as the spirit which is breathed into the womb of Mary

(Q.21:19). It is also referred to as a divine secret 'say (that) the spirit (cometh) by the command of my Lord (*qul al-ruh min amr rabbi*)' (Q.17:85). It also refers to certain angels as *al-ruh al amin*, the faithful spirits who came to Muhammad (Q.26:193) or *ruh al-qudus*, who is mainly known as the spirit which sends down revelation (Q.16:102). Sufis such as Junayd and al-Ghazali (in his late work *Kimiya' al-Sa'ada*) identified the human soul mainly with the Qur'anic esoteric *ruh* and believed that the human spirit is a divine secret within the human body so that it may acknowledge its divine origin through its earthly experience.

References

Abdul Quasem (1983).

MAHA EL-KAISY FRIEMUTH

NAHARA

See: **sacrifice**

NAHJ AL-BALAGHA

Among Shi'i Muslims, this book (*The Way of Eloquence*) is accepted without demur as a collection of sermons, letters and statements from the Imam 'Ali Ibn Abi Talib, the Prophet's cousin and son-in-law, and in their eyes his rightful successor as leader of the Muslim community. It is, thus, among Shi'is a crucial source of teachings and inspiration, as well as an exemplar of verbal accomplishment. This certainty, however, has not been shared by Sunni commentators, and there has been a sustained debate over its origins almost since the time it appeared. It is often accepted that the *Nahj al-Balagha* was assembled by a certain Abu 'l-Hasan Muhammad al-Sharif al-Ra'i (d. AD 1016), who came

from a distinguished Shi'i family of Baghdad. Comments in his name appear in many places throughout the book, usually as explanations of rare terms that occur in the compositions attributed to the imam, a few of them containing references to works that al-Ra'i is known to have composed. But as early as the thirteenth century the suspicion was raised that al-Ra'i was not so much the compiler of the work from earlier sources as its actual author. The biographer Ibn Khallikan (d. AD 1283) says as much in the *Wafayat al-A'yan*, and adds that it was not even certain whether al-Ra'i or his brother al-Murta'a was actually responsible. This was repeated by a succession of authors, down to modern times.

In favour of the Imam's possible authorship of at least some of the material, collections of his sermons dating from a few centuries after his time are listed by al-Nadim in the *Fihrist*, and also by others. In addition, a number of individual passages from the *Nahj al-Balagha* can be paralleled in earlier works, where they are attributed to 'Ali. So recent scholarship has judged that at least a proportion of the material in the work can be traced back to him with some likelihood. In favour of al-Ra'i's role as compiler rather than author are the evident signs in the work of his conservative approach to his task, presenting fragments of 'Ali's sermons as he found them rather than combining them together, including variant forms of the same sermon, and ignoring the chronology of 'Ali's life in the order of his material. These are strong circumstantial signs that he was compiling pieces from earlier sources as he came across them rather than composing them himself. Of course, it cannot be ruled out that there are apocryphal elements in the work, or that some or much of it has been through a process of revision by those who preserved the original speeches and writings.

The *Nahj al-Balagha* comprises more than 200 sermons, nearly eighty letters, and almost 500 sayings attributed to 'Ali. The sermons offer in part a virtual commentary on the Imam's political career, including remarks when some Muslims tried to make him Caliph after the Prophet's death, criticisms of Talha and Zubayr, orations after the Battle of the Camel, and after the Battle of Siffin, and the Sermon of the Shiqshiqiyya in which he scorns his predecessors in the caliphate. They also include sermons on morality and doctrine, notably the importance of the Qur'an and Muhammad, and a number on the witness of the created order to the power and sovereignty of God. Many of these are in the kind of heightened, poetic language that is appropriate for a congregation or group of listeners.

The letters likewise reflect 'Ali's political career, and come ostensibly from the period of his caliphate. They include instructions to army commanders, to individual followers and the inhabitants of towns such as Kufa and Basra, and a great many addressed to Mu'awiya b. Abi Sufyan. Last, the individual sayings include advice to other Muslims, replies to questions, reflective comments, moral aphorisms and religious exhortations. Together, the different pieces offer a source of teachings and guidance, and for Shi'is an invaluable continuation of the sacred texts themselves.

Numerous commentaries have been written on the *Nahj al-Balagha*, mainly by Shi'is but also by some Sunnis, including in recent times Muhammad 'Abduh. There have also been many editions, of which that by 'Abd al-Hamid (1983) is among the most useful. The most accessible translation is by Reza (1996).

DAVID THOMAS

AL-NAJAF

Place of pilgrimage and capital of governorate (*muhafazah*) in open desert, near the Euphrates, one of two Shi'ite holy cities in Iraq. In pre-Islamic times the graves of Adam and Noah were venerated there. The tomb of the spiritual founder of the Shi'i sect, the fourth Muslim caliph, 'Ali ibn Abi Talib (*c.* AD 600–61), son-in-law and cousin of Prophet Muhammad is venerated by the Shi'ites in al-Najaf. Shi'ites consider him to be the temporal successor to Prophet Muhammad, their divinely designated *imam*. According to a Shi'ite tradition, 'Ali mortally wounded Kufa, ordered his followers to place his body on a camel and allow it to wander freely; where the camel stopped, there he was to be buried. Under Umayyad rule the burial spot was concealed. The shrine and first mosque in al-Najaf were erected, according to tradition, when the city was founded by Harun al-Rashid (AD 793–809). However, 'Ali's mausoleum was probably erected by the Shi'i Buyid 'Adud al-Dawla (AD 979–80) who is also buried there, with his sons. The city has a high town wall reinforced by massive round towers built by Hasan b. al-Fadl (d. AD 1023–4) and deep cellars (*sirdabs*) where political dissidents may hide. Just before Malik Shah visited the town (AD 1086), it was burnt by fanatical Sunnis from Baghdad (AD 1051–2), then restored. Sulayman the Magnificent visited al-Najaf (1534–5). It was temporarily conquered by Persians (AD 1623), but restored to Ottoman control (AD 1638–9), despite Bedouin and Wahhabi raids. The shrine in al-Najaf retained a virtual monopoly under the Ottomans and maintained its function as a Shi'ite place of pilgrimage.

The focus of anti-British opposition in 1920, it opposed King Faisal. Ayatallah Khomeini lived in al-Najaf (1965–78), reviving the role of the shrine and using it as a centre for Persian clerical opposition to the Shah of Iran. In the 1980s, there was a Shi'i college and with monasteries nearby. Yet Shi'ites were forbidden to celebrate in al-Najaf under Saddam Husayn and it was the scene of violent clashes between Shi'i, Sunnis and US forces (2003–6) when Shi'i celebrated the first ten days of Muharram. Unrest has continued since 2004.

References

Bosworth (1998: I, 78), Kimber (1998: I, 273–4), Litvak (1998), Nakash (2003).

JANET STARKEY

NAJAT

'Salvation'. Guaranteed on the Day of Judgement if one's good deeds outweigh one's bad deeds, and the alternative to Hell (*al-Nar*) (Q.40:41, also, Q.23:102, Q.28:67, Q.39:61, Q.85:11).

See also: **Hell; judgement on the *yawm al-qiyama*; scales, judgement with**

ANDREW J. NEWMAN

NAJD

Central upland region of Saudi Arabia on an arid rocky plateau with no perennial streams, from al-Hijaz and al-Tihama to Rub 'al-Khali, with sand deserts of al-Nafud and al-Dahna' to north and south. The capital is al-Riyadh, other towns being Burayda, 'Anayza, Ha'il, Tharmala, Shaqra, Majma'a, Huraymala, al-Hufhuf and al-Qatif. The only densely populated oases (al-Kharj, al-Mahmal, as-Sudayr, al-'Arid, and al-Qasim), produce cattle, dates, wheat and barley. Mountain ranges include Jabal Salma and Aja'. Famous for its pre-Islamic poetry, the highlands of Najd became and archetype for paradise in Arabo-Islamic poetry.

The early caliphs, 'Umar I and 'Uthman, had great grazing grounds (*hima*) in Dar'iya, al-Rabadha, Fayd, al-Nir, Dhu'l-Shara and Naqi', in the district of al-Sharaf, but these were neglected under the 'Abbasids. Najd is dominated by Bedouin tribes (al-'Awazim, Mutayr, Harb, Bani Murra, Dawasir). Najd is mainly Wahhabi, a movement founded by Muhammad ibn 'Abd al-Wahhab and Al Sa'uds. The Ottomans seized the provincial capital of Dar'iya, but the Al Sa'uds rapidly regained control, establishing Riyadh as their capital (1824), though the Rashid dynasty, based in Ha'il, briefly controlled Najd (1900s). 'Abd al-'Aziz b. 'Abd al-Rahman Al Sa'ud, Sultan of Najd, became King of al-Hijaz in 1926, and six years later he unified al-Hijaz, Najd and other districts to form the Kingdom of Saudi Arabia, based in Riyadh, with Jidda as his diplomatic capital. From the 1950s, petroleum products were readily available in Najd: Riyadh grew rapidly and Ibn Sa'ud established Bedouin rural settlements.

References

Al-Juhany (2002), Stetkevych (1993).

JANET STARKEY

NAMING CEREMONY OF A CHILD (*'AQIQA*)

The sacrifice offered on the seventh day after the birth of a child, the day on which the new born is given a name, is known as *'aqiqa*. It is the occasion of a ritual that expresses joy and happiness, during which the child's hair is cut and the value of the equivalent weight in silver or gold of the shorn lock is then offered for distribution as alms. It is customary for an animal sacrifice to be made on this occasion, although it may be left until later. Traditionally, sacrifice is made of two sheep or goats for a boy, one for a girl. The personal circumstances of the parents dictate the kind of offering made. In some cases the sacrifice is made by the child when he or she has grown up. In each case, however, the meat is distributed as food for the poor. The sacrifice, regulated by tradition and law, carries the sanction of the Prophet Muhammad, who is recorded as saying: 'if anyone wishes to offer a sacrifice for his newly born child, he may do so'. The sacrifice of an animal made at this time is one of the two such sacrifices made by Muslims. The other is made throughout the Islamic world to mark the conclusion of the annual pilgrimage (hajj) to Mecca.

References

Omran (1992: 27–39), Tritton (1968: 135).

EDWARD D. A. HULMES

NAQSHBANDIYYA

One of the largest Sufi orders, the Naqshbandiyya is influential in central Asia (where it originated in the fourteenth century), the Indian subcontinent, the Arab world and also among Muslims in the West. Notable features of this order include a markedly Sunni flavour, strict adherence to the shari'a, and an attempt to draw the ruling classes towards an appropriate form of Islam. Eminent Sufis including 'Abd al-Rahman Jami (d. 1492) and Ahmad Sirhindi (d. 1624) were Naqshibandis.

References

Algar (1976), Nizami (1991a).

LLOYD RIDGEON

AL-NAR

See: Hell

AL-NASAFI, AHMAD

Abu al-Hasan Muhammad b. Ahmad al-Nasafi, also known as al-Nakhshabi, was an Isma'ili da'i and is considered to be the founder of Isma'ili philosophy. He succeeded in converting the Samanid ruler Nasr Ibn Ahmad and some important men of his court to Isma'ilism. However, this success did not last long and Nuh, the successor of Nasr, reversed Nasr's policies. As a result, Al-Nasafi along with other Isma'ilis was assassinated in AD 942/3.

Unfortunately, al-Mahsul (The Outcome), al-Nasafi's most important work, which apparently presented his theological and cosmological concepts, is lost. However, his main doctrines and contributions to Isma'ilism are to be found in the books of many Isma'ili critics, such as Abu Hatim al-Razi in his book al-Islah. His main contribution to the study of metaphysics lies in his cosmological doctrines, which attempt to combine the Neoplatonic theory of emanation with Isma'ili theology and the Islamic concept of creation ex nihilo. He interprets the process of creation as involving two different procedures: first in creation ex nihilo (ibda') through the word of God, which caused the existence of the Intellect, al-'aql the first created thing. The second procedure takes place through the Intellect but this time through emanation. The Intellect produces the Soul and the Soul produces matter and form. However, instead of applying the Neoplatonic word fada (emanate) al-Nasafi uses the Mu'tazilite terms tawlid, tawallada, which imply a necessary relationship between the cause and its effect. However, it is not clear here whether he wants to emphasise the Islamic concept of creation ex nihilo or to present a theory of creation through divine will and knowledge by implying creation through God's word. However, the latter seems

480

more likely because of his refusal to apply Neoplatonic terminology to God, such as 'first cause' because of its association with the image of eternal cause and effect. Al-Nasafi has influenced many other Isma'ili philosophers such as Abu Ya'qub al-Sijistani al-Kirmani and al-Hamidi.

References

Netton (1989: 210–14).

See also: **al-Hamidi, Ibrahim b. al-Husayn; al-Sijistani, Abu Ya'qub**

MAHA EL-KAISY FRIEMUTH

AL-NASAFI, 'AZIZ AL-DIN
(d. ca. 1300)

'Aziz al-Din al-Nasafi is one of the great Persian mystics of the thirteenth century. Writing all of his works in simple Persian prose, he did much to popularise metaphysical concepts such as the Perfect Man, the relationship between prophecy and friendship of God, and the nature of existence. There is some speculation that Nasafi had Shi'-ite inclinations, although these are certainly not pronounced in his works. Recently there has been some debate over his connection with Ibn al-'Arabi.

References

Ridgeon (1998; 2002).

LLOYD RIDGEON

AL-NASA'I, ABU 'ABD AL-RAHMAN AHMAD IBN 'ALI (d. AD 915)

Author of one of the recognised collections of *hadith* who died in AD 915. As with all compilers of *hadith*, Abu 'Abd al-Rahman Ahmad ibn 'Ali al-Nasa'i is said to have left his home in Khurasan and travelled widely in the Middle East in search of traditions before settling in Egypt and then Damascus. His collection called *al-Sunan* is divided into fifty-one chapters and is distinctive for its coverage, adding some topics, and omitting others, compared to other recognised collections. He pays a great deal of attention to variant transmissions of reports and applies rigid criteria in his *isnad* criticism.

References

Siddiqi (1993: 67–8).

ANDREW RIPPIN

NASER-E KHOSROU
(AD 1001–*c.* 1075)

Persian poet and prose writer, born in Qobadiyan, in the district of Balkh. Doubt surrounds some details of the early life of Naser-e Khosrou, not least because he was confused by some biographers with the later scholar Nasir-oddin Tusi. He belonged to a family of Shi'ite officials, whose profession he initially adopted. After a period in official service at Balkh, however, he appears to have received a vision in 1045, telling him to give up his post and to make the pilgrimage to Mecca. Following his visit to the Holy Places, he travelled on to Palestine and Egypt, which was ruled at the time by the Isma'ili Fatimids. At some stage, Naser-e Khosrou converted to the Isma'ili sect and attained the rank of *hujjat*, the fourth in the spiritual hierarchy, but he failed to achieve his apparent ambition to become a missionary and retired to Badakhshan, where he spent the remainder of his life.

Naser-e Khosrou's most important work is his *Safarnameh*, an account of his journey to Mecca from AD 1045 to 1052 through Marv, Nishapur, Tabriz,

Aleppo and Jerusalem. In addition to its topographical and geographical interest, the work is valuable for the information it provides on contemporary social and political conditions and for the author's accounts of meetings with famous personalities of the time, including the Arabic poet al-Ma'arri. The work is written in a lucid and straightforward style and is generally held to be one of the best examples of early Persian prose. The author's Isma'ili tendencies, which are scarcely noticeable in the *Safarnameh*, are more apparent in his poetic *diwan*, which was said to have consisted of over 30,000 verses, of which around 11,000 are now extant. The collection is composed largely of lengthy *qasidas* (odes). Among several other works, in both prose and verse, mention may be made of the *Rowshana'inameh*, a lengthy didactic poem in rhyming couplets that anticipates the *Bustan* of Sa'di, and a prose work *Jami' al-Hikmatayn*, an extended essay in which he attempted to reconcile Greek philosophy with Isma'ili theology.

References

Arberry (1958: 65–71), Le Strange (1888).

PAUL STARKEY

NASIKH AND *MANSUKH*

The 'abrogator' and the 'abrogated', in reference to verses of the Qur'an with legal importance. Given that the Qur'an was revealed over the period of twenty-three years and that it responded to individual situations related to the life and the context of Muhammad, classical Muslim jurists and exegetes reasoned that abrogation of specific laws in the Qur'an was possible. Thus, a hermeneutical tool designed to resolve inner-Qur'anic conflict became available. There were two specific rulings which

provoked such considerations: the matter of drinking wine (see Q.2:219 and 5:90) and the odds which combatants must be prepared to face in battle (see Q.8:65 and 8:66).

While not all Muslims agreed (or agree) with the application of the notion of abrogation in these situations, many did, and the use of the principle became quite widespread through the Qur'anic text. The 'Sword Verse' was seen to abrogate as many as 200 different verses that might otherwise have suggested that non-aggressiveness or patience was the appointed approach.

The question of whether the *sunna*, or custom, of Muhammad could abrogate the Qur'an was a vexed one. For the most part, the jurists upheld the absolute authority of the Qur'an above the *sunna* and used other hermeneutical tools (such as 'specification') as a method of resolving apparent conflict between twin sources of law.

References

Rippin (2000: 213–31).

ANDREW RIPPIN

AL-NASIR, AHMAD B. AL-MUSTADI, ABU'L-'ABBAS (AD 1180–1225)

Al-Nasir succeeded his father al-Mustadi as 'Abbasid caliph in Baghdad. His forty-five year reign was the longest in the 'Abbasid dynasty. Dissension and rivalries among the Saljuqs enabled al-Nasir to continue restoring some power and dignity to the caliphate, and he managed to consolidate control over Iraq and even extend this into neighbouring territories. In an attempt to destroy the last vestiges of Saljuq influence, al-Nasir allied himself with the Turkish ruler of Khwarizm, Takash, and urged him to attack the Saljuqs who ruled Baghdad. The ensuing battle resulted in the defeat of the sultan Tughril, thus ending the Saljuq line in Iraq and Kurdistan. Rather than allowing the caliph to recover the conquered territory, however, Takash himself adopted the title sultan, asserted his own authority in Baghdad and left the caliph ruler in name only. Takash's son 'Ala' al-Din went further, desiring to abolish the 'Abbasid regime and to replace it with a Shi'ite one. To counter this, the caliph al-Nasir is alleged to have sought the assistance of Jenghiz Khan, the leader of the Mongol hordes. 'Ala' al-Din fled, and the Mongol advance towards the west continued.

al-Nasir also endeavoured to reassert the secular authority of the caliphate and to restore political unity within the Muslim community on the basis of *fatuwwa*. These chivalric orders, which encouraged high moral standards and emphasised mutual loyalty and assistance, were popular and influential in Baghdad. In al-Nasir's declaration that he was to be head of the *fatuwwa* and that all *fatuwwa* that did not recognise his leadership were to be banned, he hoped to control the orders and in this way to control Baghdad and give himself a more central place in society. He also attempted to extend his influence by encouraging other rulers of the Islamic world to enrol in them. As a sign of the increased independence of the caliphate, al-Nasir was able to designate his own successor, his son Muhammad al-Zahir.

References

Boyle (1968: 168–9), Gibb and Bosworth (1960–2003: VII, 996–1003), Hitti (1970: 481–3), Hodgson (1974: 279–86), Ibn al-Tiqtaqa (1860: 370–9), Le Strange (1924: 240, 273–95 *passim*, 333, 335), Muir (1915: 587–8).

RONALD PAUL BUCKLEY

NASRIDS (1232–1492)

From the mid-thirteenth century, the progress of the Christian *Reconquista* confined the Muslims of Spain to Granada, under a line of *amirs*, the Nasrids. With intermittent but, in the end, ineffective support from the Muslim powers of the Maghrib, they survived for over two centuries, though under increasing pressure from Castile-Leon. The union of this last with the kingdom of Aragon spelt the end for them, but Granada had been a significant centre for Arabic culture, having, for example, associations with the great historian Ibn Khaldun and a leading literary figure in the Vizier Ibn al-Khatib.

References

Arié (1990), Bosworth (1996: No. 7), Gibb and Bosworth (1960–2003), Makki (1992: 77–84).

C. E. BOSWORTH

NASS

'Designation', 'appointment', referring to the designation of a successor. The Sunnis believed a *shura* (council) could be called to determine the caliph (successor) after the death of Muhammad, where the Shi'a contend that such designation could not be subject to election as the Prophet's role could only be assumed by his descendants through 'Ali.

References

Momen (1985: 153–5).

ANDREW J. NEWMAN

NASSERISM

The brand of Arab nationalism forged by Colonel Gamal Abdul Nasser (1918–70). In 1952, Nasser led the so-called

Free Officers in a *coup d'état* against the pro-British regime of King Farouk. Nasserism was as much defined by the actions of the man as any system of thought, but a number of themes developed: it promoted the interests of the Third World, advocated pan-Arab nationalism and moved towards socialism. It was influential in many Arab states, competing with other strands of Arab nationalism and more traditional belief systems. In 1958, the merger of Egypt and Syria into the United Arab Republic (UAR) represented a great breakthrough, but resentment of Egyptian dominance prompted Syrian secession in 1961. The failure of the UAR, the faltering of economic development, and defeat in the Six Day War of June 1967 undermined the prestige of Nasserism. Even by Nasser's death in 1970, Nasserism was a fading force, although his reputation endured longer.

References

Bill and Springborg (1994: 207–18), Hourani (1991: 405–15), Nasser (1955), St. John (1976: 844–5).

SIMON W. MURDEN

NATIQ

An important term in the Isma'ili tradition, the *natiq* (pl. *nutaqa'*) was a spokesman who came to the creatures with a revelation. Each *natiq* initiated a cycle of which there were seven in total (the first cycle was that of Adam and the last was the Muhammadan cycle), and these seven cycles were mirrored by the seven imams of the Isma'ili tradition.

References

Khusraw (1998).

LLOYD RIDGEON

NATURE

Muslim philosophers had developed the doctrine of nature from Aristotelian concepts, which hold that the movement of a thing is due to its specific nature. Aristotle uses the word 'nature' in order to explain the power that inheres in things and initiates their movement – this could also be understood as their form. Moreover, the movement from potentiality to actuality, for Aristotle, is due to the nature of things. Thus the term 'nature' here can be understood as the power of actuality that comes from within a thing and is not borrowed from a higher being (God). For Muslim theologians, in contrast, all movements and events are initiated by accidents that come to inhere in the atom and both atoms and accidents are created by God. They criticise the concept of nature, which they attribute to the groups called *ahl al-tabia'* in their terminology. They also mention that this concept was taken up by the group called *ahl al-'ada*, who related the repetition of events to certain natural laws. The Arab natural philosophers discussed the concept of nature under the question of causality. They considered that all events are initiated by a series of causes which are connected with each other through a natural power and which demonstrate the necessary relationship between a cause and its effect. In their metaphysical studies, the series of causes ends with the first cause, but in their physical sciences the causes are independent initiators of event. This means, in their view, that although God is the first cause and the initiator of the first movement, once He started the world, all things began to move by their own natural power which inheres in them all. Al-Ghazali in his *Tahafut al-Falasifa* criticised the philosophers for this concept, which leads to a rejection of miracles and doubt about the ability of God to reverse events.

References

Ibn Sina (1960), Wolfson (1976).

MAHA EL-KAISY FRIEMUTH

AL-NAWAWI, YAHYA IBN SHARAF MUHYI 'L-DIN (d. AD 1277)

Prominent *hadith* scholar and jurist. Born in the village of Nawa, 100 kilometres south of Damascus, Yahya ibn Sharaf Muhyi 'l-Din al-Nawawi moved to Damascus where he spent most of the rest of his life as a student and teacher of the religious sciences. Al-Nawawi died in AD 1277. Through his teaching post, al-Nawawi was an influential figure. He was a *Shafi'i* jurist and a commentator on *hadith*. He produced an important introductory text on the law, the *Kitab Minhaj al-Talibin*, a multivolume commentary on the *Sahih* of Muslim, and other works of commentary. His *Kitab al-Arba'in* or *Forty Hadith* is a small collection of *hadith* that serves as a fundamental collection whose implications cover all the basic principles of the Muslim religion. He also wrote a short and accessible commentary on the *Forty Hadith*.

References

Ibrahim (1976).

ANDREW RIPPIN

AL-NAZZAM (?–AD 846)

One of the outstanding thinkers of the school of thought known as the Mu'tazila. He was born a slave in Basra but was freed and was educated there, including some time spent in the circle of his maternal uncle Abu'l-Hudhayl al-Allaf. He was summoned to Baghdad by the Caliph al-Ma'mun around AD 818, and his views seem to have diverged from those of Abu'l-Hudhayl in that he made greater use of Greek philosophical reasoning. Only fragments of his works survive, but on the basis of these it is clear that he argued for the strict unity and utter transcendence of God, that God cannot do evil (so that as a result human beings must have free will), and that while the Qur'an is miraculous, the basis for this view is not its inimitability (*i'jaz*) but rather the predictions which it contains. He also composed some notable poetry, and was viewed with some suspicion by some of his contemporaries because of his love of wine and young boys.

References

Caspar (1998: Chapter 7), Watt (1973: Chapter 8).

HUGH GODDARD

NEW YEAR, ISLAMIC

A new Islamic year is marked by the festivities of *ra's al-sana* ('the head, or beginning, of the year'), which are celebrated on the first day of the first lunar month, Muharram (which is known as 'the sacred month'). Like all the special days in the Islamic calendar, this one begins at sunset on the day preceding the feast itself. Celebrations at the turn of the year tend to be more restrained in Islamic communities than they are in the increasingly secular parts of the Western world. It is not surprising that the new year is often celebrated with a measure of quiet thanksgiving, given the fact that the month of Muharram follows the month of Dhu'l-Hijja (the twelfth month of the lunar calendar) during which many Muslims throughout the world have made the arduous Pilgrimage to Mecca (the *hajj*). The New Year festivities vary in different parts of the world, but everywhere there is the same spirit of unity among Muslims who strive to live in the service of God. Appropriate quotations from the Qur'an (such as excerpts from Q.9, Q.22, Q.24, Q.47, Q.102, and from other religious texts that speak of the need for all Muslims to approach God with praise and humility and of Muhammad's exemplary obedience to God) are read in mosques after the appearance of the new moon signals the beginning of the new year. Special prayers are recited. Visits are made to members of the family and to friends. Hospitality, with specially prepared food and drinks, is freely offered and thankfully accepted. It is a time for a fresh start, for reconciliation, and for rededication to the beliefs and duties of Islam. The retelling of the story of the Prophet Muhammad's move from Mecca to Medina in the year AD 621/2 (the *hijra*) is given prominence in mosques and homes. The story is often brought to listeners and viewers by means of radio and television.

See also: **calendar, Islamic (*al-taqwim al-islami, al hijri*); months, Islamic**

EDWARD D. A. HULMES

NIFAQ

'Hypocrisy', but also 'dissent'. Hypocrisy is severely attacked in the Qur'an (Q.2:8–20) and is said to be worse than unbelief (Q.4:145–6). The Shi'a sanction a form of dissimulation (*taqiyya*) in the face of overwhelming opposition.

References

Gibb and Bosworth (1960–2003).

See also: *munafiqun*; *taqiyya*

ANDREW J. NEWMAN

NIGER, THE RIVER

The Niger is the third longest river in the continent of Africa, extending for 4,185 kilometres (2,600 miles) from its source on the Futa Jallon plateau in the south-west of the Republic of Guinea, bordering Sierra Leone, to the Niger Delta on the Bight of Biafra. It begins its journey flowing north-east through Guinea into the Republic of Mali. In central Mali the river forms a large inland delta, a complex maze of lakes and channels measuring 77,000 square kilometres. The dispersal of sand from the Sahara has affected the flow of the river in its central reaches, leaving it sluggish and brown coloured. At other times, it overflows its banks, although continuing drought during the past three decades has reduced water levels considerably. The French began an irrigation project in the 1930s, which allowed for the building of a dam at Sansanding. The project made available 40,000 hectares for farming, notably rice. At Timbuktu, in Mali, the river begins a great bend, flowing first to the east and then south-east out of Mali and through the Republic of Niger, where it forms part of the border with Benin. Thence it flows into Nigeria, emerging finally into the Bight of Biafra, after passing through the Niger Delta. This delta is the largest in Africa, with innumerable lagoons, swamps and navigable channels. From north of the delta to Lokoja, and thence to Baro, the Niger is seasonally navigable for river steamers and barges. At Lokoja the Niger meets the River Benue. During the rainy season the Benue is also navigable to the east by such vessels for much of its course. At Onitsha the river rises and falls 40 feet between the dry and rainy seasons of the year. The western upper reaches of the Niger played an important economic role in the history of the former empires of Mali and Songhay.

References

Hourani (1991: 94, 111, 244).

EDWARD D. A. HULMES

NIGHT JOURNEY, THE

This episode in the life of the Prophet Muhammad – whether actual or visionary – is described in Arabic by the phrase *laylat al-isra' wa'l-mi'raj*, literally, 'the Night Journey and the Ascent [into Heaven]' (cf. Q.17:1). Islamic tradition furnishes details of these events that took place before the Prophet moved from Mecca to Medina in AD 621/2. It appears that he was asleep at night near the *ka'ba* in Mecca when he was aroused by the Angel Jibr'il (Gabriel), who took him to the miraculous winged steed, al-Buraq, an animal described by the ninth-century traditionist Bukhari as 'smaller than a mule but bigger than an ass'. The word *buraq* is derived from a root that suggests the flash of lightning. The animal is depicted in India with the face of a woman and a peacock's tail. Mounting this animal alongside the angel, Muhammad was taken in the air to Jerusalem, where he joined in *salat* (ritual prayer and worship) on the ruined site of Solomon's Temple with some of the Prophets who had preceded him: Ibrahim (Abraham), Musa (Moses), 'Isa (Jesus) and others. Muhammad was next refreshed by a drink of some milk, which he chose in preference to the wine that was also offered. The significance of his choice became clear when he was praised for choosing the better course. The Temple Mount was the place from which he was then taken up into Heaven by the angel. Since that day, the place is part of 'the Farthest Mosque' (*al-masjid al-aqsa'*), which stands near to the oratory known as the Dome of the Rock (*qubbat al-sakhra*), built in the seventh century AD. The latter encloses the sacred rock that is said to mark 'the navel of the world'. Muhammad then ascended through the seven heavens to the Presence of God, encountering as he did so other celestial figures in their spiritual forms (cf. Q.53:7–18). Accounts of these experiences record that when he returned to Mecca he was mocked for his presumption by the unbelieving Quraysh, to whom Muhammad is reputed to have said nothing about his exaltation directly. Abu Bakr accepted his account without question, however, affirming that the Prophet would not lie about such a thing. His reputation as a truthful witness earned Muhammad the sobriquet *al-Siddiq*. The Night Journey is celebrated on the twenty-seventh day of the month of Rajab.

References

Hitti (1973: 114, 352), Tritton (1968: 186).

EDWARD D. A. HULMES

NIGHT OF THE DESCENT OF THE QUR'AN

The Arabic phrase referring to this event in the history of Islam is *laylat al-qadr*, literally, 'the Night of Power'. During the course of a night in the year AD 610, the year in which the Prophet Muhammad received the Call to be the Messenger (*rasul*) of God, it is claimed that the Qur'an was revealed to him, through the mediation of the Angel Jibr'il (Gabriel). The Night of Power is said to have been one of the last ten nights in the month of Ramadan, which is why this period is considered by Muslims to be especially holy each year. Just as the soul of the Prophet received the Divine Revelation, so should the individual Muslim be receptive to that which God has revealed as 'the Straight Path' of Islam (cf. Q.1:6). 'The Night of Power' is the title given to Q.97: '[God] revealed this on the Night of Power. If only you knew what that Night is like. It is better than a thousand months. On that Night the Angels and the Spirit [Gabriel] descended by God's permission with every

487

command. Peace, until the break of day'
(Q.97:1–5).

References

Hitti (1973: 112).

Edward D. A. Hulmes

NIKAH

See: **marriage**

NILE, THE RIVER

Measuring some 6,695 kilometres (4,160 miles), the river Nile is the longest river in the world. From its distant headwaters in Burundi in central Africa to its vast sprawling delta in north-eastern Egypt, the river snakes its way north, gathering water drained from over 1 million square miles (3 million square kilometres) of Africa, from parts of Tanzania, Kenya, Uganda, the Democratic Republic of the Congo (Zaire), the Central African Republic, Ethiopia, the Sudan and Egypt. After his only visit to Egypt, the fifth-century BC Greek historian Herodotus described the country as 'an acquired country, the gift of the river'. The description was, and is, justified, because the fertility of the soil has been assured for centuries by the annual inundation of floodwater from the Nile, which is channelled year after year into the narrow strips of land adjoining the river on either side of its lower course. By means of improved irrigation schemes, these strips have been widened on parts of the lower Nile in the region of Cairo. From earliest times the crops grown have included wheat, barley and grapes, for the making of bread, beer and wine, beans, lentils, leeks, onions, cabbages, radishes, lettuce, cucumbers, melons, dates and figs. Papyrus was used for making boats

and for the paper on which the story of a civilisation was written. North of Cairo is the great Nile delta, 160 kilometres (100 miles) long and up to 185 kilometres (115 miles) wide. The extensively cultivated parts of Egypt provide a marked contrast with the barrenness of the surrounding desert.

The Nile consists of two lengthy river systems. The *White Nile* maintains a steady flow throughout the year, fed by water coming from *Victoria Nyanza* (Lake Victoria) above the Owen Falls in Uganda. The *Blue Nile* rises far to the east in Ethiopia. In the dry season its flow of water falls to a trickle in places. The heavy rain, which falls in the Ethiopian Highlands between June and September each year, flows into Lake Tana and thence westwards through a great gorge in the mountains, increasing the flow to a torrent by a factor of 50. The White Nile, *c.* 3,700 kilometres (2,300 miles) long and the Blue Nile, *c.* 1,610 kilometres (1,000 miles) long meet at Khartoum, the capital of the Republic of the Sudan. The two watercourses then merge and flow together northwards to the Mediterranean. Khartoum is situated 2,988 kilometres (1,857 miles) from the sea. The 'Island' (*jazira*) formed by the confluence of the two river systems at Khartoum forms the Sudan's most fertile agricultural area. The course of the White Nile from Lake Victoria leads through several rocky rapids along an entrenched valley, which affords little cultivable land on either side. In places the waters spread to form lakes. The river has been given various names, including: *Bahr al-Abyad*, *Bahr al-Jabal*, the *Victoria Nile*, the *Albert Nile*. Commercial and tourist river-cruise services operate from Alexandria in the north (at first by canal) to Aswan. Further south, the White Nile is navigable throughout the year from Khartoum to Juba, and from Nimule to the Kabalega (Murchison) Falls. From June to December the Blue Nile is navigable from Sannar as far as al-Rusayris.

In earlier times, the vital silt, deposited on the floodplain by the annual inundation of the Nile, increased the fertility of the land. Each year over 100 million tons of fertile soil, scooped by the floodwaters from the volcanic rock in the Ethiopian highlands, are carried by the Blue Nile. More recently, the silt lodges behind the High Dam at Aswan, some 960 kilometres (600 miles) due north of Khartoum. A problem of erosion arose in the delta area when the dam prevented the alluvial silt and dissolved minerals from passing downstream. As a result, the delta began to be eroded by the incursion of the sea. There was also an impact on the fishing industry in the delta. The High Dam at Aswan, completed in 1971, stores water for irrigation in one of the world's largest artificial lakes, Lake Nasser, which also stores excess water for other purposes, notably, the development of hydro-electric power. The lake extends some 560 kilometres (350 miles) behind the dam to Wadi Halfa. The control that it is now possible to exercise over the level of the water also affords protection to people who have often experienced the more unfortunate consequences of flooding in the past. Nevertheless, the construction of the dam led to the flooding of huge areas of the Nile valley, and required the relocation of 90,000 people living nearby, the raising of the Nubian temples of Abu-Simbel to a cliff 200 feet above the original site, and the removal of other ancient archaeological treasures.

For millennia, the Nile has flowed through lands that have seen the rise and fall of different civilisations. The Old, Middle and New Kingdoms of ancient lower Egypt, dating from the middle of the third millennium to the middle of the first millennium BC, saw the construction of pyramids, temples, tombs and artefacts under the Pharaohs. In 525 BC Egypt became part of the Persian empire. The Greeks under Alexander the Great assumed control in 325 BC. They were followed by the Romans under Augustus in 30 BC. By AD 324, the ancient temples were being replaced by Coptic churches. It was not until AD 641, when a force of some 10,000 Muslims captured most of Lower Egypt, that Islam began to play a dominant part in Egypt. Islam became the state religion and Arabic became the official language. The new city of Cairo became the capital. In the centuries that followed, a number of Islamic dynasties flourished and fell. Although the fame of the civilisations that flowered alongside the lower reaches of the Nile in Egypt was widespread, comparatively little was known in Europe about the regions of the Upper Nile and the Sudan. Formerly a dependency of Egypt, the Sudan was to be ruled as a condominium by Britain and Egypt, by which time Islamic revivalists had established themselves in the region. The Republic of the Sudan became an independent state in 1956.

After his visit to Egypt, Herodotus could only speculate about the river that appeared from the south. He wrote: 'of the sources of the Nile no one can give any account. It enters Egypt from parts beyond'. It was not until the nineteenth century that the source of the river became widely known in the western world after the travels into the interior of central Africa by European explorers such as Richard Burton, John Speke, Sam Baker and his wife, David Livingstone and H. M. Stanley.

References

Holmes *et al.* (2004), Moorehead (1960, 1962).

See also: **agriculture (*al-filaha, al-zira'a*); Cairo; gardens, Islamic; irrigation (*al-siyaqa*); Khartoum (al-Khurtum)**

EDWARD D. A. HULMES

NI'MATULLAHIYYA

A Sufi order that traces its origins to Ni'mat Allah Wali who lived in the Middle East during the fourteenth century. The order attracted followers in Iran until the fifteenth century when it became popular in the Deccan, India, but its fortunes were revived in Iran during the nineteenth century. Towards the end of this period, the order suffered some disputes concerning its leadership but, nevertheless, it is still the largest Sufi order in modern Iran, and it has managed to establish thriving followings in the West. It emphasises a well-defined code of Sufi ethics and strict obedience to the *shaykh*.

References

Lewisohn (1998, 1999), Nurbakhsh (1991).

LLOYD RIDGEON

NINETY-NINE NAMES OF GOD

The Arabic definite article *al* when added to *ilah* becomes *Allah*, literally 'The God', a term already referring to the single, supreme deity prior to the commencement of the revelation of the Qur'an. The ninety-nine names are those referring to Allah's essence and attributes and qualities mainly found in the Qur'an, but also those deriving therefrom, and others traditionally ascribed.

References

Waines (1995: 25, 139–40).

See also: **anthropomorphism; attributes of God**

ANDREW J. NEWMAN

NIYYA

An important concept in Islam, which expresses the *intention* of a Muslim who is about to fulfil a specific religious duty or obligation. The statement of such intent helps to concentrate the mind and to ensure that the repetition of familiar tasks (such as those required by ritual prayer and worship) is not merely perfunctory. To this end an expression of *niyya* precedes each act of faith and witness performed *fi sabil-llah*, that is, 'in the Way of God'.

EDWARD D. A. HULMES

NIZAM AL-MULK, HASAN IBN 'ALI (AD 1018–92)

Persian statesman and administrator. Born in Tus, Nizam al-Mulk became Vizier to the Seljuk sultan Alp Arslan (d. AD 1072) and his son Malik Shah (d. AD 1092) after him. He played a leading role in furthering the educational and cultural life of the period through the foundation of the famous college in Baghdad called after him the Nizamiyya – part of his aim being to discredit the Isma'ilis and re-establish traditional Sunni doctrine. He was murdered by the Assassins in October AD 1092.

Nizam al-Mulk's reputation as a writer rests primarily on his *Siyasatname*, a work written during the last year of his life, partly on the basis of his own experience. It describes the art of governing a large empire, and is made up of fifty chapters of advice to rulers, illustrated with appropriate anecdotes. In addition to historical and administrative information, the work is rich in accounts of events from the author's own life. After Nizam al-Mulk's murder, the work was completed by Mohammad Maghrebi, who added further information on contemporary political and religious conditions.

References

Darke (1960).

PAUL STARKEY

NIZARIS (AL-NIZARIYYA)

A subsect of the Shi'ite Isma'ili grouping who were named as such due to their support of Abu Mansur Nizar (AD 1045–95). After the death of his father, the Fatimid ruler al-Mustansir (AD 1036–94), Nizar's claim to the throne was refuted by the powerful vizier al-Afdal. Thus, Abu 'l-Qasim Ahmad, Nizar's much younger half brother was crowned caliph with the title of al-Musta'li bi-llah. Consequently, Nizar disputed this claim but was captured, imprisoned and eventually killed by al-Afdal. The supporters of Nizar were consequently known as Nizaris (al-Nizariyya) and were headed by Hasan al-Sabbah (AD 1090–1124) who preached the Fatimid *da'wa* in Persia. Al-Sabbah had followed an independent policy against the Seljuk Turks and upon seizing the mountain fortress of Alamut in AD 1090 he began the establishment of an Isma'ili Nizari state, which had no effective caliph since he had been executed. Despite this, the State spread throughout Persia and parts of Syria and lasted for many generations, until the onslaught of the Mongol hordes. In spite of this setback the Nizari Isma'ilis have maintained their lineage and continued to develop over the years from mountain revolutionaries to a highly organised mercantile class, spread throughout the world, most notably in the form of the followers of their most recent imams, the Aga Khans.

References

Daftary (1998: 106–8, 120–209), al-Johani (1999: 383–6), Netton (1997: 194), Tabataba'i (n.d.: 81–3).

GAVIN PICKEN

NOAH

See: **Nuh**

NUBUWWA

'Prophecy', the source of whose inspiration (*wahy*, Q.42:51–2) or revelation (*tanzil*, Q.69:40–3) can be angels or, for false prophets, demons (Q.26:220–6). *Jinn* can be a source for good or bad revelation (Q.6:111). The onset of prophecy is accompanied by distinctive 'signs' like the ones that affected Muhammed, such as an apparent loss of consciousness. True prophets are also marked by moral rectitude, if not infallibility, piety, and noble descent. Announcements of their arrival precede them.

References

Gibb and Bosworth (1960–2003), Rahman (1979, 13–14).

See also: **angels**; *jinn*; **messengers**; *nabi*; *rasul*

ANDREW J. NEWMAN

NUH (NOAH)

Considered a *rasul* (messenger) in Islam. The story of the Flood is found in various places of the Qur'an (Q.71:25, Q.34:16 for example). Also, the title of Q.71.

See also: *nabi*; *rasul*

ANDREW J. NEWMAN

NUKUL

Failure to take an oath, a simple refusal that cannot be enforced by law except in *li'an* where married couples are expected to exchange curses on their partner when there is no proof of sin but his or her own word. *Qasama* is another occasion when it is mandatory to ask the people of the village or locality to swear an oath when a person is found dead that they know nothing relevant to the case. Failure to swear an oath may lead to punishment by imprisonment.

References

Izzi Dien (1997: 139).

MAWIL IZZI DIEN

NUR AL-DIN 'ALI B. YUSUF

Styled al-Malik al-Afdal, eldest son of Salah al-Din (Saladin) and his deputy and then successor in Damascus (r. 1186–96). After the latter's death, Egypt eventually passed to another of his sons, al-Malik al-'Aziz 'Uthman, so that Ayyubid rule, like that of the Buyids and Saljuqs before them, rapidly became a family rather than a unitary one. Al-Malik al-Afdal was in fact driven out of Damascus by the senior and most forceful member of the dynasty, Saladin's brother al-Malik al-'Adil, ruler in northern Syria and Mesopotamia, who four years later was able to add Egypt to his dominions, proclaiming himself Sultan.

References

Gibb and Bosworth (1960–2003), Humphreys (1977).

C. E. BOSWORTH

NUSAYRIS/'ALAWIS (AL-NUSAYRIYYA/ AL-'ALAWIYYA)

An extremist Shi'ite pseudo-Islamic sect that believes in the divinity of the fourth caliph 'Ali b. Abu Talib (d. AD 661). The name is said to be derived from the sect's founder Muhammad b. Nusayr al-Namiri, who was a supporter of the tenth Imam 'Ali al-Hadi (d. AD 868) and consequently proclaimed divinity and prophethood for himself. According to Nusayri tradition, al-Namiri was the favourite disciple of the eleventh imam al-Hasan al-'Askari (d. AD 874), who sanctioned him with a new revelation, which would become the essence of the Nusayri faith. The Nusayris are also known as 'Alawis (al-'Alawiyya), a name which they are proud of and which was given to them by the French colonialist powers upon granting them a state at the beginning of the twentieth century in Syria. Nusayris can also be found in Turkey and Lebanon but it is in Syria that they are strongest and where they were instrumental in taking power in the early 1970s and where the current ruling family is said to be Nusayri.

References

al-Johani (1999: 390–96), Netton (1997: 195).

See also: **Shi'ism; Sunnism**

GAVIN PICKEN

O

OLIGARCHY AND ISLAM

Oligarchy, a term of political science describing a situation where power is restricted to a small cadre of persons, can be applied to a number of the political theories of Muslim thinkers of both the classical and contemporary period. The Qur'an itself refers to 'the people who know', or 'the people of remembrance'. The believer is commanded to ask these people on matters of which they are uncertain. These locutions have been interpreted differently by different traditions of thought. The Shi'a hold that they refer to the imams, though the Shi'i concept of imamate does not really equate to an oligarchic understanding of power and authority. For most Shi'i groups, the imam has absolute power, since he is the one blessed with perfect knowledge of God's will for humanity. In some theories, this knowledge is such as to make the imam a representation (or perhaps even 'manifestation') of God on earth. The only Shi'i theory which might be classed as having

oligarchic tendencies is the Zaydiyya, where the imam is blessed with political power, but emerges from the scholarly cadre of descendents of the Prophet Muhammad. In the Sunni tradition, the Qur'anic phrases might be seen as elements of an oligarchic political theory in Islam. The references mentioned above are normally interpreted as alluding to the scholarly elite (the *'ulama'*), whose authority in religious matters is thereby asserted. However, religious authority and political power are not always seen as identical in Sunni political theory: the *'ulama'* are charged with guiding and cajoling the caliph into a more perfect obedience to the *shari'a*.

The Prophet himself did not, if historical reports are to be believed, assert any role for an oligarchy who ruled in the political sphere. Some modern Muslim thinkers have tried to assert that the Prophet consulted with his companions (or more broadly, the believers) over public policy, though it is anachronistic to try and enforce contemporary ideas such as 'democracy' and 'public consultation' on seventh-century Medina. The caliphs also did not really express an oligarchic understanding of politico-religious rule. As caliphs (viceregents) of the Prophet of God (or more directly, as the Caliph of God himself), their political rule was to be obeyed by the population, and theoretically the caliph (or 'imam' as the post was termed in legal texts) had supreme power in these matters. This political theory was tempered by the jurists, who attempted to eek out a role for the *'ulama'* in the political process. Ibn Taymiyya (d. AD 1328) argued that the rule of the political authority – *siyasa* – should be in line with the law (*fiqh*) of the scholars. The political ruler is then subject to the regulation of the law, as laid down by the jurists (*fuqaha'*). This, in a sense, produces an oligarchic theory whereby the rules of the state are laid down by the cadre of jurists and implemented by the caliph or sultan. But Ibn Taymiyya's thought was not the only model of how the ruler should relate his control to the rules of the *shari'a*. Al-Mawardi (d. AD 1058) had, before Ibn Taymiyya, described certain state officials as having the power to rule outside of the jurists' interpretation of *fiqh*. Military and administrative leaders had the powers to rule in general obedience to the law of God, but could, if the occasion demanded it, transgress the regulations of the jurist's *fiqh*. This conception of political rule is no less oligarchic, it is merely that a different oligarchy is considered as controlling the political process.

In the modern period, Ibn Taymiyya's model has emerged as more popular. The logic of movements such as the Wahhabiyya is that if a state is to operate in accordance with God's law (the *shari'a*), then the experts in that law should be part of the ruling class. To allow anything less, such as an autono-mous jurisdictional power for traditional custom (*'urf*), and to cede power to leaders who base their authority on non-religious bases, is to deviate from the *shari'a*. Hence the famed concept of those 'who loose and bind' (*ahl al-hall wa'l-'aqd*) finds a role within, say, the Sa'udi state. The great *'ulama'* form a council which 'represents' Islam to the monarch. This, it could be argued, constitutes an oligarchic political theory, though the power of the *ahl al-hall* has always been in tension with the power of the Sa'udi monarch.

Mawdudi's (d. 1979) theory of the Islamic state, which influenced his involvement in the early years of Pakistan's independence, can also be seen as oligarchic. The state is the representative (*khalifa*) of God and is organised with a ruler at its head, who rules in conjunction with a consultative assembly (*majlis*). How these leaders were to be selected was never laid out by Mawdudi in great detail, though they should be at once obedient to the *shari'a* and enjoy the confidence of the people. Similarly, the ideas of the early Muslim Brotherhood, before their accommodation with Egyptian power in the 1970s, could be seen as oligarchic. Hasan al-Banna' (d. 1949), the founder of the Brotherhood was influenced by Hanbalism, and in particular Ibn Taymiyya. Whilst for the Brotherhood, the caliph was leader of the state, he was responsible to the *ahl al-shura'*, the 'people of consultation', who were elected by the people generally.

The Twelver Shi'i community has, in the twentieth century, produced a number of political thinkers whose ideas can be classified as oligarchical. Whilst Ayatallah Khomeini (d. 1989) posited an individual as the supreme power (the jurist, or *faqih*), the implementation of his theory after the Iranian revolution of 1979 in the form of a constitution envisaged a 'Council of Guardians' (*shura-yi negahban*), chosen by the supreme jurist and the parliament, to oversee legislation and ensure it was in line with the *shari'a*. Even more oligarchical was the theory of 'Ali Shari'ati (d. 1977). Shari'ati did not produce a coherent political theory as such, though his anti-clerical Shi'ism is clear in his writings. He views Shi'ism to have been corrupted by too close an association with power, and hence both political authorities and the *'ulama'* are to blame. Shi'ism is in need of reform, and this can only come from the 'enlightened thinkers' (*rawshanfikran*) who are open to rationalism (on a Western model) and are not touched by the obscurantism of either popular religion or clerical legalism. To the extent that Shari'ati devised a model of a particular political system, it is oligarchic as it sees the desires of the *rawshanfikran* over-ruling (or at least taking precedence over) the unenlightened ideas of the masses and the clergy. The role of democracy in Shari'ati's thought is not, then, entirely clear, though he too produces the predictable rhetoric concerning the confluence between a 'true' Islam and the will of the people.

Different Muslim theorists have, then, produced oligarchic schemes for government, and these have been merged with theocracy, nomocracy and democracy. The oligarchy may be elected to rule according to the *shari'a*, though the populace has no right to determine the content of the law, they may be elected because they stand for a particular conception of the *shari'a*, and they not be elected at all, since the populace is unqualified to make such a judgement. Indeed, many of the various forms of oligarchy present in Western political philosophy have reflections in the Islamic tradition; there is nothing inherently oligarchic or anti-oligarchic in Islam.

References

Lambton (1981), Marlow (1997), Walbridge (2001).

ROBERT GLEAVE

ORGANISATION OF THE ISLAMIC CONFERENCE (OIC)

The OIC is the organisation of Muslim states, with a permanent secretariat in Jidda, supporting regular summits, ministerial meetings, and working groups. The OIC was set up amid the Muslim outrage which followed an arson attack by a Christian fundamentalist on the Al-Aqsa Mosque in Jerusalem in 1969. Saudi Arabia was its principal backer. By 2000, the OIC was composed of fifty-six states, the Palestinian National Authority and a number of observer states and bodies.

References

Murden (2002: 197–200). The official website of the OIC Permanent Mission to UN is at <http://www.oic-un.org>.

SIMON W. MURDEN

ORHAN (r. 1324?–62)

Ottoman ruler, son of Osman I. Orhan conquered Bursa in AD 1326, Iznik in 1331 and Izmit in 1337. The annexation of the Turkish principality of Karesi in the 1340s brought his territories to the Dardanelles. In 1346, he married Theodora, daughter of John Kantakouzenos and, as allies of Kantakouzenos in the Byzantine civil war, his troops crossed to Europe and, in 1354, occupied Gallipoli. By his death in 1362, Orhan's territory extended to Ankara in the east to Dhidhimoteichon in the west.

References

Imber (1990: 19–26).

COLIN IMBER

ORIENTALISM

'Orientalism' refers to a particular tradition of Western scholarship of 'the Orient'. Orientalism is defined in a broad fashion to mean the study of the culture, languages and peoples east of the Mediterranean (though many commentators include all Arabo-Muslim peoples and, hence, African Muslims – both Arabs and non-Arabs – are also included). The American-Palestinian literary critic Edward Said, in his famous work *Orientalism: Western Conceptions of the Orient*, is principally responsible for the development of an industry of criticism of 'Orientalism'. Said argued that the work of Western 'Orientalists' concerning the 'Orient' (particularly the Muslim world) during the eighteenth and nineteenth centuries formed part of the imperial project of the Western powers (particularly Britain and France). Orientalists claimed to be working in an 'objective' and 'unbiased' fashion, but this claim, Said argued, was itself part of the rhetoric of Empire, an attempt to objectify the 'Orient'. Orientalists argued that, whilst Western scholars were objective and detached, 'Orientals' were unavoidably biased and unreasonable. Hence, Orientalists claimed that their scholarship was superior to that of the indigenous people of the Orient. What was true of scholarship was also true of Western culture generally, and hence the imperial projects of the Western nations in the Orient were (indirectly, or at times directly) justified.

According to Said's analysis, Orientalist scholarship may appear dry and irrelevant to the imperial designs of the western European powers, concerned as it was with philology, obscure religious texts or the minutiae of the life of 'Orientals'. However, this body of knowledge was, in Said's view, a major element of the rational justification for imperialism and colonialism. Imperial and colonial rule was effective, in part, because of the knowledge it utilised for the rule and subjugation of 'Orientals'. This was one direct use of Orientalist scholarship, but, Said argues, Orientalist scholarship did more that merely provide useful snippets of information for the imperial powers which they could then use. Scholarship is not merely a mine from which the dictators can pick their jewels. Rather scholarship is intimately formed by, and helps to form, a particular culture – academics are not divorced from the society in which they live. Hence, the Orientalists were inspired by, and helped to solidify, a particular conception of the 'Orient', and in so doing reflected (or helped create) a certain conception of the 'West' which stood in opposition to the 'Orient'. Oriental scholarship was part of a power structure in which the West dominated the East (in particular, the Muslim East). The West was objective, dispassionate and rational, the Orient was biased, guided by emotions and irrational. The cultural superiority of the West, according to these 'Enlightenment' criteria, was obvious. Hence, Orientalism helped to create both a view of the Orient, but also the self-view of the West.

A large part of Said's work concentrates on how scholars of Islam created a certain image of Muslims and Muslim tradition, how this image has infiltrated Western culture and how it contributes to any full explanation of Western political involvement in the Middle East. Western attitudes towards Arabs and Muslims is infected by the view that Arabs/Muslims are exotic, backward, passionate and, ultimately, closed to rational engagement. Hence, colonialism (or, after independence, neo-colonialism) is the only 'appropriate' response from the West. Through this lens, Said says, one can understand, for example, US policy in Palestine/Israel. This, of course, is an inaccurate depiction of the Arab and Muslim world. There is no 'Arab mind' or 'Oriental attitude' or 'Muslim mentality'. These are inaccurate generalisations of the multifarious and complex societies and communities of Muslims, who hold a variety of different self- (and other-) perceptions. Hence, for Said, the academic tradition of 'Orientalism' does a disservice to scholarship, Western culture and the 'Oriental' peoples and traditions (the subject of 'Oriental Studies'). It harms scholarship because it establishes paradigms of understanding which exclude the participation of 'Oriental' scholars, it harms Western culture because it contributes to imperialism (and ultimately racism), and it harms the traditions of 'the Orient' because it fails to respect their integrity and worth independent of being a counterweight to the excellence of Western culture. The validity of Said's views continue to be an important academic debate in Islamic studies: to what extent can Western notions of empiricism and scientific proof be applied to religious phenomena as texts (such as the Qur'an) or mystical experiences? If a scholar criticises, for example, the Muslim version of a series of historical phenomena, does this make the scholar an Orientalist? Can a non-Muslim scholar study Islam in the same way that a Muslim scholar studies Islam? These debates have had a variety of different effects on how (and which) academics are hired at Western universities, how the discipline of Islamic studies is taught there and, ultimately, how Islam is understood in Western culture.

References

King (1999), Said (2003), Turner (1984).

ROBERT GLEAVE

ORNAMENT

The most obvious feature of Middle Eastern ornament is that it enfolds, wraps, and drapes the building or object that it decorates but is not integral to its structure. It is essentially a brilliant and versatile pattern of a rich vocabulary of designs easily transferred between contrasting media such as wall surfaces, vaults of domes, ceramic tiles and dishes, metalwork and textiles. Islamic ornament inherited the decorative repertoire of late Classical Antiquity – acanthus leaves and vine scroll – and of the ancient Middle East – formal palmettes, pine cones, stylised birds and fantastic beasts – which contributed to a stylistic interpretation based on a balance of geometric and foliate forms. Within this profusion, a disciplined order emerges which classifies Islamic ornament into three main divisions – calligraphy, geometry and botany.

Calligraphy has a unique place in Islamic ornament both as a means of recording Arabic, the language of the Qur'an, and for its remarkable variations and flexibility. From relatively austere beginnings in the angular Kufic script of early monuments and Qur'anic manuscripts, many cursive and supple forms evolved which contribute to the decorative repertoire. Kufic itself, by the tenth century AD, had grown into an exuberant variation where the vertical strokes of letters interlaced before terminating in spiralling foliage in a style much used in manuscripts of North Africa and Spain. *Naskh* and *thuluth*, which are more fluent scripts, apart from their use in administrative documents, acquired an independent ornamental life in the bands and medallions of inscriptions which framed *mihrabs*, ran along colonnades and enfolded minarets. Spectacular decorative effects were achieved in polychrome Iranian tilework by entwining rows of calligraphy in different colours against a background of spiralling foliage or interlocking geometrical forms. Ottoman Turkish ornament stretches the boundaries of calligraphy to create individual monograms – *tughras* – for each sultan in *divani* script and birds, lions, etc., all shaped from the letters of inscriptions.

The importance of calligraphy is inseparable from geometry and mathematics, which were required to calculate the proportions of individual letters and their position in a decorative scheme. Geometry also made the most striking contribution to the dominance of surface pattern in Islamic ornaments through the creation of infinitely repetitive and extended combinations of triangles, hexagons, octagons and radial stars which were particularly effective in borders and panels of polychrome mosaic tilework, carved and inlaid wooden doors and frontispieces of illuminated manuscripts picked out in blue and gold. Geometric calculations are essential for the construction of the honeycomb or stalactite *muqarnas*, the ideal design for continuous surface pattern which are seen to great effect in the lacelike stucco version that lines the domes and arches of the Alhambra.

Geometry is both softened and texturally enriched through the inclusion of plant motifs which are often present as a dynamic background to calligraphy and as contrasting borders and panels beside formal arrangements of hexagons and octagons and as compositions in their own right. The niches of an otherwise sharply angled *muqarnas* in polychrome tile mosaic can be concealed by intricate foliage designs. Here the arabesque is the most successful motif, capable of interpretation in all media, trained into borders, friezes, roundels and medallions to suit architecture or object. It is an accomplished fusion of the vine and a split palmette, which allows stems and tendrils to scroll and interweave in all directions. Later motifs of Chinese inspiration – peonies, lotus, cloud bands and dragons – enter the repertoire, which again is further increased by the naturalistic carnations, tulips and hyacinths of Ottoman Turkish decoration from the sixteenth century onwards. Brilliant and confident examples of total Islamic ornament may be seen in the Alhambra, the *madrasas* of medieval Fez and the mosques of seventeenth-century Isfahan.

References

Baer (1998), Critchlow (1976), Golombek (1988: 25–30).

JENNIFER SCARCE

OSMAN I (r. 1281– 1324)

Osman I was the son of Ertugrul. In about AD 1300, he established a principality in north-western Anatolia. By the time of his death, he controlled the countryside between the Sakarya valley and the Sea of Marmara.

References

Beldiceanu-Steinherr (2000), Imber (1990: 18–19).

COLIN IMBER

OSMAN I (r. 1618–22)

Ottoman sultan, son of Ahmed I. He tried to restore the fortunes of the Ottoman Empire by leading a campaign against Poland in 1621, and reforming institutions. Fearing that he was plotting to abolish the Corps, the Janissaries murdered him in 1623, reinstating Mustafa.

References

Imber (2002: 78–9), Mantran (1989a: 233–4), Piterberg (2003).

COLIN IMBER

OSMAN III (r. 1754–7)

Ottoman sultan, son of Mustafa II. He ascended the throne in old age. His most significant appointment was of the reforming Grand Vizier, Koca Ragib Pasha.

References

Mantran (1989b: 269).

COLIN IMBER

OTTOMAN EMPIRE

The Ottoman Empire began as a small state in Bithynia, Anatolia in the late thirteenth century, one of many buffer states between the area previously under Saljuq rule and the Byzantine empire. The former had been under Mongol Il-Khanid control, at first as a vassal state and later under direct rule. The latter had lost its Anatolian lands to the Muslims. Between these two great empires, a number of small Turkish Muslim states emerged, one of which was to expand and form the Ottoman Empire.

Sögud (in modern Turkish Söğut), in north-western Anatolia, was settled by Turks during the Saljuq period, and, according to Ottoman historians, the area was given as a fiefdom to a Turkish military hero, Ertoghrul. Ertoghrul's son, 'Othman inherited the fiefdom on his father's death, in around 1281. From there, he began to expand the area under his control. Ottoman historical tradition attributes victories over the Byzantines to 'Othman, after whom the 'Othmanli (or in European sources, Ottoman) dynasty is named. These marked the beginnings of Ottoman expansion into Byzantine lands, for the Muslim lands to the east were more heavily fortified and, hence, unavailable for immediate capture. Whether these conquests are best characterised as raids (*ghazi*) against the Byzantine 'infidels', or were part of a more developed expansionist plan is a matter of dispute amongst historians. Some have even suggested that much of the information in the chronicles is designed to legitimise subsequent Ottoman power, and, hence, cannot be used as an uncritical source for 'Othman's activities. Whichever of the various versions proves most convincing, 'Othman is considered the founder of the Ottoman royal lineage, and his exploits mark the founding of the Ottoman Empire.

'Othman's son Orkhan perhaps did more than his father to shape the future direction of the empire, through his subjugation of the Byzantine areas of eastern Greece. He came to power in AD 1324, and proceeded to capture Byzantine strongholds one by one. This was done either by treaty or through military action. By the 1330s, Ibn Battuta visited the area and described Orkhan's military state as one of the strongest in Anatolia. Orkhan's power was to grow as he intervened in the Byzantine civil war of AD 1341–7. His troops were allowed to pillage the Greek countryside, and Orkhan's military experts were to gain first-hand knowledge of Byzantine territory. This latter was to prove useful in subsequent campaigns.

Orkhan was clearly not worried about forming alliances with Christian nations when the military need arose. In AD 1351 he allied himself with the Genoese in their war with the Venetians, leading to a treaty with Genoa. Meanwhile Orkhan's son, Sulayman, embarked on military operations on European soil, taking the fortress of Kallipolis (Gallipoli), and further pushing back the boundaries of Ottoman control. When Orkhan died in AD 1360 and his son Murad became Sultan, the Ottomans were clearly the greatest threat to both the Muslim kingdoms of Anatolia, and the Byzantines. Murad I continued his father's (and grandfather's) remarkable gains by conquering land to the west of the Byzantine capital, Constantinople. The Byzantines were being surrounded and strangled by the Ottoman advances, and it was only a matter of time before the Ottomans would decide to bring a permanent end to the Byzantine empire. Murad, however, was content to allow the Byzantines limited control of an ever-decreasing area. He had his eyes on the greater prize of the Balkans. In AD 1371, he fought the Serbians at Maritsa, inflicting a blow on Serbian power and forcing them to pay a tribute to the Ottomans. They were further defeated in the battle of Kosovo in AD 1389, though Murad fell in battle. Bulgarian lands also fell to Ottoman military control. In time Murad's son, Bayazid I was forced to turn his attention to the Muslim areas of eastern Anatolia. After quelling uprisings in parts of Ottoman Anatolia, he embarked on expansionist expeditions into Asia Minor. He did not ignore the European Ottoman lands though, and in AD 1396, he engineered the great victory over the Christian allied forces of Hungary, France and Germany. However, his policy of conquest in Asia Minor provoked Timur, the Mongol ruler of central Asia and eastern Iran. Timur invaded eastern Anatolia and inflicted a defeat upon the Ottoman forces at the battle of Ankara in 1402. Bayazid was captured and committed suicide in captivity in 1403.

The disaster of the Mongol victory left the Ottoman Empire in some disarray, divided between the European lands, under the rule of one of Bayazid's sons, Sulayman, and the remaining Anatolian possessions under the rule of another son, Mehmet. Only in 1413 was the Empire restored to unity, when Mehmet (Muhammad I) regained control of the European lands. Mehmet's

death in 1421, gave his son Murad II the throne. Murad continued military activity in Serbia, defeating the Hungarians at Varna in 1444 and again later at Kosovo in 1448. His son, Mehmet (Muhammad II), known as 'al-Fatih' (the Conqueror), was to assume the throne in 1451 (having held it briefly previously when his father had prematurely retired in 1444). He immediately prepared for the conquest of Constantinople and the final extermination of the Byzantine Empire. When his forces entered the city in 1453, they took it with relative ease. Some date the Ottoman Empire from this point as it was now that Mehmet established Istanbul (formerly Constantinople) as the new capital of the Empire and the great political and cultural achievements of the Ottomans began in earnest.

The capture of Constantinople was an event that had been recorded in the *hadith* of the Prophet Muhammad with apocalyptic connotations. Mehmet having achieved this feat, also acquired greatly increased charisma amongst both the Turks and other Muslim ethnic groups. His rule became intimately associated with Islam and the Muslim interest. Muslim enemies to Ottoman rule were at best misguided and at worst heretics. The Ottoman Empire became the embodiment of true Islam for its supporters.

In Istanbul, the Ottomans established all the elements of imperial rule. Administration (including an elaborate royal court system), law, military infrastructure, communications and education all became crucial parts of the Ottoman machinery. Mehmet, and his son Bayazid II were instrumental in this endeavour. Whilst they were interested in military expansion, they were also concerned to encourage internal stability. Under Bayazid's successor, Selim (Salim 'the Grim') Syria, Egypt and the rest of Asia Minor were incorporated into the Empire. Under Sulayman ('the Magnificent'), who came to the throne in 1520, the Ottoman's moved north-wards against the Hungarians. In 1521, Sulayman took Belgrade in his first European campaign. In his second cam-paign in 1526, he reached Buda. On yet another campaign in 1528, he pushed on for Vienna. There he laid siege to the city, but was forced to return because of the early arrival of winter weather. The siege of Vienna was the high water mark of Ottoman designs in Europe, and is remembered in Christian sources as a narrow escape from the imposition of the infidel rule of the Turk upon the Christian heartlands of Europe. Sulay-man did try, once more, to penetrate the European arena in his fourth campaign (1529–33), but this was not nearly as threatening as his previous attempt.

Sulayman is also known for his reform of the legal system of the Empire, and for his imposition of a reli-gious, *shari'a*-based system of laws. Sulayman made Abu'l-Su'ud his *shaykh al-Islam* in 1545. This classically trained scholar was responsible for the imple-mentation of the law within the Otto-man domains. He held this post after Sulayman's death, and into the reign of Selim II. Abu'l-Su'ud's achievements are the stuff of academic legend – his literary prowess, his learning, his great diplomatic skill and his persuasive argumentation. He is credited with the supposed marriage of the *qanun* (the administrative law of Ottoman Empire) with the *shari'a* – or rather the adoption of the *shari'a* as the *qanun* of the Empire. To what extent this elevated reputation is justified is a matter of dispute. It is clear though that the legal reforms under Abu'l-Su'ud greatly enhanced the 'Islamic' nature of the Ottoman Empire, and confirmed the Hanafi *madhhab* as the law school of the

Empire. The sultans, without embar-rassment, saw themselves as the caliphs of all Muslims.

In addition to a sophisticated legal system, the Ottomans also developed an impressive administrational infra-structure. The population as a whole was divided into two distinct classes: the *re'aya* was the population at large who were defined really by their ability (and duty) to pay taxes. The *'askari* were descended from army stock and were viewed as servants of the Sultan. They were exempt from taxes and hence, over time, acquired much imperial wealth. They were employed by the Sultan and owed their livelihood (and life) to his whim. The administration system reflected this division of the population, which was only seriously reformed in the nineteenth century.

The cultural achievements, more nar-rowly defined, of the Ottomans are worthy of note. Architecture, carpets, literature and other fine arts flourished. The distinctive Ottoman-style mosque design, consisting of a small cube with a slender minaret, was probably devel-oped in Anatolia prior to the rise of the Ottomans, but its development into multi-domed complexes, such as the famous mosques of Istanbul, was the result of an imperial confidence which imbued most Ottoman architecture after 1453. Similarly, Ottoman carpets were much exported and prized, though per-haps they did not reach the high demand of Persian carpets. In literature, one finds Ottoman scholars writing extensively in Arabic and Persian – the former for the religious sciences and the latter used for poetry. Indeed, the Otto-man literati were heavily influenced by the high Persian culture of the Timurid courts of Herat and Samarqand. But the scholars of the Ottoman Empire also used Ottoman Turkish to compose offi-cial correspondence, histories, poetry and occasionally used it even for religious works also.

Finally, recognition should be made of the diversity of religious belief within the Ottoman territory. Apart from minorities such as Jews and Christians found throughout the Ottoman provinces, there were large numbers of 'heterodox' Muslim groups. Anatolia was famous as a breeding ground for wayward, extremist (*ghali*) Shi'i groups. Indeed the Safavids were originally an Anatolian Shi'i Sufi Order before assuming power in Iran in 1501. The heterodox nature of the Safavids (they were not only Twelver Shi'a, they were accused of being *ghulat* as well) played a role in the conflicts between the two empires. The Ottoman period also saw the enrichment and proliferation of Sufi groups – the *madrasas*, the Sufi lodges and the Khaniqahs of the Balkans and Asia Minor are testament to the vigorous activity of Sufi groups under Ottoman rule. Most famous amongst these are the Mevlavi order (taking its teaching from Mawlana Jalal al-Din Rumi, who was buried at Konya) and the less high-brow Bektashiyya (founded by Hajji Bektash Wala and with definite Shi'i elements). The importance of the latter can be traced to their influence within the Janissaries, the imperial elite troop.

In the seventeenth and eighteenth centuries, the Ottoman Empire reached the height of its geographical area and its political power. The Empire had expanded to its maximum limit and was enforcing its rule in most areas with mixed effectiveness. Inevitably, decadence and decline began to appear. Increasingly, Sultans stayed in Istanbul and did not accompany their armies into battle, becoming divorced from one key element of their legitimacy – their Ottoman military prowess. Viziers and statesmen became more important. The vizier Soqollu Mehmet Pasha, for example, served under three sultans and succeeded in maintaining the aura of veneration around the monarch, whilst gradually developing his own power. The Janissaries became a power base separate from the Sultan (though they remained theoretically loyal to him). The Janissaries and Sipahis (cavalrymen) often directed the crucial events within the Empire, including the deposition of Mehmet (Muhammad IV) in 1687 after his disastrous campaigns in Europe.

The eighteenth century saw further decline in the power of the court at Istanbul. In 1730, the Janissaries rebelled, causing the Ahmed III to leave the throne, the statesmen of the court began to seek ways of reforming the Empire in such a way as to guarantee its survival. Foreigners were brought in to try and reinvigorate discipline within the army. Claude-Alexander Comte de Bonneval, a French nobleman who had converted (for convenience, it seems) to Islam, was hired by Sultan Mahmud I (r. 1730–54). François de Tott worked with a similar brief under Mustafa III (r. 1757–74). The lack of success of these hirelings was obvious, and when Selim III (r. 1789–1807) attempted to institute a 'new order' (*nizam-i*) of troops, the Janissaries rebelled again.

In the nineteenth century, the need for reform gained further momentum, and on the succession of 'Abd al-Majid to the throne in 1839, a royal rescript signalling the start of the Tanzimat reforms was issued. Egyptian forces were breaking away from the Ottoman Porte and the financial difficulties of the Empire were apparent to both the court officials and the Western powers. The 'Beneficial Reforms', as they were called, initially appeared vague or haphazard – to secure the life and property of all classes of society, a reform of the taxation system and a reduction in length of compulsory military conscription. Within them, however, was a promise of a system of government modelled on Western methods, championed by Rashid Pasha, the Foreign Minister, who had spent much time in Europe as an Ottoman ambassador. The sultans themselves had little influence on the course of reform, as they had long become restricted in their personal power by viziers and other court officials. It was only with Sultan 'Abd al-Hamid II (r. 1874–1909) that the sultan once again dominated proceedings.

The Tanzimat reforms included educational reforms (such as the establishment of schools and universities), local parliaments (*majlis*) were instituted and mixed tribunals for disputes between Christians (foreigners) and Muslims were established. Reforms of the financial system proceeded at a slower pace, but the standardisation of coinage in 1844 brought some economic security. In 1850, the first law statute (a commercial code on a French model) was promulgated. The Crimean War of 1853–6 demonstrated to many the further need for reform, and actually quickened the pace of change. In 1856, a modern bank was established in Istanbul. In 1858, a criminal code of law was introduced, reducing the power of traditional classes like the *'ulama'*. Whilst there was a conservative backlash (an opposition movement in 1859 was uncovered and quashed), the reforms generally continued throughout the 1860s with the internal organisation of the different religious communities regularised and set down in constitutions. The 'Mejelle' civil code was introduced in 1869. Whilst the Mejelle contained elements of Islamic legal rulings, taken mainly from the Hanafi school, the process of codification robbed the *shari'a* of its dynamic *qadi*-court system.

Hand in hand with the reforms came an increase in public debate and the publication of newspapers and journals. This intellectual activity gave rise to the foundation of reform-minded societies and institutes. Members of these groups pushed for greater reform, often facing resistance from the Court. The 'Young Turks' association, for example, was founded in 1865, consisting of civil servants. They were beneficiaries of the new education system, and were pushing for reform in the Ottoman Empire, preaching pan-Islamism and constitutionalism. The constitution promulgated by Sultan 'Abd al-Hamid II of 1876 was a reflection of this general mood, and was modelled, once again, on Western constitutions. Documents such as this were supposed to ensure that the discourse of 'rights' (*huquq*) became embedded in the Ottoman system. The constitution which envisaged a parliament being established was only really activated in 1908, following the period of 'despotism' (*istibdad*) of 'Abd al-Hamid.

The Ottomans' decision to support the Central Powers during the First World War was a fatal error. The Empire came under increased pressure from both Russia and Britain, who began to sponsor independence movements in various parts of the crumbling Ottoman Empire. By the end of the war, and the armistice of 1918, the Ottomans were roundly defeated and Istanbul was occupied by Allied forces. Former provinces of the Empire were formed into mandates of the Allied powers, most conspicuously Mesopotamia, Jordan and Palestine came under British control, Syria under the French, and Greece and Italy also claimed their share. As the Istanbul government failed, a national movement emerged, centred around the military figure of Mustafa Kemal. Kemal argued for a secular, modern Turkish republic to arise from the ashes of the Ottoman Empire. Turkey consisted of Anatolia for Kemal, the provinces (Arab and Balkan) of the Ottoman Empire had held back the modernisation of the Turkish people. His argument, made as it was in the ruins of the Empire, was persuasive. At the first Great National Assembly in April 1920, he was elected president by Turkish military and political luminaries. He led a programme of resistance to the occupying powers and in October 1922 succeeded in winning an armistice with the Allied powers of Great Britain, France and Italy. In November he called a second Great National Assembly, which abolished the Ottoman sultanate, and at the Lausanne Conference he secured Turkey's independence. The Ottoman Empire was formally disbanded on 3 March 1924, when the Assembly abolished the caliphate of the Muslims, a title held by the Ottoman sultan. There were pleas to retain the caliphate, and for the caliph/sultan to operate as a symbolic head of the Muslim people, but Kemal (or Ataturk as he became known) was primarily concerned with the secularisation of the Turkish nation. He had no interest in maintaining symbols of Muslim unity. The last holder of the post of sultan, Mehmet VI, fled Turkey in 1922. The last caliph, 'Abd al-Majid II, appointed when Mehmet VI fled, left Turkey and died in Paris in 1944.

The end of the Ottoman Empire was a disaster for those Muslims who had hopes of Muslim unity and the establishment of a trans-national Islamic *umma*. The abolition of the caliphate, however, was a more serious blow to the classical theory of Muslim political organisation. The caliphs of the past, even when they have been weak and dominated by viziers and sultans, had represented the unity of all (Sunni) Muslim peoples. Many wondered whether the loss of the caliphate indicated the end of the possibility of a Muslim nation. As subsequent history has shown, Islam generally, and Sunni Islam specifically, does not require a central caliph to survive, as Roman Catholicism needs a pope. Certainly, Muslim religious authorities have emerged and proved themselves necessary since the end of the caliphate, but none has commanded the single, 'papal' authority supposedly vested in the caliph of classical theory. The diversity of belief within the Sunni Muslim community is clearly one of its strengths, and a central caliphate, in which religious orthodoxy is decreed by diktat, would probably, over time, have hindered the health of Islam. Orthodoxy always produces heretics who, by the logic of system, must be excommunicated. It could be argued that the end of the Ottoman Empire and the caliphate ensured the survival of Islam as a vibrant faith in the modern period, since the possibility of a single, authoritarian religious authority was definitively abolished.

References

Imber (1990), Inalcik (1973), Parry (1976).

ROBERT GLEAVE

OTTOMANS (late thirteenth century–1924)

The Ottomans arose out of bands of Turkish *ghazis* or raiders coming westwards in the wake of the Saljuqs. From a base in north-western Anatolia, they subdued rivals and crossed over into Europe and began the conquest of the Balkans, the beginning of a process which, many centuries later when the Ottoman tide had long receded, was to leave significant Muslim communities in regions like Albania, Bosnia and western

Thrace. Sultan Muhammad II captured Constantinople in 1453, and rulers like Sulayman the Magnificent penetrated deep into central Europe, overthrowing local powers such as the Serbian and Hungarian monarchies, with a high point in the abortive attempt to capture Vienna in 1683. Ottoman power now receded. They began a protracted rear-guard action against resurgent Christian powers such as Austria and Russia, nationalist revolts took place in Serbia, Greece and Bulgaria and, by 1914, they were reduced to only a small foothold in Europe. The Empire had, however, been the standard-bearer of a rich, composite Turkish–Persian–Arabic culture, with the sultans assuming the position of moral heads of Sunni Islam and, lat-terly, tacitly being regarded as caliphs, the patrons of peripheral communities of Muslims as far away as India, China and sub-Saharan Africa, although impotent to provide any material help for them. Turkey's disastrous decision in 1915 to enter the First World War on the side of the Central Powers led to the dismemberment of the empire, with the new nationalist leader Kemal Ataturk abolishing the Ottoman sultanate and caliphate by 1924.

References

Bosworth (1996: No. 130), Gibb and Bosworth (1960–2003), Inalcik (1973), Mantran (1989).

C. E. BOSWORTH

P

PAHLAVIS (1925–79)

The commander Rida Khan, who assumed the family name of Pahlavi, became Shah by a vote of the Persian National Assembly after the collapse of the Qajars. He introduced modernisation after the example of Kemal Ataturk in Turkey, including women's education and the discouragement of veiling, but inevitably made enemies among the Shi'ite clergy. Similar policies were pursued by his son Muhammad after 1941, but by the 1970s, political opposition and religious reaction overwhelmed the Pahlavi monarchy, which was succeeded by the Islamic Republic.

References

Gibb and Bosworth (1960–2003), Lenczowski (1978), Hambly (1991: 213–93).

C. E. BOSWORTH

PALACE

Few palaces have survived in the Islamic world, most probably because there was no religious and communal justification for building them. A ruler would construct a palace that also combined the functions of administrative centre, fortification and family residence at a strategic site. Evidence for early and medieval palaces is fragmentary depending on the results of archeological excavation and contemporary literary evidence. The best example of an Islamic palace is the Topkapi Saray at Istanbul begun by Mehmet II (1451–81), which functioned as the centre of Ottoman power. The superb location at the tip of the Golden Horn cut off by water and retaining wall from the city, while ensuring maximum security for the ruler, his court and family, ensured a long period of occupation from the late fifteenth to the mid-nineteenth century. Within high walls the palace was a complex of four courts with accommodation for soldiers, government officials, personal servants and retainers and the members of the ruler's extensive family in a sequence of barracks, audience chambers, cloisters and individual pavilions which also illustrate the main forms of Ottoman architecture and decoration.

References

Necipoglu (1991), Penzer (1936).

JENNIFER SCARCE

PANTHEISM

Belief in many gods. At the heart of Islam is the notion of the oneness, unity (*tawhid*) and singular nature of the Divine. The *shahada*, the most important of Islam's five pillars – 'I witness that there is no god except Allah and I witness that Muhammad is the messenger of Allah' – affirms this principle and its utterance affirms one's faith. *Mushrikun* (those who associate) is the term given to those idolators and pagans who associate something with Allah. In the pre-Islamic period there were acknowledged to be other gods even as there was a notion of an ultimately supreme divinity. Islam also admits the existence of *jinn* and angels, but Allah himself is the supreme, indivisible creator in the universe and so unique. Hence, Allah has no equals or partners. Thus, pantheism is a sin. *Shirk* (the act of this associating) has been attributed to certain philosophers and especially some Sufis, and especially 'folk' Sufism, in so far as the latter is identified with quest for union with the Divine. See Q.4:116.

References

Rahman (1979: 11–12, 30–31).

See also: **Allah; angels; Islam and Indian religions;** *jinn; mushrikun; shirk*

ANDREW J. NEWMAN

PERIPLUS OF THE ERYTHRAEAN SEA

This brief work from classical antiquity is a guide to the main harbours and trading settlements along the coasts of the Indian Ocean and connected seas as they would probably be known and of interest to navigators and merchants who traded from the Egyptian Red Sea ports. It belongs to a number of such guides to various coasts and harbours, all of which bear the Greek title περίπλουσ, 'circumnavigation'.

The author of the *Periplus* is not known. It used to be ascribed to the second-century AD historian Arrian, primarily because it came next to a *Periplus* by him in the better of the two manuscripts in which it is preserved. But its language and style are quite different from his and rule out his authorship. No more can be said about the author than that he spoke and wrote in demotic Greek, lived in Egypt and was probably intimately connected with the sea and trade. Whether he was Greek or Egyptian by birth is difficult to decide.

Internal evidence, most clearly references to 'Manbanos' (Chapter 41), 'Saraganes' and 'Sandanes' (Chapter 52), who were rulers in parts of western India in the early second-century AD, points to a date for the *Periplus* of around AD 100, and the period between 95 and AD 130 has been suggested as likely. However, there is no consensus on this point, and dates as early as AD 50 have also been put forward. This being so, the work, with its catalogue of ports, lists of trading stuffs available in various regions, and passing mentions of significant places in the hinterland of the shorelines it plots, is best seen as affording an insight into the coastal navigational networks of the early common era in the Red Sea, Arabian Gulf and Indian Ocean, and of the trading patterns and social relations then obtaining.

The *Periplus* comprises sixty-six short paragraphs or chapters that can be grouped into three general sections. The first, Chapters 1–18, begins from the classical port of Muos Hormos at the northern end of the Red Sea and traces the western coast down around the Horn of Africa and south along the east African coast as far as Rhapta (probably south of Zanzibar), after which 'the unexplored ocean curves round to the west, and ... mingles with the western sea' (Chapter 18). The second part, Chapters 19–36, begins again from the northern end of the Red Sea and traces its eastern coast down along the Hijaz, southern Arabia and then round to the southern shore of the Arabian Gulf to 'an established mart called Apologou, lying near Pasinou Kharax and the river Euphrates' (Chapter 35). And the third part, Chapters 37–66, continues along the northern shore of the Arabian Gulf and the western coast of India, round Cape Comorin and up into the Bay of Bengal as far as the Ganges, with beyond little-known 'Thina' which 'is said to border on the ports of Pontos and the Caspian Sea' (Chapter 64). It ends by looking further to places that 'on account of excessive winters, hard frosts, and inaccessible country, are unexplored – perhaps also on account of some divine power of the gods' (Chapter 66).

The *Periplus of the Erythraean Sea* has been edited many times. The standard edition is by Frisk (1927). An excellent English translation is by Huntingford (1980) (from which the quotations above have been taken). There is also a parallel text and English translation by Casson (1989). For what light may be cast by the work on trading patterns in Arabia before the rise of Islam, see Crone (1987).

DAVID THOMAS

PICKTHALL, MARMADUKE (1875–1936)

Marmaduke Pickthall was the first native speaker of English to translate the Holy Qur'an into English. But he was also a successful novelist, a journalist and a propagandist for the Ottoman Empire. For the last ten years of his life he had a number of posts serving the Nizam of Hyderabad.

Pickthall was born in London in 1875, one of twelve children of a Suffolk Anglican priest. He went to Harrow School and developed an early skill in languages. He failed in attempts to enter the Royal Engineers and then the Levant Consular Service and was at a loss what to do. A family contact gave him the opportunity in 1894 of a trip to Jerusalem. He stayed for two years – two years that changed his life.

During these two years he travelled extensively in Palestine and Syria, staying in villages and *khans*, 'followed the customs of the people of the land in all respects' and acquired fluency in spoken Arabic. During a visit to Damascus he was dissuaded from embracing Islam by the *shaykh al-'ulama'* of the Umayyad mosque.

He returned to England just short of his twenty-first birthday and married a childhood sweetheart, Muriel Smith. They had no children. For the next twenty years he worked as a journalist and writer, publishing first short stories. His first novel, *All Fools*, published in 1900, was a gauche social novel based on a London cramming school. He was simultaneously writing his second published novel that was a masterpiece. *Saïd the Fisherman* was published in 1903 and tells the story of a Palestinian fisherman who gets caught up in the massacres of Damascus in 1860. In it he draws on a storehouse of sensitive observation about dialect, behaviour and popular attitudes.

In England he alternated novels of the Near East with novels of social life of contemporary England, and especially East Anglia. In the years before the

First World War he was writing in a number of journals. He was alarmed at ill-informed criticism of the Ottoman Empire, and in 1913 went to live in Constantinople for seven months. He brushed up his Turkish and his regular reports for *The New Age* were published in 1914 as *With the Turk in Wartime*.

When war broke out between Britain and Turkey, Pickthall was heartbroken. He became a ferocious spokesman for Turkey, arguing for a separate peace, and deploring the hostility against Turkey and Islam. During the war he became associated with the London Muslim community, at that time mostly Indian expatriates and a few British converts. In November 1917 he gave a lecture on 'Islam and Progress' at the Muslim Literary Society, and declared his acceptance of Islam. The occasion was deeply moving, one eyewitness recording:

> With his hands folded on his breast, and an expression of serene contentment on his face, he recited that famous prayer which concludes the second chapter of the Holy Qur'an. When he sat down, every one of his hearers felt that they had lived through, during that one short hour, the most remarkable period in his or her life.

Immediately Pickthall became one of the leaders of British Islam. He regular lectured on aspects of Islam. He led the prayers at the Woking Mosque for 'Id al-Fitr in 1919 and was for several months editor of the *Islamic Review*.

When the war was over, Pickthall was at a loss. His creativity in producing novels and stories was diverted to writing about Islam. With his record of apostasy from Christianity and his sympathy for a belligerent enemy of his own country, Britain had little to offer. Fortunately, Indian contacts helped to find

him a job as editor of the *Bombay Chronicle*. He emigrated in September 1920 and spent the next fifteen years in India. Pickthall was welcomed by the Bombay Khilafat Committee and was invited all over India to lecture. In 1924 he was invited to work for the Nizam of Hyderabad. There he spent over ten happy years working in several capacities. First he was Principal of Chadarghat High School for Boys, and then was in charge of training staff for the Nizamate's public service.

But his greatest work was literary. In 1928 the Nizam gave Pickthall leave of absence to complete his translation of the Qur'an. This was published by A. A. Knopf of New York in 1930 and has been in print in numerous editions ever since. Pickthall acknowledged that the Qur'an, as the word of God, could not be 'translated'. He thus called his work, *The Meaning of the Glorious Koran*, as if it were an extended *tafsir* in the English language. He made himself familiar with Eastern and Western scholarship on the Qur'an and prefaced the work with a concise biography of the Prophet Muhammad.

For ten years Pickthall also edited a new journal, *Islamic Culture*. The journal was in English and included articles by authorities, both Muslim and non-Muslim, of a high academic standard. As Editor, Pickthall was in touch with Muslims all over the world. Shortly before he died, he wrote

> Our Hyderabad is a sort of capital for all Muslims. All kinds of people come there from afar, attracted by the fabled wealth of His Exalted Highness. And many of them used to call on me at my office, or greet me in the mosque, and tell me things.

Pickthall left Hyderabad and returned to England at the beginning of 1935. A year later, in May 1936, he died in Cornwall and is buried in the Muslim Cemetery, Brookwood, south of London.

Pickthall's Islam was open and liberal. Conservative in habits and in (British) politics, he found an anchor in pan-Islam. His translation of the Holy Qur'an is the best-known among anglophone Muslims. His liberal teachings are remembered in regular reprints of lectures he gave in Madras in 1925, *The Cultural Side of Islam*. His novels, though praised by H. G. Wells, D. H. Lawrence and E. M. Forster, are today remembered by only a handful of discriminating critics.

References

Clark (1986).

PETER CLARK

PILGIMAGE (*ZIYARAT AL-AMKAN AL-MUQADDASA*)

See: **al-Hajj**; **'umra.**

PILLARS OF ISLAM (*ARKAN AL-DIN*)

There are five pillars, or 'supports' (*arkan*) of Islam. They constitute the universally accepted religious obligations and duties of a Muslim. Separate entries on each of the following are included in this volume.

1. *al-shahada*: This is the testimony, the act of bearing witness, to the two central beliefs of every Muslim, namely, 'There is no god but God (*Allah*), and Muhammad is the Messenger (*rasul*) of God'. These words are whispered by Muslim parents into the ear of every newborn child, repeated daily by every practising Muslim throughout life, and uttered finally by the faithful on the point of death.

2. *al-salat*: This refers to the ritual prayer and worship in Islam, to the five daily sequences of obligatory prayers prescribed for all Muslims, to be performed either congregationally in a mosque or individually, as circumstances allow, and after the necessary preliminary ablutions have been performed.

3. *al-zakat*: This is the obligation to give alms (usually on the basis of an annual payment of 2.5 per cent of one's gross personal resources of wealth or income) for specific charitable purposes, notably for the promotion of Islamic ideals, projects, and the alleviation of poverty in the community.

4. *al-sawm*: The word refers to the fast from dawn until dusk, undertaken annually by Muslims during the thirty days of the month of Ramadan.

5. *al-hajj*: For Muslims who are in a sufficiently good state of health to make the journey and to endure the physical rigours, this is the pilgrimage to Mecca and its environs. The *hajj*, made each year in the month of pilgrimage, is to be undertaken at least once in one's lifetime. Those who make it are expected to have sufficient personal resources to undertake the journey without neglecting their existing fiscal and other responsibilities.

What is sometimes called 'the sixth of the five pillars', should be mentioned in this context, although it is neither universally accepted in Islam nor considered as obligatory for all Muslims. Commonly assumed in the non-Islamic world to mean 'Holy War', *jihad* may also be interpreted as 'personal effort', 'striving', *fi sabil llah*, 'for the cause of' or 'on behalf of' God. In this spiritual sense *jihad* is identified as a continuing struggle to maintain the beliefs and values of Islam, and to extend the influence of these values and beliefs in areas of the world where they are not yet acknowledged.

References

Hourani (1991: 65–6, 147–51, 169), Momen (1985: 176–83).

EDWARD D. A. HULMES

PIR

A Persian term (also used in the Indian sub-continent) used for a Sufi guide. The respect accorded to the Sufi guide has led to some excesses so that Muhammad Iqbal referred to pirism in a derogatory fashion, hinting at the exploitation of followers.

References

Jahanbakhsh (1998: 129–47).

See also: *murshid*; *shaykh*

LLOYD RIDGEON

PIRI REIS B. HAJJI MEHMED (*c.* 1470–1553/4)

Turkish traveller, cartographer and author. Born, probably in Gallipoli, into a seafaring family, Piri Reis initially learned the art of navigation from his uncle, Kemal Reis, who between *c.* 1481 and 1495 appears to have earned a living as a corsair in the Mediterranean. In 1495, his uncle was summoned to serve in the Ottoman fleet, and from then until Kemal Reis's death in 1510 or 1511, Piri Reis participated in various naval assignments in the Mediterranean,

including the 1499–1502 war with Venice. Following the death of his uncle, Piri Reis returned to Gallipoli and devoted himself to cartography and the art of navigation.

Piri Reis's present reputation turns on two principal achievements: his 'world map', dated 1513, of which only about one-third has survived, preserved in the Istanbul Topkapi Saray Library, and a major navigational work, the *Kitab-i Bahriyye*, of which two versions exist, the first completed in 1521, the second reworked in 1526.

Of these two works, it is the world map that has deservedly attracted the more attention since its rediscovery in 1929, though some descriptions of it (including that of 'the oldest map of America') are clearly inaccurate. The extant portion of the map, for which Piri relied largely on Portuguese charts, shows the Atlantic Ocean with part of the coasts of Europe and Africa and a portion of the New World mainly consisting of South America; the remainder of the map, which included the remainder of Europe and Africa and all of Asia, was lost in unknown circumstances. The map was presented to Sultan Selim I in Egypt in 1517.

The main purpose of the *Kitab-i Bahriyye*, which was presented to Sultan Sulayman in 1525/6, was to provide a complete manual for Turkish navigators in the Aegean and Mediterranean seas. Based in the European tradition of portolans, the work consists of detailed descriptions, clearly derived from the author's own voyages, each chapter of the work being accompanied by a related chart.

In 1528/9, Piri Reis produced a second world map, of which only a fragment again survives, covering the north-western part of the Atlantic and the eastern coastal regions of the northern Americas. He appears then to have returned to naval duties, recapturing Aden in 1549 and besieging Hurmuz in 1552. He is said by the Ottoman historians to have been executed in Cairo for dereliction of duty, though some doubts have been raised over the likelihood of this fate, in view of his advanced age.

References

Afetinan (1975), Piri Reis (1935).

PAUL STARKEY

PLINY THE ELDER (AD 23–79)

Roman author, Gaius Plinius Secundus. Much of his wide-ranging work was lost, but *Historia Naturalis* (AD 77), a work divided into thirty-seven books, survived largely intact. Its lucid observations about astronomy, zoology, biology, botany and medicine continued to have a significant influence throughout the medieval period. His work contained many factual inaccuracies, but it has remained one of the principal sources on the ancient world as well as on other ancient scholars whose work has been lost. His accounts of the European landscape are detailed, and drawing on earlier Greek texts he also gave an account of the flora and fauna of the Middle East. He died as a result of the eruptions of Mount Vesuvius in August AD 79 while organising rescue efforts. His adopted son, Pliny the Younger, was a notable administrator and commentator.

References

Purcell (1998: 545–6), Stannard (1976: 572–3).

SIMON W. MURDEN

POTENTIALITY AND ACTUALITY

Potentiality and actuality are Aristotelian concepts that explain the movement of the thing from its possible existence (the potential stage) to its real existence in actuality. Aristotle also uses these terms to clarify the relationship between matter and form. Matter, the material part of a thing, can only exist when the thing takes shape through its form. In this sense matter is potential existence, while form is the actual power which transfers it from having potential existence to having a shape and existing in actuality. Arab and Muslim philosophers translated these both terms as *mumkin* (for potentiality) and *wajib* (for actuality). Ibn Sina was the first of the Arab philosophers to challenge this formula of Aristotle's and argue for the existence of two different types of actuality: actuality in itself and actuality through another. The former is attributed only to the Necessary Existence (God) and the latter to all other existents. In this theory, Ibn Sina considers the Aristotelian relationship between potentiality and actuality as illogical because there is no ground for attributing actuality (in itself) to form through which all things can be actualised. One has only to differentiate between the actual which has the power to perform this process and the actual that borrows its actuality and exists as a result. Thus, instead of the Aristotelian dualistic division of the possible and the actual, Ibn Sina makes a great contribution with his argument for the need for a third element (actual in itself) which bestows the power of actuality on form and consequently on all existing things. As a result, he transformed the Aristotelian formula of potentiality and actuality to a formula of essence (matter + form) and existence.

References

Ibn Sina (1960), Rahman (1981).

MAHA EL-KAISY FRIEMUTH

PRE-ISLAMIC ARABIA

The emerging picture of the geographical, economic, social and religious conditions in pre-Islamic Arabia is far from monochrome. Muslims describe pre-Islamic Arabia, especially the 100 years or so before the birth of the Prophet of Islam, Muhammad, in Mecca (*c.* AD 570), as the time of 'the Days of Ignorance' (*al-jahiliya*). This phrase reflects the belief of Muslims that their predecessors were in ignorance of the One True God, that they had no divinely inspired Prophet and no divinely revealed 'Book' of their own. To the west of the Arabian peninsula, al-Hijaz, an impressive barrier of mountains, runs north–south close to and parallel with the Red Sea. To the east and south lie the deserts of al-Nafud, al-Dahna', al-Harra, and al-Rub' al-Khali ('the Empty Quarter'). To the south-west lies the Yemen, a region of comparative fertility. Settled life in Arabia was virtually impossible outside the few oases and centres of trade such as Mecca and Medina.

The nomadic culture of the Bedouin was centred on the needs of small self-contained family units, owing allegiance to their elected *shaykhs*. In pre-Islamic Arabia there was neither religious nor political unity in Arabia, 'the Island of the Arabs' (*jazirat al-'arab*). Even so, the city of Mecca had long been visited by pilgrims from many parts of Arabia. In the weeks of truce, when the warring factions laid down their arms and when blood-feuds were temporarily suspended, pilgrims converged on the Ka'ba in Mecca to fulfil rites of pilgrimage and to honour or propitiate the gods, goddesses, whose benign or malign influence was believed to affect the course of daily life. These deities had their images inside the Ka'ba. Visitors came to participate in the vigorous life of the fairs that were held in and around the city. The cele-brations during these gatherings were often far from pious or decorous. In the city of Mecca, the annual influx of visitors presented logistical problems as well as commercial opportunities for the local residents. The Quraysh, the tribe into which Muhammad was to be born, had grown prosperous in Mecca as a result of their dominance of the camel caravans that passed through the city, halfway along the route to Damascus in the north or to the Yemen in the south. The prosperity of the Quraysh was increased by their position as guardians of the Ka'ba and by their control of the facilities provided for visiting pilgrims. Polytheism, self-indulgence, promiscuity and drunkenness characterised the activity to which Muhammad subsequently took exception in the name of Islam. His father's name was 'Abdallah, 'slave or servant of God'. After the revelations entrusted to Muhammad in the opening decades of the seventh century AD, this name was to receive a meaning which, according to Islamic belief, was obscured rather than unknown in pre-Islamic Arabia. Monotheism, however, was not unknown in pre-Islamic Arabia. Small communities of Jews, Monophysite Christians and individual *hanifs*, (solitaries who rejected polydaemonism) were among the first to be approached by Muhammad in his mission to deliver Arabia from the errors of polytheism.

In pre-Islamic Arabia, the peoples of the south established kingdoms in which trade rather than conquest was their preoccupation. Their economic prosperity was enhanced by trade in exotica from India, China and Somalia. Frankincense (a much-demanded aromatic), spices and silks were transported northwards along the ancient camel caravan routes to Damascus in Syria and thence into Mesopotamia in return for oils and grain. Inscriptions on stone and metal are the earliest records of their activity. The Sabaean and Minaean kingdoms, which flourished from the eighth to the first centuries BC, were the first to leave their mark on the history of the region. In the south-western parts of Arabia, the natural rainfall was conserved for centuries in pre-Islamic times by the construction of dams and elegant systems of irrigation. The best known was the dam built in Saba (biblical Sheba) at the capital, Ma'rib. Its ruins are visible today. These engineering projects made it possible for settled communities to prosper, and for the civilisations of south Arabia to develop and flourish. These ancient city-states enjoyed levels of civilisation not known elsewhere in the island of the Arabs prior to the rise of Islam, although they fell into decline before the birth of Muhammad. In the sixth century AD it was the Abyssinians who came to southern Arabia, 'arriving as helpers and staying as conquerors'. In their capital, San'a' they erected a cathedral of which nothing now remains. In the year of Muhammad's birth, 'The Year of the Elephant', their expedition against Mecca was repulsed. A generation later his mission was to transform the religious, political, social, and economic life of the peninsula, and far beyond its borders.

References

Doughty (1926), Hitti (1973: 3–108), Stark (1945: 1–43), Thesiger (1959).

See also: *jahiliya*; **Mecca; Medina; Muhammad ibn 'Abdallah, the Prophet of Islam**
EDWARD D. A. HULMES

PROFESSION OF FAITH, ISLAMIC (*AL-SHAHADA*)

The word *shahada* means 'testimony' in two senses: the first religious, the second legal. In the first sense, it refers to the 'bearing witness' (*al-shahada*) to the central beliefs of Islam in a daily act of religious obligation required of every Muslim. This 'testimony', like all the religious duties performed by a Muslim, is validated by a preliminary declaration of intention (*niyya*), which serves to guard the worshipper from acts of merely thoughtless or perfunctory remembrance. The profession of faith consists of two brief credal affirmations. The first expresses the rigorous monotheism of Islam: *la ilaha illa llah* (there is no god other than Allah). The second expresses belief in the uniqueness of Muhammad, serving at the same time to emphasise that he is a created human being and in no circumstances to be 'associated' with God, the Creator: *muhammadun rasul llah* (Muhammad is the Messenger of God). Taken together, these two statements constitute what may reasonably be called the creed (*'aqida*) of Islam. To recite it with conviction in the presence of two Muslim witnesses is to become a Muslim. Once this has been done, there can be no retraction without apostasy and the risk of incurring the appropriate penalty according to Islamic law. In its legal sense, *shahada* is the statement of an eyewitness (*shahid*) in cases where a civil contract between parties is being arranged (for example, a marriage) or where an infringement of the law is under investigation (for example, a case of suspected adultery).

References

Hitti (1973: 130), Tritton (1968: 23).
EDWARD D. A. HULMES

PROPHECY

Islamic philosophers explored both the nature and function of a prophet.

Establishing the characteristics of a prophet explains the rational possibility of prophecy, and as part of this project al-Farabi, building on interpretations of Aristotle by Alexander of Aphrodisias, amongst others, developed a Neoplatonic emanationist cosmology. In this scheme, a descending series of immaterial intellects emanates from the First Source (God), until the tenth, the Active Intellect, is reached. This Active Intellect is the conduit for prophetic inspiration to human beings and continuously emits revelation. The person with a highly developed imaginative faculty can receive representations of transcendent intelligibles, which al-Farabi terms prophecy.

Ibn Sina adapts and develops al-Farabi's framework in line with his understanding of faculties of the soul. He speaks of intellectual and imaginative prophecy, and adds a further kind of prophecy deriving from the motive faculty. Intellectual prophecy describes the ability of someone supremely gifted with intuition (hads), the capacity to intuit the middle term of a syllogism in a more spontaneous way than is found in normal intellectual reasoning. This psychological theory is central to Ibn Sina's understanding of prophecy. Imaginative prophecy concerns the prophet's capacity for receiving visions during waking life which most people can receive only when asleep. This type of prophecy depends on the imaginative faculty, which organises sensory data. There is a further type, in which the noble soul can influence matter outside its own body so as to produce miracles involving, for example, healing, causing illness, or producing rain. This type of prophecy depends on an inborn capacity of the soul, assisted by leading a virtuous life, rather than on empowering through encounter with the Active Intellect. The naturalistic element of this notion of prophecy led to its frequent rejection by Christian scholastic theologians even when they embraced other aspects of Ibn Sina's thought.

Turning to the function of a prophet, a Platonic concept of the philosopher-king is evident. For al-Farabi, the prophet has the ability both to receive abstract truths and to recast them into symbolic forms comprehensible to the majority. In this way he becomes the law-giver. The Ikhwan al-Safa' focus primarily on the ability of prophecy to set souls free from this world, but the political dimension is still present. Ibn Sina shares the view that the prophet is sent to guide the community by combining the ability to receive truths with the ability to recast them in symbolic form for mass consumption.

Regarding prophecy as the symbolic representation of hidden truths naturally assumes the need for interpretation (ta'wil) of the Qur'an. The philosophers regard themselves as best equipped for this task and, therefore, see the philosophically gifted as the necessary leaders of society for two reasons. They are the true interpreters of prophetic books, and, furthermore, the prophet is in fact a supreme philosopher. This stance implicitly questions the unique position of Muhammad, and establishes a pre-eminent role for philosophy in a community basing itself on prophecy. With Ibn Rushd, however, a balance is sought, the primacy of Muhammad is reasserted, while the philosopher is the one most able to interpret the revelation correctly.

References

Al-Farabi (1985), Hasse (2000: 154–76), Ibn Sina (1959: 173–82), Mahdi (2001: 147–70).

MARIN WHITTINGHAM

PROPHETS

Divided into two classes, messenger (rasul) and prophet (nabi), the former bearing a new revelation or religion and the latter whose mission involves an existing religion.

References

Amir-Moezzi (1994: 190n340).

See also: **messengers;** *nabi; nubuwwa; rasul*
ANDREW J. NEWMAN

PROVIDENCE OF GOD

The question of God's providence is usually connected with the discussion about evil and the need for prophecy. In the eyes of the Muslim theologians, God created evil in order that humans could be tested and sent either to hell or to paradise. For the Mu'tazilites, God's *taklif*, the imposition of divine law has the main importance of allowing humans to recognise what is good and what is evil and of providing the way to follow one and reject the other. Prophecy for them is a duty on the part of God, if He imposes His *taklif* on men and women, to send out prophets throughout the earth in order to declare his divine law. The Ash'arites, though believing that God creates evil in order to test humans, consider that God is not obliged to send prophets. God's revelation is an act of pure grace, which He could have abstained from. Thus, for the theologians, God shows His providence by sending His laws which guide humans to choose good and abstain from doing evil. The Arab philosophers, however, consider that evil is a result of the nature of our world and a part of it. As God is considered the pure and highest good, at the other end of the spectrum exists evil, which is the furthest point away from God. Evil has its own function in nature and can be considered good in many cases: fire, for example, can burn the clothes of a poor man but also can cook his food. Thus evil is admitted, as they see it, when humans use something intentionally to abuse others. The importance of prophecy as an aspect of divine providence is to provide a divine law that protects humanity from evil humans. However, although prophecy seems to Ibn Sina an aspect of God's providence, he considers it a natural phenomenon. A prophet is a person who, by his nature, has the kind of strong imagination and intellect that is able to receive messages from angels and introduce the divine law to humanity. Thus the providence of God is represented to Ibn Sina by the provision of the highest kind of Goodness and a perfect natural system.

References

Ormsby (1984).
MAHA EL-KAISY FRIEMUTH

PTOLEMY (CLAUDIUS PTOLOMAEUS) (*c.* AD 90–168)

Egyptian astronomer and geographer. Ptolemy worked in the city of Alexandria. He built upon the work of Hippocrates (*c.* 460–370 BC) and Hipparchus (*c.* 170–126 BC). The Ptolemaic System was an early attempt to formulate the motions of the celestial bodies on the assumption that the Earth is at the centre of the Universe. Ptolemy's *magnum opus* on mathematical syntax was hailed by the Greeks as 'the greatest *megisté*' work yet written on the subject. Arab astronomers borrowed the description, calling it the *Almagest*. This work contained detailed tables of the motions of the Sun and the Moon, together with predictions of eclipses. It also included the positions and the magnitudes of over 1,000 stars. His *Geography*, though inaccurate, showed the longitude and latitude of the places listed. Ptolemy's influence on his successors was lasting and even inhibiting, in the sense that his cosmology was deemed to be so elegant that its intellectual power seems to have been unchallenged up to the dawn of the new scientific age in the seventeenth century AD.

References

Schacht and Bosworth (1979: 464).

See also: **astrology (*'ilm al-tanjim*); astronomy (*'ilm al-falak*, *'ilm al-nujum*); mathematics**

EDWARD D. A. HULMES

Q

AL QA'IM, 'ABDALLAH B. AL-QADIR, ABU JA'FAR (AD 1031–75)

The 'Abbasid caliph al-Qa'im was the son and successor of al-Qadir. Al-Qa'im's reign is notable for having witnessed the arrival from the east of the Saljuqs led by Tughril Beg who entered Baghdad in December 1055. This event heralded the end of the already considerably weakened dynasty of the Buyids and the beginning of a new era for the caliphate under the tutelage of the Saljuqs. With the territories of the Islamic empire almost wholly dismembered between local dynasties and independent rulers, the caliphate could nevertheless still claim to be the spiritual head of the Muslim community. It was, however, Tughril who possessed the military power and who thus became effective ruler. In an official ceremony (AD 1058) al-Qa'im acknowledged Tughril as sultan and conferred on him the honorific titles *Rukn al-Dawla* ('Pillar of the State') and *Malik al-Mashriq wa'l-Maghrib* ('King of the East and West'). al-Qa'im was succeeded by 'Abdallah b. Muhammad al-Muqtadi.

References

Boyle (1968: 44–9 *passim*, 60–1), Ibn al-Jawzi (1938: 295), Ibn al-Tiqtaqa (1860: 337–42), Kennedy (1996: 243, 212), Le Strange (1924: 99, 239), Muir (1915: 579–60).

RONALD PAUL BUCKLEY

AL-QA'IM, HAMZA AL-B. AL-MUTAWAKKIL I, ABU AL-BAQA' (AD 1451–5)

al-Qa'im was the fourth son of al-Mutawakkil I to accede to the 'Abbasid caliphate in Cairo under the Mamluks. He was chosen to succeed his brother al-Mustakfi II by Sultan Jaqmaq. Al-Qa'im was implicated in an unsuccessful *coup d'état* against the Sultan Aynal al-Ajrud, as a result of which he was deposed and exiled to Alexandria where he died a few years later. A replacement caliph was found in his brother Yusuf b. al-Mutawakkil al-Mustanjid.

References

Gibb and Bosworth (1960–2003: III, 1198), Ibn Iyas (1975: 287–349 *passim*), Petry (1998: 303), Salim (1965: 37–8), al-Suyuti (1969: 513).

RONALD PAUL BUCKLEY

QADAR

'Evaluation and judgement', a reference to the timeless knowledge of Allah and His power to plan and execute His plans.

ANDREW J. NEWMAN

QADARISM (AL-QADARIYYA)

An early theological school whose name is derived from the word '*qadar*' meaning Divine 'predestination' or 'pre-ordainment' and refers to the sixth pillar of faith in Islam, which is belief in this concept. However, the term 'Qadarism' is a misnomer as it is used quite ironically to denote a sectarian view actually opposed this concept, which proposed that human beings could in fact determine their own actions. Consequently, they believe that Allah has no power, will or decree in changing their actions and, as a result, they claimed that He has no previous knowledge of such actions until they actually take place. In addition, they believe that Allah only created good, whereas it is the human being who creates evil. These early proposals were later adopted and developed by the Mu'tazilites, who were consequently referred to as the 'second Qadarites' (*al-Qadariyya al-thaniyya*) and, as such, the Qadarite no longer exist in the modern era as an independent theological school, as their views were assimilated by others.

References

al-Johani (1999: 1114–15), Netton (1997: 200–1), Watt (1948: 49–57, 1997: 25–30, 2002: 82–118).

See also: **Sunnism**

GAVIN PICKEN

QADHDHAFI, MU'AMMAR (1942–)

Libyan revolutionary leader. Qadhdhafi was born to a Bedouin family in a tent near the coastal town of Surt. He was a talented student and graduated from the University of Libya in 1963. He showed himself to be a devout Muslim and a committed Arab nationalist. He went on to graduate from the Libyan Military Academy in 1965. He was soon promoted and together with a small number of fellow officers began plotting to overthrow the monarchical regime of King Idris. Afer the coup of 1969 as a colonel he became Commander-in-Chief of the Libyan armed forces and, a year later, Chairman of the Revolutionary Command Council. He immediately closed the large British and US military bases in the country and expelled all Italian and Jewish residents. In 1973, he nationalised foreign-owned oil companies. In keeping with his strict Islamic principles he banned alcohol and gambling.

In his politics and foreign affairs, Qadhdhafi has been a maverick eccentric. In 1977 he ostensibly gave up direct power to become Leader of the Revolution and he established a Libyan *jamahiriya* (sing. *jumhuriya* – republic), a so-called populist government with a people's congress, labour unions and other mass organisations. He adopted a form of Islamic socialism whose principles he expounded in two *Green Books*. Many houses, schools and hospitals were built with oil money and free social services were provided.

Qadhdhafi sought to spread his influence and ideas abroad. He made several unsuccessful attempts at unity with neighbouring Arab states. World leaders denounced him for his interference and in 1986 the US bombed his headquarters near Tripoli in retaliation, killing or wounding several of his children and narrowly missing him. In 1993 the UN imposed sanctions on Libya for refusing to hand over men suspected of being responsible for blowing up the PanAm jumbo aircraft over Lockerbie. In 1999 two Libyans were handed over to the UN to be tried by a Scottish court in the Netherlands. One was found guilty. UN sanctions were lifted.

In practice, Qadhdhafi remains absolute ruler of Libya, often receiving foreign visitors in his tent in the desert.

References

Bearman (1986), Bianco (1975).

DEREK HOPWOOD

QADHF

Qadhf is an Arabic term designating 'slander'. It generally refers to the offence committed by an individual who falsely accuses a third party of *zina'* or of being born out of wedlock. The punishment for proven *qadf* is eighty lashes and the non-acceptance of the offender as a witness in the future. If someone claims to have been slandered, he or she must confront the alleged offender personally and verify the occurrence of the slander. If the offence is denied, then the claimant can request the swearing of an oath to this effect, refusal to do this being considered as an admission of guilt and thus punishable.

References

al-Dhahabi (n.d.), Al-Zuhayli (1985: 6, 70–91).

MAWIL IZZI DIEN

QADI

A judge in all forms of law. There is now division between secular and religious law. In Muslim countries where there is a division between the two laws, the *qadi* deals with only religious matters, family law, and inheritance. The *qadi* is a Muslim scholar who must lead a blameless life and be conversant in sacred law. The title could be also given popularly to an arbitrator, and he could also be a specialised judge such as a military *qadi*, which was one of the army officials created by the Umayyad administration.

References

Coulson (1964: 28–9), al-Dhahabi (n.d.: 129), Izzi Dien (1997: 137), .

MAWIL IZZI DIEN

AL-QADIR, AHMAD B. ISHAQ, ABU'L-'ABBAS (AD 991–1031)

The 'Abbasid caliph al-Qadir was chosen by the Buyid *amir* Baha' al-Dawla to replace his cousin the disposed al-Ta'i'. Like his predecessors, al-Qadir initially had little function but to lend legitimacy to the Shi'ite Buyid rulers and formally to sanction their policies. In order to strengthen his position in Baghdad, however, al-Qadir assumed the role of defender of Sunnism and made an attempt to codify Sunni doctrine and ritual in opposition to that of the Shi'ites. The death of Baha' al-Dawla in AD 1012 and the general weakness of the Buyid dynasty encouraged al-Qadir to issue a decree in which he condemned Shi'ism (AD 1018). In such a way,

'Abbasid legitimacy, which was initially based on their being from the Family of the Prophet, changed and the caliph emerged as the champion of Sunnism. Although the 'Abbasid caliphs no longer intervened in affairs of government, through al-Qadir's initiatives they now had a religious role to perform which was henceforth to be the *raison d'être* of the 'Abbasid caliphate. With the strengthening of al-Qadir's position he was able to nominate his own successor, something which had not been done since al-Muktafi (r. AD 902–8). He was succeeded by his son 'Abdallah al-Qa'im.

References

Ibn al-Jawzi (1938: 160–1), Ibn al-Tiqtaqa (1860: 337), Kennedy (1996: 241–3), Le Strange (1924: 125), Muir (1915: 579).

RONALD PAUL BUCKLEY

QADIRIYYA

This Sufi order traces its roots to 'Abd al-Qadir (d. AD 1166), the Hanbali scholar and head of a Sufi lodge in Baghdad who became 'the most universally popular saint'. Today there is great diversity in the beliefs of its communities, which have been found in Iraq, Anatolia, India, Indonesia, Malaysia and North and West Africa. Some communities stress a seemingly Shi'ite form of Qadiri Sufism which stands in contrast to 'Abd al-Qadir's standard 'traditional' Sunni worldview.

References

Nizami (1991b).

LLOYD RIDGEON

AL-QADISIYA, BATTLE OF

With the intention of pre-empting any military efforts to halt the expansion of Islamic interests in Iraq and Persia, the caliph 'Umar ibn al-Khattab despatched reinforcements to Iraq under the command of Sa'd ibn Abi-Waqqas, a trusted soldier who had fought at Badr. Sa'd deployed 10,000 men against the forces of Rustum, the Persian administrator, at al-Qadisiya near to al-Hira in AD 637. Rustum was killed in the ensuing battle. The bulk of the Sasanid army fled the field, leaving Iraq vulnerable to further incursions by the Muslims, who pressed on, crossed the Tigris, and took Ctesiphon a few weeks later without loss of life. Victory for the Arab armies in the Battle of al-Qadisiya against those of the Persians was to have a lasting symbolic significance.

References

Hitti (1973: 155–7), Momen (1985: 263).

See also: **Bridge, Battle of the; Yarmuk, Battle of**

EDWARD D. A. HULMES

AL-QAHIR, MUHAMMAD B. AL-MU'TADID, ABU MANSUR (AD 929 AND 932–4)

During the troubled reign of the 'Abbasid caliph al-Muqtadir (AD 908–32) a military coup in AD 929 resulted in his deposition and the inauguration of his brother Muhammad b. al-Mu'tadid with the honorific 'al-Qahir'. However, an army mutiny a few days later led to the reinstatement of al-Muqtadir. Following al-Muqtadir's death in an encounter with the military commander Mu'nis al-Muzaffar (AD 932), al-Qahir was once again declared caliph. Further dissatisfaction within the army eventually resulted in another coup and al-Qahir's final deposition in AD 934. The military leaders replaced him with a son of al-Muqtadir, Ahmad (or

Muhammad) al-Radi. Al-Qahir died in AD 950.

References

Bowen (1928: 284–6, 322–53 *passim*, 391), Ibn al-Jawzi (1938: 241), Ibn al-Tiqtaqa (1860: 323–4), Kennedy (1996: 193, 195–6), Muir (1915: 566, 568, 575), Shaban (1971: 155–6).

RONALD PAUL BUCKLEY

QAJARS (1779–1925)

Continuing the tradition that Iran was ruled mainly by non-Persians, the Turkmen Qajars, from the Caspian Sea region, established firm control after the anarchy of the eighteenth century. Tehran now became the capital, but the religious life of Shi'ism within Persia continued to be focused on, above all, the shrine of the Eighth Imam 'Ali al-Rida at Mashhad and, to a lesser extent, Qum. Such shrines continued to be enriched and beautified by the Qajars, and in the mid-nineteenth century the shahs lent the full support of the state against the new religious movements of Babism and Baha'ism, regarded as threatening the fabrics of religion and state. It was during their rule that Iran became increasingly drawn into the diplomacy of the European Powers; towards the end of their rule, petroleum was increasingly being extracted in southwestern Persia. Tensions within state and society resulted in a constitutionalist movement from 1906 onwards, which involved both secularising politicians and Shi'ite religious leaders. The dynasty, now identified with reaction, was abolished in 1925, and replaced by the rule of Rida Khan, later Shah.

References

Bosworth (1996: No. 151), Gibb and Bosworth (1960–2003), Hambly (1991), Keddie and Amanat (1992).

C. E. BOSWORTH

QANDAHAR

Commercial centre (1,000 m above sea level) surrounded by fertile irrigated farmland in south-central Afghanistan on the Tarnak Rud, at a strategic position on the Kabul–Qandahar–Harat triangle, on a crossroads with Central Asia and India. Kandahar is now a Pashto-speaking region, with strict orthodox attitudes to the veiling of women, and fanatically intolerant of foreigners.

Greeks founded Alexandria of Arachosia (30–305 BC) here. 'Kandahar' is connected with Gandhara. Subsequently it was ruled by a succession of Central Asia rulers. In the seventh century AD it was controlled by Arab Muslims, by Zunbils, Saffafids (ninth century AD), Ghaznavids (AD 962–1186), but is infrequently mentioned in early Islamic sources. It was destroyed by the Mongols, then by Timur; it was fought over by the Mughals, Afghans and Persians (sixteenth to seventeeth centuries). In 1738, Qandahar, then called Husaynabad, was destroyed by Nadir Shah. After Nadir's assassination (1747), Ahmad Shah Durrani built a new city, Ahmad-Sham, nearby, the first capital of a unified Afghanistan, though its subsequent history was still turbulent. His tomb is venerated by the Durranis, and is next to a mosque containing the 'sacred cloak'. In the mid-1980s the city witnessed heavy fighting between Soviets and Afghan guerillas and in the twenty-first century has been the scene of battles between Taliban and US troops.

References

Adamec (1972–85), Griffin (2003).

JANET STARKEY

AL-QANUN FI 'L-TIBB

Abu 'Ali al-Husayn Ibn Sina (AD 980–1037), the greatest Islamic philosopher of the East, was also acknowledged as the greatest medical expert of the Middle Ages. His reputation in the field of medicine remained unrivalled for centuries after his death, not only in the Islamic world but also in Europe and beyond, because of his compendium of medical knowledge *al-Qanun fi 'l-Tibb*, 'The Canon of Medicine'. This was a standard in European medical curricula as late as the seventeenth century, and its authority continued long after that in some parts of the world.

Ibn Sina was a philosopher, politician and also a medical doctor. In his autobiography, he refers to the beginnings of his study of medicine: 'Medicine is not one of the difficult sciences, and therefore I excelled in it in a very short time, to the point that distinguished physicians began to read the science of medicine under me'. He adds significantly: 'I cared for the sick and there opened to me some of the doors of medical treatment that cannot be described and can be learned only from practice'. This was when he was sixteen, showing that if he was not boasting, from an early age he carried the knowledge and intellectual authority with which to command mature minds, and the practical accomplishments with which to reassure and treat sick and anxious patients.

Armed with this practical and theoretical knowledge, he was admitted into the service of the Sultan of Bukhara at the age of eighteen, and so began his career as physician to a series of rulers who sought him for his skills throughout his life. He continued his interests in the branches of medicine even when his duties as vizier to more than one ruler took up his time. His disciple and friend Abu 'Ubayd al-Juzjani in his continuation of Ibn Sina's autobiography records how his master was still experimenting with cures late on in life, packing his own head with crushed ice to try

and reduce a swelling, and prescribing sugar-based rose preserve as a possible cure for tuberculosis.

Ibn Sina wrote down his comments and observations on his medical work in a number of tracts and volumes throughout his life. Some of these were probably occasional pieces written for particular people or groups of his students, while others had the character of academic treatises. But none approached the *Qanun fi 'l-Tibb* in length or conception.

According to al-Juzjani, Ibn Sina began the *Qanun* in Jurjan, where he lived between AD 1014 and 1023. He kept on with it when he moved to Rayy and gradually completed it when he settled in Hamadhan between AD 1015 and 1023. Al-Juzjani gives some insight into the frenetic manner of its composition in his description of Ibn Sina's nightly gatherings:

> Every night pupils would gather at his house, while by turns I would read from the *Shifa'* and someone else would read from the *Qanun*. When we were finished, different kinds of singers appeared, a drinking party was prepared with its utensils, and we set to. The instruction took place at night, because of the lack of free time during the day on account of his service to the Amir.

There seems an element of bravado, or even recklessness here. And it is ironic that the composition of the bulk of such a great and authoritative work on matters of health should be squeezed into snatches of time when Ibn Sina was not being driven by the political and managerial duties of vizier to the amir Shams al-Dawla and the composition of the encyclopaedic philosophical masterpiece known as 'The Cure'. Either of these would have been a full-time activity, and the completion of the *Qanun* appears to be an additional self-induced imposition.

Ibn Sina was occupied in writing the *Qanun* for about twelve years, continuing and completing it while beginning the *Shifa'*. In one sense, the two works complement each other, since together they cover all the branches of what was accepted as science in Ibn Sina's day, though there are no evident signs that he self-consciously looked on them as components of a single project. It appears from al-Juzjani that he later intended to write a commentary, *sharh*, on his work, and to carry out experiments for the purpose. Nothing seems to have come of this, though his plan signals that he did not regard the great compendium as by any means his last word on medical matters. He was, after all, only in his thirties when he completed it.

The *Qanun fi 'l-Tibb* consists of five books, each comprising a number of divisions, *funun*, which are subdivided into instructions, *ta'alim*, and further into chapters, *fusul* (this nomenclature is not consistent throughout). The unity of the whole has often been remarked upon as a reason for its continuing authority in medical schools, even though its coverage of some topics is scattered through several parts and not easy for practitioners to turn up readily.

Book One, *Fi 'l-Umur al-Kulliyya min 'Ilm al-Tibb*, 'On General Matters concerning Medicine', comprises four *funun*: medicine and anatomy, forms and causes of sickness, their symptoms, the pulse and excreta as aids to diagnosis, means of maintaining health at various stages in life and when travelling, and the illnesses that befall those in these various circumstances, forms of treatment, including emetics, blood-letting and cauterising.

Book Two, *Fi 'l-Adawiya al-Mufrada*, 'On Individual Drugs', comprises two parts: the use of drugs in combination, experimenting with them together and hypothesising about them, their properties, and collecting and storing them, the action of drugs, and their specific effects on parts of the body, listed alphabetically.

Book Three, *Fi 'l-Amrad al-Juz'iyya al-Waqi'a bi-A'da' al-Insan 'Udw 'Udw min al-Ras ila 'l-Qadam*, 'On the Minor Illnesses that Affect the Human Organs, from the Head to the Foot', in twenty-two *funun*: the condition of the major organs, and the ailments specific to each of them.

Book Four, *Fi al-Amrad allati la takhtass bi-'Udw bi-'aynihi wa'l-Zina*, 'On Illnesses Not Specific to Particular Organs, and Hygiene', in seven *funun*: fevers of various kinds, the symptoms and climax of a fever, tumours and ulcers and their treatments, fractures and dislocations, bone-setting, poisons, hygiene.

Book Five, *Fi 'l-Adawiya al-Murakkaba wa-huwa al-Aqrabadhin*, 'On Drug Compounds, the Pharmacology', in two collections, *jumlatan*: the preparation of medicinal compounds, drugs known to alleviate particular complaints.

The work concludes with a listing of medicine and a prosopography from Asclepius to Ibn Sina's own time.

Many of these subdivisions are further divided into one or more smaller divisions. The whole comprises a vast collection of medical knowledge in all the branches practised in the eleventh century AD, and the culmination of earlier advances in medical knowledge. In recognition of its size and of the use its contents would be to practitioners, Ibn Sina summarised its essentials in his *Alfiyya*, a thousand-verse (actually 1,326 verses long) mnemonic poem in *rajaz* metre.

The *Qanun fi 'l-Tibb* remained an essential part of medical knowledge for hundreds of years, both within the

Islamic world and outside. In European universities, for example, both before and after the Renaissance, parts of it were incorporated into the medical curriculum as fundamental textbooks. As late as 1600, lecturers at Leipzig insisted that whoever wished to become a good medical practitioner must become a good 'Avicennista'. Its continuing stature was acknowledged as recently as 1930 by O. Cameron Gruner, who declared that 'Ideas are to be found in his work which provide suggestions for useful research in the future'.

Many editions of the *Qanun* exist, though there is no standard critical text, a workable edition is that of al-Lahham (1994). Translations of parts have been made into many languages, Gruner (1930) translates Book One into English.

DAVID THOMAS

QANUN 'URFI

Customary law: is based on the prevailing custom of any particular society. Custom can contribute to the formulation of law in both a practical and verbal form, however specific conditions are outlined prior to actual implementation of this. A custom must be constantly recurring, in common usage and valid at the time of the legal injunction in reference to a case. It should not violate the principles of Islamic law and only when all these conditions are fulfilled can the custom become law. It can be observed that there exists an interactive relationship between custom and the law, whereby custom may be valid when it does not violate the legal text, unless the textual law itself was established on custom and is thus a customary law that can be altered in the face of a new prevailing social custom. For example, if a specified amount of measured payment has been legislated based on weight, then this can be chan-ged at a later date if it has become custom to base it on volume. In this case, the measure of volume has overridden that of weight and a new customary law can be formulated accordingly.

References

al-Zarqa (1968: 874–90).

MAWIL IZZI DIEN

QARAMITA (CARMATIANS)

The Qaramita were an Isma'ili Shi'ite sect which flourished in southern Iraq and eastern Arabia between the ninth and (at the latest) the thirteenth centuries AD. According to heresiographical reports, the Qaramita took their name from their founder Hamdan Qarmat (who disappeared in the late ninth century AD). Hamdan was aided by his brother-in-law 'Abdan (d. AD 899). Hamdan and 'Abdan were converted by an Isma'ili missionary some time in the 870s in or around Kufa. When the missionary left, they continued to propagate the Isma'ili version of Shi'ism amongst the tribes of the area with great success. Their message included early Isma'ili and Shi'ite ideas such as the leadership of the descendants of the Prophet Muhammad, the sixth apostle of God, with the seventh Isma'ili imam, Muhammad b. Isma'il as seventh apostle of God. Muhammad b. Isma'il, who was concealed, was about to usher in a new era, abolishing the trappings of the old religions (including the *shari'a* of Islam) and establishing his rule of justice. Because of these messianic characteristics, Muhammad b. Isma'il was termed 'al-Mahdi' (the 'rightly guided one') by the Qaramita. The missionary who had converted Hamdan was most likely sent from the Isma'ili centre in Salamiyya in Syria. In Salamiyya, the Isma'ilis had established a hierarchy of religious authorities, at the head of which was 'the Proof' (*al-hujja*), the representative of the concealed imam Muhammad b. Isma'il. The *hujja* organised missionary activities throughout the Sunni Muslim Empire. Hamdan was, it seems, in close contact with the authorities in Salamiyya, and deferred to them. In AD 899, however, he heard that the newly incumbent *hujja*, 'Ubaydallah (or 'Abdallah according to Isma'ili sources), had claimed the position of 'manifest Imam' (*al-imam al-Zahir*) rather than merely proof of the concealed (*mastur*) imam. Perplexed by this, Hamdan sent 'Abdan to investigate, and when the rumours turned out to be true, the Qaramita refused to recognise 'Ubaydallah and ceased all missionary activity. Soon after, Hamdan himself disappeared. The faction of 'Ubaydallah was later to form the Fatimid dynasty in north Africa.

One follower of Hamdan, Zikrawayh seized his opportunity to lead the Qaramita movement before it disintegrated. He killed 'Abdan (the natural successor to Hamdan), and began to proselytise amongst the tribes of the Syrian desert. In this his missionaries had some success. They built up sufficient forces to carry out a number of attacks on the nascent Fatimid Isma'ilis of Syria. Zikrawayh now went into hiding, but a succession of his agents claimed to be the descendents of the imam Muhammad b. Isma'il, and therefore the harbingers of the imam's (or Zikrawayh's) *parousia*. In one revolt Zikrawayh's supporters attacked Salamiyya, massacring members of 'Ubaydallah's family. The raids from Qaramita forces continued to trouble Damascus and parts of rural Syria, in AD 906, his supporters in southern Iraq captured Kufa and entered into battle with the 'Abbasids. At first they were successful, and Zikrawayh came out of hiding to lead his

army. Ultimately the 'Abbasids were able to quell the rebellion and in AD 907 they captured Zikrawayh. He died soon after capture from wounds suffered in battle.

Hamdan, before his disappearance, had not restricted his network of missionaries to Iraq. Whilst he was still working with the Salamiyya hierarchy, he had supervised some missionary activity in eastern Arabia and Bahrayn. In AD 886–7, Hamdan sent one Abu Sa'aid al-Jannabi to Bahrayn as a missionary and after the internal dispute between the Qaramita and 'Ubaydallah, al-Jannabi began to agitate against the claims of 'Ubaydallah, securing Qaramita control of Bahrayn. The Isma'ili communities of the east (Iran and Transoxania) were probably similarly divided between Qaramita supporters and those who recognised 'Ubaydallah's claims. Amongst the earliest Isma'ili theological works we possess are those of Abu Hatim al-Razi (d. AD 933–4), an Isma'ili who was in close contact with the leaders of the Qaramita movement. A contemporary Muhammad al-Nasafi (d. AD 943) in Transoxania also seems to have supported the Qaramita position.

The Qaramita gained their most significant success in Bahrayn. After Abu Sa'id al-Jannabi was killed AD 913, his son Abu Tahir al-Jannabi consolidated his Qaramita supporters, and in AD 923, began to organise raids in southern Iraq from Bahrayn. Abu Tahir, by all accounts, saw himself as the *khalifa* (viceregent) of Muhammad b. Isma'il, the Mahdi, and the authority engendered by this claim was used to wage a campaign aimed at capturing 'Abbasid Baghdad in AD 927–9. Having retaken Kufa, they were repelled and many of the local supporters of Abu Tahir returned with him to Bahrayn on their defeat. Abu Tahir shifted his attention to the Arabian peninsula and in AD 930, he captured Mecca. This was a great psychological blow to the 'Abbasids, partly because of the religious significance of Mecca, but also because it demonstrated their inability to protect the holy places. The Qaramita had been attacking pilgrim caravans for some time, and had successfully barred Muslims from some areas from attending the *hajj*. Once he had captured Mecca, Abu Tahir massacred the inhabitants, and removed the Black Stone of the Ka'ba. This affront to Muslim sensibilities was probably calculated to demonstrate the unimportance of the symbols of 'Abbasid Islam and the establishment of the new (Qaramita) era of Muslim rule. It had the added benefit of enabling the Qaramita to extract later a significant amount of money from the 'Abbasids for the stone's return to Mecca. The stories that Abu Tahir removed the stone on the orders of the Fatimids are most probably part of the anti-Isma'ili propaganda of the 'Abbasids who naturally linked the Fatimids and the Qaramita. It is clear, however, that the two movements were quite separate.

The Bahrayni Qaramita lost most of their credibility amongst the rest of the Isma'ili community (both Fatimid and Qaramita) when in AD 931 Abu Tahir declared that the Mahdi had come in the form of a Persian immigrant, and Abu Tahir gave him the reigns of power. The 'Mahdi' turned out to be a disaster: he killed leaders of the Qaramita, proclaimed the worship of fire, suspended any resemblance of Muslim ritual and called for the cursing of all Muslim prophets. Abu Tahir was forced to retake control, promptly putting the impostor to death. The episode was deeply distressing, and outside of Bahrayn, Abu Tahir's project began to be viewed with some embarrassment.

There were attempts by the Fatimids to bring the disparate Isma'ili communities of the east under the Fatimid wing. Certain excesses of Fatimid doctrine were toned down by the caliph al-Mu'izz li-Din Allah (r. AD 953–75) – the Fatimid imams became viceregents (*khulafa'*) of the messianic Qa'im ('the one who is to rise up' – meaning here, Muhammad b. Isma'il). Al-Mu'izz permitted the inclusion of the Neoplatonic works of al-Nasafi – the influential scholar in the east – into the Fatimid canon of Isma'ili literature. One great scholar who was successfully recruited to the cause was Abu Ya'qub al-Sijistani, who developed al-Nasafi's philosophical theology. Whilst many communities in the East did forsake their Qaramita heritage and convert to Fatimid Isma'ilism, it is clear that not all did, and in particular, caliph al-Mu'izz was unsuccessful in converting the Qaramita of Bahrayn to their cause. The Qaramita of Bahrayn continued to agitate against the Fatimids. In the 970s, this hostility resulted in a series of Fatimid–Qaramita battles in Syria, where the Qaramita were supported by the Buyids and Hamdanids. Peace was eventually established in AD 977, but on terms that greatly favoured the Qaramitas as the Fatimid caliph al-'Aziz agreed to pay a large tribute in return for a meaningless pledge of allegiance.

Ten years later, the Buyids, together with tribal units in southern Iraq, began to push the Qaramita back in the Arabian peninsula. This began the period of steady decline in Qarmati power in the area. Relations with the Fatimids continued to be at best uneasy, at worst, the differences were settled on the battlefield. A local rebellion (led supposedly in the name of the Fatimid caliph al-Mustansir) by a tribe under the protection of the Isma'ili Sulayhids of Yemen (themselves owing allegiance to the Fatimids) deposed the Qaramita in al-Ahsa' in AD 1076, crushing a counter rebellion a year later. The Bahrayni

Qaramita eventually lost control of al-Ahsa' in AD 1077–8, marking the end of their rule. Isma'ilis who survived the battle became incorporated into the Fatimid mission (*da'wa*). Little is known about the Qaramita communities outside of the Bahrayn Qarmati state. Most had already probably converted to Fatimid Isma'ilism by the time of the Qaramita collapse. From then on, the Isma'ili tradition was to be dominated by the Fatimid line, whether through the Musta'li or Nizari lines of succession.

References

Ibn Malik (1939), Ivanow (1940: 43–55), Madelung (1996: 21–74), Stern (1961: 98–108).

ROBERT GLEAVE

QARUN

The Biblical Korah of Numbers 16. He is mentioned by name three times in the Qur'an (Q.28:76–82, Q.29:39 and Q.40:24). In the latter two verses, he simply appears alongside Fir'awn (Pharaoh) and his minister Haman, and the three of them call Moses a sorcerer and a liar. In the first passage (Q.28:76–82), Qarun is one of Moses' people, but he treats them arrogantly because of his wealth, which he feels he deserves. In the end, he, along with his home, is swallowed up by the earth, providing an example of those who prefer the wealth of this world to the rewards of God in the next world by believing and doing good works. The story alludes to the biblical account of the rebellion of Korah and his punishment in Numbers 16:31–3, and 26:10). In order to account for the riches of Qarun, Islamic tradition pictures him as one of the founders of alchemy.

References

Gibb and Bosworth (1960–2003: IV, 673).

ANDREW RIPPIN

QATABAN

A pre-Islamic people of south-west Arabia, known through South Semitic inscriptions in four main dialects and through classical geographers who described them living between the Red Sea and Indian Ocean. In Wadi Bayhand is ancient *Tmn'*, main town of Qataban, possibly founded by the Sabaeans (*c.* 400 BC). They were also in Wadi Harib in the township Harbat (Hajar Hinu al-Zurayr, near Ta'izz), and into Dathina. They were farmers in village communities organised into confederations (*sha'b*) at various levels, ruled by a chief executive (*malik*) who collected taxes, oversaw the markets and irrigation system with its *corvée* labour. They traded in aromatics, with coins and art influenced by the Greeks. Polythestic, the Qatabani pantheon was dominated by the lunar god ('Amm), 'Athtar (venus star), and a solar goddess. The Sirwah inscription (RES 3945) records that Saba' defeated Awsan, thus liberating Qataban. The Qataban may have existed from the sixth or fourth century BC to the first century AD, but disappeared from inscriptions from the fourth century AD so Muslim writers do not mention Qataban. They may have been overthrown by a Sabaean–Hadrami alliance, to be controlled by Hadramawt.

References

Phillips (1955), Simpson (2002).

JANET STARKEY

QAWWAL, QAWWALI

This is a form of Sufi devotional music during which religious poetry is sung. It was popularised in the Indian subcontinent among the Chishtiyya order, but is now widespread throughout the world. Nusrat Fateh Ali Khan was a *qawwali* singer who enjoyed particular fame in the West. Sufi literature argues that performance of devotional music induced mystical states. However, performance of such music remains a contentious issue among Islamic communities typified by the opposition from the Deobandi school.

References

Ernst (1997: 179–98).

LLOYD RIDGEON

QAYIT BAY, SAYF AL-DIN, CALLED AL-MALIK AL-ASHRAF (r. 1468–96)

One of the last Burji Mamluk rulers in Egypt and Syria. Conscious of a desperate need for more economic resources and finance, he encouraged Italian merchants to trade with Egypt, but the State's wealth was swallowed up in financing armies to protect his northern frontiers. His rival, the Aq Qoyunlu leader Uzun Hasan, met his match in the Ottomans, but it was now these latter who pressed heavily on Cilicia and north-western Syria, especially as the Mamluks were sheltering the Ottoman pretender Prince Jem, Sultan Bayezid II's brother. Qayit Bay took the offensive in central Anatolia and defeated the Ottomans in 1490, but was wise enough to make peace. His reign was the last great one of the Mamluks. After his death, economic recession deepened in the State, leaving it ill equipped to ward off the Ottomans.

References

Garcin (1998: 295–7), Gibb and Bosworth (1960–2003), Holt (1986: 195–8).

C. E. BOSWORTH

AL-QAYRAWAN (KAIROUAN, QAIROUAN)

A town in north-central Tunisia, founded in AD 570 by 'Uqba ibn Nafi' and built upon the site of the Byzantine fortress of Kamouinia. It served as one of the military bases from which the Islamic subjugation of the *maghrib* was conducted. In the ninth century AD it became the capital of the Aghlabids. When they were overthrown in the early years of the tenth century AD, it became the first capital of the Fatimids under whom it began to flourish as a religious, administrative and commercial centre. In the eleventh century AD it became the capital of the Zirid dynasty. By the fifteenth century it was an administrative centre under the Almoravids. Its importance declined after repeated incursions from Bedouin nomads and the emergence of Tunis as the capital city. Qayrawan is famous for its Grand Mosque and its Islamic University. Known as 'the city of 100 mosques' it remains one of the holiest places in the Islamic world. It is a centre for the production and marketing of carpets, ceramics, cereals, copperware, leather goods, olives, rose oil and wool.

References

Hitti (1973: 170n, 267, 452, 618–19), Michell (1984: 220).

See also: **Almohads; Almoravids; Berbers**

EDWARD D. A. HULMES

AL-QAZWINI, ZAKARIYYA IBN MUHAMMAD
(*c.* AD 1203–83)

Geographer and cosmographer. Born in Qazwin, he served as a *qadi* in Wasit and al-Hilla, and later at the court of 'Ata-Malik Juvayni (d. AD 1283), the Ilkhanid governor of Baghdad.

Al-Qazwini's fame rests on two works: the cosmography, *'Aja'ib al-Makhluqat wa-ghara'ib al-Mawjudat*, and the geographical dictionary, *Athar al-Bilad* wa-*Akhbar al-'Ibad*, the latter of which exists in two different versions. Although both his cosmography and his geographical work are essentially compilations of information assembled by previous authors, the degree of originality of al-Qazwini's contribution differs significantly. In his geographical work, *Athar al-Bilad*, he essentially relies, without acknowledgement, on Yaqut's *Mu'jam al-Buldan*, rearranging Yaqut's entries in alphabetical order within the Ptolemy–Khuwarazmi system of seven latitudinal climes. His *'Aja'ib*, however, despite the fact that it contains little if anything in the way of new information, represents the first genuine attempt to compile a comprehensive account of the cosmographical ideas of the day. In particular, the author's arrangement appears to be wholly original: the work is arranged in two parts, the first dealing with supraterrestrial matters; the second with terrestrial ones. The first part deals with the celestial bodies (the moon, sun and stars), with the inhabitants of heaven (the angels), and with problems of chronology. The second part deals with matters relating to climate, to the seven 'climes', to seas and rivers, and to the three natural kingdoms: animal, vegetable and mineral. The section on the animal kingdom includes a description of man, and of the *jinn* and *ghul*s who in traditional Islamic belief occupy a position between man and the lower animals. Al-Qazwini's most frequently quoted sources in the *'Aja'ib* are Abu Hamid al-Gharnati and the anonymous author of the Persian *Tuhfat al-Ghara'ib*.

Al-Qazwini's work has been criticised for its lack of originality and he has frequently been accused of plagiarism, in particular for his unacknowledged reliance on Yaqut's *Mu'jam al-Buldan* in his *Athar al-Buldan*. Despite this, al-Qazwini's work had a significant influence on later writers in the field. The popularity of his *'Aja'ib* in particular is attested by its rapid translation into Persian and Turkish and the production of a large number of manuscript copies of the work, often richly illustrated.

References

Young *et al.*. (1990: 319–21).

PAUL STARKEY

QIBLA

The direction of prayer towards the Black Stone of the Ka'ba at Mecca. Originally the *qibla* faced towards the Temple in Jerusalem, but the Prophet Muhammad changed it to Mecca in the second year of the Hijra, AD 624. Traditionally the *qibla* also commemorates the place where the Prophet stood in prayer in his house in Medina. All mosques must be orientated towards Mecca, which means that their alignment varies regionally throughout the Islamic world. The need to calculate the direction of the *qibla* accurately contributed to the development of the sciences of mathematics and geometry.

References

Frishman (1994: 17–41).

JENNIFER SCARCE

QIMAR (GAMBLING)

An Arabic term describing the action of two parties who are engaged in a game that concludes in the financial gain of one participant. The Qur'an specifies certain prohibited actions including gambling, termed *maysir* (Q.5.:90–219). *Qimar* is considered to be one of the methods by which the Devil creates friction between people: 'the devil causes animosity to take place among you by using intoxicants and gambling' (Q.5.:91).

This concept is closely related to the Muslim attitude that wealth should be generated through personal endeavour or other means prescribed by Islamic law, such as inheritance or in some cases donation. Islam draws a clear line between what is a legal contract and what is not, by clarifying that exchanges of property or valuable commodities must have a meritorious background. Any donation that lacks such an attribute may be regarded as unlawful, such as the offering of a bribe, this act being strongly denounced in Islam. The Prophet is reported to have said, 'persons giving or taking bribery are cursed'.

References

al-Dhahabi (n.d.: 88).

Mawil Izzi Dien

QISAS

Qisas is an Arabic term meaning 'retaliation' and referring to the issue of an apostate punishment. In Islamic law this signifies that a criminal may be punished in a manner reflecting the committed offence. *Qisas* is particularly relevant to cases of murder and is prescribed in the Qur'an as follows, 'And there is life for you in retaliation, O men of understanding, that ye may ward off (evil)' (Q.2:179).

An ongoing theological debate surrounds *qisas* regarding whether or not the individual who incurs the death penalty for murder will be absolved from sin after death. Excluding the Hanafis, the majority of scholars maintain that the executed murderer would have his sin expiated, based on the *hadith* narrated by Muslim that, 'the grave sins, killing, adultery and theft, would be expiated by their punishments'. However, the Hanafis perceive that the implementation of punishment is for the purpose of maintaining social order and is thus intended to be beneficial to the living and not the dead. As an Islamic penalty, *qisas* is unique because it is not viewed as a specific right of God, but rather as a personal right that is granted to benefit the individual. Also *qisas* may be waived by the relatives of the victim, whereas *hudud*, being the right of God, may not. A parent of either gender who kills a son may not be subject to *qisas* because it is expected that a father or mother would treat their own child with charity. Islamic law would generally permit a family member to resort to retaliation if this would remove emotional turmoil, such as anger, from his/her heart. Nevertheless, it is strongly recommended that the family of the victim should forgive the murderer and accept blood money instead. 'And we prescribed for them therein, the life for the life, and the eye for the eye, and the nose for the nose, and the tooth for the tooth. ... But whosoever forgiveth it (in the way of charity) it shall be expiation for him' (Q.5:45). This Qur'anic statement indicates the nature of *qisas* and the recommendation to bestow charity as a beneficial alternative. However, if the family of the victim do forgive the perpetrator, this may not prevent a legislative body from applying a discretionary penalty such as a prison sentence.

References

Coulson (1964: 18), al-Zuhayli (1985: 261–2).

Mawil Izzi Dien

QUMM

Also known as Kumandan, Qom and Ghom, Qumm is the ninth city in Iran on the river Qumm, and a district capital, near Masila, a salt lake, one of seven sacred Shi'ites cities. The district is agriculturally impoverished, with a wide range of crops dependent on irrigation via *qanats*, though there were crown properties under the Qajars and *waqf* estates associated with Fatima's shrine. The population is ethnically and linguistically diverse.

Qumm has pre-Islamic Sasanid origins, was destroyed by Alexander the Great and restored by Sasid Qubad I (AD 488–531). According to legend, Qumm was founded by Takmorubh, a king of the mythical Pishdadan dynasty. Al-Baladhuri (AD 892) claimed that Qumm was conquered by Arabs (AD 644), whereas the *Qumm Nameh* (*Book of Qumm*) records that the town was founded by Ash'ari Arabs of Kufa, fleeing persecutions of Shi'ites (AD 712–13): many Shi'i *hadiths* praise Qumm as a place of refuge for believers, as is reflected in its many honorific names (Dar al-Mu'minin, Dar al'Ilm, Dar al'Ibada, etc.). In contrast, the Sunni Caliph Harun al-Rashid resorted to force to obtain Qumm's taxes (AD 800–4) and there were also conflicts with Sunni Isfahan. Qumm became prosperous, a great theological centre that preceded al-Najaf, with hundreds of Shi'i (and a few Sunni) *'ulama'*, including Shaykh Saduq. In AD 816, Fatima, sister of the Shi'i leader, *imam* 'Ali al-Rida, died in Qumm. She is revered as the embodiment of feminine virtue. A sanctuary was dedicated to her and became an important Shi'i shrine (*c.* AD 965) patronised by the Buyids and the Saljuqs. Hasan ibn Sabah was born in Qumm (AD 1052) and founded the Isma'ili sect there.

Qumm suffered massacres by the Mongols (AD 1224) possibly urged on by Sunnis. Qumm was still recovering when the Persian historian, Mustawfi, visited in AD 1340. Timur besieged the city for a long period (end fourteenth century) but respected the holy city. It enjoyed patronage from Turkoman sultans who used it as a winter capital for hunting. Qumm's mosques often combined *madrasa* and mausolea (*Imam-Zadeh* 'Ali ibn Jaffar (AD 1339), Shazadeh Ahmad). In the sixteenth century, Shah Isma'il, ruler of the new Safavid dynasty, championed its Shi'i shrines, as did Shah Safi I and Shah 'Abbas I, who also rebuilt Fatima's sanctuary. Qumm attracted scholars, pilgrims and burials of the faithful in its sacred soil: tombs of ten rulers including Safavid Shah Safi (d. AD 1642), 'Abbas II (d. AD 1666), and Suleiman (d. AD 1694) and 400 Islamic saints and *'ulama'*. Markets and crafts flourished.

Around 1722, Qumm was pillaged by Afghans and later by Uzbeks. Fath-'Ali Shah, the second Qajar ruler, restored Fatima's sanctuary, covering its dome in gold. The Qajars restored the royal monuments, endowed *madrasa*s and the sanctuary library. Qajar royal tombs are still venerated, especially during Muharram, to commemorate the tragedy of Karbala'.

The largest theological college in Iran (established 1920), specialising in Islamic law, philosophy, theology and logic, is in Qumm and attracts eminent religious theologians. Several *madrasa* are run by Ayatallahs, and there are numerous private libraries including some of its Ayatallah Mar'ashi Najafi. Soe *'ulama'* have assumed national political positions, including Kashani (under Musaddiq) and Khomeini who led Islamic opposition to the Shah from France then Qumm (1 March 1979), following uprisings there in 1978. Millions of pilgrims continue to reinforce Qumm's spiritual role.

References

Babayan (2002), Kimber (1998: I, 273–4), Lambton (1990: 322–39), Savory (1980).

JANET STARKEY

QUR'AN, ALLEGORICAL INTERPRETATION OF THE

Often termed *ta'wil* (literally meaning 'going to the beginning'), the allegorical interpretation of the Qur'an is supported by the hermeneutical structure of the *zahir* and the *batin*, the 'outer' and the 'inner' senses of the text. Its counterpart is *tafsir*, which is seen to concentrate on the grammatical, philological and juristic aspects of the text. Such symbolic interpretation is especially emphasised in Sufi circles but finds its place among many Shi'i, especially Isma'ili, as well as some Sunni exegetes. Most exegetes held that *ta'wil* cannot replace *tafsir* but can only supplement it.

References

Lazarus-Yafeh (2003: 366–75).

ANDREW RIPPIN

QUR'AN, FIRST REVELATION OF THE

There are various traditions about which section of the Qur'an was first revealed, but most opinions hold that the Q.96:1–5, derive from the occasion of Muhammad's sojourn in the cave at the summit of Mount Hira, outside Mecca, and Gabriel's first visit to him. This is held to have been in Ramadan (because of the reference in Q.2:181, 'The month of Ramadan in which the Qur'an was brought down as a guidance to men') in AD 610. The passage reads: 'In the Name of your Lord who created, created man of a blood-clot. And your Lord is the most generous, who taught by the pen, taught man what he did not know'.

According to the stories told, this revelation came to Muhammad during his retreat. Gabriel showed him a piece of cloth, on which this *sura* was written, saying, 'Recite!' When Muhammad protested that he could not read, the angel pressed him so strongly that he nearly suffocated. At the third repetition, the angel pronounced the verses which Muhammad then retained and later repeated.

References

Guillaume (1955: 104–11).

ANDREW RIPPIN

QUR'AN, THE

For the Muslims, the Qur'an is the word of God preserved in a well-guarded tablet (Q.85:22) revealed through the Angel Gabriel to the Prophet Muhammad who was forty years old in the early part of the seventh century (AD 610) when he was meditating in a cave on Mount Hira', 3 miles from Mecca, during the night of al-Qadr (the Night of Power) one of the last ten nights in the month of Ramadan. The revelation was intermittent and lasted between twenty to twenty-five years. The Qur'an consists of 114 *suras* (chapters) which vary in length from just three *ayas* (Q.108 and Q.110) to 286 *ayas* (Q.2) apart from the first sura which is the opening of the Qur'an, and consists of seven ayas. The *suras* of the Qur'an are divided into Meccan (because they were revealed in or around Mecca), and Medinan (because they were revealed in or around Medina). Muslim scholars' views differ as to whether these *suras* were arranged by the Prophet Muhammad or were done by his companions after he passed away in AD 632. For non-Muslim scholars such as Richard Bell (1953: 41), the *suras'* arrangement was done after the Prophet's death. The constituents of each *sura* are called *ayas* whose arrangement is believed by Muslim scholars to have been done by the Prophet himself (cf. al-Zarkashi [1988:

64], al-Suyuti [1996:175], al-'Asqalani [1997:50]). The Qur'an claims in Q.3:3, Q.6:38, and Q.16:64, 89 that it is a reaffirmation of and complementary to previous scriptures (Q.5:44, Q.41:43). The Qur'an describes itself as 'enlightenment for the people, guidance, and mercy' (Q.28:43), 'a healer' (Q.10:57), and stresses in Q.5:43–4, Q.6:91, Q.7:157, Q.41:43 that it includes all that has been mentioned in the previous two scriptures (the Old Testament and the Bible), that it has perfected these scriptures and, most importantly, it has abrogated their legal rulings. For this reason, Bell (1953: 172) claims that there is an indirect influence of Judaism and Christianity upon the Qur'an. Pedersen (1984: 13) is also of the view that the Old Testament and the New Testament have the same idea about what happens in heaven and on earth, the fate of men and their good and evil deeds which the Qur'an refers to. While Muslim scholars claim that the Qur'an is free from editing and stands as it was literally revealed to the Prophet Muhammad, non-Muslim scholars, such as Bell (1953), are of the opinion that the Qur'an had undergone some additions by the companions after the Prophet's death. Cragg (2001: 10) is also of the opinion that Muhammad was consciously involved in the composition of the Qur'an. This is strongly disputed by Muslims. For Muslim scholars, the Qur'an is Muhammad's eternal miracle that is beyond human faculty to be imitated, this is referred to as *i'jaz al-Qur'an* (inimitability of the Qur'an).

The word 'qur'an' means 'recitation, reading' and the first word of the first *sura* revealed to the Prophet was also 'read' (*iqra'*). It can also be morphologically derived from the verb *qarana* 'to put something together', or from the plural noun *qara'* in whose singular form is *qarina* (linguistic consonance,

conceptual connectivity) which means that the Qur'an's constituent *ayas* are coherently connected and logically sequenced. However, al-Qurtubi claims that the word 'qur'an' is derived from the verb *qara'a* (to read, recite) but al-Shafi'i is of the view that the word 'qur'an' is not derived from this verb and that it is one of the names of the Book of God. This view is supported by Ibn Kathir who also used to recite the word 'qur'an' without the *hamzah* (glottal stop) as 'quran'. From an intertextuality point of view, the derivation of the word 'qur'an' from 'qara'in' is more appropriate. Etymologically, this word is linked to Syriac *qeryana* (scripture reading, lection) and to Hebrew *miqra'* (recitation, scripture). The word 'qur'an' occurs sixty-eight times in the Qur'an and has been given over thirty attributes. The Qur'an is divided into four parts: Part I includes *suras* 1–6, Part II includes *suras* 7–18, Part III includes *suras* 19–35, and Part IV includes *suras* 36–114. It is interesting to note that the first *sura* of the Qur'an refers to lordship while the last *sura* refers to divinity.

The Qur'an recurrently highlights four major tenets of faith (usul al-iman), these are:

(i) monotheism (*tawhid*) which refers to the oneness or unity of God and is the antonym of polytheism (*al-shirk*), which means the association of others with God, as in Q.2:22, 255, Q.3:2, Q.25:2, Q.59:23;

(ii) prophethood (*al-nubuwwa*), which confirms the prophethood of Muhammad and that the Qur'an is the word of God, as in Q.25:1, Q.3:31–2, Q.16:64, Q.28:85–7, Q.36:2–3;

(iii) eschatology (*al-ma'ad*) which refers to resurrection and the day of judgement, as in Q.7:187, Q.20:124, Q.36:51, Q.42:9, Q.50:42–3; and

(iv) reward and punishment (*al-thawab wa'l-'Iqab*) which is usually presented in the form of an antithesis where the believers are rewarded with the garden (*al-janna*) while the unbelievers are rewarded with the fire (*al-nar*) in the hereafter, as in Q.2:81–2, Q.30:15–16, Q.56:88–94, Q.64:9–10.

The Qur'an recurrently refers to various leitmotifs such as the believers as in Q.2:227, Q.98:7, the People of the Book, i.e.: the scripturists, as in Q.2:105, Q.3:64; the polytheists as in Q.2:105, Q.3:151; the hypocrites as in Q.8:49, Q.9:67; the prophets as in Q.4:163, Q.13:27, Q.20:13; parables of various Prophets as in Q.2:40–93, Q.12; parables of previous nations as in Q.36:31, Q.40:82–3; Islamic legal rulings as in Q.2:226–37, Q.4:19–25; justice as in Q.5:42, Q.7:29, Q.49:9; fighting in the cause of God as in Q.2:190, Q.9:38; spending in charity as in Q.2:254, Q.64:16; looking after the orphans and the needy as in Q.9:60, Q.22:28; patience as in Q.3:200, Q.103:3; righteousness as in Q.6:153, Q.7:26; admonition and morality as in Q.4:112, Q.6:151–2; respect for parents Q.2:83, Q.31:14; enjoining what is right and forbidding what is wrong as in Q.3:114, Q.9:112; and God's omnipotence as in Q.23:12–22, Q.36:36–42.

References

Abdul-Raof (2001a, 2001b, 2003), al-'Asqalani (1997), al-Baqillani (1994), Bell (1953), Cornell (1995: 387–94), Cragg (1991, 2001), Esack (2004: 562–8), Pedersen (1984), al-Qurtubi (1997), al-Razi (1990), Robinson (1996), al-Suyuti (1996), al-Zarkashi (1988)

HUSSEIN ABDUL-RAOF

QUR'AN, TRADITIONAL ACCOUNT OF THE COMPILATION OF THE

Muslim tradition preserves a large mass of material devoted to the compilation of the Qur'an. While there are many contradictory elements in the various accounts, a certain consensus emerged that combines a number of different elements into one coherent package. The following outline is taken from Ibn 'Atiyya (d. AD 1147).

At the time of Muhammad, the Qur'an was dispersed in the hearts of people. People wrote some of it on sheets, on palm-leaf stalks, on pumice stone, on baked clay, and on other items like that. When the killing of the Qur'anic reciters intensified during the Battle of al-Yamama, 'Umar ibn al-Khattab suggested to Abu Bakr al-Siddiq that the Qur'an should be collected. He feared that the important Qur'an reciters such as Ubayy, Zayd, Ibn Mas'ud and others like them might die. So the two of them delegated that task of collection to Zayd ibn Thabit. He collected it with great difficulty, without organising the *suras*. It is reported that, in this collection, verses from the end of *Surat al-Bara'a* (9) were omitted until they were found in the possession of Khuzayma ibn Thabit. Those sheets remained in the possession of Abu Bakr and were transferred to 'Umar ibn al-Khattab after him. Then Hafsa, his daughter, kept them during the rule of 'Uthman. When Hudhayfa returned from the military expedition in Armenia, he also considered the factors just mentioned. 'Uthman then authorised the collection of the codex and appointed Zayd ibn Thabit to the task of collecting it.

It is reported that 'Uthman said to this group collecting the Qur'an that if they disagreed about something, they

535

should write it in the dialect of the Quraysh. Thus, the arrangement of the *suras* today is that of Zayd and the associates of 'Uthman who were with him. The arrangement of the verses in the suras and the placement of the *basmala* (In the name of God, the All-merciful, the All-compassionate) at the beginning of the *suras* are said to derive from the prophet. As for the vowelling and diacritical markings of the codex, it is reported that 'Abd al-Malik ibn Marwan (r. AD 685–705) ordered this to be done and the task was completed by al-Hajjaj (d. AD 714).

References

Calder *et al.* (2003: § 4.5).

ANDREW RIPPIN

QUR'ANIC LINGUISTICS

The Qur'anic text represents a distinctive genre, and it merits an account that draws on a rainbow of linguistic approaches in order to appreciate the multi-faceted linguistic and stylistic aspects of this sensitive text. Although the Qur'anic text has been the major focal point for traditional analysis for the past fifteen centuries, there has not been an attempt to investigate Qur'anic discourse in a systematic fashion that deals with the major units of language. Muslim exegetes, grammarians and rhetoricians have dealt with the Qur'anic text through several traditional approaches which are linguistic or grammatical in orientation in some way or another, yet these investigations are independent of each other and, obviously, their aims and objectives remain distinct. As a result, the Qur'anic text remains unaccounted for in a holistic way. The major thesis of the present discussion is to lay the foundation for a new branch in Arabic linguistics, namely Qur'anic linguistics, which has been developed by the author of this article.

Qur'anic linguistics is a branch of theoretical linguistics that investigates the Qur'anic text from a variety of discoursal perspectives. It provides an indepth analysis of Qur'anic discourse based on modern European linguistic theories. Qur'anic linguistics attempts to investigate the three different but interrelated aspects of the Qur'anic text: linguistic, stylistic and phonetic features. Qur'anic linguistics examines the deliberate linguistic manipulation of the linguistic features of discourse such as grammar, lexis, and phonetics that are employed to achieve a Qur'an-specific conceptual thrust. The manipulation of linguistic and stylistic mechanisms is to achieve communicative functions. Qur'anic linguistics, therefore, accounts for stylistic shifts that are recurrent in Qur'anic discourse. Qur'anic linguistics is also concerned with the analysis of the Qur'anic text from a micro and macro level, thus, its unit of analysis is the word, the sentence, and the text in order to arrive at a comprehensive linguistic investigation of a given Qur'anic linguistic phenomenon. The present analysis, therefore, draws on text linguistics in order to take into account both the linguistic and the textual elements embedded in the Qur'anic text. From a text linguistics point of view, the Qur'anic text is cross-examined to uncover the linguistic features of textuality, intertextuality, textual progression, and conceptual interrelatedness.

Conceptual allusions and textual chaining are dominant discoursal features in the Qur'anic text and apply to its micro and macro levels. On these levels, this kind of linguistic anlaysis aims to provide a grammatical, semantic, and phonetic analysis of Qur'anic discourse. On the micro level, the lexicogrammatical selections, for instance, that contribute in the attainment of intertextual meaning relations will be analysed, on this level, the analysis also attempts to explore whether an *aya* (statement, sentence) is independent from or attuned to the one before it or after it.

Textual progression, therefore, can only be achieved if the text is intertextually and conceptually interrelated. As a result, Qur'anic text-processing and its explication can be realised. Similarly, on the macro level, textual progression explores the conceptual and intertextual connectivity that exists between a given *sura* (chapter) and the following one. In the light of this text linguistic approach, we take the Qur'anic text as a unit of description, and the semantic deep structure of the text can be interpreted as its topic, theme, or gist. According to Qur'anic text linguistics, the notions of context and co-text are paramount. The network of meaning relations echoes conceptual and intertextual chaining which can be accounted for through the analysis of the co-text which is the linguistic and textual environment in which a given word or *aya* occurs. The deep structure of meaning relations can also be accounted for through their context, which is the wider linguistic and situational elements surrounding a given text. The text, according to text linguistics, can be a word, a sentence, a chapter or the whole book. Qur'anic linguistics also accounts for the problem of applied semantics and their impact on applied and theoretical translation studies. This holistic linguistic approach, therefore, aims to provide insight into the Qur'anic text and thus be of great value to the exegesis of the Qur'an. Qur'anic linguistics also accounts for different levels of analysis; these are grammatical, semantic, phonetic and stylistic levels, which are expounded in the following discussion.

The Qur'anic text is marked by a number of linguistic features, the most interesting of these are left/right dislocation and the Qur'an-specific linguistic mechanism of simple or complex modification.

We encounter, in Qur'anic discourse, word-order change as a stylistic mechanism for communicative functions. A lexical constituent can be dislocated and placed to the left or right of its original sentence position, as in *yas'alunaka ka'annaka hafiyyun 'anha* (They ask you as if you are familiar with it) (Q.7:187), where the prepositional phrase (*'anha*, about it) is left dislocated as can be noticed by the unmarked (common) sentence structure *'yas'alunaka 'anha ka'annaka hafiyyun'*. Also in *iyyaka na'budu* (It is You we worship) (Q.1:5) where the second person singular pronoun (*iyyaka*, you) is right dislocated as can be shown by the unmarked sentence structure *na'budu iyyaka*.

Linguistically, Qur'anic statements vary in length. Grammatically, however, these can be simple or complex structures. The syntactic mechanism of cyclical modification is characterised by embedded modifying sentences, as in Q.37:40–49:

illa 'ibada allahi al-mukhlasin. ula'ika lahum rizqun ma'lum. fawakihu wahum mukramun. fi jannati al-na'im. 'ala sururin mutaqabilin. yutafu 'alayhim bika'sin min ma'in. bayda'a ladhdhatin lilsharibin. la fiha ghawlun wala hum 'anha yanzifun. wa 'indahum qasiratu al-tarfi 'in. ka'annahunna baydun maknun. (Not so however, God's true servants: in the hereafter, theirs shall be a sustenance which they will recognise as the fruits of their life on earth, and they shall be honoured in gardens of bliss, facing one another in love upon thrones of happiness. A cup will be passed round them with a drink from unsullied springs, clear, delightful to those who drink it: no headiness will be in it, and they will not get drunk thereon. And with them will be mates of modest gaze, most beautiful of eye, as free of faults as if they were hidden ostrich eggs).

(Q.37:40–9)

In the above extract, we have a list of modifications with inbuilt embedding, there are five modifying and four embedded clauses. The cyclical modifying clauses are:

1. *ula'ika lahum rizqun ma'lum* (theirs shall be a sustenance which they will recognise);
2. *fi jannati al-na'im* (in gardens of bliss);
3. *'ala sururin mutaqabilin* (facing one another in love upon thrones of happiness);
4. *yutafu 'alayhim bika'sin min ma'in* (a cup will be passed round them with a drink from unsullied springs); and
5. *'indahum qasiratu al-tarfi 'in* (with them will be mates of modest gaze, most beautiful of eye).

All of the above five modifying clauses describe the same noun phrase *'ibada allahi al-mukhlasin* (God's true servants). There are also four embedded clauses in various places modifying different noun phrases, these are:

1. *fawakihu wahum mukramun* (fruits of their life on earth, and they shall be honoured) which is embedded in the modifying clause number 1 and modifies the noun (*rizqun*, sustenance).
2. *bayda'a ladhdhatin lilsharibin* (clear, delightful to those who drink it) which is embedded in the modifying clause number 4 and modifies the noun (*ka'sin*, a cup).

3. *la fiha ghawlun wala hum 'anha yanzifun* (no headiness will be in it, and they will not get drunk thereon) which is embedded in an embedded clause number 2 and modifies the noun phrase *fi jannati al-na'im* (gardens of bliss), which is the modifying clause number 2.
4. *ka'annahunna baydun maknun* (as free of faults as if they were hidden ostrich eggs), which is embedded in the modifying clause number 5 and describes the noun phrase *qasiratu al-tarfi 'in* (mates of modest gaze, most beautiful of eye).

Qur'anic discourse is characterised by various rhetorical features such as embellishments and figures of speech, the most recurrent rhetorical features, however, are assonance and polyptoton.

In Arabic, this is referrd to as *al-saj'* whose major objectives are to achieve rhyme and musical rhythmical flow, the latter is a prerequisite for the realisation of cadence in Qur'anic discourse, as in

wal-shamsi waduhaha/wal-qamari 'idha talaha/wal-nahari 'idha jallaha. wal-layli 'idha yaghshaha. wal-sama'i wama banaha. wal-ardi wama tahaha (Consider the sun and its radiant brightness, and the moon as it reflects the sun. Consider the day as it reveals the world, and the night as it veils it darkly. Consider the sky and its wondrous make, and the earth and all its expanse)

(Q.91:1–6)

Here we have parallelistic structures rhyming together through the coreferential pronoun (*ha*, its) which has the phonetic features of a voiceless glottal fricative /h/ marked by a long vowel /a/ to accomplish cadence.

This is called in Arabic rhetoric *jinas al-ishtiqaq* that refers to the morphologically related lexical items which share the same root, as in *wama zalamnahum walakin kanu hum al-zalimin* (It is not We who will be doing wrong unto them, but it is they who will have wronged themselves) (Q.43:76) where the verb (*zalama*, to do wrong) is morphologically related to the noun (*zalim*, wrongdoer).

The notions of intertextuality, conceptual and textual allusions fall within the theory of text linguistics which accounts for the occurrence of lexical items and concepts at both micro and macro levels. Intertextuality in Qur'anic discourse provides a useful source for literary semiotics of the Qur'anic text. It is a linguistic investigation that examines how a given Qur'anic text is made in relation to other Qur'anic texts and the intertextual meaning relations among these texts.

Intertextual and conceptual relatedness runs throughout the Qur'anic text via the hook themes which provide textual cohesiveness and maintain textual progression. Therefore, an exhaustive account of this linguistic phenomenon needs to be provided at both the consecutive sura level as well as at an individual sura level.

This form of chaining takes a variety of forms as it is expounded by Q.17 and Q.18. First, hook motifs shared by Q.17 and Q.18. These two chapters are intertextually and conceptually linked by eleven major leitmotifs which hark back to each other:

(a) disbelief in the Prophet Muhammad's story of his night journey in Q.17 followed by an answer to the unbelievers scepticism and provides four stories of the companions of the cave, the wealthy man with two gardens, Moses and al-Khidr, and Dhu 'l-Qarnayn;

(b) Satan's rebellion as in Q.17:61 and Q.18:50;

(c) straightness and healing as in Q.17:9, 82 and Q.18:65;

(d) prophethood as in Q.17:15 and Q.18:65;

(e) polytheism as in Q.17:40 and Q.18:4–5;

(f) promise of the hereafter as in Q.17:104 and Q.18:98–100;

(g) contention as in Q.17:41 and Q.18:54;

(h) truth and falsehood as in Q.17:81 and Q.18:56;

(i) fogged minds and clogged ears as in Q.17:45–6 and Q.18:57;

(j) books and deeds as in Q.17:13–14 and Q.18:49; and

(k) the miracle as in Q.17:1 and Q.18:9.

Second, chaining between the beginning of Q.17 and Q.18. This is established through the prefatory ayas of Q.17 and Q.18, both suras begin with a statement glorifying God, as in Q.17:1 and Q.18:1. Third, chaining between the end of Q.17 and Q.18. This is established by the last statement of Q.17:111 and Q.18:110 in which the same notion of monotheism is highlighted. Fourth, chaining between the end of Q.17 and beginning of Q.18. This is achieved by the final aya of Q.17:111 which praises God and is intertextually and conceptually related to the first statement of Q.18:1 of the same notion.

Textual progression is realised through textual and conceptual allusions throughout a given text. Therefore, chaining can also be established at the macro level of a given Qur'anic chapter as in Q.2, for instance, which exhibits a number of intertextually and conceptually related notions. In Q.2, the recurrent leitmotifs are acceptance of repentance (*al-tawba*), mercy (*al-rahma*), favour (*al-ni'ma*), forgiveness (*al-'afwa*), arrogance (*al-istikbar*) which we encounter in Q.2:34, 37, 40, 47, 49, 52,

539

87, 122, 128, 143, 163, 182, 192, 207, 218, 225, and 235. Adam's sin, for example, is forgiven (Q.2:30–8). The prefatory statement (Q.2:2) refers to the Book as a source of guidance which leads to forgiveness. This is also related to the story of the Children of Israel who are urged to accept the revelation in order to attain forgiveness. In Q.2:36, the notion of forgetfulness is presented. Adam and his wife forget what their Lord has ordered them to do but they forget and fall victim to Satan's trap. In the transaction *aya* Q.2:282, we are urged to write contracts in transactions so that we do not forget what we have agreed before. Thus, forgetfulness which led to Adam's sin is again reiterated by the last statement Q.2:286 which is a kind of supplication (Our Lord do not condemn us if we forget or fall into error). The notion of clinging to the worldly life (*hub al-dunya wa karahiyyat al-mawt*) is another hook leitmotif which is shared by Q.2:94–5 and Q.2:212. Similarly, the notion of patience is also referred to recurrently as in Q.2:45, 61, 153, 155, 175, 249, and 250.

Texual allusions that contribute towards the attainment of texual chaining are also achieved through the notions of monotheism (Q.2:21, 22, 58, 107, 163, 255, 284–5), suppression of the truth (Q.2:42, 146, 159, 174), keeping the covenant (Q.2:27, 40, 63, 83, 84, 93) and spending in charity (Q.2:177, 195, 215, 254, 261–8, 270–71, 274). On the word level, the word 'God (Allah)' occurs 107 times and mankind in general are addressed for the first time in Q.2:21 (*ya ayyuha al-nasu* – O Mankind) and has not been repeated elsewhere in the Qur'an. We can also find an intertextual and conceptual link between the beginning and the end of Q.2 where textual allusions have been made to the believers in Q.2:2–6 and in Q.2:286.

Stylistic variation is a major linguistic characteristic of Qur'anic discourse. This linguistic feature, however, is both co-text and context-sensitive. In Q.2, for instance, we encounter a number of stylistic shifts as in the following examples:

First, word order shift, as in Q.2:48 and Q.2:123:

Wala yuqbalu minha shafa'atun wala yu'khadhu minha 'adlun (Nor shall intercession be accepted from any of them, nor ransom taken from them) (Q.2:48) and *wala yuqbalu minha 'adlun wala tanfa'uha shafa'atun* (Nor shall ransom be accepted from any of them, nor shall intercession be of any use to them) (Q.2:123), where in Q.2:48, the word *shafa'atun* (intercession) occurs first and *'adlun* (ransom) occurs sentence-finally but the order of these two words is changed in Q.2:123. This difference in word order results from their respective context of situation. In other words, stylistic variation is context sensitive. The context of Q.2:48 is Q.2:45 whose major leitmotif signifies the character traits of perseverance, patience and righteousness. Therefore, both Q.2:45 and Q.2:48 are intertextually and conceptually linked. The character traits referred to by Q.2:45 qualifies the individual to attain intercession on the day of judgement, due to the influence of context, the lexical item *shafa'atun*) occurs first in Q.2:48. The occurrence of *'adlun*, however, sentence-finally in Q.2:48 is to signify that even the availability of wealth and cash which are of great importance in the present life will be of no value in the hereafter. However, the semantic deep structure meaning of Q.2:123 is quite different due to its different context. Q.2:123 is conceptually related to Q.2:116 whose leitmotif is polytheism and refers to polytheists in the present world. Usually people resort to diplomatic effort and use intercession to settle down a serious problem. If the diplomatic effort of good offices fails, one may resort to financial means as a carrot to please the other party involved in the dispute, in other words, a ransom may be paid. To highlight the seriousness of polytheism referred to by Q.2:116, the word *'adlun* is placed sentence-initially in Q.2:123 to signify that even a huge *'adlun* (ransom) will not bring about forgiveness for polytheism, i.e., cash cannot buy God's forgiveness.

Second, lexical shift, as in Q.2:60 and Q.7:162: *fanfajarat minhu 'ithnata 'ashrata 'aynan* (Twelve springs gushed forth from it) (Q.2:60) and *fanbajasat minhu 'ithnata 'ashrata 'aynan* (Twelve springs gushed forth from it) (Q.7:160), where in Q.2:60, the verb *infajara* (to gush forth) is used but in Q.7:160 a different verb *inbajasa* (to gush forth) is employed. The two verbs have different semantic componential features: *infajara* signifies the gushing forth of water in huge quantities while *inbajasa* signifies the gushing forth of water in small quantities. The reason for this stylistic lexical shift is the context of situation in which each sentence is embedded. Q.2:60 occurs in a context in which reference to eating and drinking is made, in other words, there is a linguistic environment of hyperbole within Q.2:60, also, the occurrence of the expression *rizq Allah* (the sustenance provided by God) carries the semantic signification of abundance and infinite bounties of God. Thus, the employment of *infajara* which signifies abundance achieves lexical consonance and semantic compatibility. The verb *inbajasa*, however, occurs in a context of situation which refers to eating only and does not signify hyperbole, moreover, the expression *tayyibat* (good things) does not signify abundance, rather, there is a sense of the availability of finite things. Thus, the use of *inbajasa* achieves lexical

consonance and semantic harmony for Q.7:160.

We also encounter another case of lexical stylistic shift at word level, as in: *tilka hudud Allahi fala taqrabuha* (These are the limits set by Allah, so do not approach them) (Q.2:187) and *tilka hudud Allahi fala ta'taduha* (These are the limits of Allah, so do not transgress them) (Q.2:229), where in Q.2:187, the verb *taqrabu* (to approach the limits) is used but a different verb *ta'tadu* (to transgress the limits) occurs in Q.2:229. The stylistic variation between Q.2:187 and 229 is attributed to their respective instructional contexts of situation. The verb *taqrabu* in Q.2:187 is embedded in a context of very serious prohibition which is presented by the statement *wala tubashiruhunna wa'antum 'akifuna fi al-masajid* (Do not cohabit with your wives while you are in retreat in the mosques) where the negated verb *la tubashiruhunna* (do not cohabit with your wives) signifies the serious prohibition of not allowing the husband and wife to have a sexual intercourse in the mosque, the verb *taqrabu* is employed as a mytonymy. Also, the serious prohibition signalled by this verb is intertextually related to the same verb that has occurred in Q.2:35 *wala taqraba hadhhi al-shajarata* (Do not approach this [prohibited] tree) which also signals serious prohibition for Adam and Eve.

The second verb *ta'tadu*, however, is linked to a different context of situation which signifies a command expressed by the same statement Q.2:229 and which also signals specific Islamic legal rulings related to divorce and what is lawful for the husband and wife to take back the gifts reciprocated before divorce, etc. These details entail flexibility signalled by the additive conjunctive particles *fa ... 'aw* (either ... or) mentioned in Q.2:229. The verb *ta'tadu*, however, warns the husband and wife not to take advantage of this flexibility and transgress beyond the allowed bounds set by their Lord.

Third, case marking shift, as in Q.2:221: *wala tankihu al-mushrikati hatta yu'minna* (Do not marry polytheistic women until they believe) (Q.2:221), and *wala tunkihu al-mushrikina hatta yu'minu* (Do not marry polytheistic men [to your women] until they believe) (Q.2:221) where in the first part of Q.2:221, we encounter the verb *tankihu* (to marry) whose initial letter /ta/ is marked by two case markings /al-fatha/ (the vowel point /a/) and /tu/ (the vowel point /u/). Although the two verbs are transitive, the first verb with the vowel point /a/ is a transitive verb that takes one direct object, its direct object is *al-mushrikati* (the polytheistic women). However, the second verb with the vowel point /u/ is a transitive verb that takes two objects, its first object is *al-mushrikina* (the polytheistic men) and the second object is *al-mu'minati* (the believing women) which is ellipted from the sentence, i.e., implicitly understood.

Fourth, co-text-sensitive stylistic shift, as in Q.2:271: *wayukaffiru 'ankum min sayyi'atikum* (It will remove from you some of your misdeeds) (Q.2:271), where we have an additional preposition *min* (from) which is not usually found in this particular Qur'anic idiomatic expression as in Q.3:193, Q.8:29, Q.39:35, Q.48:5, Q.64:9, Q.65:5 and Q.66:8 (*wayukaffiru 'ankum sayyi'atikum*) which do not have the preposition (*min*). The reason why Q.2:271 is stylistically different from other statements elsewhere is due to the impact of its co-text which is represented by the two statements Q.2:272, 273 in which the preposition (*min*) occurs three times in the expression *wama tunfiqu min khayrin* (and whatever you spend of good) which occurs three times. To achieve stylistic symmetry, the preposition (*min*) is employed in Q.2:271.

This is a recurrent linguistic feature of Qur'anic discourse where two statements are intertextually and conceptually linked and echo exactly the same motif but are expressed in different stylistic ways, as in: *qala rabbi anna yakunu li ghulamun waqad balaghani al-kibaru wa imra'ati 'aqirun* (He said: 'My Lord, How will I have a boy when I have reached old age and my wife is barren?') (Q.3:40) and *qala rabbi anna yakunu li ghulamun wakanat imra'ati 'aqiran waqad balaghtu min al-kibari 'itiyya* (He said: 'My Lord, How will I have a boy when my wife has been barren and I have reached extreme old age?') (Q.19:8), which both express the same leitmotif but through more details and use of different word order.

Presentation technique is a stylistic mechanism concerned with the systematic presentation of Qur'anic notions. For instance, when the tenets of faith (*usul al-iman*) which are monotheism (*al-tawhid*), prophethood (*al-nubuwwa*), eschatology (*al-ma'ad*) and reward and punishment (*al-thawab wal-'iqab*) are referred to, they are presented in a systematic sequence, as in Q.2:21–2 (monotheism), Q.2:23 (prophethood), Q.2:24 (eschatology) and Q.2:25 (reward and punishment).

Another technique of presentation is related to substantiation and refutation where a thesis is presented and then either substantiation is provided for it or an anti-thesis is given as a rebuttal. For instance, when the notion of monotheism is presented, it is usually followed by statements substantiating it, as in Q.2:21 and Q.2:163 which refer to monotheism followed by Q.2:22 and Q.2:164 designating God's omnipotence. Similarly, whenever a thesis of polytheism is mentioned as in Q.2:28 and Q.2:116, an anti-thesis is provided as in Q.2:29 and Q.2:117 respectively which refer to God's omnipotence and aims to rebut the polytheists' thesis. In some cases, however, the two opposite notions of polytheism and monotheism occur in the same statement as in Q.39:4 followed by statements highlighting God's omnipotence as in Q.39:5–6 and concluding with reference to monotheism as in Q.39:6.

This is also part of the macro-level textual analysis that provides a comprehensive exegetical account of a given sura in terms of its leitmotifs, as in the following examples.

First, *Surat al-Nisa'* (Sura of the Women) (Q.4). This *sura* consists of 176 sentences. It was revealed in Medina and addresses Islamic law, the rights of women, social issues and human relations. It mainly focuses on women's rights in marriage, family and inheritance. The *sura* highlights the interrelationship between faith and social behaviour and stresses that the law cannot be upheld without the fear of God. Its prefatory statement appeals to mankind and reminds them that they are descendents of a single common father, Adam. The *sura* can be divided into two parts. Part I deals with Islamic legal rulings, such as the laws of inheritance, marriage and divorce, the rights of orphans and the weak-minded, and men's role after divorce. Part II deals with theological matters, such as husband–wife relationships, equality between men and women, kindness to parents, marital disputes, asylum seekers and other behavioural issues such as conceit, arrogance, prejudice, suicide, evil talk in public, hypocrisy, helping the poor and needy, and public relations.

Second, *Surat al-'Alaq* (Sura of the Germ-Cell) (Q.96). This *sura* was revealed in Mecca and was the first revelation made to the Prophet Muhammad when he was in his habitual seclusion in the cave of Mount Hira near Mecca in July or August AD 610. It is the first direct message to him to start his mission of preaching. The *sura*'s major thematic focus is the favour of knowledge bestowed upon man, reference about this particular motif is made through the initial word 'read' and the word 'pen'. We are told about the creation of mankind from a clot of congealed blood. It also highlights the moral lessons of arrogance as the source of evil, transgression against others, and righteousness. It consists of nineteen ayas.

Third, the *Surat al-Qadr* (Sura of the Night of the Decree) (Q.97)

This *sura* was revealed in Mecca and refers to the night of decree or power which is thought to be the 26th or the 27th of Ramadan and which is the night that Q.96 was revealed, that is, the night of the revelation of the Qur'an. We are told that this night is worth more than 1,000 months. This means the worshipping of God during this night is better than worshipping Him 1,000 months (eighty-three years and four months). The night of the decree holds special spiritual powers during which the angels and Gabriel descend by God's permission, and is also a blessed night during which supplication (requests) will be granted. The *sura*'s main leitmotif urges mankind to worship their Lord extensively and seek His forgiveness during this blessed night. It consists of five *ayas*.

Fourth, the *Surat al-Nasr* (Sura of the Help) (Q. 110). This is a Medinan revelation and consists of three ayas only. Its leitmotif is the guaranteed help of God to the righteous. Victory, we are told, is not an occasion for exultation, boasting and self-complacency; rather, it should be a factor that cements the believer's righteousness. The *sura* refers to the historical bloodless conquest of Mecca and predicts the prevalence of Islam. Traditions hold that this *sura* is equal to a quarter of the Qur'an and that it was the last *sura* revealed before the Prophet passed away. He lived seventy days after its revelation.

Micro-level intertextual and conceptual chaining is an account of conceptual connectivity at sentence level in which textual progression is investigated at intra-*aya* and inter-*aya* levels.

Intra-*aya* chaining is a semantically based exegetical account which aims to explore the built-in cohesion network within a given Qur'anic statement and how the logical relationship is established within a given statement. This linguistic analysis investigates the selection of a given lexical item or the phonological features of a given word that has been selected and their contribution in the overall meaning of the statement.

Let us consider the following examples:

First, *innakum lata'tuna al-rijala shahwatan min duni al-nisa'i bal antum qawmun musrifun* (Verily, with lust you approach men instead of women: nay, but you are people given to excesses!) (Q.7:81). In this sentence, the word *musrifun* (you are given to excesses or transgressed beyond bounds) is conceptually linked to Lot's advice to his people who were indulged in *al-fahisha* (abominations, i.e., homosexuality). The literal meaning of *musrifun*, however, is *those who waste*. Thus, the employment of the active participle (*musrifun*) is to establish semantic compatibility and lexical consonance within the constituents of the sentence. This can be appreciated by examining the semantic componential features of this word:

(i) going beyond what is ethically and religiously acceptable and is a kind of *israf khuluqi* (transgression beyond moral bounds);

(ii) wasting one's sexual energy in an unproductive sexual process: the valuable sperm is wasted;

(iii) the semen is the source of continuity of human civilisation on this earth; however, it is deposited in a place that does not reproduce. Thus, no investment is achieved in this kind of sexual process; and

(iv) the sexual energy and the semen should be given to a female counterpart; if homosexuality prevails as an acceptable practice, the female's womb will also be wasted, and women will no longer be able to reproduce.

Second, *wala tamudanna 'aynayka ila ma matta'na bihi azwajan minhum zahrata al-hayati al-dunya* (And never turn your eyes [with longing] towards whatever splendour of this world's life We may have allowed so many others to enjoy) (Q.20:131), where the lexical item *zahrata* is used whose literal meaning is flower, rose. In order to arrive at the semantic deep structure of Q.20:131, we need to explore the semantic componential features of the word *zahrata* which are 'attractive', 'aroma' and 'lasting'. What Q.20:131 attempts to emphasise is that people think only of the first two componential features of the word *zahrata* without taking into consideration the significant third feature which signifies that *the beauty and the aroma of the flower do not last for ever*. The admonition one gets from this is that one needs to focus on things that are everlasting and rewarding, namely, righteousness which leads to the everlasting happiness in the hereafter. The glitter of the nice things and other luxuries of this fleeting life may make an attractive show to us but their splendour will be coming to an end sooner or later, like the life of a flower.

Inter-aya chaining: textual progression and textuality can be established through the intertextuality and conceptual connectivity that hold between consecutive sentences, without this intertextual and conceptual link, any stretch of sentences cannot constitute a text. Let us consider the following example: *yuriduna an yakhruju min al-nari wama hum bikharijina minha wala-hum 'adhabun muqim* (They will wish to come out of the fire, but they shall not come out of it) (Q.5:37) and *wal-sariqu wal-sariqatu faqta'u aydiyahuma jaza'an bima kasaba nakalan min Allah* (Now as for the man who steals and the woman who steals, cut off the hand of either of them in requital for what they have wrought, as a deterrent ordained by God) (Q.5:38). On the surface level, the above two sentences are not related conceptually, therefore, Q.5:38 makes a sharp U-turn from Q.5:37. To arrive at their deep structure meaning and be able to establish conceptual connectivity between them, we need to explore the macro context surrounding them. Q.5:37 refers to the unbelievers who are trying in vain to get out of the hell fire while Q.5:38 refers to the Islamic legal injunction related to the punishment of those who steal. Earlier, however, we have encountered in Q.5:33 the legal injunction of those who endeavour to spread corruption on earth and that their hands and feet should be cut off from opposite sides. Later on, reference is made to the unbelievers in the hell fire and then to those who commit robbery. Since robbery is tantamount to hostile opposition to God's commands and His Prophet's teachings, as well as a criminal act that leads to the spread of corruption on earth, therefore, it deserves the same severe sentence of hand-cutting. Conceptual consonance and connectivity between Q.5:37 and 38 are further cemented by reference to the notion of repentence in Q.5:39 and that God is Oft-Forgiving and Most Merciful (*inna Allaha ghafurun rahim*).

A good translation is one that renders accurately the semantic features of the source language (SL) into the target language (TL). It, therefore, attempts to achieve equivalence in both meaning and response. Since Arabic and English are linguistically and culturally incongruous languages, there are limits of translatability that hamper the rendering of the Qur'anic text effectively. This is due to the various kinds of void. A void is a gap in the TL lexicon and the only way to render the meaning of the SL expression is through periphrastic translation, as in the Qur'anic expression (*tayammum*). Lexical items like these are marked by semantic compression which require lengthy details in order to convey their semantic features: 'to strike your hands on the earth and then pass the palm of each on the back of the other and then blow off the dust from them and then pass (rub) them on your face' (Q.4:43). The effect which the SL expression has left on the SL reader is not equivalent to that on the TL audience due to paraphrase. Similarly, the emotive verb *shaghafa* in *qad sha-ghafaha huban* (Her love for him has pierced her heart) (Q.12:30) is a lexical gap in the TL which needs to be paraphrased as *to pierce the heart*. The noun *al-shaghaf*, however, is the outer skin surrounding the heart, i.e., 'his love has penetrated her body and reached the outer surface and the core of her heart'. Second, this Qur'anic expression is a metonymy for being passionately in love. An interesting example of a lexical gap (delexicalisation) in the TL is the Qur'anic expression (*daha*) which most importantly signifies *shape*, as in: *wal-arda ba'da dhalika dahaha* (And after that, the earth: wide has He spread its expanse) (Q.79:30) where the verb (*daha*) in fact means 'to flatten something but to give it at the same time a round shape like a pizza base'.

Phonological features are language-specific and cannot be easily maintained in the TL. This, however, constitutes a translation problem when the sounds of a SL expression are an integral component of the semantic features of a lexical item, as in: *wakhasha'at al-aswatu lil-rahmani fla tasma'u illa hamsa* (And all sounds will be hushed before the Most Gracious, and you will hear nothing but a faint sough in the air) (Q.20:108)

Where the voiceless sounds /h/ and /s/ in *hamsa* (a faint sound in the air) are semantically effective in conveying the meaning of an atmosphere of awe and utter silence. The selection of this specific word is to achieve consonance of sound and semantic signification at the same time.

References

Abdul-Raof (2001a, 2001b), Andrews (1986: 62–154), Asad (1980), Beaugrande and Dresseler (1981), al-Biqa'i (1995), al-Razi (1990), Saheeh International (1997), Thilbault (1994: 1751–4).

HUSSEIN ABDUL-RAOF

QUR'ANIC STUDIES

Qur'anic studies (*'ulum al-Qur'an*) is a discipline that has developed after the death of the Prophet and is concerned with the investigation of various Qur'anic topics such as the compilation of the Qur'an, reasons for revelation, abrogating and abrogated *ayas*. The historical jouney of Qur'anic studies began when Muslim scholars' attention was attracted by Qur'anic calligraphy during and after the caliphate of 'Uthman b. 'Affan (d. AD 656) which later became known as Uthmani calligraphy. In the middle of the seventh century, during the Caliphate of 'Ali b. Abi Talib (d. AD 661), Muslim scholars were concerned with the grammatical analysis of Qur'anic discourse whose objective was to preserve the linguistic accuracy of the Qur'an and to facilitate its exegesis. During the second half of the first cen-

tury of the *hijra*, the focus on Qur'anic studies was shifted to other topics such as abrogation, the semantic ambiguities in the Qur'an, exegesis, and Meccan and Medinan revelations. Muslim scholars were more interested in exegesis than anything else during the second century of the *hijra*. Their research effort was culminated by the emergence of a comprehensive exegesis of the whole Qur'an by a distinguished scholar known as Ibn Jarir al-Tabari (d. AD 924). The third to seventh centuries of the Hijra were characterised by thorough research of specific topics of Qur'anic studies and the appearance of thesauruses of many volumes. The eighth century of the *hijra* was marked by the thesaurus of Badr al-Din al-Zarkashi (AD 1344–91) and the ninth century was marked by work of Jalal al-Din al-Suyuti (d. 1505). Research continued in Qur'anic studies, but the focus was mainly on exegesis until the present time. Among the major topics of Qur'anic studies are the following:

First: Meccan and Medinan Revelations. Qur'anic *suras* and *ayas* are classified as Meccan and Medinan. The leitmotifs of these two categories of revelation are different. As priority in Mecca was the establishment of a sound faith, the pivotal themes of the Meccan revelations were the belief in God, monotheism, eschatology and reward and punishment. The Meccan revelations lasted for thirteen years until the Prophet migrated to Medina in AD 622. The main focus of the Meccan revelations was to set the scene for a cohesive bond between the created and the Creator, and for the substitution of people's heedlessness towards their Lord for gratitude to His infinite favours through the total submission to God. The Meccan revelations included all the *ayas* and *suras* that were revealed in or around Mecca. The first revelation in Mecca was Q.96 and the last revelation was either Q.23 or Q.29. There are eighty-five Meccan *suras*. However, it is interesting to note that within a Meccan *sura*, we may encounter some Medinan *ayas*, and vice versa. Meccan revelations are characterised by a number of theological and linguistic features such as monotheism, prophethood, eschatology, reward and punishment, argumentation and refutation of unbelievers' theses, exhortation through reference to parables about previous Prophets and unbelieving nations, God's wrath, reference to Adam and Iblis (except for Q.2), onomatopoeic sounds, *sura*-initial cryptic letters (except for Q.2 and Q.3), concise sentence structure, and the occurrence of expressions such as 'prostration', 'O mankind' (except for the last part of Q.22:77).

The Medinan revelations, however, included all the *suras* and *ayas* that were revealed after the *hijra* in AD 622 in or around Medina, for this reason, they included revelations that were in Mecca or 'Arafa (thirteen miles from Mecca) because they were revealed after the *hijra*. The Medinan revelations lasted for about ten years; there are twenty-nine Medinan suras which are marked by leitmotifs such as the Scripturists (*ahl al-kitab*), Islamic legal rulings, social constitution, economic and family affairs, struggle for the sake of God (*jihad*), martyrdom, and the hypocrites. The Medinan revelations also focused on the regulation of religious duties such as the daily prayers, fasting, charity, and inheritance.

Second: inimitability of the Qur'an. Modern and traditional Muslim scholars have held the view that the Qur'an is inimitable and established their view on the Qur'anic reference in Q.2:23–4, 11:13–14 and Q.17:88 in which the Arabs and the rest of mankind are challenged to produce a book like the Qur'an. The inimitability of the Qur'an

(*i'jaz al-Qur'an*) as a discipline was developed by Abu Bakr al-Baqillani (d. AD 1012) who argued that the Qur'an was the Prophet's eternal miracle beyond human faculty to be imitated. Some of the aspects of inimitability are:

(a) the linguistic and aesthetic features which are Qur'an-specific such as the Qur'an's propositions, linguistic coherence, stylistic shift, presentation technique, semantically oriented phonetic features, and simple and complex modification;
(b) ethical values relevant to past, present and future generations;
(c) historical facts that were told by the Qur'an before they actually took place;
(d) scientific facts that have been approved by various modern sciences; and
(e) legislative information which includes details designed to regulate scio-economic affairs relevant to present and future generations.

Third: consonance in the Qur'an. This linguistic discipline emerged as a category of exegesis developed by exegetes like al-Razi (d. AD 1209) and al-Biqa'i (d. 1480) which investigates the cohesive semantic links between consecutive *ayas* and *suras*. According to this field of Qur'anic studies, there are thematic connectivity and textual progression between the beginning, the end, the beginning and the end, or the end and the end of *suras*. Cohesive semantic bonds and sequentiality also apply to the constituent *ayas* of a given *sura*. Although Muslim scholars unanimously agree on the arrangement of the *ayas*, they differ on the sequential order of the *suras* and whether the *suras* were divinely ordained.

Fourth: Argumentation in the Qur'an. This is a discipline that is concerned with the presentation of a Qur'anic argument that aims to refute opponents' thesis. For instance, a thesis (an opponent's view) is given first, then the anti-thesis which deals with monotheism is presented, followed by substantiation through detailed reference to God's omnipotence, and then the conclusion of the argument which provides further back-up to the anti-thesis, as in Q.30:16–31.

Fifth: reasons for revelation. This field is directly related to exegesis as it provides the scenario for each revelation. Reasons for revelation reflect the daily life of the Prophet and provide guidelines for unmasking the underlying message of a given revelation, as in Q.4:105 which highlights that justice is paramount regardless of faith, race, or colour of the accused.

Sixth: abrogating and abrogated. This is to do with the replacement of an *aya* with another as it is confirmed by Q.2:106. Since the revelation of the Qur'an was gradual and at different stages, there are some Islamic legal rulings that were enforced first but were later abolished by other revelations. Thus, the Islamic law was implemented in stages in order not to alienate people taking into consideration man's weakness and people's pre-Islamic habits and customs. For instance, the abolition of alcohol and gambling was phased in through the *ayas* Q.2:219, Q.4:43, and finally by Q.5:90–1. However, to non-Muslim scholars, this shows that within the Prophet's lifetime the contradictions, corrections, and qualifications that occur in the Qur'an began to attract attention and to arouse discussion.

Seventh: clear and ambiguous. Although Qur'anic *ayas* have accessible meanings as we are told by Q.11:1, some *ayas* are ambiguous either theologically or linguistically as we are informed by Q.39:23. The clear *ayas* refer to what is allowed and what is prohibited, the leg-islative limits, and compulsory actions. Ambiguous *ayas*, however, refer to theological matters such as God's attributes, and cryptic letters whose meanings are not known yet. Other *ayas* that are linguistically similar but stylistically different are also ambiguous as in Q.6:32, Q.7:169 and Q.12:109.

Eighth: parables and similitudes. These are employed in the Qur'an for morale-boosting and faith-strengthening, as we are told by Q.11:20. They are narrated in a simple manner without the use of flowery description. Qur'anic parables illustrate the life and experience of previous prophets such as Noah, Hud, Salih, Abraham, Lot, Moses and Jesus as in Q.2 and Q.3; previous nations such as 'Ad and Thamud as in Q.7:65–79; righteous people such as Luqman as in Q.31; the suffering of righteous people such as the Sleepers of the Cave as in Q.18 and Q.85; the life of evildoers like Pharaoh as in Q.20 and Q.26 and Gog and Magog in Q.18:94. A parable may occur at length in one *sura* but it can also occur in various other *suras* in brief complementing the same theme. For instance, the parable of the creation of Adam occurs in ten different *suras* as in Q.2:30–9, Q.3:59, Q.4:1, Q.7:11–25, Q.38:67–88. Although these parables are repeated elsewhere, they are presented in completely different styles and narrative techniques. The only complete parable is that of Joseph which occurs only in Q.12. Qur'anic similitudes, however, are used as a short, sharp shock for the reader to contemplate on their underlying morality as we are told by Q.59:21. These similitudes also occur in different *suras* as in Q.2:261, 264, Q.24:35, and Q.48:29.

Ninth: the Seven Modes. This field of Qur'anic studies is concerned with the study of the various dialects spoken by the Arab tribes in the Arab peninsula before and after the revelation of the

Qur'an. A mode is, therefore, a prestigious form of Arabic and the dialect of Quraish was the standard one. For Muslim scholars, the Qur'an was revealed in seven different forms of language spoken by the major Arab tribes. The seven modes represent different interpretations such as differences in grammatical categories as in Q.2:37; a change in grammatical category may lead to a change in meaning as in Q.12:31; differences in letters with or without dots as in *al-sirat* and *al-sirat* in Q.1:6 where both have the same meaning (straight path), singular or plural forms as in Q.23:8, differences in the morphological form as in Q.34:19, and differences in the employment of synonyms as in Q.101:5.

References

Abdul-Raof (2003), 'Atar (1988), al-Baqillani (1994), Donaldson (1953), al-Salih (1997), al-Suyuti (1996), al-Wahidi (1984), al-Zarqani (1988).

See also: **style in the Qur'an (*uslub al-Qur'an*)**

HUSSEIN ABDUL-RAOF

QURAYSH

Islamic tradition records that in the fifth century AD, 'five generations before the Prophet Muhammad', ancient Bedouin groups of camel drivers and caravan guides in central Arabia claiming descent from Quraysh were brought together by Qusayy, known as 'the Unifier' (*al-mujammi'*). These descendants of their eponymous ancestor, Quraysh, were divided into ten main clans. Muhammad belonged to one of them, the clan of Hashim. In time the Quraysh became the most powerful tribal group in the region. They developed extensive commercial interests in trading along the caravan routes that led north from Mecca into the Fertile Crescent, and south to the Yemen. As the leading family in Mecca they acquired the right to guard the central polytheistic shrine of the Ka'ba in the centre of the city and to provide for the pilgrims gathering there from all parts of the Arabian Peninsula. These commercial activities provided a source of revenue that was threatened when Muhammad began to preach the rigorously monotheistic message of Islam. As a result, the Quraysh were bitter opponents of the Prophet at the start of his mission in Mecca. They became his devoted followers. The Ka'ba became the central sanctuary of Islam after the Prophet had cleansed it of its multiplicity of pagan gods and goddesses. The city of Mecca was designated as a place of sanctuary in which inter-tribal feuding was forbidden. Non-Muslims were forbidden access to its environs. The founders of the great Islamic dynasties, the Umayyads, the 'Abbasids, the Fatimids, and the Hashimite rulers of Jordan claimed descent from the Quraysh.

EDWARD D. A. HULMES

AL-QUSHAYRI (d. AD 1074)

A Sufi from Khurasan, al-Qushayri was involved in the political intrigues between the Hanafis and Shafi'is during the eleventh century. However, he is known chiefly as the author of his *al-risala fi 'l-tasawwuf* (*Treatise on Sufism*). This work attempts to show the compatibility of Sufism with the *shari'a*, and it also contains biographies of famous Sufis, an explanation of Sufi terms, and discussions of Sufi miracles and conduct among Sufis.

References

Al-Qushayri (1990).

LLOYD RIDGEON

QUTB

Meaning the pole, or the axis, the *qutb* was the figure believed by Sufis to occupy the pinnacle of the spiritual hierarchy in the world. This hierarchy of saints, or friends of God, also included three *nuqaba'* (substitutes), four *awtad* (pillars), seven *abrar* (pious ones), forty *abdal* (substitutes) among other rankings. These individuals assist in the order of the universe which continues in existence until the *qutb* is no longer present.

LLOYD RIDGEON

R

RABAT

Administrative capital of the Sherifian Empire, situated on the north-western Atlantic coast of Morocco on the west bank of the Wadi Bou Regreg, opposite the twin town of Sale. To protect Sale in the tenth century, the Ifranids had fortified the other bank of the *wadi* with a *ribat* – a military-religious fortification. The Almohads established a permanent military camp there in the twelfth century that grew into a small town, the main feature of which was the Hassan Tower, the remains of a large unfinished mosque. A monumental gate from the period still gives access to the *kasbah*. Rabat remained less important than Sale, but on the expulsion of the Moors from Spain in 1610, some of them settled in Rabat and began its development. Sale began to decline and by the beginning of the twentieth century, Rabat, like Sale, had lost any real importance. However, in 1911 the occupying French chose Rabat as their administrative capital and it, together with Sale, grew to be the second largest urban area in Morocco after Casablanca. The French developed a large new town outside old Rabat with wide roads, green spaces and apartment and other blocks. It was French policy to build the modern European city separately to distinguish it from the traditional Islamic one. Rabat continued as official capital after independence in 1956 with Casablanca as economic and commercial capital. Rabat is the centre of government activities with a royal palace and numerous administrative institutions.

References

Abu-Lughod (1980), Findlay (1986).

DEREK HOPWOOD

RABI'A AL-'ADAWIYYA (d. AD 801)

Rabi'a was a female mystic from Basra who lived in the late eighth century and whose life is enwrapped in legend and

551

myth. She is characterised by later mystics for her intense love for God, epitomised in the saying attributed to her: 'I want to throw fire into Paradise and pour water into Hell so that these two veils disappear, and it becomes clear who worships God out of love, not out of fear of Hell or hope for Paradise'.

References

Smith (1928).

LLOYD RIDGEON

RADA'A

Rada'a is an Arabic word denoting 'breast-feeding', which refers to the legal status of a woman when she feeds a child in this manner. Islamic law perceives that any female adult who breastfeeds a child shall have a similar status to that of the child's mother. Breastfeeding is acknowledged as a duty of the birth mother, however, if for some medical or psychological reason this is not feasible, then a wet nurse can step in and assume the status of a mother. In this case, when the child is male, he is prohibited from marrying her or any of her other children, the proviso for this law being that he was suckled from an early age, i.e., during the first two years of his life and also that he had been fed in this way a minimum of five times.

References

Ibn Manzur (n.d.), Al Zuhayli (1985: 697–9).
MAWIL IZZI DIEN

AL-RADI, AHMAD (OR MUHAMMAD) B. AL-MUQTADIR, ABU'L-'ABBAS (AD 934–40)

When the 'Abbasid caliph al-Qahir was deposed in a military coup, al-Radi, a son of al-Muqtadir, was elected by the army as his replacement. The caliphate at this time had already entered a period of severe and terminal decline. Many of the most important provinces within the once united Islamic empire were slipping out of 'Abbasid control and were in the hands of semi-autonomous rulers. These provinces, which included Khurasan, North Africa, Egypt, Syria and parts of Iraq, no longer sent any revenues to the caliph. In an attempt to deal with the acute financial crisis facing the caliphate, al-Radi effectively relinquished his administrative duties by giving responsibility for all civil and military affairs to Muhammad b. Ra'iq, the military governor of Wasit, who took the title *amir al-umara'* ('commander of commanders'). When al-Radi died, it was the current *amir al-umara'* who appointed his brother Ibrahim b. al-Muqtadir as the new representative of the 'Abbasid regime with the honorary title al-Muttaqi.

References

Bowen (1928: index), Hitti (1970: 469–70), Ibn al-Jawzi (1938: 265–71), Ibn al-Tiqtaqa (1860: 328–32), Kennedy (1996: 196–8), Muir (1915: 569–72), Shaban (1971: 156–8).
RONALD PAUL BUCKLEY

RAHMAN, FAZLUR (b. 21 October 1919, in Hazara area (now in Pakistan), d. 26 July 1988)

Major Muslim thinker of the twentieth century. His father, *'alim* Maulana Shihab al-Din, an Islamic scholar, studied Islamic law at Deoband. Fazlur studied Arabic at Punjab University, then at the University of Oxford where he wrote a D.Phil. thesis on Ibn Sina (Avicenna), and was taught by H. A. R. Gibb and Van Der Bergh. He taught Persian and

Islamic philosophy at Durham University, then at McGill (Montreal) until 1961, when he was appointed by President Ayub Khan to be Director of the Central Institute of Islamic Research in Pakistan. In Pakistan he attempted to reform the university-level Islamic syllabus by returning to the basic elements of Islamic scholarly thought (Qur'an, sunna, *ijtihad* and *ijma'*), but his radical ideas led to hostile reactions from Pakistani *'ulama'* in the 1960s and, aggravated by the Pakistani political situation, he resigned. Subsequently, Rahman returned to university teaching in the West, where he re-evaluated his own religious heritage. He served first as Visiting Professor at UCLA, then in 1969 was appointed to the University of Chicago, where he built up an international centre for Near Eastern Studies until his death in 1988. In 1983 he received the prestigious Giorgio Levi Della Vida prize.

Fazlur Rahman was widely respected by both Western and Muslim scholars as a committed Muslim intellectual, attempting to reformulate the Islamic heritage by reassessing its successful manifestations in the past. He was a prolific author, producing a large number of articles and books on Islam, including *Islamic Methodology in History* (1965), *Islam* (1979), and *Islam and Modernity: Transformation of an Intellectual Tradition* (1982), in which he re-evaluated Muslim intellectual relationships with the sources of Islam, and explored the philosophical possibilities of Qur'anic hermeneutics. His approach was to attempt to understand the historical processes that lay behind the forms of modern Islam and, thereby, to distinguish essential principles based upon the Qur'an, whose central concern he saw as the 'conduct of man' (1982: 14). His attempts to apply the essential principles of Islam in a contemporary context included his book, *Major Themes in the Qur'an* (1989). *Revival and Reform in Islam: A Study of Islamic Fundamentalism*, edited by Ebrahim Moosa (1999) provided a comprehensive insight into the inconsistencies of modern Islamic fundamentalism. Fazlur Rahman's other contributions to scholarship included a reconsideration of major Islamic thinkers such as al-Ghazali and Ibn 'Arabi.

References

Armajani (2005), Berry (2003), Waugh and Denny (1998).

PAUL STARKEY

RAK'A

Literally 'bowing', the Arabic word refers to the sequence of the gestures made and the bodily positions adopted that accompany the words spoken during *salat*, the five daily prayers offered by Muslims in their ritual prayer and worship. Each period of ritual prayer requires Muslims to make the required number of such sequences (*raka'at*). A *rak'a* consists of the following succession of actions:

1. Facing Mecca, and having completed the prerequisite ablution, a Muslim raises the hands to the level of the ears and repeats the words *Allahu akbar* (God is most great).
2. The hands are lowered to the waist. The right hand is placed over the left. The words of the opening sura (*al-Fatiha*) of the Qur'an are recited.
3. The hands are raised once more to the level of the ears, and the words *Allahu akbar* repeated.
4. This is followed by a low bow from the hips so that the back is

horizontal. With the fingers spread, the hands are placed on the knees. The words 'Glory be to my Lord' are said three times.

5. After this bowing, the body is raised to the upright position. The worshipper says: 'God listens to those who thank Him' and 'Our Lord, thanks be to Thee'.

6. A full obeisance follows, in which the forehead and nose touch the ground between the supporting arms and hands. This is a mark of submission to God. The words 'Glory be to my God' are said three times.

7. After this prostration the body is set back in a sitting position on the ankles, with the legs tucked in beneath the body. The words 'God is most great' are repeated.

8. A second prostration, as in 6 above, is made.

9. The standing position is resumed and the *rak'a* is completed.

When this is done, the worshipper sits and recites words of praise to God, and repeats the *Shahada*: 'There is no god but God (*Allah*), and Muhammad is the Messenger (*rasul*) of God'. Having finished the sequence, the worshipper, still sitting, turns the head first to the right and then to the left, repeating the greeting: 'Peace be upon you, and the mercy of God'.

See also: **ritual prayer and worship.**

EDWARD D. A. HULMES

RAMADAN

The ninth month of the Islamic calendar, throughout which Muslims observe the annual period of fasting. The word *ramadan* does not mean 'fast' or 'fasting', however. It is derived from an Arabic root that suggests 'ground scor-

ched by excessive heat', 'aridity'. Such meanings are not inappropriate for the fast itself, which is often observed in periods of intense heat, although like all the months of the Islamic year, Ramadan retrogresses through the seasons.

See also: **calendar, Islamic; fasting**

EDWARD D. A. HULMES

RA'S AL-SANA

See: **New Year, Islamic**

RASHID, HARUN B. AL-MAHDI, ABU JA'FAR (AD 786–809)

Harun al-Rashid acceded to the 'Abbasid caliphate after his brother al-Hadi. The dynasty, which had been largely consolidated under al-Mansur, reached the height of its power and glory during al-Rashid's reign, this being in marked contrast to the troubles that were to befall the caliphate under subsequent rulers. Under al-Rashid, the caliph's administrative responsibilities were mainly limited to his being a court of final appeal, while the actual running of government was left to the Barmakid family and their secretaries (*kuttab*). Al-Rashid's main preoccupation was with the Holy War (*jihad*) against the Byzantines which was resumed during his reign, he himself taking personal charge of the army. Al-Rashid decreed that after his death the empire was to be divided between his two sons Muhammad al-Amin and 'Abdallah al-Ma'mun. This restructuring of government soon led to the Muslim community becoming once again embroiled in civil war.

References

Hodgson (1974: 291–300), Kennedy (1996: 141–8; 1981: 115–35), Muir (1915: 475–86),

Shaban (1971: 27–40), al-Tabari (1985–95: XXX, index).

RONALD PAUL BUCKLEY

AL-RASHID, AL-MANSUR B. AL-MUSTARSHID, ABU JA'FAR (AD 1135–6)

Al-Rashid succeeded his father al-Mustarshid as 'Abbasid caliph under the tutelage of the Saljuqs. Al-Rashid assumed the role of avenger of his father who had been murdered while prisoner of Mas'ud b. Muhammad and thus refused to send the tribute customarily paid to the Sultan. As a result, Mas'ud entered Baghdad causing the Caliph to flee to Mawsil. Mas'ud subsequently had the *'ulama'* in Baghdad issue a *fatwa* that deposed the Caliph on the grounds that he had opposed the Sultan and had therefore broken his vow of allegiance. Although al-Rashid made an attempt to rally support for his return to office, this proved unsuccessful and he was finally killed near Isfahan, probably with the involvement of the Saljuqs. He was succeeded by his uncle Muhammad b. al-Mustazhir al-Muqtafi.

References

Boyle (1968: 127, 128–9), Ibn al-Jawzi (1938: 50–1), Ibn al-Tiqtaqa (1860: 355–7), Le Strange (1924: 120, 204, 327), Muir (1915: 585).

RONALD PAUL BUCKLEY

AL-RASHIDUN ('THE RIGHTLY GUIDED CALIPHS')

See: **Abu Bakr al-Siddiq; 'Ali ibn Abi Talib; 'Umar ibn al-Khattab; 'Uthman ibn 'Affan**

RASUL

'Messenger', and sometimes translated into English as 'apostle'. One of the two classes of prophets, usually the bearer of a new revelation or faith or the head of a community (*umma*). Among those classed as 'messengers' in the Qur'an are Nuh, Lut, and 'Isa (Jesus). Angels are also accorded this status (Q.35:1). Muhammad himself is referred to as both a *rasul*, before whom there were other messengers (Q.3:144), and a *nabi*.

References

Gibb and Bosworth (1960–2003).

See also: **'Isa; messengers; Musa;** *nabi*; **prophets**

ANDREW J. NEWMAN

RASULIDS (AD 1228–1454)

The founder of this line was a commander, probably a Turk, in the service of the Ayyubids who, from a base in the Yemen formed an impressive state, the most powerful in south Arabia during later medieval times. It was strongly Sunni in ethos, hence hostile to the Zaydi Shi'ite Imams of highland Yemen. The Rasulid sultans were great encouragers within their lands of fine architecture and of culture and literature, the economic florescence of their kingdom benefiting from the proceeds of Indian Ocean trade.

References

Bosworth (1996: No. 49), Gibb and Bosworth (1960–2003).

C. E. BOSWORTH

RATIONALISM

In Islamic theology, rationalism is most closely identified with the Mu'tazilite school that arose in the aftermath of the death of the Prophet in the midst of debates about the nature of the community, the succession and the need for theological nuances between opposing, but dogmatic, positions. A particular point of contention, for example, concerned the issue of the punishment of a grave sinner, the early Mu'tazila arguing, against the two extreme arguments, that such a person was neither a non-believer nor a hypocrite, thus adopting 'a position between the two positions'. Their name 'Mu'tazila', 'those who go out/leave', originated with Hasan al-Basri (d. AD 728), an early Sufi who had argued for a sinner's status as a hypocrite. Mu'tazili rationalism in theology and jurisprudence experienced its heyday during the 'Abbasid dynasty in the early ninth century. During the later Saljuq period Ash'arism surpassed Mu'tazilism as Sunni Islam's premier school of theology and, in Sunni jurisprudence, *ijtihad* was subsequently formally ended. Nevertheless, Sunni Muslims consider the sources of the law to be the Qur'an, tradition (*sunna*), consensus (*ijma'*) and analogy (*qiyas*); in the last especially the jurisprudential process permits considerable recourse to personal legal reasoning. Shi'ism, if formally also wary of too much reliance on non-textual and especially philosophical tools of analysis, in their substitution of reason (*'aql*) for *qiyas*, formally incorporated recourse to the rationalist religious disciplines (including logic, grammar and *kalam*, for example) as among the sources of jurisprudence.

References

Rahman (1979: 43–4, 68–9, 85–6).

See also: *'adl*; **anthropomorphism; attributes of God;** *bila kayfa*; **free will and predestination;** *ijtihad*; **kalam and the** *mutakallimun*; *mujtahid*; **science**

ANDREW J. NEWMAN

AL-RAZI, ABU BAKR MUHAMMAD IBN ZAKARIYYA (AD 865–925/32)

Abu Bakr Muhammad Ibn Zakariyya al-Razi (Rhazes in the medieval Latin West) is best known as one of the very great physicians of Islam, noted for his empirical approach and for his voluminous medical writings. He was also a philosopher of note, quite unique in the annals of Islamic philosophy. Little is known about his life. Born in the Persian city of Rayy in AD 865, he served as a physician in a newly built hospital in Rayy and then in a hospital in Baghdad. He died either in 925 or AD 932. It is related that shortly before his death he developed a cataract but refused to have it operated on, exclaiming that he has seen enough of this world.

Of his philosophical writings few have survived. These include the ethical, *The Spiritual Physics*, the brief biographical apologia, *The Philosophic Way of Life*, the short, *A Treatise on Metaphysics*, whose authenticity is not certain, and a short political essay, *Portents of Advancement and Auspicious Rule*. Although helpful in reconstructing his philosophical position, they are insufficient. Much of what we know about his philosophy has been extracted from citations and the accounts of others, for the most part critical and unsympathetic. Moreover, most of these accounts were written after his death, the notable exception being the criticism of his contemporary, the Isma'ili theologian/philosopher, Abu Hatim al-Razi (d. AD 932). Despite the critical approach of most of them, these accounts tend to complement each other, yielding a discernable philosophical outlook.

Al-Razi's metaphysics rests on his doctrine of the five eternal principles, *al-qudama' al-khamsa*. Related to this metaphysics are his eschatology, ethics and his rejection prophets and revealed religions. The discernable influences on his thought are Plato's *Timaeus* (known in Islam through Galen's summary), Greek atomism, and Neoplatonic writings. Other influences suggested by some of the medieval sources remain in the realm of uncertainty.

Al-Razi's five eternal principles are matter, space, time, soul and the creator. Matter consists of the eternal atoms. These before divine intervention existed in chaos, lacking orderly arrangement, which for al-Razi meant lack of form. At a moment in time, God imposed order on the atoms, and with this act, as we shall indicate, the world as we know it came to be.

Space as one of the five eternal principles is absolute, infinite. Al-Razi distinguishes this from particular space, which is akin to the Aristotelian concept of place as the surface boundary, containing particular bodies. Particular space cannot exist without bodies. But since particular bodies come into existence with creation, absolute space transcends them. Absolute, eternal space, extend infinitely beyond the universe. Moreover, atoms, in both their chaotic state and their orderly state after creation, exist within absolute space. Absolute space allows for the existence of empty spaces between the atoms, vacuums. Hence, when organised, the atoms vary in their arrangements and proximities to each other, resulting in the respective densities of bodies, their differences in weight, texture and so on.

In a similar vein, al-Razi distinguishes between absolute universal time and particular time. Absolute time, one of the five eternal principles, is infinite, independent of motion, and not subject to enumeration. Particular time, dependent on bodies and motion, is subject to enumeration and is finite. Its finitude applies to its beginning and to its end.

For al-Razi, the created world comes to an end at a finite time in the future.

Turning to the fourth eternal principle, soul, in al-Razi's system it is not an emanation from God, but it is the principle of life and the driving force for the creation of the world. Al-Razi's resorts to myth to answer two questions: why was the world created at all, and why was it created at a particular moment of time.

According to this myth, soul became infatuated with matter and wanted to unite with it. It could only unite with it if matter was orderly, when it had form. The soul attempted to give form to the chaotic atoms, but these resisted its attempt. This left the soul in great affliction. Then the fifth principle, the creator, who is compassionate, intervened on behalf of soul, imposing order on the atoms. Soul joined matter. This resulted into its individuation at various levels, resulting in the bringing about of plant, animal and human life. God in His compassion endowed man with reason, an emanation from his essence, so that at some future time, soul will realise that its true abode is not this world, and will return to its original state. This is where philosophy comes in. It is through philosophy that the soul attains virtue and gets to know its true destiny, namely that it belongs to its original state. Unlike his philosopher successors in Islam, al-Razi believed that all humans are capable of philosophy, which led to virtue. Prophets and religions are not necessary, in fact, he held, religions have been the source of strife.

Going back to the question of why was the world created at a particular moment of time, not earlier nor later, al-Razi indicates that this is because God is a free agent. His acts are not determined, by any particular moment of time. Thus, in absolute time, each and every moment is similar to another. It is the choice between similar things that defines freedom of choice. This is how al-Razi, in effect, argues for the divine attribute of will.

It is not surprising that al-Razi's critics charged him with unorthodoxy. For in addition to his criticisms of prophethood and religions, he believed that during the world's finite duration, transmigration of souls takes place. Moreover, his system does not allow for individual reward and punishment in the hereafter. For once the soul realises that the created world is not its true abode, it returns to its original state as one entity. With its return, the atoms also return to their chaotic state.

Al-Razi's system, however, is not entirely devoid of Islamic religious components for it affirms two of the Qur'anic divine attributes, the attributes of compassion and of will.

References

Butterworth (1993: 227–36, 238–57), Druart (1997: 47–71), Goodman (1975: 25–2), Kraus (1936).

Michael E. Marmura

RECONQUISTA (CHRISTIAN RECONQUEST OF SPAIN)

The campaign by the Christian monarchs to retake Spain began soon after it had fallen to Muslim hands in the eighth century, though the first to declare the effort a 'Crusade' was Pope Urban II in AD 1095. The Muslim occupation of the Iberian Peninsula (al-Andalus) began in AD 711 when the freedman Tariq b. Ziyad landed with Muslim forces at the place later to be known as Gibraltar, followed the next year by his governor Musa b. Nusayr. The rapid success of the Muslim occupation of Spain reflects the inability of the Visigoths to defend the area after years of decay. Within twenty years, the Muslim forces had reached southern France, suffering defeat only in the Battle of Poitiers in AD 732. The governors of al-Andalus were responsible to the governor in Qayrawan and, ultimately, to the Umayyad caliphate in Damascus. When the Umayyad caliphate collapsed, members of the family fled to Spain where they established themselves as a rival caliphate to the 'Abbasids. Under this Andalusian Umayyad dynasty, the area under Muslim control was strengthened and expanded within the Iberian peninsula. The chamberlain al-Mansur was particularly successful, commanding over fifty campaigns against the Christians. The *Reconquista* was not showing much sign of success at this stage.

After al-Mansur's death in AD 1002, the Muslim kingdom began to fragment. Without his powerful hand, the ethnic and political tensions within the kingdom led to the establishment of a number of smaller Muslim states (the *tawa'if*), each with particular ethnic identities (Berber, Andalusian, Slav, Arab). This disunity amongst the Muslims presented the Castilian king Alfonso VI, eighty years later, an opportunity to launch the *Reconquista* in earnest. In AD 1079, he captured the fortress of Coria from the Sevillian Muslim ruler al-Mutawakkil. In 1085 he recaptured Toledo, and began to act as an arbiter amongst the *tawa'if*. He was only stopped in 1086 when the Muslim kingdoms asked the Almoravid Yusuf b. Tashufin to intervene and protect them. The forces met at al-Zallaqa, and Alfonso's army was soundly beaten. The *Reconquista* had been checked, though only temporarily.

The twelfth century saw a more determined and united effort by the Christian powers to retake Muslim Spain. Success by Ramon Berenguer IV, Count of Barcelona, in taking Tortosa,

Fraga and Lerida, and the campaigns of Alfonso VIII of Castile in the late twelfth to early thirteenth century lead to the recapture of much the area under Muslim control. The battle of Las Navas de Tolossa in AD 1212 was probably decisive when Muslim forces under the Almohad Muhammad al-Nasir were beaten by a coalition of Christian forces. The rival kingdoms of Navarre, Aragon and Castile united under the command of Alfonso VIII. The effort was further enhanced by a papal bull declaring the need for a crusade against the Muslims in Spain. The bull called on people to join the Christian forces, promising absolution in return. From then, Muslim power in Spain was reduced year on year: Cordoba fell in 1236, Valencia in 1238, Seville in 1248. The only Muslim territory to remain after this rather rapid collapse was the Nasrid 'Kingdom of Granada'. This was to survive for a further two centuries, during which time it became a mere vassal state of Castile, functioning in an almost identical manner to Castile's Christian vassal states. This balance between Granadan alliance with Muslim North Africa, and its treaty obligations to its Christian overlords was successful in the short term, but eventually proved impossible to maintain. The Catholic monarchs Ferdinand and Isabella eventually secured the surrender of Granada in 1492 and the Christian *Reconquista* of Spain was eventually completed.

References

Harvey (1990), al-Maqqari (1949), Watt (1965).

ROBERT GLEAVE

RED FORT, DELHI

The Mughal emperors Akbar (1556–1605) and Shah jahan (1627–58) were patrons of ambitious building programmes which included the construction of palace-cities at their capitals of Agra, Delhi and Lahore. Shah Jahan built a splendid new city Shahjahanabad between 1638 and 1648 in north Delhi within a fortification wall that originally had fourteen gates. A palace complex, the Lala Qila or Red Fort, within its own retaining wall of red sandstone is located on the north-eastern side of the city and consists of a sequence of public and private areas. An entrance gate on the west in the form of a red sandstone pavilion gives access to a large square and audience hall where the emperor heard public petitions and received important visitors seated on a white marble throne under an ornate canopy. Framing this public area are gardens, pavilions for private receptions and prayer and family life. Stylistically, the palace combines sandstone and white marble into modules of domed chambers linked by a colonnade of cusped arches on columns all decorated with carved and inlaid flowering motifs in a fusion of Indian and Islamic influences.

References

Nicholson (1989), Tillotson (1990).

JENNIFER SCARCE

REPRESENTATION OF THE HUMAN FORM, PROHIBITION ON

It is commonly reported that Islam holds that the human form should not be represented, for to do so would be in imitation of God and against the divine unity for which Islam stands. Muslims discussed the issue extensively and certainly hold to a doctrine that insists on non-representational art in all religio-ritual contexts. Yet from early times, the representation of the human (and animal) form in both sculpture and painting was widely undertaken, although it is often felt that the Arabs did not undertake such activities to the same extent as other conquered populations.

The basis for the rejection of representational art is often traced to the Qur'an, citing both God's unique power to create (as in Q.3:43) and the rejection of idols (in Q.5:92 and 6:74 for example). Unlike the biblical prohibition which is quite explicit ('Thou shall not make unto thee any graven image or likeness of anything that is in heaven or that is in the earth beneath or that is in the water under the earth', Exod. 2:4), the Qur'an does not deal with the issue in any direct manner. It is in the *hadith* material that a clearer picture emerges with statements such as 'The angels will not enter a house in which there is a picture of a dog'. Clearly, such material set the tone for later Islamic centuries, which, while the appreciation of the representational arts was certainly present, certainly did not encourage such artistic endeavours. The avoidance of such art in religious settings has thus created a particular identifying mark of Islamic society.

References

Grabar (1973: esp. Chapter 4).

ANDREW RIPPIN

RESURRECTION OF THE DEAD

The doctrine of the rising of the dead from their graves to face Judgement.

See also: **'Isa; judgement on the *yawm al-qiyama***

ANDREW J. NEWMAN

RIBAT

In early Islamic history, the *ribat* was a military fortification established on the frontier of the Islamic world. It has been suggested that there was a connection between the *ribat* and Sufism as some volunteers who participated in propagating Islam on these territorial boundaries also engaged in an ascetic lifestyle. As the Islamic boundaries stretched further into non-Islamic lands, the Sufis adopted the *ribats*, some of which became large lodges for itinerant Sufis.

LLOYD RIDGEON

RIDA, RASHID (1865–1935)

Born in Tripoli (now in Lebanon), Rida moved to Egypt after meeting Muhammad 'Abduh, and he then became 'Abduh's leading associate and biographer, helping in the production of the journal *Al-Manar* (*The Lighthouse*), with its new style of commentary on the Qur'an. After 'Abduh's death, however, and partly as a result of increased Western direct involvement in the affairs of the Middle East after the First World War, Rida's political views became more critical of the West, and his religious views, partly under the influence of the revived Wahhabi movement in Su'udi Arabia, became more conservative. He thus came to insist more vigorously that it was only the Islam of the first generation of Muslims, the *salaf*, that was reliable and, therefore, an example for modern Muslims. He was particularly concerned about the abolition of the institution of the caliphate by the new republican government of Kemal Ataturk in Turkey in 1924, and he organised an international conference in Cairo in 1926 to try to bring about its restoration, even if in a different form, but this came to nothing.

References

Badawi (1978: Chapter 3), Kerr (1966), Shahin (1993).

HUGH GODDARD

RIDDA

Ridda is a term denoting 'apostasy' and literally meaning 'going back on faith'. A person guilty of *ridda* would be allowed up to three days in which to return to Islam and after that period he would be executed. For *ridda* to be proven as an offence, the usual Islamic conditions such as sanity and maturity must be applicable to the offender. According to the Hanafis, a woman is exempt from capital punishment in a case of *ridda*. Due to the gravity of the offence and the potential punishment, it is advisable for the offender to receive three warnings to return to the fold of Islam before a final judgement is pronounced. This crime must only be considered as valid in an Islamic state where the offender openly declares his apostasy. The punishment should not be applied lightly and a thorough investigation of the offender's intention is crucial prior to the implementation of any judicial decision.

References

Al-Zuhayli (1997: 8:60, 6:186).

See also: **apostasy**

MAWIL IZZI DIEN

RIFA'IYYA

This Sufi order is known for its *dhikr* rituals during which the participants performed feats with burning coals and fire. The Rifa'iyya Sufis claim the founder of the order was Ahmad ibn 'Ali al-Rifa'i (d. AD 1182) who lived in south Iraq. The order spread into Egypt, and related groups were also found in Iran. At its greatest extent, the Rifa'iyya was the most widespread order, but its popularity has diminished since the fifteenth century.

References

Schleifer (1991).

LLOYD RIDGEON

RIHLA FI TALAB AL-'ILM

'Journey in search of knowledge', spoken of by Muhammad in the traditions as worthy of Paradise, where 'the learned' (*'ulama'*) are spoken of as 'heirs of the Prophets'.

References

Waines (1995: 38–40, 288).

ANDREW J. NEWMAN

RISALA

'Message', in reference to the mission of a *rasul*, to which the word is related in Arabic. Also, a treatise or essay.

See also: **rasul**

ANDREW J. NEWMAN

RITUAL PRAYER AND WORSHIP (*AL-SALAT*)

Motivated by right intention (*niyya*) and with a mature understanding of what they do, Muslims turn to face Mecca five times each day before performing this act of ritual prayer and worship, the second of their five religious duties (*'ibadat*). The word *salat* is probably derived from Aramaic. In its verbal form, it signifies God's disposition 'to bless', and mankind's readiness 'to worship God in prayer'. *Salat* is obligatory (*fard*), to be undertaken at dawn (*salat al-subh*), at noon (*salat al-zuhr*), in the late-afternoon (*salat al- 'asr*), immediately after sunset (*salat al-maghrib*), and at night (*salat al-'isha'*). To guard against a lapse into sun worship, once common among unbelievers, there are three times of the day when *salat* is not to be performed: at sunrise, when the sun is at the meridian, and at sunset.

During menstruation, and after postnatal bleeding, women are excused from this otherwise obligatory religious duty. Children are encouraged to pray at seven years of age and to follow the prescribed ritual from the age of ten. In any case it becomes obligatory at the age of puberty (*bulugh*). The Qur'an refers to *salat* in several places: Q.31:14 'Say to my faithful servants to observe *salat*', Q.2:43, Q.2:83, Q.2:110, Q.22:78. It is a duty to be performed by believers at fixed times (Q.4:103). 'Establish prayer at the two ends of the day and at the approaches of the night' (Q.11:114). 'Celebrate the praises of thy Lord before the rising of the sun and before its setting, celebrate them for parts of the hours of the night and at the sides of the day' (Q.20:130).

The five periods of prayer and worship (not specifically mentioned as five in the Qur'an) are given times, names and forms, on the authority of Islamic tradition. Despite minor local differences, Muslims everywhere perform essentially the same prescribed ritual. The prerequisites for the proper performance of *salat* are two, ritual cleanliness (*tahara*) and right intention (*niyya*). Without the preliminary statement of intention, acts of devotion may become perfunctory and thus without value. Before *salat* the body, the clothing, and the place of prayer are to be cleansed – so far as conditions allow. There are three kinds of ritual ablution: *ghusl*, *wudu'*, *tayammum*.

The five daily prayers are as follows: *fajr*, the morning prayer at dawn, recited at any time from dawn (about an hour and a quarter before sunrise) until sunrise. Next comes *zuhr* (prayer at noon), which may be performed shortly after midday until the time in the afternoon when the shadow of everything becomes its equal (according to *shafi'i* law) or its double (according to *hanafi* law). The third of the prayers, *'asr*, is recited in the afternoon between the end of the time for *zuhr* and just before sunset. The fourth prayer, *maghrib* immediately after sunset and ends quickly at the setting of the red twilight. The fifth hour of prayer, *'isha'* (night prayer) begins when darkness overtakes the horizon and may continue until the middle of the night. If one of the times of prayer is missed, it can be made up at another time. As Islam began to move beyond the confines of Arabia these rules have been modified in the light of local conditions and circumstances.

Salat is performed in community or privately in a mosque, but it may be performed anywhere, provided that the location is not deemed to be impure. So, for instance, the environs of an abattoir, a cemetery, or a bath house, are excluded for the purpose. The correct performance of ritual prayer requires a Muslim to complete the prescribed cycles of 'bowings' (*raka'at*, sing. *rak'a*) and prostrations whilst the appropriate sequence of sacred words is uttered in Arabic. A Muslim must be in a state of ritual purity (*tahara*, *ihram*) before beginning to pray. This involves ablution. Standing to face the direction of Mecca, the worshipper first raises the hands to the ears and says: *Allahu akbar* ('God is greater'). Lowering the arms to meet in front of the body, with the right hand over the left, the worshipper then recites the *fatiha* (the opening sura of the Qur'an). The hands are raised again to the ears and the words *Allahu akbar* repeated. This is followed with a bow, with hands on knees, fingers spread, and the upper body bent forward to a horizontal position. The words: 'Glory be to God the Almighty One' is said three times. Standing upright after the bow, the worshipper next says: 'God hears those who thank him', and 'Our Lord, thanks be to thee'. Next comes the prostration (*sujud*), as a mark of submission to God. Forehead and nose are placed on the ground between the hands. The words 'Glory to my God, the Most High' are then spoken three times. In the next position (*jalsa*) the worshipper sits back and rests on the heels, hands on knees, repeating *Allahu akbar*. A second prostration follows. The *rak'a* is completed by resuming the standing position. The words of the *Shahada* are recited afterwards in a sitting position: 'There is no god but God, and Muhammad is the Messenger of God'. Still sitting, a Muslim turns the head first to the right and then to the left, repeating the greeting: 'Peace be upon you, and the mercy of God'. The performance of this daily religious duty is a primary obligation for all Muslims, although according to some Islamic traditions, those whose circumstances are such as to make prayer at the appointed times difficult (travellers, for instance) are permitted to perform some of the prayers at the same time, shortening the sequence of four *raka'at* to two, in a concession known as *qasr*.

References

Hitti (1973: 131–2), Hourani (1991: 66, 148,169), Smart (1969: 383–4).

EDWARD D. A. HULMES

RITUAL SLAUGHTER OF ANIMALS

See: **sacrifice**

ROBERTS, DAVID (1796–1864)

Scottish painter. Born to a poor family in Edinburgh, David Roberts showed early talent as an artist. He moved to London where he became a scene painter at the Drury Lane Theatre. He soon began to travel in Europe and further afield and his journeys inspired many of his best-known paintings. His views of the forum in Rome, of Gothic cathedrals in Spain and most of all his impressive depictions of ancient Egypt are familiar to art lovers and specialists. He owes his present fame as an Orientalist painter mostly to his lithographs of the Middle East, perhaps in particular those of the Holy Land. These latter are the fruit of his travels through the Sinai Peninsula to Jerusalem and as far as Ba'labak. They were published in three volumes in 1843 and 1849 under the title *The Holy Land, Syria, Idumea, Egypt, Nubia*. His style is recognisable by its mixture of grandeur and attention to detail. His paintings are an invaluable record of the Middle East of his time.

References

Guiterman (1978).

DEREK HOPWOOD

ROSARY, ISLAMIC

See: **misbaha**

ROYAL MOSQUE, ISFAHAN

The spectacular Royal Mosque built between 1613 and 1630 is an integral building in Shah Abbas I's (1587–1629) ambitious master plan to establish a new political, religious and commercial centre in Isfahan. The heart of this scheme is a vast square begun in about 1590, dominated on each side by a major building. The monumental portal of the

Royal Mosque dominates the south side. This impressive structure is based on the classic Iranian mosque plan of an open court with four *iwans* and a domed square chamber towards the *qibla* that extends into a winter prayer hall and adjoining *madrasas*. The portal, entire interior surface and the dome are covered in mosaic and overglaze painted tilework in a profusion of geometric design and panels of peony and palmette scrollwork in a brilliant palette of blue, turquoise, yellow, green, white and black.

References:

Blunt (1966), Seherr-Thoss and Seherr-Thoss (1968).

JENNIFER SCARCE

RUMI, JALAL AL-DIN
(AD 1207–73)

Perhaps the most famous of all Persian mystic poets, Rumi was born in Balkh but settled in Konya to escape the Mongols. His chief works include a didactic *mathnawi* of some 25,000 verses, and over 3,000 *ghazals* collected in the *Diwan-i Shams-i Tabrizi*. It is difficult to find a systematic framework in Rumi's verses, but his works contain most of the elements contained in the Persian Sufi worldview of the thirteenth century AD, including the idea of 'everything is He', the need for a spiritual guide, to pass from the exterior to the interior meaning of things, and to engage in specific Sufi practices. Rumi is famous for his association with his own spiritual guide, Shams-i Tabrizi, who was probably killed because of the jealousy some of Rumi's followers felt towards him.

Rumi is often associated in the West with the Mawlawiyya Sufi order, which has become known for its mystical dancing, or whirling. This whirling is accompanied by music and the recitation and singing of Rumi's verses. It has been remarked that in recent years English translations of Rumi's works are among the best-selling books of poetry in the West.

References

Rumi (1924–40, 1991).

LLOYD RIDGEON

RUSTAMIDS (AD 778–909)

The Rustamid imams of Tahert, in what is now north-western Algeria, represent an enduring strain in North African Islam, that of the Ibadi sect of the Kharijites. Ibadi communities were scattered all over the Maghrib from the Moroccan Sahara to Tripolitania and Fezzan, and these acknowledged the Rustamids as their spiritual heads. Ethnically, they were predominantly Berber, and their stance represented a protest against the political hegemony of the Arabs and their promotion of Sunni Islam. The Rustamids succumbed to the Fatimids, but isolated pockets of Ibadism have survived in the eastern Maghreb countries till today.

References

Bosworth (1996: No. 9), Gibb and Bosworth (1960–2003).

C. E. BOSWORTH

RU'YAT ALLAH

The conflict around the concept of witnessing God is a theological controversy on interpreting the Qur'anic verse: 'Some faces that day will beam (in brightness and beauty) looking towards their Lord' (Q.75:23). The idea here is that the believers will see God at the

Day of Judgment, this belief was mainly adopted by the Sunni Ash'arites, who, however, could not agree about the nature of this vision. Al-Ghazali and many Ash'arite Sufis believed that it would be a vision of the heart rather than a sensible vision. In his book *Kitab al-'Arba'in*, al-Ghazali considered the possibility of a vision of God also in this life. Sufis such as al-Hallaj and al-Bistami did not only claim to have seen God but also to have been in full unity with Him. The Mu'tazilite school, on the contrary, rejected in general the whole concept and argued for the impossibility of such a vision either in this life or in the next. Their disagreement is based on their concept of the absolute immateriality of the nature of God. Since God is immaterial, He cannot be seen by the senses and therefore the above verse must be interpreted as an attempt to convey an image of the highest happiness in paradise for souls directing themselves wholly towards God. Although the philosophers shared this concept with the Mu'tazilites, some, like Ibn Sina, believed that the goal of the after-life is to be in connection with the light of God and that the whole idea of paradise should rather be perceived as a state of spiritual happiness than a material pleasure.

References

Arberry (1966), al-Ghazali (1952).

MAHA EL-KAISY FRIEMUTH

S

SA'A

Sa' is a term used to designate a legal measure (quantity) and the instrument that is normally used to measure the payment of *Zakat*. Its value was 4 *mudd* (*modius*) according to the custom of Medina. The value of the *sa'* was, from the shari'a point of view, fixed in Islamic law by the Prophet in the year AD 623–4 when he laid down the ritual details of the Islamic feast of *id al fitr*. This carried with it the compulsory giving of alms called *zakat al fitr*, the value of which in grain represented one *sa'* for each member of a family. The *sa'* of Medina was subsequently chosen as the standard measure.

References

Izzi Dien (2004: 165).

MAWIL IZZI DIEN

SABA'

Biblical Sheba, pre-Islamic Sabaean kingdom, flourished *c.* 750–*c.* 115 BC.

Minaean and Sabaean civilisations were the earliest recorded in south Arabia and mentioned in Akkadian texts, the Bible, in classical texts and their own Semitic Sabaic inscriptions in *musnad* script. The Sabaeans migrated from the north and ruled through kings and 'high priest-princes' (*mukarribs*). Its capital after *c.* 600 BC was at Maryab (later Ma'rib in Yemen), on a natural land route from Qana to Wadi Hadramawt.

An ever-changing series of wars, alliances and coalitions were made between Saba' and the nearby kingdoms of Qataban, Ma'in and Hadramawt and other minor city-states, including Najran, and Awsan. Saba' controlled the Bab al-Mandab and straits into the Red Sea and set up colonies in east Africa as late as the first century BC. The Himyarites, who followed the Sabaeans, were conquered by the Romans (first century BC), then the Ethiopians (*c.* AD 340–78). Until the third century AD, the prosperity of Saba' depended on trade in frankincense and spices by caravan into ancient Israel and Syria and across the Red Sea. The powerful Shamir Yuhar'ish became king of Saba', Dhu Raydan, Hadramawt and Yamanat (third century AD). Although the kings of Aksum claimed to be kings of Saba' and Dhu Raydan (fourth century AD), Saba' regained control of the four provinces. In the fourth to sixth centuries, Saba' was ruled by Himayrites. The fourth-century Sabeans were polytheistic pagans worshipping principal deities including their (local national patron, sun, moon and Venus-star), and Christian by the sixth century. In AD 628 Badhan, the Persian governor of Yemen, converted to Islam.

The significance of Saba' for the Islamic world lay partly in establishing an Arab tradition of pre-Islamic secular art, through legends of its splendid tall palaces and copper lions, for Ma'rib and Sirwah contained impressive buildings. From the eighth century BC the famous Ma'rib dam provided a stable, highly organised, vast irrigated agricultural economy until the late sixth century AD, when Saba' disappeared after the dam collapsed. Saba' is mentioned in Q.34:15–16 as a warning against worldly pride after the resulting devastation of Ma'rib oasis.

Islamic, Ethiopian, and Jewish traditions contain many references to the 'Queen of Sheba' (Bilqis) who possibly flourished (tenth century BC) and visited King Solomon in Israel. Bilqis appears in the Qur'an (27:26ff), unnamed, and her story has been recounted by Muslim commentators. Arabs gave her a southern Arabian genealogy and she appears in Persian tradition as daughter of a Chinese king and a *peri*. In Ethiopian tradition, in which she is called Makeda, she married King Solomon and their son, Menelik I, founded the royal dynasty of Ethiopia, the line continuing to King Haile Selassie.

References

Schippmann (2001), Simpson (2002).

JANET STARKEY

SABIL

The fourth pillar of Islam is charity, which can range from providing funds for the construction of a mosque, hospital or school to modest donations. One of the most common forms of charity was to commission a *sabil* – a public drinking fountain – to distribute free water. The *sabil* (from the Arabic, *fi sabil Allah* 'in the path of God') took many forms. In the mausoleum of Qa'it Bey, built in Cairo in 1474, it is located behind a window grille in the outer wall. In Ottoman Turkey, the *sabil* is related in charitable intention and function to the more elaborate *cesme* – street fountain. The grandest here is the fountain built in 1728 for Ahrnet III in front of the Topkapi Palace in the form of a square kiosk with a deep overhanging roof. Comparably ornate street fountains are located in the medina of Fez, such as the Nejjarine fountain, of eighteenth-century date, decorated with mosaic tilework and carved stucco, which supplies water to the craftsmen and residents of the neighbourhood.

References

Burckhardt (1992).

JENNIFER SCARCE

SACRIFICE

In a religious context, a sacrifice is an act intended to make sacred to deity the offerings provided by the worshipper. In Islam this involves the ritual slaughter of animals offered for a specific and declared purpose. Several words are used in Arabic to refer to the sacrifice of a slaughtered animal. The verb *dahha* means 'to sacrifice by immolation', the verb *dhabaha* means 'to slaughter by slitting the throat', the verb *nahara* means 'to butcher by slitting the throat'. The first two verses of Q.108 (*al-Kawthar*, 'the Abundance'), may be rendered in English thus: 'We [God] have granted you abundance, so turn to your Lord in prayer and offer sacrifice'. From an Islamic point of view, it is God who provides abundantly for the welfare of those obedient to his revealed will. Because of the generosity of the Provider, the injunction to make the sacrifice elicits a response of gratitude. The sacrifice is not intended to appease an offended God nor does it serve as atonement for sin. Sacrifice may be made at any time but the Feast of the Sacrifice, *'id al-adha*, is celebrated throughout the Islamic world at the end of the *hajj*, the annual pilgrimage to Mecca. Animals acceptable for sacrifice include sheep, goats, cows and camels. They must be ritually slaughtered in order to be consumed as food. In the process they become *halal*, i.e., 'released from prohibition'. A declaration of intent (*niyya*) to perform an act of ritual slaughter is followed by the invocation of the Divine name: 'In the Name of God, God is Most Great'. The two 'Names of Mercy', *al-rahman*, *al-rahim*, are omitted. The animal's throat is swiftly cut by a Muslim in a way that severs both the jugular vein and the windpipe. The blood, which is not acceptable as a food in Islam, must be drained from the animal. As in Judaism, the blood is identified with the life force and is not to be consumed.

References

Hulmes and Sykes (1991: 265–69, 276–9).

See also: **Feast of the Sacrifice (*'Id al-adha*); food and drink; naming ceremony of a child (*'aqiqa*)**

EDWARD D. A. HULMES

SADAQA

See: **alms-giving (*zakat*, *sadaqa*, *waqf*)**

SADAT, ANWAR (1918–81)

Egyptian statesman and president. Sadat was born into a poor family in a village north of Cairo. He spent the first seven years of his life in his village, went to the local school and enjoyed life amongst the peasants. In 1925, he moved with his father to Cairo where he went to secondary school and was drawn into the political atmosphere of demonstrations against the British presence. He then entered the Military Academy and graduated as an officer in 1938. He was posted to Upper Egypt together with Jamal 'Abd al-Nasir, and the two of them, with one or two others, formed an informal group of officers who were dissatisfied with the existing government. During the Second World War, Sadat showed pro-Nazi sympathies and was arrested by the British and imprisoned until October 1944. After the war, he was active on the fringes of political violence and terrorism. Surprisingly, he did not take part in the Palestine war with 'Abd al-Nasir and his comrades but rejoined the army only in 1950 as captain. The other officers did not quite trust him and he was not given a leading role in the 1952 coup, although from then on he was a faithful son of the revolution, working loyally for 'Abd al-Nasir, even at times being mocked for his assiduous self-effacing sycophancy. He held a number of minor posts and to most people's surprise he was appointed 'Abd al-Nasir's deputy in 1969 and was able to take over on his master's death in 1970.

Emerging from the shadows, he quickly showed himself to be his own man with policies radically different from those of his predecessor. He broke ties with the Soviet Union and mended fences with the West. He then turned on the real enemy, Israel, and launched in October 1973 the attack across the Suez Canal. This was well planned and kept secret, and it raised Sadat's prestige. Although the war ended in stalemate and even Israeli victory, with American help the Israelis were forced to withdraw across the canal, which was reopened to shipping for the first time since 1967.

At home, Sadat was not so successful. The withdrawal of food subsidies in 1977 caused widespread rioting and numerous casualties. Sadat was stunned and looked around for scapegoats. He blamed the Left and the Marxists and made hundreds of arrests. He had over-reacted and it marked the beginning of a decline in his popularity. He introduced strict censorship and declared a state of emergency. Sadat had to look abroad for new moves and astonished the world when he made a dramatic visit to Jerusalem in November 1977. In a speech to the Knesset he made clear his commitment to peace and later at Camp David he signed a peace treaty with Menachem Begin. Most other Arabs believed that he had been hoodwinked by the Israelis, as he had obtained no real concessions from them. He was ostracised and the more extreme Muslim groups were particularly bitter in their criticism of him for his 'betrayal'. In October 1981 at a military parade, members of one such group, *Jihad*, assassinated him for having behaved in their eyes as a corrupt tyrant.

References

Hirst and Beeston (1981), Sadat (1978).

DEREK HOPWOOD

SA'DI, SHEYKH MOSLEHODDIN
(*c.* AD 1208–92)

Persian poet and prose writer, born in Shiraz, where he also died. Sa'di's pen name was probably derived from the name of the family of Abu Bakr Sa'd ibn Zangi, who ruled Fars in the early thirteenth century. He studied at the Nizamiyya College in Baghdad and travelled extensively in the Islamic world for around thirty years before returning to Shiraz in AD 1256. The frequent references to dervishes in his works have led some scholars to suggest that at some stage he had been initiated into a Sufi order.

Sa'di's two most celebrated works, the *Bustan*, a didactic poem in ten chapters, and his *Golestan*, in mixed prose and poetry, were composed in AD 1257 and AD 1258 respectively. Both works cover much the same ground, their purpose being to provide advice and to illustrate, often through the use of anecdotes, such virtues as justice, good government, humility, contentment, and earthly and mystical love; of the two works, the *Golestan* has the lighter touch. Sa'di also composed love lyrics in the *ghazal* form, as well as *qasida*s in honour of the Zangid and other rulers, and a collection of *mutayabat* containing obscene poems, after the fashion of the time. After AD 1260, Shiraz began to be affected by the arrival of the Mongols, and the poet dedicated to Shamsoddin Joveyni, an influential official, a collection of lyrical and didactic poems known as the *Sahebnameh*.

Sa'di's work, both prose and verse, is characterised by a freshness and simplicity of approach, and he has traditionally been regarded as a master of classical Persian style, widely read by students beginning the study of written Persian. These qualities have given his work a more immediate appeal than that of many other Persian authors; numerous commentaries on the *Golestan* and *Bustan* have appeared in various languages, and many manuscripts of his works are richly illustrated. Many of his verses have achieved the status of proverbs. The respect accorded him has led to his frequently being called 'Shaykh Sa'di'.

References

Arberry (1945, 1958: 186–213), Massé (1919).

PAUL STARKEY

SAFA

See: *al-Hajj*

SAFAVIDS (1501–1722)

Although arising from a local, originally Sunni Sufi order in Azerbaijan, the Turkish Safavids speedily became the vigorous upholders of Shi'ism, with the shahs elevated to a status as divinely inspired leaders for the imams. The founder Shah Isma'il began the process of turning the Persians and Turks of Iran, by brute force, from Sunnis largely to Shi'ites. Sufi orders were persecuted and Shi'ite '*ulama*' encouraged to emigrate to Iran from outside, hence it is the Safavid period that sees the elaboration, in its final form, of Twelver Shi'ite law and theology. There also evolved a distinctive school of philosophical mysticism based on the capital, Isfahan – a city adorned with fine buildings and gardens, the wonder of visiting European travellers and traders. In the early eighteenth century, however, the Safavids succumbed to the attacks from Afghan bands, the last Safavids being puppets and pretenders.

References

Bosworth (1996: No. 148), Gibb and Bosworth (1960–2003), Roemer (1986: 189–350), Savory (1980).

See also: **al-Shirazi, Mulla Sadra**

C. E. BOSWORTH

AL-SAFFAH, 'ABDALLAH AL-B. MUHAMMAD, ABU'L-'ABBAS (AD 749–54)

Abu'l-'Abbas al-Saffah was the founding caliph of the 'Abbasid dynasty, the longest lasting and most celebrated dynasty in Islam. Shortly after the arrival of the Khurasanian army in Kufa in AD 749, Abu'l-'Abbas was declared Caliph and was acknowledged as such by most of the Muslim community. The bases of al-Saffah's power included the Khurasanian army and members of the 'Abbasid family who were given military commands and governorships in the provinces. He adopted a policy of reconciliation with former enemies, but the remaining members of the Umayyad family were sought out and many were executed.

The 'Abbasids, who were from the House of the Prophet, were proclaimed to replace the secular kingship (*mulk*) of the Umayyads with a rule whose foundation was primarily religious, thus marking a return to the original conception of the caliphate as a religious institution. The one fundamental difference between them, however, was that whereas the Umayyad regime had ruled a largely Arab empire, the 'Abbasids ruled an empire that was more international and in which the Arabs formed only a constituent part.

The ill-defined principle of hereditary succession inaugurated by the first Umayyad caliph Mu'awiya b. Abi Sufyan was continued under the new dynasty, and al-Saffah nominated his brother 'Abdallah b. Muhammad al-Mansur as his successor.

References

Kennedy (1981: 46–57, 1996: 128–30), Muir (1915: 437–45), Shaban (1971: 187–8), al-Tabari (1985–95: XXVII, 145–212 *passim*).

RONALD PAUL BUCKLEY

SAFFARIDS (AD 861–1003)

Whereas the Samanids represented the aristocratic Perso-Islamic tradition and are therefore praised in the Arabic and Persian sources, the Saffarids were of plebeian origin (lit. 'sons of the copper-smith') from Sistan in eastern Iran. They seem to have arisen out of anti-Kharijite volunteer bands there, but since they built up a vast military empire from lands that were theoretically under 'Abbasid caliphal authority, and even threatened Baghdad with capture, they incurred orthodox disapproval. In the tenth century, Saffarid power shrank, but the last *amir*, Khalaf b. Ahmad, achieved a reputation as patron of scholars and theologians, from whom he commissioned a 100-volume compendium of the Qur'anic science. Not surprisingly, this has failed to survive.

References

Bosworth (1975: 106–35, 1994: 1–361, 1996: No. 84), Gibb and Bosworth (1960–2003).

See also: **Kharijism**

C. E. BOSWORTH

AL-SAHABA

Two prominent groups assisted the Prophet Muhammad in Medina after the *hijra*. The 'Emigrants' (*al-Muhajirun*) were those who moved from Mecca to help him in establishing the Islamic community in Medina. The 'Supporters' (*al-Ansar*) already lived in Medina and joined his cause when he arrived there in CE 621. Muhammad was obliged to use his skills to reconcile the differences that arose between the Emigrants (who maintained that they had supported him from the outset of his mission in Mecca) and the Supporters (who asserted that if they had not given him asylum when he arrived in Medina, he would not have survived). The Prophet succeeded in bringing both groups together in the common cause, after which they were known collectively as *al-sahaba*, 'the Companions'.

EDWARD D. A. HULMES

SAHIH AL-BUKHARI

After the Qur'an, the *Jami' al-Sahih* of Abu 'Abdullah Muhammad b. Isma'il al-Bukhari (AD 810–70) is arguably the most revered book of Sunni Islam. Together with the *Jami' al-Sahih* of Muslim b. al-Hajjaj, it is generally considered to contain the fullest collection of *hadiths* that can reliably be traced back to the Prophet Muhammad. As such, it is one of the foundations of legal and theological thinking in Islam, as well as religious practice and everyday morality.

As might be thought requisite for a *hadith* specialist, al-Bukhari is credited with a formidable memory. He was the son of a traditionist, and studied traditions in his native Bukhara while still a teenager. From the age of sixteen, when he performed the *hajj*, he travelled through many parts of the Islamic world in pursuit of *hadiths* and wrote a number of works on aspects of their transmission. He was celebrated for his immense knowledge and attracted great audiences of the interested, among them Muslim b. al-Hajjaj and Abu 'Isa al-Tirmidhi, the author of another of the *Kutub al-Sitta*.

Al-Bukhari conceived the idea for his greatest work when he heard the wish expressed for a collection comprising the reliable *hadiths* alone. He is quoted as confessing that it took him sixteen years to complete, though the result has stood the test of time among Muslims, and for Sunnis it remains the most widely used source of prophetic sayings.

The method that al-Bukhari followed in compiling the *Sahih* traditions was to establish the complete soundness of an *isnad*, the chain of transmitters, by investigating the biographies of the individual members to ensure their complete honesty and that they could have heard the preceding member reciting the *hadith*. Here al-Bukhari was particularly strict, because he imposed the requirement not only that any pair of individuals in a chain should be contemporaries and so could have met, but that there must be positive evidence that they actually did meet.

The result of his precise and painstaking application was a collection of more than 2,700 individual traditions (the precise count varies, though the figure of 2,762 is accepted by many), less than 0.5 per cent of the original mass of 600,000 he reputedly collected. They are arranged in ninety-seven books, *kutub*, which are each divided into chapters, *abwab*. The number of these varies widely, from nearly 380 separate comments on the Qur'an in Book 65, the *Kitab al-Tafsir*, and 199 chapters in Book 56, the *Kitab al-Jihad*, to as few as three in Book 36, the *Kitab al-Shuf'a*, and Book 38, the *Kitab al-Hawalat*, and a single chapter in Book 31, the *Kitab Salat al-Tarawih*. Similarly, the number of *hadiths* in each chapter varies, and some have none. In all, a total of 7,563 traditions are included in the *Sahih* (again the precise number varies), though many of these are repetitions of the 2,700 or so that al-Bukhari admitted as reliable.

This arrangement of books and chapters, and the repetition of *hadiths* in more than one place explains al-Bukhari's intentions in composing the *Sahih*. Although he does not explicitly state what he was about, one can see in this structure an attempt to order the traditions according to legal and spiritual requirements. In cases where *hadiths* exemplified and commented on more than one of these, he repeated them as he thought appropriate. It has been inferred from the widely differing number of *hadiths* in various chapters, and from the fact that some chapters contain none, that he was actually fitting traditions into a predetermined scheme, and leaving chapters empty when he found nothing to illustrate their scheme. Thus, far from being a mere list of the *hadiths* that could be regarded as reliable, the *Sahih* can be regarded as a guide to questions of *fiqh* and *iman*, embracing all the major aspects of Islam.

The range of subjects comprised in the ninety-seven chapters of the *Sahih* is striking. It starts with the biographical topic of the Prophet's first experience of revelation, and ranges through such matters as faith, the five pillars and questions of their observance, issues of life in the community and of relations between the community and those outside, creation, pre-Islamic prophets, the Prophet Muhammad himself, the companions, expeditions, comments on the Qur'an, divorce, medicine, manners, religious duties, penalties, and finally the oneness of God. From such richness and variety, it is not difficult to understand how Sunnis can claim to be able to follow the Prophet's teachings and enacted example in all aspects of their individual and communal life.

Such an ambitious and elaborate undertaking has inevitably met with criticism. Some Muslim scholars have questioned al-Bukhari's judgement about the standing of certain transmitters in *isnad*s and of a few of the *hadiths*, and have also doubted his whole method of examining *isnad*s to the neglect to the *matn*s. But the overall reliability of his collection was generally accepted within a century of al-Bukhari's death, and for many Muslims it has long been assumed that if a *hadith* appears in the *Sahih* it can be taken as originating from the Prophet.

Among the numerous editions of the *Jami' al-Sahih*, the *Sahih al-Bukhari* (Riyadh, 1999) is a recent single-volume publication with useful indexes. There is an edition with parallel English, translated by Khan (1996). The chapters concerning historical matters are edited and translated by Asad (1993).

DAVID THOMAS

SAHIH MUSLIM

Together with the *Sahih* of al-Bukhari, the *Jami' al-Sahih* of Muslim Ibn al-Hajjaj (AD 821 [in some reports 817]–75) is regarded as the most reliable collection of *hadiths* from the Prophet Muhammad. It is habitually mentioned together with its companion work, and throughout Islamic history comparisons between the two have frequently been made. While al-Bukhari has generally been accepted as superior, in such areas as the Maghrib, Muslim has often been given precedence. And it is generally agreed that of the two his collection is the more readily accessible.

Muslim's *sahih* is unusual in compilations of *hadiths* in having an introduction. Here the author reveals that he set about the project in response to a friend's request, and also says that he intends his compilation for lay-people, because 'there is no point in their searching through the majority, since they are unable to understand even a little'.

In this introduction, Muslim explains his method in accepting and rejecting certain transmitters, quotes a number of *hadiths* from both the Prophet and Companions concerning forgery and the reliability of transmitters, and lastly defends the acceptability of *isnad*s in which the relationship between certain individuals cannot be fully known. Overall, he makes it clear that he was writing in an uncertain situation in which he believed it was imperative to provide a body of prophetic sayings that believers could trust. The unanimous consensus of Muslims in the following centuries has been that he succeeded entirely.

The *Sahih* contains over 7,400 individual *hadiths*, a tiny fraction of the 300,000 sayings that Ibn Khallikan says Muslim originally collected. The precise total is 7,479 according to the 1996 Beirut edition, and 7,190 according to Siddiqi's translation. Allowing for repetitions, however, the number of *hadiths* has been computed at about 3,000 (though 4,000 is often given). They are arranged in fifty-four books, *kutub* (this is according to the numeration of al-Nawawi, who edited and commented on the *sahih* in the thirteenth century, in his *Tuhfat al-Ashraf*; Jamal al-Din al-Mizzi [d. AD 1341] lists forty-two books), which are each divided into dramatically differing numbers of chapters, from ninety-six in Book 1, the *Kitab al-Iman*, which is one of the longest, to a mere two in Book 41, *Kitab al-Shi'r*. Within each chapter the number of *hadiths* likewise differs considerably.

The accessibility of Muslim's arrangement has frequently been commented upon. Whereas al-Bukhari repeats *hadiths* according to their relevance to the themes of his chapter divisions, Muslim gathers related *hadiths* on the same point of teaching in the same chapter. A good example of this occurs in Book 6, *Kitab Salat al-Musafirin wa-Qasriha*, Chapter 48 on the seven readings of the Qur'an. This chapter comprises nine separate *hadiths*, though they all refer to the same subject of the seven readings. The first is the most explicit, in which 'Umar Ibn al-Khattab brings before the Prophet someone he has heard reciting differently from the way he himself was taught, and the Prophet informs him of the *ahruf* in which the Qur'an was revealed, 'so recite the one that is easy'. The second contains a slight difference in the *matn*, and the third has a different *isnad*. Then the remaining six offer variants of another version of the story containing different characters and motivations, but still sanctioning seven readings.

This method of organisation suggests that he was guided by the core message of similar *hadiths*, and brought them together so that they enforce one another. He was thus saved from providing long introductory headings to his chapters in the manner of al-Bukhari, since the contents presumably speak for themselves.

The order of the books in the *Sahih* begins with the five pillars, continues with marriage, business transactions and other elements of individual and communal concerns, and concludes with repentance, judgement day, paradise, the end time and piety. The last book of all is a Qur'an commentary, though it was never completed. If this order conforms to any principle of arrangement, this seems to be doctrinal, beginning with the bases of faith, then the elements of the good life, and finally the prospects of the life to come.

The reliability of Muslim's work was recognised early, and it was accepted together with al-Bukhari's *Sahih* as the best compilation of authentic traditions, so much so that for Sunni Muslims it has long had an almost canonical status.

A mark of the high regard in which it has been held is that the great thirteenth century traditionist Muhyi 'l-Din Yahya b. Sharaf al-Nawawi (d. AD 1277) wrote a commentary on it with which it is regularly published.

The best edition of the *Jami' al-Sahih* is by 'Abd al-Baqi (1955–6). It has been published with al-Nawawi's commentary many times, most recently in Beirut, 1996. There is an English translation by Siddiqi (1976). This lacks Muslim's Introduction which is, however, supplied by Juynboll (1984).

DAVID THOMAS

SAHIH AL-TIRMIDHI

The *Kitab al-Jami' al-Sahih*, 'The Reliable Collection', one of the Sunni *Kutub al-Sitta*, is the major work of Abu 'Isa Muhammad b. 'Isa al-Tirmidhi (d. AD 892), who was born in Mecca and, after extensive travels, died in Tirmidh. Despite its title, it is regarded as one of the four *sunan* works, and conventionally placed below the *Kitab al-Sunan* of Abu Da'ud in importance.

Al-Tirmidhi learned from both al-Bukhari and Abu Da'ud, and like the latter he wrote notes to many of the 3,956 *hadiths* he included in his *sahih*. This comprises forty-six books (fifty in some editions), beginning with cleanliness and prayer and ranging through the main observances and requirements of religion to commentary on verses of the Qur'an and details about the life and virtue of the Prophet. It includes books on theological matters (like the *sahih*s of al-Bukhari and Muslim) as well as legal and ritual matters.

In his comments on the *hadiths*, al-Tirmidhi categorises them with some precision into: *sahih* 'sound', *hasan* 'fair', *sahih hasan* 'fair–sound', etc., going as far as *hasan sahih gharib* 'fair–sound–rare', and the like. This system permits clear differentiation between individual traditions, and it proved influential among later *muhaddith*s. He also frequently identifies individuals in an *isnad*, compares a tradition with others which may be fuller or transmitted differently and, in general, reveals something of the process by which he came to admit a tradition. His comments often display the differences between legal groups of his own time and earlier, and thus preserve valuable information about the regional diversity in legal thinking. He concludes his work with the *Kitab al-'Ilal*, 'The Book of Reasons', in which he explains his methods, and in particular defends his system of categorising and defines what he means by *hasan* when applied to a *hadith*.

Al-Tirmidhi's *Sahih* was accepted as an authoritative collection of traditions in the centuries after the *muhaddith*'s death and was given its place in the *Kutub al-Sitta* among the four *sunan* works. Many commentaries have been written on it, including Ibn 'Arabi's *Sharh Sahih al-Tirmidhi*. An accessible edition of the work is by Nassar (2000).

DAVID THOMAS

SAID, EDWARD WILLIAM (1935–2003)

Palestinian American scholar. Said was born in Jerusalem and was educated in Western schools there and in Cairo. He moved to the USA and received his BA from Princeton and a doctorate from Harvard. He combined at least two careers as a scholar and critic in English literature (and in music) and as a committed spokesman and writer for the Palestinian cause. His most famous work *Orientalism* (1978) combines both these interests and is also in a different field. It is a stinging critique of the approach to their subject of European and American Orientalists, whom he sees as using their knowledge to further the cause of imperial domination and colonialism. He defines Orientalism as a style of thought based on a feeling of superiority over others on the part of Europeans and Americans and on a false distinction between an imagined Orient and the Occident. The book has had immense success and its followers have changed the course of Oriental studies. He wrote numerous other works including *Culture and Imperialism* (1993) on a similar theme. In the field of Palestinian studies he published *The Politics of Dispossession* (1993) and many articles on contemporary problems. For many years he was Professor of Comparative Literature at Columbia University.

References

Said (1999).

DEREK HOPWOOD

SAKK

A legal document is called *sakk* in Arabic (pl. *sukuk*). The branch of legal science that deals with documents is called the science of *shurut* (sing. *shart*), 'stipulations'. The word is used today to designate a variety of legal documents ranging from that which contains a judge's decision on a tribunal to simply an everyday bank cheque.

References

Izzi Dien (1997: 52, 140).

MAWIL IZZI DIEN

SALAF

'Ancestors', referring to the earliest, usually the first three, generations of

575

Muslims believed to be the most reliable sources of issues of doctrine and practice.

References

Waines (1995: 47, 228–30).

Andrew J. Newman

SALAFIS (AL-SALAFIYYA)

This term is derived from the word *salaf* meaning predecessor and is used specifically to refer to the first three generations after the Prophet, i.e., his companions (*al-sahaba*), their students, termed 'successors' (*al-tabi'un*) and their students the 'successors' successors' (*atba' al-tabi'un*), who were termed *al-salaf al-salih* ('the Pious Predecessors'). Thus, those Muslims who affiliate themselves with these early generations and try to imitate them in their religious practice were known as 'Salafis' (lit. those who follow the *salaf*). This has developed further in the contemporary period to represent a specific group within the Muslim community who claim this title for themselves to the exclusion of those who do not conform to their particular views. As such, the Salafis conform to a specific methodology (*manhaj*), which can be summarised in the following three points: first, their view with regard to creed (*'aqida*) is that only the position of the *salaf* is acceptable, by this they mean that all that is mentioned in the revealed sources of the Qur'an and the *sunna* should be understood as they are, without resorting to esoteric or metaphorical interpretation (*ta'wil*) or anthropomorphic comparison with the creation (*tashbih*). As such, they reject the method of scholastic theology of the Ash'aris and the Maturidis, considering it to be an innovated approach (cf. Ash'arism, Maturidism, Sunnism). Second, they oppose the blind following of juristic schools (*madhahib*, sing. *madhhab*), suggesting that Islamic law should be understood from its original sources of the Qur'an and the *sunna* and be derived via a process of independent reasoning (*ijtihad*). Third, Salafis entirely reject the concept of Sufism (*tasawwuf*) and in particular the method of the Sufi orders (*turuq*, sing. *tariqa*), also considering it be an innovated approach. As an alternative, they suggest that spiritual improvement be achieved through a process of self-development and purification (*tasfiya wa tarbiya*) by emulating the practice of the *salaf*. In addition to giving great reverence to the earliest generations, the Salafis also give credence to the opinions of scholars of the classical period such as Ahmad b. Hanbal (AD 780–855) and Ibn Taymiyya (1263–1328) and are represented in the modern period by the late *mufti* of Saudi Arabia 'Abd al-Aziz b. Baz (1912–2000) and the renowned *hadith* scholar Muhammad Nasir al-Din al-Albani (1914–2000).

References

Hanafi (1980: 77–84), al-Johani (1999: 36–46, 1072–6), Netton (1997: 221–2), Sirriyeh (1999: 86–108).

Gavin Picken

SALAH AL-DIN (SALADIN), YUSUF B. AYYUB, styled AL-MALIK AL-NASIR (r. AD 1169–93)

Ayyubid ruler first in Egypt and then in Damascus and southern Syria, and founder of the dynasty. Stemming from a Kurdish family in the service of the Saljuqs and then of their Atabegs, the Zangids, his career was to give him great fame as the foe of the Latin Crusaders in Palestine and the Syrian littoral. In fact, Salah al-Din spent most of his career fighting other Muslim rivals, who regarded him as being as opportunistic and self-centred as other princes of the age. In AD 1174, he took over Damascus, considering himself as the true heir of the great Zangi himself, and extended his power over central Syria. He campaigned against the remaining Zangids in Aleppo and secured his northern frontiers in Mesopotamia. Only in AD 1187 was he free to attack the Franks. He won a major victory at Hattin, capturing Acre and a large stretch of the Palestinian coastland, and then Jerusalem, although Acre was soon regained by the Third Crusaders. Saladin did keep together a disparate coalition of Muslim forces, surmounting the usual problems of maintaining armies in the field for lengthy period of campaigning. His ability to secure loyalty, his military successes and his devotion to strict observance of the prescriptions of the Islamic *shari'a*, seem to show that he was indeed by now recognised as the spearhead of *jihad* and an outstanding figure in his age. Outside the Islamic world, Saladin also became a mythic figure within medieval European chivalry, with a reputation buttressed by such works as the romantic novels of Sir Walter Scott.

References

Chamberlain (1998: 214–19), Gibb and Bosworth (1960–2003), Holt (1986: 48–59), Lyons and Jackson (1982).

C. E. BOSWORTH

SALAT

See: **ritual prayer and worship**

SALAT AL JANAZA

The funeral prayer, which is said not at the graveyard but either at a mosque or in an open space near the home of the deceased. The *niyya* is made to perform four *takbiras*. The imam says, 'God is great', and then he and the congregation recite the *subhan* in a low voice with their hands folded right over left below the navel. Then follows the second *takbir*, 'God is great', followed by the *du'a*; the third 'God is great' is followed by the *du'a* for God to grand mercy upon the deceased, and finally the fourth *takbir* which consists of 'God is great' and then turning the head to the right, 'Peace and mercy be to Thee', and then to the left, 'Peace and mercy be to Thee'.

References

Ibn Manzur (n.d.).

MAWIL IZZI DIEN

SALJUQS (AD 1040–1194)

The line of great Saljuq sultans in Iran and Iraq arose out of Turkish tribesmen attracted from the central Asian steppes into the richer lands of the Islamic Middle East. They expanded at the expense of existing powers in Iran, and the founder Toghril Beg was able to pose as the Sunni rescuer of the 'Abbasid Caliph from Shi'ite Buyid tutelage. The establishment of their extensive empire certainly meant a check for the previous successes of political Shi'ism, as exemplified by the Buyids and Fatimids, and the Saljuq period was notable for the consolidation of Sunni theology and education, aided by the impetus given to the already-existing *madrasa*-building programme, providing institutions in which orthodox officials and scholars could be trained, by the vizier Nizam al-Mulk. One outstanding figure associated with these Nizamiyyas was the theologian al-Ghazali. There were other minor lines of Saljuqs, including a long-lasting one, the Saljuqs of Rum or

Anatolia (AD 1081–1307), at whose court in Konya there flourished scholars and literary men fleeing before the Mongols, notably the mystic Jalal al-Din Rumi.

References

Bosworth (1968: 11–184, 1996: No. 91), Cahen (1968), Gibb and Bosworth (1960–2003).

C. E. BOSWORTH

SALSABIL

A fountain in Paradise. See Q.76:18.

See also: **Tasnim**

ANDREW J. NEWMAN

SAMA'

The *sama'* is the Sufi ritual of listening and dancing to music and poetry that glorifies God. It has caused much controversy within the Islamic world as it is seen by its opponents as being un-Islamic. One of the most well-known forms of *sama'* is perhaps that performed by the 'whirling dervishes' of the Mawlawiyya order.

References

Michon (1991).

LLOYD RIDGEON

SAMANIDS (AD 819–1005)

These were the last ethnically Persian power to rule in medieval Transoxania and eastern Iran. In its time, their state formed the north-eastern bastion of Islam against Inner Asia, and across their lands came the greater part of the large numbers of Turks necessary, for military and domestic purposes, to medieval Islamic society. The Samanids led raids against the pagan Turks of the steppes, whilst, more peacefully, dervish missionaries went out from their lands to evangelise. The Samanids themselves were strong Sunnis, and an effort in the mid-tenth century to implant Isma'ilism in their territories was stamped out. They succumbed to attacks from the steppes by a newly Islamised Turkish people, the Qarakhanids, whose rule in Transoxania now began the process of Turkicisation in what had hitherto been an essentially Iranian land.

References

Barthold (1968), Bosworth (1996: No. 83), Frye (1975), Gibb and Bosworth (1960–2003).

C. E. BOSWORTH

SAMARQAND

Samarqand, known in Arabic as Ma'wara al-Nahr, is an administrative centre, Uzbekistan, from 1938, one of the oldest cities in Central Asia, on trade routes from Afghanistan, Persia and India.

As Maracanda it was occupied by Alexander the Great (329 BC), then capital of Sogdiana 323 BC, and mentioned in T'ang annals. Qutham, the Prophet's cousin, may have been in Samarqand in AD 676. The city engaged in wars with Qutayba (AD 704–10) who built a mosque and an Arab garrison there but Arabs were not in authority until the late 730s and Islamisation was slow. Travellers describe Buddhists, Manichaeans and Nestorian Christians (tenth century). In the early 'Abbasid period, the Neo-Mazdakites led by al-Muqanna' were suppressed; Abu Muslim built the outer wall and Harun al-Rashid restored it. Conquered by the Samanids (ninth to tenth centuries AD) who made Bukhara their capital, it had a fortress, town with suburbs, bazaars, mosques and an aqueduct. It became famous for Turkish slaves, paper and Islamic scholars, including the Hanafi theologian al-Maturidi (d. *c.* AD 944) and Abu'l-Layth al-Samarqandi.

Invaded by Qarakhanids (AD 992) and by various Turkic peoples (eleventh to thirteenth centuries AD), including the Khwarazmians (AD 1212), it flourished as a cultural and artistic centre, with a sizeable Jewish population. Sacked by the Mongols under Čingiz Khan (AD 1220), Samarqand revived after becoming capital of Timur's empire (AD 1369), as an important economic and splendid cultural centre. Timur built the Friday mosque of Bibi Khanom and his own mausoleum, the Gur-e Amir. His fourth son, Shah Rokh Miza, was born in Samarqand in AD 1377 (d. 1447 in Iran). Timur's grandson, Ulugh Beg (d. AD 1449), built its famous observatory (AD 1420) and for producing astronomical tables (*zij*). Many shrines including the *Shah-i Zinda* complex and the Khawaja Ahrar complex of mausolea, *madrasas* (Muhammad Sultan), mosques (Hadrat Khidr) and wonderful gardens (Dilgusha in AD 1396) were created.

In 1500, the city was conquered by Uzbeks and subjugated to Bukhara. Samarqand declined and was deserted in the eighteenth century but revived as a provincial capital of the Russian Empire from 1868 with railway connections after 1871. It was capital of the Uzbek Soviet Socialist Republic (1924–30) and within the Uzbekistan Republic after 1990.

References

Creswell (1989: 112), Degeorge (2001), Naumkin (1992).

JANET STARKEY

AL-SANUSI (d. 1859)

Founder of the Sanusiyya order in North Africa, Muhammad al-Sanusi composed a major work on the *dhikr* called *'Salsabil al-mu'in fi 'l-tara'iq al-arba'in* (*The Clear Fountain on the Forty Paths*). The book explains the *dhikrs* of forty different Sufi brotherhoods (although the number may be in conformity with the literary genre of describing forty initiations), and al-Sanusi claimed that his own brotherhood was the successor of the forty.

References

Vikor (1995).

LLOYD RIDGEON

SANUSIYYA

A relatively modern Sufi order founded by Muhammad b. 'Ali al-Sanusi (d. 1859), the Sanusiyya is popular in north and central Africa. It is an order that spearheaded the rejection of European imperialism.

References

Vikor (1995), Ziadeh (1958).

LLOYD RIDGEON

AL-SARRAJ (d. AD 988)

A Sufi from Khurasan, al-Sarraj is celebrated for his Sufi manual *Kitab al-Luma'*. In this work, Sufism is portrayed as the pristine version of Islam lived by the Prophet and his companions, and also the practices and beliefs of existing Sufi schools are detailed. Although he defended some of the more 'ecstatic' Sufis, al-Sarraj is generally considered an exponent of 'sober' Sufism.

References

Al-Sarraj (1914).

LLOYD RIDGEON

579

SASSANIAN EMPIRE

The Sasan family established an empire, the borders of which were in constant flux, but was based for most of its imperial rule in Ctesiphon (in Arabic, 'al-Mada'in'). They ruled from 224 until AD 651, when the empire finally fell to the Arab-Muslim armies. The heart of the empire was in Fars province, and the Sasanids took their role of Achaemenid successors seriously, adding inscriptions and reliefs to Achaemenid monuments such as those at Naqsh-i Rustam and generally exploiting the Achaemenid legacy.

The exact origins of the Sasanid dynasty are still uncertain. Early in the third century AD (probably around AD 205–6), Papak, a Persian leader in Fars, overthrew the Parthian sponsored ruler of the province, establishing his own rule from Istakhr, near to the ruins of Persepolis. Sasan was either the name of Papak's father, or his son-in-law and was supposedly descended from the last Achaemenid king Darius. This connection gave the Sasanids a royal heritage, though its historical accuracy is difficult to confirm. Shapur, Papak's son, was responsible for the first expansion of the empire. Shapur's brother Ardashir (the Artaxerxes of the Greek and Latin sources) was the real founder of the empire, conquering a larger part of southern Iran and Mesopotamia and expanding the empire into the Arabian peninsula. The extensive area under Sasanid control was to fluctuate throughout the next 400 years, as Sasanid kings battled with the Romans (latterly the Byzantines) to the west and smaller rebellious powers to the east.

Ardashir's son Shapur co-ruled with his father until the latter's death in AD 242. Shapur was sufficiently confident of his power to claim the title 'Shahenshah [king of kings] of Iran and non-Iran', taking Armenia in AD 242, and Antioch from the Romans in AD 256. Shapur developed his role as head of the imperial religion, Zoroastrianism, and through inscriptions from the time, we know of his adoption of the title 'The Mazda-Worshipping Shah'. Mani, the founder of the dualist religion Manichaeism, is also reported to have converted members of the Sasanid royal family. The religious tolerance of Shapur also allowed Christians and Jews to become a permanent feature of Sasanid society in Iran. He is famous for establishing a stable and hierarchically organised state, with Kirdir, the Mazdaean high priest, maintaining the orthodox nature of the State. The idea, proffered in some secondary literature that he favoured some sort of universalist, syncretistic religion seems, however, unlikely.

Shapur's son Hormizd Ardeshir came to the throne in AD 270, and promoted a similar policy of religious tolerance. However, Bahram I, the next Sasanid king, was more closely allied with the Mazdaean Zoroastrianism of Kirdir, as were his son (Bahram II) and grandson (Bahram III). Kirdir, who had maintained his position through the changes of monarch, ceased this opportunity to suppress Mani and his new cult. Mani was imprisoned and died in AD 276. Manichaeism did not die out, though, and managed to survive the death of its founder, partly because of a well-organised clergy hierarchy. Bahram III's claim to the title was challenged by the remaining son of Shapur, Narseh. Narseh attempted to obliterate the reigns of the three Bahrams from imperial memory, replacing their name with his own on some monuments. His descendants made up the next tranche of Sasanid monarchs.

Narseh continued to war with the Christian forces to his west, attempting to maintain the boundaries of the empire. One of his sons, Shapur II, assumed the throne in AD 309, ruling for seventy years. He fought in the east and the west at different points during his reign, and he exemplifies the nature of Sasanid legitimacy: the warrior king. The idea of a divine king, which had been prominent in the early stages of Sasanid rule, was under religious pressure, primarily from the various Zoroastrian reform movements, but also from the priestly class themselves. Shapur II was probably the last to be widely considered of 'divine descent' or having a divine nature, and a monotheistic belief, or at least Ohrmazd-centred Zoroastrianism began to emerge.

Apart from the Zoroastrians (with all their various subgroups), other religious communities lived under the authority of their own leaders – whether bishops for the Christians or the Exilarch of the Jews. The leaders of non-Zoroastrian religious communities played a central role in maintaining the well-being of their community in a potentially hostile society. The various classes of society were seemingly fixed: the elite, consisting of nobles, monarchs and priests, was sharply distinguished from the rest of the population. Other religious communities operated as separate entities, exerting pressure on the elite at crucial times and suffering bouts of oppression from the Sasanid rulers at others. This structure seems to have stayed in place for much of the fifth century, during which time the Shah can be clearly said to have lost his divine status. Instead, the Sasanids traced their lineage back to Kayanids, who were said to have fathered the Achaemenids – this became their legitimising ideology.

Zoroastrianism orthodoxy was to be challenged in the late fifth century by the rise of Mazdakism. Kubadh (Kavad) I, who reigned from the late fifth century until AD 531, was undoubtedly influenced by this movement, which had its roots in reformist views within Zoroastrianism before this date. Mazdakism promoted an egalitarian Zoroastrianism, whereby material wealth was to be enjoyed in moderation by all; justice was to be distributed evenly throughout society, as was wealth. This would readdress the wrongs that existed in a society where the rich were powerful and preyed on the weak. The movement also had certain gnostic elements, which seem to have been derived from Manichaeism. The most notorious accusation, found in later Islamic sources, is that Mazdakism advocated the sharing of women and, hence, transgressed a Muslim sexual taboo. The accuracy of this depiction, however, is doubtful, filtered as it is through at least one hostile lens (the early Muslim denunciations of Zoroastrianism) and possibly two (as the Muslim writers used Mazdaean sources for their understanding of Mazdakism).

The conflict between the Mazdaean Zoroastrianism of the priestly hierarchy and egalitarian Mazdakism was transformed into a conflict over succession to Kavad when he died in 531. Mazdakites wished to install his son Kawus. The priests, eager to prevent the Mazdakites from controlling the appointment, advocated Khusraw. The latter was successful and was named Anushirwan ('the immortal soul'), and Sasanid Iran witnesses a reassertion of traditional Zoroastrianism and a suppression of Mazdakism. Society became, once again, more stratified; the bureaucratic classes began to come to the fore and nobility moved into the background. The State remained highly class based, but become rationalised, with an impressive administrative network whereby Sasanid rule might be maintained both at court and in the provinces. A more structured legal system, with the promulgation of standard legal works, was established. The society in these times is depicted as stable and ordered, with each class of the population knowing their place and performing their allotted role, for the betterment of all. The picture may be tinged with hyperbole, but Zoroastrian tradition remembers Khusraw Anushirvan as a great king who re-established the moral values of Zoroastrianism that had been lost to the Mazdakite heresy. The conflicting emphases of egalitarianism and elitism dogged the rule of Khusraw's successor Hormazd IV, and the brief reign of Bahram VI (AD 590–91).

Khusraw II, having been forced from the throne by Bahram VI in AD 590, returned to power in part by help from the Byzantines. His rule (AD 591–628) was absolutist, and he styled himself as a divine being. His achievements almost lived up to his propaganda. He set himself the demanding task of eliminating the Byzantine empire and, though unsuccessful, he did have some success. With the help of local rebels, he conquered Damascus, Antioch and eventually Jerusalem in AD 614. There followed a period of suppression of Christianity (the creed of the vanquished Byzantines), as Jews hailed him as a precursor to the messiah. He was to perform similar persecution in AD 625, when pressurised by the Byzantines in Azerbaijan and Armenia. Khusraw Parviz (as Khusraw II was known) was supposedly a lover of music and the arts, but he was also suspicious of his court personnel. Following a defeat by the Byzantines in AD 627–8, he had his officers imprisoned and executed. This lead to resentment at court, and eventually there was a revolt in his army resulting in the proclamation of his son, Kavad II, as Shah, and the execution of Khusraw Parviz. The Sasanid empire, though, was unravelling. The Byzantine defeat of Khusraw had opened up fissures in the ruling classes, as monarchs were unable to unify the empire.

Dynastic crises meant that the throne changed hands a number of times over the next three years until Yazdagird III, the grandson of Khusraw Parviz, was placed on the throne in AD 632, the year of the Prophet Muhammad's death.

Yazdagird was to be the last Sasanid monarch: Sasanid possessions in Arabia had already been lost; now he lost his allies there also. Previously loyal governors of major Arabian cities converted to Islam and threw in their lot with Muhammad. In AD 633 and AD 634, Muslim armies began to capture Sasanid outposts in Iraq. Eventually in AD 636 at al-Qadisiyya, the Sasanids were forced out of Iraq, and Yazdagird fled back to Iran proper, making his base at Rayy. Determined to regain the glories of the empire, and conscious of the loss of his administrative heart, Yazdagird raised an army to confront the Muslims at Nihavand in AD 642. His forces were defeated, and he was forced to flee once more. He eventually reached the desert oasis of Marv, where local rulers, aware of his weakness, made their own grab for power, forcing him to flee once again. He was killed near Marv in AD 651. The lands of the Sasanid empire were available for Muslim conquest, a conquest that was performed with some alacrity by the organised and skilled Muslim armies.

The end of the Iranian Sasanid dynasty removed a major obstacle for the Muslims: after the successes against Yazdagird's forces, the Muslims were able to move almost effortlessly across the land of Iran, and into central Asia and India. However, the Persian bureaucrats, who had contributed so much to the stability and success of the Sasanid empire were to prove a useful resource for the Muslim empire. Many families subsequently converted to Islam and the skills present within them, developed through years of service under the Sasanids, made them indispensable for the operation of the new Muslim empire. Whether or not the Muslim conquests over the Sasanids were the result of a desire for converts or wealth is a disputed point amongst historians. It seems that there was no organised Muslim proselytism, and the invading forces were happy to claim booty and, in the longer term, collect taxes from the former Sasanid subjects. Many of the converted nobility became rulers of Muslim dynasties in their own right, proud of their Sasanid heritage, and other Iranian dynasties claimed descent from the Sasanids, demonstrating that their legacy had some legitimising currency amongst the populace well after their eventual fall to Arabs.

References

Boyce (1975), Taqizadeh (1970), Yarshater (1968–91).

ROBERT GLEAVE

SASANIDS (AD 254–651)

The Sasanid emperors were the last line of indigenous Persian emperors of Iran before the Arab invasions of the seventh century and what became the almost complete Islamisation of Iran. Until then, Zoroastrianism or Magianism had been the state religion of Iran, with a powerful and persecuting Zoroastrian priesthood. This was toppled almost totally by the Arab Muslims, and Zoroastrian communities survived only vestigially within Iran and, as an implantation into western India, as the Parsee community. But much of the governmental ethos, and the customs and practices of Sasanid society survived the demise of the dynasty and was imported into the nascent Muslim society, Persian ways and attitudes were a considerable component of what became the Arabic concept of *adab*, polite learning and refined social

practice. These and Sasanid administrative traditions were incorporated into what became, in the Muslim East, a composite Perso-Islamic culture that was to make an immense contribution to Islamic civilisation in general, though at times arousing the suspicions and opposition of Muslim rigorists, upholders of what they conceived as the pure Arabic tradition against heretical Persian innovations.

References

Christensen (1944), Frye (1983), Gibb and Bosworth (1960–2003).

C. E. BOSWORTH

SAWM, SIYAM

See: **fasting; Ramadan**

SAYF AL-DAWLA (r. AD 944–67)

Hamdanid ruler in northern Syria and western Mesopotamia from his capital at Aleppo. The family's original centre was in northern Iraq, but Sayf al-Dawla took over northern Syria in the teeth of Ikhshidid opposition and made Aleppo the base for a holding operation against Byzantine pressure, punctuated by retaliatory raids into Anatolia, being involved in some forty battles there. His reputation as a *ghazi* or fighter for the faith was enhanced by his panegyrist, the poet al-Mutanabbi.

References

Gibb and Bosworth (1960–2003), Kennedy (1986: 275–82).

C. E. BOSWORTH

SAYYID AHMAD KHAN (1817–98)

The most important representative of Islamic reform in the Indian context in

583

the nineteenth century. Born in the context of expanding British influence and rule in India, as a young man Ahmad Khan was employed by the British East India Company. In the aftermath of what the British called the Indian Mutiny in 1857, he attempted to articulate the best way forward for the Muslim community under direct British rule, and his recommendation was that, as a minority of the population, Muslims should seek to establish their loyalty to the British and seem to gain the maximum benefit from what British rule offered, particularly in the sphere of education. He therefore adopted Western dress and, in 1878, joined the Viceroy's Council for governing India. He established a number of organisations devoted to the translation and dissemination of Western texts for the improvement of Muslim education, among both men and women. He also, in 1875, opened the Muhammadan Anglo-Oriental College at Aligarh, with English as the language of instruction and based on the model of a Cambridge college, as an avenue of advancement for young Muslims. His religious views were controversial as he challenged a number of traditional beliefs, suggesting that the only reliable source of guidance for Muslims was the Qur'an (not the *hadith* as well), that the Qur'an needed careful historical interpretation in order to distinguish permanently valid principles from time-specific details, and that there were no essential clashes between Islamic and Western ideas because they both, with Judaism, had a common ancestry in Abraham, and each of the three had also had a deep engagement with the Greek tradition during the course of their history.

References

Baljon (1949), Malik (1980), Troll (1978).

HUGH GODDARD

SAYYID QUTB (1906–66)

The most important intellectual ancestor of the radical wing of the modern Islamic revivalist movement. Qutb was born in Musha, a small village in Upper Egypt, from which he moved to Cairo to study, and during his time there he was heavily influenced by the liberal intellectual figures of the day, becoming very interested in English literature. In 1933 he became an employee of the Ministry of Education, and in 1948 he was sent by the Ministry to the USA in order to study Western methods of education. The three years he spent in the USA were a turning point in his life, resulting in complete disillusionment with the West because of its sexual immorality and its uncritical support for the new state of Israel in the Middle East. When he returned to Egypt he therefore sought an alternative intellectual outlook, which he located in the Muslim Brotherhood, which had been founded in 1928 in order to make Egypt a more truly Islamic society. In addition some of the works of A. A. Mawdudi were translated into Arabic in 1951, and here Qutb found an understanding of Islam as an ideology, distinct from both capitalism and communism and in sharp opposition to Western materialism, which was deeply attractive. He therefore joined the Brotherhood. Shortly afterwards, however, relations between the Government and the Brotherhood deteriorated sharply and Qutb was arrested. Maltreatment in prison heightened his sense of contrast between the ideals of Islam and the current situation in Egypt and when, in 1964, he was released and published *Signposts* (or *Milestones*) *on The Way*, in which he completely rejected all forms of government that did not correspond to what he believed to be the ideals of Islam and argued that they should be overthrown he was rearrested and then, in 1966, executed. He is therefore the main ideologue of the revolutionary (as opposed to the gradualist) stream of the contemporary Islamic revival, and provides much of the theoretical underpinning for the views of Usama bin Laden. He was also the author of a very influential commentary on the Qur'an, *Fi Zilal al-Qur'an* (*In the Shade of the Qur'an*).

References

Kepel (1985), Moussalli (1992), Shepard (1996), Sivan (1990).

HUGH GODDARD

SCALES, JUDGEMENT WITH

A Qur'anic reference (Q.7:8–9, Q.21:47, Q.23:102–3, Q.101:6–7) to the scales set up on the Day of Judgement, and one of two types of judgement exercised on this day.

See also: **books, judgement with; judgement on the** *yawm al-qiyama*; *najat*; *yawm al-qiyama*

ANDREW J. NEWMAN

SCEPTICISM

Scepticism is the notion of doubting the ability of human beings either to have real knowledge of the material world or to reach any reality behind the sensible world. This kind of thinking appeared first among some Greek thinkers who doubted the ability of philosophy and of the human intellect to reach any kind of truth. Arab thinkers knew these Greek ideas, according to the report of the biographer al-Qifti in his book *Akhbar al-Hukama'*. From 'Abd al-Jabbar's refutation of an Arabic group under the name *munkiri al-haqa'iq*, we can trace the presence of such scepticism among Arab thinkers. Their main question was: how can we be confident of reality and

the authenticity of our knowledge? This tendency to doubt all kinds of realities led to the danger of spreading doubt and uncertainty about the existence of the prophets, revelations and God. Therefore, most theologians and philosophers of the medieval period constructed arguments refuting the concepts of these groups. 'Abd al-Jabbar, for example, devoted a section in his encyclopaedic work *al-Mughni* to presenting the arguments of different Mu'tazilite scholars against scepticism. Some of the Muslim philosophers attempted to solve this problem through their study of psychology. Ibn Sina was the first to deal with the problem in this way. In his parable of the floating man he explained that if a human had all his limbs cut off and was deprived of his senses, he would still acknowledge his inner self, the 'I'. In the same way philosophers recognise that the only reliable notion which one cannot doubt is one's inner self, the 'I'. Through our assurance of our own existence and our inner perceptions we are able to acknowledge the existence of true objects. Thus, the belief in the 'I' is a belief in the existence of a certain reality which is undoubted and therefore is the first step in releasing oneself from scepticism.

References

Leaman (1999: 69–72).

MAHA EL-KAISY FRIEMUTH

SCIENCE

Though perceived as inimically hostile thereto, in the premodern period Islamic civilisation was in fact generally more open than the West to scientific inquiry especially as such inquiry sought to understand the manner in which the Creator established life and the nature of that life. Islamic scientific inquiry easily incorporated and added to the Hellenic scientific and philosophical legacy as this became available in Arabic beginning especially in the ninth and tenth centuries. It is usually held that via these Arabic-language scientific writings the West, emerging from the Middle Ages, reacquainted itself with the tradition of scientific inquiry. Both Galenic and prophetic theory and practice informed the Islamic medical tradition itself and the latter was also sufficiently eclectic to sanction aspects of 'germ theory' prior to the latter's appearance in the West. In the nineteenth and twentieth centuries, the incursion of 'modern', i.e., Western, scientific theory and practice, as increasingly both humanistic and secularised and identified with Western imperial ambitions alone or in partnership with local autocratic elites, was deemed suspect, especially by local religious elements. Local autocrats sent delegations of government officials and students to Europe to absorb aspects of 'modern' Western civilisation, including 'the scientific method', as a means to reorganise society at home along 'Western lines' and so enhance their own authority against the various opponents of the growing authority of the central state structure, including religious elements. The region's socialist proponents identified secular humanist discourse and the scientific method as the means to attaining 'modernity' and a standard of development and living similar to that of the West and the study of 'scientific' disciplines such as medicine, engineering and the like was popular in the Middle East from the 1960s especially. These disciplines' graduates populated the growing secular left and liberal intelligentsia in this period. The failure of socialism presaged the questioning of the secular humanist dimensions of science and scientific theory and prac-

tice. The importance of acquaintance with the body of knowledge and practice these disciplines, if compromised by the political failures of Arab socialism, was never questioned, and, having readopted the notion of the Divine as the Prime Mover behind earthly phenomena, students and graduates of various scientific disciplines have played an important role in the more recent formulation of Islamist discourse.

References

Hourani (1970: esp. 34–5, 1991: esp. 299–300), Savage-Smith (1996).

See also: **modernity; secularism; socialism;** *tibb nabawi*

ANDREW J. NEWMAN

SECOND WORLD WAR (1939–45)

The global war that stemmed from the expansionism of Germany, Italy and Japan (the Axis powers). The principal fronts were in western Europe, the Soviet Union, China and the Pacific, but significant fighting took place in the Middle East. In North Africa, the first Italian offensive in mid-September 1940 was checked at Sidi Barrani in Egypt by British forces. Hitler supported his ally by dispatching the Afrika Korps under Erin Rommel. The campaign ebbed and flowed across North Africa for two years, but the decisive moment came at El Alamein in November 1942, when over-extended Axis forces were defeated by the British 8th Army under Lt. Gen. Bernard Montgomery. Anglo-American landings in Morocco and Algeria on 8 November 1942 cornered the Axis forces in Tunisia. The Afrika Korps was finally defeated in spring 1943. Meanwhile, British forces were active elsewhere. In

1941, they overthrew the pro-Axis regime of Rashid Ali al-Gailani in Iraq and marched on to conquer the Vichy French forces in Syria and Lebanon. In coordination with the Soviet Union, Britain also invaded Iran in 1941, forcing the abdication of Reza Shah in favour of his son. The war killed over 50 million people, including 6 million Jews murdered in Nazi extermination camps.

References

Gilbert (1989: 188–97, 350–64, 419–27), Liddell-Hart (1997: 128–34, 178–89, 277–357).

SIMON W. MURDEN

SECULARISM

Although such secular concepts as that of free will are acceptable in Islam, secular emphases on absence of Divine Will are not. Secular political ideologies and movements in the Islamic world can be dated to the mid-twentieth century especially, and the aftermath of the Second World War in particular, as Middle Eastern intellectuals especially struggled to formulate a response to Western efforts to re-establish pre-war colonial relationships with the region. These movements and ideologies were, for the most part, at least loosely associated with interpretations of Marxist-Leninist and socialist thought and often associated with the efforts of the USSR to influence, if not control, such movements throughout the third world. These discourses, given added impetus by their establishment as those of the region's ruling parties following anti-monarchy coups, promoted Islam as the chief impediment to the attaining of 'modernity' in the region. As the product of overtly atheist thought, such discourse was anathema to traditional

Islam. The military defeats of 1956, 1967, 1973 and 2003 however, tarnished the various manifestations of Arab socialism and encouraged increasingly greater interest in Islamist discourses as better suited to address and develop a response to issues of modernity, especially as these were perceived as indigenous responses thereto. In Iran the equation of modernity with the shah's increasingly autocratic rule and pro-Western policies coupled with the inability of a secular/socialist discourse to attract any audience beyond the narrow, usually well-educated, middle and upper middle class, left the way open for the discourse of scholar clerics and lay persons which addressed issues of modernity from an Islamic axis.

References

Abrahamian (1989), Ayubi (1993), Keddie (1981), Kerr (1971), Munson (1988).

See also: **free will and predestination; Marxism and Islam; materialism; modernity; socialism**

ANDREW J. NEWMAN

SELIM I (r. 1512–20)

Ottoman sultan, son of Bayezid II. He succeeded to the throne after forcing his father to abdicate and defeating and executing his brothers Korkud and Ahmed. He next undertook a campaign against the Safavid Shah Isma'il of Iran, defeating him at Chaldiran in 1514. Between 1514 and 1516, Selim overran Safavid territories in south-eastern Anatolia by military conquest and by negotiation with local Kurdish lords. In 1516–17, he conquered the Mamluks of Cairo, annexing to his realms Egypt, Syria and the Hijaz. An addition to his Empire came in 1519 when the regent of

Algiers and Tunis, Hayreddin Barbarossa, voluntarily submitted to Selim.

References

Bacqué-Grammont (1989: 139–45), Imber (2002: 44–8).

COLIN IMBER

SELIM II (r. 1566–74)

Ottoman sultan, son of Süleyman I. Throughout his reign, affairs of state remained largely in the hands of his grand vizier and son-in-law, Sokollu Mehmed Pasha. Sokollu's plans to dig canals across the isthmus of Suez and between the Don and Volga rivers in order to give the Ottomans maritime access to the Red Sea and Caspian both failed. However, the conquest of Cyprus between 1570 and 1573 succeeded, despite the Holy League's naval victory off Lepanto in 1571. The conquest of Tunis from Spain followed in 1574.

References

Bacqué-Grammont (1989: 155–8), Imber (2002: 61–3).

COLIN IMBER

SELIM III (r. 1789–1807)

Ottoman sultan, son of Mustafa III. Selim came to the throne at the time of war with Russia. The peace of Jassy concluding the hostilities recognised the Russian occupation of Georgia and the Crimea. To strengthen the army, Selim established a new military corps, recruited in Anatolia and trained by European officers. His efforts, however, met with resistance, especially in Rumelia, where local notables feared that the corps was intended to undermine their power. After the Russian war, the Ottoman empire suffered the Napoleonic occupation of Egypt between 1798 and 1801 and the invasion of Palestine in 1799. War with France brought temporary alliances with Russia and England. A later rapprochement with France allowed Selim to prevent any power dominating his realms. Opposition came primarily from within his realms, especially Rumelia where lords such as Tepedelenli Ali Pasha of Ioannina or Pazvanoğlu of Vidin ruled virtually independently. In 1807, a Janissary rebellion seeking to reverse his reforms forced Selim to abdicate. He was assassinated in the following year.

References

Mantran (1989: 425–33), Shaw (1971).

COLIN IMBER

SEVERIN, (GILES) TIMOTHY (1940–)

British historian, adventurer and prolific author, who recreated many historic journeys. In 1961, he led a motorcycle team along the route taken by Marco Polo. Many journeys followed, including one in the footsteps of the first crusade to Jerusalem (1987–8) as well as recreations of the mythical journeys of St Brendan (Ireland to America, 1977), Sinbad (Oman to China, 1980–1), Jason (Iolkos to Colchis, 1984), and Ulysses (Troy to Ithaca, 1985).

References

Severin (1964, 1978, 1983, 1985, 1987, 1989, 1991).

SIMON W. MURDEN

SEVILLE

The capital city of Seville Province in Andalusia is located in southern Spain, some 75 miles (120 kilometres) southwest of Cordoba and 64 miles (102 kilometres) north of Cadiz on the Atlantic coast. Seville's port on the Guadalquivir River is accessible to ocean-going vessels by river and canal. Known as Hispalis in the ancient world, it was taken by the Romans under Julius Caesar in 45 BC. From the fourth to the eighth century it was ruled successively by Vandals and Visigoths. From AD 712–1248 it flourished as a centre of Islamic civilisation under the Moors, who built the royal palace, Alcazar (Ar. *al-Qasr*), in AD 1181. From AD 1093–91 it was the capital of an independent emirate under the 'Abbasids, during whose rule the city became famous, *inter alia*, for the manufacture of musical instruments. Traces of Moorish influence remain to be seen in the courtyards, fountains, narrow streets and the ruins of the wall that once surrounded the city. After Seville fell to the Christian king Ferdinand III of Castile in AD 1248 following a long siege, some 300,000 Moors were said to have left the city. The Gothic cathedral, with its works of art by El Greco and Murrillo and the tomb of Christopher Columbus, was built between 1401 and 1519. It occupies the site on which a twelfth-century mosque once stood. Two parts of the old mosque remain, the *Giralda* tower, once a minaret rising to a height of of 300 feet (91 metres), now the cathedral's bell-tower, and the Court of Oranges. The European discovery of the Americas in 1492 promoted lucrative commercial opportunities for Spain, from which Seville benefited.

References

Hitti (1973: 502–3), Michell (1984: 214–15).

See also: **Almohads; Almoravids; al-Andalus; Cordoba; Granada**

EDWARD D. A. HULMES

AL-SHADHILI (1187–1258)

Born in Morocco, al-Shadhili founded the brotherhood known as the Shadhiliyya. Famous for his ascetic lifestyle and preaching, al-Shadhili became popular in North Africa, and he established a lodge in Alexandria. He left no systematic writings, although his disciples were active in the propagation of his teachings. These teachings emphasised the pragmatic dimension of Sufism rather than the metaphysical, and the need to observe the *shari'a* is paramount.

References

Knysh (2000: 207–12).

LLOYD RIDGEON

SHADHILIYYA

A Sufi order that traces its origins back to al-Shadhili (d. AD 1258), the Shadhiliyya has been popular in Egypt and other parts of North Africa, although followings have been found in areas as far off as China. A Sunni order, the Shadhiliyya has stressed strict adherence to the *shari'a* and promotes a 'sober' form of Sufism that advises affiliates to adopt a low public profile while remaining active on social issues.

References

Danner (1991).

LLOYD RIDGEON

SHAFA'A

'Intercession'. In the Qur'an, intercession at the Day of Judgement is disavowed for non-believers (Q.2:48, Q.123, Q.254, Q.19:87, Q.20:109, Q.34:23, Q.36:23, Q.43:86, Q.53:26, Q.74:48).

References

Wensinck (1996).

See also: **judgement on the *yawm al-qiyama*; najat; *yawm al-qiyama***

ANDREW J. NEWMAN

SHAFI'I (AD 767–820)

Shafi'i, originally Muhammad b. Idris, was born in the Gaza strip in the year of Abu Hanifa's death and from childhood he was known for his sharp intelligence. He began his academic career as a man of literature and poetry before progressing to study under the Mufti of Mecca. The actual date of this is unspecified; however, it is known that he was still a young man and it has been recorded that he completed his learning at the age of fifteen and was duly given a licence to issue *fatwas*. Perhaps it was his background in Arabic language study that gave rise to his skill in articulating his legal knowledge, this manifesting itself later in his prolific works.

Shafi'i represents a milestone in the history of Islamic law, because he initiated its shift from the level of an oral culture to one of documentation and methodical organisation of concepts. Influencing factors for this phenomenon were his early move from Mecca to Medina and his visits to Yemen and Iraq in his quest to seek and digest as much knowledge as possible. There are conflicting narrations as to exact dates, but it is accepted that at the age of fifteen, Shafi'i spent some time in the dessert.

Having completed his first studies with Muslim Khalid al-Zunji in Mecca, he made his early trip to Medina and found the environment and culture there to be very different. The majority of the Prophet's companions resided in the town and Shafi'i gained much of benefit from them, although the main scholar with whom he wished to study was Malik b. Anas. At their first meeting, Malik realised that he was facing a young man with great scholastic potential, particularly as Shafi'i had memorised Malik's work, the *Muwatta'*, in preparation. Their relationship was to continue until Malik's death in *c.* AD 795.

Shafi'i made a statement that summarised the ethos of Medina as opposed to that of Mecca: 'In Medina I experienced four wonders. I saw a grandmother who was twenty-one years old. I saw a man who had been declared bankrupt for a tiny debt of 2 *mudd* measures of dates stones. I saw a very old man who was over ninety and he spent all day barefoot, teaching girls to sing. When the time for prayer came, he would pray in a sitting position because he was so old. I saw a holy man who had been ostracised by the community and when he asked the people why they only visited leaders and nobility? they replied, "you don't harm or hit people as they do". The holy man was so desperate to have visitors that he began to use the same threatening behaviour as the noblemen so that he might resume contact with others'.

Shafi'i's time in Yemen was spend as an advisor to the judge Mus'ab b. al-Zubayr and, undoubtedly, his practical life there provided a solid background that aided in the formulation of his own jurisprudence. His initial trip to Iraq was not made out of choice, as he was sent there accused of rebelling against the Government. When the Caliph actually met him, he was so impressed by Shafi'i's eloquence and knowledge that he granted his freedom and gave him a large sum of money as a gift. Whilst there, he began studying Iraqi knowledge and benefited from the teachings of Muhammad b. al-Hasan, a student of Abu Hanifa. He returned to Mecca with some of al-Hasan's books and from this point Shafi'i combined his knowledge of the text with the analytical and deductive methodology of Abu Hanifa, subsequently producing highly skilled works such as *al-Umm* and *al-Risala*, which represent the foundation of Islamic jurisprudence.

Shafi'i is recorded to have made two further trips to Iraq, in 810/11 and AD 814/15. It appears that he was attempting to examine the Iraqi society that was so different from Mecca and Medina. During his second visit, he composed *al-Hujja*, wherein he analysed various aspects of the Islamic legal views of both Medina and Iraq. His third visit lasted for eight months, but there is little documentation to indicate the purpose of his stay and one can only assume that Shafi'i intended to fill any missing gaps in his knowledge.

His journey to Egypt (*c.* 815/16) represents a further formative period that contributed to his creation of many new ideas. These however, were considered by some to delineate a marked change in his scholastic principles, although it was doubtless inevitable that the new Egyptian environment would require the production of a set of new injunctions. Shafi'i's study circle in Cairo became a distinguished seminar that was attended by hundreds of students and friends. Some of these went on to become scholars in their own right.

References

Coulson (1964: 52–7), al-Diqr (1996), Izzi Dien (2004: 19–23).

MAWIL IZZI DIEN

SHAH WALIULLAH
(AD 1702–62)

Important Muslim reformer in India. After studying in Delhi Shah Waliullah spent some time in Mecca, which was an important meeting place for Muslims from all corners of the world. When he returned to India, he called for the reform

of a number of areas of Islamic belief and practice, suggesting that of the traditional four sources of Islamic law only two, the Qur'an and the *hadith* had ongoing validity, and that these needed creative interpretation (*ijtihad*) in order to make their message applicable in the Indian context. He therefore translated the Qur'an into Persian, the cultured language of Indian Muslims, and his sons translated it into Urdu. He also suggested that the *hadith* needed careful review, in order to clarify which sections were unreliable, this work thus serving as an early example of *hadith* criticism. And he also argued that the different schools of *shari'a* law were no longer valid, and that what was needed was a return to the situation before their emergence, so that there could be one school for all Muslims.

References

Baljon (1986), Hermansen (1996), Rizvi (1980).

HUGH GODDARD

SHAHADA

See: **profession of faith, Islamic**

SHAHJAHAN B. JAHANGIR
(r. 1628–57)

Mughal emperor. By vigorous campaignings he maintained the integrity of his realm against the Safavids in the west and the Ozbegs in the north. In religion, he largely continued the tolerant policy of his predecessors, patronising Hindi poets, whilst his son Dara Shikoh associated with Hindu scholars and holy men, held ecumenical attitudes regarding religion and patronised the translation of Sanskrit scriptures, inevitably attracting obloquy from pious, traditionalist Muslim circles. But Shahjahan is chiefly famed as a patron of architecture; he laid out the town of Shahjahanabad at Delhi and, above all, built the superlative mausoleum for his wife Mumtaz Mahall at Agra, the Taj Mahal.

References

Gibb and Bosworth (1960–2003), Richards (1993: 119–50).

C. E. BOSWORTH

AL-SHAHRASTANI
(AD 1086–1153)

Best known for his descriptions of the whole range of religious beliefs present in his day, both within and outside the Islamic community, on the strength of which his work was described by E. J. Sharpe as 'the first history of religion in world literature'. He was born in eastern Iran and studied in Nishapur. After going to Mecca on pilgrimage in AD 1116, he taught for three years in Baghdad before returning to eastern Iran. His theological views were basically Ash'ari, but he was readier than some of his predecessors in that school to take full account of the views of the philosophers, and even if he ultimately sought to refute their views he did so on the basis of the use of philosophical concepts and with considerable philosophical sophistication.

References

Cureton (1842, 1846), Kazi and Flynn (1984), Lawrence (1976), Madelung and Mayer (2001), Watt (1985: Chapter 13).

HUGH GODDARD

SHARI'A

The word *shari'a* is to be interpreted in two complementary senses. In general terms, it refers to the way of life ordained by God for the whole of mankind. This 'Path' is *al-sirat al-mustaqim*, 'the Straight Path' of Islam (see Q.1:6). In specific terms it refers to the canonical law of Islam, which is developed from principles contained in the Qur'an, on example provided by the *sunna* of the Prophet Muhammad, and on analysis made subsequently in the four major schools of Islamic jurisprudence. The introduction (or reintroduction) of *shari'a* law in Islamic communities had led in recent years to profound disagreements (and even to violence) between Muslims and non-Muslims. Such disagreement has not been limited to non-Muslim critics, however. In Europe, in particular, many Muslims are seeking to reinterpret Islamic law in ways that allow for an adaptation of Islam to the needs and problems of an essentially secular Western environment, without compromising the distinctive revelation that is at the heart of Islam. In the course of this adaptation, *shari'a* law is in process of being interpreted in a spirit of cooperation between Muslims and non-Muslims, by means of which common aspirations about freedom and democracy (for instance) are acknowledged. The much publicised penalties for infractions of *shari'a* law, especially amputation for cases of theft and stoning for proven adultery, continue to provoke discussion inside as well as outside Islamic communities.

References

Gibb (1955: 72–84), Tritton (1968: 58–71).

EDWARD D. A. HULMES

SHATAHAT

The *shatahat* (sing. *shath*) are the ecstatic statements made by the Sufis at the height of their mystical experiences. Such statements have been regarded with the utmost suspicion by many Muslims because they smack of *shirk*. Among the most (in)famous *shatahat* are al-Hallaj's 'I am the Truth' and Abu Yazid al-Bistami's 'Glory be to me! How great is my majesty'.

References

Ernst (1985).

LLOYD RIDGEON

SHAYKH

The *shaykh* is a Sufi guide or master who is otherwise known as the *pir* or *murshid*. Such individuals existed from the earliest period of mystical Islam, but the position of the *shaykh* became formalised with the establishment of 'orders' by the twelfth century. Absolute obedience to the *shaykh* by the disciple was a prerequisite in the Sufi path.

References

Jahanbakhsh (1998: 129–47).

LLOYD RIDGEON

SHIFA'

The *Shifa'*, '*The Cure*', is the most important philosophical work of Abu 'Ali al-Husayn Ibn Sina (AD 980–1037), the greatest of the eastern Islamic philosophers. It had immense influence within both the Islamic world and Christian Europe. A token of its significance among Muslims is that when Abu Hamid al-Ghazali in his *Tahafut al-Falasifa* criticised the entire philosophical tradition, he focused mainly on the teachings contained within it. And a token of its significance in the West is that it was systematically translated into Latin so that it could be studied in the colleges and schools of medieval Europe.

We know more about the process of composition of the *Shifa'* than most other works by Muslim authors of its time. According to Ibn Sina's devoted disciple and friend Abu 'Ubayd al-Juzjani, he began it when he was Vizier to the Samanid ruler Shams al-Dawla in Hamadhan. This would be sometime before about AD 1020. In addition to coping with the administration of the State and the political chicanery of the court, he was also engaged in writing the *Qanun fi 'l-Tibb*, his great systematic medical work. Al-Juzjani prevailed on him to write a work on Aristotle, but rather than writing a commentary he undertook to compose a work 'in which I would set forth what, to me, is sound in these sciences, without debating with those who disagree or busying myself with refuting them', the 'sciences' he had in mind being the Neoplatonic Aristotelian tradition passed down through late antiquity and the *falsafa*.

Al-Juzjani goes on to say that Ibn Sina began his writing with 'The Physics', *al-Tabi'iyyat*, the second of the four *jumal* of the complete work. Each night his pupils would gather to listen to what he had written that day of the *Shifa'* and the *Qanun*, amid all his duties for Shams al-Dawla, and afterwards (not surprisingly) would relax and celebrate with drinking and singers. But a change of ruler and loss of favour at court upset this pattern, and Ibn Sina continued his composition in hiding. There he drew up the subject list of the *Shifa'*, 'without the presence of a book or source to consult, but entirely from his memory and by heart'. He then began the work of commenting on each of these topics in turn, writing about fifty pages a day according to al-Juzjani, until he had completed 'The Physics', except for the last part on 'Animals', and 'The Metaphysics', *al-Ilahiyyat*, the fourth *jumla* in the final arrangement.

Ibn Sina's political fortunes continued to change: he was incarcerated for four months, and then rehabilitated and moved to a house in Hamadhan, all the time continuing to write. He composed most of the Logic, *al-Mantiq*, and the Metaphysics, *al-Ilahiyyat*, the first and fourth *jumal* of the complete *Shifa'*, as well as a number of other works at this time. Then he moved to Isfahan to the protection of the Kakuyid *amir* 'Ala' al-Dawla, and over a period until about AD 1032 he finished the remaining parts of the work, writing last the concluding sections of 'The Physics', the 'Plants', *al-Nabat*, and the 'Animals', *al-Hayawan*, once again amid the administrative tasks brought to him as Vizier, this time at the court in Isfahan.

The composition of the *Shifa'* thus took more than twelve years, and was completed in a mixture of conditions. But it seems clear from al-Juzjani's account of his master listing the topics he intended to include that Ibn Sina held a clear conception of what the compendium was to contain from the start, and was thus able to compose the different elements when and as he was able. He was also, in part, covering subjects he had already written about in earlier works. Portions from these and other earlier treatises are quoted at length in some parts of the *Shifa'*.

The work is demonstrably Aristotelian in conception, and it resumes the outline of Aristotle's *oeuvre* in many of its contents. But it is far from being a reproduction of the Greek philosopher in Arabic, not only because his teachings had come down to Ibn Sina through Neoplatonic intermediaries, but also and rather more importantly, Ibn Sina had a much larger vision and an original intention in composing the work. It covers not only Aristotle's writings but also those of the mathematician Euclid and astronomer Ptolemy,

among others, as well as themes covered nearer home by Islamic thinkers themselves. And here, even in additions noted by al-Juzjani, Ibn Sina's more obvious innovations can be seen: 'In every book of the "Mathematics" he presented additional materials, the need for which he thought to be compelling. In the *Almagest* he presented ten figures illustrating parallax. And elsewhere in the *Almagest* on the science of astronomy he presented materials that were unprecedented. In Euclid he presented some geometrical figures, in the Arithmetic some excellent numerical properties, and in the Music some problems which the ancients had neglected'. It bears the character of an encyclopaedia of all branches of knowledge except medicine, and has not inappropriately been called 'the first medieval summa which can be said to have signalled the beginning of scholastic philosophy'. While antecedents can be cited, the *Shifa'* is undeniably one of the earliest comprehensive attempts to systematise the various branches of knowledge in the Islamic tradition. Its title aptly sums up this purpose, suggesting a cure for intellectual and spiritual ignorance, the remedying of which provided the only sure means for the soul to regain its true home.

The *Shifa'* comprises four *jumal*, compendia, divided between Logic, Physics, Mathematics and Metaphysics. Each of the first three is subdivided into books, *funun*, as follows:

I. Logic, *al-Mantiq*, nine books: Isagoge, *al-Madkhul*, Categories, *al-Maqulat*, Hermeneutics, *al-'Ibara*, Analytics, *al-Qiyas*, Apodictics, *al-Burhan*, Dialectic, *al-Jadal*, Sophistics, *al-Safsata*, Rhetoric, *al-Khataba*, Poetics, *al-Shi'r*.

II. Physics, *al-Tabi'iyyat*, eight books: Scope of Physics, *al-Sama' al-tabi'i*, the Heavens and the Earth, *al-Sama' wa'l-'Alam*, Generation and Corruption, *al-Kawn wa'l-Fasad*, Actions and Passions, *al-Af'al wa'l-Infi'alat*, Meteors and Minerals, *al-Athar al-'Ulwiyya wa'l-Ma'daniyyat*, the Soul, *al-Nafs*, Plants, *al-Nabat*, Animals, *al-Hayawan*.

III. Mathematics, *al-'Ilm al-Riyadi*, four books: Geometry, *Usul al-Handasa*, Arithmetic, *al-Hisab*, Music, *Jawami' 'Ilm al-Musiqa*, Astronomy, *'Ilm al-Hay'a*.

IV. Metaphysics, *al-Ilahiyyat*, ten parts, *maqalat*.

The *funun* are divided into parts (*maqalat*), and each part into chapters (*fusul*). In each of these Ibn Sina methodically summarises the main views on the topic in hand, for and against, and then works through them demonstrating their weaknesses and strengths until he reaches his conclusion. So the *Shifa'* is the product of his own reflection upon the thought of major thinkers before him, more than a commentary or straightforward explanation.

This characteristic of the work is evident as much as anywhere in the fourth *jumla*. While this is based on Aristotle's *Metaphysics*, it has distinctively Islamic elements, and owes as much to Ibn Sina's insights as to external influences. The first part is concerned with general questions of the nature of metaphysics and its relationship with other branches of knowledge, and in the second Ibn Sina examines substance in its various forms (in Chapters 6 and 7 he discourses on the Necessary Existent, *al-wajib al-wujud*). Then in the third and fourth parts he discusses the accidental concomitants of substance that give it qualities and bring it into relation, in the fifth he examines definitions, and in the sixth

questions of cause and effect. In the seventh part he debates with Aristotle's detractors, and then in the eighth part he turns from questions of the ordering and interpretation of the phenomenal world to establish the existence of the First Principle and the mode of his knowing particulars. In all these parts, the structure and influence of Aristotle's *Metaphysics* is traceable as the informing principle of much of Ibn Sina's procedure and comments. But at this point the influence of the Islamic context and his own beliefs become more evident though never prevalent. In the eighth part his characterisation of the First Principle bears some resemblances to Qur'anic depictions of God. And in the ninth part, on the relationship between the One and the contingent order, which he conceives of as a series of causal links effected through emanation, he treats the problem of evil in a universe that flows entirely from God, and also the question of the life to come. Last, in the tenth part he discusses further explicitly religious issues such as revelation, prophethood, the purpose of forms of worship, life in the community, the family and marriage, and finally the importance of obeying the Government.

In this progression can be seen Ibn Sina's own fashioning of the metaphysical issues raised by Aristotle and his later exponents, and also the theological issues raised by the practitioners of *kalam*, in a single discussion that bears the mark of his own mind and spirit. Some Muslims who came after, such as al-Ghazali and Abu 'l-Fath al-Shahrastani, found fault with it. But its breadth of conception made it impossible to ignore, and a number of key later Muslim theological works show clear marks of its influence. It is maybe no exaggeration to say that the *Ilahiyyat*, and the *Shifa'* as a whole, contributed towards reconstructing Islamic religious thought from the time it was written. Among both Sunni and Shi'i scholars, notably in the Ishraqi school among the latter, as well as in Sufism from the time of Ibn 'Arabi onwards, its influence is unmistakable.

This influence was also felt in Europe, first in Sicily and Spain and later further north, where parts were translated by the end of the twelfth century and the whole work by 1400. Among others, Roger Bacon regarded it as the supreme exposition of Aristotle, and Thomas Aquinas borrowed from it, even though he came to criticise Ibn Sina where he differed from the teachings of the Church. Its influence continued in later centuries, and has been detected in the thought of Descartes and Pascal.

The best critical edition of the *Shifa'* is that made to celebrate the millennium of Ibn Sina's birth. This was published in separate parts by various editors under the general oversight of Ibrahim Madkour (1952–83). Parts have been translated into various European languages, notably the *Ilahiyyat* into French by Anawati (1985) and into English by Marmura (2005). Information about its composition is given by Ibn Sina's companion al-Juzjani in his continuation of his master's autobiography Gohlman (1974) (the quotations above have been taken from this work).

References

Fakhry (1983, Chapter 4), Netton (1989: Chapter 4).

DAVID THOMAS

SHI'ISM (AL-SHI'A)

Shi'ism is the second largest denomination in Islam, being identified by its emphasis on and reverence for, the spiritual authority of the Prophet's family (*Ahl al-Bayt*), in particular his daughter Fatima, his son-in-law/cousin 'Ali b. Abu Talib and their descendants in terms of this particular lineage. The crux of the dispute between Sunnism and Shi'ism is the issue of succession of the Prophet after his death – a right that belongs exclusively to 'Ali from the Shi'ite perspective. From the Shi'ite viewpoint, those who recognised the validity of 'Ali's claim after the death of the Prophet were only a handful of his companions, including Salman al-Farisi, Abu Dharr and Miqdad b. al-Aswad, the remainder of the companions falling outside the pale of the religion as a result. Consequently, those who supported 'Ali's accession to power were known as 'the Party of 'Ali' (*shi'at 'Ali*), which gave this group its name. At this stage however the dispute was very much a political division, which later developed into a theological sect. From the theological perspective then, Shi'ism has five principles of religion (*usul al-din*), namely belief in Divine Unity (*tawhid*), prophethood (*nubuwwa*), resurrection (*ma'ad*), the Imamate (*imama*) and Divine Justice (*'adl*). In the first three they agree with their Sunni counterparts although there is a heavy emphasis on intellectual interpretation similar to that of the Mu'tazilites. However, it is in the last two articles of faith that the Shi'ites define themselves and their unique identity. The concept of imam is central to Shi'ite belief and revolves around the idea that the 'Divine light of prophethood' was 'shone' upon the Prophet Muhammad and continues to be 'reflected' in his direct descendants, giving them esoterical knowledge of the religion, which qualifies them as imams. As such, each imam is divinely appointed and specifically mentions his successor upon his death by designation (*nass*), through which the process continues. Having such inspirational, esoterical knowledge derived from a divine source makes the imam infallible (*ma'sum*) and, as a consequence, Divine justice will not prevail until the Imam takes his rightful position, 'filling the earth with justice in the same way it was filled with tyranny'. Thus, it is clear that succession of the Prophet was not merely an issue of succession from the Shi'ite perspective, as the first three caliphs were not imams in the Shi'ite sense, this being reserved exclusively for 'Ali. Despite this, however, the very nature of the imamate system has been characterised by sectarianism and schisms due to the various claims of succession put forward. In addition, this has given rise to a characteristic of melancholy and 'passion' in the Shi'ite tradition, as many of the imams were killed whilst supporting their claims to power, which is often celebrated in annual events, such as the feast of 'Ashura' held on the 10th of Muharram to remember the death of 'Ali's son al-Husayn at Karbala' in AD 680. This in turn has given rise to another characteristic concept in Shi'ite theology that of occultation/concealment (*ghayba*), which usually means that the Imam in question did not actually die and will return under the messianic concept of al-Mahdi, to right all wrongs and re-establish justice on the planet. It is also worth mentioning that although the Shi'ite doctrine has a tradition of *hadith* literature, it differs entirely from that of the Sunnis as in their view, the majority of the companions of the Prophet apostatised, by not recognising 'Ali's position as imam and, therefore, their narrations are not to be considered trustworthy. In addition, since Shi'ism has often been the religion of the disaffected and, as a consequence, the persecuted, the Shi'ites developed the concept of dissimulation (*taqiyya*),

which in essence allows them to deceive to hide their true religious convictions. Many Shi'ites also consider temporary marriage (*mut'a*) to be permissible if the time period is known and the dowry (*mahr*) has been paid. In addition, they have a unique jurisprudential (*fiqh*) system, which has marked differences from that of their Sunni counterparts, not only in the complex discussion regarding matters of inheritance but even in basic practices such as prayer (*salat*) and fasting (*sawm*). Three main Shi'ite groups exist: the majority Ithna 'Asharis, the Isma'ilis and the Zaydis.

References

Daftary (1998: 23–5), Hanafi (1980: 46–53), Netton (1997: 230–1), Tabataba'i (n.d.: 9–16), Watt (1997: 14–18, 56–62, 122–30).

See also: **Sunnism**

GAVIN PICKEN

SHIRAZ

Capital of Fars Province (*ostandar*) in a great plain in the central Zagros mountains, southern Iran, its gardens irrigated by *qanats*, one of the leading medieval Islamic cities, with the title *dar al-'ilm*, Fars. Shiraz was founded by the mythical Pishdadhid dynasty. The city (1,486 metres above sea level), near Persepolis, was important under the Seleucid, Parthian and Sasanian empires.

The Muslim city (founded AD 684) and surrounding plain were used by the Arabs during the siege of Istakhr, the Sasanian capital of Fars. In AD 875, the Saffarid 'Amr ibn Layth built its Friday Mosque. Adherence to Islam by rulers, *qadis*, *'ulama'* and Sufis was vigorous: Ibn Khafif (d. AD 982) founded a *riba* here. A provincial centre under the Shi'i Buyids (AD 949–77), and Shiraz attracted Islamic theologians, mystics and poets in search of patronage from 'Adud al-Dawla (r. AD 978–83), including al-Mutanabbi (*c.* AD 915–65). 'Adud al-Dawla developed a flourishing town, building a great library, hospital, mosques, elaborate gardens, markets and the palace-barracks, Kard Fana Khosrow, reputedly with 360 rooms. Samsam al-Dawla built a robust city wall. Under the Saljuqs the city was repeatedly plundered, though several *madrasa*s were endowed. Under the Salghurids (mid-twelfth century), Shiraz flourished: the Sunquriyya mosque-*madrasa* and many other shrines were built. The great Persian poet, Sa'di (AD 1207–91), was born there and died in Shiraz after many travels. His poems are delicately lyrical and eloquent. His *Bustan* (AD 1257) illustrated Muslim virtues such as liberality, justice, modesty and contentment as well as reflecting the ecstatic behaviour of Sufis, whilst his *Gulistan* (AD 1258) discusses Muslim morals.

The benevolent Abu Bakr (d. AD 1261) and his Il-Khan followers made many charitable bequests, built hospitals, and mosques including the New Mosque (now the Martyrs' Mosque), possibly the largest mosque in Iran. The late thirteenth century was turbulent with Shiraz affected by drought, measles and famine. Al-Mustawfi (AD 1281/2–1339/40) noted that Shirazis were strictly traditional and addicted to holy poverty. Ibn Battuta visited Shiraz (AD 1347) during the reign of Abu Ishaq (r. AD 1342–3) and noted their piety and pure manners. He described the bazaar, palaces, mausolea and tax-revenues; also the Shah Čiragh mausoleum-shrine, college and hospice erected (1344–9; rebuilt 1506; nineteenth century) at the tomb of Ahmad b. Musa (d. AD 835) by Tash Khatun, Abu Ishaq's mother. He describes her visits there on Monday evenings to meet assembled jurists and *sharifs*, with over 14,000 *sharifs* receiving stipends and where the Qur'an was recited daily. The shrine is still venerated by Shi'ite pilgrims.

There was a cultural, artistic and commercial revival under the Timurids. The Shirazi Hafiz (AD 1324–89), master of lyric poetry of exceptional symbolic complexity, was probably visited by Timur. His tomb (*aramgah'i-Hafiz*) is venerated. In the sixteenth century Shiraz prospered under the Safawid ruler Imam Quli Khan and it became a Muslim centre of learning that rivalled Baghdad. The Great Library (built AD 1615) later became an important theological college (Madrasé-i-khan); mosques, palaces, city walls, and the Khan Madrasa were built but terrible floods (1630, 1668) damaged many buildings. Many European travellers and traders visited Shiraz including Della Valle (1612–21) and Thévenot (1663). The Dhahabiyya order was based in Shiraz (early seventeenth century AD).

After the fall of the Safawids (1722), Afghans sacked Shiraz and Nadir Shah (d. 1747) besieged it several times though he attempted to restore its mosques and gardens. In 1766–7, Karim Khan Zand (d. 1782) made Shiraz the Persian capital and prosperity returned; glass, ceramics and wine (chiefly made by Jews and Armenians) were exported. His massive building programme included a new wall and fortress-citadel, town-quarters, a reception hall, the Masjid-i-Vakil (1773, restored 1825–6), Wakil bazaar and his mausoleum, an octagonal tiled kiosk.

In the eighteenth century, the Qajars built gardens to reflect Islamic concepts of paradise, including the Bagh-i-Aram, Bagh-i-Ali, Bagh-i-Delgosha. Aqa Muhammad Khan (d. 1797) moved the Qajar capital to Tehran, with Shirazi Hajji Ibrahim (d. 1801) his first minister. Ibrahim's descendants became leaders of the Khamsa tribal federation. Shiraz declined in the nineteenth to twentieth centuries under effects of damaging earthquakes (1824, 1853), plague, heavy taxes, social disorder, riots, famine and family rivalries.

References:

Arberry (1960), Hillenbrand (1994: 403), Meisami (1998: 8).

JANET STARKEY

AL-SHIRAZI, MULLA SADRA (d. 1641)

Sadr al-Din Muhammad ibn Ibrahim Shirazi, better known as Mulla Sadra and given the title of *Sadr al-Muta'allihin* (Master of those who would be divine) is arguably the most significant Islamic philosopher after Avicenna. He became famous as the thinker who revolutionised the doctrine of existence in Islamic metaphysics and extended the shift from Aristotelian substance metaphysics to (Neoplatonic) process metaphysics of change. He was the sole child, born into a courtly family in Shiraz in around 1571. A bright young man, his interest in intellectual pursuits was indulged by his father and he moved first to Qazvin and then to Isfahan, successive capitals of the Safavid empire to pursue his inquiry into philosophy, theology and hermeneutics with the two pre-eminent teachers of his age, Mir Muhammad Baqir Damad (d. 1621), the grandson of the powerful *mujtahid* 'Ali al-Karaki, and Shaykh Baha' al-Din al-'Amili (d. 1621), who was Shaykh al-Islam in Isfahan during the reign of Shah 'Abbas I. Completing his training, he returned to Shiraz to work and teach, but failing to find an adequate patron, he retreated to Kahak, a small village outside the holy city of Qumm to meditate upon his inquiries and initiate the composition of his main works, especially his philoso-phical and theological summa, *al-Hikma al-Muta'aliyya fi'l-Asfar al-'Aqliyya al-Arba'a* (Transcendent Wisdom of the Four Journeys of the Intellect), popularly known as *al-Asfar al-Arba'a* (The Four Journeys). Having acquired a patron in the form of Imamquli Khan (d. 1612), a notable Georgian *ghulam* who was in charge of the Safavid military administration and the governor of Sadra's home province of Fars, he moved to Shiraz and began to teach at the Madrasa-yi Khan, founded by Imamquli with the main purpose of providing Sadra with a place to teach the intellectual sciences. There, he trained a generation of philosophers, the most significant were Muhsin Fayz Kashani (d. 1680) and 'Abd al-Razzaq Lahiji (d. 1661) both of whom became his sons-in-law. After an illustrious and prolific career, he died in Basra on the return from his seventh pilgrimage to Mecca in 1641. It is not clear if his gravesite has survived.

Mulla Sadra's *magnum opus* is a large compendium of philosophy and theology that, instead of following the traditional divisions of logic, physics and metaphysics, maps intellectual inquiry upon a mystical metaphor of the soul's journey in this world. Hence, it is popularly known as the *Four Journeys*. The first journey from this world to God provides the seeker with the intellectual principles for understanding philosophy such as the basic definition of philosophy and metaphysics, the significance of metaphysics and the question of being for this study. In this journey, the seeker moves away from multiplicity and phenomenal deception towards unity and an awareness of the underlying nature of reality. The second journey in God with God is a discourse on the nature of God, the divine attributes and significantly including his famous proof for the existence of God. It is the stage of the mystic's absorption in the divine essence and his effacement of the self. The third journey from God to this world explains the God–world relationship, nature, time and creation and ontological categories in this world. For the mystic, this is the return to sobriety and a realisation of the duties of moral agency in this world. The final journey in this world with God is a description of human psychology focusing on soteriology and eschatology and reveals most clearly the significance of Twelver Shi'ism to his thought. This is the final stage of the mystic's journey, a recognition that everything as a unified whole reflects the ontological unity of the divine and that the realised human recognises a desire to return to the principle, the one who is the source of being, God.

His other works mainly deal with philosophical theology such as *al-Hikma al-'Arshiyya* (Wisdom of the Throne) and *al-Shawahid al-Rububiyya* (*Divine Witnesses*). One work, *al-Masha'ir* (*Inspired Recognitions*) stands out as a dense epitome of his doctrine of being as expressed in the first part of the *Four Journeys*. As a religious thinker, Mulla Sadra was also keen to come to terms with his scriptural heritage and he wrote three works on the hermeneutics of the Qur'an, *Mafatih al-Ghayb* (*Keys to the Unseen*), *Asrar al-Ayat* (*Secrets of the Verses/Signs*), and *Mutashabihat al-Qur'an* (*Allegories of the Qur'an*) as a preparation for his own incomplete mystical and philosophical commentary on the text. As a Shi'i thinker, he also wrote an incomplete commentary on the main doctrinal collection of tradition, *Usul al-Kafi* of al-Kulayni, as an attempt to grapple with the question of what it means to be an intuitive philosopher in the Shi'i tradition.

Mulla Sadra is often described as a metaphysical revolutionary because of his uniquely posited doctrine of exis-

tence. Existence is ontologically prior, a unified reality graded in degrees of intensity and an elusive reality that cannot be fully grasped. Any attempt to conceptualise existence falsifies it through reification. A reified, fixed concept cannot capture the nature of existence, which is dynamic and in flux. Unpacking this metaphysical package, one can discern three distinct doctrines of existence that draw upon his intellectual influences, which include Avicennan philosophy, the intuitive philosophy of the Ishraqi school associated with Suhrawardi and the Sufi metaphysics of being of Ibn 'Arabi. The first doctrine is the ontological primacy of existence (*asalat al-wujud*), a doctrine that is located within the debate on the Avicennan distinction between existence and essence in contingent beings as seen through the prism of the Sufi metaphysics of ontological monism (*wahdat al-wujud*). If contingents are composites, then one element of the composition is active and ontologically prior. Is it the case that there are essences in some of being such as humanity that wait for a divine agent to actualise and individuate them through the bestowal of existence, an essentialist doctrine that posit a rather paradoxical existence of an essence before it comes to exist? Or as Mulla Sadra suggests, the divine agent produces existences in this world that take on the 'garb' of some particular essence. Existence must be ontologically prior not only because of the absurdity of an existence before existence, but also because God is devoid of essence and his causal link to the world can only be existential if one wishes to avoid the contamination of the divine nature with essences that are composites of different and multiple properties and features. Mulla Sadra uses this doctrine as part of his own ontological proof for the existence of God known as the Proof of the Veracious (*burhan al-siddiqin*). The monism of the doctrine is expressed in the phrase *basit al-haqiqa kull al-ashya'* (The Simple is all things): God, the One is simple and Pure Being and thus as such is all existence. The second doctrine is the modulation and gradation of existence (*tashkik al-wujud*). Existence is a singular reality as the phenomenal experience of existence as multiple is illusory. But multiplicity in this world still needs to be explained. Different existents in this world are thus different intense degrees of a single whole. Thus, there is a horizontal and a vertical hierarchy of existence that is connected and involved in a whole chain of existence. The particular degrees of existence are not stable substances in the Aristotelian sense and thus neither is Sadrian ontology concerned with a multiplicity of substances or the problem that would be raised by the objection: how can all things be one substance? This leads us to the third doctrine that all individuals in existence undergo motion and flux (*haraka jawhariyya*). An existing entity is not a stable substance constant in time to which change occurs as an accident such as a young Zayd becoming old and greying, rather, it is a structure of unfolding, dynamic events of existence. The young Zayd is thus literally not the same existent as the old Zayd since the change in him is substantial and existential. One implication of this doctrine is that at every instance each existent is renewed and thus provides a solution to the old problem of time and creation by asserting that the world is created in time because at each instant, all existence is new in time.

He applies his metaphysics to problems in psychology and eschatology as well. Just as the totality of existence is singular with degrees of intensity, similarly intellect and the soul are singular realities with grades of intensity since there is an intimate connection between existence, the intellect and the soul as the concrete, intellectual and psychic aspects of being. This entails a thorough-going pan-psychism in which for Mulla Sadra all existents are sentient beings that aspire to be 'more intense' than they are, to a higher ontological level. Since all levels of intellect are connected, knowledge is an existential relationship of identity and the cognition of certainty in which the intellecting subject becomes identified with the intellected object (*ittihad al-'aqil wa'l-ma'qul*). Further, he uses his doctrine of modulation to explain physical resurrection, a theological doctrine that traditionally could not be philosophically demonstrated. He distinguishes two levels of resurrection that involve two 'types' of body, a purely physical one and an 'imaginal' body that is as real as the physical. The imaginal body is at first resurrected and can be demonstrated. This is predicated upon the existence of an ontological state of being known as the imaginal (*mithali*) that mediates between an intelligible world of concepts and the sensible world of things. It is used to explain those traditions that discuss abstract concepts such as fear and desire as having physical or corporeal features in resurrection. Concepts from the intelligible world can mimic physicality of this world through the mediation of the imaginal realm of being.

Mulla Sadra has become the dominant philosopher of the Islamic East. His commentary on the peripatetic work *al-Hidaya* (*The Guidance*) of Athir al-Din al-Abhari became the cornerstone of the rationalist curriculum of the Indian *madrasa* from the eighteenth century. In Iran, the study of Islamic philosophy takes its cue from the study and commentary on his major works at least from the nineteenth century. The revival of Islamic philosophy in Isfahan ushered by 'Ali Nuri (d. 1836) and later Hadi Sabzawari (d. 1873), described as the 'last great Islamic philosopher', established Mulla Sadra as the ultimate philosopher whose thought and arguments 'transcended' discursive peripatetic philosophy and also intuitive and allusive mystical arguments and discourse in favour of a higher synthesis that combined ratiocinative arguments with mystical insight, complete syllogistic demonstrations with narrative, allusion and allegory. In more recent times, some of the key thinkers involved in the Iranian revolution of 1979 such as Ayatallah Khomeini and Murtaza Mutahhari were profoundly influenced by the thought of Mulla Sadra and some have even attempted to appropriate Mulla Sadra as the philosopher of the revolution despite the distinct lack of an engagement with political philosophy in his work.

References

Ashtiyani (1998), Cooper (1998), Corbin (1964, 1972: IV, 54–122, 1986: 439–669), Jambet (2000, 2002), Khamanehi (2000), Morris (1981), Rahman (1975), Rizvi (2006, 2007, 2008), Yad (1998).

SAJJAD H. RIZVI

SHIRK

The 'association' of something other than Allah himself with Allah. This is the sole sin that cannot be forgiven.

References

Waines (1995: 105).

See also: *muskrikun*; **pantheism**

ANDREW J. NEWMAN

SHUBHA

Lexically, the word designates similarity. In Islamic law, similarity of objects of articles may lead to doubt or uncertainty. One may perceive the resemblance of an unlawful act that was been committed, to another, lawful one and, therefore, subjectively speaking, the presumption of a bona fides in the accused. Duress is widely recognised, particularly in the case of drinking wine or unlawful sexual intercourse.

MAWIL IZZI DIEN

SHUHADA' (sing. *shahid*)

'Martyrs', believers who die for the faith, in its defense or from persecution and who are guaranteed a place in Heaven (Q.3:169).

ANDREW J. NEWMAN.

SHURA

'Consultation', 'council' in early Islamic history referring the process whereby a group of beleivers determined the successors to the Prophet after his death. Also the title of Q.42.

See also: *majlis*; *nass*

SHU'UBIYYA

Shu'ubiyya, in classical Islamic literature, refers to a movement (or series of movements) – mainly literary, but with political aspects – in which Arabs and non-Arabs were proclaimed as equal. At times, the *shu'ubi* sentiment expressed itself in the rebuttal of Arab claims to superiority by a denigration of Arab culture, language and race. Literally, *shu'ubiyya* means 'of the people' (that is 'people', undifferentiated by race). Some scholars argue that the expansion of the Muslim empire in the seventh and eighth centuries was primarily ethnic (rather than religious) in character: the Arab armies that conquered non-Arab neighbouring states intended to establish

Arab political domination, not any new religious state. This was expressed in doctrines such as the superiority of Arabs generally, the exclusive right of the Quraysh (the tribe of the Prophet Muhammad) to the caliphate and the lack of marriage equality (*kafa'a*) between an Arab and a non-Arab. The common means whereby a non-Arab joined the Arab community (or converted to Islam) was for the non-Arab to affiliate (*wala'*) himself to a tribe, becoming a client (*mawla*) of a particular Arab grouping. The Muslim polity, it seems, operated along the lines of Arab tribal organisation, with the inbuilt Arab superiority that such a system assumes.

This lead to a reaction by many of the converted (or dominated) peoples who resented the power of the Arabs – particularly that manifest during the Umayyad period. Little attempt was made to incorporate the clients (*mawali*) into the political structure. One political movement which reflected elements of *shu'ubiyya* sentiment were the Kharijites, who did not recognise the inherent right of the Quraysh to rule the Muslim community, and advocated a regime of justice which was equally severe on both Arab and non-Arab. The 'Abbasid revolution drew on the support of 'disenfranchised' *mawali* and had a certain *shu'ubi* character. The *shu'ubiyya* itself is considered by Goldziher to be a purely literary movement made up of secretaries and scribes in the new 'Abbasid government. The *shu'ubiyya* were almost entirely Persians (*'Ajam*) who had been incorporated into 'Abbasid state structures and were reflecting their new-found confidence in literary expression. Translating the epics of their pre-Arab civilisation into Arabic, or developing 'new Persian' (the Persian language in Arabic script) were expressions of a confidence in non-Arab traditions of learning. At times, this confidence was expressed in criticism of Arab-Muslim learning. In some poetry of the early 'Abbasid period, for example, Arabs are portrayed as illiterate camel herders with little conception of the civilised culture of the court. Little *shu'ubiyya* literature has survived from the period – most of our information comes from anti-*shu'ubi* criticisms, such as those of the famous *litterateur*, al-Jahiz (d. AD 868). This, of course, makes it difficult to be confident about even the most sketchy portrait of the movement. It seems that the early impetus to the *shu'ubiyya* created by the 'Abbasids did not last, and whilst the *shu'ubiyya* did secure a place and role for non-Arab culture within Islamic culture generally (and a theoretical recognition of the religious equality of Arabs and non-Arabs), Arab lineage continued to be accompanied by privileges throughout the classical period in the central Islamic lands.

One finds the term '*shu'ubi*' being used in reference to a number of movements later in Muslim history. After the 'Abbasids when the *shu'ubiyya* seem to have disappeared, the term was used again to describe anti-Arab sentiments amongst the Berbers and Europeans of the Andalusian Muslim empire. The descendents of Arabs had claimed superiority over non-Arab Muslims (the *saqaliba* – or 'Slavs' who had converted to Islam). There was a literary movement aimed at denigrating the Arabs, and upholding the universality of Islam. The motifs of the earlier *shu'ubiyya* (the backward nature of pre-Islamic Arabian culture and the relative sophistication of the Persians and Byzantines) are evident in the *Risala* of the eleventh-century Andalusian Ibn Gharsiya. There is no historical link between the 'Abbasid and Andalusian *shu'ubiyyas*, though there is clear literary influence on Ibn Gharsiya of the earlier anti-Arab polemic. Both also share the interesting feature of a general acceptance of (and in some cases strong attachment to) the Arabic language as the mode of communication. From this period onwards, *shu'ubi* is better understood as a description of the literary characteristic of a text, or possibly a broader social phenomenon, rather than the description of a single movement which rears its head at particular points in time. Under some analyses, any individual who aims to invalidate Arab claims of Muslim precedence might be termed *shu'ubi*, and this could include the (Turkish) Ottoman Empire, or modern *shu'ubiyya* such as the attempted nationalism of Iraq or Syria (where the populations are ethnically mixed and nationalism is seen as a cure to rivalry between Arabs and non-Arabs). Popularist anti-Arabism, (which could, at a stretch, be considered *shu'ubi*) was used by Muhammad Reza Shah of Iran (d. 1980), as he tried to elevate Iran's pre-Islamic past. A *shu'ubi*-style rejection of Arab culture and language continues to play a major role in modern Persian culture. Arab nationalism could be seen as a reaction against these more recent manifestations of *shu'ubiyya*: it is an attempt to reassert the distinctive (and in some ways, superior) character of Arab culture.

References

Gibb (1962), Goldziher (1961: I, 177–218), Mottahedeh (1976: 161–82).

ROBERT GLEAVE
ANDREW J. NEWMAN

SICILY

Largest island in the Mediterranean, an autonomous region of Italy with the islands of Egadi, Lipari, Pelagie and Panteleria. Colonised by Phoenicians and Greeks (eighth century BC), by the third century BC Sicily was the first province of Rome. It was conquered by a succession of invaders from the early Middle Ages (Vandals, Ostrogoths, Byzantines, Arabs).

The Aghlabids under jurist Asad b. al-Furat invaded Sicily from Ifriqiya (AD 1212), the last major *futuh* of Islam combining *jihad* and conquest, ironically initiated by a Byzantine appeal for support. Messina was conquered by the poet Mujbar ibn Sufyan (AD 843), and Syracuse destroyed (AD 878). The Fatimid general, Jawhar, who captured Cairo in AD 970 was a eunuch slave from Sicily. Sicily became a province of Ifriqiya and a way station for pilgrims to Mecca.

Arabs supported the arts and built palaces, castles and exotic gardens. The Shi'i Kalbite *amirs* (AD 947–1053) ruled a culturally prosperous Sicily and the spread of Islam accompanied perceived economic benefits. Maliki poets, grammarians and jurists fleeing the spread of Shi'ism in the Maghrib were patronised in Sicily. Schools of thought developed in Sicily that became renowned in the Mediterranean. The geographer Ibn Hawqal (visited AD 972–3) described Palermo's water supply, 300 mosques and Sufi *ribats*.

By the tenth century, Byzantines, Normans and Arabs were in dispute over control. By the eleventh century, Sicily was in a state of anarchy and in danger of conquest from a revived Western Christian world. Robert d'Hauteville and his brother Robert le Guiscard seized Sicily (AD 1060–91) despite resistence from Benavert, the last Islamic leader in Sicily.

The Normans found Islamic culture so congenial that they did little to change it or convert the Arabs to Christianity: the Sicilian Islamicist Ibn Zafar (AD 1104–70/3) described these Arab communities in Christian Sicily. Many Sicilian churches and cathedrals were later built on Muslim holy sites, such as Palermo cathedral, built in AD 1170 on the site of a sixth-century basilica that had been converted into a mosque. Magnificent Arab-Norman palaces in Palermo included Ziza (AD 1154–80 built by William I), Favara and Cuba (AD 1180). The Norman Palace in Palermo was originally built by the Arabs (ninth century AD) on the ruins of a Roman fortress. It has a Palatine chapel (AD 1132–40) and wooden ceiling in Sicilian Arab-Norman style. Evidence of Arab rule is still reflected in Sicilian place and family names, in its lexicon, its road network, in architectural features, gardens and fountains. The most Sicilian of words, *mafia*, is derived from Arabic *mafya'*, 'place of shade' or 'refuge'.

Ibn Sharaf (*c.* AD 1000–67) spent his later years in Sicily but many Muslim Sicilians fled after attack from the Normans, including the poet Ibn Hamdis (AD 1056–1133) who fled to Seville after fighting the Normans. Yet Norman kings encouraged Maghribi scholars, such as the geographer al-Idrisi (AD 1100–*c.* 1162), who systematically surveyed Sicily under the Norman patronage, dedicating *Kitab al-Rujjar* to Roger II. Al-Idrisi's maps are among the great achievements of Islamic science. Ibn Jubayr wrote an account of his visit in AD 1184–5. In the thirteenth century, a school was founded in Palermo to translate Arabic manuscripts on mathematics, philosophy and natural sciences, and many are now lodged in the Vatican Library in Rome. Scholars included royal astrologers Michel Scorns of Toledo and Theodore of Antioch (with his treatise on falcons), who were translators for Frederick II, a sympathiser of Arabo-Islamic civilisation. Jewish scholars, Moses of Palermo and Moses Farachi, translated major medical Arab treatises in the 1270s into Latin. Sicilio-Arabic poetry influenced Italian Renaissance poetic tradition.

References

Ahmad (1975), Corrao (1998: 719–20), Metcalfe (2003).

JANET STARKEY

SIDRAT AL-MUNTAHA

'The lot tree on the boundary', where Muhammad saw the angel Gabriel. See Q.53:13–18.

ANDREW J. NEWMAN

SIFFIN, BATTLE OF

The battle was fought in AD 657, near the Syrian–Iraqi border on the west bank of the Euphrates, between Iraqi troops of the fourth Rightly Guided Caliph, 'Ali ibn abi Talib, and a force of Syrians led by Mu'awiya. Instead of recognising the legitimacy of 'Ali's succession to the caliphate in AD 656, Mu'awiya (the Governor of Syria) vowed vengeance for the murder of his kinsman, the third of the Rightly Guided Caliphs, 'Uthman ibn 'Affan in that year. 'Ali's forces promptly invaded Syria. A series of indecisive engagements and temporary truces followed. Legend has it that Mu'awiya's troops went into the battle with copies of the Qur'an fixed to the tips of their lances. The implication was that 'the Word of God' should decide the outcome, but it was arbitration in the following year rather than the passage of arms that decided the issue in the long term. Had 'Uthman betrayed the principles of Islam? If so, he deserved death at the hands of his killer, and 'Ali's succession to the caliphate was valid. If 'Uthman was innocent of breaking Islamic law, Mu'awiya was justified in seeking vengeance and in pressing his own claims to the caliphate. In AD 658, arbitration supported the innocence of 'Uthman. Mu'awiya's star was henceforward in the ascendant. 'Ali, who had been advised to press his military advantage from the outset and not to agree to arbitration, retired to his capital, Kufa, where he was assassinated on his way to prayer in the mosque in AD 661. Mu'awiya became the first of the Umayyad caliphs in AD 660.

References

Momen (1985: 25).

EDWARD D. A. HULMES

AL-SIJISTANI, ABU SULAYMAN

Muhmmad b. Tahir b. Barham, known as Abu Sulayman al-Mantiqi al-Sijistani, was born in Sijistan, probably at the turn of the tenth century. The details of his life are obscure to us but probably he lived in Sijistan until AD 939 and then moved to Baghdad. Soon, he became a member of the philosophical school of al-Farabi. He studied under Yahya Ibn 'Adi and became the master of the school after his death. The details of al-Sijistani's activities and works are known to us through the writings of his colleague and friend Abu Hayyan al-Tawhidi. His both works al-Imta' wa al-Mu'anasa and al-Muqabasat disclose many aspects of al-Sijistani's philosophy. The only work of al-Sijistani that has survived, however, is the famous *Siwan al-Hikma*. It is an important work on the history of philosophy. Al-Sijistani's writings seem to have followed the encyclopaedic Aristotelian curriculum moving from logic, mathematics, physics and metaphysics. It is not clear whether he produced important works in all those subjects but al-Tawhidi reports, in his both works mentioned above, the interesting and vivid discussions around those sciences which Abu Sulayman led among his students and the attendees of his *majlis*. Although he directed the Farbian School for some time, he does not seem to be a strict follower of al-Farabi's system. His master can be rather identified with Plotinus, however in his natural physics he was a sincere follower of Aristotle. His discussion on the theological part of metaphysics, follows the Poltinian trinity of the One, the Universal Intellect and the Universal Soul. Emanation, for him, is the eternal process through which existence flows from the unknowable and mysterious One to the Intellect and the Soul. Al-Tawhidi also reports the interesting discussion which al-Sijistani led on the concept of the human soul. Unlike many philosophers of his time and after him, he made a clear distinction between the spirit, *al-ruh*, and the soul, *al-Nafs*. He seems to identify the spirit with a very thin material spreading in the body and causing its life, while the soul is the intellectual principle that provides the power to the spirit and gives rise to the rational ability of the human. The soul has three faculties: the vegetation, the animal, and the rational. The spirit is connected to the animal soul and it is the mediator between the human soul and body.

In his life, al-Sijistani could win the patronage of the governor of Sijistan Ja'far and the Buyid prince of Baghdad 'Adud al-Dawla. He considered the death of the latter to be a great loss for the culture life in Baghdad and sadly recited 'who is going to remember me after him?' The date of AD 985, which is two years after the death of 'Adud al-Dawla, is usually given as the date of Abu Sulayman's death.

References

Kraemer (1992).

MAHA EL-KAISY FRIEMUTH

AL-SIJISTANI, ABU YA'QUB

Very little is known about the life of this 'pillar' of the so-called 'Persian school of Isma'ilism' in the tenth century. But his works, especially *Kashf al-Mahjub* (*Unveiling the Hidden*), and doctrines aroused controversy both inside and outside the Isma'ili community and were subject to criticism in polemics by the anti-Isma'ili Zaydi polemicist Abu'l-Qasim al-Busti (d. AD 1030), the scientist and philosopher al-Biruni in his work on India (written AD 1030) and the Isma'ili philosopher Nasir-i Khusraw (d. after AD 1052). What we do know is that an active Isma'ili missionary called Abu Ya'qub Ishaq ibn Ahmad Sijistani was operating in his home province of Sistan in eastern Iran from roughly AD 934 (when he reported from Baghdad to the head of the mission on his return from the pilgrimage to Mecca) to AD 971 (when he wrote the latter part of his work *al-Iftikhar* or the *Boast*). Sometime after this date, the Saffarid ruler of Khurasan and Sistan, Khalaf ibn Ahmad executed him for heresy, thus making him a martyr to the Isma'ili cause. He had never visited the Isma'ili Fatimid state in North Africa but remained a loyal operative and supported the imam-caliphs, unlike other earlier or contemporary Isma'ili missionaries in Iran who were Qarmatians such as Abu Hatim al-Razi and al-Nasafi.

All of his works were composed in Arabic and one of them (*The Wellsprings*) also survives in an archaic Persian paraphrase. His two earliest works were *Kitab al-Yanabi'* (*The Wellsprings*) and *Ithbat al-Nubuwwa* (*Prophecy's Proof*). The former discusses forty points of Isma'ili philosophy concerning the nature and source of knowledge and addresses the relationship between nature and prophecy and the role of prophets as sources of spiritual knowledge and life. *Prophecy's Proof* is a standard defence of the need for prophecy (against some philosophical reservations on the issue) and the continuing need for imams as executors of the prophetic testament and mission. But unlike other works in the genre of his time, he attempts to provide a philosophical demonstration for the necessity of prophecy. *Kitab al-Maqalid* (*The Keys*), divided into seventy chapters, is also a philosophical work on some key cosmological doctrines. His two later works, *Kitab al-Iftikhar* (*The Boast*) and *Sullam al-Najat* (*Ladder of Salvation*) are polemics and apologetics that defend Isma'ili theological doctrines through a hermeneutics of reading the Qur'an and other key Muslim texts to tease out justifications for the Isma'ili mission. His most significant work is *Kashf al-Mahjub* (*Unveiling the Hidden*), a philosophical justification of Isma'ili cosmology that is divided into seven books.

What is interesting about al-Sijistani's work is that it represents an early phase in the intellectual encounter of Isma'ilism and Neoplatonism. The core problems and issues in his texts do not deal solely with the Shi'i notion of the imamate but with aspects of cosmogony, prophecy and history. They reveal the complementarity of approach between an intellectual quest for the truth and the imparting of truth from an infallible imam who is the trustee and successor of the prophet. Already in *The Wellsprings*, this reconciliation is visible. Al-Sijistani argues that there are four sources and ways to truth: the intellect, the soul, legislating prophecy, and infallible interpretation of the imam. Each of these sources has a function in guiding a believer. The first source provides support (*ta'yid*), the second composes and forms a higher synthesis (*tarkib*), the third composes a scripture and law (*ta'lif*) and the fourth expounds and glosses on these compositions and explains the truth (*ta'wil*). The imam as wielder of *ta'wil*, as sole authorised interpreter, has a critical role in bringing these sources together. Apart from this epistemological harmonisation, al-Sijistani also draws upon the apophatic theology of Neoplatonism in his 'double-negating' description of the divine nature and the scheme of emanative cosmogony. The first three creations in *Unveiling the Hidden* are the standard Neoplatonic triad of the hypostases of intellect, soul and nature.

However, the most controversial aspect of al-Sijistani's thought is his eschatology. In Chapter 7 (significantly) of *Unveiling the Hidden*, he reinterprets and criticised the Muslim notion of resurrection as an end of time revival of humanity to be judged at the end of linear history. Consonant with the Isma'ili notion of the cyclical nature of sacred history, resurrection (*al-ba'th*) for al-Sijistani is a process of continuous re-creation through the transmigration of souls. This cyclical recreation is a continuation of the process of emanation from the Intellect that prepares the way for the creation of the cosmos. The Intellect thus is constantly involved in creation in this universe and does not suspend its connection after the first impetus at the beginning of the chain of emanation. It is clear, nevertheless, that al-Sijistani insists that metempsychosis (*al-tanasukh*) does not entail a change but rather a preservation of species and he condemns the 'vulgar' notion of the transmigration of souls. This did not prevent criticism as metempsychosis had already become anathema to the Isma'ili mission and his work was condemned by Nasir-i Khusraw and others.

References

Alibhai (1983), Corbin (1994), Hirji (1995), Landolt (2000: II, 81–124), Madelung (1990:

131–43, 1996: 85–8), Marquet (1994: 5–28), al-Sijistani (1949), Walker (1993, 1996, 1999).

SAJJAD H. RIZVI

SILSILA

The *silsila* is a term used by the Sufis to denote the chain of mystics that connect them back to Muhammad. In other words, it is a spiritual genealogy. Some *silsilas* are very long but this is not always the case, as there have been some Sufis who have claimed initiation into the secrets of the mystical world directly through Muhammad in the form of a dream. The *silsila* became very crucial in establishing the identity of the Sufi orders that took place in the medieval period.

References

Trimingham (1971).

LLOYD RIDGEON

SIN

In Islam there are two categories of sin. The first is a fault or shortcoming that causes sanction not punishment per se, as opposed to a willful infraction that does merit punishment. There is no concept of original sin in Islam, as the Fall was not the fault of Adam but of Satan.

References

Waines (1995: 29–30).

See also: **Adam; Iblis**

ANDREW J. NEWMAN

SINAN

Sinan (*c.* 1491–1588), the chief architect to Sultan Suleyman I (1520–66) is the most famous Islamic architect for the many works which he built and the plans which his staff and local builders used throughout the Ottoman provinces for religious and civil buildings. His output was prolific, well over 100 buildings. He transformed the Ottoman mosque into a great harmonious structure based on a disciplined interplay of domes and semidomes, courts and minarets, which owed much to the technical expertise he acquired during his early career as an engineer in the Janissery corps. His masterpieces are the Suleymaniye Mosque built from 1550 to 1557 in Istanbul and the Selimiye Mosque built from 1569 to 1575 at Edirne.

References

Goodwin (1993), Necipoglu (2005).

JENNIFER SCARCE

AL-SIRAT

'The way', as well as a bridge in Hell.

See also: *al-sirat al-mustaqim*

ANDREW J. NEWMAN

SIRAT AL-JAHIM

The bridge in Hell (Q.61:23). By tradition, the bridge is said to have seven arches.

See also: *al-Jahim*

ANDREW J. NEWMAN

AL-SIRAT AL-MUSTAQIM

The Arabic phrase means 'the Straight Path' of Islam: 'Guide us along the Straight Path, the Path of those whom you [*Allah*] have blessed, not of those with whom you are displeased, nor of those who go astray' (Q.1:6–7).

EDWARD D. A. HULMES

SIRAT RASUL ALLAH

The first Arabic works in the field of Islamic historiography contain pre-Islamic stories and legends from the 'Days of Ignorance' (*al-jahiliyya*), which were based on collections of oral and written traditions. These were then used as prolegomena for accounts of the Prophet Muhammad's life and mission. The first biography of the Prophet was the *Sirat Rasul Allah* (*The Life of the Messenger of God*), written by Muhammad ibn-Ishaq of Medina, who died in Baghdad in AD 767. This biography survived only in the later recension of ibn Hisham, who died in Cairo in AD 834. Some Muslim scholars, including the jurists and traditionalists, Malik ibn-Anas (*c.* AD 715–95) and Ahmad ibn-Hanbal (AD 780–855) declined to accept ibn-Ishaq's work as authoritative on the grounds that he was insufficiently meticulous in naming his legal and religious sources.

References

Guillaume (1955).

EDWARD D. A. HULMES

SIRHINDI, AHMAD (1564–1624)

Muslim reformer in the context of the Moghul Empire in India. Living as he did through the start of the second millennium of Islamic history, which fell in 1592, Sirhindi was extremely concerned about a number of threats to the Muslim community that he perceived as existing in India. These were, first, extreme Sufism, which he thought compromised the transcendence of God by suggesting that it was possible for Sufis to become united with God; second, the new movement of Sikhism, which drew on elements of both the Hindu and the Islamic traditions, and, third, the *din-i-ilahi* (literally 'religion of God'), espoused by the Moghul Emperor Akbar, which combined elements from the whole variety of religions then found in India. All of these things Sirhindi perceived to be threats to the purity of the Islamic faith and the identity of the Muslim community, and he therefore campaigned against them by all means available, including military ones against the Sikhs.

References

Ansari (1986), Friedmann (1971).

HUGH GODDARD

SLAVERY AND THE SLAVE TRADE IN WEST AFRICA

In many parts of the world, slavery goes back to prehistoric times. The practice was widespread in ancient Mesopotamia, Egypt, in Homer's Greece, in the Roman Empire, and it was familiar to the Biblical Hebrews. The institution of slavery was acknowledged, if not condoned, by the early Christians, who were encouraged to make the manumission of their slaves an evangelical duty. This example was not followed as a matter of principle by the entrepreneurs of medieval Europe. The Portuguese, the Spanish, the French, the Dutch and the British were all to engage in the African slave trade. In the fifteenth and sixteenth century the Portuguese began to develop a trade in slaves seized in the interior of Africa. The first African slaves were taken to Portugal as early as 1440. In support of this lucrative trade, Muslim raiders and local African chiefs were only too ready to cooperate with their European contacts. King Alvare of Congo was selling African slaves to the Portuguese at the end of the seventeenth century. King Tegbesu of Dahomey is said to have made the almost unbelievable sum of 250,000 pounds a year in the mid-1750s from selling fellow Africans into slavery. The Muslim groups involved in the trafficking of slaves included the Tuareg. Muslims, though forbidden to enslave fellow Muslims, did not extend the proscription to non-Muslims when the slave trade was at its height. In 1821, for instance, the town of Oshogun in south-west of what is now Nigeria was attacked by Yoruba Muslims. Men, women and children were taken by their captors into slavery, roped together by the neck. One of them was Samuel Ajayi Crowther. The captives were herded south to the coast to Popo (Dahomey), then the centre of the Portuguese slave trade. In 1822, the Portuguese ship on which the slaves were being shipped to the Americas was intercepted by an anti-slavery patrol ship of the British navy. The slaves, including Crowther, were liberated and taken to the recently founded haven for freed slaves, Sierra Leone.

For almost 500 years the inhuman trade in West African slaves continued to provide lucrative business for European merchant venturers, many of whom operated out of ports such as Lisbon, Nantes, Bristol and Liverpool. The latter was the largest slaving port in Europe, from which 4,000 slaving voyages to Africa were sent out between the years 1700 and 1807. Europe was not the principal market for African slaves, however. It was from the Americas that the chief demand for African slave labour came. In the nineteenth century, the port of Havana in Cuba was the largest slave port in the world. Native American Indians were the first to be used as slave labour by the Portuguese and Spanish in the West Indies and Latin America but their resistance to oppression increased the demand for African slaves to replace them. African slaves were introduced in the British settlements along the Atlantic coast of America. In 1619, they appeared in Virginia. Slaves were shipped across the Atlantic in fearfully overcrowded transports such as the *Enterprize*, a vessel that worked out of Liverpool. The captives were forced to labour in the plantations across the Atlantic, working to produce coffee, tobacco, sugar, rice and later cotton on the islands of the Caribbean and in the southern states of America. Countless numbers of captives perished on board ship during the Atlantic crossing. These ships were first loaded in the commissioning ports of Europe with goods, including alcohol and guns, for West Africa. On the west coast of Africa the goods were exchanged for slaves, who were then packed on board and subjected to the horrors of the transatlantic passage. In the Americas the slaves were sold or exchanged for goods, which filled the holds of the ships for the return voyage to Europe.

Moves to abolish slavery and the slave trade began in earnest in the eighteenth century, in the Age of Enlightenment. The ideas of Jean-Jacques Rousseau and the pro-democratic sentiments of the French Revolution gave impetus to humanitarian initiatives to end the trade in slaves. There was little enthusiasm in the USA for abolition until after the end of the American Civil War (1863–5). Christians worked in Britain to bring about the abolition of the slave trade in 1807. The leading figures in the campaign were William Wilberforce, Thomas Clarkson, Zachary Macaulay and Lord Brougham, who continued to work for the total abolition of the slave trade throughout the British empire. This was achieved in 1833. It has to be noted, however, that there are still parts of Africa in which the scourges of slavery and the slave trade have not yet been completely eliminated.

References

Thomas (1997).

EDWARD D. A. HULMES

SOCIALISM

In the context of the decolonialisation process after the Second World War, many newly emerging states sought a middle path between the socio-economic and political ideologies and practices of the capitalist West, whose countries had, in fact been the chief colonising powers, and the communism of the USSR. In 1955 representatives of some twenty-nine African and Asian nation met in Bandung, Indonesia, to promote economic and cultural cooperation and to oppose colonialism. Stemming from that meeting, in 1961 Yugoslavia, India, and Indonesia were instrumental in founding the Non-Aligned Movement. Many of the latter's members promoted identification with non-Stalinist forms of 'socialist' and materialist discourse and Middle Eastern and other states adopted names for themselves intended to express identification with the movement, including 'socialist' and 'democratic' but which, in practice, meant the centralisation of political life around a single party, with the latter controlling the state and the State acting as the nation's key economic and political player. The latter presupposed state ownership of a country's chief 'public' and, especially, economic institutions, the development of economic planning and a limited range of 'democratic' institutions. In the process, in the atmosphere of the Cold War and the demands of 1950s and 1960s US foreign policy, many of these countries found themselves turning to the USSR and China for assistance and advice on issues of economic and political development. Thus, Egypt sought and received Soviet aid in the construction of the Aswan High Dam (1960–70) after the USA and UK withdrew their assistance in 1956. Egypt, Syria and other Middle Eastern states evolved their own varieties of 'socialist' discourse centred on pan-Arabism. The Ba'ath Party, founded in 1941, focusing on secularism, socialism and pan-Arab union, played a prominent role in the evolution of such discourse in the 1950s and the 1958–61 United Arab Republic, made up of Egypt and Syria – whose foreign minister had helped found the party – and, briefly, North Yemen, with Egypt's Nasser as president, was the product of such discourse. A 1963 coup brought the Iraqi branch of the party to power.

References

Abrahamian (1989), Ayubi (1993), Hourani (1991: esp. 416–17), Keddie (1981), Kerr (1971), Munson (1988).

See also: **Marxism and Islam; materialism; modernity; secularism**

ANDREW J. NEWMAN

SOKOTO

A city on the Sokoto river. Sokoto state is the second largest in Nigeria and contains Sokoto and Gwandu, former Fulani emirates, on a traditional caravan route across the Sahara. In the eighteenth century Sokoto was ruled by Hausa states (Gobir, Zamfara, Kebbi, Yauri). Predominantly Muslim, the main ethnic groups are the Fulani, Hausa, Dakarki (Dakarawa) and Kamberi. Shaykh 'Uthman b. Fudi (d. 1817) led a *jihad* against Muslim and non-Muslim Gobi (1804–8). By 1808 the sultanate of Sokoto (*aka* the Fulani empire) emerged with Sokoto, then a *ribat*, as capital (1809) of the Sokoto caliphate. His distinctive Islamic doctrine became the focus of greater political unity for the Fulani and his tomb became a place of local pilgrimage, especially for pious women. His son, Muhammad Bello, became the second spiritual leader (*amir al-mu 'minin* or *sarkin musulmi*) of the Fulani empire and first Sultan of Sokoto (1817–37), despite intermittent uprisings of Hausa. The mud-walled city centred on Muhammad Bello's house facing west, on an open forum in front, surrounded by officials' houses, mosques to its south and the market to the north. Two large mosques (Masallacin Shehu, Masallacin Bello) were built in Sokoto in the 1820s (restored in the 1960s). From 1812 Sokoto was divided into a series of emirates. Muhammad Bello was ruler of the north and east, with the Shaykh's brother, 'Abd Allah b. Fudi, in charge of emirates in the west and south, ruling from Gwandu.

Sokoto gained influence not through taxes, trade or military strength but through its reputation for scholarship and poetry: 300 books were written by leaders of the *jihad*. Sokoto is also famous for 'morocco leather' made from the Sokoto red goat and traditionally traded with North Africa to be used as binding for the Qur'an and other Islamic texts. They were practising Sufis, adhering to the Qadiriyya and the Tijaniyya (after 1830–8). Many expected the end of the world was nigh and awaited the Mahdi, so many migrated eastwards into Sudan where their descendants are called 'Fellata'.

Pressures from European imperialism also added to the pressures to migrate east. The British signed a treaty in 1885 for additional trade privileges, defeating Sokoto in 1903 to incorporate it into colonial Nigeria, with Muhammad al-Tahir II as Sultan of Sokoto. From 1933 the Sultan (*sardauna*) was also the leading Muslim in Nigeria. Sultan Abubakar (1938–88) remained an influential political and spiritual leader. Violent uprisings occurred in 1966 when the *sardauna*, Sir Ahmadu Bello, was assassinated, thus ending the dream of a caliphate based on common Islamic morality.

References

Last (1977), Stilwell (2004).

JANET STARKEY

SOKOTO CALIPHATE

The Sokoto caliphate was founded in 1809 by Shehu Usuman dan Fodio, a Fulani leader. The name *fodio* means 'religious teacher' (cf. Arabic *faqih*). On his return from Mecca after completing the pilgrimage (*hajj*) he felt inspired by Wahhabi ideas to preach to the Fulani (Fulbe, Peulh) people about the need for reform within Islam, and then to declare holy war (*jihad*) against the local pagans in Hausaland. He established a large Islamic empire that eventually stretched from Chad to Niger, which included much of what is now northern Nigeria. The city of Sokoto became the capital of the empire, which was built up after dan Fodio's death in 1816 by his two sons Muhammadu Bello and 'Abdullah. The tomb of dan Fodio in Sokoto remains a place of pilgrimage for Muslims. In the second half of the nineteenth century the Sokoto caliphate fell into decline as a result of the continuing incursions of other belligerent groups such as the Tuareg, and not least because of the growing opposition of the population to the strict interpretation of the teachings and ethical practices of Islam preached by the founder. In 1903, British troops took the city on the orders of Sir Frederick (later Lord) Lugard, whose policy of delegated indirect rule under British supervision effectively deprived local Islamic leaders of the powers they had formerly wielded. The following year saw the start of British occupation. The city of Sokoto, situated on the Sokoto river, continues to thrive as a commercial centre in the northern Nigerian state that bears its name. Hides, skins and groundnuts are among the local products. Industries include the manufacture of cement, dyeing, pottery and tanning.

References

Adeleye (1971), Hiskett (1973), Last (1967).

See: **Fodio, Shehu Usuman dan;** *jihad*

EDWARD D. A. HULMES

SOLOMON

See: **Sulayman**

SONGHAY, EMPIRE OF

The Empire of Songhay eventually became the largest of the ancient empires of West Africa. Its origins date back to the early eighth century, when the State was founded by Berbers near the central reaches of the river Niger. In the early years of the eleventh century the King, Dia Kossoi, was converted to Islam. At this stage it appears that most of his people retained their beliefs in their ancient traditional animist religious beliefs. The King may have seen conversion to Islam as helpful in his dealings with the Muslim Berbers, whose cooperation in the lucrative trans-Saharan caravan trade he no doubt wished to secure. The power of Songhay increased under Sunni 'Ali, 'the Great' (sometimes known as 'Ali Ber, or as the Shi), who ruled from 1464 to 1492. He transformed his territories into a multi-ethnic Islamic empire, which replaced the empire of Mali as the most important power in the western savannah. The success of his military campaigns extended the borders of the empire. New royal residences were required. New subsidiary capitals were established: Gao, Kabara and Warra in

Tindirma. Within a period of thirty years, the empire stretched from the borders of Kebbi in the south-east, past the Great Bend of the river Niger to Jenné. At the height of its power the empire occupied parts of present day Guinea, Burkina Faso, Senegal, the Gambia, Mali, Mauritania, Niger, and Nigeria. Sunni 'Ali took Timbuktu in 1468 in an attack that led to the persecution of many leading Islamic scholars. Many of these cultured teachers, 'men of the desert', were forced to leave the city.

The Songhay empire reached its greatest extent under Muhammad Turay, who was to be known as Askia Muhammad I (1493–1528), 'Askia the Great'. He was deposed by his son, and in the subsequent conflicts between his successors the empire began to decline. Its demise was hastened by the Moroccan invasion of 1591.

References

Davidson (1977: 68–85), Hiskett (1994: 94–101).

EDWARD D. A. HULMES

STARK, FREYA (1893–1993)

British traveller and writer. Stark was born in Paris and spent her childhood in England and Italy. She served as a nurse on the Italian front during the First World War after which she studied Arabic at the School of Oriental and African Studies in London. She went out to Baghdad where she worked for a while on the *Baghdad Times*, the local English-language newspaper. She then began to undertake her numerous travels in the Middle Eastern region, which she described in a long series of travel books together with several works of autobiography. Titles range from the early *Valley of the Assassins* to *The Coast of Incense* describing travel in

Arabia, Yemen, Persia and the Fertile Crescent. During the Second World War, Stark worked for the Ministry of Information in Aden and Cairo. She founded a brotherhood there to spread anti-Nazi propaganda and to encourage support for Britain amongst certain classes of Arabs. She was named a dame of the British Empire in 1972.

References

Izzard (1993).

DEREK HOPWOOD

STONING VERSE

A verse (*ayat al-rajm*) of the Qur'an which contains the penalty of stoning for adultery, no longer found in the text of the Qur'an but held by some still to be legally binding. The text, held to have been omitted from the Qur'an, was remembered by some as reading, 'The man and the woman, when they fornicate, stone them outright as an exemplary punishment from God. God is All-mighty, All-wise'. Variants to the text exist. The verse was accommodated within the legal structures of Islam through means of the notions of *al-nasikh wa'l-mansukh*, 'the abrogator and the abrogated' which held that it was possible for a verse of the Qur'an not be read in the text today but still be legally valid. The stoning verse has continued to have legal validity in some Muslim circles.

References

Burton (1977).

ANDREW RIPPIN

STRABO (*c.* 64 BC – AD 23)

Greek geographer and historian. He travelled widely in the Roman world, moving to Rome in 44 BC. His *Geographical Sketches*, a work in seventeen books, described the peoples and landscapes of western Europe, the Mediterranean, Iberian Peninsula, northern Africa, the Balkans, Black Sea, Mesopotamia, Persia and India. He drew on many sources, including the accounts of Alexander's campaigns, but also on his own travels and contacts. He was a friend of the Roman Prefect of Egypt, Aelius Gallus, and during a visit there in circa 25–24 BC travelled up the Nile as well as receiving first-hand accounts of an ill-fated expedition to Arabia. Strabo made particular note of the spice trade in Arabia and the wealth that flowed from it.

References

Purcell (1998: 692, 596).

SIMON W. MURDEN

STYLE IN THE QUR'AN (*USLUB AL-QUR'AN*)

Rafael Tamlon (2002: 220) draws our attention to the linguistic mechanism of Qur'anic Arabic and informs us that linguistic studies specific to the Qur'an are few but not detailed enough. Our present work, however, attempts to provide a glance at the stylistic and linguistic peculiarities of Qur'anic discourse. Western scholars who have been intrigued by these peculiarities are like Fleischer, Reckendorf, Brockelmann, Ewald, and Nöldeke (Tamlon 2002: 348).

The Qur'an is characterised by Qur'an-bound stylistic features such as stylistic shift and presentation technique. Stylistic shift is a major linguistic property of Qur'anic discourse and is interrelated to exegesis. It takes different forms and is conditioned by various factors. The variation in Qur'anic style occurs at different levels of language such as word level or sentence level. The Qur'an also adopts the stylistic mechanism of presentation of leitmotifs and tenets of faith which are referred to as *mabadi' al-iman*. Let us first investigate some of the major stylistic features of the Qur'an.

In Qur'anic discourse, we encounter two ayas whose linguistic structure is different due to the different word order in each of them, as in: *qul la amliku linafsi naf'an wala dharran* [Say, 'I do not possess for myself any benefit or harm] (Q.7:188); *qul la amliku linafsi darran wala naf'an* [Say, 'I do not possess for myself any harm or benefit] (Q.10:49).

The stylistic variation is represented by the occurrence of the word (*naf'an* – benefit) first in Q.7:188 and its occurrence at the end in Q.10:49. This change in word order is attributed to the surrounding lexical environment of each aya. The word (*naf'an*) signifies a positive meaning, it has occurred first because other positive meaning words have also occurred first as in Q.7:178 and 188 where positive meaning words also occur before negative meaning words such as (*yahdi*, to guide) comes before (*yadhlil*, to misguide), and (*khayr*, welfare, wealth) occurs before (*su'*, harm). Similarly, the word (*darran*, harm) occurs first in Q.10:49 because of the lexical influence of other ayas such as Q.10:18 and 107 in which (*darran*) has occurred four times before the word (*naf'an*).

The concept of word form refers to the grammatical function of the word and has a direct impact on the underlying meaning of the aya. For instance, some words occur in the verb form while others occur in the active participle form as in Q.53:59–61. The stylistic change lies in the occurrence of the verbs (*'ajaba*, to wonder; *dahika*, to laugh; *baka*, to cry) in ayas 59–60, while the active participle (*samid*, heedless, lost in vain amusements) is used in aya

61, the active participle is referred to in Arabic as *ismu al-fa'il*. In order to highlight the continuity of the action of heedlessness and that this group of people are repeatedly wasting their time in vanities, the active participle is employed to echo this meaning. However, this same group of people do occasionally other things such as wondering curiously with a strange feeling against something, laughing at times, and not crying, i.e., not feeling sorry for their negative curiosity. These occasional actions are stylistically best represented by a verb rather than by any other linguistic form.

Shift is referred to in Arabic as *iltifat* which is a recurrent linguistic property of Qur'anic discourse used as rhetorical ornamentation in the Qur'an. The most common form is pronoun shift, as in: *alam tara ila rabbika kayfa madda al-zilla ... thumma ja'alna al-shamsa ... thumma qabadnahu ilayna ... wahuwa alladhi ja'ala lakum ... linuhyi bihi ... wahuwa alladhi maraja al-bahrayn ...* [Have you not considered your Lord how He extends the shadow ... Then We made the sun ... Then We held it in hand ... It is He who has made for you ... that We may bring to life thereby ... It is He who has released the two seas ...] (Q.25:45–53) where a stylistic shift in pronoun has taken place from the second person pronoun in (*rabbika*, your Lord), to first person plural in *ja'ala* (We made) and in *qabadna* (We held), to third person singular pronoun in *huwa* (He), to first person plural in *nuhyi* (We bring to life), to third person singular pronoun in *huwa* (He).

Some ayas are structurally identical but stylistically different due to the employment of different words, as in *tilka hududu Allahi fla taqrabuha* [These are the limits set by Allah, so do not approach them] (Q.2:187); *tilka hududu Allahi fla ta'taduha* [These are the limits of Allah, so do not transgress them] (Q.2:229) where the stylistic variation is attributed to the selection of the verb *taqrabu* (to approach) in Q.2:187 and the employment of a different verb *ta'tadu* (to transgress) in Q.2:229. This stylistic change is conditioned by the context of each aya. In aya 187, the context refers to a serious prohibition stated by the Islamic legal ruling *wala tubashiruhunna wa'antum 'akifuna fi al-masajid* [Do not cohabit with your wives as long as you are staying for worship in the mosques] (Q.2:187) which does not allow the husband to cohabit with his wife in the mosque. This serious warning is introduced by the verb *taqrabu*. However, the context of aya 229 also refers to a warning but of a less serious nature. Aya 229 highlights the command that urges the divorced couple to be fair with each other regarding the presents given by the husband to his wife and that they both should not transgress beyond the allowed bounds, therefore, the verb *ta'tadu* is stylistically more appropriate.

The context of situation also has an impact upon the selection of words that occur at the end of the aya, as in: *dhalikum wassakum bihi la'allakum ta'qilun* [This has He instructed you that you may use reason] (Q.6:151); *dhalikum wassakum bihi la'allakum tadhakkarun* [This has He instructed you that you may use remember] (Q.6:152); *dhalikum wassakum bihi la'allakum tattaqun* [This has He instructed you that you may use become righteous] (Q.6:153).

These three ayas undergo stylistic shift where three different words occur (*ta'qilun*, to use reason; *tadhakkarun*, to remember; *tattaqun*, to become righteous) at the end due to their different contexts of situation and their relevant moral lesson. The word *ta'qilun* is employed in Q.6:151 urging the reader to use his or her intellect pertaining the five commandments (to observe monotheism, to respect own parents, not to kill own children, to avoid shameful deeds, and not to commit murder), i.e., these can be observed by people with sound reasoning. The context of aya 152 refers to four different commandments (not to take away the orphan's property, to be just, to give just witness, and to fulfill the covenant of God), i.e., these have to be remembered. Aya 153, however, highlights the leitmotif of righteousness and urges the reader to observe it and avoid what goes against it, therefore, the word (*tattaqun*) is stylistically and semantically most appropriate for this aya.

Stylistic shift also occurs in the Qur'an due to the different phonetic co-text (which is the surrounding textual environment) of the two ayas. Let us consider the following examples: *rabbi musa wa harun* (Q.7:122) and *rabbi harun wa musa* (Q.20:70).

Although the two ayas have the same meaning, each aya ends with a different name, Q.7:122 ends with *harun* which is the same for Q.26:48, while Q.20:70 ends with *musa*. This is attributed to the phonetic co-text where in Q.7 the assonance, i.e., the rhyme of the ayas, is the /un/, while the rhyme of Q.20 is the long vowel /a/.

Phonetic co-text also applies to the following examples: *wa'indahum qasiratu al-tarfi 'in* [With them will be women limiting their glances, with large, beautiful eyes] (Q.37:48) and *wa'indahum qasiratu al-tarfi atrab* [With them will be women limiting their glances and of equal age] (Q.38:52), where the macro-phonetic environment surrounding each of the above ayas has influenced the lexical variation from *'in* (large, beautiful eyes) in Q.37:48 to *atrab* (of equal age) in Q.38:52 in order to achieve symmetrical rhyme and

phonetic compatibility at aya-final level that can match the previous rhyme of each aya.

Stylistic variation can also result from the different wording of different ayas which have an identical meaning, as in: *man dha alladhi yashfa'u 'indahu illa b'idhnih* [Who is that can intercede with Him except by His permission] (Q.2:255); *ma min shafi'in illa min ba'di idhnih* [There is no intercessor except after His permission] (Q.10:3); *wala tanfa'u al-shafa'atu 'indahu illa liman adhina lahu* [Intercession does not benefit with Him except for one whom He permits] (Q.34:23)

These stylistically different ayas signify the same leitmotif of intercession that cannot be accepted without God's leave. These different ayas are expressed in different styles but designate the same signification. The following examples demonstrate the same stylistic phenomenon in the Qur'an: *thumma tuwaffa kullu nafsin ma kasabat* [Then every soul will be compensated for what it earned] (Q.2:281); *watuwaffa kullu nafsin ma 'amilat* [And every soul will be fully compensated for what it did] (Q.16:111); *wawuffiyat kullu nafsin ma 'amilat* [And every soul will be fully compensated for what it did] (Q.39:70); *walitujza kullu nafsin bima kasabat* [So that every soul may be recompensed for what it has earned] (Q.45:22).

The above four ayas are stylistically distinct but semantically identical. They all signify the same leitmotif of divine justice on the day of judgement and that every individual will only reap the fruit of his/her deeds.

Grammaticality in the Qur'an is at times broken. This means that the grammatical form of some ayas does not conform to the grammatical norms of Arabic, as in *wa akhadha alladhina zalamu al-sayhatu* [The shriek seized those who had wronged] (Q.11:67).

According to Arabic grammar, this aya is grammatically inaccurate because the subject noun *al-sayhatu* (the shriek, the mighty blast) is in the feminine form while its verb *akhadha* (to seize) occurs in the masculine form. According to Arabic grammar, there has to be a gender agreement between the subject and its verb, i.e., when the subject is masculine, its verb should occur in the masculine form, and when it is feminine, its verb needs to take the feminine form. In Qur'anic discourse, however, some ayas violate Arabic grammar because they employ false feminine nouns which are referred to in Arabic as *mu'annath ghayr haqiqi*. Therefore, the feminine subject noun *al-sayhatu* has an underlying meaning of a masculine noun which is *al-sawtu* (the mighty blast).

Another example of ungrammaticality is found in the following aya: *wa'in ta'ifatani min al-mu'minina iqtatalu* [If two factions among the believers should fight each other] (Q.49:9) where the subject noun *ta'ifatani* (two factions) is employed in *al-muthanna* (the dual form) while its verb *iqtatalu* (to fight each other) occurs in the plural form, this is counter to the grammatical norms of Arabic and the verb should, therefore, be in the dual form as well, i.e. *iqtatalata*. However, Q.49:9 is stylistically acceptable because the underlying meaning of the plural verb *iqtatalu* designates an implicit pronoun *hum* (they) which can be grammatically used to refer to either plural or dual.

There is an interesting presentation style of the four major tenets of faith: monotheism, prophethood, eschatology, and reward and punishment. These tenets of faith can occur in one of the following forms:

1. A single tenet of faith is presented within an individual aya, such as Q.35:23.

2. More than one tenet of faith is presented within an individual aya, such as Q.40:3 where reward and punishment, monotheism, and eschatology are presented.

3. More than one tenet of faith is presented in a series of interrelated ayas, such as Q.2:21–5, where monotheism is presented by ayas 21–2, prophethood by aya 23, and reward and punishment by ayas 24–5.

4. Some tenets of faith are followed by specific leitmotifs, such as God's omnipotence and His creative power, or reference to evocation, i.e., reference to previous disbelieving nations and God's wrath, as in Q.54:17 which refers to prophethood which is followed by evocative ayas 18–21 that refer to the people of 'Ad, and as in Q.57:1–3 that highlight monotheism which is followed by ayas 4–6 that refer to the leitmotif of God's omnipotence and is followed by ayas 7–9 that highlight prophethood,

5. Asseverative ayas are followed by a given tenet of faith, as in Q.53 which starts off with an asseverative aya Q.53:1 followed by ayas 2–4 that highlight prophethood.

6. The tenets of faith can be found in a single short sura, as in Q.101 where eschatology is presented by ayas 1–5, and reward and punishment are introduced by ayas 6–11.

7. One tenet of faith dominates a single sura, as in Q.112 where monotheism is the only tenet of faith.

References

Abdul-Raof (2000: 37–51), al-Qurtubi (1997), Talmon (2002), al-Zamakhshari (1995).
HUSSEIN ABDUL-RAOF

SUHBA

Meaning the association or the companionship that a disciple has with a master, *suhba* became a vital element in the Sufi tradition, and elaborate rules were established for correct conduct between master and disciple.

References

Hujwiri (1911).

LLOYD RIDGEON

AL-SUHRAWARDI, ABU HAFS

Shihab al-Din Abu Hafs 'Umar al-Suhrawardi born in AD 1145 in the Persian town Suhraward. He is one of the important Sufis who attempted to combine traditional Sufism with Ash'ari theology and Neoplatonic and Isma'ili philosophy. However, he should not be confused with the illuminationist philosopher Shihab al-Din Yahya al-Suhrawardi, known as al-Maqtul. Abu Hafs studied in Baghdad under his uncle Abu al-Najib al-Suhrawardi, who founded a Sufi school in Baghdad, and under the Hanbli 'Abd al-Qadir al-Jilani. This produced in Abu Hafs a critical attitude to theologians and philosophers, but he, nevertheless, assimilated and adopted many of their concepts. The 'Abbasid caliph al-Nasir, who showed an interest in Sufism, invited al-Suhrawardi to his court. This friendship enabled the caliph to use Sufism as an instrument at the service of the caliphate. As a result, al-Suhrawardi adopted a political doctrine which stated that the caliph, as the Sufi teacher, mediates between God and the people, and therefore the caliph must show superiority by his internal and external ethics. Al-Suhrawardi also played an important political role in dealing with the problems of the caliphate under the rulers of various pro-

vinces. He was also the founder of the *Suhrawadiyya tariqa*, which flourished mainly in India. He lived a long and productive life and died in Baghdad at the age of ninety in November AD 1234.

He left a considerable amount of writings of which the most important are: *'Awarif al-Ma'arif* and *Rashf al-Naasa'ih al-Imaniyya wa Kashf al-Fada'ih al-Yunaniyya*. The latter is his most important work, which criticises theology and Greek philosophy. However, he adopted a metaphysical system which combined creation with emanation in the line of the Isma'ili cosmology.

References

Ibn al-Futi (1932).

MAHA EL-KAISY FRIEMUTH

AL-SUHRAWARDI, ABU AL-NAJIB

Abu al-Najib Ibn Abd al-Qahir b. 'Abdallah al-Bakri al-Suhrawardi, was born in AD 1097 in Suhraward in the Jibal region of Persia. He moved to Baghdad where he studied *Shafi'i* law, and Arabic grammar. He was influenced by 'Umar b. Muhammad who had a Sufi house in Baghdad and became a faithful follower of Sufism. Later, he also founded a Sufi house and was appointed in 1145 to teach *fiqh* in the famous Baghdadi Nizamiyya school, but soon was dismissed due to problems between the caliph and the Saljuq sultan. Abu al-Najib was the teacher of the well known Sufi 'Ammar al-Bidlisi (d. AD 1207). Among his important disciples was also his nephew Abu Hafs al-Suhrawardi, who was the founder of the *Suhrawrdiyya tariqa*, which flourished in India.

Abu al-Najib did not leave many writings. His most important work was *Adab al-Muridin* which was widely known and used by Sufis. In 1161 he wanted to travel to Jerusalem but the political conditions made it impossible to travel further than Damascus and he returned to Baghdad. He died there some years later and was buried in his *madrasa*.

MAHA EL-KAISY FRIEMUTH

AL-SUHRAWARDI, SHIHAB AL-DIN 'AL-MAQTUL' (THE MARTYR)

Shihab al-Din Abu'l-Futuh Yahya ibn Habash ibn Amirak Suhrawardi founded an independent non-Aristotelian school of philosophy that was critical of the dominant Avicennism of his time and relied upon intuition and illumination as philosophical methods of inquiry. He named his method the Philosophy of Illumination (*Hikmat al-Ishraq*) after his main work and is often known as *shaykh-i ishraq*. As a thinker, he refused to be constrained by Aristotelianism and felt that the dictates of Aristotelian science were not universally applicable, and needed to be subjected to critique. Born in Suhraward in north-western Iran in AD 1154, he first moved to Maragha to study philosophy and theology with Majd al-Din Jili, where his co-students included Fakhr al-Din al-Razi. He later went to Isfahan to study with Fakhr al-Din al-Maridini (d. AD 1198). He also studied logic with Zahir al-Farisi who introduced him to *al-Basa'ir* (*Observations*), a key non-Aristotelian logic text of the twelfth century Persian logician 'Umar ibn Sahlan al-Sawi. He sought out a series of patrons, finally settling in Aleppo in AD 1183, indulged by the Ayyubid governor al-Malik al-Zahir ibn Salah al-Din. Whether as a result of court intrigue or political machinations or even Suhrawardi's claims for his own political authority (and even prophethood), he was exe-cuted on the order of Salah al-Din for heresy in 1191. Perhaps because of the circumstances of his end, no disciples of his are mentioned and it was only around a generation later that his works (somehow preserved) began to circulate and were discussed and explained, beginning with Shams al-Din Shahra-zuri (d. after AD 1288).

In a short career, Suhrawardi was quite prolific and his works fill four large volumes. His wide-ranging critique of peripatetic philosophy envisaged a curriculum of philosophical study in which students would engage with his works that explained and then criticised peripatetism such as *al-Talwihat* (*Intimations*), *al-Mashari' wa'l-Mutarahat* (*Paths and Havens*), and *al-Muqawamat* (*Apposites*). Once having mastered these works, they would study his major exposition *Hikmat al-Ishraq* (*Philosophy of Illumination*), completed in Aleppo in 1186. Other texts such as *Hayakil al-Nur* (*Temples of Light*) that became popular in Iran and India through the commentaries of philosophers such as Jalal al-Din Davani (d. 1501) complemented the core curriculum. His Arabic and Persian allegories were further complements in which he uses symbolic narrative to portray philosophical issues. What the corpus reveals is a systematic intent at literally reorienting philosophy as a committed way of life and inquiry that utilised both intuitive non-propositional thought based on experience (*dhawq*) with discursive reason (*bahth*). The use of the term *ishraqi* (illuminationist) is clearly intended by Suhrawardi to distinguish a particular doctrine or mode of argumentation as belonging to himself or as distinct from Aristotelianism. In his works, he often explicitly genu-flects to the authority of Platonism and other 'Greek sages' such as Empedocles and Pythagoras. He also claims that his philosophy is a revival of an ancient

Persian wisdom but this is difficult to assess.

Suhrawardi followed the Stoic and late antique model of dividing philosophy into logic, physics and metaphysics. His logical innovations were both structural and substantive. He reformed the Aristotelian *Organon* into a more coherent tripartite of semantics, formal logic and material logic. The semantics of his major work includes a critique of the reference of the term 'existence' which for him is a meaningless concept and, somewhat like Kant, not a predicate. Hence, Suhrawardi is often described as an essentialist. His critique of Aristotelian logic not only attacks the theory of definition and its inability to render knowledge, which for him must be certain and intuitive, but also holds that the laws of science are not universal since they do not yield propositions that are always necessary and always true.

The totality of being is a hierarchy of lights. The ultimate principles and source of light is the Light of Lights, or God who bestows light upon things in a descending scale of decreasing intensity. The opposite of light is darkness that describes base matter. Things in this phenomenal world are thus composites of light and darkness, of necessity and value derived from light and contingency from darkness. Functionally, the relationship between God and lesser lights in this system sounds remarkably like the Avicennan distinction between the modalities of necessity and contingency. But one complication is that contingents are not mental composites of existence and essence, since for Suhrawardi existence is not a real concept that has reference in reality, but are essences composed of light and darkness. Platonism provides the metaphor of light but also the angelology of this metaphysics. The deities

and demiurges of the Platonic world are translated in this Muslim context into commanding angels who control aspects of this hierarchy. Suhrawardi also accepts the Platonic distinction between an intelligible higher world of being and forms and a lower sensible world of becoming and shadows. But he adds an intermediary, the imaginal realm (*'alam al-mithal*) that mediates and as such circumvents the age-old problem of the third man argument in the platonic theory of forms. It is significant that the place of the active intellect of Avicennan philosophy, which is a static substance in the cosmological chain of intellects, is taken by a commanding light and angel (*al-nur al-isfahbud*) in the imaginal realm. It inspires the imagination of the philosopher with forms.

Knowledge for Suhrawardi is based on certain principles and he is famous for the doctrine of immediate knowledge by presence (*'ilm huduri*). Self-consciousness is the prime requisite for intuitive knowledge. This theory unequivocally posits primacy to a temporal, pre-inferential and immediate mode of knowledge, which, in contemporary terms, is non-propositional intuitive knowledge prior to dyadic differentiation of subject-object. Knowledge is thus not based on the duality of representation. The *ishraqi* theory of definition is thus experiential and features of an object of knowledge can only be ascertained once the object has been ascertained. To take the example of humanity, the essence underlying the term can only be ascertained by the subject through an act of recovery that translates the term (or symbol) 'human' into its equivalent in the consciousness of the subject.

The *ishraqi* school came to dominate in the Islamic East and increasingly Avicennan philosophy was viewed as a background to *ishraq*. Later commentaries on Avicenna thus could not fail to incorporate the objections and critiques made by Suhrawardi. Nevertheless, the illuminationist tradition was often divided into those with more discursive tastes and others who preferred to focus upon the allegorical, the inspirational and the fantastic. The holism of Suhrawardi's approach remains supremely attractive. Yet his neglect in standard histories of philosophy is no doubt occasioned by the Eurocentrism of accounts that consider 'Arabic philosophy' to be a moment in the history of medieval thought made significant through translation into Latin. Suhrawardi never 'suffered the fate' of being translated into Latin.

References

Aminrazavi (1997), Corbin (1972: Vol. II, 1976), Ibrahimi-yi Dinani (1996), Rizvi (1999: 219–27), Suhrawardi (1998, 1999a, 1999b), Walbridge (2000, 2001), Ziai (1991, 1992: 304–44).

SAJJAD H. RIZVI

SUHRAWARDIYYA

This Sufi order traces its foundation to Abu 'l-Najib al-Suhrawardi (d. AD 1168), although his nephew Abu Hafs 'Umar al-Suhrawardi did much to formalise the order. The latter was the spiritual advisor to the 'Abbasid Caliph of the time and was instrumental in promoting the *futuwwa* chivalry guilds. The Suhrawardiyya order was popular in Arab areas and India and promoted a 'sober' form of Sufism that avoided excess in piety and ritual performance.

References

Nasr (1991), Rizvi (1978).

LLOYD RIDGEON

SULAYMAN

The Old Testament 'Solomon', as in Q.27:15–16.

See also: **nabi**

ANDREW J. NEWMAN

SULAYMAN B. 'ABD AL-MALIK (AD 715–17)

Sulayman was the brother and successor of the Marwanid (Umayyad) caliph al-Walid b. 'Abd al-Malik. During his reign the third and final unsuccessful siege of Constantinople (AD 716–17) began (the previous two occurred under the rule of Mu'awiya b. Abi Sufyan). With Sulayman, the capital of the Umayyad dynasty Damascus ceased to be the home of the caliphs, he himself residing in Ramla, Palestine. Although Sulayman had a reputation for being a pleasure-seeker, he also appears to have been very devout. He was thus persuaded to change the order of succession from the sons of 'Abd al-Malik, which would have resulted in Sulayman's brother Yazid b. 'Abd al-Malik becoming caliph, in favour of 'Umar b. 'Abd al-'Aziz, a pious cousin.

References

Hodgson (1974: 267–8), Muir (1915: 364–8), Shaban (1971: 127–30), al-Tabari (1985–95: XXIV, 3–93 *passim*).

RONALD PAUL BUCKLEY

SULAYMAN B. QUTALMISH/ QUTLUMUSH B. ARSLAN ISRA'IL (r. AD 1081–6)

Member of the Saljuq dynasty and founder of the branch that had a lengthy, largely independent history as the Saljuqs of Rum or Anatolia. He headed a Turkmen band, apparently operating independently of the Great

Saljuq sultanate further east, which seized Nicaea in north-western Anatolia, intervened in Byzantine internal affairs and overran most of central and western Asia Minor. He then turned eastwards with the aim of expanding into Syria, but came up against his kinsman already established there, Tutush, who defeated him in battle and killed him.

References

Cahen (1968: 72–8), Gibb and Bosworth (1960–2003).

C. E. BOSWORTH

SÜLEYMAN (r. 1402–11, RUMELIA)

Ottoman prince, eldest son of Bayezid I. After his father's defeat at Ankara in 1402, he established his rule in Rumelia and, between 1404 and 1409, in western Anatolia. From 1409, his brother Musa challenged his rule in Rumelia, leading to his flight and assassination in 1411.

References

Imber (1990: 55–69), Zachariadou (1983).

COLIN IMBER

SÜLEYMAN I (r. 1520–66)

Ottoman Sultan, known in Europe as 'the Magnificent', son of Selim I. His reign opened with the conquests of Belgrade in 1521 and Rhodes in 1522. In 1526, he defeated and killed the King of Hungary at Mohács. The Hungarian Diet elected John Szapolyai as successor, and Süleyman confirmed the appointment. However, the Habsburg Ferdinand of Austria, brother of Charles V, the Holy Roman Emperor and King of Spain, also claimed the crown, and occupied the western and northern parts of the kingdom, forcing Süleyman to undertake further expeditions, in 1529 and 1532, to enforce Szapolyai's rights.

Between 1533 and 1536, Süleyman campaigned against Iran. The Shah did not confront his army, but used scorched-earth tactics to force Süleyman to withdraw from Tabriz. Nonetheless, by 1536 Süleyman had conquered Baghdad, Erzurum and, temporarily, Van. In 1533, he had appointed Hayreddin Barbarossa as Admiral in expectation of war in the Mediterranean. This materialised in 1535 when Charles V conquered Tunis, forcing Süleyman into an alliance with Charles V's enemy, Francis I of France. In 1537, Süleyman unsuccessfully attacked the Venetian island of Corfu, an act that precipitated a Habsburg–Venetian–Papal alliance. Barbarossa however defeated the allied fleet at Prevesa in 1538. By 1540 Barbarossa had taken most of the Venetian possessions in the Aegean and the Peloponnesos.

The peace with Venice concluded the period of Süleyman's large-scale conquests although warfare continued uninterruptedly. The death of Szapolyai reactivated Ferdinand's claims to Hungary, forcing Süleyman to annex central Hungary and despatch Szapolyai's infant son as king to Transylvania. As Ferdinand besieged Buda in 1541, his brother Charles attacked Algiers. Both operations failed, and in 1543 Suleiman led a campaign to Hungary to restore Ottoman authority, while in the Mediterranean a combined Franco-Ottoman fleet stormed Nice. Despite a treaty of 1547 between Süleyman and Charles V and Ferdinand, Ferdinand's continuing claim to Transylvania prolonged hostilities in Hungary, leading to the Ottoman occupation of Temesvár and Lipova in 1552. Hostilities also continued in North Africa. In 1551 the

Ottomans took Tripoli from the Knights of St John, in 1556–7 they occupied Wahran and Bizerta and in 1560 expelled the Spaniards from Jerba. Süleyman himself led expeditions against the Safavids in 1548–9 and 1553–4. The treaty of Amasya of 1555 concluded hostilities by confirming the existing border.

Süleyman's infirmities after 1550 led to a struggle among his sons for succession. In 1553, he executed his son Mustafa on suspicion of plotting his overthrow. In 1558, following the death of their mother Hurrem, his sons Selim and Bayezid came into conflict and Bayezid into open revolt. Bayezid's defeat, flight to Iran and, in 1562, execution ended the rebellion.

In 1565, Süleyman's fleet failed to take Malta, but in 1566 captured the Genoese island of Chios, while Süleyman himself led a campaign to Hungary. He died during the siege of Szigetvár.

References

Bacqué-Grammont (1989: 145–55), Imber (2002: 48–61).

COLIN IMBER

SÜLEYMAN II (r. 1687–91)

Ottoman Sultan, son of Ibrahim. Suleyman came to the throne at a time of severe crisis. In 1688, the Austrians captured Belgrade. However, Süleyman and his Grand Vizier Köprülü Mustafa Pasha retook Belgrade and restored losses in Serbia and Transylvania. Their reforms gave the empire new financial and administrative stability.

References

Mantran (1989a : 248).

COLIN IMBER

SUNAN

This *hadith* collection is the best-known work of Abu Muhammad 'Abdallah b. 'Abd al-Rahman b. al-Fadl b. Bahram al-Darimi (AD 797–869), and is regarded as second only to the Sunni *Kutub al-Sitta* in reliability. Its author was known for his piety and learning, leading to his being pressed into office as *qadi* of Samarkand, though he relinquished this after giving only one judgement.

Al-Darimi was the older contemporary of the collectors of the recognised books of *hadith*, and, in fact, Muslim and al-Tirmidhi transmitted *hadiths* in his name. His collection was sometimes regarded as equal to the recognised *sunan* works, and superior to Ibn Maja's *sunan*. But it never attained the authority of those works, because it was thought to include more weak traditions. It came to be regarded as commendable but not as important as the six books.

The *Sunan* is often regarded as a *musnad* work, though it is arranged in the same manner as the *musannaf* collections, with the individual *hadiths* organised according to theme. It comprises twenty-three books, together with an Introduction, and is estimated to contain 3,550 traditions. These cover the same topics as many of the *sunan* works: prayer, cleanliness, fasting, charity tax, food, dress, marriage, business dealings, warfare, and ending with the excellences of the Qur'an. The Introduction outlines the Prophet's character and the miracles that attended him, and then the danger of forming incorrect judgements and the means of arriving at true knowledge.

There are a number of published editions of the *Sunan*, and also an alphabetical index of *hadiths* and transmitters edited by al-Rafa'i (1988).

DAVID THOMAS

SUNNISM (*AHL AL-SUNNA WA 'L-JAMA'A*)

The majority or mainstream branch of Islam, known as Sunnis and often also referred to as 'the people of tradition and community' (*Ahl al-Sunna wa 'l-Jama'a*). This latter term came into usage with the advent of the various sects in Islamic history and was used to distinguish the earliest community of Muslims and those who followed their method from these later groups. The term *sunna*, from which the word 'Sunnis' originates means 'an established practice' and is used here to denote the established practice of the Prophet Muhammad, in terms of his statements, actions and tacit approval, which in itself is considered a form of revelation. The second term *jama'a* refers to the earliest community of Muslims, i.e., the prophetic companions, and so the whole phrase means in very simple terms that Sunnis are Muslims who adhere strictly the prophetic practice of Islam as understood by the earliest and most righteous generation, following their method and teaching implicitly. This is not to say that Sunnis only rely on the *sunna*, they also adhere strictly to the primary source of revelation, the Qur'an, as well as the consensus of the Muslim community (*al-ijma'*) as a whole. Consequently, Sunnis believe in all that is presented in the Qur'an and *sunna* whether it be in terms of acts of worship, commonly referred to as 'the five pillars of Islam' or doctrinal teachings commonly referred to as 'the six pillars of faith'. As such Sunnis believe their religion to be from revealed sources and therefore complete (*kamil*) having been perfected by Allah through His Prophet, thus additions to it are considered innovations (*bid'a*) and infallibility (*'isma*) in religious matters is for the Prophet alone. With regard to matters of faith and in particular to the nature of divinity, Sunnis believe that there is no contradiction between revelation and the intellect and as such, whatever has been revealed in the Qur'an and *sunna* must be understood as it is, without esoterical interpretation, distortion, modification or invalidation. As such, the nature of Allah is perfection and this includes His attribute of being The Creator, consequently it is He who creates not only His creation but also their actions. They also believe that Muhammad is the final prophet sent to mankind and that the revelation given to him, i.e, the Qur'an is the final revelation to be revealed until the end of time. In addition, the Qur'an is the direct speech of Allah and as such is uncreated and eternal. With regard to divine predestination (*qadar*) Sunnis believe that Allah has knowledge of all that will be before its occurrence and that this has been written down on a 'preserved tablet' (*al-lawh al-mahfuz*) that is with Him and that nothing will come into being unless He wills it. As for events in the hereafter, Sunnis believe in both the intercession of the Prophet, the angels and the pious on the Day of Judgement, as well as the Beatific Vision in the hereafter. With regard to the nature of faith (*iman*) Sunnis consider it to consist of three elements: belief in the heart, affirmation of the tongue and its manifestation in taking action. As such those who commits a major sin (*murtakib al-kabira*) are not excluded from the religion by doing so but are regarded as being of 'weak faith' and will be left to the mercy of Allah on the Day of Judgement – he may forgive them or punish them as He wills. At a political level, Sunnis believe that imamate/caliphate is established either by the consensus of the community (*ijma' al-u'mma*) or a pledge of allegiance from those charged with authority and once a legitimate imam-caliph takes office then it is impermissible to remove him from power unless he displays clear disbelief. As such the first four caliphs are all considered legitimate and in fact 'rightly guided' (*rashidun*). In addition, the Sunnis believe that all the Companions of the Prophet were just and reliable, special reverence being given to his family (*Ahl al-Bayt*) and in particular his wives, who are considered to be the 'mothers of the believers' (*ummahat al-mu'minin*). Sunnis are represented in the earliest generations by the *salaf*, i.e., the prophetic companions (*al-sahaba*), their students termed successors (*al-tabi'un*) and their students the successors' successors (*atba' al-tabi'un*), and in the later generations (*al-khalaf*) by schools such as the Ash'aris and the Maturidis.

References

al-'Aql (1991: 13–16), al-Johani (1999: 36–42), Netton (1997: 23, 238).

See also: **Ahmadis (al-Ahmadyya); Babism (al-Babiyya); Druzes (Duruz); 'Ibadism (al-'Ibadiyya); Isma'ilism/Batinism (al-Isma'iliyya/al-Batiniyya); Jahmism (al-Jahmiyya); Kharijism (al-Khawarij); Murji'ism (al-Murij'a); Mu'tazilism (al-Mu'tazila); Nusayris/'Alawis (al-Nusayriyyala/al-'Alawiyya); Qadarism (al-Qadariyya); Shi'ism (al-Shi'a)**

GAVIN PICKEN

SUQ

The *suq* is the principal commercial centre throughout the Islamic world. It exists in many forms from the small *suq* selling basic goods alongside the teahouses and inns that serviced travellers on the main trade routes to the well-planned complexes of capital cities. Certain features are always present – a network of small shops grouped together according to their stock along streets and alleys, awnings and roofs to provide shelter from sun and rain, and gates which are locked at night time. Within the busy streets are special areas for the sale of precious items – silks, gold jewellery, the courtyards of large caravanserais where merchants and imported goods are lodged, mosques and *madrasas*, and the workshops of dyers, weavers and metalsmiths. The Kapili Carsi (covered market) of Istanbul begun in the late fifteenth century combines function with architectural form. It is a well-planned small town whose vaulted streets and domed squares are laid out in a rectangular grid. The heart of the market is the Bedestan where valuables are still sold. There are also temporary weekly country *suqs* still seen in Morocco, where villagers come to sell their surplus produce, to buy goods that they cannot make themselves and to exchange news. They may well be derived from the pre-Islamic Suq al-'Arab, held annually in the Hejaz, where poets came to recite their odes. This fair, a gathering opportunity for scattered Arab tribes, was abolished by the Prophet Muhammad as a pagan institution.

References

Brotton (2002), Weiss and Westermann (1998).

JENNIFER SCARCE

SURA

A 'chapter' of the Qur'an. The Qur'an consists of 114 chapters; there is very little history of variation in this number within the history of Islam. Each chapter is divided into verses and all except Q.9 start with the *basmala*, 'In the name of God, the Merciful, the Compassionate'. Each *sura* has a name and it is by those names Muslims have traditionally referred to each *sura*, rather than by number as has become more common in recent times. There is a good deal of discrepancy in the naming of the *suras*, with most *suras* having more than one name, and some having as many as six names (or even more). Among the most common variations is Q.17 called *Surat Bani Isra'il* or *Surat al-Isra'*. The sura titles are not considered a part of the revelation of the Qur'an and are mnemonic tags derived from prominent words, unique words, or the beginning words of the chapter.

References

Kandil (1992: 44–60), Paret (1977: 539–47).

See also: **aya**

ANDREW RIPPIN

SURAT AL-A'RAF

The seventh chapter of the Qur'an. The *a'raf* of the title are the 'ramparts' or 'battlements', and the reference is often taken to be to a place between Heaven and Hell which serves as a kind of purgatory. It is referred to in Q.7:46–8:

> And between them is a veil, and on the ramparts are men knowing each by their mark, who shall call to the inhabitants of paradise: 'Peace be upon you! They have not entered it, for all their eagerness'. And when their eyes are turned towards the inhabitants of the fire they shall say, 'Our Lord, do not assign us with the people of the evildoers'. And the dwellers on the battlements shall call to certain men they know by their sign: 'Your amassing has not availed you, neither your waxing proud'.

The historical context of the *sura* as a whole is generally understood to be from shortly before Muhammad's emigration to Medina. The content of the chapter is focused on an invitation to Islam accompanied by a typical Qur'a-

nic warning of pending doom for those who resist the message. The stubbornness of the Meccans and the Jews in their attitude towards Muhammad's message is isolated for censure. The advice of continued patience on the part of Muhammad is also clear.

References

Yusuf Ali (1968: 352–3).

ANDREW RIPPIN

SURAT AL-FATIHA

The 'opening' chapter of the Qur'an. The *sura* is distinctive within the scriptural text for being one of the passages which is phrased as a prayer of humans rather than in the voice of God:

> In the Name of God, the Merciful, the Compassionate / Praise belongs to God, the Lord of all being, / the all-Merciful, the all-Compassionate, / The master of the day of judgement. / You only do we serve, to You alone do we pray for succour. / Guide us in the straight path / The path of those whom You have blessed / Not of those against whom You are wrathful, nor of those who are astray.

The switch from the omniscient narrator in verse 1 to the human speaking voice in verse 4 created a good deal of discussion by the exegetes who tended to interpret the chapter as a dialogue between God and His creation.

The *sura* is a central ritual, symbolic, and emblematic unit in Islam. It is the constant focus of Muslim devotion by being featured prominently in art, being recited constantly within the ritual prayer, and serving as a summary of all the key tenets of Islam. The *sura* is recited at each standing phase of the ritual prayer and is one of the key elements which all Muslims must know in Arabic in order to fulfil the ritual requirements of the faith. It also features in individual prayer, marriage, visits to holy sites, funerals, and so forth.

References

Ayoub (1979: 635–47), Renard (1998: 29–34).

ANDREW RIPPIN

SURAT AL-FIL

The 'Chapter of the Elephant' (Q.105) in reference to a pre-Islamic invasion of Mecca by forces from the south of Arabia. The reference and the entire *sura* is brief:

> In the Name of God, the All-Merciful, the All-Compassionate. / Hast thou not seen how thy Lord did with the Men of the Elephant? / Did He not make their guile to go astray? / And He loosed upon them birds in flights, hurling against them stones of baked clay / and He made them like green blades devoured.

Each element of this chapter is attached to the overall story of the sixth-century south Arabian leader Abraha and his attempted invasion of Mecca with an elephant in the lead. The troops were repulsed by a flock of birds who threw stones at the troops and killed them all. The birds were sent by God to protect his holy house in Mecca. The story is important for accounting for some of Muhammad's ancestors and also for establishing the birth date of Muhammad himself in the 'Year of the Elephant', understood to be AD 570.

References

Calder *et al.* (2003: §4.3).

ANDREW RIPPIN

SURAT AL-IKHLAS

The 'Chapter of Sincerity' or 'Purity', Q.112. A feature of ritual prayer alongside *surat al-fatiha*, the chapter emphasises the absolute oneness of God: 'In the Name of God, the All-Merciful, the All-Compassionate. Say: "He is God, One, God, the Everlasting Refuge, who has not begotten, and has not been begotten, and equal to Him is not any one"'. Both anti-polytheist and anti-Christian sentiment have been seen in the rejection of God having offspring. The word *samad*, here translated as 'everlasting refuge', is lexically uncertain.

References

Rubin (1984: 197–217).

ANDREW RIPPIN

SURAT AL-KAHF

The 'Chapter of the Cave', the eighteenth chapter of the Qur'an, which is framed as a response to testing questions put to Muhammad by the Jews and the inhabitants of Mecca prior to his emigration to Medina. The questions were: 'Who were the Seven Sleepers in the cave (*ashab al-kahf*)?', 'What is the real story of al-Khidr?' and 'What do you know about Dhu 'l-Qarnayn (generally understood to be Alexander)?' The answers to the questions are allusive stories, each of which has provoked extensive commentary and speculation within Islam.

References

Netton (2000: 67–87).

ANDREW RIPPIN

SURAT MARYAM

The 'Chapter about Mary' (Q.19), that is, the mother of Jesus, which contains, among other themes, the story of the birth and childhood of Jesus. The chapter is placed in the context of the period of emigration to Abyssinia by a group of Meccan Muslims. After relating the story of prophets John and Jesus in verses 1–40 (an account seen to be relevant to those emigrating to Christian Abyssinia), the story of Abraham is told in verses 41–50 as an example of someone who had also been forced to leave his country because of persecution. Other prophets are mentioned in verses 51–65 to emphasise Muhammad's connection to the prophets of the past, and the conclusion of the chapter (verses 66–98) makes a strong criticism of the evil ways of the Meccans, while the Believers are reassured of success in the end.

References

Calder *et al.* (2003: §4.1, includes an interpretation of verses 16–31).

ANDREW RIPPIN

SURAT YUSUF

The 'Chapter about Joseph', the twelfth chapter of the Qur'an, which contains the longest cohesive narrative of the Qur'an in its recounting of the story of the patriarch Joseph. As a story, it parallels the biblical account in the book of Genesis fairly closely, although it does presume some knowledge of the biblical story for all the elements to make sense to the reader (e.g., the elements related to Joseph's brother Benjamin). However, the story also reflects the general Qur'anic conception of prophethood in its understanding of Joseph as a messenger to his people.

References

Beeston (1963), Nwyia (1977: 407–23).

ANDREW RIPPIN

SU'UD III B. 'ABD AL-'AZIZ

Successor of the great Ibn Su'ud (r. 1952–64). During his reign, the simple way of life and the great achievements of his father seemed endangered by the growth of materialism and corruption within the ruling Su'udi family. The oil revenues were recklessly spent, leading to a financial crisis in 1957. There were external pressures caused by the growth of nationalism in neighbouring Arab countries, in particular, in Nasserite Egypt, combined with resentment at the tight grip on power of the immediate Su'udi royal family. An ultimatum was presented to Su'ud in 1958, leading to a temporary transfer of ruling power to the Crown Prince Faysal. The King's declining health plus continuing pressure for reform led to his enforced abdication and exile in 1964.

References

Gibb and Bosworth (1960–2003), Vassiliev (1998: 335–6, 354–68).

See also: **'Abd al-'Aziz II b. 'Abd al-Rahman**

C. E. BOSWORTH

SU'UDIS (SAUDIS) (1735–)

The Su'udi sheikhs arose in central Arabia as, in effect, the political wing of the puritanical reform movement of Muhammad b. 'Abd al-Wahhab. Surviving attacks by the Egyptian armies of Muhammad 'Ali's house, they eliminated local rivals and in the early twentieth century wrested control of the Holy Places in western Arabia from the Hashimites, thereby constituting the Su'udi Arabian kingdom controlling three-quarters of the peninsula. The dynasty continues to be closely identified with Wahhabism and, as such, is hostile towards such manifestations of popular piety as the veneration of local saints at their tombs and towards the Shi'ite communities of eastern Arabia.

References

Bosworth (1996: No. 55), Gibb and Bosworth (1960–2003), Vassiliev (1998), Winder (1965).

See also: **Wahhabism**

C. E. BOSWORTH

AL-SUYUTI, JALAL AL-DIN (1445–1505)

Shafi'ite religious scholar and encyclopaedist. Born in Cairo and orphaned at an early age, he received his basic education and spent most of his life there, serving for a time as *shaykh* of the Sufi Baybarsiyya *khanqah*. His arrogance, however, made him unpopular with his fellow teachers, and after quarrelling with them, he retired from teaching and spent much of the remainder of his life in scholarly seclusion, though he remained an advocate of the Sufi approach to Islam.

One of the most prolific authors in Islamic history, al-Suyuti's works run to some 550 titles, of which about 450 still survive. They range over the entire field of literary and religious studies, including Qur'anic exegesis, *hadith*, law, philosophy, history, philology and rhetoric. Although a number of his works are no more than a few pages in length, he also composed a number of substantive volumes, among the most important of which are: a treatise on Qur'anic exegesis entitled the *Itqan*; a commentary on the Qur'an known as the *Tafsir al-Jalalayn* (*The Commentary by the two Jalals*), begun by Jalal al-Din al-Mahalli and completed by al-Suyuti; a historical work on the caliphs entitled *Tarikh al-Khulafa'*, and a history of Cairo, *Husn al-Muhadara*. Al-Suyuti's best work probably lay in the field of *hadith* studies, which he

considered the 'noblest of sciences', and he appears to have had a particular fascination for theological minutiae, writing on such abstruse topics as the legality of wearing fur, whether the Prophet wore trousers, and how many persons constituted a congregation at Friday prayers. Disappointingly, his autobiography, *al-Tahadduth bi-ni'mat Allah*, is little more than an account of the teachers with whom he had studied and a list of the books and *fatwas* he had issued himself.

With such a vast output, it is hardly surprising that al-Suyuti's works are characterised by inclusiveness rather than originality, and he was accused of plagiarism, not without some justification, by his contemporary al-Sakhawi. Al-Suyuti's works nevertheless quickly gained a wide following throughout the Islamic world and did much to spread a knowledge of the Islamic sciences among his contemporaries.

References

Jarret (1881), Sartain (1975), Sprenger *et al.* (1857).

PAUL STARKEY

SWORD VERSE

The fifth verse of the ninth chapter of the Qur'an. The verse is often held to abrogate many of the Meccan period verses which suggest patience in facing the unbelievers. 'Then, when the sacred months are drawn away, slay the idolaters wherever you find them, and take them, and confine them, and lie in wait for them at every place of ambush. But if they repent, and perform the prayer, and pay the alms, then let them go their way, God is All-forgiving, All-compassionate'.

The verse has especially become a focal point of modern Muslim discussion in which activist radical Muslims wish to see the verse as supporting acts of violence which are conceived to help the spread of Islam while other Muslims see the verse as limited in its application to the context of Muhammad's lifetime.

References

Firestone (1997: 14–16).

ANDREW RIPPIN

SYED AMEER ALI (1849–1928)

A significant reformer of Islamic thought in the Indian context. Following in the footsteps of Sayyid Ahmad Khan, Ameer Ali sought to reformulate traditional Islamic teachings in order to make them both more easily applicable in the modern world and more easily understood and appreciated by non-Muslims. His most famous book *The Spirit of Islam,* and also his *A Short History of the Saracens* were both published in London, in English, and served a basically apologetic purpose, arguing that Islam was essentially a progressive force, for example with respect to the position of women in society, and that it was fundamentally sympathetic to reason.

References

Ahmad (1967: Chapter 4), Ali (1922).

HUGH GODDARD

SYKES–PICOT AGREEMENT (1916)

The Anglo-French agreement signed by diplomats Sir Mark Sykes and François Picot in 1916 to divide the Ottoman empire into British, French and Russian zones. It contradicted undertakings given to those Arabs assisting Britain in its war against Turkey. With revisions, it formed the basis of the new state system in the Middle East after the First World War.

References

Hourani (1991: 318, 955–6), James (1997: 358, 398, 404), Lapidus (1999: 596–7, 642–3), Owen (2000: 9–11).

SIMON W. MURDEN

SYNCRETISM

Syncretism refers to the attempts of Muslim philosophers to reconcile different ideas which seem to be in conflict. Therefore, they attempted to provide a study reconciling the ideas of various Greek philosophers by devising a central concept which could connect them with one another. Al-Farabi was one of the first Arab philosophers who attempted to reconcile the thought of Aristotle and Plato in his book *The Reconciliation between the Two Sages*.

In the same way, the Muslim philosophers also attempted to reconcile philosophy with religion. This reconciliation was mainly based on the concept of *ta'wil*, the allegorical interpretation of scripture. Philosophers such as al-Farabi and Ibn Sina considered that philosophy in its demonstrative methods is the only way of perceiving the truth of this world. Religion, however, presents the truth in symbolic and figurative language in order that the masses can know God, but only in simplified way. Therefore, al-Farabi, and Ibn Sina after him, adopted the method of *ta'wil* in order to restore the religious Qur'anic truth to its philosophical formulation. However, it was Ibn Rushd's book *Fa l al-Maqal* that presented systematic arguments in this discipline. It is considered by many Muslim, Jewish and Christian scholars to have introduced the strongest argument for the reconciliation between philosophy and religion.

References

Leaman (1999: 3–5).

See also: **Averroism; Double truth**

MAHA EL-KAISY FRIEMUTH

T

AL-TABARI, ABU JA'FAR MUHAMMAD IBN JARIR (d. AD 923)

Historian, Qur'an commentator, jurist. The first landmark in the vast library of books providing comprehensive interpretations of the Qur'an was written by Abu Ja'far Muhammad ibn Jarir al-Tabari, who died in AD 923. Born in the area near the Caspian sea, al-Tabari studied first in Iran and then went to Baghdad where he spent most of his life. He developed a sufficient following as a teacher and a jurist to have a law school named after him, the Jaririyya, although it disappeared within a couple of generations after his death. He left behind several books dealing with aspects of law. Al-Tabari also achieved considerable fame as a historian, writing a massive universal history.

Al-Tabari's commentary on the Qur'an, *Jami' al-Bayan fi ta'wil ay al-Qur'an*, provides a detailed discussion of most every interpretational trend by means of a verse-by-verse analysis. Ideas are documented by the transmission of the opinions said to derive from Muhammad or his closest companions, who are pictured as having the best information regarding the understanding of the text. However, al-Tabari is certainly willing to express his own opinion when there is a lack of reports or even when faced with contradictory reports. Grammar along with theological perspective were his main guiding tools for constructing his exegesis.

References

Calder (1993: 101–40), Cooper (1987).

ANDREW RIPPIN

AL-TABI'UN

A comprehensive collection of, biographical detail about the Prophet Muhammad, his companions, and his successors (*al-tabi'un*), was prepared by Ibn-Sa'd, who died in Baghdad in AD 845.

EDWARD D. A. HULMES

TABLIGH

See: **Faith Movement**

TABUK

Tabuk is situated some 600 kilometres north of Medina. In the days of the Prophet Muhammad it was a strategically placed oasis town near the Syrian border. Today it is one of Saudi Arabia's developing industrial centres. In the ninth year after the *hijra*, AD 630, the 'Year of Delegations' (*sanat al-wufud*), Muhammad moved to Tabuk against his enemies, actual and potential, with a force that was intended to subdue them. His reputation preceded him, so much so that no armed conflicts were needed before he was able to conclude peace treaties with local and neighbouring Christian and Jewish tribes. Jews and Christians became protected 'clients' (*dhimmis*), in return for payment of a tax that was to become known as the *jizya*.

References

Momen (1985: 13).

EDWARD D. A. HULMES

TAFSIR

The interpretation of scripture, an activity that fundamentally expresses the Muslim devotion to the text. As a scholastic disciple, the writing of works of exegesis, *tafsir,* has been central and such products have always formed the basis of religious education in Islam.

The practice of exegesis of the Qur'an is usually seen to have a scriptural prop, even if the technical term for the activity, *tafsir,* is not used in the text itself in precisely that sense. Central to the pursuit of the understanding of the Qur'an has been the passage in Q.3:7, which provides the hermeneutical separation between the 'clear' and the 'ambiguous' verses.

Fundamentally, a work of *tafsir* provides an interpretation of the Arabic text of scripture and is defined by a number of formal characteristics: it will follow the text of the Qur'an from beginning to end and will provide an interpretation of the text segmented either into words, phrases or verses. While exceptions are found to these characteristics in some works that would be accepted as *tafsir*s, the vast majority of works fit into this pattern. Works of exegesis are written in virtually every language in which Islam manifests itself, although by far most of the works are themselves in Arabic.

The earliest period of exegesis for which we have direct textual evidence probably stems from 150 to 200 years after the death of Muhammad, although some of the material collected in works of *tafsir* in general claims to be transmitted from the earliest generations and even from Muhammad himself. Early works tend to focus on certain tendencies in interpretation. Some pursue the narrative aspects of the Qur'an, developing the text into an entertaining and edifying whole, paying attention to the needs of the reader who will approach the text of scripture with a curious and speculative mind. Thus, providing the historical background to the various pieces of revelation (in a format which later becomes known as *asbab al-nuzul,* the 'occasions of revelation') and identifying people, places and things that are only alluded to become important aspects. The work of Muqatil ibn Sulaymam (d. AD 767), *Tafsir al-Qur'an,* provides a typical example. Other works pursue the legal aspects of the text, focusing on the early community's need to support legal practice by reference to the text of scripture. One example of this comes again from Muqatil, *Tafsir Khams Mi'a Aya*, a work which organised the text of scripture into topics rather than follow the text *ad seriatim*. Yet other works examine textual matters, including lexicographical issues. Al-Farra' (d. AD 822), *Ma'ani 'l-Qur'an*, provides an example of a work which is grammatical in focus and with detailed attention to textual niceties. Abu 'Ubayda (d. AD 825), *Majaz al-Qur'an*, provides an example of a fourth type of approach that focuses on literary figures and expressions, laying the basis for later arguments about the miraculous character (*i'jaz*) of the text. Finally, mystical approaches to the Qur'an in which the text provides a starting point for inspirational meditations are seen to start in works such as al-Tustari (d. AD 896).

The classical period of exegesis is often seen to commence with al-Tabari (d. AD 923), whose work *Jami' al-Bayan fi Tawil Ay al-Qur'an* brings together all the various tendencies of early *tafsir* into one body of material. There, it becomes clear that grammar along with theological perspective became the main guiding tools for constructing an exegesis of the Qur'an. Grammar served to assert the scholar's status and authority within the whole discipline of *tafsir* such that the ability to pursue the minutiae of Arabic constructions became a focal point of argumentation over how the meaning of the text could be derived. Theology tends to play a lesser role, usually subsumed under grammatical or legal wranglings. All such issues continue to play their role in the exegesis of later centuries, with major works being produced with great regularity, generally each one building upon the work of its predecessors (either implicitly or explicitly) such that a work such as that of al-Qurtubi (d. AD 1273), *Jami' al-Ahkam*, represents the consolidation of

centuries of discussion in the attempt to demonstrate that the Qur'an encompasses a broad range of meanings and as such must be celebrated for its never-ending potential. Other writers, however, such as Ibn Taymiyya (d. AD 1327) and Ibn Kathir (d. AD 1373), saw a loss of authority for the learned classes in such excess of meaning and attempted to reverse the tendency by asserting a more limited range of meanings. The legacy of that attitude survives until today within revivalist circles of Islam.

The historicisation of the text of the Qur'an was another important element in the production of exegesis. The integration of the text with the stories of the prophets of the past (primarily biblical) in the material known as the *qisas al-anbiya'*, 'stories of the prophets', and with the story of the life of Muhammad as embedded in books of *sira* ('life story'), such as that of Ibn Ishaq (d. AD 767), was designed both to prove the theological fact of the reality of revelation and to provide a context for interpretation for an otherwise historically opaque text. The result was a text that was grounded in day-to-day human existence with an emphasis on the formative Muslim community. Not all Muslims pursued such ends, however, for mystical (Sufi) *tafsir* was very much a flight from the constraints of sacred history into interpretations derived from and legitimated by mystical experience. A work such as al-Kashani (d. AD 1330), containing the teachings of the famous mystic Ibn 'Arabi (d. AD 1240), and usually known as *Tafsir ibn al-'Arabi*, is typical.

Exegesis of the Qur'an is a flourishing field in the modern Muslim world. New works are being produced and new editions of classical works are appearing with regularity. Major modern Muslim thinkers such as Muhammad 'Abduh, Rashid Rida, and Sayyid Qutb have put their thoughts down in the form of *taf-sir*, if somewhat altered compared to the classical model, especially in their rejection of the earlier grammatical bias. The historical-critical method, so closely associated with nineteenth-century biblical scholarship, has made very limited inroads in *tafsir*, with few authors interested in seeing the meaning of the text constrained by the historical circumstances of Muhammad, whose life story still mainly provides an interpretational framework for the derivation of universal meaning.

References

Rippin (2001).

See also: **muhkamat** and **mutashabihat**

ANDREW RIPPIN

TAFWID

The belief that Allah has delegated complete free will to man.

References

Momen (1985: 66).

See also: **jabr**

ANDREW J. NEWMAN

TAHAFUT AL-FALASIFA

This is a searching refutation of philosophy by the theologian and jurist Abu Hamid al-Ghazali (AD 1058–1111), which exposes the heretical and non-Islamic principles held by leading philosophers in the Islamic tradition. Its title, which means 'collapse', 'inconsistency' and 'disintegration', is usually translated as 'The Incoherence of the Philosophers'.

Al-Ghazali wrote the *Tahafut* in his period as professor at the Nizamiyya College in Baghdad, AD 1091–5, being one of a number of related works he composed on philosophy at this time: the *Maqasid al-Falasifa* (*The Intentions of the Philosophers*), an exploration of Islamic philosophical teachings, the *Mi'yar al-'Ilm* (*The Standard of Knowledge*), an exposition of philosophical logic, and the *Iqtisad fi 'l-I'tiqad* (*Moderation in Believing*), a treatise of Ash'ari dogmatics. The *Tahafut* fits in with these as an intentionally destructive exposure of the inadequacy of philosophical principles in religious terms, and an invalidation of *falsafa* as an alternative to traditional Qur'an-based belief.

Al-Ghazali's declared intention in writing the *Tahafut* was to demonstrate the shortcomings and dangers of philosophy to fellow Muslims who were so enamoured of it that they no longer followed the requirements of religion. But this takes him into the much wider enterprise of showing that some of the key teachings of the most fashionable philosophers have no more rational solidity or logical completeness than those of religion.

The philosopher whose thought exerted most influence in the time of al-Ghazali was Ibn Sina (d. AD 1037) who had died about sixty years before the *Tahafut* was written. He had developed a form of Neoplatonic philosophy in which the observable and inferential cosmos was understood as an emanation from the Necessary Being, who did not create in time or have knowledge of particular events, since these would necessitate change within him. This Necessary Being was seductively different from the active interventionist God of the Qur'an, and it is this sublimely remote and indifferent Being that al-Ghazali was concerned to overthrow.

Typical of his writings, the *Tahafut* is very clearly set out and much more accessible than many works of the opponents who are its targets. It is divided into twenty discussions or problems, *masa'il*, the first sixteen being concerned with metaphysical matters, such as the eternity of the world, the existence and character of God, and the nature of the spiritual beings that supervise the cosmos, and the last four being concerned with physical matters, such as miracles, the nature of the human soul, and the possibility that the body as well as the soul may be resurrected from the dead. Al-Ghazali is not concerned with differences in terminology, or indeed with teachings that do not actually undermine Islam since they do not bear directly on faith, but ultimately with three issues that contradict the received truths of religion and amount to unbelief.

The first of these major points of contention is whether the universe is eternal or originates in time. In Ibn Sina's system it is necessarily pre-eternal, because it is the effect of an eternal cause, but al-Ghazali shows at some length in the first discussion (this makes up almost a quarter of the whole work) that there is no compelling reason to accept this, and in fact there are empirical reasons to reject it. As he presents the case, the philosophers cannot provide any persuasive argument in favour of the eternity of the world, and so al-Ghazali's own position that it was created in time by God actively choosing to do this can be upheld.

The second major point of contention is whether Ibn Sina's God can know individuals and the particulars of their existence. Ibn Sina contended that God knew in a universal way, which is to say that his knowledge was not limited by times or places and did not extend beyond the general categories in which all individuals were included. In the thirteenth discussion, al-Ghazali rejects this concept as not proven: God's knowledge may be universal and unconditioned by specifics, but this need not rule out his knowing particulars, and any change in them need not entail change in him.

The third major point in which al-Ghazali detects a direct contradiction of the Qur'an is whether there can be a bodily resurrection. Ibn Sina held that the human soul as immaterial was distinct from the body, and the only part of the individual that survived death. But in the eighteenth discussion, al-Ghazali shows that the philosophers' purely rational arguments in favour of the soul's self-subsistence are not convincing, and in the twentieth discussion he contends that they have no justification to deny the resurrection of the body as the Qur'an teaches it.

Throughout the twenty discussions, al-Ghazali repeatedly seeks to show that the philosophers' suppositions about God are no more than that, and thus have no firmer claim to acceptance than the teachings of Islam. But the matter is more serious in these three discussions, because the points under examination actually contradict the Qur'an. So he concludes that on these points the philosophers are not only guilty of innovation, *bida'*, but convicted of unbelief, *kufr*, and liable to the penalties that may follow.

While the *Tahafut* shows clearly the growth of the theologian's scepticism with purely intellectual means of arriving at certainly, it did not have the crushing effect for which al-Ghazali might have hoped. The Andalusian philosopher Ibn Rushd (d. AD 1198) replied to it in the succinctly descriptive *Tahafut al-Tahafut* (*The Incoherence of the Incoherence*), and the Shi'i philosopher and theologian Nasir al-Din al-Tusi (d. AD 1274) in the less well-known *al-Dhakira*. It did have the effect of alerting traditional believers to the danger of Avicennan philosophy, but at the same time it made the main teachings of philosophy accessible to a non-specialist audience through the clarity of its exposition.

References

Bouyges (1927), Fakhry (1983: Chapter 7), Marmura (2000).

DAVID THOMAS

TAHAFUT AL-TAHAFUT

As is intimated by its succinct title, this work is a rejoinder to Abu Hamid al-Ghazali's *Tahafut al-Falasifa* (*The Incoherence of the Philosophers*). It was written by the great Andalusian philosopher, jurist and physician Abu al-Walid Muhammad b. Ahmad Ibn Rushd (AD 1126–98) in about 1180, when he was *qadi* of Seville, and thus dates from about eighty-five years after al-Ghazali's work had originally appeared. It is generally translated as '*The Incoherence of The Incoherence*'.

Ibn Rushd's *Tahafut* is thematically related to two other works which he composed just before. The first of these is the *Fasl al-Maqal wa-Taqrib ma bayn al-Shari'a wa'l-hikma min al-Ittisal*, (*The Authoritative Treatise and Exposition of the Convergence between the Law and Wisdom*), a treatise on the essential harmony of the teachings of the Qur'an and philosophy, and the *Kitab al-Kashf 'an Manahij al-Adilla fi 'Aqa'id al-Milla*, (*The Exposition of the Methods of Demonstration concerning the Dogmas of the Congregation*), a treatise on the errors of theology and the reliability of philosophical methods to arrive at true knowledge of God. These two linked works (the latter refers to the former) both justify philosophy on Qur'anic grounds and promote it as a method by which the few can achieve the sublime, abstract knowledge that the Qur'an presents pictorially for the many. The *Tahafut* continues from and complements them to show that al-Ghazali's refutation did not in fact produce decisive criticisms or arguments that affected philosophy as it should properly be conducted.

Al-Ghazali had assembled twenty discussions on the main elements in the philosophical systems of the Neoplatonic Aristotelians al-Farabi (d. AD 950) and Ibn Sina (d. AD 1037). Employing only arguments that would be accepted in philosophy, as he says, he attempted to expose contradictions and inconsistencies in these twenty elements and to show where they threatened the faith of the Qur'an. Ibn Rushd recognised the importance of replying in detail to this, and so constructed his defence on al-Ghazali's work, dividing his *Tahafut* into twenty discussions, in each quoting al-Ghazali's arguments and commenting upon them in minute detail.

As might be expected, Ibn Rushd countered each of al-Ghazali's points with arguments that display his technical mastery over both philosophy and theology. But his *Tahafut* is not simply an exercise in polemic, rejecting all that his opponent said by any means at his disposal. Ibn Rushd is distinguished among Islamic philosophers as the exponent of Aristotle's pure thought divested of the Neoplatonic accretions of late antiquity through which earlier philosophers in the Islamic east had access to it. By the time he wrote the *Tahafut* he had already produced summaries of many of Aristotle's treatises and was engaged in the middle commentaries upon them at the very time of writing. Thus he was as concerned to point out errors and shortcomings in the philosophical ideas which al-Ghazali attacks as he was to rebut the theologian's refutations.

With no more than an opening statement of the book's intention, which is to prove that most of al-Ghazali's arguments have 'not reached the degree of evidence and of truth', Ibn Rushd immediately begins his examination by quoting his opponent's first argument and replying to it. This sets the tone for the whole work, which is direct and business-like, and also open in both its dismissal of errors in earlier philosophers and its rejoinders to the theologian. Ibn Rushd sometimes hardly conceals his impatience with either.

The *Tahafut* is, then, more than a straightforward refutation of al-Ghazali's work. In his own contributions to the debate Ibn Rushd shows his detachment from both the discipline of theology and the composite versions of earlier philosophy, and presents himself as the upholder of a form of philosophy that stands invulnerable to attacks as a cogent means of reaching the truth.

References

Bouyges (1930), Fakhry (1983: Chapter 9), Van den Bergh (1987).

DAVID THOMAS

TAHANNUTH

The term is derived from the Arabic *hanitha,* meaning 'to perform works of devotion', 'to practise piety'. The practice of penance is said to have been performed by the Quraysh in pre-Islamic times by spending one month each year on Mount Hira', with the intention of seeking religious cleansing.

EDWARD D. A. HULMES

TAHARA

See: **ritual prayer and worship**

TAHMASP I B. ISMA'IL (r. 1524–76)

The second shah of the Safavid dynasty in Iran. The first decade of his reign was spent mastering the ambitions in the state of the Qizilbash ('red heads', from the red caps they wore), the Turkmen tribesmen who had been the original, fervidly inspired partisans of the Safavids and with whose support Shah Isma'il had achieved the throne. Only then was he able to undertake warfare against the Ottomans, increasingly with the military backing of Georgian, Armenian and Circassian slave troops rather than the unreliable Qizilbash. Tahmasp had the reputation in his own time, confirmed by the experience of Western vistors to his court, of being a particularly fanatical Shi'ite; thus when the fugitive Mughal Humayun sought refuge at his court, he was compelled to make a tactical conversion to Shi'-ism before the Shah would extend his protection.

References

Gibb and Bosworth (1960–2003), Savory (1980: 50–68), Roemer (1986: 233–50).

C. E. BOSWORTH

TAHRIF

The 'alteration' of scripture, a polemical charge within the Qur'an and Muslim tradition levelled against Jews and Christians. On most occasions when this charge of 'alteration' is made the reference is to the description of Muhammad which either is to be found, or should be found, in the Bible. The Jews and Christians have either erased the reference, removed from its proper place, distorted it, or wilfully misinterpreted the statements.

References

Lazarus-Yafeh (1992: Chapter 2).

ANDREW RIPPIN

AL-TA'I', 'ABD AL-KARIM B. AL-MUTI', ABU'L-FADL (AD 974–91)

The 'Abbasid caliph al-Ta'i'was chosen by the Buyid *amir* to succeed his father the deposed al-Muti'. Al-Ta'i' receives scant attention by Muslim historians, generally being referred to in connection with certain ceremonial duties he was called upon to perform. He subsequently married a daughter of the *amir* 'Adud al-Dawla, while 'Adud married a daughter of the caliph, the *amir* hoping in this way to have a descendant of his accede to the caliphate. Al-Ta'i' was, however, eventually deposed by the Buyid Baha' al-Dawla who replaced the caliph with his cousin Ahmad b. Ishaq al-Qadir. Al-Ta' died in AD 1003.

References

Hitti (1970: 471–3), Kennedy (1996: 241), Le Strange (1924: 118, 162, 270, 271), Muir (1915: 579), Ibn al-Jawzi (1938: 66–7), Ibn al-Tiqtaqa (1860: 336–7).

RONALD PAUL BUCKLEY

AL-TA'IF

Principal summer resort and fourth largest town of Saudi Arabia, in Makka province, al-Hijaz region. Linked to a pre-Islamic shrine for the pagan goddess al-Lat, it was then ccupied by Jews expelled from Yemen and Ma'rib. Its pre-Islamic fortress is linked to Mas'ud b. Mu'attib, father of the Prophet's Companion, 'Urwa. One *hadith* notes fertile land from Palestine was transferred by God to al-Ta'if after prayers from Abraham (Q.14:37). Known as 'the orchard of the *haram*' (that is for Mecca), Qurayshi estates nearby produced fruit, pomegranates, grapes and honey. Literacy levels were high so many al-Ta'ifis worked in administration in the early Islamic world. Poets included al-Samawwa'al (sixth century AD), Durayd ibn al-Simma (d. AD 630), Umayya ibn Abi al-Salt (d. *c*. AD 631). Al-Ta'if oriented around the tombs and mosque of 'Abdallah ibn 'Abbas, cousin of the Prophet Muhammad, and two of the Prophet's infant sons. The Treaty of Tayif (1934) was signed to demarcate part of the Saudi-Yemeni border. A modern highway links al-Ta'if with Makka and Jiddah.

References

Creswell (1989: 4), Gelder (1998: I, 285–6).

JANET STARKEY

TAJ MAHAL

The Taj Mahal at Agra, commissioned by the Mughal Emperor Shah Jahan (AD 1628–57) as a tomb for his wife Mumtaz Mahal was begun in 1632 and completed only by 1647. This remarkable building, justifiably famous in its own right, is also part of the well-established tradition of the monumental mausoleum in Islamic culture. While traditional Islamic doctrine proscribes ostentatious rituals of mourning and burial, popular opinion encouraged the placing of a special structure to mark the grave of the Prophet Muhammad in his house. Following this practice, mausolea were built over the graves of the companions of the Prophet, Shi'a martyrs such as the Imam Husayn at Karbala. Later mausolea became associated with wealth and power and assumed accordingly monumental proportions. The direct ancestor of the Taj Mahal is the tomb of the Ilkhanid ruler Uljaitu (AD 1304–16) at Sultaniyeh in north Iran. This is an imposing brick structure built between 1307 and 1313 with a dome rising over an octagonal tomb chamber surrounded with eight purely decorative minarets and an external gallery. Decoration in moulded, carved and painted stucco, and glazed tile mosaic in turquoise, blue and white forms designs of Arabic inscriptions, geometric and foliate motifs. The plan resembles that of the Dome of the Rock and of the mausolea of local rulers of Bukhara and Samarkand. The Taj Mahal interprets the basic principles of a domed chamber flanked by supporting structures in a garden complex, which creates an image of Paradise. The white marble tomb is set on a terrace at the north end of a rectangular garden crossed by watercourses that intersect at a pool reflecting the four rivers of Paradise. It is constructed of finely cut and dressed blocks of white marble to a square plan opening into a pavilion at each corner. The central dome is flanked by four small domes on open colonnades. Symmetry is further stressed by four marble minarets one at each corner of the terrace and identical three-domed buildings in sandstone to the west and east. The decoration combines Qur'anic inscriptions with graceful compositions of flower sprays carved or inlaid in semiprecious stones.

References

Begley and Desai (1989), Tillotson (1990).

JENNIFER SCARCE

TAJWID

The rules that govern the art of reciting of Qur'an. The word itself is not found in the Qur'an but it became applied to recitation of scripture in the early Islamic period. The term denotes not only the performance of recitation but all the technical aspects of how to pronounce the text in recitation as well. Letters, words and phrases are to be produced in particular ways, with shading, lengthening, assimilation, and nasalisation of certain sounds in certain places being dictated.

As such, *tajwid* consists of the application of phonetic principles that are a part of Arabic. Also governed within *tajwid* are the punctuation of the text – stopping, starting, brief pauses, and so forth.

References

Denny (1989: 5–26).

ANDREW RIPPIN

AL-TAKFIR WA'L-HIJRA

Al-Takfir wa'l-Hijra (literally, 'excommunication and emigration') is the name given to an Egyptian underground political movement that was officially formed in 1971 as a schism from the Muslim Brotherhood. The group called themselves Jama'at al-Muslimin ('the Muslim society'). The Brotherhood (al-Ikhwan) had become the principal Islamist opposition movement to the Egyptian political establishment both under the monarchy, and (after 1952) under the Free Officers and Nasser. The Brotherhood, like many modern Muslim political movements, proposed a return to the Islam of the early Muslims – the Islam of the *salafiyya* (hence the Brotherhood, along with many other movements are termed *salafi*).

Following a period of state suppression in the early 1960s, culminating in the execution of a number of Brotherhood leaders (the most famous being Sayyid Qutb who was executed in 1965), divisions amongst the members of the Brotherhood began to emerge. Some moderate *ikhwan* contemplated a compromise with the Egyptian regime in order to gain an influence on political affairs. Other Brothers advocated a continuation of the underground, secretive campaign in order to establish an Islamic state through the destabilisation the regime. The former went on to change the Brotherhood into a political party with representatives in the Egyptian

Parliament, the latter went on to form a number of 'terrorist' movements. It was from this latter group that al-Takfir wa'l-Hijra drew its early participants. What is particularly interesting about al-Takfir wa'l-Hijra is that they appear to have completely rejected Islamic law (*fiqh*) as it was classically understood and instead advocated a law based almost entirely on the Qur'an. Not even the *sunna* of the Prophet (considered by the group's founder Shukri Ahmad Mustafa as 'unreliable') was an acceptable source of law.

Al-Takfir wa'l-Hijra, as their name suggests, advocated the 'excommunication' of all of Egyptian society, and an 'emigration' to a place where they would not be under its influence. For them, Egyptian society was irredeemably corrupt and un-Islamic. This referred not only to the upper echelons of society, but also to all levels from the political elite to the peasant class. Egyptians were not true Muslims due to their involvement in this un-Islamic society; true Muslims should withdraw and live in separate communities, even establishing a separate political state from where they could wage *jihad* against the unbelieving world. In this they were influenced by the Brotherhood thinker, Sayyid Qutb, who had argued in his various works that modern Egyptian society was not Muslim (though it may claim to be) but in fact *jahilii* (that is, ignorant of the true nature of Islam, as the Arabs before the coming of Islam had been). *Takfir* refers to this doctrine (common to Qutb and the later movement), as society and its members are 'declared unbelievers (*kafirs*)'. In their *hijra* (emigration) from society, the group claimed to be following the Prophet's example (the Prophet migrated from Mecca to Medina when he perceived Meccan society to be beyond reform). More pertinently, they were adopting the legacy of the Kharijites of early Islam, who had withdrawn from Muslim society, establishing smaller 'pure' communities and embarking on attacks on non-Kharijite Muslims. Central to this tendency was a belief that Islam is not simply a profession of faith, but must be reflected in societal action. Those who do not act as Muslims lose the right to be considered such. This position justified al-Takfir wa'l-Hijra's doctrine that Egyptian society could be attacked as part of a *jihad* since it constituted an enemy of Islam.

Al-Takfir wa'l-Hijra gained some notoriety through their covert operations. Since they considered themselves as the only true Muslims, anyone who left the organisation has 'apostatised' (*irtidad*). They carried out raids, attacking defectors from al-Takfir wa'l-Hijra to other Islamist opposition groups. From what we know of the internal organisation of the group, it was heavily dependent on the personality cult of Shukri himself. In 1977, they abducted and killed an Egyptian minister. The regime's response was severe, and there is some indication that the regime used the activities of al-Takfir wa'l-Hijra (or rather the news of their activities) to justify the further repression of other Islamist groups. Shukri was captured and executed in 1978. With their charismatic leader gone, the group appears to have dispersed and petered out. Some members may have joined other groups in the 1980s. Whilst al-Takfir wa'l-Hijra may no longer operate, their interpretation of Qutb's ideas has been influential and has been employed in a number of radical Islamist groups in the past two decades.

References

Ansari (1984: 123–44), Ibrahim (1988: 632–57), Kepel (1985).

ROBERT GLEAVE

TALAQ, INFISAL

See: **divorce**

TALFIQ

talfiq is an Arabic term derived from *laffaqa*, to fabricate. This term is used to indicate the adherence to one school of thought regarding a particular issue, whilst following a different school's opinion that is related to the same matter. According to the Hanafi school, *talfiq* is unacceptable. If a person prays after making *wudu'* by wiping part of the head, then he cannot nullify the prayer on the ground that Imam Malik maintains the necessity of wiping the whole head.

References:

Ibn Manzur (n.d.), al-Zuhayli (1985: 1: 59).

MAWIL IZZI DIEN

TALIBAN (AFGHANISTAN)

Of Afghanistan's estimated 28.5 million people (in 2004), 99 per cent are Muslim, 80 per cent being Sunnis and around 19 per cent Shi'ites (Hazaras and Isma'ilis). Afghanistan is divided between a number of ethnic groups including the Pashtuns of the south, the Tajiks, Uzbeks and Turkmen to the north, and others including the Hazaras in the central areas. Therefore it has often been suggested that only Islam binds the majority of Afghans together. In Afghanistan, Islam has traditionally found a number of expressions, none of which are mutually exclusive: (i) the popular religion of the masses, which combines magical elements and tribal customs; (ii) the orthodox Sufism of the medieval mystical orders (the Qadiriyya, Chistiyya and especially the Naqshabandiyya); and (iii) the (relatively

flexible) Hanafi law school of the *'ulama'*. However, during the resistance to the Soviet occupation of the 1980s especially, there was a growth in the influence of Islamist and Wahhabi movements, all sponsored by regional and world powers. The Islamists were instrumental in forming *mujahidin* (armies of holy warriors) which, together with traditional tribal and religious leaders, eventually saw the declaration of an Islamic state in 1992.

The main supply of arms to the *mujahidin* came through General Zia's Pakistan (1977–88), funded, amongst others, by Saudi Arabia, the USA and Pakistan itself. Pakistan recognised only seven Sunni *mujahidin* parties, which together formed an alliance from 1985 onwards. Thereafter, the tide began to turn in favour of the resistance and it became clear the new Soviet Premier, Gorbachov, wanted to withdraw his troops. Amongst the alliance were three broadly traditionalist groupings that were Sufi and *'ulama'* led. However, it was the hitherto marginal Islamists and their urban, university-educated, leadership, which benefited most from outside intervention. The two best-known Islamist parties were the 'moderate' Jami'at-i Islami led by the Tajik former professor of Islamic Studies, Burhanuddin Rabbani, and the more 'radical' Hizb-i Islami, led by the Pashtun student of engineering, Gulbuddin Hekmatayar. The war also brought other influences to bear on Afghanistan in the form of a trans-national force of Islamic militants, the so-called 'Arab-Afghans', which included Usama Bin Laden. Finally, of two Shi'ite *mujahidin* parties, the largest was funded by Iran.

While the Soviets eventually withdrew from Afghanistan in 1989, it was a further three years before the communist government fell and an Islamic state was established. However, as foreign patrons withdrew their interest, and victory gave way to distrust, civil war broke out. Kabul, the capital city, was carved up between the different ethnic and sectarian factions with the rest of the country separated into the fiefdoms of various warlords. Moreover, under Rabbani as President and Hekmatayar as Prime Minister, the Islamists of Afghanistan failed to sustain any coherent ideology. There was Islamisation of personal law, in terms of women wearing veils, bans on the consumption of alcohol and so on. However, law and order had effectively broken down, so much so that the way was left open for the Taliban, a neo-traditionalist alternative to the Islamists, to enforce their own severely puritanical vision. Seeking to disassociate themselves from party politics, on their own web site they projected themselves as wanting to promote virtue and abolish vice.

The Taliban first came to prominence in 1994 by enforcing a measure of stability on the southern city of Kandahar. They found support amongst the war-weary Pushtuns as corruption and banditry was stamped out and trade began to revive. Because they might protect important trade routes and oil pipelines running across Afghanistan, they were also supported by Pakistan, Saudi Arabia and the USA. Iran, Turkey, India and Russia supported their opponents. By 1996 the movement had advanced to Kabul and by 1998, the Taliban controlled 90 per cent of Afghanistan. However, some have suggested that their *jihad* was effectively directed against non-Pushtuns. For example, thousands of Hazara Shi'ites were killed when the Taliban captured Mazar-i Sharif.

Only a small proportion of the Taliban's number had actually been involved in resistance to the Soviets. Rather, they were orphans of the war, literally the *taliban* (students) of the *madaris* (religious schools). These institutions had mushroomed in number during Pakistan's own period of Islamisation during the 1980s. Established along the Afghan/Pakistan border in NWFP and Baluchistan, they provided one of the few sources of education and shelter to many of the conflict's three million refugees. One school, in particular, Madrasa Haqqaniyya in Akora Kathak near Peshawar trained many of the Taliban's key leaders. The majority of these institutions, and certainly the Taliban themselves, identified with a traditionalist *'ulama'*-led movement founded in nineteenth-century India known as Deobandism. In India, the Deobandis have remained largely moderate and apolitical, so the *madaris* that produced the Taliban, often run by semi-illiterate religious functionaries, were hardly representative of the movement's mainstream. Nevertheless, all Deobandis do share an emphasis on the centrality of correct ritual and personal behaviour to Islamic law, which includes the seclusion of women. Indeed, it was the extreme rigour of their interpretations of *shari'a*, heavily influenced by patriarchal Pushtun tribal codes, that first drew criticism from the outside world.

Under the Taliban, there were public executions and amputations in Afghanistan. Girls were forbidden to attend school and women to work. Giant statues of the Buddha, carved into the mountains of central Afghanistan, were destroyed and television, music and cinema were all banned even in cities with a cosmopolitan heritage such as Kabul and Herat. For all the controversy surrounding the Taliban rule in Afghanistan, however, it was the regime's association with Usama Bin Ladin that proved to be their downfall. There had been little or no contact between the Taliban and the Arab-Afghans before 1996. Though the former did not share the latter's vision of a global *jihad*, or their absolute abhorrence of the West, Bin Ladin was a valuable asset. Because of his networks, wealth and charisma, he was offered Taliban protection in 1997. However, when Bin Ladin was linked to terrorist attacks in east Africa during 1998, and the Taliban refused to hand him over, the USA responded by launching missile attacks on the suspected terrorist's bases. This was followed in 1999 by United Nations' sanctions.

After 9/11, and further attempts to extradite Bin Laden, Allied forces finally resorted to air strikes in October 2001, precipitating the fall of the Taliban government by the end of the year. Since then, the remnants of Taliban and al-Qa'ida forces have been pursued in the south-east of Afghanistan. However, their leaderships have so far evaded capture and clashes with guerrilla forces and sympathisers are ongoing. Signs of social change in Afghanistan today include women on television and the return of the Sikh minority to Kabul.

References

Griffin (2001), Maley (1998), Marsden (1998), Metcalf (2002), Rashid (2000).

See also: **Deobandism**

SEÁN MCLOUGHLIN

TANZIL

Literally 'descent', used to refer to the mode of revelation of the Qur'an within the mythic picture of the pre-existent 'heavenly tablet' being brought down to earth by Gabriel. This is complemented by the notion of 'revelation', *wahy*, which is often seen as closer to 'inspiration'.

References

Gibb and Bosworth (1960–2003: XI, 53–6).

ANDREW RIPPIN

TANZIMAT

The period of legal and governmental reforms in mid-nineteenth century Ottoman Turkey.

References

Hourani (1991: 272).

ANDREW J. NEWMAN

TAQIYYA

'Dissimulation', affirmed in Q.16:106, whereby a believer masks his true religious beliefs to avoid persecution and a practice traditionally associated with the Shi'a.

References

Momen (1985: 39), Waines (1995: 169–70).

See also: **nifaq**

ANDREW J. NEWMAN

TAQLID

This Arabic term designates 'imitation' and normally refers to the practice of following the legal judgements of one particular school of thought, without understanding its legal or conceptual reasoning. Generally, a person who is a *muqallid* is not expected to be appointed as a judge, unless through dire necessity. The practice of *taqlid* became very common after the fall of Baghdad in AD 1258 when scholars became unable to sustain the dynamism that had prevailed prior to this point. This coupled with the ready availability of numerous detailed legal texts, led scholars to follow *taqlid* or judgements that had been applied in the past in a bid to avoid errors. The alleged closing of the gate of *ijtihad* constituted a prime reason for the emergence of *taqlid*, which was perhaps a natural sequel to the degradation and loss of self-confidence felt by the Islamic world after losing its main capital to the Mongols.

References

Al-Zuhayli (1985: 6:122–4).

MAWIL IZZI DIEN

TARIQA

In the Sufi tradition, the *tariqa* denotes a Sufi order. The orders came into existence during the medieval period and each has developed its own unique devotional rituals (other than those required by Islamic law) although many orders have practices that are very similar, such as the *dhikr*. At the head of the *tariqa* is a master, known as the *shaykh* (or *pir* or *murshid*). Some *tariqas*, such as the Naqshbandiyya, have grown to such an extent that they have branches in many countries within the Islamic and non-Islamic world.

References

Trimingham (1971).

LLOYD RIDGEON

TARIQAT IN WEST AFRICA

See: **Almohads**

TASHBIH

'Drawing comparisons', the term by which analogous references are made to aspects of Allah especially based on, and starting from, the various names given Him in the Qur'an and references to His sitting on a throne, having a hand, etc.

References

Momen (1985: 66), Rahman (1979: 90).

See also: **al-'arsh, istawa 'ala; ninety-nine names of God**

ANDREW J. NEWMAN

TASHKENT

Tashkent ('stone village' in Uzbek) is a region in north-east Uzbekistan and a town in the Čirčik oasis, the main industrial and cultural centre of Central Asia on caravan routes to Europe and China. The population is diverse (Uzbek, Russian, Tatars, Jews, Ukrainians). Known from the eleventh century as Chachkent, Shashk or Binkent, the town dates from the second or fifteenth century BC. Chinese rulers were conquered by Arabs sent by Abu Muslim (AD 751), an event that established Islamic political supremacy in central Asia. Under the 'Abbasids, Tashkent was the frontier of Islam against the Turks. It was ruled by Samanids and other Muslim rulers until the Mongols occupied the town (thirteenth century), then fought over by Timurids, Uzbeks (after 1503), Shaybanids, Kazaks, and Kalmucks (1723). A few fifteenth- and sixteenth-century religious buildings and mausoleums survive, including the Barakkan *madrasa* (theological school) and the headquarters of the Spiritual Board of Muslims of Central Asia and Kazakhastan (established 1943). Independent for a while, in 1809 Tashkent was annexed as part of the khanate of Kokand. In 1865, it was captured by the Russians who made it the administrative capital of the new governorate of Turkistan. Muslim reformists fled repression from 1902, Orthodox churches were built and an 'anti-Muslim' mission opened. In November 1917 Tashkent became capital of the Turkistan Autonomous Soviet Socialist Republic. Soviet forces bombarded the Muslim 'state' of Khoband (1918), which led to civil war (1918–22). In 1924, Samarqand became

645

the first capital of the Uzbek Soviet Socialist Republic until 1930 when Tashkent became capital. In 1966 it suffered a major earthquake making over 400,000 people homeless. Rebuilding incorporated modern techniques and Uzbek styles. In 1971, a Higher Islamic Institute was opened and in the 1990s numerous mosques were reopened. In 1991 Tashkent became capital of the independent Republic of Uzbekistan.

References

Allworth (1990), Gibb (1923).

JANET STARKEY

TASMIYYA

'The naming', a reference to the recitation of the formula 'In the Name of Allah the Merciful, the Beneficent', which begins every Qur'anic sura except 9.

References

Waines (1995: 78).

ANDREW J. NEWMAN

TASNIM

Name of a fountain in Paradise.

See also: **Salsabil.**

ANDREW J. NEWMAN

TATFIF

Paying less for a commodity than it is worth. It can also mean any kind of cheating in weights and measures. The Qur'an rebuked those who cheat in Q.83 whose title is derived from the same word.

References

Ibn Manzur (n.d.: 11:126), Izzi Dien (1997: 135).

MAWIL IZZI DIEN

TA'TIL

In debates about anthropomorphism, removing the attributes of Allah.

ANDREW J. NEWMAN

TAWBA

Literally 'turning' that is to the truth and thus 'repentance', one of the names of the ninth chapter of the Qur'an. According to the Qur'an, God turns to those who turn to Him.

References

Gibb and Bosworth (1960–: X, 384–5).

ANDREW RIPPIN

TAWFIQ

A reference to Allah's grace and helpfulness to humanity, e.g. Q.4:35.

ANDREW J. NEWMAN

TAWHID (MONOTHEISM)

Tawhid is the cornerstone of Islam. As it is their fundamental doctrine, the Muslims are described as 'the nation of *tawhid*' (*ahl al-tawhid*). The doctrine of *tawhid* signifies the total obedience and submission to God in worship and deeds. *Tawhid* designates the oneness of God (divine unicity), His absolute existence, and that He has no equal. It is embodied in the first profession of faith in Islam 'there is no god but Allah' (*la ilaha illa Allah*). Although the word *tawhid* does not occur in the Qur'an, this tenet of faith has occurred recurrently throughout the Qur'an. *Tawhid* occurs as substantiation to God's omnipotence, the prophethood of Muhammad, and eschatology. *Tawhid*, therefore, occurs in refutation to the argument of the Scripturists as in Q.2:116, 255, Q.3:3, 62–4, Q.171, Q.73:31, the dualists as in Q.5:116, Q.16:51, Q.23:91, the trinitarians as in Q.5:73, and the polytheists as in Q.22:5–6 and Q.72:2.

The notion of *tawhid* is characterised by three main features:

(i) Oneness of lordship (*tawhid al-rububiyya*) which refers to the belief in one God who is the creator and sustainer of every thing, and that He is one and without a partner in His dominion and actions.

(ii) Oneness of worshipping God (*tawhid al-iluhiyya*) which signifies that only God is worthy of worship and that He has no rival in His divinity.

(iii) Oneness of God's names and attributes (*tawhid al-asma' wal-sifat*) which refers to God's names and attributes that none of us can be named by or be equal to.

Tawhid has been examined by Muslim scholars in terms of divine unicity, divine immutability and divine essence. Although Muslim scholars stress the absolute unicity of God and that the divine essence is beyond human comprehension, they understood *tawhid* from different perspectives. For traditional Muslim scholars, rational theology (*'ilm al-kalam*) was synonymous with divine unicity (*'lm al-tawhid*). While the traditionalist Muslim scholars adopted the same early Islamic community non-rationalist approach to God's attributes, al-Mu'tazila, during the seventh century, adopted a rationalist approach to the same theological issue. The Mu'tazila was a school of thought which began during al-Hasan al-Basri's lifetime (d. AD 738). They also claimed that the Qur'an was created, was not part of the divine essence since the Qur'an can be comprehended by humans while God's essence is inaccessible to human reason, and that God's

attributes and names in the Qur'an were allegorical, i.e., references to God in the Qur'an were not real, such as God has hands and eyes as in Q.5:64 and Q.20:39 or that God is actually above His throne as in Q.7:54 and Q.20:5. For them, the essence of God was unitary, eternal, and unchanging. Their opponents, however, believed that the Qur'an was uncreated, part of the essence of God, and that God's attributes and names are not allegorical. In other words, they adopted a literal exegesis to God's references in the Qur'an. During the middle of the ninth century, al-Ash'ari Muslim scholars also claimed that the Qur'an was uncreated and also believed in the literal meanings of God's arrtibutes and names. For them, God's attributes are befitting to Him alone as we are told by Q.42:11 that there is nothing like unto Him. In Qur'anic studies, God's attributes are referred to as *ambiguous* (*mutashabihat*). Imam Malik (d. AD 790) held the view that all the anthropomorphic expressions of the Qur'an, i.e., God's references, must be believed *without questioning how*. This has been known in Arabic as (*bila kayf*). He stressed that the notion of rising above the throne as it occurs in Q.20:5 is not known, the how of it is not intelligible, asking about it is an innovation (*bid'a*), and to believe in it is a duty. Al-Tabari (d. AD 924) was particularly sensitive in refuting the Mu'tazila's rationalist interpretation of God's attributes. Other traditional Muslim scholars such as al-Zarkashi (AD 1344–91) and al-Suyuti (d. 1505) also emphasised that God's attributes had subtle definitions and sensitive theological semantic significations that were inaccessible to human comprehension. However, at the end of the ninth century, the Mu'tazila were accused of innovation.

In the middle of the thirteenth century, Ibn Taymiyya rejected both the

Mu'tazila's allegorical interpretation and the traditionalist's literal understanding of God's attributes. He highlighted the absolute unity of God and that God was reflected in His creation. Ibn Taymiyya argued for accepting the attributes of God without indulging into their underlying meanings.

During the middle of the nineteenth century, the notion of God's omnipotence and omniscience was stressed by Muhammad 'Abdu (1849–1905) who was influenced by Ibn Taymiyya. 'Abdu later on stressed *tawhid* from a socio-political perspective where he directed *tawhid* to religious pluralism, i.e., the unity of religion regardless of diversity. Similarly, Sayyid Qutb in the middle of the twentieth century also linked *tawhid* to politics and urged Arab and Muslim governments to adopt Islamic law.

As *tawhid* is the central message of the Qur'an, this notion reiterates several underlying meanings such as:

(i) abandoning the worship of any god except Allah as in Q.1:5, Q.2:22, Q.17:23;

(ii) putting one's trust in Allah only: a true monotheist firmly believes that his/her success or failure can be given only by Allah, that his/her supplication and personal request should be made only to Allah; this is expressed by Q.2:45, 165, Q.5:35, Q.27:62, Q.40:60, and Q.65:3.

(iii) intercession (*al-shafa'a*) on our behalf to God for a personal request is not allowed as it is reiterated by Q.6:51, 94, Q.17:56–7, and Q.82:19;

(iv) intercession between Allah and us can only be achieved by His permission as we are told by Q.2:255, 20:109, Q.21:28, and Q.53:26;

From socio-political and economic contexts, the ultimate Qur'anic message of *tawhid* is to emancipate people, eliminate inferiority to one another, and establish a positive bondage with their Creator. The notion of mankind emancipation and the direct link between the created and the Creator is interrelated to Q.49:13 which highlights the monotheistic message that the most noble of us in the sight of God is the most righteous, and to Q.65:3 which highlights the message that God is sufficient for anyone who puts his/her total trust in Him.

The reverse side of *tawhid* in the Qur'an is polytheism (*al-shirk*) which is the association of partners with God or the worship of others in addition to God. While *tawhid* stresses total reliance on God, polytheism refers to the belief that other human or non-human creatures can influence our life, have the power to make us prosperous or poor, have the power to make us live or die, and can do good or bad to us; these polytheistic beliefs are referred to by Q.39:38. There are three categories of polytheism:

(i) Major polytheism (*al-shirk al-akbar*) which is related to any act of worship that is directed to other than God such as idolatory. It represents a gross rebellion against the Lord and is a major sin. There are four aspects of major polytheism:

(a) polytheism of supplication (*shirk al-du'a'*) which is to invoke, supplicate or pray to other deities besides Allah;

(b) polytheism of intention (*shirk al-niyya*) which is to have the intention to worship not for the sake of Allah but for the sake of other deities;

(c) polytheism of obedience (*shirk al-ta'a*) which is to be obedient to the authority of others other than Allah;

(d) polytheism of love (*shirk al-mahabba*) which is to show your love to others other than Allah.

(ii) Minor polytheism (*al-shirk al-asghar*) refers to acts of worship or religious deeds just to gain praise, fame or wordly gains.

(iii) Covert polytheism (*al-shirk al-khafiyy*) refers to dissatisfaction with what one has been given by his/her Lord. It also applies to anyone who assumes that had he/she done this or that, he/she would have got what he/she aspired for.

References

Abdul-Raof (2003), al-Maqdisi (1995), al-Shaykh (1992), Sonn (1995).

HUSSEIN ABDUL-RAOF

AL-TAWHIDI, 'ALI B. MUHAMMAD B. AL-'ABBAS ABU HAYYAN

Abu Hayyan al-Tawhidi was born in 922 or AD 932. His birthplace is not certain and may have been in Nishapur, Shiraz or Iraq. He was a professional scribe, secretary and courtier. He received his education under the most famous philosophers who took part in the important literary salons of the day. However his criticism of many of his teachers and colleagues created many enemies who caused him much trouble later and were the reason for the pessimism of his writing.

Al-Tawhidi's most important work is his *Kitab al-Imta'* which reports the lessons and discussions at some important *majalis* (salons or meetings) of wazirs and scholars which took place in the Buyid period. He presented these reports as occurring on different nights and wrote about them in an informal and vivid style, not so much historical reports but as literary stories which

could be compared with the *Arabian Thousand and One Nights*. Beside the different reports, he also explored a number of philosophical and religious themes. This work is considered one of the main sources of the life and philosophy of his friends and colleagues such as Abu Sulayman al-Sijistani.

Al-Tawhidi probably became a Sufi and was accused of heresy because of his book, *The Spiritual Pilgrimage when Legislated Pilgrimage is Impossible*, which was written in Hallajian style. Massignon, considers him to have influenced the Sufi Abu 'l-Hasan al-Daylami (d. AD 1030).

Al-Tawhidi lived for many years but towards the end of his life he became very poor and suffered great hardship. He died in AD 1023 and was buried alongside the Sufi Shaykh al-Shirazi (d. AD 981).

References

Kraemer (1992).

MAHA EL-KAISY FRIEMUTH

TA'WIL

See: **Qur'an, allegorical interpretation of the**

TAWQ AL-HAMAMA

This is one of the best-known works of the Andalusian jurist, theologian and controversialist Abu Muhammad 'Ali b. Ahmad Ibn Hazm (AD 994–1064), among whose other works, and particularly the sober and polemical *Kitab al-Fisal fi 'l-Milal wa'l-Ahwa' wa'l-Nihal*, it sits rather uncomfortably. For it is a work dedicated to love, with few references to religion or disagreements over it.

Ibn Hazm points out a number of times in the *Tawq al-Hamama fi Ulfa wa'l-Ullaf*, (*The Collar of the Dove, on Love and Lovers*), that he wrote it while he was resident in Jativa. This would date it to about AD 1027, when he is known to have settled there after an eventful ten years in which he had served caliphs as vizier and also been imprisoned at least twice when they were overthrown. It is therefore a work of his thirties, when he had experienced love, as he candidly recounts at various points in the book, and was also old enough to reflect on its meaning.

The *Tawq*, which is technically a letter, consists of thirty chapters together with a preface. Here Ibn Hazm expresses his misgivings about the subject since 'it behoves us rather, considering the brief duration of our lives, not to expend them save upon those enterprises which we may hope will secure for us a spacious destination and a fair homecoming upon the morrow', though he is comforted to know that even the Prophet himself advised his followers to 'rest your souls from time to time'. And after this hint of moralising he is off, warning his readers that he will divulge confidences, some of them shameful, and insinuating that there is gossip and scandal in what follows, and he does not disappoint.

The book proper begins with a preliminary discourse on the nature of love, in which Ibn Hazm calls it 'a conjunction between scattered parts of souls that have become divided in this physical universe'. But rather than analysing its nature too minutely, he declares simply that 'love is in truth a baffling ailment, and its remedy is in strict accord with the degree to which it is treated, it is a delightful malady, a most desirable sickness'. And he moves on to map its progress.

The main body of the *Tawq* comprises chapters on the first stages of love, how people betray that they are in love, how they fall in love through descriptions, at first sight, after long association, and hints with the eyes, then chapters on the development of love, with its successes assisted by messengers and keeping secrets, and its failures caused by betraying secrets, listening to people who criticise the beloved, spies and slanderers, until the moment of vision, and then chapters on the disappearance of love, through breaking off, betrayal, separation, forgetting and death, and lastly two chapters on sinning and continence. The whole traces a virtual journey through the experience of love, from its first awakening through its mounting passion and then its decline and ceasing.

The enjoyment of the work derives from the means Ibn Hazm uses to depict this journey. Without abandoning his moral tone, he mixes ethical and occasional didactic maxims and exhortations with personal reminiscences and stories about his contemporaries and earlier lovers. Together, these afford a mixture of delightful indiscretions and pictures of medieval Andalusian customs. Thus, we are told about his own youthful passion for Nu'm, a slave-girl he owned in his teens, and about his preference for blondes because of an early love. We are introduced to Muhammad b. 'Amir, 'our dear friend', who never rested until he possessed any slave-girl he had seen, but having done so, 'love turned to revulsion, intimacy to aversion'. We hear of the young man who is hindered in his love-making by a spy who will not go away: 'If you could only have seen the young lover, and the mixture of evident despair and anger on his face, you would have witnessed a truly wonderful spectacle'. These are individuals whom the original readers would have known or enjoyed guessing at, but the truthfulness of their actions and sentiments lends them a timeless character and makes them recognisable to readers of all periods.

From time to time Ibn Hazm spices his discourse with stories that reach beyond entertaining gossip to the edge of salaciousness. There is the account from faraway Baghdad, told by 'a man naturally wise, intelligent and understanding', of a man who undressed on his wedding night to see his bride rush back home to her mother because 'she took fright at his virility'. There is the incident of the Mu'tazili scholar Ibrahim al-Nazzam 'for all his eminence in scholastic theology' composing a treatise in praise of the Trinity in order to have his way with a boy from a Christian household. These and other stories of adulterers and men pursuing one another give a deeper tinge to the *Tawq*, presenting the more varied forms that love takes and giving readers samples of the forbidden to heighten their titillation and indignation.

If, however, the *Tawq* provides smiles, sighs of sympathy and the odd gasp, it is essentially a book that upholds the morality of love. For it never sanctions unrestrained indulgence, and points towards the highest virtues of selfless dedication to the beloved. Written for an audience who did not need reminding of what is taught by Islam, it could introduce some of the very human realities that populate the boundaries of the faith and sometimes exceed them.

The *Tawq* is written in a heightened prose style and contains extensive extracts from the author's own poems, some composed for this work and others quoted from earlier pieces. It is an example of *adab* literature, intended to give pleasure as much through the form of its expression as its contents. It is the only example of this genre that is known from Ibn Hazm, and as such has been recognised as one of his major works and one of the finest written by an Andalusian Muslim. Many of its themes resemble those in the literature of courtly love that flourished in France and elsewhere in Europe in the century after it was written, causing some to

wonder about a line of influence, though no direct connection has been established. Ibn Hazm himself was quite probably inspired by the *Kitab al-Zahra* (*The Book of the Flower*), of Abu Bakr Muhammad Ibn Dawud al-Isfahani, whom he names, the son of the founder of the Zahiri law school of which he became an adherent.

The *Tawq al-hamama* has survived in a single manuscript, which is a cut down version of the original. This was first edited by Petrof (1914), and has been republished many times. The most readable translation is by Arberry (1953), from which the quotations above are taken.

DAVID THOMAS

AL-TAWRAT

The five books of Moses, of the Old Testament, accepted as divine revelation in Islam (e.g. Q.3:3). The Qur'an says the Jews both distorted these and used them poorly (e.g. Q.2:75, Q.3:78, Q.4:46, Q.5:14, Q.62:5).

See also: **al-Injil**; **al-Zabur**

ANDREW J. NEWMAN

TAYAMMUM

See: **ablution**

TA'ZIR

Ta'zir is a punishment intended to prevent the culprit from relapsing. Many crimes now punished as *ta'zir* were counted as sins in the Qur'an for which there was no specified punishment. The kind and amount of *ta'zir* is left to the discretion of the judge.

References

Izzi Dien (1997: 49, 138), Al-Zuhayli (1985: 6:18, 175).

MAWIL IZZI DIEN

TEHRAN

Located in the southern foothills of the Elburz mountains, Tehran is the capital and the largest city of Iran. It is situated 62 miles (100 kilometres) south of the Caspian Sea and north of the Central Plateau. It replaced Isfahan as the capital of Persia in AD 1788. The shrines of a number of Shi'i saints are to be found in and near the city. Close by the modern city is the old settlement of al-Rayy, which was the birthplace of 'the most original of all the Muslim physicians', Abu Bakr Muhammad ibn Zakariya' al-Razi (AD 865–925). In 1943, at the height of the Second World War, the city was the venue for the Conference attended by the leaders of the USA, the United Kingdom and the Soviet Union. One of the decisions taken there guaranteed the post-war independence of Iran. Under Mohammed Reza Shah Pahlevi (AD 1941–79) the city was modernised. The manufacture of textiles, carpets, and motor vehicles was increased. Petroleum products boosted the economy further. After the overthrow of the Shah in 1979, an Islamic republic was established. The spiritual leader of the revolution was the Shi'i Muslim Imam Ayatollah Khomeini (AD 1900–89).

References

Arberry (1953: 263–91), Browne (1921), Momen (1985: 246–56).

See also: **Isfahan**

EDWARD D. A. HULMES

THABIT IBN QURRA

Abu 'l-Hasan b. Zahrun al-Harrani, known as Thabit b. Qurra, mathematician, scientist and translator. He was born in Harran in AD 826 and was fluent in Syriac, Greek and Arabic. Originally a moneychanger in Harran, the turning point of his life was when he met some members of the famous scientific family Banu Musa in Harran. They recognised his intelligence and took him to Baghdad. There he received teaching in mathematics, astronomy and philosophy. He succeeded the Banu Musa as head of their school. He himself composed many works of astronomy and mathematics and translated many Greek works in these fields into Arabic. His real contribution was in the dispute between physical and mathematical astronomy, we possess about eight works on this theme written by Ibn Qurra. He also taught science to many important scholars of this period, one being his grandson the great mathematician Ibrahim b. Sinan. Thabit lived in Baghdad leading the scientific work in Banu Musa's school until his death in AD 901.

MAHA EL-KAISY FRIEMUTH

THAMUD

See: **'Ad and Thamud**

THEOLOGIA ARISTOTELIS

Kitab al-Uthulujiya, translated into Latin as *Theologia Aristotelis*, the so-called 'Theology of Aristotle' is in fact an Arabic paraphrastic epitome of Plotinus' *Enneads* IV–VI produced by the Nestorian translator 'Abd al-Masih b. 'Abdallah b. Na'ima al-Himsi (d. AD 835) for the circle of al-Kindi (d. AD 870) in Baghdad. This composition was part of the wider cultural translation movement that was both a politically and ideologically motivated strategy of appropriating the other envisioned by the 'Abbasid caliphate. There seem to be two recensions of the text: a standard or short version that has been edited and was the subject of commentary in the main Islamic philosophical traditions, and a longer version that is extant in Hebrew and seemed to have been appropriated by the early Isma'ili philosophers such as Abu Ya'qub al-Sijistani. The *Theology* is also part of a larger corpus of *Plotiniana Arabica* drawing upon the *Enneads* that includes fragmentary sayings attributed to the 'Greek Sage' (*al-Shaykh al-Yunani*) and an Epistle on Divine Science (*Risala fi'l-'Ilm al-Ilahi*).

The text purports to be a translation of a theological text of Aristotle with the commentary of Porphyry (d. AD 270) and certainly is a valuable expression of the Neoplatonic heritage of classical Islamic philosophy. The misattribution appealed to the taste of early Islamic philosophy that perpetuated the late antique Neoplatonic reconciliation of the philosophies of Plato and Aristotle and filled a perceived lacuna in the system of Aristotle that the Arabs inherited, providing doctrines about the nature of God and eschatology. Nevertheless, the text was adapted to suit the needs of its audience and was always more than a translation, incorporating material akin to Aristotelianism and even drawing upon pseudo-Dionysian doctrines on the 'profession of ignorance'. The *Theology* is divided into ten *mayamir* (sing. *mimar*), the Syriac Christian word for a chapter of a theological treatise. It is prefaced by a prologue that mentions the author, the translator, the editor (al-Kindi) and the patron (Ahmad the son of the Caliph al-Mu'tasim). It may have been modelled upon a text of Porphyry that sets out some of the key issues to be tackled in the text concerning the nature of the nature of the soul, its descent into the world of matter and its reversion to its principle. The *Theology* became the impetus for philosophical speculation and established some of the key features of Islamic Neoplatonism. Commentaries and glosses upon the text were written by Christian, Jewish and Muslim philosophers including Ibn Sina and 'Abd al-Latif al-Baghdadi (d. AD 1231) in the classical period and Qadi Sa'id Qummi (d. 1696) in the later Safavid period.

The doctrines of the *Theology* mainly concern the nature of the soul. The soul descends, like all other beings, from a causal chain of emanation that is produced by a purely good and loving principle, the One or the Creator (*al-Bari'*). It descends from a higher intelligible world to reside within a material body that is part of the sensible world. The cosmos is thus a natural and logical consequence of the One and not a volitional result of a theistic creator. Unlike the Aristotelian doctrine, the soul is not a perfection or entelechy of the body (although in at least one instance this view is approved) but is independent of the body as an eternal, immaterial substance capable of separating itself and ascending momentarily to experience the beatitude of its intelligible origin. This possibility is expressed in the famous 'doffing metaphor' of *Theology mimar* I (cf. *Enneads* IV.8.1). The soul alienated in this world desires to taste the freedom of its origins, transcending the material cage of this world and wishes to revert to its principle. Philosophers such as Suhrawardi and Sufis such as Ibn 'Arabi later cited this metaphor. Other doctrines and issues broached include time and creation, the nature of God and His agency, the nature of knowledge and the end of the soul.

References

Adamson (2002), Aouad (1989), Brague (1997: 365–87), D'Ancona (1999: 47–88, 2001a, 2001b), Endress (1997: 43–76), Genequand (1996: 103–13), Gutas (1998), Kraye *et al.* (1986), Langermann (1999: 247–59), Pines (1954: 7–20), Rizvi (2005), Rosenthal

(1952: 461–92, 22; 1953: 370–400, 24; 1955: 42–66), Rowson (1992: 478–84).

SAJJAD H. RIZVI

THRONE VERSE

Ayat al-kursi, Q.2:255, contains the image of God's throne which has become a central focus of devotion and speculation in Islam with regard to the nature of God.

> God! There is no god but He, the living, the self-subsisting, eternal. No slumber can seize Him nor sleep. His are all things in the heavens and on earth. Who is there can intercede in His presence except as He permits? He knows what is before or after or behind them. Nor shall they understand any of His knowledge except as He wills. His throne extends over the heavens and the earth, and He feels no fatigue in guarding and preserving them for He is the most high, the supreme.
> (A. Yusuf Ali translation, modified).

The verse is held to have protective value in that one's soul is entrusted to God. It is often written on amulets.

References

Yusuf Ali (1968: 102–3).

ANDREW RIPPIN

TIBB NABAWI

'Prophetic medicine', that tradition of healing and wellness in Islam derived from the Qur'an and the *sunna* of Muhammad which, in fact, encompassed aspects of Galenic medical theory and practice as well as 'traditional' theories of disease and their cures rooted in magic, the evil eye, as well as the intervention of both Allah and the *jinn*.

References

Savage-Smith (1996).

ANDREW J. NEWMAN

AL-TIBRIZI, WALI 'L-DIN IBN 'ABDALLAH (d. AD 1348)

Wali 'l-Din ibn 'Abdallah al-Tibrizi (d. AD 1348), compiler of *Mishkat al-Masabih*, a late reworking of the *hadith* collection of al-Baghawi (d. AD 1122), *Masabih al-Sunna*. Little is known of al-Tibrizi himself but his work was considered a significant improvement on its sources. Al-Tibrizi added 1,511 reports to the original compilation of al-Baghawi, raising the total from 4,434 to 5,945. He organised his text into twenty-nine books and a total of 327 chapters. Al-Baghawi's work is divided into two sections, the first having reports from al-Bukhari and Muslim, and the second from other sources. Al-Tibrizi added a third section to most of the chapters in al-Baghawi's work, recording additional reports from the works of al-Bukhari, Muslim and other sources which he deemed relevant to the topics. As well, al-Tibrizi identifies the sources from which the reports were taken, whereas al-Baghawi omitted the *isnad* altogether. The work attracted a good deal of attention through the centuries and became a standard textbook for *hadith* and jurisprudence. The book became a substitute for the larger collections of *hadith* and was popular among all strata of Muslim society. Many commentaries were written on it and it has been translated into Persian, Urdu and English.

References

Osman (2003).

ANDREW RIPPIN

TIHAMA

Coastal plain in southwest Saudi Arabia and Yemen, about 64 kilometres in width between mountain ranges and the Red Sea, divided into the Tihamat 'Asir and the Tihamat al-Yaman by international boundaries. Largely unproductive salt flats near the coast to 200 metred but the upper terraces are productive agriculture land in Saudi Arabia south of Haly. In parts of Hajjah, al-Hudaydah and Ta'izz provinces, Yamani Tihama (13,520 square kilometres) produces about half the country's agricultural output, with cultivation along seven *wadis* including Maur, Surdud, and Zabid. Salt is mined at as-Salif. Fishing is important from the Red Sea ports of al-Luhayyah, al-Hudaydah, al-Ghulay-figah and Mocha using *sambuk* (small boats). Though not strictly speaking part of al-Hijaz, it is often included in that region, with Makka called 'Tiha-miyya' and al-Madina 'half-Tihamiyya/half-Hijaziyya'. The Tihama has historical connections from pre-Islamic times with the East African coast and its history is linked with Abyssinia as well as al-Hijaz. For example, 'Ali b. Muhammad (r. AD 1047–67), the Fatimid *da'i* of the Sulayhid dynasty in Yemen, defeated the Abyssinian slave dynasty of the Najahids in the Tihama.

The main towns of the Tihama are Zabid, al-Makna, Bayt al-Faqih and al-Hudayda. Zabid was established in AD 820 by Muhammad ibn 'Abdallah ibn Zayad, founder of the Ziyadid dynasty that ruled southern Tihama from AD 819 to 1012, then by the Najahids. Ibn Zayad brought at-Taghlabi from Baghdad to found an Islamic university that had over 5,000 students in the Rasulid era (1229–1454), but it declined under Tahirid rule (1454–1526). Ahmad Abu Musa al-Jaladi, founded the al-Jabr algebraic system there. Islamic law, grammar, poetry, history, and mathematics were studied in 200 or more Qur'anic schools and 236 mosques. Only eighty-six mosques remain including the al-Asha'ir Mosque (the great mosque), the Iskandar mosque with a 60-metre-high minaret and the Turkish Mustafa Pasha mosque. Al-Makha in south Tihama was a prosperous coffee-exporting port in the 1500s, with its Zabidi-influenced architecture including the ash-Shadhli Mosque. Bayt al-Faqih, about 37 kilometres north of Zabid was a market centre for coffee from the early 1700s. The Ottoman Turks and Mamluk Egyptians ruled the Tihama from 1513 until 1636 when they were expelled by the Zaydis who ruled until the eighteenth century. The Tihama became part of Turkish Arabia from 1849 and in 1909 several north Tihama tribes under the leadership of Sayyid Muhammad al-Idrisi rebelled against Turkish rule until the Ottoman Turks finally withdrew in 1919. Yemen was then ruled by Zaydis under Imam Yahya ibn Muhammad (d. AD 1948) and Idrisi forces retreated to 'Asir in 1920. Al-Hudayda, an Ottoman fishing port, developed after 1934. Under Imam Ahmad Yahya (d. 1962) only 5 per cent of children were educated and then only in traditional Qur'anic schools and Legislation was determined by *shari'a* law until the 1960s.

References

Bosworth (1967: 74), Durrani (2001), Stone (1999).

JANET STARKEY

AL-TIJANI, AHMAD (d. 1815)

Ahmad al-Tijani was a Sufi from Morocco and founder of the Tijaniyya Sufi brotherhood. He demanded strict adherence to the spiritual master (himself) and denied his followers the right to affiliate with other Sufi orders. The disciples only required the spiritual master for access to the divine, and particular spiritual exercises were to no avail.

References

Abun-Nasr (1965).

LLOYD RIDGEON

TIJANIYYA

A Sufi order that has become popular in North and North-West Africa from the beginning of the nineteenth century. Like many other North African Sufi orders, the Tijaniyya actively opposed European imperialism, and recently the order has been successful in establishing mass followings in Senegal, Nigeria and Ghana.

References

Abun-Nasr (1965).

LLOYD RIDGEON

TILES

Glazed ceramic tilework is one of the most important forms of decoration in Islamic architecture especially in Iran, Turkey, central Asia and Morocco. It is first seen in lustre tiles of the ninth century which adorned the palace of Samarra and the *mihrab* of the Great Mosque at Qairouan in Tunisia, but the first period of real experimentation took place in Iran in the eleventh century where glazed turquoise bricks pick out mosaic designs in minarets and domes of mosques. Three main techniques evolved: mosaic, overglaze painting and more rarely underglaze painting, each with their own advantages. Mosaic tiles of turquoise, yellow, black and white in geometric designs and inscriptions covered mosque domes and minarets. Overglaze painting in blue, turquoise,

yellow, green, yellow, white and black was a rapid means of covering surfaces with panels of foliate motifs notably in the seventeenth-century Isfahan and nineteenth-century Tehran. Underglaze painting in an equally brilliant scheme was the chosen medium for the tiles which introduced colour to the grey stone mosques of Ottoman Istanbul. Morocco fully exploited the potential for geometric design in the mosaic technique.

References

Porter (1995), Scarce (1989: 271–94).

JENNIFER SCARCE

TILES, IZNIK

The major ceramic centre of Ottoman Turkey, which was based at Iznik since the fifteenth century, produced a range of polychrome wares of high aesthetic and technical quality both for the court and for export to Europe. From about 1550 onwards, however, the main product was tilework for the building projects of Suleyman I (1520–66). Tiles of a hard white ceramic paste were decorated in bright colours – blue, turquoise, red – under a transparent colourless glaze with fluent designs based on Arabic calligraphy, interlacing foliage, tulips, carnations and peony palmettes. Outstanding examples cover the interior of the mosque of Rustem Pasha of 1561 and frame the *mihrab* of the mosque of Sokullu Mehmet Pasha of 1571 both in Istanbul.

References

Atasoy and Raby (1989), Carswell (1998).

JENNIFER SCARCE

TIMBUKTU

A region of and a city in northern Mali in the Sahara created in 1977 and occupied by Tuareg and Fulbe, Arabs, Berbers, Soninke and Dyala merchants and scholars. Songhay is the dominant language, though Arabic is spoken. Salt is mined in Taoudenni and transported by camel to Timbuktu, 13 kilometred north of the Niger River, on the trans-Saharan caravan route to Morocco.

The city was founded as a seasonal camp by Tuareg nomads (*c.* AD 1100) and was part of the Mali empire when Ibn Battuta visited Timbuktu (AD 1353). Mansa Musa employed a Maliki scholar Abu Ishaq whom he met in Makka, to build the Great Mosque (Djingerey-ber) and a palace (Madugu), now lost. Timbuktu was a centre of Islamic culture (1400–1600), with Maghribi *'ulama'* and notable scholarly families. The Sankore mosque was the focus of learning. Moroccan merchants bought gold and slaves in exchange for salt, Venetian glass and horses. Tuareg dominated the city (1433) but remained desert nomads. In 1468 Sunni 'Ali, the Songhai ruler, conquered the city and disturbed the *'ulama'*. Muhammad I Askiya (r. AD 1493–1528), first of the Askiya dynasty that ruled the Songhay empire from 1493–1591, respected the *'ulama'* as his legal and moral advisors. Many Muslim intellectuals studied in Makka or Egypt and attracted students from a large area.

In 1591 Timbuktu was captured by the Sa'dian ruler of Morocco, Mawlay Ahmad al-Mansur (1578–1603), nicknamed 'Edh Dhahabi', who sought gold, slaves, ostrich feathers, ebony and rhino horn. His Sa'dian 'pashas' ruled the Western Sahara and Mauritania as part of a protectorate based in Timbuktu. In 1593 many scholars were arrested, killed or exiled to Marrakesh. Descendants of slaves taken by the Sa'dians to Morocco formed the Black Guard, that controlled Morocco under Mawlay Isma'il (d. 1727). Timbuktu went into decline, suffering famine and

droughts and attacked by Bambara, Fulbe and Tuareg. French troops captured the city in 1863 and ruled until Malian independence (1934). The French established a *madrasa* (1911) where Islamic sciences were taught in Arabic and restored some religious buildings. In 1960 Timbuktu became an administrative centre for the independent Republic of Mali. Drought and the Tuareg rebellion affected the region until 1996. Though there is still a tradition of Islamic scholarship and it has a library with over 6,000 Arabic manuscripts, Timbuktu survives mainly as a tourist attraction: its mud-brick mosques are studded with projecting palm beams and their minarets resemble truncated cones.

References

Conrad (1998: I, 318–19), Hunwick (1999), Saad (1983).

JANET STARKEY

TIME

The question of defining what time is has mainly been connected with the study of movement and change, since movement and change are the basis on which the existence of the material world is inferred. Time is, therefore, the measure of the movement and change, which are always taking place. Motion, change and time are three universal concepts that must happen simultaneously, because motion generates change and motion is measured by time. For the Muslim theologians, however, time is a finite concept because it is bound up with the creation of the world. Al-Ghazali argues against the philosophers who believed in the eternity of the world and as a consequence considered that time is infinite. For al-Ghazali, an act must have a beginning and an end which means that all actions must be finite, therefore time, which is the duration of an act, is also finite.

References

Al-Ghazali (1990: 81–9).

See also: **time and eternity**

MAHA EL-KAISY FRIEMUTH

TIME AND ETERNITY

Although the concept of eternity, for the Arab philosophers, refers to whatever is unchangeable and unmoveable they attributed eternity to time. The reason is that the philosophers, following Aristotle, considered the circular movement as an eternal act by the immoveable mover that has existed eternally. This consequently attributed eternity to 'time', which is the measure of motion. In their Neoplatonic concept of emanation, however, they explain that the world emanates from God in an infinite process. However, although the existence of the world is fully dependent on God's act of emanation, thus satisfying the Qur'anic criterion of creation, this creation–emanation process has happened over an infinite period of time. Consequently, time is a measure of an infinite process that is always happening and will never reach an end. In this way the Arab philosophers view time in its relationship to the metaphysical process of the existing of the world.

References

Leaman (1999: 26–33), Wolfson (1973).

MAHA EL-KAISY FRIEMUTH

TIMUR (TAMERLANE) (r. 1370–1405)

Called *Lang* 'the Lame', founder of the Timurid dynasty. Stemming from the Turkish Barlas tribe in central Asia, Timur never assumed the Turco-Mongol royal title of Khan but did style himself *güregen* 'royal son-in-law' from his marriage with a Chingizid princess. From his capital at Samarqand, which he adorned with monumental buildings, he took over what had been the Chaghatayid territories or *ulus* and embarked on an expansionist policy, which seemed consciously to aim at reconstituting the Mongol empire. There were campaigns into south Russia, against the Mamluks in Syria and into Muslim India, whilst, at his death, he was planning an attack on China. The vast empire that he assembled by military conquest and terror failed to survive his death, and his successors were local rulers in Khurasan and Transoxania.

References

Gibb and Bosworth (1960–2003), Forbes Manz (1989), Grousset (1970: 409–56), Roemer (1986: 42–97).

C. E. BOSWORTH

TIMURIDS (1370–1507)

These were the last great dynasty within Islam of Turkish steppe origin. The founder, Timur (Tamerlane), who had a tenuous connection with the old Mongol ruling house, built up his power in Transoxania, established his capital at Samarqand and made it the centre of a great military empire covering central Asia and the Iranian lands. His descendants settled down as local rulers in Transoxania and Khurasan, with their courts at Samarqand and Herat especially notable for literary and artistic splendour. The period also saw a considerable florescence of central Asian Sufism, which continued the older traditions of the Yasawi order and developed the new ones of the Naqshbandis, who were to be influential in central Asia, Muslim India and China, also notable under the later Timurids was a great increase in *waqf* endowments for central Asian shrines, madrasas, mosques and other charitable purposes.

References

Bosworth (1996: No. 144), Gibb and Bosworth (1960–2003), Grousset (1970: 409–65), Roemer (1986: 42–146).

C. E. BOSWORTH

AL-TIRMIDHI, ABU 'ISA MUHAMMAD IBN 'ISA (d. AD 892)

Abu 'Isa Muhammad ibn 'Isa al-Tirmidhi, one of the collectors of a traditional/recognised book of *hadith* who died in AD 892. Born in Mecca, he travelled widely through Khurasan, Iraq and the Hijaz in search of authentic traditions; he was a student of another prominent collector, al-Bukhari. His *al-Jami' al-Sahih* is considered the fourth most valuable book of the six collections (after al-Bukhari, Muslim and Abu Da'ud) and contains almost 4,000 traditions. He made a special effort to identify and assess every transmitter as fully as possible and expresses his opinion about many of the traditions that he includes in his work. He also provides comments about the legal implications of various traditions and how the jurists use them to support various points of law.

References

Siddiqi (1993: 64–7).

ANDREW RIPPIN

TRANSLATION MOVEMENT

The translation movement is usually considered to have flourished in the reign of the 'Abbasid caliph al-Ma'mun but its origins are much older. It can indeed, be connected with the older translation movement that aimed, as early as the fifth century, to present Greek works to Syriac scholars. Greek philosophy and the sciences were taught in Alexandria, Syria and Persia in centres such as Antioch, Harran and Edessa, and from AD 557 in Jundishapur. Harran and Jundishapur, in Persia, were the best-known Arab schools. They taught medicine, astronomy, natural sciences and also Greek philosophy. Many of the Greek sources were translated into Syriac and mostly were known to Arab translators only in their Syriac version.

Arabic translations of the many scientific treatises, especially medical and astronomical works, started probably as early as the end of the seventh century when Arabic became the official language of the Muslim empire instead of Syriac and Persian. Ibn al-Nadim in his *al-Fihrist* considers that the Umayyad prince Khalid b. Yazid (d. AD 704) should be credited with the title of initiator of Arabic translation. The early translations mainly touched on matters of practical concern to the Arabs, such as works of medicine, alchemy and astronomy. One of the earliest known translators of this period is the Iranian scholar 'Abdallah b. al-Muqaffa' (d. AD 757), who translated the fable of the Indian sage Bidpai *Kalila wa Dimna*. However, the translation movement began its greatest period in the reign of the second Abbasid Caliph al-Mansur, and his successors Harun al-Rashid and al-Ma'mun. Yahya Ibn al-Batriq, who lived during the reigns of al-Rashid and al-Ma'mun, is the first known translator of some of the philosophical works of

Aristotle and Plato. (For the later development of this movement see Hunayn b. Ishaq and Thabit b. Qurra.).

References

Fakhry (1983: 4–19).

MAHA EL-KAISY FRIEMUTH

TRANSMIGRATION

Metempsychosis, or reincarnation, the process by which the soul of a dead person is reborn in another. The practice is absolutely denied in Islam, as the life of an individual is the Allah-given opportunity for acknowledging one's created and ultimately contingent relationship with the Divine.

References

Momen (1985: 66).

ANDREW J. NEWMAN

TRIPOLI, LEBANON
(TARABULUS AL-SHAM)

Lebanese port and city on the north western Mediterranean coast. It lies on a peninsula that terminates at al-Mina – the harbour. It was founded in 700 BC as capital of a Phoenician federation, its name unknown. It then became Greek Tripolis of 'Syria' and was the seat of a bishopric. Its site was that of the present harbour. The town fell to the Arabs in AD 638 but was attacked several times by the Byzantines until the tenth century. It was used as the port for Damascus and was defended by troops from that city until it fell to the Fatimids. In the centre was built the great mosque. Under the Crusaders a county of Tripoli was created and the town itself fell to them in AD 1109. It held out as an important Christian base until taken by the Mamluks in AD 1289. Under the Ottomans it

was made chief town of a province but it declined in importance as the fortunes of Beirut, Sidon and Acre rose. In 1876 it entered the age of modernity when new roads and railways were constructed. After the creation of Greater Lebanon by the French Tripoli became a Lebanese port. It remained, however, rather separate from the rest of Lebanon still looking towards Damascus. By 1995 (after the Lebanese civil war) Tripoli had developed as the second economic city of the country, a rail and road centre and a base for oil refining.

References

Gulick (1967).

DEREK HOPWOOD

TRIPOLI, LIBYA
(TARABULUS AL-GHARB)

Capital of the Libyan Arab Jamahiriyya situated in the west of the country on the Mediterranean coast. The ancient city of Oea was established on the site by the Phoenicians in the seventh century BC and enlarged by the Greeks, Romans and Byzantines. The Arch of Marcus Aurelius still remains there from Roman times. It was a busy port that fell to the Arabs in AD 710 only after stiff resistance. It then had a chequered history of being ruled by numerous local North African dynasties, interrupted from 1145 to AD 1158 by a period of rule under the Normans of Sicily. The Almohad dynasty from Morocco occupied Tripoli in AD 1159 and integrated it into a unitary state in the Maghrib. Europeans appeared once more in the shape of Filippo Doria from Genoa but he quickly sold it to a local who recognised the sovereignty of the Marinid sultans. In AD 1398 the Hafsid sultan from Tunis occupied the town for over 100 years. Tripoli's close connection with Europe continued in 1510 with the conquest by the Spanish who in 1539 offered it the Knights of Malta. They rebuilt and enlarged the castle (still standing) but were too weak to resist the power of the Ottoman fleet in 1551. Tripoli became one of the bases of the corsairs (the Barbary pirates – notorious in European history). The local governors, some of whom were quasi-independent, permitted or encouraged piracy and kept European captives in the city. A local family of the Karamanlis seized power for over 100 years (1711–1835) and the corsairs were allowed free reign.

In 1835 the Ottomans were strong enough to reassert their authority and Tripoli became a *wilaya*. It was not until 1911 that they were again threatened by Europe when Italy invaded in a desperate search for colonies. Tripoli became capital of the Italian colony of Tripolitania. The city was rebuilt and expanded, garden suburbs, a modern port, and a large cathedral were built all to the south-west of the *madina*. After independence in 1951 (and after suffering in the Second World War) Tripoli became joint capital of Libya (together with Benghazi) and then sole capital after Qadhdhafi's revolution. It has expanded continuously and is now the country's largest city and port and leading commercial and manufacturing centre.

References

Ward (1969).

DEREK HOPWOOD

TUAREGS

The Tuaregs are members of a group of nomadic stock-breeding peoples who live in the West and central Sahara, the *sahil* (the North African littoral), Algeria, Burkina Faso, Libya, Mali, Niger, and Nigeria. In the Middle Ages they were the undisputed lords of the desert and the masters of the trans-Saharan caravan routes. In the fifteenth century they traded with Portuguese West Africa, controlling the transport of salt, gold and slaves. The French authorities eventually subdued their local power and influence. In 1917 they rose against the French, who were increasingly threatening their interests, but the uprising was quelled. In the ensuing struggle the numbers of Tuaregs were systematically reduced. Thousands fled to northern Nigeria. Their language, Tamashek, belongs to the Berber branch of the Hamito-Semitic family. They are predominantly Muslims. In earlier times, when the feudalistic structure of society allowed for nobles, vassals, and slaves, nobility passed through the mother's line, not the father's. The men shunned modern weapons of war, preferring to engage in individual combat with swords, daggers, and shields. They ruled with a harsh desert code of honour. Tuaregs have their own written language. Known as *tifinagh*, it is a non-cursive script, based upon an alphabet related to that used by the ancient Libyans. In the Middle Ages their culture was feudalistic, with nobles, vassals, and slaves.

Tuareg society is traditionally matriarchal. Tuareg women are determinedly independent. They wear a garment that covers the whole body. It is usually made up from material coloured indigo or black. It is light in the desert heat and keeps out driving sand. One end of it goes over the head and is thrown over the shoulder. A decorative weight keeps the head covering in place even in high winds. The weights may be made of iron, copper, brass or silver. The metal edges and wooden weights are elaborately designed. The indigo dye is pounded into the cloth with stones so as not to waste precious water. The pounding imparts a metallic sheen to the cloth. The dye rubs off on the skin of the wearer. The men wear dark blue robes, turbans, and veils, which have given rise to stories about 'the Blue Men of the Sahara'.

It is the Tuareg male who wears the face-veil as a symbol of adulthood. Only among close family members will he remove it. At mealtimes he raises the veil from his mouth. Veils are worn until they disintegrate. Tuareg nomads, their camels, goats, and other animals find shelter and sustenance in the mountains of the Sahara wherever there is a sufficient supply of water to produce vegetation. Today the glory of their past has disappeared and they exist in comparative poverty, although retaining their characteristic culture. Their traditional dwellings are hand-woven goatskin tents. In recent times some Tuareg have opted for an urban life, although drought and famine continue to make the choice a difficult one to sustain.

References

Fuchs (1956), Rennell (1926).

EDWARD D. A. HULMES

TUGHLUQIDS (1320–1412)

The Turco-Indian Tughluqids formed one of the component lines of the Delhi Sultans, who stabilised Muslim power in northern India, establishing there a distinctive style of Indo-Muslim architecture and a flourishing Persian and Turkish culture. They also gave enthusiastic patronage to the Sufi orders, adorning such shrines as the tomb of the Chishti founder at Ajmer, and, as strong Sunnis, cultivated links with the 'Abbasid caliphs. The most conspicuous ruler of the dynasty, Muhammad b. Tughluq, failed to retain conquests in the Deccan, and the line was fatally weakened by Timur's invasion of India in 1398–9, to be replaced by those of the Sayyids and the Lodis.

References

Bosworth (1996: No. 160), Gibb and Bosworth (1960–2003), Jackson (1999: 151–325).

C. E. BOSWORTH

TULUNIDS (AD 868–905)

This short-lived local line of Turkish governors of Egypt and Syria was the first there to achieve autonomy from Baghdad. The founder, Ahmad b. Tulun, inaugurated what was later regarded as golden age for Egypt, enlarging his capital Fustat, in the south of what is modern Cairo, by laying out a military quarter and constructing a famous mosque for the troops. But his weaker successors were unable to contain attacks from the radical Shi'ite Qaramita or Carmathians of the Syrian desert, and the 'Abbasids were able to re-assert direct control.

References

Bianquis (1998: 91–108), Bosworth (1996: No. 25), Gibb and Bosworth (1960–2003).

C. E. BOSWORTH

TUNIS

Capital of the Republic of Tunisia situated in the north east of the country on the lake of Tunis. Nearby Carthage was founded by the Phoenicians in the ninth century BC, Tunis by the Arabs at the end of the seventh century AD. It took its name from an older settlement called Tunes that perhaps dated from the beginning of the fourth century BC. It was destroyed at the end of the third

Punic war but was reborn under the Romans in 14 BC. It was the seat of a bishop but was always under the shadow of Carthage. The Arabs settled in Tunis rather than Carthage in AD 699 and built it up. It was part of the Umayyad and 'Abbasid empires and then fell under the Aghlabids who built the Great Mosque there – the Zaytuna – and the kasbah. It fell under the Zirids for a while and then the Banu Khurasan – a tribe from the east that built up the city walls. It became part of the North African empire of the Almohads in 1159 but flourished under the Hafsids for over three centuries, 1227–1574, who made it their capital. Many different industries were developed there and it became a flourishing intellectual centre. Although officially part of the Ottoman Empire from 1574, local military chiefs often seized power. One such founded the Husaynid dynasty that lasted until 1956. Many newcomers settled in Tunis including immigrants from Andalusia and Europe. In 1830 it was opened to wide European influence that culminated in the French occupation of 1881. The French in their colonial fashion built a new city alongside the old with modern buildings, wide straight streets and parks, a modern port and railways. The city has continued to expand since independence and is a large commercial and industrial centre.

References

Findlay (1986).

DEREK HOPWOOD

AL-TUSI, NASIR AL-DIN
(AD 1201–74)

Persian Shi'ite scholar, writing in Persian and Arabic. Al-Tusi's early career was spent as court astrologer to the Isma'ili Governor of Kuhistan and at the Isma'ili stronghold of Alamut. When the Mongol Hulagu sacked Alamut, he defected to the Mongols and accompanied Hulagu on his expedition to Baghdad. He subsequently served in various administrative capacities under Hulagu (AD 1256–65) and his successor Abaka (AD 1265–83), founding an observatory at Maragha in Azerbaijan.

Nasir al-Din's writings include works on astronomy, mathematics, ethics and philosophy. His most significant work is the *Akhlaq-i Nasiri*, a work on ethics divided into three parts, written in Persian for Naseroddin 'Abdorrahim b. Abi Mansur, the Governor of Kuhistan. This work, which builds on a previous work of Miskawayh known as the *Tahdhib al-Akhlaq*, has been generally considered to be among the most important works of its type in medieval Islam; among the diverse subjects covered are 'moral refinement', 'knowledge of policy and the administration of revenues', good manners, and the art of government and laws governing human relations.

Among al-Tusi's other works are: the *Tajrid al-Kalam*, an outline of Shi'ite philosophy, in Arabic; the Persian *Zije ilkhani*, astronomical tables drawn up for the Ilkhan Hulagu; the Persian *Bist bab dar astorlab*, on the astrolabe, and a commentary on Ibn Sina's *al-Isharat wa'l-Tanbihat*, in which he defended Ibn Sina against the criticisms of Fakhr al-Din al-Razi.

Despite al-Tusi's close links with the Isma'ilis, the precise nature of his beliefs has remained somewhat ambiguous: his best-known work, *Akhlaq-i Nasiri*, has two prefaces, the first lauding his Isma'ili patron, the second thanking a benevolent prince for rescuing him from the hands of 'these heretics'. Questions have also been raised about his behaviour during the Mongol incursions, when he is said to have betrayed his Isma'ili master to the Mongols, and even to have been instrumental in ensuring his death.

References

Fakhry (1991), Ragib (1953), Wickens (1964).

PAUL STARKEY

TWELVER IMAMS

See: 'Ali al-Hadi; 'Ali Al-Rida; Hasan Al-'Askari, Abu Muhammad Hasan ibn 'Ali; imam; Isma'ilism/Batinism (al Isma'iliyya/al-Batiniyya); Isma'il ibn Ja'far al Sadiq; Ithna'asharism (al-Ithna'ashariyya); Ja'far al-Sadiq; Muhammad al-Taqi; Musa al-Kazim (Abu'l-hasan Musa ibn Ja'far)

U

'UBAYDALLAH OR 'ABDALLAH B. HUSAYN AL-MAHDI (r. 909–34)

Founder of the Fatimid dynasty in North Africa, so that hostile Sunni and Twelver Shi'ite sources often referred to the line as 'Ubaydiyyun. His origins remain mysterious, and a genealogical connection with Isma'il, son of the Sixth Imam of the Twelver Shi'ites, Ja'far al-Sadiq, is unproven. He certainly made his way from Isma'ili circles in Syria to the Maghrib, where he started a separate Isma'ili da'wa or propagandist movement. Triumphing over the Aghlabids in Ifriqiya, he publicly assumed the titles of Mahdi and Commander of the Faithful, putting his movement in direct rivalry with the 'Abbasids, combatting local Kharijites and Maliki Sunnis of the Maghrib and the Byzantines in the Mediterranean basin. Founding a new capital, al-Mahdiyya, in Ifriqiya, he had by the time of his death set the Fatimids on a firm footing, ready to expand eastwards.

References

Dachraoui (1981: 115–60), Gibb and Bosworth (1960–2003).

C. E. Bosworth

UHUD, BATTLE OF

If the military victory of the Muslims against the Meccans at the Battle of Badr in AD 624 confirmed the Prophet Muhammad's temporal authority, the Battle of Uhud the following year questioned his leadership, the motivation of his troops and the discipline of his followers. In AD 625 the Meccans returned under Abu Sufyan to avenge the defeat suffered at Badr. They marched towards Medina and met Muhammad's army at the hill of Uhud. The battle started well for the Muslims, but at a critical moment large numbers of them deserted and returned to Medina. Others broke off from the fighting in search of booty. The Meccans rallied. The remaining Muslim troops were forced to withdraw. The Meccans won the day but, having suffered considerable losses, were unable to press home their advantage before returning to Mecca. The Prophet was wounded in battle, but he escaped with a remnant of his troops. His prestige suffered in consequence of this reverse. Neighbouring tribes were emboldened to challenge his authority, but he was successful in a series of subsequent campaigns against them. From the Battles of Badr and Uhud, the Islamic community learned that success is achieved by strict discipline and obedience to the Prophet and that defeat comes through indiscipline and the pursuit of individual interests.

References

Q.3:121–9, 8:1–19, 42–8, Watt (1956): 2–39

See also: **Badr, Battle of; al-Khandaq, Battle of; Khaybar;** *umma*

EDWARD D. A. HULMES

'ULAMA'

'Ulama' is the plural of *'alim*, 'scholar'. It is used as a title for Muslim doctors of theology or law. They form the theocratic element of the government and their *fatwas* or decisions regulate life.

MAWIL IZZI DIEN

References

Izzi Dien (2004: 167).

'UMAR B. 'ABD AL-'AZIZ B. MARWAN (AD 717–20)

'Umar II, a grandson of 'Umar b. al-Khattab and a man of great piety, asceticism, and humility, succeeded his cousin Sulayman b. 'Abd al-Malik as caliph of the Umayyad state. 'Umar's main focus was internal policy. Thus, as soon as he acceded to power, he put a stop to all the military campaigns currently taking place, including those on the eastern front and the siege of Constantinople, which had begun under Sulayman. 'Umar based his rule on the ideals of Islam, believing that Islamic ideology should be the uniting factor of the State rather than authoritarian might, and that all Muslims, both Arab and non-Arab, had equal rights and responsibilities. He also considered that it was only through the assimilation of the *mawali* (non-Arab converts to Islam) that there could emerge a single united community.

'Umar earned the reputation of being the best of the Umayyad caliphs, subsequent Muslim historians exempting him from the general opprobrium and impiety that they attach to the dynasty. Upon 'Umar's death, the office of caliph reverted to Sulayman b. 'Abd al-Malik's brother, Yazid.

References

Gibb (1955: 1–16), Hodgson (1974: 268–73), Kennedy (1996: 106–7), Shaban (1971: 130–5, 176–7), al-Tabari (1985–95: XXIV, 37–150 *passim*).

RONALD PAUL BUCKLEY

'UMAR IBN AL-KHATTAB

Born in Mecca *c.* AD 586 into the relatively uninfluential clan of the Bano 'Adi of the tribe of Quraysh. Possessed of great determination and singleness of mind, he was to be one of the greatest figures in the Islamic community in Medina. Some traditions claim that after the name of Muhammad, his is the greatest name in the early days of Islam. Many stories and legends have arisen about his life and achievements. Among them are those that describe his conversion from unbelief (and vigorous opposition to the mission of the Prophet

Muhammad) to acceptance of Islam. The extent and manner of his persecution of the first Muslims in Mecca have probably been exaggerated in order to show the measure of the change brought about by his conversion, which is generally believed to have taken place in the year AD 615. His change of heart is said to have occurred when he happened to overhear the recitation of some verses of the Qur'an in the house of his sister, Fatima. The simplicity and frugality of life he experienced when young was characteristic of his later life as well. Even after his succession to the caliphate he is said to have lived in the simple fashion of a Bedouin shaykh and to have continued to support himself by trading. He was an austere figure and a firm, even a fearsome, disciplinarian. Two stories illustrate this side of his character. The first tells of his decision to beat his son to death for immorality and drunkenness. The second records an occasion during his caliphate, when he struck a suppliant Bedouin in anger and thus broke ancient tribal custom. 'Umar quickly acknowledged the injustice of his action, repented and invited his victim to beat him instead. The Bedouin declined to do so. Tradition records 'Umar's unusual height, his physical strength and his baldness. He is reported to have taken part in the Battles of Badr and Uhud. In Medina his influence was advisory and personal. He was not appointed to any official position. During this period in Medina, he became a close associate of Abu Bakr. Tradition holds that their relationship was exemplary for its friendship, for the absence of personal rivalry between them, and for the lack of jealousy on either side. Both men became fathers-in-law to the Prophet. In AD 625, the Prophet Muhammad married 'Umar's daughter, Hafsa. A few years earlier, shortly before the *hijra*, Muhammad had married Abu

Bakr's six-year-old daughter, 'A'isha. On the death of Muhammad in AD 632, 'Umar insisted on the election of Abu Bakr as the first successor (*khalifa*) of the Prophet. Two names were put forward, those of 'Umar and Abu 'Ubayda. Pressed to enter his own claims to the succession, 'Umar is recorded as addressing Abu Bakr like this: 'While you still live? No, It is not for anyone to hold you back from the position in which the Messenger of God placed you. Stretch out your own hand'. At this 'Umar took Abu Bakr's hand and pledged allegiance to him. The incident may be legendary, in which case it cannot be cited as evidence that Muhammad ever designated anyone as his successor. On the death of Abu Bakr two years later, 'Umar became the second of the 'Rightly Guided Caliphs' (*rashidun*) and ruled with the support of most of the leading figures in Medina for the next ten years. Whether or not Abu Bakr actually designated 'Umar as his successor is open to question.

'Umar was the first caliph to use the title 'Commander of the Faithful' (*Amir al-Mu'minin*). He sent his armies to conduct successful campaigns that led to the expansion of Islam into Syria, the Fertile Crescent, Persia and Egypt, far beyond the borders of Arabia. For this he is recognised as the founder of the Islamic Empire. His concerns were not only for Islamic expansion and conquest, however. He also developed a system for administering the newly conquered territories which, as parts of the Islamic Empire, belonged henceforward to the Islamic community. He continued to organise the Islamic community under an elite, with himself as the unrivalled head. He appointed competent individuals to manage the developing trading commitments. He relied on proven military commanders such as Khalid ibn Walid, until the two quarrelled.

Khalid was then dismissed. He died in obscurity. The world that was opening up to Islamic influence was explicitly divided into the *dar al-Islam* ('the Abode of Islam') and the *dar al-harb* ('the Abode of War'). The distinction placed a continuing obligation on Muslims to 'strive to the utmost' (cf. *jahada*) 'in the way of God' (*fi sabil Allah*), in order to extend the borders of the *dar al-Islam* at the expense of the borders of the *dar al-harb*. Muslims everywhere were identified by their distinctive religious beliefs and obligations, by their dietary laws, by their abstinence from alcohol, by their loyalty to the supra-national Islamic community, and by their readiness to engage in *jihad*. In AD 637, the Caliph 'Umar decided to date the Islamic era from the *hijra*. The year 621/2 *Anno Domini* thus became the year 1 *Anno Hegirae*. 'Umar appointed six men, including his opponent, 'Ali ibn Abi Talib, as electors to a consultative board (*al-shura*), to decide who should be the next caliph. 'Umar insisted that his son was not to be considered for election. At this stage, leadership of the Islamic community was not to be by means of dynastic succession. 'Umar transformed a community with a local habitation (in Medina) with a name (Islam) into a significant force among the nations. He was admired for many personal qualities and achievements, but finally feared rather than loved. His achievements inevitably brought him detractors and enemies. Whilst still in his prime in AD 644, he was assassinated by a Persian slave (reputedly a Christian), who inflicted a fatal wound on him with a poisoned dagger. The third caliph, elected in the same year, was 'Uthman ibn 'Affan.

References

Hitti (1973: 175–78).

See also: **Abu Bakr; 'Ali ibn Abi Talib; calendar, Islamic;** *umma*; **'Uthman ibn 'Affan; wives of the Prophet**

EDWARD D. A. HULMES

UMAYYADS (661–750 AD.)

This was the first line of caliphs in Islam, descendants of a clan notable amongst the pre-Islamic merchant elite of Mecca who established their power in the capital Damascus. They despatched Muslim arms as far as Morocco and Spain in the west, central Asia in the north and Afghanistan and Sind in the east, so that under them, the caliphate acquired virtually its fullest extent, whilst warfare with the Byzantines involved two abortive attempts to capture Constantinople. In their time, the Muslim cult and Islamic doctrine were still fluid, and later, the circles of pious theologians and traditionists, especially those centred on Medina and the cities of Iraq, were to regard the Umayyads as secular kings rather than as divinely buttressed theocratic rulers, though in fact, the Umayyads seem to have been fully conscious of their responsibilities as heads of the community of the faithful and extenders of the borders of Islam. However, it is true that it was only under their supplanters and successors, the 'Abbasids, that Islam was to receive a firmer, more developed basis.

References

Bosworth (1996: No. 2), Gibb and Bosworth (1960–2003), Hawting (1986), Kennedy (1986: 50–81).

C. E. BOSWORTH

UMAYYADS OF SPAIN (AD 756–1031)

Muslim troops crossed from Morocco in AD 711 and overthrew the Visogothic monarchy in Spain, driving its remnants into the mountainous north of the Iberian peninsula and even raiding into western France. Members of the Umayyad family who had escaped slaughter by the 'Abbasids made their way to Spain and assumed power in what the Muslims came to call al-Andalus, building up a powerful state under the Amirs, who latterly styled themselves 'caliphs' in rivalry with the 'Abbasids. A flourishing Arabic literary culture grew up, with the capital Cordova rivalling in splendour Baghdad in the east, but in the eleventh century, for reasons which are still not yet clear, the Umayyad caliphate (as it had come to style itself, in rivalry with the 'Abbasids), collapsed, and Muslim Spain dissolved into a welter of petty city-states and princedoms.

References

Bosworth (1996: No.4), Gibb and Bosworth (1960–2003), Lévi-Provençal (1950–67), Makki (1992: 19–49).

See also: **Muluk al-Tawa'if**

C. E. BOSWORTH

UMMA

The Arabic word means 'community', 'nation', 'a people'—and specifically, the community of Islam. The opening words of Q.3:110 may be rendered in English as: 'You [that is, members of the *umma*] are the best of peoples to be raised up for mankind'. The community in question is not defined by race or ethnicity but by acceptance of the will of God as revealed in the Qur'an and by the exemplary life of the Prophet Muhammad. This means that membership of the Islamic community of the elect is not limited by nationalistic considerations. Acceptance of Islam is the criterion for membership, which

is, thus, open to all. In Sunni Islam, it is the *umma* that provides the consensus (*ijma'*) for the interpretation and the application of Islamic Law (*shari'a*).

References

Brown and Palmer (1987: 206–9), Hitti (1973: 173).

EDWARD D. A. HULMES

'UMRA

This is 'the Lesser Pilgrimage' to Mecca, which may be undertaken at any time of the year, as distinct from 'the Greater Pilgrimage', the *hajj*, which takes place annually at the prescribed time during the month of pilgrimage. The *'umra* may also be performed during the *hajj*. All the ceremonies associated with it are completed within a few hours in the precincts of the Grand Mosque in Mecca (*al-masjid al haram*). They may be performed by proxy for someone who is unable to do it personally. As with the *hajj*, the male pilgrim enters into a state of ritual purity and consecration (*ihram*) by exchanging normal dress for two pieces of unsewn woollen or linen white cloth, one wrapped around the lower part of the body and the other draped over the shoulders. Women wear simple white gowns, which leave their faces unveiled. The dress symbolises the equality of all before God, irrespective of their personal wealth and position. The dress is worn until the pilgrimage is completed. It is forbidden in the interim to have sexual intercourse, to hunt animals, to engage in disputation or to trim nails or hair. The *'umra* is performed in four consecutive ceremonies. First comes *al-tawaf*, the seven circumambulations of the *ka'ba* at the centre of the Grand Mosque's precincts. Prayers are said, involving two ritual 'bowings' (*raka'at*). Pilgrims then drink from the nearby well of Zamzam. Pilgrims then perform *al-sa'y*, hastening seven times between the hills of Safa and Marwa. The clipping of a lock of hair, a beard, or the shaving of the head completes the pilgrimage.

See also: **al-Hajj**

EDWARD D. A. HULMES

UNIVERSALS

Universals are concepts that have an abstract nature and, though they can be attributed to material beings, they are in themselves non-figurative. They can denote a certain power possessed by things – such as motion, duration or space – or a moral quality such as justice, goodness or evil. Plato discussed the nature of universal concepts in reference to the world of ideas. These ideas are, in his eyes, universal concepts such as goodness, justice, unity, etc., which he believed had a real existence (unlike the material world, which is illusory) and could influence the material world.

Aristotle, in contrast, considered these concepts to be part of the nature of things but without any separate existence outside the material thing or the intellect. Some of the Arab philosophers such as Ibn Sina tried to combine the two theories by explaining that universal concepts developed through three different stages. At the first stage they were part of the nature of God and of different intellects but combined with the existence of the material world, in the second stage, they were separated from the divine world and became a part of nature of each thing that they characterised. On the third level, they were drawn out of the things and became abstracted universal concepts through the power of the human intellect. Al-Ghazali in his concept of *ta'wil* used this theory of Ibn Sina and considered that the scriptural text has both a symbolic and a real interpretation. The real meaning of a text declares the ideas as they existed in the Divine Mind. In the second stage, they were expressed in the symbolic and figurative language of the scriptures. *Ta'wil* thus restores, in the third stage, the true meaning and unveiling of the divine origin of these universals.

References

Goodman (1992), Wolfson (1973: 143–52).

MAHA EL-KAISY FRIEMUTH

'UQUBA

Punishment or chastisement, a legal term for punishment which includes punishments of all kinds of crimes whether specified by the text or at the discretion of the magistrate.

MAWIL IZZI DIEN

'URF

A custom. Derives from the root that indicates knowledge. The Arabic term normally refers to the common 'known' daily practices of a social group and denotes both verbal and practical custom. Customary use of language may create ambiguities in certain contexts, such as the word *walad*, which can be used to indicate either a male or female child. However, it is customary to use the term in reference to boys. Custom is considered to be one of the sources of Islamic law and the implications of this can alter the concept and application of law within differing environments. For this reason, a variation in legislative practice can be observed from country to country.

References

Izzi Dien (1997: 46–49), Khallaf (1986: 89), Zaydan (1991: 257–8).

MAWIL IZZI DIEN

USUL AL-DIN

'The bases of the faith', the essential theological principles that form the bases for Islamic theological discourse.

References

Momen (1985: 175).

ANDREW J. NEWMAN

'UTHMAN IBN 'AFFAN

After the murder in AD 644 of the second Rightly Guided Caliph, 'Umar ibn al-Khattab, 'Uthman was elected to succeed him. He ruled as Caliph for the next twelve years with varying degrees of success in expanding and unifying the Islamic community. His election by the members of the consultative council (al-shura), appointed by 'Umar shortly before he died to decide on the succession, was probably a compromise. Other candidates, including one of the electors, 'Ali ibn Abi Talib, had greater claims to the caliphate, but it was the outsider, 'Uthman, who was finally chosen. It was a classic case of the success of an apparent also-ran, after the main candidates had failed to agree about the election of one of their own number. Born c. AD 574, 'Uthman belonged to the Umayyad family, the members of which occupied prominent positions in Meccan society. Unlike 'Umar, whose social origins were humble, and whose private means were modest, 'Uthman was a member of the Meccan aristocracy and a wealthy merchant with a lifestyle to match. He was renowned for his elegance and for the fastidiousness of his personal habits.

His reputation, as a man who disliked armed conflict and who avoided it whenever possible, is probably based on little more than the malice of his enemies. He, like other members of his family, had at first opposed the Prophet Muhammad's mission, but several years before the hijra he converted to Islam. In doing so, he was the first prominent Meccan to become a Muslim. No doubt Muhammad welcomed the conversion at a time when converts to Islam in Mecca were mostly from the poorer classes, and when the embryonic Islamic community was experiencing vilification and persecution at the hands of 'Uthman's more privileged pagan kinsmen. 'Uthman's marriage to one of Muhammad's daughters, Ruqayya, may have led to his change of heart. After her death, he married another of the Prophet's daughters, Umm Kulthum. He is reported to have been among the number of Muslims in Mecca who took refuge in Abyssinia. He is said to have joined the Muhajirun in Medina at a later date. In the event, 'Uthman, whose temperament and talents were different from those of 'Umar, continued the policies established by his predecessor. He went ahead with the centralisation of administration in the caliphate, although his approach to leadership was less energetic and decisive than 'Umar's had been. The appointment of members of his own family to important posts in the Islamic Empire, including provincial governorships, offended those who sensed nepotism and were suspicious of a resurgence of Meccan power. There were to be further military campaigns during 'Uthman's caliphate, which were designed to add conquered territory to the empire. In economic terms, however, they were subject to the law of diminishing returns. The cost of these ventures was not always covered by the amount of booty seized, or by the sums of money exacted in tax, not least because many of those appointed to positions of authority diverted the spoils of war into their own coffers. Neither the soldiers (who had once been officially allotted a share in these perquisites) nor the central government (which was entitled to the rest) were happy with this state of affairs, but 'Uthman was incapable of using his authority as Caliph to control what was happening. Compliant rather than indolent or lacking in initiative, he lived to supervise a period of efficient government during the first years of his caliphate, but the final years were marked by intrigue, dissension and open rebellion. Another apparently unrelated matter contributed to his growing unpopularity. The revelations of the Qur'an, first received by the Prophet Muhammad, had been written down by those who heard them on whatever materials were available. No further revelations were to come after the Prophet died. It was time to review these miscellaneous collections and to produce an officially authorised version of the Holy Book of Islam, one that would end disagreements about the text and be used throughout the empire. The aim was well intentioned, but many outside the narrow circle of centralised authority saw it as provocative. It seemed to them as if the Caliph had taken a unilateral decision to impose a standardised text of the title deeds of Islam on all Muslims, thus offending local susceptibilities and already-established preferences. The process of collecting the scattered fragments of the revelations had begun under the first two caliphs, Abu Bakr and 'Umar. 'Umar had bequeathed a collection of *suhuf* ('written pages') to his daughter Hafsa, the Prophet's widow. These pages were handed on to 'Uthman, who was aware that incomplete collections

of the Qur'anic revelations were to be found in different parts of the empire. 'Uthman thus inherited the task of producing a scripture that would materially help to preserve the unity of the Islamic community. Arguments had begun to arise about variant readings of the text, about the arrangement of the individual *suras,* and about the kind of script in which an accurately pointed text would be able to eliminate, or at least reduce, uncertainty in interpreting what was intended to be unambiguous. In an effort to end these disputes and to avoid the kind of disagreements about sacred texts that divided Jews and Christians, 'Uthman appointed a special commission to complete the task he had inherited, using the fragments originally brought together by the Prophet Muhammad' s secretary, Zayd ibn Thabit of Medina. Copies of the newly produced final text kept in Medina were made. They were sent to Mecca, to Damascus, to Hums, to Kufa, to Basra and no doubt to other centres of Islamic importance. All other copies of the revelations were to be destroyed. This action was taken as proof of 'Uthman's high-handedness. It may only have been a contributory factor in deciding 'Uthman's fate, however. Dissent was growing. Revolts subsequently broke out in Mesopotamia and Egypt. In CE 656, a group of dissidents besieged 'Uthman's house in Medina. They eventually broke in and one of them (Muhammad, the son of the first caliph Abu Bakr) struck him down whilst he was reading a copy of the Qur'an. It is reported that 'Uthman's blood stained the page on which the words of Q.2:131 appear. His assassination in CE 656, the first of a caliph at the hands of a fellow Muslim, led to serious political and religious disagreements within the Islamic community, which eventually caused the lasting rift between Shi'i and Sunni Muslims following the assassination of his immediate successor, 'Ali.

References

Hitti (1973: 176–77), Hourani (1991: 25, 31, 60), Momen (1985: 21–22).

See also: **Abu Bakr al-Siddiq; 'Ali ibn Abi Talib;** *umma*; **'Umar ibn al-Khattab; wives of the Prophet**

EDWARD D. A. HULMES

V

VEILING OF WOMEN

See: *burqu'*; *hijab*

WAHB IBN MUNABBIH

Wahb ibn Munabbih (AD 654–c. AD 730), a Yemeni, probably of Persian and possibly Jewish descent, who served as a judge in San'a. Considerable controversy has surrounded his background and biography, including the story of his conversion to Islam. There are also enigmatic references to his having held Qadarite views. However, a large number of works are attributed to him by later scholars and historians, and he is frequently quoted by later writers, including Ibn Hisham and al-Tabari, as a source of information on pre-Islamic Arabia and on Jewish and Christian tradition. As such, he is responsible for many of the fabulous *Awa'il* which Islamic chroniclers commonly prefixed to their historical chronicles. His references to the Prophet and his companions, which now exist only in papyrus fragments, are a blend of truth and legend that have been interpreted as perhaps the earliest *sira* compilation of all; many of Wahb's stories, which frequently included mir-

aculous elements, were incorporated into later *sira*s, including that of Ibn Ishaq.

A number of other titles are also attributed to Wahb ibn Munabbih by later writers, of which only fragments are now extant: they include *Kitab al-Mubtada' wa-Qisas al-Anbiya'*, *Kitab al-Isra'ilyyat*, *Zabur* (or *Mazamir*) *Dawud*, *Maghazi Rasul Allah*, *Kitab al-Qadar*, and *Tafsir Wahb*.

Medieval Islamic scholars were divided in their opinion on Wahb ibn Munabbih's reliability. He certainly misquoted biblical verses, but in the absence of any complete texts, the accuracy of the more general information provided in his works is difficult to evaluate with any certainty. He remains, in any event, an important source, linking the Judaeo-Christian and pre-Islamic Yemenite traditions with the early development of mainstream Islamic scholarship.

References

Khoury (1972).

PAUL STARKEY

WAHDAT AL-SHUHUD

This is an early term that is used to explain the mystical experience of the union of everything with the divine. The first Muslim thinkers who talked about the possibility of union with the divine were al-Bistami and al-Hallaj. This experience of union is attained after a period of the total annihilation of oneself, when the Sufi saint experiences God as the only existent being. According to al-Ghazali in his work *Mishkat al-Anwar,* the Sufi will experience the world, which is also called *'alam al-shuhud* or *al-shahid*, as a shadow and a reflection of God and therefore is experienced as an illusion. This experience is also known as *tawhid,* meaning the unity of God that includes the whole world. Real existence is only the existence of God. This Sufi experience was the first sign of the pantheistic tendency of Islamic Gnostic mysticism. This tendency was developed by later philosophers such as Ibn al-'Arabi, in his concept of unity of existence, *wahdat al-wujud.* This latter concept, however, confirms the real existence of the divine in all things in the world and therefore differs from the *wahdat al-shuhud*, which is a consequence of the Sufi experience of union.

References

Al-Ghazali (1952), Schimmel (1975).

MAHA EL-KAISY FRIEMUTH

WAHHABISM

'Wahhabism' (Wahhabiyya) is the name routinely given to the eighteenth-century movement of Islamic revival that first emerged on the Arabian frontier of the Ottoman Empire. In the early twentieth century, it became the religious ideology that legitimated the ultraconservative 'Islamic' monarchy of Saudi Arabia.

However, since the events of '9/11' especially, Western public discourse has come to identify 'Wahhabism' with any attempt to combine religious 'purification' with violent *jihad.* As Esposito suggests, such a tendency obscures the significance of other, more contemporary, influences on Islamic revolutionaries. It also elides the important differences between groupings. Moreover, the appellation 'Wahhabi' has often been used polemically by opponents in order to de-legitimate adherents as deviant extremists. For their part, the adherents of 'Wahhabism' are likely to refer to themselves as *muwahhidun* (Unitarians), or, as increasingly, and problematically, seems the case, *salafiyya* (those who follow the paradigm of the generation after Muhammad).

Muhammad Ibn 'Abd al-Wahhab (1703–92), the eponymous founder of 'Wahhabism', was born in the small settlement of 'Uyaina, in the region of Najd. Raised in a family of Hanbali scholars, he was also a follower of the Sufi path, and as a youth had no objections to the common practice of *ziyara* ('visitation' at the tombs of saints). However, after a period of study in Medina, Ibn 'Abd al-Wahhab became aware of reformist trends in Sufism although, ultimately, he would go much further than his teachers in denying that mysticism had any value whatsoever. On leaving Medina, Ibn 'Abd al-Wahhab continued to study, travelling widely outside Arabia to modern-day Iraq and Iran. It is in Qumm that he is said to have become a determined follower of Hanbali literalism.

On returning to his homeland, Ibn 'Abd al-Wahhab began to preach the doctrines set out in his *Kitab al-Tawhid* (Book of Unity). His mission was to purge Arabia of the various 'innovations' (*bid'a*) which he maintained had compromised God's absolute oneness, uniqueness and sovereignty, in effect returning the peninsula to a state of polytheistic *jahiliyya* (pre-Islamic 'ignorance'). Under the influence of popular Sufism, Muslims were said to make intercession (*tawassul*) to the Prophet and the saints, as well as venerating shrines and even trees and stones. For Ibn 'Abd al-Wahhab, only that given sanction in the Qur'an, *hadith* or by the first generation of Islam, the pious ancestors (*al-salaf al-salih*), could be considered authentically 'Islamic'.

Wahhabism, then, is an expression of the Hanbali *madhhab* (school of law), as interpreted by Ibn Taymiyya (d. 1328) and others. There is a stress on *hadith* rather than *fiqh* (jurisprudence). *Taqlid* (imitation) of the medieval law schools – including the Hanbali school – was rejected in cases where a ruling could not be squared with the fundamental sources of Islam. In the last resort, there could be reference to the *ijma'* (consensus) of scholars in the first three centuries only, anything not found in these sources was considered *bid'a*. Moreover, there was no notion of *bid'a hasana* (a 'good' innovation) such as the celebration of *mawlid al-nabi* (the Prophet's birthday), which was rejected outright. Ibn 'Abd al-Wahhab also rejected the idea that the 'gates of *ijtihad*' (reinterpretation) were closed. Voll considers that, initially at least, Wahhabism made it an obligation on believers to think for themselves rather than blindly accept the words of others. Indeed, given his overall methodology, Rahman sees Ibn 'Abd al-Wahhab's support for *ijtihad* in matters not covered directly by the key texts as rather ironic. The literalist position on the Qur'an and *sunna*, which marginalised *qiyas* (analogy) in favour of *ijtihad*, ultimately opened the door for more liberalising forces to interpret texts more freely than the medieval jurists.

Despite some success, Ibn 'Abd al-Wahhab attracted much criticism in his homeland and eventually left the area as a result of feuding. Indeed, his interpretation of Islam would have had very little effect without the backing of chieftain Muhammad Ibn Sa'ud. In the village of Dar'iyya, near modern Riyad, Ibn Sa'ud accepted the reformer's doctrines and undertook to defend and propagate them. All the time expanding his political control and legitimacy amongst the tribes, he was able to claim that he was recreating the Islam of the seventh century. Like the Khawarij of early Islamic history, the Wahhabis saw themselves as the only 'true' believers. *Shirk* (polytheism) exposed Muslims to the charge of *takfir* (unbelief) and the Wahhabis believed that unbelievers and idolaters should be fought and killed in the name of Islam. This was the beginning of Wahhabism as an activist social and political movement. However, as Rahman argues, while both the Wahhabis and the Khawarij intended to unify the Muslim community, they actually took up arms against the *umma* and created divisions within it. Nevertheless, as Sirriyeh maintains, while Ibn 'Abd al-Wahhab is routinely seen as being especially severe in his interpretation of Islam, many of his concerns (including *jihad*) were held in common with Sufi reformers of the nineteenth century. One important difference, however, was that Ibn 'Abd al-Wahhab was quickly able to implement his vision.

In 1773, the Wahhabi movement took Riyad after a war of twenty-eight years and made it the movement's capital. In 1801, Karbala' was invaded and Shi'ite Muslims were attacked while the tomb of al-Hasan, grandson of the Prophet, was sacked. In 1803, Wahhabi iconoclasm spread to Mecca where the graves of the *sahaba* were destroyed. Medina was taken in 1804 and Mecca in 1806.

Thereafter, Wahhabi raiders advanced beyond the bounds of Arabia, uniting many diverse tribes that would conquer most of the peninsula by 1811. Some have seen a proto-Arab nationalism in the movement. However, Wahhabi expansionism was eventually checked by Muhammad 'Ali, Pasha of Egypt, who forced their surrender to a weakening Ottoman Empire in 1818.

During most of the nineteenth century, the Wahhabis were simply a small tribal principality in the interior of Arabia. However, a second phase of political prominence began in 1902 under 'Abd al-Aziz Ibn Sa'ud with the assistance of the so-called Ikhwan (brotherhood). These zealous Bedouin tribesmen emigrated to newly Islamised agricultural settlements from which they sought to make converts to Wahhabism by force. During the 1920s, 'Abd al-Aziz became first the sultan of Najd and then proclaimed his guardianship of the holy places. However, he was more pragmatic than his fervent Ikhwani supporters and, when Medina fell in 1925, he prevented them from destroying the tomb of the Prophet. The Kingdom of Saudi Arabia was proclaimed in 1932 and, while Hanbali *fiqh* has pride of place, the country is very much a monarchy and not a theocracy. 'Abd al-Aziz was certainly criticised by the Ikhwan for allowing 'un-Islamic' inventions such as cars, telephones and radios in the kingdom. However, during the twentieth century, 'flexibility' in Hanbali religious interpretation has allowed the rulers of the Saudi state to 'modernise' with a minimum of opposition from the Wahhabi *'ulama'*. As Mortimer suggests, Wahhabism today is a religious ideology that selectively sanctions both the removal of bars to development and the promotion of bars to democracy.

Oil was discovered in Saudi Arabia in 1938, and since the increase in oil revenues in the 1970s especially, both the Saudi Government and wealthy businessmen have sought to export Wahhabism on a global scale in the shape of aid, mosques, libraries, publications and scholars. Islamic revivalist movements, from the Muslim Brethren in the Middle East to the Jama'at-i Islami of south Asia, but also the Arab Afghan *mujahidin*, have benefited from their largesse. However, in Mecca during 1979, armed Islamic activists captured al-Masjid al-Haram, using the siege to publicly accuse the Saudi royal family of corruption and a hypocritical betrayal of 'Wahhabi' ideology. A decade later, during the Gulf War of 1991, the Saudi rulers were also criticised for allowing non-Muslim forces to defend the kingdom when Iraq invaded Kuwait. Foremost amongst the critics was veteran of the Arab–Afghan *jihad* in the 1980s, Usama Bin Ladin. However, as Esposito maintains, the challenge of understanding contemporary Wahhabism is to distinguish between an ultra-conservative theology on the one hand and militant extremism on the other. This problem is reinforced by the current tendency of authoritarian governments around the world to label any religiously based opposition as Wahhabi and so justify their repression with impunity.

References

Algar (2002), Esposito (2002), Mortimer (1982), Rahman (1979), Sirriyeh (1999), Voll (1994).

See also: **Muslim World League**

SEÁN MCLOUGHLIN

WAHY (REVELATION)

Wahy is a special instance of God's speech in the Qur'an by which there is communication of knowledge about the unseen world. In the Qur'an, *wahy* frequently means a communication, without linguistic formulation and without an intermediary, which conveys the will of God, as in Q.7:117, 'And we revealed (*awhayna*) to Moses: "Cast thy staff". And lo, it forthwith swallowed up their lying invention'. On other occasions, it suggests the speech of God to be shared as a message, as in Q.18:27, 'Recite what has been revealed [*uhiya*] to thee of the book of thy Lord'. Prophets are not the only recipients of this *wahy*: a bee (Q.16:68) and heaven and earth (Q.41:12) are also spoken of. Nor is God the only source of *wahy*: the genies and the satans who lurk among humans also inspire via *wahy,* as in Q.6:121, 'The Satans inspire (*yuhuna*) their friends to dispute with you, if you obey them, you are idolaters'. But it is *wahy* that inspires the prophets, as in Q.4:163, 'We have revealed (*awhayna*) to thee as We revealed to Noah and the prophets after him, and we revealed to Abraham, Ishmael, Isaac, Jacob, and the Tribes, Jesus and Job, Jonah and Aaron, and Solomon, and we gave (*atayna*) to David Psalms'. Q.42:7 speaks of an Arabic Qur'an as the final product of this revelation, 'And so we have revealed to you an Arabic Qur'an'. In this usage, the word may be seen to be functionally equivalent to *tanzil*, the word frequently used with the image of a literal 'bringing down' of a message.

In dealing with *wahy*, it has been common for scholars to resort to ideas of historical development in Muhammad's thought, with 'internal' inspiration being early, reflecting ideas native to the Arabs, and 'external' revelation being later, physical scriptural notion. This is tied into Muhammad's relationship to his contemporaries, especially the poets, such that a separation is seen between a notion of internal 'inspiration', which is similar to that claimed by the pre-Islamic Arabian poets, and a revelation from outside, which is seen to emerge later in Muhammad's career as the distinction between himself and poets became clearer to him.

Fundamentally, the Qur'an shares in a Near Eastern value of inspiration, but it was one that became transformed through the history of Islam out of the desire to protect Muhammad (and the Arabic language) from contemporary and necessarily secular (since prophecy had ceased) ideals of 'inspiration'.

References

Jeffery (1952).

ANDREW RIPPIN

WALI

In ordinary use, it can mean protector, benefactor, companion or friend. In a religious connection the equivalent would be 'saint'. A person meriting this title is thought to be free from passion, to have influence with God, and to be able to work miracles. If the word was put in a genitive form with *amr*, it designates the ruler who is in charge of the government *Wali al-Amr*.

MAWIL IZZI DIEN

AL-WALID B. 'ABD AL-MALIK (AD 705–15)

al-Walid I was the first of four sons of the Marwanid (Umayyad) caliph 'Abd al-Malik b. Marwan (r. AD 685–705) to accede to the caliphate. Due to the efforts of his father and the redoubtable governor al-Hajjaj b. Yusuf, the state was well established and largely stable. Al-Walid's ten-year period in office was more or less a continuation of his father's, and he continued the process of the Arabicisation of the administration that 'Abd al-Malik had begun. Al-Walid was the greatest of the Umayyad builders and inaugurated an extensive programme of construction, erecting numerous magnificent mosques in addition to building roads, schools and hospitals. His reign was, however, most notable for the further expansion of the Islamic empire, which saw the geographical boundaries of the Marwanid state attain their greatest extent. Al-Walid's designation of his brother Sulayman as his successor was accepted without opposition.

References

Hitti (1970: 206, 217, 221), Hodgson (1974: 223–6), Shaban (1971: 117–19), al-Tabari (1985–95: XXIII, 109–228 *passim*).

RONALD PAUL BUCKLEY

AL-WALID B. YAZID
(AD 743–4)

al-Walid II was the nephew and heir of Hisham b. 'Abd al-Malik to the Marwanid (Umayyad) caliphate, possibly as a result of a pre-arrangement made by al-Walid's father Yazid b. 'Abd al-Malik. During his brief reign, he proved to be an ineffectual and negligent ruler and later Muslim historians refer to his dissolution and debauchery. Al-Walid was eventually murdered during a *coup d'état* orchestrated by generals of the Syrian army with the support of members of the Marwanid family. He was replaced by Yazid b. al-Walid, a son of al-Walid b. 'Abd al-Malik. The consequences for the ruling dynasty were more serious than the murder of the caliph, however, since it exposed serious divisions within the Marwanid family in addition to signalling the loss of support of the Syrian army, both of them pillars of the regime.

References

Kennedy (1996: 112–13), Muir (1915: 403–5), Shaban (1971: 153–5), al-Tabari (1985–95: XXVI, 51–271 *passim*).

RONALD PAUL BUCKLEY

WAQF

See: **alms-giving**

AL-WAQIDI, MUHAMMAD IBN 'UMAR (AD 797–874)

Muhammad ibn 'Umar al-Waqidi was a biographer of the Prophet Muhammad, whose chronological treatment of Muhammad's career is considered by many to be second in importance only to the *Sira* of Ibn Ishaq that has come down in the recension of Ibn Hisham. The contribution made by al-Waqidi to the criticism of the traditionists, as well as the collections of the traditions about the Prophet, has earned him recognition as a pioneer in the study of 'the men of distinction' (*'ilm al-rijal*).

See also: **al-Maghazi**; **Sirat Rasul Allah**; **al-tabi'un**

EDWARD D. A. HULMES

WARAQA IBN-NAWFAL

In Pre-Islamic Arabia, religious belief and worship were focused on a multiplicity of local gods and goddesses. There is evidence that some Jews and some Christians were to be found in the towns of the region, but the prevailing religion among the scattered tribes of Arabia was polytheistic. By the time the Prophet Muhammad was born in the second half of the sixth century AD, a different kind of spirituality had already emerged. It was not institutionalised into any organised religion. It attracted individuals who professed belief in a vaguely defined monotheism. They became known as *hunafa'* (sing. *hanif*). Waraqa ibn-Nawfal, a cousin of the Prophet's first wife, Khadija, was reputed to be among their number, although some traditions describe him as a Christian. His monotheistic ideas may have influenced those of Muhammad.

References

Hitti (1973: 108, 113).

See also: **Bahira;** *hanif*

EDWARD D. A. HULMES

WASIL IBN 'ATA' (AD 699–748)

One of the leading early figures of the important school of Islamic theology, the Mu'tazila. He was born in Medina and from there migrated to the Iraqi town of Basra, where he became a member of the circle of Hasan al-Basri, whose sermons addressed the whole range of aspects of piety, political, theological and spiritual. In his own thinking, Wasil subscribed to the view that God's attributes should be understood metaphorically rather than literally, that human beings have genuine free will, that a grave sinner was neither a believer nor an unbeliever (the so-called 'intermediate position' on this question) and that in the first civil war in the Islamic community, one of the protagonists was in the wrong, but Wasil refused to make a categorical statement concerning which one it was. These views were taken up and developed further by later members of the Mu'tazila.

References

Caspar (1998: Chapter 7), Watt (1973: Chapters 7 and 8).

HUGH GODDARD

AL-WATHIQ, HARUN B. AL-MU'TASIM, ABU JA'FAR (AD 842–7)

al-Wathiq succeeded his father al-Mu'tasim as 'Abbasid caliph in Iraq. Muslim historians have little to say about his activities, but al-Wathiq seems generally to have maintained the policies of his father, including the Mu'tazilite *mihna* ('inquisition'). The Turkish ruling elite that had surrounded al-Mu'tasim was similarly left largely intact. After a rule of five years, al-Wathiq died without designating a successor.

References

Muir (1915: 519–22), Shaban (1971: 69–71), al-Tabari (1985–95: XXXIV, see index).

RONALD PAUL BUCKLEY

AL-WATHIQ I, IBRAHIM B. MUHAMMAD AL-MUSTAMSIK, ABU ISHAQ (AD 1340–1)

The previous 'Abbasid caliph in Cairo, al-Mustakfi, designated his son Ahmad b. al-Mustakfi to succeed him, but the Mamluk Sultan al-Nasir b. Muhammad b. Qalawun rejected this and, instead, installed al-Wathiq I. When al-Nasir died in the same year that the oath of allegiance was given to al-Wathiq, the Sultan's son Abu Bakr al-Mansur is said to have convened a committee of judges to decide whether al-Wathiq should remain as caliph or be replaced by Ahmad b. al-Mustakfi. The result was the deposition of al-Wathiq and the inauguration of Ahmad.

References

Salim (1965: 26–7), al-Suyuti (1969: 488–90), Ibn Iyas (1975: 475, 487).

RONALD PAUL BUCKLEY

AL-WATHIQ II, 'UMAR B. AL-WATHIQ I, ABU HAFS
(AD 1383–6)

The Mamluk Sultan Barquq installed al-Wathiq II as 'Abbasid caliph in Cairo to replace his brother, the deposed al-Mutawakkil I. Al-Wathiq's reign was of no historical importance being restricted to largely ceremonial duties. He remained in office until his death and was succeeded by another brother, Zakariyya' b. al-Wathiq al-Musta'sim.

References

Salim (1965: 33), al-Suyuti (1969: 505), Ibn Iyas (1975: 333, 377, 382).

RONALD PAUL BUCKLEY

WAZIR

'Vizier' or minister of government, sometimes governor.

References

Hodgson (1974: 286, 292).

ANDREW J. NEWMAN

WEST AFRICA

The term 'West Africa' is used to refer to an extensive area in the land mass of the continent of Africa, in which there is considerable geographical, religious and cultural diversity. The region is bordered to the north by the Sahara desert, to the west and south by the Atlantic Ocean, and to the east by the Cameroons, in which stand the mountains and highlands that separate West from Central Africa. The scramble for Africa in the nineteenth century by European colonial powers, notably Britain and France, led in several cases to the imposition of arbitrary borders that cut across ancient tribal and political boundaries. For the most part, the map of West Africa retains the geographical divisions imposed by expatriate administrators, although the days of colonial dependency have ended. West Africa today consists of fifteen independent states. In alphabetical order, the name of each, with the date when independence from colonial rule was achieved, is as follows: Benin (formerly Dahomey), 1960, Burkina Faso (formerly Upper Volta), 1960, the Gambia, 1965, Ghana, 1957, Guinea, 1958, Guinea Bassau, 1973, Ivory Coast, 1960, Liberia, 1847, Mali, 1960, Mauritania, 1960, Niger, 1960, Nigeria, 1960, Senegal, 1960, Sierra Leone, 1961, Togo, 1960. The history of Islam in this region cannot be restricted to what may conveniently be known geographically as West Africa, however. Other entries in this volume consider aspects of the origin and development of Islamic communities under headings of name and place.

References

Ajayi and Crowder (1977–8: *passim*).

EDWARD D. A. HULMES

WIRD

The *wird* (pl. *awrad*) is a ritual litany that is usually performed at specific times each day. A particular *wird* is often given by the Sufi *shaykh* to the disciple, which reflects the spiritual level of the disciple.

References

Waley (1993: 511–13).

LLOYD RIDGEON

WIVES OF THE PROPHET MUHAMMAD

The Prophet Muhammad contracted eleven marriages. The first was to

Khadija, the wealthy and twice-widowed Meccan Qurashi whose entrepreneurial activities included the organisation of trading caravans north into Syria and south into the Yemen. It was she who arranged for Muhammad to accompany some of her trading expeditions along those ancient caravan routes. On their marriage (*c.* AD 595) she was forty years old, Muhammad fifteen years her junior. In many ways, this was the most fruitful of his marriages. Khadija was the only one of his wives who bore him children. The sons died in infancy. The four daughters, Umm Kulthum, Ruqayya, Zaynab and Fatima all married, but only Zaynab and Fatima survived their father. Until she died in the year AD 619, 'the Year of Sadness', Khadija was Muhammad's only wife. She was the first to accept the message of Islam and the prophethood of her husband. After her death, at a time when polygamy was common, he contracted further marriages. The Qur'anic injunction (4:3) limited the number of wives a man may take to four, with the proviso that this may be done only if each woman can be treated equally and justly. This condition, impossible to fulfil as some have argued, suggests that monogamy is the Islamic ideal. Reasons have been given for Muhammad's not observing this restriction. The number of concubines associated with the Prophet, including Rayhana, a Jewess from the Banu Qurayza, and the Coptic Christian slave, Mary, is not precisely known. Some of his subsequent marriages were contracted to help widows whose previous husbands had died in the service of Islam. Others were contracted to help seal alliances as Islam spread throughout the region. Following the death of Khadija, Muhammad married Sawda, the thirty-five-year-old widow of Sakran, one of the companions (*sahaba*) of

the Prophet. Muhammad next married the six-year-old 'A'isha in Mecca, who is said to have become his favourite wife. She was the daughter of Abu Bakr, the first of the 'Rightly Guided Caliphs'. In AD 625, after the Battle of Badr, Muhammad married the eighteen-year-old Hafsa, daughter of 'Umar, the second of the 'Rightly Guided Caliphs'. She was the widow of Khunays, who had gone to Abyssinia in AD 615 with a small number of other Muslims to seek asylum under the protection of the Christian Negus after persecution in Mecca. In Ramadan a year later, the Prophet married Zaynab bint Khuzayma, the widow of 'Ubayda, who was among those killed at Badr. Known as *Umm al-Masakin* (Mother of the Poor) for her generosity, she died shortly after the marriage. In AD 625, at Uhud, one of those to fall in the battle was Abu Salama. Muhammad subsequently married Abu Salama's widow, Umm Salama. This union was followed by a marriage to Zaynab bint Jahsh, divorced from the Prophet's forty-year-old adopted son and freedman, Zayd ibn Haritha. She became his fifth living wife. Questions were raised about the legitimacy of this marriage, although for the Prophet it appears that the union was a true 'marriage of affinity'. Juwariyya bint Harith, the daughter of the leader of a clan against whom the Muslims fought, was Muhammad's former enemy in Mecca, Abu Sufyan, was the father of Umm Habiba, whom the Prophet married next. Then came Safiyya, the widow of Kinana, the Jewish leader in Khaybar. She converted to Islam. The eleventh marriage of Muhammad was to Maymuna after the Prophet's successful return to Mecca on pilgrimage.

See also: **'A'isha; Khadija; Muhammad ibn Abdallah, the Prophet of Islam**

EDWARD D. A. HULMES

WOLOF

The Wolof are a black African ethnic group who inhabit the Atlantic coast of West Africa. Most of them live in modern Senegal, but a substantial minority live in the Gambia. Wolof society was characterised by a threefold division of the population into classes. At the top were the aristocracy (nobles who elected the king) and freeborn farmers. The latter worked arable farms, but there were also cattle-herders. Beneath them were the artisans and labourers (including musicians). The lowest class included the slaves of the community. A small state called Jolof began to grow in the central region of Senegal in the early fourteenth century. A separate Wolof state was established in the same century. Conversions to Islam continued in the eighteenth century, although there are accounts that by the start of the nineteenth century there was a movement away from Islam, especially in the royal courts. Open hostility to Muslims was expressed, despite the fact that Islam had been a familiar feature of the region since the eleventh century.

> This did not, however, mean that Islam had been wiped out. Among the Wolofs in the sixteenth century, Islam seems to have been only a court religion, represented by a few marabouts, often of foreign extraction (Moors) living under the protection of the sovereign and giving him the benefit of their religious, or, even better, magic powers (making charms out of written extracts from the Qur'an). It seems that during the seventeenth and eighteenth centuries an indigenous Muslim group grew up, under the guidance of Moor or Wolof marabouts, political in intent and acting as a focus for the discontent of a section of the peasant masses (the *badalos*) who were victims of more and more exacting demands on the part of princes.
> Suret-Canale and Barry (1977: 466)

By the end of the fifteenth century, the Wolof gained control of the greater part of modern Senegal. A Wolof ruler was called *burba*. He was elected to his office by the members of the aristocracy. After visiting the Wolof in 1455, Cadamosto, a Portuguese, recorded that '*Burba* Jollof' boasted an army of 10,000 cavalrymen and 100,000 soldiers. He added that the *Burba* Jolof did not rule by heredity: 'Three or four lords, of whom there are many in this country, choose a king whom they like, who reigns as long as he pleases them. They often dethrone their kings by force. The kings often try to make themselves so powerful that they can not be dethroned'. The State grew powerful and prosperous on the basis of its trans-Saharan trade and its commercial links with the Atlantic coast. This latter trade weakened as European entrepreneurs developed the Atlantic coast sea trade. The Wolof Empire was controlled by *burbas* until the middle of the sixteenth century and lasted until the nineteenth century when the French invaded, bringing Wolof control effectively to an end. The failure of the Wolof Empire may be attributed at least in part to the refusal of the aristocratic class to relieve the lower classes of the social and economic burdens placed on them. This resulted in a growing conflict of interest between the social groups. Residual elements of the ancient social divisions are still to be seen. The Wolof language belongs to the Niger-Congo family of languages.

References

Hiskett (1994: 107–12).

EDWARD D. A. HULMES

WOMEN IN ISLAM

It has always been the claim of Muslims that Islam brings true freedom and liberation from oppression for women as for men. They point to the prevailing social conditions in pre-Islamic Arabia, which were challenged by the mission of the Prophet Muhammad. He not only forbade the exposure of infant females left to die but preached a message of the equality before God of women and men. This does not mean, however, that the divinely established equality of men and women is interpreted in Islam in a way that can easily be appreciated in a Western secular cultural milieu, in which 'equal rights for women' are demanded in the name of feminism. It is averred that in Islam there is no need for women's rights to be fought for because they have already been inalienably established by God in the title deeds of Islam.

The best introduction to the Islamic approach to the equality of the sexes is found in Q.4 (*al-Nisa'*, 'the Women'), which begins with an appeal to the unity of all human kind, created from a single 'soul' (*nafs*). The point is made again in Q.39:6. The fourth sura proceeds to identify the rights of women, children and orphans, the nature of peaceable family relationships and the appropriate distribution of goods and property after death. Parents are to work together for the common good of the family. Women are to be held in high esteem. Their role at the heart of the family is unique. Their rights in marriage and divorce, their share in property, and their entitlements with regard to inheritance are outlined in principle. These Qur'anic injunctions about the rights and duties of women were subsequently codified into Islamic law, thus giving rise to the claim that Muslim women were granted legal rights long before the nineteenth century, when women in Britain first enjoyed the benefits guaranteed to them in the provisions of the Married Women's Property Acts (1870, 1882, 1884).

Despite these claims from the Islamic side, non-Muslims point to the differentiation of roles between Muslim women and Muslim men, which subordinate the female to the male. With regard to conjugal rights, for example, it is the husband who is entitled to the submissive response of the wife. The penalties for infidelity in marriage and for adultery are particularly harsh for women. The veiling of women, though acknowledged to be a pre-Islamic custom, is still insisted upon in fundamentalist Islamic communities because of the protection it offers to women. The separation of the sexes in public worship and prayer is common. Both sexes are called to follow the Straight Path of Islam in the hope that they may enjoy the privileges of entering Paradise. In theory, if not always in practice, women have the same rights as men in performing the statutory religious duties, although when it comes to making the *hajj*, the annual pilgrimage to Mecca, women must be accompanied by a male member of the family.

The inculturalisation of Islam over centuries in very different parts of the world has not limited the ancient freedoms enjoyed by women in parts of Africa and the Far East, where a matriarchal society has not been displaced by the Islamic patriarchal norm. From a Western secular point of view, there is something to be learned about the integrity of family relationships from the spirit of Islam. The reinterpretation of Islamic scripture and tradition by Muslims in the light of the comparatively recent expansion of Islamic life and thought in Europe will help to promote a renewed exploration of Islamic ideals in the West. A case in point, which relates specifically to the rights of women in Islam, is raised by

685

Islamic attitudes to monogamy and polygamy.

References

Bouhdiba (1985: 14–18, 19–29, 30–42, 233–7), Omran (1992: 15–26, 27–39, 40–58).

See also: **abortion (*ijhad, isqat*); birth control; *burqu'* (*burqa*); children (*atfal,*** *awlad*); **circumcision; divorce (*talaq, infisal, khul'*); *hijab*; marriage**

EDWARD D. A. HULMES

WUDU

See: **ablution**

Y

YAHYA (JOHN THE BAPTIST)

Mentioned in Qur'an (e.g. Q.6:85) and accepted as a *nabi* in Islam.

See also: *nabi*; **Zakariyya (Zechariah)**
ANDREW J. NEWMAN

YA'QUB

The Biblical patriarch Jacob, mentioned especially in the story of Joseph in Q.12 and in Q.2:132–40. Jacob's role as Joseph's father mirrors the biblical portrait with him being perceived to favour Joseph over his other sons. In common with the other biblical patriarchs, Jacob is seen as fitting within the Islamic prophetic model.

References

Gibb and Bosworth (1960–2003: XI, 254).
ANDREW RIPPIN

AL-YA'QUBI, AHMAD IBN ABI YA'QUB [IBN WADIH] (d. *c.* AD 900)

Arab historian and geographer. Few details of al-Ya'qubi's life are known to us. Born into a family that may possibly have been partly at least of Egyptian origin, he spent most of his life in Iraq and Iran, but following the fall of the Tahirid dynasty in the East, he settled in Egypt, where he died. His universal history, known simply as al-Ta'rikh, deals with the peoples and civilisations of the pre-Islamic period, and with the history of the Islamic caliphate until AD 872. The first volume, which lacks any precise chronology, discusses the classical civilisations of Greece and Rome, other ancient peoples of the Middle East (Syrians, Assyrians, Babylonians, Persians, Israelites and early Christians), North Africa (Egyptians, Berbers and the peoples of Sudan and Ethiopia), China, India, the Turks and the pre-Islamic Arabs. In the course of this account, he cites both the Old and the New Testaments, and indeed the work is notable for its use of non-Islamic sources generally. The second volume, the organisation of which appears more systematic then the first, is an account of the early history of Islam, beginning with the life of Muhammad, and subsequently organised by the reigns of individual caliphs. It is notable for the attention given to the Shi'ite imams. This has led to considerable debate about whether al-Ya'qubi was himself a Shi'ite – a debate that remains unresolved.

Towards the end of his life, al-Ya'qubi also composed a geographical treatise, *Kitab al-Buldan*, the parts of which relating to Byzantium, India and China have unfortunately been lost. The work, which, like that of Ibn Khurradadhbih begins with a description of Baghdad, covers the then Islamic world and is notable for the author's evident interest in historical detail. Like the *Ta'rikh*, this work displays features such as the selective, anthological approach to knowledge, that place it square in the *adab* genre of medieval Arabic literature.

A third work of al-Ya'qubi, *Mushakalat al-Nas li-Zamanihim*, discusses some of the ways by which people are influenced by the tastes of the particular caliphs under whom they live.

References

de Goeje (1892).

YAQUT IBN 'ABDALLAH AL-HAMAWI (AD 1179–1229).

Arab biographer and geographer. Also known as Yaqut al-Rumi by way of reference to his non-Arab, Anatolian origins, Yaqut was sold in his youth as a slave to a Baghdad merchant, who employed him on trading visits in the eastern Islamic world. After being freed in AD 1199, he worked as a copyist in Baghdad but continued to travel widely in the eastern part of the Islamic world. Following the first Mongol incursion in AD 1219, he fled to Mosul and Aleppo, where he died in 1229.

Yaqut al-Hamawi made important contributions both to the Arabic biographical dictionary and to the geographical tradition. His *Irshad al-Arib ila Ma'rifat al-Adib* is a biographical dictionary of literary figures, past and present, including entries of considerable length on well-known authors such as al-Jahiz and al-Ma'arri. Its scope, combined with the author's scholarly and critical approach to his material and his telling use of anecdotes, has ensured that it has continued to be an essential scholarly tool until this day. Yaqut's main geographical work, *Mu'jam al-Buldan*, remains equally invaluable. The first attempt at a 'world gazetteer' in the Arab world, this vast compilation not only lists place names in alphabetical order and establishes their correct spelling and locations, but also goes on to provide historical and geographical information about each place and, in many cases, the famous people associated with it. The work, which is often illustrated with appropriate verse quotations, is characterised by the same systematic and methodical approach as the author's *Irshad al-Arib* and was used as a source by many later Arab geographers and other writers. It is particularly informative on places such as Aleppo in which the author had himself resided for some time.

In addition to these two major works, Yaqut wrote a book on places sharing the same name, *Kitab al-Mushtarik Wad'an wa'l-muftariq suq'an*. A number of titles of works now lost are also recorded, in particular a dictionary of poets, *Mu'jam Akhbar al-Shu'ara'*.

References

Margoliouth (1907–31), Wüstenfeld (1846, 1866–73).

PAUL STARKEY

YARMUK, BATTLE OF

The battle took place in AD 636 south of the Yarmuk River in Syria. A Muslim army led by Khalid ibn Walid met a powerful Byzantine army of Christian Arabs, Armenians and their auxiliaries, who had marched up from Palestine. Khalid's force was strengthened by reinforcements from Medina. His position was strengthened further by the desertion of large numbers of men on the Byzantine side. Khalid chose the right moment to attack and gained the victory, pursuing the remnants of the enemy down the Yarmuk valley. During the course of the battle, which helped to open up the rest of Palestine for Islamic conquest, some 50,000 Byzantine troops are said to have been killed.

See also: **'Umar ibn al-Khattab**

EDWARD D. A. HULMES

YATIM

Yatim is the Arabic word for 'orphan', and refers to an individual who has become fatherless before the age of puberty. A child cannot be considered as *yatim* after this age. The Muslim attitude towards orphans is grounded in the Qur'anic verses that state an orphan's entitlement to kindness and charity. The text highlights the importance of donating funds and insists that orphans should never be mistreated or cheated out of their dues by relatives or guardians. However, as there are so many pertinent textual rules, guardians have often found difficulty in controlling the property of orphans. Perhaps for this reason the Qur'an states 'do not take the property of orphans, except with care' (Q.6:152). This indicates that to do so is acceptable so long as the intention is to reduce hardship, however, the guardian must remain vigilant not to misuse or take unjustifiably from an orphan. Islamic ethics dictate that the *yatim* has particular value since he or she should be neither oppressed nor humiliated.

References

Al-Zuhayli (1997: 4–7, 79).

MAWIL IZZI DIEN

YAWM AL-QIYAMA (YAWM AL-DIN)

The day on which a trumpet is blown and the dead rise from their graves to be reunited with their bodies in readiness for judgement of their deeds and belief.

References

Waines (1995: 130).

See also: **day of judgement; judgement on the** *yawm al-qiyama*; **najat;** *shafa'a*

ANDREW J. NEWMAN

YAZD

Capital of a province, western central Persia, founded in the fifth century AD in a remote sandy desert plain (1,200 metres above sea level) between the Great Salt Desert (Dasht-i-Kavir) and the Great Sand Desert (Dasht-i-Lut) with water supplied from Shir Khu mountains via *qanat*s and its houses ventilated by wind towers (*badgir*s). At the intersection of trade between central Asia and India, Fars and Khurasan, Yazd has been famous for carpets, silk and cotton, and sweetmeats.

Originally called Kathah (from the Persian *kandan*, 'to hollow out'), after the deep moat around the city walls, it was important as a religious centre in pre-Islamic times. According to legend, the mythical heroes Rustum and Zal stayed in Yazd *en route* to Fars from Seistan. According to tradition, Yazd was occupied by Arabs (AD 642) but probably converted to Islam only gradually, initially fanatical Sunni then devoted Shi'i. An important Zoroastrian centre from the Sasanian period, the name may derive from Yezdegerd (a Sasanian king) or *yezd-i-khast* ('God willed it'). The city has the largest number of Zoroastrians in Iran and a sacred flame (AD 470) that is continually burning. There were communities of Jews and Baha'is until the nineteenth century.

The historian Ibn Hawqal (fl. AD 943–88) described Yazd as fairly prosperous with strong fortifications. It was called *dar al-ibada* because of its many religious buildings, many of them finely ornamented with stucco and polychromes. The fine Davazdah Imam mausoleum (AD 1037) has a Saljuq inscription listing the Shi'ite leaders. The Friday mosque was built in AD 1119 (rebuilt AD 1375, refurbished 1416) and its minarets are the highest in Iran. Marco Polo noted 'the noble city of Yazd' in the thirteenth century. Many monuments, including over fourteen *madrasa*s were built when Yazd came under the Muzaffarids (fourteenth century).

*Sayyid*s were numerous and physicians, *'ulama'*, poets, painters, craftsmen and calligraphers were also influential over the centuries and Muslim merchants had connections with India. The *masjid-i-Vaqt-o-Saat* complex (AD 1326), with a mosque, *madrasa*, pharmacy and observatory (*rasad*), was built by the prominent Sayyid Rukn al-Din (d. AD 1332–3). Other religious buildings were built by the Muzaffarids including

libraries, the Shamsiya *madrasa* and Mir Shams al-Din mausoleum that combined *madrasa* and *khanqab* (AD 1365). In 1392 Yazd submitted to Timur and new fortifications were built (1396–7).

Under the Safavids the city was a prosperous commercial centre with the expansion of the silk trade. Amir Čaqmaq (r. 1427/8–1446/7), his wife Bibi Fatima and other benefactors built many mosques, including a new Friday mosque (1436–7). From 1501, Yazd was a province of the Safavid Empire and continued to flourish until a decline in security in 1722 when Yazd was besieged by Afghans. The bodies in mass burial pits by the ramparts were preserved for over 120 years in the dry climate. Yazd's history in the eighteenth century was turbulent until Muhammad Taqi took control (1748) and held office for fifty-two years, developing charitable trusts and religious buildings. Yazd was besieged in the 1830s, and in 1846 around 8,000 people died from cholera. By 1872, Yazd was a walled city with bazaars, caravanserais, fifty mosques and eight *madrasa*, and was surrounded by gardens and cultivated fields.

References

Boyce (1977), Nobuaki (2003).
JANET STARKEY

YAZID B. 'ABD AL-MALIK (AD 720–4)

After the death of 'Umar b. 'Abd al-'Aziz (AD 720), the Marwanid caliphate reverted to Yazid II, the third son of 'Abd al-Malik b. Marwan to hold the office. Yazid's reign was of little consequence, he being a ruler of little energy or ability and possessing none of the asceticism and devotion to religion of his cousin 'Umar. He was succeeded by his considerably more able brother Hisham.

References

Kennedy (1996: 107–8), Muir (1915: 375–82), Shaban (1971: 135–7), al-Tabari (1985–95: XXIV, 70–196 *passim*).

RONALD PAUL BUCKLEY

YAZID B. MU'AWIYA
(AD 680–3)

Yazid I was the son and successor of Mu'awiya b. Abi Sufyan, the founder of the Umayyad dynasty. The delicate balance of relationships that Mu'awiya had been able to maintain soon began to disintegrate during Yazid's reign and it witnessed the beginning of the second *fitna* (civil war) in Islam, which continued until the defeat of 'Abdallah b. al-Zubayr in AD 692. The first threat to Yazid's position came from 'Ali b. Abi Talib's younger son al-Husayn, who refused to acknowledge the new caliph. This culminated in the massacre of al-Husayn and most of his small group of followers at Karbala' in AD 680 at the hands of the Umayyad forces. Ibn al-Zubayr similarly refused to give Yazid his oath of allegiance and was proclaimed Caliph in the Hijaz, Iraq, Egypt, and parts of Syria. Yazid died while the Syrian forces were still attempting to regain control. He left no obvious successor and, with his death, most Muslims began to support Ibn al-Zubayr.

References

Hitti (1970: 190–2), Hodgson (1974: 219–21), Shaban (1971: 91–2), al-Tabari (1985–95: XIX, see index).

RONALD PAUL BUCKLEY

YAZID B. AL-WALID (AD 744)

Yazid III was chosen by Syrian generals as the new Marwanid (Umayyad) caliph to succeed his murdered predecessor al-Walid b. Yazid. During Yazid's short reign, continued Arab rivalries in Spain and North Africa were to lead to the eventual loss of Marwanid control there. Yazid died suddenly after ruling for only six months and was succeeded by his brother Ibrahim b. al-Walid.

References

Muir (1915: 405–8), Shaban (1971: 155–60), al-Tabari (1985–95: XXVI, 126–263 *passim*), Wellhausen (1963: 362–84 *passim*).

RONALD PAUL BUCKLEY

YUNUS

'Jonah' of the Old Testament, accepted as a *rasul* in Islam (Q.4:163, 6:86), who was swallowed by a fish (37:142), praised Allah, and was delivered therefrom (21:87–8).

ANDREW J. NEWMAN

YUSUF

'Joseph' of the Old Testament, whose story is told in the sura of the same name.

ANDREW J. NEWMAN

YUSUF B. TASHUFIN
(r. 1061–1106)

Sanhaja Berber, lieutenant of the Berber chiefs inspired by the militant religiosity of 'Abdallah b. Yasin and the real founder of the strict Maliki Almoravid power in North Africa. He completed the conquest of Morocco and what is now central Algeria, founded the new capital of the dynasty at Marrakesh, and in 1086 answered a summons from the demoralised Muslim princes of al-Andalus for help against the Christians, who had just regained Toledo. He won a great victory at Zallaqa near Badajoz which slowed down the Reconquista, giving Muslim Spain a breathing space and in effect a further century and a half of existence.

References

References: Bosch J. Vilá (1956), Gibb and Bosworth (1960–2003), Norris (1982: 131–40).

See also: **Muluk al-Tawa'if**

C. E. BOSWORTH

Z

ZAB, BATTLE OF THE

The defeat of the last Umayyad caliph Marwan II in the battle of the Greater Zab in AD 750 signalled the end of the Umayyad dynasty and the rise of the 'Abbasids. Marwan II came to power through the infighting within the Umayyad Empire amongst the Arab tribal factions of Qays and Kalb and members of the Umayyad house. When he assumed the caliphate in AD 744, Marwan II had already gained a reputation for his military prowess in the campaigns of Azerbaijan and Iraq. In both places he had acted as governor and built for himself a power base.

Soon after accepting the oath of allegiance (*bay'a*), Marwan II was faced with internal dissent in Syria, which occupied his time in the early part of the reign. Meanwhile, in the east, the 'Alid movement (which was to later become the 'Abbasid military force) was growing. The famed work of Shi'ite missionaries (in particular Abu Muslim)

had gained much success in the Iranian provinces. Abu Muslim assembled forces in Khurasan, and began to move west to challenge Umayyad power in the name of an unspecified Shi'ite imam.

When the movement had taken Kufa, 'Abdallah b. Muhammad al-Saffah, a descendent of the Prophet's uncle al-'Abbas, was proclaimed the new caliph in AD 749. One wing of the new 'Abbasid army moved into northern Mesopotamia from the Persian Zagros mountains. Marwan II, perceiving the threat to Umayyad power from the 'Abbasid forces too late, engaged the force under the control of al-Saffah's uncle at the Greater Zab in January AD 750.

The battle was short, and the 'Abbasid victory decisive. Marwan's army certainly outnumbered the 'Abbasid forces, though even with this advantage, Marwan made a fatal tactical error. He built a bridge and ordered that his troops move over to the south bank of the Zab. He advocated restraint amongst his commanders, but one, too eager to defend the Caliph, broke ranks and began the attack. 'Abdallah b. 'Ali, the 'Abbasid commander, also feared insubordination amongst his men, and was worried about deserters. He ordered his men to adopt a kneeling position in close formation, with their spears pointed out in defence. This, apparently, scared the Syrians and they turned and fled. Marwan, also fleeing, destroyed the bridge in his retreat, leaving many of his forces on the south bank. Many more of his men drowned trying to escape the 'Abbasids than were actually killed in the battle.

Marwan II fled the battlefield, retreating to Syria and then to Egypt where he was eventually killed by pursuing 'Abbasid forces. The battle of the Greater Zab, then, was the beginning of the end of Umayyad power and the end of their dynastic system, portrayed as nepotistic and corrupt in the Arabic sources. The battle also gave prominence to the 'Abbasid General 'Abdallah b. 'Ali (d. AD 764), a particularly bloodthirsty pursuer of the remnants of the house of the Banu Umayya during the early 'Abbasid period.

References

Hawting (1986), Sharon (1983), al-Tabari (1879–1901: III, 38–45), al-Ya'qubi (1883: 418–20).

ROBERT GLEAVE

AL-ZABUR

'The Psalms', as received by the king and prophet David (Da'ud) and accepted as divine revelation in Islam, along with the five books of Moses and the Gospels. See Q.4:163.

See also: **Da'ud**; *al-Injil*; *al-Tawrat*

ANDREW J. NEWMAN

ZACHARIYA

See: **Zakariyya**

ZAGHLUL, SA'D (1860–1927)

Egyptian statesman. Zaghlul was born into a prosperous landowning family in the Nile delta and followed a traditional Islamic education after which he studied law. He became interested in nationalist politics and took up a modernist position opposed to the more traditional Islamic trend. He quickly became well known and made his way in politics. He was appointed Minister of Education in 1906 and of Justice in 1910. He resigned from the latter post in 1913 in order to head the opposition in the Legislative Assembly. By the end of the First World War he had assumed the leadership of the nationalist movement that was totally opposed to the British presence in Egypt. In November 1918, he lead a delegation (*wafd*) to the British to demand independence. The Wafd political party evolved from this delegation in 1919. At this time, the nationalist movement erupted into a countrywide uprising against the British and, in an effort to emasculate it, the British exiled Zaghlul first to Malta in 1919 and then to Aden and Gibraltar in 1922. He could not be ignored, however, and in 1923 he took part in the first election campaign in nominally independent Egypt. The Wafd gained a large majority and he was appointed Prime Minister in January 1924.

On the assassination of Sir Lee Stack (the *sirdar* or commander of the Egyptian army), Lord Allenby, the British High Commissioner, attempted to impose humiliating conditions on the Egyptians. Zaghlul refused to accept these and resigned. In 1925 he was elected speaker of the new parliament, and in 1926 the Wafd again won elections, but the British refused to allow him to become Prime Minister. He was again elected Speaker, but his death in 1927 robbed Egyptian politics of its outstanding leader.

References

Yeghen (1927).

DEREK HOPWOOD

AL-ZAHIR, MUHAMMAD B. AL-NASIR, ABU NASR
(AD 1225–6)

The 'Abbasid caliph al-Zahir was the son and designated successor of al-Nasir. Although al-Zahir acquired a reputation for his integrity, high moral standards and generosity, he played no significant role in government and exercised little influence on the course of events. His short reign of a little over nine months was largely spent watching the inexorable advance of the Mongol hordes under the leadership of Jenghiz Khan towards the west and the capital of the caliphate, Baghdad. He was succeeded by his son al-Mansur b. al-Zahir al-Mustansir.

References

Ibn al-Tiqtaqa (1860: 379), Le Strange (1924: 163), Muir (1915: 589).

RONALD PAUL BUCKLEY

ZAHIRISM

Followers of the school of law formed around the ideas of Da'ud ibn Khalaf (d. AD 884). The Zahiris hold to limiting the sources of law to the Qur'an and the *sunna*, rejecting the use of independent reasoning and analogy, and holding that consensus could only be binding if it stemmed from the companions of the Prophet. Da'ud ibn Khalaf emphasised the literal or apparent meaning (*zahir*) of the text of the Qur'an and the *sunna*. The end result of the legal position is a combination of a very liberal and a very strict imposition of the law. By restricting the law to the specifics mentioned in the Qur'an, the application of a law was frequently restricted rather than applied more generally as in the majority case. The Zahiris saw no need for the investigation into the reasons for any given law, so the extension of the law to parallel situations was not entertained. But at the same time, rules which were interpreted as merely recommendations or simple disapprovals by the other schools of law were often taken as absolute commands.

Zahirism had limited historical success, having a moment of political influence under one of the Almohads in the twelfth century. This approach to law became a position that was generally incorporated into summaries of law, and individuals would sometimes appeal to its principles even if not being adherents of the school. Ibn Hazm (d. AD 1064) was the school's major intellectual supporter.

References

Goldziher (1971b).

ANDREW RIPPIN

ZAKARIYYA (ZECHARIAH)

The father of John the Baptist of the New Testament. Zakariyya is reckoned in the Qur'an (Q.6:85) along with John, Jesus, and Elias as among the righteous. The Qur'an gives the substance of the biblical Luke 1:5–25, as it summarises the story in Q.3:37–41, Q.19:2–11, and Q.21:89–90. Zakariyya guards Mary, the mother of Jesus, in the temple and always finds fresh fruits there. He prays to God, and angels announce to him that a son will be born to him who is to be named Yahya (John), a name never previously given to anyone. John is foretold to be a pious man, a prophet, Jacob's heir, and someone who will be pleasing to God. Zakariyya thinks he is too old to have a son and as a sign of the truth of the promise, he is struck dumb for three days.

References

Gibb and Bosworth (1960–2003: XI, 405–6).
ANDREW RIPPIN

ZAKAT

See: **alms-giving**

AL-ZAMAKHSHARI
(d. AD 1144)

Qur'an commentator, grammarian, linguist. Abu'l-Qasim Mahmud ibn 'Umar al-Zamakhshari (d. AD 1144) lived most of his life in the region of his birth, Khwarizm in central Asia, although he did spend some time studying in Bukhara and Baghdad, and twice he visited Mecca. Motivated by a great appreciation of Arabic (although he was a native Persian speaker) and influenced by rationalist Mu'tazilite theology, al-Zamakhshari wrote one of the most widely respected commentaries on the Qur'an called *al-Kashshaf an Haqa'iq Ghawamid al-Tanzil*, 'The Unveiler of the Realities of the Sciences of the Revelation'. Despite what came to be regarded as a heretical theological slant, the work has been an essential part of the curriculum of religious education throughout the Muslim world for centuries. It attracted many super-commentaries that attempted to explain its terse style and intricacies, as well as refutations (for example, by Fakhr al-

Din al-Razi [d. AD 1209]) and bowdlerised versions (for example, by al-Baydawi [d. *c.* AD 1286 or later]). Al-Zamakhshari commented on each phrase of the Qur'an in sequence, providing philosophical, lexicographical, and philological glosses while displaying a concern for the rhetorical qualities of the text. His text is also imbued with his theological vision which is characterised by a thorough-going de-anthropomorphisation and support for the doctrines of human free will and the 'created Qur'an'. Al-Zamakhshari also wrote a number of other works, including works on Arabic grammar, rhetoric, and lexicography, and a collection of proverbs.

References

Goldziher (1920: 117–77), Ibrahim (1980).
ANDREW RIPPIN

ZANADIQA

The most precise meaning of *zanadiqa* (sing. *zindiq*) is 'Manichaeans', though the term is used in Muslim literature to refer to 'heretics' and 'unbelievers' more generally. The term was present in non-Arabic vocabularies before Islam (Pahlavi and Armenian), where it meant Manichaeans specifically. When the term was transferred into Arabic literature, it was originally used to describe the followers of the prophet and founder of Manichaeanism, Mani (d. AD 277), it later came to refer to heretics more generally, and occasionally even Muslim apostates. The term is not found in the Qur'an, though the Prophet is reported to have talked of the *zanadiqa* in uncomplimentary terms. The Manichaeans were dualists, believing in the eternal opposition of Good and Evil: God is good and a devil figure is evil. In this sense they shared some beliefs with the Zoroastrians, though

Mani was condemned as a heretic by the Zoroastrian priests (the Magi) on account of the fact that he advocated celibacy. He also asserted that evil was somehow manifest in matter, and that true believers had to disassociate themselves from attachment to matter. In these latter beliefs, one may see the influence of Indic philosophies (Mani is said to have travelled to India). On the other hand, Manichaean belief in a line of prophets, ending with Mani, who had contact with the supernatural through his 'twin' spirit, has some similarity to Muslim and Jewish conceptions of God and his communication with humanity through angels. Similarly, the advocacy of Jesus as a prophet, who did not die on the cross may be derived from Gnostic Christianity. St Augustine, most famously, was a Manichaean before his conversion to Christianity.

The term *zindiq*, even before Islam, was loaded with these connotations in the Middle Eastern milieu, and it is, therefore, not so surprising that its use in Arabic literature covered not only those who were members of the Manichaean religious community (which survived, despite persecutions, until the sixteenth century), but also to any community, Muslim or otherwise, whose religious beliefs displayed a similarity with those of the *zanadiqa*.

References

Chokr (1993), Lieu (1997, 1998).

ROBERT GLEAVE

ZANZIBAR

An island in the Indian Ocean, some 600 square miles (1550 square kilometres) in area, situated 22 miles (35 kilometres) off the east coast of Tanzania. The name 'Zanzibar' appears to be a corruption of the Arabic word *Zanjabar*, which is derived most probably from the Persian word for Ethiopia (*Zang*). In the seventeenth century, the island was controlled by Omani Arabs, for whom it gave access to the interior of central Africa as well as a location for ocean-going commercial activity with India and other points to the east. Together with the islands of Latham and Pemba, Zanzibar became a sultanate in AD 1856. In 1885, as part of the European scramble for Africa, it was annexed by Germany. Five years later, the island became a British protectorate, having been handed over to Britain by Germany in exchange for Heligoland. The trade in African slaves as well as in ivory thrived there until the nineteenth century, when the port in Zanzibar was used by the British navy to suppress the slave trade. Independence was gained in 1963. Zanzibar became a republic one year later, after the rule of the Sultan was overthrown. Following this change of power, Zanzibar joined with Tanganyika to create the United Republic of Tanzania. Several languages are spoken today in communities whose ethnic origins are not only in the Gulf States but in Asia. Kiswahili, a form of the Arabised lingua franca Swahili, is spoken by many.

References

Hitti (1973: 247, 391, 448, 467).

See also: **Ibadism; slavery and the slave trade in West Africa**

EDWARD D. A. HULMES

ZAQQUM, TREE OF

A tree that grows in Hell and whose bitter fruit the damned must eat (e.g., Q.44:43).

ANDREW J. NEWMAN

697

ZAWAJ

See: **marriage**

ZAWIYA

Meaning a corner, the *zawiya* is another kind of Sufi *khanaqah*. Generally however, the *zawiya* was smaller than the Sufi *khanaqah* or *ribat*, and housed just a master and a few of his disciples.

References

Trimingham (1971).

LLOYD RIDGEON

ZAYD B. THABIT (d. between AD 662/3 and 675/6)

A companion of Muhammad who served as his secretary and who played a central role in the collection of the Qur'an. Zayd was born eleven years before the *hijra* into the tribe of Quraysh and worked as a scribe for Muhammad during his lifetime, he is credited with having written letters to the kings of the time, inviting them to Islam. He continued in this role under the first three caliphs especially. He was also famed for his ability at arithmetic, becoming an authority on the Islamic system of inheritance as well as calendar reckoning. His role in the collection of the Qur'an was as a literate individual who represented the interests and language of Quraysh which figured highly in the criteria for establishing the authentic text of the scripture. Zayd's date of death is uncertain, it is said that he died somewhere between AD 662/3 and 675/6.

References

Gibb and Bosworth (1960–2003: XI, 475–6).

ANDREW RIPPIN

ZAYD IBN-'ALI

A jurist of the Madina School, whose compendium of Islamic laws is one of the oldest to have been compiled. He was a contemporary of the better-known Malik ibn Anas (*c.* AD 715–95) whose work, *al-Muwatta,* 'The Paved Path', became the standard work of reference for the School of Islamic jurisprudence that bears his name. Zayd ibn-'Ali died in AD 743.

See also: **Almohads**

EDWARD D. A. HULMES

ZAYD IBN-HARITHA

The adopted son of the Prophet Muhammad. In AD 629 there was a military skirmish at Mu'ta, east of the southern shore of the Dead Sea in Jordan, between a Christian force and a raiding party of Muslims under the command of Zayd. The raid was probably carried out with the intention of securing the famous Mashrafiya swords manufactured in Mu'ta. It failed. Zayd was killed in the fighting. The vanquished Muslims were led back to Medina by Khalid ibn Walid.

EDWARD D. A. HULMES

ZAYDISM (AL-ZAYDIYYA)

A Shi'ite group taking its name from Zayd b. 'Ali b. al-Husayn, a grandson of al-Husayn b. 'Ali b. Abu Talib. Zayd was the first to make an abortive attempt to seize the caliphate for the House of the Prophet since the disaster at Karbala' but was deserted by his troops when he refused to reject the caliphate of the first three caliphs. This left him with only 500 men to face the Umayyad army of Hisham b. 'Abd al-Malik and, as a consequence, he was killed. The Zaydis are considered moderate due to their acceptance of the early caliphate before 'Ali, as they consider it acceptable to have an imam in power while there is a more suitable candidate, in their opinion this being 'Ali. They also accept that the Imam can be any descendant of Fatima, regardless if he be from the lineage of al-Hasan or al-Husayn and do not stipulate that the imam be designated by his predecessor. They also differ from their Shi'ite co-religionists in that they reject the concept of temporary marriage (*mut'a*) but agree with their approach to theological matters tending to a Mu'tazilite type doctrine. The Zaydis have their own jurisprudential (*fiqh*) and *hadith* tradition, said to be from Zayd b. 'Ali himself, which is comparable to that of the Sunnis, differing only in secondary issues (*furu'*). The Zaydis established two states historically, one near the Caspian Sea and the other in Yemen, which was still intact until 1962, when the Yemeni revolution took place. Nevertheless, these two regions still remain the abodes of considerable communities until today.

References

al-Johani (1999: 76–82), Netton (1997: 264–5), Tabataba'i (n.d.: 76–83), Watt (1997: 128–30).

See also: **Ithna'asharism (al-Ithna'ashar-iyya); Shi'ism; Sunnism**

GAVIN PICKEN

ZAYNAB

See: **Zenobia**

ZENOBIA

The self-styled 'Queen' of Palmyra (modem Tadmur) was a woman of Arab origin, who ruled the ancient city situated to the north of the Syrian desert in central Syria in the name of her sons, after the murder of her husband, Septimius Odaenathus, in AD 266. His position was weakened by internal intrigues, in which his wife probably played a willing part. Having won back the eastern parts of the Roman Empire from the Persians, Odaenathus became the client ruler of the Roman colony, the borders of which he was able to extend to form what was effectively a semi-autonomous state that included large tracts of Syria, Mesopotamia and Armenia. Zenobia increased the area over which she had control, not least in Asia Minor and Egypt, after her accession to power in AD 266. She declared independence from Rome and pronounced her son Emperor. Her arrogance and ambition provoked the Romans to attack six years later. In AD 272, the Emperor Aurelian besieged Palmyra, captured and partly destroyed it. Zenobia was taken captive to Rome and paraded in public as Aurelian's handsome trophy. She was later granted a pension and ended her life in retirement near Tibur (modern Tivoli) after marrying a Roman senator. Posterity associates her name with the beauty, the intelligence and the ruthlessness for which she is celebrated.

EDWARD D. A. HULMES

ZINA'

See: **adultery and fornication; divorce**

AL-ZUBAYR, 'URWA IBN

The son of one of the companions of the Prophet Muhammad, 'Urwa ibn al-Zubayr (AD 643–712) was among the earliest of the redactors of the traditions, men who laid the foundations for the writing of the biography, or 'Life' (*sira*) of the Prophet.

See also: **Sirat Rasul Allah**

EDWARD D. A. HULMES

ZUHD

'Asceticism', the renouncing of worldly goods and comforts in favour of a life of personal spiritual searching and contemplation.

References

Hodgson (1974: 394), Waines (1995: 135–7).

ANDREW J. NEWMAN

ZULAYKHA'

Traditional name given to the wife of a prominent Egyptian (Aziz) in the story of Joseph, unnamed in the Qur'an. In the recounting of the story of the biblical patriarch Joseph in Q.12, the role of the wife of the Egyptian who owned him as a slave is well developed and has become a focus of significant interest in Islam. The wife is captivated by the beauty of Joseph and she seeks to seduce him, but Joseph rejects her. The wife's lies afterwards about the events are discovered and Joseph's innocence is proven. When word of this attempted seduction circulates in the town, the wife invites her neighbours to view Joseph in order to show them why she felt the way she did. Cunningness and seductiveness are characteristics of the portrayal of the wife in the story. Medieval developments of the story, in which the wife gains the name Zulaykha, construct a plot line of romantic love and mutual devotion, emphasising Zulaykha's repentance as it is found at the end of the Qur'anic account, and having her and Joseph married with children by the end of the story. The most popular rendition is that of Jami (d. 1492) in his *Mathnawi*. The story is capable of being interpreted on the symbolic level with Zulaykha as the senses or 'lower world', and Joseph as the heart or the 'spiritual world', displaying his longing for God.

References

Stowasser (1994: Chapter 4).

ANDREW RIPPIN

General bibliography

Entries by Abdul-Raof

Abdul-Raof, H. (2000) 'The Linguistic Architecture of the Qur'an', *Journal of Qur'anic Studies*, 2 (2): 37–51.

—— (2001a) *Qur'an Translation: Discourse, Texture and Exegesis*. Richmond: Curzon.

—— (2001b) *The Qur'an Outlined: Theme and Text*. London: Ta-Ha.

—— (2003) *Exploring the Qur'an*. Dundee: Al-Maktoum Institute Academic Press.

Andrews, A. (1986) 'The Major Functions'of the Noun Phrase', in Timothy Shopen (ed.) *Language Typology and Syntactic Description*. Cambridge: Cambridge University Press, pp. 62–154.

Asad, Muhammad (1980) *The Message of the Qur'an*. Gibraltar.

al-'Asqalani, b. Hajar (1997) *Fathu al-Bari Sharhu Sahih al-Bukhari*. vols. 1–13. Riyadh: Maktabat Dar al-Salam.

'Atar, Hasan Diya' al-Din (1988) *al-Ahruf al-Sab'a wa Manzilat al-Qira'at Minha*. Beirut: Dar al-Basha'ir al-Islamiyya.

al-Baqillani, Abu Bakr Muhammad (1994) *I'jaz al-Qur'an*. Beirut: Dar Ihya' al-'Ulum.

Beaugrande, R. de and Dressler, W. (1981) *Introduction to Text Linguistics*. London and New York: Routledge.

Bell, R. (1953) *Introduction to the Qur'an*. Edinburgh: Edinburgh University Press.

al-Biqa'i, Burhan al-Din Abi al-Hasan (1995) *Nazm al-Durar fi Tanasub al-Ayat wa al-Suwar*, 8 vols. Beirut.

Cornell, V. J. (1995) 'The Qur'an as Scripture', in *The Oxford Encyclopedia of the Modern Islamic World*. Oxford: Oxford University Press, pp. 387–94.

Cragg, K. (2001) *Muhammad in the Qur'an: The Task and the Text*. London: Melisende.

—— (1991) *A Commentary on the Qur'an*. vols. 1–2. Manchester: The Victoria University of Manchester.

Donaldson, D. M. (1953) *Studies in Muslim Ethics*. London: SPCK.

Esack, F. (2004) 'Qur'an', in R. C. Martin (ed.) *Encyclopedia of Islam and the Muslim World*. New York: Macmillan, pp. 562–8.

al-Maqdisi, Abu Abd Allah Muhammad (1995) *Manaqib al-A'imma al-'Arab*. Beirut: Dar al-Mu'ayyad.

Pedersen, J. (1984) *The Arabic Book*. Princeton, NJ: Princeton University Press.

al-Qurtubi, Abu 'Abd Allah Muhammad (1997) *al-Jami'li Ahkam al-Qur'an*, vols. 1–20. Beirut: Dar al-Kitab al-'Arabi.

al-Razi, Fakhr al-Din (1990a) *al-Tafsir al-Kabir*. 32 vols. Beirut.

—— (1990b) *Mafatih al-Ghayb*. vols. 1–32. Beirut: Dar al-Kutub al-'Ilmiyya.

Robinson, N. (1996) *Dicovering the Qur'an: A Contemporary Approach to a Veiled Text*. London: SCM Press.

Saheeh International (1997) *The Qur'an: Arabic Text with Corresponding English Meanings*. Riyadh.

al-Salih, Subhi (1997) *Mabahith fi 'Ulum al-Qur'an*. Beirut: Dar al-'Ilm li al-Malayin.

al-Shaykh, 'Abd al-Rahman b. Hasan (1992) *Fath al-Majid*. Riyadh: Maktabat Dar al-Salam.

Sonn, T. (1995) 'Tawhid', in John L. Esposito (ed.) *The Oxford Encyclopedia of the Modern Islamic World*. Oxford: Oxford University Press, pp. 190–8.

al-Suyuti, Jalal al-Din (1996) *al-Itqan fi 'Ulum al-Qur'an*. vols. 1–2. Beirut: Dar Ihya' al-'Ulum.

Talmon, R. (2002) 'Grammar and the Qur'an', in *Encyclopedia of the Qur'an*, pp. 345–67.

Thilbault, P. J. (1994) 'Intertextuality', in *The Encyclopedia of Language and Linguistics*, vol. IV. pp.1751–4.

al-Wahidi, Abu al-Hasan 'Ali (1984) *Asbab Nuzul al-Qur'an*. Riyadh: Dar al-Qibla li al-Thaqafa al-Islamiyya.

al-Zamakhshari, Abu al-Qasim Jar Allah (1995) *al-Kashshaf*, vols. I–IV. Beirut: Dar al-Kutub al-'Ilmiyyah.

al-Zarkashi, Badr al-Din (1988) *al-Burhan fi 'Ulum al-Qur'an*. vols. I–IV. Beirut: Dar al-Kutub al-'Ilmiyya.

al-Zarqani, Muhammad 'Abd al-'Azim (1988) *Manahil al-'Irfan fi 'Ulum al-Qur'an*. vols. I–II. Beirut: Dar al-Kutub al-'Ilmiyya.

Entries by Bosworth

Arié, R. (1990) *L'Espagne musulmane au temps des Nasrides (1232–1492)*. Paris: Boccard.

Barthold, W. (1968) *Turkestan down to the Mongol Invasion*. 3rd edn. London: Luzac & Co.

Bianquis, Th. (1998) 'Autonomous Egypt from Ibn Tulun to Kafur, 868–969,' in C. F. Petry (ed.) *The Cambridge History of Egypt*, vol. I. Cambridge: Cambridge University Press, pp. 86–119.

Bosch, J. Vilá (1956) *Los Almorávides*. Tetuan: Editora Marroqui.

Bosworth, C. E. (1968) 'The Political and Dynastic History of the Iranian World,' in J. A. Boyle (ed.) *The Cambridge History of Iran*, vol. V. Cambridge: Cambridge University Press, pp. 1–202.

—— (1973) *The Ghaznavids, their Empire in Afghanistan and Eastern Iran 994–1040*. 2nd edn. Beirut: Librairie du Liban.

—— (1975) 'The Tahirids and Saffarids,' in R. N. Frye (ed.) *The Cambridge History of Iran*, vol. IV. Cambridge: Cambridge University Press, pp. 90–135.

—— (1975) 'The Early Ghaznavids,' in R. N. Frye (ed.) *The Cambridge History of Iran*, vol. IV. Cambridge: Cambridge University Press, pp. 162–97.

—— (1977) *The Later Ghaznavids: Splendour and Decay. The Dynasty in Afghanistan and Northern India 1040–1186*. Edinburgh: Edinburgh University Press.

—— (1994) *The History of the Saffarids of Sistan and the Maliks of Nimruz (247/861 to 949/1542–3)*. Costa Mesa, CA and New York.

—— (1996) *The New Islamic Dynasties: A Chronological and Genealogical Manual*. Edinburgh: Edinburgh University Press.

Brunschvig, R. (1940–7) *La Berbérie orientale sous les Hafsides des origines à la fin du XVeme siècle*, 2 vols. Paris: Adren-Maisonneuve.

Busse, H. (1969) *Chalif und Grosskönig. Die Buyiden im Iraq (945–1055)*. Beirut and Wiesbaden: In Kommission bei F. Steiner.

—— (1975) 'Iran under the Buyids,' in R. N. Frye (ed.) *The Cambridge History of Iran*, vol. IV. Cambridge: Cambridge University Press, pp. 250–304.

Cahen, C. (1968) *Pre-Ottoman Turkey: A General Survey of the Material and Spiritual Culture and History c. 1071–1330*. London: Sidgwick & Jackson.

Canard, M. (1951) *Histoire de la dynastie des H'amdanides de Jazira et de Syrie*, vol. I. Algiers: La Typo-Litho.

Chamberlain, M. (1998) 'The Crusader Era and the Ayyubid Dynasty,' in C. F. Petry (ed.) *The Cambridge History of Egypt*, vol. I. Cambridge: Cambridge University Press, pp. 211–41.

Christensen, A. (1944) *L'Iran sous les Sassanides*. Copenhagen: E. Munksgaard.

Dachraoui, F. (1981) *Le Califat fatimide au Maghreb (296–362 H./909–973 JC.): histoire politique et institutions*. Tunis.

Fahmy, K. (1998) 'The Era of Muhammad 'Ali Pasha,' in M. W. Daly (ed.) *The Cambridge History of Egypt*, vol. II. Cambridge: Cambridge University Press, pp. 136–79.

Forbes Manz, B. (1989) *The Rise and Rule of Tamerlane*. Cambridge: Cambridge University Press.

Frye, R. N. (1975) 'The Samanids,' in R. N. Frye (ed.) *The Cambridge History of Iran*, vol. IV. Cambridge: Cambridge University Press, pp. 136–61.

—— (1983) 'The Political History of Iran under the Sasanians,' in E. Yarshater (ed.) *The Cambridge History of Iran*, vol. III. Cambridge: Cambridge University Press, pp. 116–80.

Garcin, J.-C. (1998) 'The Regime of the Circassian Mamluks,' in C. F. Petry (ed.) *The Cambridge History of Egypt*, vol. I. Cambridge: Cambridge University Press, pp. 290–317.

Gaury, G. de (1951) *Rulers of Mecca*. London: Barnes & Noble.

Gibb, H. A. R. and Bosworth, C. E. (eds) (1960–2003) *Encyclopaedia of Islam. 2nd edn.* Leiden: E. J. Brill.

Grousset, R. (1970) *The Empire of the Steppes. A History of Central Asia*, Eng. tr. New Brunswick, NJ: Rutgers University Press.

Hambly, G. R. G. (1991) 'Agha Muhammad Khan and the establishment of the Qajar Dynasty,' in P. Avery, G. Hambly and C. Melville (eds) *The Cambridge History of Iran*, vol. VII. Cambridge: Cambridge University Press, pp. 104–43.

—— (1991) 'Iran during the Reigns of Fath 'Ali Shah and Muhammad Shah,' in P. Avery, G. Hambly and C. Melville (eds) *The Cambridge History of Iran*, vol. VII. Cambridge: Cambridge University Press, pp. 144–73.

—— (1991) 'The Pahlavi Autocracy: Riza Shah, 1921–1941,' in P. Avery, G. Hambly and C. Melville (eds) *The Cambridge History of Iran*, vol. VII. Cambridge: Cambridge University Press, pp. 213–43.

—— (1991) 'The Pahlavi Autocracy: Muhammad Riza Shah, 1941–1979,' in P. Avery, G. Hambly and C. Melville (eds) *The Cambridge History of Iran*, vol. VII. Cambridge: Cambridge University Press, pp. 244–96.

Hawting, G. R. (1986) *The First Dynasty of Islam. The Umayyad Caliphate AD 661–750.* London: Routledge.

Hodgson, M. G. S. (1955) *The Order of Assassins. The Struggle of the Early Nizari Isma'ilis against the Islamic World.* The Hague: Mouton.

Holt, P. M. (1966) *Egypt and the Fertile Crescent 1516–1922. A Political History.* Ithaca, NY and London: Cornell University Press.

—— (1986) *The Age of the Crusades. The Near East from the Eleventh Century to 1517.* London: Addison Wesley Longman.

Huici Miranda, A. (1956–7) *Historia politica del imperio Almohade*, 2 vols. Tetuan: Editorial Universidad de Granada.

Humphreys, R. S. (1977) *From Saladin to the Mongols. The Ayyubids of Damascus, 1193–1260.* Albany, NY: State University of New York Press.

Hunter, F. R. (1998) 'Egypt under the Successors of Muhammad 'Ali,' in M. W. Daly (ed.) *The Cambridge History of Egypt*, vol. II. Cambridge: Cambridge University Press, pp. 180–97.

Inalcik, H. (1973) *The Ottoman Empire. The Classical Age 1300–1600.* London: Weidenfeld & Nicholson.

Irwin, R. (1986) *The Middle East in the Middle Ages. The Early Mamluk Sultanate 1250–1382.* London: Croom Helm.

Jackson, P. (1999) *The Delhi Sultanate. A Political and Military History.* Cambridge: Cambridge University Press.

Keddie, N. and Amanat, M. (1992) 'Iran under the Later Qajars,' in P. Avery, G. Hambly and C. Melville (eds) *The Cambridge History of Iran*, vol. VII. Cambridge: Cambridge University Press, pp. 174–212.

Kennedy, H. (1981) *The Early Abbasid Caliphate. A Political History.* London: Barnes & Noble.

—— (1986) *The Prophet and the Age of the Caliphs: The Islamic Near East from the Seventh to the Eleventh Century.* London: Longman.

Khadra Jayyusi, S. (ed.) (1992) *The Legacy of Muslim Spain.* Leiden: E. J. Brill.

Lenczowski, G. (ed.) (1978) *Iran under the Pahlavis.* Stanford, CA: Stanford University Press.

Le Tourneau, R. (1969) *The Almohad Movement in North Africa in the Twelfth and Thirteenth Centuries.* Princeton, NJ: Princeton University Press.

Lévi-Provençal, E. (1950–67) *Histoire de l'Espagne musulmane*, 3 vols. Paris and Leiden: E. J. Brill.

Lyons, M. C. and Jackson, D. E. P. (1982) *Saladin: The Politics of the Holy War.* Cambridge: Cambridge University Press.

Makki, M. (1992) 'The Political History of al-Andalus,' in Jayyusi, Salma Khadra/ Marin, Manuela (ed.): *The Legacy of Muslim Spain*, London: E.J. Brill. pp. 3–87.

Mantran, R. (ed.) (1989) *Histoire de l'empire Ottoman.* Paris.

Morgan, D. O. (1986) *The Mongols.* Oxford: Blackwell.

Norris, H.T. (1982) *The Berbers in Arabic Literature.* London: Longman.

Northrup, L. S. (1998) 'The Bahri Mamluk Sultanate, 1250–1390,' in C. F. Petry (ed.) *The Cambridge History of Egypt*, vol. I. Cambridge: Cambridge University Press, pp. 242–89.

Ratchnevsky, P. (1991) *Genghis Khan: His Life and Legacy*, Eng. tr. Oxford: Blackwell.

Richards, J. F. (1993) *The New Cambridge History of India. Vol V. The Mughal*

Empire. Cambridge: Cambridge University Press.

Rizvi, S. A. A. (1975) *Religious and Intellectual History of the Muslims in Akbar's Reign ... (1556–1605)*. New Delhi:

Roemer, H. R. (1986) 'Timur in Iran,' in P. Jackson and L. Lockhart (eds) *The Cambridge History of Iran*, vol. VI. Cambridge: Cambridge University Press, pp. 42–97.

—— (1986) 'The Successors of Timur,' in P. Jackson and L. Lockhart (eds) *The Cambridge History of Iran*, vol. VI. Cambridge: Cambridge University Press, pp. 98–146.

—— (1986) 'The Safavid Period,' in P. Jackson and L. Lockhart (eds) *The Cambridge History of Iran*, vol. VI. Cambridge: Cambridge University Press, pp. 189–350.

Sanders, P. A. (1998) 'The Fatimid State, 969–1171,' in C. F. Petry (ed.) *The Cambridge History of Egypt*, vol. I. Cambridge: Cambridge University Press, pp. 151–74.

Savory, R. M. (1980) *Iran under the Safavids*. Cambridge: Cambridge University Press.

Shahid, I. (1995–2002) *Byzantium and the Arabs in the Sixth Century*, 2 vols. Washington, DC: Dumbarton Oaks Pub Service.

Spuler, B. (1955) *Die Mongolen in Iran. Politik, Verwaltung und Kultur der Ilchanzeit' 1220–1350*, 4th edn. Leiden: E. J. Brill.

Talbi, M. (1966) *L'æmirat aghlabide*. Paris: Librairie d'Amérique et d'Orient.

Terrasse, H. (1949–50) *Histoire du Maroc des origines à l'établissement du Protectorat français*, 2 vols. Casablanca: n.p.

Vasiliev, A. A. (1952) *History of the Byzantine Empire*, 2nd edn. 2 vols. Madison, WI: University of Wisconsin Press.

Vassiliev, A. (1998) *The History of Saudi Arabia*. London and New York: New York University Press.

Vatikiotis, P. J. (1980) *The History of Egypt from Muhammad Ali to Sadat*, 2nd edn. Baltimore, MD, and London: Johns Hopkins University Press.

Walker, P. E. (1998) 'The Isma'ili Da'wa and the Fatimid Caliphate,' in C. F. Petry (ed.) *The Cambridge History of Egypt*, vol. I. Cambridge: Cambridge University Press, pp. 120–50.

Wasserstein, D. (1985) *The Rise and Fall of the Party Kings: Politics and Society in Islamic Spain 1002–1086*. Princeton, NJ: Princeton University Press.

Winder, R. B. (1965) *Saudi Arabia in the Nineteenth Century*. New York: St. Martin's Press.

Entries by Buckley

Arnold, T. W. (1924) *The Caliphate*. Oxford: Clarendon Press.

Ayalon, D. (1960) 'Studies on the Transfer of the 'Abbasid Caliphate to Cairo', *Arabica* vii: 41–59.

Bowen, H. (1928) *The Life and Times of 'Ali b. 'Isa*. Cambridge.

Boyle, J. A. (ed.) (1968) *The Cambridge History of Iran*. Cambridge: Cambridge University Press.

Gibb, H. A. R. (1955) 'The Fiscal Rescript of Umar II', *Arabica*?: 1–16.

Gibb and Bosworth (1960–2003) *The Encyclopaedia of Islam*. Leiden: E. J. Brill.

Hitti, P. K. (1970) *History of the Arabs*. London: Palgrave Macmillan.

Hodgson, M. G. S. (1974) *The Venture of Islam*. Chicago, IL: University of Chicago Press.

—— (1984) 'Some Observations on the 'Abbasid Caliphate of Cairo', *Bulletin of the School of African and Oriental Studies* 47: 501–7.

Ibn Iyas, Muhammad b. Ahmad (1975) *Bada'i' al-Zuhur fi Waqa'i' al-Duhur*. Wiesbaden.

Ibn al-Jawzī, Abū al-Faraj, 'Abd al-Raḥmān (1938). *al-Muntaẓam fī Tārīkh al-Mulūk wa al-Umam*. Hayderabad: Matba'at Da'irat al-Ma'arif al-Uthmaniyya.

Ibn al-Ṭiqṭaqā, Muḥammad b. (1860) *'Alī al-Fakhrī fī al-Ādāb al-Sulṭaniyya wa al-Duwal al-Islāmiyya*. Greifswald: al-Madrasa al-Kulliyya al-Malakiyya.

Kennedy, H. (1981) *The Early Abbasid Caliphate*. London: Barnes & Noble.

—— (1996) *The Prophet and the Age of the Caliphs*. London: Longman.

Le Strange, G. (1924) *Baghdad during the Abbasid Caliphate*. Oxford: Kessinger Publishing.

Muir, W. (1915) *The Caliphate*. Edinburgh: n.p.

Petry, C. (ed.) (1998) *The Cambridge History of Egypt, vol. I: Islamic Egypt 640–1517*. Cambridge: Cambridge University Press.

Salim, M. R. (1965) *'Asr al-Saladin al-Mamalik*. Cairo.

Shaban, M. A. (1971) *Islamic History: A New Interpretation*. Cambridge: Cambridge University Press.

al-Suyuti, Jalal al-Din (1969) *Tarikh al-Khulafa'*. Cairo.

al-Tabari, Muhammad b. Jarir. (1985–95) *The History of al-Tabari*. Albany, NY: State of New York University Press.

Wellhausen, J. (1963) *The Arab Kingdom and its Fall*, trans. M. G. Weir. Beirut.

Entries by Clark

Clark, P. (1986) *Marmaduke Pickthall: British Muslim*. London: Quartet Books.

Gibbon, Edward (1986) *Memoirs of My Life*. Harmondsworth: Penguin.

Low, D. M. (1937) *Edward Gibbon*. London: Chatto & Windus.

Porter, R. (1988) *Edward Gibbon: Making History*. Basingstoke: Palgrave Macmillan.

Entries by Friemuth

Abdul Quasem, M. (1983) *Salvation of the Soul and Islamic Devotion*. London: Kegan Paul.

Arberry, A. J. (1966) *Muslim Saints and Mystics*. London: Routledge & Kegan Paul.

Badawi, A. (1971) *Madhahib al-Islamiyyn*, vol. II. Beirut: Dar al-'ilm lil-Malaiyyn.

—— (1977) *al-Aflatuniya al-Muhdatha 'Ind al-'Arab*. Kuwait: Wikala al-Matbu'at.

Broandie, A. (1996) 'Maimonides', in S. H. Nasr and O. Leaman (eds), *History of Islamic Philosophy*, vol. I. London: Routledge.

Corbin, Henry (1986) *Les Livres du glorieux de Jabir Ibn Hayyan: L'Alchimi comme l'art hiératique*. Paris: Herne.

Davidson, H. A. (1992) *al-Farabi, Avicenna and Averroes on the Intellect*. Oxford: Oxford University Press.

Dhanani, A. (1994) *The Physical Theory of Kalam: Atoms, Space, and Void in Basrian Mu'tazili Cosmology*. Leiden: E. J. Brill.

Fakhry, M. (1983) *A History of Islamic Philosophy*. New York: Columbia University Press.

al-Farabi (1985) *Ara' Ahl al-Madina al-Fadila*, R. Walzer (ed.). Oxford: Oxford University Press.

Genequand, C. (1996) 'Metaphysics', in S. H. Nasr and O. Leaman (eds), *History of Islamic Philosophy*, vol. I. London: Routledge.

al-Ghazali, Abu Hamid (1952) *Mishkat al-Anwar*, trans. W. H. T. Gairdner. Lahore: Ashraf.

—— (1961) *Tahafut al-Falasifa*, S. Dunya (ed.). Cairo: Dar al-Ma'arif.

—— (1990) *Tahafut al-Falasifa*, M. Fakhry (ed.), Beirut: Dar al-Shuruq, pp. 81–9.

—— (2000) *Tahafut al-Falasifa*. Provo, UT: Brigham Young University Press, 2000.

Gibb, H. A. R. and Bosworth, C. E. (eds) (1960–2003) *Encyclopaedia of Islam*, 2nd edn. Leiden: E. J. Brill.

Goodman, L. (1992) *Avicenna*. London and New York: Routledge.

—— (1996a) 'Ibn Bajjah', in S. H. Nasr and O. Leaman (eds), *History of Islamic Philosophy*, vol. I. London: Routledge.

—— (1996a) 'Ibn Masarrah', in S. H. Nasr and O. Leaman (eds), *History of Islamic Philosophy*, vol. I. London: Routledge.

Gutas, D. (1988) *Avicenna and the Aristotelian Tradition*. Leiden: E. J. Brill.

Ibn al-Futi (1932) *al-Hawadith al-Jami'a*. Baghdad.

Ibn Rushd (1972) *Fasl al-Maqal*. Cairo: Dar al-Ma'arif.

Ibn Sab'in (1978) *Budd al-'Afif (Escape of the Gnostic)*, G. Kattura (ed.). Beirut: Dar al-Andalus.

Ibn Sina (1960) *Al-Shifa', al-Ilahiyyat*, 2 vol., G. C. Anwati. (ed.), Cairo: Dar al-Kitab al-'Arabi lil-Tiba'ah wa-al-Nashr.

Kraemer, J. L. (1992) *Humanism in Renaissance of Islam: The Culture Revival During the Buyid Age*. Leiden: E. J. Brill.

Lancaster, I. (1996) 'Ibn Gabirol', in S. H. Nasr and O. Leaman (eds), *History of Islamic Philosophy*, vol. I. London: Routledge, pp. 712–18.

Leaman, O. (1996) 'Jewish Everroism', in S. H. Nasr and O. Leaman (eds), *History of Islamic Philosophy*, vol. I. London: Routledge, pp. 769–79.

—— (1999) *A Brief Introduction to Islamic Philosophy*. Cambridge: Polity Press.

Netton, I. R. (1989) *Allah Transcendent*. Richmond: Curzon.

—— (1992) *Al-Farabi and His School*. London: Routledge.

Ormsby, E. L. (1984) *Theodicy in Islamic Thought*. Princeton, NJ: Princeton University Press.

Peters, J. R. T. M. (1976) *God's Created Speech*. Leiden: E. J. Brill.

Rahman, F. (1981) 'Essence and Existence in Ibn Sina: The Myth and Reality', *Hamdard Islamicus*. 4 (1).

Rosenthal, F. (1937) 'Die Arabische Autobiography', *Studia Arabica*. I: 15–19,

Rowson, E. (1996) 'Al-'Amiri', in S. H. Nasr and O. Leaman (eds), *History of Islamic Philosophy*. London: Routledge.

Schimmel, A. M. (1975) *Mystical Dimensions of Islam*. Chapel Hill, NC: University of North Carolina Press.

Taftazani and Leaman (1996) 'Ibn Sab'in', in S. H. Nasr and O. Leaman (eds), *History of Islamic Philosophy*, vol. I. London: Routledge, pp. 346–9.

Ullmann, M. (1978) *Islamic Medicine*. Edinburgh: Edinburgh University Press.

Wolfson, H. A. (1973) *Studies in the History of Philosophy and Religion*. Cambridge, MA: Harvard University Press.

—— (1976) *The Philosophy of the Kalam*. London: Harvard University Press.

Entries by Gleave

Abrahamian, E. (1982) *Iran Between Two Revolutions*. Princeton, NJ: Princeton University Press.

Algar, H. (1969) 'The Revolt of. Agha Khan Mahalati and the transference of the Isma'ili Imamate to India', *Studia Islamica*. 29: 55–81.

Amir-Moezzi, M. (1994) *The Divine Guide in Early Shi'ism*. Albany, NY: SUNY Press.

Ansari, H. (1984) 'The Islamic Militants in Egyptian Politics', *International Journal of Middle East Studies* 16: 123–44.

Arjomand, S. A. (1988) *The Turban for the Crown*. Oxford: Oxford University Press.

Babinger, F. (1978) *Mehmet the Conqueror and his time*. Princeton, NJ: Princeton University Press.

Bamyeh, M. (1999) *The Social Origins of Islam*. Minneapolis, MN: University of Minnesota Press.

Boyce, M. (1975) *A History of Zoroastrianism*. Leiden: E. J. Brill.

Boyle, J. A. (1977) *The Mongol World Empire, 1206–1370*. London: Variorum Reprints.

Bravmann, M. (1972) *The Spiritual Background of Early Islam: Studies in Ancient Arabian Concepts*. Leiden: E. J. Brill.

Calder, N. (2000) 'The Limits of Islamic Orthodoxy', in F. Daftary (ed.) *Intellectual Traditions in Islam*. London: I. B. Tauris, pp. 66–86.

Chokr, M. (1993) *Zandaqa et zandiqs en islam au second siècle de l'hégire*. Damascus: Institut Français de Damas.

Crone, P. (1987) *Roman, Provincial and Islamic Law*. Princeton, NJ: Princeton University Press.

—— (1994) 'Were the Qays and Yemen of the Ummayyad Period Political Parties?', *Der Islam* 76: 1–57.

Crone, P. and Hinds, M. (1986) *God's Caliph*. Cambridge: Cambridge University Press.

Dabashi, H. (1993) *Theology of Discontent: The Ideological Foundation of the Islamic Revolution in Iran*. New York: New York University Press.

Daftary, F. (1990) *The Isma'ilis*. Cambridge: Cambridge University Press, pp. 435–548.

—— *The Assassin Legends: Myths of the Isma'ilis*. London: I.B. Tauris.

Donner, F. (1981) *The Early Islamic Conquests*. Princeton, NJ: Princeton University Press, pp. 24–126

Dumasia, N. M. (1903) *A Brief History of the Agha Khan*. Bombay: Times of India Press.

Fischer, M. (1980) *Iran: From Religious Dispute and Revolution*. Cambridge MA: Harvard University Press.

Fredegarius Scholasticus (1888) *Chronicarum quae dicuntur Fredegarii libri IV*. Hanover: Monumenta Germania Historica Scriptores Rerum Merovingicarum.

Freidmann, Y. (1989) *Prophecy Continuous*. Berkeley, CA: University of California Press.

Gibb, H. A. R. (1962) 'Pre-Islamic Monotheism in Arabia', *Harvard Theological Review*. 55: 269–80.

—— (1962) 'The Social Significance of the Shu'ubiyya' in *Studies on the Civilisation of Islam*. London: Routledge & Kegan Paul.

Gieling, S. (1999) *Religion and War in Revolutionary Iran*. London: I. B. Tauris.

Goitein, S. D. (1967–93) *A Mediterranean Society*, 3 vols. Berkeley, CA: University of California Press.

Goldziher, I. (1961) 'Die Shu'ubijja und ihre Bekundung in der Wissenschaft' in *Muhammedenische Studien*, vol. I. Hildesheim: Olms, pp. 177–218.

Gutas, D. (1988) *Greek Thought, Arabic Culture*. London: Routledge.

Harvey, L. P. (1990) *Islamic Spain 1250–1500*. Chicago, IL, and London: University of Chicago Press.

Hawting, G. (1986) *The First Dynasty of Islam*. London: Croom Helm.

—— (1999) *Idolatory and the Emergence of Islam*. Cambridge: Cambridge University Press.

Hinnells, J. (1981) *Zoroastrianism and the Parsees*. London: Ward Lock Educational.

Hodgeson, M. G. S. (1955) *The Order of the Assassins*. The Hague: Mouton.

Ibn Malik al-Hammadi al-Yamani (1939) *Kashf al-Asrar al-Batiniyya wa Akhbar al-Qaramita*. Cairo: n.p.

Ibrahim, S. E. (1988) 'Egypt's Activism in the 1980s', *Third World Quarterly*. 10: 632–57.

Imber, C. (1990) *The Ottoman Empire 1300–1481*. Istanbul: Isis Press.

Inalcik, K. (1973) *The Ottoman Empire: The Classical Age 1300–1600*. London: Weidenfeld & Nicolson.

Ivanow, V. (1960) *Alamut and Lamasar: Two Mediaeval Ismaili Strongholds in Iran*. Tehran: Ismaili Society.

Ivanow, W. (1940) 'Ismailis and Qarmatians', *Journal of the Bombay Branch of the Royal Asiatic Society* 16: 43–55.

Kepel, G. (1985) *The Prophet and the Pharaoh*. London: Al Saqi.

King, R. (1987) *The Iran–Iraq War: The Political Implications*. London: International Institute for Strategic Studies.

—— (1999) *Orientalism and Religion*. London: Routledge.

Kister, M. (1980) *Studies in Jahiliyya and Early Islam*. Aldershot: Variorum.

Lambton, A. K. S. (1981) *State and Government in Medieval Islam*. Oxford: Oxford University Press.

Lévi-Provençal, E. (1950) *Histoire de l'Espagne musulmane*. Paris: G.-P. Maisonneuve.

Lewis, B. (1968) *The Assassins*. New York: Basic Books.

—— (1984) *Jews of Islam*. Princeton, NJ: Princeton University Press.

Lieu, S. (1997) *Manichaeism in Mesopotamia and the Roman East*. Leiden: E. J. Brill.

—— (1998) *Manichaeism in China and Central Asia*. Leiden: E. J. Brill.

Madelung, M. (1985) *Religious Schools and Sects in Medieval Islam*. London: Variorum.

Madelung, W. (1996) 'The Fatimids and the Qarmatis of Bahrayn', in F. Daftary (ed.) *Mediaeval Isma'ili History and Thought*. Cambridge: Cambridge University Press, pp. 21–74.

Mahdi, Muhsin (1957) *Ibn Khaldun's Philosophy of History*. London: Allen and Unwin.

al-Maqqari, Ahmad b. Muhammad (1949) *Nafh al-Tib*, 10 vols. Cairo: al-Maktaba al-Tijariya al-Kubr.

Marlow, L. (1997) *Hierarchy and Egalitarianism in Islamic Thought*. Cambridge: Cambridge University Press.

Melchert, C. (199) *The Formation of the Sunni Schools of Law, 9th–10th Centuries C.E.* Leiden: E. J. Brill.

Morgan, D. (1986a) 'The "Great Yasa" of Chingiz Khan and the Mongol Law of the Ilkhanate', *BSOAS* 44: 163–76.

—— (1986b) *The Mongols*. Oxford: Blackwell.

Mottahedeh, R. (1976) 'The Shu'ubiyya Controversy and the Social History of Early Islamic Iran', *International Journal of Middle East Studies*. 7: 161–82.

Nasr, S. H. *et al*. (eds) (1988) *Expectation of the Millennium*. Albany, NY: SUNY.

Nicol, Donald (1993) *The Last Centuries of Byzantium, 1261–1453*. Cambridge: Cambridge University Press.

Parry, V. J. (1976) *A History of the Ottoman Empire to 1730*. Cambridge: Cambridge University Press.

Reif, S. C. (2000) *A Jewish Archive from Old Cairo: The History of Cambridge University's Genizah Collections*. Richmond: Curzon.

Runciman, S. (1977) *The Byzantine Theocracy*. Cambridge: Cambridge University Press.

Sachedina, A. (1981) *Islamic Messianism*. Albany, NY: SUNY Press.

Said, E. (2003) *Orientalism*. London: Penguin.

Sharon, M. (1983) *Black Banners from the East*. Leiden: E. J. Brill.

Stern, S. M. (1961) 'Ismailis and Qarmatians', in *L'Élaboration de l'Islam*. Paris: Presses Universitaires de France, pp. 98–108.

al-Tabari, Muhammad b. Jarir (1879–1901) *Tarikh al-Rasul wa'l-Muluk*. Leiden: E. J. Brill.

Taqizadeh, S. H. (1970) *Az Parviz ta Changiz*. Tehran: Furughi.

Turner, B. (1984) *Orientalism, Postmodernism and Globalism*. London: Routledge.

Walbridge, L. (ed.) (2001) *The Most Learned of the Shi'a*. Oxford: Oxford University Press.

Walzer, R. (1962) *Greek into Arabic*. Oxford: Oxford University Press.

Wansbrough, J. (1977) *Quranic Studies: Sources and Methods of Scriptural Interpretation*. Oxford: Oxford University Press.

Wassertrom, S. (1995) *Between Muslim and Jew*. Princeton, NJ: Princeton University Press.

Watt, W. M. (1965) *A History of Islamic Spain*. Edinburgh: Edinburgh University Press.

—— (1973) *The Formative Period of Islamic Thought*. Edinburgh: Edinburgh University Press.

al-Ya'qubi, Ahmad b. Abi Ya'qub (1883) *Tarikh*, vol. II. Leiden: E. J. Brill, pp. 418–20.

Yarshater, E. (eds) (1968–91) *Cambridge History of Iran*, vol. III. Cambridge: Cambridge University Press.

Zaehner, R. C. (1955) *Zurvan, A Zoroastrian Dilemma.* London: Weidenfeld & Nicolson.

Entries by Goddard

'Abduh, M. (1966) *The Theology of Unity*, trans. I. Musa'ad and K. Cragg. London: George Allen & Unwin.

Abun-Nasr, J. M. (1987) *A History of the Maghreb in the Islamic Period.* Cambridge: Cambridge University Press.

Ahmad, A. (1964) *Studies in Islamic Culture in the Indian Environment.* Oxford: Oxford University Press.

—— (1967) *Islamic Modernism in India and Pakistan 1857–1964.* Oxford: Oxford University Press.

Ahmad, K. and Ansari, Z. I. (eds) (1980) *Islamic Perspectives: Studies in Honour of Mawlana Sayyid Abul A'lā Mawdudi.* Leicester: Islamic Foundation.

Algar, H. (2002) *Wahhabism: A Critical Essay.* Oneonta, NY: Islamic Publications International.

Ali, A. (1922) *The Spirit of Islam.* London: Christophers.

Amin, A. (1968) *My Life*, trans. I. J. Boullata. Leiden: E. J. Brill.

Amin, Q. (2000) *The Liberation of Women* and *The New Woman: Two Documents in the History of Egyptian Feminism*, trans. S. S. Peterson. Cairo: American University in Cairo Press.

Ansari, M. A. H. (1986) *Sufism and Shar'ah: A Study of Shaykh Ahmad Sirhindi's Effort to Reform Sufism.* Leicester: Islamic Foundation.

Badawi, M. A. Z. (1978) *The Reformers of Egypt.* London: Croom Helm.

Baljon, J. M. S. (1949) *The Reforms and Religious Ideas of Sir Sayyid Ahmad Khan.* Leiden: E. J. Brill.

—— (1986) *Religion and Thought of Shah Wali Allah Dihlawi 1703–1762.* Leiden: E. J. Brill.

Black, A. (2001) *The History of Islamic Political Thought.* Edinburgh: Edinburgh University Press.

Burrell, D. B. (ed.) (1992) *Al-Ghazali: the Ninety-Nine Beautiful Names of God.* Cambridge: Islamic Texts Society.

Caspar, R. (1998) *A Historical Introduction to Islamic Theology.* Rome: Pontifical Institute for Arabic and Islamic Studies.

Cureton, W. (ed.) (1842, 1846) *The Book of Religious and Philosophical Sects.* London: The London Society for the Publication of Oriental Texts.

al-Faruqi, I. R. (ed.) (1979) *The* Kitab al-Tawhid *of Shaykh Muhammad ibn 'Abd al-Wahhab.* Beirut and Damascus: Holy Koran Publishing House.

Friedmann, Y. (1971) *Shaykh Ahmad Sirhindi: An Outline of His Thought and a Study of His Image in the Eyes of Posterity.* Toronto: McGill University Press.

Haddad, W. Z. (1995) 'A Tenth-Century Speculative Theologian's Refutation of the Basic Doctrines of Christianity: al-Baqillani (d. A.D. 1013)' in Y. Y. Haddad and W. Z. Haddad (eds) *Christian-Muslim Encounters.* Gainesville, FL: University Press of Florida, pp. 82–94.

Hallaq, W. B. (1993) *Ibn Taimiyya Against the Greek Logicians.* Oxford: Oxford University Press.

Haq, M. A. (1972) *The Faith Movement of Mawlana Muhammad Ilyas.* London: George Allen & Unwin.

Hermansen, M. K. (ed.) (1996) *The Conclusive Argument from God: Shah Wali Allah of Delhi's Hujjat Allah al-Baligha.* Leiden: E. J. Brill.

Hourani, A. H. (1983) *Arabic Thought in the Liberal Age, 1798–1939*, 2nd edn. Cambridge: Cambridge University Press.

Hourani, G. F. (1971) *Islamic Rationalism: the Ethics of 'Abd al-Jabbar.* Oxford: Oxford University Press.

Iqbal, M. (1934) *The Reconstruction of Religious Thought in Islam*, first published in London and reprinted many times, e.g. Lahore: Ashraf, 1954.

Jackson, S. A. (ed.) (2002) *On the Boundaries of Theological Tolerance in Islam.* Oxford: Oxford University Press.

Johnstone, P. (ed.) (1998) *The Medicine of the Prophet.* Cambridge: Islamic Texts Society.

Kazi, A. K. and Flynn, J. G. (1984) *Muslim Sects and Divisions.* London: Kegan Paul.

Keddie, N. R. (1972) *Sayyid Jamal al-Din 'al-Afghani': A Political Biography.* Berkeley, CA: University of California Press.

—— (1983) *An Islamic Response to Imperialism: Religious and Political Writings of Sayyid Jamal al-Din 'al-Afghani'*, 2nd edn. Berkeley, CA: University of California Press.

Kedourie, E. (1966) *Afghani and Abduh: An Essay on Religious Unbelief and Political Activism in Modern Islam.* London: Frank Cass.

Kepel, G. (1985) *The Prophet and Pharoah*. London: al-Saqi Books.

Kerr, M. H. (1966) *Islamic Reform: The Political and Legal Theories of Muhammad 'Abduh and Rashid Rida*. Cambridge: Cambridge University Press.

Khan, Q. (1983) *The Political Thought of Ibn'Taymiyah*. Lahore: Islamic Book Foundation.

Lambton, A. K. S. (1981) *State and Government in Medieval Islam*. Oxford: Oxford University Press.

Lawrence, B. B. (1976) *Shahrastani on the Indian Religions*. The Hague: Mouton.

Macdonald, D. B. (1903) *The Development of Muslim Theology, Jurisprudence and Constitutional Theory*. New York: Russell & Russell.

McCarthy, R. J. (ed.) (1953) *The Theology of al-Ash'ari*. Beirut: Imprimerie Catholique.

—— (ed.) (1957) *Kitab al-Tamhid*. Beirut: Imprimerie Catholique.

—— (ed.) (2001) *Deliverance from Error*. Louisville, KY: Fons Vitae.

Madelung, W. and Mayer, T. (eds) (2001) *Struggling with the Philosopher: A Refutation'of Avicenna's Metaphysics*. London: I. B. Tauris.

Makari, V. E. (1983) *Ibn Taimiyya's Ethics: The Social Factor*. Chico, CA: Scholars Press.

Makdisi, G. (ed.) (1962) *Ibn Qudama's Censure of Speculative Theology*. London: E. J. W. Gibb Memorial Series.

Malik, H. (ed.) (1971) *Iqbal: Poet-Philosopher of Pakistan*, New York: Columbia University Press.

—— (1980) *Sir Sayyid Ahmad Khan and Muslim Modernization in India and Pakistan*. New York: Columbia University Press.

Marmura, M. E. (ed.) (1997) *The Incoherence of the Philosophers*. Provo, UT: Brigham Young University Press.

Martin, R. C., Woodward, M. R. and Atmaja, D. S. (1997) *Defenders of Reason in Islam: Mu'tazilism from Medieval School to Modern Symbol*. Oxford: Oneworld.

al-Mawardi, (1996) *The Ordinances of Islamic Government*. Reading: Garnet.

Mawdudi, A. A. (1955) *Islamic Law and Constitution*. Lahore: Islamic Publications.

Memon, M. U. (1976) *Ibn Taimiyya's Struggle Against Popular Religion*. The Hague: Mouton.

Metcalf, B. D. (1982) *Islamic Revival in British India: Deoband 1860–1900*. Princeton, NJ: Princeton University Press.

—— (1994) '"Remaking Ourselves": Islamic Self-Fashioning in a Global Movement of Spiritual Renewal', in M. E. Marty and R. S. Appleby (eds) *Accounting for Fundamentalisms*. Chicago, IL: University of Chicago Press, pp. 706–25.

Michel, T. (1984) *A Muslim Theologian's Response to Christianity*. Delmar, NY: Caravan Books.

Mikhail, H. (1995) *Politics and Revelation: Mawardi and After*. Edinburgh: Edinburgh University Press.

Moosa, E. (forthcoming) *Al-Ghazali of Tus: His Life and Thought*. Oxford: Oneworld.

Moreh, S. (ed.) (1993) *Napoleon in Egypt: Al-Jabarti's Chronicle of the French Occupation, 1798*. Princeton, NJ: Markus Wiener.

Moussalli, A. S. (1992) *Radical Islamic Fundamentalism: The Ideological and Political Discourse of Sayyid Qutb*. Beirut: American University of Beirut Press.

Nadwi, A. H. A. (1983) *Life and Mission of Maulana Mohammad Ilyas*. Lucknow: Academy of Islamic Research and Publications.

Nasr, S. V. R. (1994) *The Vanguard of the Islamic Revolution: the Jama'at-i Islami of Pakistan*. London: I. B. Tauris.

—— (1996) *Mawdudi and the Making of Islamic Revivalism*. Oxford: Oxford University Press.

Peters, J. R. T. M. (1976) *God's Created Speech: A Study of the Speculative Theology of the Mu'tazilite Qadi'l-Qudat Abu'l-Hasan 'Abd al-Jabbar ibn Ahmad al-Hamadani*. Leiden: E. J. Brill.

Raschid, M. S. (1986) *Iqbal's Concept of God*. London: Kegan Paul.

Rizvi, S. A. A. (1980) *Shah Wali Allah and His Times: A Study of Eighteenth Century Islam, Politics and Society in India*. Canberra: Ma'rifat.

Rosenthal, E. I. J. (1958) *Political Thought in Medieval Islam*. Cambridge: Cambridge University Press.

Schimmel, A. (1963) *Gabriel's Wing: A Study into the Religious Ideas of Sir Muhammad Iqbal*. Leiden: E. J. Brill.

Shahin, E. E. (1993) *Through Muslim Eyes: M. Rashid Rida and the West*. Herndon, VA: International Institute of Islamic Thought.

Shepard, W. E. (1996) *Sayyid Qutb and Islamic Activism*. Leiden: E. J. Brill.

Sikand, Y. (2002) *The Origins and Development of the Tablighi Jama'at (1920–2000):*

A Cross-Country Comparative Study. Hyderabad: Orient Longman.

Sivan, E. (1990) *Radical Islam: Medieval Theology and Modern Politics*, 2nd edn. New Haven, CT: Yale University Press.

Troll, C. W. (1978) *Sayyid Ahmad Khan: A Reinterpretation of Muslim Theology.* Delhi: Vikas. Reprinted Karachi: Oxford University Press, 1979.

Vassiliev, A. (2000) *The History of Saudi Arabia.* London: Saqi Books.

Von Grunebaum, G. E. (1950) *A Tenth-Century Document of Arabic Literary Theory and Criticism: the Sections on Poetry of al-Baqillani's I'jaz al-Qur'an.* Chicago, IL: University of Chicago Press.

Walker, P. E. (ed.) (2000) *A Guide to Conclusive Proofs for the Principles of Belief.* Reading: Garnet.

Watt, W. M. (1963) *Muslim Intellectual: A Study of al-Ghazali.* Edinburgh: Edinburgh University Press.

—— (1973) *The Formative Period of Islamic Thought.* Edinburgh: Edinburgh University Press. Reprinted Oxford: Oneworld, 1998.

—— (1985) *Islamic Philosophy and Theology*, 2nd edn. Edinburgh: Edinburgh University Press.

—— (1994) *The Faith and Practice of al-Ghazali.* Oxford: Oneworld.

Williams, J. A. (1994) *The Word of Islam.* Austin, TX: University of Texas Press.

al-Yassini, A. (1985) *Religion and State in the Kingdom of Saudi Arabia.* Boulder, CO: Westview Press.

Entries by Hopwood

Abu-Lughod, J. (1971) *Cairo: 1001 Years of the City Victorious.* Princeton, NJ: Princeton University Press.

—— (1980) *Rabat: Urban Apartheid in Morocco.* Princeton, NJ: Princeton University Press.

Ahmed, L. (1978) *Edward Lane: A Study of his Life and Work.* London: Longman.

Asher, M. (1998) *Lawrence: The Uncrowned King of Arabia.* London: Penguin.

Ayalon, D. (1960) 'The Historian al-Jabarti and His Background', *Bulletin of the School of Oriental and African Studies* 23: 217–49.

Baghdad (1969) *Baghdad: An Illustrated Historical Survey.* Baghdad.

Bar-Zohar, M. (1978) *Ben-Gurion: A Biography.* New York: Weidenfeld & Nicolson.

Bearman, J. (1986) *Qadhafi's Libya.* London: Palgrave Macmillan.

Bianco, M. (1975) *Gadhafi: Voice from the Desert.* New York: Longman.

Burrowes, R. D. (1995) *Historical Dictionary of Yemen.* Lanham, MD: Scarecrow Press.

Cachia, P. (1956) *Taha Husayn: His Place in the Egyptian Literary Renaissance.* London: Gorgias Press.

Cockburn, A. (2002) *Saddam Hussein: An American Obsession.* London: Verso.

Debbas, F. C. (1986) *Beirut: Our Memory; a Guided Tour with Postcards from the Collection of Fouad C. Debbas.* Beirut: Garnet Publishing.

De Gaury, G. (1951) *Rulers of Mecca.* London: Barnes & Noble.

Devlin, J. (1976) *The Ba'th Party: A History from its Origins to 1966.* Stanford, CA: Stanford University Press.

Diehl, G. (1967) *Delacroix.* Paris: Flammarion.

Dodwell, H. (1931) *The Founder of Modern Egypt.* Cambridge: Cambridge University Press.

Egypt (1976) *Egypt.* Paris: Editions Marcus.

El-Enany R. (1993) *Naguib Mahfouz: the Pursuit of Meaning.* London: Routledge.

Findlay, A. M. (1986) *Planning the Arab City: The Cases of Tunis and Rabat.* Oxford: Elsevier.

Fugelstad-Aumenier, V. (ed.) (1991–4) *Alep et la Syrie du Nord.* Aix-en-Provence.

Guiterman, H. (1978) *David Roberts R.A.* London: n.p.

Gulick, J. (1967) *Tripoli: A Modern Arab City.* Cambridge, MA: Harvard University Press.

Hart, A. (1989) *Arafat: A Political Biography.* Bloomington, IN: Indiana University Press.

Hirst, D. and Beeston, I. (1981) *Sadat.* London: Faber&Faber.

Hitti, P. K. (1973) *Capital Cities of Arab Islam.* Minneapolis, MN: University of Minnesota Press.

Hopwood, D. (1989) *Syria 1945–1986: Politics and Society.* London: Unwin Hyman.

—— (1992) *Habib Bourguiba of Tunisia: The Tragedy of Longevity.* New York: St. Martin's Press.

Izzard, M. (1993) *Freya Stark: A Biography.* London: Hodder & Stoughton.

Jidejian, N. (1973) *Beirut through the Ages.* Beirut: Dar el-Machreq.

—— (1980) *Tripoli through the Ages.* Beirut: Dar el-Machreq.

Kinross, Lord (1964) *Ataturk: The Rebirth of a Nation*. London: Weidenfeld & Nicholson.

Mango, A. (2000) *Ataturk: The Biography of the Founder of Modern Turkey*. London: Overlook Press.

Marsot, A. L. and Marsot, S. (1986) *Egypt in the Reign of Muhammad Ali*. New York: Columbia University Press.

Michell, G. (ed.) (1995) *Architecture of the Islamic World: its History and Social Meaning with a Complete Survey of its Monuments*. London: Thames & Hudson.

Mitchell, R. (1969) *The Society of Muslim Brothers*. Oxford: Oxford University Press.

Murphy-O'Connor, J. (1992) *The Holy Land: An Archaeological Guide from Earliest Times to 1700*. Oxford: Oxford Archaeological Guides.

Northedge, A. (1992) *Studies on Roman and Islamic Amman*. Oxford: Oxford University Press.

Perlmutter, A. (1987) *The Life and Times of Menachem Begin*. New York: Doubleday.

Rihawi, A. (1977) *Damascus: Its History, Development and Artistic Heritage*. Damascus: Dar al-Bashar

Sadat, A. (1978) *In Search of Identity: An Autobiography*. London: HarperCollins.

Said, E. W. (1999) *Out of Place: A Memoir*. London: Knopf.

Seale, P. (1990) *Assad of Syria*. Berkeley, CA: University of California Press.

Somekh, S. (1973) *The Changing Rhythm, a Study of Najib Mahfuz's Novels*. Leiden: E. J. Brill.

Stephens, R. (1971) *Nasser: A Political Biography*. New York: Simon & Schuster.

Temko, N. (1987) *To Win or Die: A Personal Portrait of Menachem Begin*. New York: Morrow.

Walkley, C. E. (1935/6) 'The Story of Khartoum', *Sudan Notes and Records*, vols. 18, 19.

Wallach, J. (1996) *Desert Queen: The Extraordinary Life of Gertrude Bell*. London: Anchor.

Ward, P. (1969) *Tripoli: Portrait of a City*. Stoughton, WI: Oleander.

Wendell, C. (1978) *Five Tracts of Hasan al-Banna (1906–1949)*. Berkeley, CA: University of California Press.

Wilson, J. (1990) *Lawrence of Arabia: The Authorized Biography of T. E. Lawrence*. London: Atheneum.

Winstone, H. V. F. (1993) *Gertrude Bell*. London: Constable.

Yeghen, F. (1927) *Saad Zaghloul: le 'pere du peuple' egyptien*. Paris: Les Cahiers de France.

Entries by Hulmes

Abboud, P. F. *et al.* (1976) *Elementary Modern Standard Arabic*. Ann Arbor, MI: University of Michigan Press.

Abdul-Rauf, M. (1977) *Arabic for English-Speaking Students*. London: Shorouk International.

—— (1978) 'Pilgrimage to Mecca', *National Geographic Magazine* November, 154 (5): 581–607.

Achebe, Chinua (1964) *Things Fall Apart*. London: Heinemann.

—— (1978) *Arrow of God*. London: Heinemann.

Adeleye, R. A. (1971) *Power and Diplomacy in Northern Nigeria: The Sokoto Caliphate and its Enemies*. London: Longman.

Ahmad, K. (1968) *Principles of Islamic Education*. Lahore: Islamic Publications.

Ajayi, J. F. A. (1967) 'Samuel Crowther of Oyo', in P. D. Curtin (ed.) *Africa Remembered: Narratives by West Africans from the Era of the Slave Trade*. Madison, WI: University of Wisconsin/ Ibadan University Press.

—— (1977) *Christian Missions in Nigeria, 1841–1891*. London: Longman.

Ajayi, J. F. A. and Crowder, M. (eds) (1977–8) *History of West Africa*, 2 volumes. London: Longman.

Ali, A. Y. (1968) *The Holy Qur'an: Text, Translation and Commentary*, first published 1934. Beirut : Dar al-Arabia.

Anderson, J. D. (1972) *West Africa since 1800*. London: Heinemann Educational.

Anderson, J. D. with Ikime, O. (1972) *West Africa and East Africa in the Nineteenth and Twentieth Centuries*, Book 1. London.

Arberry, A. J. (ed.) (1953) *The Legacy of Persia*. Oxford: Oxford University Press.

—— (1964) *The Koran Interpreted*. Oxford: Oxford University Press.

Arnold, T. and Guillaume, A. (eds) (1931) *The Legacy of Islam*. Oxford: Oxford University Press.

Ayandele, E. A. (1966) *The Missionary Impact on Modern Nigeria, 1842–1914*. London: Longman.

Blyden, E. W. (1905) *West Africa before Europe*. London: C. M. Phillips.

—— (1967) *Christianity, Islam and the Negro Race*, first published 1887. Edinburgh: Edinburgh University Press.

Bosworth, C. E. (1967) *The Islamic Dynasties*, Islamic Survey No. 5. Edinburgh: Edinburgh University Press.

Bosworth, C. E. and Richardson, M. E. J. (eds) (1991) *Richard Bell's Commentary on the Qur'an*, 2 vols. Journal of Semitic Studies Monograph 14. Manchester: University of Manchester Press.

Bouhdiba, A. (1985) *Sexuality in Islam*. London: Routledge & Kegan Paul.

Brown, K. and Palmer, M. (1987) *The Essential Teachings of Islam*. London: Rider.

Browne, E. G. (1921) *Arabian Medicine*. Cambridge: Cambridge University Press.

—— (1926) *A Year Among the Persians*, first published by A. & C. Black Ltd. 1893. Cambridge: Cambridge University Press.

Burland, C. A. (1967) *The Arts of the Alchemists*. New York: Macmillan.

Burton, R. (2004) *A Secret Pilgrimage to Mecca and Medina*, first published 1855–6. London: Folio Society.

Cohen, R. (1967) *The Kanuri of Bornu*. New York: Holt, Rinehart & Winston.

Crowder, M. (1977) *West Africa: An Introduction to its History*. London: Longman.

Crowther, S. A. (1892) *Experiences with Heathens and Mohammedans in West Africa*. London: SPCK.

Davidson, B. (1977) *A History of West Africa 1000–1800*. London: Longman.

Dawood, N. J. (1991) *The Koran*. London: Penguin Classics.

Doughty, C. M. (1926) *Travels in Arabia Deserta*, first published 1883. London: Jonathan Cape and The Medici Society.

Earthy, E. D. (1955) 'The Impact of Mohammedanism on Paganism in the Liberian Hinterland', *Numen* 2 (3): 206–16.

Esposito, John L. (ed.) (1995) *The Oxford Encyclopaedia of the Modern Islamic World*. New York: Oxford University Press.

Fage, J. D. (1959a) *Ghana: An Historical Interpretation*. London: Green Apple Books.

—— (1959b) *Ghana: A New Interpretation*. Madison, WI: Wisconsin University Press.

Fisher, H. J. (1963) *Ahmadiyyah: A Study in Contemporary Islam on the West African Coast*. Oxford: Oxford University Press.

—— (1969) *Islam in Africa*. New York:

—— (1970) 'The Western and Central Sudan and East Africa', in *Cambridge History of Islam*, vol. II. Cambridge: Cambridge University Press, pp. 345–405.

Friedlander, S. (1977) *Submission: Sayings of the Prophet Muhammad*. New York: Harper Colophon Books.

Fuchs, P. (1956) *The Land of Veiled Men*. London: Weidenfeld & Nicolson.

Gibb, H. A. R. (1955) *Islam: An Historical Survey*. New York: Mentor Books.

Gibb, H. A. R. and Bosworth, C. E. (eds) (1960–2003) *Encyclopaedia of Islam*, 2nd edn. Leiden: E. J. Brill.

Gibb, H. A. R. and Kramers, J. H. (eds) (1961) *Shorter Encyclopaedia of Islam*. Leiden: E. J. Brill.

Glasse, C. (ed.) (2001) *The Concise Encyclopaedia of Islam*. London: Stacey International.

Gray, R., *et al.* (eds) (1978) *The Cambridge History of Africa*. Cambridge: Cambridge University Press.

Gray, Richard, Fashole-Luke, Edward, Hastings, Adrian and Tasie, Godwin (eds) (1978) *Christianity in Independent Africa*. Bloomington, IN: Indiana University Press.

Guillaume, A. (1954) *Islam*. London: Penguin.

—— (1955) *The Life of Muhammad: A Translation of Ibn Isbaq's 'Sirat Rasul Allah'*. London: Oxford University Press.

Haleem, Abdel M. A. S. (2004) *The Qur'an: A New Translation*. Oxford: Oxford University Press.

Hiskett, M. (1973) *The Sword of Truth: the Life and Times of Shehu Usuman dan Fodio*. New York: Oxford University Press.

—— (1994) *The Course of Islam in Africa*, Islamic Surveys 15. Edinburgh: Edinburgh University Press.

Hitti, P. K. (1973) *History of the Arabs from the Earliest Times to the Present*. London: Macmillan.

Holmes, M., Maxwell, G. and Scoones, T. (2004) *Nile*. London: BBC.

Holt, P. M., Lambton, A. K. S. and Lewis, B. (eds) (1970) *Cambridge History of Islam*, 2 vols. Cambridge: Cambridge University Press.

Hourani, A. (1962) *Arabic Thought in the Liberal Age 1798–1939*. Oxford: Oxford University Press.

—— (1991) *A History of the Arab Peoples*. London: Faber & Faber.

Houtsma, M. T. (ed.) (1913–34) *Encyclopaedia of Islam*. Leiden: E. J. Brill.

Hughes, T. P. (1976) *Dictionary of Islam*, first published 1885. New Delhi: Oriental Books Reprint Corp.

Hulmes, E. (1988) 'Walter Miller and the *Isawa*: An Experiment in Christian–Muslim Relationships', *Scottish Journal of Theology* 41: 233–46.

—— (1989) *Education and Cultural Diversity*. London: Longman.

—— (1990) 'Edward Wilmot Blyden's Understanding of Christianity and Islam as Instruments of Black Emancipation', *Islam and Christian-Muslim Relations*. 1 (1): 44–65.

—— (1991) Sykes, S. (ed.) *Sacrifice and Redemption: Durham Essays in Theology*, Cambridge: Cambridge University Press.

Idowu, E. B. (1962) *Oludumare: God in Yoruba'Belief*. London: A. & B. Book Publishers.

—— (1973) *African Traditional Religion: A Definition*. London: SCM Press.

Jackson, J. G. (1820) *An Account of Timbuctoo and Housa by el Hage Abd Salam Shabeeny*. London: Longman.

Johnson, P. (1987) *A History of the Jews*. London: Weidenfeld & Nicolson.

Kapliwatsky, J. (1975) *Arabic Language and Grammar*. Jerusalem: Rubin Mass.

al-Khaysi, Marwan I. (1996) *Morals Manners and Islam: A Guide to Islamic Adab*. Leicester: Kazi Publications.

Kirk-Greene, (1970) *Teach Yourself Hausa*. London: English Universities Press.

Kritzeck, J. and Lewis, W. H. (eds) (1969) *Islam in Africa*. New York: Van Nostrand Reinhold.

Last, M. (1967) *The Sokoto Caliphate*. London: Longman.

Levtzion, N. (1973) *Ancient Ghana and Mali*. London: Methuen.

Levtzion, N., and Pouwels, R. L. (eds) (2000) *The History of Islam in Africa*. Norman, OH: Ohio University Press and Oxford: James Currey.

Linden, I. (1974) 'The *Isawa* Mallams c.1850–1919: Some Problems in the Religious History of Northern Nigerian', Occasional Paper. Ahmadu Bello University, Nigeria.

Lord, P. (trans.) (1979) *A Moorish Calendar: from the Book of Agriculture of Ibn al-Awwam*. Wantage: The Black Swan Press.

Lynch, H. (1970) *Edward Wilmot Blyden, Pan Negro Patriot 1832–1912*. London: Oxford University Press.

—— (ed.) (1978) *The Selected Letters of Edward Wilmot Blyden*. New York: US Division of Kralis-Thompson Organisation.

Marty, P. (1926) *Études sur l'Islam au Dahomey*. Paris: E. Leroux.

Mbiti, J. S. (1975) *Introduction to African Religion*. London: Heinemann.

—— (1975) *Concepts of God in Africa*. London: SPCK.

McKenzie, P. R. (1976) *Inter-Religious Encounters in West Africa*. Leicester: Study of Religion Sub-Department, University of Leicester.

Michell, George (ed.) (1984) *Architecture of the Islamic World: Its History and Social Meaning*. London: Thames & Hudson.

Middle East Centre for Arab Studies (MECAS) (1974) *Word List, Grammar of Modern Literary Arabic* and *The Way Prepared*. Shemlan: Middle East Centre for Arab Studies.

Miller, W. R. S. (1936) *Reflections of a Pioneer*. London: Church Missionary Society.

Momen, M. (1985) *An Introduction to Shi'i Islam: The History and Doctrines of Twelver Shi'ism*. New Haven, CT: Yale University Press.

Moorehead, A. (1960) *The White Nile*. London: Hamish Hamilton.

—— (1962) *The Blue Nile*. London: Hamish Hamilton.

Mostyn, T. and Hourani, A. (eds) (1988) *The Cambridge Encyclopaedia of the Middle East and North Africa*. Cambridge: Cambridge University Press.

Neill, S. (1975) *A History of Christian Missions*. London: Penguin.

Nicholson, R. A. (1953) *A Literary History of the Arabs*. Cambridge: Cambridge University Press.

Noss, J. B. (1974) *Man's Religions*. New York: Collier Macmillan.

Omran, A. R., (1992) *Family-Planning in the Legacy of Islam*. London: Routledge.

Padwick, C. (1969) *Muslim Devotions: A Study of Prayer-Manuals in Common Use*. London: SPCK.

Page, J. (1908) *The Black Bishop, Samuel Adjai Crowther*. London: Hodder & Stoughton.

Rennell, F. J. (1926) *People of the Veil*. London: Macmillan.

Rosander E. E. and Westerlund, D. (eds) (1997) *African Islam and Islam in Africa: Encounters between Sufis and Islamists*. London: C. Hurst & Co.

Runciman, S. (1951–4) *A History of the Crusades*, 3 vols. Cambridge: Cambridge University Press.

Sanneh, L. (1983) *West African Christianity: The Religious Impact*. Maryknoll, NY: Orbis Books.

Schacht, J. and Bosworth C. E. (1979) *The Legacy of Islam*, 2nd edn. Oxford: Oxford University Press.

Smart, N. (1969) *The Religious Experience of Mankind*. New York: Charles Scribner's Sons.

Spear, P. (1965) *A History of India*, vol. II. Harmondsworth: Penguin.

Stark, F. (1945) *East is West*. London: Jonathan Cape.

Sykes, S. (ed.) (1991) *Sacrifice and Redemption: Durham Essays in Theology*. Cambridge: Cambridge University Press.

Thapar, R. (1966) *A History of India*, vol. I. Harmondsworth: Penguin.

Thesiger, W. (1959) *Arabian Sands*. Harmondsworth: Penguin.

Thomas, H., (1997) *The Slave Trade: The History of the Atlantic Slave Trade 1440–1870*. New York: Picador, Macmillan.

Tibawi, A. L. (1972) *Islamic Education: Its Traditions and Modernisation into the Arab National Systems*. London: Luzac & Co.

Trimingham, J. S. (1962a) *A History of Islam in West Africa*. London: Oxford University Press.

—— (1962b) *Islam in West Africa*. Oxford: Clarendon Press.

—— (1980) *The Influence of Islam upon Africa*. Harlow: Longmans.

Tritton, A. S. (1951) *Islam*. London: Hutchinson University Library.

—— (1968) *Islam*. London: Hutchinson.

Watt, W. M. (1953) *Muhammad at Mecca*. Oxford: Oxford University Press.

—— (1956) *Muhammad at Medina*. Oxford: Oxford University Press.

Wehr, Hans (1961) *A Dictionary of Modern Written Arabic*, (ed.) J. Milton Cowan. Wiesbaden: Otto Harrasowitz.

Entries by Imber

Ahmad, F. (1969) *The Young Turks: the Committee of Union and Progress in Turkish Politics*. Oxford: Oxford University Press.

Babinger, F. (1978) *Mehmed the Conqueror and his Time*, trans. R. Manheim, ed. W. Hickman. Princeton, NJ: Princeton University Press.

Bacqué-Grammont, J.-L. (1989) 'L'apogée de l'Empire Ottoman: les événements (1512–1606)' in Robert Mantran (ed.) *Histoire de l'Empire Ottoman*. Paris: Fayard, pp. 139–58.

Beldiceanu-Steinherr, I. (2000) 'La conquête de la Bythinie maritime, étape décisive dans la fondation de l'ætat ottoman' in Belke, Hild, Koder, Souster (eds) *Byzanz als Raum*. Vienna: Verlag der Österreichischen Akademie der Wissenschaften, pp. 21–36.

Deringil, S. (1998) *The Well-Protected Domains: Ideology and the Legitimation of Power in the Ottoman Empire, 1876–1909*. London: I. B. Tauris.

Dumont, P. (1989) 'La Période des *Tanzîmât* (1839–1878)', in Robert Mantran (ed.) *Histoire de l'Empire Ottoman*. Paris: Fayard, pp. 459–522.

Dumont, P. and Georgeon, F. (1989) 'La Mort d'un empire (1908–1923)', in Robert Mantran (ed.) *Histoire de l'Empire Ottoman*. Paris: Fayard, pp. 577–647.

Flemming, B. (1994) 'The Reign of Murad II: A Survey', *Anatolica* XX: 249–67.

Georgeon, F. (1989) 'Le Dernier sursaut (1878–1908)', in Robert Mantran (ed.) *Histoire de l'Empire Ottoman*. Paris: Fayard, pp. 523–76.

Griswold, W. J. (1983) *The Great Anatolian Rebellion, 1591–1611*. Berlin: Klaus Schwartz Verlag.

Imber, C. (1990) *The Ottoman Empire, 1300–1481*. Istanbul: Isis Press.

—— (2002) *The Ottoman Empire, 1300–1650: The Structure of Power*. Basingstoke: Palgrave Macmillan.

Mantran, R. (1989a) 'L'ætat ottoman au XVIIe siècle: stabilisation ou déclin?', in Robert Mantran (ed.) *Histoire de l'Empire Ottoman*. Paris: Fayard, pp. 227–86.

—— (1989b) 'L'ætat ottoman au XVIIIe siècle: la pression européenne', in Robert Mantran (ed.) *Histoire de l'Empire Ottoman*. Paris: Fayard.

—— (1989c) 'Les Débuts de la question d'orient (1774–1839)', in Robert Mantran (ed.) *Histoire de l'Empire Ottoman*. Paris: Fayard, pp. 421–58.

Piterberg, G. (2003) *An Ottoman Tragedy: History and Historiography at Play*. Berkeley, CA: University of California Press.

Quataert, D. (2000) *The Ottoman Empire, 1700–1922*. Cambridge: Cambridge University Press.

Reinert, S. W. (1993) 'From Niš to Kosovo Polje: Reflections on Murad I's final years' in E. A. Zachariadou (ed.) *The Ottoman Emirate (1300–1389)*. Rethymnon: Crete University Press, pp. 169–211.

Shaw, S. J. (1971) *Between Old and New: The Ottoman Empire under Selim III, 1789–1807*. Cambridge, MA: Harvard University Press.

Vatin, N. (1989) 'L'Ascension des Ottomans (1451–1512)', in Robert Mantran (ed.) *Histoire de l'Empire Ottoman*. Paris: Fayard, pp. 79–116.

Yasamee, (1996) *Ottoman Diplomacy: Abdulhamid II and the Great Powers, 1878–1888*. Istanbul: Isis Press.

Zachariadou, E. A. (1983) 'Suleyman Celebi in Rumili and the Ottoman Chronicles', *Der Islam* 60: 268–96.

Entries by Izzi Dien

Al-Bustani, Salim Rustum Baz, *Majallat al-Ahkam al-'Adliyya*, 3rd rpt. First published 1886-7. Beirut.

Coulson, N. J. (1964) *A History of Islamic Law*. Edinburgh: Edinburgh University Press.

al Dhahabi, Muhammad ibn 'Uthman (n.d.) *Kitab al Kaba'ir*. Beirut: Dar al-Raid al'Arabi.

al-Diqr, 'Abd al-Ghani (1988) *al-Imam Malik*. Damascus.

—— (1996) *al-Imam al Shafi'i*. Damascus.

—— (1999) *al-Imam Ahmad ibn Hanbal*. Damascus.

Izzi Dien, M. (1997) *The Theory and Practice of Market Law in Medieval Islam*, London: E. J. W. Gibb Memorial Trust.

—— (2000) *The Environmental Dimensions of Islam*. Cambridge: Cambridge University Press.

—— (2004) *Islamic Law*. Edinburgh: Edinburgh University Press.

Ibn Manzur (n.d.) *Lisan al-'Arab*. Beirut: Dar Sadir.

Khallaf, 'Abd al-Wahhab (1986) *'Ilm Usul al Fiqh al-Islami*. Cairo.

Mawardi, Muhammad bin Habib (1973) *Al-Ahkam al-Sultaniyya*. Cairo.

Schacht, J. and Bosworth, C. E. (1974) *The Legacy of Islam*. Oxford: Oxford University Press.

Subhi Al-Salih (1982) *Ma 'Alim al-shari'a al-Islamiyya*. Beirut.

Wahabi Sulayman Ghawji (1999) *Abu Hanifa al-Nu'man*. Damascus.

al-Zarqa, Mustafa (1968) *al Madhkal al-Fiqhi al-Islami*. Damascus.

Zaydan, 'Abd al Karim (1991) *Madkhal li Dirasat al-shari'al-Islamiyya*. Beirut.

al-Zuhayli, Wahba (1985) *Al-Fiqh al Islami*. Damascus.

Zuhayli, Wahba (1985) *Usul al-Fiqh al-Islami*. Damascus.

—— (1997) *Nazariyat al-Darura al-Shar-i'iyya*. Beirut.

Entries by Leslie McLoughlin

Asali, K. J. *Jerusalem in History*. Buckhurst Hill: Scorpion.

Cresswell K. A. C. (1932/40) *Early Muslim Architecture*, 2 vols. Oxford: Clarendon Press.

Hamilton, R. W. (1949) *The Structural History of the Aqsa Mosque*. Jerusalem: Published for the Govt. of Palestine by Oxford University Press.

Richmond, E. T. (1924) *The Dome of the Rock in Jerusalem*. Oxford: Clarendon Press.

Entries by Seán McLoughlin

Ahmed, A. S. (1997) *Jinnah, Pakistan and Islamic Identity: The Search for Saladin*. London: Routledge.

Akhtar, S. (1989) *Be Careful with Muhammad!* London: Bellew.

Algar, H. (2002) *Wahhabism: A Critical Essay*, Oneonta, NY: Islamic Publications International.

Anwarul Haq, M. (1972) *The Faith Movement of Mawlana Muhammad Ilyas*. London: Allen & Unwin.

Bhatt, C. (1997) *Purity and Liberation: Race, New Religious Movements and the Ethics of Postmodernity*. London: University College London Press.

Burgat, F. (2003) *Face to Face with Political Islam*. London: I. B. Tauris.

Calder, N. (1993) 'Tafsir from Tabari to Ibn Kathir: Problems in the Description of a Genre', in G. R. Hawting and Abdul-Kader A. Shareef (eds) *Approaches to the Qur'an*. London and New York: Routledge, pp. 101–40.

Esposito, J. L. (2002) *Unholy War: Terror in the Name of Islam*. Oxford and New York: Oxford University Press.

Gray, J. (2003) *Al Qaeda and What it Means to be Modern*. London: Faber & Faber.

Griffin, M. (2001) *Reaping the Worldwind: The Taliban Movement in Afghanistan.* London: Pluto Press.

Jalal, A. (1994) *The Sole Spokesman: Jinnah, the Muslim League and the Demand for Pakistan.* Cambridge: Cambridge University Press.

Kepel, G. (1994) *The Revenge of God.* Oxford: Polity in association with Blackwell Publishers.

Maley, W. (ed.) (1998) *Fundamentalism Reborn? Afghanistan and the Taliban.* New York: New York University Press.

Marsden, P. (1998) *The Taliban: War, Religion and the New Order in Afghanistan.* London: Zed Books.

Masud, Muhammad Khalid (2000) *Travellers in Faith: Studies of the Tablighi Jama'at as a Transnational Islamic Movement for Faith Renewal.* Leiden: E. J. Brill.

Metcalf, B. (1982) *Islamic Revival in British India: Deoband, 1860–1900.* Princeton, NJ: Princeton University Press.

—— (1996) 'Islam and Women: The Case of the Tablighi Jamaat'. Available on-line at <http://www.stanford.edu/group/SHR/5–1/text/metcalf.html>.

—— (2002) 'Traditionalist Islamic Activism: Deoband Tablighis and Talibs', *Social Science Research Council/After September 11*, 810 Seventh Avenue New York, NY 100019, USA. Available on-line at: <http://www.ssrc.org/sept11/essays/metcalf_text_only.htm>.

Mortimer, E. (1982) *Faith and Power.* New York: Random House.

Parekh, B. (1992) *The Concept of Fundamentalism.* Warwick: The Centre for Research in Asian Migration, The University of Warwick.

Rahman, F. (1979) *Islam*, 2nd edn. Chicago, IL: Chicago University Press.

Rashid, A. (2000) *Taliban: Islam, Oil and the New Great Game in Central Asia.* London: I. B. Tauris.

Rippin, A. (2005) *Muslims: The Religious Beliefs and Practices*, 3rd edn. London: Routledge.

Robinson, F. (1997) 'The Muslims and Partition', *History Today.* September: 40–6.

Roy, O. (n.d.), 'Neo-Fundamentalism', available on-line at <http://www.ssrc.org/sept11/essays/roy/htm>.

Sanyal, U. (1996) *Devotional Islam and Politics in British India: Ahmad Riza Khan Barelwi and His Movement, 1870–1920.*

Oxford and Delhi: Oxford University Press.

Sayyid, S. (2003) *A Fundamental Fear: Eurocentrism and the Emergence of Islamism*, 2nd edn. London: Zed.

Shepherd, W. (1987) 'Fundamentalism Christian and Islamic', *Religion* 17 (4): 355–68.

Sirriyeh, E. (1999) *Sufis and Anti-Sufis.* London: Curzon.

Taji-Farouki, S. (1996) *A Fundamental Quest: Hizb al-Tahrir and the Search for the Islamic Caliphate.* London: Grey Seal.

Voll, J. O. (1994) *Islam: Continuity and Change in the Modern World*, 2nd edn. Syracuse, NY: Syracuse University Press.

Zakariyya, M. (1987) *Teachings of Islam* (*Tablighi Nisab*). Chicago, IL: Kazi Publications.

Zaman, M. Q. (2002) *The Ulama in Contemporary Islam: Custodians of Change.* Princeton, NJ: Princeton University Press.

Entries by Marmura

Ahwani, F. (ed.) (1950) *Talkhis Kitab al-Nafs* [Epitome on the Soul incorrectly titled as a tafsr, i.e. Middle Commentary]. Cairo.

Anawati, G. C. (French trans.) (1978–85) *Le Metaphysique du 'Shifa'*, 2 Vol., Paris: J. Vrin, 210 ff.

Amin, U. (ed.) (1958) *Talkhis Kitub Māba'da al-Ṭabi'ah* [Epitome of the Metaphysics], Cairo.

Arberry, A. J. (trans.) (1950) *The Spiritual Physick of Rhazes.* London.

Atiya, G. N. (1966) *Al-Kindi: The Philosopher of the Arabs.* Rawalpindi: Islamic Research Institute.

Black, D. L. (1999) 'Conjunction and Identity of Knower and Known in Averroes', *American Catholic Philosophical Quarterly.* 73:159–84.

Bouyges M. (ed.) (1930) Averroes (Ibn Rushd) *Tahufut al-Tahufut.* English translation S. Van Den Bergh as *The Incoherence of the Incoherence* (1954). 2 vols. London.

—— (1938-52) *Tafsir Ma ba'd al-tabi'a* (Commentary on Aristotle's *Metaphysics*), 4 vols. Beirut: Imprimarie Catholique.

—— (1938) (ed.) *Risala fi al-'aql* (*Treatise on the Intellect*). Ed. as *Al-Farabi'sRisala fi'l Aql.* Beirut: Imprimarie Catholique.

Butterworth, C. E. (trans.) (1986) *Averroes Middle Commentary on Aristotle's Poetics.* Princeton, NJ: Princeton University Press.

—— (1993) 'The Origins of al-Razi's Political Philosophy', *Interpretation* 20:238–57.

—— (1993) 'The Book of Philosophic Life', trans. of al-Razi's *Al-Sira al-Falsafiyya*, *Interpretation* 20:227–36.

—— (1993) (trans.) 'The Philosophic Life, in "The Book of Philosophic Life"', *Interpretation* 20:227-236.

—— (2001) (trans.) *Kitab Fasl al-Maqal (The Book of Decisive Treatise)*, text and annotated translation. Provo, UT.

Conrad, L. (1996) *Ibn Tufayl, interdisciplinary perspectives on Hayy Ibn Yaqzan*. Leiden, New York.

Davidson, H. A. (1992) *Alfarabi, Avicenna and Averroes, on Intellect*. New York, Oxford: Oxford University Press.

Druart, Th-. A. (1944) 'Averroes on God's Knowledge of God's Being Qua Being', *Anaquel de Estudios Arabes* 5:35–57.

—— (1997) 'The Ethics of al-Razi', *Medieval Philosophy and Theology* 6:47–71.

—— (1998) 'Gawami' Kitab al-Nawamis li-Aflatun: Le Sommaire des "Lois" de Platon,' edition critique et introduction par . *Bulletin D'Etudes orientales, Tome L, Institut francais de Damas* pp. 109–55;

Endress, G. (1973) *Proclus Arabus*. Beirut.

—— (1995) 'Averroes *de Caelo*, Ibn Rushd's Cosmology in his Commentaries on Aristotle's *On the Heavens*', *Arabic Sciences and Philosophy* 5: 9–49.

Endress, G. and Aersten, J. A. (eds) (1996) *Averroes and the Aristotelian Tradition*. Cologne.

Fakhry, M. (1958) *Islamic Occasionalism and its Critique by Averroes and Aquinas*. London: George Allen & Unwin.

—— (1968) 'A Tenth Century Arabic Interpretation of Plato's Cosmology', *Journal of the History of Ideas* 6: 15-22.

—— (2001) *Averroes (Ibn Rushd); his Life, Works and Influence*. Oxford: One World Publications.

Galston, M. (1990) *Politics and Excellence: The Political Philosophy of Alfarabi*. Princeton, NJ: Princeton University Press.

Al-Ghazali, A. H. (2000) *Tahafut al-Falasifa (The Incoherence of the Philosophers)*, trans. M. E. Marmura, 2nd edn. Provo, UT: Brigham Young University Press.

Gauthier, L. (1936) Ibn Tufayl *Hayy Ibn Yaqzan*. Arabic text, critical edition and French translation, 2nd edn. Beirut: Imprimerie Catholique.

Goodman, L. E. (1972) *Ibn Tufayl's Hayy Ibn Yaqzan*. New York: Twain Publishers.

—— (1975) 'Razi's myth of the Fall of the Soul,' in G. F. Hourani (ed.) *Essays in Islamic Philosophy and Science*. Albany, NY: State University of New York Press, pp. 25–40.

Hawi, S. E. (1974) *Islamic Naturalism and Mysticism*. Leiden: Brill.

Hourani, G. F. (1956) 'The Principle Subject of Ibn Tufyal's *Hayy Ibn Yaqzan*', *Journal of Near Eastern Studies* XV 1: 40–46,

—— (1961) (trans.) *Averroes on the Harmony of Religion and Philosophy*. London.

Hyman, A. (1973) 'The Letter Concerning the Intellect', trans. of al-Farabi's *Risala fi al-'Aql*, in A. Hyman and Walsh, J. J. (eds) *Medieval Philosophy: The Christian, and Jewish Traditions*. Indianapolis, IN: Hackett Publishing Company, pp. 215–21.

Ivry, A. L. (1966) 'Averroes on Intellect and Conjunction', *Journal of the American Oriental Society* 86: 76–85.

—— (1974) *Al-Kindi's Metaphysics*, trans. of al-Kindi's *On First Philosophy*. Albany, NY: State University of New York Press.

—— (1994) *Middle Commentary on the De Anima (Talkhs Kitub al-Nafs)*. Cairo.

Jayyusi-Lehn, Gh. (2002) 'The Epistle of Ya'qub ibn Ishaq al-Kindi on the Device of Dispelling Sorrows', *British Journal of Middle Eastern Studies* 29, 2: 137–51.

Jolivet, J. (1971) *L'intellect selon Kindi*. Leiden: Brill.

Kogan, B. S. (1985) *Averroes and the Metaphysics of Causality*. Albany, NY: State University of New York Press.

Kraus, P. (1939) *al-Razi's Opera Philosophica*. Cairo.

Kutch, K., S. J., and Morrow, S., S. J., (eds) (1960) *Alfarabi's Commentary on Aristotle's De interpretatione*. Beirut: Imprimerie Catholique.

Lerner, M. (1974) *Averroes on Plato's Republic*. Ithaca, NY: The Free Press of Glencoe.

Lerner, M. and Mahdi. M. (1963) *Medieval Political Philosophy: A Source Book*. New York: Cornell University Press.

Madkour, I. (ed.) (1960) Ibn Sina (Avicenna) *al-Shifa'Healing: al-Ilahiyyat (Metaphysics)*. Cairo.

Mahdi, M. (1961) Falsafat Aristūtālīs (al-Fārābī's Philosophy of Aristotle). Beirut: Dar Majahual Shi'i.

—— (1962) *Alfarabi's Philosophy of Plato and Aristotle*. New York: The Free Press of Glencoe.

717

—— (1965) 'Ghazali and Demonstrative Science,' *Journal of the History of Philosophy* III, 2 (October): 183–204

—— (1968a) Kitab al-Alfaz al-Musta'mala fi al-Mantiq (*Utterances Employed in Logic*). Beirut: Dar al-Mashriq.

—— (1968b) *Kitab al-Milla (Alfarabi's Book on Religion and Related Texts)*. Beirut: Dar al-Mashriq.

—— (1969) *Kitab al-Huruf (Alfarabi's Book of Letters)*. Beirut.

—— (1994) 'Ghazali's Chapter on Divine Power in the Iqtiṣād', *Arabic Sciences and Philosophy* vol. 4: 279–315.

—— (2000) *Alfarabi and the Foundation of Islamic Political Philosophy*. Chicago, IL: University of Chicago Press.

Marmura, M. E. (1965) 'Ghazali and Demonstrative Science' *Journal of the History of Philosophy* III, 2 (October): 183–204.

—— (1979) 'The Philospher and Society: Some Medieval Arabic Discussions', *Arab Studies Quarterly* 1, 4: 309–52.

—— (1981) 'Avicenna on Causal Priority', in Morewedge, P. (ed.) *Islamic Philosophy and Mysticis*. Delmar, NY, pp. 65–83.

—— (1984) 'The Metaphysics of Efficient causality in Avicenna (Ibn Sina)', in M. E. Marmura (ed.) *Islamic Theology and Philosophy: Studies in Honor of George F. Hourani*. Albany, NY: State University of New York Press, pp. 172–87.

—— (1994) 'Ghazali's Chapter on Divine Power in the Iqtiṣād', *Arabic Sciences and Philosophy*, vol. 4:279–315.

—— (2004) *Probing in Islamic Philosophy: Studies in the Philosophies of Ibn Sina, al-Ghazali and Other Major Muslim Thinkers*. (The Studies include discussions of the thought of al-Kindi, al-Razi, al-Farabi and Ibn Tufayl). Binghamton, NY: Global Academic Publishing.

—— (2005) (trans.) Ibn Sina (Avicenna) *The Metaphysics of the Healing*. Provo, UT: Brigham Young University Press.

Marmura, M. E. and Rist, J. M. (1963) "Al-Kindi's "Discussion on Divine Existence and Oneness"', *Mediaeval Studies* vol. 25: 338–54.

Morewedge, P. (ed.) (l992) 'Al-Farabi, Emanation and Metaphysics', in *Neoplatonism and Islamic Thought*. Albany, NY: State University of New York Press, pp. 127–48.

Najjar, I. Y. (trans.) (1963) *The Political Regime* in Lerner, R. and Mahdi, M. (eds) *Medieval Political Philosophy: A Source Book*. New York: Cornell University Press, pp. 24–57.

—— (1964) *Kitab al-Siyasa al-Madaniyya* (The Political Regime). Beirut: Imprimerie Catholique.

—— (2001) *Faith and Reason in Islam: Averroes' Exposition of Religious Arugments* (trans. of Averroes' *Al-Kashf 'an Manahij al-Adilla*). Oxford: Oneworld Publications.

Netton, I. R. (1992) *Al-Farabi and His School*. London and New York: Routledge.

Qasim, M. (ed.) (l964) *Al-Kashf 'an Manahij al-Adilla*. Cairo. English annotated translation.

Rashed and Jolivet, J. (eds) (1998) *Oeuvres philosopiques et scientifique d'al-Kindi, vol. II: métaphysique et cosmologie*. Leiden.

Rescher, N. (1964) *Al-Kindi: An Annotated Bibliography*. Pittsburgh.

Rosenthal, F. and Walzer, R. (eds) (1943) *Falsafat Aflatun (The Philosophy of Plato)*. Ed. as *Alfarabius de Platonis philosophia*. London: Warburg Institute.

Taylor, R. C. (1998) 'Averroes on Psychology and the Principles of Metaphysics,' *Journal of the History of Philosophy*, 4 (October): 507–523.

Van Den Bergh, S. (1954) *The Incoherence of the Incoherence*. London.

Walker, P. E. (1992) 'The Political Implications of al-Razi's Philosophy,' in Butteroworth, C. E. (ed.) *The Political Aspects of Islamic Philosophy. Essays in Honor of Muhsin Mahdi, Harvard Middle Eastern Monographs*, 27, Cambridge, MA, pp. 61–65.

Walzer R. (ed. e trans.) (1985) *On the Perfect State. Abu Nasr al-Farabi's Mabadi' Ahl al-Madina al-Fadila (The Principle Opinions of the Virtuous City)*. Oxford: Great Books of the Islamic World.

Zimmerman, F. W. (1981) *Alfarabi's Commentary on Aristotle's De Interpetatione*. English translation with Introduction and Notes. Oxford.

Entries by Murden

Ayubi, N. (1995) *Over-stating the Arab State: Politics and Society in the Middle East*. London: I B Tauris.

Bill, J. and Springborg, R. (1994) *Politics in the Middle East*. 4th edn. New York: Harper Collins College Publishers.

Bosworth, A. B. (1998) in S. Hornblower and A. Spawforth (eds.) *The Oxford Companion to Classical Civilization*. Oxford: Oxford University Press.

Bulloch, J. and Morris, H. (1991) *Saddam's War*. London: Faber & Faber.

Fernandez-Armesto, F. (1995) *Millennium: A History of the Last Thousand Years*. London: Free Press.

Gilbert, M. (1989) *Second World War*. London: Owl Books.

Hiro, D (1996) *Dictionary of the Middle East*. London: Palgrave Macmillan.

Hourani, A. (1991) *A History of the Arab Peoples*. London: Faber & Faber.

James, L. (1997) *The Rise and Fall of the British Empire*. London: St. Martin's Griffin.

Keay, J. (2000) *India: A History*. London: Harper Collins.

Lapidus, I. M. (1999) *A History of Islamic Societies*. Cambridge: Cambridge University Press.

Lawrence, T. E. (1955) *Seven Pillars of Wisdom*. London: Jonathan Cape.

Liddell-Hart, B. (1997) *History of the First World War*. London: Papermac.

—— (1997) *History of the Second World War*. London: Papermac.

Maraini, F. (1976) 'Polo, Marco', in *Encyclopaedia Britannica*, Macropaedia, 14: 757–60.

Masonen, P. (2002) 'Leo Africanus: The Man with Many Names', *Al-Andalus-Magreb* vol.VII-IX: 115–43.

Murden, S. (1995) *Emergent Regional Powers and International Relations in the Gulf 1988–91*. Reading: Ithaca Press.

—— (2002) *Islam, the Middle East and the New Global Hegemony*. Boulder, CO: Lynne Rienner Publishers.

Nasser, G. A. (1955) *Falsafat al-Thawra*, (Cairo, 1955); English trans. *Philosophy of Revolution* (Washington, 1955).

Norton, A. R. (1991) 'Lebanon after Ta'if', *Middle East Journal* 45, 3: 457–73.

Owen, R. (2000) *State, Power and Politics in the Making of the Modern Middle East*. 2nd edn. London: Routledge.

Perrett, B. (1996) *The Battle Book: Crucial Conflicts in History from 1469 BC to the Present*. London: Brockhampton Press.

Polo, M. (1968) *The Travels of Marco Polo*. Intro. and trans. R. Latham. London: The Folio Society.

Purcell, N. (1998) 'Pliny the Elder' and 'Strabo', in S. Hornblower and A. Spawforth (eds) *The Oxford Companion to Classical Civilization*. Oxford: Oxford University Press, pp. 545–46.

Ralling, C. (1990) *Kon-Tiki Man: Thor Heyerdahl*. London: BBC Books.

Roy, O. (1994) *The Failure of Political Islamism*. London: I. B. Tauris.

Salibi, K. S. (1976) 'History of Syria and Palestine', *Encyclopaedia Britannica*, 15th edn. Macropaedia, 17: 926–65.

Severin, T. (1964) *Tracking Marco Polo*. London: Routledge & Kegan Paul.

—— (1978) *The Brendan Voyage*. London: Hutchinson.

—— (1983) *The Sinbad Voyage*. London: Arrow Publishers.

—— (1985) *The Jason Voyage*. London: Hutchinson.

—— (1987) *The Ulysses Voyage*. London: Hutchinson

—— (1989) *Crusader: By Horse to Jerusalem*. London: Hutchinson.

—— (1991) *In Search of Genghis Khan*. London: Hutchinson.

Sharoni, S. and Abu-Nimer, M. (2000) 'The Israel-Palestinian Conflict' in D. Gerner (ed.) *Understanding the Contemporary Middle East*. Boulder, CO: Lynne Rienner Publishers, 6: 420.

Spencer, C. (1996) 'The Roots and Future of Islamism in Algeria', in A. S. Sidahmed and A. Ehteshami (eds.) *Islamic Fundamentalism*. Boulder, CO: Westview Press.

Stannard, J. (1976) 'Pliny the Elder' in *Encyclopaedia Britannica*, Macropaedia, 14: 572–73.

St. John, R. (1976) 'Nasser' in *Encyclopaedia Britannica*, Macropaedia, 12: 844–45.

Sweetman, J. (1984) *A Dictionary of European Land Battles*. London: Spellmount Publishers.

Usher, G. (1997) 'What Kind of Nation: The Rise of Hamas in the Occupied Territories', in Beinin and Stork (eds), *Political Islam: Essays from Middle East Report*. Washington, DC: University of California Press.

Zisser, E. (1997) 'Hizballah in Lebanon', in Maddy-Weitzman and Inbar (eds), *Religious Radicalism in the Greater Middle East*. London: Frank Cass, pp. 90–110, 264.

Official Website of the League of Arab States: http://www.arableagueonline.org/las/index.jsp

Official Website of the Organization of the Islamic Conference Permanent Observer Mission to United Nations Offices at Geneva and Vienna: http://www.oic-un.org/

Entries by Netton

Diwald, S. (1975) *Arabische Philosophie und Wissenschaft in der Enzyklopadie Kitab Ihwan as-Safa' III: Die Lehre von Seele und Intellekt.* Wiesbaden: Harrassowitz.

Goodman, L. E. (1978) *The Case of the Animals versus Man Before the King of the Jinn.* Boston, MA: Twayne Publishers.

Ikhwan al-Safa' (1957) *Rasa'il Ikhwan al-Safa'*, 4 vols. Beirut: Dar Sadir.

Marquet, Y. (1975) *La Philosophie des Ihwan al-Safa'.* Algiers: Société Nationale d'Edition et de Diffusion.

Nasr, S. H. (1978) *An Introduction to Islamic Cosmological Doctrines*, rev. edn. London: Thames & Hudson.

Netton, I. R. (1991) *Muslim Neoplatonists: An Introduction to the Thought of the Brethren of Purity (Ikhwan al-Safa').* London: Allen & Unwin.

—— (1996) 'The Brethren of Purity', in S. H. Nasr and O. Leaman (eds) *History of Islamic Philosophy.* London: Routledge, pp. 222–30.

Tibawi, A. L. (1955) 'Ikhwan as-Safa' and their Rasa'il: A Critical Review of a Century and a Half of Research', *Islamic Quarterly* 2 (1): 28–46.

Entries by Newman

Abrahamian, E. (1989) *Radical Islam, the Iranian Mojahedin.* London: Yale University Press.

Al Ahmad, J. (1997) *Gharbzadegi: Weststruckness.* Costa Mesa, CA: Mazda Publishers.

Amir-Moezzi, M. A. (1994) *The Divine Guide in Early Shi'ism: The Sources of Esotericism in Islam*, trans. David Streight. Albany, NY: State University of New York Press.

Ayubi, N. (1993) *Political Islam, Religion and Politics in the Arab World.* London: Routledge.

Binder, L. (1965) 'The Proofs of Islam: Religion and Politics in Iran', in George Makdisi (ed.) *Arabic and Islamic Studies in Honor of Hamilton A. R. Gibb.* Leiden: E. J. Brill, pp. 118–40.

Boroujerdi, M. (1996) *Iranian Intellectuals and the West: The Tormented Triumph of Nativism.* Syracuse, NY: Syracuse University Press.

Cole, J. (2002) *Sacred Space and Holy War: The Politics, Culture and History of Shi'ite Islam.* London: I. B. Tauris.

Cook, M. A. (2000) *Commanding Right and Forbidding Wrong in Islamic Thought.* Cambridge: Cambridge University Press.

Fakhry, M. (1983) *A History of Islamic Philosophy.* London and New York: Columbia University Press.

Gibb, H. A. R. and Bosworth, C. E. (eds) (1960–2003) *Encyclopaedia of Islam*, 2nd edn. Leiden: E. J. Brill.

Hallaq, W. (1997) *A History of Islamic Legal Theories.* Cambridge: Cambridge University Press.

Halm, H. (1991) *Shiism.* Edinburgh: Edinburgh University Press.

Hodgson, M. (1974) *The Venture of Islam*, vol. I. Chicago, IL: Chicago University Press.

Hourani, A. (1970) *Arabic Thought in the Liberal Age, 1798-1939.* Cambridge: Cambridge University Press.

—— (1991) *A History of the Arab Peoples.* Cambridge, MA: Warner Books.

Keddie, N. (1981) *Roots of Revolution: An Interpretive History of Modern Iran.* New Haven, CT: Yale University Press.

Kerr, M. (1971) *Arab Cold War.* London: Oxford University Press.

Madelung, W.

Momen, M. (1985) *An Introduction to Shi'i Islam.* New Haven, CT: Yale University Press.

Munson, H. (1988) *Islam and Revolution in the Middle East.* New Haven, CT: Yale University Press.

Newman, A. J. (2000) *The Formative Period of Twelver Shi'ism: Hadith as Discourse Between Qum and Baghdad.* London: RoutledgeCurzon.

Rahman, F. (1979) *Islam.* Chicago, IL: University of Chicago Press.

Said, E. (1978) *Orientalism.* New York: Vintage.

Sadowski, Y. (1991) *Political Vegetables.* Washington, DC: The Brookings Institution.

Savage-Smith, E. (1996) 'Medicine', in R. Rashed (ed.) *Encyclopedia of the History of Arabic Science*, vol. III. London: Routledge, pp. 903–62.

Schimmel, A. (1980) *Islam in the Indian Subcontinent.* Leiden: E. J. Brill.

Waines, D. (1995) *An Introduction to Islam.* Cambridge: Cambridge University Press.

Watt, W. M. (1961) *Muhammad, Prophet and Statesman*. Oxford: Oxford University Press.

—— (1973) *The Formative Period of Islamic Thought*. Edinburgh: Oneworld.

Wehr, H. (1974) *A Dictionary of Modern Written Arabic*, (ed.) M. Cowen. Beirut: Spoken Language Services

Entries by Picken

Al-'Aql, N. 'A. (1991) *Mabahith fi 'Aqida Ahl al-Sunna wa al-Jama'a wa Mawqif al-Harakat al-Islamiyya al-Mu'asira minha*. London: Dar al-Ifta'.

—— (1996) *al-Khawarij: Awwal al-Firaq fi Tarikh al-Islam*. Riyadh: Dar al-Watan.

Arberry, A. J. (1990) *Sufism: An Account of the Mystics of Islam*. London: Unwin Hyman Ltd.

al-Ash'ari, 'A. (1997) *Maqalat al-Islamiyyin*, 2 vols. Beirut: al-Maktaba al-'Asriyya.

al-Baghdadi, 'A. T. M. (2001) *al-Farq bayn al-Firaq*. Beirut: Dar al-Ma'rifa.

Daftary, F. (1998) *A Short History of the Ismailis*. Edinburgh: Edinburgh University Press

Al-Hamawi, A. S. (1983) *al-Qadiyaniyya*. Riyadh: Maktabat 'l-Sharawat.

Hanafi, M. A. (1980) *A Survey of Muslim Institutions and Culture*. Lahore: Sh. Muhammad Ashraf.

Ibn al-Mundhir, M. I. (1993) *al-Awsat fi 'l-Sunan wa 'l-Ijma' wa 'l-Ikhtilaf*, (ed.) Saghir, Ahmad Muhammad Hanif, 2nd edn. 5 vols. Riyadh: Dar ayyibah.

—— (1997) *al-Iqna'*, 3rd edn. 2 vols. edited by 'Abdullah b. 'Abd al-'Aziz al-Jibrin. Riyadh: Maktabat 'l-Rushd.

Al-Johani, M. H. (ed.) (1999) *al-Mawsu'a al-Muyassara fi 'l-Adyan wa al-Madhahib wa 'l-Ahzab al-Mu'asira*, 2 vols. Riyadh: al-Nadwa al-'Alamiyya li 'l-Shabab al-Islami.

Knysh, A. (1999) *Islamic Mysticism: A Short History*. Leiden: E. J. Brill.

Mahmud, 'A. (1973) *Ustadh al-Sa'irin – al-Harith b. Asad al-Muhasibi*. Cairo: Dar al-Kutub al-Hadithah.

al-Muhasibi, H. A. (1982) *al-'Aql wa Fahm al-Qur'an*, 3rd edn. ed. Husayn al-Quwwatli. Beirut: Dar al-Kindi.

Netton, I. R. (1997) *A Popular Dictionary of Islam*. Richmond: Curzon.

Picken, G. N. (1999) 'The Life and Works of Ibn al-Mundhir with Special Reference to the Methodology of His Book al-Awsat',

unpublished MA thesis, Leeds: University of Leeds.

al-Shahrastani, M. A. (2002) *al-Milal wa 'l-Nihal*. Beirut: al-Maktaba al-'Asriyya.

al-Shami, S. A. (ed.) (1999) *Mawa'idh al-Imam al-Harith al-Muhasibi*. Beirut: al-Maktabat 'l-Islami.

Sirriyeh, E. (1999) *Sufis and Anti-Sufis: The Defence, Rethinking and Rejection of Sufism in the Modern World*. Richmond: Curzon.

Smith, M. (1935) *An Early Mystic of Baghdad*. London: Sheldon Press.

Tabataba'i, M. H. (n.d.) *Shi'ite Islam*, trans. Seyyed Hossein Nasr. Houston, TX: Free Islamic Literatures.

'Uwayda, K. M. (1994) *al-Harith ibn Asad al-Muhasibi: al-'Alim, al-Zahid, al-Faqih*. Beirut: Dar al-Kutub al-'Ilmiyyah.

Van Ess, J. (1961) *Die Gedankenwelt des Harit al-Muhasibi*. Bonn: Selbstverlag des Orientalischen Seminars der Universität Bonn.

Watt, W. M. (1948) *Free Will and Predestination in Early Islam*. London: Luzac & Co.

—— (1997) *Islamic Theology and Philosophy*. Edinburgh: Edinburgh University Press.

—— (2002) *The Formative Period of Islamic Thought*. Oxford: Oneworld.

Zahir, A. I. (n.d.) *al-Babiyya: 'Ard wa Naqd*. Lahore: Idara Turjuman al-Sunna.

—— (n.d.) *al-Qadiyaniyya: Dirasat wa Tahlil*. Lahore: Idara Turjuman al-Sunna.

Entries by Ridgeon

Abdel-Kader (1976) *The Life, Personality and Writings of Al-Junayd*. London: Oxbow.

Abu Talib al-Makki (1893) *Qut al-qulub* (in Arabic). Cairo.

Abun-Nasr (1965) *The Tijaniyya*. Oxford: Oxford University Press.

Addas, C. (1993) *Quest for the Red Sulphur*, translated by Peter Kingsley. Cambridge: Islamic Texts Society.

Algar, H. (1976) 'The Naqshbandi Order', *Studia Islamica*. 44: 123–52.

Arberry, A. J. (trans.) (1935) *The Doctrine of the Sufis* (translation of Al-*Kalabadhi's Kitab al-ta'arruf*). Cambridge: Suhail Academy.

—— (trans.) (1964) *Muslim Saints and Mystics* (excerpts from *Tadhkirat al-awliya'*). London: Arkana.

—— (trans.) (1969) *A Sufi Martyr* (a translation of 'Ayn al-Qudat's *Apology*). London: Allen & Unwin.

GENERAL BIBLIOGRAPHY

Avery, P. (1998) *The Speech of the Birds: Mantiqu't-Tair*. Cambridge: Islamic Texts Society.

Avery, P. and Heath-Stubbs, J. (1989) *Rubaiyat of Omar Khayyam*. London: Penguin.

Birge, J. K. (1937) *The Bektashi Order of Dervishes*. London: Luzac & Co.

Chittick, W. (1989) *The Sufi Path of Knowledge*. Albany, NY: State University of New York Press.

—— (1991) 'Rumi and the Mawlawiyyah' in S. H. Nasr (ed.) *Islamic Spirituality: Manifestations*. London: SCM, pp. 105–26.

Danner, V. (1991) 'The Shadhiliyyah and North African Sufism' in S. H. Nasr (ed.) *Islamic Spirituality: Manifestations*. London: SCM, pp. 26–48.

Elias, J. J. (1995) *The Throne Carrier of God*. Albany, NY: State University of New York Press.

Ernst, C. (1985) *Words of Ecstasy in Sufism*. Albany, NY: State University of New York Press.

—— (1996) *Ruzbihan Baqli*. Richmond: Curzon.

—— (1997) *The Shambhala Guide to Sufism*. Boston, MA: Shambhala.

Al-Ghazali, A. (1986) *Sawanih*, trans. N. Pourjavady. London: Kegan Paul.

Goodwin, G. (1994) *The Janissaries*. London: Saqi.

Heer, N. (ed.) (1979a) *The Precious Pearl*. Albany, NY: State University of New York Press.

—— (ed.) (1979b) 'Al-Jami's Treatise on Existence' in P. Morewedge (ed.) *Islamic Philosophical Theology*. Albany, NY: State University of New York Press.

Hujwiri (1911) *Kashf al-mahjub*, trans. R.A. Nicholson. London: Luzac & Co.

Ibn al-'Arabi (1980) *The Bezels of Wisdom*, trans. Ralph Austin. New York: Paulist Press.

Izutsu, T. (1994) *Creation and the Timeless Order of Things*. Ashland, OR: White Cloud Press.

Jahanbakhsh, F. (1998) 'The Pir-Murid Relationship in the Thought of 'Ayn al-Qudat Hamadani' in S. J. D. Ashtiyani, Matsubara, Iwami and Matsumoto (eds) *Consciousness and Reality*. Leiden: E. J. Brill.

Al-Jilani (n.d.) 'Abd al-Qadir. *Futuh al-Qayb*, trans. M. Aftab ud-Din Ahmad. Lahore.

Khusraw, N. (1998) *Knowledge and Liberation*, (ed.) and trans. Faquir M. Hunzai. London: I. B. Tauris.

Kiyani, M. (1369/1990–91) *Tarikh-i khanaqah dar Iran*. Tehran.

Knysh, A. (2000) *Islamic Mysticism*. Leiden: E. J. Brill.

Lewisohn, L. (1993) 'In Quest of Annihilation', in L. Lewisohn (ed.) *Classical Persian'Sufism: From its Origins to Rumi*. Oxford: Oneworld, pp. 285–336.

—— (1998) 'An Introduction to the History of Modern Persian Sufism, Part I', *Bulletin of the School of Oriental and African Studies* 61 (3): 437–64.

—— (1999) 'An Introduction to the History of Modern Persian Sufism, Part II', *Bulletin of the School of Oriental and African Studies* 62 (1): 36–59.

Massignon, L. (1982) *The Passion of Hallaj*, trans. H. Mason. Princeton, NJ: Princeton University Press.

Michon, J.-L. (1991) 'Sacred Music and Dance in Islam,' in S. H. Nasr (ed.) *Islamic Spirituality: Manifestations*. London: SCM, pp. 469–505.

Momen, M. (1985) *An Introduction to Shi'i Islam*. New Haven, CT: Yale University Press.

Nakamura, K. (1990) *Invocations and Supplications*. Cambridge: Islamic Texts Society.

Nasr, S. H. (1991) 'Spiritual Chivalry' in S. H. Nasr (ed.) *Islamic Spirituality: Manifestations*. London: SCM, pp. 304–18.

Netton, I. (1993) 'Adab, Ahwal and Maqamat in Suhrawardi', in L. Lewisohn (ed.) *Classical Persian Sufism: From its Origins to Rumi*. Oxford: Oneworld, pp. 457–82.

Nicholson, R. A. (1921) *Studies in Islamic Mysticism*. London: Kegan Paul.

Nizami, K. A. (1957) 'Some Aspects of Khanaqah Life in Medieval India', *Studia Islamica* 8.

—— (1991a) 'The Naqshibandiyyah Order', in S. H. Nasr (ed.) *Islamic Spirituality: Manifestations*. London: SCM, pp. 162–93.

—— (1991b) 'The Qadiriyyah Order', in S. H. Nasr (ed.) *Islamic Spirituality: Manifestations*. London: SCM, pp. 6–25.

Nurbakhsh, J. (1991) 'The Nimatullahi' in S. H. Nasr (ed.) *Islamic Spirituality: Manifestations*. London: SCM, pp. 144–61.

Al-Qushayri (1990) *The Principles of Sufism by al-Qushayri*, trans. B. R. Von Schlegell. Berkeley, CA: Islamic Publications International.

Radtke, B and O'Kane, J. (1996) *The Concept of Sainthood in Early Islamic Mysticism*. Richmond: Curzon.

Ridgeon, L. (1998) *'Aziz Nasafi*. Richmond: Curzon.

—— (2002) *Persian Metaphysics and Mysticism: Selected Treatises of Aziz Nasafi*. Richmond: Curzon.

Ritter, H. (1931) 'Hasan al-Basri', *Der Islam*, 21.

Rizvi, S. A. A. (1978) *A History of Sufism in India*. New Delhi: Munshiram Manoharlal Publishers.

—— (1991) 'The Chishtiyyah', in S. H. Nasr (ed.) *Islamic Spirituality: Manifestations*. London: SCM, pp. 127–43.

Rumi, Jalal al-Din (1924–40) *The Mathnawi of Jalalu'ddin Rumi*, trans. and ed. R. A. Nicholson. London: Luzac & Co.

—— (1991) *Mystical Poems of Rumi*, 2 vols. trans. A. J. Arberry. Chicago, IL: University of Chicago Press.

Al-Sarraj (1914) *Kitab al-Luma'* (Arabic Text) edited by R. A. Nicholson. London: Luzac & Co.

Schimmel, A. (1975) *Mystical Dimensions of Islam*. Chapel Hill, NC: University of North Carolina Press.

Schleifer, A. (1991) 'Sufism in Egypt and the Arab East,' in S. H. Nasr (ed.) *Islamic Spirituality: Manifestations*. London: SCM, pp. 194–205.

Smith, M. (1928) *Rabi'a the Mystic and Her Fellow Saints in Islam*. San Francisco, CA: Rainbow Press.

—— (1931) *Studies in Early Mysticism in the Near and Middle East*. London: Kessinger Publishing.

Sviri, S. (1997) 'Dhikr: The Experience of Remembrance of God,' *Sufi*, 33 (spring): 22–30.

Takeshita, M. (1987) *Ibn 'Arabi's Theory of the Perfect Man and its Place in the History of Islamic Thought*. Tokyo: Institute for the Study of Languages and Cultures of Asia and Africa.

Trimingham, J. S. (1971) *The Sufi Orders in Islam*. Oxford: Oxford University Press.

Vikor, K. (1995) *Sufi and Scholar on the Desert Edge*. London: Hurst.

Waley, M. I. (1993) 'Contemplative Disciplines in Early Persian Sufism,' in L. Lewisohn (ed.) *Classical Persian Sufism: From its Origins to Rumi*. Oxford: Oneworld, pp. 497–548.

Zaehner, R. C. (1960) *Hindu and Muslim Mysticism*. London: Athlone Press.

Ziadeh, N. (1958) *Sanusiyah*. Leiden: E. J. Brill.

Entries by Rippin

Abdel Haleem, M. (1999) *Understanding the Qur'an: Themes and Styles*. London: I. B. Tauris.

Amjad, M. (2003) 'Explanation of *Iman, Islam, Ihsan*: Some Signs of the Day of Judgment, The *Hadith* of Jibreel'. Available online at <http://www.understanding-islam.org/related/text.asp?type=article&aid = 156>. Accessed 23 August, 2003.

Ayoub, M. M. (1979) 'The Prayer of Islam: A Presentation of Surat al-Fatiha in Muslim Exegesis', *Journal of the American Academy of Religion* 47: 635–47.

Beeston, A. F. L. (trans.) (1963) *Baidawi's Commentary on Surah 12 of the Qur'an*. Oxford.

Böwering, G. (2003) 'The Scriptural "Senses" in Medieval Sufi Qur'an Exegesis', in J. Dammen McAuliffe, B. D. Walfish, J. W. Goering (eds) *With Reverence for the Word: Medieval Scriptural Exegesis in Judaism, Christianity, and Islam*. New York: Oxford University Press, pp. 346–65.

Bukhari (1974) *al-Sahih*, trans. Muhammad Muhsin Khan. Ankara.

Burton, J. (1977) *The Collection of the Qur'an*. Cambridge: Cambridge University Press.

Calder, N. (1993) 'Tafsir from Tabari to Ibn Kathir: Problems in the Description of a Genre, Illustrated with Reference to the Story of Abraham', in G. R. Hawting, Abdul-Kader A. Shareef (eds) *Approaches to the Qur'an*. London: Routledge, pp. 101–40.

Calder, N., Mojaddedi, J., Rippin, A. (eds and trans.) (2003) *Classical Islam: A Sourcebook of Religious Literature*. London: Routledge.

Cooper, J. (trans.) (1987) *The Commentary on the Qur'an by Abu J'far Muhammad b. Jarir al-Tabari*. Oxford: Oxford University Press.

Denny, F. M. (1989) 'Qur'an Recitation: A Tradition of Oral Performance and Transmission', *Oral Tradition* 4: 5–26.

Firestone, R. (1997) 'Disparity and Resolution in the Qur'anic Teachings on War: A Reevaluation of a Traditional Problem', *Journal of Near Eastern Studies* 56: 1–19.

Gibb, H. A. R. and Bosworth, C. E. (eds) (1960–2003) *Encyclopaedia of Islam*, 2nd edn. Leiden: E. J. Brill.

Goldziher, I. (1920) *Die Richtungen der islamischen Koranauslegung*. Leiden: E. J. Brill.

—— (1971a) *Muslim Studies*. London: George Allen & Unwin.

—— (1971b) *The Zahiris: Their Doctrine and their History*. Leiden: E. J. Brill.

Grabar, O. (1973) *The Formation of Islamic Art*. New Haven, CT: Yale University Press.

Graham, W. A. (1977) *Divine Word and Prophetic Word in Early Islam: A Reconsideration of the Sources with Special Reference to the Divine Saying or Hadith Qudsi*. The Hague and Paris: Mouton.

Guillaume, A. (trans.) (1955) *The Life of Muhammad: A Translation of Ibn Ishaq's Sirat Rasul Allah*. Oxford: Oxford University Press.

Heinrichs, W. (1984) 'On the Genesis of the *Haqiqa–Majaz* Dichotomy', *Studia Islamica*, 59: 111–40.

Husayn, Saha (1981) *An Egyptian Childhood: The Autobiography of Taha Hussein*, trans. E. H. Paxton. London: Passeggiata.

Ibrahim, E. (1976) *An-Nawawi's Forty Hadith. An Anthology of Sayings of the Prophet Muhammad*, trans. Denys Johnson-Davies. Damascus: Islamic Texts Society.

Ibrahim, L. (1980) 'Al-Zamakhshari: His Life and Works', *Islamic Studies*. 19: 95–110.

Jeffery, A. (1952) *The Qur'an as Scripture*. New York: R. F. Moore Co.

Johns, A. (1990) 'Let my People Go! Sayyid Qutb and the Vocation of Moses', *Islam and Christian Muslims Relations*, 1: 143–70.

Jung, C. G. (1959) 'Four Archetypes: Mother/Rebirth/Spirit/Trickster', *Collected Works*, vol. IX. Part I. Princeton, NJ: Princeton University Press.

Juynboll, G. H. A. (1984) 'Muslim's Introduction to his *Sahih*, Translated and Annotated with an Excursus on the Chronology of the *Fitna* and *Bid'a*', *Jerusalem Studies in Arabic and Islam* 5: 263–302.

Kandil, L. (1992) 'Die Surennamen in der offiziellen Kairiner Koranausgabe und ihre Varianten', *Der Islam* 69: 44–60.

Kane, C. H. (1972) *Ambiguous Adventure*, trans. by Katherine Woods. London: Heinemann.

Lassner, J. (1993) *Demonizing the Queen of Sheba: Boundaries of Gender and Culture in Postbiblical Judaism and Medieval Islam*. Chicago, IL: Chicago University Press.

Lazarus-Yafeh, H. (1992) *Intertwined Worlds: Medieval Islam and Bible Criticism*. Princeton, NJ: Princeton University Press.

—— (2003) 'Are there Allegories in Sufi Qur'an Interpretation?', in J. Dammen McAuliffe, B. D. Walfish, J. W. Goering (eds) *With Reverence for the Word: Medieval Scriptural Exegesis in Judaism, Christianity, and Islam*. New York: Oxford University Press, pp. 366–75.

Nelson, K. (2001) *The Art of Reciting the Qur'an*. Cairo: The American University of Cairo Press.

Netton, I. R. (2000) 'Towards a Modern *Tafsir* of Surat al-Kahf: Structure and Semiotics', *Journal of Qur'anic Studies* 2: 67–87.

Nwyia, P. (1977) 'Un cas d'exégèse soufie: l'historie de Joseph', in S. H. Nasr (ed.) *Mélanges offerts à Henry Corbin*. Tehran: Institute of Islamic Studies, pp. 407–23.

Osman, M. Y. (2003) *Mishkat al-Masabih: An Exposition*. Available online at <http://www.jamiat.org.za/isinfo/mishkat.html>. Accessed 23 August 2003.

Paret, R. (1977) *Der Koran. Kommentar und Konkordanz*. Stuttgart: Kohlhammer.

Qutb, S. (1979) *In the Shade of the Qur'an*. London: Islamic Foundation.

Renard, J. (ed.) (1998) *Windows on the House of Islam*. Berkeley, CA: University of California Press.

Rippin, A. (1988) 'The Function of *Asbab al-Nuzul* in Qur'anic Exegesis', *Bulletin of the School of Oriental and African Studies* 51: 1–20.

—— (2000) 'The Exegetical Literature of Abrogation: Form and Content', in G. Hawting, J. Modaddedi, A. Samely (eds) *Studies in Islamic and Middle Eastern Texts and Tradition in Memory of Norman Calder*. Oxford: Oxford University Press, pp. 213–31.

—— (2001) *The Qur'an and its Interpretative Tradition*. Aldershot: Ashgate.

Rubin, U. (1984) 'Al-Samad and the High God: An Interpretation of Sura CXII', *Der Islam* 61: 197–217.

Siddiqi, M. Z. (1993) *Hadith Literature: Its Origin, Development and Special Features*, revised edn. Cambridge: Islamic Texts Society.

Siddiqui, A. H. (1976) *Sahih Muslim, Being Traditions of the Sayings and Doings of the Prophet Muhammad*. Lahore: Sh. Muhammad Ashraf.

Spitaler, A. (1935) *Die Verszählung des Koran nach islamicher Überlieferung*. Munich: Bayerischen Akademie der Wissenschaften.

Stowasser, B. F. (1994) *Women in the Qur'an, Traditions, and Interpretation*. New York: Oxford University Press.

Tottoli, R. (2002) *Biblical Prophets in the Qur'an and Muslim Literature*. Richmond: Curzon.

Watt, W. M. (1970) *Bell's Introduction to the Qur'an*. Edinburgh: Edinburgh University Press.

—— (1974) 'The Queen of Sheba in Islamic Tradition', in James B. Pritchard (ed.) *Solomon and Sheba*. London: International Thomson Publishing, pp. 85–103.

Wild, S. (2003) 'The Self-Referentiality of the Qur'an: Sura 3:7 as an Exegetical Challenge', in J. Dammen McAuliffe, B. D. Walfish, J. W. Goering (eds) *With Reverence for the Word: Medieval Scriptural Exegesis in Judaism, Christianity, and Islam*. New York: Oxford University Press, pp. 422–36.

Yusuf Ali, A. (1968) *The Holy Qur'an: Text, Translation and Commentary*. Beirut: Dar Al Furqan.

Entries by Rizvi

Abu Zayd, N. H. (1983) *Falsafat al-Ta'wil: Dirasa fi'l-Ta'wil al-Qur'an 'ind Muhyi al-Din ibn 'Arabi*. Beirut: Dar al-Tanwir.

Adamson, P. (2002) *The Arabic Plotinus: A Philosophical Study of the 'Theology of Aristotle'*. London: Duckworth.

—— and Taylor, R. J. (eds) (2005) *The Cambridge Companion to Arabic Philosophy*. Cambridge: Cambridge University Press.

Addas, C. (1989) *Ibn 'Arabi ou La quête du Soufre Rouge*. Paris: Gallimard.

—— (1993) *The Quest for the Red Sulphur*, trans. P. Kingsley. Cambridge: The Islamic Texts Society.

—— (2000) *The Voyage of No Return*. Cambridge: The Islamic Texts Society.

Afnan, S. M. (1964) *Philosophical Terminology in Arabic and Persian*. Leiden: E. J. Brill.

Alibhai, M. A. (1983) *Abu Ya'qub al-Sijistani and his Kitab Sullam al-Najat: A Study in Islamic Neoplatonism*, unpublished Ph.D. dissertation, Harvard University.

Aminrazavi, M. (1997) *Suhrawardi and the Illuminationist School*. Richmond: Curzon Press.

D'Ancona, C. (1999) 'Porphyry, Universal Soul and the Arabic Plotinus', *Arabic Sciences and Philosophy*, 9:47–88.

—— (2001a) *Plotino: La discesa dell'anima nei corpi (Plotiniana Arabica, pseudo-Teologia de Aristotele cap. 1 e 7)*. Padua: Il Poligrafico Editore.

—— (2001b) 'Pseudo-*Theology of Aristotle* chapter 1 and structure', *Oriens* 36: 78–112.

Aouad, M. (1989) 'La "Théologie d'Aristote" et autres texts du Plotinus Arabus', in R. Goulet (ed.) *Dictionnaire des philosophes antiques*. Paris: CNRS, i: 541–90.

Arnaldez, R. (1972) 'Un précédent avicennien du cogito cartésien?', *Annales Islamologiques* 11: 341–49.

Ashtiyani, S. J. (1966) *Sharh-i muqaddima-yi Qaysari bar Fusus al-Hikam*. Mashhad: Mashhad University Press.

—— (1974) *Muntakhabati az athar-i hukama'-yi ilahi-yi Iran*, Volume i. Tehran: L'Institut Franco-Iranien.

—— (1998) *Sharh-i hal u ara'-yi Mulla Sadra Shirazi*, repr. Qum: Daftar-i Tablighat-i Islami.

Austin, R. J. (1971) *Sufis of Andalusia*. London: Allen and Unwin.

—— (1982) *The Bezels of Wisdom*. New York: Paulist Press.

Badawi, A. (1946) *Al-Turath al-Yunani fi'l-Hadara al-Islamiyya*. Cairo: L'Institut Français.

Brague, R. (1997) 'La philosophie dans la Théologie d'Aristote. Pour un inventaire', *Documenti e Studi sulla Tradizione Filosofica Medievale* 8: 365–87.

De Bustinza, V. J. (1999) *Las iluminaciones de la Meca: textos escogidos*. Barcelona: Siruela.

Chittick, W. C. (1989) *The Sufi Path of Knowledge [SPK]*. Albany, NY: The State University of New York Press.

—— (1998) *The Self-Disclosure of God [SDG]*. Albany, NY: The State University of New York Press.

Chittick, W. C. *et al.* (trans.) (1988) *Les illuminations de la Mecque (Selections from al-Futuhat al-Makkiyya)*. Paris: Sindbad.

Chodkiewicz, M. (1986) *Le Sceau des saints*. Paris: Editions du Seuil.

—— (1993a) *The Seal of Saints*, trans. L. Sherrard. Cambridge: The Islamic Texts Society.

—— (1993b) *An Ocean without Shore*. Albany, NY: The State University of New York Press.

Cooper, J. (1998) 'Mulla Sadra Shirazi', in *Routledge Encyclopaedia of Philosophy*, 6: 595–99.

Corbin, H. (1961) *Avicenna and the Visionary Recital*. Princeton, NJ: Princeton University Press.

—— (trans.) (1964) *Livre des pénétrations métaphysiques (Kitab al-Masha'ir)*. Tehran: L'Institut Franco-Iranien.

—— (1964) *Histoire de la philosophie islamique*. Paris: Gallimard.

—— (1969) *Creative imagination in the Sufism of ibn 'Arabi*. Princeton, NJ: Princeton University Press.

—— (1972) *En islam iranien*, 4 vols. Paris: Gallimard.

—— (1976), *L'archange empourpré*. Paris: Fayard.

—— (trans.) (1986) *Commentaire (Ta'liqa) de Molla Sadra Shirazi sur Le Livre de la Sagesse Orientale (Kitab Hikmat al-ishraq) de Sohravardi*. Paris: Verdier, pp. 439–669.

—— (1994) *Trilogie ismaélienne*. Paris: Verdier.

Cornell, V. (1996) *The Way of Abu Madyan*. Cambridge: The Islamic Texts Society.

Crabbe, J. C. (ed.) (1999) *From Soul to Self*. London: Routledge.

Dabashi, H. (1996) 'Mir Damad,' in S. H. Nasr & O. Leaman (eds) *History of Islamic Philosophy* London: Routledge I: 597–634.

Daiber, H. (1999) *A Bibliography of Islamic Philosophy*. Leiden: Brill.

De Smet, D. (1995) *La quiétude de l'intellect: Néoplatonisme et gnose ismaélienne dans l'œuvre de Hamid al-Din Kirmani*. Leuven: Peeters.

Druart, T. -A. (1988) 'The Soul and Body problem: Avicenna and Descartes', in T-A. Druart (ed.) *Arabic Philosophy and the West* Washington, DC: The Catholic University of America, pp. 27–48.

Elmore, G. (1999) *Islamic Sainthood in the Fullness of Time: Ibn al-'Arabi's Book of The Fabulous Gryphon ('Anqa Mughrib)*. Leiden: E. J. Brill.

Endress, G. (1990), 'The defence of reason: The plea for philosophy in the religious community', *Zeitschrift für der Arabisch-islamischen Wissenschaften* 6: 1–49.

—— and Kruk, R. (eds) (1997) *The Ancient Tradition in Christian and Islamic Hellenism*. Leiden: CNRW.

—— (1997) 'The circle of al-Kindi', in G. Endress and R. Kruk (eds) *The Ancient Tradition in Christian and Islamic Hellenism* Leiden: CNRW pp. 43–76.

Fakhry, M. (1983) *A History of Islamic Philosophy*. New York: Columbia University Press.

Furlani, G. (1927) 'Avicenna e il cogito ergo sum di Cartesio', *Islamica* 3: 53–72.

Galindo-Aguilar, E. (1958) 'L'Homme Volant d'Avicenne et le cogito de Descartes', *Bulletin des belles lettres arabes* (Tunis) 21: 279–95.

Genequand, C. (1996) 'La mémoire de l'âme: Porphyry et la *Théologie d'Aristote*', *Bulletin d'études orientales* 48: 103–13.

Gohlman, W. E. (1974) *The Life of Ibn Sina*. Albany, NY: The State University of New York Press.

Goodman, L. (1992) *Avicenna*. London: Routledge.

Gutas, D. (1988) *Avicenna and the Aristotelian Tradition*. Leiden: Brill.

—— (1998) *Greek Thought, Arabic Culture*. London: Routledge.

—— (2002) 'The Study of Arabic Philosophy in the Twentieth Century', *British Journal of Middle Eastern Studies* 29:5–25.

—— and Endress, G. (1992–) *A Greek and Arabic Lexicon*. Leiden: Brill.

Hadi, A. (1984) *Sharh-i hal-i Mir Damad va Findiriski*. Tehran: Tehran University Press.

Hadot, P. (1995) *Philosophy as a Way of Life*, trans. M. Chase. Oxford: Blackwell's.

Haeri Yazdi, M. (1992) *The Principles of Epistemology in Islamic Philosophy*. Albany, NY: The State University of New York Press.

Haji, H. (1999) *A Distinguished Da'i under the Shade of the Fatimids*. London: Hamid Haji.

Al-Hakim, S. (1981) *Al-Mu'jam al-Sufi*. Beirut: Dandara.

Hasse, D. (2000) *Avicenna's De Anima in the Latin West*. London: The Warburg Institute.

Hirji, B. (1995) *A Study of al-Risalah al-Bahirah*, unpublished Ph.D. dissertation, McGill University.

Hirtenstein, S. and Tiernan, M. (eds) (1993) *Muhyiddin ibn 'Arabi: A Commemorative Volume*. Shaftesbury: Element Books.

Ibn 'Arabi (1946) *Fusus al-Hikam*, A. al-'Afifi (ed.). Cairo: L'Institut Français.

Ibn Sina (1952) *Avicenna's Psychology: An English Translation of Kitab al-Najat Book II, Chapter VI*, trans. F. Rahman. London: Oxford University Press.

—— (1954) *Livre des remarques et directives (al-Isharat wa'l-Tanbihat)*, trans. A-M. Goichon. Paris: Maisonneuve.

—— (1972) *The Metaphysica of Avicenna (ilahiyyat-i Danishnama-yi 'Ala'i)*, trans. P. Morewedge. New York: The State University of New York Press.

—— (2000) *Lettre au Vizir Abu Sa'd*, ed. and trans. Y. Michot. Paris: al-Bouraq.

—— (2004) *The Metaphysics (al-ilahiyyat min al-Shifa')*, trans. M. Marmura. Provo, UT: Brigham Young University Press.

Ibrahimi-yi Dinani, G. (1996) *Shu'a'-yi andisha va shuhud dar falsafa-yi Suhravardi.* Tehran: Intisharat-i Amir Kabir.

Iskandar Beg (1971) *Tarikh-i 'alam-ara'-yi 'Abbasi*, ed. I. Afshar. Tehran: Intisharat-i Ittila'at.

Izutsu, T. (1984) *Sufism and Taoism.* Berkeley, CA: University of California Press.

Al-Jabiri, M. A. (1982–98) *Naqd al-'Aql al-'Arabi*, 3 vols. Beirut: al-Saqi.

Jambet, C. (2000) *Se rendre immortel suivi du Traité de la resurrection (Risalat al-Hashr) de Molla Sadra Shirazi.* Paris: Fata Morgana.

Jambet, C. (2002) *L'acte d'être: la philosophie de la revelation chez Mollâ Sadrâ.* Paris: Fayard.

Janssens, J. (1991–99) *An Annotated Bibliography of Avicenna*, 2 vols. Louvain: Brill/Peeters.

—— and de Smet, D. (eds) (2002) *Avicenna and his Heritage.* Louvain: Peeters.

Khamanehi, M. (2000) *Mulla Sadra: zindagi, shakhsiyyat va maktab-i Sadr al-muta'allihin.* Tehran: SIPRIn.

Kirmani (2000) *Al-Risala al-Durriyya (The Brilliant Epistle)*, trans. Faquir M. Hunzai in *An Anthology of Philosophy in Persia.* New York: Oxford University Press, II:192–200.

Knysh, A. (1999) *Ibn 'Arabi in the Later Islamic Tradition.* Albany, NY: The State University of New York Press.

Kraye, J. *et al.* (eds) (1986) *Pseudo-Aristotle in the Middle Ages.* London.

Kuspinar, B. (1996) *Isma'il Anqaravi on the Illuminative Philosophy.* Kuala Lumpur: ISTAC.

Landolt, H. (trans.) (2000) *Kashf al-mahjub*, in Nasr, S. H. and Aminrazavi, M. (eds) *An Anthology of Philosophy in Persia.* II: 81–124.

Langermann, Y. (1999) 'A new Hebrew passage from the Theology of Aristotle', *Arabic Sciences and Philosophy* 9: 247–59.

Leaman, O. (1985) *An Introduction to Medieval Islamic Philosophy.* Cambridge: Cambridge University Press.

Madelung, W. (1990) 'Abu Ya'qub al-Sijistani and metempsychosis', in *Iranica Varia: Papers in Honor of Professor Ehsan Yarshater.* Leiden: Brill, pp. 131–43.

—— (1996) 'Abu Ya'qub al-Sijistani and the seven faculties of the intellect', in F. Daftary (ed.) *Medieval Isma'ili History and Thought.* Cambridge: Cambridge University Press, pp. 85–88.

Marmura, M. (1986) 'Avicenna's flying man in context', *The Monist* 69: 384–95.

Marquet, Y. (1994) 'La revelation par l'astrologie selon Abu Ya'qub al-Sijistani et les ikhwan al-Safa', *Studia Islamica*, 80: 5–28.

Mattock, J. N. (1989) 'The early translations from Greek into Arabic: An experiment in comparative assessment', in *Symposium Graeo-Arabicum II.* Amsterdam: B. R. Grüner, pp. 73–102.

McTighe, T. P. (1988) 'Further remarks on Avicenna and Descartes', in Druart, T. -A. (ed.) *Arabic Philosophy and the West*, Washington DC: Center for Contemporary Arab Studies, Georgetown University, pp. 51–54.

Michot, Y. (1986) *La destinée de l'homme selon Avicenne.* Brussels.

Mir Damad (1977) *Kitab al-Qabasat* M. Mohaghegh and T. Izutsu (eds). Tehran: Tehran University Press.

Morris, J. W. (trans.) (1981) *The Wisdom of the Throne: a Translation of al-Hikma al-'Arshiyya.* Princeton, NJ: Princeton University Press.

—— (1986, 1987) 'Ibn 'Arabi and his interpreters', *Journal of the American Oriental Society* 106: 539–51, 733–56 and 107: 101–19.

Musavi-Bihbahani, M. (1998) *Hakim-i Astarabad.* Tehran: Tehran University Press.

Nadir, A. (1998) *Al-Nafs al-Bashariyya 'ind Ibn Sina.* Beirut: Dar el-Machreq.

Nasr, S. H. and Leaman, O. (eds) (1996) *History of Islamic Philosophy.* London: Routledge.

Nettler, R. (2004) *Sufi Metaphysics and Quranic Prophets.* Cambridge: The Islamic Texts Society.

Perlmann, M. (1967–71) *Ibn Kammuna's Examination of the Inquiries into the Three Faiths.* Berkeley, CA: University of California Press.

Peters, F. E. (1968) *Aristotle and the Arabs.* New York: New York University Press.

Peterson, C. (1990) *Cosmogony and the Ten Separated intellects in the Rahat al-'aql of Hamid al-Din al-Kirmani*, unpublished Ph.D. dissertation, UCLA.

Pines, S. (1954) 'La Longue Recension de la Théologie d'Aristote dans ses rapports avec la doctrine ismaélienne', *Revue des etudes islamiques* 22: 7–20.

Plotinus (1947) *Kitab al-Uthulujiya*, 'A. Badawi (ed.). Cairo: L'Institut Français.

—— (1951–73) *Plotini Opera*, P. Henry and H. Schwyzer (eds). Paris, Brussels: Desclée de Brouwer.

Rahman, F. (1975) *The Philosophy of Mulla Sadra*. Albany, NY: The State University of New York Press.

—— (1980) 'Mir Damad's concept of *huduth dahri*: a contribution to the study of God–world relationship in Safavid Iran', *Journal of Near Eastern Studies* 39: 139–51.

Reisman, D. (2002) *The Making of the Avicennan Tradition*. Leiden: Brill.

Reisman, D. and al-Rahim, A. (eds) (2003) *Before and After Avicenna*. Leiden: Brill.

Rizvi, S. A. A. (1975) *Religious and Intellectual History of the Muslims in Akbar's Reign*. Agra: Munshiram Manoharlal.

Rizvi, S. H. (1999) 'An islamic subversion of the existence–essence distinction: Suhrawardi and the Philosophy of illumination', *Asian Philosophy* 9: 219–27.

—— (2005) 'Ibn 'Arabi and Mulla Sadra', in R. Taylor and P. Adamson (eds) (2005) *The Cambridge Companion to Arabic Philosophy*. Cambridge: Cambridge University Press, pp. 224–46.

—— (2006) *Mulla Sadra: His Life, Works and the Sources for the Intellectual History of Safavid Iran*. Oxford: Oxford University Press.

—— (2007a) 'Qadi Sa'id Qummi's reception of the Theology of Aristotle', in P. Adamson and C. Burnett (eds) *Classical Arabic Philosophy: Sources and Reception*. London: The Warburg Institute.

—— (2007b) *Mulla Sadra Shirazi: Philosopher for Mystics?* Cambridge: The Islamic Texts Society.

—— (trans.) (2008) *Divine Theophanies (al-Mazahir al-ilahiyya)*. Tehran: SIPRIn.

Rosenthal, F. (1952, 1953, 1955) 'Ash-Shaykh al-Yunani and the Arabic Plotinus source', *Orientalia* 21: 461–92, 22: 370–400, 24: 42–66.

—— (1975) *The Classical Heritage in Islam*. London: Routledge and Kegan Paul.

—— (1988) 'Ibn 'Arabi between philosophy and mysticism', *Oriens* 31: 1–35.

Rowson, E. K. (1992) 'The *Theology of Aristotle* and some other pseudo-Aristotelian texts reconsidered', *Journal of the American Oriental Society* 112: 478–84.

Schmidtke, S. (2000) *Theologie, Philosophie und Mystik in zwölferschiitischen islam des 9./15. Jahrhunderts: Die Gedankenwelt des ibn Abi Jumhur al-Ahsa'i*. Leiden: Brill.

Sells, M. (1994) *Mystical Languages of Unsaying* Chicago, IL: University of Chicago Press.

Al-Sijistani, A. (1949) *Kashf al-Mahjub (Dévoilement des choses caches)* H. Corbin (ed.). Tehran: L'Institut Franco-Iranien.

—— (1992) *al-Risala al-Bahira fi'l-Ma'ad*, *Tahqiqat-i islami* 7: 21–62.

—— (1994) *Yanabi' al-hikma (Wellsprings of Wisdom)*, trans. P. Walker. Salt Lake City, UT: University of Utah Press.

Steinschneider, M. (1960) *Die Arabischen Übersetzungen aus dem Griechischen*. Graz: Akademische Druck-u. Verlagsanstalt.

Street, A. D. (2004) *Avicenna*. Cambridge: The Islamic Texts Society.

Suhrawardi, S. (1998) *Partownama (The Book of Radiance)*, (ed.) and trans. H. Ziai. Costa Mesa, CA: Mazda Publishers.

—— (1999a) *Hikmat al-ishraq (The Philosophy of Illumination)*, (ed.) and trans. H. Ziai and J. Walbridge. Provo, UT: Brigham Young University Press.

—— (1999b), *The Philosophical Allegories and Mystical Treatises*, (ed.) and trans. W. M. Thackston. Costa Mesa, CA: Mazda Publishers.

Takeshita, M. (1987) *Ibn 'Arabi's Theory of the Perfect Man and its Place in the History of Islamic Thought*. Tokyo: Oriental Institute.

Tarabishi, G. (1998) *Naqd Naqd al-'Aql al-'Arabi*. Beirut: al-Saqi.

Walbridge, J. (1992) *The Science of Mystic Lights: Qutb al-Din Shirazi and the Illuminationist Tradition in Islamic Philosophy*. Cambridge, MA: Harvard University Press.

—— (2000) *The Leaven of the Ancients: Suhrawardi and the Heritage of the Greeks*, Albany, NY: The State University of New York Press.

—— (2001) *The Wisdom of the Mystic East: Suhrawardi and Platonic Orientalism*, Albany, NY: The State University of New York Press.

Walker, P. (1993) *Early Philosophical Shiism: The Ismaili Neoplatonism of Abu Ya'qub al-Sijistani*. Cambridge: Cambridge University Press.

—— (1996) *Abu Ya'qub al-Sijistani: Intellectual Missionary*. London: Institute of Ismaili Studies.

—— (1999) *Hamid al-Din al-Kirmani: Ismaili Thought in the Age of al-Hakim.* London: The Institute of Ismaili Studies.

Walzer, R. (1962) *Greek into Arabic.* Oxford: Bruno Cassirer.

Winkel, E. (1997) *Ibn 'Arabi and the Living Law.* Karachi: Oxford University Press.

Wisnovsky, R. (ed.) (2001) *Aspects of Avicenna.* Princeton, NJ: Markus Wiener.

—— (2003) *Avicenna's Metaphysics in Context.* London: Duckworth.

Yad, M. H. (1998) *Mulla Sadra ka qabil-e 'amal falsafa.* Lahore: al-Firaq.

Yahia, O. (1984) *Histoire et classification de l'œuvre d'ibn 'Arabi.* Damascus: L'Institut Français.

'Avicenna', *Encyclopaedia Iranica*, II:66–110. (possibly: Yarshater, Ehsan (ed.) (2003) Herat and New York: Encyclopaedia Iranica Foundation.)

Ziai, H. (1991) *Knowledge and illumination.* Atlanta, GA: Scholars Press.

—— (1992), 'Source and nature of authority: A study of Suhrawardi's illuminationist political doctrine', in C. Butterworth (ed.) *The Political Aspects of Islamic Philosophy.* Cambridge. MA: Harvard University Press, pp. 304–44.

—— (1996) 'The illuminationist tradition', in S. H. Nasr and O. Leaman (eds), *History of Islamic Philosophy.* London: Routedge, I:465–96.

Entries by Scarce

Atasoy, N. and Raby, J. (1989) *Iznik: the Pottery of Ottoman Turkey.* London.

Atasoy, N., Denny W. B., Mackie, L. W., Tezcan, H., Ipek (2001) *Imperial Ottoman Silks and Velvets.* London: Azimuth Editions Limited.

Baer, E. (1998) *Islamic Ornament.* Edinburgh: Edinburgh University Press.

Begley, W. E., and Desai, Z. A. (1989) *Taj Mahal.* Cambridge, MA.

Behrens-Abouseif, D. 'Mukarnas' in *Encyclopaedia of Islam* (second edition 1960), vol. 7, Leiden: E.J. Brill. pp. 501–6.

Bloom, J. (1989) *Minaret, Symbol of Islam.* Oxford: Oxford Studies in Islamic Art VII.

Blunt, W., Isfahan (1966) *Pearl of Persia.* London.

Brend, B. (1991) *Islamic Art.* London: British Museum Press.

Brotton, J. (2002) *The Renaissance Bazaar from the Silk Road to Michelangelo.* Oxford: Oxford University Press.

Burckhardt, T. (1992) *Fez, City of Islam.* Cambridge: The Islamic Texts Society.

Campbell, D. (1926) *Arabian medicine and its Influence on the Middle Ages.* 2 vols. London: Kegan Paul, Trench, Trubner and Co.

Carswell, J. (1998) *Iznik pottery.* London: British Museum Press.

Critchlow, K. (1976) *Islamic patterns. An Analytical and Cosmological approach.* London.

El-Said, I. and Parman, A. (1976) *Geometric concepts in Islamic art.* London.

Endress, G. (1988) *An Introduction to Islam,* trans. Carole Hillenbrand, Edinburgh: Edinburgh University Press.

Frishman, M. and Khan, H.-U. (eds) (1994), *The Mosque, History Architectural Development and Regional Diversity.* London, Thames and Hudson.

Golombek, L. (1988) 'The draped universe of Islam', in Priscilla P. Soucek (ed.) *Content and Context of Visual Arts in the Islamic World.* Pennsylvania and London, pp. 25–30.

Goodwin, G. (1971) *A History of Ottoman Architecture.* London: Thames and Hudson (paperback edition 1987).

—— (1993) *Sinan, Ottoman Architecture and its Value today.* London: Saqi Books.

Grabar, O. (1978) *The Alhambra.* London.

—— 'The Earliest Islamic Commemorative Structures' in *Ars Orientalis VI*, pp. 1–46.

—— 'La Grande Mosquee de Damas et les origines architecturales de la mosquee' in *Synthronon Art et Archéologie de la Fin de l'Antiquité et du Moyen âge.* Paris: Receuil d'Etudes, pp./ 107–14.

—— (1990) *The Great Mosque of Isfahan.* London and New York.

Gye, D. (1988) 'Arches and Domes in Iranian Islamic buildings: an Engineer's Perspective', *Iran (Journal of the British Institute of Persian Studies)* XXVI. 129–44.

Hasan-Uddin (eds) (1994) in *The Mosque, History Architectural Development and Regional Diversity.* London: Thames and Hudson, pp. 17–41.

Hautecoeur, L. Y. and Wiet, G. (1932–4) *Les mosques du Caire.* 2 vols. Paris.

Hillenbrand, R. (1982) 'La dolce vita in Early Islamic Syria, the Evidence of late Ummayad Palaces'. *Art History* 5/1: 1–35.

—— (1994) *The Mosque in Islamic Architecture,* Edinburgh: Edinburgh University Press, Chapter 2, pp. 31–128.

Irwin, R. (2004) *The Alhambra*. London: Profile Books.

Lane, E. (1908) *Manners and Customs of the Modern Egyptians*. London: Dent, pp. 60–63.

Lewis, R. (1971) 'Family life', Chapter 5, in Lewis, Raphaela, *Everyday life in Ottoman Turkey*. London: Batsford, pp. 96–7.

Makdisi, G. (1981) *The Rise of Colleges and Institutions of Learning in Islam and the West*. Edinburgh: Edinburgh University Press.

Necipoglu, G. (1991) *Architecture, Ceremony and Power. The Topkapi Palace in the Fifteenth and Sixteenth Centuries*. Cambridge, MA, and London.

—— (2005) *The Age of Sinan, Architectural Culture in the Ottoman Empire*. London: Reaktion Books.

Nicholson, L. (1989) *The Red Fort, Delhi*. London: Tauris Park Books.

Penzer, N. M. (1936) *The Harem*. London: George Harrap.

Peretic, A. (1912) 'Medersas de Fez'. *Archives marocaines* XVIII, 257–372.

Porter, V. (1995) *Islamic Tiles*. London: British Museum Press.

Al-Qaradawi (1985) *The Lawful and the Prohibited in Islam*. London: Shorouk International.

Rosintal, J. (1928) *Pendentifs, trompes and stalactitites dans l'architecture oriental*. Paris.

Roxburgh, D. (ed.) (2005) *Turks, a Journey of a Thousand Years 600–1600*. Catalogue of an Exhibition held at the Royal Academy London, 22 January –12 April 2005, London.

Safadi, Yasin (1978) *Islamic Calligraphy*. London.

Scarce, J. M. (1987) *Women's Costume of the Near and Middle East*. London: Unwin Hyman (paperback edition Routledge Curzon 2002).

—— (1989) 'Tilework', Chapter 18 in Ferrier, Ronald W. (ed.) *The Arts of Persia*. New Haven and London: Yale University Press, pp. 271–94.

Scarce, J., Bray, J. and Ezzy, W. (1976) *'Wood' in the Arts of Islam*, Catalogue of an Exhibition held at the Hayward Gallery 8 April –4 July 1976, London: Arts Council, pp. 273–274.

Seherr-Thoss, S. and Seherr-Thoss, H. (1968) *Design and Colour in Islamic Architecture*. Washington.

Serjeant, R. B. (1939) 'Mihrab', *Bulletin of the School of Oriental and African Studies* XXII: 439–52.

Stillman, Y. K. (2000) *Arab Dress from the Dawn of Islam to Modern Times*. Leiden: E. J. Brill.

Synthronon (1968) *Art et archéologie de la fin de l'Antiquité et du Moyen âge*. Paris: Receuil d'Etudes, pp. 107–14.

Tillotson, G. H. R. (1990) *Mughal India, Architectural Guides for Travellers*. London: Viking.

Weiss, W. M. and Westermann, K.-M. (1998) *The Bazaar, Markets and Merchants of the Islamic world*. London: Thames & Hudson.

Welch, A. (1979) *Calligraphy in the Arts of the Muslim World*. New York, Asia Society.

Entries by Janet Starkey

Adamec, L. W. (ed.) (1972–85) *Historical and Political Gazetteer of Afghanistan*. Graz: Akademische Druck-u. Verlagsanstalt.

Ahmad, A. (1975) *History of Islamic Sicily*. Edinburgh: Edinburgh University Press.

Allworth, E. (1990) *The Modern Uzbeks: From the Fourteenth Century to the Present: a Cultural History*. Stanford, CA: Hoover Institution Press, Stanford University Press.

Arberry, A. J. (1960) Shiraz: *Persian City of Saints and Poets*. Norman, OK: University of Oklahoma Press.

Babayan, K. (2002) *Mystics, Monarchs and Messiahs: Cultural Landscape of Early Modern Iran*. London: Harvard University Press.

Bosworth, C. E. (1998) 'Ali ibn Abi Talib', in J. Scott Meisami and P. Starkey (eds) *Encyclopaedia of Arabic Literature*, vol. I. London and New York: Routledge, p. 78.

—— (1967) *The Islamic Dynasties*. Edinburgh: Edinburgh University Press, p. 74.

Boyce, M. (1977) *A Persian Stronghold of Zoroastrianism*. Oxford: Clarendon Press.

Braudel, F. (1975) *The Mediterranean and the Mediterranean World in the Age of Philip II*. London: Fontana.

Brett, M. (1999) *Ibn Khaldun and the Medieval Maghrib*. Aldershot: Ashgate.

Broadhurst, R. J. C. (transl.) (1952) *The Travels of Ibn Jubayr*. London: Jonathan Cape.

Brody, L. A. (1955) 'The School of Medicine at Jundishapur: the Birthplace of Arabic Medicine', *Trans Stud Coli Physicians Phila*. 23 (1): 29–37.

Bruinessen, M. van, (2000) *Mullas, Sufis and Heretics: The Role of Religion in Kurdish Society*. Istanbul: Isis Press.

Bujra, Abdulla A. (1971) *The Politics of Stratification: A Study of Political Change in a South Arabian Town*. Oxford: Clarendon Press.

Burckhardt, J. L. (1968) *Travels in Arabia*. First published 1829. London: H. Colburn.

Clancy-Smith, J. (ed.) (2001) *North Africa, Islam, and the Mediterranean World: From the Almoravids to the Algerian War*. London: Frank Cass.

Conrad, L. I. (1998) 'Ibn Battuta', in J. Scott Meisami and P. Starkey (eds) *Encyclopaedia of Arabic Literature*, vol. I. London and New York: Routledge, pp. 318–19.

Corrao, F. M. (1998) 'Sicily, Siculo-Arabic poets', in J. Scott Meisami and P. Starkey (eds) *Encyclopaedia of Arabic Literature*, vol. II. London and New York: Routledge, pp. 719–20.

Crane, H. (transl.) (2000) *The Garden of the Mosques: Hafiz Hüseyin al-Ayvansarayi's Guide to the Muslim monuments of Ottoman Istanbul*. Leiden: E. J. Brill.

Creswell, K. A. C. (1989) *A Short Account of Early Muslim Architecture*, (ed.) James W. Allan. First published 1958. Cairo: American University in Cairo Press, pp. 9–10, 261–4.

Cross, T. M. and Leiser, G. (2000) *A Brief History of Ankara*. Vacaville, CA: Indian Ford Press.

Degeorge, G. (2001) *Samarkand, Bukhara, Khiva*. Paris: Flammarion.

al-Deihani, M. S. (1993) 'Al-Kufa: The City and the Society in the Early Islamic Period (c17–671c. 638–87)'. Ph.D. thesis, University of Manchester.

Dodge, B. (1967) 'The Sabians of Harran', in Fuad Sarruf and Suha Tamin (eds) *American University of Beirut Festival Book*. Beirut: American University of Beirut, pp. 59–85.

Durrani, N. (2001) 'The Tihamah Coastal Plain of South West Arabia in its Regional Context (c. 6000BC–AD600)', Ph.D. thesis, University of London.

—— (2004) 'Merv', *Current World Archaeology*, 3 (January/February): 18–30.

Farhfidi, A. G. (1996) '*Abdullah Ansari of Her at (1006–89 CE.): An Early Sufi Master*. Richmond: Curzon.

Gelder, G. J. H. van (1998) 'Hijaz', in J. Scott Meisami and P. Starkey (eds) *Encyclopaedia of Arabic Literature*, vol. I.

London and New York: Routledge, pp. 285–6.

Gibb, H. A. R. (1923) *The Arab Conquests in Central Asia*. London: The Royal Asiatic Society.

—— (1971) *The Travels of Ibn Battuta*. First published in 1958. Cambridge, Cambridge University Press.

Golliday, J. (1988) *Morocco*. London: A. & C. Black.

Green, T. M. (1992) *The City of the Moon God: Religious Traditions of Harran*. Leiden: E. J. Brill.

Griffin, M. (2003) *Reaping the Whirlwind: Afghanistan, Al-Qa'ida, and the Holy War*. London: Pluto Press.

Hashmi, S. M. A. (1989) *Muslim Response to Western Education: A Study of Four Pioneer Institutions*. New Delhi: Commonwealth Publishers.

Herrmann, G. and Kennedy, H. (1999) *Monuments of Merv: Traditional Buildings of the Karakum*. London: Society of Antiquaries of London.

Herrmann, G. *et al.* (2002) *The Monuments of Merv: A Scanned Archive of Photographs and Plans*. London: Institute of Archaeology, University College, London and the British Institute of Persian Studies.

Hillenbrand, R. (1994) *Islamic Architecture: Form, Function and Meaning*. Edinburgh: Edinburgh University Press, pp. 414–15.

Hunwick, J. O. (transl.) (1999) *Timbuktu and the Songhay Empire: Al-Sadi's Tarikh al Sudan down to 1613, and other Contemporary Documents*. Boston, MA: Brill.

Ivanov, V. A. (ed. and transl.) (1953) *The Truth-Worshippers of Kurdistan: Ahl-i haqq Texts*. Leiden: E. J. Brill.

Al-Juhany, U. M. (2002) *Najd before the Salafi Reform Movement: Social, Political and Religious Conditions during the Three Centuries Preceding the Rise of the Saudi State*. Reading: Ithaca Press.

Kimber, R. A. (1998) 'Harlin ai-Rashid', in J. Scott Meisami and P. Starkey (eds) *Encyclopaedia of Arabic Literature*, vol. I. London and New York: Routledge, pp. 273–4.

King, G. (1998) *The Traditional Architecture of Saudi Arabia*. London: I. B. Tauris, pp. 32–51.

Knysh, A. (1998) 'Maghrib', in J. Scott Meisami and P. Starkey (eds) *Encyclopaedia of Arabic Literature*, vol. II. London and New York: Routledge, pp. 484–8.

731

Lambton, A. K. S. (1990) 'Qum: The Evolution of a Medieval City', *Journal of the Royal Asiatic Society* 2: 322–39.

Last, M. (1977) *The Sokoto Caliphate*. London: Longman.

Litvak, M. (1998) *Shi'i Scholars and Patrons of Nineteenth-Century Iraq: The Ulama of Najaf and Karbala*. Cambridge: Cambridge University Press.

Mansel, P. (1997) *Constantinople: City of the World's Desire 1453–1924*. London: Penguin.

Maxwell, G. (1966) *Lords of the Atlas*. London: Longman.

Meisami, J. S. (1998) "Abbasids', in J. Scott Meisami and P. Starkey (eds) *Encyclopaedia of Arabic Literature*, vol. I. London and New York: Routledge, p. 8.

Meisami, J. S. and Starkey, P. (eds) (1998) *Encyclopaedia of Arabic Literature*, London and New York: Routledge.

Metcalf, B. D. (2002) *Islamic Revival in British India: Deoband, 1860*. New Delhi: Oxford University Press.

Metcalfe, A. (2003) *Muslims and Christians in Norman Sicily: Arabic Speakers and the End of Islam*. London: Routledge Curzon.

Montgomery, S. L. (2000) *Science in Translation: Movements of Knowledge through Cultures and Time*. Chicago, IL: University of Chicago Press.

Nagamia, H. F. (1998) 'Islamic Medicine: History and Current Practice'. Available on-line at <http://www.iiim.org/islamed3.html>.

Nakash, Y. (2003) *The Shi'is of Iraq*. First published 1994. Princeton, NJ: Princeton University Press.

Naumkin, V. (1992) *Samarkand*. Reading: Garnet.

Naval Intelligence Division (1943) *Turkey Geographical Handbook*, BR 507, II, 28–34.

Nobuaki, K. (ed.) (2003) *Persian Documents: Social History of Iran and Turan in Fifteenth to Nineteenth Centuries*. London: RoutledgeCurzon.

Ochsenwald, W. (1984) *Religion, Society, and the State in Arabia: The Hijaz under Ottoman Control, 1840–1908*. Columbus, OH: Ohio State University Press.

Pesce, A. (1974) *Jiddah, Portrait of an Arabian City*. Cambridge: Oleander Press.

Phillips, W. (1955) *Qataban and Sheba: Exploring Ancient Kingdoms on the Biblical Spice Routes of Arabia*. London: V. Gollancz.

Powers, D. S. (2002) *Law, Society, and Culture in the Maghrib*. Cambridge: Cambridge University Press.

Rasanayagam, A. (2003) *Afghanistan, a Modern History: Monarchy, Despotism or Democracy? The Problems of Governance in the Muslim Tradition*. London: I. B. Tauris.

Raudvere, C. (2002) *The Book and the Roses: Sufi Women, Visibility, and Zikir in Contemporary Istanbul*. Istanbul: Swedish Research Institute in Istanbul.

Robinson, C. F. (2000) *Empire and Elites after the Muslim Conquest: The Transformation of Northern Mesopotamia*. Cambridge: Cambridge University Press.

Roy, O. (1990) *Islam and Resistance in Afghanistan*. First published in 1986. Cambridge: Cambridge University Press.

Saad, E. N. (1983) *Social History of Timbuku: The Role of Muslim Scholars and Notables, 1400–1900*. Cambridge: Cambridge University Press.

Sachs, M. (1970) *Marv*. New York: Doubleday.

Savory, R. (1980) *Iran under the Safavids*. Cambridge: Cambridge University Press.

Schippmann, K. (2001) *Ancient South Arabia: From the Queen of Sheba to the advent of Islam*. Princeton, NJ: Markus Wiener.

Schubel, V. J. (1993) *Religious Performance in Contemporary Islam: Shii Devotional Rituals in South Asia*. Columbia, SC: University of South Carolina Press.

Searight, S. (2005) 'Jiddah in the Nineteenth Century: The Role of European Consuls', in Janet Starkey (ed.) *People of the Red Sea, Proceedings of the Red Sea Project II, 2004*. Oxford: Archaeopress.

Simpson, St John (ed.) (2002) *Queen of Sheba: Treasures from Ancient Yemen*. London: British Museum.

Smith, G. R. (1997) *Studies in the Medieval History of the Yemen and South Arabia*. Brookfield, VT: Ashgate.

Stark, F. (2003) *The Southern Gates of Arabia: A Journey in the Hadhramaut*. First published 1936. London: John Murray.

Stetkevych, J. (1993) *The Zephyrs of Najd: The Poetics of Nostalgia in the Classical Arabic Nasib*. London: University of Chicago Press.

Stewig, R. (2004) *Proposal for Including Bursa, the Cradle City of the Ottoman Empire, in the UNESCO World Heritage*. Kiel: Geographisches Institut der Universitat Kiel.

Stilwell, S. A. (2004) *Paradoxes of Power: The Kano 'Mamluks' and Male Royal Slavery in the Sokoto Caliphate, 1804– 1903*. Portsmouth, NH: Heinemann.

Stone, F. L. (1999) *Tihamah Gazetteer, the Southern Red Sea Coast of Arabia to 923/ 1517*. Manchester: University of Manchester.

Wasserstein, D. J. (1998) 'Ibn Jubayr', in J. Scott Meisami and P. Starkey (eds) *Encyclopaedia of Arabic Literature*, vol. I. London and New York: Routledge, p. 340.

Watt, W. M. (1968) *Islamic Political Thought*. Edinburgh: Edinburgh University Press, p. 43.

White, J. B. (2002) *Islamist Mobilization in Turkey: A Study in Vernacular Politics*. Seattle, WA: University of Washington Press.

Wohaibi, A. (1973) *The Northern Hijaz in the Writings of the Arab Geographers, 800 1150*. Beirut: al-Risalah.

Yamani, Mai (2004) *Cradle of Islam: The Hijaz and the Quest for an Arabian Identity*. London: I. B. Tauris.

Yarshater, Ehsan (ed.) (2003) *Encyclopaedia Iranica*, vol. XII: 2–3. Herat and New York: Encyclopaedia Iranica Foundation.

Entries by Paul Starkey

Abdur Rahman, K.M. (1938) 'Sources of Yaqut's geographical dictionary', *Dacca University Studies*, 2ii, 81–3.

—— (1958) 'The Arab geographer Yaqut al-Rumi', *JAS Pakistan*, 3, 23-8.

—— (1965) *Islamic Methodology in History*. Karachi.

—— (1979) *Islam*. Chicago.

—— (1982) *Islam and Modernity: Transformation of an Intellectual Tradition*. Chicago.

Abu Deeb, K. (1969) 'Towards a structural analysis of pre-Islamic poetry, II. The eros vision' *Edebiyat*, 1, 3–69.

Afetinan, A. (1975) *Life and Works of Piri Reis: The Oldest Map of America*, tr. by L. Yola and E. Uzmen, Ankara.

Amir Arjomand, Said (1994) 'Abd Allah ibn al-Muqaffa and the 'Abbasid revolution', *Iranian Studies* 27, 9–36

Armajani, Jon (2005) *Dynamic Islam: Liberal Muslim Perspectives in a Transnational Age*. Dallas, TX, and Oxford

Arberry, A. J. (trans.) (1945) *Gulistan. Kings and Beggars*. London.

—— (1947) *Fifty Poems of Hafiz: Texts and Translations collected and made, introduced*

and annotated by. Cambridge & New York, repr. 1968.

—— (trans.) (1957) *The Seven Odes*. London.

—— (1958) *Classical Persian Literature*. London.

Ashtiany J. *et al.* (eds) (1990) *Cambridge History of Arabic Literature: 'Abbasid Belles Lettres*. Cambridge: Cambridge University Press

Auchterlonie, P. (1987) *Arabic Biographical Dictionaries: a Summary Guide and Bibliography*. Durham.

Bat, Mansur Ahmad (1998) *Muhammad 'Ali Jinnah*. Lahaur.

Beeston, A. F. L. (1980) *The Epistle on Singing-Girls by Jahiz*, (ed. and trans.), Warminster.

—— (1990) 'Al-Hamadhani al-Hariri and the *maqamat* genre', in Julia Ashtiany *et al.* (eds) *Cambridge History of Arabic Literature: 'Abbasid Belles Lettres*. Cambridge: Cambridge University Press, pp. 125–35.

Berry, D. L. (2003) *Islam and Modernity through the Writings of Islamic Modernist Fazlur Rahman*. Lewiston, NY: Lampeter.

Bombaci, A. *et al.* (eds) (1978) *Opus Geographicum*. Naples.

Bosworth, C. E. (1983) 'The Persian impact on Arabic literature', in Beeston, A.F.L., *et al.* (eds) *Cambridge History of Arabic Literature: Arabic Literature to the End of the Umayyad Period*. Cambridge: Cambridge University Press, pp. 483–96.

Broadhurst, R. J. C. (trans.) (1952) *The Travels of Ibn Jubayr*. London.

Cachia, P. J. E. (1970) 'The Dramatic Monologues of al-Ma'arri', *Journal of Arabic Literature* 1: 129–36,

Chenery, T. and Steingass, F. (eds and trans.) (1867–98) *The Assemblies of Al Hariri*. London, reprinted 1969.

Collins, B. A. (trans.) (1994) *The Best Divisions for Knowledge of the Regions*. Reading.

Dankoff, R. (1991) *The Intimate Life of an Ottoman Statesman: Melek Ahmed Pasha (1588–1662: as Portrayed in Evliya Celebi's Book of Travels (Seyahatname)*. Translation and commentary. Albany.

Dankoff, R. and Elsie, R. (2000) *Evliya Celebi in Albania and Adjacent Regions: (Kosovo, Montenegro, Ohrid): the Relevant Sections of the Seyahatname*. Edited with translation, commentary and introduction. Leiden.

Darke, H. (trans) (1960) *The Book of Government, or Rules for Kings: the Siyasatnama or Siyar al-Muluk.* London & New Haven.

Davis, D. (1993) *Epic and Sedition: the case of Ferdowsi's Shahnameh.* Fayetteville.

Dodge, B. (trans.) (1970) *The Fihrist of al-Nadim.* New York.

Duri, A. A. (1983) *The Rise of Historical Writing among the Arabs,* trans. L.I. Conrad. Princeton, NJ.

Fakhry, Majid (1991) *Ethical Theories in Islam.* Leiden.

Ferrand, G. (ed.) (1921) 'Kitab al-Fawa'id' in *Instructions nautiques et routiers arabes et portugais, I.* Paris.

Gaudefroy-Demombynes (ed. and trans.) (1947) *Introduction au Livre de la poesie et des poete.* Paris.

de Gayangos, P. (1840–3) *The History of the Mohammedan Dynasties in Spain,* (with partial translation of *Nafh al-tib*) 2 vols. London.

de Goeje, M. J. 'Die Istahri Balhi Frage', *ZDMG* XXV: 42–58.

—— (ed.) (1870) *Kitab al-Masalik waal-Mamalik.* Leiden.

—— (ed.) (1889) *Kitab al-Masalik waal-Mamalik.* Leiden.

—— (ed.) (1906) *Ahsan al-Taqasim.* Leiden.

Gibb, H. A. R. (1962) "al-Mawardi's Theory of the Caliphate' in *Studies in the Civilization of Islam,* Boston, pp. 151–65.

Gibb, H. A. R. and Beckingham, C.F. (trans) (1994) *The Travels of Ibn Battuta.* 4 vols. London.

el-Hajji, A. A. (ed.) (1968) *Jughrafiya al-Andalus wa-Urubba.* Beirut.

Hashim, Salah al-Din 'Uthman (ed.) (1963–5), *Ta'rikh al-Adab al-Jughrafi al-'Arabi.* Cairo.

Hawting, G. R. (1986) *The First Dynasty of Islam: The Umayyad Caliphate AD 661–750.* London: Routledge.

Haydar, A. (1977) 'The Mu'allaqa of Imru' al-Qays: its structure and meaning', *Edebiyat* 2: 227–61. 3 (1978): 51–82.

—— (1978) 'The Mu'allaqa of Imru' al-Qays: its structure and meaning', *Edebiyat* 3: 51–82.

Hawting, G.R., Gibb and Bosworth (1960–2003) '*al-Mukhtar b. Abi 'Ubayd*', *Encyclopedia of Islam,* second edn. Leiden: E.J. Brill.

Hitti, Philip K. and Murgoten, Francis C. (trans.) (1916–24) *The Origins of the Islamic State.* New York.

Hopkins, J.F.P. (1990) 'Geographical and Navigational Literature', in M.J.L. Young, J.D. Latham and R.B. Serjeant

(eds) *Religion, Learning and Science in the 'Abbasid period,* Cambridge History of Arabic Literature. Cambridge: Cambridge University Press, pp. 319–21.

Humphreys, R. S. (1991) *Islamic History: a Framework for Enquiry.* Princeton, NJ.

Hyderabad (1929-31) *al-Durar al-Kamina.*

Jarret, H. S. (trans.) (1881) *History of the Caliphs.* Calcutta, repr. Amsterdam, 1971.

Kennedy, H. (1981)*The Early 'Abbasid Caliphate.* London.

Khalidi, Tarif (1994) *Historial Thought in the Classical Period.* Cambridge.

Khan, Q. (trans.) (1983) *al-Mawardi's Theory of the State.* Lahore.

Khoury, R. G. (1972) *Wahb b. Munabbih.* Wiesbaden: Der Heidelberger Papyrus P.S.R. Heid. Arab. 23.

Killito, A. (1978) 'Contribution a l'etude de l'ecriture a litteraire classique: l'exemple de Hariri', *Arabica.* 25: 18–47.

Kilpatrick, Hilary (2002) *Making the Great Book of Songs: Compilation and the Author's Craft in Abu l-Faraj al-Isbahani's Kitab al-Aghani.* New York.

Krachkovsky, I. J. (1957) *Arabskaya Literatura Geograficeskaya.* Moscow/Leningrad.

—— (1960-61) 'Les Geographes arabes des XIe et XIIe siecles en Occident', (trans.) M. Canard, *AIEO* 18–19, 1-72

Kramers, J. H. (ed.) (1938-9) *Kitab Surat al-ard.* Leiden and Leipzig

Latham, J. D. (1990), 'Ibn al-Muqaffa' and early 'Abbasid prose', in J. Ashtiany, *et al.* (eds) *Cambridge History of Arabic Literature: 'Abbasid Belles Lettres.* Cambridge: Cambridge University Press, pp. 48–77.

Lecomte, G. (1965) *Ibn Qutayba (mort en 276/889), l'homme, son oeuvre et ses idees.* Damascus.

Le Strange, G. (trans.) (1888) *Diary of a Journey through Syria and Palestine.* London.

Levy, R. (1969), *An Introduction to Persian Literature,* New York & London, pp. 116–34.

Lewis, G. L. (1957) *The Balance of Truth.* London.

McGuckin de Slane (ed.) (1842–71) *Biographical Dictionary.* 4 vols. Paris.

—— (1857) *Description de l'Afrique septentrionale.* Algiers.

Mackintosh-Smith, T. (2001) *Travels with a Tangerine: a Journey in the Footnotes of Ibn Battutah.* London.

—— (2002) *The Travels of Ibn Battuta, abridged, introduced and annotated.* London.

Margoliouth, D. S. (ed.) (1907–31) *Irshad al-Arib ila Ma'rifat al-Adib or Dictionary of Learned Men.* 6 vols. Leiden.

Massé, H. (1919) *Essai sur le poete Saadi.* Paris.

—— (1935) *Firdousi et l'epopee nationale.* Paris.

Miller, K. (1926–7) *Mappae Arabicae.* Stuttgart.

Miquel, A. (1967) *La Geographie humaine du monde musulman jusq 'au milieu du XIe siecle,* Paris/The Hague.

—— (1967–80) *La Geographie humaine du monde musulman jusqu 'au milieu du XIe siecle.* Paris.

—— (1967–88) *La Geographie humaine au monde musulman jusqu'au milieu du 11e siecle.* Paris.

Mitchell, J. (1831) *The History of the Maritime Wars of the Turks,* London.

Monroe, J. T. (1983) *The Art of Badi' az-Zaman al-Hamadhani as Picaresque Narrative.* Beirut.

Moosa, E. (ed.) (1999) *Revival and Reform in Islam: A Study of Islamic Fundamentalism.* Oxford.

Nicholson, R. A. (ed. and trans.) (1900–02) 'The Risalat al-Ghufran'. *Journal of the Royal Asiatic Society*

Oman, G. (1961) 'Notizie bibliografiche sul geografo arabo al-Idrisi (XII secolo) e sulle sue opere', *AIUON* n.s., 11, 25–61.

Pallis, A. (1951) *In the Days of the Janissaries: Old Turkish Life as Depicted in the 'Travel-book' of Evliya Chelebi.* London.

Pellat, C. (1953) *Le milieu basrien et la Formation de Gahiz.* Paris.

—— (1990) ''Al-Janiz', in J. Ashtiany *et al.* (eds), *Cambridge History of Arabic Literature: 'Abbasid Belles Lettres.* Cambridge: Cambridge University Press, pp. 78–95.

Perier, J. (1904) *Vie d'al-Hadjdjaj ibn Yousof.* Partis.

Piri Reis (1935) *Kitab-i Bahriyye.* Istanbul.

—— (1935) *Haritasi.* Istanbul.

Popper, W. (1954–60) *History of Egypt, 1382–1469 A.D., translated from the Arabic Annals of Abu'l-Mahasin ibn Taghri Birdi.* Berkeley.

Predergast, W. J. (trans.) (1915) *The Maqamat of Badi al-Zaman al-Hamadhani,* London and Madras, repr. London and Dublin, 1973

Ragib, F. J. (ed. and trans.) (1953) *Nasir al-Din Tusi's Memoir on Astronomy (al-Tadhkira fi 'Ilm al Hay'a).* New York.

Rashed, R., (1996) 'Algebra', in Roshdi Rashed (ed.) *Encyclopaedia of Arabic Science,* vol. 2. London, pp. 349–55.

Rosenfeld, B. A. (1983) *Muhammad ibn Musa al-Khorezmi.* Moscow.

Rosenthal, E. J. (1958) *Political Thought in Medieval Islam.* Cambridge.

Rosenthal, F. (1968) *A History of Muslim Historiography,* 2nd edn. Leiden.

Rosenthal, Franz (1952, 2nd ed.1968) A History of Muslim Historiography, Leiden: Brill.

—— (1964) *Configuration de la terre,* J. H. Kramers and G. Wiet (trans), 2 vols. Beirut and Paris.

Sachau, E. (trans.) (1879) *The Chronology of Ancient Nations.* London.

—— (trans.) (1888) *Alberun's India.* London.

Saliba, G. (1990) ''Al-Biruni and the Sciences of his Time', in M.J.L. Young *et al.* (eds) *Cambridge History of Arabic Literature: Religion, Learning and Science in the 'Abbasid Period.* Cambridge: Cambridge University Press.

Samad, Y. (1995) *A Nation in Turmoil: Nationalism and Ethnicity in Pakistan, 1937-58.* New Delhi and London: Thousand Oaks.

Sartain, E. M. (1975) *Jalal al-Din al-Suyuti,* vol. 1: *Biography and Background,* vol. 2: *al-Tahadduth bi-ni'mat Allah.* Cambridge.

Sawa, G. D. (1989) *Music Performance Practice in the Early 'Abbasid Era 132–320 AH/750–932 AD.* Toronto.

Shaban, M.A. (1970) *The 'Abbasid Revolution,* Cambridge.

—— (1971) *Islamic History A.D. 600–750 / A.H. 132: A New Interpretation.* Cambridge

Somogyi, J. de (1932) 'The Ta'rikh al-islam of adh-Dhahabi', *JRAS* 815-55

Sourdel, D. (1959-60) *Le vizirat 'Abbaside.* Damascus.

Sperl, S. (1989) *Mannerism in Arabic Poetry.* Cambridge.

Sprenger, A. *et al.* (eds) (1857) *Suyuti's Itqan on the Exegetic Sciences of the Qur'an.* Calcutta.

Stetkevych, J. (1993) *The Zephyrs of Najd: the Poetics of Nostalgia in the Classical Arabic Nasrib.* Chicago, IL, University of Chicago Press.

—— (1993) *The Mute Immortals Speak: Pre-Islamic Poetry and the Poetics of Ritual.* Ithaca, NY, pp. 241–85.

Tibbetts, G.R. (1971) *Arab Navigation in the Indian Ocean Before the Coming of the Portuguese, being a Translation of Kitab al-Fawa'id of Ahmad ibn Majid al-Najdl.* London.

Waugh, E. H. and Denny, F. M. (eds) (1998) *The Shaping of an American Islamic Discourse: a Memorial to Fazlur*. Atlanta, GA.

Wellhausen, J. (1963) *The Arab Kingdom and its Fall*, trans. by M. G. Weir. Beirut.

Wickens, G. M. (trans.) (1964) *The Nasirean Ethics*. London.

Wiistenfeld, F. (ed.) (1846) *Kitab al-Mushtarik*. Gottingen.

—— (1866–73) *Mu'jam al-Buldan, Jacut's geographisches Worterbuch*. 6 vols. Leipzig, also later editions.

—— (1876–7) *Das geographische Worterbuch*. Gottingen.

Young, M. J. L., Latham, J. D. and Serjeant, R.B. (eds) (1990) 'Science in the 'Abbasid period' in Young *et al.* (eds) *Cambridge History of Arabic Literature: Religion, Learning and Science in the 'Abbasid Period*. Cambridge: Cambridge University Press.

Entries by Street

Averroes (1983) *Rasa'il Falsafiyya*, (ed.) J. D. Alawi. Casablanca.

Avicenna (1964) *Al-Shifa', al-Qiyas*, (ed.) S. Zayed. Cairo.

Corbin, H. (1993) *History of Islamic Philosophy*, trans. L. Sherrard. London: Kegan Paul.

Goldziher, I. (1981) 'The attitude of orthodox Islam toward the "ancient sciences", in M. L. Swartz (ed. and trans.) *Studies on Islam*. Oxford: Oxford University Press, pp. 185–215.

Gutas, D. (1999) 'The "Alexandria to Baghdad" complex of narratives. A contribution to the study of philosophical and medical historiography among the Arabs', in *Documenti e studi sulla tradizione filosofica medievale* 10: 155–93.

—— (1988) *Avicenna and the Aristotelian Tradition*. Leiden, E. J. Brill.

Hallaq, W. B. (1993) *Ibn Taymiyya against the Greek Logicians*. Oxford: Clarendon.

Lagerlund, H. (2000) *Modal Syllogistics in the Middle Ages*. Leiden, E. J. Brill.

Lameer, J. (1994) *Al-Farabi and Aristotelian Syllogistics: Greek Theory and Islamic Practice*. Leiden, E. J. Brill.

Peters, F. E. (1968) *Aristotle and the Arabs*. New York: New York University Press.

Rescher, N. and Van Der Nat, A. (1974) 'The theory of modal syllogistic in medieval Arabic philosophy', in Rescher *et al.* *Studies in Modality*. Oxford, pp. 17–54.

Shehaby, N. (1973) *The Propositional Logic of Avicenna*. Dordrecht.

Street, T. (2002) 'An outline of Avicenna's syllogistic', *Archiv fur Geschichte der Philosophie* 84: 129–60.

Wisnovsky, R. (2003) *Avicenna's Metaphysics in Context*. London: Duckworth.

Entries by Thomas

'Abd al-Baqi, 'A. (ed.) (1993) Ahmad Ibn Hanbal, *Musnad*. First published Cairo 1896. Beirut: Dar al-kutub al-'ilmiyya.

'Abd al-Baqi, M. F. (ed.) (1995) Abu 'Abdallah Muhammad Ibn Maja, *Kitab al-Sunan*. First published 1954. Beirut: Dar al-kutub al-'ilmiyya.

—— (ed.) (1996) Muslim b. al-Hajjaj *Jami' al-Sahih*. Beirut: Dar al-ma'arifa.

'Abd al-Hamid, M. M. (ed.) (1983) *Nahj al-Balagha*. Beirut: n.p.

Abu Rida, M. (ed.) (1950) Abu Yusuf al-Kindi, *Fi 'l-Falsafat al-Ula*, in *Rasa'il al-Kindi al-Falsafiyya*, vol. I. Cairo: Dar al-fikr al-'arabi.

'Afifi, A. 'A. (ed.) (1946) Muhyi al-Din Ibn 'Arabi, *Fusus al-Hikam*. Beirut: Dar al-kitab al-'arabi.

Aminrazavi, M. (1996) *Suhrawardi and the School of Illumination*. Richmond: Curzon.

'Amrush, A. R. (ed.) (1984) Malik Ibn Anas, *Al-Muwatta'*. Beirut: n.p.

Anawati, G. (trans.) (1978) Abu 'Ali al-Husayn Ibn Sina, *La Métaphysique du Shifa'*, Livres I-V. Paris: Librairie Metaphysique J. Vrin.

—— (trans.) (1985) Abu 'Ali al-Husayn Ibn Sina, *La Métaphysique du Shifa'*, Livres VI-X. Paris: Librairie Metaphysique J. Vrin.

Arberry, A. J. (trans.) (1953) Abu Muhammad 'Ali Ibn Hazm, *The Ring of the Dove*. London: Luzac and Co.

Asad, M. (ed. and trans.) (1993) *Sahih al-Bukhari, the Early Years of Islam*. First published 1938. Gibraltar: Dar al-Anadalus.

Al-Ash'ari, Abu al-Hasan 'Ali (1980) *Maqalat al-Islamiyyin wa 'khtilaf al-Musallin*, H. Ritter (ed.). First published Istanbul, 1930. Wiesbaden: Franz Steiner.

Atil, E. (trans.) (1981) 'Abdallah Ibn al-Muqaffa', *Kalila wa Dimna, Fables from a Fourteenth-Century Arabic Manuscript*. Washington, DC: Smithsonian Institution Press.

Atiyeh, G. N. (1966) *Al-Kindi, the Philosopher of the Arabs*. Rawalpindi: Islamic Research Institute.

Austin, R. W. J. (trans.) (1980) Muhyi al-Din Ibn al-'Arabi, *Ibn al-'Arabi, the Bezels of Wisdom*. London: SPCK.

Al-Azmeh, A. (1982) *Ibn Khaldun: An Essay in Reinterpretation*. London: Frank Cass.

Badr, M. (ed.) (1910) Abu Mansur al-Baghdadi, *Al-Farq bayn al-Firaq*. Cairo: Matba'at al-Ma'arif.

Badran, M. (ed.) (1951 and 1955) Abu 'l-Fath Muhammad al-Shahrastani, *Kitab al-Milal wa'l-Nihal*, 2 vols. Cairo: n.p.

Al-Bandari, 'A. S. and Hasan, K. (eds) (1991) Abu 'Abd al-Rahman Ahmad al-Nasa'i, *Kitab al-Sunan al-Kubra*. Beirut: Dar al-kutub al-'ilmiyya.

Barbier de Meynard, C. and Pavet de Courteille, A. (eds and trans.) (1861–77) Abu 'l-Hasan al-Mas'udi, *Muruj al-Dhahab, Maçoudi, les prairies d'or*, 9 vols. Paris: Societé asiatique.

Bewley, A. 'A. (trans.) (1989) Malik Ibn Anas, *Al-Muwatta', Al-Muwatta of Imam Malik ibn Anas*. London and New York: Kegan Paul International.

Bosworth, C. E. (1963) 'A Pioneer Arabic Encyclopaedia of the Sciences: al-Khwarizmi's Keys of the Sciences', *Isis* 54: 97–111.

Bousquet, G.-H. (1955) *Ihya' ou Vivification des sciences de la foi, analyse et index*. Paris: M. Besson.

Bouyges, M. (ed.) (1927) Abu Hamid al-Ghazali, *Tahafut al-Falasifa*. Beirut: Imprimerie Catholique.

— (ed.) (1930) Muhammad Ibn Ahmad Ibn Rushd, *Tahafut al-Tahafut*. Beirut: Imprimerie Catholique.

Al-Bukhari, Abu 'Abdallah Muhammad (1999) *Jami' al-Sahih*. Riyadh: Dar al-Salam.

Casson, L. (ed. and trans.) (1989) *The Periplus Maris Erythraei*. Princeton, NJ: Princeton University Press.

Cheikho, L. (ed.) (1905) 'Abdallah Ibn al-Muqaffa' *Kalila wa Dimna, la Version arabe de Kalilah et Dimnah d'après le plus ancien manuscript arabe*. Beirut: Al-matba'at al-kathuwliqiyya li'l-Aba' al-Yasuwiyyin.

Chodkiewicz, M. (1993) *Seal of the Saints*. Cambridge: Islamic Texts Society.

—— and Chittick, W. (eds and trans.) (1988) Muhyi al-Din Ibn al-'Arabi, *Les Illuminations de La Mecque*. Paris: Sindbad.

Conrad, L. (1996) *The World of Ibn Tufayl, Interdisciplinary Perspectives on Hayy ibn Yaqzan*. Leiden: E. J. Brill.

Crone, P. (1987) *Meccan Trade and the Rise of Islam*. Oxford: Basil, Blackwell.

Culme-Seymour, A. (trans. from the French of Titus Burckhardt) (1975) Muhyi al-Din Ibn al-'Arabi, *The Wisdom of the Prophets*. Aldsworth: Beshara Publications.

Cureton, W. (ed.) (2002) Abu 'l-Fath Muhammad al-Shahrastani, *Kitab al-Milal wa'l-Nihal, Book of Religions and Philosophical Sects*, 2 vols. First published London: James Madden, 1842 and 1846. Piscataway, NJ: Gorgias Press.

Dawood, N. (trans.) (1973) *Tales from the Thousand and One Nights*. Harmondsworth: Penguin.

Dodge, B. (trans.) (1970) Abu 'l-Faraj Muhammad al-Nadim, *The Fihrist of al-Nadim*, 2 vols. New York: Columbia University Press.

Dutton, Y. (2002) *The Origins of Islamic Law, the Qur'an and the Muwatta', and Medinan 'Amal*. Richmond: Curzon.

Fagnan, E (trans.) (1915) Abu 'l-Hasan al-Mawardi, *Les Status gouvernementaux ou règles de droit public et administratif (Al-Ahkam al-Sultaniyya wa'l-Wilayat al-Diniyya)*. Algiers: Typ. A. Jourdan.

Fakhry, M. (1983) *A History of Islamic Philosophy*, 2nd edn. New York: Columbia University Press.

Faslul-Karim, M. (trans.) (1978–79) Abu Hamid al-Ghazali, *Ihya' 'Ulum al-Din*. Delhi: Taj Company.

Frisk, H. (ed.) (1927) *Le Périple de la Mer Érythrée*. Goteburg: Elanders Boktryckeri Aktiebolag.

Gauthier, L. (ed. and trans.) (1936) Abu Bakr Ibn Tufayl, *Hayy Ibn Yaqzan*. Beirut: Imprimerie Catholique.

Gimaret, D. and Monnot, G. (trans.) (1986), *Shahrastani, Livre des religions et des sectes I*. Louvain: Peeters.

Gohlman, W. E. (ed. and trans.) (1974) *The Life of Ibn Sina*. Albany, NY: State University of New York Press.

Goodman, L. E. (trans.) (1972) *Ibn Tufayl's Hayy Ibn Yaqzan*. New York: Twayne Publishers.

Gruner, O. C. (trans.) (1930) Abu 'Ali al-Husayn Ibn Sina, *The Canon of Medicine of Avicenna*. London: Luzac and Co.

Guidi, I. (1895–1900) *Tables alphabétiques du Kitab al-Aghani*. Leiden: Brill.

Haddawy, H. (trans.) (1990) *The Arabian Nights*. New York: Norton.

Halkin, A. S. (trans.) (1935) Abu Mansur al-Baghdadi, *Moslem Schisms and Sects, Part II*. Tel Aviv: Palestine Publishing.

Hill, D. R. (1979) *The Book of Ingenious Devices (Kitab al-Hiyal) by the Banu (sons of) Musa bin Shakir*. Dordrecht, Boston and London: D. Reidel.

—— (1993) *Islamic Science and Engineering*. Edinburgh: Edinburgh University Press.

Hirtenstein, S. and Miernan, M. (eds) (1993) *Muhyiddin Ibn 'Arabi, a Commemorative Volume*. Shaftesbury, Rockport and Brisbane: Element.

Huntingford, G. W. B. (trans.) (1980) *Periplus of the Erythraean Sea*. London: Hakluyt Society.

Al-Hurini, N. (ed.) (1858) 'Abd al-Rahman Ibn Khaldun, 'Muqaddima', in *Kitab al-'Ibar wa Diwan al-Mubtada' wa'l-Khabar fi Ayyam al-'Arab*. Cairo: Bulaq.

Husayn, T. and 'Azzam, 'A. (eds) (1941) 'Abdallah Ibn al-Muqaffa', *Kalila wa Dimna*. Cairo: Matba'at al-ma'arif wa-maktabatuha.

Ibn al-'Arabi (1911) *Al-Futuhat al-Makkiyya*. Cairo: Bulaq.

Ibn Hazm (1926) *Al-Fisal fi 'l-Milal*. Cairo: Al-Matba'at al-adabiyya.

Ibn Qudama, M. 'A. (1985) *Al-Mughni*. Beirut: Dar al-Fikr.

Ibrahim, E. and Johnson-Davies, D. (ed. and trans.) (1976) Abu Zakariyya' Yahya al-Nawawi, *Kitab al-Arba'in*, in *Al-Nawawi's Forty Hadith*. Damascus: Holy Koran Publishing House.

Al-Isbahani, 'Ali Ibn al-Husayn (1927–74) *Kitab al-Aghani*, 24 vols. Cairo: Matba'a dar al-kutub al-'arabiyya.

Ivry, A. L. (trans.) (1974) Abu Yusuf al-Kindi, *Fi 'l-Falsafat al-Ula*, in *Al-Kindi's Metaphysics*. Albany, NY: State University of New York Press.

Jeffrey, A. (trans.) (1962) Abu 'Abdallah Muhammad al-Busiri, *Qasidat al-Burda*, in *A Reader in Islam*. Gravenhage: Mouton.

Jolivet, J. and Monnot, G. (trans.) (1993) *Shahrastani, Livre des religions et des sectes II*. Louvain: Peeters.

Juynboll, G. H. A. (1984) 'Muslim's Introduction to his *Sahih*, Translated and Annotated with an Excursus on the Chronology of *Fitna* and *Bid'a'*, *Jerusalem Studies in Arabic and Islam*, 5: 263–311. Repr. 1996, G. Juynboll, *Studies on the Origins and Uses of Islamic Hadith*. Aldershot: Variorum.

Kazi, A. K. and Flynn, J. G. (trans.) (1984) *Muslim Sects and Divisions, the Section on Muslim Sects in Kitab al-Milal wa'l-Nihal*. London and Boston: Kegan Paul International.

Al-Khalidi, M. 'A. (ed.) (1996) Abu Da'ud Sulayman al-Sijistani, *Kitab al-Sunan*, 3 vols. Beirut: Dar al-kutub al-'ilmiyya.

Khalidi, T. (1975) *Islamic Historiography, the Histories of Mas'udi*, Albany, NY: State University of New York Press.

Khan, M. M. (ed. and trans.) (1996) *The Translation of the Meanings of Sahih al-Bukhari*, 9 vols. Lahore: Kazi Publications.

Kilpatrick, H. (2003) *Making the Great Book of Songs, Compilation and the Author's Craft in Abu al-Faraj al-Isbahani's* Kitab al-Aghani. London: RoutledgeCurzon.

Al-Kulini, Abu Ja'far Muhammad (1955–58) *Al-Kafi fi 'Ilm al-Din*. Tehran: Dar al-kutub al-islamiyya.

Al-Lahham, S. (ed.) (1994) Abu 'Ali al-Husayn Ibn Sina, *Al-Qanun fi 'l-Tibb*. Beirut: Dar al-Fikr.

Lunde, P. and Stone, C. (trans.) (1989) Abu 'l-Hasan 'Ali al-Mas'udi, *Muruj al-Dhahab*, in *Meadows of Gold: The Abbasids*. London: Kegan Paul International.

McCarthy, R. J. (trans.) (1980) Abu Hamid al-Ghazali, *Freedom and Fulfillment*. Boston, MA: Twayne Publishers.

Mahdi, M. (1957) *Ibn Khaldun's Philosophy of History: A Study in the Philosophical Foundations of the Science of Culture*. London: Allen & Unwin.

—— (ed.) (1984) *The Thousand and One Nights (Alf Layla wa Layla) from the Earliest Known Sources*, 2 vols. Leiden: E. J. Brill.

Madkour, I., Ahwani, A. F., Al-Khudayri, M. M. and Anawati, G. C. (eds) (1952–83) Abu 'Ali al-Husayn Ibn Sina, *Al-Shifa'*. Cairo: al-Matba'a al-amiriyya.

Marmura, M. (ed. and trans.) (2000) Abu Hamid al-Ghazali, *Al-Ghazali, the Incoherence of the Philosophers*. Provo, UT: Brigham Young University Press.

—— (ed. and trans.) (2004) Abu 'Ali al-Husayn Ibn Sina, *The Metaphysics of The Healing: a parallel English-Arabic text*. Provo, UT: Brigham Young University Press.

Marzolph, U., van Leewen, R. and Wassouf, H. (2004) *The Arabian Nights Encyclopaedia*, 2 vols. Santa Barbara, CA: ABC-CLIO.

Matar, N. (1998) *Islam in Britain 1558–1685*. Cambridge: Cambridge University Press.

Meisami, J. S. and Starkey, P. (eds) (1998) *Encyclopaedia of Arabic Literature*, 2 vols. London and New York: Routledge.

Miquel, A. (trans.) (1957) 'Abdallah Ibn al-Muqaffaʻ, *Ibn al-Muqaffaʻ, Le Livre de Kalila et Dimna*. Paris: C. Klincksieck.

Monnot, G. (1972) 'Les Écrits musulmans sur les religions non-bibliques', *Mélanges de l'Institut dominicain d'études orientales*, 11: 5–48. Repr. 1986 in G. Monnot, *Islam et Religions*. Paris: Maisonneuve et Larose, pp. 39–82.

Al-Nasaʼi, Abu ʻAbd al-Rahman Ahmad (1988) *Kitab al-Sunan al-Sughra*. Beirut: Dar al-kutub al-ʼilmiyya.

Nassar, M. M. M. (ed.) (2000) Abu ʻIsa Muhammad al-Tirmidhi, *Al-Jamiʻ al-Sahih wa-huwa Sunan al-Tirmidhi*. Beirut: Dar al-kutub al-ʻilmiyya.

Netton, I. (1989) *Allah Transcendent: Studies in the Structure and Semiotics of Islamic Philosophy, Theology and Cosmology*. Richmond: Curzon Press.

Pellat, C. (trans.) (1962–89) Abu ʼl-Hasan ʻAli al-Masʻudi, *Prairies d'or*. Paris: Société asiatique.

—— (ed.) (1966–74) Abu ʼl-Hasan ʻAli al-Masʻudi, *Muruj al-Dhahab*. Beirut: Manshurat al-jamiʻa al-Lubnaniyya.

Petrof, D. K. (ed.) (1914) ʻAli Ibn Ahmad Ibn Hazm, *Tawq al-Hamama*. Leiden: E. J. Brill.

Pouzet, L. (ed. and trans.) (1982) Abu Zakariyyaʻ Yahya al-Nawawi, *Kitab al-Arbaʻin*, in *Le Commentaire des Arbaʻin al-Nawawiya de Muhyi al-Din Yahya al-Nawawi (m. 676/1277)*. Beirut: Dar al-Mashriq.

Al-Rafaʻi, A. ʻA. (ed.) (1988) *Fahras Ahadith wa-Athar Sunan al-Darimi*. Beirut: ʻAlam al-kutub.

Rashed, R. and Jolivet, J. (ed. and trans.) (1998) Abu Yusuf al-Kindi, *Fi ʼl-Falsafat al-Ula*, in *Oeuvres philosophiques et scientifiques d'al-Kindi: vol. II. Métaphysique et cosmologie*. Leiden: E. J. Brill.

Reza, S. A. (trans.) (1996) *Nahjul Balagha, Peak of Eloquence*. First published 1980. Bombay: Iman Foundation.

Rida-Tajaddud, M. (ed.) (1971) Abu ʼl-Faraj Muhammad al-Nadim, *Fihrist*. Tehran: Matbaʻa-i Danishgah.

Ritter, H. (ed.) (1931) Abu Muhammad al-Hasan al-Nawbakhti, *K. Firaq al-Shiʻa*.

Istanbul: Matbaʻa al-dawla li-jamiya al-mustashriqin al-Almaniyya.

Robson, J. (1956) 'The Transmission of al-Nasaʼi's "Sunan"', *Journal of Semitic Studies* 1: 38–59.

—— (trans.) (1963–65) Muhammad Ibn ʻAbdallah al-Tibrizi, *Mishkat al-Masabih*. Lahore: Shaykh Muhammad Ashraf.

Rosenthal, F. (trans.) (1958) ʻAbd al-Rahman Ibn Khaldun, *Ibn Khaldun. The Muqaddimah, an Introduction to History*, 3 vols. London: Routledge and Kegan Paul.

Schimmel, A. (1985) *And Muhammad is his Messenger*. Chapel Hill, London: University of North Carolina Press.

Seelye, K. C. (trans.) (1920) Abu Mansur al-Baghdadi, *Moslem Schisms and Sects, Part I*. New York: Columbia University Press.

Shakir, A. M. (ed.) (1954) Ahmad Ibn Hanbal, *Musnad*. Cairo: Dar al-maʻarif.

Shboul, A. (1979), *Al-Masʻudi and his World, a Muslim Humanist and his Interest in non-Muslims*. London: Ithaca Press.

Siddiqi, A. H. (trans.) (1976) Muslim b. al-Hajjaj, *Sahih Muslim*, 4 vols. New Delhi: Kitab Bhavan.

Thomas, D. (1996) 'Abu ʻIsa al-Warraq and the History of Religions', *Journal of Semitic Studies*, 41: 275–90.

Van den Bergh, S. (trans.) (1987) Abu ʼl-Walid Muhammad Ibn Rushd, *Averroes' Tahafut al-Tahafut*. First published 1954. Cambridge: E. J. W. Gibb Memorial Series.

Van Ess, J. (1991–97) *Theologie und Gesellschaft im 2. und 3. Jahrhundert Hidschra, eine Geschichte des religiösen Denkens im frühen Islam*. Berlin and New York: Walter de Gruyter.

Van Vloten, G. (ed.) (1895) Abu ʻAbdallah Muhammad al-Khuwarizmi, *Mafatih al-ʻUlum*. Leiden: E. J. Brill.

Wahba, W. H. (trans.) (1996) Abu ʼl-Hasan al-Mawardi, *Al-Ahkam al-Sultaniyya waʼl-Wilayat al-Diniyya* in *Al-Mawardi: The Ordinances of Government*. Reading: Garnet.

Walbridge, J. and Ziai, H. (ed. and trans.) (1999) Abu ʼl-Futuh Yahya al-Suhrawardi, *Hikmat al-Ishraq, Suhrawardi. The Philosophy of Illumination*. Provo, UT: Brigham Young University Press.

Watt, W. M. (1973) *The Formative Period of Islamic Thought*. Edinburgh: Edinburgh University Press.

—— (trans.) (1994) Abu Hamid al-Ghazali, *The Faith and Practice of al-Ghazali*. First published 1953. Oxford: Oneworld Publications.

Wensinck, A. J. (1932) *The Muslim Creed, its Genesis and Historical Development*. London: Frank Cass.

Wood, R. (trans.) (1980) 'Abdallah Ibn al-Muqaffa', *Kalila and Dimna. Tales for Kings and Commoners, Selected Fables of Bidpai*. Rochester, VT: Inner Traditions International.

Yahya, O. (ed.) (1972–) Muhyi al-Din Ibn al-'Arabi, *Al-Futuhat al-Makkiyya*. Cairo: Al-hay'a al-misriyya al-'amma li'l-kitab.

Zarabozo, J. M. (ed. and trans.) (1999) *Commentary on the Forty Hadith of al-Nawawi*, 3 vols. Boulder, CO: Al-Basheer Publications and Translations.

Ziai, H. (1990) *Knowledge and Illumination: A Study of Suhrawardi's Hikmat al-Ishraq* Atlanta, GA: Scholar's Press.

Entries by Whittingham

Brewster, D. P. (1975) 'Philosophical Discussions of Prophecy in Medieval Islam'. Unpublished D.Phil. thesis, University of Oxford.

Al-Farabi (1985) *Al-Farabi on the Perfect State: Abu Nasr al-Farabi's* Mabadi' Ara' Ahl al-Madina al-Fadila, ed. and trans. R. Walzer. Oxford: Clarendon.

Hasse, D. N. (2000) *Avicenna's* De Anima *in the Latin West*. London: The Warburgh Institute/Turin: Nino Aragno Editore.

Ibn Rushd (1998) *Al-Kashf 'an manahij al-adilla*, (ed.) M. Hanafi. Beirut: Markaz Dirasat al-Wahdat al-'Arabiyya.

—— (2001) *Faith and Reason in Islam*, trans. Ibrahim Najjar. Oxford: Oneworld.

Ibn Sina (1959) *De Anima*, (ed.) F. Rahman. Oxford: Oxford University Press.

—— (1968) *Fi Ithbat al-Nubuwwat*, (ed.) M. Marmura. Beirut: Dar al-Nahar.

—— (1972) *On the Proof of Prophecies* in *Medieval Political Philosophy: A Sourcebook*, trans. M. Marmura, eds. R. Lerner and M. Mahdi. Ithaca, NY: Cornell University Press.

Mahdi, M. (2001) *Al-Farabi and the Foundations of Islamic Political Thought*. Chicago, IL: University of Chicago Press.

Rosenthal, E. (1953) 'The Place of Politics in the Philosophy of Ibn Rushd', *BSOAS* 15: 246–78.

Thematic bibliography
compiled by Patrick S. O'Donnell

I General

Ahmed, Akbar (1999) *Islam Today: A Short Introduction to the Muslim World*. London: I. B. Tauris.

Ahmed, Akbar (2002) *Discovering Islam: Making Sense of Muslim History and Society*, rev. edn. New York: Routledge.

Ali, Syed Ameer (1978) *The Spirit of Islam: A History of the Evolution and Ideals of Islam, with a Life of the Prophet*. London: Chatto & Windus.

Armstrong, Karen (2002) *Islam: A Short History*, rev. edn. New York: Modern Library.

Awde, Nicholas (trans. and ed.) (2000) *Women in Islam: An Anthology from the Qur'an and Hadiths*. New York: Palgrave Macmillan.

Bloom, Jonathan and Blair, Sheila (2002) *Islam: A Thousand Years of Faith and Power*. New Haven, CT: Yale University Press.

Bowker, John (1999) *What Muslims Believe*. Oxford: Oneworld.

Brown, Daniel W. (2003) *A New Introduction to Islam*. Malden, MA: Blackwell.

Calder, Norman, Mojaddedi, Jawid and Rippin, Andrew (eds) (2003) *Classical Islam: A Sourcebook of of Religious Literature*. New York: Routledge.

Daniel, Norman (2000) *Islam and the West: The Making of an Image*, rpt edn. Oxford: Oneworld.

Davies, Merryl Wyn and Sardar, Zia (2004) *The No-Nonsense Guide to Islam*. London: Verso.

Denny, Frederick Mathewson (1994) *An Introduction to Islam*. New York: Macmillan.

Elias, Jamal J. (1999) *Islam*. Upper Saddle River, NJ: Prentice Hall.

Endress, Gerhard (2002) *Islam: An Historical Introduction*, 2nd edn. New York: Columbia University Press.

Ernst, Carl W. (2003) *Following Muhammad: Rethinking Islam in the Contemporary World*. Chapel Hill, NC: University of North Carolina Press.

Esposito, John L. (1995) *The Oxford Encyclopedia of the Modern Islamic World*, 4 vols. Oxford: Oxford University Press.

—— (1998) *Islam: The Straight Path*, 3rd edn. New York: Oxford University Press.

Esposito, John L. (ed.) (2003) *The Oxford Dictionary of Islam*. Oxford: Oxford University Press.

Esposito, John L. and John Obert voll (2001) *Makers of Contemporary Islam*. Oxford: Oxford University Press.

Gibb, Hamilton A. R. and Kramers, J. H. (eds) (1997) *Shorter Encyclopedia of Islam*, rpt edn. Leiden: E. J. Brill.

Gilsenan, Michael (1982) *Recognising Islam: An Anthropologist's Introduction*. London: Croom Helm.

Glassé, Cyril (2003) *The New Encyclopedia of Islam*. Lanham, MD: AltaMira Press.

Guillaume, Alfred (1924) *The Traditions of Islam: An Introduction to the Study of Hadith Literature*. Oxford: Clarendon Press.

Hodgson, Marshall G. S. (1974) *The Venture of Islam*, 3 vols. Chicago, IL: University of Chicago Press.

Keller, Nuh Ha Mim (trans.) (1996) *Al-Nawawi's Manual of Islam*. Cambridge: The Islamic Texts Society.

Lewis, Bernard (ed.) (1992) *The World of Islam: Faith, People, Culture*. New York: Thames & Hudson.

Murata, Sachiko (1992) *The Tao of Islam: A Sourcebook on Gender Relationships in Islamic Thought*. Albany, NY: State University of New York Press.

Murata, Sachiko and Chittick, William C. (1994) *The Vision of Islam*. New York: Paragon House.

Murphy, Caryle (2002) *Passion for Islam – Shaping the Modern Middle East: The Egyptian Experience*. New York: Scribner.

Nasr, Seyyed Hossein (1966) *Ideals and Realities of Islam*. London: Allen & Unwin.

—— (1981) *Islamic Life and Thought*. Albany, NY: State University of New York Press.

—— (1987) *Islamic Spirituality I: Foundations*. New York: Crossroad.

—— (1991) *Islamic Spirituality II: Manifestations*. New York: Crossroad.

—— (2002a) *The Heart of Islam: Enduring Values for Humanity*. San Francisco, CA: Harper SanFrancisco.

—— (2002b) *Islam: Religion, History, and Civilization*. San Francisco, CA: Harper SanFrancisco.

Netton, Ian Richard (1992) *A Popular Dictionary of Islam*. London: Curzon.

Newby, Gordon D. (2002) *A Concise Encyclopedia of Islam*. Oxford: Oneworld.

Nigosian, S. A. (2003) *Islam: Its History, Teaching, and Practices*. Bloomington, IN: Indiana University Press.

Peters, F. E. (1994) *A Reader on Classical Islam*. Princeton, NJ: Princeton University Press.

Rahman, Fazlur (1979) *Islam*, 2nd edn. Chicago, IL: University of Chicago Press.

Rejwan, Nissim (ed.) (2000) *The Many Faces of Islam: Perspectives on a Resurgent Civilization*. Gainesville, FL: University Press of Florida.

Renard, John (1992) *In the Footsteps of Muhammad: Understanding the Islamic Experience*. New York: Paulist Press.

—— (1996) *Seven Doors to Islam: Spirituality and the Religious Life of Muslims*. Berkeley, CA: University of California Press.

—— (1998a) *Responses to 101 Questions on Islam*. Mahwah, NJ: Paulist Press.

—— (ed.) (1998b) *Windows on the House of Islam: Muslim Sources on Spirituality*. Berkeley, CA: University of California Press.

Riddell, Peter G. and Cotterell, Peter (2003) *Islam in Context: Past, Present, and Future*. Grand Rapids, MI: Baker Academic.

Rippin, Andrew (2000) *Muslims: Their Religious Beliefs and Practices*, 2nd edn. London: Routledge.

Rippin, Andrew and Knappert, Jan (eds) (1986) *Textual Sources for the Study of Islam*. Chicago, IL: University of Chicago Press.

Robinson, Francis (1982) *Atlas of the Islamic World since 1500*. New York: Facts on File.

Robinson, Neal (1999) *Islam: A Concise Introduction*. Richmond: Curzon.

Ruthven, Malise (2000a) *Islam: A Very Short Introduction*. New York: Oxford University Press.

—— (2000b) *Islam in the World*, 2nd edn. New York: Oxford University Press.

Savory, R. M. (ed.) (1976) *Introduction to Islamic Civilization*. Cambridge: Cambridge University Press.

Schimmel, Annemarie (1992) *Islam: An Introduction*. Albany, NY: State University of New York Press.

Schulze, Reinhard (2000) *A Modern History of the Islamic World*. New York: New York University Press.

Schuon, Frithjof (1963) *Understanding Islam*. Trans. D. M. Matheson. London: George Allen & Unwin.

—— (1976) *Islam and the Perennial Philosophy*. London: World of Islam Festival Publ. Co.

Sonn, Tamara (2004) *A Brief History of Islam*. London: Polity Press.

Tayob, Abdulkader (1999) *Islam: A Short Introduction*. Oxford: Oneworld.

Waines, David (2003) *An Introduction to Islam*, 2nd edn. Cambridge: Cambridge University Press.

Watt, William Montgomery (1970) *What is Islam?* London: Longman.

—— (1996) *Islam: A Short History*. Oxford: Oneworld.

Williams, John Alden (ed.) (1994) *The Word of Islam*. Austin, TX: University of Texas Press.

II Muhammad

Abbott, Nabia (1998) *Aishah: The Beloved of Mohammad*. London: Al-Saqi.

Andrae, Tor (1936) *Mohammed: The Man and His Faith*. London: George Allen & Unwin.

Armstrong, Karen (1993) *Muhammad: A Biography of the Prophet*. San Francisco, CA: HarperSanFrancisco.

Asani, Ali *et al.* (1996) *Celebrating Muhammad: Images of the Prophet in Popular Muslim Poetry*. Columbia, SC: University of South Carolina Press.

Cook, Michael (1983) *Muhammad*. New York: Oxford University Press.

Forward, Martin (1997) *Muhammad: A Short Biography*. Oxford: Oneworld.

Guillaume, Alfred (1955) *The Life of Muhammad: A Translation of Ibn Ishaq's Sirat Rasul Allah*. London: Oxford University Press.

Kahn, Muhammad Zafrulla (1981) *Muhammad, Seal of the Prophets*. New York: Viking Press.

Lings, Martin (1983) *Muhammad: his life based on the earliest sources*. New York: Inner Traditions International.

Motzki, Harald (ed.) (2000) *The Biography of Muhammad: The Issue of the Sources*. Leiden: E. J. Brill.

Nasr, Seyyed Hossein (1995) *Muhammad: Man of God*. Chicago, IL: Kazi.

Newby, Gordon (1989) *The Making of the Last Prophet: A Reconstruction of the Earliest Biography of Muhammad*. Columbia, SC: University of South Carolina Press.

Nurbakhsh, Javad (1981) *Traditions of the Prophet: Ahadith*. New York: Khaniqahi Nimatullahi.

Peters, Francis E. (1994) *Muhammad and the Origins of Islam*. Albany, NY: State University of New York Press.

Robinson, Neal (1991) *The Sayings of Muhammad*. London: Duckworth.

Rodinson, Maxime (1980) *Muhammad*. New York: Pantheon Books.

Rubin, Uri (1995) *The Eye of the Beholder: The Life of Muhammad as Viewed by the Early Muslims*. Princeton, NJ: Darwin Press.

—— (ed.) (1998) *The Life of Muhammad*. Aldershot: Ashgate.

Schimmel, Annemarie (1985) *And Muhammad is His Messenger: The Veneration of the Prophet in Islamic Piety*. Chapel Hill, NC: University of North Carolina Press.

Warraq, Ibn (ed. and trans.) (2000) *The Quest for the Historical Muhammad*. Amherst, NY: Prometheus Books.

Watt, William Montgomery (1953) *Muhammad at Mecca*. Oxford: Clarendon Press.

—— (1956) *Muhammad at Medina*. Oxford: Clarendon Press.

—— (1961) *Muhammad: Prophet and Statesman*. London: Oxford University Press.

III The Qur'an (translations, commentaries, studies)

Abu-Hamdiyyah, Mohammad (2000) *The Qur'an: An Introduction*. New York: Routledge.

Ali, Abdullah Yusuf (1989) *The Holy Qur'an: Text, Translation and Commentary*. Washington, DC: Amanah.

Ali, Ahmed (1988) *Al-Qur'an: A Contemporary Translation*. Princeton, NJ: Princeton University Press.

Arberry, Arthur J. (trans.) (1955) *The Koran Interpreted*. New York: Macmillan,

Asad, Muhammad (1980) *The Message of the Qur'an*. Gibraltar: Dar al-Andalus.

Ayoub, Mahmoud (1984) *The Qur'an and Its Interpreters*, 2 vols. Albany, NY: State University of New York Press.

Baljon, Jon M. S. (1961) *Modern Muslim Koran Interpretation (1880–1960)*. Leiden: E. J. Brill.

Barlas, Asma (2002) *'Believing Women' in Islam: Unreading Patriarchal Interpretations of the Qur'an*. Austin, TX: University of Texas Press.

Bell, Richard (trans.) (1939) *The Qur'an Translated, With a Critical Rearrangement of the Surahs*. Edinburgh: T. & T. Clark.

—— (1960) *The Qur'an Translated*, 2 vols. Edinburgh: T. & T. Clark.

—— (1963) *Introduction to the Qur'an*. Edinburgh: Edinburgh University Press.

Burton, John (1977) *The Collection of the Quran*. Cambridge: Cambridge University Press.

Cook, Michael (2000) *The Koran: A Very Short Introduction*. Oxford: Oxford University Press.

Cragg, Kenneth (1971) *The Event of the Quran: Islam in its Scripture*. London: George Allen & Unwin.

—— (1973) *The Mind of the Quran: Chapters in Reflection*. London: George Allen & Unwin.

Dawood, N. J. (1956) *The Koran*. Harmondsworth: Penguin.

Esack, Farid (1997) *Qur'an, Liberation and Pluralism*. Oxford: Oneworld.

—— (2002) *The Qur'an: A Short Introduction*. Oxford: Oneworld.

Fakhry, Majid (trans.) (2002) *An Interpretation of the Qur'an*. New York: New York University Press.

Farooq-i-Azam Malik, Muhammad (trans.) (1997) *English Translation of the Meaning of Al-Qur'an: The Guidance for Mankind*. Houston, TX: The Institute of Islamic Knowledge.

Gätje, Helmut (1976) *The Quran and Its Exegesis*, trans. and ed. Alford T. Welch. Berkeley, CA: University of California Press.

Hawting, G. R. *et al.* (eds) (1993) *Approaches to the Quran*. London: Routledge.

Izutsu, Toshihiko (2002) *Ethico-Religious Concepts in the Quran*. Montreal: McGill-Queens University Press.

—— (1980) *God and Man in the Koran*. Salem, NH: Ayer Co.

Jansen, J. J. G. (1974) *The Interpretation of the Koran in Modern Egypt*. Leiden: E. J. Brill.

Kassis, Hanna E. (1998) *A Concordance of the Qur'an*. Berkeley, CA: University of California Press.

Khalifa, Rashad (2000) *Quran, Hadith, and Islam*. Fremont, CA: Universal Unity.

al-Khu'i, Abu'l Qasim (1998) *The Prolegomena to the Qur'an*. Oxford: Oxford University Press.

Madigan, Daniel A. (2001) *The Qur'an's Self-Image: Writing and Authority in Islamic Scripture*. Princeton, NJ: Princeton University Press.

McAuliffe, Jane Dammen (ed.) (2001) *The Encyclopedia of the Qur'an*, vol. 1. Leiden: E. J. Brill.

Mir, Mustansir (1987) *Dictionary of Qur'anic Terms and Concepts*. New York: Garland.

Nelson, Kristina (1985) *The Art of Reciting the Qur'an*. Austin, TX: University of Texas Press.

Rahman, Fazlur (1980) *Major Themes of the Qur'an*. Minneapolis, MN: Bibliotheca Islamica.

Rippin, Andrew (ed.) (1988) *Approaches to the History of the Interpretation of the Qur'an*. Oxford: Clarendon Press.

—— (ed.) (2000) *The Qur'an: Formative Interpretation*. Aldershot: Ashgate/Variorum.

—— (ed.) (2001) *The Qur'an: Style and Contents*. Aldershot: Ashgate.

—— (2002) *The Qur'an and Its Interpretive Tradition*. Aldershot: Ashgate.

Robinson, Neal (1996) *Discovering the Qur'an: A Contemporary Approach to a Veiled Text*. London: SCM Press.

Rodwell, J. M. (trans.) (1974) *The Koran*, first published 1909. London: J. M. Dent & Sons.

Sells, Michael (1999) *Approaching the Qur'an: The Early Revelations*. Ashland, OR: White Cloud Press.

Sher Ali, Maulavi (trans.) and Ghulam Farid, Malik (ed.) (1994) *The Holy Qur'an: Arabic Text with English Translation and Short Commentary*. Tilford: Islam International.

Stowasser, Barbara Freyer (1994) *Women in the Qur'an: Traditions and Interpretations*. New York: Oxford University Press.

Turner, Colin (trans.) (1998) *The Quran: A New Interpretation*, with textual exegesis by Mohammad Baqir Behbudi. Richmond: Curzon.

Wadud-Muhsin, Amina (1999) *Qur'an and Woman: Reading the Sacred Text from a Woman's Perspective*, rpt edn. New York, Oxford University Press.

Wansbrough, John (1977) *Qur'anic Studies: Sources and Methods of Scriptural Interpretation*. Cambridge: Cambridge University Press.

Wansbrough, John and Rippin, Andrew (2004) *Quranic Studies: Sources and Methods of Scriptural Interpretaion*. Amherst, NY: Prometheus Books.

Warraq, Ibn (ed.) (1998) *The Origins of the Koran: Classic Essays on Islam's Holy Book*. Amherst, NY: Prometheus Books.

—— (ed.) (2002) *What the Koran Really Says: Language, Text, and Commentary*. Amherst, NY: Prometheus Books.

Watt, William Montgomery (1994) *Companion to the Qur'an*. Oxford: Oneworld.

Watt, William Montgomery and Bell, Richard (1970) *Introduction to the Qur'an*. Edinburgh: Edinburgh University Press.

Wild, S. (ed.) (1997) *The Qur'an as Text: Islamic Philosophy, Theology, and Science*. Leiden: E. J. Brill.

Zafrulla Khan, Muhammad (trans.) (1997) *The Qur'an* (with Arabic text). Northampton, MA: Olive Branch Press.

IV Shi'i Islam

Abdul-Jabar, Faleh (ed.) (2002) *Ayatollahs, Sufis, and Ideologues: State, Religion and Social Movements in Iraq*. London: Saqi.

Amir-Moezzi, Mohammad Ali (1994) *The Divine Guide in Early Shi'ism: The Sources of Esotericism in Islam*. Albany, NY: State University of New York Press.

Arjomand, Said Amir (1984) *The Shadow of God and the Hidden Imam*. Chicago, IL: University of Chicago Press.

—— (ed.) (1988) *Authority and Political Culture in Shi'ism*. Albany, NY: State University of New York Press.

Ayoub, Mahmoud (1978) *Redemptive Suffering in Islam*. The Hague: Mouton.

Bill, James A. and John Alden Williams (2003) *Roman Catholics and Shi'i Muslims: Prayer, Passion, and Politics*. Chapel Hill, NC: University of North Carolina Press.

Blichfeldt, Jan-Olaf (1985) *Early Mahdism: Politics and Religion in the Formative Period of Islam*. Leiden: E. J. Brill.

Brunner, Ranier and Ende, Werner (eds) (2001) *The Twelver Shia in Modern Times: Religious Culture and Political History*. Leiden: E. J. Brill.

Chelkowski, Peter J. (ed.) (1979) *Ta'ziyah: Ritual and Drama in Iran*. New York: New York University Press.

Chittick, William (1980) *A Shi'ite Anthology*. London: Muhammadi Trust of Great Britain and Northern Ireland.

Cole, Juan (2002) *Sacred Space and Holy War: The Politics, Culture and History of Shi'ite Islam*. London: I. B. Tauris.

Cole, Juan R. I. and Nikki R. Keddie (1986) *Shi'ism and Social Protest*. New Haven, CT: Yale University Press.

Corbin, Henry (1977) *Spiritual Body and Celestial Earth: From Mazdean Iran to Shi'ite Iran*. Princeton, NJ: Princeton University Press.

—— (1985) *Cyclical Time and Ismaili Gnosis*. London: The Institute of Ismaili Studies Ltd/Kegan Paul with Islamic Publications.

Daftary, Farhad (1990) *The Isma'ilis: Their History and Doctrines*. Cambridge: Cambridge University Press.

—— (1994) *The Assassin Legends: Myth of the Isma'ilis*. London: I. B. Tauris.

—— (ed.) (1996) *Mediaeval Isma'ili History and Thought*. Cambridge: Cambridge University Press.

Fuller, Graham E. and Rend Rahim Francke (2001) *The Arab Shi'a: The Forgotten Muslims*. New York: Palgrave Macmillan.

Halm, Heinz (1992) *Shiism*. Edinburgh: Edinburgh University Press.

—— (1997) *Shi'a Islam: From Religion to Revolution*. Princeton, NJ: Markus Wiener.

—— (2001) *The Fatimids and their Traditions of Learning*. London: I. B. Tauris.

Hollister, John N. (1953) *The Shi'a of India*. London: Luzac & Co.

Jabar, Faleh A. (2003) *The Shi'ite Movement in Iraq*. London: Saqi.

Jafri, S. Husain M. (2002) *The Origins and Early Development of Shi'a Islam*. Oxford: Oxford University Press.

Kholberg, Etan (1991) *Belief and Law in Imami Shi'ism*. Aldershot: Variorum/Ashgate.

—— (ed.) (2003) *Shi'ism*. Aldershot: Ashgate.

Khumayni, Ayatallah Seyyid Ruhullah (1981) *Islam and Revolution: Writings and Declarations of Imam Khomeini*, trans. and ed. Hamid Algar. Berkeley, CA: Mizan Press.

Kramer, Martin S. (ed.) (1987) *Shi'ism, Resistance, and Revolution*. Boulder, CO: Westview Press.

Litvak, Meir (2002) *Shi'i Scholars of Nineteenth-Century Iraq*. Cambridge: Cambridge University Press.

Mallat, Chibli (1988) *Shi'i Thought from the South of Lebanon*. Oxford: Centre for Lebanese Studies.

Modarressi, Hossein (2003) *Tradition and Survival: A Bibliographical Survey of Early Shi'ite Literature*, vol. 1. Oxford: Oneworld.

Momen, Moojan (1985) *An Introduction to Shi'i Islam: The History and Doctrines of Twelver Shi'ism*. New Haven, CT: Yale University Press.

Nakash, Yitzhak (2003) *The Shi'is of Iraq*. Princeton, NJ: Princeton University Press.

Nasr, Seyyed Hossein, Hamid Dabashi and Seyyed Vali Reza Nasr (eds) (1988) *Shi'ism: Doctrines, Thought and Spirituality*. Albany, NY: State University of New York Press.

—— (eds) (1989) *Expectation of the Millennium: Shi'ism in History*. Albany, NY: State University of New York Press.

Newman, Andrew J. (2001) *The Formative Period of Twelver Shi'ism: Hadith as Discourse Between Qum and Baghdad*. Richmond: Curzon.

Pinault, David (1993) *The Shiites: Ritual and Popular Piety in a Muslim Community*. New York: Palgrave.

Sachedina, Abdulaziz A. (1981) *Islamic Messianism: The Idea of the Mahdi in Twelver Shi'ism*. Albany, NY: State University of New York Press

Tabatabai, 'Allamah Sayyid Muhammad Husain (1975) *Shi'ite Islam*, trans. and ed. Seyyed Hoseyn Nasr. London: George Allen & Unwin.

Walker, Paul E. (1993) *Early Philosophical Shiism: The Isma'ili Neoplatonism of Abu Ya'qub al-Sijistani*. Cambridge: Cambridge University Press.

—— (1998) *Abu Ya'qub al-Sijistani: Intellectual Missionary*. London: I. B. Tauris.

—— (1999) *Hamid al-Din al-Kirmani: Ismaiili Thought in the Age of al-Hakim*. London: I. B. Tauris.

Wiley, Joyce N. (1992) *The Islamic Movement of Iraqi Shi'as*. Boulder, CO: Lynne Rienner.

V Sufism

Abbas, Shemeem Burney (2003) *The Female Voice in Sufi Ritual: Devotional Practices of Pakistan and India*. Austin, TX: University of Texas Press.

'Abd al-Qadir al-Jilani (1997) *Fifteen Letters (Khamsata 'Ashara Maktuban)*, trans. Muhtar Holland. Hollywood, FL: Al-Baz.

—— (1998) *The Sublime Revelation (Al-Fath ar-Rabbani)*, 2nd edn. trans. Muhtar Holland. Fort Lauderdale, FL: Al-Baz.

—— (1996 – 7) *Sufficient Provision for Seekers of the Path of the Truth (Al-Ghunya li-Talibi Tariq al-Haqq)*, 5 vols. trans. Muhtar Holland. Hollywood, FL: Al-Baz.

—— (1998) *Utterances of Shaikh 'Abd al-Qadir al-Jilani (Malfuzat)*, 2nd edn. trans. Muhtar Holland. Fort Lauderdale, FL: Al-Baz.

—— (2000) *The Book of the Secret of Secrets and the Manifestation of Lights (Kitab Sirr al-Asrar wa Mazhar al-Anwar)*, trans. Muhtar Holland. Fort Lauderdale, FL: Al-Baz.

Abdel-Kader, Ali Hassan (1976) *The Life, Personality and Writings of al-Junayd: A Study of a Third/Ninth Century Mystic with an Edition and Translation of his Writings*. London: Luzac & Co.

Abrahamov, Binyamin (2002) *Divine Love in Islamic Mysticism: The Teachings of al-Ghazali and al-Dabbagh*. London: RoutledgeCurzon.

Abun-Nasr, Jamil M. (1965) *The Tijaniyya: A Sufi Order in the Modern World*. London: Oxford University Press.

Addas, Claude (1993) *Quest for the Red Sulphur: The Life of Ibn 'Arabi*. Cambridge: The Islamic Texts Society.

Affifi, Abu'l-A'la (1936) *The Mystical Philosophy of Muhyid'Din Ibnul-'Arabi*. Cambridge: Cambridge University Press.

Andrae, Tor (1987) *In the Garden of Myrtles: Studies in Early Islamic Mysticism*. Albany, NY: State University of New York Press.

Andreyev, Sergei (2000) *Sufi Illuminati: The Rawshani Movement in Muslim Mysticism, Society and Politics*. London: Curzon.

Arberry, Arthur John (1950) *Sufism: An Account of the Mystics of Islam*. London: Allen & Unwin.

—— (1961a) *Discourses of Rumi*. London: John Murray.

—— (1961b) *Tales from the Masnavi*. London: George Allen & Unwin.

—— (1963) *More Tales from the Masnavi*. London: George Allen & Unwin.

—— (1968) *Mystical Poems of Rumi*. Chicago, IL: University of Chicago Press.

—— (1969) *A Sufi Martyr: The Apologia of 'Ain al-Qudat al-Hamadhani*. London: George Allen & Unwin.

—— (trans.) (1977) *The Doctrine of the Sufis* (translation of Kalabadhi's *Kitab al-ta'arruf*). Cambridge: Cambridge University Press.

—— (1979) *Mystical Poems of Rumi, 2: Second Selection*. Chicago, IL: University of Chicago Press.

Attar, Farid ud-Din (1984) *The Conference of the Birds*, trans. Dick Davis and Afkham Darbandi. London: Penguin Books.

Awn, Peter J. (1983) *Satan's Tragedy and Redemption: Iblis in Sufi Psychology*. Leiden: E. J. Brill.

Baldick, Julian (1989) *Mystical Islam: An Introduction to Sufism*. New York: New York University Press.

—— (1993) *Imaginary Muslims: The Uwaysi Sufis of Central Asia*. New York: New York University Press.

Banani, Amin, Hovannisian, Richard and Sabagh, George (eds) (1994) *Poetry and Mysticism in Islam: The Heritage of Rumi*. New York: Cambridge University Press.

Baqli, Ruzbihan (1997) *The Unveiling of Secrets: Diary of a Sufi Master*, trans. Carl W. Ernst. Chapel Hill, NC: Parvardigar Press.

Bashir, Shahzad (2003) *Messianic Hopes and Mystical Visions: The Nurbakhshiya between Medieval and Modern Islam*. Columbia, SC: University of South Carolina Press.

Bennigsen, Alexandre, *et al.* (1986) *Mystics and Commissars: Sufism in the Soviet Union*. Berkeley, CA: University of California Press.

Birge, John K. (1937) *The Bektashi Order of Dervishes*. London: Luzac & Co.

Böwering, Gerhard (1980) *Mystical Vision of Existence in Classical Islam: The Qur'anic Hermeneutics of the Sufi Sahl al-Tustari*. Berlin: Walter de Gruyter.

Brenner, Louis (1984) *West African Sufi: The Religious Heritage and Spiritual Search of Cerno Bokar Saalif Taal*. London: C. Hurst & Co.

de Bruijn, J. T. P. (1997) *Persian Sufi Poetry*. Richmond: Curzon.

Buehler, Arthur F. (1998) *Sufi Heirs of the Prophet: The Indian Naqshbandiyya and the Rise of the Mediating Sufi Shaykh*. Columbia, SC: University of South Carolina Press.

Burckhardt, Titus (1995) *Introduction to Sufism*. London: Thorsons.

—— (2001) *Mystical Astrology According to Ibn 'Arabi*. Louisville, KY: Fons Vitae.

Chittick, William C. (trans. and ed.) (1983) *The Sufi Path of Love: The Spiritual Teachings of Rumi*. Albany, NY: State University of New York Press.

—— (1989) *The Sufi Path of Knowledge: Ibn al-'Arabi's Metaphysics of Imagination*. Albany, NY: State University of New York Press.

—— (ed.) (1992) *Faith and Practice of Islam: Three Thirteenth Century Sufi Texts*. Albany, NY: State University of New York Press.

—— (1995) *Imaginal Worlds: Ibn al-'Arabi and the Problem of Religious Diversity*. Albany, NY: State University of New York Press.

—— (1997) *The Self-Disclosure of God: Principles of Ibn al-'Arabi's Cosmology*. Albany, NY: State University of New York Press.

—— (2000) *Sufism: A Short Introduction*. Oxford: Oneworld.

Chittick, William C. and Lamborn Wilson, Peter (trans.) (1982) *Fakhruddin 'Iraqi: Divine Flashes*. Mahwah, NJ: Paulist Press.

Chodkiewicz, Michel (1993a) *An Ocean Without Shore: Ibn 'Arabi, The Book, and The Law*. Albany, NY: State University of New York Press.

—— (1993b) *The Seal of the Saints: Prophethood and Sainthood in the Doctrine of Ibn 'Arabi*. Cambridge: The Islamic Texts Society.

Coates, Peter (2002) *Ibn 'Arabi and Modern Thought: The History of Taking Metaphysics Seriously*. Oxford: Anqa.

Corbin, Henri (1978) *The Man of Light in Iranian Sufism*, trans. Nancy Pearson. Boulder, CO: Shambhala.

—— (1998a) *Creative Imagination in the Sufism of Ibn 'Arabi*. Princeton, NJ: Princeton University Press.

—— (1998b) *The Voyage and the Messenger: Iran and Philosophy*, trans. Joseph H. Rowe. Berkeley, CA: North Atlantic Books.

Cornell, Rkia E. (intro. and trans.) (1999) *Early Sufi Women (Dhikr an-niswa al-muta'abbidat as- Suffiyat)*. Louisville, KY: Fons Vitae.

Cornell, Vincent J. (1996) *The Way of Abu Madyan*. Cambridge: The Islamic Texts Society.

—— (1998) *Realm of the Saint: Power and Authority in Moroccan Sufism*. Austin, TX: University of Texas Press.

Cragg, Kenneth (1976) *The Wisdom of the Sufis*. New York: W. W. Norton.

Currie, P. M. (1989) *The Shrine and Cult of Mu'in al-Din Chishti of Ajmer*. Delhi: Oxford University Press.

Danner, Victor and Thackston, Wheeler M. (trans.) (1988) *Ibn 'Ata' Illah (The Book of Wisdom)/Kwaja Abdullah Ansari (Intimate Conversations)*. Mahwah, NJ: Paulist Press.

Eaton, Richard M. (1978) *Sufis of Bijapur, 1300–1700: Social Roles of Sufis in Medieval India*. Princeton, NJ: Princeton University Press.

Elias, Jamal J. (trans.) (1998) *The Sufi Poems of Sultan Bahu*. Berkeley, CA: University of California Press.

Elmore, Gerald T. (ed.) (1999) *Islamic Sainthood in the Fullness of Time: Ibn al-'Arabi's Book of the Fabulous Gryphon*. Leiden: E. J. Brill.

Ernst, Carl W. (1984) *Words of Ecstasy in Sufism*. Albany, NY: State University of New York Press.

—— (1992) *Eternal Garden: Mysticism, History, and Politics at a South Asian Sufi Center*. Albany, NY: State University of New York Press.

—— (1996) *Ruzbihan Baqli: Mystical Experience and the Rhetoric of Sainthood in Persian Sufism*. London: Curzon.

—— (1997) *The Shambhala Guide to Sufism*. Boston, MA: Shambhala.

Ernst, Carl W. and Lawrence, Bruce B. (2002) *Sufi Martyrs of Love: The Chishti Order in South Asia and Beyond*. London: Palgrave Macmillan.

Farhadi, A. G. Ravan (1996) *Abdullah Ansari of Herat: An Early Sufi Master*. Richmond: Curzon.

Friedlander, Shems (2003) *Rumi and the Whirling Dervishes*, rev. edn. New York: Parabola Books.

Gilsenan, Michael (1973) *Saint and Sufi in Modern Egypt*. Oxford: Clarendon Press.

Hammarlund, Anders *et al.* (eds) (2001) *Sufism, Music and Society in Turkey and the Middle East*. Richmond: Curzon.

Heer, Nicholas and Honerkamp, Kenneth L. (intro. and trans.) (2003) *Three Early Sufi Texts*. Louisville, KY: Fons Vitae.

Helminksi, Camille Adams (ed.) (2003) *Women of Sufism, A Hidden Treasure: Writings and Stories of Mystic Poets, Scholars & Saints*. Boston, MA: Shambhala.

Hoffman, Valerie (1995) *Sufism, Mystics, and Saints in Modern Egypt*. Columbia, SC: University of South Carolina Press.

Homerin, Th. E. (1994) *From Arab Poet to Muslim Saint: Ibn al-Farid, His Verse, and His Shrine*. Columbia, SC: University of South Carolina Press.

Huda, Qumar-ul (2003) *Striving for Divine Union: Spiritual Exercises for Suhrawardi Sufis*. New York: RoutledgeCurzon.

Ibn 'Abbad of Ronda (1982) *Letters on the Sufi Path*, trans. John Renard. Mahwah, NJ: Paulist Press.

Ibn al-'Arabi, Muhyiddin (1971) *Sufis of Andalusia: The Ruh al-quds and Al-Durrat al-fakhirah*, trans. R. W. J. Austin. London: George Allen & Unwin.

—— (1980) *Bezels of Wisdom*, trans. R. W. J. Austin. New York: Paulist Press.

—— (1981) *Journey to the Lord of Power: A Sufi Manual on Retreat*, trans. Rabia Harris. Rochester, VT: Inner Traditions.

—— (1983) *The Seals of Wisdom (ten selections from the Fusus al-Hikam)*, Ragha-van Iyer (ed.), (with introductory essay by Elton Hall). Santa Barbara, CA: Concord Grove Press.

—— (2000) *The Seven Days of the Heart: Prayers for the Days and Nights of the Week*, trans. Pablo Beneito and Stephen Hertenstein. Oxford: Anqa.

—— (2001) *Contemplation of the Holy Mysteries*, trans. Cecilia Twinch and Pablo Beneito. Oxford: Anqa.

Ibn 'Ata' Allah al-Iskandari (1996) *The Key to Salvation: A Sufi Manual of Invocation*, trans. Mary Ann Koury-Danner. Cambridge: The Islamic Texts Society.

Ibn al-Farid, 'Umar (2001) *Sufi Verse, Saintly Life*, trans. Th. Emil Homerin. Mahwah, NJ: Paulist Press.

Ingram, Harold *et al.* (1997) *Studies in Islamic Mysticism*. New York: Columbia University Press.

'Iraqi, Fakhruddin (1982) *Divine Flashes*, trans. William Chittick and Peter Wilson. Mahwah, NJ: Paulist Press.

Islam, Riazul (2002) *Sufism in South Asia: Impact on Fourteenth Century Muslim Society*. Karachi: Oxford University Press.

al-Jilani, Hadrat 'Abd al-Qadir (1992) *The Secret of Secrets*, interpretative trans. by Shaykh Tosun Bayrak al-Jerrahi al-Halveti. Cambridge: The Islamic Texts Society.

Jurji, Edward J. (1937) *Illumination in Islamic Mysticism*. Princeton, NJ: Princeton University Press.

Karamustafa, Ahmet T. (1994) *God's Unruly Friends: Dervish Groups in the Islamic Later Middle Period, 1200–1550*. Salt Lake City, UT: University of Utah Press.

Karrar, Ali S. (1992) *The Sufi Brotherhoods in the Sudan*. Evanston, IL: Northwestern University Press.

Keshavarz, Fatemeh (1998) *Reading Mystical Lyric: The Case of Jalal al-Din Rumi*, Frederick M. Denny (ed.). Columbia, SC: University of South Carolina Press.

Knysh, Alexander (2000) *Islamic Mysticism: A Short History*. Leiden: E. J. Brill.

Lawrence, Bruce B. (1978) *Notes from a Distant Flute: Sufi Literature in Pre-*

Mughal India. Tehran: Imperial Iranian Academy of Philosophy.

—— (ed.) (1992) *Nizam ad-din Awliya: Morals for the Heart*. New York: Paulist Press.

Lewis, Franklin D. (2000) *Rumi: Past and Present, East and West: The Life, Teachings and Poetry of Jalal al-Din Rumi*. Oxford: Oneworld.

Lewisohn, Leonard (1995) *Beyond Faith and Infidelity: The Sufi Poetry and Teachings of Mahmud Shabistari*. Richmond: Curzon.

—— (ed.) (1999a) *The Heritage of Sufism, vol. I: Classical Persian Sufism from its Origins to Rumi (700–1300)*. Oxford: Oneworld.

—— (ed.) (1999b) *The Heritage of Sufism, vol. II: The Legacy of Medieval Persian Sufism (1150–1500)*. Oxford: Oneworld.

—— (ed.) (2001) *The Wisdom of Sufism*. Oxford: Oneworld.

Lewisohn, Leonard and Morgan, David (eds) (1999) *The Heritage of Sufism, vol. III: Late Classical Persianate Sufism (1501–1750)*. Oxford: Oneworld.

Lings, Martin (1971) *A Sufi Saint of the Twentieth Century, Shaikh Ahmad al-'Alawi: His Spiritual Heritage and Legacy*, 2nd edn. London: George Allen & Unwin.

Lings, Martin (1993) *What is Sufism?*, rpt edn. Cambridge: The Islamic Texts Society.

Maneri, Sharafuddin (1980) *The Hundred Letters*, trans. Paul Jackson. Mahwah, NJ: Paulist Press.

Mason, Herbert W. (1991) *The Death of al-Hallaj: A Dramatic Narrative*, first published 1979. Notre Dame, IN: University of Notre Dame Press.

—— (1995) *Al-Hallaj*. Richmond: Curzon.

Massignon, Louis (1982) *The Passion of al-Hallaj, Mystic and Martyr of Islam*, 4 vols., trans. Herbert Mason. Princeton, NJ: Princeton University Press.

—— (1997) *Essay on the Origins of the Technical Language of Islamic Mysticism*, trans. Benjamin Clark. Notre Dame, IN: University of Notre Dame Press.

Meier, Fritz (1999) *Essays on Islamic Piety and Mysticism*, trans. John O'Kane. Leiden: E. J. Brill.

Meisami, Julie (1987) *Medieval Persian Court Poetry*. Princeton, NJ: Princeton University Press.

Milson, Menahem (trans.) (1973) *A Sufi Rule for Novices: Kitab Adab al-muridin of Abu Najib al-Suhrawardi*. Cambridge, MA: Harvard University Press.

Mojaddedi, Jawid A. (2001) *The Biographical Tradition in Sufism: The Tabaqat Genre from al-Sulami to Jami*. Richmond: Curzon.

Murata, Sachiko (2000) *Chinese Gleams of Sufi Light: Wang Tai-Yu's Great Learning of the Pure and Real and Liu Chih's Displaying the Concealment of the Real Realm*. Albany, NY: State University of New York Press.

Nasr, Seyyed Hossein (1991) *Sufi Essays*, 2nd edn. Albany, NY: State University of New York Press.

Netton, Ian Richard (2000) *Sufi Ritual: The Parallel Universe*. Richmond: Curzon.

Nicholson, Reynold A. (1921) *Studies in Islamic Mysticism*. Cambridge: Cambridge University Press.

—— (1923) *The Idea of Personality in Sufism*. Cambridge: Cambridge University Press.

—— (ed. and trans.) (1977) *Mathnawi of Jalaluddin Rumi*. London: E. J. W. Gibb Memorial Trust/Luzac & Co.

—— (2000) (ed. and trans.) *A Rumi Anthology*. Oxford: Oneworld.

Nizam, ad-Din Awliya' (1992) *Morals for the Heart*, trans. and ed. Bruce B. Lawrence. Mahwah, NJ: Paulist Press.

Nurbakhsh, Javad (1981) *Sufism: Meaning, Knowledge and Unity*. New York: Khaniqahi Nimatullahi.

—— (1984) *Spiritual Poverty in Sufism*. London: Khaniqahi Nimatullahi.

—— (1984–95) *Sufi Symbolism*, 5 vols. London: Khaniqahi Nimatullahi.

—— (1989) *Dogs from a Sufi Point of View*. London: Khaniqahi Nimatullahi.

—— (1990) *Sufi Women*, 2nd edn. London: Khaniqahi Nimatullahi.

—— (1992a) *The Psychology of Sufism*. New York: Khaniqahi Nimatullahi.

—— (1992b) *In the Tavern of Ruin: Seven Essays on Sufism*, 2nd edn. New York: Khaniqahi Nimatullahi.

O'Fahey, R. S. (1990) *Enigmatic Saint: Ahmad Ibn Idris and the Idrisi Tradition*. Evanston, IL: Northwestern University Press.

Özdalga, Elisabeth (ed.) (1999) *The Naqshbandis in Western and Central Asia*. London: Curzon.

Pendlebury, David (trans. and ed.) (1980) *Yusuf and Zulaikha: An Allegorical Romance, by Hakim Abdurrahman Jami*. London: Octagon Press.

al-Qushayri (1990) *Principles of Sufism*, trans. B. R. von Schlegell. Berkeley, CA: Mizan Press.

Radtke, Berndt *et al.* (trans. and eds) (1999) *The Exoteric Ahmad Ibn Idris: A Sufi's Critique of the Madhahib and the Wahhabis – Four Arabic Texts with Translation and Commentary*. Leiden: E. J. Brill.

Radtke, B. and O'Kane, J. (1996) *The Concept of Sainthood in Early Islamic Mysticism*. Richmond: Curzon.

Ramakrishna, Lajwanti (1938) *Panjabi Sufi Poets*. London: Oxford University Press.

Renard, John, S. J. (trans.) (1988) *Ibn 'Abbad of Ronda: Letters on the Sufi Path*. New York: Paulist Press.

—— (1994) *All the King's Falcons: Rumi on Prophets and Revelation*. Albany, NY: State University of New York Press.

—— (ed.) (2004) *Knowledge of God in Classical Sufism*. Mahwah, NJ: Paulist Press.

Roberts, Allen F. and Nooter Roberts, Mary (with Gassia Armenian and Ousmane Gueye) (2003) *A Saint in the City: Sufi Arts of Urban Senegal*. Los Angeles, CA: UCLA Fowler Museum of Cultural History.

el-Sakkakini, Widad (1982) *First Among Sufis: The Life and Thought of Rabia al-Adawiyya, the Woman Saint of Basra*. London: Octagon Press.

Sanai, Hakim (1974) *The Walled Garden of Truth*, abridged edn. trans. D. L. Pendlebury. London: Octagon Press.

Schimmel, Annemarie (1975) *Mystical Dimensions of Islam*. Chapel Hill, NC: University of North Carolina Press.

—— (1978) *The Triumphal Sun: A Study of the Works of Jalaloddin Rumi*. London: Fine Books.

—— (1982) *As Through a Veil: Mystical Poetry in Islam*. New York: Columbia University Press.

—— (1992a) *I Am Wind, You Are Fire: The Life and Work of Rumi*. Boston, MA: Shambhala.

—— (1992b) *A Two-Colored Brocade: The Imagery of Persian Poetry*. Chapel Hill, NC: University of North Carolina Press.

—— (trans.) (1996) *Look! This is Love: Poems of Rumi*. Boston, MA: Shambhala.

Sedgwick, Mark J. (2001) *Sufism: The Essentials*. Cairo: American University in Cairo Press.

Sells, Michael A. (1996) *Early Islamic Mysticism: Sufi, Qur'an, Mi'raj, Poetic and Theological Writings*. Mahwah, NJ: Paulist Press.

Shah, Idries (intro.) (1980) *Four Sufi Classics: Salaman and Absal; The Niche for Lights; The Way of the Seeker; The Abode of Spring*, various trans. London: Octagon Press (for The Sufi Trust).

Siraj ad-Din, Abu Bakr (2002) *The Book of Certainty: The Sufi Doctrine of Faith, Vision and Gnosis*. Cambridge: The Islamic Texts Society.

Sirriyeh, Elizabeth (1999) *Sufis and Anti-Sufis: The Defence, Rethinking and Rejection of Sufism in the Modern World*. Richmond: Curzon.

Smith, Grace Martin and Ernst, Carl W. (eds) (1994) *Manifestations of Sainthood in Islam*. Istanbul: Isis Press.

Smith, Margaret (1928) *Rabi'ah the Mystic and Her Fellow-Saints in Islam*. Cambridge: Cambridge University Press.

—— (1995) *Studies in Early Mysticism in the Near and Middle East*. Oxford: Oneworld.

—— (2001) *Muslim Women Mystics: The Life and Work of Rabi'a and Other Women Mystics in Islam*. Oxford: Oneworld.

as-Sulami, Abu 'Abd ar-Rahman (1999) *Early Sufi Women: Dhikr an-niswa al-muta 'abbidat as sufiyyat*, trans. R. E. Cornell. Louisville, KY: Fons Vitae.

Thackston, W. M., Jr. (trans.) (1999a) *Suhrawardi: The Philosophical Allegories and Mystical Treatises*. Costa Mesa, CA: Mazda.

—— (trans.) (1999b) *Signs of the Unseen: The Discourses of Jalaluddin Rumi*. Boston, MA: Shambhala.

Trimingham, J. Spencer (1971) *The Sufi Orders in Islam*. Oxford: Clarendon Press.

Trix, Frances (1993) *Spiritual Discourse: Learning with an Islamic Master*. Philadelphia, PA: University of Pennsylvania Press.

de Vitray-Meyerovitch, Eva (1987) *Rumi and Sufism*, trans. Simone Fattal. Sausalito, CA: Post Apollo.

Wilson, Peter Lamborn and Pourjavady, Nasrollah (trans. and eds) (1987) *The Drunken Universe: An Anthology of Persian Sufi Poetry*. Grand Rapids, MI: Phanes Press.

Wolper, Ethel Sara (2003) *Cities and Saints: Sufism and the Transformation of Urban Space in Medieval Anatolia*. University Park, PA: Pennsylvania State University Press.

VI Theology and philosophy

Abed, Shukri (1991) *Aristotelian Logic and the Arabic Language in Alfarabi*. Albany, NY: State University of New York Press.

Abrahamov, Binyamin (1996) *Anthropomorphism and Interpretation of the Qur'an in the Theology of al-Qasim ibn Ibrahim-Kitab Al-Mustarshid*. Leiden: E. J. Brill.

—— (1998a) *Islamic Theology*. Edinburgh: Edinburgh University Press.

—— (ed.) (1998b) *Islamic Theology: Traditionalism and Rationalism*. Edinburgh: Edinburgh University Press.

Algar, Hamid (2002) *Wahhabism: A Critical Essay*. Oneonta, NY: Islamic Publishing.

Aminrazavi, Mehdi (1997) *Suhrawardi and the School of Illumination*. Richmond: Curzon.

Arberry, Arthur J. (1977) *Revelation and Reason in Islam*. London: George Allen & Unwin.

Arkoun, Mohammed (2002) *The Unthought in Contemporary Islamic Thought*. London: Saqi/The Institute of Ismaili Studies.

Arnaldez, Roger (2000) *Averroes: A Rationalist in Islam*. Notre Dame, IN: University of Notre Dame Press.

Averroes (1956) *Commentary on Plato's 'Republic'*, trans. and ed. Erwin Rosenthal. Cambridge: Cambridge University Press.

—— (1961) *Averroes: On the Harmony of Religion and Philosophy*, trans. George F. Hourani, London: Luzac & Co.

—— (2001) *Faith and Reason in Islam: Averroes' Exposition of Religious Arguments*, trans. Ibrahim Najjar. Oxford: Oneworld.

Bakar, Osman (1999) *The History and Philosophy of Islamic Science*. Cambridge: The Islamic Texts Society.

Baljon, J. M. S. (1949) *The Reforms and Religious Ideas of Sir Sayyid Ahmad Khan*. Leiden: E. J. Brill.

Bayrak (al-Jerrahi al-Halveti), Shaykh Tosun (2001) *The Name and the Named: The Divine Attributes of God*. Louisville, KY: Fons Vitae.

Bell, Joseph N. (1978) *Love Theory in Later Hanbalite Islam*. Albany, NY: State University of New York Press.

Bello, Iysa A. (1989) *The Medieval Islamic Controversy between Philosophy and Orthodoxy: Ijma'and Ta'wil in the Conflict between al-Ghazzali and Ibn Rushd*. Leiden: E. J. Brill.

Bravmann, M. M. (1997) *The Spiritual Background of Early Islam*. Leiden: E. J. Brill.

Brockopp, Jonathan E. (ed.) (2003) *Islamic Ethics of Life: Abortion, War, and Euthanasia*. Columbia, SC: University of South Carolina Press.

Brown, Daniel (1999) *Rethinking Tradition in Modern Islamic Thought*. Cambridge: Cambridge University Press.

Burrell, David B. (1986) *Knowing the Unknowable God: Ibn-Sina, Maimonides, Aquinas*. Notre Dame, IN: University of Notre Dame Press.

—— (1993) *Freedom and Creation in Three Traditions*. Notre Dame, IN: University of Notre Dame Press.

Butterworth, Charles (ed.) (1971) *Averroes' Three Commentaries on Aristotle's 'Topics,' 'Rhetorics,' and 'Poetics.'* Albany, NY: State University of New York Press.

—— (ed.) (1992) *The Political Aspects of Islamic Philosophy: Essays in Honor of Muhsin Mahdi*. Cambridge, MA: Harvard University Press.

—— (trans.) (2001) *Alfarabi – The Political Writings: 'Selected Aphorisms' and Other Texts*. Ithaca, NY: Cornell University Press.

Chittick, William C. (2001) *The Heart of Islamic Philosophy: The Quest for Self-Knowledge in the Teachings of Afdal al-Din Kashani*. Oxford: Oxford University Press.

Conrad, Lawrence I. (ed.) (1996) *The World of Ibn Tufayl: Interdisciplinary Perspectives on Hayy ibn Yaqzan*. Leiden: E. J. Brill.

Cook, Michael (1981) *Early Muslim Dogma*. Cambridge: Cambridge University Press.

—— (2000) *Commanding Right and Forbidding Wrong in Islamic Thought*. Cambridge: Cambridge University Press.

Corbin, Henry (1960) *Avicenna and the Visionary Recital*, trans. W. R. Trask. New York: Pantheon Books.

—— (1986) *Temple and Contemplation (Islamic Texts and Contexts)*. New York: Columbia University Press.

—— (1993) *History of Islamic Philosophy*, trans. Liadain Sherrard. London: Kegan Paul.

—— (1994) *The Man of Light in Iranian Sufism*. New Lebanon, NY: Omega.

Craig, William L. (1979) *The Kalam Cosmological Argument*. New York: Harper & Row.

Crone, Patricia and Zimmermann, Fritz (eds) (2001) *The Epistle of Salim Ibn Dhakwan*. Oxford: Oxford University Press.

Daiber, Hans (1999) *Bibliography of Islamic Philosophy:* Leiden: E. J. Brill.

Daftary, Farhad (1990) *The Isma'ilis: Their History and Doctrines*. Cambridge: Cambridge University Press.

—— (ed.) (2000) *Intellectual Traditions in Islam*. London: I. B. Tauris.

Davidson, Herbert A. (1992) *Alfarabi, Avicenna, and Averroes on Intellect: Their Cosmologies, Theories of the Active Intellect, and Theories of Human Intellect*. New York: Oxford University Press.

Dhanani, Alnoor (1994) *The Physical Theory of Kalam: Atoms, Space, and Void in Basrian Mu'tazili Cosmology*. Leiden: E. J. Brill.

Druart, Therese-Anne (ed.) (1988) *Arabic Philosophy and the West: Continuity and Interaction*. Washington, DC: Center for Contemporary Arab Studies, Georgetown University.

Fakhry, Majid (1958) *Islamic Occasionalism and its Critique by Averroes and Aquinas*. London: George Allen & Unwin.

—— (1983) *A History of Islamic Philosophy*, 2nd edn. London: Longman.

—— (1991) *Ethical Theories in Islam*. Leiden: E. J. Brill.

—— (1994) *Philosophy, Dogma, and the Impact of Greek Thought in Islam*. Aldershot: Ashgate/Variorum.

—— (1997) *A Short Introduction to Islamic Philosophy, Theology and Mysticism*. Oxford: Oneworld.

—— (2002a) *Al-Farabi, Founder of Islamic Neoplatonism*. Oxford: Oneworld.

—— (2002b) *Averroes: His Life, Works, and Influence*. Oxford: Oneworld.

al-Farabi, Abu Nasr (1998) *On the Perfect State (Mabadi' ara' al-madinat al-fadilah)*, rev. edn. trans. Richard Walzer. Chicago, IL: Kazi.

Firestone, Reuven (1990) *Journeys in Holy Lands: The Evolution of the Abraham-Ishmael Legends in Islamic Exegesis*. Albany, NY: State University of New York Press.

Frank, Richard M. (1978) *Beings and Their Attributes: The Teaching of the Basrian School of the Mu'tazila in the Classical Period*. Albany, NY: State University of New York Press.

—— (1994) *Al-Ghazali and the Ash'arite School*. Durham, NC: Duke University Press.

Galston, Miriam (1990) *Politics and Excellence: The Political Philosophy of Alfarabi*. Princeton, NJ: Princeton University Press.

al-Ghazali, Abu Hamid Muhammad (1984) *The Jewels of the Qur'an*, trans. Muhammad Abul Quasem. London: Kegan Paul.

—— (1989) *Al-Ghazali on the Remembrance of Death and the Afterlife: Book XL of the Revival of the Religious Sciences*, trans. T. J. Winter. Cambridge: The Islamic Texts Society.

—— (1990) *Al-Ghazali on Invocations and Supplications: Book IX of the Revival of the Religious Sciences*, trans. Kojiro Nakamura. Cambridge: The Islamic Texts Society.

—— (1992) *Al-Ghazali on the Ninety-nine Beautiful Names of God*, trans. David B. Burrell and Nazih Daher. Cambridge: The Islamic Texts Society.

—— (1995) *Al-Ghazali on Disciplining the Soul and on Breaking the Two Desires: Books XII and XIII of the Revival of the Religious Sciences*, trans. T. J. Winter. Cambridge: The Islamic Texts Society.

—— (2000a) *Deliverance from Error – Five Key Texts, Including His Spiritual Autobiography, al-Munqidh min al-Dalal*, 2nd edn. trans. Richard Joseph McCarthy. Louisville, KY: Fons Vitae.

—— (2000b) *The Incoherence of the Philosophers*, trans. Michael E. Marmura. Provo, UT: Brigham Young University Press.

—— (2000c) *Al-Ghazali on the Manners Relating to Eating: Book XI of the Revival of the Religious Sciences*, trans. Denys Johnson-Davies. Cambridge: The Islamic Texts Society.

—— (2001) *On Faith in Divine Unity and and Trust in Divine Providence*, trans. David B. Burrell. Louisville, KY: Fons Vitae.

—— (2002) *Al-Ghazali on Poverty and Abstinence: Book XXXIV of the Revival of the Religious Sciences*, trans. Asaad F.

Shaker. Cambridge: The Islamic Texts Society.

—— (forthcoming) *Al-Ghazali on Intention, Sincerity and Truthfulness: Book XXXVII of the Revival of the Religious Sciences*, trans. Asaad F. Shaker. Cambridge: The Islamic Texts Society.

—— (forthcoming) *Al-Ghazali on Patience and Thankfulness: Book XXXIII of the Revival of the Religious Sciences*, trans. Henry T. Littlejohn. Cambridge: The Islamic Texts Society.

Gianotti, Timothy J. (2001) *Al-Ghazali's Unspeakable Doctrine of the Soul: Unveiling the Esoteric Psychology and Eschatology of the Ihya'*. Leiden: E. J. Brill.

Gohlman, William E. (trans.) (1974) *The Life of Ibn Sina: A Critical Edition and Annotated Translation*. Albany, NY: State University of New York Press.

Goldziher, Ignaz (1971) *The Zahiris, Their Doctrine and Their History: A Contribution to the Study of Islamic Theology*, trans. Wolfgang Behn. Leiden: E. J. Brill.

—— (1981) *Introduction to Islamic Theology and Law*. Princeton, NJ: Princeton University Press.

Goodman, Lenn E. (1992) *Avicenna*. New York: Routledge.

—— (1999) *Jewish and Islamic Philosophy: Crosspollinations in the Classic Age*. New Brunswick, NJ: Rutgers University Press.

—— (2003) *Islamic Humanism*. Oxford: Oxford University Press.

Graham, William A. (1977) *Divine Word and Prophetic Word in Early Islam*. The Hague: Mouton.

Gutas, Dimitri (1988) *Avicenna and the Aristotelian Tradition*. Leiden: E. J. Brill.

—— (1998) *Greek Thought, Arabic Culture: The Graeco-Arabic Translation Movement in Baghdad and Early 'Abbasid Society*. London: Routledge.

—— (2001) *Greek Philosophers in the Arabic Tradition*. Aldershot: Ashgate.

Haddad, Yvonne Yazbeck and Idleman Smith, Jane (1981) *The Islamic Understanding of Death and Resurrection*. Albany, NY: State University of New York Press.

Hahn, Lewis Edwin, Auxier, Randall E. and Stone, Lucian W. Jr. (eds) (2001) *The Philosophy of Seyyed Hossein Nasr*. La Salle, IL: Open Court.

Hallaq, Wael B. (trans.) (1993) *Ibn Taymiyya against the Greek Logicians*. Oxford: Clarendon Press.

Hamid, Abdul Ali (ed.) (2003) *Moral Teachings of Islam: Prophetic Traditions from Al-Adab al-mufrad by Imam al-Bukhari*. Lanham, MD: Rowman & Littlefield.

Hasse, Dag Nikolaus (2000) *Avicenna's De Anima in the Latin West*. London: The Warburg Institute.

Hawting, G. R. (2002) *The Idea of Idolatry and the Emergence of Islam: From Polemic to History*. Cambridge: Cambridge University Press.

Heath, Peter (1992) *Allegory and Philosophy in Avicenna: With a Translation of the Book of the Prophet Muhammad's Ascent to Heaven*. Philadelphia, PA: University of Pennsylvania Press.

Heemskerk, Margaretha T. (2000) *Suffering in Mu'tazilite Theology: 'Abd al-Jabbar's Teaching on Pain and Divine Justice*. Leiden: E. J. Brill.

Hourani, Albert (1993) *Arabic Thought in the Liberal Age: 1798–1939*. Cambridge: Cambridge Cambridge University Press.

Hourani, George F. (1971) *Islamic Rationalism: The Ethics of 'Abd al-Jabbar*. Oxford: Oxford University Press.

—— (ed.) (1975) *Essays on Islamic Philosophy and Science*. Albany, NY: State University of New York Press.

—— (1985) *Reason and Tradition in Islamic Ethics*. Cambridge: Cambridge University Press.

Fitzgerald, Michael Abdurrahman and Slitine, Moulat Youssef (trans.) (2000) *Ibn Qayyim al-Jawziyya: The Invocation of God*. Cambridge: The Islamic Texts Society.

Ibn Rushd (2000) *The Distinguished Jurist's Primer, 2 vols*, trans. Imran Ahsan Khan Nyazee. Reading: Ithaca Press.

Inati, Shams Constantine (1996) *Ibn Sina and Mysticism: Remarks and Admonitions*. London: Kegan Paul.

Iqbal, Muhammad (1932) *The Reconstruction of Religious Thought in Islam*. Oxford: Oxford University Press.

Izutsu, Toshihiko (1980) *Concept of Belief in Islamic Theology*. Salem, NH: Ayer Co.

Jackson, Sherman A. (2002) *On the Boundaries of Theological Tolerance in Islam: Abu Hamid al-Ghazali's Faysal al-Tafriqa*. Oxford: Oxford University Press.

Kelsay, John (1993) *Islam and War: The Gulf War and Beyond – A Study in Comparative Ethics*. Louisville, KY: Westminster John Knox Press.

Kelsay, John and Turner Johnson, James (eds) (1991) *Just War and Jihad: Historical and Theoretical Perspectives on War and Peace in Western and Islamic Traditions*. Westport, CT: Greenwood Publ. Group.

Kemal, Salim (1991) *The Poetics of Alfarabi and Avicenna*. Leiden: E. J. Brill.

—— (2003) *The Philosophical Poetics of Alfarabi, Avicenna, and Averroes: The Aristotelian Reception*. New York: RoutledgeCurzon.

Kennedy-Day, Kiki (2003) *Books of Definition in Islamic Philosophy: The Limits of Words*. London: RoutledgeCurzon.

Kindi, Abu Yusuf Ya'qub (1974) *On First Philosophy*, trans. Alfred Ivry. Albany, NY: State University of New York Press.

Knysh, Alexander D. (1998) *Ibn 'Arabi and the Later Islamic Tradition: The Making of a Polemical Image in Medieval Islam*. Albany, NY: State University of New York Press.

Kogan, Barry S. (1985) *Averroes and the Metaphysics of Causation*. Albany, NY: State University of New York Press.

Kraemer, Joel L. (1986) *Philosophy in the Renaissance of Islam: Abu Sulayman al-Sijistani and his Circle*. Leiden: E. J. Brill.

Lawrence, Bruce B (ed.) (1979) *The Rose and the Rock: Mystical and Rational Elements in the Intellectual History of South Asian Islam*. Durham, NC: Duke University Comparative Program in Comparative Studies on Southern Asia.

Leaman, Oliver (1997) *Averroes and His Philosophy*. Oxford: Clarendon Press.

—— (1999) *A Brief Introduction to Islamic Philosophy*. Malden, MA: Blackwell.

—— (2001) *An Introduction to Classical Islamic Philosophy*, 2nd edn. Cambridge: Cambridge University Press.

Mahdi, Muhsin (2001) *Alfarabi and the Foundation of Islamic Political Philosophy*. Chicago, IL: University of Chicago Press.

Marmura, Michael E. (ed.) (1984) *Islamic Theology and Philosophy: Studies in Honor of George F. Hourani*. Albany, NY: State University of New York Press.

Martin, Richard C. and Woodward, Mark R. (with Dwi S. Atmaja) (1997) *Defenders of Reason in Islam: Mu'tazilism from Medieval School to Modern Symbol*. Oxford: Oneworld.

Mashita, Hiroyuki (ed.) (2003) *Theology, Ethics and Metaphysics: Royal Asiatic Society Classics of Islam*, 5 vols. London: RoutledgeCurzon.

Mitha, Farouk (2002) *Al-Ghazali and the Ismailis: A Debate on Reason and Authority in Medieval Islam*. London: I. B. Tauris.

Morewedge, Parviz (ed.) (1979) *Islamic Philosophical Theology*. Albany, NY: State University of New York Press.

—— (ed.) (1981) *Islamic Philosophy and Mysticism*. New York: Caravan.

—— (ed.) (1992) *Neoplatonism and Islamic Thought*. Albany, NY: State University of New York Press.

—— (1997) *Essays in Islamic Philosophy, Theology, and Mysticism*. Binghamton, NY: Global, Binghamton University, State University of New York.

—— (2001) *The Mystical Philosophy of Avicenna*. Binghamton, NY: Global, Binghamton University, State University of New York.

Morris, James W. (1981) *The Wisdom of the Throne: An Introduction to the Philosophy of Mulla Sadra*. Princeton, NJ: Princeton University Press.

Motzki, Harald (ed.) (2004) *Hadith: Origins and Developments*. Aldershot: Ashgate.

Mulla Sadra (1992) *The Metaphysics of Mulla Sadra*, trans. Parviz Morewedge. Binghamton, NY: Institute of Global Cultural Studies.

Nasr, Seyyed Hossein (1964) *Three Muslim Sages: Avicenna, Suhrawardi, Ibn 'Arabi*. Cambridge, MA: Harvard University Press.

—— (1975) *The Philosophy of Mulla Sadra*. Albany, NY: State University of New York Press.

—— (1978) *Sadr al-Din Shirazi and his Transcendent Theosophy*. Tehran: Imperial Iranian Academy of Philosophy.

—— (1993) *An Introduction to Islamic Cosmological Doctrines*. Albany, NY: State University of New York Press.

—— (1996) *Religion and the Order of Nature*. Oxford: Oxford University Press.

—— (1997) *The Islamic Intellectual Tradition in Persia*. London: Curzon.

Nasr, Seyyed Hossein and Leaman, Oliver (eds) (1996) *History of Islamic Philosophy*. London: Routledge.

Nasr, Seyyed Hossein and Razavi, Mehdi Amin (eds) (2000) *An Anthology of Philosophy in Persia*. Oxford: Oxford University Press.

Nasr, Seyyed Hossein *et al.* (eds) (2000) *The Philosophy of Seyyed Hossein Nasr.* La Salle, IL: Open Court.

Netton, Ian Richard (1989) *Allah Transcendent: Studies in the Structure and Semiotics of Islamic Philosophy, Theology and Cosmology.* New York: Routledge.

—— (1992) *Al-Farabi and His School.* London: Routledge.

—— (1996) *Seek Knowledge: Thought and Travel in the House of Islam.* Richmond: Curzon.

—— (2002) *Muslim Neoplatonists: An Introduction to the Thought of the Brethren of Purity.* London: RoutledgeCurzon.

Ormsby, Eric L. (1984) *Theodicy in Islamic Thought: The Dispute Over al-Ghazali's 'Best of All Possible Worlds.'* Princeton, NJ: Princeton University Press.

Padwick, Constance E. (1996) *Muslim Devotions: A Study of Prayer-Manuals in Common Use.* Oxford: Oneworld.

Parens, Joshua (1995) *Metaphysics as Rhetoric: Alfarabi's Summary of Plato's 'Laws.'* Albany, NY: State University of New York Press.

Peters, F. E. (1968) *Aristotle and the Arabs: The Aristotelian Tradition in Islam.* New York: New York University Press.

Peters, J.R.T.M. (1976) *God's Created Speech: A Study in the Speculative Theology of ... 'Abd al-Jabbar.* Leiden: E. J. Brill.

Peters, Rudolph (1996) *Jihad in Classical and Modern Islam: A Reader.* Princeton, NJ: Markus Wiener.

Rahman, Fazlur (1958) *Prophecy in Islam.* London: Allen & Unwin.

—— (1975) *The Philosophy of Mulla Sadra (Sadr al-Din al-Shirazi).* Albany, NY: State University of New York Press.

—— (1982) *Islam and Modernity: Transformation of an Intellectual Tradition.* Chicago, IL: University of Chicago Press.

Raschid, M. S. (1981) *Iqbal's Concept of God.* London: Kegan Paul.

Razavi, Mehdi Amin (1997) *Suhrawardi and the School of Illumination.* Richmond: Curzon.

Rescher, Nicholas (1967) *Studies in Arabic Philosophy.* Pittsburgh, PA: University of Pittsburgh Press.

Reinhart, A. Kevin (1995) *Before Revelation: The Boundaries of Muslim Moral Thought.* Albany, NY: State University of New York Press.

Rosenthal, Franz (1970) *Knowledge Triumphant: The Concept of Knowledge in Medieval Islam.* Leiden: E. J. Brill.

—— (1990) *Greek Philosophy in the Arab World: A Collection of Essays.* Aldershot: Ashgate/Variorum.

—— (1997) *Sweeter than Hope: Complaint and Hope in Medieval Islam.* Leiden: E. J. Brill.

Saleh, Fauzan (2001) *Modern Trends in Islamic Theological Discourse in 20th Century Indonesia: A Critical Study.* Leiden: E. J. Brill.

Schimmel, Annemarie (1994) *Deciphering the Signs of God: A Phenomenological Approach to Islam.* Albany, NY: State University of New York Press.

Sherif, M. A. (1975) *Ghazali's Theory of Virtue.* Albany, NY: State University of New York Press.

Smith, Jane I. and Haddad, Yvonne (1981) *The Islamic Understanding of Death and Resurrection.* Albany, NY: State University of New York Press.

Street, Tony (forthcoming) *Avicenna: Intuitions of the Truth.* Cambridge: The Islamic Texts Society.

Stroumsa, Sarah (1999) *Freethinkers of Medieval Islam: Ibn al-Rawandi, Abu Bakr al-Razi and Their Impact on Islamic Thought.* Leiden: E. J. Brill.

Suhrawardi, Shihab al-Din Yahya (1998) *The Book of Radiance: Partaw-Nama,* trans. Hossein Ziai. Costa Mesa, CA: Mazda.

—— (1999) *The Philosophy of Illumination (Hiqmat al-ishraq),* trans. John Walbridge and Hossein Ziai. Provo, UT: Brigham Young University Press.

Thackston, W. M., Jr. (1982) *The Mystical and Visionary Treatises of Shihabuddin Yahya Suhrawardi.* London: Octagon Press.

Thomas, David (ed.) (2002) *Early Muslim Polemic against Christianity: Abu 'Isa al-Warraq's 'Against the Incarnation'.* Cambridge: Cambridge University Press.

Troll, Christian W. (1978) *Sayyid Ahmad Khan: A Reinterpretation of Muslim Theology.* New Delhi: Vikas.

Wahba, Mourad and Abousenna, Mona (eds) (1996) *Averroës and the Enlightenment.* Amherst, NY: Prometheus Books.

Walbridge, John (1992) *The Science of Mystic Lights: Qutb al-Din Shirazi and the Illuminationist Tradition in Islamic Philo-*

sophy. Cambridge, MA: Harvard University Press.

—— (1999) *The Leaven of the Ancients: Suhrawardi and the Heritage of the Greeks*. Albany, NY: State University of New York Press.

—— (2001) *The Wisdom of the Mystic East: Suhrawardi and Platonic Orientalism*. Albany, NY: State University of New York Press.

Walker, Paul E. (1998) *Abu Ya'qub al-Sijistani: Intellectual Missionary*. London: I. B. Tauris.

Walzer, Richard (1962) *Greek into Arabic: Essays on Islamic Philosophy*. Oxford: B. Cassirer.

Watt, William Montgomery (1948) *Free Will and Predestination in Early Islam*. London: Luzac.

—— (1963) *Muslim Intellectual: A Study of al-Ghazali*. Edinburgh: Edinburgh University Press.

—— (1985) *Islamic Philosophy and Theology: An Extended Survey*, 2nd edn. Edinburgh: Edinburgh University Press.

—— (trans.) (1995) *The Faith and Practice of Al-Ghazali*. Oxford: Oneworld.

—— (1998) *The Formative Period of Islamic Thought*. Oxford: Oneworld.

Wheeler, Brannon M. (1996) *Applying the Canon in Islam: The Authorization and Maintenance of Interpretive Reasoning in Hanafi Scholarship*. Albany, NY: State University of New York Press.

—— (2002) *Moses in the Qur'an and Islamic Exegesis*. London: RoutledgeCurzon.

Wisnovsky, Robert (ed.) (2002) *Aspects of Avicenna*. Princeton, NJ: Markus Wiener.

—— (2003) *Avicenna's Metaphysics in Context*. Ithaca, NY: Cornell University Press.

Wolfson, Harry A. (1976) *The Philosophy of the Kalam*. Cambridge, MA: Harvard University Press.

Yazdi, Mehdi Ha'iri (1992) *The Principles of Epistemology in Islamic Philosophy: Knowledge by Presence*. Albany, NY: State University of New York Press.

Ziai, Hossein (1990) *Knowledge and Illumination: A Study of Suhrawardi's 'Hikmat al-Ishraq.'* Atlanta, GA: Scholar's Press.

VII Jurisprudence

Abou El Fadl, Khaled (2001) *Speaking in God's Name: Islamic Law, Authority and Women*. Oxford: Oneworld.

—— (2002) *Rebellion and Violence in Islamic Law*. Cambridge: Cambridge University Press.

Ahmad, Kassim (1997) *Hadith: A Re-evaluation*. Fremont, CA: Universal Unity.

El-Alami, Dawoud S. (1992) *The Marriage Contract in Islamic Law*. London: Graham & Trotman.

Algar, Hamid, trans. (1980) *Constitution of the Islamic Republic of Iran*. Berkeley, CA: Mizan Press.

Anderson, J. N. D. (1976) *Law Reform in the Muslim World*. London: Athlone Press.

An-Na'im, Abdullahi Ahmed (1996) *Toward an Islamic Reformation: Civil Liberties, Human Rights, and International Law*. Syracuse, NY: Syracuse University Press.

Arabi, Oussama (2001) *Studies in Modern Islamic Law and Jurisprudence*. The Hague: Kluwer Law International.

Asad, Muhammad (1980) *Principles of State and Government in Islam*. London: Islamic Book Trust.

Azami, M. M. (1985) *On Schacht's Origins of Muhammadan Jurisprudence*. New York: John Wiley.

al-Azmeh, Aziz (ed.) (1988) *Islamic Law: Social and Historical Contexts*. London: Routledge.

Bakhtiar, Laleh (trans. and ed.) (1996) *Encyclopedia of Islamic Law: A Compendium of the Major Schools*. Chicago, IL: Kazi.

Bowen, John R. (2003) *Islam, Law and Equality in Indonesia: An Anthropology of Public Reasoning*. Cambridge: Cambridge University Press.

Brockopp, Jonathan E. (2000) *Early Maliki Law: Ibn 'Abd al-Hakam and his Major Compendium Jurisprudence*. Leiden: E. J. Brill.

Burton, John (1990) *The Sources of Islamic Law: Islamic Theories of Abrogation*. Edinburgh: Edinburgh University Press.

—— (1994) *An Introduction to the Hadith*. Edinburgh: Edinburgh University Press.

Calder, Norman (1993) *Studies in Early Muslim Jurisprudence*. Oxford: Clarendon Press.

Christelow, Alan (1985) *Muslim Law Courts and the French Colonial State in Algeria*. Princeton, NJ: Princeton University Press.

Cotran, Eugene (ed.) (2002) *Yearbook of Islamic and Middle Eastern Law: 1999–2000*. The Hague: Kluwer Law International.

Cotran, Eugene and Adel Omar Sherif (eds) (1999) *Democracy: the Rule of Law and Islam*. London: Kluwer Law International.

Cotran, Eugene and Mai Yamani (eds) (2000) *The Rule of Law in the Middle East and Islamic World: Human Rights and the Judicial Process*. London: I. B. Tauris.

Coulson, Noel J. (1964) *A History of Islamic Law*. Edinburgh: Edinburgh University Press.

—— (1969) *Conflicts and Tensions in Islamic Jurisprudence*. Chicago, IL: University of Chicago Press.

—— (1971) *Succession in the Muslim Family*. Cambridge: Cambridge University Press.

Crone, Patricia (2002) *Roman, Provincial and Islamic Law: The Origins of the Islamic Patronate*. Cambridge: Cambridge University Press.

Dahlén, Ashk P. (2003) *Islamic Law, Epistemology and Modernity: Legal Philosophy in Contemporary Iran*. New York: Routledge.

Dutton, Yasin (1999) *The Origins of Islamic Law: The Qur'an, the Muwatta' and Medinan 'Amal*. Richmond: Curzon.

Eisenman, Robert H. (1978) *Islamic Law in Palestine and Israel: A History of the Survival of Tanzimat and Shari'a in the British Mandate and the Jewish State*. Leiden: E. J. Brill.

Esposito, John L. with DeLong-Bas, Natana J. (2002) *Women in Muslim Family Law*, 2nd edn. Syracuse, NY: Syracuse University Press.

Fareed, Muneer Goolam (1996) *Legal Reform in the Muslim World: The Anatomy of a Scholarly Dispute in the 19th and the Early 20th Centuries on the Usage of Ijtihad as a Legal Tool*. Bethesda, MD: Austin & Winfield.

Ferrari, Silvio and Bradney, Anthony (eds) (2000) *Islam and European Legal Systems*. Aldershot: Ashgate.

Fluehr-Lobban, Carolyn (1987) *Islamic Law and Society in the Sudan*. London: Frank Cass & Co.

Forte, David F. (1999) *Studies in Islamic Law*. Bethesda, MD: Austin & Winfield.

Gerber, Haim (1994) *State, Society, and Law in Islam: Ottoman Law in Comparative Perspective*. Albany, NY: State University of New York Press.

—— (1999) *Islamic Law and Culture, 1600–1840*. Leiden: E. J. Brill.

Gleave, Robert (2000) *Inevitable Doubt: Two Theories of Shi'i Jurisprudence*. Leiden: E. J. Brill.

Gleave, Robert and Kermeli, Eugenia (eds) (2001) *Islamic Law: Theory and Practice*. London: I. B. Tauris.

Haddad, Yvonne Yazbeck and Freyer Stowasser, Barbara (eds) (2004) *Islamic Law and the Challenges of Modernity*. Lanham, MD: AltaMira Press.

Haeri, Shahla (1989) *Law of Desire: Temporary Marriage in Shi'i Iran*. Syracuse, NY: Syracuse University Press.

Haleem, M. Abdel *et al.* (eds) (2003) *Criminal Justice in Islam: Judicial Procedure in the Shari'ah*. London: I. B. Tauris.

Haleem, M. Abdel, Sharif, Adel Omar and Edge, Ian (eds) (2003) *Criminal Justice in Islam: Judicial Procedure in the Shari'ah*. London: I. B. Tauris.

Hallaq, Wael B. (1995) *Law and Legal Theory in Classical and Medieval Islam*. Aldershot: Ashgate/Variorum.

—— (1997) *A History of Islamic Legal Theories: an introduction to Sunni usul al-fiqh*. Cambridge: Cambridge University Press.

—— (2001) *Authority, Continuity and Change in Islamic Law*. Cambridge: Cambridge University Press.

—— (ed.) (2004) *The Formation of Islamic Law*. Aldershot: Ashgate.

Heer, Nicholas L. (ed.) (1990) *Islamic Law and Jurisprudence: Studies in Honor of Farhat J. Ziadeh*. Seattle, WA: University of Washington Press.

Hooker, Michael B. (1991) *Islamic Law in Southeast Asia*. Oxford: Oxford University Press.

Ibrahim, Ezzedin and Johnson-Davies, Denys (trans.) (1997a) *An-Nawawi's Forty Hadith*. Cambridge: The Islamic Texts Society

—— (trans.) (1997b) *Forty Hadith Qudsi*. Cambridge: The Islamic Texts Society.

Imber, Colin (1997) *Ebu's-Su'd: The Islamic Legal Tradition*. Stanford, CA: Stanford University Press.

Johansen, Baber (1988) *The Islamic Law on Land Tax and Rent: The Peasants' Loss of Property Rights as Interpreted in the Hanafite Legal Literature of the Mamluk and Ottoman Periods*. London: Croom Helm.

—— (1999) *Contingency in a Sacred Law: Legal and Ethical Norms in Muslim Fiqh*. Leiden: E. J. Brill.

Juynboll, G. H. A. (1983) *Muslim Tradition: Studies in Chronology, Provenance and Authorship of Early Hadith*. Cambridge: Cambridge University Press.

Kamali, Mohammad Hashim (2000) *Principles of Islamic Jurisprudence*, rev. edn. Cambridge: The Islamic Texts Society.

Kelsay, John (forthcoming) *War and the Imperatives of Justice in Islamic Law*. Cambridge: Cambridge University Press.

Khadduri, Majid (1955) *War and Peace in the Law of Islam*. Baltimore, MD: Johns Hopkins University Press.

—— (1984) *The Islamic Conception of Justice*. Baltimore, MD: Johns Hopkins University Press.

—— (1999) *Al-Shafi'i's Risala: Treatise on the Foundations of Islamic Jurisprudence*. Cambridge: Islamic Texts Society.

Khadduri, Majid (trans.) (2002) *The Islamic Law of Nations: Shaybani's Siyar*. Baltimore, MD: Johns Hopkins University Press.

Khare, R. S (ed.) (1999) *Perspectives on Islamic Law, Justice, and Society*. Lanham, MD: Rowman & Littlefield.

Kusha, Hamid Rez (2003) *The Sacred Law of Islam: A Case Study of Women's Treatment in the Islamic Republic of Iran's Criminal Justice System*. Aldershot: Ashgate.

Lindholm, Tore and Vogt, Kari (eds) (1993) *Islamic Law Reform and Human Rights: Challenges and Rejoinders*. Copenhagen: Nordic Human Rights Publications.

Makdisi, George (1991) *Religion, Law and Learning in Classical Islam*. Aldershot: Ashgate/Variorum.

Mallat, Chibli (2003) *The Renewal of Islamic Law*. Cambridge: Cambridge University Press.

Masud, Muhammad Khalid, Messick, Brinkley and Powers, David S. (eds) (1996) *Islamic Legal Interpretation: Muftis and their Fatwas*. Cambridge, MA: Harvard University Press.

Mehdi, Rubya (1994) *The Islamization of the Law in Pakistan*. Richmond: Curzon.

Melchert, Christopher (1997) *The Formation of the Sunni Schools of Law, 9th–10th Centuries*. Leiden: E. J. Brill.

Mir-Hosseini, Ziba (2001) *Marriage on Trial: A Study of Islamic Family Law – Iran and Morocco Compared*. London: I. B. Tauris.

Moors, Annelies (1996) *Women, Property and Islam: Palestinian Experiences, 1920–1990*. Cambridge: Cambridge University Press.

Motzki, Harald (2001) *The Origins of Islamic Jurisprudence: Meccan Fiqh before the Classical Schools*. Leiden: E. J. Brill.

Omran, Abdel Rahim (ed.) (1992) *Family Planning in the Legacy of Islam*. New York: Routledge.

Peletz, Michael G. (2002) *Islamic Modern: Religious Courts and Cultural Politics in Malaysia*. Princeton, NJ: Princeton University Press.

Peters, Rudolph (1996) *Jihad in Classical and Modern Islam: A Reader*. Princeton, NJ: Markus Wiener.

—— (forthcoming) *Islamic Criminal Law: Theory and Practice from the Sixteenth to the Twentieth Century*. Cambridge: Cambridge University Press.

Powers, David S. (1986) *Studies in Qur'an and Hadith: The Formation of the Law of Inheritance*. Berkeley, CA: University of California Press.

Rosen, Lawrence (1989) *The Anthropology of Justice: Law as Culture in Islamic Society*. Cambridge: Cambridge University Press.

—— (2000) *The Justice of Islam: Comparative Perspectives on Islamic Law and Society*. Oxford: Oxford University Press.

Sachedina, Abdulaziz Abdulhussein (1998) *The Just Ruler in Shi'ite Islam: The Comprehensive Authority of the Jurist in Imamite Jurisprudence*. Oxford: Oxford University Press.

as-Sadr, Muhammad Baqir (2003) *Lessons in Islamic Jurisprudence*, trans. Roy Mottahedeh. Oxford: Oneworld.

Saeed, Abdullah (1997) *Islamic Banking and Interest: A Study of the Prohibition of Riba and Its Contemporary Interpretation*, 2nd edn. Leiden: E. J. Brill.

Saeed, Abdullah and Saeed, Hassan (2004) *Freedom of Religion, Apostasy and Islam*. Aldershot: Ashgate.

Schacht, Joseph (1950) *The Origins of Muhammadan Jurisprudence*. Oxford: Clarendon Press.

—— (1984) *An Introduction to Islamic Law*, rpt edn. first published 1964. Oxford: Clarendon Press.

Schirazi, Asghar (1998) *The Constitution of Iran: Politics and the State in the Islamic Republic*. London: I. B. Tauris.

Serajuddin, Alamgir Muhammad (2001) *Shari'a Law and Society: Tradition and Change in South Asia*. Oxford: Oxford University Press.

Serjeant, R. B. (1991) *Customary and Shar-i'ah Law in Arabian Society*. Aldershot: Ashgate/Variorum.

Shaham, Ron (1997) *Family and the Courts in Modern Egypt: A Study Based on Decisions by the Shari'a Courts, 1900–1955*. Leiden: E. J. Brill.

Siddiqi, Muhammad Zubayr (1993) *Hadith Literature: Its Origin, Development & Special Features*. Cambridge: The Islamic Texts Society.

Sonbol, Amira El-Azhary (ed.) (1996) *Women, The Family, and Divorce Laws in Islamic History*. Syracuse, NY: Syracuse University Press.

—— (2003) *Women of Jordan: Islam, Labor and the Law*. Syracuse, NY: Syracuse University Press.

Starr, June (1992) *Law as Metaphor: From Islamic Courts to the Palace of Justice*. Albany, NY: State University of New York Press.

Stewart, Devon J. (1998) *Islamic Legal Orthodoxy: Twelver Shiite Responses to the Sunni Legal System*. Salt Lake City, UT: University of Utah Press.

Tucker, Judith E. (2000) *In the House of the Law: Gender and Islamic Law in Ottoman Syria and Palestine*. Berkeley, CA: University of California Press.

Vogel, Frank E. (2000) *Islamic Law and Legal Systems: Studies of Saudi Arabia*. Leiden: E. J. Brill.

Vogel, Frank E. and Hayes, Samuel L. (1998) *Islamic Law and Finance: Religion, Risk, and Return*. The Hague: Kluwer Law International.

Weiss, Anita M. (1986) *Islamic Reassertion in Pakistan: The Application of Islamic Laws in a Modern State*. Syracuse, NY: Syracuse University Press.

Weiss, Bernard G. (1992) *The Search for God's Law: Islamic Jurisprudence in the Writings of Sayf al-Din al-Amidi*. Salt Lake City, UT: University of Utah Press.

—— (1998) *The Spirit of Islamic Law*. Athens, GA: University of Georgia Press.

—— (ed.) (2002) *Studies in Islamic Legal Theory*. Leiden: E. J. Brill.

Welchman, Lynn (2000) *Beyond the Code: Muslim Family Law and the Shari'a Judiciary in the Palestinian West Bank*. The Hague: Kluwer Law International.

Zubaida, Sami (2003) *Law and Power in the Islamic World*. London: I. B. Tauris.

VIII The Arts

Alexander, David (1992) *The Arts of War: Arms and Armour of the 7th to 19th Centuries (The Nasser D. Khalili Collection of Islamic Art, vol. XXI)*. London: The Nour Foundation.

Ali, Wijdan (1997) *Modern Islamic Art: Development and Continuity*. Gainesville, FL: University Press of Florida.

Ali, Wijdan and Bisharat, S. (eds) (1990) *Contemporary Art from the Islamic World*. Northampton, MA: Interlink.

Allan, James W. (1981) *Metalwork from the Early Islamic Period*. New Haven, CT: Yale University Press.

—— (ed.) (1995) *Islamic Art in the Ashmolean Museum*. Oxford: Oxford University Press.

Allan, James *et al.* (eds) (2001) *Persian Steel: The Tanavoli Collection* (Oxford Studies in Islamic Art). Oxford: Oxford University Press.

Amin, Mohamed (2000) *The Beauty of Makkah and Madinah*. Northampton, MA: Interlink.

Arberry, A. J. (2001) *Islamic Art of Persia*. New Delhi: Goodword Books.

Ardalan, Nader and Bakhtiar, Laleh (1973) *The Sense of Unity: The Sufi Tradition in Persian Architecture*. Chicago, IL: University of Chicago Press.

Arnold, Sir Thomas (1928) *Painting in Islam*. Oxford: Clarendon Press.

Asani, Ali A. and Abdel-Malek, Kamal (1995) *Celebrating Muhammad: Images of the Prophet in Popular Muslim Poetry*. Columbia, SC: University of South Carolina Press.

Asher, Catherine B. (1992) *Architecture of Mughal India*. Cambridge: Cambridge University Press.

Atil, Esin (2000) *Levni and the Surname: The Story of an Eighteenth-Century Ottoman Festival*. Seattle, WA: University of Washington Press.

Baer, Eva (1998) *Islamic Ornament*. New York: New York University Press.

Baker, Patricia L. (2003) *Islam and the Religious Arts*. London and New York: Continuum.

Barry, Michael (2003) *Figurative Art in Medieval Islam and the Riddle of Bizhad of Heart*. New York: Flammarion.

Bates, Michael and Savage, Elizabeth (2003) *Dinars and Dirhams, Coins of the Islamic*

759

Lands: The Early Period. Oxford: Oxford University Press.

Bayani, Manijeh *et al.* (1998) *The Decorated Word: Qur'ans of the 17th to 19th Centuries (The Nasser D. Khalili Collection of Islamic Art, vol. IV)*. London: The Nour Foundation.

Beach, Milo Cleveland (1987) *Early Mughal Painting*. Cambridge, MA: Harvard University Press.

—— (1993) *Mughal and Rajput Painting*. Cambridge: Cambridge University Press.

Beach, Milo Cleveland, Koch, Ebba and Thackston, Wheeler M. (1997) *The King of the World – The Padshahnama: An Imperial Mughal Manuscript from the Royal Library, Windsor Castle*. New York: Thames & Hudson.

Becker, Judith (1993) *Gamelan Stories: Tantrism, Islam, and Aesthetics in Central Java*. Tempe, AZ: Arizona State University Program for Southeast Asian Studies.

Behrens-Abouseif, Doris (1997) *Islamic Architecture in Cairo: An Introduction* (Studies in Islamic Art and Architecture, vol. 3). Leiden, E. J. Brill.

Bellamy, James A. *et al.* (eds) (1993) *Literary Heritage of Classical Islam: Arabic and Islamic Studies in Honor of James A. Bellamy*. Princeton, NJ: Darwin Press.

Blair, Sheila S. (1991) *The Monumental Inscriptions from Early Islamic Iran and Transoxiana (Studies in Islamic Art and Architecture, vol. V)*. Leiden: E. J. Brill.

—— (1995) *A Compendium of Chronicles: Rashid al-Din's Illustrated History of the World (The Nasser D. Khalili Collection of Islamic Art, vol. XXVII)*. London: The Nour Foundation.

—— (1998) *Islamic Inscriptions*. New York: New York University Press.

Blair, Sheila S. and Bloom, Jonathan M. (1991) *Images of Paradise in Islamic Art*. Austin, TX: University of Texas Press.

—— (1994) *The Art and Architecture of Islam, 1250–1800*. New Haven, CT.: Yale University Press.

Bloom, Jonathan M. (ed.) (2002) *Early Islamic Art and Architecture*. Aldershot: Ashgate.

Bloom, Jonathan and Blair, Sheila S. (1997) *Islamic Arts*. London: Phaidon Press.

Bravmann, René (1994) *Islam and Tribal Art in West Africa*. New York: Cambridge University Press.

Brend, Barbara (1991) *Islamic Art*. London: British Museum of Art.

Burckhardt, Titus (1976) *The Art of Islam: Language and Meaning*. London: World of Islam Festival.

Bürgel, J. C. (1988) *The Feather of Simurgh: The 'Licit Magic' of the Arts in Medieval Islam*. New York: New York University Press.

Carboni, Stefano (2001) *Glass from Islamic Lands: The Al-Sabah Collection, Kuwait National Museum*. London: Thames & Hudson.

Carboni, Stefano *et al.* (2001) *Glass of the Sultans*. New Haven, CT: Yale University Press.

Clévenot, Dominique and Degeorge, Gérard (2000) *Splendors of Islam: Architecture, Decoration and Design*. New York: The Vendome Press.

Contadini, Anna (1998) *Fatimid Art at the Victoria and Albert Museum*. London: Victoria & Albert Museum.

Creswell, K. A. C. (1932–40) *Early Muslim Architecture*, 2 vols. Oxford: Clarendon Press.

Critchlow, Keith (1999) *Islamic Patterns: An Analytical and Cosmological Approach*. Rochester, VT: Inner Traditions.

Degeorge, Gerard and Porter, Yves (2002) *The Art of the Islamic Tile*. Paris: Flammarion.

Deroche, François (1992) *The Abbasid Tradition: Qur'ans of the 8th to 10th Centuries AD (The Nasser D. Khalili Collection of Islamic Art, vol. I)*. London: The Nour Foundation.

Diba, Layla S., Ekhtiar, Maryam and Robinson, B. W. (eds) (1998) *Royal Persian Paintings: The Qajar Epoch, 1785–1925*. London: I. B. Tauris.

El-Said, Issam and Parman, Ayse (1990) *Geometric Concepts in Islamic Art*. London: Scorpio.

Ettinghausen, Richard, Grabar, Oleg and Jenkins-Madina, Marilyn (2001) *The Art and Architecture of Islam, 650–1250*, 2nd edn. New Haven, CT: Yale University Press.

Farsi, Hani M. S. (1991) *Jeddah, City of Art: The Sculptures and Monuments*. Boston, MA: Interlink.

Fehérvári, Géza (2000) *Ceramics of the Islamic World in the Tareq Rajab Museum*. London: I. B. Tauris.

Field, Robert (1999) *Geometric Patterns from Islamic Art and Architecture*. Norfolk: Tarquin.

Flood, Finbarr Barry (2001) *The Great Mosque of Damascus: Studies on the Making of an Umayyad Visual Culture*. Leiden: E. J. Brill.

Frishman, Martin and Khan, Hasan-Uddin (eds) (1994) *The Mosque*. New York: Thames & Hudson.

Gonzalez, Valerie (2001) *Beauty and Islam: Aesthetics in Islamic Art and Architecture*. London: I. B. Tauris.

Goodwin, Godfrey (2003) *A History of Ottoman Architecture*. New York: Thames & Hudson.

Grabar, Oleg (1987) *The Formation of Islamic Art*, 2nd edn. New Haven, CT: Yale University Press.

—— (1988) *Muqarnas: An Annual on Islamic Art and Architecture*. Leiden: E. J. Brill.

—— (1990) *The Great Mosque of Isfahan*. New York: New York University Press.

Grube, Ernst J. (1995) *Cobalt and Lustre: The First Centuries of Islamic Pottery (The Nasser D. Khalili Collection of Islamic Art, vol. IX)*. London: The Nour Foundation.

Grube, Ernst J. and Sims, Eleanor G. (eds) (1997) *Islamic Art: A Biennial Dedicated to the Art and Culture of the Muslim World, 1990–1991*. Oxford: Oxford University Press.

—— (eds) (2001) *Islamic Art 5: Studies on the Art and Culture of the Islamic World*. Oxford: Oxford University Press.

Helms, Svend (1990) *Early Islamic Architecture of the Desert: A Bedouin Station in Eastern Jordan*. Edinburgh: Edinburgh University Press.

Hillenbrand, Robert (1994) *Islamic Architecture: Form, Function, and Meaning*. New York: Columbia University Press.

—— (1998) *Islamic Art and Architecture*. London: Thames & Hudson.

Hoag, John D. (1975) *Islamic Architecture*. New York: Rizzoli.

Howard, Deborah (2000) *Venice and the East: The Impact of the Islamic World on Venetian Architecture, 1100–1500*. New Haven, CT: Yale University Press.

Hutt, Antony (1998) *North Africa: Islamic Architecture*. Northampton, MA: Interlink Publishing Group.

Hutt, Antony and Harrow, Leonard (1990) *Islamic Architecture: Iran*, 2 vols. Northampton, MA: Interlink.

Irwin, Robert (1997) *Islamic Art in Context: Art, Architecture and the Literary World*. New York: Harry N. Abrams.

James, David (1992a) *After Timur: Qur'ans of the 15th and 16th Centuries (The Nasser D. Khalili Collection of Islamic Art)*. London: The Nour Foundation.

—— (1992b) *The Master Scribes: Qur'ans of the 11th to 14th Centuries AD (The Nasser D. Khalili Collection of Islamic Art, vol. II)*. London: The Nour Foundation.

Kalter, Johannes (1985) *The Arts and Crafts of Turkestan*. New York: Thames & Hudson.

Kasam, Kutub (ed.) (1996) *Shimmering Light: An Anthology of Ismaili Poetry*. London: I. B. Tauris with The Institute of Ismaili Studies.

Khalili, Nasser D., Robinson, B. W. and Stanley, Tim (1996) *Lacquer of the Islamic Lands, Part One (The Nasser D. Khalili Collection of Islamic Art, vol. XXII)*. London: The Nour Foundation.

Khalili, Nasser D., Robinson, B. W. and Lands *Part Two (The Nasser D. Khalili Collection of Islamic Art, vol. XXII)*. London: The Nour Foundation.

Khatibi, Abdelkebir and Sijelmassi, Mohammed (1996) *The Splendor of Islamic Calligraphy*. London: Thames & Hudson.

Koch, Ebba (2001) *Mughal Art and Imperial Ideology: Collected Essays*. New Delhi: Oxford University Press.

Kritzeck, James (ed.) (1964) *Anthology of Islamic Literature: From the Rise of Islam to Modern Times*. New York: Holt, Rinehart & Winston.

—— (ed.) (1970) *Modern Islamic Literature from 1800 to the Present*. New York: Holt, Rinehart & Winston.

Kröger, Jens (1995) *Nishapur: Glass of the Early Islamic Period*. New Haven, CT: Yale University Press.

Leach, Linda (1998) *Paintings from India (The Nasser D. Khalili Collection of Islamic Art, vol. VIII)*. London: The Nour Foundation.

Lifchez, Raymond (ed.) (1992) *The Dervish Lodge: Architecture, Art, and Sufism in Ottoman Turkey*. Berkeley, CA: University of California Press.

Lowry, Glenn D. (1988) *An Annotated and Illustrated Checklist of the Vever Collection, a Jeweler's Eye: Islamic Arts of the Book from the Vever Collection*. Seattle, WA: University of Washington Press.

761

Meinecke, Michael (1996) *Patterns of Stylistic Changes in Islamic Architecture: Local Traditions versus Migrating Artists*. New York: New York University Press.

Michell, George (ed.) (1984) *The Islamic Heritage of Bengal*. Paris: United Nations Educational, Scientific and Cultural Organization (UNESCO).

—— (ed.) (1995) *Architecture of the Islamic World: Its History and Social Meaning*. New York: Thames & Hudson.

Michell, George and Zebrowski, Mark (1999) *Architecture and Art of the Deccan Sultanates*. Cambridge: Cambridge University Press.

Mir, Mustansir (trans. and ed.) (2000) *Tulip in the Desert: A Selection of the Poetry of Muhammad Iqbal*. Montreal: McGill-Queen's University Press.

Moynihan, Elizabeth B. (1980) *Paradise as a Garden: In Persia and Mughal India*. New York: George Braziller.

Nasr, Seyyed Hossein (1987) *Islamic Art and Spirituality*. Albany, NY: State University of New York Press.

Necipoglu, Gülru (1992) *Architecture, Ceremonial, and Power: The Topkapi Palace in the Fifteenth and Sixteenth Centuries*. Cambridge, MA: MIT Press.

—— (ed.) (1997) *Muqarnas: An Annual on the Visual Culture of the Islamic World*. Leiden: E. J. Brill.

Nelson, Kristina (1986) *The Art of Reciting the Qur'an*. Austin, TX: University of Texas Press.

Nicholson, R. A. (1921) *Studies in Islamic Poetry*. Cambridge: Cambridge University Press.

Parker, Ann and Neal, Avon (1995) *Hajj Paintings: Folk Art of the Great Pilgrimage*. Washington, DC: Smithsonian Institution Press.

Pedersen, Andrew (1996) *Dictionary of Islamic Architecture*. New York: Routledge.

Petruccioli, Attilio (ed.) (1997) *Gardens in the Time of the Great Muslim Empires: Theory and Design*. Leiden: E. J. Brill.

Pickett, Douglas (1997) *Early Persian Tilework: The Medieval Flowering of Kashi*. Madison, NJ: Fairleigh Dickinson University Press.

Prussin, Labelle (1986) *Hatumere: Islamic Design in West Africa*. Berkeley, CA: University of California Press.

Renard, John (1993) *Islam and the Heroic Image: Themes in Literature and the Visual Arts*. Columbia, SC: University of South Carolina Press.

Rice, David Talbot (1999) *Islamic Art*, rev. edn. London: Thames & Hudson.

Ruggles, D. Fairchild (2003) *Gardens, Landscapes, and Vision in the Palaces of Islamic Spain*. University Park, PA: Pennsylvania State University Press.

Safadi, Yasin Hamid (1987) *Islamic Calligraphy*. London: Thames & Hudson.

Safwat, Nabil F. (1996) *The Art of the Pen: Calligraphy of the 14th to 20th Centuries (The Nasser D. Khalili Collection of Islamic Art, vol. V)*. London: The Nour Foundation.

—— (2000) *Golden Pages: Qur'ans and Other Manuscripts from the Collection of Ghassan I. Shaker*. Oxford: Oxford University Press.

Salameh, Khader (2001) *The Qur'an Manuscripts in the Al-Haram Al-Sharif Islamic Museum, Jerusalem*. Paris: United Nations Education, Scientific and Cultural Organization (UNESCO).

Schimmel, Annemarie (1982) *Islam in India and Pakistan*. Leiden: E. J. Brill.

—— (1984) *Calligraphy and Islamic Culture*. New York: New York University Press.

Sells, Michael A. (2000) *Stations of Desire: Love Elegies from Ibn 'Arabi and New Poems*. Jerusalem: Ibis Editions.

Shokoohy, Mehrdad (1988) *Bhadresvar: The Oldest Islamic Monuments in India*. Leiden: E. J. Brill.

Simakoff, N. (1993) *Islamic Designs in Color*, first published by the Imperial Society for the Encouragement of the Fine Arts, St. Petersburg, 1883. New York: Dover.

Soucek, P. P. (ed.) (1988) *Content and Context of Visual Arts in the Islamic World*. University Park, PA: Pennsylvania State University Press.

Soudavar, Abou and Beach, Milo Cleveland (1993) *Art of the Persian Courts: Selections from the Art and History Trust Collection*. New York: Rizzoli.

Stierlin, Henri and Stierlin, Anne (1996) *Islam: Early Architecture from Baghdad to Jerusalem and Cordoba*. New York: Taschen America.

—— (1997) *Splendors of an Islamic World*. New York: St. Martin's Press.

—— (2002) *Islamic Art and Architecture: From Isfahan to the Taj Mahal*. London: Thames & Hudson.

Stronge, Susan (2002) *Painting for the Mughal Emperor: The Art of the Book,*

1560–1660. London: Victoria & Albert Museum.

Tabbaa, Yasser (2002) *The Transformation of Islamic Art during the Sunni Revival.* Seattle, WA: University of Washington Press.

Vernoit, Stephen (1997) *Occidentalism: Islamic Art in the 19th Century (The Nasser D. Khalili Collection of Islamic Art, vol. XXIII).* London: The Nour Foundation.

—— (ed.) (2000) *Discovering Islamic Art: Scholars, Collectors and Collections.* London: I. B. Tauris.

Ward, Rachel (1993) *Islamic Metalwork.* London: Thames & Hudson.

Welch, Anthony (1979) *Calligraphy in the Arts of the Muslim World.* Austin, TX: University of Texas Press.

Welch, Stuart Cary (1987) *The Islamic World.* New York: The Metropolitan Museum of Art.

Wilkinson, Charles K. (1974) *Nishapur: Pottery of the Early Islamic Period.* New Haven, CT: Yale University Press.

IX History

Abun-Nasr, Jamil M. (1987) *A History of the Maghrib in the Islamic Period,* 3rd edn. Cambridge: Cambridge University Press.

Afary, Janet (1996) *The Iranian Constitutional Revolution, 1906–1911: Grassroots Democracy, Social Democracy, and the Origins of Feminism.* New York: Columbia University Press.

Afsaruddin, Asma (2002) *Excellence and Precedence: Medieval Islamic Discourse on Legitimate Leadership.* Leiden: E. J. Brill.

Allison, Robert J. (2000) *The Crescent Obscured: The United States and the Muslim World 1776–1815.* Chicago, IL: University of Chicago Press.

Armstrong, Karen (2000) *Islam: A Short History.* New York: Modern Library.

Austin, Allan D. (1997) *African Muslims in Antebellum America: Transatlantic Stories and Spiritual Struggles,* rev. edn. New York: Routledge.

Ayoub, Mahmoud M. (2003) *The Crisis of Muslim History: Religion and Politics in Early Islam.* Oxford: Oneworld.

Bailey, Harold (ed.) (1993) *The Cambridge History of Iran,* 8 vols. Cambridge: Cambridge University Press.

Barnes, John Robert (1986) *An Introduction to Religious Foundations in the Ottoman Empire.* Leiden: E. J. Brill.

Bayat, Mangol (1982) *Mysticism and Dissent: Socioreligious Thought in Qajar Iran.* Syracuse, NY: Syracuse University Press.

—— (1997) *Iran's First Revolution: Shi'ism and the Constitutional Revolution of 1905–1909.* Oxford: Oxford University Press.

Beinin, Joel and Lockman, Zachary (1987) *Workers on the Nile: Nationalism, Communism, Islam, and the Egyptian Working Class, 1882–1954.* Princeton, NJ: Princeton University Press.

Bennison, Amira K. (2002) *Jihad and its Interpretation in Pre-Colonial Morocco: State–Society Relations during the French Conquest of Algeria.* New York: Routledge Curzon.

Berg, Herbert (2000) *The Development of Exegesis in Early Islam: The Authenticity of Muslim Literature from the Formative Period.* Richmond: Curzon.

Berkey, Jonathan P. (1992) *The Transmission of Knowledge in Medieval Cairo: A Social History of Islamic Education.* Princeton, NJ: Princeton University Press.

—— (2001) *Popular Preaching and Religious Authority in the Medieval Islamic Near East.* Seattle, WA: University of Washington Press.

—— (2003) *The Formation of Islam: Religion and Society in the Near East, 600–1800.* Cambridge: Cambridge University Press.

Black, Antony (2001) *The History of Islamic Political Thought: From the Prophet to the Present.* New York: Routledge.

Blanks, David R. and Frassetto, Michael (eds) (1999) *Western Views of Islam in Medieval and Early Modern Europe.* New York: Palgrave Macmillan.

Bloom, Jonathan M. (2001) *Paper before Print: The History and Impact of Paper in the Islamic World.* New Haven, CT: Yale University Press.

Bosworth, Clifford E. (1967) *The Islamic Dynasties.* Edinburgh: Edinburgh University Press.

—— (1996a) *The Arabs, Byzantium and Iran: Studies in Early Islamic History and Culture.* Aldershot: Variorum/Ashgate.

—— (1996b) *The New Islamic Dynasties,* rev. edn. New York: Columbia University Press.

—— (1997) *The Mediaeval Islamic Underworld: The Banu Sasan in Arabic Society and Literature*, Part One. Leiden: E. J. Brill.

Brann, Ross (2002) *Power in the Portrayal: Representations of Jews and Muslims in Eleventh- and Twelfth-Century Islamic Spain*. Princeton, NJ: Princeton University Press.

Brett, Michael (2001) *The Rise of the Fatimids: The World of the Mediterranean and the Middle East in the Tenth Century CE*. Leiden: E. J. Brill.

Browne, Edward G. (1902–24) *A Literary History of Persia*, 4 vols. Cambridge: Cambridge University Press.

—— (1910) *The Persian Revolution of 1905–1909*. Cambridge: Cambridge University Press.

Bulliet, Richard W. (1979) *Conversion to Islam in the Medieval Period: An Essay in Quantitative History*. Cambridge, MA: Harvard University Press.

Cameron, Averil and Conrad, Lawrence I. (eds) (1992) *The Byzantine and Early Islamic Near East: Problems in the Literary Source Materials*. Princeton, NJ: Darwin Press.

Chamberlain, Michael (1994) *Knowledge and Social Practice in Medieval Damascus, 1190–1350*. Cambridge: Cambridge University Press.

Chaudhuri, K. N. (1990) *Asia before Europe: Economy and Civilisation of the Indian Ocean from the Rise of Islam to 1750*. Cambridge: Cambridge University Press.

Chew, Samuel C. (1937) *The Crescent and the Rose: Islam and England during the Renaissance*. New York: Oxford University Press.

Choksy, Jamsheed K. (1997) *Conflict and Cooperation: Zoroastrian Subalterns and Muslim Elites in Medieval Iranian Society*. New York: Columbia University Press.

Clancy-Smith, Julia A. (1994) *Rebel and Saint: Muslim Notables, Populist Protest, Colonial Encounters (Algeria and Tunisia, 1800–1904)*. Berkeley, CA: University of California Press.

Commins, David Dean (1990) *Islamic Reform: Politics and Social Change in Late Ottoman Syria*. New York: Oxford University Press.

Conrad, Lawrence I. (ed.) (2003) *History of Historiography in Early Islamic Times: Studies and Perspectives*. Princeton, NJ: Princeton University Press.

—— (ed.) (2004) *Reflections on Islamic History and Civilization: The Complete Collected Essays of Sir Hamilton Gibb*. Princeton, NJ: Darwin Press.

Cook, Michael (2004) *Studies in the Origins of Early Islamic Culture and Tradition*. Aldershot: Ashgate.

Cooperson, Michael (2000) *Classical Arabic Biography: Heirs of the Prophet in the Age of al-Ma'mun*. Cambridge: Cambridge University Press.

Courbage, Youssef and Fargues, Philippe (1997) *Christians and Jews Under Islam*. London: I. B. Tauris.

Crone, Patricia (1980) *Slaves on Horses: The Evolution of the Islamic Polity*. Cambridge: Cambridge University Press.

—— (1987) *Meccan Trade and the Rise of Islam*. Princeton, NJ: Princeton University Press.

—— (2004) *God's Rule: Government and Islam – Six Centuries of Medieval Islamic Political Thought*. New York: Columbira University Press.

Crone, Patricia and Cook, Michael (1977) *Hagarism: The Making of the Islamic World*. Cambridge: Cambridge University Press.

Crone, Patricia and Hinds, Martin (1986) *God's Caliph: Religious Authority in the First Centuries of Islam*. Cambridge: Cambridge University Press.

Dabashi, Hamid (1989) *Authority in Islam: From the Rise of Muhammad to the Establishment of the Umayyads*. New Brunswick, NJ: Transaction.

Daly, M. W. and Petry, Carl F. (eds) (1998) *The Cambridge History of Egypt*, 2 vols. Cambridge: Cambridge University Press.

Dennett, Daniel (1950) *Conversion and the Poll Tax in Early Islam*. Cambridge, MA: Harvard Press.

Divine, Donna Robinson (1994) *Politics and Society in Ottoman Palestine: The Arab Struggle for Survival and Power*. Boulder, CO: Lynne Rienner.

Donner, Fred McGraw (1981) *The Early Islamic Conquests*. Princeton, NJ: Princeton University Press.

—— (1998) *Narratives of Islamic Origins: The Beginnings of Islamic Historical Writing*. Princeton, NJ: Darwin Press.

Doumani, Beshara (1995) *Rediscovering Palestine: Merchants and Peasants in Jabal Nablus, 1700–1900*. Berkeley, CA: University of California Press.

Eaton, Richard Maxwell (1993) *The Rise of Islam and the Bengal Frontier, 1204–1760*.

Berkeley, CA: University of California Press.

—— (2001) *Essays on Islam and Indian History*. Oxford: Oxford University Press.

Echevarria, Ana (1999) *The Fortress of Faith: The Attitude Toward Muslims in Fifteenth Century Spain*. Leiden: E. J. Brill.

Ehrenkreutz, Andrew S. and Arbor, Ann (1992) *Monetary Change and Economic History in the Medieval Islamic World*. Aldershot: Ashgate/Variorum.

El-Hibri, Tayeb (2000) *Reinterpreting Islamic Historiography: Harun al-Rashid and the Narrative of the 'Abbasid Caliphate*. Cambridge: Cambridge University Press.

Ephrat, Daphna (2000) *A Learned Society in Transition: The Sunni 'Ulama' of Eleventh-Century Baghdad*. Albany, NY: State University of New York Press.

Faroqhi, Suraiya (2000) *Subjects of the Sultan: Culture and Daily Life in the Ottoman Empire*. London: I. B. Tauris.

Feraoun, Mouloud (2000) *Journal, 1955–1962: Reflections on the French–Algerian War*, trans. Mary Ellen Wolf and Claude Fouillade, ed. James D. Le Sueur. Lincoln, NE: Bison Books.

Fleet, Kate (1999) *European and Islamic Trade in the Early Ottoman State: The Merchants of Genoa and Turkey*. Cambridge: Cambridge University Press.

Fletcher, Richard (1993) *Moorish Spain*. Berkeley, CA: University of California Press.

—— (2004) *The Cross and the Crescent: Christianity and Islam from Muhammad to the Reformation*. New York: Viking Press.

Flood, Finbarr B. (2001) *The Great Mosque of Damascus: Studies on the Makings of an Umayyad Visual Culture*. Leiden: E. J. Brill.

Fortna, Benjamin C. (2002) *Imperial Classroom: Islam, the State, and Education in the Late Ottoman Empire*. Oxford: Oxford University Press.

Frank, Allen J. (2001) *Muslim Religious Institutions in Imperial Russia: The Islamic World of Novouzensk District and the Kazakh Inner Horde, 1780–1910*. Leiden: E. J. Brill.

Fuchs, Barbara (2001) *Mimesis and Empire: The New World, Islam, and European Identities*. Cambridge: Cambridge University Press.

Gabrieli, Francesco (1969) *Arab Historians of the Crusades*. Berkeley, CA: University of California Press.

Gershoni, Israel, Erdem, Hakan and Woköck, Ursula (eds) (2002) *Histories of the Modern Middle East: New Directions*. Boulder, CO: Lynne Rienner.

Gilmartin, David (1988) *Empire and Islam: Punjab and the Making of Pakistan*. Berkeley, CA: University of California Press.

Goitein, S. D. (1966) *Studies in Islamic History and Institutions*. Leiden: E. J. Brill.

Goodman, Lenn E. (2003) *Islamic Humanism*. Oxford: Oxford University Press.

Goodwin, Jason (1999) *Lords of the Horizons: A History of the Ottoman Empire*. New York: Henry Holt & Co.

Gregorian, Vartan (1969) *The Emergence of Modern Afghanistan: Politics of Religion and Modernization, 1880–1946*. Stanford, CA: Stanford University Press.

von Grunebaum, G. E. (1953) *Mediaeval Islam: A Study in Cultural Orientation*. Chicago, IL: University of Chicago Press, 2nd edn,

—— (1970) *Classical Islam: A History, 600–1258*, trans. Katherine Watson. London: George Allen & Unwin.

Haj, Samira (1997) *The Making of Iraq, 1900–1963: Capital, Power, and Ideology*. Albany, NY: State University of New York Press.

Hambly, Gavin R. G (ed.) (1998) *Women in the Medieval Islamic World*. New York: Palgrave Macmillan.

Hardy, Peter (1972) *The Muslims of British India*. Cambridge: Cambridge University Press.

Harrison, Christopher (1988) *France and Islam in West Africa, 1860–1960*. Cambridge: Cambridge University Press.

Hathaway, Jane (2002) *The Politics of Households in Ottoman Egypt: The Rise of the Qazdaglis*. Cambridge: Cambridge University Press.

Hawting, G. R. (1999) *The Idea of Idolatry and the Emergence of Islam: From Polemic to History*. Cambridge: Cambridge University Press.

—— (2000) *The First Dynasty of Islam: The Umayyad Caliphate, AD 661–750*, 2nd edn. London: Routledge.

Hillenbrand, Carole (2000) *The Crusades: Islamic Perspectives*. New York: Routledge.

Hinds, Martin, *et al.* (eds) (1997) *Studies in Early Islamic History*. Princeton, NJ: Darwin Press.

Hitti, Philip K. (2002) *History of the Arabs: From Earliest Times to the Present*, 10th edn. London: Macmillan.

—— (trans.) (2000) *An Arab-Syrian Gentleman and Warrior in the Period of the Crusades: Memoirs of Usamah ibn-Munqidh*. New York: Columbia University Press.

Hodgson, Marshall G. S. (1955) *The Order of the Assassins*. The Hague: Mouton.

—— (1974) *The Venture of Islam: Conscience and History in a World Civilization*, 3 vols. Chicago, IL: University of Chicago Press.

—— (1993) *Rethinking World History: Essays on Europe, Islam, and World History*, Edmund Burke III (ed.). Cambridge: Cambridge University Press.

Holt, P. M. *et al.* (eds) (1970) *Cambridge History of Islam*, 2 vols. Cambridge: Cambridge University Press.

Hourani, Albert H. (1991) *A History of the Arab Peoples*. London: Faber & Faber.

Hovannisian, Richard G. and Sabagh, Georges (eds) (2000) *Religion and Culture in Medieval Islam*. Cambridge: Cambridge University Press.

Humphreys, R. Stephen (1977) *From Saladin to the Mongols: The Ayyubids of Damascus, 1193–1260*. Albany, NY: State University of New York Press.

—— (1991) *Islamic History: A Framework for Inquiry*, rev. edn. Princeton, NJ: Princeton University Press.

—— (1999) *Between Memory and Desire: The Middle East in a Troubled Age*. Berkeley, CA: University of California Press.

Ibn Khaldun (1969) *The Muqaddimah: An Introduction to History*, trans. Franz Rosenthal, 3 vols. Princeton, NJ: Princeton University Press.

Inalcik, Halil *et al.* (1994) *An Economic and Social History of the Ottoman Empire, 1300–1914*, 2 vols. Cambridge: Cambridge University Press.

Irwin, Robert (1986) *The Middle East in the Middle Ages: The Early Mamluk Sultanate, 1250–1382*. London: Croom Helm.

Itzkowitz, Norman (1972) *Ottoman Empire and Islamic Tradition*. Chicago, IL: University of Chicago Press.

Jackson, Peter (1999) *The Delhi Sultanate: A Political and Military History*. Cambridge: Cambridge University Press.

Jankowski, James (2002) *Nasser's Egypt, Arab Nationalism, and the United Arab Republic*. Boulder, CO: Lynne Rienner.

Jaschok, Maria and Jingjun, Shui (2000) *The History of Women's Mosques in Chinese Islam*. Richmond: Curzon.

Jayyusi, Salma Khadra (ed.) (1994) *The Legacy of Muslim Spain*, 2 vols. Leiden: E. J. Brill.

Juynboll, G. H. A (ed.) (1982) *Studies on the First Century of Islamic Society*. Carbondale, IL: Southern Illinois University Press.

Kaegi, Walter E. (1992) *Byzantium and the Early Islamic Conquests*. Cambridge: Cambridge University Press.

Karpat, Kemal H. (2001) *The Politicization of Islam: Reconstructing Identity, State, Faith and Community in The Late Ottoman State*. Oxford: Oxford University Press.

Karsh, Efraim and Irani (1999) *Empires of the Sand: The Struggle for Mastery in the Middle East, 1789–1923*. Cambridge, MA: Harvard University Press.

Kasaba, Resat (1988) *The Ottoman Empire and the World Economy: The Nineteenth Century*. Albany, NY: State University of New York Press.

Kayali, Hasan (1997) *Arabs and Young Turks: Ottomanism, Arabism, and Islamism in the Ottoman Empire, 1908–1918*. Berkeley, CA: University of California Press.

Keddie, Nikki R (ed.) (1972) *Scholars, Saints and Sufis: Muslim Religious Institutions in the Middle East since 1500*. Berkeley, CA: University of California Press.

Keddie, Nikki R. and Baron, Beth (eds) (1991) *Women in Middle Eastern History: Shifting Boundaries in Sex and Gender*. New Haven, CT: Yale University Press.

Keller, Shoshana (2001) *To Moscow, Not Mecca: The Soviet Campaign Against Islam in Central Asia, 1917–1941*. Westport, CT: Praeger.

Kennedy, Hugh (1981) *The Early Abbasid Caliphate: A Political History*. London: Croom Helm.

—— (2001a) *The Armies of the Caliphs: Military and Society in the Early Islamic State*. London: Routledge.

—— (ed.) (2001b) *The Historiography of Islamic Egypt (*c. 950–1800*)*. Leiden: Brill Academic.

—— (ed.) (2002) *An Historical Atlas of Islam*. Leiden: Brill Academic.

Khalidi, Rashid (1980) *British Policy Towards Syria and Palestine, 1906–1914*. London: Ithaca Press.

Khalidi, Tarif (1994) *Arab Historical Thought in the Classical Period*. Cambridge: Cambridge University Press.

Khoury, Philip (2003) *Urban Notables and Arab Nationalism: The Politics of Damascus, 1860–1920*. Cambridge: Cambridge University Press.

Kingston, Paul W. T. (2002) *Britain and the Politics of Modernization in the Middle East, 1945–1958*. Cambridge: Cambridge University Press.

Kister, M. J. (1997) *Concepts and Ideas at the Dawn of Islam*. Aldershot: Ashgate/Variorum.

Kohlberg, Etan (1992) *A Medieval Muslim Scholar at Work: Ibn Tawus and his Library*. Leiden: E. J. Brill.

Kostiner, Joseph (1993) *The Making of Saudi Arabia, 1916–1936: From Chieftaincy to Monarchical State*. New York: Oxford University Press.

Kraemer, Joel L. (1992) *Humanism in the Renaissance of Islam: The Cultural Revival during the Buyid Age*, 2nd edn. Leiden: E. J. Brill.

Kramer, Martin (1986) *Islam Assembled: The Advent of the Muslim Congresses*. New York: Columbia University Press.

Laiou, Angeliki E. and Mottahedeh, Roy P. (eds) (2001) *The Crusades from the Perspective of Byzantium and the Muslim World*. Washington, DC: Dumbarton Oaks Center Studies.

Lambton, Ann K. (1988) *Continuity and Change in Medieval Persia: Aspects of Administrative, Economic and Social History, 11th–14th Century*. London: I. B. Tauris.

Lane-Pool, Stanley (2002) *Saladin: All-Powerful Sultan and the Uniter of Islam*. New York: Cooper Square Press.

Lapidus, Ira M. (1967) *Muslim Cities in the Later Middle Ages*. Cambridge, MA: Harvard University Press.

—— (2002) *A History of Islamic Societies*. Cambridge: Cambridge University Press, 2nd edn,

Laremont, Ricardo René (1999) *Islam and the Politics of Resistance in Algeria, 1783–1992*. Lawrenceville, NJ: Africa World Press.

Lassner, Jacob (1980) *The Shaping of Abbasid Rule*. Princeton, NJ: Princeton University Press.

—— (1986) *Islamic Revolution and Historical Memory: An Inquiry into the Art of Abbasid Apologetics*. New Haven, CT: American Oriental Society.

Lazarus-Yafeh, Hava *et al.* (eds) (1999) *The Majlis: Interreligious Encounters in Medieval Islam*. Wiesbaden: Harrassowitz.

Lecker, Michael (1998) *Jews and Arabs in Pre- and Early Islamic Arabia*. Aldershot: Ashgate/Variorum.

Lelyveld, David (1978) *Aligarh's First Generation: Muslim Solidarity in British India*. Princeton, NJ: Princeton University Press.

Lesch, Ann Mosely (1979) *Arab Politics in Palestine, 1917–1937: The Frustration of a Nationalist Movement*. Ithaca, NY: Cornell University Press.

Lewis, Bernard (1967) *The Assassins: A Radical Sect in Islam*. London: Weidenfeld & Nicolson.

—— (1985) *The Muslim Discovery of Europe*, reissue edn. New York: W. W. Norton & Co.

—— (1987a) *The Jews of Islam*. Princeton, NJ: Princeton University Press.

—— (ed.) (1987b) *Islam from the Prophet Muhammad to the Capture of Constantinople: Politics and War*. Oxford: Oxford University Press.

—— (1989) *Istanbul and the Civilization of the Ottoman Empire*. Norman, OK: University of Oklahoma Press.

—— (1990) *Race and Slavery in the Middle East: An Historical Inquiry*. Oxford: Oxford University Press.

—— (2001) *Islam in History: Ideas, People, and Events in the Middle East*, rev. edn. La Salle, IL: Open Court.

Louis, William Roger (1984) *The British Empire in the Middle East, 1945–1951: Arab Nationalism, the United States, and Postwar Imperialism*. Oxford: Oxford University Press.

Lowick, Nicholas (1990) *Islamic Coins and Trade in the Medieval World*. Aldershot: Ashgate/Variorum.

Lyons, Malcolm Cameron and Jackson, David E. P. (1984) *Saladin: The Politics of the Holy War*. Cambridge: Cambridge University Press.

Mack, Rosamond E. (2001) *Bazaar to Piazza: Islamic Trade and Italian Art, 1300–1600*. Berkeley, CA: University of California Press.

Madelung, Wilferd (1985) *Religious Schools and Sects in Medieval Islam*. London: Variorum.

—— (1988) *Religious Trends in Early Islamic Iran*. Albany, NY: State University of New York Press.

—— (1992) *Religious and Ethnic Movements in Medieval Islam*. Aldershot: Ashgate/ Variorum.

—— (1997) *The Succession to Muhammad: A Study of the Early Caliphate*. Cambridge: Cambridge University Press.

Madelung, Wilferd and Walker, Paul E. (trans. and eds) (2000) *The Advent of the Fatimids: A Contemporary Shi'i Witness*. London: I. B. Tauris.

Makdisi, George (1989) *The Rise of Humanism in Classical Islam and the Christian West*. Edinburgh: Edinburgh University Press.

Malti-Douglas, Fedwa (2001) *Power, Marginality, and the Body in Medieval Islam*. Aldershot: Ashgate/ Varorum.

Mandel, Neville J. (1976) *The Arabs and Zionism before World War I*. Berkeley, CA: University of California Press.

Marcus, Abraham (1989) *The Middle East on the Eve of Modernity: Aleppo in the Eighteenth Century*. New York: Columbia University Press.

Marsot, Afaf Lutfi al-Sayyid (1984) *Egypt in the Reign of Muhammad Ali*. Cambridge: Cambridge University Press.

Marsot, Afaf Lutfi al-Sayyid (1985) *A Short History of Modern Egypt*. Cambridge: Cambridge University Press.

Massell, Gregory J. (1974) *The Surrogate Proletariat: Moslem Women and Revolutionary Strategies in Soviet Central Asia, 1919–1929*. Princeton, NJ: Princeton University Press.

Masters, Bruce (1988) *The Origins of Western Economic Dominance in the Middle East: Mercantilism and and the Islamic Economy in Aleppo, 1600–1750*. New York: New York University Press.

Matar, Nabil (1998) *Islam in Britain, 1558–1685*. Cambridge: Cambridge University Press.

Mattar, Phillip (1992) *The Mufti of Jerusalem*. New York: Columbia University Press.

Mazzaoui, Michel (1972) *The Origin of the Safawids: Shi'ism, Sufism, and the Gulat*. Wiesbaden: Franz Steiner.

McChesney, R. D. (1991) *Waqf in Central Asia: Four Hundred Years in the History of a Muslim Shrine, 1480–1889*. Princeton, NJ: Princeton University Press.

Meri, Josef W. (2003) *The Cult of Saints among Muslims and Jews in Medieval Syria*. Oxford: Oxford University Press.

Meriwether, Margaret L. and Tucker, Judith E. (eds) (1999) *A Social History of Women and Gender in the Modern Middle East*. Boulder, CO: Westview Press.

Mernissi, Fatima (1993) *The Forgotten Queens of Islam*. Minneapolis, MN: University of Minnesota Press.

Morris, Benny (1987) *The Birth of the Palestinian Refugee Problem, 1947–1949*. New York: Cambridge University Press.

Mottahedeh, Roy P. (1980) *Loyalty and Leadership in an Early Islamic Society*. Princeton, NJ: Princeton University Press.

Nashat, Guity and Tucker, Judith E. (1999) *Women in the Middle East and North Africa: Restoring Women to History*. Bloomington, IN: Indiana University Press.

Nicolle, David (2003) *Warriors and their Weapons around the Time of the Crusades: Relationships between Byzantium, the West, and the Islamic World*. Aldershot: Ashgate/Variorum.

Noonan, Thomas S. (1998) *The Islamic World, Russia, and the Vikings, 750–900: The Numismatic Evidence*. Aldershot: Ashgate/Variorum.

Ouyang, Wen-Chin (1997) *Literary Criticism in Medieval Arabic-Islamic Culture: The Making of a Tradition*. Edinburgh: Edinburgh University Press.

Owen, E. Roger (1993) *The Middle East in the World Economy, 1800–1914*, rev. edn. London: I. B. Tauris.

Özcan, Azmi (1997) *Pan-Islamism: Indian Muslims, the Ottomans and Britain (1877–1924)*. Leiden: E. J. Brill.

Peirce, Leslie P. (1993) *The Imperial Harem: Women and Sovereignty in the Ottoman Empire*. Oxford: Oxford University Press.

Perry, Glenn E. (1996) *The Middle East: Fourteen Islamic Centuries*, 3rd edn. Upper Saddle River, NJ: Prentice-Hall.

Peters, F. E. (1972) *Allah's Commonwealth: A History of Islam in the Near East, 600–1100 AD*. New York: Simon & Schuster.

—— (ed.) (1999) *The Arabs and Arabia on the Eve of Islam*. Aldershot: Ashgate.

Petry, Carl F. (1981) *The Civilian Elite of Cairo in the Later Middle Ages*. Princeton, NJ: Princeton University Press.

—— (ed.) (1998) *The Cambridge History of Egypt: vol. I, Islamic Egypt, 640–1517.* Cambridge: Cambridge University Press.

Pipes, Daniel (1981) *Slave Soldiers and Islam: The Genesis of a Military System.* New Haven, CT: Yale University Press.

Quataert, Donald (2000) *The Ottoman Empire, 1700–1922.* Cambridge: Cambridge University Press.

Rahman, Fazlur (1984) *Islam and Modernity: Transformation of an Intellectual Tradition.* Chicago, IL: University of Chicago Press.

al-Rasheed, Madawi (2002) *A History of Saudi Arabia.* Cambridge: Cambridge University Press.

Repp, R. C. (1986) *The Mufti of Istanbul: A Study in the Development of the Ottoman Learned Hierarchy.* London: Ithaca Press.

Richards, John F. (1993) *The Mughal Empire.* Cambridge: Cambridge University Press.

Ricklefs, M. C. (2002) *A History of Modern Indonesia since c. 1200,* 3rd edn. Stanford, CA: Stanford University Press.

Robinson, Chase F. (2000) *Empires and Elites after the Muslim Conquest: The Transformation of Northern Mesopotamia.* Cambridge: Cambridge University Press.

—— (ed.) (2002) *A Medieval Islamic City Reconsidered: An Interdisciplinary Approach to Smarra.* Oxford: Oxford University Press.

—— (2003) *Islamic Historiography.* Cambridge: Cambridge University Press.

Robinson, David (2000) *Paths of Accommodation: Muslim Societies and French Colonial Authorities in Senegal and Mauritania, 1890–1920.* Athens, OH: Ohio University Press.

—— (2004) *Muslim Societies in African History.* Cambridge: Cambridge University Press.

Robinson, Francis (1997) *Separatism Among Indian Muslims: The Politics of the United Provinces' Muslims, 1860–1923.* Oxford: Oxford University Press.

Rogan, Eugene L. (1999) *Frontiers of the State in the Late Ottoman Empire: Transjordan, 1850–1921.* Cambridge: Cambridge University Press.

Rogan, Eugene L. and Shlaim, Avi (eds) (2001) *The War for Palestine: Rewriting the History of 1948.* Cambridge: Cambridge University Press.

Rosenthal, Franz (trans. and ed.) (1975) *The Classical Heritage in Islam.* Berkeley, CA: University of California Press.

—— (1990) *Muslim Intellectual and Social History: A Collection of Essays.* Aldershot: Ashgate/Variorum.

Sabra, Adam (2000) *Poverty and Charity in Medieval Islam: Mamluk Egypt, 1250–1517.* Cambridge: Cambridge University Press.

Salibi, Kamal (1988) *A House of Many Mansions: The History of Lebanon Reconsidered.* Berkeley, CA: University of California Press.

Sanders, Paula (1994) *Ritual, Politics and the City in Fatimid Cairo.* Albany, NY: State University of New York Press.

Saunders, J. J. (1990) *A History of Medieval Islam.* New York: Routledge.

Savage, Elizabeth (1997) *A Gateway to Hell, a Gateway to Paradise: The North African Response to the Arab Conquest.* Princeton, NJ: Darwin Press.

Searing, James F. (2002) *'God Alone is King': Islam and Emancipation in Senegal – The Wolof Kingdoms of Kajoor and Bawol, 1859–1914.* Portsmouth, NH: Heinemann.

Sertima, Ivan Van (ed.) (1991) *Golden Age of the Moor.* Piscataway, NJ: Transaction.

Shaban, M. A. (1971) *Islamic History: A New Interpretation, vol. 1: AD 600–750 (AH 132).* Cambridge: Cambridge University Press.

—— (1978) *Islamic History: A New Interpretation, vol. 2: AD 750–1075 (AH 132–448).* Cambridge: Cambridge University Press.

Shaikh, Farzana (1989) *Community and Consensus in Islam: Muslim Representation in Colonial India, 1860–1947.* Cambridge: Cambridge University Press.

Shaked, Shaul (1995) *From Zoroastrian Iran to Islam.* Aldershot: Ashgate/Variorum.

Shatzmiller, Maya (ed.) (1993) *Crusaders and Muslims in Twelfth-Century Syria.* Leiden: E. J. Brill.

—— (1997) *Labour in the Medieval Islamic World.* Leiden: E. J. Brill.

Shaw, Stanford J. (1977) *History of the Ottoman Empire and Modern Turkey, vol. 1: Empire of the Gazis – The Rise and Decline of the Ottoman Empire, 1280–1808.* Cambridge: Cambridge University Press.

Shoshan, Boaz (1993) *Popular Culture in Medieval Cairo*. Cambridge: Cambridge University Press.

Sibai, Mohamed M. (1987) *Mosque Libraries: An Historical Study*. London: Mansell.

Siddiq, Mohammed (2003) *The Epigraphy of Muslim Bengal: Religious, Cultural and Historical Aspects of Arabic and Persian Inscriptions of West Bengal and Bangladesh, 1205–1707*. New York: Routledge.

Smith, Wilfred Cantwell (1957) *Islam in Modern History*. Princeton, NJ: Princeton University Press.

Stora, Benjamin (2001) *Algeria, 1830–2000: A Short History*. Ithaca, NY: Cornell University Press.

al-Tabari (1987–99) *The History of al-Tabari*, various trans., 40 vols. Albany, NY: State University of New York Press.

Tabbaa, Yasser (1997) *Constructions of Power and Piety in Medieval Aleppo*. University Park, PA: Pennsylvania State University Press.

Taylor, Christopher Schurman (1998) *In the Vicinity of the Righteous: Ziyara and the Veneration of Muslim Saints in Late Medieval Egypt*. Leiden: E. J. Brill.

Tessler, Mark (1994) *A History of the Israeli–Palestinian Conflict*. Bloomington, IN: Indiana University Press.

Tolan, John V. (2002) *Saracens: Islam in the Medieval European Imagination*. New York: Columbia University Press.

Tripp, Charles (2002) *A History of Iraq*, 2nd edn. Cambridge: Cambridge University Press.

Tritton, Arthur Stanley (1970) *The Caliphs and their Non-Muslim Subjects: A Critical Study of the Covenant 'Umar*. London: Frank Cass.

Tucker, Judith E. (2002) *Women in Nineteenth-Century Egypt*. Cambridge: Cambridge University Press.

Turner, Colin (2001) *Islam without Allah? The Rise of Religious Externalism in Safavid Iran*. Richmond: Curzon.

Udovitch, Abraham L. (1970) *Partnership and Profit in Medieval Islam*. Princeton, NJ: Princeton University Press.

—— (ed.) (1981) *The Islamic Middle East, 700–1900: Studies in Economic and Social History*. Princeton, NJ: Darwin Press.

Van Leeuwen, Richard (1999) *Waqfs and Urban Structures: The Case of Ottoman Damascus*. Leiden: E. J. Brill.

Vatikiotis, P. J. (1991) *The History of Modern Egypt: From Muhammad Ali to Mubarak*, 4th edn. Baltimore, MD: Johns Hopkins University Press.

voll, John O. (1994) *Islam: Continuity and Change in the Modern World*, 2nd edn. Syracuse, NY: Syracuse University Press.

Walker, Paul E. (2002) *Exploring an Islamic Empire: Fatimid History and Its Sources*. London: I. B. Tauris.

Wasserstrom, Steven M. (1995) *Between Muslim and Jew: The Problem of Symbiosis under Early Islam*. Princeton, NJ: Princeton University Press.

Watt, William Montgomery (1972) *The Influence of Islam on Medieval Europe*. Edinburgh: Edinburgh University Press.

—— (1974) *The Majesty that was Islam: The Islamic World, 661–1100*. London: Sidgwick & Jackson.

—— (1991) *Early Islam: Collected Articles*. Edinburgh: Edinburgh University Press.

Wheatley, Paul (2001) *The Places Where Men Pray Together: Cities in Islamic Lands, Seventh Through the Tenth Centuries*. Chicago, IL: University of Chicago Press.

Wilson, Mary C. (1987) *King Abdullah, Britain, and the Making of Jordan*. Cambridge: Cambridge University Press.

Wink, André (2002) *Al-Hind: The Making of the Indo-Islamic World, vol.1. Early Medieval India and the Expansion of Islam, 7th–11th Centuries*, 2nd edn. Amherst, NY: Prometheus Books.

Woods, John E. (1999) *The Aqquyunlu: Clan, Confederation, and Empire*, rev. edn. Salt Lake City, UT: University of Utah Press.

Yemelianova, Galina M. (2002) *Russia and Islam: A Historical Survey*. New York: Palgrave Macmillan.

Zaman, Muhammad Qasim (1997) *Religion and Politics under the Early 'Abbasids: The Emergence of the Proto-Sunni Elite*. Leiden: E. J. Brill.

X Geographic regions and nation-states

Abdo, Geneive (2000) *No God but God: Egypt and the Triumph of Islam*. Oxford: Oxford University Press.

Abdo, Geneive and Lyons, Jonathan (2003) *Answering Only to God: Faith and Freedom in Twenty-First Century Iran*. New York: Henry Holt & Co.

Abir, Mordechai (1993) *Saudi Arabia: Government, Society, and the Gulf Crisis*. New York: Routledge.

Abrahamian, Ervand (1982) *Iran Between Two Revolutions*. Princeton, NJ: Princeton University Press.

—— (1993) *Khomeinism: Essays on the Islamic Republic*. Berkeley, CA: University of California Press.

—— (1999) *Tortured Confessions: Prisons and Public Recantations in Modern Iran*. Berkeley, CA: University of California Press.

Abu-'Amr, Ziyad (1994) *Islamic Fundamentalism in the West Bank and Gaza: Muslim Brotherhood and Islamic Jihad*. Bloomington, IN: Indiana University Press.

Abu-Lughod, Ibrahim (ed.) (1987) *The Transformation of Palestine: Essays on the Origin and Development of the Arab-Israeli Conflict*, 2nd edn. Evanston, IL: Northwestern University Press.

Abu-Lughod, Janet (1971) *Cairo: 1001 Years of the City Victorious*. Princeton, NJ: Princeton University Press.

Aburish, Saïd K. (1996) *The Rise, Corruption and Coming Fall of the House of Saud*. New York: St. Martin's Press.

Adamson, Kay (1998) *Algeria: A Study in Competing Ideologies*. New York: Continuum.

Adelkhah, Fariba (2000) *Being Modern in Iran*. New York: Columbia University Press.

Afkhami, Mahnaz and Friedl, Erika (eds) (1994) *In the Eye of the Storm: Women in Post-Revolutionary Iran*. Syracuse, NY: Syracuse University Press.

Ahmad, Aziz (1967) *Islamic Modernism in India and Pakistan*. London: Oxford University Press.

—— (1969) *An Intellectual History of Islam in India*. Edinburgh: Edinburgh University Press.

—— (1999) *Studies in Islamic Culture in the Indian Environment*. Oxford: Oxford University Press.

Ahmad, Aziz and von Grunebaum, G. E. (eds) (1970) *Muslim Self-Statement in India and Pakistan, 1857–1968*. Wiesbaden: Harrassowitz.

Ahmad, Feroz (2003) *Turkey: The Quest for Identity*. Oxford: Oneworld.

Ahmida, Ali Abdullatif (ed.) (2000) *Beyond Colonialism and Nationalism in the Maghreb: History, Culture and Politics*. New York: Palgrave.

Akhavi, Shahrough (1980) *Religion and Politics in Contemporary Iran: Clergy–State Relations in the Pahlavi Period*. Albany, NY: State University of New York Press.

Akiner, Shirin (1987) *Islamic Peoples of the Soviet Union*, 2nd edn. London: Kegan Paul.

Algar, Hamid (1969) *Religion and State in Iran 1785–1906: The Role of the Ulama in the Qajar Period*. Berkeley, CA: University of California Press.

—— (1980) *The Islamic Revolution in Iran*. London: Open Press.

Alizadeh, Parvin (ed.) (2000) *The Economy of Iran: The Dilemma of an Islamic State*. London: I. B. Tauris.

Allievi, Stefano *et al.* (eds) (2003) *Muslim Networks and Transnational Communities in and across Europe*. Leiden: E. J. Brill.

Allworth, Edward *et al.* (eds) (1994) *Muslim Communities Reemerge: Historical Perspectives on Nationality, Politics, and Opposition in the Former Soviet Union and Yugoslavia*. Durham, NC: Duke University Press.

al-'Amri, Husayn 'Abdullah (1985) *The Yemen in the 18th and 19th Centuries: A Political and Intellectual History*. London: Ithaca Press.

Amin, Galal (2000) *Whatever Happened to the Egyptians?* Cairo: American University in Cairo Press.

Amin, Qasim (2000) *The Liberation of Women and The New Woman: Two Documents in the History of Egyptian Feminism*. Cairo: American University in Cairo Press.

Anderson, Lisa (1986) *The State and Social Transformation in Tunisia and Libya, 1830–1980*. Princeton, NJ: Princeton University Press.

Ansari, Ali M. (2003a) *Iran, Islam, and Democracy: The Politics of Managing Change*, rev. edn. London: Royal Institute of International Affairs.

—— (2003b) *Modern Iran Since 1921: The Pahlavis and After*. London: Longman.

Ansari, Hamied (1986) *Egypt: The Stalled Society*. Albany, NY: State University of New York Press.

Antoun, Richard and Donald Quataert (eds) (1991) *Syria: Society, Culture, and Polity*. Albany, NY: State University of New York Press.

Arjomand, Said Amir (1988) *The Turban for the Crown: The Islamic Revolution in Iran*. Oxford: Oxford University Press.

Badran, Margot (1994) *Feminists, Islam, and Nation: Gender and the Making of Modern Egypt*. Princeton, NJ: Princeton University Press.

Baker, Raymond William (2003) *Islam without Fear: Egypt and the New Islamists*. Cambridge, MA: Harvard University Press.

Bakhash, Shaul (1990) *The Reign of the Ayatollahs: Iran and the Islamic Revolution*. New York: Basic Books.

Barakat, Halim (ed.) (1988) *Toward a Viable Lebanon*. London and Washington, DC: Croom Helm and the Center for Contemporary Arab Studies, Georgetown University.

Bargach, Jamila (2002) *Orphans of Islam: Family, Abandonment, and Secret Adoption in Morocco*. Lanham, MD: Rowman & Littlefield.

Barkey, Henri J. and Fuller, Graham E. (1998) *Turkey's Kurdish Question*. Lanham, MD: Rowman & Littlefield.

Baron, Beth (1997) *The Women's Awakening in Egypt: Culture, Society, and the Press*, rpt edn. New Haven, CT: Yale University Press.

Barton, Greg (2002) *Abdurrahman Wahid: Muslim Democrat, Indonesian President*. Honolulu, HI: University of Hawaii Press.

Batatu, Hanna (1978) *The Old Social Classes and the Revolutionary Movements of Iraq: A Study of Iraq's Old Landed and Commercial Classes and of Its Communists, Ba'thists, and Free Officers*. Princeton, NJ: Princeton University Press.

Baxter, Craig and Kennedy, Charles (eds) (1998) *Pakistan 1997*. Boulder, CO: Westview Press with the American Institute of Pakistan Studies.

Bayat, Asef (1997) *Street Politics: Poor People's Movements in Iran*. New York: Columbia University Press.

Behrman, Lucy C. (1970) *Muslim Brotherhoods and Politics in Senegal*. Cambridge, MA: Harvard University Press.

Benard, Cheryl (2002) *Veiled Courage: Inside the Afghan Women's Resistance*. New York: Broadway Books/Random House.

Bennigsen, Alexandre A. and Broxup, Marie (1983) *The Islamic Threat to the Soviet State*. New York: St. Martin's Press.

Bennison, Amira K. (2002) *Jihad and its Interpretation in Pre-Colonial Morocco: State–Society Relations during the French Conquest of Algeria*. New York: Routledge Curzon.

Bennoune, Mahfoud (1988) *The Making of Contemporary Algeria, 1830–1987: Colonial Upheavals and Post-Independence Development*. Cambridge: Cambridge University Press.

Berkes, Niyazi (1964) *Development of Secularism in Turkey*. Montreal: McGill University Press.

Bibars, Iman (2001) *Victims and Heroines: Women, Welfare and the Egyptian State*. London: Zed Books.

Binder, Leonard (1978) *In a Moment of Enthusiasm: Political Power and the Second Stratum in Egypt*. Chicago, IL: University of Chicago Press.

Blank, Jonah (2002) *Mullahs on the Mainframe: Islam and Modernity among the Daudi Bohras*. Chicago, IL: University of Chicago Press.

Boland, B. J. (1982) *The Struggle of Islam in Modern Indonesia*. The Hague: Martinus Nijhoff.

Bonine, Michael E. and Keddie, Nikki R. (eds) (1981) *Modern Iran: The Dialectics of Continuity and Change*. Albany, NY: State University of New York Press.

Bourqia, Rahma and Miller, Susan Gilson (eds) (1999) *In the Shadow of the Sultan: Culture, Power, and Politics in Morocco*. Cambridge, MA: Harvard Center for Middle Eastern Studies and the Harvard University Press.

Bowen, John R. (2003) *Islam, Law and Equality in Indonesia: An Anthropology of Public Reasoning*. Cambridge: Cambridge University Press.

Boyle, Francis Anthony (2003) *Palestine, Palestinians, and International Law*. Atlanta, GA: Clarity Press.

Bozdogan, Sibel and Kasaba, Resat (eds) (1997) *Rethinking Modernity and National Identity in Turkey*. Seattle, WA: University of Washington Press.

Bringa, Tone (1995) *Being Muslim the Bosnian Way: Identity and Community in a Central Bosnian Village*. Princeton, NJ: Princeton University Press.

Browne, Edward G. (1910) *The Persian Revolution, 1905–1909*. Cambridge: Cambridge University Press.

Brumberg, Daniel (2001) *Reinventing Khomeini: The Struggle for Reform in Iran*. Chicago, IL: University of Chicago Press.

Bukharaev, Ravil (2000) *Islam in Russia: The Four Seasons*. New York: St. Martin's Press.

Bulloch, John and Morris, Harvey (1992) *No Friends but the Mountains: The Tragic History of the Kurds*. Oxford: Oxford University Press.

Burgat, François and Dowell, William (1997) *The Islamic Movement in North Africa*. Austin, TX: Center for Middle Eastern Studies, University of Texas.

Callaway, Barbara and Creevey, Lucy (1994) *The Heritage of Islam: Women, Religion, and Politics in West Africa*. Boulder, CO: Lynne Reinner.

Carapico, Sheila (1998) *Civil Society in Yemen: The Political Economy of Activism in Modern Arabia*. Cambridge: Cambridge University Press.

Cardini, Franco (2001) *Europe and Islam*. Malden, MA: Blackwell.

Charrad, Mounira M. (2001) *States and Women's Rights: The Making of Postcolonial Tunisia, Algeria, Morocco*. Berkeley, CA: University of California Press.

Cockburn, Andrew and Cockburn, Patrick (2000) *Out of the Ashes: The Resurrection of Saddam Hussein*. New York: HarperCollins.

Cole, Juan (1988) *Roots of North Indian Shi'ism in Iran and Iraq: Religion and State in Awadh, 1722–1859*. Berkeley, CA: University of California Press.

Connelly, Matthew (2002) *A Diplomatic Revolution: Algeria's Fight for Independence and the Origins of the Post-Cold War Era*. New York: Oxford University Press.

Cooley, John (2002) *Unholy Wars: Afghanistan, America and International Terrorism*, 3rd edn. London: Pluto Press.

Cruise O'Brien, Donal B. (1975) *Saints and Politicians: Essays in the Organization of Senegalese Peasant Society*. London: Cambridge University Press.

Cruise O'Brien, Donal B. and Coulon, Christian (eds) (1988) *Charisma and Brotherhood in African Islam*. Oxford: Clarendon Press.

Crystal, Jill (1995) *Oil and Politics in the Gulf: Rulers and Merchants in Kuwait and Qatar*, rev. edn. Cambridge: Cambridge University Press.

Dabashi, Hamid (1993) *Theology of Discontent: The Ideological Foundations of the Islamic Revolution in Iran*. New York: New York University Press.

Dale, Stephen F. (1994) *Islamic Society on the South Asian Frontier*. Oxford: Oxford University Press.

Dann, Uriel (1984) *Studies in the History of Transjordan, 1920–1949: The Making of a State*. Boulder, CO: Westview Press.

—— (1989) *King Hussein and the Challenge of Arab Radicalism: Jordan, 1955–1967*. New York: Oxford University Press.

Davison, Andrew (1998) *Secularism and Revivalism in Turkey: A Hermeneutic Reconsideration*. New Haven, CT: Yale University Press.

Dawisha, Adee (1980) *Syria and the Lebanese Crisis*. London: Macmillan.

Deweese, Devin (1994) *Islamization and Native Religion in the Golden Horde: Baba Tukles and Conversion to Islam in Historical and Epic Tradition*. University Park, PA: Pennsylvania State University Press.

Dhofier, Zamakhsyari (1999) *The Pesantren Tradition: The Role of the Kyai in the Maintenance of Traditional Islam in Java*. Tempe, AZ: Arizona State University Program for Southeast Asian Studies.

Dillon, Michael (1996) *China's Muslims (Images of Asia)*. Oxford: Oxford University Press.

Diouf, Sylviane A. (1998) *Servants of Allah: African Muslims Enslaved in the Americas*. New York: New York University Press.

Dresch, Paul (2000) *A History of Modern Yemen*. Cambridge: Cambridge University Press.

Dudoignon, Stéphane A. and Hisao, Komatso (eds) (2002) *Islam in Politics in Russia and Central Asia*. London: Kegan Paul.

Eaton, Richard M. (ed.) (2003) *India's Islamic Traditions, 711–1750*. Oxford: Oxford University Press.

Ehteshami, Anoushiravan (1995) *After Khomeini: The Iranian Second Republic*. New York: Routledge.

Eickelman, Dale (1976) *Moroccan Islam*. Austin, TX: University of Texas Press.

—— (1985) *Knowledge and Power in Morocco: The Education of a Twentieth Century Notable*. Princeton, NJ: Princeton University Press.

El-Ghonemy, M. Riad (1998) *Affluence and Poverty in the Middle East*. London: Routledge.

d'Encausse, Helene Carrere (1989) *Islam and the Russian Empire: Reform and Revolution in Central Asia*. Berkeley, CA: University of California Press.

Entelis, John P (ed.) (1997) *Islam, Democracy, and the State in North Africa*. Bloomington, IN: Indiana University Press.

Entessar, Nader (1992) *Kurdish Ethnonationalism*. Boulder, CO: Lynne Rienner.

Esfandiari, Haleh (1997) *Reconstructed Lives: Women and Iran's Islamic Revolution*. Baltimore, MD: Johns Hopkins University Press.

Fandy, Mamoun (2001) *Saudi Arabia and the Politics of Dissent*. New York: Palgrave Macmillan.

Farouk-Sluglett, Marion and Sluglett, Peter (2001) *Iraq Since 1958: From Revolution to Dictatorship*. New York: Palgrave.

Farsoun, Samih K. (1992) *Iran: Political Culture in the Islamic Republic*. London: Routledge.

Farsoun, Samih K. (with Christina Zacharia) (1997) *Palestine and the Palestinians*. Boulder, CO: Westview Press.

Federspiel, Howard M. (1993) *The Usage of Traditions of the Prophet in Contemporary Indonesia*. Tempe, AZ: Arizona State University Program for Southeast Asian Studies.

—— (1995) *A Dictionary of Indonesian Islam*. Athens, OH: Ohio University Press.

—— (1998) *Indonesia in Transition: Muslim Intellectuals and National Development*. Hauppauge, NY: Nova Science.

—— (2001) *Islam and Ideology in the Emerging Indonesian State: The Persatuan Islam (Persis), 1923–1957*. Leiden: E. J. Brill.

Fischbach, Michael R. (2000) *State, Society and Land in Jordan*. Leiden: E. J. Brill.

Fischer, Michael M. J. (1980) *Iran: from Religious Dispute to Revolution*. Cambridge, MA: Harvard University Press.

Fisk, Robert (2002) *Pity the Nation: The Abduction of Lebanon*, 4th edn. New York: Thunder's Mouth Press/Nation Books.

Foran, John (1993) *Fragile Resistance: Social Transformation in Iran from 1500 to the Revolution*. Boulder, CO: Westview Press.

—— (ed.) (1994) *A Century of Revolution: Social Movements in Iran*. Minneapolis, MN: University of Minnesota Press.

Freedman, Lawrence and Karsh, Efraim (1993) *The Gulf Conflict, 1990–1991: Diplomacy and War in the New World Order*. Princeton, NJ: Princeton University Press.

Friedman, Francine (1996) *The Bosnian Muslims: Denial of a Nation*. Boulder, CO: Westview Press.

Friend, Theodore (2003) *Indonesian Destinies*. Cambridge, MA: Belknap Press of Harvard University Press.

Gaffney, Patrick D. (1994) *The Prophet's Pulpit: Islamic Preaching in Contemporary Egypt*. Berkeley, CA: University of California Press.

Gallagher, Nancy Elizabeth (2002) *Medicine and Power in Tunisia, 1780–1900*. Cambridge: Cambridge University Press.

Geertz, Clifford (1971) *Islam Observed: Religious Development in Morocco and Indonesia*. Chicago, IL: University of Chicago Press.

Gelvin, James (1998) *Divided Loyalties: Nationalism and Mass Politics in Syria at the Close of Empire*. Berkeley, CA: University of California Press.

George, Alan (2003) *Syria: Neither Bread nor Freedom*. London: Zed Books.

Gershoni, Israel and Jankowski, James P. (1986) *Egypt, Islam and the Arabs: The Search for Egyptian Nationhood, 1900–1930*. New York: Oxford University Press.

Ghani, Cyrus (1987) *Iran and the West: A Critical Bibliography*. London: Kegan Paul.

—— (2000) *Iran and the Rise of Reza Shah: From Qajar Collapse to Pahlavi Power*. London: I. B. Tauris.

Ghareeb, Edmund (1981) *The Kurdish Question in Iraq*. Syracuse, NY: Syracuse University Press.

Gilsenan, Michael (1996) *Lords of the Lebanese Marches: Violence and Narrative in an Arab Society*. Berkeley, CA: University of California Press.

Gohari, M. J. (2001) *The Taliban: Ascent to Power*. Oxford: Oxford University Press.

Goodson, Larry P. (2001) *Afghanistan's Endless War: State Failure, Regional Politics, and the Rise of the Taliban*. Seattle, WA: University of Washington Press.

Gunter, Michael M. (1993) *The Kurds of Iraq: Tragedy and Hope*. London: Palgrave Macmillan.

—— (1997) *The Kurds and the Future of Turkey*. London: Palgrave Macmillan.

—— (1999) *The Kurdish Predicament in Iraq: A Political Analysis*. London: Palgrave Macmillan.

Hadawi, Sami (1998a) *Bitter Harvest: A Modern History of Palestine*, 4th edn.

Northampton, MA: Interlink Publ. Group.

—— (1998b) *Palestinian Rights and Losses in 1948: A Comprehensive Study*. London: Saqi Books.

Haddad, Yvonne Yazbeck (ed.) (1993) *The Muslims of America*. New York: Oxford University Press.

—— (ed.) (2002) *Muslims in the West: From Sojourners to Citizens*. New York: Oxford University Press.

Haghayeghi, Mehrdad (1996) *Islam and Politics in Central Asia*. London: Palgrave Macmillan.

Hairi, Abdu'l-Hadi (1977) *Shi'ism and Constitutionalism in Iran*. Leiden: E. J. Brill.

Halawi, Majed (1992) *A Lebanon Defied: Musa al-Sadr and the Shi'a Community*. Boulder, CO: Westview Press.

Hale, Sondra (1996) *Gender Politics in Sudan: Islamism, Socialism, and the State*. Boulder, CO: Westview Press.

Hamidi, Muhammad al-Hashimi (1998) *The Politicization of Islam: A Case Study of Tunisia*. Boulder, CO: Westview Press.

Hammoudi, Abdellah (1997) *Master and Disciple: The Cultural Foundations of Moroccan Authoritarianism*. Chicago, IL: University of Chicago Press.

Hart, David M. (2000) *Tribe and Society in Rural Morocco*. London: Frank Cass.

Hasan, Mushirul (1997) *Legacy of a Divided Nation: India's Muslims since Independence*. Boulder, CO: Westview Press.

—— (2000) *Islam in the Subcontinent: Muslims in a Plural Society*. New Delhi: Munshiram Manoharlal.

Hefner, Robert W. (2000) *Civil Islam: Muslims and Democratization in Indonesia*. Princeton, NJ: Princeton University Press.

Hefner, Robert W. and Horvatich, Patricia (eds) (1997) *Islam in an Era of Nation-States: Politics and Religious Renewal in Muslim Southeast Asia*. Honolulu, HI: University of Hawaii Press.

Henry, Clement M. (1996) *The Mediterranean Debt Crescent: Money and Power in Algeria, Egypt, Morocco, Tunisia, and Turkey*. Gainesville, FL: University Press of Florida.

Hillebrand, Carole (ed.) (1999) *The Sultan's Turret: Studies in Persian and Turkish Culture*. Leiden: E. J. Brill.

Hinnebusch, Raymond A. (1990) *Authoritarian Power and State Formation in Ba'thist Syria: Army, Party, and Peasant*. Boulder, CO: Westview Press.

Hinnebusch, Raymond and Ehteshami, Anoushiravan (eds) (2002) *The Foreign Policies of Middle East States*. Boulder, CO: Lynne Rienner.

Hiro, Dilip (1991) *The Longest War: The Iran-Iraq Military Conflict*. New York: Routledge.

—— (1995) *Between Marx and Muhammad: The Changing Face of Central Asia*. London: Harper-Collins.

—— (2001) *Neighbors, Not Friends: Iraq and Iran after the Gulf Wars*. New York: Routledge.

Hiskett, Mervyn (1984) *The Development of Islam in West Africa*. London: Longman.

—— (1994) *The Course of Islam in Africa*. Edinburgh: Edinburgh University Press.

Hitchcock, Michael (1996) *Islam and Identity in Eastern Indonesia*. Hull: Hull University Press.

Hooglund, Eric (ed.) (2002) *Twenty Years of Islamic Revolution: Political and Social Transition in Iran since 1979*. Syracuse, NY: Syracuse University Press.

Horne, Alistair (1977) *A Savage War of Peace: Algeria, 1954–1962*. London: Macmillan.

Hourani, Albert H. (1946) *Syria and Lebanon*. London: Oxford University Press.

Houston, Christopher (2001) *Islam, Kurds and the Turkish Nation State*. Oxford: Berg.

Howe, Marvine (2000) *Turkey Today: A Nation Divided Over Islam's Revival*. Boulder, CO: Westview Press.

Hunter, Shireen T (ed.) (2002) *Islam, Europe's Second Religion: The New Social, Cultural and Political Landscape*. Westport, CT: Praeger.

Hurewitz, Jacob C. (ed.) (1975–9) *The Middle East and North Africa in World Politics: A Documentary Record*, 2 vols. New Haven, CT: Yale University Press.

Irfani, Shuroosh (1983) *Revolutionary Islam in Iran: Popular Liberation or Religious Dictatorship?* London: Zed Books.

Israeli, Raphael (1994) *Islam in China: A Critical Bibliography*. Westport, CT: Greenwood.

—— (2002) *Islam in China: Religion, Ethnicity, Culture, and Politics*. Lanham, MD: Lexington Books.

Jackson, Karl D. (1980) *Traditional Authority, Islam, and Rebellion: A Study of*

Indonesian Political Behavior. Berkeley, CA: University of California Press.

Jahanbakhsh, Forough (2001) *Islam, Democracy and Modernism in Iran, 1953–2000: From Bazargan to Soroush*. Leiden: E. J. Brill.

Jalal, Ayesha (1985) *The Sole Spokesman: Jinnah, The Muslim League and The Demand for Pakistan*. Cambridge: Cambridge University Press.

—— (2000) *Self and Sovereignty: Individual and Community in South Asian Islam since 1850*. London: Routledge.

Jankowski, James (2000) *Egypt: A Short History*. Oxford: Oneworld.

Jawad, Saad (1981) *Iraq and the Kurdish Question, 1958–1970*. London: Ithaca Press.

Jawed, Nasim A. (1999) *Islam's Political Culture: Religion and Politics in Pre-divided Pakistan*. Austin, TX: University of Texas Press.

Johnson, Douglas H. (2003) *The Root Causes of Sudan's Civil Wars*. Bloomington, IN: Indiana University Press.

Johnson, Nels (1982) *Islam and the Politics of Meaning in Palestinian Nationalism*. London: Kegan Paul.

Jones, Owen Bennett (2002) *Pakistan: Eye of the Storm*, 2nd edn. New Haven, CT: Yale University Press.

Kamrava, Mehran (1990) *Revolution in Iran: The Roots of Turmoil*. London: Routledge.

Karmi, Ghada and Cotran, Eugene (eds) (2000) *The Palestinian Exodus: 1948–1998*. London: Ithaca Press.

Karpat, Kemal H. (2002) *The Politicization of Islam: Reconstructing Identity, State, Faith and Community in the Late Ottoman State*. Oxford: Oxford University Press.

Kassem, Maye (2004) *Egyptian Politics: The Dynamics of Authoritarian Rule*. Boulder, CO: Lynne Rienner.

Kayali, Hasan (2003) *A History of Modern Turkey*. Cambridge: Cambridge University Press.

Kazemi, Farhad (1981) *Poverty and Revolution in Iran: The Migrant Poor, Urban Marginality, and Politics*. New York: New York University Press.

Keddie, Nikki R. (1966) *Religion and Rebellion in Iran: The Tobacco Protest of 1891–1892*. London: Frank Cass.

—— (1980) *Iran: Religion, Politics and Society*. London: Frank Cass.

—— (1981) *Roots of Revolution: An Interpretative History of Modern Iran*. New Haven, CT: Yale University Press.

—— (ed.) (1983) *Religion and Politics in Iran: Shi'ism from Quietism to Revolution*. New Haven, CT: Yale University Press.

—— (1995) *Iran and the Muslim World: Resistance and Revolution*. New York: New York University Press.

—— (2003) *Modern Iran: Roots and Results of Revolution*. New Haven, CT: Yale University Press.

Kelly, J. B. (1959) *Sultanate and Imamate in Oman*. London: Chatham House.

Kennedy, Charles H. and Baxter, Craig (eds) (2000) *Pakistan 2000*. Lanham, MD: Lexington Books.

Kennedy, Charles H. *et al.* (eds) (forthcoming) *Pakistan at the Millennium*. Oxford: Oxford University Press.

Kennedy, Hugh (1997) *Muslim Spain and Portugal: A Political History of al-Andalus*. Boston, MA: Addison-Wesley.

Kepel, Gilles (2003) *Muslim Extremism in Egypt: The Prophet and Pharaoh*. Berkeley, CA: University of California Press.

Khadduri, Majid (1969) *Republican Iraq*. London: Oxford University Press.

—— (1978) *Socialist Iraq: A Study in Iraqi Politics Since 1968*. Washington, DC: Middle East Institute.

Khadduri, Majid and Ghareeb, Edmund (2001) *War in the Gulf, 1990–91: The Iraq–Kuwait Conflict and Its Implications*. Oxford: Oxford University Press.

Khalaf, Samir (2002) *Civil and Uncivil Violence: The Internationalization of Communal Conflict in Lebanon*. New York: Columbia University Press.

Khalid, Adeeb (1999) *The Politics of Muslim Cultural Reform: Jadidism in Central Asia*. Berkeley, CA: University of California Press.

Khalid, Mansour (2002) *War and Peace in Sudan: A Tale of Two Countries*. London: Kegan Paul.

Khalidi, Omar (1995) *Indian Muslims Since Independence*. New Delhi: Vikas.

Khan, M. A. Muqtedar (2002) *American Muslims: Bridging Faith and Freedom*. Beltsville, MD: Amana.

Khoury, Dina Rizk (1998) *State and Provincial Society in the Ottoman Empire: Mosul, 1540–1834*. Cambridge: Cambridge University Press.

Khoury, Philip (1987) *Syria and the French Mandate: The Politics of Arab National-*

ism, 1928–1945. Princeton, NJ: Princeton University Press.

Kienle, Eberhard (2000) *Ba'th v. Ba'th: The Conflict Between Syria and Iraq, 1968–1989*. London: I. B. Tauris.

Kimmerling, Baruch and Migdal, Joel S. (2003) *The Palestinian People: A History*. Cambridge, MA: Harvard University Press.

King, Stephen J. (2003) *Liberalization against Democracy: The Local Politics of Economic Reform in Tunisia*. Bloomington, IN: Indiana University Press.

Kinzer, Stephen (2002) *Crescent and Star: Turkey Between Two Worlds*. New York: Farrar, Straus & Giroux.

Kirisci, Kemal and Winrow, Gareth M. (1997) *The Kurdish Question and Turkey: An Example of a Trans-state Ethnic Conflict*. London: Frank Cass.

Knezys, Stasys and Sedlickas, Romanas (1999) *The War in Chechnya*. College Station, TX: Texas A&M University Press.

Kostiner, Joseph (ed.) (2000) *Middle East Monarchies: The Challenge of Modernity*. Boulder, CO: Lynne Rienner.

Kucuk, Hulya (2002) *The Role of the Bektashis in Turkey's National Struggle*. Leiden: E. J. Brill.

Kuri, Fuad I. (1980) *Tribe and State in Bahrain*. Chicago, IL: University of Chicago Press.

Kupferschmidt, Uri M. (1987) *The Supreme Muslim Council: Islam under the British Mandate for Palestine*. Leiden: E. J. Brill.

Laffan, Michael Francis (2002) *Islamic Nationhood and Colonial Indonesia: The Umma below the Winds*. New York: RoutledgeCurzon.

Latifa, with Shékéba Hachemi (2002) *My Forbidden Face – Growing Up Under the Taliban: One Woman's Story*, trans. Linda Coverdale. New York: Miramax/Hyperion.

Launay, Robert (1992) *Beyond the Stream: Islam and Society in a West African Town*. Berkeley, CA: University of California Press.

Lawrence, Bruce B. (2002) *New Faiths, Old Fears: Muslims and Other Asian Immigrants in American Religious Life*. New York: Columbia University Press.

Layachi, Azzedine (1998) *State, Society and Democracy in Morocco: The Limits of Associative Life*. Washington, DC: Center for Contemporary Arab Studies.

Lebor, Adam (2001) *A Heart Turned East: Among the Muslims of Europe and America*. New York: St. Martin's Press.

Lesch, Ann Mosely (1998) *The Sudan: Contested National Identities*. Bloomington, IN: Indiana University Press.

Levtzion, Nehemia (1994) *Islam in West Africa: Religion, Society and Politics to 1800*. Aldershot: Ashgate/Variorum.

Levtzion, Nehemia and Pouwels, Randall L. (eds) (2000) *The History of Islam in Africa*. Athens, OH: Ohio University, Center for International Studies.

Lewis, Bernard (2001) *The Emergence of Modern Turkey*, 3rd edn. Oxford: Oxford University Press.

Lewis, Bernard and Schnapper, Dominique (eds) (1994) *Muslims in Europe*. London: Pinter.

Lewis, Philip (1994) *Islamic Britain: Religion, Politics and Identity among British Muslims*. London: I. B. Tauris.

Liel, Alon (2001) *Turkey in the Middle East: Oil, Islam, and Politics*, trans. Emanuel Lottem. Boulder, CO: Lynne Rienner.

Lindholm, Charles (2002) *The Islamic Middle East: Tradition and Change*, 2nd edn. Malden, MA: Blackwell.

Lipman, Jonathan N. (1998) *Familiar Strangers: A History of Muslims in Northwest China*. Seattle, WA: University of Washington Press.

Löffler, Rheinhold (1988) *Islam in Practice: Religious Belief in a Persian Village*. Albany, NY: State University of New York Press.

Logan, Harriet (2002) *Unveiled: Voices of Women in Afghanistan*. New York: Regan Books.

Long, David E. (1997) *The Kingdom of Saudi Arabia*. Gainesville, FL: University Press of Florida.

Lynch, Marc (1999) *State Interests and Public Spheres: The International Politics of Jordan's Identity*. New York: Columbia University Press.

McAmis, Robert Day (2002) *Malay Muslims: The History and Challenge of Resurgent Islam in Southeast Asia*. Grand Rapids, MI: William B. Eerdmans.

Mackey, Sandra (1998) *The Iranians: Persia, Islam and the Soul of a Nation*. New York: Plume/Penguin.

—— (2003) *The Reckoning: Iraq and the Legacy of Saddam Hussein*. New York: W. W. Norton & Co.

Magnus, Ralph H. and Naby, Eden (2002) *Afghanistan: Mullah, Marx, and Mujahid.* Boulder, CO: Westview Press.

Majul, Cesar Adib (1985) *The Contemporary Muslim Movement in the Philippines.* Berkeley, CA: Mizan Press.

—— (1999) *Muslims in the Philippines.* Quezon City: University of the Philippines Press.

Makiya, Kanan (1998) *Republic of Fear: The Politics of Modern Iraq*, updated edn. Berkeley, CA: University of California Press.

Maley, William (1998) *Fundamentalism Reborn? Afghanistan and the Taliban.* New York: New York University Press.

—— (2002) *The Afghanistan Wars.* New York: Palgrave Macmillan.

Malik, Hafeez (1980) *Sir Sayyid Ahmad Khan and Muslim Modernism in India and Pakistan.* New York: Columbia University Press.

—— (ed.) (1994) *Central Asia: Its Strategic Importance and Future Prospects.* New York: St. Martin's Press.

—— (ed.) (2000a) *Pakistan: Founders' Aspirations and Today's Realities.* Karachi: Oxford University Press.

—— (ed.) (2000b) *Russian-American Relations: Islamic and Turkish Dimensions in the volga-Ural Basin.* New York: Palgrave Macmillan.

Malik, Iftikhar Haider (1999) *Islam, Nationalism, and the West: Issues of Identity in Pakistan.* New York: Palgrave Macmillan.

Malik, Jamal (1998) *Colonialization of Islam: Dissolution of Traditional Institutions in Pakistan.* New Delhi: Munshiram Manoharlal.

Malley, Robert (1996) *The Call from Algeria: Third Worldism, Revolution and the Turn to Islam.* Berkeley, CA: University of California Press.

Mardin, Serif (2000) *The Genesis of Young Ottoman Thought: A Study in the Modernization of Turkish Political Ideas.* Syracuse, NY: Syracuse University Press.

—— (2002) *Religion, Society and Modernity in Turkey.* Syracuse, NY: Syracuse University Press.

Maréchal, Brigette *et al.* (eds) (2003) *Muslims in the Enlarged Europe.* Leiden: E. J. Brill.

Marr, Phebe (1985) *The Modern History of Iraq.* Boulder, CO: Westview Press.

Martin, Vanessa (2000) *Creating an Islamic State: Khomeini and the Making of a New Iran.* London: I. B. Tauris.

Martinez, Luis (2000) *The Algerian Civil War, 1990–1998.* New York: Columbia University Press.

Massad, Joseph A. (2001) *Colonial Effects: The Making of National Identity in Jordan.* New York: Columbia University Press.

Matinuddin, Kamal (1999) *The Taliban Phenomenon: Afghanistan, 1994–1997.* Karachi: Oxford University Press.

Menashri, David (2001) *Post-Revolutionary Politics in Iran: Religion, Society and Power.* London: Frank Cass & Co.

Metcalf, Barbara Daly (ed.) (1984) *Moral Conduct and Authority: The Place of Adab in South Asian Islam.* Berkeley, CA: University of California Press.

Millard, Mike (2004) *Jihad in Paradise: Islam and Politics in Southeast Asia.* Armonk, NY: M. E. Sharpe.

Milton-Edwards, Beverly (1996) *Islamic Politics in Palestine.* London: Tauris Academic Studies.

Minault, Gail (1998) *Secluded Scholars: Women's Education and Muslim Social Reform in Colonial India.* Oxford: Oxford University Press.

—— (1999) *The Khilafat Movement: Religious Symbolism and Political Mobilization in India*, 2nd edn. Oxford: Oxford University Press.

Mir-Hosseini, Ziba (1999) *Islam and Gender: The Religious Debate in Contemporary Iran.* Princeton, NJ: Princeton University Press.

Mitchell, Timothy (1988) *Colonising Egypt.* Cambridge: Cambridge University Press.

—— (2002) *Rule of Experts: Egypt, Technopolitics, Modernity.* Berkeley, CA: University of California Press.

Moaddel, Mansoor (1992) *Class, Politics, and Ideology in the Iranian Revolution.* New York: Columbia University Press.

Morony, Michael G. (1984) *Iraq After the Muslim Conquest.* Princeton, NJ: Princeton University Press.

Moslem, Mehdi (2002) *Factional Politics in Post-Khomeini Iran.* Syracuse, NY: Syracuse University Press.

Mottahedeh, Roy (2000) *The Mantle of the Prophet: Religion and Politics in Iran.* Oxford: Oneworld.

Mumtaz, Khawar (1987) *Women of Pakistan: Two Steps Forward, One Back?* London: Zed Books.

Munson, Henry, Jr. (1989) *Islam and Revolution in the Middle East.* New Haven, CT: Yale University Press.

—— (1993) *Religion and Power in Morocco.* New Haven, CT: Yale University Press.

Murphy, Emma C. (1999) *Economic and Political Change in Tunisia: From Bourguiba to Ben Ali.* New York: St. Martin's Press.

Murshid, Tazeen M. (1995) *The Sacred and the Secular: Bengal Muslim Discourses, 1871–1977.* Calcutta: Oxford University Press.

Mutalib, Hussin (1990) *Islam and Ethnicity in Malay Politics.* New York: Oxford University Press.

Nabavi, Negin (2003a) *Intellectuals and the State in Iran: Politics, Discourse and the Dilemma of Authenticity.* Gainesville, FL: University Press of Florida.

—— (ed.) (2003b) *Intellectual Trends in 20th Century Iran.* Gainesville, FL: University Press of Florida.

Najem, Tom Pierre (2003) *Lebanon: The Politics of a Penetrated Society.* New York: Routledge.

Nasr, Seyyed Vali Reza (1994) *The Vanguard of the Islamic Revolution: The Jama'at-i Islami of Pakistan.* Berkeley, CA: University of California Press.

Nawid, Senzil K. (2000) *Religious Response to Social Change in Afghanistan, 1919–1929: King Aman-Allah and the Afghan Ulama.* Costa Mesa, CA: Mazda.

Niblock, Tim (2003) *Saudi Arabia.* New York: Routledge.

Nielsen, Jorgen S. (1999) *Towards a European Islam.* New York: Palgrave Macmillan.

Nivet, Anne (2001) *Chienne de Guerre: A Woman Reporter Behind the Lines of the War in Chechnya.* New York: Public Affairs/Perseus.

Norton, Augustus Richard (1987) *Amal and the Shi'a: Struggle for the Soul of Lebanon.* Austin, TX: University of Texas Press.

Norris, Harry T. (1994) *Islam in the Balkans: Religion and Society between Europe and the Arab World.* Columbia, SC: University of South Carolina Press.

Nyang, Sulayman S. (1999) *Islam in the United States of America.* Chicago, IL: ABC International. Group/Kazi.

O'Ballance, Edgar (1999) *Civil War in Lebanon, 1975–92.* New York: Palgrave Macmillan.

Olcott, Martha Brill (ed.) (1992) *Everyday Islam: Religion and Tradition in Rural Central Asia.* New York: M. E. Sharpe.

Olson, Robert W. (1998) *The Kurdish Question and Turkish-Iranian Relations: From World War I to 1998.* Costa Mesa, CA: Mazda.

—— (2001) *Turkey's Relations with Iran, Syria, Israel, and Russia, 1991–2000: The Kurdish And Islamist Questions.* Costa Mesa, CA: Mazda.

Owtram, Francis (2003) *A Modern History of Oman: Formation of the State since 1920.* London: I. B. Tauris.

Özbudun, Ergun (2000) *Contemporary Turkish Politics: Challenges to Democratic Consolidation.* Boulder, CO: Lynne Rienner.

Ozdalga, Elisabeth (ed.) (1999) *Naqshbandis in Western and Central Asia: Change and Continuity.* Richmond: Curzon.

Özdemir, Adil and Kenneth Frank (2000) *Visible Islam in Modern Turkey.* New York: Palgrave Macmillan.

Palumbo, Michael (1991) *The Palestinian Catastrophe: The 1948 Expulsion of a People from Their Homeland.* New York: Olive Branch Press.

Pampanini, Andrea H. (1997) *Cities from the Arabian Desert: The Building of Jubail and Yanbu in Saudi Arabia.* Westport, CT: Praeger.

Peacock, James L. (1978) *Purifying the Faith: The Muhammadiyah Movement in Indonesian Islam.* Menlo Park, CA: Benjamin/Cummings.

Peck, Malcolm C. (1986) *The United Arab Emirates: A Venture in Unity.* Boulder, CO: Westview Press.

—— (1996) *Historical Dictionary of the Gulf Arab States.* Lanham, MD: Scarecrow Press.

Pennell, C. R. (2003) *Morocco: From Empire to Independence.* Oxford: Oneworld.

Perry, Glenn E. (2004) *The History of Egypt.* Westport, CT: Greenwood.

Perthes, volker (1997) *The Political Economy of Syria under Asad.* London: I. B. Tauris.

Petterson, Donald (1999) *Inside Sudan: Political Islam, Conflict, and Catastrophe.* Boulder, CO: Westview Press.

Pilkington, Hilary and Galina M. Yemelianova (eds) (2002) *Islam in Post-Soviet Russia.* New York: RoutledgeCurzon.

Politkovskaya, Anna (2001) *A Dirty War: A Russian Reporter in Chechnya*. London: Harvill Press.

Pope, Hugh and Pope, Nicole (2000) *Turkey Unveiled: A History of Modern Turkey*. Woodstock, NY: Overlook Press.

Porter, Donald J. (2002) *Managing Politics and Islam in Indonesia*. New York: Routledge Curzon.

Poulton, Hugh and Taji-Farouki, Suha (eds) (1997) *Muslim Identity and the Balkan State*. New York: New York University Press.

Quandt, William B. (1998) *Between Ballots and Bullets: Algeria's Transition from Authoritarianism*. Washington, DC: The Brookings Institution.

Quinn, Charlotte A. and Quinn, Frederick (2003) *Pride, Faith, and Fear: Islam in Sub-Saharan Africa*. Oxford: Oxford University Press.

Qureshi, M. Naeem (1999) *Pan-Islam in British Indian Politics: A Study of the Khilafat Movement, 1918–1924*. Leiden: E. J. Brill.

Rahman, Tariq (1997) *Language and Politics in Pakistan*. Oxford: Oxford University Press.

—— (2002) *Language, Ideology and Power: Language-Learning among the Muslims of Pakistan and North India*. Oxford: Oxford University Press.

Rajaee, Farhang (ed.) (1993) *The Iran–Iraq War: The Politics of Aggression*. Gainesville, FL: University Press of Florida.

Ramage, Douglas E. (1995) *Politics in Indonesia: Democracy, Islam and the Ideology of Tolerance*. New York: Routledge.

Rasanayagam, Angelo (2003) *Afghanistan: A Modern History*. London: I. B. Tauris.

Rashid, Ahmed (1994) *The Resurgence of Central Asia: Islam or Nationalism?* London: Zed Books.

—— (2000) *Taliban: Militant Islam, Oil and Fundamentalism in Central Asia*. New Haven, CT: Yale University Press.

—— (2002) *Jihad: The Rise of Militant Islam in Central Asia*. New Haven, CT: Yale University Press.

Rath, Jan (ed.) (2001) *Western Europe and Its Islam*. Leiden: E. J. Brill.

Reiter, Yitzhak (1997) *Islamic Institutions in Jerusalem: Palestinian Muslim Organization under Jordanian and Israeli Rule*. Boston, MA: Kluwer Law International.

Reynolds, Jonathan T. (2001) *The Time of Politics (Zimanin Siyasa): Islam and the Politics of Legitimacy in Northern Nigeria, 1950–1966*, 2nd edn. Lanham, MD: University Press of America.

Ricklefs, M. C. (1998) *The Seen and Unseen Worlds in Java, 1726–1749: History, Literature and Islam in the Court of Pakubuwana II*. Honolulu, HI: University of Hawaii Press.

Riddell, Peter G. (2001) *Islam and the Malay-Indonesian World: Transmission and Responses*. Honolulu, HI: University of Hawaii Press.

Roberts, Hugh (2003) *The Battlefield: Algeria, 1988–2002 – Studies in a Broken Polity*. London: Verso.

Robins, Philip (2002) *A History of Jordan*. Cambridge: Cambridge University Press.

Rogan, Eugene L. (2000) *Frontiers of the State in the Late Ottoman Empire: Transjordan, 1850–1921*. Cambridge: Cambridge University Press.

Rogers, Alisdair and Vertovec, Steven (eds) (1998) *Muslim European Youth: Reproducing Religion, Ethnicity, and Culture*. Aldershot: Ashgate.

Ro'i, Yaacov (2000) *Islam in the Soviet Union: From World War II to Perestroika*. New York: Columbia University Press.

—— (ed.) (2002) *Democracy and Pluralism in the Muslim Regions of the Former USSR*. London: Frank Cass.

Roy, Asim (1983) *The Islamic Syncretistic Tradition in Bengal*. Princeton, NJ: Princeton University Press.

Roy, Olivier (1990) *Islam and Resistance in Afghanistan*, 2nd edn. Cambridge: Cambridge University Press.

—— (1995) *Afghanistan: From Holy War to Civil War*. Princeton, NJ: Princeton University Press.

Rubin, Barnett R. (2002) *The Fragmentation of Afghanistan*, 2nd edn. New Haven, CT: Yale University Press.

Rubin, Barry and Kirisci, Kemal (eds) (2001) *Turkey in World Politics: An Emerging Multiregional Power*. Boulder, CO: Lynne Rienner.

Ruedy, John (ed.) (1994) *Islamism and Secularism in North Africa*. New York and Washington, DC: St. Martin's Press/Center for Contemporary Arab Studies.

Ryan, Curtis R. (2002) *Jordan in Transition: From Hussein to Abdullah*. Boulder, CO: Lynne Rienner.

Sabbagh, Suha (ed.) (1998) *Palestinian Women of Gaza and the West Bank*.

Bloomington, IN: Indiana University Press.

Saeed, Javaid (1994) *Islam and Modernization: A Comparative Analysis of Pakistan, Egypt and Turkey*. Westport, CO: Praeger.

Sagdeev, Roald and Eisenhower, Susan (eds) (2000) *Islam and Central Asia: An Enduring Legacy or an Evolving Threat?* Washington, DC: Eisenhower Institute/The Center for Political and Strategic Studies.

Said, Edward W. (1994) *The Politics of Dispossession: The Struggle for Palestinian Self-Determination, 1969–1994*. New York: Pantheon Books.

Saikal, Amin and Maley, William (1991) *Regime Change in Afghanistan: Foreign Intervention and the Politics of Legitimacy*. Boulder, CO: Westview Press.

Salibi, Kamal (1999) *The Modern History of Jordan*. New York: St. Martin's Press.

Sanasarian, Eliz (1982) *The Women's Rights Movement in Iran: Mutiny, Appeasement, and Repression from 1900 to Khomeini*. New York: Praeger.

Satlof, Robert (1994) *From Abdullah to Hussein: Jordan in Transition*. New York: Oxford University Press.

Savory, Roger M. (1980) *Iran under the Safavids*. Cambridge: Cambridge University Press.

Sayari, Sabri and Esmer, Yilmaz (eds) (2002) *Politics, Parties, and Elections in Turkey*. Boulder, CO: Lynne Rienner.

Sayigh, Yezid (1999) *Armed Struggle and the Search for State: The Palestinian National Movement, 1949–1993*. Oxford: Oxford University Press.

Schirazi, Asghar (1997) *The Constitution of Iran: Politics and the State in the Islamic Republic*, trans. John O'Kane. London: I. B. Tauris.

Seale, Patrick (1987) *The Struggle for Syria: A Study of Post-War Arab Politics, 1945–1958*. New Haven, CO: Yale University Press.

Schimmel, Annemarie (1980) *Islam in the Indian Subcontinent*. Leiden: E. J. Brill.

Schulz, Helena Lindholm (1999) *The Reconstruction of Palestinian Nationalism: Between Revolution and Statehood*. Manchester: Manchester University Press.

Shahin, Emad Eldin (1998) *Political Ascent: Contemporary Islamic Movements in North Africa*. Boulder, CO: Westview Press.

Shankland, David (2003) *The Alevis in Turkey: The Emergence of a Secular Islamic Tradition*. London: Curzon.

Sharoni, Simona (1995) *Gender and the Israeli-Palestinian Conflict: The Politics of Women's Resistance*. Syracuse, NY: Syracuse University Press.

Shatzmiller, Maya (ed.) (2002) *Islam and Bosnia: Conflict Resolution and Foreign Policy in Multi-Ethnic States*. Montreal: McGill-Queen's University Press.

Sidahmed, Abdel Salam (1996) *Politics and Islam in Contemporary Sudan*. New York: St. Martin's Press.

Siegel, James T. (2000) *The Rope of God*. Ann Arbor, MI: University of Michigan Press.

Silverfarb, Daniel (1997) *Britain's Informal Empire in the Middle East: A Case Study of Iraq, 1929–1941*. Oxford: Oxford University Press.

Simon, Reeva S. (1996) *Iraq Between the Two World Wars: The Creation and Implementation of a Nationalist Ideology*. New York: Columbia University Press.

Sisson, Richard and Rose, Leo E. (1990) *War and Secession: Pakistan, India, and the Creation of Bangladesh*. Berkeley, CA: University of California Press.

Skaine, Rosemarie (2001) *The Women of Afghanistan under the Taliban*. London: McFarland & Co.

Smith, Jane I. (1999) *Islam in America*. New York: Columbia University Press.

Smith, Jane I. and Haddad, Yvonne Y. (eds) (1994) *Muslim Communities in North America*. Albany, NY: State University of New York Press.

Sonbol, Amira Al-Azhary (2000) *The New Mamluks: Egyptian Society and Modern Feudalism*. Syracuse, NY: Syracuse University Press.

Starrett, Gregory (1998) *Putting Islam to Work: Education, Politics, and Religious Transformation in Egypt*. Berkeley, CA: University of California Press.

Stone, Martin (1998) *The Agony of Algeria*. New York: Columbia University Press.

Sukma, Rizal (2003) *Islam in Indonesian Foreign Policy*. New York: Routledge-Curzon.

Sullivan, Denis J. and Abed-Kotob, Sana (1999) *Islam in Contemporary Egypt: Civil Society vs. the State*. Boulder, CO: Lynne Rienner.

781

Tabari, Azar and Yeganeh, Nahid (1982) *In the Shadow of Islam: The Women's Movement in Iran*. London: Zen Press.

Talbott, John E. (1980) *The War without a Name: France in Algeria, 1954–1962*. New York: Alfred A. Knopf.

Tapper, Richard (ed.) (1994) *Islam in Modern Turkey: Religion, Politics, and Literature in a Secular State*. New York: Palgrave Macmillan.

Tauber, Eliezer (1995) *The Formation of Modern Syria and Iraq*. London: Frank Cass & Co.

Tavakoli-Targhi, Mohamad (2001) *Refashioning Iran: Orientalism, Occidentalism and Historiography*. New York: Palgrave Macmillan.

Tayob, Abdulkader I. (1999) *Islam in South Africa: Mosques, Imams, and Sermons*. Gainesville, FL: University Press of Florida.

Toprak, Binnaz (1981) *Islam and Political Development in Turkey*. Leiden: E. J. Brill.

Trimingham, J. S. (1959) *Islam in West Africa*. Oxford: Clarendon Press.

—— (1965) *Islam in Ethiopia*. London: Frank Cass & Co.

Troll, Christian W (ed.) (2003) *Muslim Shrines in India*. Oxford: Oxford University Press.

Uwaysi, Abd al-Fattah Muhammad (1998) *The Muslim Brothers and the Palestine Question, 1928–1947*. London: Tauris Academic Studies.

Van Dam, Nikolaos (1996) *The Struggle for Power in Syria: Politics and Society under Asad and the Ba'th Party*. London: I. B. Tauris.

Van Den Bos, Matthijs (2002) *Mystic Regimes: Sufism and the State in Iran, from the late Qajar Era to the Islamic Republic*. Leiden: E. J. Brill.

Van Dijk, Cornelius (1981) *Rebellion under the Banner of Islam: The Darul Islam in Indonesia*. The Hague: Martinus Nijhoff.

Vassiliev, Alexei (2000) *The History of Saudi Arabia*. New York: New York University Press.

Vertovec, Steven and Peach, Ceri (eds) (1997) *Islam in Europe: The Politics of Religion and Community*. London: Palgrave Macmillan.

Villalón, Leonardo A. (1995) *Islamic Society and State Power in Senegal: Disciples and Citizens in Fatick*. Cambridge: Cambridge University Press.

voll, John O (ed.) (1991) *Sudan: State and Society in Crisis*. Bloomington, IN: Indiana University Press.

volpi, Frederic (2003) *Islam and Democracy: The Failure of Dialogue in Algeria, 1988–2001*. London: Pluto Press.

Von Der Mehden, Fred R. (1993) *Two Worlds of Islam: Interaction Between Southeast Asia and the Middle East*. Gainesville, FL: University Press of Florida.

Wedeen, Lisa (1999) *Ambiguities of Domination: Politics, Rhetoric, and Symbols in Contemporary Syria*. Chicago, IL: University of Chicago Press.

Westerlund, David and Rosander, Eva (eds) (1997) *African Islam and Islam in Africa: Encounters Between Sufis and Islamists*. Athens, OH: Ohio University Press.

White, Jenny B. (2003) *Islamist Mobilization in Turkey: A Study in Vernacular Politics*. Seattle, WA: University of Washington Press.

Wickham, Carrie Rosefsky (2002) *Mobilizing Islam: Religion, Activism, and Political Change in Egypt*. New York: Columbia University Press.

Wiktorowicz, Quintan (2001) *The Management of Islamic Activism: Salafis, the Muslim Brotherhood and State Power in Jordan*. Albany, NY: State University of New York Press.

Wilkinson, John Craven (1987) *The Imamate Tradition of Oman*. Cambridge: Cambridge University Press.

Willis, Michael (1999) *The Islamist Challenge in Algeria: A Political History*. New York: New York University Press.

Wing, Adrien K. (1994) *Democracy, Constitutionalism and the Future of Palestine*. Jerusalem: Palestinian Academic Society for the Study of International Affairs.

Wirsing, Robert G. (1994) *India, Pakistan, and the Kashmir Dispute: On Regional Conflict and Its Resolution*. New York: St. Martin's Press.

Wolpert, Stanley A. (1984) *Jinnah of Pakistan*. New York: Oxford University Press.

—— (1993) *Zulfi Bhutto of Pakistan: His Life and Times*. New York: Oxford University Press.

—— (2000) *A New History of India*, 6th edn. New York: Oxford University Press.

Woodward, Mark R (ed.) (1996) *Toward a New Paradigm: Recent Developments in Indonesian Islamic Thought*. Tempe, AZ: Arizona State University Program for Southeast Asian Studies.

Wright, Robin (2001) *The Last Great Revolution: Turmoil and Transformation in Iran*. New York: Vintage Books.

Al-Yassini, Ayman (1985) *Religion and State in the Kingdom of Saudi Arabia*. Boulder, CO: Westview Press.

Yavuz, M. Hakan (2003) *Islamic Political Identity in Turkey*. Oxford: Oxford University Press.

Zaheer, Hasan (1994) *The Separation of East Pakistan: The Rise and Realization of Bengali Muslim Nationalism*. Karachi: Oxford University Press.

Ziring, Lawrence (1996) *Bangladesh: From Mujib to Ershad. An Interpretive Study*. Oxford: Oxford University Press.

—— (1998) *Pakistan in the Twentieth Century: A Political History*. Karachi: Oxford University Press.

—— (2003) *Pakistan: At the Crosscurrent of History*. Oxford: Oneworld.

Zisser, Eyal (2001) *Asad's Legacy: Syria in Transition*. New York: New York University Press.

Zoubir, Yahia (ed.) (1999) *North Africa in Transition: State, Society, and Economic Transformation in the 1990s*. Gainesville, FL: University Press of Florida.

Zürcher, Erik (1997) *Turkey: A Modern History*. London: I. B. Tauris.

XI Culture, economics and politics

Abaza, Mona (2002) *Debates on Islam and Knowledge in Malaysia and Egypt: Shifting Worlds*. London: Routledge Curzon.

Abootalebi, Ali Reza (2000) *Islam and Democracy: State-Society Relations in Developing Countries, 1980–1994*. London: Garland.

Abou El Fadl, Khaled (2001) *And God Knows the Soldiers: The Authoritative and Authoritarian in Islamic Discourses*. Lanham, MD: University Press of America.

Abou El Fadl, Khaled *et al.* (2002) *The Place of Tolerance in Islam*. Boston, MA: Beacon Press.

Abou El Fadl, Khaled *et al.* (2004) *Islam and the Challenge of Democracy*. Princeton, NJ: Princeton University Press (A *Boston Review* Book).

Abu-Lughod, Lila (ed.) (1998) *Remaking Women: Feminism and Modernity in the Middle East*. Princeton, NJ: Princeton University Press.

Abu-Nimer, Mohammad (2003) *Nonviolence and Peace Building in Islam*. Gainesville, FL: University Press of Florida.

Afkhami, Mahnaz (ed.) (1995) *Faith and Freedom: Women's Human Rights in the Muslim World*. Syracuse, NY: Syracuse University Press.

Afkhami, Mahnaz and Friedl, Erika (eds) (1997) *Muslim Women and the Politics of Participation: Implementing the Beijing Platform*. Syracuse, NY: Syracuse University Press.

Afsaruddin, Asma (ed.) (2000) *Hermeneutics and Honor: Negotiating Female 'Public' Space in Islamiclate Societies*. Cambridge, MA: Harvard University Press.

Ahmad, Hisham H. (1994) *Hamas: From Religious Salvation to Political Transformation*. Jerusalem: Palestinian Academic Society for the Study of International Affairs.

Ahmed, Akbar S. (1992) *Postmodernism and Islam: Predicament and Promise*. New York: Routledge.

—— (1997) *Jinnah, Pakistan and Islamic Identity: The Search for Saladin*. London: Routledge.

—— (2003) *Islam under Siege: Living Dangerously in a Post-Honour World*. London: Polity Press.

Ahmed, Leila (1993) *Women and Gender in Islam: Historical Roots of a Modern Debate*. New Haven, CT: Yale University Press.

Ajami, Fouad (1992) *The Arab Predicament: Arab Political Thought and Practice since 1967*. Cambridge: Cambridge University Press.

Akbar, M. J. (2003) *The Shade of Swords: Jihad and the Conflict Between Islam and Christianity*, 2nd edn. New York: Routledge.

Akbarzadeh, Shahram and Saeed, Abdullah (eds) (2003) *Islam and Political Legitimacy*. London: Routledge Curzon.

Al-Ali, Najde (2000) *Secularism, Gender, and the State in the Middle East: The Egyptian Women's Movement*. Cambridge: Cambridge University Press.

Al-Azmeh, Aziz (1986) *Arabic Thought and Islamic Societies*. London: Routledge & Kegan Paul.

—— (1997) *Islams and Modernities*, 2nd edn. London: Verso.

Ali, Tariq (2002) *Clash of Fundamentalisms: Crusades, Jihads, and Modernity*. London: Verso.

Allain, Jean (2004) *International Law in the Middle East: Closer to Power than Justice.* Aldershot: Ashgate.

Al-Sayyad, Nezar and Castells, Manuel (eds) (2002) *Muslim Europe or Euro-Islam: Politics, Culture, and Citizenship in the Age of Globalization.* Lanham, MD: Lexington Books.

Al-Sulami, Mishal (2004) *The West and Islam: Western Liberal Democracy versus the System of Shura.* London: RoutledgeCurzon.

Ansari, Ali M. (2000) *Iran, Islam and Democracy: The Politics of Managing Change.* London: Royal Institute of International Affairs.

Antoun, Richard (1989) *Muslim Preacher in the Modern World: A Jordanian Case Study in Comparative Perspective.* Princeton, NJ: Princeton University Press.

Aruri, Naseer H. (1995) *The Obstruction of Peace: The United States, Israel, and the Palestinians.* Monroe, ME: Common Courage Press.

Asad, Talal (1993) *Genealogies of Religion: Discipline and Reasons of Power in Christianity and Islam.* Baltimore, MD: Johns Hopkins University Press.

—— (2003) *Formations of the Secular: Christianity, Islam, Modernity.* Stanford, CA: Stanford University Press.

Ashrawi, Hanan (1996) *This Side of Peace.* New York: Simon & Schuster.

Ask, K. and Tjomsland, Marit (eds) (1998) *Women and Islamization: Contemporary Dimensions of Discourse on Gender Relations.* Oxford: Berg.

Aswad, Barbara C. and Bilge, Barbara (eds) (1996) *Family and Gender among American Muslims: Issues Facing Middle Eastern Immigrants and their Descendants.* Philadelphia, PA: Temple University Press.

El-Awaisi, Abd al-Fattah Muhammad (1998) *The Muslim Brothers and the Palestine Question, 1928–1947.* London: Tauris Academic Studies.

Ayalon, David (1988) *Outsiders in the Land of Islam: Mamluks, Mongols, and Eunichs.* Aldershot: Ashgate/Variorum.

Ayoub, Mohammed (1981) *The Politics of Islamic Reassertion.* London: Croom Helm.

Ayubi, Nazih N. (1991) *Political Islam: Religion and Politics in the Arab World.* London: Routledge.

Azumah, John (2001) *The Legacy of Arab-Islam in Africa: A Quest for Inter-religious Dialogue.* Oxford: Oneworld.

Baaklini, Abdo, Denoeux, Guilain and Springborg, Robert (1999) *Legislative Politics in the Arab World: The Resurgence of Democratic Institutions.* Boulder, CO: Lynne Rienner.

Bamyeh, Mohammed (1999) *The Social Origins of Islam.* Minneapolis, MN: University of Minnesota Press.

Bannerman, Patrick J. (1988) *Islam in Perspective: A Guide to Islamic Society, Politics, and Law.* New York: Routledge & Kegan Paul.

Barakat, Halim (1993) *The Arab World: Society, Culture and State.* Berkeley, CA: University of California Press.

Barazangi, Nimat Hafez, Raquibuz Zaman, M. and Afzal, Omar (eds) (1996) *Islamic Identity and the Struggle for Justice.* Gainesville, FL: University Press of Florida.

Barnett, Michael N. (1992) *Confronting the Costs of War: Military Power, State, and Society in Egypt and Israel.* Princeton, NJ: Princeton University Press.

—— (1998) *Dialogues in Arab Politics: Negotiations in Regional Order*, 2nd edn. New York: Columbia University Press.

Beck, Lois Grant and Keddie, Nikki (eds) (1978) *Women in the Muslim World.* Cambridge, MA: Harvard University Press.

Beeman, William O. (1986) *Language, Status, and Power in Iran.* Bloomington, IN: Indiana University Press.

Beinin, Joel (2001) *Workers and Peasants in the Modern Middle East.* Cambridge: Cambridge University Press.

Beinin, Joel and Stork, Joe (eds) (1997) *Political Islam: Essays from Middle East Report.* Berkeley, CA: University of California Press.

Bennis, Phyllis, *et al.* (eds) (1998) *Beyond the Storm: A Gulf Crisis Reader.* Northampton, MA: Interlink.

Bill, James A. (1988) *The Eagle and the Lion: The Tragedy of American–Iranian Relations.* New Haven, CT: Yale University Press.

Bin Sayeed, Khalid (1995) *Western Dominance and Political Islam.* Albany, NY: State University of New York Press.

Binder, Leonard (1988) *Islamic Liberalism: A Critique of Development Ideologies.* Chicago, IL: University of Chicago Press.

—— (ed.) (1999) *Ethnic Conflict and International Politics in the Middle East*. Gainesville, FL: University Press of Florida.

Blank, Jonah (2001) *Mullahs on the Mainframe: Islam and Modernity among the Daudi Bohras*. Chicago, IL: University of Chicago Press.

Bodman, Herbert and Tohidi, Nayereh (eds) (1998) *Women in Muslim Societies: Diversity within Unity*. Boulder, CO: Lynne Rienner.

Boroujerdi, Mehrzad (1996) *Iranian Intellectuals and the West: The Tormented Triumph of Nativism*. Syracuse, NY: Syracuse University Press.

Bowen, Donna Lee and Early, Evelyn A. (eds) (2002) *Everyday Life in the Muslim Middle East*, 2nd edn. Bloomington, IN: Indiana University Press.

Brand, Laurie A. (1998) *Women, the State and Political Liberalization: Middle Eastern and North African Experiences*. New York: Columbia University Press.

Brann, Ross (ed.) (1997) *Languages of Power in Islamic Spain*. Bethesda, MD: CDL Press.

Brooks, Geraldine (1996) *Nine Parts of Desire: The Hidden World of Islamic Women*. New York: Anchor Books.

Brown, L. Carl (1984) *International Politics and the Middle East: Old Rules, Dangerous Game*. Princeton, NJ: Princeton University Press.

—— (2000) *Religion and State: The Muslim Approach to Politics*. New York: Columbia University Press.

—— (2001) *Diplomacy in the Middle East: The International Relations of Regional and Outside Powers*. New York: Palgrave.

Brown, Nathan (1997) *The Rule of Law in the Arab World*. Cambridge: Cambridge University Press.

Brynen, Rex (1990) *Sanctuary and Survival: The PLO in Lebanon*. Boulder, CO: Westview Press.

Brynen, Rex, Korany, Bahgat and Noble, Paul (eds) (1995–8) *Political Liberalization and Democratization in the Arab World*, 2 vols. Boulder, CO: Lynne Rienner.

Bukhari, Zahid J. *et al.* (eds) (2004) *Muslims' Place in the American Public Square*. Lanham, MD: AltaMira Press.

Bulliet, Richard W. (1995) *Islam: The View from the Edge*. New York: Columbia University Press.

Bunt, Gary (2000) *Virtually Islamic: Computer-Mediated Communication and Cyber-Islamic Environments*. Cardiff: University of Wales Press.

Burckhardt, Titus (1999) *Fez, City of Islam*. London: I. B. Tauris.

Burke, Edmund and Lapidus. Ira M. (eds) (1988) *Islam, Politics, and Social Movements*. Berkeley, CA: University of California Press.

Butterworth, Charles E. and Zartman, I. William (eds) (2001) *Between the State and Islam*. Cambridge: Cambridge University Press.

Charnay, Jean-Paul (1981) *Islamic Culture and Socio-Economic Change*. Leiden: E. J. Brill.

Chaudhry, Kiren Aziz (1997) *The Price of Wealth: Economies and Institutions in the Middle East*. Ithaca, NY: Cornell University Press.

Chelkowski, Peter and Dabashi, Hamid (1999) *Staging a Revolution: The Art of Persuasion in the Islamic Republic of Iran*. New York: New York University Press.

Cheshin, Amir S., Hutman, Bill and Melamed, Avi (1999) *Separate and Unequal: The Inside Story of Israeli Rule in East Jerusalem*. Cambridge, MA: Harvard University Press.

Chomsky, Noam (1999) *The Fateful Triangle: The United States, Israel and the Palestinians*, 2nd edn. Boston, MA: South End Press.

—— (2003) *Middle East Illusions*. Lanham, MD: Rowman & Littlefield.

Choueiri, Youssef M. (2000) *Arab Nationalism: A History*. Oxford: Blackwell.

Citino, Nathan J. (2002) *From Arab Nationalism to OPEC: Eisenhower, King Sa'ud, and the Making of U.S.– Saudi Relations*. Bloomington, IN: Indiana University Press.

Cleveland, William L. (1985) *Islam against the West: Shakib Arslan and the Campaign for Islamic Nationalism*. London: Saqi Books.

Cobban, Helena (1984) *The Palestinian Liberation Organization: People, Power and Politics*. Cambridge: Cambridge University Press.

Cohn-Sherbok, Dan and El-Alami, Dawoud (2001) *The Palestine–Israeli Conflict: A Beginner's Guide*. Oxford: Oneworld.

Cole, Juan R. I (ed.) (1992) *Comparing Muslim Societies: Knowledge and the*

State in a World Civilization. Ann Arbor, MI: University of Michigan Press.

Cooke, Miriam (2000) *Women Claim Islam: Creating Islamic Feminism through Literature.* New York: Routledge.

Cotran, Eugene, Mallat, Chibli and Stott, David (eds) (1996) *The Arab–Israeli Accords: Legal Perspectives.* Boston, MA: Kluwer Law International.

Crow, Ralph E., Grant, Philip and Ibrahim, Saad E. (eds) (1990) *Arab Nonviolent Political Struggle in the Middle East.* Boulder, CO: Lynne Rienner.

Curtis, Edward E. IV (2002) *Islam in Black America: Identity, Liberation, and Difference in African-American Islamic Thought.* Albany, NY: State University of New York Press.

Curtis, Michael (ed.) (1981) *Religion and Politics in the Middle East.* Boulder, CO: Westview Press.

Daniel, Norman (1966) *Islam, Europe, and Empire.* Edinburgh: Edinburgh University Press.

—— (1993) *Islam and the West: The Making of an Image.* Oxford: Oneworld.

Davies, Merryl Wyn (1988) *Knowing One Another: Shaping an Islamic Anthropology.* London: Mansell.

Davies, Merryl Wyn and Pasha, Adnan Khalil (eds) (1989) *Beyond Frontiers: Islam and Contemporary Needs.* London: Continuum.

Davis, Joyce M. (1997) *Between Jihad and Salaam: Profiles in Islam.* New York: Palgrave Macmillan.

—— (2003) *Martyrs: Innocence, Vengeance and Despair in the Middle East.* New York: Palgrave Macmillan.

Dawisha, Adeed (2003) *Arab Nationalism in the Twentieth Century: From Triumph to Despair.* Princeton, NJ: Princeton University Press.

Decasa, George C. (1999) *The Qur'anic Concept of Umma and its Function in Philippine Muslim Society.* Rome: Gregorian University Press.

Dekmejian, R. Hrair (1995) *Islam in Revolution: Fundamentalism in the Arab World,* 2nd edn. Syracuse, NY: Syracuse University Press.

Diamond, Larry, Plattner, Marc F. and Brumberg, Daniel (eds) (2003) *Islam and Democracy in the Middle East.* Baltimore, MD: Johns Hopkins University Press.

Dien, Mawil Izzi (2000) *The Environmental Dimensions of Islam.* Cambridge: Lutterworth Press.

Djait, Hichem (1985) *Europe and Islam.* Berkeley, CA: University of California Press.

Dodge, Toby and Higgott, Richard (eds) (2002) *Globalization and the Middle East: Islam, Economy, Society and Politics.* London: Royal Institute of International Affiars (Chatham House).

Donaldson, William J. (2000) *Sharecropping in the Yemen: A Study in Islamic Theory, Custom and Pragmatism.* Leiden: E. J. Brill.

Donnan, Hastings (ed.) (2002) *Interpreting Islam,* abridged edn. London: Sage.

Doumato, Eleanor A. and Pripstein Posusney, Marsha (eds) (2003) *Women and Globalization in the Arab Middle East: Gender, Economy and Society.* Boulder, CO: Lynne Rienner.

Dumper, Michael (2002) *The Politics of Sacred Space: The Old City of Jerusalem in the Middle East Conflict.* Boulder, CO: Lynne Rienner.

Dwyer, Kevin (1991) *Arab Voices: The Human Rights Debate in the Middle East.* Berkeley, CA: University of California Press.

Eickelman, Dale F. and Anderson, Jon W. (eds) (2003) *New Media in the Muslim World: The Emerging Public Sphere,* 2nd edn. Bloomington, IN: Indiana University Press.

Eickelman, Dale F. and Piscatori, James (1996) *Muslim Politics.* Princeton, NJ: Princeton University Press.

El Guindi, Fadwa (1999) *Veil: Modesty, Privacy, and Resistance.* New York: Berg.

El Saadawi, Nawal (1980) *The Hidden Face of Eve: Women in the Arab World.* Boston, MA: Beacon Press.

Enayat, Hamid (1982) *Modern Islamic Political Thought.* Austin, TX: University of Texas Press.

Erickson, John (1998) *Islam and Postcolonial Narrative.* Cambridge: Cambridge University Press.

Esack, Farid (1997) *Qur'an, Liberation, and Pluralism.* Oxford: Oneworld.

Esfandiari, Haleh and Udovitch, A. L. (eds) (1990) *The Economic Dimensions of Middle Eastern History: Essays in Honor of Charles Issawi.* Princeton, NJ: Darwin Press.

Esposito, John L. (ed.) (1980) *Islam and Development: Religion and Sociopolitical*

Change. Syracuse, NY: Syracuse University Press.

—— (1984) *Islam and Politics*. Syracuse, NY: Syracuse University Press.

—— (ed.) (1997) *Political Islam: Revolution, Radicalism or Reform?* Boulder, CO: Lynne Rienner.

—— (1999) *The Islamic Threat: Myth or Reality?* 3rd edn. New York: Oxford University Press.

—— (2002) *Unholy War: Terror in the Name of Islam*. New York: Oxford University Press.

Esposito, John L. and Burgat, François (eds) (2003) *Modernizing Islam: Religion in the Public Sphere in Europe and the Middle East*. New Brunswick, NJ: Rutgers University Press.

Esposito, John L. and voll, John O. (eds) (1996) *Islam and Democracy*. Oxford: Oxford University Press.

—— (2001) *Makers of Contemporary Islam*. New York: Oxford University Press.

Everest, Larry (2003) *Oil, Power and Empire: Iraq and the U.S. Global Agenda*. Monroe, ME: Common Courage Press.

Ewing, Katherine Pratt (1997) *Arguing Sainthood: Modernity, Psychoanalysis and Islam*. Durham, NC: Duke University Press.

Falk, Richard (2003) *Unlocking the Middle East: The Writings of Richard Falk*, ed. Jean Allain. Northampton, MA: Olive Branch Press/Interlink.

Feldman, Noah (2003) *After Jihad: America and the Struggle for Islamic Democracy*. New York: Farrar, Straus, Giroux.

Fernea, Elizabeth Warnock (1969) *Guests of the Sheik: An Ethnography of an Iraqi Village*, reissue edn. New York: Anchor.

—— (1988) *A Street in Marrakech*. Prospect Heights, IL: Waveland Press.

—— (ed.) (1995) *Children in the Muslim Middle East*. Austin, TX: University of Texas Press.

—— (1998) *In Search of Islamic Feminism: One Woman's Global Journey*. New York: Bantam Books.

Fernea, Elizabeth Warnock and Bezirgan, Basima Qattan (eds) (1978) *Middle Eastern Muslim Women Speak*. Austin, TX: University of Texas Press.

Finkelstein, Norman G. (1995) *Image and Reality of the Israel-Palestine Conflict*. London: Verso.

Fischer, Michael M. J. and Abedi, Mehdi (1990) *Debating Muslims: Cultural Dialogues in Postmodernity and Tradition*. Madison, WI: University of Wisconsin Press.

Firestone, Reuven (2002) *Jihad: The Origin of Holy War in Islam*. Oxford: Oxford University Press.

Fleischmann, Ellen L. (2003) *The Nation and Its 'New' Women: The Palestinian Women's Movement, 1920–1948*. Berkeley, CA: University of California Press.

Fluehr-Lobban, Carolyn (2004) *Islamic Societies in Practice*, 2nd edn. Gainesville, FL: University Press of Florida.

Friedland, Roger and Richard Hecht (2000) *To Rule Jerusalem*. Berkeley, CA: University of California Press.

Friedmann, Yohanan (2001) *Shaykh Ahmad Sirhindi: An Outline of His Thought and Study of His Image in the Eyes of Posterity*, first published 1971. Delhi: Oxford University Press.

—— (2003) *Tolerance and Coercion in Islam: Interfaith Relations in the Muslim Tradition*. Cambridge: Cambridge University Press.

Fuller, Graham (2003) *The Future of Political Islam*. New York: Palgrave Macmillan.

Fuller, Graham E. and Lesser, Ian O. (1995) *The Geopolitics of Islam and the West*. Boulder, CO: Westview Press.

Garnham, David and Tessler, Mark (eds) (1995) *Democracy, War and Peace in the Middle East*. Bloomington, IN: Indiana University Press.

Gasiorowski, Mark (1991) *U.S. Foreign Policy and the Shah: Building a Client State in Iran*. Ithaca, NY: Cornell University Press.

Gellner, Ernest (1981) *Muslim Society*. Cambridge: Cambridge University Press.

Gendzier, Irene L. (1998) *Notes from the Minefield: Unites States Intervention in Lebanon and the Middle East, 1945–1958*. Boulder, CO: Westview Press.

Gerber, Haim (1987) *The Social Origins of the Modern Middle East*. Boulder, CO: Lynne Rienner.

—— (1988) *Islam, Guerilla War, and Revolution*. Boulder, CO: Lynne Rienner.

Gerges, Fawaz A. (1999) *America and Political Islam: Clash of Cultures or Clash of Interests?* Cambridge: Cambridge University Press.

Gerner, Deborah J. and Schwedler, Jillian (eds) (2003) *Understanding the Con-*

temporary Middle East, 2nd edn. Boulder, CO: Lynne Rienner.

Ghadbian, Najib (1997) *Democratization and the Islamist Challenge in the Arab World*. Boulder, CO: Westview Press.

Ghanem, As'ad (2001) *The Palestinian Regime: A 'Partial Democracy'*. Brighton: Sussex Academic Press.

Ghoussoub, Mai and Sinclair-Webb, Emma (2000) *Imagined Masculinities: Male Identity and Culture in the Modern Middle East*. London: Saqi Books.

Giacaman, George *et al.* (eds) (1998) *After Oslo: New Realities, Old Problems*. London: Pluto Press.

Gibb, H. A. R. (1982) *Studies on the Civilization of Islam*. Princeton, NJ: Princeton University Press.

Gibb, H. A. R. and Harold Bowe (eds) (1957) *Islamic Society and the West: A Study of the Impact of Western Civilization on Moslem Culture in the Near East*. Oxford: Oxford University Press.

Gillette, Maris Boyd (2000) *Between Mecca and Beijing: Modernization and Consumption Among Urban Chinese Muslims*. Stanford, CA: Stanford University Press.

Goodwin, Jan (1995) *Price of Honor: Muslim Women Lift the Veil of Silence on the Islamic World*. New York: Plume/Penguin.

Gorny, Josef (1987) *Zionism and the Arabs, 1882–1948: A Study in Ideology*. New York: Oxford University Press.

Griffin, Michael (2003) *Reaping the Whirlwind: Afghanistan, Al Qa'ida and the Holy War*. London: Pluto Press.

Guazzone, Laura (ed.) (1995) *The Islamist Dilemma: The Poltical Role of Islamist Movements in the Contemporary Arab World*. Reading: Ithaca Press.

Haddad, Yvonne Yazbeck (2002) *Muslims in the West: From Sojourners to Citizens*. New York: Oxford University Press.

Haddad, Yvonne Yazbeck and Esposito, John L. (eds) (1997) *Islam, Gender, and Social Change*. New York: Oxford University Press.

—— (eds) (2000) *Muslims on the Americanization Path?* New York: Oxford University Press.

Haddad, Yvonne Yazbeck and Smith, Jane I. (eds) (2002) *Muslim Minorities in the West: Visible and Invisible*. Lanham, MD: AltaMira Press.

Haeri, Shahla (2002) *No Shame for the Sun: Lives of Professional Pakistani Women*. Syracuse, NY: Syracuse University Press.

Hafez, Kai (ed.) (2000) *Islam and the West in Mass Media: Fragmented Images in a Globalizing World*. Mount Waverly: Hampton Press.

Hafez, Kai *et al.* (eds) (2000) *The Islamic World and the West: An Introduction to Political Cultures and International Relations*. Leiden: E. J. Brill.

Hafez, Mohammed M. (2003) *Why Muslims Rebel: Repression and Resistance in the Islamic World*. Boulder, CO: Lynne Rienner.

Halliday, Fred (1996) *Islam and the Myth of Confrontation: Religion and Politics in the Middle East*. London: I. B. Tauris.

—— (2000) *Nation and Religion in the Middle East*. London: Saqi Books.

Halliday, Fred and Alavi, Hamza (eds) (1988) *State and Ideology in the Middle East and Pakistan*. New York: Monthly Review Press.

Hamdi, Mohamed Elhachmi (1999) *The Making of an Islamic Political Leader: Conversations with Hasan al-Turabi*. Boulder, CO: Westview Press.

Harik, Judith Palmer (2004) *Hezbollah: The Changing Face of Terrorism*. London: I. B. Tauris.

Hasan, Mushirul (ed.) (1998) *Islam, Communities and the Nation: Muslim Identities in South Asia and Beyond*. New Delhi: Munshiram Manoharlal.

Hashmi, Sohail H (ed.) (2002) *Islamic Political Ethics: Civil Society, Pluralism and Conflict*. Princeton, NJ: Princeton University Press.

Hassan, Riaz (2002) *Faithlines: Muslim Concepts of Islam and Society*. Oxford: Oxford University Press.

Hatina, Meir (2001) *Islam and Salvation in Palestine: The Islamic Jihad Movement*. Syracuse, NY: Syracuse University Press (The Moshe Dayan Center for Middle Eastern and African Studies).

Henry, Clement M. and Springborg, Robert (2001) *Globalization and the Politics of Development in the Middle East*. Cambridge: Cambridge University Press.

Herold, Marc (2003) *Blown Away: The Myth and Reality of Precision Bombing In Afghanistan*. Monroe, ME: Common Courage Press.

Hijab, Nadia (1988) *Womanpower: The Arab Debate on Women at Work*. Cambridge: Cambridge University Press.

Hiltermann, Joost R. (1991) *Behind the Intifada: Labor and Women's Movements in the Occupied Territories*. Princeton, NJ: Princeton University Press.

Hiro, Dilip (1989) *Holy Wars: The Rise of Islamic Fundamentalism*. New York: Routledge.

—— (2002) *War without End: The Rise of Islamist Terrorism and the Global Response*. New York: Routledge.

Hoexter, Miriam, Shmuel N. Eisenstadt and Nehemia Levtzion (eds) (2002) *The Public Sphere in Muslim Societies*. Albany, NY: State University of New York Press.

Hopkins, Nicholas S. and Ibrahim, Saad Eddin (eds) (1998) *Arab Society: Class, Gender, Power and Development*, 3rd edn. Cairo: American University in Cairo Press.

Hopwood, Derek (ed.) (2000) *Arab Nation, Arab Nationalism*. New York: St. Martin's Press.

Hourani, Albert H. (1983) *Arabic Thought in the Liberal Age, 1798–1939*. Cambridge: Cambridge University Press.

Hroub, Khaled (2000) *Hamas: Political Thought and Practice*. Washington, DC: Institute for Palestine Studies.

Huband, Mark (1998) *Warriors of the Prophet: The Struggle for Islam*. Boulder, CO: Westview Press.

Hudson, Michael E. (1977) *Arab Politics: The Search for Legitimacy*. New Haven, CT: Yale University Press.

—— (1999) *Middle East Dilemma: The Politics and Economics of Arab Integration*. New York/Washington, DC: Columbia University Press/Center for Contemporary Arab Studies.

Hunter, Shireen T. (1998) *The Future of Islam and the West: Clash of Civilizations or Peaceful Coexistence?* Westport, CT: Praeger.

Ibrahim, Mahmood (1990) *Merchant Capital and Islam*. Austin, TX: University of Texas Press.

Ibrahim, Saad Eddin (1996) *Egypt, Islam, and Democracy: Twelve Critical Essays*. Cairo: American University in Cairo Press.

Insoll, Timothy (1999) *The Archaeology of Islam*. Oxford: Basil Blackwell.

Issawi, Charles (1982) *An Economic History of the Middle East and North Africa*. New York: Columbia University Press.

Jaber, Hala (1997) *Hezbollah: Born with a Vengeance*. New York: Columbia University Press.

Jankowski, James and Gershoni, Israel (eds) (1997) *Rethinking Nationalism in the Arab Middle East*. New York: Columbia University Press.

Jansen, Johannes J. G. (1996) *The Neglected Duty: The Creed of Sadat's Assassins and Islamic Resurgence in the Middle East*. New York: Macmillan.

Jawad, Haifaa A. (1998) *The Rights of Women in Islam: An Authentic Approach*. New York: St. Martin's Press.

Joseph, Suad (ed.) (2000) *Gender and Citizenship in the Middle East*. Syracuse, NY: Syracuse University Press.

Kahf, Mohja (1999) *Western Representations of the Muslim Woman: From Termagant to Odalisque*. Austin, TX: University of Texas Press.

Kaiser, Paul J. (1996) *Culture, Transnationalism, and Civil Society: Aga Khan Social Service Initiatives in Tanzania*. Westport, CT: Praeger.

Kamalipour, Yahya R. and Mowlana, Hamid (eds) (1994) *Mass Media in the Middle East: A Comprehensive Handbook*. Westport, CT: Greenwood.

Kamrava, Mehran (1998) *Democracy in the Balance: Culture and Society in the Middle East*. New York: Chatham House.

Kapchan, Deborah (1996) *Gender on the Market: Moroccan Women and the Revoicing of Tradition*. Philadelphia, PA: University of Pennsylvania Press.

Karawan, Ibrahim A. (1998) *The Islamist Impasse*. Oxford: Oxford University Press.

Kawar, Amal (1997) *Daughters of Palestine: Leading Women in the Palestinian National Movement*. Albany, NY: State University of New York Press.

Kedar, Mordechai (2003) *Asad in Search of Legitimacy: Messages and Rhetoric in the Syrian Press, 1970–2000*. Brighton: Sussex Academic Press.

Keddie, Nikki R. (1972) *Sayyid Jamal ad-Din 'al-Afghani': A Political Biography*. Berkeley, CA: University of California Press.

—— (1983) *An Islamic Response to Imperialism: Political and Religious Writings of*

Sayyid Jamal ad-Din 'al-Afghani'. Berkeley, CA: University of California Press.

Kedourie, Elie (1966) *Afghani and 'Abduh: An Essay on Religious Unbelief and Political Activism in Modern Islam*. London: Frank Cass & Co.

—— (1992) *Politics in the Middle East*. Oxford: Oxford University Press.

—— (1994) *Democracy and Arab Culture*, 2nd edn. London: Frank Cass & Co.

Kepel, Gilles (2002) *Jihad: The Trail of Political Islam*. Cambridge, MA: Harvard University Press.

Kerr, Malcolm (1966) *Islamic Reform: The Political and Legal Theories of Muhammad 'Abduh and Rashid Rida*. Berkeley, CA: University of California Press.

Khalidi, Rashid (1998) *Palestinian Identity: The Construction of Modern Consciousness*. New York: Columbia University Press.

Khalidi, Rashid *et al.* (eds) (1993) *The Origins of Arab Nationalism*. New York: Columbia University Press.

Khan, Shahnaz (2000) *Muslim Women: Crafting a North American Identity*. Gainesville, FL: University Press of Florida.

Khuri, Fuad I. (1990) *Imams and Emirs: State, Religion and Sects in Islam*. London: Saqui Books.

Kienle, Eberhard (2001) *A Grand Delusion: Democracy and Economic Reform in Egypt*. London: I. B. Tauris.

Kimmerling, Baruch (2003) *Politicide: Ariel Sharon's War Against the Palestinians*. London: Verso.

Kipper, Judith and Saunders, Harold H. (eds) (1991) *The Middle East in Global Perspective*. Boulder, CO: Westview Press.

Kramer, Martin S. (1996) *Arab Awakening and Islamic Revival: The Politics of Ideas in the Middle East*. New Brunswick, NJ: Transaction.

—— (ed.) (1997) *The Islamism Debate*. Syracuse, NY: Syracuse University Press.

Kuran, Timur (2004) *Islam and Mammon: The Economic Predicaments of Islamism*. Princeton, NJ: Princeton University Press.

Kurzman, Charles (ed.) (1998) *Liberal Islam: A Sourcebook*. Oxford: Oxford University Press.

Lambton, Ann K. S. (1981) *State and Government in Medieval Islam; An Introduction to the Study of Islamic Political Theory: The Jurists*. Oxford: Oxford University Press.

Landau, Jacob M. (1992) *The Politics of Pan-Islam: Ideology and Organization*. Oxford: Clarendon Press.

Laroui, Abdullah (1977) *The Crisis of the Arab Intellectual*. Berkeley, CA: University of California Press.

Lawrence, Bruce B. (1998) *Shattering the Myth: Islam beyond Violence*. Princeton, NJ: Princeton University Press.

Lee, Robert D. (1997) *Overcoming Tradition and Modernity: The Search for Islamic Authenticity*. Boulder, CO: Westview Press.

Lesch, Ann Mosely (1989) *Israel, Egypt, and the Palestinians: From Camp David to Intifada*. Bloomington, IN: Indiana University Press.

Lesch, Ann Mosely (1993) *Transition to Palestinian Self-Government: Practical Steps Toward Israeli- Palestinian Peace*. Bloomington, IN: Indiana University Press.

Lewis, Bernard (1993) *Islam and the West*. Oxford: Oxford University Press.

—— (2002) *The Political Language of Islam*. Oxford: Oxford University Press.

Lia, Brynjar (1998) *The Society of the Muslim Brothers in Egypt: The Rise of an Islamic Mass Movement, 1928–1942*. Reading: Ithaca Press.

Lincoln, C. Eric (1973) *The Black Muslims in America*, rev. edn. Boston, MA: Beacon Press.

Little, Douglas (2002) *American Orientalism: The United States and the Middle East since 1945*. Chapel Hill, NC: University of North Carolina Press.

Lockman, Zachary and Joel Beinin (eds) (1989) *Intifada: The Palestinian Uprising against Israeli Occupation*. Boston, MA: South End Press (A Middle East Research and Information Project/ MERIP Book).

Long, David (1979) *The Hajj Today*. Albany, NY: State University of New York Press.

Lustick, Ian (1980) *Arabs in the Jewish State: Israel's Control of a National Minority*. Austin, TX: University of Texas Press.

McCloud, Aminah Beverly (1995) *African American Islam*. London: Routledge.

Mack, Beverly B. and Jean Boyd (2000) *Nana Asma'u, Scholar and Scribe*. Bloomington, IN: Indiana University Press.

Majid, Anouar (2000) *Unveiling Traditions: Postcolonial Islam in a Polycentric World.* Durham, NC: Duke University Press.

Makdisi, George (1981) *The Rise of Colleges: Institutions of Learning in Islam and the West.* Edinburgh: Edinburgh University Press.

Malik, Hafeez (ed.) (1971) *Iqbal: Poet-philosopher of Pakistan.* New York: Columbia University Press.

Mannan, M. A. (1987) *Islamic Economics: Theory and Practice.* Boulder, CO: Westview Press.

Marlow, Louise (1997) *Hierarchy and Egalitarianism in Islamic Thought.* Cambridge: Cambridge University Press.

Martin, Richard C. (1982) *Islam, a Cultural Perspective.* Englewood Cliffs, NJ: Prentice-Hall.

Mayer, Ann Elizabeth (1999) *Islam and Human Rights: Tradition and Politics*, 3rd edn. Boulder, CO: Westview Press.

Meddeb, Abdelwahab (2003) *The Malady of Islam.* New York: Basic Books.

Mernissi, Fatima (1987) *Beyond the Veil: Male–Female Dynamics in Modern Muslim Society*, rev. edn. Bloomington, IN: Indiana University Press.

—— (1989) *Doing Daily Battle: Interviews with Moroccan Women.* New Brunswick, NJ: Rutgers University Press.

—— (1992) *The Veil and the Male Elite: A Feminist Interpretation of Women's Rights in Islam.* New York: Perseus Books.

—— (1993) *The Forgotten Queens of Islam.* Minneapolis, MN: University of Minnesota Press.

—— (1996) *Women's Rebellion and Islamic Memory.* London: Zed Books.

—— (2002) *Islam and Democracy: Fear of the Modern World*, 2nd edn. Cambridge, MA: Perseus.

Messaoudi, Khalida (interviews with Elisabeth Schemla) (1998) *Unbowed: An Algerian Woman Confronts Islamic Fundamentalism.* Philadelphia, PA: University of Pennsylvania Press.

Messick, Brinkley (1993) *The Calligraphic State: Textual Domination and History in a Muslim Society.* Berkeley, CA: University of California Press.

Metcalf, Barbara Daly (ed.) (1996) *Making Muslim Space in North America and Europe.* Berkeley, CA: University of California Press.

Minns, Amina and Hijab, Nadia (1991) *Citizens Apart: A Portrait of Palestinians in Israel.* London: I. B. Tauris.

Mirsepassi, Ali (2000) *Intellectual Discourse and the Politics of Modernization: Negotiating Modernity in Iran.* Cambridge: Cambridge University Press.

Mishal, Shaul and Sela, Avraham (2000) *The Palestinian Hamas: Vision, Violence, and Coexistence.* New York: Columbia University Press.

Mitchell, Richard P. (1969) *The Society of the Muslim Brothers.* Oxford: Oxford University Press.

Moaddel, Mansoor and Talattof, Kamran (eds) (2002) *Modernist and Fundamentalist Debates in Islam: A Reader.* New York: Palgrave Macmillan.

Moghadam, Valentine M. (ed.) (1996) *Gender and National Identity: Women and Politics in Muslim Society.* London: Zed Press.

—— (2003) *Modernizing Women: Gender and Social Change in the Middle East*, 2nd edn. Boulder, CO: Lynne Rienner.

Moghissi, Haideh (1999) *Feminism and Islamic Fundamentalism: The Limits of Postmodern Analysis.* London: Zed Books.

Mohammadi, Ali (ed.) (2002) *Islam Encountering Globalization.* London: RoutledgeCurzon.

Monk, Daniel Bertrand (2002) *An Aesthetic Occupation: The Immediacy of Architecture and the Palestine Conflict.* Durham, NC: Duke University Press.

Monshipouri, Mahmood (1998) *Islamism, Secularism, and Human Rights in the Middle East.* Boulder, CO: Lynne Rienner.

Moussalli, Ahmad S. (1999) *Moderate and Radical Islamic Fundamentalism: The Quest for Modernity, Legitimacy and the Islamic State.* Gainesville, FL: University Press of Florida.

—— (2001) *The Islamic Quest for Democracy, Pluralism, and Human Rights.* Gainesville, FL: University Press of Florida.

Mowlana, Hamid, Gerbner, George and Schiller, Herbert I. (eds) (1992) *Triumph of the Image: The Media's War in the Persian Gulf – A Global Perspective.* Boulder, CO: Westview Press.

Mufti, Malik (1996) *Sovereign Creations: Pan-Arabism and Political Order in Syria and Iraq.* Ithaca, NY: Cornell University Press.

al-Mughni, Haya (2001) *Women in Kuwait: The Politics of Gender*. London: Saqi Books.

Munoz, Gema Martin (ed.) (1999) *Islam, Modernism and the West: Cultural and Political Relations at the End of the Millenium*. London: I. B. Tauris.

Murden, Simon W. (2002) *Islam, the Middle East, and the New Global Hegemony*. Boulder, CO: Lynne Rienner.

Musallam, Basim (1983) *Sex and Society in Islam: Birth Control before the Nineteenth Century*. Cambridge: Cambridge University Press.

Muslih, Muhammad Y. (1988) *The Origins of Palestinian Nationalism*. New York: Columbia University Press.

An-Na'im, Abdullahi Ahmed (1990) *Toward an Islamic Reformation: Civil Liberties, Human Rights and International Law*. Syracuse, NY: Syracuse University Press.

Nasr, Seyyed Vali Reza (1996) *Mawdudi and the Making of Islamic Revivalism*. New York: Oxford University Press.

—— (2001) *The Islamic Leviathan: Islam and the Making of State Power*. Oxford; Oxford University Press.

Nassar, Jamal Raji (1991) *The Palestine Liberation Organization: From Armed Struggle to the Declaration of Independence*. New York: Praeger.

Niblock, Tim and Rodney Wilson (eds) (2000) *The Political Economy of the Middle East*, 6 vols. Cheltenham: Edward Elgar.

Noorani, A. G. (2003) *Islam and Jihad: Prejudice Versus Reality*. London: Zed Books.

Norton, Augustus Richard (ed.) (1995–7) *Civil Society and the Middle East*, 2 vols. Leiden: E. J. Brill.

Noyon, Jennifer (2002) *Islam, Politics, and Pluralism: Turkey, Jordan, Tunisia, and Algeria*. Washington, DC: Brookings Institution Press.

Nusse, Andrea (1998) *Muslim Palestine: The Ideology of Hamas*. Amsterdam: Harwood Academic.

Oren, Michael B. (2002) *Six Days of War: June 1967 and the Making of the Modern Middle East*. Oxford: Oxford University Press.

Owen, Roger (2000) *State, Power and Politics in the Making of the Modern Middle East*, 2nd edn. New York: Routledge.

Ozdalga, Elisabeth (1998) *The Veiling Issue, Official Secularism and Popular Islam in Modern Turkey*. Richmond: Curzon.

Ozdalga, Elisabeth and Sune Persson (eds) (1997) *Civil Society, Democracy, and the Muslim World*. Richmond: Curzon.

Pedersen, Lars (1999) *Newer Islamic Movements in Western Europe*. Aldershot: Ashgate.

Peled, Alisa Rubin (2001) *Debating Islam in the Jewish State: The Development of Policy toward Islamic Institutions in Israel*. Albany, NY: State University of New York Press.

Peters, Rudolph (1984) *Islam and Colonialism: The Doctrine of Jihad in Modern History*. Berlin: Mouton de Gruyter.

Pirzada, Sayyid A. S. (2000) *The Politics of the Jamiat Ulema-I-Islam Pakistan, 1971–1977*. Karachi: Oxford University Press.

Piscatori, James P (ed.) (1983) *Islam in the Political Process*. Cambridge: Cambridge University Press and the Royal Institute of International Affairs.

—— (1986) *Islam in a World of Nation-States*. Cambridge: Cambridge University Press and the Royal Institute of International Affairs.

Podeh, Elie (1999) *The Decline of Arab Unity: The Rise and Fall of the United Arab Republic*. Brighton: Sussex Academic Press.

Poole, Elizabeth (2002) *Reporting Islam: Media Representations of British Muslims*. London: I. B. Tauris.

Potter, Lawrence G. and Sick, Gary G. (eds) (2002) *Security in the Persian Gulf: Origins, Obstacles, and the Search for Consensus*. New York: Palgrave.

Poya, Maryam (1999) *Women, Work and Islamism: Ideology and Resistance*. London: Zed Books.

Price, Daniel E. (1999) *Islamic Political Culture, Democracy and Human Rights: A Comparative Study*. Westport, CT: Praeger.

Quandt, William B. (1986) *Camp David: Peacemaking and Politics*. Washington, DC: The Brookings Institution.

—— (2001) *Peace Process: American Diplomacy and the Arab–Israeli Conflict since 1967*, rev. edn. Berkeley, CA: University of California Press.

Rahman, Fazlur (1999) *Revival and Reform in Islam: A Study of Islamic Fundamentalism*, ed. Ebrahim Moosa. Oxford: Oneworld.

Rahnema, Ali (ed.) (1994) *Pioneers of Islamic Revival*. London: Zed Books.

—— (1998) *An Islamic Utopian: A Political Biography of Ali Shari'ati*. London: I. B. Tauris.

Rejwan, Nissim (1998) *Arabs Face the Modern World: Religious, Cultural, and Political Responses to the West*. Gainesville, FL: University Press of Florida.

—— (ed.) (2000) *The Many Faces of Islam: Perspectives on a Resurgent Civilization*. Gainesville, FL: University Press of Florida.

Rai, Milan (and Noam Chomsky) (2002) *War Plan – Iraq: Ten Reasons against War on Iraq*. London: Verso.

Ramadan, Tariq (2003) *Western Muslims and the Future of Islam*. Oxford: Oxford University Press.

Richards, Alan and Waterbury, John (1996) *A Political Economy of the Middle East*, 2nd edn. Boulder, CO: Westview Press.

Riddell, Peter G., Street, Tony and Johns, Anthony H. (eds) (1997) *Islam: Essays on Scripture, Thought and Society – A Festschrift in Honour of Anthony H. Johns*. Leiden: E. J. Brill.

Roald, Anne-Sofie (2001) *Women in Islam: The Western Experience*. New York: Routledge.

Roberson, B. A. (2003) *Shaping the Current Islamic Reformation*. London: Frank Cass.

Robinson, Francis (2000) *Islam and Muslin History in South Asia*. Oxford: Oxford University Press.

—— (2003) *Islam in South Asia*. Cambridge: Cambridge University Press.

Robinson, Glenn E. (1997) *Building a Palestinian State: The Incomplete Revolution*. Bloomington, IN: Indiana University Press.

Rodinson, Maxime (1978) *Islam and Capitalism*. Austin, TX: University of Texas Press.

—— (1979) *Marxism and the Muslim World*. London: Zed Books.

—— (2002) *Europe and the Mystique of Islam*. London: I. B. Tauris.

Rogan, Eugene (ed.) (2002) *Outside In: On the Margins of the Modern Middle East*. London: I. B. Tauris.

Rosen, Lawrence (1984) *Bargaining for Reality: The Construction of Social Relations in a Muslim Community*. Chicago, IL: University of Chicago Press.

—— (2003) *The Culture of Islam: Changing Aspects of Contemporary Muslim Life*. Chicago, IL: University of Chicago Press.

Rosenthal, Erwin (1958) *Political Thought in Medieval Islam*. Cambridge: Cambridge University Press.

Roy, Olivier (1994) *The Failure of Political Islam*. Cambridge, MA: Harvard University Press.

Rubenberg, Cheryl A. (2001) *Palestinian Women: Patriarchy and Resistance in the West Bank*. Boulder, CO: Lynne Rienner.

Rubin, Barry (ed.) (2003) *Revolutionaries and Reformers: Contemporary Islamist Movements in the Middle East*. Albany, NY: State University of New York Press.

Ruggles, D. Fairchild (ed.) (2000) *Women, Patronage, and Self-Representation in Islamic Societies*. Albany, NY: State University of New York Press.

Rugh, William A. (2004) *Arab Mass Media: Newspapers, Radio, and Television in Arab Politics*. Westport, CT: Praeger.

Ruthven, Malise (2002) *A Fury for God: The Islamist Attack on America*. London: Granta Books.

Saad-Ghorayeb, Amal (2002) *Hizbu'llah: Politics and Religion*. London: Pluto Press.

Sabbagh, Suha (ed.) (1998) *Palestinian Women of Gaza and the West Bank*. Bloomington, IN: Indiana University Press.

—— (ed.) (2002) *Arab Women: Between Defiance and Restraint*. Northampton, MA: Interlink.

Sachedina, Abdulaziz (2001) *The Islamic Roots of Democratic Pluralism*. Oxford: Oxford University Press.

Sadri, Mahmoud and Sadri, Ahmad (trans. and eds) (2002) *Reason, Freedom, and Democracy in Islam: Essential Writings of Abdolkarim Soroush*. Oxford: Oxford University Press.

Safi, Omid (ed.) (2003) *Progressive Muslims: On Gender, Justice, and Pluralism*. Oxford: Oneworld.

Said, Abdul Aziz *et al.* (eds) (2001) *Peace and Conflict Resolution in Islam: Precept and Practice*. Lanham, MD: University Press of America.

Said, Edward W. (1995) *Peace and its Discontents: Essays on Palestine in the Middle East Peace Process*. New York: Vintage.

—— (1997) *Covering Islam: How the Media and the Experts Determine How We See the Rest of the World*, rev. edn. New York: Vintage.

—— (2000) *The End of the Peace Process: Oslo and After*. New York: Pantheon Books.

Said, Edward W. and Hitchens, Christopher (eds) (1988) *Blaming the Victims: Spurious Scholarship and the Palestinian Question*. London: Verso.

Saikal, Amin (2003) *Islam and the West: Conflict or Cooperation?* New York: Palgrave Macmillan.

Saikal, Amin and Schnabel, Albrecht (eds) (2003) *Democratization in the Middle East: Struggles, Challenges*. Paris: United Nations.

Sajoo, Amyn B (ed.) (2002) *Civil Society in the Muslim World: Contemporary Perspectives*. London: I. B. Tauris.

Sakr, Naomi (2002) *Satellite Realms: Transnational Television, Globalization and the Middle East*. London: I. B. Tauris.

Salame, Ghassan (ed.) (1994) *Democracy Without Democrats? The Renewal of Politics in the Muslim World*. London: I. B. Tauris.

Saliba, Therese, Allen, Carolyn and Howard, Judith A. (eds) (2002) *Gender, Politics, and Islam*. Chicago, IL: University of Chicago Press.

Salvatore, Armando (1997) *Islam and the Political Discourse of Modernity*. London: Ithaca Press.

Salvatore, Armando and Eickelman, Dale F. (eds) (2003) *Public Islam and the Common Good*. Leiden: E. J. Brill.

Sanasarian, Eliz (2000) *Religious Minorities in Iran*. Cambridge: Cambridge University Press.

Schwedler, Jillian (ed.) (1995) *Toward Civil Society in the Middle East?: A Primer*. Boulder, CO: Lynne Rienner.

Segal, Ronald (2002) *Islam's Black Slaves: The Other Black Diaspora*. New York: Hill & Wang.

Sells, Michael A. (1996) *The Bridge Betrayed: Religion and Genocide in Bosnia*. Berkeley, CA: University of California Press.

Shadid, Anthony (2001) *Legacy of the Prophet: Despots, Democrats and the New Politics of Islam*. Boulder, CO: Westview Press.

Shadid, W. A. R. and van Koningsveld, P. S. (eds) (2002) *Religious Freedom and the Neutrality of the State: The Position of Islam in the European Union*. Louvain: Peeters.

Sharabi, Hisham (1988) *Neopatriarchy: A Theory of Distorted Change in Arab Society*. Oxford: Oxford University Press.

—— (ed.) (1990) *Theory, Politics and the Arab World*. London/Washington, DC: Routledge/Center for Contemporary Arab Studies.

Shari'ati, Ali (1979) *On the Sociology of Islam: Lectures by Ali Shari'ati*, trans. Hamid Algar. Berkeley, CA: Mizan Press.

Sheikh, Naveed S. (2003) *The New Politics of Islam: Pan-Islamic Foreign Policy in a World of States*. New York: Routledge Curzon.

Shepard, William (1996) *Sayyid Qutb and Islamic Activism*. Leiden: E. J. Brill.

Shirazi, Fagheh (2001) *The Veil Unveiled: The Hijab in Modern Culture*. Gainesville, FL: University Press of Florida.

Sidahmed, Abdel Salam and Ehteshami, Anoushiravan (eds) (1996) *Islamic Fundamentalism*. Boulder, CO: Westview Press.

Simons, Thomas W., Jr. (2003) *Islam in a Globalizing World*. Stanford, CA: Stanford University Press.

Singerman, Diane (1996) *Avenues of Participation: Family, Politics, and Networks in Urban Quarters of Cairo*. Princeton, NJ: Princeton University Press.

Singerman, Diane and Hoodfar, Homa (eds) (1996) *Development, Change, and Gender in Cairo: A View from the Household*. Bloomington, IN: Indiana University Press.

Sivan, Emmanuel (1990) *Radical Islam: Medieval Theology and Modern Politics*. New Haven, CO: Yale University Press.

Smith, Charles D. (2000) *Palestine and the Arab–Israeli Conflict: A History with Documents*, 4th edn. New York: Bedford/St. Martin's Press.

Sonn, Tamara (1990) *Between Qur'an and Crown: The Challenge of Political Legitimacy in the Arab World*. Boulder, CO: Westview Press.

—— (1996a) *Interpreting Islam: Bandali Jawzi's Islamic Intellectual History*. Oxford: Oxford University Press.

—— (ed.) (1996b) *Islam and the Question of Minorities*. Lanham, MD: University Press of America.

Spaulding, Jay *et al.* (1994) *The Enigmatic Saint: Ahmad Ibn Idris and the Idrisi Tra-*

dition. Evanston, IL: Northwestern University Press.

Spellberg, Denise A. (1996) *Politics, Gender, and the Islamic Past: The Legacy of 'A'isha bint Abi Bakr*. New York: Columbia University Press.

Stetkevych, Suzanne Pinckney (2002) *The Poetics of Islamic Legitimacy: Myth, Gender, and Ceremony in the Classical Arabic Ode*. Bloomington, IN: Indiana University Press.

Stowasser, Barbara Freyer (ed.) (1989) *The Islamic Impulse*. Washington, DC: Center for Contemporary Arab Studies.

Taheri, Amir (1986) *The Spirit of Allah: Khomeini and the Islamic Revolution*. Bethesda, MD: Adler & Adler.

Tamadonfar, Mehran (1989) *The Islamic Polity and Political Leadership: Fundamentalism, Sectarianism, and Pragmatism*. Boulder, CO: Westview Press.

Tamimi, Azzam S. (2001) *Rachid Ghannouchi: A Democrat Within Islamism*. New York: Oxford University Press.

Tamimi, Azzam and Esposito, John L. (eds) (2000) *Islam and Secularism in the Middle East*. New York: New York University Press.

Tauber, Eliezer (1993) *The Emergence of the Arab Movements*. London: Frank Cass & Co.

Telhami, Shibley and Barnett, Michael (eds) (2002) *Identity and Foreign Policy in the Middle East*. Ithaca, NY: Cornell University Press.

Tessler, Mark A. (ed.) (with Jodi Nachtwey and Anne Banda) (1999) *Area Studies and Social Science: Strategies for Understanding Middle East Politics*. Bloomington, IN: Indiana University Press.

Tibi, Bassam (1988) *The Crisis of Modern Islam*. Salt Lake City, UT: University of Utah Press.

—— (1990) *Islam and the Cultural Accommodation of Social Change*. Boulder, CO: Westview Press.

—— (1997) *Arab Nationalism: Between Islam and the Nation-State*, 3rd edn. New York: Palgrave Macmillan.

—— (2002a) *The Challenge of Fundamentalism: Political Islam and the New World Disorder*, updated edn. Berkeley, CA: University of California Press.

—— (2002b) *Islam between Culture and Politics*. New York: Palgrave Macmillan.

Turner, Bryan S. and Akbar Ahmed (eds) (2003) *Islam: Critical Concepts in Sociology*, 4 vols. New York: Routledge.

Turner, Richard Brent (1997) *Islam in the African-American Experience*. Bloomington, IN: Indiana University Press.

Vatikiotis, P. J. (1987) *Islam and the State*. London: Croom Helm.

Viorst, Milton (1998) *In the Shadow of the Prophet: The Struggle for the Soul of Islam*. New York: Anchor Books.

Waardenburg, Jacques (2003) *Muslims and Others: Relations in Context*. Berlin: Walter de Gruyter.

Waltz, Susan E. (1995) *Human Rights and Reform: Changing the Face of North African Politics*. Berkeley, CA: University of California Press.

Warde, Ibrahim (2000) *Islamic Finance in the Global Economy*. Edinburgh: Edinburgh University Press.

Watson, Andrew W. (1983) *Agricultural Innovation in the Early Islamic World*. Cambridge: Cambridge University Press.

Watt, William Montgomery (1961) *Islam and the Integration of Society*. London: Routledge & Kegan Paul.

Wendell, Charles (trans.) (1978) *Five Tracts of Hasan al-Banna', 1906–1949*. Berkeley, CA: University of California Press.

Winckler, Onn (forthcoming) *The Political Demography of the Modern Arab World*. Brighton: Sussex Academic Press.

Wright, Robin B. (2001) *Sacred Rage: The Crusade of Modern Islam*, rev. edn. New York: Simon & Schuster.

Yamani, Mai (ed.) (1996) *Feminism and Islam: Legal and Literary Perspectives*. New York: New York University Press.

Zaman, Muhammad Qasim (2002) *The Ulama in Contemporary Islam: Custodians of Change*. Princeton, NJ: Princeton University Press.

Zebiri, Kate (1993) *Mahmud Shaltut and Islamic Modernism*. Oxford: Clarendon Press.

Ziadeh, Nicol A. (1958) *Sanusiyah: A Study of a Revivalist Movement in Islam*. Leiden: E. J. Brill.

Zubaida, Sami (1993) *Islam, the People and the State: Essays on Political Ideas and Movements in the Middle East*. London: I. B. Tauris.

Zunes, Stephen (2002) *Tinderbox: U.S. Middle East Policy and the Roots of Terrorism*. Monroe, ME: Common Courage Press.

XII Miscellany

Abbott, Nabia (1942) *Aishah: The Beloved of Mohammad*. Chicago, IL: University of Chicago Press.

Abdallah, Anouar (ed.) (1994) *For Rushdie: Essays by Arab and Muslim Writers in Defense of Free Speech*. New York: George Braziller.

Abou El Fadel, Khaled (2001) *Conference of the Books: The Search for Beauty in Islam*. Lanham, MD: University Press of America.

Abu-Izzeddin, Nejla M. (1993) *The Druzes: A New Study of their History, Faith and Society*, 2nd edn. Leiden: E. J. Brill.

Ahmad, Barakat (1979) *Muhammad and the Jews: A Re-examination*. Delhi: Vikas.

Allen, Roger (1995) *The Arabic Novel: An Historical and Critical Introduction*. Syracuse, NY: Syracuse University Press.

—— (1998) *The Arabic Literary Heritage: The Development of its Genres and Criticism*. Cambridge: Cambridge University Press.

Anees, Munawar Ahmad (1990) *Islam and Biological Futures: Ethics, Gender and Technology*. London: Mansell.

Arberry, Arthur John (1964) *Aspects of Islamic Civilization*. London: Allen & Unwin.

Asad, Mohammad (2001) *The Road to Mecca*, rpt edn. Louisville, KY: Fons Vitae.

Baljon, Jon M. S. (1953) *The Reforms and Religious Ideas of Sayyid Ahmad Khan*. Lahore: Ashraf.

Bangura, Ahmed S. (2000) *Islam and the West African Novel: The Politics of Representation*. London: Lynne Rienner.

Beinin, Joel (1990) *Was the Red Flag Flying There? Marxist Politics and the Arab–Israeli Conflict in Egypt and Israel, 1948–1965*. Berkeley, CA: University of California Press.

Berg, Herbert (2000) *The Development of Exegesis in Early Islam: The Authenticity of Muslim Literature from The Formative Period*. Richmond: Curzon.

Betts, Robert Brenton (1988) *The Druze*. New Haven, CT: Yale University Press.

Birkeland, Harris (1955) *The Legend of the Opening of Muhammad's Breast*. Oslo: Nordske Videnskaps Academi.

Bowen, John R. (1993) *Muslims through Discourse*. Princeton, NJ: Princeton University Press.

Bradway, Becky (ed.) (2003) *In the Middle of the Middle East: Literary Nonfiction from the Heartland*. Bloomington, IN: Indiana University Press.

Brass, Paul R. (2003) *The Production of Hindu–Muslim Violence in Contemporary India*. Seattle, WA: University of Washington Press.

Buck-Morss, Susan (2003) *Thinking Past Terror: Islamism and Critical Theory on the Left*. London: Verso.

Bulliet, Richard W. (1990) *The Camel and the Wheel*. New York: Columbia University Press.

Burton, Richard (1853) *Personal Narrative of a Pilgrimage to El Medinah and Meccah*. New York: G. P. Putnam & Co.

Campo, Juan Eduardo (1991) *The Other Sides of Paradise: Explorations into the Religious Meanings of Domestic Space in Islam*. Columbia, SC: University of South Carolina Press.

Combs-Schilling, M. E. (1989) *Sacred Performances: Islam, Sexuality, and Sacrifice*. New York: Columbia University Press.

Corbin, Henry (1995) *Swedenborg and Esoteric Islam*, trans. Leonard Fox. West Chester, PA: Swedenborg Foundation.

Cragg, Kenneth (1956) *The Call of the Minaret*. New York: Oxford University Press.

Daniel, Norman (1958) *Islam and the West: The Making of an Image*. Edinburgh: Edinburgh University Press.

Dannin, Robert (2002) *Black Pilgrimage to Islam*. New York: Oxford University Press.

Donaldson, William J. and Naim, Mashary Abdullah (2000) *Sharecropping in the Yemen: A Study in Islamic Theory, Custom and Pragmatism*. Leiden: Brill Academic.

Doumato, Eleanor Abdella (2000) *Getting God's Ear: Women, Islam and Healing in Saudi Arabia and the Gulf*. New York: Columbia University Press.

Dundes, Alan (2003) *Fables of the Ancients? Folklore in the Qur'an*. Lanham, MD: Rowman & Littlefield.

Dunn, Ross E. (1990) *The Adventures of Ibn Battuta: A Muslim Traveler of the Fourteenth Century*. Berkeley, CA: University of California Press.

Easwaran, Eknath (2000) *Nonviolent Soldier of Islam: Badshah Khan, A Man to Match His Mountain s*, 2nd edn. Tomales, CA: Nilgiri Press.

Eickelman, Dale and James Piscatori (eds) (1990) *Muslim Travelers: Pilgrimage, Migration, and the Religious Imagination*. Berkeley, CA: University of California Press.

Esack, Farid (1999) *On Being a Muslim*. Oxford: Oneworld.

Firro, Kais M. (1997) *A History of the Druzes*. Leiden: E. J. Brill.

Foltz, Richard C., Denny, Frederick M. and Baharuddin, Azizan (eds) (2003) *Islam and Ecology: A Bestowed Trust*. Cambridge, MA: Harvard University Press.

Gallagher, Nancy Elizabeth (ed.) (1997) *Approaches to the History of the Middle East: Interviews with Leading Middle East Historians*. Reading: Ithaca.

Gaudefroy-Demombynes, Maurice (1984) *Muslim Institutions*. Westport, CT: Greenwood Press.

Gibb, Hamilton A. R. (1932) *Whither Islam?* London: Gollancz.

—— (1972) *Modern Trends in Islam*. New York: Octagon Books.

Goldschmidt, Arthur, Jr. (2000) *Biographical Dictionary of Modern Egypt*. Boulder, CO: Lynne Rienner.

Grunebaum, Gustave E. von (1958) *Muhammadan Festivals*. Leiden: Brill.

Hallaq, Wael B. and Little, Donald P. (eds) (1991) *Islamic Studies Presented to Charles J. Adams*. Leiden: E. J. Brill.

al-Hassan, Ahmad Y. and Donald R. Hill (1986) *Islamic Technology: An Illustrated History*. Cambridge: Cambridge University Press.

Hassan, Hassan (2000) *In the House of Muhammad Ali: A Family Album, 1805–1952*. Cairo: American University in Cairo Press.

Hawting, Gerald (ed.) (2004) *The Development of Islamic Ritual*. Aldershot: Ashgate.

Hill, Donald R. (1998) *Studies in Medieval Islamic Technology: From Philo to al-Jazari, from Alexandria to Diyar Bakr*, ed. David A. King. Aldershot: Ashgate.

Hiro, Dilip (1996) *Dictionary of the Middle East*. New York: Palgrave Macmillan.

Hogendijk, J. P. and Sabra, A. I. (eds) (2003) *The Enterprise of Science in Islam: New Perspectives*. Cambridge, MA: MIT Press.

Hoodbhoy, Perez (1991) *Islam and Science: Religious Orthodoxy and the Battle for Rationality*. London: Zed Books.

Hourani, Albert (1991) *Islam in European Thought*. Cambridge: Cambridge University Press.

Huff, Toby E. (1995) *The Rise of Early Modern Science: Islam, China, and the West*. Cambridge: Cambridge University Press.

Husain, Ali Akbar (2000) *Scent in the Islamic Garden: A Study of Deccani Urdu Literary Sources*. Karachi: Oxford University Press.

Jaschok, Maria and Jinjin, Shui (2000) *The History of Women's Mosques in Chinese Islam*. Richmond: Curzon.

Jayyusi, Salma Khadra (ed.) (1987) *Modern Arabic Poetry: An Anthology*. New York: Columbia University Press.

Jayyusi, Salma Khadra and Allen, Roger (eds) (1995) *Modern Arabic Drama: An Anthology*. Bloomington, IN: Indiana University Press.

Johnstone, Penelope (trans.) (1998) *Ibn Qayyim al-Jawziyya: Medicine of the Prophet*. Cambridge: The Islamic Texts Society.

Joseph, Suad (ed.) (2003) *The Encyclopedia of Women and Islamic Cultures*, vol.I. Leiden: Brill Academic.

Kahera, Akel Ismail (2002) *Deconstructing the American Mosque: Space, Gender and Aesthetics*. Austin, TX: University of Texas Press.

Kanaaneh, Rhoda (2002) *Birthing the Nation: Strategies of Palestinian Women in Israel*. Berkeley, CA: University of California Press.

Kassam, Tazim R. (1995) *Songs of Wisdom and Circles of Dance: Songs of the Satpanth Isma'ili Muslim Saint, Pir Shams*. Albany, NY: State University of New York Press.

Kennedy, Edward S. (1998) *Astronomy and Astrology in the Medieval Islamic World*. Aldershot: Ashgate/Variorum.

Khalidi, Tarif (trans. and ed.) (2001) *The Muslim Jesus: Sayings and Stories in Islamic Literature*. Cambridge, MA: Harvard University Press.

Khan, Gabriel Mandel (2001) *Arabic Script: Styles, Variants, and Calligraphic Adaptations*. New York: Abbeville Press.

Kimball, Michelle and von Schlegell, Barbara R. (1997) *Muslim Women throughout the World: A Bibliography*. Boulder, CO: Lynne Rienner.

King, David A. (1993) *Astronomy in the Service of Islam*. Aldershot: Ashgate/Variorum.

—— (1999) *World Maps for Finding the Direction and Distance to Mecca: Innovation and Tradition in Islamic Science*. Leiden: E. J. Brill.

Kritzek, James (1964) *Peter the Venerable and Islam*. Princeton, NJ: Princeton University Press.

Kueny, Kathryn (2001) *The Rhetoric of Sobriety: Wine in Early Islam*. Albany, NY: State University of New York Press.

Lamoreaux, John C. (2002) *The Early Muslim Tradition of Dream Interpretation*. Albany, NY: State University of New York Press.

Lane, E. W. (1984) *Arabic–English Lexicon*, 2 vols. Cambridge: The Islamic Texts Society.

Laurance, Robin (2002) *Portrait of Islam A Journey through the Muslim World*. New York: Thames & Hudson.

Lorch, Richard (1995) *Arabic Mathematical Sciences: Instruments, Texts and Transmission*. Aldershot: Ashgate/Variorum.

Macfie, A. L. (ed.) (2000) *Orientalism: A Reader*. Edinburgh: Edinburgh University Press.

Malcolm X (1992) *The Autobiography of Malcolm X (as told to Alex Haley)*, reprint edn. New York: Ballantine.

Martin, Richard C. (1995) *Islamic Studies: A History of Religions Approach*, 2nd edn. Upper Saddle River, NJ: Prentice-Hall.

—— (ed.) (2001) *Approaches to Islam in Religious Studies*. Oxford: Oneworld.

Masri, Al-Hafiz Basheer Ahmad (1989) *Animals in Islam*. Petersfield: Athene Trust.

Mattar, Philip (ed.) (2000) *Encyclopedia of the Palestinians*. New York: Facts on File.

Nafisi, Azar (2003) *Reading Lolita in Tehran: A Memoir in Books*. New York: Random House.

Naipaul, V. S. (1981) *Among the Believers: An Islamic Journey*. New York: Alfred A. Knopf.

Nasr, Seyyed Hossein (1993) *The Need for a Sacred Science*. Albany, NY: State University of New York Press.

Nettler, Ronald L. and Taji-Farouki, Suha (eds) (1998) *Muslim–Jewish Encounters: Intellectual Traditions and Modern Politics*. New York: Routledge.

Netton, Ian Richard (ed.) (1993) *Golden Roads: Migration, Pilgrimage and Travel in Mediaeval and Modern Islam*. Richmond: Curzon.

Nimer, Mohamed (2002) *The North American Muslim Resource Guide*. New York: Routledge.

Nimni, Ephraim (ed.) (2003) *The Challenge of Post-Zionism: Alternatives to Israeli Fundamentalist Politics*. London: Zed Books.

Nomachi, Ali Kazuyoshi and Nasr, Seyyed Hossein (1997) *Mecca the Blessed, Medina the Radiant: The Holiest Cities of Islam*. New York: Aperture.

Peled, Alisa Rubin (2001) *Debating Islam in the Jewish State: The Development of Policy toward Islamic Institutions in Israel*. Albany, NY: State University of New York Press.

Peters, Francis E. (1994a) *The Hajj: The Muslim Pilgrimage to Mecca and the Holy Places*. Princeton, NJ: Princeton University Press.

—— (1994b) *Mecca: A Literary History of the Muslim Holy Land*. Princeton, NJ: Princeton University Press.

Piamenta, Moshe (1979) *Islam in Everyday Arabic Speech*. Leiden: E. J. Brill.

Rahman, Fazlur (1987) *Health and Medicine in the Islamic Tradition: Change and Identity*. New York: Crossroad.

Riddell, Peter G. and Street, Tony (eds) (1997) *Islam: Essays on Scripture, Thought and Society*. Leiden: E. J. Brill.

Ridgeon, Lloyd V. J. (2001) *Crescents on the Cross: Islamic Vision of Christianity*. Oxford: Oxford University Press.

Robinson, Francis (ed.) (1999) *The Cambridge Illustrated History of the Islamic World*. Cambridge: Cambridge University Press.

Robinson, Neal (1991) *Christ in Islam and Christianity*. Albany, NY: State University of New York Press.

Rosenthal, Franz (1956) *Humour in Early Islam*. Leiden: E. J. Brill.

—— (1991) *Science and Medicine in Islam: A Collection of Essays*. Aldershot: Ashgate/Variorum.

Samsó, Julio (1994) *Islamic Astronomy and Medieval Spain*. Aldershot: Ashgate/Variorum.

Sardar, Ziauddin (1977) *Science, Technology, and Development in the Muslim World*. London: Croom Helm.

—— (1987) *The Future of Muslim Civilization*, 2nd edn. London, Mansell.

—— (1989) *Explorations in Islamic Science*. London: Mansell.

Savage-Smith, Emilie (ed.) (2004) *Magic and Divination in Early Islam*. Aldershot: Ashgate.

Shaheen, Jack G. (2001) *Reel Bad Arabs: How Hollywood Vilifies a People*. New York: Olive Branch Press.

Shariati, Ali (1993) *Hajj: Reflections on its Rituals*, trans. Laleh Bakhtiar. Chicago, IL: Kazi.

Shirazi, Faegheh (2001) *The Veil Unveiled*. Gainesville, FL: University Press of Florida.

Simon, Reeva S., Mattar, Philip and Bulliet, Richard W. (eds) (1996) *The Encyclopedia of the Modern Middle East*, 4 vols. New York: Macmillan.

Smith, Wilfred Cantwell (1981) *On Understanding Islam: Selected Studies*. The Hague: Mouton.

Suleiman, Yasir (2004) *A War of Words: Language and Conflict in the Middle East*. Cambridge: Cambridge University Press.

Turner, Bryan S. (1974) *Weber and Islam: A Critical Study*. London: Routledge & Kegan Paul.

—— (1978) *Marx and the End of Orientalism*. London: George Allen & Unwin.

Turner, Howard R. (1997) *Science in Medieval Islam: An Illustrated Introduction*. Austin, TX: University of Texas Press.

Ullmann, Manfred (1997) *Islamic Medicine*. Edinburgh: Edinburgh University Press.

van der Veer, Peter (1994) *Religious Nationalism: Hindus and Muslims in India*. Berkeley, CA: University of California Press.

von Grunebaum, G. E (ed.) (1955) *Unity and Variety in Muslim Civilization*. Chicago, IL: University of Chicago Press.

—— (1961) *Islam: Essays in the Nature and Growth of Cultural Tradition*, 2nd edn. London: Routledge & Kegan Paul.

Wang, Jianping (2001) *A Glossary of Chinese Islamic Terms*. Richmond: Curzon.

Warraq, Ibn (ed.) (2003) *Leaving Islam: Apostates Speak Out*. Amherst, NY: Prometheus Books.

Webb, Gisela (ed.) (2000) *Windows of Faith: Muslim Women Scholar-Activists in North America*. Syracuse, NY: Syracuse University Press.

Wheeler, Brannon M. (2002a) *Moses in the Quran and Islamic Exegesis*. New York: Routledge.

—— (ed.) (2002b) *Teaching Islam* (American Academy of Religion). Oxford: Oxford University Press.

Wolfe, Michael (1993) *The Hadj: An American's Pilgrimage to Mecca*. New York: Grove Press.

—— (ed.) (1997) *One Thousand Roads to Mecca: Ten Centuries of Travelers Writing about the Muslim Pilgrimage*. New York: Grove Press.

—— (ed.) (2002) *Taking Back Islam: American Muslims Reclaim their Faith*. Emmaus, PA: Rodale Press.

Index

INDEX

Muhammad B. Tumart 434–5;
see also Reconquista
Almoravids **47**, 51, 81, 100, 194;
in Maghrib 375;
see also 'Abdallah b. Yasin; Yusuf b.
Tashufin
alms-giving **47–8**;
see also al-zaqat; Pillars of Islam
Alp Arslan B. Chaghri Beg Dawud **48**
'am al-fil 11, 435, **514**;
see also Surat al-Fil
Amal **48**
Amin, Ahmad **48–9**
Amin, Qasim **49**
Amina **49**;
see also Muhammad ibn 'Abdallah, the
Prophet of Islam
Aminrazavi, M. 233, 622
Amir al-Hajj **49**
Amir al-Mu'minin **49**, 390, 394, 446, 667;
see also mu'minin
Amir Arjomand, Said 251
Amir-Moezzi, M. 290, 414, 516
al-'Amiri, Abu al-Hasan Muhammad **49–50**
Amjad, M. 204
Amman **50**
al-Amr bi'l-ma'ruf **50–1**
'Amr ibn al-'As 239
Anawati, G. C. 123
D'Ancona, C. 653
al-Andalus **51–2**;
see also Almohads, Almoravids, Cordoba,
Granada, Reconquista; Sevilla;
Umayyads of Spain
Andrews, A. 546
angels 24, **52,** 126, 133, 225, 377, 476–7, 491,
516, 555;
Harut and Marut 217;
Iblis 245;
Israfil 316;
'Izra'il 319;
Jibril 331;
Malik 385;
Mikha'il 414;
Munkar and Nakir 447
Ankara **52**, 72
al-Ansar **52–3**, 431, 437;
see also Companions under Muhammad
ibn 'Abdallah, the Prophet of Islam; al-
Sahaba
Ansari, M. A. H. 610, 641
anthropomorphism 46, **53**, 64, 73, 100;
see also Allah; tashbih
Anti-Christ see al-Dajjal
Antun, Farah **53**
Anwarul, Haq 160
Aouad, M. 653
apostasy **53–4**, 282;
see also hudud; ilhad; ridda
'Aqaba, Pledges of **54**

'aqa'id **54**
aqalim **54–5**
'aqida 175, **514**;
see also creed, Islamic
'aqila **55**
'aqiqa see naming ceremony of a child
'aql 55, 68, 126, 556
al-'Aql, N. 'A. 245, 626
al-Aqsa Mosque see al-Masjid al-Aqsa;
Jerusalem
Arab Bulletin 364
Arab Nationalism 22–3, 92, 134, 183, 461, 483–4;
Egyptian Nationalism 84
Pan-Arab Nationalism 23, 65, 92, 183, 461,
483–4, 612;
see also 'Abd al-Nasir, Jamal; Hizb al-
Tahrir; Nasserism; socialism
Arab Revolt **55**, 219, 365
Arab socialism 5, 587;
Arab Socialist Union 5
Arabia Deserta 149
Arabic coinage 4
Arabic language 3, 77, 659;
alphabet 59;
Arabic-speaking population 55, 58–59;
classical Arabic 56–7, 59;
colloquial Arabic 57, 59;
dialectal Arabic 56–7;
educated spoken Arabic 57
elements of 58, **59**;
grammar 45;
as international language 55;
and Islam 55–6;
as liturgical language 55–6, 58–9;
majaz 380–1;
in the modern world **55–9;**
modern written Arabic and its spoken form
56–7;
as official language, 55;
origins 58;
and the Qur'an 56–9;
and science 59, 240–1;
script 55, 56;
as Semitic language 55, 56, 58, 59;
translations into Arabic 240–1, 246, 251,
652–3;
translations from Arabic 605;
Translation Movement 659–60;
written Arabic 57–8, 59;
maghribi writing 374–5;
see also Hausa language; calligraphy
Arabic syllogism **59–61**;
Analysis of juristic arguments in terms of
syllogism 60;
Avicennan School 59–61;
Farabian School 59–61;
matter of syllogisms 60;
modal syllogistic 61;
relation between categorical and
hypothetical syllogistics 60–1

804

INDEX